AN ENCYCLOPEDIA OF CONTINENTAL WOMEN WRITERS

edited by
KATHARINA M. WILSON

VOLUME TWO · L - Z

Garland Publishing, Inc.
New York and London, 1991

Library of Congress Cataloging-in-Publication Data

An Encyclopedia of continental women writers /
    edited by Katharina M. Wilson.
        p.   cm.—(Garland reference library of the
    humanities ; vol. 698)
        ISBN 0-8240-8547-7 (acid-free paper)
        1. Women authors—Biography—Dictionaries.
    2. Women in literature—Biography—Dictionaries.
    3. Literature, Modern—Women authors—History
    and criticism—Dictionaries. I. Wilson, Katharina M.
    II. Series.
    PN481.E5   1991
    809'.89287'03—dc20   [B]   91-6930

Printed on acid-free, 250-year-life paper

Manufactured in the United States of America

AN ENCYCLOPEDIA OF CONTINENTAL WOMEN WRITERS

VOLUME TWO

L

L.A.V.G.

(see: Luise Adelgunde Victoria
Gottsched)

Louise Labé

*Born April 1522 (?), Lyons, France; died
Lyons, April 1566*
Genre(s): débat, elegy, sonnet
Language(s): French

In the sixteenth century Lyons was a major
commercial and intellectual center that rivalled
Paris in importance. Close to Italy, frequented by
Italian traders and bankers, serving as occasional
residence for the king and his court, it welcomed
the intellectual contributions of the Renaissance.
Labé's father, a wealthy cordier or rope-maker,
allowed his daughter to profit from the more
liberated trends in feminine education that prevailed among some of the French and Italian
aristocracy. She learned Latin, Spanish, Italian
and became an accomplished musician. Biographers indicate that she also mastered fencing and
amazed more conservative members of Lyons
society by riding horseback in male costume.
Her marriage to Ennemond Perrin, thirty-five
years her senior, did not prevent her from pursuing her interest in literature and the arts. The
Belle Cordiére, as she was called, entertained
intellectuals and writers, among them Maurice
Scève and Olivier de Magny. The latter is rumored
to have been her partner in a brief but tempestuous love affair that inspired some of Labé's
most celebrated poetry. In 1555 a small volume
consisting of the *Débat de Folie et Amour* in prose,

three elegies, and 24 sonnets appeared in Lyons
as the *Euvres de Louize Labé lionnoize*. Although
there are occasional references to some Latin
verses by Labé, these have apparently been lost,
and her literary reputation depends exclusively
upon the sonnets and the *Débat*.

In the prefatory letter to her friend Clémence
de Bourges, Labé argues that the time has come
for women to look beyond mere domestic duties
and show what they can do in the field of
humanistic learning. This includes publishing
their literary works so that Labé is, herself, an
example of the enlightened Renaissance woman.
The *Débat de Folie et Amour* suggests a rapport
with the medieval *débat*, but Labé renews the
genre through her light and sophisticated manipulation of prose style and reveals the influence
of Leo Ebreo and other Renaissance Neoplatonists
as well as such Italian literary models as Bembo
and Sannazaro. She is also indebted to Plutarch,
Lucian, Erasmus, and Ovid, but the myth that
provides the substance of the *Débat* is her own
invention. Labé shows similar originality in the
sonnets where she transforms the Petrarchan
discourse of male poets into a vehicle for feminine desire and feminine emotion.

Labé's sonnets are remarkable for both technical mastery and passionate intensity, qualities
that make her one of the more accessible poets of
the School of Lyons and that have sustained her
literary reputation from Ronsard to Rilke. In the
sixteenth century the sensuous character of her
love, the frank expression of longing for physical
union, combined with her liberated lifestyle to
place her in a difficult social position. Insulting
songs and verses suggested that she was little

better than a prostitute. Contemporaries like François de Billon, Antoine du Verdier and Jean Calvin openly referred to her as a courtesan or worse. She was also accused of assisting her cousin Antonia Rosset to poison her husband Jean Yvard, but Yvard's death in Geneva prevented the case from coming to trial and spared her further scandal.

Labé apparently withdrew from Lyons society following the publication of her book and spent the remaining years of her life at her villa of Parcieu en Dombes. The *Oeuvres*, accompanied by laudatory verses from contemporaries like Scève and Pontus de Tyard, enjoyed considerable success, with a second and third edition published in Lyons by Jean de Tournes in 1556 and a fourth edition appearing the same year in Rouen. It is not likely that Labé's departure from Lyons was occasioned by the reception accorded her poetry or even the legend of the "Belle Cordière." Lyons was in financial decline and suffered from the political and military turmoil occasioned by the outbreak of religious warfare. The city was also ravaged by plague, and a great many of the Lyons intelligentsia had died in the 1550s. The brilliant and refined Lyonese society that had surrounded and nourished the Belle Cordiére no longer existed.

Works

Euvres de Louize Labé lionnoize (1555). Oeuvres complètes, ed. Enzo Giudici (1981).

Translations: *Sonnets*, tr. Graham Dustin Martin (1973). *The Debate Between Folly and Cupid*, tr. Edwin Marion Cox (1925).

Bibliography

Giudici, E., *Louise Labé e "l'Ecole lyonnaise"* (1964). Harvey, L. E., *The Aesthetics of the Renaissance Love Sonnet* (1962). O'Connor, D., *Louise Labé: sa vie et son oeuvre* (1926). Jondorf, G., "Petrarchan Variations in Pernette du Guillet and Louise Labé." *Modern Language Review* 71 (1976). Jones, R., "Assimilation with a Difference: Renaissance Women Poets and Literary Influence." *Yale French Studies* 62 (1981). Poliner, S. M., "'Signes d'Amante' and the Dispossessed Lover: Louise Labé's Poetics of Inheritance." BHR 46 (1984). Schulze-Witzenrath, E., *Die Originalität der Louise Labé* (1974). Sibona, C., *Le Sens qui résonne: une étude sur le sonnet français à travers l'oeuvre de Louise Labé* (1984). Wiley, K., "Louise Labé's Deceptive Petrarchism." *Modern Language Studies* 9 (1981). Zamaron, F., *Louise Labé Dame de franchise* (1968). General references: *Dictionnaire des lettres françaises*, pp. 407–408. McFarlane, I. D., *A History of French Literature: Renaissance France*, pp. 162–165.

Paula Sommers

Clemencia Laborda Medir

Born 1908, Lérido, Spain; died 1980
Genre(s): poetry, drama, novel
Language(s): Spanish

Also known as Clemencia Laborda, she was best known for her poetry. Largely self-educated, she read Jiménez and Lorca in her youth, and her own verse was praised by Machado, Alonso, and Carmen Conde, who commended her ". . . impeccable mastery" of form and her intimate, committed, profound poetry. She preferred the classic verse forms and cultivated the sonnet in particular. Her lyricism penetrates into the world of dreams and nostalgia. Her themes are varied. Her first collection of poetry was well received critically, but with the exception of her Catholic play *La sacristía* (The Sacristy), which was produced in Madrid in 1953, her works are not readily available. Several of her volumes of poetry are reported to have been unpublished at the time of her death in 1930.

Works

Poetry: *Caudal* [Torrent] (n.d.). *Ciudad de soledades* [City of Solitudes] (1948). *En busca de los recuerdos perdidos* [In Search of Lost Memories] (n.d.), reportedly unpublished at the time of her death. *Niños y jardines* [Children and Gardens] (n.d.). *Poesías religiosas* [Religious Poems] (n.d.). *Retorno a la provincia* [Return to the Province] (1961). *Tiempo del hombre, tiempo de Dios* [Time of Man, Time of God] (1972). *Vacaciones bajo los árboles* [Vacation Under the Trees] (n.d.), reportedly unpublished at the time of her death. Plays: *Aniversario de bodas* [Wedding Anniversary] (n.d.). *Don Juan en la niebla* [Don Juan in the Fog].[With Concha Suárez de Otero], En media hora de sueño [In a Half-Hour of Sleep] (n.d.), *Fachada a la calle* [Looking Toward the Street] (n.d.). *Una familia ideal* [An Ideal Family] (n.d.), inspired by Jane Austen's *Pride and Prejudice. Laura y el ángel* [Laura and the Angel] (n.d.). *La sacristía: comedia dramática en tres actos* [The Sacristy: Drama in Three Acts] (1957). Novels: *Historia de una niña* [History of a Girl] (n.d.). *El sobrino* [The Nephew](n.d.).

Bibliography

Conde, C., *Poesía femenina española viviente* (1954). Miró, E., "Poetisas españolas contemporáneas." *Revista de la Universidad Complutense* XXIV, No. 95 (enero-febrero 1975): 271–310. *Women Writers of Spain*, ed. C. Galerstein (1986).

Paula T. Irvin

María Elvira Lacaci

*Born 1934, El Ferrol del Caudillo, Galicia,
    Spain*
Genre(s): poetry, short story
Language(s): Spanish

From a family of mariners, Lacaci now lives in Madrid. She is married to the novelist Miguel Buñuel. Although she has written a number of brief narratives, she is best known as a poet. Her style has been described as very intuitive rather than formal or traditional, the result of a somewhat limited literary education.

The source of much of her poetry is her own personal and subjective experiences, particularly in a collection like *Humana voz* (1957), which was awarded the Premio Adonais, and *Sonido de Dios* (1962), in which she revealed the restlessness of a religious spirit longing for inner peace and equilibrium. In the poetry in which more objective elements seem to dominate, Lacaci may be termed a realist but without any socialist influences. The sorrow and anguish she reveals in the face of the wretched spectacle of poverty are a reflection of her own sensitivity and Christian beliefs.

Works

Humana voz (1957). *Sonido de Dios* (1962). *Al este de la ciudad* (1963). *Molinillo de papel.*

Bibliography

Cano, José Luis, *Antología de la nueva poesía española*, 3rd ed. (Madrid, 1968). *Diccionario de la literatura española.* Vol I, Autores (Barcelona, 1975). Torrente Ballester, G., *Panorama de la literatura española contemporánea*, 3rd ed. (Madrid, 1965).

Carol Stos

Cristina Lacasa

Born 1929, Tarrasa, Spain
Genre(s): poetry, short story
Language(s): Spanish

Lacasa writes testimonial poetry that is among the most significant of contemporary Spain, in spite of her lack of association with any particular generational group of writers. Her verse is profoundly lyrical in nature, and she is conscious of her insistent demand for peace and brotherhood. In addition to decrying the injustice and sorrow of human life, she also gives voice to the hope within the soul of humankind, and the limitless joy of human experience. Lacasa's works have been considered for several literary prizes, and she was awarded the "Ciudad de Barcelona" prize for Castilian Poetry in 1964 for her collection entitled *Poemas de la muerte y de la vida* (Poems of Death and Life).

Works

Poetry: *La voz oculta* [The Hidden Voice] (1953). *Los brazos en estela* [Trailing Arms] (1958). *Un resplandor que no perdonó la noche* [Splendor Unforgiven by the Night] (1961). *Con el sudor alzado* [With Raised Sweat] (1964). *Poemas de la muerte y de la vida* [Poems of Death and Life] (1966). *Encender los olivos como lámparas* [Light the Olive Trees Like Lamps] (1969). *Ha llegado la hora* [The Time Has Come] (1971). *Opalos del instante* [Opals of the Moment] (1982). *En un plural designio* [In a Plural Design] (1983). *Ramas de la esperanza* [Branches of Hope] (1984). Short Stories: *Jinetes sin caballo* [Riders Without Horses] (1979). *Los caballos sin bridas* [Horses Without Reins] (1981).

Bibliography

Women Writers of Spain, ed. C. Galerstein (1986). Miró, E., "Poetisas españolas contemporáneas." *Revista de la Universidad Complutense* XXIV, No. 95 (enero-febrero 1975): 271–310.

Paula T. Irvin

Claire (Rose) Lacombe

Born March 4, 1765, Ariège, France; died (?)
Genre(s): political and feminist pamphlets,
speeches
Language(s): French

Claire Lacombe, known as "Red Rosa" for her radical social and economic ideas, was one of the most active and vocal feminists of the French Revolution. Nothing is known about her early life except she was an actress in southern France before she arrived in Paris in 1792. She was soon affiliated with the radical Enragés, including Théophile Leclerc, a journalist and deputy from Lyon, with whom she lived. Her first public appearance was before the Legislative Assembly in July 1792; she demanded that Lafayette be replaced as French Chief of Staff and that women be allowed to serve the nation in the same capacity as men: "abolish the privileges of the male sex. . . . Thirteen million slaves are shamefully dragging the chains of thirteen million despots," she declared. Women should be armed to fight in defense of *la patrie* and crush counterrevolution at home; most deputies scoffed at these would-be "grenadiers in greasy skirts." That women could fight was proven on August 10, 1792 when Lacombe, at the head of a male corps of Fédéres, stormed the Tuileries Palace in Paris; this bloody attack by enemies of monarchy overthrew the King. Lacombe was wounded and received a civic crown from the government. To educate women about their rights and role in the new France, Lacombe and several other feminists founded the Society of Revolutionary Republican Woman (May 1793) which eventually claimed 170 members. These women were to be at least eighteen years old, virtuous and of good moral character. It was the first club organized for lower class women with an interest in their concerns such as adequate food supplies and inflation. Lacombe was committed to bettering their lives through pressure on the government. The Society was partially responsible for the victory of the Montagnards in 1793, but a rift among members soon diminished their effectiveness. Lacombe was secretary, then president of the Society, and she favored the more radical Enragés over the Montagnards and the Jacobins.

Under her leadership the club demanded that women be allowed in the military, that national workshops be established, and all nobles be excluded from public office. The radicalism of many feminists alienated the working class women whom they were trying to organize and lead. Dissension over wearing the cockade and dressing in trousers and the caps of liberty caused an irreparable breach in the Society. When the Jacobins consolidated their power, Lacombe and others were targeted as enemies of the state. Lacombe especially disliked Robespierre and accused him of being a coward and an "ordinary man." Moreover, the market women of Paris sided with the Jacobins and petitioned the National Convention to abolish the Society. On October 28, 1793, members of the club were attacked by a mob of market women at their meeting hall in Saint-Eustache. This marked the end of the feminist movement in France—the Jacobins disbanded all women's clubs. The women were ordered to return to their homes and their traditional roles as wives and mothers.

Lacombe was a victim of the very women she hoped to aid and of the Jacobins' anti-feminism. She was accused of being a counter-revolutionary and of immorality (for living with Leclerc), arrested on April 2, 1794, and imprisoned. By 1795 women were barred from attending meetings of the assembly and lost their right to organize clubs and petition the government. The activist revolutionary women were silenced. When she was released from prison on August 20, 1795, Lacombe became a proprietress of a tobacco shop before resuming her acting career and fading into obscurity. The efforts of Lacombe and others on behalf of women's rights failed to win the support of the leading revolutionaries, but in the nineteenth century they were lauded for their attacks on aristocratic and middle-class privilege and their efforts on behalf of the working class.

Works

Discours prononcé à la barre de l'Assemblée nationale par Madame Lacombe, le 25 juillet 1792, l'an 4, de la liberté (n.d.). Rapport fait par la Citoyenne Lacombe à la Société des républicaines révolutionaires [sic] de qui s'est passé le 16 septembre à la Société des Jacobins concernant celle des Républicaines révolutionaires [sic] séante à S. Eustache; et les dénonciations faites contre la Citoyenne Lacombe personnellement (n.d.).

Bibliography

Archives nationales, F⁷ 4756, dossier 2 (Claire Lacombe). Aulard, F.-A., *La Société des Jacobins: Recueil de documents pour l'histoire du Club des Jacobins de Paris*, 6 vols. (1889–1897). Cerati, Marie, *Le Club des citoyennes républicaines révolutionnaires* (1966). Lacour, Leopold, *Trois femmes de la Révolution . . . Claire Lacombe* (1900). Latour, Thérèse-Louis, *Princesses, Ladies, and Republicans of the Terror* (1930). Levy, Darline G. et al., *Women in Revolutionnary Paris, 1789–1795* (1979). *Réglement de la Société des citoyennes républicaines révolutionnaires de Paris* (n.d.). Roussel, Pierre-J.-A., *Le Château des Tuileries*, vol. 2 (1802). Sokolnikova, Galina O., *Nine Women: Drawn from the Epoch of the French Revolution* (1969). Whale, Winifred Stephens, *Women of the French Revolution* (1922).

Jeanne A. Ojala

Monique Laederach

Born 1938, Les Brenets, Switzerland
Genre(s): poetry, novel, drama, translation
Language(s): French

The Swiss-French writer Monique Laederach was born in Les Brenets, near Neuchâtel. She studied at the Music Conservatory of Neuchâtel, then, in 1960–1961, at the Academy of Music in Vienna. She has taught since 1962 and completed studies in modern languages at the Université de Neuchâtel in 1974. Active in literary, publishing, political, and various media groups from 1958 onwards, she published her first book in 1970. Apart from her poetry and, more recently, her novels, she has prepared a good number of translations from the German, done some musical composition, and written numerous pieces of theatre for radio, television, and the stage.

L'Etain la source (1970; Spring Pewter) is a beautifully intense reflection on death and desire, loss and memory. A book of mourning like other poetic collections to come, it wrestles with the tensions of revolt and consent, grief and song, presence and the unconscious, the need both for continuing attachment and personal renewal.

Pénélope (1971) takes up the above meditation and centers it on the emblematic myth of Penelope and her absent Ulysses. It is a poem of fidelity in death, elaborating in measured poetic prose the earlier obsessions. *Pénélope*, however, delves further into the problematics of language, its place of tombal memory, closure, ambivalence, and hollowed beauty.

Monique Laederach's next-but-one collection, *J'habiterai mon nom* (1977; I Shall Inhabit My Name), takes not only its dedication but also its title from Perse. It is written at the intersection of self-questioning and affirmation, deprivation, and desire. Language, then, is both fraught with vulnerability and filled with possibility, and the volume is the long poem of a threshold consciousness. In a not dissimilar way, *Jusqu'à ce que l'été devienne ma chambre . . .* (1978; Until Summer Becomes My Room) is a poem of expectation and spiritual traversal demanding an effort to live with the slowly spreading bounds of song.

1982 saw the publication both of *La Femme séparée* (The Separated Woman), the first fully fledged novel of Monique Laederach, and of *La Partition*, her latest collection of poems. Both books demonstrate new awakening, burgeoning consciousness and energy. *La Femme séparée* depicts a young woman's search for her identity, for the establishment of a specifically feminine locus, and the emotional and spiritual firmness of this woman's (re)discovery of the difficulties and the freedoms of her adult separateness. Somewhat related factors are explored also in Monique Laederach's latest novel, *Trop petits pour Dieu* (1986; Too Small for God) which, while complicated by the war context, remains centered upon a woman's fragile sense of becoming, thrust willingly or unwillingly up against the others. *La Partition* (The Score) is a collection that tells of new adaptations; of sensitive, profound, and felt feminism; of questions of the body: its "wealth" and its distortion; of the horrors and the waste of misogyny; of the ownership and identity of the female self; of the role of language in all of this. It seems to offer a radical break, on the surface, with the early poetry, and certainly the collection is more publicly combative. But, essentially, the lines of continuity of purpose and emotion remain quite visible in this powerful and original writer.

Works

Poetry: *L'Etain la source* (1970). *Pénélope* (1971). *La Ballade des faméliques baladins de la Grande*

Tanière (1974). *J'habiterai mon nom* (1977). *Jusqu'à ce que l'été devienne une chambre*, ill. de Raymond l'Epée (1978). *La Partition* (1982).

Novels: *Stéphanie* (1978). *La Femme séparée* (1978). *Trop petits pour Dieu* (1986).

Bibliography

Bevan, David, "Monique Laederach." *La Littérature romande en vingt entretiens*, Coll. "Ecrivains d'aujourd'hui." (Lausanne, 1986), pp. 111–119. Bofford, Jacques, "Monique Laederach: *La Femme séparée*." *Magazine Littéraire* 189 (nov. 1982): 47. Brindeau, Serge, "Monique Laederach." *La Poésie contemporaine de langue française depuis 1954* (Paris, 1973), pp. 343–344. Fauré, Gabrielle, "Des poèmes de Monique Laederach." *Tribune de Genève* (sept. 1977). Garzarelli, Richard, "Monique Laederach: *Ballade des faméliques baladins de la grande tanière*." *Tribune de Lausanne* (May, 1974). Jakubec, Doris, "Monique Laederach: comment concilier liberté et don de soi." *Gazette de Lausanne* (March, 1979). Jakubec, Doris, "Monique Laederach (Prix Schiller 1977): une méditation très personnelle sur le mystère de l'identité." *Journal de Genève* (1977). K., J.-L, "*J'habiterai mon nom* par Monique Laederach." *Construire* (Switzerland) (nov. 1977): 11. "Monique Laederach: *La Partition*." *Verso* (Lyon) (1983). Pache, Jean, "Monique Laederach." *24 heures* (Switzerland) (oct. 1977). Z., J.J. "La poétesse Monique Laederach: Plainchant d'amour." *Construire* (oct. 1978).

Michael Bishop

María de los Reyes Lafitte y Pérez del Pulgar

(a.k.a. Condesa de Campo Alange)

Born 1902, Sevilla, Spain
Genre(s): short story, essay, criticism, biography, memoirs
Language(s): Spanish

Born to an aristocratic family, Lafitte resided in her native Sevilla until her marriage in 1922 to the Count of Campo Alange, a Grandee of Spain. Later (1931–1934), she and her husband lived in Paris, where she studied art and art history, leading to her first book, a critical biography of the painter María Blanchard. Campo Alange's contributions to art history and criticism have been recognized with membership in several academies of art and of literature. She is equally well known as a historian and sociologist of Spanish women and essayist on feminist themes.

La guerra secreta de los sexos (1948; The Secret War Between the Sexes), Campo Alange's second book-length essay, presents a study of women throughout history. As philosophical as it is historical, the work emphasizes feminine psychology and examines woman's position in society throughout the ages as well as her relationship with and reactions toward men. *De Altamira a Hollywood* (1953; From Altamira to Hollywood) and *La magia natural en Velázquez* (1960; Natural Magic in Velazquez) both belong to her work in the area of aesthetics and art history.

La flecha y la esponja (1959; The Arrow and the Sponge) is a short story collection whose title evinces the author's awareness of Freudian symbolism. The seven tales provide a fictional development of themes introduced in *The Secret War Between the Sexes*, presented via emotional and sexual elements that become symbols of masculine and feminine characteristics of the present age. With her personal style and gifted use of irony as well as her creation of dramatic effects and sensitive interpretations of feminine psychology, Campo Alange stands almost alone in the feminist short story of this period. Sexual conflicts are recreated with imagination and sensitivity, with certain unexpected problems verging upon the pathological.

Additional important feminist essays by Campo Alange include *La mujer como mito y como ser humano* (1961; Woman as Myth and as Human Being) and *La mujer en España, cien años de su historia (1860–1960)* (1963; Woman in Spain: One Hundred Years of History, 1860–1960), in which Spanish womanhood becomes the subject of a study whose focus is both historical and literary. The writer utilizes articles, interviews, letters, published and unpublished memoirs, polls, statistics, and even oral tradition in her attempt to reconstruct feminine social and cultural evolution, always with emphasis upon the collective rather than the individual phenomena. *Concepción Arenal 1820–1893*, also of interest for women's studies, is a detailed biography of Spain's pioneering feminist, underscoring Arenal's work for reform of the penitentiary system and her activities as educator and novelist.

Mi atardecer entre dos mundos: Memorias y cavilaciones (1983; My Twilight Between Two Worlds: Memoirs and Doubts) continues the autobiographical memoir begun in *Mi niñez y su mundo (1906–1917)* (1956; My Childhood and Its World). Campo Alange portrays her adolescence in Sevilla, her marriage and subsequent move to Madrid, stays in Paris and Biarritz and return to Spain following the Civil War. Her personal and public life thereafter, especially her cultural activities and acquaintance with prominent intellectual, artistic and literary personalities of the day, is the basis of incisive judgments of Spanish cultural currents and figures to which Campo Alange has been a witness.

Several sources refer to novels by Campo Alange, but none have been located; Spanish printings are characteristically very small and usually go out of print rapidly even in the case of more or less successful works. Campo Alange's significance is perhaps more sociological and psychological than purely literary in the belletristic sense of imaginative creation, but her skilled handling of the relationship of the sexes and sensitive interpretation of feminine emotions stand apart as a distinctive contribution to Spain's short fiction.

Works

Concepción Arenal 1820–1893(1973). De Altamira a Hollywood (1953). La flecha y la esponja (1959). María Blanchard (1944). Metamorphosis del arte (1953). Mi atardecer entre dos mundos: Memorias y cavilaciones (1983). Mi niñez y su mundo (1906–1917) (1956). La mujer en España, cien años de su historia 1860–1960 (1963–64). La mujer como mito y como ser humano (1961). La poética ingenuidad de Papi Sánchez (1959). La secreta guerra de los sexos (1958).

Bibliography

General references: *Women Writers of Spain*, ed. C.L. Galerstein (Westport, CT, 1986).

Janet Perez

Carmen Laforet

Born 1921, Barcelona, Spain
Genre(s): novel, short story
Language(s): Spanish

Carmen Laforet grew up and lived in the Canary Islands until after the Spanish Civil War when she went to study law in Barcelona and Madrid. She became an instant celebrity when at 22 years of age she won the first Nadal Prize of 1944 for her novel *Nada* (Nothing). She married Manuel Cerezales, a journalist, and they had five children. She visited the United States in 1965, and presently she lives in Rome.

Laforet has written four novels, many short stories and several short novels. Most of them deal with life in Spain in the "posguerra" years and in particular with the woman's place in society. *Nada*, 1945, is told in first person by Andrea, a young girl going to Barcelona in the 1940s to study and live with her strange, violent relatives. Despite some melodramatic scenes, this novel is Laforet's best and, by far, the most studied. Several interpretations are possible: as a *Bildüngsroman* or as an initiation story, and as a mythical fairy tale; a feminist perspective as well as a social or psychological approaches are valid. Its interest lies in the complexity of the characters and the ability to capture a crucial time in Spanish life. This novel has been translated into many languages, including English (*Andrea* by Charles F. Payne, 1964).

Roberta Johnson studies her three other novels together: *La isla y los demonios* (1952; The Island and the Devils), *La mujer nueva* (1955; The New Woman), and *La insolación* (1963; Sunstroke), because they have many common characteristics. Marta, the protagonist of the first of these novels, is an adolescent would-be writer who suffers some changes when her relatives join her family in the Canary Islands during the Spanish Civil War.

Paulina, an adult married woman, converts to Catholicism in *La mujer nueva* after a mystical experience. This novel, which received the "Premio Menorca," is somewhat more complex structurally than Laforet's previous novels with effective use of the flashback technique to cover from the 1930s—during the Spanish Republic— to the 1950s in the midst of Franco's regime. A strong current of social criticism permeates this novel as well as a disapproving view of Catholic Spain.

La insolación is the first volume of the trilogy Tres pasos fuera del tiempo (Three Steps Out of Time) which was never finished and the only novel by Laforet told from a masculine perspective. Martín is a complex adolescent who, like Andrea of Nada, seeks his self-identity in the midst of uncaring relatives. In fact, these three novels share with the award-winning Nada the theme of loneliness and isolation as well as similar family structures that affect the development of the young protagonists.

Most of Carmen Laforet's short works collected in La muerta (1952; The Dead Woman) and La llamada (1954; The Call), are interesting because of their feminist themes. Some of the best known—"La muerta," "Rosamunda," "El veraneo" (The Summer Vacation), "Un matrimonio" (A Marriage), "El regreso" (The Homecoming), "La fotografía" (The Photograph), "Al colegio" (Off to School), "En la edad del pato" (The Awkward Age), "Un noviazgo" (An Engagement) and "El piano" (The Piano)—are also included in the first volume of her Novelas (1977).

Although Laforet's production has been considered to be of uneven quality, she had a prominent role in the development of the Spanish novel during the "posguerra" generation. Roberta Johnson points out her influence in the female novelists who followed her, not only because of the impact of winning the first Nadal prize but because of the representation of diverse female characters. Her insight into the psychological development of the families who grow up in the repressed society of Franco's Spain is most valuable as well.

All of the translations of Carmen Laforet's works into different languages—Nada in particular—are not easily traced and are not included in the bibliography.

Works

Nada (Barcelona: Destino, 1945). La isla y los demonios (1952). La muerta (1952). La llamada (1954). La mujer nueva (1955). La insolación (1963). La niña y otros relatos [The Young Girl and Other Narratives] (1970) Un noviazgo, ed. Carolyn L. Galerstein (1973).

Bibliography

Alborg, Juan Luis, Hora actual de la novela española. Vol. I (Madrid, 1958). Cerezales, Agustín, Carmen Laforet (Madrid, 1982). Feal Deibe, Carlos, "Nada de Carmen Laforet: la iniciación de una adolescente," in Analysis of Hispanic Texts: Current Trends in Methodology, ed. by Mary Ann Beck et al. (New York, 1976), pp. 221–241. Glenn, Kathleen M., "Animal Imagery in Nada." Revista de Estudios Hispánicos 11 (1977): pp. 381–394. Illanes Adaro, Graciela, La novelística de Carmen Laforet (Madrid, 1971). Jones, Margaret E.W., "Dialectical Movement as Feminist Technique in the Works of Carmen Laforet." Studies in Honor of Gerald E. Wade (Madrid, 1979), pp. 109–120. Newberry, Wilma, "The Solstitial Holidays in Carmen Laforet's Nada: Christmas and Mid Summer." Romance Notes 17 (1976): 76–81. Ordóñez, Elizabeth, "Nada: Initiation into Bourgeois Patriarchy," in Analysis of Hispanic Texts: Current Trends in Methodology, ed. by Mary Ann Beck et al. (New York 1976), pp. 61–78. Spires, Robert C., "La experiencia afirmadora de Nada." La novela española de posquera (Madrid, 1978), pp. 51–73. Thomas, Michael D., "Symbolic Portals in Laforet's Nada." Anales de la Novela de Posguerra 3 (1978): 57–74. Villegas, Juan, "Nada de Carmen Laforet o la infantilización de la aventura legendaria." La estructura mítica del hérde (Barcelona, 1973), pp. 177–201.

Concha Alborg

Gina Lagorio

Born 1930, Bra (Cuneo), Italy
Genre(s): criticism, novel, journalism, drama, children's literature
Language(s): Italian

Born in the Piedmont region, Gina Lagorio lived many years in Liguria, where she taught Italian literature and history in Savona. The wife of publisher Livio Garzanti, she now lives in Milan, where she collaborates with the national broadcasting system, RAI, and writes for many newspapers and journals.

Lagorio's career as an essayist began with a study of the correspondence of the critic Renato Serra (1966) and a book on neo-realist Beppe Fenoglio (1970), followed by separate studies on poets Camillo Sbarbaro and Angelo Barile (1973). She later returned to the Ligurian poet Sbarbaro, writing his biography, which was published in 1981 and awarded the prize for criticism, "Città di Messina." She has written plays and children's books, but is best known as a novelist. Her first novel, *Un ciclone chiamato Titti* (1969; A Cyclone called Titti), tells the story of a middle-class family surprised by the birth of a child when the parents are getting on in years and do not expect one. As is true of her later novels, this work reveals great psychological richness and sensitivity to everyday surroundings.

Lagorio's 1971 novel, *Approssimato per difetto* (Failing All Else), is the story of a man dying of a malignant tumor. Both he and his wife narrate his internal struggle, he during his illness, his wife after his death. Her third novel, *La spiaggia del lupo* (Wolf's Beach) paints a vivid portrait of the Italian Riviera, both as it is remembered by the female protagonist and as it has become in the wake of tourism and pollution. In *Fuori scena* (1979; Offstage), Lagorio's protagonist is a famous actress who discovers that solitude is a mature choice rather than merely an anguishing burden. Her 1983 novel, *Tosca dei gatti* (Tosca of the Cats), which won the "Viareggio" literary prize, recounts the life of a solitary "cat lady" whose story is told by a journalist. As he writes about Tosca, he becomes more and more drawn into her reality and better understands the importance of every individual's truth, no matter how humble. Lagorio's latest novel, the 1987 *Golfo del Paradiso* (Gulf of Paradise), is set once more on the Italian Riviera, and has as protagonist an old painter named Michele.

Lagorio's fiction is in the tradition of realistic prose, which seeks to capture both the external and internal details of life as it is lived. It is marked, moreover, by great psychological subtlety and is imbued with the author's obvious belief in the power of fiction to communicate and enrich the reader's understanding of the lives of others. Often indirectly autobiographical in inspiration, Lagorio's works go beyond mere confession or self-analysis, attaining the richness and variety of authentic narrative art.

Works

Narrative: *Il polline* (1966). *Un ciclone chiamato Titti* [A Cyclone called Titti] (1969). *Approssimato*

per difetto [Failing All Else] (1971, 1976). *La spiaggia del lupo* [Wolf's Beach] (1977). *Fuori scena* [Offstage] (1979, 1980). *Tosca dei gatti* [Tosca of the Cats] (1983). *Golfo del paradiso* (1987).

Books for Children: *Le novelle di Simonetta* (1960). *Attila re degli Unni* (1964). *Qualcosa nell'aria* (1975). *Schitimiro e Mamma Nasella* (1980). *Giotto, la storia di Gesù* (1982). *La terra negli occhi* (1984).

Scholarly Works: *L'espistolario di Serra* (1966). *Fenoglio* (1970). *Cultura e letteratura ligure del '900* (1972). *Sbarbaro controcorrente* (1973). *Sui racconti di Sbarbaro* (1973). *Angelo Barile o la poesia dell'intima transparenza* (1973). *Sbarbaro, un modo spoglio di esistere* (1981).

Journalism: *Penelope senza tela*, Franco Mollia, ed. (1984).

Bibliography

Farina, Lorenza, "Gina Lagorio, scrittrice di sentimenti e di personaggi." *Letture* 40 (1985): 691–708. Frassica, Pietro, "Gina Lagorio and Tosca's Solitude." *Italica* 4 (1988): 329–343. Merola, Nicola, "Per Gina Lagorio." *Letteratura ultima scorsa* (Naples, 1984). Mollia, Franco, "Tosca dei gatti: Un romanzo compromettente di Gina Lagorio." *Il lettore di provincia* 57–58 (1984): 80–83. Ruffilli, Paolo, "La scrittura al femminile di Gina Lagorio." *Il lettore di provincia* 49–50 (1982): 82–87.

General references: Luti, Giorgio, ed., *Narratori italiani del secondo Novecento: la vita, le opere, la critica* (Rome, 1985). Manacorda, Giorgio, *Storia della letteratura italiana contemporanea* (Rome, 1977).

Rebecca West

Concha Lagos

(a.k.a. Concepción Gutiérrez Torrero)

Born 1909, Córdoba, Spain
Genre(s): poetry, novel, short story
Language(s): Spanish

Concha Lagos, born Concepción Gutiérrez Torrero, belongs both by birth and by poetic tradition to the Andalusian School of personal poetry (as opposed to such major movements as the Spanish "Generation of 1927" [vanguardists], or the "Mid-Century Generation" or postwar "social" poets). Lagos came rather late to poetry and to literature, first entering Madrid's literary scene in the mid 1950s, when she was associated with well-known poets and critics including Gerardo Diego, José Hierro, Jorge Campos, and José García Nieto. She became important in the publishing field, founding the journal *Cuadernos de Agora* (1956–1964), which was a major outlet for poetic creativity and criticism, and the "Colección Agora," one of relatively few specialized series open to poets.

The first collection by Lagos, *Balcón* (1954; Balcony), consists of 59 brief poems on such traditional themes as love, nature, and philosophical inquiry. In the same year, she published one of her rare prose collections, *El pantano (del diario de una mujer)* (The Swamp [From a Woman's Diary]). The forty-nine brief, lyric fragments recount the impact on the writer—an Andalusian woman like the poet—of life on Spain's boggy northern coast. The collection constitutes an early indication of Lagos' interest in women's perspectives and sensibilities. *Los obstáculos* (1955; Obstacles), two dozen short rhythmic lyrics, presents a more disillusioned attitude, somewhat offset by the lighter vein found in *Al sur del recuerdo* (1955; To the South of Memory), a short novel in fragments, much like the earlier prose collection, which evokes the author's youth in Andalusia, drawing upon her memories of villagers, animals, and a more unspoiled nature. *El corazón cansado* (1957; The Weary Heart) utilizes the unpretentious style and quotidian vocabulary characteristic of Spanish social poets of the day to comment upon women's roles and special perceptions, deepening the emphasis on the feminine perspective already perceived in Lagos' early prose.

This poet is fond of trilogies, and *Arroyo claro* (1958; Clear Stream) is part of a trilogy whose titles and images emphasize water symbolism (the associations with time, with purification and transformation), also including *Agua de Dios* (1958; Water of God), a brief and somber collection which emphasizes the theme of children, and *Canciones desde la barca* (1962; Songs from the Boat), in which the sailing motif prevails as a metaphor for the journey of life. *Campo abierto* (1959; Open Field) is dedicated to eleven poets of the Mid-Century Generation and may be considered Lagos' closest approach to the social

poetry movement. It is also a collection dealing with poetics in which the nature of poetry becomes a major focus. *Luna de enero* (1960; January Moon) centers upon the sentiment that remains after renunciation of a passionate love, while *Tema fundamental* (1961; Fundamental Theme) traces the theme of spiritual growth through the stage of religious plenitude.

Golpeando el silencio (1961; Striking the Silence) is one of two works by Lagos published outside Spain, in Caracas, perhaps because the Spanish censors did not authorize printing in Spain. It includes elegies to a group of exiled poets (who were political anathema to the regime) and a leader of the opposition poets within Spain, Gabriel Celaya. While the compositions themselves are not "protest poetry," Lagos undoubtedly intended some statement of solidarity with the poets who opposed the regime more openly and actively than she. This is not necessarily her best or most typical collection, but it is one of the few that contains a useful introduction to the poet and a study of her work by Manuel Mantero, another poet in exile. *Para empezar* (1963; To Begin) is a collection of miscellany which includes a reprinting of *Campo abierto*.

In *Los anales* (1966; Annals), the poet returns to religious themes, treating mysteries of Christianity, faith and despair, the anguish of mortality, and the theological virtues. Deep seriousness and maturity contrast with the simplicity and down-to-earth style of *La vida y otros sueños* (1969; Life and Other Dreams), a collection of sixteen narrative vignettes treating everyday life in Spanish villages or the existences of other simple people, including the young. The tranquility prevailing is in contrast to the melancholy questioning and reflection of human foibles and deficiencies that appears in her next poetic collection, *Diario de un hombre* (1970; Diary of a Man). *El cerco* (1971; The Fence) repeats the theme of human shortcomings and defects but introduces the concept of the poet as prophet, a role made necessary by mortal limitations. It initiates another trilogy, which includes *La aventura* (1973; Adventure) and *Fragmentos en espiral desde el pozo* (1974; Spiral Fragments from the Wellspring), works in which the poet continues to develop the themes of human defects and shortcomings, as well as to treat the religious quest theme and a search for vaguer metaphysical origins.

Gótico florido (1976; Flowering Gothic) evokes architectural features with varied historical associations as a point of departure for more transcendent metaphysical reflections and an undercurrent of existentialist concerns. In *Elegías para un álbum* (1982; Elegies for an Album), the poetic pretext is a family album whose photographs—figures from the past—are revived to create intersecting time planes in which nostalgia blends with the poet's metaphysical and existential concern with time. *Teoría de la inseguridad* (Theory of Insecurity) and *Por las ramas* (Along the Branches), both published in 1980, employ the extended metaphor of life as a journey, already present in the earliest collections but with increased emphasis on the presence of God—a silent God, the object of impassioned search—as essential to the voyage. Returning to an earlier theme somewhat unexpectedly, Lagos ends this collection with the portrayal of woman as an unheeded prophet. *La paloma* (1982; The Dove), a collection of traditional songs, is divided into five sections, each with a common theme.

Although little criticism exists on her work, Lagos is among the most prolific and best-known of Spain's living women poets. Her nearly thirty works offer both depth and breadth, and she is definitely worthy of study. *Antología 1954–1976/ Concha Lagos* (1976), an anthology with selections representing all works up to and including *Gótico florido*, provides the best introduction, and includes a useful prologue by Emilio Miró.

Works

Agua de Dios (1958). Al sur del recuerdo (1955). Los anales (1966). Arroyo claro (1958). La aventura (1973). Balcón (1954). Campo abierto (1959). Canciones desde la barca (1962). El corazón cansado (1957). El cerco (1971). Diario de un hombre (1970). Elegías para un álbum (1982). Fragmentos en espiral desde el pozo (1974). Golpeando el silencio (1961). Gótico florido (1976). Luna de enero (1960). Los obstáculos (1955). La paloma (1982). El pantano (diario de una mujer) (1954). Para empezar (1963). Por las ramas (1980). La soledad de siempre (1958). Tema fundamental (1961). Teoría de la inseguridad (1980). La vida y otros sueños (1969).

Janet Perez

Catherine Meurdrac de La Guette

Born February 20, 1613, Mandres en Brie, France; died ca. 1680, The Netherlands (?)

Genre(s): memoir
Language(s): French

All that is known about Madame de La Guette comes from her memoirs. Their authenticity, however, is beyond question, and scholars have been able to verify many of the events and persons mentioned there. She was born in Normandy in 1613 and married in 1635, without her father's knowledge or consent, to one captain Jean Marius (or Mariot) de La Guette, by whom she had ten children. Madame de La Guette describes in precise and sober language, sometimes reminiscent of that of her contemporary Madame de Lafayette, her own life, particularly her experiences during the Fronde (1649–1653). Although she was loyal to the King—"une mazarine"—her husband was in the service of the Prince du Condé. Scholars have cast doubt on her role in the negotiations conducted between Louis XIV and the princes in 1653, but her account of the events she witnessed during the Fronde, which takes up over half of her memoirs, is nevertheless both vivid and immediate. She was conscious of how unusual it was for a woman to write of her own experiences, remarking at the beginning of her work:

> Ce n'est pas une chose fort extraordinaire de voir les histoires des hommes qui, par leurs beaux faits ou par leurs vertus éminentes, se sont rendus recommendables à la posterité ou qui ont été élevés ou abaissés selon les caprices de la fortune; mais il se trouve peu de femmes qui s'avisent de mettre au jour ce qui leur est arrivé dans leur vie. Je serai de ce petit nombre.
> [It is not very extraordinary to see the histories of men, who, by their great deeds or outstanding virtues have commended themselves to posterity or who have been raised or lowered according to the whims of fortune, but there are few women who have striven

to bring to light what has happened to them in life. I will be one of this small number.]

Her work also speaks eloquently of her deep love for her husband. She resented their separations and often chose to share his military life. In fact, her attachment to such a "masculine" sphere had prompted some (male) scholars to have their doubts regarding the authenticity of the memoirs. This "virago" herself noted:

En effet j'ai toujours été d'une humeur plus portée à la guerre qu'aux exercices tranquilles de mettre les poules à couver et de filer la quenouille, quoique l'on dise qu'une femme ne doit savoir que cela. [In fact I have always been more inclined to war than to the tranquil exercises of putting the hens in their nests and spinning at the distaff, although it is said that a woman should only know these things.]

Works

Mémoires, escrits par elle-meme (1681). Her memoirs have been reedited three times since, in 1856 by M. Moreau; in 1929 by Pierre Viguié; and in 1982 by Michéline Cuénin. They have never been translated into English.

Bibliography

Freudmann, Félix, *The Memoirs of Madame de La Guette, A Study* (Geneva/Paris, 1957).

Earl Jeffrey Richards

Maria Laina

Born 1947, Athens, Greece
Genre(s): poetry
Language(s): Greek

Maria Laina lives in Athens. She has published five books of poetry, beginning with her 1968 collection, *Enēlikiosē* (Coming of Age).

Laina attracted attention very early, for her writing showed unusual depth and sensitivity. Her poems are short (sometimes too short) and prosaic. In fact, many of them (including most of the ones in *Sēmeia stixeōs*) are prose-poems. There is a lightness about her poetry, but her language is metaphorical, and her meanings more complex than one would suspect at first.

All the poems in *Allagē topiou* revolve around the general subject of love. There is no perceptible movement within this collection, however, and thus many of the poems become repetitive and monotonous. In many cases there is a lack of cohesiveness. The best poems in the collection are the last seven beginning with "Gia dyo phōnes kai tampourlo" (For Two Voices and a Drum). In these poems Laina succeeds in blending imagery and theme and achieves a unified vision.

Love (eros) and death (thanatos) are Laina's major preoccupations, and she deals with the latter extensively in *Epekeina* and *Sēmeia stixeōs*. Her death poems are quiet reflections on a topic that "makes the words heavier" (*Epekeina*).

Diko tēs (Hers) is her most mature work in both design and execution although it lacks the spontaneous insights of her earlier poetry. The persona traces the life of a woman in eight stages, beginning with the youthful awakening to love and ending with the eventual loss of love and "death." Referring to this woman as Maria, which is also the name of the poet, the persona appears to be pointing to the autobiographical nature of this work while suggesting that the poet is at the same time attempting to distance herself from this "other" person.

Works

Enēlikiosē [Coming of Age] (1968) *Epekeina* [Beyond] (1970). *Allagē topiou* [Change of Scenery] (1975). *Sēmeia Stixeōs* [Punctuation Marks] (1979). *Diko tēs* [Hers] (1985).

Translations: *Twenty Contemporary Greek Poets*, ed. Dinos Siotis and John Chioles (1979).

Bibliography

Decavalles, Andonis, "Modernity: The Third Stage, the New Poets." *The Charioteer* 20 (New York, 1958). Frangopoulos, Th., Review. *Books Abroad. Bulletin analytique de bibliographie hellènique, 1970.* Vol. 46. (Athens, 1973), p. 525. Rexine, J.E., Review. *World Literature Today* 55, 1: 158.

Helen Dendrinou Kolias

Natasha Lako

Born May 13, 1948, Koçë, Albania
Genre(s): poetry, novel
Language(s): Albanian

Lako is one of the best-known women writers of the younger generation in Albania, particularly as a poetess. She studied at the University of Tiranë, concentrating on journalism. On last report, she was working at the "New Albania" Film Studios in Tiranë.

Works

Marsi brenda nesh [March Within Us] (1972). *E para fjalë e botës* [The World's First Word] (1979). *Këmisha e pranverës* [The Spring Shirt] (1984). She has also published a novel, *Stinët e jetës* [The Seasons of Life] (1977).

Philip Shashko

La Latina

(see: Beatriz Galindo)

Félix Lamb

(see: Jenny P. d'Héricourt)

Juliette Lamber

(see: Juliette Adam)

Anne-Therese de Marguenat de Courcelles, Marquise de Lambert

Born 1647, Paris, France; died July 12, 1733, Paris
Genre(s): essay, narrative fiction, letters
Language(s): French

Born to a family of old nobility, Lambert lost her father at an early age. Her stepfather, the amateur writer Bachaumont, encouraged her penchant for reading and reflection and urged her to keep journals of her readings. This the marquise continued to do after marriage to Henri de Lambert, marquis de Saint-Bris (1666). Al-though the son of a distinguished army commander and himself an able man, Lambert's career progressed slowly up to a final short tenure as governor of Luxembourg. Widowhood (1686) left Lambert with complicated and extended litigation to safeguard the fortunes of her two surviving children: Henri-François (b. 1677) and Marie-Thérèse (comtesse de Saint-Aulaire, 1679–1731).

Short essays like the comparison of Diogenes and Alexander published posthumously may have been written much earlier. Only three of Lambert's writings were published during her lifetime, all without her prior consent. Of these, the two *Avis d'une mère*, to his son and to her daughter, became her best known works (the former circulated widely in English translation, going through seven printings alone with the letters of Lord Chesterfield to his son). After the unauthorized publication of the letter to her son (1726), Lambert supervised the appearance of the two (1728 and republished them in Holland in 1729 under the title *Lettres sur la véritable éducation*). Both were composed at the turn of the century. Linked by the common concern of education, this time a "continuing" one, *Réflexions nouvelles sur les femmes* (1728) was published only to counter an unauthorized printing (1727; rpt. in 1729 in part as *Métaphysique de l'amour*).

Both the letters of advice to her children and the reflections on women have given Lambert a place in the early history of feminism, the so-called theoretical, élite phase, in which education had become central. The education proposed for Mlle de Lambert, like that of her brother, is pragmatic, an education whose end is happiness in the world and whose basis is self-reliance. As for the son's letter, the title given the pirated printing, "On True Glory," gives the tone. Heroism (worthy of his grandfather), however, is to be tempered by conscience and a sensitivity to humanity that adds the claims of others to those of self-worth. Although Lambert's correspondent Fénelon found ambition here to be too exalted, seemingly at the expense of religion that is nowhere literally invoked, he found nothing to criticize in that to the daughter. Religion in it is commended as guide to a woman's duties but also as consolation for the situation in which men's institutions have placed that duty. Education for an independent judgment and broad culture goes well beyond the program Fénelon had proposed. Although attention to religion here, a stoic tone, and insistence on decorum have made Lambert seem conservative, there is no doubt of her belief in the equality of women once their self-identity is achieved through proper education. The more personal and original *Réflexions*, whose program remains individual ethical feminism, convey a message of the need for reenforcement of female identity, which will come in a felt community but must first be found in individual self-esteem, consciously cultivated in terms of the positive differences of imagination, sensibility, and love that constitute that identity.

Lambert's posthumously published treatises on friendship and on old age, like her educational reflections, show continuous meditation on modern texts, on Montaigne and Descartes especially, but also on Pascal and Nicole, Malebranche, La Rochefoucauld and Saint Evremond. Her readings of Plato, the Stoics, Cicero and Horace are also direct and formative. From the writings on education, several times declared as useful to herself as to her children, through those on old age, it becomes apparent that Lambert's writing reflects a conscious shaping by the humanist tradition that strives through reflection to live fittingly and that her mind was deeply affected by Cartesian rationalism. Her single narrative fiction, *La Femme hermite*, a sustained confession by a woman of quality ("qui s'est retirée du monde"), narrates the consequences of the sin of not having reflected on life and may seem an enactment of Horace's wisdom on the vanity of travel when introspection is lacking. Lambert's embodiment of this honored tradition, in an elegant *style coupé*, drew tributes at her death (notably by Fontenelle) as it had during her lifetime frequently in her own drawingroom.

For more than two decades, after it began in 1710, Lambert's salon retained its preeminence in Parisian society. She realized in it long-held desires for good discussion. Society gathering simply for diversion was assigned one day, whereas afternoon discussions on specific topics—sometimes from prepared texts—was set for Tuesdays (in an "enlightened" development D'Alembert later praised the two soon com-

mingled to their mutual profit). Gaming and literary parlor games, like those of Mme du Maine at Sceaux, were not allowed. Nor were explicitly polemical discourses on religion and politics. Both certainly entered into discussion that was predominantly centered in moral philosophy and moved across a broad range of topics including aesthetics (with Houdar de la Motte, Du Bos), mathematics and science (Mairan, Fontenelle), and economies both political (Saint-Pierre) and hedonistic (Lassay). Playwrights like Dancourt and Marivaux, and the actress Adrienne Lecouvreur, met learned classicists like Buffier, Mongault, Louis de Sacy. And Marivaux, who left a more flattering evocation of his hostess in *La Vie de Marianne* than did the outsider Le Sage in his satirical character portrait of Marquise de Chaves, found at least one topic for a play (*La Colonie*)— and perhaps the tone for another (*La Voiture embourbée*), as did Mme. de Staal (*L'Engouement, La Mode*). Staal's accounts of the court at Sceaux and communications read from the duchesse must have caught the ear of the novelists Crébillon and Duclos, as well as Mlles La Force, Murat, Saintonge. Their worldly texts, like the *vers badins* of Chaulieu and Saint-Aulaire, refracted the Tuesdays' conversation.

In retrospect, Lambert's salon takes its place as the first of the great Enlightenment salons. Although classicists like Mme Dacier, Fraguier, Valincour were regulars, and Lambert toyed momentarily with the rôle of mediator in the Querelle des Anciens et des Modernes, her preference was for the modern. Fontenelle remained central for her, as his broad interests did for the salon. Discussing and filtering the Moderns' positions, as it were communicating with the Club de l'Entresol, Lambert's salon seemed also an "antechamber" to a renaissant Académie française. Beyond direct and fictionalized accounts of its life, Lambert's enlivening dialogue may be rediscovered in certain dialogic readings of her writings: the treatise on old age in dialogue with Sacy, her paraphrase of Montesquieu— *Discours sur la différence qu'il y a de la réputation à la considération*—as a revealing woman's rewriting that the author himself highly valued.

Works

Oeuvres (1808). *Avis d'une mère à son fils* (1726). *Réflexions nouvelles sur les femmes, par une dame* de la cour de France (1727). Avis d'une mère à son fils et à sa fille (1728). Traité de la viellesse (posth., 1747). "Réflexions sur le goût" (posth., 1747). La Femme hermite, nouvelle nouvelle (posth., 1747). "Reflexions sur les richesses" (posth., 1747). "Dialogue entre Alexandre et Diogène sur l'égalité des biens" (posth., 1747). "Discours sur la différence qu'il y a de la réputation à la considération" (posth., 1747). Lettres (posth., 1747, 1754).

Translations: The Works of the Marchioness de Lambert, tr. anon. (1749; rpt. 1769, 1781). A Mother to Her Son and Daughter: On True Education and Dialogue Between Alexander and Diogenes on the Equality of Happiness, tr. Rowell (1749). New Reflections on the Fair Sex, tr. J. Lockman (1729, 1737). Essays on Friendship and Old Age, tr. by a Lady (E.H.) (1780). The Fair Solitary, or Female Hermit, tr. anon. (1790).

Bibliography

Fassiotto, Marie-José, Madame de Lambert (1647–1733) ou le féminisme moral (1984; reprints Réflexions nouvelles). Granderoute, Robert, "Madame de Lambert et Montaigne." Bulletin de la Société des Amis de Montaigne 7–8 (1981): 97–106. "De L'Education des filles aux Avis d'une mère à sa fille: Fénelon et Mme de Lambert." Revue d'Histoire Littéraire de la France 87 (1987): 15–30. Hine, Ellen, "Madame de Lambert, Her Sources and Her Circle: on the Threshold of a New Age." Studies on Voltaire and the Eighteenth Century 102 (1973): 173–190. Hoffman, Paul, "Madame de Lambert et l'exigence de dignité." Travaux de Linguistique et de Littérature 11 (1973): 19–32. Kryssing-Berg, Ginette, "La Marquise de Lambert ou l'ambivalence de la vertu." Revue Romane 17 (1982): 35–45. Marchal, Robert, "Deux paraphrases de Madame de Lambert," In Le Génie de la forme. Mélanges de langage et de littérature offerts à Jean Mourot (1982), pp. 257–266. Zimmerman, J.-P., "La Morale laïque au commencement du XVIIIe siècle. Madame de Lambert." Revue d'Histoire Littéraire de la France 24 (1917): 42–64; 440–466.

Charles G.S. Williams

Juliette La Messine

(see: Juliette Adam)

Monique Lange

Born 1926, Paris, France
Genre(s): novel, biography
Language(s): French

Monique Lange's fiction depicts a search for self-identification and an endeavor to integrate the female personality in a world that seems generally alien. With wit as well as emotion, she shows heroines, who for the most part resemble one another strongly even if they may be at different stages in their lives, either against the background of a family in Indochina, where she spent the war years, or else in the context of their dealings with men in France, particularly in Paris, where she has pursued her career, first in publishing with Gallimard and then as a script writer. Colonial experiences, Jewishness and a haunting suspicion that bourgeois values are basically unsound in a world racked by poverty and class injustice lead her heroines, like the novelist herself, it would appear, to feel at odds with society in general and to be ill at ease in their sexual relationships in particular. Childhood is a time of questioning, as well as of discovery, and no definitive solutions are discovered in adolescence. We see couples who try hard to make their marriages work again after periods of separation; divorce and infidelity are always possibilities, and male homosexuality too is taken into account, in a notably sympathetic way. The various novels explore different phases of female life. Une Petite Fille sous une Moustiquaire (A Little Girl under a Mosquito Net) tells of a girl growing up, first in Saigon, then coming back to Paris and flirting with Catholicism, while a young woman's early experiences of sexuality are treated in a fashion that is both frank and amusing in Les Poissons-Chats (Cat-Fish). Marriage breakdown, an affair and subsequent reconciliation are the theme of both L'Enterrement (The Burial) with the wife finding her husband again after the death of her lover, and Cannibales en Sicile (Cannibals in Sicily), in which a woman recovers her composure after the death of her mother when her husband takes her on holiday. Again using the characteristic motif of a trip away from home, Les Cabines de bain (The Bathing Huts) finds fresh hope for a middle-aged woman whose mistake, as she sees at the end, was to regard herself all the time as younger than she really was.

Like many French women of her generation, Monique Lange is occupied by the question of abortion: what is more surprising is a recurrent interest in bullfighting which stems from Hemingway's *Death in the Afternoon*. All her fiction is short, and it often takes the form of a first-person narrative, generally told by the heroine. There is persuasive psychological insight, and past and present are intermingled in a vivid jostle of facts, feelings, beliefs and opinions that cry out to be set in order. Descriptions are precise and compelling, though commonly very succinct, and dialogues are deft and laconic, as might be expected from an author who has worked as a script writer. What are sometimes less satisfying are the conclusions that Monique Lange provides for her stories. *Rue d'Aboukir*, named after a street in Paris, has compelling characterization in a tale told largely in dialogue, but the final twist is just too contrived. *L'Enterrement* (The Burial), with its fascinating bi-focal interior monologue, has a happy ending that appears conventional after the creation of a complex dilemma, unless, of course, we are to take it as a double irony. *Une Drôle de Voix* (A Funny Sort of Voice) relates the death of Monique Lange's mother from throat cancer that necessitated tracheotomy; a moving, non-fictional account that possibly owes something to Simone de Beauvoir's *Une Mort très douce*, it also confirms the impression that much in the novels is autobiographical. *Histoire de Piaf* (translated as *Piaf*) is a good, sympathetic illustrated biography of the great cabaret star.

Works

Les Poissons-Chats (1959). Les Platanes (1960). Rue d'Aboukir, with L'Enterrement and La Plage espagnole (1962). Une Drôle de Voix (1966). Cannibales en Sicile (1967). Une Petite Fille sous une Moustiquaire (1972). Histoire de Piaf (1979). Les Cabines de Bain (1982).
Translations: Catfish [Les Poissons-Chats], tr. Barbara Wright (1961). Plane Trees [Les Platanes], tr. J.M. Calder (1961). Cannibals in Sicily [Cannibales en Sicile (with Cabines de Bain)], tr. B.J. Beaumont (1988). Piaf [Histoire de Piaf], tr. R.S. Woodward (1979).

Christopher Smith

Katja Lange-Müller

Born February 13, 1951, Berlin, East Germany
Genre(s): short prose, novel
Language(s): German

Katja Lange-Müller was raised in the DDR. After graduating from the prestigious Johannes R. Becher Institute, Leipzig, in 1982, she travelled to Mongolia as the employee of a publishing house to scout for new and unusual works. She moved to West Berlin, where she currently resides, in 1984.

Lange-Müller's stories sparkle with wit. Wisecracks, outrageous situations, flippant humor, and brilliant wordplay chase each other across the pages in a contemporary renewal of the proverbial Berlin sense of humor. Yet the laughter in these stories has deep roots, and the alert reader will detect that, like much genuine humor, it is a form of sublimated anger and mourning. Lange-Müller recently published a novel, "Kaspar Mauser—Die Feigheit vorm Freund," based on the text which won her the Ingeborg Bachmann prize for literature in 1986.

Works

Wehleid—wie im Leben [Self-pitying Sighs—Just Like Life], short stories (1986). "Kaspar Mauser—Die Feigheit vorm Freund." *Klagenfurter Texte zum Ingeborg-Bachmann-Preis 1986*, ed. Humbert Fink and Marcel Reich-Ranicki [Kaspar Mauser—Cowardice in the Face of Friendship] (1986). "Einige Paare." *Reise durch die Gegenwart. Ein Lesebuch der Collection*, ed. Thomas Beckermann [Some Couples] (1987) . *Kaspar Mauser. Die Feigheit vorm Freund*, novel (1988).

Bibliography

Klagenfurter Texte zum Ingeborg-Bachmann-Preis 1986, ed. Humbert Fink and Marcel Reich-Ranicki (München, 1986). [Press reviews and reactions to the 1986 competition].

Ann Marie Rasmussen

Marianne Langewiesche

Born November 16, 1908, Irschenhausen/
Bavaria; died September 4, 1979, Munich
Genre(s): novel, short story, travel literature,
radio journalism
Language(s): German

The daughter of the innovative publisher Wilhelm Langewiesche-Brandt, Marianne Langewiesche moved to Munich as a child, where she completed her schooling and worked for a time as a social worker and journalist. She married the writer and dramatist Heinz Coubier in 1935. Their connections made it possible for Langewiesche to overcome the double handicap of her mother's part-Jewish ancestry and Coubier's "Schreibverbot" (ban on writing imposed by the Nazis) and continue writing. In 1938 she published her first book, *Die Ballade der Judith von Loo*, a historical novel set during the Thirty Years' War (1618–1648). The themes and settings of her later work often reflect her fascination with the Mediterranean. Venice, for example, is not only the hero of the novel *Königin der Meere* (1940) but also the subject of excellent and informative guidebooks from 1955 and 1973. In the 1950s, Langewiesche turned from fiction to cultural, geographical, and religious studies. Her radio broadcasts about her worldwide travels made Langewiesche a well-known figure of the Bavarian cultural scene.

Works

Die Ballade der Judith von Loo [The Ballad of Judith von Loo], novel (1938). *Die Dame in Schwarz* [The Lady in Black], short story (1940). *Königin der Meere. Roman einer Stadt* [The Queen of the Seas. A Novel of a City], novel (1940, 1953, 2nd ed., 1985). *Die Allerheiligen-Bucht* [All-Saints Bay], novel (1942). *Castell Bò. Odysseus und seine Ruder* [Castell Bò. Odysseus and His Oars], short stories (1947). *Die Bürger von Calais* [The Citizens of Calais], novel (1949). *Der Ölzweig* [The Olive Branch] novel, (1952). *Der Garten des Vergessens* [The Garden of Forgetting], story (1953). (Co-editor) *Psalter und Harfe. Lyrik der Christenheit* [Psalter and Harp. Christian Poetry], poetry anthology (1955). *Mit Federkiel und Besenstiel. Poetische Gedanken einer Hausfrau* [With Quill and Broom. The Poetic Musings of a Housewife]

(1956, 1973). Ed., Simone de Beauvoir, *Das andere Geschlecht* [The Second Sex], shortened, revised edition (1961). *Venedig. Geschichte und Kunst. Eine Bildungsreise.* Updated as *Venedig. Geschichte und Kunst* (1955; 1962). *Erlebnis einer einzigartigen Stadt.* [Venice. History and Art] (1973, 3rd ed. 1979). *Ravenna, Stadt der Völkerwanderung. Eine Bildungsreise* [Ravenna, the City of the Germanic Migration. An Educational Journey], travel literature (1964). *Spuren in der Wüste? Heilige und Verräter in der biblischen Geschichte* [Traces in the Desert? Saints and Traitors in Biblical History] (1970). *Wann fing das Abendland zu denken an? Jüdischer Glaube und griechische Erkenntnis* [When Did the West Begin to Think? Jewish Faith and Greek Knowledge] (1970). *Jura-Impressionen* [Impressions from the Jura] (1971). Over fifty radio programs for the Bavarian State Radio (Bayrischer Runkfunk) including *Diesseits der hundert Tore* [This Side of the Hundred Gates] (1977), *Albanien* [Albania] (1978), and *Togo* [Togo] (1979).

Bibliography

DLL. Vol. 9, p. 927. Koenig-Warthausen, Gabriele Freiin von, "M.L." *Neue Deutsche Biographie,* Vol. 13 (Berlin, 1953–1985), pp. 595–596. LdS. pp. 171–172. Mechtel, Angelika, *Alte Schriftsteller in der Bundesrepublik. Gespräche und Dokumente* (München, 1972), pp. 68–77. [Interview] Wilhelm, Gertraude, "M.L." *Handbuch der deutschen Gegenwartsliteratur,* ed. Hermann Kunisch (München, 1965), p. 379.

Ann Marie Rasmussen

Elisabeth Langgässer

Born February 23, 1899, Alzey, Rheinhessen,
Germany; died July 25, 1950,
Rheinzabern
Genre(s): poetry, short story, novel
Language(s): German

Elisabeth Langgässer was the daughter of an architect. She attended the university at Darmstadt and was a teacher for ten years in her own province. She married the philosopher, Dr. Wilhelm Hoffmann. In 1929 they moved to Berlin where Elisabeth joined the literary circle and literary journal "Die Kolonne" ("The Column"). In 1936 Elisabeth Langgässer, who was half-Jewish, was forbidden to continue writing. She was forced to work in a factory, and her oldest daughter was incarcerated at Auschwitz.

Elisabeth Langgässer was a member of the PEN-Central of Germany, of the German Academy for Language and Poetry and of the Academy of Science and Literature. In 1932 she received the German Citizens' Literature prize for her short stories; posthumously in 1950 she received the Georg-Büchner prize.

Elisabeth Langgässer's recurrent theme throughout her fiction is the tension between the unredeemed natural world and the world of grace, between Catholicism and classical mythology. In the supra-naturalism of Elisabeth Langgässer's Rhineland the fusion of past and present is extreme and extravagant. For her the Here and the Now are one with the Always and the Eternal. The unity of all life is her concern in her writings. Langgässer combines pagan antiquity as found in Greece with the Middle Ages and with the modern world. Thus, her poetry explores the correspondence between the pagan mysteries and the mysteries of the Catholic faith. She is a master of interior monologue. Her novel *Proserpina* (1933), a personal myth of childhood, was followed by *Das Triptichon des Teufels* (The Triptych of the Devil) and *Der Gang durch das Ried* (Stroll Through the Marsh). The theme of *Die Rettung im Rhein* (Rescue on the Rhine) is grace abounding, as it is declaredly of the masterpiece that made her famous, *Das unauslöschliche Siegel* (The Indelible Seal). It is a highly complex prose structure composed of visionary images of the nightmarish dissolution of our physical world, of allegorical configurations and hallucinatory dialogues transcending all limitations of time and space, the story of the converted Jew, Lazarus Belfontaine, who rebels against and finally succumbs to the curse and the grace inherent in the sacrament of baptism. *Märkische Argonautenfahrt* (The Quest) is an allegory and legend of our age. Seven people, strangers to each other, leave war-ruined Berlin together in search of an unharmed monastery to which they will not be admitted, but they discover on the way their deep involvement in guilt and, through endless conversations, reminiscences and soul-baring confessions, the impossibility of

escaping the unavoidable great "trapper: God." The same brooding qualities, the same struggle for divine grace through absolute faith mark the poems also.

Works

Der Wendekreis des Lammes [The Tropic of the Lamb] (1924). *Grenze, besetztes Gebiet* [The Border, Occupied Area] (1932). *Das Triptychon des Teufels* [The Triptych of the Devil] (1932). *Proserpina* [Proserpina] (1933). *Die Tierkreisgedichte* [Poems of the Zodiac] (1935). *Der Gang durch das Ried* [Stroll Through the Marsh] (1936). *Rettung am Rhein* [Rescue on the Rhine] (1938). *Das unauslöschliche Siegel* [The Indelible Seal] (1946). *Der Torso* [The Torso] (1947). *Der Laubmann und die Rose* [The Foliage Man and the Rose] (1947). *Kölnische Elegie* [Cologne Elegy] (1948). *Das Labyrinth* [The Labyrinth] (1949). *Die märkische Argonautenfahrt* (1950).
Translation: *The Quest* [*Die märkische Argonautenfahrt*], tr. J.B. Greene (1953).

Bibliography

Alker, Ernst, *Profile und Gestalten der Deutschen Literatur nach 1914* (Stuttgart, 1977). *Autorenlexikon deutschsprachiger Literatur des 20. Jahrhunderts*, ed. Manfred Brauneck (Hamburg, 1984). Closs, August, *Twentieth Century German Literature* (New York, 1969). *Kindlers Literaturgeschichte der Gegenwart: Die Literatur der Bundesrepublik Deutschland*, ed. Dieter Lattmann (Munich, 1973). Lennartz, Franz, *Deutsche Dichter und Schriftsteller unserer Zeit* (Stuttgart, 1959). Rinser, L., *Mägische Argonautenfahrt: Eine Einführung in die gesammelten Werke von Elisabeth Langgässer* (Hamburg, 1959). Welzig, Werner, *Der Deutsche Roman im 20. Jahrhundert* (Stuttgart, 1967).

Brigitte Archibald

Adelheid Langmann

Born Nuremberg (Bavaria); died November 22, 1375
Genre(s): vernacular letter
Language(s): German

Adelheid Langmann was born into a Nuremberg patriciate family. She entered the Dominican convent at Engelthal (Bavaria) between 1325 and 1330. Her literary contribution consists of her revelations in the form of a diary written between 1330 and 1347, and three surviving letters of the correspondence with her spiritual adviser Ulrich von Kaisheim, abbot at Kaisheim, between 1340 and 1360. Ulrich's documented friendship with Heinrich von Nördlingen and Margarethe Ebner suggests that Adelheid Langmann may have been part of the large intellectual religious community of women and men that apparently flourished in twelfth and thirteenth century Germany, Switzerland, and Alsace.

Bibliography

Buber, Martin, *Ekstatische Konfessionen* (Leipzig, 1921), pp. 100–103. Oehl, Wilhelm, *Deutsche Mystikerbriefe des Mittelalters 1100–1550* (Darmstadt, 1972), pp. 393–396. Prestel, Josef, *Die Offenbarungen der Margaretha Ebner und der Adelheid Langmann* (Weimar: Hermann Bölhaus, 1939).

Secondary References: Bauerreiss, Romuald, *Kirchengeschichte Bayerns* 4 (1953): 71. Krebs, Engelbert, "Adelheid Langmann." *Verfasserlexikon* 3, pp 22ff. Preger, W., *Geschichte der deutschen Mystik* 2 (1881), pp. 274ff. *Reallexikon der deutschen Literaturgeschichte* 2 (1965), pp. 550–551. Strauch, Philipp, "Die Offenbarungen der Adelheid Langmann." *Quellen und Forschungen zur Sprach- und Kulturgeschichte der Germanischen Völker* 25 (1878), pp. 11–12. Wilms, P. Hieronymus, "Das Tugendstreben der Mystikerinnen." *Dominikanisches Geistesleben* 2 (1927), pp. 181ff. Wilms, P. Hieronymus, "Das älteste Verzeichnis der deutschen Dominikanerklöster." *Quellen und Forschungen zur Geschichte des Dominikanerordens in Deutschland* 24 (1928), pp. 70–71.

Gabriele L. Strauch

Ilse Langner

Born May 21, 1899, Breslau, Germany; died January 16, 1987, Darmstadt
Genre(s): drama, novel, poetry
Language(s): German

Ilse Langner's early dramas, which were performed during the last years of the Weimar Republic, were critical and popular successes. For the most part silenced during the Nazi years, she published several works in the late 1940s, but in spite of a few laudatory reviews and an occasional literary prize she was not able to reestablish herself as a major figure on the German literary scene. Only in the 1980s did her works again begin to receive attention.

Langner was the daughter of the teacher Erdmann Langner and his wife, Helene. She began to write while attending school in Breslau, but her career began only after moving to Berlin in 1928, the year before her marriage to the scientist Werner Siebert and the premiere of her first drama, *Frau Emma kämpft im Hinterland* (Emma Fights on the Home Front). She lived in Berlin until 1963, and her experiences toward the end of the war are reflected in the novel *Flucht ohne Ziel: Tagebuch-Roman Frühjahr 1945* (1984; Flight Without Goal: A Diary Novel, Spring 1945). The remainder of her life was rich and active, as she traveled extensively, giving lectures and supporting the cause of peace throughout the world.

In virtually all of Langner's dramas the protagonist is a woman, and some aspect of her attitude toward and relationship with a patriarchal society is at the core of the action. In *Frau Emma kämpft im Hinterland* the struggles of a German housewife while her husband is at the front during the First World War are realistically portrayed; after the husband's return the couple arrive at a *modus vivendi* based on equality and mutual respect. A similar theme, if in a totally different setting and with a totally different ending, is taken up in *Klytämnestra* (1947; Clytaemnestra), a reworking of the traditional myth in which the heroine is rather positively portrayed. In other dramas the heroine achieves success in a material sense but at the cost of human values. The protagonist of *Die Heilige aus USA* (The Saint from the USA, performed 1931, published in *Dramen I*, 1983), a hostile portrayal of the life of Mary Baker Eddy, is consumed by avarice and lust for power; and the "widow" of the drama of that title—*Die Witwe* (1973), in *Drei Pariser Stücke* (Three Parisian Plays)—is consumed by jealousy.

The dangers of science and technology constitute the themes of the drama *Cornelia*

Kungström (performed 1955, published in *Dramen I*, 1983) and the novel *Die Zyklopen* (1960; The Cyclopes), two of Langner's more controversial works. In the former, a prominent woman scientist kills her son to prevent him from misusing her discoveries, and the latter portrays a world dominated by "one-eyed" people, i.e., those who focus their attention only on progress in the field of atomic research to the exclusion of human values and human dignity. Although the novel won a minor literary prize, both works were generally found to be artistically flawed by reviewers in spite of the timely themes.

Langner consistently portrays variations of the archetypal dichotomy between nature and intellect. She accepts the traditional conception that women are intrinsically more in tune with nature and emotions—especially love, in all its manifestations—and that men are more inclined to abstraction and action. In her view each gender must attempt to integrate the positive aspects of the other. When this takes place, happiness and harmony, for the individual and society in general, are the result. When men fail to deviate from their pursuit of material success or women (as in the case of Mary Baker Eddy) succumb to its allure, individuals and society alike suffer the consequences. In an essay in 1946 Langner summarized her position on women's liberation, a view that remained essentially unchanged: "Women had begun to free themselves from male dominance, only in a twist of fateful irony to fall victim to the male mentality that they were in the process of fighting."

Works

Die purpurne Stadt: Roman (1937). *Klytämnestra: Tragödie in drei Akten* (1947). *Rodica: Eine Pariser Novelle* (1947). *Das Gionsfest. Kyoto* (1948). *Iphigenie kehrt heim: Dramatische Dichtung* (1948). *Zwischen den Trümmern: Gedichte* (1948). *Sonntagsausflug nach Chartres: Roman* (1956). *Geboren 1899: Biographische Gedichte* (1959). *Chinesisches Tagebuch: Erinnerung und Vision* (1960). *Die Zyklopen: Roman* (1960). *Japanisches Tagebuch: Erinnerung und Vision* (1961). *Ich lade Sie ein nach Kyoto ins alte Japan von heute* (1963). *Drei Pariser Stücke* (1974). *Heimkehr: Ein Berliner Trümmerstück* (1974). *Mein Thema und mein Echo*, ed. Ernst Johann (1974). *Frau Emma kämpft im Hinterland: Chronik in drei Akten* (1979). *Dramen I* (1983). *Flucht ohne Ziel: Tagebuch-Roman Frühjahr 1945* (1984).

Bibliography

Glenn, Jerry, "An Introduction to the Dramas of Ilse Langner." *University of Dayton Review* 15, No. 3 (1982): 17–30. Johann, Ernst, ed., *Ilse Langner: Mein Thema und mein Echo* (Darmstadt, 1979).

Jerry Glenn

Contessa Lara

(see: Eva Cattermole Mancini)

Berta Lask

(a.k.a. Berta Jacobsohn-Lask, Gerhard Wieland)

Born November 17, 1878, Wadowice (Galicia); died March 28, 1967, East Berlin
Genre(s): drama, short story, poetry, children's literature, essay
Language(s): German

The daughter of a paper manufacturer, Berta Lask was raised in Pomerania in the humanistic tradition. She married the physician and lecturer L. Jacobsohn in 1901 and moved to Berlin, where she became politically active, particularly in the women's movement. In 1923 she joined the Communist Party (KPD), and in October 1928 she became a founding member of the *Bund Proletarisch-Revolutionärer Schriftsteller* (Confederation of Proletarian-Revolutionary Writers, 1928–1935), serving also as one of its leading functionaries. In the 1920s Lask wrote a number of short stories, dramas, and poetry as well as essays that appeared mainly in leftist journals and newspapers such as the *Rote Fahne* (KPD daily). She also participated in the activities of the *Arbeitertheaterzirkel* (Workers' Theater Circle). When the Nazis took power in 1933, she was arrested and consequently immigrated to the Soviet Union where she worked primarily as a contributor to newspapers and radio. In 1953 she returned to the GDR and lived until her death in East Berlin.

While her earlier works reveal her social and ethical engagement (*Auf dem Hinterhof, vier Treppen links*, 1912; her first social drama) and a pacifist stand (1915; anti-war poems), Lask became one of the most noted representatives of German proletarian-revolutionary literature during the era of the Weimar Republic, particularly in the field of drama, in which she developed an epic-documentary form incorporating revue-like sequences of scenes and a chorus intended to increase the immediate political appeal to the audience. In her efforts to present the working class as a collective entity by reducing the individualistic depiction of the single person, she approached the aesthetic concept of "Proletkult."

Lask's best known plays of this time period are *Thomas Münzer* (1925), written in commemoration of the 400th anniversary of the peasant wars, *Leuna 1921—Drama der Tatsachen* (Drama of Facts), a "kaleidoscope" of scenes from the struggle of the workers in Central Germany based on interviews and files of the authorities, and *Giftgasnebel über Sowjetruland* (Poisonous Gas Cloud Over the Soviet Union), a "revue" drama staged in 1927 that deals with the war threats against Soviet Russia at that time. Beginning with *Thomas Münzer*, Lask and her plays were subjected to censorship, *Leuna 1921* being performed illegally.

Lask's greatest achievement probably lies in her contributions to the new genre of proletarian children's literature that emerged in close connection with the proletarian education movement during the Weimar Republic. In her stories and fairy tales she skillfully relates to the horizon of understanding and experience of young readers and listeners and distributes and personifies social differences in her characters. In *Auf dem Flügelpferd durch die Zeiten* (1924; On the Winged Horse through Time), a working class boy undertakes a fantastic journey through the major periods of repression and class struggle; her last youth book, *Otto und Elsa* (1956), which consists of four stories, centers around the struggle of German working class youths.

After 1933, during her years of exile, Lask turns, in shorter narrative texts "Januar 1933 in Berlin" (1935) and "Ein Dorf steht auf" (1935; A Village Rebels), and in plays, to the subject of antifascism. In her autobiographical trilogy *Stille und Sturm* (1955; Calm and Storm), an "Entwicklungs"-novel, she traces the development of the daughter of a Jewish manufacturer, Gertrud Weygand-Bernary, and her sons to becoming devoted socialists, and at the same time presents a panorama of the times from the turn of the century to the dawn of fascism. Lask must be considered one of the major writers of German proletarian-revolutionary literature, particularly regarding her plays into which she introduced an array of innovative forms, thus creating a distinct type of documentary epic theater. Insofar as her plays as well as her children's books were closely related to the social movement of her times, they necessarily reveal a forced depiction of sociopolitical and historic forces and constellations in black and white.

Works

Dramatic Works: *Die Päpstin* (1911). *Auf dem Hinterhof, vier Treppen links* (1912, revised 1932). *In Jehudas Stadt* (1914). *Senta* (1921). *Die Toten rufen* (1923). *Mitternacht* (1923). *Der Obermenschenfresser Weltkapitalismus und die Internationale Arbeiterhilfe* (1924). *Die Befreiung—Bilder aus dem Leben der deutschen und russischen Frauen 1914–1920* (1925). *Thomas Münzer* (1925). *Leuna 1921* (1927). *Johann der Knecht* (1936). *Vor dem Gewitter* (1938).

Narrative Texts: *Die Radfahrerkolonne aus dem Unstruttal* (1928). Gerhard Wieland /Ps./, *Junge Helden* (1934). Gerhard Wieland /Ps./, *Januar 1933 in Berlin* (1935). *Ein Dorf steht auf. Johann der Knecht* (1935). *Die schwarze Fahne von Kolbenau* (1939). *Stille und Sturm* (2 volumes, 1955). *Aus ganzem Herzen* (1961).

Poetry Collections: *Stimmen* (1919). *Rufe aus dem Dunkel. Auswahl 1915–1921* (1921).

Children's Literature: *Proletarischer Kindergarten* (1921). *Weihe der Jugend. Sprechchordichtungen für proletarische Jugendweihen* (1922; revised 1956). *Auf dem Flügelpferd durch die Zeiten* (1925). *Wie Franz und Grete nach Ruland kamen* (1926). *Spartakus* (1928). *Otto und Elsa* (1956). *Unsere Aufgabe an der Menschheit. Aufsätze* (1923). *Kollektivdorf und Sowjetgut. Ein Reisetagebuch* (1932).

Bibliography

"Berta Lask." *Das Wort* 2 (1937): 178. Dt. Ak. Der Künste zu Berlin, GDR, ed., *Zur Tradition der sozialistischen Literatur in Deutschland* (Berlin and Weimar, 1967). Dt. Ak. der Künste zu Berlin, GDR, ed. *Veröffentlichungen deutscher sozialistischer Schriftsteller in der demokratischen und revolutionären Presse 1918–1945*. (Berlin and Weimar, 1966, 1969), pp. 323–331. Introduction to *Leuna 1921* (Münster, 1973), pp. I-III. Kändler, Klaus, *Drama und Klassenkampf* (Berlin and Weimar, 1970), pp. 129–142. Melzwig, Brigitte, *Deutsche sozialistische Literatur 1918–1945* (Berlin and Weimar, 1975), pp. 225–228. Schellenberger, Johannes, Introduction to *Leuna 1921* (Berlin, 1961), pp. 145–150.

Cornelia Petermann

Else Lasker-Schüler

Born February 11, 1869, Wuppertal-Elberfeld,
   Germany; died January 22, 1945,
   Jerusalem
Genre(s): poetry, novel, essay
Language(s): German

Else Lasker-Schüler was the daughter of a well-to-do Jewish family who married the physician Berthold Lasker but was divorced after nine years. However, even before her divorce, Else lived independently in Berlin, where she joined a circle of literary-minded friends, one of whom was Peter Hille. Hille greatly influenced her writing, and she dedicated many of her works to him. In 1903 she married George Lewin, who assumed the name of Herwarth Walden to please her. Else Lasker-Schüler was the chief editor for Walden's magazine, *Der Sturm* (The Storm), from its inception and for its first three years. Else Lasker-Schüler was responsible for recruiting Paul Baum and Peter Zech for the literary circle. Else Lasker-Schüler's works were published in the major magazines and books of the Expressionists.

In 1912 Lasker-Schüler divorced Walden and led the life of a Berlin bohemian. She joined the Expressionist circles in and around Berlin at that time: Gottfried Benn, Theodor Däubler, O. Kokoschka, Franz Marc, Georg Trakl, Franz Werfel. In 1932 she received the Kleist Prize for Literature, but in 1933 she was forbidden to publish any of her works. She immigrated to Switzerland and travelled to Egypt and finally, in 1937 she settled in Jerusalem where she died in poverty and isolation.

Else Lasker-Schüler had a tendency to cover up biographical data, and some of the autobiographical material contained in her work is misleading. She was an eccentric.

Else Lasker-Schüler was at the very center of the Berlin Expressionists as the wife of Herwarth Walden. It is said that she had no ethics of any sort, and, for that reason, could not be considered an Expressionist herself. In both her prose and her poetry, Else Lasker-Schüler is the main protagonist. Almost all her poetry demonstrates a high degree of subjectivity, strange moods and fancies, exotic dream visions, and shadow images. What emerges in her works is an Oriental princess—Princess Tino of Bagdad—who has the tales of Scheherazade to tell. Her protagonist is often sunk in harem silks and cushions or in a moonlight halt among the sheiks of the desert. Often her protagonist is on a pilgrimage to the New Jerusalem and is, in some strange way, herself the angel before the gates of Paradise, with his star glittering on her brow and his broken pinion on her shoulder. Her most poignant book is her last, *Das Hebräerland*, travel impressions of the Holy Land and at the same time a vision of the poetry and tragedy of Jewish history in the homeland.

All her books are adorned by her own illustrations and drawings, and this alone makes them prizes for collectors.

Works

Styx [Styx], her first collection of poems (1902). *Das Peter Hille Buch* [The Peter Hille Book] (1906–1907). *Die Nächte der Tino von Bagdad* [The Nights of Tino of Bagdad] (1908). *Meine Wunder* [My Wonder] (1911). *Mein Herz* [My Heart] (1912). *Hebräische Balladen* [Hebrew Ballads], considered by the author to be her major work (1913). *Essays* [Essays] (1913). *Gesichte* [Faces] (1913). *Der Malik* [The Malik], novel (1916–1917). *Gesammelte Gedichte* [Collected Poems] (1917). *Gesamtausgabe* [Complete Works] (1919–1920), 10 vols. *Briefe Peter Hilles an Else Lasker-Schüler* [Peter Hilles' Correspondence with Else Lasker-

Schüler] (1921). *Ich räume auf: Meine Anklage gegen meine Verleger* [I Clarify: My Accusation Against My Publishers] (1925). *Arthur Aronymus. Geschichte meines Vaters* [Arthur Aronymus. History of my Father] (1932). *Hebräerland* [The Land of the Hebrews] (1937).

Bibliography

Alker, Ernst, *Profile und Gestalten der Deutschen Literatur nach 1914* (Stuttgart, 1977). *Autorenlexikon deutschsprachiger Literatur des 20. Jahrhunderts*, ed. Manfred Brauneck (Hamburg, 1984). Closs, August, *Twentieth Century German Literature* (New York, 1969). Ginsberg, E., ed. *Lasker-Schüler: Dichtungen und Dokumente* (1951). Kemp, F. and W. Kraft, eds., *Gesammelte Werke* (1959–1962). Kesting, M., "Zur Dichtung Else Lasker-Schülers." *Akzente* III (1956). *Kindlers Literaturgeschichte der Gegenwart: Die Literatur der Bundesrepublik Deutschland*, ed. Dieter Lattmann (Munich, 1973). Lennartz, Franz, *Deutsche Dichter und Schriftsteller unserer Zeit* (Stuttgart, 1959).

Brigitte Archibald

Patricia Lasoen

Born September 25, 1948, Brugge, Belgium
Genre(s): poetry
Language(s): Dutch

The sole woman in a group of contemporary poets who call themselves the "New Realists," Patricia Lasoen's poetry embodies a realism that stresses common, down-to-earth subjects expressed in a simple, unadorned style that seeks to overcome modern poetry's "inaccessibility."

The banalities of life—peeling potatoes, making coffee, etc.—are the topics of poems that attempt to transmute the mundane through a simple, repetitive elegance that lives life through the daily encounters with the uneventful. Lasoen divides her work into two different types of poetry, objective-descriptive poems, and those which lean towards surrealism, as in *Landschap met Roze Hoed* (1981; Landscape with Pink Hat). Most of the poems of her early objective-descriptive period, as well as the recent *De Witte Binnenkant* (1985; The White Inside), are clearly influenced by Brian Patten, a British poet of the

Mersey Sound Group, who was the subject of Lasoen's Master's thesis.

Her best works are undoubtedly *Een Zachte, Wrede Okerbruine Dood* (1975; A Soft, Cruel, Mustard-colored Death) in which Lasoen deals with the death of her father and the deepening of her own bourgeois sensibilities, and *Veel ach en een Beetje O* (1978; Much Ah and a Bit of Oh) in which "body work" is the achievement of mundane life (cooking, giving birth, growing old, etc.). In her most recent work Lasoen's orienting question is, "what shall I write about?," and she has turned to writing poems whose titles are taken from punk and heavy rock music. Overall, Lasoen's poetry seeks to transcend the insignificance of the mundane through a poetry in search of a subject, and which ultimately remains limited only by the question(s) it asks.

Works

Ontwerp van een Japanse Houtgravure (1968). *Een Verwarde Kalender* (1969). *Recepten en Verhalen* (1971). *Het Souvenirswinkeltje van Lucas* (1972). *Een Zachte, Wrede Okerbruine Dood* (1975). *Veel ach en een Beetje O* (1978). *Landschap met Roze Hoed* (1981). *De Witte Binnenkant* (1985).
Translations: Wolf, Manfred, *The Shape of Houses. Women's Voices from Holland and Flanders* (San Francisco, 1974). Decorte, Bert, ed., *Boeket. Fifty Dutch poems in English or French Translation* (Brugge, 1975). Hopkins, Konrad and Ronald van Roekel, eds., *Quartet. An Anthology of Dutch and Flemish Poetry* (Paisley, 1978).

Bibliography

Brems, H., in *Kritisch Literatuur Lexicon* (Maart, 1981). Deflo, L., in *Bij Nader Inzien* (Antwerpen, 1985).

An Lammens

Anna Margrethe Lasson (Lassen)

Born 1659, Copenhagen, Denmark; died 1738, Odense, Denmark
Genre(s): novel, poetry, letters
Language(s): Danish

Anna Margrethe Lasson deserves a special place in Danish literature as the author of the very first Danish novel, *Den beklædte Sandhed* (1715; The Truth in Disguise, published anonymously, 1723). Lasson also wrote several honorary poems and letters of recognition and acknowledgment, most notably an honorary poem (and defense of women) for the significant Norwegian poet, Dorothe Engelbretsdatter. This poem was included in Engelbretsdatter's longer poetic work, *Taareoffer for bodfærdige Syndere* (1685; Offering of Tears for Penitent Sinners). Lasson's other verses include *Et Æreminde paa adskillige Vers over Familiens gamle Ven Oluf Borck* (1696; A Remembrance in Several Verses for an Old Friend of the Family, Oluf Borck), and the *Gratulations Vers til den Glorværdigste Danske Konge, Friderich den Fierde* (Verse in Honor of the Most Excellent Danish King, Frederik the Fourth), which Lasson wrote in her youth. Lasson has secured her position in Danish literature as an "early advocate of Danish, her mother tongue [and as a defender] of women who have dedicated themselves to scholarly matters, study and writing, which many consider uncommon, indeed improper and inadmissible concerns for women" (Friderich Schönau, *Samling af danske lærde Fruentimmer*, p. 962). Lasson advocated "true love for the mother tongue" (Fredrick Bajer, "En dansk Roman," 366), and, in the preface to her novel, she once again defended her contemporaries, literate, well-educated women. In Denmark, Anna Margrethe Lasson is remembered as the first Danish novelist, "our lovely Danish Aminda . . . who has given us the beautiful novel" (Schönau, p. 977). Modern literary critics have often taken a dimmer view of *Den beklædte Sandhed*, but the work remains important as the very first novel in Danish.

Anna Margrethe Lasson, the Aminda of *Den beklædte Sandhed*, was born in 1659 and christened on March 6, 1659, in Holmens Church, Copenhagen. She was the daughter of a gifted, avaricious, and very eccentric legal officer and country judge, Jens Lassen (1625–1706), and of Margrethe Christensdatter Lund (who died about 1690). Anna Margrethe Lasson never married. For a time, she administered the office and estate of the Dean of Our Lady Church and Parish (Vor Frue Sogn), Odense, on Fyn. She lived a humble, rather isolated life in Odense, until her death in 1738. Her writings reveal, however, an individual in close touch with the events and society of her day.

Anna Margrethe Lasson's major work is the novel, *Den beklædte Sandhed* (1715, 1723). The novel is very reminiscent of the precious, baroque *romans à clef* ("key" novels) of the seventeenth-century Madeleine de Scudery. In the novel, Lasson refers to places on Fyn, the island where she spent her life, and she exhibits intimate, detailed knowledge of "the Danish royal family and nobility . . . she had occasion to know of society's most prominent circles, if not directly, then at least through very good sources" (*Dansk biografisk Leksikon*, 614). *Dansk biografisk Leksikon* further suggests that *Den beklædte Sandhed* is a very pompous, disjointed, complicated, and improbable story about knights and fair damsels; the novel is a retelling in flowery style of contemporary intrigues and scandals, possibly a fictional account of the marriage of Christian V's brother Jørgen and the English princess, Anne. In contrast to F.C. Schönau's (1753) glowing assessment of the work, modern literary historians have viewed *Den beklædte Sandhed* skeptically and critically, with little enthusiasm and interest; there have been "many assurances of the book's poor quality and insignificance in comparison with the classics" (Dalager, p. 90). The novel seems to be a rather curious *mélange* of "high baroque, *galant-heroic, pastorale,* and late baroque, semi-historical elements" (DbL, 614). Even the full title of the novel immediately suggests its complexity, its flowery, flamboyant language, and its *roman à clef* precedents: *Den fordum i Ronne Bogstavs Kaabe nu i Danske Tunge-Maals Klæde iførte liden Roman kaldet "Den beklædte Sandhed," fremviist alle Liebhavere til Fornøyelse af en det danske Sprogs inderlige Elskerinde Aminda, Trykt 1723* ("The Truth in Disguise," a Little Novel, Formerly Written in the Cape of Runic Letters Now Clad in the Danish Language, Written for the Enjoyment of All Lovers by a Passionate Lover of the Danish Language, Aminda, Published 1723). However, the literary historians Stig Dalager and Anne-Marie Mai have recently taken a more positive approach to the first Danish novel. Dalager and Mai admit that the novel suggests "many impulses . . . [from] the pastorale's love-universe [and] the courtly novel's heroism,

[to] rococo's affected descriptions of nature" (Dalager, p. 90), but they also suggest that the novel "creates an inner unity . . . [that] it points to the future . . . [and] that it contains much more than the conventional love-story: [it is] a multi-faceted love-story, sensual and spiritual, tragic and haunting, an element in a social utopia, rococo's elegant utopia" (Dalager, pp. 90–93). To Dalager and Mai, *Den beklædte Sandhed* reflects "a new opposition between rationalism and complexity of feeling, a new pensive relationship to nature, and a new interest for the emotional and passionate as something fine, intimate, and tempestuous" (Dalager, p. 93). The novel suggests a new prose wave, a turning point in Danish literature and letters; perhaps it merits more critical acclaim on that basis.

Anna Margrethe Lasson's contribution to Danish letters and literature cannot be measured in terms of wide acclaim, European recognition, and a multitude of celebrated works. We must, instead, consider Lasson a prose pioneer, one who suggested a new direction for Danish literature, enhanced the Danish language immeasurably with her "exceptionally well-composed letters" (Gustav Wad, *Fra Fyns Fortid*, p. 80), and one who asserted the worth and significant role of literate, well-educated women, both in her poems to Engelbredtsdatter and Frederik IV and in her notable preface to the very first Danish novel, *Den beklædte Sandhed*.

Works

Taareoffer for bodfærdige Syndere: Vers(1685). *Et Æreminde paa adskillige Vers over Familiens gamle Ven Oluf Borck* (1696). *Gratulations Vers til den Glorværdigste Danske Konge, Friderich den Fierde* (n.d.). *Den beklædte Sandhed* (1715, 1723).

Bibliography

Bajer, Fredrik, "En dansk roman fra 1723." *Danske Samlinger* 2, nr. 5 (1876–1877): 359–366. Dalager, Stig, and Anne-Marie Mai, *Danske dvindelige forgattere. Bind I. Sophie Brahe—Mathilde Fibiger. Udvikling og perspektiv* (København, 1982). *Dansk biografisk Leksikon. Bind 8* (København, 1981), pp. 614–615. *Dansk Litteraturhistorie. Bind 3. Stænderkultur og Enevælde 1620–1746* (København, 1983), p. 310. Schönau, Friderich Christian, *Samling af danske lærde Fruentimmer, som ved deres Lærdom, og Udgivne eller efterladte Skrifter, have gjort deres Navne i den lærde Verden bekiendte, med adskillige mest historiske Anmerkninger forøget og udgivet. 2. Bind* (København, 1753), pp. 934–977. Wad, Gustav Ludvig, *Fra Fyns fortid: Samlinger og Studier* IV (Kjøbenhavn, 1924), pp. 77–80.

Lanae Hjortsvang Isaacson

Anna László

Born January 5, 1926, Budapest, Hungary;
* died March 19, 1981, Budapest*
Genre(s): novel, short story, radio drama
Language(s): Hungarian

László published extensively in the 1960s and 1970s. Her main concern is with middle-class and professional women of her time.

She received a degree from the College of Theatrical Art. Her novels, such as We *Are Expecting You on Tuesday* (1963), portray life among the intelligentsia. Her numerous short stories appeared in four volumes. In her short fiction, she manages to capture the tragedy of insignificant everyday events. Her lonely heroines, such as those in the stories "Mourning in Colorful Clothes" or "The Enlightened or Rather: The Dumb" are surrounded by roughness and vulgarity in a male-dominated, intolerant world. They often lack privacy and independence and their prospects for a better future are bleak since they do not fit into the model of which society approves.

As a psychological realist, she utilizes short and unadorned but carefully selected sentences. She particularly excels in creating atmosphere.

Works

Szilveszter éjszakája (1959). *Nincs mindenre paragrafus*(1961). *Várjuk kedden* (1963). *Harkály a vizen* (1965). *A hitehagyott* (1967). *Zárójelentés* (1969). *Gyász tarkában* (1973). *Felépítjük Bábel tornyát* (1976). *Vaspólya* (1979).

Bibliography

Pomogáts, Bela, *Az ujabb magyar irodalom története* (Budapest, 1982).

Peter I. Barta

Madeleine de L'Aubespine

(a.k.a. Madame de Villeroy)

Born 1546, France; died 1596, France
Genre(s): poetry
Language(s): French

Although there is no problem identifying Madeleine de L'Aubespine and her literary acquaintances, her works are the basis of a continuing controversy. The outlines of her life are fairly clear. Born in 1546 to Claude de L'Aubespine and Jeanne Bochetel, Madeleine's life would always be linked to the political turmoil of the period. In 1562, she married Nicolas de Neufville, marquis of Villeroy, who would later succeed his father-in-law as Secretary of State. Her presence at the court was not solely dependent upon the high office of her father or her husband. As lady-in-waiting to Catherine de Medici, she had access to its many intrigues. Her husband's fortunes as well as hers would vary with the political climate in the struggles between Catholics and Protestants. For a time the couple lived in disgrace, but their return to power and prestige was assured when they sided with the followers of Henry IV who would reinstate Villeroy as Secretary of State. Madeleine's death two years later in 1596 cut short her enjoyment of their regained status.

Villeroy was a noted patron of poets and the likes of Ronsard, DuBellay, and Philippe Desportes were no strangers to his country house. Madeleine, too, was known as a patron and, more importantly, as a writer. It is here that the source of the problem lies. Numerous contemporary records refer to her talent as a writer of original poetry and prose as well as a translator of Ovid. Indeed, Ronsard lauds her gifts in a sonnet he dedicates to her and Desportes, who served for a while as secretary to Villeroy, praises her in a number of his poems, the *Sonnets à Callianthe* (Sonnets to Callianthe). But was Desportes the first of the many lovers Madeleine was reputed to have, and is she the author of the some twenty poems found in MS. 1718 at the Bibliothèque Nationale and of a translation of Ovid in a manuscript at the Protestant Library in Paris? Of the works attributed to her in 1926 and published as *Les Chansons de Callianthe* (Songs of Callianthe), only the Ovid seems indisputable.

As for the other poems, they have also been attributed to Héliette de Vivonne.

The liaison between Desportes and Madeleine would have begun sometime in 1573 and ended in 1577 when he left for Poland. In a period when a poet's praise for his patron's wife was frequently couched in amorous rhetoric, it is difficult to establish the extent of a relationship. In this case, the problem is two-fold: Are the anonymous sonnets by a female poet expressions of real sentiments or are they a mere formulaic exchange of poetry with another poet? Are they the work of Madeleine de L'Aubespine? While the sonnets do seem to be inspired by a real affair, it is not possible to be absolutely certain that Madeleine is their author. Perhaps the strongest elements favoring her candidacy are the renown she enjoyed during her lifetime as a women of letters and a reference to a collection of her poems. While this collection is now lost, its one-time existence lends support to the case for Madeleine.

Works

Les Epitres d'Ovide (n.d., lost). Les Chansons de Callianthe (posthumous, 1926).

Bibliography

Lavaud, Jacques, *Philippe Desportes (1546–1606)* (Paris, 1936).

Edith J. Benkov

Marie Laurencin

Born October 1885, Paris, France; died June 8, 1956, Paris
Genre(s): poetry
Language(s): French

The illegitimate child of an elegant Creole, Marie Laurencin always showed an interest for drawing and painting. After having completed her education, her mother reluctantly allowed her to go to the Academy Humbert. There she met Georges Braque, one of her fellow-students in 1905. Braque recognized her talent and introduced her to the Bateau-Lavoir, where she befriended many members of the intelligentsia: Gertrude Stein was to patronize her; Max Jacob, Picasso and Guillaume Apollinaire were to become her friends. She engaged in an intimate relationship with the poet that lasted for six years. Much of the praise attributed to Laurencin as a painter is said to owe much to Apollinaire's taste for her work: he gave her a most flattering appraisal in his *Méditations esthétiques, les peintres cubistes* (Aesthetic Meditations, the Cubist Painters). Apollinaire found great inspiration in the person of his mistress, and numerous allusions to her can be found in his writings. The liaison came to an end between 1912 and 1914, the year in which she married the German artist Otto von Waëtken, a few weeks before the outbreak of World War I. The couple had to spend the war in Spain, and after a year in Dusseldorf, Marie Laurencin came back to Paris in 1920. She then filed for divorce and was to spend the remainder of her life in Paris. She was by then a well-established artist and her work included not only paintings but also book illustrations (for Katherine Mansfield's *The Garden Party*, André Gide's *La Tentative amoureuse* [An Attempt at Love], and Lewis Carroll's *Alice in Wonderland*, among others). She also worked in the theater and in 1923 designed the décors and costumes of the ballet *Les Biches*, by Francis Poulenc.

In 1926, she published her first collection of poems, *Le Petit Bestiaire* (The Little Bestiary). Bestiaries were in vogue then, Apollinaire also having published one, illustrated by Picasso. In 1946, she published *Le Carnet des Nuits* (The Notebook of Nights). The *Carnet* is constituted of two parts: the first of unpublished notes, the second of *Le Petit Bestiaire*, her poems already published in 1926.

Le Petit Bestiaire is composed of short prose poems (four or five sentences each) of no great literary merit. The unedited part of *Le Carnet* is of historical value for those interested in the generation of the 1920s, even though Laurencin-style is deliberately unexplicit and, at times, confused.

Works

Le Petit Bestiaire (1926). Le Carnet des Nuits (1946).

Bibliography

Apollinaire, Guillaume, *Méditations esthétiques, les peintres cubistes* (Paris, 1913). Day, George, *Marie Laurencin* (Paris, 1947).

Valerie Lastinger

Nicole Laurent-Catrice

Born 1937, Hem, France
Genre(s): poetry, literary criticism
Language(s): French

In the context of mainly intellectually-geared poetry in present day France, Laurent-Catrice sees herself as going "against the stream": she seeks a balance of body, spirit, and heart, and believes that the "fundamental issues have become too poignant to occupy oneself with mere linguistic experimentation."

Mother of five children, occasional painter, M.A. in Spanish with a dissertation on Juan Ramón Jiménez, she has always lived in tension between her duties as wife and mother and her creative impetus. She participates in numerous poetry festivals in France and outside (Conversano, Fano), is the producer of a weekly radio program on poetry at Rennes since 1984 and one of the principal directors of International Poetry Week in Bretagne since 1983. Since 1984 she has been in charge of all poetry programs at the Rennes festival. She has widely lectured about the blind poet Angèle Vannier and has written about her poetry. Her poems have been translated into Italian (by Gina Labriola) and Spanish. She herself has translated works of Pedro Salinas, Gabriela Mistral, J.R. Jiménez, Miguel Hernández, Gabriel Celaya, five Latin-American poets, and several Lithuanian poets in collaboration, published in *Arpa, Artus, Les Cahiers de l'Archipel, Jalons, Journal des Poètes, Nord, Pierre Eclatée, Poésie Présente, Tessons*.

The poetry of Laurent-Catrice has evolved considerably since 1959 (date of some poems included in *Poèmes au vent*). In her first book (1974; Poems to the Wind) the presence of Symbolist poets as well as a late-Romantic note are evident. She adheres to strict form, often that of a sonnet, and incorporates certain traditional rhetorical elements. The attention is geared to herself and her feelings. In *Paysages intérieurs* (1980; Interior Landscapes), the lines flow more freely, the strictures of rhyme have been abandoned. The "I" still constitutes the center, but without romantic undertones. The language operates on a different level from that spoken every day. In some poems a mythic ambience is created. In all, symbolism has an important place.

Amour-Miroir (1986; Love-Mirror) falls almost within the tradition of medieval mystery plays or allegories, to be presented on stage. Built on the theme of the original unity of man/woman, it explores in symbolic sequence the ways to recuperate that ancient harmony. There is a strong philosophical-psychological undercurrent in it; the dialogue is in blank verse. The significance of poetry is enhanced by having "the Poet" deliver the prologue and the epilogue and also enter as a character in the only act. *Deuil m'est seuil* (1987; Sorrow, My Threshold) re-elaborates the all-pervasive theme of the necessity of suffering. The poems have become very short here—bare notations—the word, more essential, and the direct presence of I has vanished. The symbolic note and the ambiguity persist. The whole book is an affirmation of human experience, where body and spirit merge to produce a new being. This can be considered the most constant and original aspect of Laurent-Catrice's poetry: a conscious striving to not "purify" it to the point of becoming abstract, to not lose touch with palpable reality. In her last book, *Liturgie des pierres*, she has reached full maturity. The lines are terse, the message condensed: she is really sculpting the stone, hewing eternal truths from it.

Laurent-Catrice sees poetry as "a gift to give visibility to that which is invisible to the uninitiated: the unusual turn of a situation, the hidden significance of a gesture, the ultimate meaning of the world of appearances." Her great themes are love, questioning of the reasons for failure, death. She believes in the plenitude and meaningfulness of the universe—hence the affirmative closing in most of her books. Very consciously, she wants to write as a woman. Her goal is to achieve a "metaphysical poetry that would yet be tangible; sensitive and spontaneous while being well structured; and profoundly rooted in present-day life."

Works

Poèmes au vent (1974). Paysages intérieurs (1980). Amour-Miroir (1986). Deuil m'est seuil (1987). Liturgie des pierres [The Liturgy of Stones] (1989).

Birutė Ciplijauskaitė

Madame de Lauvergne

Flourished 1680, France
Genre(s): poetry
Language(s): French

Mme de Lauvergne is a poet without a biography; even her first name is unknown. Her *Collected Poems*, published in 1680 and dedicated to Mme de Neuville, is presented by "your obedient servant Leroux." Viollet-le-Duc, speculating that Leroux was the author's maiden name, thought that she might have enjoyed the patronage of Mme de Neuville's mother. Several poems are addressed to a Mme and Mlle Godefroy, who belonged perhaps to the Godefroy family known for its jurists and historiographers.

Although published near the end of the French vogue for *precieux* poetry, most of Mme de Lauvergne's poems fit comfortably into that category. She is fond of those minor poetic forms popular in seventeenth-century salons: the madrigal, chanson, elegy, stanzas, and quatrains. She is also concerned with the topics of *precieux* poetry, particularly love's trials and tribulations, which she explores from both masculine and feminine perspectives. In one elegy addressed to an inconstant lover, the female speaker suffers typically Petrarchan pains; her spirit "disturbed by deadly displeasure," her "eyes bathed with tears," and her "heart heavy with sighs," she grows pale and shivers whenever she remembers that she has devoted herself to an unfaithful lover. After analyzing her pain and convincing herself that her passion might still be reciprocated, the speaker finds her love renewed but still suffers. The poem ends with an appeal to her "faithless shepherd." Mme de Lauvergne generally avoids the sentimentality and excessive hyperbole that can mar *precieux* poetry. Some of her most powerful statements come from the madrigals and chansons, where strictures of form seem to curb excesses of exclamation. In one "Quatrain," for instance, she asserts quietly the power of a true love: "I love you more than my life,/ And I have told you so more than a hundred times,/ Nothing pleases me but you; apart from you everything bores me,/ And I enjoy no happy days but those shared with you."

The *Collected Poems* contains a few long pieces, including a mythological poem about

Venus and Adonis. In Mme de Lauvergne's version Venus and Adonis enjoy a mutual, satisfying passion. But although they indulge freely in love's physical pleasures, the love also has a spiritual dimension, since the two reveal to one another the "secrets of their souls." In her final lament over Adonis' mangled body, Venus chides Adonis for insisting on hunting the boar. But Adonis rouses himself to affirm his love—"I die because I am a lover, and I die joyfully"—and pledges to carry his "deathless" passion for Venus faithfully to the grave. The poem concludes with Venus' lament. She curses the "harsh fates" and Mars, then considers whether she might join Adonis in death by renouncing her godhead. Her desire thwarted by her own immortality, Venus finally decides to revenge herself by translating Adonis into a blood-red flower, which will stand as a tribute to their eternal love. "Adonis's Poem" contains some pleasant scene-painting and a rhythmically-charged account of the boar's attack. The poem's most powerful sections, however, are Venus' lament (characterized by clear logic) and the conversations between Venus and Adonis (characterized both by passion and mutual respect). Structurally, Venus' final lament bears some resemblance to her lament in La Fontaine's "Adonis" (1669), although Mme de Lauvergne's Venus is psychologically more credible.

Mme de Lauvergne's collection contains one satire, "The Invalid's Caprice," a dialogue between the ailing speaker's heart and soul. The heart, seeking to put his affairs in order, wants to will his hoard of untouched virtues, such as love and faithfulness, to Fulvance, a "miserable flirt." The soul objects, arguing that fame is fleeting and that the "remains of a dead heart do not touch the heart of a living beauty." After the heart assents and decides to fight for life, the speaker taunts Fulvance, who has helped him indirectly by her indifference.

Viollet-le-Duc, the only source for description and evaluation of Mme de Lauvergne's *Collected Poems*, ranks her poetry higher than that of Desmarets and Dassoucy. Although limited in scope and occasionally prone to artificial diction, her poems at their best provide sharply focused and intuitively just glimpses of love's moods and effects.

Works

Recueil de Poésies (1680).

Bibliography

Grente, G. et al., eds., *Dictionnaire des Lettres Françaises*, III, p. 594. *Nouvelle Biographie Generale*. Viollet-le-Duc, Emmanuel Louis Nicholas, *Catalogue des Livres Composant La Bibliothèque Poétique* (1843), p. 574.

Christy Desmet

Christine Lavant

Born 1915, St. Stefan in the Lavant valley,
    Austria
Genre(s): poetry, short story
Language(s): German

Born as ninth child of a miner, in the valley whose name she uses as a pseudonym, Christine Lavant had a childhood affected by poverty and illness, especially the danger of losing her eyesight. She has remained in her home village all her life, working as a knitter. Her three early stories, "Das Kind," "Die Rosenkugel," and "Das Krüglein," capture with intense clarity the feelings of childhood: girls taking refuge in dreams. More important, however, is Lavant's poetry. While her first volume *Unvollendete Liebe* is still inspired by Rilke and Trakl, she has become something of a unique cult figure since her *Bettlerschale* of 1956, winning many prizes: the Trakl Prize in 1954 and 1964; the Wildgans Prize in 1964; and in 1956, a stipend of the state of Austria.

With its striking images and a language that is artistically and deliberately arch and archaic, Lavant's poetry is almost mystically religious, yet it moves unbelievers. Although she uses traditionally rhymed verse, she is conscious of twentieth-century poetic devices, but more than anything else, her poems have been called "a witch's spell spun out endlessly, as well as the powerful confession of a tormented soul" (Gerhard Fritsch about *Spindel im Mond*). And Robert Schwarz has said of the stories united in *Nell*: "the common leitmotif . . . is the bitterness of the human condition and the forlornness of unlived people, but also the arcane and inspired communication that, in the end, God is the only refuge."

Works

"Das Kind," story (1948). *Die unvollendete Liebe,* poetry (1949). "Das Krüglein" story (1949). "Die Rosenkugel," story (1956). *Die Bettlerschale,* poetry (1956). *Spindel im Mond,* poetry (1959). *Lumpensammler* (1961). *Der Pfauenschrei,* poetry (1962). *Hälfte des Herzens,* poetry (1967). *Nell,* stories (1969).

Bibliography

Brinker-Gabler, Gisela, *Deutsche Dichterinnen* (Frankfurt, 1986).

Ute Marie Saine

Maribel Lázaro

Born 1948, Córdoba, Spain
Genre(s): drama
Language(s): Spanish

Although born in Andalusia, Lázaro lives in and is associated with Madrid. She is almost completely self-taught, having dropped out of school at a very early age (about twelve). Enormously talented and versatile, Lázaro has been an active painter, actress, and singer before concentrating her efforts on playwriting. *Humo de Beleño* (Witches' Smoke) won the Calderón de la Barca Prize in 1985, and *La fosa* (The Grave) was performed in Madrid in 1986.

Works

Humo de Beleño [Witches Smoke] (1986). *La fosa* [The Grave] (1986). *La fuga* [The Getaway] (1989).

Bibliography

O'Connor, Patricia W., *Dramaturgas españolas de hoy* (Madrid, 1989).

Patricia W. O'Connor

Zinaīda Lazda

Born June 6, 1902, Vidzeme, Latvia; died
November 7, 1957, Salem, Oregon
Genre(s): lyric poetry
Language(s): Latvian

Zinaīda Lazda, whose real name was Zinaīda Zelma Šreibere, is one of the best known modern Latvian poets. She was born into a farmer's family, and as a child became steeped in the traditions of Latvian folklore, especially the folk song, or *daina*, which thereafter deeply influenced her own poetry. In 1939 she received from the Latvian University a master's degree in folklore. During most of her adult life in her home country she taught Latvian language and literature at the secondary school level as well as at a school for kindergarten teachers. In 1944, caught between Russian and German battle lines, she became separated from most of her family and barely saved herself by escaping into Germany. After the war, she lived there until 1949 in a Latvian displaced persons' camp near Nürnberg. At that point she immigrated to the United States, where she found employment as a domestic servant and then as a nurse's aide, first in Salem, Oregon, later in Berkeley, California. Her profound sense of exile gives much of her poetry a somber cast; its virtue lies in its powerful simplicity. She has also written numerous essays, articles, and reviews.

Works

Zaļie vārti (1936). *Staru viesulis* (1942). *Tālais dārzs* (1946). *Bēgle* (1949). *Saules koks* (1956). *Pazeme* (a major unfinished work). Numerous essays, articles, and reviews, as well as separate poems. "Da'i vārdi par manu dzīvi," in *Trimdas rakstnieki* II, ed. Pēteris ērmanis (Kempten, 1947) (an autobiographic account).

Translations: Samples of her work in *A Century of Latvian Poetry,* ed. and tr. W.K. Matthews (London, 1957); also a selection of poems, *A Green Leaf.*

Bibliography

Kārkliņš, Valdemārs and Kārlis Rabācs, ed., *Zinaīda Lazda: dzejnieces piemiņai veltīts rakstu krājums* (Chicago, 1963). Also see Benjamiņš Jēgers, *Latviešu trimdas izdevumu bibliografija–Bibliography of Latvian Publications Published Outside Latvia, 1940–1960* (Sundbyberg, 1972); *1961–1970* (Sundbyberg, 1977); and *1971–1980* (Stockholm, 1988).

Zoja Pavlovskis

Leana

(see: Elena Farago)

Adrienne Lecouvreur

*Born April 5, 1692, Damey, near Epernay,
France; died March 1730, Paris*
Genre(s): letters
Language(s): French

Adrienne Lecouvreur, the greatest French actress of the first third of the eighteenth century, was the daughter of a not very prosperous provincial hatter called Robert Couvreur and his second wife. She owed her formal education to the Soeurs de l'Instruction chrétienne in Paris and is said to have first made her mark as an actress when at the age of thirteen she played the taxing role of Pauline in Corneille's religious tragedy *Polyeucte* in a private performance. She became a pupil of Marc-Antoine Le Grand of the Comédie-Française and made her début on the professional stage at Lille at the age of fifteen, changing her surname to Lecouvreur to give it a more aristocratic ring. Her career was interrupted for a while when a liaison with an army officer left her pregnant, and a son was born on September 3, 1710. Soon she returned to the stage, playing at Lunéville and Strasbourg, where in 1714 Voltaire saw her acting.

On May 14, 1717 she took Paris by storm in the role of the eponymous heroine of Crébillon's *Electre*, at the Comédie-Française. She went on to delight audiences by her interpretation of the female leads in the whole classical repertory, and she also distinguished herself in one of the runaway successes of the period, Houdar de la Motte's *Inès de Castro*. In thirteen years she performed over a thousand times in a hundred different roles, in comedy as well as tragedy, and took part in twenty-two premières. Of medium height, with a slightly aquiline nose and quite full cheeks, Adrienne Lecouvreur was always admired above all for the naturalness of her delivery; precisely what was meant by that praise is hard to say, but it is certain that she turned away from the elevated tone that had been thought especially suitable for tragedy since the seventeenth century when, for instance, Racine had taken the trouble to rehearse his leading lady, La Champmeslé, in what was called her "chant." Instead, her speech combined nobility with frank simplicity. She also took unusual pains to choose costumes suitable for her roles.

Adrienne Lecouvreur was also famous for her amours, and in particular her liaison with Maurice de Saxe (1691–1750), then at the start of what was to prove a brilliant career culminating in his elevation to the rank of Marshal of France, attracted much attention. She died suddenly— so suddenly that poisoning was suspected— with Voltaire and Maurice de Saxe at her bedside in March 1730. Because she refused to make a formal repentance for her connection with the "sinful" profession of acting and, no doubt, also because her life had been tainted with scandal, the curé of Saint-Sulpice, Languet de Gergy, refused her Christian rites and burial in consecrated ground. Instead she was laid to rest, wrapped only in a sheet, at night in a hastily dug grave in waste ground not far from the present-day Quai d'Orsay in Paris. Voltaire, who had been her constant admirer and had praised her abilities in a number of poems, expressed his fury at the attitude of the church in his poem on "La Mort de Mlle Lecouvreur." In the twenty-eighth of his *Lettres philosophiques* in which he contrasts English and French customs, he did not let slip the opportunity of contrasting the ignominious burial of Adrienne Lecouvreur with the funeral of the celebrated English actress Anne Nance Oldfield in Westminster Abbey, though he conveniently overlooked the fact that the ecclesiastical authorities had drawn the line at allowing her lover to erect a monument to her memory.

It was, of course, in the theatre that Adrienne Lecouvreur gave her best, but her personal letters have an easy style and great spirit. Her brilliant career and tragic end caught the imagination of Eugène Scribe and Ernest Legouvé whose melodramatic *Adrienne Lecouvreur, comédie-drame* was first performed on April 14, 1849 with Rachel, the star of the age, in the title role which Sarah Bernhardt was later to take up with great success. A. Colautti fashioned a libretto from the play, and Francesco Cilea set it to music; with Angelica Pandolfini as Adrianna and Enrico Caruso as Murizio its première at the Teatro lirico, Milan on November 6, 1902 was a great success, and the opera remains on the fringes of the standard repertoire to the present day.

Works

Lettres, ed. Georges Monval (1892). "Lettres à Maurice de Saxe," in *Revue des Deux Mondes*, ed. Marquis d'Argenson (December 15, 1926), pp. 814–842; (January 1, 1927), pp. 104–128; (January 15, 1927), pp. 349–371. Marquis d'Argenson, *Adrienne Lecouvreur et Maurice de Saxe: leurs lettres d'amour* (1926).

Bibliography

Germain, Pierre, *Adrienne Lecouvreur, tragédienne* (Paris, 1983). Sainte-Beuve, C.A., *Causeries du lundi*, I (Paris, 1857), pp. 199–220. Voltaire, "La Mort de Mlle Lecouvreur (1730)." *Oeuvres complètes*, IX (Paris, 1877).

Christopher Smith

Denise Le Dantec

Born 1937, Brittany, France
Genre(s): poetry, essay
Language(s): French

Denise Le Dantec is a poet, philosopher and painter. She obtained the Grand Prix de la Poésie en Bretagne in 1980 and the Prix de Poésie de la Société des Gens de Lettres in 1986.

Le Jour (Daylight), published with the Editions des Femmes in 1975, was Denise Le Dantec's second book, after *Métropole* (1970; Metropolis). It offers a series of prose texts upon the feminine condition, of which the last, "Notes pour un scénario imaginaire (Notes for an Imaginary Scenario) is perhaps the most well known. As a whole, the book explores (a) woman's agoraphobia, the "madness" of her entrapments. It is feminist only in the most powerfully and delicately positive sense: it is about women, their minds, their oppression, and it endeavors to discover whether feminine perception and feeling exist *per se*. It is "an ethical reflection on feminine experience, but also a call for transgression, for political transition and fulguration."

Mémoire des dunes (Memory of Dunes) appeared in 1985, eight years after her third book, *Les Joueurs de Go* (The Go Players). It is a slim, elliptically eloquent collection, at once centered upon the world, presence, and self-reflexively concerned with the questionableness of its own links with the real. The world relent-

lessly ciphers itself, constant and shifting, falling prey to the senses, especially sight, and consciousness, especially via memory. In this sense writing for Denise Le Dantec is doubly lucid, beyond hope, beyond stupor, yet it does move towards some fullness in the midst of its marred and holed condition.

Les Fileuses d'étoupe (The Cotton Spinners) also appeared in 1985 and together with *Mémoire des dunes* heralds a period of intense creative and critical activity, with books to appear soon with Plon, PUF, Qui Vive and Folle Avoine. *Les Fileuses d'étoupe* is a much more extensive and complicated collection than *Mémoire des dunes*. Predicated upon a desire to match the "dimensions of the world" in its ecstatic-convulsive spasms, the collection articulates a taut serenity at the intersection of near-mystical feminine principles and extreme alertness to all that threatens to overwhelm. On the one hand, Denise Le Dantec plunges into the simple and the profound in being, sensitive to the shadow within the shadow, the other within what appears to be. On the other hand, her writing can be "confounded" with a consciousness of all that is wretched, poisoned and hurt, by a sense of invading darkness, restlessness and nervous wear. A "Black Angel" may thus impose its presence, rendering love a hell, exchange mutual enmity. The collection achieves some reconciliation, however, in balancing combat with prayer, in fusing "visible and invisible/In the filthy gentleness of our earth."

Works

Métropole (1970). *Le Jour* (1975). *Les Joueurs de Go* (1977). *Le Bar aux oiseaux* (libretto), musique de Patrice Fouillaud (1980). *Mémoire des dunes* (1985). *Les Fileuses d'étoupe* (1985).

Bibliography

Bishop, Michael, "Contemporary Women Poets." *Contemporary French Poetry, Studies in Twentieth-Century Literature* (Fall 1988). Marks, Elaine, and Courtivron, Isabelle de, *New French Feminisms* (New York, 1981).

Michael Bishop

Violette Leduc

Born 1907, Arras, France; died 1972
Genre(s): novel, autobiography
Language(s): French

Violette Leduc was born in Arras in 1907 and grew up in Valenciennes, in the close atmosphere described in *La Bâtarde* (1964; The Bastardess), in which her mother and grandmother played such decisive roles, her father not recognizing his daughter. The latter book, firmly autobiographical like nearly all her books, also evokes her early life as a *pensionnaire*, her high school days in Paris and her work as editorial secretary and publicity writer with Plon, a major French publishing house, and, later, as a journalist. *La Bâtarde* and *La Folie en tête* (1970; Madness in Mind) describe in intimate detail and with her characteristic admixture of intensity and detachment her various friendships with Maurice Sachs, Jean Genet, Simone de Beauvoir, and others and the respect earned, with difficulty and yet certainty, from them and other writers such as Sartre, Jouhandeau, and Camus. Violette Leduc died in 1972 in Faucon, in the Alps of Upper Provence.

In 1946, Camus welcomed the manuscript of *L'Asphyxie* (Asphyxia) into the collection *Espoir* he was then editing. It was clearly an auspicious start for Violette Leduc although it would take many years, until the publication of *La Bâtarde* in 1964, for widespread public success. Simone de Beauvoir argued that all of Violette Leduc's books could assume the title of *L'Asphyxie*.

After *L'Affamée* (1948; Famished), which speaks, through the typical blatancy of its title, of the deep yearnings and desires that, inevitably, peopled the gaping holes of emotional and aesthetic deprivation and frustration of Violette Leduc's private and public lives, came *Ravages* (1955; Ravages). This powerful book, linked to all the others in its fundamental obsessions and aspirations (and perhaps especially to *Thérèse et Isabelle*), proceeds to narrate, with the most transparent of novelistic veils, the reciprocally ravaging effect of a double possessive passion. Jealousy, the tensions of exclusion and sharing, blindness and lucidity, the gentleness and the (self-)destructiveness of love, the wonders and the horrors of high emotion: these are the principal elements of a book as profoundly confessional as any of the great books of self-revelation by contemporaries such as Maurois, Mauriac, de Beauvoir, Malraux, and many others.

La Vieille Fille et le mort (1958; The Old Woman and the Corpse), which also offers us "Les Boutons dorés," recounts the moving, pathetic gestures of a woman desperately wishing to reveal her love, incapable of finding that delicate equilibrium of giving and receiving with men, thrust up against her loneliness, her age, her inhibitions. It is a short novel of quiet tragedy and, typically, resistant, even if intransitive, hope. "Les Boutons dorés" is a short novel of youth and love, loss and "floating." Less flagrantly centered upon the self, it nevertheless partakes of the essential paradoxes and struggles at the heart of all Violette Leduc's work.

Trésors à prendre (1960; Treasures for the Taking) is, perhaps, the most splendidly resilient and, in a sense, serene of all of her works. Relating her wanderings on foot through Southern France in 1951, it demonstrates with supreme clarity Violette Leduc's passion for life. The emotional gamut is a full one: despair, solitude, fear, vulnerability, inadequacy, victimization, courage, persistence, vigor, recovery, and love. The "centers of interest" are as endless as the things of the world, and as rich, as profound, as significant. The style is characteristically telegraphic, staccato, never predictable, sharply observant.

La Bâtarde, according to Simone de Beauvoir, offers "a temperament, a style." The book depicts with intensity the strife in Violette Leduc's life, it treats her "ugliness," the stiflements and humiliations, the ambivalences and tensions of her many human interchanges. She also finds in love a crucial "instinct of self-preservation" and shows, in S. de Beauvoir's celebrated phrase, "that a life is the taking up of a destiny by a freedom." *La Folie en tête* (1970) ekes out a salvation by its intense interest in the world and deep cherishing of people. It, too, is searingly authentic, audacious, and rarely judgmental. Violette Leduc continues to be the misfit, the outsider, mistrustful yet desiring, dazzled yet lucid when faced with the literary "stars" of her epoch. This book, like all her books, bears the mark of love's burning trace upon her body and her soul.

Works

Prose: *Ma mère ne m'a jamais donné la main* (1945). *L'Asphyxie* (1946). *L'Affamée* (1948). *Ravages* (1955). *La Chasse à l'amour* (1973). *La vieille fille et le mort* (1958). *Trésors à prendre* (1960). *La Bâtarde*, préf. de Simone de Beauvoir (1964). *La Femme au petit renard* (1965). *La Folie en tête* (1970). *Thérèse et Isabelle* (1970). *Le Taxi* (1971).

Bibliography

Aury, Dominique, "VL." *NRF* 255 (March, 1974): 114–116. Balakian, Anna, "*Mad in Pursuit* by VL." *Saturday Review* (Sept. 1971): 47. Beauvoir, Simone de, Preface to *La Bâtarde* (Paris, 1964). Beauvoir, Simone de, "VL: La passion de vivre." *Nouvel Observateur* 395 (June, 1972): 68. Bishop, Thomas, "A Light on Loneliness." *Saturday Review* 49, 48 (Nov. 1976): 44–45. Bliven, Naomi, "Unhappy as the Day Is Long." *New Yorker* (Mar. 1972): 11–13. Brooks, Peter, "Escaping the Inner Prison Through the Solitary Labour of Writing." *NY Times Book Review* (Oct. 1971): 4, 41. Burns, Robert, "The Fourth Sex." *Nation* (Sydney) 186 (Jan. 1966): 21–22. Chalon, Jean, "Les dernières béatitudes de VL." *Figaro Littéraire* 1437 (déc. 1973): III, 15. Courtivron, Isabelle de, "VL's *L'Affamée*: The Courage to Displace." *Contemporary Women Writers in France, L'Esprit Créateur* (1979), pp. 95–106. Evans, Martha Noël, "La mythologie de l'écriture dans *La Bâtarde* de VL." *Graphies* (Paris, 1982), pp. 82–92. Faabre-Luce, Anne, "A la proue du silence." *Quinzaine littéraire*, 178 (jan. 1974): 15. Galey, Matthieu, "Extravagante Violette." *Réalités* 334 (nov. 1973): 120–121. Josselin, Jean-François, "VL, suite et fin. . . ." *Nouvel Observateur* 467 (oct. 1973): 59. Kikkert, Marja, "VL et l'écriture." *Analyses de textes* (Groningen, 1982). Kyria, Pierre, "La 'sincérité intrépide' de VL." *Combat* 8668 (June, 1972): 7. Lacey, Nicola, "Asphyxia." *Observer* 9331 (May 1970): 31. Lange, Monique, "*Le Taxi*, par VL." *Nouvel Observateur* 350 (August, 1971): 37. Lorier, Carry, "VL et la bâtardise." *Analyses de textes* (Groningen), 110–132. Marchessault, Jovette, *La Terre est trop courte, VL* (Montréal, 1982). "Mort de la romancière VL." *Monde* 8514 (May, 1972): 29. Poirot-Delpech, Bertrand, "Le salut par l'écriture." *Monde des livres* 8940 (oct. 1973): 19. Prior, Maurice, "A Crackle of Satire." *Illustrated London News* 252, 6722 (June 1968): 32. Rule, Jane, "VL: 1907–1972." *Lesbian Images* (New York, 1975): pp. 139–146. Schoenfeld, Jean Snitzer, "*La Bâtarde*, or Why the Writer Writes." *French Forum* 7, 3 (sept. 1982): 261–268. "Utterly unhappy." *TLS* 3764 (Apr. 1974): 442. Van Dyke, Anne, "Léon et Emma." *NY Times Book Review* (Aug. 1972): 28. Weightman, John, "Blushing Violette." *Observer* 9390 (July 1971): 28. Wood, Michael, "Squish." *NY Review of Books* 19, 2 (Aug. 1972): 14–16.

Michael Bishop

Anne Charlotte Leffler

(a.k.a. Carlot, Anne Charlotte Edgren, f. Leffler)

Born October 1, 1849, Stockholm, Sweden;
died October 21, 1892, Naples, Italy
Genre(s): drama, novellas, novels, biography
Language(s): Swedish

In the wake of August Strindberg's novel *Röda Rummet* (1879; The Red Room), Anne Charlotte Leffler became one of Sweden's most talented naturalistic writers. Leffler participated in the pan-Scandinavian social debates, inspired by Ibsen and Brandes, and created vivid portraits of her own society.

Anne Charlotte Leffler came from a family of artists and scholars. She was encouraged in her early literary efforts by her father, Rector John Olof Leffler, who published her first novellas at his own expense. In 1872, Leffler married a friend of the family, Gustaf Edgren. Although Leffler entered into the marriage willingly, the union was not a particularly happy one.

Leffler's first attempt at a play, *Skådespelerskan* (performed 1873, published 1883, The Actress) was submitted anonymously to the Dramatic Theater in Stockholm. The play tells the story of a woman who must choose between her artistic calling or love and was very well received by the public. This success was followed by other plays dealing with a woman's right to free personal development. One of the best known of these, *Sanna Kvinnor* (1883; True Women, 1885) consisted of a polemic against the notion that true women must be submissive and eternally forgiving of male vices. Despite these literary arguments on behalf of women's rights, Leffler always distanced herself from the women's movement proper, since she felt it agitated for a masculinization of women.

Leffler found her true element in the prose novella. Between the years 1882 to 1893, Leffler published six volumes of novellas under the collective title of *Ur livet* (1882–1893; From Life). In her novella "Aurora Bunge" (1883; Aurora Bunge), a young woman from high society has a tempestuous affair with a lighthouse operator but then is pushed into a marriage of convenience to conceal the consequences of this dalliance. Implicit in the tale is a critique of the social structure which requires Aurora to forsake her own passions. The novella created a furor in the morally conservative climate of Sweden. Leffler was especially fond of demasking social hypocrisy, as in "En stor man" (1882; A Great Man). In that novella, the daughter of a great man, a member of the Swedish Academy, discovers that her dying father is financially and morally bankrupt, but after his death, society conspires to conceal the sins of one of their cultural heroes.

Leffler soon became one of the foremost representatives of the "Young Sweden" literary group, and her salon was a cultural centerpoint in Stockholm. Leffler struck up a close friendship with the Russian mathematician Sonja Kovalevsky, with whom she collaborated in writing the drama *Kampen för lyckan* (1887; The Fight for Happiness). After her friend's death, Leffler wrote a well-known memoir in Kovalevsky's honor. In 1889, Leffler divorced Gustaf Edgren and shortly thereafter married for love Pasquale del Pezzo, Duke of Cajanello and Professor of Mathematics at Naples University. Not long after the birth of their daughter in 1892, Leffler died from appendicitis at the age of forty-three.

Soon after her death, Leffler's biography gained a good deal of attention as an archetypal female destiny, and she became the subject of monographs by both Ellen Key and Laura Marholm. Among literary critics, her work has often been dismissed as *kvinnlig problemliteratur* (female polemical literature), but more recently critics have displayed a renewed interest in her literary artistry and special brand of "sober realism."

Works

Händelsevis (1869). *Pastorsadjunkten* (1876). *Ur livet, 1*: En bal i "societeten," En stor man, En triumf, Dömd, Doktorns hustru, Sesam öppna dig! Tvifvel (1882). *Ur livet, 2*: Aurore Bunge, Barnet, Ett bröllop, I krig mid samhèllet (1883). *Elfvan* (1883). *Sanna kvinnor* (1883). *Skådespelerskan. Under toffeln* (1883). *Ur livet, 3:1* Kvinnlighet och erotik [1], Gusten får pastoratet (1883). *Hur man gör godt* (1885). *Ur livet, 4*: En sommarsaga 12 (1886). *Kampen för lyckan* (1887). *Ur livet, 3:2*: Gamla jungfrun, I fattigstugan, En brödkaka, Moster Malvina, Gråtande venus (1889). *Ur livet, 5*: Kvinnlighet och erotik 2 (1890). *Familjelycka* (1892). *Den kärleken* (1892). *Moster Malvina* (1892). *Sonja Kovalevsky* (1892). *Efterlämnade Skrifter 1–2*: 1: Sanningens vägar, Napolitanska bilder; 2: *Ur livet, 6*: Trång horisont, Resa utrikes, Giftermål af tycke, Utomkring äktenskapet, Ett underverk, Jämlikhet (1893).

Translations: *Sonja Kovalevsky: Biography & Autobiography*, tr. Louise von Cossel (1895). *True Women*, tr. H.L.Braekstad (1885).

Bibliography

Hennel, Ingeborg Nordin, "Aurore Bunge. Några reflexioner kring en 1880-tals-novell," in *Kvinnor och skapande*, ed. Birgitta Paget (Stockholm, 1983), pp. 163–175. Holmberg, Hans, "Några brev från Anne-Charlotte Edgren-Leffler till Herman Bang." *Nordisk Tidskrift* 59 (1983): 188–190. Palmkvist, Karin, "Hur 'skrifvande damer' bedömdes." *Tidskrift för litteraturvetenskap* 10 (1981): 115–122. Svensson, Conny, "Sommarsagan och verkligheten." *Svensk Litteraturtidskrift* 45, no. 2 (1982): 40–252. Sylvan, Maj, *Anne Charlotte Leffler. En kvinna finner sing väg* (Stockholm, 1984). Utterström, Gudrun, "Ann Charlotte Leffler. Uttrycksmedel och uttryckssätt." *Vitterhetsnöjen. Läsning för humanister och andra* (Umeå, 1980), pp. 175–196.

Susan Brantley

f. Leffler

(see: Anne Charlotte Leffler)

Luisa Castro Legazpi

Born July 11, 1966, Foz (Lugo), Spain
Genre(s): poetry
Language(s): Spanish

Luisa Castro is one of the youngest published poets in Spain. In 1986 she won the first Premio de Poesía Hiperión for her book *Los versos del eunuco* (Verses of the Eunuch). This collection, which begins with a quote from Terence's *Eunucchus*, appears to be a reckoning with history itself seen as the great castrator of humankind. In this book, Castro's verse has a rough and uncompromising dramatical quality.

Castro boldly gives herself over to each word. Many of the poems in her book *Odisea definitiva* (Definitive Odyssey) seem to be a continuous dialogue between tenderness and violence. Poems such as "Casi mediodía" (Almost Noon), "Apuntes sobre el crepúsculo" (Notes on the Twilight), and "Epílogo" (Epilogue) call attention to her subtle control of the language and her discursive ability. These are poems in which Castro presents herself as poet-narrator of her love experience.

Luisa Castro has been a precocious writer. She has a large amount of unpublished material in Galician as well as in Castilian. Currently she is a student of Hispanic Philology at the University of Santiago at Compostela, in Galicia.

Works

Odisea definitiva, libro póstumo [Definitive Odyssey] (1984). *Los versos del eunuco* [Verses of the Eunuch] (1986).

Bibliography

Las diosas blancas. Antología de la joven poesía española escrita por mujeres (Madrid, 1985), pp. 216–232.

Carlota Caulfield

Ann Tizia Leitich

Born January 25, 1896, Vienna, Austria; died
September 3, 1976, Vienna
Genre(s): novel, travel literature, biography
Language(s): German

Ann Tizia Leitich had a turbulent life as a correspondent of various German and Austrian newspapers in the United States. She studied at the High School Training Institute in Vienna, then transferred to the United States. She worked in New York, and Chicago, later again in Vienna. She married a man named Korningen, but her work only became known under her maiden name. Her American experiences dominate her novels and travel reports.

Works

Novels: *Ursula entdeckt Amerika* [Ursula Discovers America] (1926). *Amor in Wappen, Roman aus dem Wien der Kongreßzeit* [Love in Coats-of-Arms. Novel from the Time of the Viennese Congress (1815)] (1940). *Drei in Amerika* [Three in America] (1946). *Unvergleichliche Amonate, Roman einer Indianerin* [Uncomparable Amonate, Novel of a North American Indian Woman] (1947). *Der Kaiser mit dem Granatapfel, Ein Roman der Wirklichkeit* [The Emperor with the Pomegranate, A Novel about Reality] (1955). *Metternich und die Sibylle, Ein intimer Roman im hochpolitische Rahmen* [Metternich and the Sibyl, An Intimate Novel Within a Very Important Political Framework], later also under the title *Ein intimer Roman im hochpolitische Rahmen* [An Intimate Novel Within the Framework of Very Important Politics] (1960).

Studies, Essays, Travel Reports, Biographies: *Amerika, du hast es besser* [America, You Are Much Luckier] (1926). *New York* (1932). *König von Eldorado, Eine romantische Chronik* [King in Eldorado, A Romantic Chronicle] (1938). *Die Wienerin* [The Viennese Woman] (1939). *Wiener Biedermeier, Kultur, Kunst und Leben der alten Kaiserstadt vom Wiener Kongreß bis zum Sturmjahr 1848* [Viennese Biedermeier, Culture, Art and Life in the Old Imperial City from the Viennese Congress Until the Stormy Year of 1848] (1941). *Verklungenes Wien, Vom Biedermeier zur Jahrhundertwende* [Sounds Faded Away in Vienna, from Biedermeier to the Turn of the Century] (1942). *Vienna gloriosa: Weltstadt des Barock* [Glorious Vienna: World Metropole of the Baroque] (1948). *Zwölfmal Liebe, Frauen um Grillparzer* [Twelfth Time Love, Women Around Grillparzer] (1950). *Augustissima, Maria Theresia—Leben und Werk* [Augustissima, Maria Theresia—Life and Work] (1953). *Begegnung in Chicago* [Encounter in Chicago] (1954). *Die spanische Reitschule in*

Wien [The Spanish Horseback Riding School in Vienna] (1956). *Damals in Wien, Das große Jahrhundert einer Weltstadt 1800–1900* [Long Ago in Vienna, The Great Century of a World Metropole, 1800–1900] (1957). *Lippen schweigen—flüstern Geigen, Ewiger Zauber der Wiener Operette* [Lips Are Silent—Violins Are Whispering, Eternal Magic of the Viennese Operetta] (1960). *Premiere in London, Georg Friedrich Händel und seine Zeit* [Premiere in London, Georg Friedrich Händel and His Time] (1962). *Das süße Wien, Von Kanditoren und Konditoren* [The Sweet Vienna, on Candy Bakers and Tart Bakers] (1964). *Genie und Leidenschaft, Die Frauen um Grillparzer* [Genius and Passion, the Women Around Grillparzer] (1965). *Eine rätselhafte Frau, Madame Récamier und ihre Freunde* [An Enigmatic Woman, Madame Récamier and Her Friends].

Bibliography

Bigler, Ingrid, "Lingen, Ann Thekla." *Deutsches Literatur-Lexikon*, 3rd completely revised ed. by H. Rupp and C.L. Lang, vol. 9 (Bern-Munich, 1984), col. 1186.

Albrecht Classen

Lavdie Leka

Born 1935, Lushnjë, Albania
Genre(s): short story
Language(s): Albanian

Leka gained prominence as a woman writer of short stories in Albania. She studied in Moscow at the Lenin Institute for Advanced Pedagogical Studies. She is chief editor of the magazine *Shqiptarja e re* (The New Albanian Woman) and vice-president of the Albanian Union of Women.

Works

Mos e këndo atë këngë [Don't Sing That Song] (1965). *Djemtë e rrugicës me kalldrëm* [The Boys from the Paved Alley] (1976).

Philip Shashko

Ellen Gyrithe Lemche

Born April 17, 1866, Copenhagen, Denmark;
    died May 3, 1945, Lyngby
Genre(s): novel, short story, history
Language(s): Danish

Gyrithe Lemche joined the Danish women's rights movement in 1910 and soon became its first historian with *Dansk Kvindesamfunds Historie Gennem 40 Aar* (1911; History of Danish Women's Society Through 40 Years). From 1913 to 1918, she headed the Society's executive committee, and from 1913 to 1919, she edited its journal, *Kvinden og Samfundet* (Woman and Society). In 1921–1922, she was national president. Based on her experiences in the women's movement, Lemche's novels and short stories contributed to contemporary discussions of women's rights and duties.

Lemche's debut novel, *Folkets Synder* (1899; Sins of the People), is a vitriolic attack on the double standard, with an emphasis on the threat of venereal disease. The autobiographical *Tempeltjenere* I-III (1926–1928; Temple Servants) argues for a woman's movement of married women, focusing on the eternal feminine—maternity—rather than the vote. A later novel, *Vuggen Gaar* (1935; Rock the Cradle) further examines the relationship between marriage, freedom and motherhood.

Lemche's historical works more indirectly trace the origins of the gender constructs of her class. The novel cycle *Edwardsgave* (1900–1912; Edwardsgave) describes the rise and fall of the merchant bourgeoisie from the 1750s to the 1890s through the stories of two families, while the four-volume *Strømmen* (1929–1932; The Stream) follows the male protagonists' struggle to establish an industry based on water power.

Lemche's literary production explores the sexual and intellectual oppression of women that propelled the author into a political fight for protective legislation. Primarily remembered as a feminist and a historian, Lemche remains a central and controversial figure of the early women's movement in Denmark.

Works

Soedtmanns Jomfruer (1898). *Folkets Synder* (1899). *Edwardsgave* I-IV (1900–1912). *De*

Fyrstenberg Bønder (1905). *Naar Dagen, Den Kommer* (1909). *Kvindesagen i Sang, Tale og Skrift* (1910). *Anadyomene og Andre Fortaellinger* (1910). *Dansk Kvindesamfund Gennem 40 Aar* (1911). *Paa Godt og Ondt: En Bog om Ungdom* (1924). *Fru Fama: En Hofkrønike fra Det Attende Aarhundrede* (1925). *Tempeltjenere* I-III (1926–1928). *Strømmen* I-IV (1929–1932). *Bedemandens Datter* (1934). *Vuggen Gaar* (1935). *Bedeslag* (1936). *Farvergaarden* (1937). *Jeg Saa Mig Tilbage* (1943). *De Fagre Riger* (1945).

Translations: "For Dear Life," tr. W.W. Worster. *American-Scandinavian Review* 13 (August 1925).

Bibliography

Gandrup, Richardt, "Gyrithe Lemche." *Døgnet og Tiden: Kritik og Betragtning* (Copenhagen, 1926), pp. 111–120. Juncker, Beth, "Emma Gad og Gyrithe Lemche." *Danske Digtere i Det 20. Aarhundrede* I, ed. Torben Brostrøm and Mette Winge (Copenhagen, 1980), pp. 330–342.

Clara Juncker

Filipa de Lencastre

Born 1437; died 1497
Genre(s): translation/adaptation, poetry
Language(s): Portuguese

The daughter of Infante D. Pedro, Duque de Coimbra, who died tragically in 1449 at Alfarrobeira, Filipa de Lencastre, princess of the Houses of Avis and Lencastre, spent much of her life in retirement in the convent of Odievellas near Lisbon. Her sister was Queen Isabel of Portugal (d. 1455). Her brother, Infante D. Pedro (1429–1466), Constable of Portugal, was the transition poet who inaugurated the practice of writing in Castilian, a fashion that lasted two centuries. He also introduced classical allusion and allegory into poetry.

A major influence on Lencastre's work was Laurentius Justinianus, patriarch of Venice. She wrote adaptations or translations, from Latin to Portuguese, of two of his works. To *Tratado da vida solitária*, which meditates on the contemplative life, Lencastre added her own rhymed tract. *Regra dos Monges* deals with spiritual perfection and disdain for the world. There is considerable debate as to who translated or adapted this second work. Some critics credit Infanta D. Catarina, the daughter of D. Duarte and Filipa de Lencastre's cousin, but it seems reasonable to believe that each woman, writing in isolation, most probably did her own translation.

Adept at combining the pious with the literary, Lencastre's style of translation is lively, her language vibrant, strong, and beautiful. At least one of her own poems survives. The following is the complete text of her dedicatory poem to her own translation of the Gospels.

> Ao Bom Jesus
> Nam vos sirvo nem vos amo
> mas desejo vos amar,
> de sempre vossa me chamo
> sem quem nam é repousar.
> O' vida e lume e luz,
> infindo bem e inteiro,
> meu Jesus, Deus verdadeiro,
> por mim morto em a cruz.
> Se mim mesma nam desamo
> nam vos posso bem amar:
> a me ajudar vos chamo
> para saber repousar!

Works

Regra dos Monges. Tratado da vida solitária.

Bibliography

Bell, Aubrey F.G., *The Oxford Book of Portuguese Verse* (Oxford, 1925). Bell, Aubrey F.G., *Portuguese Literature* (1922; rpt. Oxford, 1970). Martins, Mario S.J., *Estudios De Literatura Medieval* (Braga, 1956).

Rosetta Radtke

Anne de Lenclos

Born January 9, 1623 (?), Paris, France; died
*   October 17, 1706, Paris*
Genre(s): letters
Language(s): French

Ninon de Lenclos, a French courtesan, who later became the legendary model of the free thinker for such French Philosophes as Voltaire, was born in Paris. Although the records of her birth were lost in a Parisian fire, from the evidence of her letters, it appears that she was born in

November of 1620 or on the ninth of January 1623. She was the daughter of Henri de Lenclos, an aristocratic scholar and soldier of fortune whose talent for lute playing is well documented. Her mother, Marie-Barbe de La Manche, was from an old and well-established French family.

When Anne was twelve, her father killed a man and was forced to flee the country. He left his daughter little more than an example of heroic rebellion and his gift for lute playing. Anne's mother, probably poverty stricken, was forced to send her daughter to the Marais when only sixteen, there to become a professional dancer and lute player in Paris' most fashionable neighborhood. The move was tantamount to pushing Anne into prostitution, and indeed, she rapidly became one after her appearance in the Marais.

Her first affair, with a man named St. Etienne, appears to have been a matter of affection rather than cash. In part, Anne seems to have valued him for his skills as a conversationalist. Whatever the attraction, however, this first affair confirmed her marginal status in French society, and, soon after the doors of the Marais were shut to her, she turned to her second lover, Jean Coulon, a noted libertine and counsellor to Parliament, who agreed to support her for five hundred livres a month. With this arrangement, she became a full-fledged courtesan. By her third lover, M. de Châtillon, she had established a life-long pattern—her need for an individual existence independent of her clients and her forceful if charming determination to satisfy her own desires as well as the desires of others.

From 1640–1656, Lenclos became an important fixture of French libertine society. She changed her name to Ninon, perhaps to establish a parallel with the older and more famous Italian courtesan, and established lasting friendships with such men as Paul Scarron, who wrote the first of many literary tributes to her. Her lovers included noted libertines such as Miossens d'Albert, Alexandre d'Elbéne, and Charlevall, men whose opinions on free love and free thought greatly influenced her and added to her earlier fascination with the writings of Montaigne. Although she was self-taught, and her learning, in many ways, remained sketchy, she displayed certain linguistic gifts, and a faculty for framing the bon mot and the witty aphorism. In addition, her artistic abilities as a lute player and a dancer, as well as her marvelous voice and her reputation as a witty conversationalist, helped to make her house the obvious gathering place for an intellectual as well as social elite. During these years, she was widely celebrated in the written and spoken word as a woman of intelligence and pleasing disposition, as an artist of talent, as a charming conversationalist who could reason on Herodotus, Plato, or Epicurus, as a witty debater of moral strictures, but always, and disconcertingly, as a courtesan. During these years too, her only idyllic love affair, with Villarceaux, produced her only surviving child, a son.

All of this heady success came to an abrupt halt in March 1656 when Ninon was incarcerated on the order of Queen Anne of Austria in the Madelonettes, an institution for women of low reputation. Her crimes were listed as debauchery and impiety—she was an open scoffer of religious tenets and indiscreet about her failure to observe the Lenten laws. After a short while, she was moved to the convent in Lagny, and while there, she was visited by Queen Christina of Sweden, another woman who conceived of her role in terms other than traditional ones. It is possible that Ninon's later release came at the request of this unusual woman.

Back in Paris Ninon attempted to reform her image and gain a position once more in respectable society. She moved back to the Marais next to her friend Paul Scarron, whose new wife, the future Madame de Maintenon, would prove an important ally. Once again she used her abilities as a lute player to open important doors, giving lessons to society women as a way of reentering respectable circles. By 1675, her transformation from Ninon the courtesan to Mlle de Lenclos was complete. Her wit and her charm, her legendary honesty, her social skills, won her admiration even from Madame de la Sablière, the estranged wife of Ninon's former lover, Antoine de Rambouillet. It was a mark of Ninon's acceptance that she became Madame de la Sablière's friend.

In her old age she met Voltaire, whose father was her accountant and to whom she left a small legacy with which to buy books. By this time, she had succeeded in transforming herself into a myth, a myth which greatly attracted the young

Voltaire and proved fertile material for further myth-making on his part. However, at the time of her death on October 17, 1706, her life really embodied an achievement far different from Voltaire's picture of the single standard for both sexes, the free-thinker, the debunker of social hypocrisy. Actually, Madame de Lenclos was one of the great social climbers of her day. Her life story is one of a slow ascent from marginal exclusion to total inclusion within the conventional society of her time. Thanks to Voltaire, she is remembered primarily as a "sage courtesan." However, it is as a "femme d'esprit" rather than an "honnête homme" that she can continue to interest us.

Numerous works have been wrongly attributed to Lenclos, including the *Coquette vengée* (1659) and *Le portrait d'un inconnu* (1659). Aside from her inspiration of Clarisse in Mlle de Scudery's novel *Célie*, and Voltaire's use of her in "Ninon," arguably his best comedy, her sole interest as a literary figure lies in her correspondence, collected and published in 1886 by Colombey. All of these letters come from the pen of an older woman, a woman who is saving herself from the encroaching ennui of respectable living by wittily mocking her own successes. The letters, dated from 1677–1697, are primarily addressed to François de Bonrepaus and Saint Evremond. They are spontaneous and flowing, written without correction or review in an easy and rapid style. References to literary works are rare—in the thirty or more epistles, one finds Seneca mentioned twice and Rabelais only once. Instead of erudite allusions, the correspondence endlessly circles the topics of her son, La Sablière, her frail health, and, perhaps most importantly for the aging beauty, the question of the separation or identity of body and mind. The letters, while not particularly noteworthy for stylistic innovations, do give a privileged look into the mind of a woman whose most lasting triumph was her conquest of the society which had sought to exclude her. Lenclos won her place in that society not by birth but by close observation, shrewd planning, and inspired calculation. Such letters have much to tell us about the courtesans of Parisian society and the place of women in the society as a whole.

Works

Correspondance authentique de Ninon de Lenclos [The Authentic Correspondence of Ninon de Lenclos] (Rpt. 1968).

Bibliography

Cohen, E.H., *Mademoiselle Libertine* (New York, 1970). Duchêne, Roger, *Ninon de Lenclos* (Paris, 1984). Jal, Auguste, *Dictionnaire Critique et Biographie et d'Histoire* (rpt. New York, 1970), p. 771. Magne, Emile, *Ninon de Lenclos* (Paris, 1948). Réaux, Tallement des, *Histoirettes* (Paris, 1961). Uglow, Jennifer, ed., *International Dictionary of Women's Biography* (New York, 1982), p. 136.

Glenda Wall

Anna Maria (Malmstedt) Lenngren

Born June 18, 1754, Uppsala, Sweden; died March 8, 1817, Stockholm
Genre(s): poetry, satire, journalism
Language(s): Swedish

"Fru Lenngren" (as she is often called in Sweden) must be included in any listing of Sweden's best poets. She ranks certainly as its best poetess. She did not care for public recognition; all of her poems and articles, save one ("Dröm" [1798; Dream]), were published anonymously. Her verse, the best of it written during Sweden's troubled 1790s, provides a bridge of sorts from the Enlightenment period to the beginnings of Romanticism, for it contains elements of both.

Anna Maria Lenngren grew up in a bourgeois household where the father, Magnus Brynolf Malmstedt, was a member of the Moravian Brethren and took the needy into his home. It has been speculated that this "turmoil" in the home gave rise to Lenngren's desire for peaceful orderliness in her own adult household. This same father, a lecturer in Latin eloquence at Uppsala University, encouraged his daughter's learning, and she received a classical education virtually unheard of for girls of her time. This schooling in the Latin classics would serve her well when she took up the pen herself; one of her greatest skills is her acute sense of stylistic propriety. Her literary debut occurred in 1772 when she published some (unoriginal) poems in a newspaper. In 1780 she married a government employee, Carl Peter Lenngren, with whom she enjoyed an ostensibly happy, if childless, marriage. Lenngren assisted her husband in editing the newborn *Stockholms-Posten* during the 1780s, where she contributed causeries and witty poems as well, it is conjectured, as articles. The 1790s saw her most mature and perfect poetic creations, and her most controversial; her most satirical poems against the nobility could not be published until the nineteenth century. She was considered for a position in the prestigious Swedish Academy, but the time was not ripe for a woman to be admitted to this literary Parnassus, no matter how gifted she might be. But Lenngren herself was always disparaging of her own poetic talents and hid her pen and paper in a special cupboard when visitors came.

Lenngren's poems were collected and published for the first time after her death. Among them, some of the best are "Porträtterne" (1796; The Portraits), in which an older gout-plagued countess deigns to describe the portraits of her illustrious forebears for her servant girl, a satiric masterpiece in miniature; "Slottet och kojan" (1800; The Castle and the Cottage), which compares the simple, happy life of the poor man to the unhappy if materially comfortable one of the wealthy. "Några ord till min dotter, ifall jag hade någon" (1798; A Few Words to my Daughter, If I Had One) has been touted by some as proof that Lenngren valued the traditional wife-mother role higher than her literary efforts; others see an ironic, closet-feministic genesis for this piece. "Den glada festen" (1796; The Jolly Party) and "Grevinnans besök" (1800; The Countess' Visit) are considered her finest idylls; "Hans nåds morgonsömn" (1796; His Grace's Morning Sleep) is one of her most tart poetic commentaries, presenting the nobleman sleeping off a night of "wine, women and song" while his middle-class creditors, some in desperate need of their payment, wait for him to leave his bed.

Lenngren's poetry has aged well; she is a standard classic even today. During her lifetime and afterward, she was accorded the admiration and respect of many readers, educated and not, female and male. Her "snapshot" style does not rule out an occasional touch of sentimentality; she writes in praise of bourgeois morality and simplicity. Even so, many scholars find it difficult to encapsulate her work into a simple, all-encompassing description, and she remains one of Sweden's most enigmatic, as well as admired, poets.

Works

Skaldeförsök [Poetic Attempts] (1819).
Translations: Nelson, Philip K., *Anna Maria Lenngren: 1754–1817*, poems (1984). "The Portraits," "The Boy and His Playthings," and "Castle and Cottage" [respectively, "Porträtterne," 1796; "Gossen och leksakerna," 1798; and "Slottet och kojan," 1800], in Charles Wharton Stork, *Anthology of Swedish Lyrics from 1750 to 1915* (New York, 1917). "Family Portraits" [Porträtterne"], in Henry Wadsworth Longfellow, *Poets and Poetry of Europe* (Philadelphia, 1845). (This version also appears, the translator's name unmentioned, in N. Clemmons Hunt [ed.], *Poetry of Other Lands*, Philadelphia, 1883.)

Bibliography

Blanck, Anton, *Anna Maria Lenngren, Poet och pennskaft jämte andra studier* (Stockholm, 1922). Böök, Fredrik, *Stridsmän och sångare* (Stockholm, 1910). Gustafson, Alrik, *A History of Swedish Literature* (Minneapolis, 1961). Kunitz, Stanley J., and Vineta Colby, eds., *European Authors 1000–1900* (New York, 1967). Olsson, Henry, *Törnrosdiktaren och andra porträtt* (Stockholm, 1956). von Platen, Magnus, *1700-tal, Studier i svensk litteratur* (Stockholm, 1963). Pleijel, Agneta, "Den kvinnliga författaren och offentligheten. Om Anna Maria Lenngren." Ardelius, Lars, and Gunnar Rydström, eds., *Författarnas litteraturhistoria* (Stockholm, 1977). Tigerstedt, E.N., *Svensk litteraturhistoria* (Stockholm, 1948). Warburg, Karl, *Anna Maria Lenngren* (Stockholm, 1887).

Kathy Saranpa Anstine

André Léo

Born 1832, Champagné Saint-Hilaire (Vienna); died 1900
Genre(s): essay, novel, polemic
Language(s): French

Born to a retired French naval officer and his wife, in 1853 Léodile Bera married Grégoire

Champceix, a disciple and lieutenant of Pierre Leroux, who had relocated to Lausanne, Switzerland, in the wake of the repression following the revolution of 1848. They had twin sons, André and Léo, and (according to one account) a daughter. The family returned to Paris following the political amnesty of 1860 and quickly became active in political causes. Champceix died in late 1863, and his widow began to publish under a pseudonym composed of the names of her twin sons. A number of her novels concerning the problem of marriage for French women appeared in *Le Siècle* in serial form. In 1866 she founded the *Société pour la Revendication du Droit de la Femme* (Society for the Pursuit of Woman's Right[s]), which merged in 1881 with a second group established in 1870 by Maria Deraismes. Throughout the late 1860s her Parisian salon served as a gathering point for radicals and women's movement figures from Europe and North America.

During the Prussian siege of Paris and the Commune of 1871, André Léo became active as a public speaker and journalist of repute. She escaped to Switzerland just before the bitter repression set in. There she became the associate and lifelong companion of Benoît Malon, who subsequently became a major leader of non-Marxian socialism in France. Little is known of André Léo's later life, although she did continue to publish fiction until the end of the century.

Works

Un Mariage scandaleux (1862; new ed. 1883). *Une vieille fille; articles de divers journaux sur un mariage scandaleux* (1864). *Observations d'une mère de famille à M. Duruy* (1865). *Les Deux filles de M. Plicohn* (1865). *Un Divorce* (1866). *La Femme et les moeurs. Liberté ou monarchie* (1869). *Aline-Ali* (1869). *Légendes corréziennes* (1870). *La Guerre sociale; discours prononcé au Congrès de la Paix à Lausanne, 1871* (1871). *Marianne* (1877). *L'Epousée du bandit* (1880). *L'Enfant des Rudière* (1881). *La Justice des choses* (1891). *La Famille Audroit et l'éducation nouvelle* (1899).

Translations: "Woman and morals," partially tr. in *The Agitator* by Kate Newell Doggett (1869).

Bibliography

Archives de la Prefecture de Police, Dossier, B/A 1008. Arnaud, Angélique, "Madame André Léo," *L'Avenir des femmes* (15 Oct. 1871). *Dictionnaire biographique du Mouvement ouvrier français*, vol. 2, pt. 5, p. 52. Lejeune, P., "Une grande journaliste communarde: Léodile Champceix, dite André Léo," *Femmes en mouvements*, no. 2 (Feb. 1978): 58–59.

Karen Offen

Leobgyda

Born c. 732, Wessex, England; died September 780, Schornsheim, Germany
Genre(s): epistle
Language(s): Latin

Leobgyda (whose Anglo-Saxon name, Leofgytha, is also modernized as Leofgyth) is also known by the shortened form of her name, Leoba/Lioba, which means "the beloved one." She is known as a writer from a letter to St. Boniface in the Boniface Collection.

Leobgyda, who was also called Thrudgeba as a child, was born in Wessex, the daughter of Boniface's kinswoman Aebbe and his friend Dynne. She studied with Eadburg, the abbess of Minster in Thanet, and with the abbess Tetta at the monastery of Wimborne, where she was in charge of the young nuns. According to Rudolf of Fulda's Life of Leoba, written around 836, St. Boniface invited her to join his mission in Germany, and he made her abbess of a double monastery in Bischofsheim (modern Baden). She was learned and wise in council, and bishops discussed church affairs with her. She also visited monasteries other than her own, including Fulda, which other women were forbidden to enter. Her influence on the public life of her time is attested by her close friendship with Charlemagne's wife Hildegard, whom she visited at court. As an elderly woman, she retired to the monastery of Schornsheim, and after her death in September 780, she was buried near Boniface at Fulda.

Only one letter by Leobgyda is extant, although the Boniface Collection includes a letter from Boniface to Leobgyda, Tecla, and Cynehild in their English monastery and another to Leobgyda after her arrival in Germany. These letters indicate that there was substantial correspondence between the two. The tone of Leobgyda's letter, in which she introduces herself to Boniface, suggests that the author is young; Michael Tangl dates it shortly after 732. She reminds Boniface of his friendship for her parents and says that she regards him as a brother. She appends four lines of poetry because she had been taught the art of composition by Eadburg and wishes to use her training. As in the case of Berhtgyth, the poem shows a tradition of women poets and teachers of the art of composition. Like many medieval poems, Leobgyda's is a *cento*; she recombines formulas borrowed from the poetry of Aldhelm to make her own metrical composition. Michael Lapidge compares this technique to that of oral-formulaic vernacular poetry and suggests that an investigation of formularity in Latin poetry like that of Leobgyda would illuminate oral-formulaic composition in Old English. Leobgyda's letter therefore sheds light on the personality of a young nun and increases our understanding of early medieval poetics.

Works

Michael Tangl, ed., *Die Briefe des heilgen Bonifatius und Lullus.* Monumenta Germaniae Historica: Epistolae Selectae, vol. 1, 2d. ed. (Berlin, 1955). Unterkircher, F., *Sancti Bonifacii Epistolae. Codex Vindobonensis 751 des österreichischen Nationalbibliothek, Codices selecti phototypice impressi XXIV* (Graz, 1971). Ephraim Emerton, tr., *The Letters of St. Boniface* (New York, 1940). Edward Kylie, tr. The English Correspondence of Saint Boniface (New York, 1966).

Bibliography

Browne, G.F., *Boniface of Crediton and His Companions* (London, 1910). Dronke, Peter, *Women Writers of the Middle Ages, A Critical Study of Texts from Perpetua (†203) to Marguerite Porete (†1310)* (Cambridge, 1984). Fell, Christine E., "Some Implications of the Boniface Correspondence," in *New Readings on Women in Old English Literature,* ed. Helen Damico and Alexandra Hennessey Olsen (Bloomington, 1989). Lapidge, Michael, "Aldhelm's Latin Poetry and Old English Verse." *Comparative Literature* 31 (1970): 209–231. Rudolf of Fulda, *Life of Leoba,* in *Monumenta Germaniae Historica, Scriptores,* ed. Georg Waitz (Hanover, 1887), vol. 15, pp. 127–131. Talbot, C.H., tr., *The Anglo-Saxon Missionaries in Germany* (New York, 1954), pp. 205–226. Stenton, F.M., *Anglo-Saxon England,* 3rd ed. (Oxford, 1971).

Alexandra Hennessey Olsen

María Teresa León

Born 1904, Logroño, Spain
Genre(s): essay, criticism, novel
Language(s): Spanish

León and her husband, poet Rafael Alberti, served as two of the greatest examples of the flourishing of Spanish letters in exile after the Spanish Civil War. Her early prose reflects the vanguardist style of the 1920s; the war serves as the theme for her memoirs and most of her fiction, written in exile in France, Argentina and Rome and during extensive travels in the Soviet Union and China. *Juego limpio* (1959; Clean Game) is an autobiographical novel based on her experience with the popular theatre she and Alberti founded during the war. Her innocent priest-hero observes many of the horrors of war and learns that a civil war is not a clean game but a jumble of varied hatreds.

Works

Cuentos para soñar, children's stories (1920s). *La bella del mal amor,* stories (1930). *Rosa-Fría, patinadora de la luna,* stories (1934). *Crónica general de la Guerra Civil* (1937). *Una estrella roja,* stories (1937; reissued with additional stories, 1979). *Contra viento y marea,* novel (1941). *Morirás lejos,* stories (1942). *La historia tiene la palabra: Noticia sobre el salvamento del tesoro artístico* (1944). *Gran amor de Gustavo Adolfo Bécquer: Una vida pobre y apasionada,* fictional biography (1946). *Las peregrinaciones de Teresa,* stories (1950). *Rodrigo Días de Vivar, el Cid Campeador,* juvenile historical fiction (1954). *El Cid Campeador* (1962). *Sonríe China* (1958). *Juego limpio,* novel (1959). *Doña Jimena Díaz de Vivar: Gran señora de todos los deberes,* historical fiction (1960). *Fábulas del tiempo amargo,* stories (1962). *Doinas y baladas populares rumanas* (1963). *Menesteos, marinero de abril,* novel (1965). *Memoria de la melancolía,* memoirs (1970). *Poesía china* (1972). *Cuentos de la España actual,* stories (1973). *Teatro de agitación política, 1933–1939* (1976). *Cervantes, el soldado que nos enseñó a hablar*, juvenile historical fiction (1978).

Translations: Russian translation of *El Cid Campeador* (Moscow: Ed. Estatal de Literatura Infantil-Ministerio de Educación, 1958).

Bibliography

Galerstein, Carolyn, "The Spanish Civil War: The View of Women Novelists." *Letras Femeninas* X, No. 2 (fall 1984): 12–18.

Carolyn Galerstein

Sapho Leondias

Born 1832, Istanbul; died 1900, Istanbul
Genre(s): poetry, historical fiction, critical
essay, school manual, translation,
women's history
Language(s): Greek

Sapho Leondias was born in 1832 in Istanbul. She was the daughter of the professor Leondios Kliridis, a major representative of Greek Enlightenment who dedicated his life to the national and intellectual "awakening" of the Greeks before and after the Independence. Kliridis transmitted to his daughter his passion for Greek, German, and French literature. From a very early age, Sapho worked with her father for the development of Greek education among the Greek diaspora and contributed to the foundation of the first schools in Cyprus and the Dodecanese. From 1852 to 1891, she was in charge of girls schools in Samos, Smyrni and Istanbul. Leondias was one of the most important pedagogues of the nineteenth century. She invented new educational methods for teaching the classics, wrote various school manuals, and dedicated all her energies to the development of women's secondary education.

Leondias was also a gifted philologist, the author of imaginative commentaries and interpretations of ancient Greek mythology and Classic drama. She gave lectures on the social world of Euripides, on the images of women in tragedy, on women in history. She translated into modern Greek the *Persans* of Aeschylus and Racine's *Esther*. In 1856, she published a volume of poems entitled *Piissis Sapfous Leondiathos* (Poetry of Sapho Leondias). She was a contributor to such cultural and literary publications of her time as *Chrysallis, Pandora, Nea Pandora, Ethnikon Imerologuion M. Vrettou* (National Almanac of M. Vrettos), *Attikon Imerologuion* (Attic Almanac), *Imerologion Constandinou Skokou* (Almanac of C. Skokos). She was also an important contributor of *Evridiki* (Euridice), a publication in favor of women's intellectual development, published in 1874, in Istanbul by her sister, Emilia Ktena Leondias. From 1887 to 1900, she was one of the main editors of *Efimeris ton Kyrion* (Ladies' Newspaper), the first Greek feminist publication.

Resenting from an early age the confined existence imposed on her gender, Leondias became a pioneer of women's emancipation. She was the first representative of a whole generation of the first educated women who were driven, by their intellectual ambitions and educational activities, to gender and/or feminist consciousness. The improvement of women's social position and the affirmation of their human value and redemptive potential are the key ideas that dominate her writings. As she herself wrote in the 1856 introduction of her *Poetry*, publication was motivated by her "desire to prove that the female race of our nation is also in the way to true civilization."

Like most of the women poets of this first generation, Leondias was too respectful of the stylistic and grammatical conventions of her time and wrote in the official puristic language (*katharevoussa*), which prejudiced the spontaneity and originality of her verse. Her poetic works are more treatises than poems and present a far bigger sociological interest than a literary one. On the contrary, her historical writings and essays, particularly those published in the *Efimeris ton Kyrion* (Ladies' Newspaper), show an originality and autonomy of thought that was difficult to find in the writings of her contemporaries, men and women. Unlike the mainstream of women's history of her time, which did not go beyond the celebration of women "worthies," Sapho Leondias proposed a critical revision of the past from the viewpoint of women. For her, sex antagonism and male domination were crucial factors of deformation or occultation of historical facts that should be taken into consideration in the interpretation of human past. In an imaginative analysis of the tradition of Athena's birth, Leondias showed that myths should not be treated as mere historical descriptions transmitted by oral tradition but rather as imaginary creations significant of human intentions, fears, and desires.

Sapho Leondias died in 1900, at the age of sixty-eight. In spite of the general recognition she enjoyed during her life, she has been completely forgotten until recently, and her writings have never been reprinted.

Works

Piïssis Saphous Leondiados [Poetry of Sapho Leondias] (1856). "Peri klisseos tis yinaikos" ["Of woman's inclination"]. *Evridiki* I, nos. 2, 3, 5, 6, 7 (1870). *Ieron ekloyion* [Sacred Anthology] (1874). *Dorassiaki Christomathia* [Young Girls Guide] (1876). *Ikiaki Ikonomia pros chrissin ton Parthenagoyion* [Domestic Economy for Women Schools] (1887). "I yini en ti archea tragothia" (Woman in Ancient Tragedy). *Ladies' Newspaper* 2 (1888). *Anir kai Yini* [Man and Woman] (1899). "Peri tou yinekiou zitimatos" (The Woman's Question), *Ladies' Newspaper* 10/400 and 10/402 (1895). "I prossefhi tis yayas" [The Grandmother's Prayers]. *Imeroloyion tis Efimerithos ton Kyrion* [Almanac of the Ladies' Journal] (Athens, 1895).

Bibliography

Aliberti, Sotiria, "Sapho Leondias, i tou yenous thithaskalos" [Sapho Leondias the Nation's Pedagogue]. *Pleias* 2/8–9 (1900). Paschalis, D.P., "Leondias Sapho." *Megali Elliniki Egkyklopedia* [Great Greek Encyclopedia], vol. 15, p. 940. Tarsouli, Athina, *Ellinithes piitries* [Greek Women Poets] (Athens, 1951).

Eleni Varikas

Dorothea Leporin

(a.k.a. Dorothea von Erxleben)

Born November 13, 1715, Quedlinburg, Germany; died June 13, 1762, Quedlinburg
Genre(s): treatise
Language(s): German, Latin

She studied science under the guidance of her father, Christian Leporin, who was himself a physician. She learned Latin from the local pastor.

Dorothea wanted to study medicine with her brother but had to postpone this plan due to his military service. However, she continued her studies, and in 1741 her father's plea that she be allowed to take the examination leading to the doctorate was granted. She did not at first take advantage of this because of her betrothal to the pastor Johann Christian Erxleben, whom she married the following year. At that time she also wrote her treatise: *Gründliche Untersuchung der Ursachen, die das weibliche Geschlecht vom Studieren abhalten* (Through Investigation into the Causes Which Prevent the Female Sex from Studying), first published in 1742 and reissued in 1749. Twelve years later she appeared before the medical faculty in Halle with her dissertation, *Quod, nimis cito ac quounde curare saepius fiat caussa minus tutae curationis* (1754; Treatise About the Too Quick and Pleasant but Therefore Often Less Than Full Cure of Sicknesses), passed the examination, and received her degree. Until her death in 1762 she practiced medicine in Quedlinburg.

Works

Gründliche Untersuchung der Ursachen, die das weibliche Geschlecht vom studieren abhalten (1742). *Quod nimis cito ac quounde curare saepius fiat caussa minus tutae curationis* (1754).

Bibliography

Billig, A.H., "Dorothee Christiane Erxleben die erste deutsche Ärztin." Diss., München, 1966. Böhm, H., *Dorothee Christiane Erxleben Ihr Leben und Wirken* (1965). Duboc, J., *Fünfzig Jahre Frauenfrage in Deutschland* (1896). Ersch, J.S., and J.G. Gruber, eds., "Dorothee Christiane Erxleben." *Allgemeine Encyclopädie der Wissenschaften und Künste I*, 37 (1842). Fischer-Defoy, W., "Die Promotion der ersten deutschen Ärztin Dorothee Christiane Erxleben und ihre Vorgeschichte." *Archiv für Geschichte der Medizin* (1911). Heindorf, H., and K. Renker, "Über Werk und Bedeutung der Dr. med. Dorothee Christiane Erxleben." *Zeitschrift für die gesamte Hygiene* (1966). Heischkel, F., "Dorothee Christiane Erxleben, eine Vorkämpferin des Frauenstudiums im 18. Jahrhundert." *Die Ärztin* (1940). Hirsch, A., "Dorothee Christiane Erxleben." *Allgemeine Deutsche Biographie* 6 (1877): 334–335. Kaiser, W., and K.-H. Krosch, "Zum 250. Geburtstag von

Dorothee Christiane Erxleben." *Wissenschaftliche Zeitschrift der Martin-Luther-Universität Halle-Wittenberg* (1965). Knabe, L., "Die erste Promotion einer Frau in Deutschland zum Dr. med. an der Universität Halle 1754," *450 Jahre Martin-Luther-Univ. Halle-Wittenberg* 2 (1952). Schelenz, H., *Frauen im Reiche Aesculaps* (1900). Zaunick, R., "Dorothee Christiane Erxleben." *Zeitschrift für ärztliche Fortbildung* (1954). Zaunick, R., "Dorothee Christiane Erxleben und ihre Schriften." *Literatur der Zeit* (1965).

Marjanne E. Goozé and Helene M. Kastinger Riley

Madame Jeanne-Marie Le Prince de Beaumont

Born April 26, 1711, Rouen, France; died 1780, Chavanod, Haute-Savoie, France
Genre(s): novels, didactic works
Language(s): French

Madame Le Prince de Beaumont was a popular novelist and a prolific writer of educational works for women and children, Christian apologetics, and moral tales that were widely read throughout Europe and America between 1750 and ca. 1830.

Coming from a large artistic family—the painter Jean-Baptiste Le Prince was her younger brother—Marie Le Prince taught at a convent school for teachers in Rouen. When her unhappy marriage was annulled in 1745, she turned to writing to supplement a meager income. Her first novel, *Le Triomphe de la Vérité*, was published in 1748, the same year as two works in which she argues that women's natural qualities are superior to those of men. Shortly after, she settled in London, where she quickly established a reputation as a governess and started a monthly magazine, the *Nouveau Magasin français*, aimed primarily at women. She also wrote full-length didactic works such as the *Éducation complète* (1753), which was used by the Princess of Wales, *Civan, roi de Bungo* (1754), which was set in Japan, and the *Anecdotes du XIVe siècle* (1759), as well as the highly popular epistolary novels, *Lettres de Madame Du Montier* (1756) and *La nouvelle Clarisse* (1767). Many of her books ran to several editions and were translated into every major European language. In 1758 she bought a house near Annecy, France, to which she retired with her second husband and where she continued writing until her death.

The most important of her works, the *Magasin des Enfants* (1756), is divided into *journées* in which a governess called Mlle. Bonne converses with seven pupils (Ladies Sensée, Spirituelle, Tempête, etc.) who are between five and thirteen in age. Each day, the lessons on history, geography, and science are alternated with Bible stories and fairy tales, including the classic version of "La Belle et la Bête" (adapted from a rambling 362-page story by Mme. de Villeneuve, q.v.). Though always present, the morality is never saccharine, and many of the tales (e.g. "Le Prince au long nez") reveal considerable humor. It is the first work written not for a specific child, but for children in general; the first to address children as children and not as mini-adults, and to do so without being condescending. She continued her success with the *Magasin des Adolescentes* (1760), which introduces the same girls and others in their teens (Miss Frivole, Lady Sincère, etc.) to philosophy, and with *Instructions pour les jeunes Dames* (1764), which outlines the duties of a wife. One of her themes throughout is that women should rely not on men but on their own inner resources and to do this they must understand religion. In *Les Américaines* (1770), Mme. Bonne asks the same young women, now her friends, to imagine how they would react in a European city if they had been transported there suddenly from the forests of America. The ensuing dialogue introduces the women to theology. In spite of her generally conservative views, Mme. Bonne is constantly respectful of her pupils' individuality: "Each Lady is made to speak according to her particular Genius, Temper and Inclination." The question-and-answer technique is designed to stimulate their independent thought, great self-awareness, and ability to conduct a reasoned debate: "Oui Messrs. les tirans, j'ai dessein de les tirer de cette ignorance crasse, à la quelle vous les avez condamnées. . . . Je veux leur apprendre à penser, à penser juste, pour parvenir à bien vivre" (1756, I, p. xi). At a time when women received virtually no formal education, this intention was revolutionary.

Mme. Le Prince de Beaumont's achievement can be measured by the success which her works enjoyed and the rapid improvement in women's education between 1760 and 1785. The *Magasin des Enfants* was frequently reprinted; in the nineteenth century, its format was much copied but never equalled. When her books fell out of fashion, except for two or three of her fairy tales—notably "La Belle et la Bête"—none was ever republished. They were the first victims of a movement that she did much to create. She was the first editor of a woman's monthly magazine, the founder of children's literature in France, and an indefatigable promoter of women's equal right learning.

Works

Le Triomphe de la Vérité, ou, Mémoires de M. de la Villette (1748), tr. *The Triumph of Truth, or, Memoirs of Mr. de la Villette* (1755). *Lettre en réponse à 'L'Année merveilleuse'* (1748). *Arrêt solennel de la nature* (1748). *Lettres diverses et critiques* (1750). *Le Nouveau Magasin français, ou, Bibliothèque instructive* (1750–1752, 1755). *Éducation complète, ou, Abrégé de l'histoire universelle, mêlée de géographie, de chronologie . . . à l'usage de la famille royale de la princesse de Galles* (1753). *Civan, roi de la famille royale de la princesse de Galles* (1753). *Civan, roi de bungo, histoire japonnoise, ou, Tableau de l'éducation d'un prince* (1754), tr. *Civan, King of Bungo* (1800). *Lettres de Mme Du Montier à la marquise de *** , sa fille, avec les réponses* (1756), tr. *The History of a Young Lady of Distinction. In a Series of Letters Which Passed Between Madame Du Montier, and the Marchioness De ***, Her Daughter* (1758). *Magasin des Enfants, ou, Dialogues entre une sage gouvernante et plusieurs de ses élèves* (1756), tr. *The Young Misses Magazine, or, Dialogues Between a Discreet Governess and Several Young Ladies of the First Rank Under Her Education* (1757). *Anecdotes du XIVᵉ siècle, pour servir à l'histoire des femmes illustres de ce temps* (1758). *Lettres curieuses, instructives et amusanntes, ou, Correspondance historique, galante, etc. entre une dame de Paris et une dame de province* (1759). *Magasin des Adolescentes . . . Pour servir de suite au 'Magasin des Enfants'* (1760), tr. *The Young*

Ladies Magazine (1760). *Principes de l'Histoire-Sainte* (1761). *Instructions pour les jeunes Dames qui entrent dans le monde et qui se marient . . . Pour faire suite au "Magasin des Adolescentes"* (1764), tr. *Instructions for Young Ladies on Their Entering into Life, Their Duties in the Married State, and Towards Their Children* (1764). *Lettres d'Émérance à Lucie* (1765), tr. *Letters from Émérance to Lucy* (1776). *Mémoires de Madame la Baronne de Batteville, ou, La Veuve parfaite* (1766), tr. *The Virtuous Widow: or, Memoirs of the Baroness de Batteville* (1768). *La nouvelle Clarisse, histoire véritable* (1767), tr. *The New Clarisse: a True History* (1768). *Magasin des Pauvres, des Artisans, des Domestiques et des Gens de la campagne* (1768), tr. *Dialogues for Sunday Evenings; Translated from a Work of Madame Le Prince de Beaumont Called "Magasin des Pauvres"* (1797). *Les Américaines, ou, La Preve de la Religion Chrétienne, par les lumières naturelles* (1770). *La Double Alliance, ou, Les heureux naturels, histoire du marquis D*** * (1772–1773). *La Mentor moderne, ou, Instructions pour les garçons et pour ceux qui les élèvent* (1772). *Manuel de la Jeunesse, ou, Instructions familières, en dialogues* (ca. 1773). *Contes moraux* (1774), tr. *Moral Tales* (1775). *Oeuvres mêlées de Mme Le Prince de Beaumont: Extraites des Journaux & Feuilles périodiques qui ont paru en Angleterre pendant le séjour qu'elle y a fait* (1775; rpt. of *Le Nouveau Magasin français*). *Nouveaux Contes moraux* (1776). *Le Dévotion éclairées, ou, Magasin des Dévotes* (1779).

Bibliography

Barchilon, Jacques, "'Beauty and the Beast': From Myth to Fairy Tale." *Psychoanalytic Review* 46 (1959): 19–29. Bettelheim, Bruno, "Beauty and the Beast," in *The Uses of Enchantment* (1976), pp. 303–310. Clancy, Patricia A., "Mme Leprince de Beaumont: Founder of Children's Literature," *Australian Journal of French Studies* 16 (1979): 281–287. Clancy, Patricia A., "A French Writer and Educator in England: Mme Le Prince de Beaumont." *Studies on Voltaire and the Eighteenth Century* 20 (1982): 195–208. Stewart, Joan Hinde, "Allegories of Difference: An Eighteenth-Century Polemic," *Romantic Review* 75 (1984): 283–293. Wilkins, Kay S., "Children's Literature in Eighteenth-Century France." *Studies on Voltaire and the Eighteenth Century* 176 (1979): 429–449.

Terence Dawson

Katherijne Lescaille

Born September 26, 1649, Amsterdam, The Netherlands; died June 8, 1711, Amsterdam
Genre(s): occasional poetry, translation
Language(s): Dutch

Katherijne was the daughter of publisher-bookseller Jacob Lescaille, a well-known figure in the literary milieu of Amsterdam. After his death, Katherijne continued his business; she never married. She started writing at an early age, viz., occasional pieces that elicited the praise (sometimes in verse) of several male colleagues and even of Joost Van den Vondel himself. Vondel was kind enough to predict a glorious poetic career for Katherijne on the basis of these early works. Later generations were less enthusiastic. Lescaille's occasional poetry (contained in Vols. I and II of the posthumously published *Mengel- en Toneel poëzy*, 1731) is lacking in spirit and originality of thought and imagery though it is formally regular and charmingly civilized. Some of the more interesting poems of this type, collected under the heading "Staatsgevallen" (State Cases), present in heroic rhyming couplets powerful interpretations of contemporary political and military encounters.

But in general, Lescaille illustrates well the validity of Basse's judgment of seventeenth-century Dutch women writers, namely that these ladies, though generally well educated, were lacking in inspiration. Basse concludes that "to us [all the activity of these female authors] seems to display mostly wit and reading culture, but otherwise far less skill than interest in literature." (o.c. 73–74; my tr.).

Lescaille deserves more appreciation for her second literary activity: translation. She made available to the actors and the patrons of the Amsterdam City Theater a significant number of contemporary French tragedies. Her rhymed translations and adaptations of some of the success pieces of the seventeenth-century tragic oeuvre

prove her a far better poet than her numerous wedding and anniversary poems would suggest.

Works

Kassandra (1684?; after P. d'Assezan). *Genserik* (1685; after Mme. Deshoulières). *Herodes en Marianne* (1685; after Tristan L'Hermite). *Wenseslaus, koning van Poolen* (1686; after J. de Rotrou). *Herkules en Dianira* (1688, 1744; after Tuillerie). *Nicomedes* (1692; after P. Corneille). *Ariadne* (1693; after Th. Corneille). *Geta, of de Broedermoord van Antoninus* (1713). Her collected edition *Mengel- en Toneel poëzy* (Amsterdam, 1731; quarto edition), in 3 volumes.

Bibliography

Basse, M., *Het Aandeel der Vrouw in de Nederlandsche Letterkunde*, I-II (Ghent, 1920), pp. 73–74.

Kristiaan P. Aercke

Rina Levinzon

Born October 18, 1945, Moscow, The Soviet Union
Genre(s): poetry, short story, journalism
Language(s): Russian, Hebrew, English

Rina Levinzon is an intensely lyrical poet. She started writing as a radio and television journalist in the USSR. Before her immigration to Israel she had published two books of poems in Russian; several of her poems appeared in Soviet periodicals, such as *Neva, Ural, Veselye kartinki* (Joyful Pictures) and others. One of her stories for children was filmed for Sverdlovsk television.

In the mid-1970s she joined the *alia* movement of Soviet Jewry, and in April 1976 she arrived in Israel. There she published four books of poems in Russian and a book of poems for children in Hebrew. Her poems appeared in many Russian-language journals and newspapers in Western Europe and America. Soon Rina Levinzon was recognized as one of the significant poets of our time. Critics note her short traditional stanzas and rhymes and also her striking lyrical originality.

The change from one poetical soil to another brought into her poetry both a sense of freedom and a sense of profound loss. Recently her poetry has also appeared in translation: one book of poems in Hebrew, and one in Arabic.

Works (including translations)

Puteshestvie [Travel] (1967). Priletai vorobushek [Fly to Me, Sparrow] (1973). Dva portreta [Two Portraits] (1977). Sneg v Ierusalime [Snow in Jerusalem] (1980). Utsutstvie oseni [Absence of Autumn] (1985). Gedichte [Poems] (1986). I Am not Alone (1987).

Bibliography

Dar, D., "Chistyj golos" (1977). Druskin, L., "Sneg nad Ierusalimom" (1982). Kolker, I., "O poezii Riny Levinzon" (1985). Kosinski, I., "Osen' ostalas' v Rosii" (1986). Radashkevich, A., "Stikhi Riny Levinzon" (1986). A.T., "O novykh stikhakh Riny Levinzon" (1987).

Katherina Filips-Juswigg

Mechthild von Lichnowsky, Princess, Duchess of Arco-Zinneberg

Born March 8, 1879, Schloß Schönburg, Bavaria; died June, 4, 1958, London
Genre(s): novel, short story, aphorism, drama, dialogue, lyric poetry, edition
Language(s): German

Mechthild von Lichnowsky was the granddaughter of Emperess Maria Theresia of Austria and the daughter of the Bavarian Duke of and at Arco-Zinneberg. She received her education at a monastic school and married the Prince Lichnowsky in 1904, whose grandfather had been the object of ridicule in Heinrich Heine's and Georg Weerth's literary works. When her husband was appointed ambassador of Germany in London in 1912 (both in his diary and his letters he warned strongly against the coming WW I), she accompanied him there and quickly gained a significant role in society and among the artists. In 1914 her husband was called back to Berlin because of the beginning of WW I. Since then Mechthild lived in Munich, Southern France and in Czechoslovakia. After her husband's death, she married an old friend from her youth, the English Major Peto. She moved to London with him in 1937 and acquired British citizenship.

She was adamantly opposed to the National Socialism under Hitler and strongly favored a democratic cosmopolitanism. Consequently her books were banned in the Third Reich. She composed a wide range of literary works including aphorisms to which she had been stimulated by her friends Karl Kraus and Alfred Kerr. Her most important narrative fiction was the novel Kindheit (Childhood), continued in the novel Der Lauf der Asdur (The Course of the Asdur), in which she reflected upon the process of maturation of a girl.

Works

Novels: Götter, Könige und Tiere in Ägypten [Gods, Kings and Animals in Egypt] (1912). Der Stimmer [The Tuner] (1915; rpt. in 1936 as Das rote Haus [The Red House]). Geburt [Birth] (1921). Das Rendezvous im Zoo [Meeting in the Zoo] (1928). An der Leine [On the Leash] (1930). Kindheit [Childhood] (1934). Der Lauf der Asdur [The Course of the Asdur] (1936). Delaide (1937).

Plays: Ein Spiel vom Tod [A Play of Death] (1915). Der Kinderfreund [The Friend of Children] (1919).

Lyric Poetry: Gott betet [God Is Praying] (1916). Halb und Halb [Half and Half] (1926). Heute und Vorgestern [Today and the Day Before Yesterday] (1958).

Essays, Aphorism, Dialogues: Der Kampf mit dem Fachmann [The Fight with the Expert] (1924). Gespräche in Sybaris [Talks in Sybaris] (1946). Worte über Wörter [Words About Words] (1949). Zum Schauen bestellt [Ordered for Looking On] (1953).

Collected editions of her work: Zum Schauen bestellt [Ordered for Looking On] (1953). Heute und Vorgestern [Today and the Day Before Yesterday] (1958).

Bibliography

Fliessbach, Holger, Mechthild von Lichnowsky, eine monographische Studie. Ph.D. Diss., University of Munich, 1973. Hildenbrand, Fred, . . . ich soll dich grüsen von Berlin. 1922–1932 (Munich, 1974). Jonas, Klaus W., "Rilke und Mechthild von Lichnowsky." Modern Austrian Literature 5, 1/2 (1972): 58–69. Mann, Golo, "Mechthild von Lichnowsky." Neue Rundschau 90 (1979): 554–560. von Haselberg, Peter, "Mechthild von Lichnowsky." M.L.: Der Kampf mit dem Fachmann (1978). Webhofer, Erika, "Zur Rezeption von Karl Kraus. Der Briefwechsel aus dem Nachlaß

Albert Bloch—Michael Lazarus—Sidonie Nadherny." *Mitteilungen aus dem Brenner Archiv* 3 (1984): 35–53.

Albrecht Classen

Sara Adela Lidman

Born 1923, Missenträsk, Jörns Parish, Sweden
Genre(s): novel, drama, short story, essay
Language(s): Swedish

A farmer's daughter, Sara Lidman grew up in a rural, isolated, religious and rather harmonious environment. Convalescing from a lung ailment at the age of fourteen, Lidman became not only interested in literature, but began writing her own stories. She continued her schooling through correspondence and then entered a private school. In 1944 she moved to Stockholm where she worked alternately as a waitress and as a drama student at a local theater. Eventually she continued her academic studies at Uppsala University and finished with her phil. cand. exam in 1949.

Lidman's literary interest concentrated to a large extent on Dostoyevsky, whose novels fascinated her. Of her own countrymen she admits to having been greatly influenced by the Norrland painters, especially Th. Jonsson. Experimenting with her own writing, she found eventually her own style by the time she wrote her first novel, *Tjärdalen* (Tar Valley), published in 1953. With this novel she began the major theme in her work. In book after book she returns to the same problem: the downtrodden of human society.

Until the sixties, the setting in Lidman's novels and plays was the Swedish countryside as she had known and experienced it as a child. However, a trip to South Africa in 1960–1961 inspired her to write about the racial problems on that continent in her continued effort to speak out on the plight of the outcasts of society.

Her concern led Lidman to engage more and more politically. Aligning herself with the anti-bourgeois political Left, she began to speak out publicly, especially on the then ongoing war in Vietnam. In 1966 she published *Samtal i Hanoi* (Conversation in Hanoi), in which she dispensed with fiction altogether in favor of so-called "reportage writing" through which she voiced her own opinions and feelings more directly. Her books did indeed help to promote public discussion and instigate political action in favor of society's oppressed and disadvantaged. In *Gruva* (Mine), published in 1968 and written in the same "reportage technique," Lidman takes on the adverse conditions under which her own countrymen, the miners in the Swedish province of Norrland, must work. The book is thought to have contributed to the ore miners' strike in 1969–1970.

Living in Stockholm, Lidman continues to write and speak out on behalf of those who live, for whatever reason, "on the other side of the tracks" of society. From 1955 until 1963 she was a member of the distinguished Swedish literary society De Nio. Many of her books have been translated into Eastern European languages such as Russian, Polish, Hungarian, Czech, Lithuanian and the language of the Albanians. Her works have also appeared in Danish, Norwegian, Icelandic, Finnish, Dutch, German, French and Italian translations. Her book *Regnspiran* was published in English translation as *The Rain Bird* in London in 1963.

Works

Tjärdalen (1953). *Hjortronlandet* (1955). *Mitt första besök i Skellefteå* (1955). *Regnspiran* (1958). *Bära mistel* (1960). *Misteldans* (1960). *Jag och min son* (1961). *Med fem diamanter* (1964). *Samtal i Hanoi* (1966). *Gruva* (1968). *Vänner och u-vänner* (1969). *Marta, Marta: En folksaga* (1970). *Fåglarna i Nam Dinh: Artiklar om Vietnam* (1972). *Din tjänare hör* (1979). *Vredens barn* (1979). *Varje löv är ett öga* (1980). *Nabotssten* (1981). *Den underbare mannen* (1983). *Järnkronan* (1985).

Plays: *Job Klockmakares dotter* (1954). *Aina* (1956). Articles: *Politisk asyl åt Vietnamkrigsvägrare*. Articles and speeches by Sara Lidman a.o. (Stockholm, 1971). "The Heart of the World." *They Have Been in Vietnam* (Hanoi, 1968), pp. 9–13.

Translations: *Ho Chi Minh*, Tr. Sara Lidman. From Ho Chi Minh's prison diary (Stockholm, 1967).

Bibliography

Gravé, Rolf, *Biblicismer och liknande inslag i Sara Lidmans Tjärdalen* (Lund, 1969). Jäger, Leif, *Sara Lidman 1953–1973: bibliografiska anteckningar* (Borås, 1976). Thygesen, Marianne, *Jan Myrdal og

Sara Lidman: Rapportgenren i svensk 60-tals litteratur (Århus, 1971).

Hanna Kalter Weiss

François Lilar

(see: Françoise Mallet-Joris)

Suzanne Lilar

Born 1901, Ghent, Belgium
Genre(s): novel, drama, essay
Language(s): French

Trained as a philosopher and lawyer, the francophone Belgian author, Suzanne Lilar, entered the world of letters at the age of forty-two as a dramatist. Her plays *Le Burlador* (1945), *Tous les chemins menent au ciel* (1947), and *Le roi lepreux* (1950) demonstrate the neo-platonism that dominates her work. As early as the *Burlador*, Lilar's reinterpretation of the Don Juan legend filtered through the perceptions of a female character, the author pleads for an amorous mystique as gateway to a lost paradise of wholeness, a path to the absolute. In the novels which follow, *Le divertissement portugais* (1960) and *La confession anonyme* (1960), Lilar examines with lucidity the spiritual enchantments that accompany profound physical experience. The erotic becomes a privileged source of knowledge in these essayistic novels in which protagonists train an analytical eye on their experience of a passion that is at once sensual and mystic. Art, like love, represents for Lilar nostalgia for another, more harmonious world. The *Journal de l'analogiste* (1954) examines the metamorphosic aspect of poetry, all art bearing the message "that there is but one dread and one desire in the world, that for God, and but a single misery, that of being held separate."

Lilar's essay, *Le couple* (1963), continues her analysis of love as the most significant mode of "deliverance from duality." Throughout the study, Lilar stresses eros as "liaison," linking source of secret interconnection, and human love as a revelation of divine love. The essays, *A propos de Sartre et de l'amour* (1967) and *Le malentendu du deuxieme sexe* (1969), are at once critiques of Sartre and Simone de Beauvoir, respectively, and explorations of the metaphysical eros, profane love being "divine love as yet unaware of itself." In these studies, Lilar also discusses biological androgyny, which determines the participation of each sex to a certain extent in the characteristics of the other, and polemicizes against overestimation of masculine values that have led to wars of extermination. Lilar's final, autobiographical works, *Une enfance gantoise* (1976) and *A la recherche d'une enfance* (1979), are investigations of memory and of significant moments of childhood that determine and reveal a life.

Suzanne Lilar's work is resonant with sincerity and a spirit of vocation, namely that of revealing the initiatory and sacral aspects of erotic love. Novels, plays, and essays detail an interior voyage, a pursuit of poetry, and a fascination with the possibility of unified experience beyond the dualities of quotidian existence. In her memoirs of childhood, Lilar has written: "It seems to me . . . that a single desire has underlined all of my most disparate experiences—that of abdicating, effacing myself, melting, allowing myself to be absorbed by something else from which I could no longer be distinguished."

Works

Novels: *La confession anonyme* (1960). *Le divertissement portugais* (1960).
Plays: *Le Burlador* (1945). *Tous les chemins menent au ciel* (1947). *Le roi lepreux* (1950).
Essays: *Le journal de l'analogiste* (1954). *Le couple* (1963). *A propos de Sartre et de l'amour* (1967). *Le malentendu du deuxieme sexe* (1969). *Une enfance gantoise* (1976). *A la recherche d'une enfance* (1979).
Translations: *Aspects of Love in Western Society* (1965). *The Burlador in Two Great Belgian Plays about Love* (1966).

Bibliography

Cahiers Suzanne Lilar (1986). *Autour de Suzanne Lilar.* Bulletin de l'Academie Royale de Langue et de Litterature Francaises (1978).

Donald Friedman

Luisa-María Linares

Born 1915, Madrid
Genre(s): novel
Language(s): Spanish

Linares developed her powers of observation in the course of extensive travel as a child with her father, dramatist Luis Linares Becerra, and began writing stories at age eight. She began publishing novels at twenty-four with *En poder de Barba Azul* (Held by Bluebeard), a work that she helped to adapt for successful stage and film versions. This work concerns a high-spirited young woman who stows away on the yacht of a handsome, wealthy, woman-hating bachelor who spends his time at sea to avoid women. Although for a time she disguises herself as a deck hand, eventually she reveals herself. The dashing bachelor tames the "shrew," and the novel suggests that the couple lives happily ever after.

Linares also assisted in the adaptations for stage and screen versions of *Doce lunas de miel* (Twelve Honeymoons) and *Un marido a precio fijo* (Fixed Price for a Husband). Among the best-known of her many (more than thirty) novels, all of which feature women protagonists, are: *Sólo volaré contigo* (I'll Only Fly with You), *Salomé la magnífica* (Salome, the Magnificent), *Casi siempre te adoro* (I Almost Always Adore You), *Mis cien últimos amores* (My Last Hundred Loves), *Juan a las ocho, Pablo a las diez* (John at Eight, Paul at Ten), *De noche soy indiscreta* (At Night, I'm Indiscreet). With their adventure-loving heroines, uncomplicated plots, witty dialogue, exotic settings, and happy endings, these novels have enjoyed wide popularity, particularly among upper middle-class women. All of Linares' popular romance novels have been made into movies, most have been translated into other languages (e.g., French, German, English, Dutch, Finnish, Swedish, etc.) and adapted for stage, film and television in various countries outside of Spain (principally France, Argentina, and Italy). *Cada día tiene su secreto* (Every Day Holds Its Secret) was selected as the "Book of the Month" in Vienna in 1955. She has collaborated on many internationally-known journals, such as *Elle, Marie Claire, Constanze, Freundin, Bunte Illustrierte, Beatijs, Grazia,* and *Woman's Own,* among others.

Works

En poder de Barba Azul [Held by Bluebeard] (1939). *Doce lunas de miel* [Twelve Honeymoons] (1944). *Marido a precio fijo* [Fixed Price for a Husband] (1955). *Sólo volaré contigo* [I'll Only Fly with You] (1956). *Salomé la magnífica* [Salome, the Magnificent] (1946). *Escuela para nuevos ricos* [School for the Nouveau Riche] (1957). *Esta noche, volveré tarde* [Tonight, I'll Come Home Late] (1958). *Imposible para una solterona* [Impossible for an Old Maid] (1959). *Casi siempre te adoro* [I Almost Always Adore You] (1960). *Mis cien últimos amores* [My Last Hundred Loves] (1963). *Juan a las ocho, Pablo a las diez* [John at Eight, Paul at Ten] (1965). *De noche soy indiscreta* [At Night I'm Indiscreet] (1965).

Translations: *Web of Fear* [*Juan a las ocho, Pablo a las diez*] (1979). *Fatal Legacy* [*No digas lo que hice ayer*] (1979).

Bibliography

O'Connor, Patrica W., *Dramaturgas españolas de hoy* (Madrid, 1989). O'Connor, Patrica W., "Women Playwrights in Contemporary Spain and the Male-Dominated Canon." *Signs: Journal of Women in Culture and Society* 15.2 (Winter 1990).

Patricia W. O'Connor

Astrid Lindgren

Born 1907, near Vimmerby, Småland
*   Province, Sweden*
Genre(s): children's and young adult literature
Language(s): Swedish

Astrid Lindgren was the second child of tenant farmer Samuel August Ericsson and his wife Hanna. They lived on the farm *Näs* in an old red house surrounded by apple trees where the four Ericsson children grew up much like the children she describes in her "Bullerbybooks." Already in school her classmates predicted that some day she would write stories and even went as far as calling her "Vimmerby's Selma Lagerlöf." But the very idea frightened her. Training as a secretary in Stockholm, she worked in an office, got married, and had two children. It is thanks to her children that her storytelling eventually developed.

In 1941 her daughter had pneumonia and wanted her mother to "tell a story . . . about 'Pippi Långstrump'" (Pippi Longstocking). The stories about Pippi were so successful with her daughter and her friends, that Astrid Lindgren had to repeat them time and again over the years. But it was not until 1944, when Astrid Lindgren was immobilized with a sprained ankle, that she finally wrote the Pippi Longstocking stories down and presented them to her daughter as a birthday present. Another copy she sent to a publisher. It was promptly rejected.

While waiting for the answer, Astrid Lindgren had worked on another story, *Britt-Marie lätter sitt hjärta* (Britt-Marie Eases Her Heart), and entered it in a prize competition for young adult literature in 1944. It received the second prize. When the same publisher announced another prize competition the following year, Astrid Lindgren entered the slightly edited Pippi manuscript, and it won her first prize.

Other Pippi stories followed in short, steady succession: *Pippi Långstrump går ombord* (1946; Pippi Goes On Board) and *Pippi Långstrump i Söderhavet* (1948; Pippi in the South Seas). The Pippi stories became the basis and cornerstone of Astrid Lindgren's international fame despite the often stormy attacks that "no normal kid" behaves the way Pippi does. But Pippi, with her strong defiance of all adult authority and undaunted by convention, became the heroine and model for young adults all over the world who saw in Pippi their dream of freedom and power fulfilled.

In 1946 Lindgren's book about master detective Bill Bergson won her a shared first prize, but it remained the last book she ever entered in a competition. The same year she also published her first book about the Bullerby children whose adventures closely resemble those of her own as a youngster at Näs with its seasonal rhythm of life lived in an old Swedish farming community.

The author of about fifty books and still going strong, Astrid Lindgren has become a popular figure as a Swedish writer for children and young adults. Since 1963 she has been a member of the distinguished literary society *Samfundet De Nio*. Her books have been translated into more than 39 languages and dialects. Her inspiration does not come from either her own or other people's children and grandchildren.

"There is no child that can inspire me as much as the child I myself was once upon a time," she maintains. All it takes is to remember how it was and felt at the time. She does not want to influence youngsters in any way. The only thing she dares to hope is that her books contribute to fostering some kind of basic philosophy of humanity, democracy and love of life in those who read them. Her major satisfaction lies in brightening the lives of children. "That's enough for me," she says. And the numerous reprints of her stories attest to her success in her chosen genre.

Works

Britt-Marie lätter sitt hjärta (1944). *Kerstin och jag* (1945). *Pippi Långstrump* (1945). *Pippi Långstrump går ombord* (1946). *Mästerdetektiven Blomkvist* (1946). *Alla vi barn i Bullerbyn* (1947). *Pippi Långstrump i Söderhavet* (1948). *Mera om os barn in Bullerbyn* (1949). *Nils Karlsson-Pyssling* (1949). *Kajsa Kavat* (1950). *Kati i Amerika* (1950). *Mästerdetektiven Blomkvist lever farligt* (1951). *Bara roligt i bullerbyn* (1952). *Kati på Kaptensgatan* (1952). *Kalle Blomkvist och Rasmus* (1953). *Mio min Mio* (1954). *Kati i Paris* (1954). *Lillebror och Karlsson på taket* (1955). *Rasmus på luffen* (1956). *Rasmus, Pontus och Toker* (1957). *Barnen på Bråkmakargatan* (1958). *Sunnanäng* (1959). *Madicken* (1960). *Lotta på Bråkmakargatan* (1961). *Karlsson på Taket flyger igen* (1962). *Emil i Lönneberga* (1963). *Vi på Saltkråkan* (1964). *Nya hyss av Emil i Lönneberga* (1966). *Karlsson på Taket smyger igen* (1968). *Än lever Emil i Lönneberga* (1970). *Kati i Italien* (1971). *Bröderna Lejonhjärta* (1973). *Madicken och Junibackens Pims* (1976). *Pippi Långstrump har Julgransplundring* (1979). *Ronja Rövardotter* (1981). *När lilla Ida skulle höra hyss* (1984). *Emils hyss nr 325* (1985).

English Translations: *Pippi Longstocking*, tr. Florence Lamborn (New York, 1950, 1969, 1973). *Pippi Goes on Board*, tr. Florence Lamborn (New York, 1957, 1973). *Pippi in the South Seas*, tr. Gerry Bothmer (New York, 1959, 1964). *The Six Bullerby Children*, tr. Evelyn Ramsden (London, 1963). *The Children of Noisy Village*, selections of Bullerby children, tr. Florence Lamborn (New York, 1962). *Happy Times in Noisy Village*, selections of Bullerby children, tr. Florence Lamborn (New York, 1963). *All About the Bullerby Children*, tr. Evelyn Ramsden and Florence Lamborn (London, 1970). *Bill*

Bergson, Master Detective, tr. Herbert Antoine (New York, 1952, 1968). *Bill Bergson Lives Dangerously*, tr. Herbert Antoine (New York, 1954). *Bill Bergson and the White Rose Rescue* tr. Florence Lamborn (New York, 1965). *Kati in America*, tr. Maianne Turner (Leicester, 1964). *Kati in Italy*, tr. Daniel Dupuy (New York, 1961). *Mio, My Son*, tr. Marianne Turner (New York, 1956). *Karlsson on the Roof*, tr. Marianne Turner (New York, 1971). *Rasmus and the Vagabond*, tr. Gerry Bothmer (New York, 1968). *The Children on Troublemaker Street*, tr. Gerry Bothmer (New York, 1964). *Lotta on Troublemaker Street*, tr. Gerry Bothmer (New York, 1963). *Mischievous Meg*, tr. Gerry Bothmer (New York, 1962). *Emil in the Soup Tureen*, tr. Lilian Seaton (Chicago, 1970). *Emil's Pranks* (Chicago, 1971). *Emil and the Piggy Beast*, tr. Michael Heron (Chicago, 1973). *Seacrow Island*, tr. Evelyn Ramsden (New York, 1969). *The Brothers Lionheart*. tr. Joan Tate (New York, 1975).

Bibliography

Holmberg, Olle, "Astrid Lindgren, låtsandet och det ensamma barnet." *Svensk litteraturtidskrift* (1963): 1–10. Klint, Liselotte, "Könsrollsuppfattningen i Astrid Lindgrens barnböcker." *Barn och kultur* 6 (1971): 176–179; Lorentz Larson comments on Klint's essay, 179. Landau, Elliott, "Quibble, Quibble: Funny? Yes; Humorous, No!" *Horn Book Magazine* 2 (1962): 154–164. Ørvig, Mary, ed., *En bok om Astrid Lindgren* (Stockholm, 1977). Includes a most detailed bibliography by Lena Törnqvist and a short summary on Astrid Lindgren in English. See also *Svenskt författerlexikon* which publishes Swedish publications in five-year intervals.

Hanna Kalter Weiss

Thekla Lingen

Born March 6 (or 8), 1866, Goldingen/
Kurland (today Lithuania); died
November 7, 1931, Eittenau
Genre(s): poetry, novel
Language(s): German

At the age of fourteen she went to St. Petersburg for a training course as an actress. She was quite successful on the stage but abandoned her career for marriage. In St. Petersburg she held a high reputation among the upper circles of the German colony there. She excelled in her poems and novels.

Works

Am Scheideweg, poems [At the Crossroad] (1898, 2nd enlarged ed., 1900). *Die schönen Frauen* [The Beautiful Women] (1901). *Aus Dunkel und Dämmerung* [Out of Dark and Dawn] (1902). *Und gestern hat er mir Rosen gebracht, Für eine Singstimme und Orchester* [Yesterday Roses He Brought, for Voice and Orchestra] (1921).

Translations: *Yesterday Roses He Brought, for Voice and Orchestra*, tr. by the poet.

Bibliography

Bigler, Ingrid, "Lingen, Thekla." *Deutsches Literatur-Lexikon*. 3rd, completely revised ed. by H. Rupp and C.L. Lang, vol. 9. (Bern-Munich, 1984), col. 1489. "Thekla Lingen." *Lexikon der deutschen Dichter und Prosaisten vom Beginn des 19. Jahrhunderts bis zur Gegenwart*, ed. F. Brümmer, 6th completely revised and enlarged ed., vol. 3 (rpt. Nendeln/Liechtenstein, 1975), p. 273.

Albrecht Classen

Věra Linhartová

Born 1938, Brno, Czechoslovakia
Genre(s): novel, poetry, criticism
Language(s): Czech

After receiving degrees in art history and aesthetics, Linhartová worked for an art gallery in Southern Bohemia from 1961 to 1966. She had started to write while in her teens, publishing her first works in 1964. In 1966 Linhartová moved to Prague during a period of relative cultural freedom and of experimentation in literature, art, theatre, and film. She worked on various joint projects with other avant-garde artists and writers and sat on the editorial board of the innovative literary journal *Tvář*. After the 1968 Soviet invasion, Linhartová left Czechoslovakia. She lives and writes in France.

In addition to fiction, Linhartová has written poetry and critical works on literature and art. Among her works published outside of Czechoslovakia are *Internalisi del fluito pressimo* (1969), *Chimäre oder Querschnitt durch die*

Zwiebel (1970), *Canon a l'écrivisse* (1970), and *Mehrstimmige Zerstreuung* (1971). She is best known for her fiction of the 1960s: *Meziprůzkum nejblíž uplynulého* (1964; Interim Investigation of the Recent Past), *Proster k rozlišení* (1964; Space for Differentiation), *Rozprava o zdviži* (1965; Discussion about the Elevator), *Preštoreč* (1966), and *Dům daleko* (1968; The Faraway House). These works have much in common with the "nouveau roman" in France, although direct influence is unlikely. Linhartová's interest in non-representational and surrealist art is reflected in her fiction. The plot is minimal, held in suspension by the narrator's word play and digressions. The fictional nature of the characters and events described is insisted upon. Language itself and the process of artistic creation come to the foreground.

Although Linhartová's work is, in many ways, part of a broader movement away from realism (and socialist realism) in the 1960s, her complex style and use of experimental forms are highly original. She is one of the outstanding contemporary Czech writers.

Works

See Brabec, Jiří, ed., *Slovník českých spisovatelů: Pokus o rekonstrukci dějin české literatury 1948–1979* (Toronto, 1982), pp. 294–295.

English Translation: Nemcova, Jeanne W., ed. and tr., *Czech and Slovak Short Stories* (1967), pp. 284–296.

Bibliography

Blackwell, Vera, "Věra Linhartová: Mirrors and Masks," in *New Writing of Eastern Europe*. George Gömöri and Charles Newman, comps.(Chicago, 1968), pp. 233–237. French, Alfred, *Czech Writers and Politics, 1945–1969* (Canberra, 1982), pp. 241–243. Pražan, Bronislav, and Oleg Sus, "Proměny kontextu a významotvorného principu v próze Věry Linhartové: Pokus o typologickou analýzu." *česká Literatura*, Vol. 18 (1970): 60–80. (English summary). Richterová, Sylvie, "Totožnost člověka ve světě znaků (Kundera—Linhartová—Hrabel)." *Proměny* 19, iss. 2 (1982); 81–90. See also Brabec, above.

Nancy Cooper

Irene Lisboa

(a.k.a. João Falco, Manuel Suares)

Born 1892, Casal de Murtinheira, Concelho de Arruda dos Vinhos, Portugal; died 1958, Lisbon
Genre(s): poetry, fiction, essay, children's literature
Language(s): Portuguese

Lisboa was an elementary school teacher who began her literary career in 1926 with *Contarelos* (Tiny Tales), a collection of thirteen children's stories. Forced to retire from teaching in 1940 because of her opposition to the Portuguese dictatorship, she thereafter dedicated herself completely to writing. In addition to her verse and fiction, she contributed to various Portuguese publications, notably *Seara Nova*. Lisboa sometimes used the pseudonyms João Falco and Manuel Soares. Her fiction, known for its originality, deals compassionately with members of the urban underclass in a unique style she called the "chronicle," or "report." Her language is simple, incorporating colloquial speech, which heightens the journalistic effect of her narrative. Her poetry, unique in its use of everyday language, focuses on similar themes.

Works

Fiction: *Solidão* [Solitude] (1939). *Começa uma vida* [A Life Begins] (1940), autobiography. *Lisboa e quem cá vive* [Lisbon and Those Who Live In It] (1940). *Esta Cidade!* [This City!] (1942). *Apontamentos* [Sketches] (1943). *Uma Mão Cheia de Nada, Outra de Coisa Nenhuma* [One Handful of Nothing, Another of Something Unimportant] (1955). *O Pouco e o Muito* [Scarcity and Abundance] (1956). *Voltar atrás para que?* [Turning Back—What For?] (1956), autobiography. *Titulo qualquer serve* [Any Title Will Do] (1958). *Crônicas da Serra* [Highland Sketches] (ca. 1961).

Poetry: *Un Dia e Otro Dia* [One Day and Another] (1936). *Outono havias de vir, latente e triste* [Autumn, You Were Bound to Come, Latent and Sad] (1937). *Folhas Volantes* [Drifting Leaves] (1940).

Children's Stories: *Contarelos* [Tiny Tales] (1926). *Queres ouvir, eu conto* [Would You Like a Story, I'll Tell You One] (1958).

Essays: *Troebel e Montessori e o Trabalho Manual na Escola* [Troebel and Montessori and Manual

Labor in the School] (1937). *Modernas Tendencias da Educação* [Modern Tendencies in Education] (1942). *Inquérito ao Livro em Portugal* [Inquiry into the Book in Portugal] (1946).

Bibliography

Bédé, J.-A., and W.B. Edgerton, eds., *Columbia Dictionary of Modern European Literature* (1940). Das Neves, J. Alves, "Irene Lisboa, Contadora de Historias." *Anhembi*, 34 (100) (1959). Klein, L., ed., *Encyclopedia of World Literature in the 20th Century* (1981). Moisés, M., ed., *Literatura Portuguesa Moderna* (1973). Sayers, R.S., "Irene Lisboa as a Writer of Fiction." *Hispania* 45 (1962).

Paula T. Irvin

Inna L'vovna Lisnianskaia

Born June 24, 1928, Baku, The Soviet Union
Genre(s): poetry
Language(s): Russian

A contemporary poet in the Soviet Union, Lisnianskaia is not a member of the Union of Writers by her own choice. Her poetry is too personal and centers on themes far removed from the official canon.

Lisnianskaia began to publish in 1949 with collections of poetry appearing in 1957, *Éto bylo so mnoi* (So It Happened to Me) and 1958, *Vernost'* (Fidelity). Her collection *Ne prosto liubov'* (1963; Not Simply Love) centered on her experiences on an arctic expedition. She continued to publish her poetry in 1966, *Iz pervykh ust* (Right from the Source) but soon became almost silent. With the appearance of *Vinogradnyj svet* (1978; Grape Light) which was harshly excoriated in official critiques, she ceased to publish in the Soviet Union altogether. She remains in "internal exile" publishing only abroad. Among her more recent works released by foreign presses, in Paris, a collection of poems called *Dozhdi i zerkala* (1983; Rains and Mirrors) and the United States, *Na opushke sna* (1984; On the Brink of Sleep).

Lisnianskaia cries for a reformation of artistic ideals, the abandoning of the perversion of expression for the sake of political meaning: "Where are the verses about love? I'm always rhyming 'war' with 'guilt'/ I'm tired of myself . . ." ("Pronzeni polovetskimi strelami russkie sny"). But most often she simply cries out her own ideas, retaining her own ideal of expression. Her themes revolve around love and the recognition of self as both good and bad. Her short lyrics are the vehicle for two or three highly-concentrated complex thoughts or images, well-balanced and expertly timed.

Lisnianskaia deserves to be recognized as one of the most important voices in contemporary Russian poetry. Her message is to transcend everyday life through the ennobling effects of poetry, the goal of all true poetry.

Works

Vernost' (1958). *Ne prosto, liubov: stikhi* (1963). *Iz pervykh ust* (1966). *Vinogradnyj svet* (1978). *Dozhdi i zerkala* (1983). *Na opushke sna* (1984).

Bibliography

Belaia, L., "Slovo ob Arktike." *Moskovskaia komsomolets* (September 11, 1963). Dymshits, A., "Vzyskatel'nost'" *Znamia*, 7 (1963). Kostrov, V., "Ne prosto—liubov." *Komsomol'skaia pravda* (October 16, 1963). Shekhter, M., "Neutolimyi gorod slova." *Literaturnaia Rossiia* (August 30, 1963).

Chris Tomei

Olga Lisovska

Born 1928
Genre(s): poetry, translation, essay
Language(s): Latvian

In addition to her skill as a lyric poet, much loved in Soviet Latvia, Olga Lisovska has also gained renown as a critic, essayist, reviewer, and editor. As a translator she has brought the works of both English and Russian writers into Latvian. Her verse is characterized by its traditional form, lyrical quality and intonation, and balance of the intellectual and emotional.

Works

Stārķu Krasts [The Storks' Shore] (1978).

Warwick J. Rodden

Gabrielle van Loenen

(see: Jeanne Gabrielle van Schaik-
Willing)

Catherina Anna Maria de Savornin Lohman

Born January 4, 1868, Assen, The Netherlands;
died September 23, 1930, The Hague
Genre(s): novel, article, essay
Language(s): Dutch

Anna de Savornin Lohman was one of a few women authors who, at the turn of the century, wrote about the social and ethical position of woman in contemporary society. Born into The Hague upper class, she passed a cheerless childhood and youth. She was thwarted in her desire to pursue higher education (a course of life only open to her brothers). She lost some of her close relatives too soon and suffered disappointment in love. When her father was financially ruined, she was forced to earn her living and turned to writing.

In her numerous novels, essays, pamphlets, and literary reviews, she took a firm and controversial stand not only on the "woman's question," as it was then called, but also on matters of literature and religion, and she used her sharp pen to relentlessly attack the fake propriety and stern Calvinism of the top circles in The Hague.

Disillusionment with the world, often culminating in bitterness, and profound doubts about the rigorous faith of her parents run through her novels. She is very effective in portraying a slice in the life of a number of closely related characters (relatives, friends, couples), often without any climax of plot line, and in observing the way in which they cope with the growing awareness that human existence is essentially flawed. Their doubts about the discrepancy between the misery of daily life and the ideals of their faith, between positive rational thinking and mystic belief are best pictured in her most successful novel, which carries the significant title *Vragensmoede* (1896; Question-weary). Central in the book is the couple Uytweerde, young ambitious Calvinists—he, politically, she

socially, active. The birth of an idiotic child upsets their blind belief in a God whom the wife especially comes to see as utterly cruel and loveless. It is typical for Lohman that the character who deals best with the imperfections of human existence is the serene and humane agnostic Dr. Vrede, an old friend of the couple and, as they see it, an unfortunate unbeliever.

Savornin Lohman's opinions on the position of woman in the social fabric are best expressed in *De liefde in de vrouwenquestie* (1898; Love in the Woman's Question) and *Vrouwenliefde in de moderne literatuur* (1902; Woman's Love in Modern Literature). *De Liefde in de vrouwenquestie* is a pamphlet partly written in response to the novel *Hilda van Suylenburg* (1898) in which the feminist author Cécile Geokoop pictured two women who combined a successful career with a happy marriage. Though Savornin Lohman was an advocate of the equal work/equal pay principle and a defender of women's education, the latter because that would make it possible for women to earn a living if they had to (think of her own plight), she considered the pursuit of a career to be chiefly a substitute for love. A successful combination of love and career is impossible, and women who wish to imitate men are ridiculous. Woman's highest aspiration is to find a man she can love with unconditional surrender.

But Savornin Lohman also fulminated against the marriages of convenience of which she professed to see too many in The Hague upper class. She exposed it as immoral for mothers to promote a union between their innocent daughters and men too much about town but blessed with wealth and title. On the other hand, she went as far as advocating free love (though she would not always admit it), curiously enough in the configuration one man/more women, her rationale being that too many women were leading a lonely life or were trapped in a loveless union.

The most extreme illustration of her conviction that woman's highest happiness is the love for a man is the novel *Het ééne noodige* (1897; The One and Only Need). It is the curious and somewhat morbid story of Katie de Reth who actually "falls in love" with and "devotes" her life to a man she never meets. On the news of his death she burns her poetry and commits suicide.

Savornin Lohman further wrote many book reviews, some of which were later collected in *Over boeken en schrijvers* (1903; On Books and Writers). She had no affinity at all with the avant-garde of her time and their art for art's sake principle, but she persistently admired writers who wrote openly about sensuality and sex, especially from the woman's point of view.

Her memoirs, *Herinneringen* (1909), were candid, personal and, at times, high-tempered. From 1903 till 1917 she edited *De Hollandsche Lelie*, a woman's weekly. In her very last book, *Levensraadselen* (1921; Life's Mysteries), published when she had been widowed after a short but happy union (during which she had given up writing), she held a much more cheerful view of her fellow human beings than in the rest of her work. Instead of perceiving God as cruel and loveless, she now saw him as loving and forgiving.

A restless and belligerent mind, Savornin Lohman was a widely read and self-made intellectual whose writing lacked discipline. Her style and language are often careless (partly due to the fact that she had to be prolific to earn a living) and larded with needless repetitions. Her nonchalance, unchecked emotions, and bitterness tended to undercut the effectiveness of her polemics, and she was an easy victim of the derision of male colleagues. She was, however, a fluent storyteller and sharp observer, who had a keen understanding of the conflicts between men and women and between children and parents. Her fiction can be read as a series of novels of manners mirroring Dutch upper-class life at the turn of the century.

Though Lohman's viewpoints on the position of woman are certainly dated today, she should be appreciated in her own time when ideas about women pursuing a career or women capable of sensual love were only slowly coming to fruition. She was also immensely popular at the time and therefore deserves a space in reference works and women's studies larger than the one usually allotted to her.

Works

Miserere (1895). Vragensmoede (1896). Het ééne noodige (1897). Levens-ernst (1897). De liefde in de vrouwenguestie (1898). Naschrift op de liefde in de vrouwenguestie (1899). Geloof (1899). Smarten (1900). Na het ontwaken (1901). Vrouwenliefde in de moderne literatuur (1902). Over boeken en schrijvers (1903). Jonge roeping (1903). Gelukswegen (1903). Letterkundig leven (1904). Van het inwendige leven (1904). Liefde (1905). Kleine levensdingen (1905). In den opgang (1906). Uit de sfeer gerukt (1908). Herinneringen (1909). Uit Christelijke kringen (1911). Zedelijkheids-apostelen (1912). Levensraadselen (1921). Wat nooit sterft (n.d.). Om de eere Gods (n.d.).

Bibliography

Basse, M., *Het aandeel der vrouw in de Nederlandse letterkunde* 2 (1921). Hartog, H., *Een eigenwijs schrijfster* (1903). Jonckbloet, G. *Jonkvrouwe Anna de Savornin Lohman in en uit hare werken* (1912). Postma, H., "Emancipatieromans rond de eeuwwisseling." *Opzij* 6 (1978). Romein-Verschoor, A., *Vrouwenspiegel* (1935). Smit Kleine, F., *Anna Lohhman (Jonkvrouwe Anna de Savornin Lohman)* (1912). Stamperius, H., *Vrouwen en literatuur* (1980).

For articles in reference works, see: *Winkler Prins Lexicon der Nederlandse letterkunde* (1986).

Ria Vanderauwera

Mirra Aleksandrovna Lokhvitskaia

Born 1869, St. Petersburg, Russia; died 1905, St. Petersburg
Genre(s): poetry
Language(s): Russian

Called the "Russian Sappho" by her contemporaries, Mirra Lokhvitskaia was an outstanding member of the Russian Symbolist movement at the end of the nineteenth century. Her poetry, which is impressive both for the ease and grace of its technique and its artistic beauty, reflects on Symbolist themes and philosophy, using colors and other motifs very much in the same manner as the poetry of Blok or Bal'mont. Particularly in her early poetry, the ideal world outside of banal reality is the power that "draws one to the heights." However, in contrast to the Divine Feminine of Blok or Bely, Lokhvitskaia, as Sam Cioran justly pointed out, invoked a "Divine masculine." Lokhvitskaia was both acclaimed and deplored for her occupation with female passions and eroticism.

Born in St. Petersburg in 1869, Lokhvitskaia was one of the two daughters of the well-known solicitor and law professor A.V. Lokhvitskii who would turn to writing as a career (the other became Nadezhda Teffi). Mirra Lokhvitskaia was first published in the journal *Sever* (The North) in 1889. She became a regular contributor to this and other journals, among them "Universal illustration," "Northern Messenger," "Russian Thought," "Labor," etc. The poem "U moria" (By the Sea), published in 1892, launched her meteoric career. Her first volume of collected poems was published to great critical acclaim in 1895; the following year it was awarded the Pushkin Prize for literature. Her second volume appeared in 1898 and her third in 1900 (when the first two were reprinted as well). Her fourth and fifth volumes appeared in 1903 and 1904, respectively. She was awarded her second Pushkin Prize (posthumously) for the fifth volume in 1905. In 1908 her family published a last collection under the title *Pered zakatom* (Before Sunset).

Lokhvitskaia was extremely popular in her own time and acclaimed by such astute critics as V. Briusov, who asserted that ten or fifteen poems of Lokhvitskaia will last throughout time. As it turned out, Lokhvitskaia has been all but forgotten in Soviet Russia. No Soviet critic can justly appreciate her art because of its "lack of social content" and, more importantly, its involvement with feminine passions. To the Soviet critic, the erotic poetry of Nadson was only tolerable, but Lokhvitskaia's was profligate. Even many of her contemporaries, notably L.N. Tolstoy, castigated her for this occupation. If Lokhvitskaia was bold in asserting, as T. Pachmuss claims, that women are free "to express their individuality, to lay bare the passionate erotic aspect of their emotions, to explore and portray elements of their nature that outmoded and stereotyped definitions of 'female' and 'femininity' had excluded" in the pre-Soviet era, she was too bold for the Soviet era, which is even more prudish and intolerant of her art than her critics had been. However, even her Soviet critics admit that she possessed "an undoubtable talent" only she wasted it stupidly on "cheap ornaments."

To a modern non-Soviet critic, her art is impressive, her power over verse form is impeccable, her flow of images and control of words is masterful—she is clearly able to combine the sound and the sense of poetic speech successfully and artistically. Her lyric imagery involves effusions of colors and fragrances—she called herself the "Queen of Flowers," a name she probably deserves. However, it would be a mistake to assert that her involvements with sensual elements constitutes the extent of her poetic creativity. She capably blended all her images and her sound patterns to create a beautiful poetic world that has a convincing and attractive appeal. Her last two volumes include primarily long poems with medieval and religious themes. She was criticized for this stage of her development, too, except for her more perceptive readers who, like the poet Minskii, realized she was evolving as an artist. Her early death cut short further evolution, but her poetry stands as a bold and mature statement of a female individuality and a Symbolist sensitivity.

Works

Stikhotvoreniia (1896). *Stikhotvoreniia*, Vol. 2 (1898). *Stikhotvoreniia*, Vols. 1–5 (1900–1904). *Pered zakatom* (1908). (For a list of articles, see V. Terras, *Handbook of Russian Literature*, 1985, p. 263.)

Translation: Pachmuss, T., *Women Writers in Russian Modernism: An Anthology* (Urbana, 1978), pp. 85–113.

Bibliography

Bialyi, G.A., *Poèty 1880–1890-kh godov* (Biblioteka poèta, 1972). Introductory article, pp. 58–62, also pp. 601–605. Cioran, S., "The Russian Sappho: Mirra Lokhvitskaia." *Russian Literature Triquarterly* 9 (1974): 317–335.

Christine Tomei

Mama Lola

(see: Margareta Miller-Verghi)

Lombarda

Flourished first half of the XIII century,
Toulouse, France
Genre(s): poetry
Language(s): Provençal

The works of Lombarda are disputed, yet it would appear from Perkal-Balinsky that she is responsible for two poems, one of which is preceded by a *razo*. As such the poems work as a sort of extended *tenso* between herself and Bernard Arnaut, since it would appear that he wrote the first to her, she the second in response. If this is so, then the editions of Schultz and Bogin are unreliable. From the *razo* we learn that Lombarda was from Toulouse, and that she became involved with the brother of the Count of Armagnac, Bernard Arnaut. Bogin thinks her name comes from the fact that her family was in banking—Lombard was a common banking name—not that she was Italian.

The two poems follow the same rhyme scheme of two *coblas singulars* of eight lines each, the first poem ending with a four-line tornada. It would certainly appear that the lyrics are by two different hands, as the first one is much more straightforward than the second. The first extols the virtues of Lombarda, playing on the eponymous aspects of her name by comparing her to Alamanda and Giscarda. The second responds to the name play but shifts it to a male-female game as she wishes that she could be Na Bernarda to his Bernard and Arnauda for his Arnaut. This poem then moves into *trobar clus* style, as she picks up the image of a mirror the first poem mentions in its *tornada* and uses it to play on images of concealment spelled out through a series of puns.

Works

Ed., Schultz, p. 22; Véran, pp. 90–92; Boutiere-Schutz, pp. 416–417; Bogin, p. 114; Perkal-Balinsky, pp. 89–95.

Bibliography

Anglade, J., *Les Troubadours et les Bretons* (Toulouse, 1928–1929; rpt. Slatkine, 1973), p. 35. Bec, P., "*Trobairitz* et chansons de femme: Contribution à la connaissance du lyrisme féminin au moyen âge." *CCM* 22 (1979); 235–262. Bogin, M., *The Women Troubadours* (New York, 1980). Boutiére, J., and A.-H. Schutz, *Biographies des troubadours*. 2d. ed. (Paris, 1964). Branciforti, F., *Il canzoniere di Lanfrancesco Cigala* (Florence, 1954). Bruckner, M., "Na Castelloza, *Trobairitz*, and Troubadour Lyric." *Romance Notes* 25 (1985): 1–15. Chabaneau, C., "Les biographies des troubadours en langue provençale." *Histoire générale de Languedoc* X (Toulouse, 1885). Dronke, P., *Women Writers of the Middle Ages* (Cambridge, 1984). Mahn, C.A.F., *Die Werke der Troubadours in provenzalischer Sprache* (Berlin, 1846). Perkal-Balinsky, D., *The Minor Trobairitz*. Diss., Northwestern University, 1986. Raynouard, M., *Choix des poésies originales des troubadours*, 6 vols. (Osnabruck, 1966). Riquer, M. de., *Los trovadores*, 3 vols. (Barcelona, 1975). Schultz, O., *Die Provenzalischen Dichterinnen* (Leipzig, 1888). Shapiro, M., "The Provençal *Trobairitz* and the Limits of Courtly Love." *Signs* 3 (1978): 560–571. Tavera, A., "A la recherche des troubadours maudits." *Sénéfiance* 5 (1978): 135–161. Véran, J., *Les poétesses provençales* (Paris, 1946).

Sarah Spence

Lucia Lopresti Longhi

(see: Anna Banti)

Cécile Ines Loos

Born February 4, 1883, Basel, Switzerland;
died January 21, 1959, Basel
Genre(s): novel, short story
Language(s): German

Loos, one of the most important recent rediscoveries in Swiss literature, grew up under the influence of death, loss, and abandonment. The fifth child of an organist, she was two when, following her mother's death, she was given to a childhood friend of her mother. Her natural father died in 1887. Her well-to-do and cultured foster home provided a few years of security. These came to an abrupt end in 1892, when her foster mother died in childbirth. Loos, a bright and imaginative child, was lodged in an orphanage near Berne run on the principles of strict religious instruction, hard work, little praise, and brutal punishment. Bereft and isolated, with an intimate knowledge of death, yet nourished by the fairy-tale-like, past years of comfort, ten-year-old Loos sustained and protected herself by writing poetry.

After leaving the orphanage in 1900, Loos worked for ten years as a governess in Switzerland and England. In 1911, she returned to Basel, and on August 22, 1911, gave birth in Milan to an illegitimate son. Loos's deeply ambivalent experience of motherhood, with its near-pathological undertones, reveals the dark and damaged side of her character. The son's childhood was largely spent in foster families and orphanages, as Loos did not have the economic means to spare him her fate. She came to bitterly blame her over-idealized son, who had disappointed her unrealistically high expectations, for her failure to marry, and in her old age, obsessed with the idea that he was not her real child, she repeatedly attempted to disinherit him.

Following the birth, Loos, who returned to Basel permanently in 1921, eked out her existence as a waitress, clerk, and secretary. During this time of crisis she also became an expert in astrology and found solace in esoteric religions. Her determination to become a successful author bore fruit in 1929, with the best-seller *Matka Boska*, a flawed but imaginative and vivid study, set in Poland, of the ignorant and defenseless peasant girl Meliska and her illegitimate daughter. Her next novel *Die Rätsel der Turandot*, a fantastic, romantic tale of the lives and loves of a dancer, was also a success, and Loos's career seemed launched.

But the period of security was short-lived. After 1933, Loos lost her German publisher and soon the German market as well. Her difficulties in placing manuscripts with Swiss publishers were enormous, for her work did not conform to Swiss tastes and the sales of her later novels rarely covered production costs. Attempts to adapt her work to the present, such as *Konradin* (1943), a patriotic tale which Loos explicitly wrote as a contribution to the "geistige Landesverteidigung" (Swiss state of preparedness during the Second World War) failed. Forgotten by all but a few constant friends, she spent the rest of her life in poverty, living from occasional translations, menial part-time jobs, tiny stipends, gifts, and handouts. That she not only continued to write but also produced her two finest works during this period is a tribute to her enormous energy, and to the unquenchable love of life attested to by her friends. Loos spent her last years in an old people's home in Basel, where she died. Her literary estate, now in the University Library at Basel, includes a number of unpublished novels (for details see the bibliographical appendix to *Verzauberte Welt. Ein Lesebuch*).

The flights of fantasy and affected, pathetic tone of Loos's weaker novels alienate today's reader. These works are most effective in evoking childhood, as in *Jehanne* (1946), a novel based on the life of Joan of Arc, or in moments of social satire (*Leute am See*, 1951). Loos is at her strongest when she stays close to autobiographical inspiration, varying motivation and outcome, transposing in time and place, recasting roles. Her best characters are innocents, abandoned to fend for themselves in the bitterest of circumstances, yet often protected by an enigmatic invulnerability. Their instinctive sense of an inviolate self gives the stories some of the charm and inner logic of a fairy tale. But Loos knows no happy endings: like Susanne in *Hinter dem Mond* (1943), her protagonists triumph by surviving intact. In this work, as well as in the artistic re-imagining of her childhood, *Der Tod und das Püppchen* (1939), realistic narration, plain, sensuous language, and the flow of destiny cohere into a whole of striking originality and mastery.

Works

Matka Boska novel (1929; 1944). *Die Rätsel der Turandot* [Turandot's Enigmas], novel (1931). *Die leisen Leidenschaften. Ein Lied der Freundschaft* [Quiet Passions. A Song of Friendship], novel (1934). *Der Tod und das Püppchen* [Death and the Doll], novel (1939; 1983; 1987). *Hinter dem Mond* [Beyond the Moon], novel (1942; 1983). *Konradin. Das summende Lied der Arbeit von Vater, Sohn und Enkel* [Konradin. The Humming Song of the Labor of Father, Son, and Grandson], novel (1943). *Jehanne* [Joan of Arc], novel (1946). *Leute am See* [People at the Lakeside], novel (1951). *Schlafende Prinzessin* [Sleeping Princess], short story (1955). *Verzauberte Welt. Ein Lesebuch* [Enchanted World. A Reader], anthology and reader (1983).
Translations: *Matka Boska* [Mother of God]. tr. Margaret Goldsmith (1930).

Bibliography

Bartlin, Elisabeth, "Cécile Ines Loos. Eine Einführung in ihre Werke." Diss., U. of Basel, 1968. Linsmayer, Charles, "Ich fand nirgends eine Heimat ausser bei mir selbst." Leben und Werk der Schriftstellerin C.I.L." Afterword to Cécile Ines Loos, Hinter dem Mond (Küsnacht/Zürich, 1983), pp. 167–232. Linsmayer, Charles, "Kindheit als Höhepunkt des Lebens." Afterword to Cécile Ines Loos, *Der Tod und das Püppchen* (Frankfurt a.M., 1987), pp. 165–184. (Rpt. from Cécile Ines Loos. *Der Tod und das Püppchen*. Küsnacht/Zürich: 1983). Matt, Beatrice von, "Von Mädchenperspektiven. Zu Cécile Ines Loos." *Lesarten. Zur Schweizer Literatur von Walser bis Muschg* (Zürich, 1985), pp. 34–39. (First published 1983). Vogt, Albert, "Die Darstellung der Kindheit bei Jakob Schaffner, Meinrad Inglin und Cécile Ines Loos." Lizentiatsarbeit. Master's Thesis, U. of Berne, 1987.

General references: DLL, Vol. 9, 1651. LdS, 204.

Ann Marie Rasmussen

Leonor López de Córdoba

Born circa 1362; died circa 1412, Spain
Genre(s): autobiography
Language(s): Spanish

Leonor López de Córdoba belonged to a noble Spanish family loyal to Pedro I ("The Cruel") of Castile, who was killed and succeeded by his bastard brother, Enrique II. This tragic event affected her life to an incredible degree. Her father, the Master of Calatrava, was executed, and most of her brothers died in prison, for defending Pedro I's daughters against Enrique II's troops in Carmona. Leonor and her husband survived the horrors of jail but lost all of their possessions and had to endure great hardship, always at the mercy of their political enemies. Leonor was given shelter by an aunt loyal to Enrique II and enjoyed some modest prosperity for a while. However, her aunt asked her to leave because of her struggles with her cousins, which culminated when she protected against their will a Jewish servant infected with the plague. After all the other servants had died as a result of taking care of the infected servant, Leonor had her own son care for him. The servant lived, but her son died. Later, Leonor became the chief advisor and protegée of Catalina de Lancaster, wife of Enrique III and granddaughter of Pedro I, enjoying enormous influence in Castile. However, due to the intrigues of some courtiers, she lost the favor of the queen and died shortly thereafter.

We know about Leonor López de Córdoba's life partly because of what some historians have written on the subject, but mostly because of her own account, her *Memorias*, the first autobiography in Spanish literature. These memoirs are a short document which she dictated to a notary in the last years of her life. After an oath to tell the truth and an introduction about her family, Leonor concentrates on two episodes in her life: the death of her father and that of her son. That of all the events in her life, she should have chosen these two is revealing, for both are cases of extreme loyalty and exemplify her intense sense of honor. What she seems to be telling us by this choice is that her family always made sacrifices to fulfill its obligations both to its superiors (the king in the first episode) and to its subordinates (the servant in the second episode) regardless of who these were. Even though the king was cruel and the servant was Jewish, her family still honored its obligations towards them.

It is interesting that Leonor López de Córdoba's memoirs do not talk about her recent falling out with Catalina de Lancaster, which must have been painfully present in her mind. Given her precarious situation, Leonor probably did not feel she could mention Catalina at all. The queen is, however, the most likely addressee of the memoirs, which can be read as a bitter complaint about disloyalty. Most critics consider the memoirs a justification, and they are, but they are also an attack. By explaining how she lost most of her family out of loyalty to superiors and subordinates, Leonor is condemning those who did not behave that way: the courtiers who abandoned the king and the queen who abandoned the courtiers. This pretty much covers the spectrum of her political enemies, old and new. It particularly applies to the queen, whom she had served faithfully and for whose family her family had sacrificed so much. After all, Leonor's father died for saving Catalina's mother, a fact that she is not about to let her forget.

As can be seen, contrary to what most critics believe, Leonor López de Córdoba's account of her own life is far from incoherent. Rather, it is a well-articulated discourse that constitutes an overt justification of the author's behavior, as well as a surreptitious attack on the behavior exhibited by her enemies. If her account seems somewhat rambling, it is because of the immense bewilderment with which she contemplates the world. The fact that her overflowing anger is communicated to the reader so forcefully is very much to her credit as a writer.

Works

Memorias (circa 1410).

Bibliography

Ayerbe-Chaux, Reinaldo, ed., "Las memorias de doña Leonor López de Córdoba." *Journal of Hispanic Philology* II (1977). Deyermond, Alan D., "Spain's First Women Writers." *Women in Hispanic Literature. Icons and Fallen Idols*, ed. Beth Miller (Berkeley, Calif., 1983). Ghassemi, Ruth, "La crueldad de los vencidos: Las *Memorias* de Leonor López de Córdoba." *La Corónica* 18, 1 (1989): 19–32. Serrano y Sanz, Manuel. *Apuntes para una biblioteca de autoras españolas*. I. Biblioteca de Autores Españoles, 168 (Madrid, 1903).

Cristina González

Louise

(see: Luise Maria Hensel)

Marie Claire Loupard

(see: Nel [Pieternella Margaretha] Noordzij)

Cecilie Löveid

Born 1951, Bergen, Norway
Genre(s): poetry, novel, drama
Language(s): Norwegian

Cecilie Löveid is among the most innovative and imaginative of Norway's young authors. Her writing is experimental, an attempt "to bring in something new, reality so to speak," as she says in one of her books. Löveid has designated her first six books as "novels," but in fact they are a combination of literary genre—poetry, short prose texts, songs, fragments of myth and fairytale and dramatic dialogue. She gives free rein to her sense of humor and sends her characters—and readers—on wonderful adventures via her ingenious use of language. Her texts are filled with unexpected and fanciful associations and an imagery which delights and surprises.

In her earliest works one detects a social consciousness. In *Most* (1972) and *Tenk om isen skulle komme* (1974; What If the Ice Should Come), Löveid demonstrates how a society in which human values are steadily losing priority can have a negative, even destructive effect on individual lives. And there are a number of segments in *Fanget villrose* (1977; Imprisoned Wild Rose) that have clear political messages. But these concerns are not allowed to overshadow the characters Löveid portrays, typically female and young, sensuous and eager for experiences. Their relationships with men are of particular interest to Löveid, but relationships among women also have an important place in her fictional world. Löveid does not intend that her characters should be eccentric or extraordinary figures; they are ordinary women depicted in everyday situations.

Sug (1979; Sea Swell) is the title of Löveid's sixth novel; it is probably her most successful work to date and has already been translated into several languages including English. It is the story of Kjersti, a young single mother, and her search to learn more about herself and how she relates to men, specifically her father and her current lover. Her father was a sailor and consequently absent from home for long periods of time. Kjersti's feelings towards him are ambivalent; on the one hand she feels a strong attraction, on the other hand, anger and resentment at being abandoned so frequently. When, as an adult woman, she enters into relationships with men her own age, there is an imperceptible merging of emotions and expectations elicited by and directed toward father and lover. At the same time Kjersti is searching for herself and an understanding of her erotic nature, the narrator is searching for a language suitable to relate this story. As the character delves into her past and glides downward toward the unconscious levels of her mind, the language becomes less and less realistic. Dream-like sequences, rich with imagery and associations, seem better suited to describe this particular reality.

In recent years Löveid's interest has turned to drama, and she has written a number of dramatic pieces for radio and stage. She has had the good fortune of being able to work closely with theater people in her native Bergen and to see her works performed, on stage, radio or television. Her radio plays have been performed in other Scandinavian countries as well, and one of them, *Måkespisere* (Gull-Eaters), was awarded the Prix Italia in 1983.

Löveid has demonstrated her affinity to music throughout her production, both with musical allusions and actual songs which appear in her prose texts and radio plays. Thus, it is no real surprise that she should write a text to be sung, namely the libretto for a short opera, *Dusj-1 opera for 2* (Shower-1 Opera for 2), which was performed at the annual music festival in Bergen in 1984.

In terms of thematic content and stylistic devices Löveid's dramatic works are an extension of her earlier prose texts. Her scripts for radio and stage can perhaps best be compared to performance theater. As a dramatist, Löveid continues to experiment and blend genre, searching for a form that can hold the reality she wishes to portray and a language to convey it.

Works

Novels: *Most* (1972). *Tenk om isen skulle komme* (1974). *Alltid skyer over Askøy* (1976). *Mörkets muligheter* (1976). *Fanget villrose* (1977). *Sug* (1979).

Drama: *Måkespisere* (1983). *Vift* (1905). *Balansedame* (1985). *Fornuftige dyr* (1986). *Dobbel nytelse* (1989).

Translations: *Sea Swell*, tr. Nadia Christensen (1986). *An Everyday Story*, in *Norwegian Women's Fiction*, ed. Katherine Hanson (1984). *New Norwegian Plays*, tr. Janet Garton and Henning Sehmsdorf (1989).

Bibliography

Christensen, Kari, "'—den særegne klangen av knust språk.' Assosiasjonsteknikken i Cecilie Löveids *Alltid skyer over Askøy.*" *Norsk Litterær Årbok.* (Oslo, 1979). Engelstad, Irene, and Överland, Janneken, *Frihet til å skrive. Artikler om kvinnelitteratur fra Amalie Skram til Cecilie Löveid* (Oslo, 1981). Smidt, Jofrid Karner, "One day we will find a path that has heart." *New from the Top of the World*, vol. 1 (Oslo, 1988). Rasmussen, Janet E., "Dreams and Discontent: The Female Voice in Norwegian Literature." *Review of National Literatures. Norway*, vol. 12 (New York, 1983). Rönning, Helge, ed., *Linjer i nordisk prosa. Norge 1965–1975* (Oslo, 1977).

Katherine Hanson

Rosalie Loveling

Born March 19, 1834, Nevele (Ghent),
Belgium; died May 4, 1875, Nevele
Genre(s): translation, anecdotal poetry,
realistic-regional novellas, essays
Language(s): Dutch

Rosalie and Virginie Loveling (see separate entry) were the daughters of an exceptionally well-educated Flemish mother (Marie Comparé) and her second husband, a gifted and versatile connoisseur of languages and literature of German origin. The girls were privately educated. After the death of her husband in 1846, Mrs. Loveling and her two daughters moved to Ghent where they became immersed in the intellectual and anticlerical francophone milieu. Yet the sisters abandoned neither their carefully cultivated interest in Flemish-Dutch literature, nor their very deep love for nature and the countryside. Already at an early age, both Rosalie and Virginie had delighted their family with their rhymed descriptions of authentic anecdotal events. Some of these have been preserved and they still sound remarkably fresh and natural in tone and diction.

The slightly naive quality of such anecdotal observations of daily events would remain characteristic of Rosalie Loveling's poetry. By virtue of her precise simplicity and natural tone, Rosalie managed to convey a deeper humanistic note than most of the more formal Flemish poetry of the time. Supposedly Rosalie's work is more pessimistic than Virginie's, but if the sisters had not carefully indicated the authorship of the poems and novellas they published jointly in their first volumes, the distinction would actually be hard to make. Some of the poems in their first collection, *Gedichten* (1870, 1889), had appeared previously in newspapers and periodicals.

The sisters are known best for their fictional prose. Again jointly, they published a collection of *Novellen* (1874, 1886). Of the twelve novellas, five were the work of Rosalie; of these, especially "Meester Huyghe," "De Baan der Kunst" (The Road of Art—about life as an artist), and "Broeder en Zuster" (Brother and Sister—about the inconstancy of love) have been praised. Both in Flemish Belgium and in the Netherlands this volume was hailed as an important work. Precise, needle-sharp observations of daily life in the city and in the country, these novellas shun superfluous imagery. An undertone of disappointment can always be detected in Rosalie's five stories, as well as in the three novellas she contributed to the third joint volume with her sister, *Nieuwe Novellen* (1875). Unlike Virginie, Rosalie never wrote a full-length novel. Her lack of constructive skill has been noted by M. Basse.

Rosalie Loveling deserves mention also for her essayistic prose and her chronicles in periodicals. She delivered a fine plea for equal education for men and women ("Iets over het Onderwijs der Vrouw," 1871), and in "Uw tweede Vrouw" (1874) she attempts in a very acute and sensitive way to deal with the inevitable problems of being a man's second wife. A *curiosum* is her essay "De Hond" ("The Dog"), in which this otherwise tolerant and sensitive woman expresses violent disgust for the canine species.

Works

[With Virginie Loveling], *Gedichten* (1870). *Novellen* (1874; Rosalie wrote: "Jan-Oom en Belle-Trezeken," "De Baan der Kunst," "Serafine," "Broeder en Zuster," and "Meester Huyghe"). *Nieuwe Novellen* (1875; Rosalie wrote: "Mijnheer Daman en zijne Erfgenamen," "Juffrouw Leocadie Stevens," and "Po en Paoletto"). *Polydoor en Theodoor, en andere novellen en schetsen* (1883).

Bibliography

See Virginie Loveling. Van Elslander, A. *Twintig Eeuwen Vlaanderen* 19 (1) (1976).

Kristiaan P. Aercke

Virginie Loveling

(a.k.a. W.G.E. Walter)

Born May 17, 1836, Nevele (Ghent), Belgium; died December 1, 1923, Ghent
Genre(s): anecdotal poetry, naturalistic novella, children's literature, novel, essay
Language(s): Dutch

For Virginie Loveling's childhood and family background as it influences her work, see the entry devoted to her (also unmarried) sister Rosalie Loveling (separate entry).

Virginie Loveling's literary production is astonishing both for its quantity and its diversity. Her first literary efforts were realistic poems, often with a sentimental tone; some of these were published together with poems by her sister Rosalie in 1870. The sisters also published two volumes of novellas together (1874, 1875), clearly indicating, however, who had written what. Unlike her sister, Virginie gradually expanded subsequent novellas in length and thematic diversity. From 1877 onward, she wrote some remarkable novels on controversial political-religious topics of the time with significant psychological depth in the characters (especially her women). Virginie Loveling's fictional prose was recognized as important and modern in style and themes by the foremost Belgian and Dutch literary personalities of her time (such as Potgieter, Busken Huet, Max Rooses, Karel van de Woestijne) and by commissions of both governments. Most of Virginie's novellas (which she continued to write during her entire career) were first published in prestigious literary periodicals in Holland (*De Gids, Nederland, Nederduytsch Tijdschrift, Leeskabinet*). In 1894 she was awarded the Five-Yearly (Belgian) Prize for Dutch Literature for her novel *Een dure Eed* (1891; A Costly Oath). Her series of *Kinderverhalen* (1863–1886; Children's Stories) won her the prize of the Royal Academy of Belgium.

Virginie Loveling combines the crisp observation of types with such themes as heredity, marriage, and the problems of and with children, in Flemish country and city settings. The narrative is often situated in the framework of contemporary political (including religious) discussions. Recurring themes and motives are family life, marriage (Virginie Loveling acknowledges that only marriages for love have a chance of success), the frustration of having children (or of not having children), poverty, death. Serious social drama, village amours, and the psychology of socially and physically crippled characters are rendered almost starkly, without the soothing wrapper of metaphor. Indeed, her careful avoidance of metaphor throughout her oeuvre is remarkable.

Virginie Loveling's first novel-length prose work was *In onze Vlaamsche Gewesten* (1877, 1882; In our Flemish Regions. Under the pseud. W.G.E. Walter); it is subtitled "Political Sketches" and treats the then-very-explosive anticlerical and liberal (in other words, conservative, in Belgium) problematics of the country in her characteristic intelligent and objective manner. Loveling recognizes the absurdity and inadequacy of black-and-white characterization and type-casting—something she carefully avoids in all her novels. Hypocrisy and extremism, goodness and understanding are to be found on both sides of a political-religious controversy and in all human beings. Another "political novel" is *Sophie* (1885). The novel dates from, and is set in, the turbulent years of Belgian history known as the era of the "School War," when the Catholic and the Liberal parties fought over fundamental issues of conflict between them. *Sophie* is about a crisis of faith; it is an *étude de moeurs* as well as a critical statement against the very strong influence of Catholicism in the Flemish countryside.

Polydoor en Theodoor (1881, 1883) is interesting as a study of a half-idiotic dwarf (Polydoor) who mercilessly tyrannizes his environment and his mother in particular—another variant of the child-theme that is so prominent with Virginie Loveling. A form of naturalism is announced in *Een Vonkje van Genie* (1883; A Spark of Genius). Jeroen, a child with a talent for painting, will never realize his dreams; he will die in prison. Heredity and milieu are to blame for the tragic—or rather: melodramatic—course of the lives of potentially gifted child and (memorably drawn) parents. This novella stands as an accusation of the world which withholds the food from the soul that craves it and thus extinguishes the spark of genius.

From now on, Loveling steers clear from happy endings! Heredity is again a major force in the novella *Onze Idealen* (1892; Our Ideals), where the melodramatic and the fantastic blend in a tale that is as gripping as any of Poe's or Maupassant's. Among Loveling's longer novellas, *Meesterschap* (1898; Mastery) deserves special mention. With this work her pessimistic, black period really begins. *Meesterschap* presents a somber view of Flemish farm life—a view that can stand as a rural equivalent of Zola's industrial city pessimism. Loveling's ugly and vicious farmers, however, become subhuman only as the result of the increasing concern with money and power in their very small economic circle, in the course of the story itself. Milieu and circumstance are thus presented as the strongest influences on personality. Money is always a negative force for Loveling. Marriage, too, it has already been noted, should exclusively be a concern of the heart. The heart, not fortune, is the condition for Love.

Together with *Sophie* and *Een Dure Eed, Een Revolverschot* (1911; A Gunshot) is generally considered one of Loveling's masterpieces. Again a study of heredity and its effects on psyche and eros, *Een Revolverschot* presents the fatal love of two sisters for the same man. Somber horror pictures and a few touches of melodrama stand out in this gruesome tale of murder and insanity.

Throughout her literary career, Virginie Loveling was also active as essayist and translator (of English and German poetry and of essays from English, French, and Swedish into Dutch and French for various Belgian periodicals). Some of her novellas have been translated into French, German, English, Italian, Danish, and Czech, even during her lifetime. Finally, Virginie Loveling was also the author of two little books for children, one on insects, the other on the solar system.

Works

Anton (1866). Detel, tr. of German novellas by Klaus Groth (1866). [With Rosalie Loveling], Gedichten (1870). Novellen (1874). Nieuwe Novellen (1875).

A selection of her major novellas and novels (dates of publication do not always correspond with date of composition): [Pseud. W.G.E. Walter]. *In onze Vlaamsche Gewesten* (1877). *Polydoor en*

Theodoor (1881, 1883). *Kinderverhalen* (1883–1886). *Een Vonkje van Genie* (1883). *Sophie* (1885). *Een Dure Eed* (1891). *Onze Idealen* (1892). *Een Idylle* (1893). *De Bruid des Heeren* (1895). *Mijnheer Connehaye* (1895). *Meesterschap* (1898). *Het Land der Verbeelding* (1896). *Madeleine* (1897). *De Twistappel* (1904). *Erfelijk belast* (1906). *Jongezellenlevens* (1907). *Een Revolverschot* (1911).

With her cousin Cyriel Buysse, another important figure in Belgian literature in Dutch, she wrote *Levensleer* (1912), a humorous novel about the francophone bourgeoisie of Ghent.

Her collected works, *Volledige Werken,* were published in 1933–1934 (10 vols.).

Bibliography

Baekelmans, L., *Vier Vlaamsche Prozaschrijvers* (Antwerpen, 1931). Basse, M., *Het Aandeel der Vrouw in de Nederlandsche Letterkunde*, II (Ghent, 1921). Piette, H., *Les Soeurs Loveling* (Bruxelles, 1942).

Kristiaan P. Aercke

Monica Lovinescu

(a.k.a. Claude Pascal, Monique Saint-Côme)

Born 1923, Bucharest
Genre(s): short story, drama, literary criticism, essay, translation
Language(s): Romanian, French

Monica Lovinescu exiled herself from Romania in 1947 and has lived since in Paris, becoming a French citizen in 1967. When she left Bucharest, at age twenty-four, she had already published a number of short stories in *Vremea*, and *Revista Fundaţiilor Regale* as well as regular drama reviews in *Democraţia*. After 1947 she continued to write in Romanian for the Romanian exile periodicals *România*, *Revista scriitorilor români*, *Contrapunct*, *Limite*, *Caiete de dor*, *Micromagazin*, *Lupta*, etc. while at the same time contributing essays to the French and English publications *Preuves*, *Les Lettres nouvelles*, *East Europe*, *L'Alternative*, *Problèmes du communisme*, *La France catholique*, and *Continent*.

Between 1951 and 1974 Lovinescu worked for the Radiodiffusion Française broadcasts in Romanian. In the sixties, she became a cultural commentator for the Romanian Desk of Radio Free Europe. Since then, she airs, with utmost regularity, two weekly programs—"Actualitatea culturală românească" (Romanian Cultural News) and "Teze şi antiteze la Paris" (Theses and Antitheses in Paris) which have the strongest impact in Romania. The Romanian public listens to far away but impeccably informed and adamantly true Monica Lovinescu more than to the local broadcasts. Lovinescu would speak the unspeakable, with poise and lucidity, denounce cultural terrorism, abuse, or institutionalized lies, rejoice at the real artistic achievements (at times slighted or ignored by the nomenklatura), keep Romanian audiences informed with respect to the art and literature of the Romanian and East European exiles and dissidents or with the main trends in contemporary Western thought. Many times, the dissatisfactions of the Romanian writers, systematically ignored or denied publicity by the local authorities, have been voiced first by Lovinescu and acknowledged in Romania only after this by now almost indispensable, though paradoxical step. This is to say that the Romanian authorities listen to Monica Lovinescu's broadcasts at least as much as the general public, though for different reasons and with infinitely less pleasure.

Since 1950 there have been many violent official campaigns against Lovinescu in the Romanian press. In 1977, the Romanian Secret Police backed a terrorist attack against this Iron Lady of Romanian literary criticism. According to the D.S.T. and to the French press—see the numerous articles published by *Le Monde*, *Le Matin*, *Le Quotidien de Paris*, *La Croix* as well as the important books by Wolton (1986) and Picaper (1987)—the aim was to prevent her from ever writing or broadcasting again. Luckily transported to the hospital in due time by a passer-by, Lovinescu was saved and continues to talk to Romania twice a week. In 1978 she published in a compact volume of 500 pages entitled *Unde scurte. Jurnal indirect* (Short Waves. An Indirect Journal) a small part of her essential analyses devoted to post-World War II Romanian literature. The volume has been considered potentially so dangerous by the Romanian authorities that the literary weekly *Luceafărul* initiated, under the name "Pseudo-cultura pe unde scurte" (Pseudo-culture on Short Waves) a special anti-Lovinescu column which lasted almost two years.

Lovinescu's physiognomy as a contemporary literary critic is most unusual. She airs her criticism more often than she publishes it. She addresses her refined analyses not to a sparse learned readership here and there but to a whole country which listens to them with a concern and a fervor no Occidental critic would ever dream to elicit. She is able to determine through her comments many a shift in the evolution of Romanian culture both at the individual creator's and at the institutional level. While doing so she faces risks few of her peaceful homologues would be prepared to confront for professional reasons and assumes extra-literary responsibilities toward her sources which complicate and severely challenge her expression. Finally, Lovinescu practices a double, schizoid reading, with one eye—as she put it—looking at the text from the point of view of strict truth which cannot be uttered in Romania (wherefrom the critic's permanent irritation and frustration) and the other from the point of view of the degree of boldness incorporated in its transgression of limits and interdictions (wherefrom the critic's interest and hope). While writing and speaking as a sober professional, literary criticism is for Lovinescu a means for survival, a way to continue to live in the essential space of the country she left but did not abandon.

Unde scurte (1978; Short Waves) is devoted to a critical examination of the 1961–1971 decade of "liberalization" (or "destalinization") in Romanian literature. It is Lovinescu's thesis that while all the other East European countries achieved their "liberalization" by means of radical contestation and as the result of a cathartic ethical quest aimed at redefining and reestablishing the abused literary contract between artists and society, Romanian writers chose to put into parentheses the Stalinist experience and outgrow it by simply refusing to express it artistically. This unusual battle of silence in which all those who had published ideological maculature between 1948–1960 were tacitly shunned from the literary memory, and a whole generation reconnected itself—over the gap of more than a decade—to the inter-war tradition and, among its immediate predecessors, only to those who had perished in political prison or abstained from publishing during the Stalinist years, resulted in an unprecedented aesthetic explosion of Romanian literature which might be considered as the most evolved and modern literature in the communist bloc. At the same time though, by hurriedly giving precedence to the aesthetic over the ethic, the Romanian writers missed the opportunity to break the ideological totalitarian taboos and thus, through their punitive silence, continued to serve the major interests of the regime. This basic misunderstanding on their behalf, combined with the misunderstanding of the regime which, unaware of the fact that aesthetic evasion functioned as a safety valve preventing the writers from attaining real freedom and asking essential questions, started a strong antimodernistic campaign. Thus, while most of the East European writers became part of an efficient intelligentsia renouncing, for a while, to a strictly professional writers' profile, their Romanian homologues hastened to function again as real contemporary writers but missed the opportunity and the duty of transforming into a unified and active intelligentsia.

Lovinescu translated from Romanian into French Virgil Gheorghiu's *La vingt-cinquième heure* (1949; The Twenty-fifth Hour) as well as Adriana Georgescu Cosmovici's novel *Au commencement était la fin* (1952; At the Beginning Was the End).

Works

Unde scurte. Jurnal indirect [Short Waves. An Indirect Journal] (1978).

Bibliography

Delaunay, Jean, *La foudre et le cancer* (Paris, 1985).
Picaper, Jean-Paul, *Le pont invisible. Ces radios que l'Est veut réduire au silence* (Paris, 1987).

Sanda Golopentia

Camila Lucinda

Born mid-1570s; died c. 1612–1613
Genre(s): poetry
Language(s): Spanish

Camila Lucinda is the almost perfect anagram of Micaela de Luján, mistress of Lope de Vega for a decade (approximately 1598 to 1608) and mother of five of his children, including Marcela and Lope Félix. The scant biographical information that survives from documentary sources is supplemented by Lope's tendency to "literaturize" his personal life. Micaela was married to the actor Diego de Díaz de Castro, who left for Peru in 1596 and continued performing there until his death in 1603. Her acquaintance with Lope probably dates from around 1598, and although Lope had married Juana de Guardo in April 1598, Micaela became his passionate and celebrated love for the next several years. In the 1610s Micaela, often accompanied by Lope, moved around between Toledo, Madrid, Sevilla, and Granada, probably on the theatrical circuit. The love between them was common knowledge, satirized by some but celebrated in Lope's verse, especially her rare beauty, her beautiful blue eyes, and her melodious voice. Other tokens of their relation are Lope's own pseudonym (Lucinda-Belardo) and the initial "M" before his signature on autograph manuscripts of that decade. The *Plaza Universal*, written by Suárez de Figueroa in 1610–1611 and published in 1615, is important contemporary corroboration of her profession. The author mentions Micaela as one of the most famous living actresses of the time, although this reference could antedate the publication date. In 1613 Lope, after the death of his second wife, took the two surviving children, Marcela and Lope Félix, to live with him in Madrid, which may suggest that Micaela was dead. The poems attributed to Camila Lucinda, who was probably illiterate, were undoubtedly by Lope, who, as other authors, sometimes prefaced his own works with self-eulogistic verses attributed to others, either real or imaginary.

Works

La Hermosura de Angélica, in *Obras Escogidas de Lope de Vega*, ed. F. Sainz de Robles, Vol. II (1953). (A redondilla among the introductory verses, attributed to Camila Lucinda, was undoubtedly written by Lope.) *Lope de Vega en las justas poéticas toledanas de 1605 y 1608*, ed. Joaquin de Entrambasaguas (1969). (Includes a "Soneto de Lucinda Serrana" and a "Romance a San Juan Baptista" by Clarinda Lisarda, Serrana del Jordán. According to Entrambasaquas, both are poetic pseudonyms of Micaela de Luján.) *El Peregrino en su patria*, ed. Juan Bautista Avalle-Arce (1971). (A prefatory sonnet, attributed to her, precedes the novel [1604], which contains many allusions to the Lope-Micaela liaison.) *Rimas de Lope de Vega*, ed. Gerardo Diego (1963), 2nd ed., 1981. (The sonnet attributed to her is undoubtedly by Lope—a profession of his love as well as a self-panegyric.)

Bibliography

Bruerton, Courtney, "Lope's Belardo-Lucinda Plays." *Hispanic Review* 5 (1937): 309–315. Castillejo, David, "Diego de Díaz: Marido de Micaela de Luján." *Boletín de la Real Academia Española* 64 (1984): 231–232, 257–275. Castro, Américo, "Alusiones a Micaela de Luján en las obras de Lope de Vega." *Revista de Filología Española* 5 (1918): 256–292. Cossío, José María de, "La patria de Micaela Luján." *Revista de Filología Española* 15 (1928): 379–381. Cossío, José María de, "La descendencia de Lope de Vega." *Boletín de la Real Academia Española* 2 (1915): 21–56, 137–172. Icaza, Francisco de, *Lope de Vega. Sus amores y sus odios* (Segovia, n.d). Morley, S.G., "The Pseudonyms and Literary Disguises of Lope de Vega." UCPMP 33, No. 5 (1951): 421–484. Rennert, Hugo A., "The Luzinda of Lope de Vega's Sonnets." *Modern Language Notes* 16 (1901): 351–356. Rennert, Hugo A., *The Life of Lope de Vega (1562–1635)* (Glasgow, 1904; rpt. New York, 1937). Rodríguez Marín, Francisco, "Lope de Vega y Camila Lucinda." *Boletín de la Real Academia Española* 1 (1914): 249–290.

Ruth Lundelius

Paula Ludwig

Born 1900, Vorarlberg, Austria; died 1974, Darmstadt
Genre(s): poetry, poetic prose
Language(s): German

Paula Ludwig was born the daughter of an Austrian mother and a Silesian carpenter father. In 1919, she moved to Munich, from 1923–1933 she lived in Berlin, and later in Tyrol. From 1931–1940, she had an intense relationship with expressionist poet Ivan Goll, of which a correspondence survives. In 1938, she immigrated to Brazil via stages in France, Spain, and Portugal. In San Paulo, she survived as a painter. When she returned to Europe in 1953, she first moved to Wetzlar and later to Darmstadt.

Inspired by Hölderlin, Rilke, and Trakl, Paula Ludwig developed a unique hymnic style. Her poetry is about nature and the supernatural, while the contemporary conflictive themes emerge more often than not as dreams. She also wrote a book of notations and essays about dreams. In 1962, Paula Ludwig received the Trakl Prize. Her oeuvre merits to be rediscovered: there have been no recent editions of her poetry.

Works

Die selige Spur (1919). *Der himmlische Spiegel* (1927). *Dem dunklen Gott* (1932). *Traumlandschaft* (1935). *Buch des Lebens* (1936). *Gedichte 1920–1958* (Anthology) (1958). *Träume. Aufzeichnungen 1920–1960* (1962). *Ich sterbe mein Leben. Briefwechsel mit Ivan Goll* (1982).

Bibliography

von Wilpert, Gero, *Deutsches Literatur-Lexikon.* 2nd ed. (1975). Brinker-Gabler, Gisela, *Deutsche Dichterinnen* (Frankfurt, 1986).

Ute Marie Saine

Ludwiga

(see: Luise Maria Hensel)

Luise

(see: Luise Maria Hensel)

Rosa Luxemburg

Born 1871, Zamosc, Russian Poland; died 1919, Berlin, Germany
Genre(s): letters, economic and political treatises
Language(s): Polish, German, Russian, French

Rosa Luxemburg is best known as a brilliant and original Marxist theoretician and political strategist ("the best brain after Marx," according to her first biographer, Franz Mehring). The author of major economic and political treatises (*Reform or Revolution* [1899]; *The Accumulation of Capital—An Anti-Critique* [1906]; *The Crisis of Social Democracy* [1916] and *Introduction to National Economy* [1925]), she became internationally known in her time as "Red Rosa," the militant fighter on the frontline of the struggle for world socialism in late nineteenth- and early twentieth-century Europe. In her letters, however, we see another, less well-known, Rosa Luxemburg: the woman, friend, and lover, who in her private writings revealed herself to be much more complex than her public persona showed.

Born in the Polish city of Zamosc in 1871 into an educated and cosmopolitan but financially struggling middle-class Jewish family, Luxemburg lived in Poland until her political activism as a high-school student in Warsaw forced her to go into exile in 1883. As an expatriate in Zurich, she engaged in a thorough study of socialist theory and organizing practice under the tutelage of Leo Jogiches, her political mentor and lover of many years, and as a student of political economy whose brilliant dissertation was immediately published as a book. Quickly rising to a position of leadership within the left wing of the international socialist movement, Luxemburg chose as her base Berlin, the capital of European Social Democracy at that time. Although she traveled much and widely as an organizer and orator in the cause of international socialism, she also cultivated life-long, intimate friendships with a small circle of people who constituted her emotional family and home: her comrades Karl and Luise Kautsky, Clara Zetkin, Karl and Sonja Liebknecht, Mathilde Wurm and Marta Rosenbaum; her secretary Mathilde Jacob; and her lovers Leo Jogiches and Hans Diefenbach. In 1919, shortly after founding, with Karl Liebknecht, the Spartacus League (precursor of the German Communist Party), Luxemburg was assassinated in Berlin by fanatical right-wing storm troopers.

In contrast to her public writings—treatises, analyses, newspaper articles and speeches—Luxemburg's private writings—her correspondence with comrades, friends and lovers—were not published in their entirety until the early 1980s. Previously published selections reflect the shifts in interest in various aspects of Luxemburg as a thinker, activist, and person. They reflect changing definitions of what constitutes the political as well.

The first letters to be published, within a year of her death, were her letters from prison, written primarily to her closest woman friend Sonja Liebknecht. In these letters Luxemburg emerges as a woman in whom the intellectual acuity of her analysis is matched by the emotional depth of her compassion. Reading, thinking, watching the clouds above the prison walls and the birds outside her window, she reflects on people's inhumanity both to other people and to the creatures over whom they exercise power. She sees the fundamental interconnectedness of all things: "I am rather surprised that Karl wants you to send him a book on bird song. For me the song of birds is inseparable from their life as a whole; it is the whole that interests me, rather than any detached detail" (Letter to Sonja Liebknecht, August 2, 1917).

This sense of the connectedness of all things, which was at the heart of Luxemburg's political vision as well, is also articulated in the letters to her friends and comrades that were published next. Finally, the publication of Luxemburg's love letters, documents of her tempestuous and life-long relationship with Leo Jogiches, was a sign of the increasing public interest in Rosa Luxemburg the woman, an interest informed by a 1970s consciousness of the political nature of personal relationships. Always insisting on the legitimacy of a person's dream for personal happiness (what else, she herself asked, is political struggle for?), Luxemburg's vision of a happy and fulfilled private life is inseparable from her vision of social change on a national and international level. Her anguish was that, in practice, she found that they were in perpetual conflict.

The style of Luxemburg's letters is consonant with her political form: an activism impelled by the vision of the infinite capacity for change within ourselves and the world we live in. Ranging in tone from sharp wit and biting sarcasm through dry, factual analysis to a tenderness that is unafraid of brushing up against sentimentality, they reveal a woman of keen intellect and deep feelings. In her letters to Jogiches the quality of her style, which appears less as writing than as words spoken on paper, is particularly palpable. Writing primarily in Polish and German (the languages of her childhood), but also intermingling Russian and French and bits of Yiddish, English and Latin, her writing is startling in its range and freedom. Considered one of the great language artists in the field of Polish literature, Luxemburg was, in her own words, "a land of boundless possibilities."

Works

Gesammelte Briefe [Collected Letters], ed. Annelies Laschitza and Günter Radczun, tr. Hildegard Bamberger and Eduard Ullman (1982–1984). *The Letters of Rosa Luxemburg*, ed. Stephen E. Bronner, tr. Stephen E. Bronner and Hedwig Pachter) (1978). *Briefe aus dem Gefängnis* [Letters from Prison], tr. Eden and Cedar Paul (1946). *Prison Letters to Sophie Liebknecht*. tr. Eden and Cedar Paul (New York: A.J. Muste Memorial Institute, 1974–1985). *Briefe an meine Freunde* [Letters to My Friends] (1985). *Briefe an Freunde* [Letters to Friends], ed. Benedikt Kautsky (1976). *Briefe an Mathilde Jacob* [Letters to Mathilde Jacob], ed. Narihiko Ito (1972). *Briefe an Karl und Luise Kautsky, 1896–1918* [*Letters to Karl and Luise Kautsky from 1896 to 1918*], ed. Luise Kautsky, tr. Louis P. Lochner (1923; rpt. 1982). *Comrade and Lover: Rosa Luxemburg's Letters to Leo Jogiches*, ed. and tr. Elzbieta Ettinger (1979).

Bibliography

Delany, Sheila, "Red Rosa: Bread and Roses." *Writing Woman: Women Writers and Women in Literature Medieval to Modern* (New York, 1983), pp. 113–134. Dunayevskaya, Raya, *Rosa Luxemburg, Women's Liberation, and Marx's Philosophy of Revolution* (New Jersey, 1982). Frölich, Paul, *Rosa Luxemburg: Her Life and Work*, New tr. Johanna Hoornweg (New York, 1972).

Angelika Bammer

Margarita Lyberaki

Born 1910, Athens, Greece
Genre(s): novel, drama, poetry
Language(s): Greek

Lyberaki studied law and painting. She wrote mainly novels and plays but also a few poems. Already in her first novel *Ta Dendra* (The Trees), published in 1945, she shows a remarkable dexterity. In it, the main character Irene, a young woman who lives in Paris, reaches maturity and strives for the fulfillment of her desires through a group of artists. Lyberaki reveals her sensitivity, lyricism, and emotionalism, especially when she talks about Irene's love affair with Alexis. The novel has been criticized for its vague character description and the unpersuasive depiction of the heroine's personality. It shows, however, the writer's promise.

Lyberaki's second novel, *Ta Psathina Kapella* (The Straw Hats), published in 1946, is her masterpiece, and it established her reputation. It focuses on the lives and various relations of three sisters, Maria, Infanta, and Katerina. Lyberaki is deeply interested in the everyday life, and the little incidents, which, she believes, contain the true significance of life; it is through these trivial events that the mythical and imaginative worlds are projected. No thrilling and breath-taking events occur, only simple and common incidents from the daily routine. This novel is largely autobiographical.

Lyberaki published her third novel *O Allos Alexandros* (The Other Alexander) in 1950. In it she shows herself capable of dealing with deeper psychological problems and also abandons the autobiographical tone dominant in her previous novels. The main figure in this novel, Alexander, leads a double family life, with both his legitimate family whose members constitute the principal characters of the novel, and his illegitimate one, which is rather vaguely depicted. Lyberaki's aim throughout the novel is to emphasize the drama of human alienation, revealed especially in the superficial dialogues, which are, as a matter of fact, monologues. She invents impossible relations between her characters and incredible situations, which she mingles with ordinary, commonplace ones, and thus creates an unusual and very original atmosphere.

Lyberaki also wrote plays, such as *I Gynaica Tou Kandavli* (Kandavli's Wife), *O Agios Pringips* (The Saint Prince) and others. In 1972, she published a collection of poems with the title *Yia Ton Aponta, Esperini Teleti* (For the Absent, An Evening Feast), on the occasion of G. Seferis' death. Her sentences are fragmented, and the prevailing tone in the poems is melancholic and depressive. Lyberaki lives in Paris and is regarded as a major figure among modern Greek women writers.

Works

Novels: *The Trees* (1945). *The Straw Hats* (1946). *The Other Alexander* (1950).

Plays: *Kandavli's Wife*, *The Saint Prince* and others.

Poetry collection: *For the Absent, an Evening Feast* (1972).

Bibliography

Despotopoulos, K.I., *Kainouryia Epochi* (1957). Dictaeos, A., *Kathimerini* (2/16/1962). Farmakis, F., "M. Lyberaki," in *The Great Encyclopaedia of Neohellenic Literature*, ed. C. Patsis, vol. 9 (Athens, 1968), pp. 540–541. Fouriotis, A., *Pnevmatiki Poreia 1900–1950* (Athens, 1952). Hatzinis, G., "The Other Alexander." *Nea Estia* 47, 551 (Athens, 1950). Karapanou, M., "The Straw Hats." Nea *Estia* 42, 484 (Athens, 1947). Politis, L., A His*tory of Modern Greek Literature* (Oxford, 1973). Sachinis, A., *New Prose Writers* (Athens, 1965). Sachinis, A., *Our Contemporary Literature* (Athens, 1951). Vitti, M., *History of Neohellenic Literature* (Athens, 1978).

Aristoula Georgiadou

H.M. Lyhne

(see: Marie Herzfeld)

Andrée Lynne

(see: Stanisława Przybyszewska)

M

Terezka M.

(see: Terézia Vansová)

Marg. M.-V.

(see: Margareta Miller-Verghi)

M.C.

(see: Wilhelmina "Minna" Ulrika [Johnson] Canth)

M.H.

(see: Margarita Hickey-Pellizzoni)

Madame d'Orléans

(see: Marie de Clèves)

Madame de BẠẠẠs

(see: Marie-Françoise Catherine de Beauvau[-Craon], marquise de Boufflers)

Mme de Maintenon

(see: Françoise d' Aubigné, Marquise de Maintenon)

Madame la baronne Caroline A . . ., née V . . . de M . . .; W . . .

(see: Caroline Wuïet, Baronne Auffdiener)

Asunción Madera

(a.k.a. Chona Madera)

Born 1901, Las Palmas de Gran Canaria
Genre(s): poetry
Language(s): Spanish

Author of seven volumes of poetry, Chona Madera did not begin her publishing career until 1944. Her style is informalist; her inner world corresponds with the poetic world of Alonso Quesada and, less directly, with the lyric works of Fernando González. Filled with nostalgia and absence, her life, like her heart, is, as she says, "kneaded with the leavening of sadness." In addition to her books, she has published widely in the newspapers and magazines of the Canary Islands.

Works

El volcado silencio (1944; 1947). *Mi presencia más clara* (1956). *Las estancias vacías* (1961). *La voz que me desvela* (1965). *Los contados instantes* (1967) received the "Tomás Morales" prize and was reprinted in Málaga in 1970. *Continuada señal* (1970). *Mi otra palabra* (1977).

Bibliography

Artiles, Joaquin, *La Literatura Canaria* (Las Palmas de Gran Canaria, 1979). Galerstein, Carolyn L., ed., *Women Writers of Spain* (Westport, CT, 1986).

Rosetta Radtke

Chona Madera

(see: Asunción Madera)

Magda

(see: Otilia Cazimir)

Mechthild von Magdeburg

Born c. 1210; died c. 1282–1294
Genre(s): mystical revelation in prose and
*   verse*
Language(s): Low German, translated into
*   Latin and Middle High German*

Mechthild von Magdeburg was a Beguine (a member of a medieval lay religious order for women) at Magdeburg, whose loosely structured book of mystical revelations, *The Flowing Light of the Divinity*, serves as one of the rare extant examples of women's writing in medieval Germany. Originally written in Low German between c. 1250–1285, her revelations are retained in Latin and Middle High German translations and consist of seven parts, first gathered by her Magdeburg Dominican confessor, Heinrich von Halle (parts 1–6), and subsequently by the sisters at the convent of Helfte (part 7), which she entered c. 1270. Her writings were translated first into Latin by Heinrich and then c. 1344 into Middle High German by Heinrich von Nördlingen, a member of the Friends of God sect, and it is this manuscript (Einsiedeln Nr. 277) upon which the bulk of subsequent complete and fragmentary translations into German and English, as well as Middle High German text editions, have been based.

Not a conventionally learned woman, she apparently was literate and raised in a household that was reasonably prosperous. While her knowledge of Latin apparently did not extend beyond the liturgy, familiarity with theological issues and the courtly language of chivalry clearly are evident in her work. While she often professed hesitancy and inadequacy at the God-given task of communicating her mystical experiences to others, she was obviously a woman of strong opinions when convinced to write or to dictate her thoughts as evinced in her criticism of the clergy of her time—she found many religious people quite materialistic and misguided—and in her willingness to use the metaphoric language associated with sexual union that appears in the secular love poetry of the time as well as in the biblical prototype, *The Song of Songs*.

Mechthild's work is notable both for its variety and depth. Her revelations take the form of allegorical visions, aphorisms, prayers, poems strongly influenced by the *Minnesang* tradition, reflections on societal behavior, and numerous cryptic references to historical and biblical personages; it should be noted that Heinrich von Halle arranged these revelations somewhat arbitrarily into "chapters" that do not necessarily reflect Mechthild's spiritual development. Nevertheless, the compiler's and subsequent editors' and translators' transmission of Mechthild's revelations cannot obscure the wonderment she experiences when shown glimpses of Heaven and Hell, the puzzlement and querulousness she expresses when dealing with fellow religious women and men who do not live up to her standards, and the ecstasy she knows in mystical union with the Trinity—and the deprivation she encounters in periods of spiritual dryness and debilitating illness.

Mechthild's imagery is striking: supernatural fluidity, light, sublimated sexuality, and color mix and mingle with mundane touches, such as Christ calling for his dinner, mad dogs running in the streets, and her own loneliness in strange, new settings. The theme of the Godhead *as Trinity* occurs repeatedly in her revelations, as does the more courtly theme of love as pursuit: "And now she beholds a complete God in three persons, and professes the three persons within one God. He greets her with courtly language, not likely to be heard in the kitchen. He dresses her in clothes fit to be worn in a palace, and puts Himself at her disposal. . . . He wants to play a game with her alone, a game not known to the body, nor to the peasants behind their plows, nor the knights in their tournaments, nor even His sweet mother Mary."

Mechthild's subjects are wide-ranging. She describes, among other things, mystical union, the composition of the nine choirs of angels, the paths that lead to righteousness or damnation, and the ways holy people ought to live in the world. She powerfully sketches the landscapes of Heaven as well as Hell and draws visionary portraits of Enoch and Elias, Lucifer, the Virgin, John the Baptist, and Christ on the cross. Mechthild constantly attempts to make sense of the revelations given to her: her intent is to find verbal "likenesses" that express not only the relationship of the Divine to the human but also the Word to the world. Her words, she insists, cannot do adequate justice to what she has experienced ("One can hardly touch [it] with words"), but she must try to show, for example, how Christ is "like" a pilgrim, how man's sufferings are "like" Christ's, how the apostles are "like" bees, and how man is "like" an animal. She utilizes parables (parable equals "gelichnis" equals likeness) and dialogues to show the gap she attempts to bridge, a gap that on the earthly plane is characterized by the limits of language and the imperfect nature of man.

Mechthild's work remains as one of the few examples in the German Middle Ages of women's writings. Yet, if it were one of many examples, it would remain unique both for the breadth and depth of her visions and for their vibrant individual expression.

Works

Offenbarungen der Schwester Mechthild von Magdeburg, oder Das fliessende Licht der Gottheit, ed. P. Gall Morel (1869; rpt. 1963). New edition based on the same Einsiedein manuscript (Nr. 277), ed. Hans Neumann, in progress. Galvani, Christiane Masch, *A Female Perspective on the Mystical Experience: Mechthild von Magdeburg's* Ein vliessendes Lieht der Gotheit *in a Complete English Translation, with Annotations and Introduction*. M.A. thesis, Rice University, 1987. Menzies, Lucy, *The Revelations of Mechthild von Magdeburg* (1953).

Bibliography

Abraham, Ruth Ann Dick, *Mechthild von Magdeburg's Flowing Light of the Godhead: An Autobiographical Realization of Spiritual Poverty*. DAI 40 (1980): 5855A. Clark, Susan L., "'Ze glîcher wîs': Mechthild von Magdeburg and the Concept of Likeness," in *The World of Medieval Women: Creativity, Influence, and Imagination*, eds. Constance H. Berman, Charles W. Connell, and Judith Rice Rothschild (Morgantown, W. V., 1985), pp. 41–50. College, Erice, "Mechthild von Magdeburg." *Month* 25 (1961): 325–336. Egres, Odo, and Lackner, Bede, "Mechthild von Magdeburg: *The Flowing Light of God*," in *Cistercians in the Late Middle Ages*, ed. Ellen Rozanne Elder (Kalamazoo, Mich., 1981). Eveland, Sandra Anne Newton, *The Divine Lover of Mira Bai and Mechthild von Magdeburg: A Study of Two Women's Literary Descriptions of a Mystical Relationship with God*. DAI 39 (1979): 6754A. Franklin, James, *Love and Transition: Water and the Imagery of Liquids in the Works of Mechthild von Magdeburg*. Diss., Case-Western Reserve, 1972. Franklin, James, *Mystical Transformations: The Imagery of Liquids in the Works of Mechthild von Magdeburg* (Rutherford, N.J., 1974). Gooday, Frances, "Mechthild von Magdeburg and Hadewijch of Antwerp: A Comparison." *Ons Geestelijk Erf* 48 (1974): 305–362. Haas, Alois M., "Mechthild von Magdeburg: Dichtung und Mystik." *Amsterdamer Beiträge zur älteren Germanistik* 2 (1972): 105–156. Koch, Regina, "Mechthild von Magdeburg, Woman of Two Worlds." *Fourteenth Century English Mystics Newsletter* 3 (1981): 111–131. Langner, Ilse, "Vorläuferinnen der Emanzipation? Drei Nonnen—drei Dichterinnen." *Neue Deutsche Hefte* 163 (1979): 497–511. Laubner, Horst, *Studien zum geistlichen Sinngehalt des Adjektivs im Werk Mechthilds von Magdeburg*. Göppinger Germanistische Arbeiten 163 (Göppingen, 1975). Margetts, John, "Latein und Volkssprache bei Mechthild von Magdeburg." *Amsterdamer Beiträge zur älteren Germanistik* 12 (1977): 119–136. McDonnell, Ernest, *The Beguines and Beghards in Medieval Culture* (New Brunswick, N.J., 1954). Mohr, Wolfgang. "Darbietungsformen der Mystik bei Mechthild von Magdeburg." *Märchen, Mythos, Dichtung: Festschrift zum 90. Geburtstag Friedrich von der Leyens am 19. August 1963* (Munich, 1963), pp. 365–399. Müller, Ulrich, "Mechthild von Magdeburg und Dantes *Vita Nuova* oder erotische Religiosität und religiöse Erotik." *Liebe als Literatur: Aufsätze zur erotischen Dichtung in Deutschland* (Munich, 1983), pp. 163–176. Neumann, Hans, "Mechthild von Magdeburg und die mittelniederländische Frauenmystik." *Medieval German Studies Presented to Frederick Norman* (London), pp. 231–246. Ruh, Kurt, "Beginenmystik: Hadewijch, Mechthild .von Magdeburg, Marguerite Porete." *Zeitschrift für Deutsches Altertum und Deutsche Literatur* 106 (1977): 265–277. Schwietering, Julius, *Mystik und höfische Dichtung im Hochmittelalter* (Tübingen, Niemeyer, 1960). Tax, Petrus W., "Die grosse Himmelsschau Mechthilds von Magdeburg und ihre Höllenvision: Aspekte des Erfahrungshorizontes, der Gegenbildlichkeit und Parodierung." *Zeitschrift für Deutsches Altertum und Deutsche Literatur* 108 (1979): 112–137. Vitzketely, András, and Gisela Kornrumpf, "Budapester Fragmente des 'Fliessenden Lichts der Gottheit.'" *Zeitschrift für Deutsches Altertum und Deutsche Literatur* 97 (1968): 278–306. Völker, Paul-Gerhard, "Neues zur Überlieferung des 'Fliessenden Lichts der Gottheit.'" *Zeitschrift für Deutsches Altertum und Deutsche Literatur* 97 (1968): 28–69.

Susan Clark

Ernestine Friederike Elisabeth Mahler

(see: Hedwig Courths-Mahler)

Maïa

(see: Callirhoe Parren)

Ella Maillart

Born February 20, 1903, Geneva, Switzerland
Genre(s): travel literature, journalism
Language(s): French, English

Born into a middle-class family in Geneva, the young Maillart acquired through sports the independence of mind and physical robustness that enabled her to make her now-classic treks across Asia. She played field hockey and skied competitively and from girlhood on sailed on Lake Geneva, later becoming the only woman entered in the 1924 Olympic single-handed sailing competition in Paris, in which seventeen countries participated. Self-supporting, she worked all over Europe as a language teacher, a deckhand (*Gypsy Afloat* recalls some of her voyages), and a film extra, until, succumbing to the lure of the unknown and her own indomitable sense of curiosity, she set out alone in 1930 for Russia.

Maillart's six-month stay in Moscow marked the beginning of her career as a writer and a traveler. She supported herself with journalism and wrote the volume *Parmi la jeunesse russe*, of special interest because of her contacts with the Russian film industry. But ever more distant horizons beckoned: in the early 1930s, at the time when enormous stretches of Central Asia were still only accessible by horse, donkey, or camel, Maillart made the journeys described in her finest travel books: the intrepid trek into Russian Turkestan in 1932 recorded in *Des Monts célestes aux Sables rouges* (in English as *Turkestan Solo*), and, in 1935, the transcontinental *Forbidden Journey* (Oasis interdites) from Peking to India, so titled because the vast northwest Chinese province of Sinkiang, racked by civil war and only nominally under the control of the Kuomintang, was strictly forbidden to foreigners.

Maillart's fascination with the dignity and strangeness of Asian ways, and her attraction to the limitless unknown, whether physical or spiritual, shaped her life. *Cruises and Caravans*—Maillart had now begun to write in English—recalls the adventuresome jaunts of the 1930s, *Ti-Puss* records the war years which Maillart spent in India, and *The Land of the Sherpas* reports briefly on her trip to Nepal. The most fascinating of her later works is *The Cruel Way*, in which the central confrontation is no longer between the author and Asia, but rather between Maillart and her beautiful, sensitive, self-destructive and drug-addicted traveling companion "Christina," a pseudonym for the Swiss writer Annemarie Schwarzenbach (see separate entry). The account of their trip to Afghanistan, undertaken in the spring of 1939, is an honest study of a troubled friendship and of the failure of Maillart's attempts to guide Christina out of her suffering.

During these years Maillart came to understand that her passion for traveling sprang from a search for real values: it was, in essence, a spiritual quest. She widened her horizons again by including in her search for knowledge the religious heritage of the East. Maillart now resides in French-speaking Switzerland, where she is something of a celebrity. She continues to travel widely; her last trip to Tibet was in 1986.

Maillart is a traveler first and a writer second. Her best books, such as *Forbidden Journey*, are direct, fresh, and modest. They are not political reports, for though Maillart often mentions the corruptive effect of Western materialism on Eastern culture, the mechanisms of political change do not interest her. Her works live on the spirit of adventure that thrilled to the myriad foreign sights and sounds and souls. Where Maillart is not yet fully aware of the ultimately spiritual origin of her zest for the physical universe, where her courageous journeys express more of herself than she recognizes, her writing, in all its simplicity, has the force of lived allegory. After resolving the tension between the outside world and the ultimate truths of life (which Maillart in any case sees as complementary rather than contradictory) her writing loses some of its color and force: the introspective view does not capture the reader as fully as the alert, outward gaze. Maillart's best work, however, embodies the paradox of the consummate individualist searching or reintegration with a lost completeness.

Works

"With Bonita to Greece." *The Yachting Monthly* 49.291 and 49.292 (1930). *Parmi la jeunesse russe. De Moscou au Caucase* (1932). "Tachkent et Samarcande." *La Revue de Paris* 41.6 (1934). *Des Monts célestes aux Sables rouges* (1934; 1971; 1986). *Oasis interdites. De Pékin au Cachemire.* (1937; 1971; 1982). "De la Mer Jaune à la Mer d'Oman par le Tibet." *L'Illustration* 96, 27.8 and 3.9 (1938). *Cruises and Caravans* (1942). *Gypsy Afloat* (1942). *The Cruel Way* (1947; 1986). *Ti-Puss* (1951). *The Land of the Sherpas* (1955).
Translations into English: *Turkestan Solo* [Des Monts célestes aux Sables rouges] (1934; 1985).

Forbidden Journey [Oasis interdites] (1937; 1949; 1983).
Translations into German: *Verbotene Reise. Von Peking nach Kaschmir* [Oasis interdites] (1938). *Turkestan solo* (1941). *Auf abenteuerlicher Fahrt durch Iran und Afganistan* [Cruel Way] (1948). *Leben ohne Rast. Eine Frau fährt durch die Welt* [Cruises and Caravans] (1952). *Ti-Puss. Drei Jahre in Süd-Indien mit einer Katze als Kamerad* (1954).
Translations into French: *Croisières et caravanes* (1951; 1984). *Ti-Puss* (1979). *La voie cruelle* (1952).
Translations (other): *The Cruel Way* has been translaʼ into Dutch (1949), Swedish (1952), and Spa.. (1955); *Oasis interdites* into Japanese (1938).

Bibliography

d'Ivernois, Roger, "E.M." *Le Globe. Bulletin et Mémoires de la Société de Géorgraphie de Genève* 120 (1980): 12–13. *Voyage vers le réel: mélanges dédiés à E.M. à l'occasion de ses 80 ans,* réalisé par Anneliese Hollmann, Felix Bollmann, Olivier Lombard (Genève, 1983). (Includes bibliography with list of Maillart's shorter contributions to anthologies.)

Ann Marie Rasmussen

Françoise d'Aubigné, Marquise de Maintenon

(a.k.a. Mme de Maintenon)

Born November 27, 1635, Niort, France; died April 15, 1719, Saint-Cyr
Genre(s): educational tract, letters, maxim
Language(s): French

Mme de Maintenon had one of the most remarkable careers of the Splendid Century, the Age of Louis XIV. Born in prison in Niort to a ne'er-do-well father and a placid, commoner mother, Françoise endured poverty and neglect during her youth and adolescence. In 1639 her family moved to Martinique where her father died six years later; Françoise was sent to live with an aunt in France. In this strict Calvinist household, the young girl became imbued with moral and religious beliefs that influenced her entire life. Another female relative received permission to educate the girl; at the convent of the Ursulines in Paris, Françoise was converted to Catholicism before leaving the convent at age fourteen. Living in poverty with her mother in Paris, the beautiful and spirited girl had no prospects for making a good marriage or for employment.

Fortunately she came to the attention of a neighbor, the crippled, satiric poet and playwright Paul Scarron, who offered to marry her or provide a dowry so she could enter a convent. Neither offer was accepted until her mother died, and Françoise was left with no alternative; in 1652, at age sixteen, she married Scarron. Though poor himself, Scarron's residence in the Marais was a gathering place for a brilliant and rather uninhibited society. The beautiful courtesan, Ninon de Lenclos, was a regular visitor along with free-thinking gentlemen from the *beau monde* of Paris. Mme Scarron used her charm and beauty to good advantage and earned a reputation for prudence and trying to please; ". . . everyone loved me," she wrote later in life, "I had seen everything, but [I] always acted so as not to sully my reputation. . . . I wanted to be part of society, to have my name said with admiration and respect, . . . and especially to be approved by people of quality." The illustrious company at Scarron's social gatherings admired his sensible, cautious, young wife. After his death in 1660, his widow continued to associate with this diverse, socially prominent group; at the fashionable hôtels d'Albret and Richelieu she mingled with distinguished women such as Mme de Sévigné, Mme de LaFayette, and Mme de Montespan. Once more reduced to penury, Mme Scarron retired to the Ursuline convent in Paris and lived on a small pension from the Queen Mother.

A dramatic change in her fortunes came about after the beautiful, sensuous, and passionate Mme de Montespan became the official mistress of Louis XIV. When they had children, Montespan proposed that Mme Scarron raise the children. Only after the king personally requested it did the impoverished widow agree to accept this unusual position. The arrangement was a poorly kept secret in Paris, especially when the king began visiting the residence on the rue de Vaugirard. Mme Scarron's discretion and her dedication to the children gradually developed into a kind of bond between this surrogate mother and the king. In 1673, Louis formally recognized his natural children, and they joined him at Court. Mme Scarron was given an apartment there and continued to supervise their upbringing. As a reward for her services Louis gave her the estate of Maintenon and the title of marquise (1674).

During the next six years the fortunes of Mme de Montespan waned as the king drew closer to Mme de Maintenon. By 1681 Montespan had left the Court and Mlle de Fontanges, the king's last mistress, had died. It is doubtful that Mme de Maintenon ever became Louis' mistress. In fact, she actually encouraged the king to be more attentive to his long-suffering Queen, and the latter was touchingly grateful to Maintenon. The true relationship between Louis and the Marquise has never been fully ascertained, but when the Queen died, it is certain that they were married morganatically in late 1684. The marriage was never openly acknowledged by either party nor by anyone at Court, and Maintenon was not Queen.

The Marquise never involved herself in affairs of state, but she did influence Louis on religious matters. She has been accused of encouraging the king's anti-Huguenot (Protestant) campaign that led to the revocation of the Edict of Nantes (1685), but this has not been proven. Her involvement with Quietism and sympathy for Jansenism have been cited as examples of her lack of firm religious principles. However, it was through her commitment to female education that Maintenon earned the admiration and respect of her contemporaries. In 1685 she persuaded Louis to found a secular school for poor noble girls. Neither she nor the king considered a convent education as adequate for living in the world. Saint-Cyr was completed in 1686; part secular, part religious, the school provided a better education for girls than was usual at the time. Maintenon personally oversaw the curriculum, hired and directed the instructors, and provided dowries for the pupils. Saint-Cyr was the focal point of her life. Often bored and tired of the stifling court life, she put her talents to good use at the school. Much of her writing concerned the education of young women, preparing them for life outside a convent. The great

Fénelon advised her on instruction, and Racine wrote plays (*Esther* and *Athalie*) which were performed by the students. After the king died, Maintenon retired to Saint-Cyr, where she died in 1719.

Most of her writings and letters were preserved in the library at Saint-Cyr. In 1756 La Beaumelle published her letters and wrote a work on Maintenon and the seventeenth century (6 vols.). This editor/author took many liberties with her style, cutting words and sentences and inserting phrases of his own. Fortunately, Lavallée used the original manuscripts, now dispersed at Versailles, the archives of Seine-et-Oise, and the Bibliothèque Nationale, for his *Oeuvres de Mme. de Maintenon. . .* (Works of Mme. de Maintenon. . .) published in the nineteenth century. Through his efforts the finesse, conciseness and restrained elegance of her writing style were aptly demonstrated. Her writings, like those of Mme de Sévigné, provide an insider's view of Paris society and the Court and are an important source for understanding the role of women in seventeenth century France.

Works

Choix d'entretiens et de lettres (1876). Conseils et instructions aux demoiselles pour leur conduits dans le monde, 2 vols. (1857). Conversations (1828). Correspondance générale de Madame de Maintenon, 4 vols. (1865–1866). Recueil des instructions que Madame de Maintenon a données aux demoiselles de St.-Cyr, d'après un manuscript original et inédit appartenant à la comtesse de Gramont d'Aster (1908).

Bibliography

Aragonnès, Claude, *Madame Louis XIV, Françoise d'Aubigné marquise de Maintenon* (1938). d'Aumale, Marie Jeanne, *Mémoire & lettres inédites* (1902). Bailly, Auguste, *Madame de Maintenon* (1942). Baudrillart, Alfred, "Madame de Maintenon: son rôle politique pendant les dernières années du règne de Louis XIV, 1700–1715." *Revue des questions historiques* 47 (1890): 101–161. Boislisle, Arthur A.G.M. de, *Paul Scarron et Françoise d'Aubigné, d'après des documents nouveaux* (1894). Boislisle, Arthur A.G.M. de. "Paul Scarron et Françoise d'Aubigné." In *Revue des questions historiques* 54 (1892): 86–144, 389–443. Boislisle, Arthur A.G.M. de, "Le Veuvage de Françoise d'Aubigné." *Revue des questions historiques* 56 (1894): 48–110. Bonhomme, Honore, *Madame de Maintenon et sa famille* (1863). Bourdaloue, Louis, *Instruction général donnée, le 30 octobre 1688, par le père Bourdaloue à Madame de Maintenon* (1819). Cadet, Felix, ed., *Education et morale; choix de lettres, entretiens et instructions* (1884). Caraccioli, Louis A., *La vie de Madame de Maintenon, institutrice de la royale maison de Saint-Cyr* (1786). Chabaud, Louis, *Mesdames de Maintenon, de Genlis et Campan. Leur rôle dans l'éducation chrétienne de la femme* (1901). Chandenagor, Françoise, *L'allée du roi: souvenirs de Françoise d'Aubigné, marquise de Maintenon, épouse du Roi de France* [King's Way: The Life of Mme de Maintenon] (1981; 1984). Cordelier, Jean, *Madame de Maintenon* (1959). Cordelier, Jean, *Madame de Maintenon, une femme au Grand Siècle* (1955). *The Correspondence of Madame de Maintenon, in Relation to Saint-Cyr,* In *The Correspondence of Madame, Princess Palatine,* vol. 2 (1899), pp. 216–321. Cruttwell, Maude, *Madame de Maintenon* (1930). Danielou, Madeleine, *Madame de Maintenon éducatrice* (1946). Dumoulin, C., *Receuil des instructions que Madame de Maintenon a données aux demoiselles de Saint-Cyr* (1908). DuPérou, Mme., *Mémoires sur Mme de Maintenon* (1846). *L'esprit de l'institut des filles de Saint Louis* (1808). Fouque, Victor, ed., *Quatre lettres inédites de Madame de Maintenon* (1864). Geffroy, Auguste, *Mme de Maintenon après sa correspondance,* 2 vols. (1884). Genlis, Stéphanie F.-D. de St Aubin, comtesse de, *Madame de Maintenon* (1843). Girard, Georges, *Madame de Maintenon, celle qui n'a jamais aimé* (1936). Gréard, O., ed., *Extraits de ses lettres, avis, entretiens, conversations et proverbes sur l'éducation, précédés d'une introduction* (1884). Guitton, Georges, "Une conflict de direction spirituelle, Mme de Maintenon et le Père de la Chaize." *XVIIe siècle* 29 (October 1955): 378–395. Haldane, Charlotte F., *Madame de Maintenon: Uncrowned Queen of France* (1970). Hastier, Louis, *Louis XIV et Madame de Maintenon* (1957). Haussonville, Gabriel Paul O. de C. and Hanotaux, G., *Souvenirs sur Mme de Maintenon,* 3 vols. (1902–1905). Jacquinet, P., ed., *Mme de Maintenon dans le monde et à Saint-Cyr* (1888). LaBeaumelle, Laurent, *Lettres de Madame de Maintenon,* 2 vols. (1752). LaBeaumelle, Laurent, *Mémoires et lettres de Madame de Maintenon,* 16 vols. (1778). LaBeaumelle, L., *Mémoires pour servir à l'histoire de Madame de Maintenon & à celle du siècle passé*, 6 vols. (1755–1756) [*Memoirs for the History of Madame de Maintenon and of the Last Age*, 5 vols. (1757)]. Langlois, Marcel, *Madame de Maintenon*, 5 vols. (1933–1939). Langlois, Marcel, "Les 'petits livres secrets' de Madame de Maintenon." *Revue d'histoire littéraire de la France* 35 (1928): 354–368. Languet de Gergy, Jean J., *Mémoires inédits sur Mme de Maintenon* (1863). Laurent, A., ed., *Madame de Maintenon; esquisse biographique et lettres choisies* (1875). Lavallée, Théophile, *Histoire de la maison royale de Saint-Cyr* (1853). Lavallée, Théophile, ed., *Lettres et entretiens sur l'éducation des filles*, 2 vols. (1861). Lavallée, Théophile, ed., *Lettres historiques et édifiantes adressées aux Dames de Saint-Louis*, 2 vols. (1856). Lavallée, Théophile, ed., *Lettres sur l'éducation des filles* (1854). *The Letters of Madame de Maintenon; and Other Eminent Persons in the Age of Lewis VIV. To Which Are Added, Characters of Some of the Principal Persons of the Court* (1754). *Letters of Mme de Maintenon*, 2 vols. (1749). *Lettres à d'Aubigné et à madame des Ursins* (1921). *Lettres choisies de mesdames de Sévigné et de Maintenon* (1812). *Lettres inédites de Mme de Maintenon et de Mme la princesse des Ursins* (1826). *Loisirs de Madame de Maintenon* (1757). *Madame de Maintenon d'après sa correspondance authentique. Choix de ses lettres et entretiens* (1887). *Maintenoniana, ou Choix d'anecdotes intéressantes, de portraits, de pensées ingénieuses, de bons mots, de maximes morales, politiques, etc.* . . . , ed. M BẠẠẠ de BẠẠẠ (1773). *Memoires sur Mme de Maintenon recueillis par les dames de Saint-Cyr* (1846). Mermaz, Louis, *Madame de Maintenon au l'amour dévot* (1966). Monmerqué, M. de, *Notice sur Mme de Maintenon* (1829). Monmerqué, M. de, ed., *Proverbes inédites* (1829). Noailles, Paul duc de, *Histoire de Madame de Maintenon et des principaux évènements du règne de Louis XIV*, 4 vols. (1849–1858). *Pièces inédites sur les règnes de Louis XIV, Louis XV et Louis XVI, ouvrage dans lequel on trouve des mémoires, des notices historiques et des lettres de Louis XIV, de madame de Maintenon* (1809). Pilastre, Edouard, *Vie et caractère de Madame de Maintenon* (1907). "Quelques lettres de vieillesse de Madame de Maintenon." *Revue de l'histoire de Versailles et de Seine-et-Oise* 27 (1925): 5–65. Saint-Beuve, Charles A., *Causeries du lundi*, vol. IV (1851–1862). Sainte-René Taillandier, Madeleine Marie Louise (Chevrillon), *Madame de Maintenon*, tr. Lady Mary Loyd (1922). *The Secret Correspondence of Madame de Maintenon, with the Princess des Ursins* (1827). Suard, Amélie (Pankoucke), *Madame de Maintenon, peinte par elle-même* (1810). Truc, Gonzague, *La Vie de Madame de Maintenon* (1929). Vogüe, M. de, ed., *Madame de Maintenon et le Marechal de Villars; correspondance inédite* (1881).

William T. Ojala and Jeanne A. Ojala

Marie Majerová

Born 1882, Uvali, Czechoslovakia; died 1967, Prague
Genre(s): novel, short story, essay
Language(s): Czech

Marie Majerová grew up in a working-class family in the mining town of Kladno (near Prague). She started working at sixteen as a servant in Budapest. Then in Prague, Paris and Vienna, she completed her education and became active in social-democratic and feminist movements. She was a member of the Czechoslovak Communist Party from its beginnings in the 1920s.

Majerová's fiction centers on social conflicts, in particular, the exploitation of workers and the oppression of women. These two themes appear, respectively, in her earliest works, *Povídky z pekla a jiné* (1907; Stories from Hell and Other Stories) and the novel *Panenství* (1907; Maidenhood). *Náměstí republiky* (1914; Republic Square) portrays Parisian revolutionaries. Feminist and socialist themes converge in the novel *Nejkrásnější svět* (1920; The Most Beautiful of Worlds), whose heroine leaves her middle-class world for revolutionary activity. The stories of *Mučenky* (1924; Passionflowers) reflect the tragedies of war as seen through women's eyes. *Přehrada* (1932; The Barrier) is a utopian vision of the future, while *Sirena* (1935; The Siren) turns to the past to follow three generations of a mining family. Majerová once again describes the hardships of mining life in the short work *Havířská balada* (1938; The Ballad of a Miner).

The Nazi occupation interrupted Majerová's work. After the Communist coup she became, through numerous short stories and journalistic pieces, a prominent spokesperson for the new regime. She is also known for her literature for children.

Among her contemporaries, Majerová was closest artistically and politically to such radical writers as Stanislav Neumann and Ivan Olbracht. She was a talented if tendentious and artistically conventional writer, officially hailed today as a founder of Czech socialist realism.

Works

Majerová, Marie, ed., *Spisy* [Works] (1952–1661) in 19 vols. For a detailed list of works, see Lantová, below and Shmel'kova, I.A., introd. and ed., *Mariia Maierova: Bibliograficheskii ukazatel'* (1962).

Bibliography

Hajek, Jiří, *Narodní umělkyně Marie Majerová* (Prague, 1958). Hajek, Jiří, *Marie Majerová aneb román a doba* (Prague, 1962). Lantová, Ludmila, "Marie Majerová," in *Slovník českých spisovatelů,* Havel, Rudolf and Opelík, Jeří, eds. (Prague, 1964), pp. 304–307. Mourková, Jarmila, ed., *Marie Majerová, 1882–1967: Literaturná pozůstalost* (Prague, 1967).

English translations: Finlayson-Samsour, Roberta, tr., *Ballad of a Miner* [Havířská balada] (1960). Urwin, Iris, tr., *The Siren, a Novel* [Sirena] (1953).

Nancy Cooper

Elena Makarova

Born 1950s
Genre(s): short story, novella
Language(s): Russian, Baku

As the daughter of two poets (her mother is Inna Lisnianskaia), Makarova grew up in a literary household full of tensions stemming from her parents' incompatibility. After receiving a degree in art and studying at the Gorky Literary Institute in Moscow, Makarova obtained a job at an experimental school teaching art to children of kindergarten age. That experience is evoked in her volume of essays entitled *Osvobodite slona* (1985; Free the Elephant). Thus far she has published only two other collections: *Katushka, Povesti* (1978; The Spool, Novellas), and *Perepolnennye dni* (1982; Overfilled Days). These contain her stories and novellas, mainly from the 1970s, accompanied by her illustrations. Drawing

heavily on her own biography, Makarova's narratives combine subtle psychological insights, originality of subject matter and perspective, and a colorful language in which slang and colloquialisms consort with philosophical aphorisms and numerous literary references.

The majority of Makarova's protagonists are adolescent girls caught in a variety of problematic situations that test their maturity. Their vulnerabilities, sense of inadequacy, or naivete provide the focal point of many Makarova stories, e.g., "Travy iz Odessy" (1975; Herbs from Odessa), "Bonzhur, papa . . . i kniksen" (1977; Bonjour, Papa . . . and a Curtsey), "Ryba-igla" (1978; Fish-Needle). Born into an artistic and highly educated environment—the world of music, literature, or painting—these heroines are raised in somewhat desultory fashion by parents who are writers, artists, or scholars. The adults' talent and intellect, however, contribute little to the establishment of a sympathetic rapport with their troubled offspring, who are prone to rash or self-destructive acts, feelings of inferiority, and self-delusion. For the most part Makarova's adolescents are cast back upon themselves as they grope their way through a world ruled by shabby values, selfishness, and impotent regret. One of the most unsettling aspects of Makarova's fiction is the spiritual isolation of its adolescents and children, the dearth of reassuring warmth among the adults populating her fictional world. Mothers, in particular, seem incapable of fulfilling the hallowed maternal role of nurturers, mainly because of their own instability, self-absorption, or physical frailty. With rather dispiriting consistency Makarova's characters bicker, harbor grudges, and cling to petty prejudices; couples marry, become disillusioned with each other, and divorce with unseemly speed, paying scant attention to the impact of their actions on their children; men drink to excess, resort to physical violence against women, and so forth. Makarova's fiction assumes that frustration, melancholy, and restlessness are the common lot of humanity, only sporadically interrupted by fleeting encounters with joy or satisfaction. Nevertheless, the majority of her protagonists seek some form of permanence, and while their search inevitably ends in disappointment, in the process they obtain a "sentimental education."

Owing to the elliptical nature of Makarova's style, which often omits logical links and gives no preparation for, or explanation of, temporal leaps and shifts in locale, her narratives proceed in spurts and bounds. Although the terseness and uneven pacing can occasionally lead to confusion, when used judiciously they lend a vitality to her prose. Makarova never bores her readers or underestimates their abilities, preferring to stimulate their curiosity with cryptic allusions rather than offer them lengthy explanations.

Makarova's attachment to first-person narration results in complex effects that she handles with considerable skill. Her choice of the thoughtful but naive adolescent as narrator achieves two related goals: it reveals the mental processes and emotional censoring mechanisms at work in the girl's psychology, which are clearly discernible in the pattern of her observations; it simultaneously creates dramatic irony, for Makarova withholds from the partly gullible yet endlessly analytical narrator the crucial insights that the reader infers from the girl's imperceptive description of events and reactions. For instance, in "Zolotse" (1979; Treasure), the five-year-old narrator never realizes that her poet-mother is a self-centered neurotic who neglects her family, contracts liaisons, and presumably tries to commit suicide, but the reader has little difficulty in deducing that her destructive behavior accounts in large measure for the girl's perpetual insecurity and her father's drinking bouts.

Although Makarova portrays primarily Moscow intelligentsia, several of her pieces are set in Baku. The setting of the Azerbaijan capital on the Caspian Sea tinges the narrative with exoticism and allows Makarova to incorporate into the text phrases in the local language as well as ethnic names of native residents, food, etc. (e.g., "Zolotse"). In similar fashion, she has characters speak in German or communicate in a jargon comprehensible only to a specific circle (e.g., "Bonzhur, papa . . . i kniksen"). Elsewhere she includes songs and poems, ostensibly composed by one of the narrative's personae (e.g., "Cherez kazhdoe shest' dnei—voskresen'e" [Every Seventh Day It's Sunday], "Takaia devochka" [1978; Such a Girl]). Such a linguistic mixture

enriches the texture of individual stories, while also suggesting the diversity of Makarova's fiction, which her repeated preoccupation with a certain type of character can obscure.

Although Makarova is too young to have produced much, the stories she has published to date show a distinct talent for psychological analysis, narrative flair, and secure command of language. After Tolstaia she is the most exciting of the younger women writing in Russia today.

Works

Collections: *Katushka* (1978). *Perepolnennye dni* (1982). *Osvobodite slona* (1985).

Translations: "Herbs from Odessa," tr. Helena Goscilo, in *HERitage and HEResy: Recent Fiction by Russian Women*, ed. Helena Goscilo (1985).

Bibliography

Nancy Condee, in *Newsletter* No. 9 to Institute of Current World Affairs, July 29, 1985, pp. 3–11.

Helena Goscilo

Desanka Maksimović

Born May 16, 1898, Rabrovica, western Serbia, Yugoslavia
Genre(s): poetry, fiction, children's literature, travel literature
Language(s): Serbian

Desanka Maksimović studied comparative literature, history, and history of art at the University of Belgrade and aesthetics at the Sorbonne until 1925. She then received an appointment as a high school teacher in Belgrade, a career that she maintained until her retirement in 1953. At this time, she gave expression to her strong conviction of a poet's didactic duty by traveling throughout Yugoslavia to read her poetry to children, soldiers, workers, academicians, or whatever other audience gathered for her. She also visited Bulgaria and the Soviet Union. In 1976, she toured the United States and Canada, two countries with large communities of Yugoslav emigrants. In 1959, Desanka Maksimović was elected to regular membership in the Serbian Academy of Arts and Sciences; in 1976, she received the prestigious Vuk Karad'ić Prize for the totality of her literary work. In addition to composing her original work, Maksimović translates poetry from French and Bulgarian.

The first collection of Desanka Maksimović's poetry appeared in 1924. The poems were youthful lyrics, full of a love of nature and a sense of wonder at life unfolding before her. During the years before World War II, she wrote more poetry, short stories, and a novel. Her writing is characterized by a great variety of themes; in fact, after an early period of personal absorption, she took all of her country as a source of inspiration, just as she took all of her countrymen as an audience. The works of Maksimović are marked by an optimistic, normative realism. Her strength and characteristic style owe much to her lifelong knowledge of Serbian folk literature, a body of poetry that is couched in language that was never modern—terse, often humorous, laced with Turkish words and imbued with a deep sense of the essential rightness of what it proclaims. The structure and voice of Desanka Maksimović's writing, as in her model, shifts freely between the epic and the lyric but to a lyricism that is typological rather than individualistic. Like the linden tree of Serbian legend, the poet has her roots deep in the earth, with her wide-reaching arms stretched out to heaven.

After World War II, the works of Desanka Maksimović grew more patriotic and more Serbian. Two works stand out. *Tra'im pomilovanje* (1964; I Plead for Mercy) is addressed to Tsar Dušan, a medieval ruler of Serbia whose code of law effectively built the nation. The cycle of short poems begs mercy for sinners of various sins and for their victims; charity is worth more than justice. *Letopis o Perunovih potomaka* (1976; Chronicle of Perun's Descendants) celebrates the uninterrupted impulses running through Serbian history. Occasionally, it is quite adamant, as in "Miracle in the Church," where a monk's Latin prayers repeatedly and ineluctably bring forth a Serbian echo.

The work of Desanka Maksimović shows mastery of an idiom, breadth of compassion, and assured craftsmanship. She did not invent a new voice, but for many years, she *was* a voice of her people. It is chiefly her poetry which has won her not only the status of a best-seller, but an august position in Serbian letters.

Works

Pesme (1924). Vrt detinjstva (1927). Zeleni vitez (1930). Gozba na livadi (1932). Kako oni 'ive (1935). Nove pesme (1936). Oslobodjenje Cvete Andrić (1945). Pesnik i zavičaj (1946). Otad'bina u prvomajkskok povorci (1949). Izabrane pesme (1950). Otad'bino, tu sam (1951). Krvava bajka (1951). Otvoren prozor (1954). Strašna igra (1954). Miris zemlje (1955). Izabrane pjesme (1958). Buntovan razred (1960). Zarobljenik snova (1960). Govori tiho (1961). Pesme (1963). Pesme (1964). Pesme (1965). Pesme (1966). Deset mojih pesama (1967). Pesme (1967). Stihovi (1967). Vratnice (1968). Ne zaboraviti (1969). Sabrana dela (1969) 7 vols. Verujem (1969). Pradevojčica (1970). Izabrane pesme (1972). Izbor iz dela (1974). Letopis Perunovih potomaka (1976). Praznici putovanja (1972). Nemam više vremena (1973). Pesme iz Norveške (1976). Pjesme (1977). Snimci iz švajčarske (1978). Ničija zemlja (1978). Izabrana dela (1980), 5 vols. Greetings from the Old Country (1976), bilingual.

Bibliography

Eekman, T., *Thirty Years of Yugoslav Literature (1945–1975)* (1978), pp. 25–26. Šljivić-Šimšić, B., *Encyclopedia of World Literature in the Twentieth Century* (1983), pp. 182–183. Surdučki, M., Preface to *Greetings from the Old Country* (1976).

Gertrud Champa

Hanna Malewska

Born 1911
Genre(s): novel, short story
Language(s): Polish

Graduate of the University of Lublin, Poland, she later taught high school and took an active part in the anti-Nazi resistance movement during the German occupation; after the war she was one of the editors of the Catholic weekly *Tygodnik Powszechny* as well as the Catholic monthly *Znak* in Cracow. She is best known for historical novels on a wide range of subjects, from ancient Greece, through Germany, Spain, France or Italy in the Middle Ages to modern Poland. Her controlled and direct technique and the disciplined construction of her story lines permit her to focus on both the larger historical background as well as the minute details of the protagonists' psychological make-up. At the core of the author's interest lie the problems of evil as studied through historical examples of power and impotence, war and peace, success and downfall. Critics ascribe the mastery of Malewska's stories to her deep knowledge of history and observation of the principles of social sciences; some point out a certain ideological pattern in her selection of historical events to be presented in her novels, where Providence is shown actively at work, both in the lives of individuals and whole countries.

Works

Wiosna grecka [Greek Spring] (1933). Zelazna korona [The Iron Crown] (1938). Kamienie wolac beda [The Stones Will Cry Out] (1939). Zniwo na sierpie [Harvest on the Sickle] (1947). Przemija postac swiata [Fleeting is the Shape of the World] (1954). Sir Thomas More odmawia [Sir Thomas More's Refusal] (1956). Spowiedz Archipoety [Confessions of the Archpoet] (1958). Opowiesci o siedmiu medrcach [Stories of Seven Sages] (1959). Panowie Leszczynscy [The Men of the Leszczynski Family] (1961). Apokryf rodzinny [Family Apocrypha] (1965).

Bibliography

Milosz, Czeslaw, The History of Polish Literature (New York, 1969). Krzyzanowski, Julian, A History of Polish Literature (Warsaw, 1978).

Maya Peretz

Marie Malézieux

(see: Marie Robert Halt)

Helena Maliřová

Born 1877, Prague, Czechoslovakia; died 1940, Prague
Genre(s): short story, novel
Language(s): Czech

Helena Maliřová (born Helena Nosková) was brought up in the midst of Prague intellectual life. After serving as a nurse and reporter in the Serbian-Turkish war in 1912, she married the "proletarian novelist" Ivan Olbracht. From the 1920s on, Maliřová was an active Communist Party member, editing and contributing to several party publications. Her political activity closely parallels that of the better-known writer, Marie Majerová.

Maliřová's fiction is strongly autobiographical in plot and setting as well as in its confessional tone. Women's search for self-fulfillment and love is pitted against societal restrictions. Examples are the short-story collections Lidské srdce (1903; A Human Heart), Křehké květiny (1907; Fragile Flowers), První polibky (1912; First Kisses), and the novels Právo na štěstí (1908; Right to Happiness), Víno (1912; Wine), and Popel (1914; Ashes). These early efforts, especially the novels, are compositionally weak. Their strongest point is their evocation of turn-of-the-century Prague, the setting of the more successful Barva krve (1932; The Color of Blood).

Maliřová's wartime experiences provide the raw material for Srdce nemá stání (1918; The Heart Knows No Peace), Vítězství (1918; Victory) and Po'ehnání (1920; The Blessing). In the 1920s she produced many fairy tales and other works for children. In the 1930s, the period of her best work, Maliřová began to experiment with nonlinear, fragmented, mosaic-like narrative forms. Written in the new mode are Deset zivotů (1937; Ten Lives) and Mariola (1940; Mariola). Deset zivotů is closely based on the author's life. In this novel, as in all her fiction, Maliřová strives to link the personal and the intimate with the political and the social.

Works

Maliřová, Helena, Vybrané spisy (1957–; Collected Works). For a detailed list of works, see Pinz, below.

Bibliography

Helena Maliřová, 1877–1940: Malá výběrová bibliografie (Znojmo, 1977). Homolová, Květa, Mojmír Otruba, and Zdeňka Pešata, eds., Čeští spisovatelé 19. a počátku 20. století: Slovníková příručka (Prague, 1982), pp. 173–175. Knězek, Libor, "Spisovateľka štedrého srdca." Slovenskeé pohľady na literature a umenie 93, xi (1977): 112–116. Pinz, Radko, "Helena Maliřová," in Slovník českých spisovatelů, Havel, Rudolf and Jiři Opelík, eds. (Prague, 1964), pp. 307–308.

Nancy Cooper

Françoise Mallet-Joris

(a.k.a. François Lilar)

Born 1930, Antwerp, Belgium
Genre(s): poetry, novel, autobiography,
*   biography, short story*
Language(s): French

Daughter of a well-known Antwerp family, her mother being the novelist Suzanne Lilar and her father a figure in public life, she was educated in the United States and in France. She now lives in Paris, having become a French citizen through her third marriage.

Her literary career began early with the publication of a volume of poetry, *Poèmes du Dimanche* (1947; Sunday Poems), under her family name. This was followed in 1951 by her first novel *Le Rampart de Béguines* (The Illusionist) and its sequel *La Chambre rouge* (1955; The Red Room), which enjoyed a marked success because of the rather scandalous nature of their subject, the seduction of a young girl by her father's strong-willed mistress, told with a detachment worthy of scientific reporting. The success of this technique set the style for later works. She was particularly interested in studying the clash of wills between characters, the difference between appearance and reality, as well as the impossibility of real communication among human beings. Self-mastery, achieved through an effort of the will, is the goal of her principal characters. These qualities were especially successful in her next two novels, *Les Mensonges* (1956; The House of Lies), which presents a power struggle between two generations of a Belgian merchant's family where a daughter revolts against the hypocrisy and willfulness of her dying father, and *L' Empire Celeste* (1958; The Café Celeste), which examines the illusions dominating a group of people whose lives center around a left-Bank Parisian café. These illusions, which make life bearable for the individuals, involve clashes of will when the existence of one illusion destroys another. Particularly striking in these novels is the author's power of description, reminiscent of the best period of Flemish painting. *Les Mensonges* was awarded the Prix des Libraires and the *L' Empire Celeste* the Prix Femina (1958).

Three historical studies followed: *Les Personnages* (1961; The Favorite), inspired by Louise de Lafayette, a favorite at the court of Louis XIII; *Marie Mancini: le premier Amour de Louis XIV* (1964); and *Jeanne Guyon* (1974). To this period also belongs the first of two autobiographical works: *Lettre à Moi-Même* (1963; Letter to Myself), awarded the Presse de Monaco Prize, to be followed by *La Maison de Papier* (1970; The Paper House). These are interesting revelations of the evolution of the writer from rebellious young girl to professional writer and devoted mother of four children, by way of a spiritual crisis and religious conversion. They greatly enhance an understanding of the ideas and experiences that have contributed to the writer's novels and short stories.

Although Mallet-Joris has not participated in experiments with the form of the novel, she has shown her interest in the nature of language in *Le Jeu du Souterrain* (1973; The Underground Game), which questions the foundations of words and their meanings. In *Allegra* (1976), the central character sacrifices her life in an attempt to give meaning to the silence of a mute boy.

More recent writings have included *Un Chagrin d'amours et Ailleurs* (1981; An Unhappy Love Affair and Elsewhere) and *Le Clin d'Oeil de l'Ange* (1983; The Angel's Wink), seven short stories about couples who could or could not take advantage of a significant moment capable of changing their lives, and *Le Rive de Laura* (1985; Laura's Laughter), in which a woman trying to save a wayward son liberates herself with an accepting and tragic laugh from the limitations of marriage and motherhood, all variations on earlier themes now approached from the viewpoint of a mature writer. Her own development is perhaps the most interesting aspect of her writing.

She was awarded the Prince Pierre de Monaco prize in 1964 for the ensemble of her work and elected to the Goncourt Academy in 1970. Curiously, her later work has not attracted the critical attention that it merits.

Works

Poèmes du dimanche [Sunday Poems] (1947). *Le Rampart de Béguines* [The Illusionist] (1951). *La Chambre Rouge* [The Red Room] (1955). *Les*

Mensonges [The House of Lies] (1956). *Cordélia: Nouvelles* [Cordelia and Other Stories] (1956). *L'Empire Céleste* [The Café Celeste] (1958). *Les Personnages* [The Favorite] (1961). *Lettre à Moi-Même* [Letter to Myself] (1963). *Les Signes et les Prodiges* [Signs and Wonders] (1966). *Marie Mancini, Le Premier Amour de Louis XIV* [Marie Mancini, the First Love of Louis XIV] (1966). *Trois Ages de la Nuit* [Three Ages of the Night] (1966). *La Maison de Papier* [The Paper House] (1970). *Le Jeu du Souterrain* [The Underground Game] (1973). *Le Roi qui Aimait Trop les Fleurs* [The King Who Loved Flowers Too Much] (1971). *Les Feuilles Mortes d'un Bel Eté* [The Dead Leaves of a Beautiful Summer] (1976). *Allegra* (1976). *J'aurais voulu jouer de l'accordion* [I Would Have Liked to Play the Accordion] (1976). *Dickie-Roi* [King Dickie] (1979). *Un Chagrin d'Amours et d'Ailleurs* [An Unhappy Love Affair and Somewhere Else] (1981). *Le Clin d'Oeil de l'Ange* [The Angel's Wink] (1983). *Le Rire de Laura* [The Laughter of Laura] (1985). *La Tristesse du Cerf-Volant* [The Sadness of the Kite] (1988).

Translations: *The Illusionist* [*Le Rempart de Béguines*] (1952). *The Red Room* [*La Chambre Rouge*] (1956). *The House of Lies* [*Les Mensonges*] (1957). *Cordelia and Other Stories* [*Cordélia: Nouvelles*] (1965). *Café Celeste* [*L'Empire Céleste*] (1959). *The Favorite* [*Les Personnages*] (1962). *Letter to Myself* [*Lettre à Moi-Même*] (1964). *Signs and Wonders* [*Les Signes et les Prodiges*] (1967). *The Uncompromising Heart: A Life of Marie Mancini, Louis XIV's First Love* [*Marie Mancini, Le Premier Amour de Louis XIV*] (1966). *The Witches, Three Tales of Sorcery* [*Trois Ages de la Nuit*] (1970). *The Paper House* [*La Maison de Papier*] (1971). *The Underground Game* [*Jeu du Souterrain*] (1975).

Bibliography

Boisdeffre, Pierre de, *Une Histoire Vivante de la Littérature d'Aujourd'hui.* 6th ed. (Paris, 1966), pp. 583–585. Crosland, M., *Women of Iron and Velvet: French Women Writers After George Sand* (New York, 1986), pp. 180–191. Delattre, G., "Mirrors and Masks in the World of Françoise Mallet-Joris." *Yale French Studies* 27 (Spring 1961): 121–126. Géoris, Michel, *Françoise Mallet-Joris* (Paris, 1964). Reck, R. D., "Mallet-Joris and the Anatomy of Will." *Yale French Studies* 24 (Winter 1959): 74–79. Soos, Emese, "The Only Motion Is Returning: The Metaphor of Alchemy in Mallet-Joris and Yourcenar." *French Forum* 4 (1979): 3–16.

Charity C. Willard

Mathilda Malling

(a.k.a. Stella Kleve)

Born January 20, 1864, Sweden; died March 21, 1942, Copenhagen, Denmark
Genre(s): novels, plays, novellas, autobiography
Language(s): Swedish

Mathilda Malling began her career writing of nervous *fin de siècle* heroines in the charged atmosphere of the sexual morality debates in the Scandinavian 1880s. Later, in the 1890s, Malling developed an interest in the historical novel, joining a trend in Swedish literature that would also include Verner von Heidenstam, Oscar Levertin, Harald Molander, and August Strindberg.

Malling was born Mathilda Ingrid Kruse on her family's estate in southern Sweden. She was considered a gifted child and was one of the first women to study at Lund University. During a stay in Switzerland, Malling came into contact with the late naturalistic literature of France, which resulted in her first novel *Berta Funke* (1885), published under the pseudonym Stella Kleve. This novel and the novella "Pyrrahussegrar" (1886; Pyrrhic Victories) caused a great public outcry in Sweden, since Malling's emphasis on female eroticism was considered immoral. Malling came to be associated with the group called "Young Skåne," whose ranks included Victoria Benedictsson, Ola Hansson, and Axel Lundegård, among others. Malling and Ola Hansson became primary conduits of French decadent literature to Sweden. Malling eventually broke with "Young Skåne," and the publication of *Alice Brandt* (1888) signaled the end of a controversial and vital phase of her early authorship.

Malling married Peter Malling, a Danish businessman, in 1890 and moved to Copenhagen. After six years of silence, she published anonymously *En roman om förste konsuln* (1894; A

Romance of the First Consul, 1898), which was the first of a long string of popular historical novels. Initially, Malling's historical novels were received well by critics and public alike. Georg Brandes praised her eloquent prose, attention to detail, and knowledge of the historical sources. However, after *Skyttes på Munkeboda* (1897; The Skyttes of Munkeboda), critics began to miss the artistic spark of her earlier works and accused her of writing mere entertainment literature. Malling was not insensitive to such criticism, which seems to have inspired *Malin Skytte* (1900), the story of a happily married woman whose domestic idyll is disturbed by a cousin who seeks to rekindle the artistic ambitions of her youth.

Critics lost interest in Mathilda Malling although the public continued to enjoy her romantic and well-told tales. She eventually came to be hailed as the Grand Old Dame of the Swedish "Miss novel." Her works had evolved from provocative immorality to recommended family reading.

Works

Berta Funke (1885). *Alice Brandt* (1888). *En roman om förste konsuln* (1894). *Fru guvernören af Paris* (1895). *Eremitage-idyllen* (1896). *Doña Ysabel* (1897). *Fru Leonora* (1897). *Skyttes på Munkeboda* (1897). *Malin Skytte* (1900). *Damerna på Markby* (1901). *Daggryning* (1902). *Nina* (1903). *Lilla Marica och hennes man* (1904). *Lady Elizabeth Percy* (1905). *Hennes hjälte* (1906). *Maria Stuart* (1907). *Ninas bröllopsresa* (1908). *Karl Skyttes hustru* (1909). *Systrarna på Ribershus 1–2* (1910). *Det hvita huset och den röda stugan* (1911). *Mannen, hustrun och Lord Byron* (1912). *Den olycklige Henry Percy* (1913). *Ebba Stjerne, Eva Skytte och de andra* (1914). *Madleine Stjerne* (1915). *Madleines hem* (1916). *Marieholm och Munkeboda* (1918). *Hemmet på Urfva* (1919). *Uppfostran och inflytande 1864–1885* (1920). *Erik Stjernes idyl* (1921). *Eva Skyttes venner* (1924). *Mina dagböcker* (1926). *Kongsager* (1928). *Många damer och en man* (1928). *Det fatala giftermålet* (1931).

Translations: *A Romance of the First Consul*, tr. Anna Molboe (1898). *The Governor's Wife. Pictures from the Imperial Court of France 1806–1807*, tr. Henriette Langaa (1904). *The Immaculate Young Minister*, tr. A.G. Chater (1913).

Bibliography

Åhlén, Bengt, *Svenskt Författar Lexikon. 1900–1940* (Stockholm, 1942). Bredsdorff, Elias, "Stella Kleve." *Den Store Nordiske Krig om Seksualmoralen* (Copenhagen, 1973), pp. 159–162. Fahlgren, Margarethe, "Kvinnor och självbiografi. En studie i Mathilda Mallings Uppfostran och inflytande 1864–1886." *Tidskrift för litteraturvetenskap* 11 (1982): 47–60. Sjöblad, Christina, "Det lagade halsbandet eller Mathilda Mallings självbiografi." *Tidskrift för litteraturvetenskap* 11 (1982): 230–235. Sjöblad, Christina, *Baudelaires väg till Sverige* (Lund, 1975).

Susan Brantley

Concepció Maluquer i González

Born 1918, Salas (Catalunya), Spain
Genre(s): poetry, novel
Language(s): Spanish

Maluquer was born in a small town in the Pyrenees, Spain's mountainous northern border with France, a relatively isolated rural area where the traditional Catalan language was preserved in rich authenticity. She is one of the earliest writers to publish in Catalan in the post-Civil War period in Spain, an undertaking rendered hazardous by the Franco regime's previous prohibition of all the vernacular languages, and made more difficult by arbitrary censorship and harassment. She moved to Barcelona, intellectual and publishing center for Catalan writers and culture, and first achieved recognition for her poetry, winning the City of Barcelona prize in 1957 for her long poem *La creu dels vents* (1959; Cross of the Winds). Barcelona is personified in extended dialogue with the four winds (representing spiritual forces of the world, as well as the spirit of the city). The "cross" of the title is drawn by the lines extending between the four cardinal points and may be interpreted symbolically as an allusion to the persecution of Catalonia by the Franco regime, which nonetheless fails to suppress the Catalan spirit and to prevent the city's spiritual contact with freer elements in the external world. *La ciutat y les hores* (1960; The City and The Hours) again utilizes the device of personification, this time presenting the twenty-four hours in feminine guise, with Barcelona as the implicit interlocutor. There is an organic unity to what constitutes in essence a single long poem, arranged around a nucleus of five-stanza lyric compositions.

Parèntesi (1962; Parenthesis), Malquer's first venture into the area of prose fiction, was followed two years later by Gent del Sud (1964; People of the South), a novel belonging to the postwar current of critical realism of political intent, euphemistically dubbed "social" literature. Set in the author's native Pyrenees region, it presents the conflict in a small village that results from the clash of mentalities between the traditional mountain people and a wave of immigrants from the South (i.e., Andalusia), who are driven by unemployment, hunger, and lack of economic opportunities to leave their homes in search of opportunity for betterment. Because the Franco regime's economic policies produced almost no postwar recovery for the first two decades, internal migration and emigration were both critical issues in Spain during the 1960s, the very mention of them implying failure of governmental programs. Que s'ha fet d'en Pere Cots (1966; What Has Become of Peter Cots) is a novel of psychological analysis whose point of departure is the unexplained disappearance of a simple, seemingly normal man. Aigua térbola (1967; Muddy Waters) belongs to the so-called "testimonial" literature of the 1950s and 1960s in Spain, a tendentious neorealist current that either exposed the social injustices and economic hardships suffered by the working class or denounced the dolce vita of the upper classes. This novel, Maluquer's longest, is especially critical of the mentality of the wealthy sector, with its prejudices, religious fanaticism and misapplication of Christian tenets, moral rigidity, and misguided social policies. Gent del nord (1971; People from the North) further evinces Maluquer's concern for the country's socioeconomic problems. Its focus is upon the phenomenon of tourism in Spain, which, beginning in the 1960s, became the country's leading industry of the 1970s and led to massive development of the Mediterranean coast along with hasty and frequently ill-advised urbanization and disastrous ecological consequences. The social, moral, and psychological impact of the influx of millions of tourists also concern the novelist.

Works

Aigua térbola (1967). La ciutat y les hores (1960). La creu dels vents (1959). Gent del nord (1971). Gent del Sud (1964). Parèntesi (1962). Que s'ha fet d'en Pere Cots (1966).

Janet Perez

Michèle Manceaux

Born February 17, 1928, Paris, France
Genre(s): novel
Language(s): French

Michèle Manceaux worked as a journalist for the magazine L'Express (1954–1964), and Le Nouvel Observateur (1971–1972). She was also a producer of the program "Cinéma," in collaboration with Frédéric Rossif, for the "Office de Radio et Télévision Françaises" (1965–1968). She is presently an editorialist for the woman's magazine Marie-Claire.

Her works include many non-fictional essays, and a few novels, in which she often uses journalistic techniques. In Grand Reportage (Grand Report), for example, she tells the story of a crisis that happened in her life in 1975. She presents it as the diary of her own psychoanalysis. Her restrained emotion, which has been compared to that of Marguerite Duras, enables her to treat this delicate and personal subject without pathos, even though one of the main themes is her mother's agony. Her rational clarity avoids theoretical jargon and ravings of the unconscious, which have been shortcomings in many books of that genre. Frederico Fellini once wished her to become the heroine of her own life: with Grand Reportage, Manceaux fulfilled this wish and won a double challenge, personal and literary.

All her other works reveal her curiosity and passion for the problems of our times and her compassion for women of all races and countries. This combination of literary sensitivity and journalistic talents has made her a chronicler and writer of exceptional awareness and perceptiveness.

Works

Un beau mariage (1962). *Catherine La Danseuse* (1966). *La nuit sera noire et blanche* (1968). *Ce n'est qu'un début* (1968; in collaboration with Philippe Labro). *Les policiers parlent* (1969). [With Madeleine Chapsal], *Les profs, pourquoi faire?* (1970). *Les maos en France* (1972). *Les femmes de Gennevilliers* (1974). *Les femmes du Mozambique* (1975). *Grand reportage* (1980). "Points Roman," collection (1981). *Pourquoi pas Venise* (1981). "Points Roman," collection (1982). *Anonymous* (1982). *Brèves* (1984). *Eloges de l'insomnie* (1985). *Le voyage en Afrique de Lara Simpson* (1985). *La zone des tempêtes* (1986).

Translations: *As mulheres de Moçambique*, tr. Manuel Joao Gomes (1976). *Der Westen wird rot: die Maos in Frankreich* (1973).

Bibliography

Le Nouvel Observateur (9/1/75). *Jeune Afrique* (10/31/75). *Le Monde Hebdomadaire* (7/10/75). *L'Express* (8/18/75). *Le Monde* (2/15/80). *Le Matin de Paris* (3/10/80).

Michèle M. Magill

Eva Cattermole Mancini

(a.k.a. Contessa Lara)

Born 1849, Florence; died 1896, Rome
Genre(s): poetry, novel, short story, children's literature
Language(s): Italian

Through her father, who was a private music teacher, Cattermole grew up in contact with the children of powerful and intellectual families, when Florence was the capital of Italy from 1860 to 1870. When she was very young, she married a lieutenant, E.F. Mancini, son of a famous statesman, Stanislao Mancini, and the poet Laura Beatrice Oliva. She separated from her husband after a sensational trial in Milan, whereby he was indicted for killing her lover, a cavalry officer, in a duel. For the rest of her days, she lived in Rome on her modest income from her writing, contributing to several journals and papers, among which were *Il Fieramosca, Nabab, Corriere di Roma, Caffaro, Fracassa, Fanfulla della domenica, Illustrazione italiana, Tribuna illustrata.* She was murdered by a young lover who resented her rejection of him.

The publication of *Canti e ghirlande* (Songs and Garlands) in 1867 had brought young Cattermole to the attention of a literary figure of the time, Francesco Dall'Ongaro. Her career, however, was not launched until 1883, when a book of poetry, *Versi* (Verses), was brought out by Angelo Sommaruga, a publisher who had been scandalizing Italian literary circles with his provocative publicity methods. The recurring themes of that collection are the domestic scene and the dramas of conjugal life: quarrels, reconciliations, suspicions, betrayals. Strains of romantic passion, with the implicit revolt against conventional society, and her talent for photographic descriptions associated Cattermole with the Milanese group of *Scapigliatura*. In a new volume, *Nuovi versi* (1886; New Verses), her constant theme, love, seems to have deepened into an exalted desire for total dedication to a man, thus reflecting her mood in a period of life when she lived with a young, and later celebrated, scholar, Giovanni Alfredo Cesareo. In her later poetry—*Ancora versi* (More Verses), published posthumously in 1897—Cattermole shows her basic psychological conflict, as she alternatively expresses a wish for a new life, quiet and sentimentally satisfying, on one side, and sudden longings for reckless self-determination, on the other. Her most successful poems are sketches of interiors, recreated with the simple, but decisive description of a few objects, with a suggestion of a color or an odor, where an erotic feeling is suddenly alluded to with delicate but vivid longing. A pronounced cult of death emerges at the end of her production, together with other decadent themes in the manner of Gabriele D'Annunzio, who then dominated the Roman literary scene. Her beauty and her sensational life in end-of-the-century Rome made Contessa Lara appear as the prototype of D'Annunzian heroines, as they were described in *Il piacere* (1889; The Pleasure) and *L'innocente* (1891; The Innocent). Throughout her career, Cattermole wrote many short stories; she published an autobiographical novel, *L'innamorata* (1892; Woman in Love) and two books for children: *Una famiglia di topi* (1895; A Family of Mice) and *Il romanzo della bambola* (1896; The Doll's Novel).

Works

Cant i e ghirlande (1867). Versi (1883). Ancora versi (1897). Nuovi versi (1886). Cosi e (1887). L'innamorata (1892). Storia d'amore e di dolore (1893). Il romanzo della bambola (1896). Una famiglia di topi (1895). Storia di Natale (1897). Novelle (1914). La Madonna di Pugliano (1917).

Bibliography:

Barbiera, R., Il salotto della contessa Maffei (Milan, 1895). Borgese, Maria, La Contessa Lara, una vita di passione e di poesia nell'Ottocento italiano (Milan, 1936). Costa-Zalessow, N., Scrittrici italiane dal XIII al XX secolo (Ravenna, 1982), pp. 235–39. Croce, B., Letteratura della nuova Italia II (Bari, 1921). Morandini, G., La voce che è in lei, Antologia della narrativa femminile italiana tra Ottocento e Novecento (Milan, 1980), pp. 200–216. Squarciapino, G., Roma bizantina (Turin, 1950), pp. 172–180, 358–361.

Nadezhda Mandelshtam

Born October 31, 1899, Saratov, Russia; died December 29, 1980, Moscow
Genre(s): memoirs
Language(s): Russian

Nadezhda Mandelshtam's two books, *Hope Against Hope* and *Hope Abandoned*, bear witness to her incredible tenacity in the face of relentless persecution under Stalin. The wife of Osip Mandelshtam, a poet of genius, she devoted her life to the preservation of her husband's *oeuvre* after his arrest and disappearance in the concentration camps in 1938.

She was born Nadezhda Yakovlevna Khazina in an educated Jewish family in the provincial town of Saratov. Living most of her early life in Kiev, she became an art student in the studio of A.A. Ekster. It was in 1919 in Kiev that she met her future husband, Mandelshtam, to whom she was officially married in 1922. The couple lived in Moscow, in the Herzen House, while looking for a place of their own to live. Her friendship with Anna Akhmatova, a great poet and fellow Acmeist of Mandelshtam, dates from 1925. Already in the 1920s Osip Mandelshtam was beginning to come under fire on account of his nonconformist attitude vis-a-vis the "social command" imposed upon literature by the new Soviet regime.

His first arrest in 1934 was occasioned by a denunciatory poem he wrote about Stalin. After his second arrest and disappearance in 1938, Nadezhda evaded the authorities on numerous occasions by moving from one provincial town to another, teaching English to earn her daily bread. From this time until Mandelshtam's official rehabilitation, she devoted herself to preserving her husband's memory and poetry, often devising ingenious ways of hiding manuscripts from the police.

Nadezhda Yakovlevna composed her two great memoirs *Hope Against Hope* (1970) and *Hope Abandoned* (1972) in the latter half of the 1960s. These works have never been published in the Soviet Union. Her first book concentrates primarily on the four years between Mandelshtam's two arrests. Although restricted to this time span, the author's style is discursive, and provides many valuable insights into the horror of Soviet life under Stalin. Indeed, to resurrect the past and to expose the moral bankruptcy of a system wherein the end justifies the means is the author's avowed purpose. This intent is even more apparent in her second book, *Hope Abandoned*, which Jane Harris has rightfully characterized as a "Book of Judgment." The author attacks the moral laxity and blindness to human suffering characteristic of those who supported Stalinism. *Hope Abandoned* in this sense is different from *Hope Against Hope*, whose focus was primarily upon Mandelshtam. In the second work greater attention is given to Nadezhda Yakovlevna's life with Mandelshtam from the beginning of their relationship up to his arrest in 1934. The author's own life, from her husband's death to the writing of the book, is also described. In this second memoir she adds "considerably to her portrait gallery of contemporaries, bringing Mandelshtam's lonely eminence into sharper relief" (Max Hayward).

In these writings Nadezhda Mandelshtam comes through to the reader as a person of great courage, whose devotion to her husband saved the works of one of the greatest poets of the twentieth century from oblivion. By virtue of her brutal honesty and powerful convictions, her moral victory over her persecutors is complete.

Works

Vospominaniya (1970). Vtoraya kniga (1972). Translations: Hope Against Hope, tr. Max Hayward, introd. Clarence Brown (1970). Hope Abandoned, tr. with forward by Max Hayward (1974). Mozart and Salieri, tr. by Robert A. McClean (1973).

Laura Jo Turner McCullough

Eglantina Mandia

Born 1936, Tiranë, Albania
Genre(s): short story, novel, reportage, drama
Language(s): Albanian

Mandia is a graduate of the University of Tiranë (1959). She has worked as a journalist and teacher.

Works

Tregime për ty [Tales for You] (1969). Lisa të mëdhenj [Great Oaks] (1984). Jeta dhe motrat e saj [Jeta and Her Sisters] (1977). Një pritje e gjatë [A Long Wait] (1984). Duke mposhtur vdekjen [Conquering Death] (1977). Në cdo pëllëmbë të tokës sime [ON Every Inch of My Land] (1981).

Philip Shashko

Erika Mann

Born November 9, 1905, Munich, Germany;
died August 27, 1969, Zurich,
Switzerland
Genre(s): journalism, biography, short story,
travel literature, children's literature
Language(s): German, English

The firstborn of the six children of Thomas Mann and Katja (Pringsheim) Mann, Erika grew up in the pleasant Bavarian surroundings of Munich and Tolz, where the family spent their summers. Among their neighbors in the city was the family of Bruno Walter, and it was in amateur theatricals with the Walter children that she got her first taste of the theater. After finishing school she studied drama for a year under Max Reinhardt in Berlin, then moved on to Bremen and Hamburg, where she met and married a young leftist actor, Gustaf Gründgens. To her dismay, Gründgens' socialism proved to be of the national rather than the international persuasion. When the Nazis came to power he got himself appointed manager of the Berlin state theater through the good offices of his friend Hermann Goering, and Erika divorced him and returned home to Munich.

She seems to have been possessed by an almost unlimited restless energy. In addition to her acting career, she wrote a boys' book, collaborated with her brother Klaus on accounts of trips to the Riviera and around the world, and participated in an automobile rally about Europe, driving over six thousand miles in ten days and phoning in daily reports to newspapers from each of her stops. She won the competition, incidentally, and received a Ford automobile as a prize.

It was soon to come in handy. Her father had long been an outspoken critic of the Nazis, and after the burning of the Reichstag in 1933, Hitler placed the Mann home in Munich under surveillance and forbade the removal of any of the author's possessions. After warning their parents, who were on a brief trip in Switzerland at the time, that "the weather in Munich was unpleasant," Erika and Klaus left Germany to join them. Discovering that her father had left the manuscript of Joseph and His Brothers in the house, Erika disguised herself in peasant costume, drove secretly back into Germany, slipped into the house in the dead of night, and returned safely to Switzerland with the manuscript hidden in the toolbox of her Ford.

Meanwhile she had been making herself unpopular with Hitler in her own right. She had founded and played the lead role in a revue called Die Pfeffermühle which included sketches lampooning the Nazis by Klaus, W.H. Auden and Aaron Copland. The revue, which was playing to packed houses in Munich when Von Epp arrived and raised the swastika, was immediately banned and Erika became a fugitive. Leaving Germany, she took the Pfeffermühle on tour in Holland, Switzerland, Austria, Czechoslovakia, Belgium and Luxembourg, then on to New York. It was a success, enjoying over a thousand performances before it was banned after formal protests from the German government and a staged gas bomb riot in Zurich. By now Erika had lost her German citizenship but became a British subject through a pro forma marriage to W. H. Auden.

In 1936 she immigrated to America and embarked on yet another career as a political activist, denouncing Nazism from the lecture platform with her father and Klaus.

Her first political work, *Zehn Millionen Kinder*, is a heavily documented indictment of the Nazi regime that describes in detail exactly what was happening to German children under Hitler. It was quickly followed by two more anti-Nazi works in collaboration with Klaus: *Escape to Life*, which documents, by means of vignettes about Albert Einstein, Rudolf Serkin, and others, the flight of the intellectual and artistic elite from Germany, and *The Other Germany*, an attempt to explain, if not to excuse, the many "civilized Germans who, through their refusal to take part in politics, made the Hitler takeover possible." Her final propaganda work, *The Lights Go Down*, relates in documentary fashion what happened to various typical German citizens under Hitler.

After the war Erika returned to Europe with her father and settled down with him in Kilchberg near Zurich. Here she edited his letters, compiled an anthology of his works, did a brief memoir of the final year of his life, wrote short stories and children's books, and worked on screenplays of *The Confessions of Felix* and *Tonio Kröger*.

Works

Political: *Zehn millionen Kinder: Die Erziehung der Jugend im Dritten Reich* (1938). *The Lights Go Down* (1940). *A Gang of Ten* (1942).

Biographical: *Das letzte Jahr: Bericht über meinen Vater* (1956). With Klaus Mann: *Rundherum*, travel (1929); *Das Buch von der Riviera*, travel (1931); *Escape to Life*, political (1939); *The Other Germany*, political (1940). [With Stephen Vincent Benét et al.], *Zero Hour: A Summons to the Free*, political (1940). Numerous children's books, 1932–1959.

Robert Harrison

Eeva-Liisa Manner

(a.k.a. Anna September)

Born December 5, 1921, Helsinki, Finland
Genre(s): poetry, drama, novel, translation
Language(s): Finnish

Eeva-Liisa Manner is one of the most important, innovative writers of modern Finnish poetry. The characteristic features of her work are philosophically analytical thinking, concise imagery, and a musical beauty of expression. These features are typical of her whole range—poetry, prose and drama—the difference between the genres largely fade in her writing.

Manner was born in Helsinki in 1921. She left secondary school to work in insurance and publishing from 1940 to 1946. Since then, she has been a freelance writer and a productive translator. She spent her childhood in Viipuri (now part of the Soviet Union); later she has lived in Tampere and Churriana (Spain).

The work that marked her breakthrough and that of modernism in Finnish poetry was her collection *Tämä matka* (1956; This Journey). It was preceded by two traditional books of poetry typical of the forties and a novel describing her childhood in the early fifties. The central problems of the poet can be seen in *Tämä matka*. The themes that run through it are loneliness—her great theme, taking part in the world's suffering ("Misericordia") and opposing violence ("Strontium"). Music has been a powerful influence, especially Bach and Mozart, but equally modern jazz. A counterforce to loneliness in this and later works is the relation with nature, an experience tinged with pantheism. Much of her imagery comes from childhood experiences, dreams, and myth (the horse is an especially frequently repeated metaphor); later the relation with nature is also linked with oriental philosophy, particularly Chinese wisdom.

High points of her later work are a verse drama, *Eros ja Psykhe* (1959; Eros and Psyche), which most purely continued the themes of *Tämä matka*, and the poetry collections *Kirjoitettu kivi* (1966; Written Stone), *Fahrenheit 121* (1968) and *Kuolleet vedet* (1977; Dead Waters). *Varokaa, voittajat* (1972; Beware, Victors), a novel in limpid style, is a significant analysis of violence. It describes a southern country not precisely identified, with a political murder as a starting point. It deals with the fate of forgotten people, the oppressed, who are seen as the plague of prosperity. The novel is dominated by the theme of shared suffering that pervades her poetry.

Kirjoitettu kivi and *Fahrenheit 121* belong to the Spanish period in Manner's poetry, containing attitudes to topical events and the state of the world. They continue the voyage of discovery of *Tämä matka* into the ego world of subjective experience: "The world is the poem of my instincts / and ceases when I die." The prose passages in these works are not poetic philosophy but philosophic poetry. Often they mock the conclusions of classical philosophy, as in the poem *Kirjoitettu kivi* (Shoes Are Polished): "You live, you have two children, a wife, a bed, a mangy dog, you live, because it is impossible, you live, because it is impossible." Collections like *niin vaihtuivat vuoden ajat* (1964; So Changed the Seasons) and *Paetkaa purret kevein purjein* (1971; Flee, Boats with Light Sails) are noteworthy above all for their sensitive, reflective nature poetry. In *Kuolleet vedet* the thematic material has definitely deepened: it presents a view of the world in recent times as a living domain of blood and destruction. All the central imagery points the same way, to the rotting of the world, and the process is shown from the point of view of the individual, the family, and the land. The images—"sourceless light," life as a "dream," with "dead waters" around—are variations on the word of the Bible, including the beginning of St. John's Gospel, and contain points of contact with medieval mysticism: "And in the light shone darkness and / the light understood it not."

Manner's most successful play *Uuden vuoden yö* (1965; New Year's Night) describes in almost naturalistic st/ "cultured misery"; *Toukokuun lumi* (1967; Snow in May) stands alongside it. *Poltettu oranssi* (1968; Burnt Orange) exploits psychoanalysis and modern dramatic language: it is a picture of a family hell and the tragedy of a sick young woman.

In a different genre and under a different name, Anna September, Manner has published a cheerful detective novel *Oliko murhaaja enkeli?* (1963; Was the Murderer an Angel?). The same sort of change of tone is seen in poetry with *Kamala kissa* (1976; The Horrible Cat), a masterly book of rhymed sequences and satirical poems in the style of T.S. Eliot's cat poems.

Manner has translated into Finnish *inter alia* the prose of Willy K. Kyrklund, Yasunari Kawabata, and Herman Hesse, Shakespeare's plays and Spanish poetry.

Works

Poetry: *Tämä matka* [This Journey] (1956). *Orfiset laulut* [Orphic Songs] (1960). *Niin vaihtuivat vuoden ajat* [So Changed the Seasons] (1964). *Kirjoitettu kivi* [Written Stone] (1966). *Fahrenheit 121* (1968). *Jos suru savuaisi* [If Sorrow Should Give Smoke] (1968). *Paetkaa purret kevein purjein* [Flee Boats with Light Sails] (1971). *Kamala kissa* [The Horrible Cat] (1976). *Kuolleet vedet* [Dead Waters] (1977). *Runoja* [Poems] (1980). *1956–1977* (1980).

Plays: *Eros ja Psykhe* [Eros and Psyche, verse drama] (1959). *Uuden vuoden yö* [New Year's Night] (1965). *Toukokuun lumi* [Snow in May] (1967). *Poltettu oranssi* [Burnt Orange] (1968). *Varjoon jäänyt unien lähde* [The Source of Dreams Left in Shadow, radio play] (1969). *Vuorilla sataa aina* [In the Mountains It Always Rains, radio play] (1970).

Other: *Kävely musiikkia pienille virtahevoille ja muita harjoituksia* [Walking Music for Small Hippopotami and Other Exercises, prose] (1957). [Anna September, pseud.], *Oliko murhaaja enkeli?* [Was the Murderer an Angel?] (1963). *Varokaa, voittajat* [Beware, Victors, novel] (1972).

Translations: Two poems from *Kamala kissa* [An Awful Cat], tr. Herbert Lomas. Books from Finland 1 (1977). Poems from *Kuolleet vedet* [Dead Waters], intro. Aarne Kinnunen, tr. Herbert Lomas. Books from Finland 4 (1978).

Bibliography

Anhava, Tuomas, "Runon uudistumisesta" [The Renewal of Poetry]. *Suomalainen Suomi* 8 (1956). Kinnunen, Aarne, "Kuolemasta" [On Death]. *Parnasso* 4 (1978). Mäenpää, Anna-Liisa, "Eeva-Liisa Mannerin hevoset" [M.'s Horses]. *Rivien takaa* (1976). Mattila, Pekka, *Anomalioiden osuus Eeva-Liisa Mannerin lyriikassa I-II* [Anomalies in the Poetry of M.] (1972–1974). Sala, Kaarina, "Yhtenäisiä kuvioita" [Combining Images]. *Parnasso* 2 (1964). Tarkka, Auli, "Vangitun muodon murtaminen" [Breaking Imprisoned Form]. *Parnasso* 7 (1968). Tarkka, Pekka, "Eeva-Liisa Manner" *Suomalaisia nykykirjailijoita*. Modern Finnish Writers (1980). Tuohimaa, Sinikka, *Empiirisen minän kokemuksia—Heijastussymboliikka Eeva-Liisa Mannerin tuotannossa* [Experiences of the Empirical Self Reflection Symbolism in the Work of Manner]

(1986). Tuurna, Margu, "Kiinalainen Manner" [Chinese M.]. *Kirjallisuudentutki jain Seuran vuosikirja* 21 [1965].

Lucia Mantu

Born 1888, Iaşi, Romania; died 1971, Bucharest
Genre(s): short story, novel, translation
Language(s): Romanian

Lucia Mantu (née Camelia Nădejde) was a natural science teacher whose lively short story volumes—*Miniaturi* (1923; Miniatures) and *Instantanee* (1945; Snapshots) brought to the readers' ears unforgettably humorous street dialogues from the old city of Iaşi. Her readers learn to appreciate the richly orchestrated monologues poured by Bulgarian, Russian or Jewish carriage drivers over the heads of their silent clients; admire the elegant exchange between talkative beggars, who obligingly deduct the rightful amount of charity from your money, giving you back the change, and the polite passers-by who never hurry; and listen to the news that the Bucovina peasant maids working in Iaşi pass to each other with the preciseness and harsh concision of a TV journal *avant la lettre*.

Her novel *Cucoana Olimpia* (1924; Ma'am Olimpia) is a lucid case study of the stereotypical existence of a provincial housewife while *Umbre chinezeşti. Romane în fragmente* (1930; Chinese Shadows. Fragment Novels) resulted from conflating novelistic and short story structures.

Lucia Mantu was a regular contributor to *Adevărul literar şi artistic*, *Revista Fundaţiilor Regale*, and *Viaţa românească* as well as a skilled translator from Russian into Romanian.

Works

Miniaturi [Miniatures] (1923). *Cucoana Olimpia* [Ma'am Olimpia] (1924). *Umbre chinezeşti. Romane în fragmente* [Chinese Shadows. Fragment Novels] (1930). *Instantanee* [Snapshots] (1945).

Bibliography

Călinescu, G., *Istoria literaturii române*. Compendiu (Bucharest, 1968), p. 300. Miller-Verghi, Margareta and Ecaterina Săndulescu, *Evoluţia scrisului feminin în România* (Bucharest, 1935), p. 441. Perpessicius, "Lucia Mantu: *Umbre chinezeşti, romane în fragmente*," In Perpessicius, *Menţiuni critice*, Vol. 3 (Bucharest, 1936), pp. 252–253. Piru, Al, *Panorama deceniului literar românesc 1940–1950*. (Bucharest, 1968), pp. 283–285.

Sanda Golopentia

Gianna Manzini

Born 1896, Pistoia, Italy; died 1974, Rome
Genre(s): novel, short story, memoirs, journalism
Language(s): Italian

Manzini graduated from the University of Florence with a degree in modern literature and soon began an active collaboration with the prestigious *Solaria* and *Letteratura*. These two Florentine journals were attentive to the new European fiction and to formal values: not surprisingly, Manzini showed an early preference for the stream-of-consciousness technique and a continued attention to style. In 1945–46, she directed *Prosa*, a review of international contemporary fiction. Throughout her long, productive career as a writer, Manzini enjoyed a continuous critical acclaim.

Her first work, *Tempo innamorato* (1928; Time of Love), revealed a novelist with a strong lyrical vein, a figurative style, and a keen perception of unusual sensations and emotions. The story line is fractured by a free association of reminiscences and by the search of spiritual affinities among characters, of correspondences between people and the landscapes in which they live. These qualities explain her preference for the shorter narrative form. In the best stories of *Incontro col falco* (1929; Encounter with the Falcon), *Boscovivo* (1932; Boscovivo), *Un filo di brezza* (1936; A Slight Breeze), *Rive remote* (1940; Distant Shores), *Venti racconti* (1941; Twenty Stories), *Forte come un leone* (1944; Strong as a Lion), we find autobiographical recollections of rare inner experiences, where a precious, metaphorical style turns the narrative line into a proliferation of dream-like, almost surrealistic images.

Manzini's capacity to harmonize symbolic effects and psychological states is well exemplified by *Il valzer del diavolo* (1953; The Devil's Waltz), in which the recurring presence of a cockroach becomes linked to the protagonist's new awareness of her morbid and overpowering dedication to others. In the novel, *La sparviera* (1956; The Sparrow-Hawk), a recurring cough that afflicts the main character over a period of many years, soon develops into a nightmarish awareness of something alive, hidden, and destructive. The man's bouts with the illness are intertwined with the occasional appearances in his life of a woman who exercises on him a strangely exhilarating effect. Finally he succumbs to his illness, willingly facing a death which takes on the mysterious face of his enchantress. Thanks to Manzini's controlled technique and her vivid description of threshold perceptions, the character's pathological state becomes emblematic of human existence, whereby a hazardous condition is transformed into an irresistible presence.

What makes Manzini's work unique is her capacity to sustain a prose style of continuous analogical transformations as well as to analyze feelings and moral states that imperceptibly turn into something unexpected. In *È un' altra cosa* (1961; Another Thing) the object of analysis is a writer's dilemma of compromising with his conscience and creativity or remaining faithful to himself and thus antagonizing his wife, who wishes him to adapt to the values of society and the tastes of the general public. Moral and psychological revelations are more explicitly handled in the autobiographical novel *Ritratto in piedi* (1971; Standing Portrait). This is the author's confession of her slowly coming to terms with her hidden affection for her father, whose character and principles are brought to life by her reminiscences. An anarchist who disapproved of private property and the exploitation of other human beings, Signor Manzini rejected all compromises with the bourgeois way of life and lived a lonely existence as a watch repairman. Later he faced Fascist persecution and death by the hand of a gang of Fascist youths. Manzini recollects her visits to the mountain village where her father was exiled, his participation in the Spanish civil war, his coming together with other anarchists in preparation of an international congress and, finally, her own college days, where new experiences blurred all concerns for her persecuted father. In all, a moving confession of filial appreciation for a downtrodden, peaceful man who had, in fact, renounced affections and comforts out of his own sense of love and social justice.

Although many Italian critics have praised her artistic achievements, Manzini has failed to capture the interest of the large public, and foreign publishers have generally ignored her. She stands out, however, as an innovative stylist and a masterful practitioner of psychological analysis.

Works

Tempo innamorato (1928). *Incontro col falco* (1929). *Boscovivo* (1932). *Un filo di brezza* (1936). *Rive remote* (1940). *Venti racconti* (1941). *Forte come un leone* (1944). *Carta d'identità* (1945). *Lettera all'editore* (1946). *Forte come un leone e altri racconti* (1947). *Ho visto il tuo cuore* (1950). *Cara prigione* (1951). *Animali sacri e profani* (1953). *Il valzer del diavolo* (1953). *Foglietti* (1954). *La sparviera* (1956). *Arca di Noè* (1960). *È un'altra cosa* (1961). *Il cielo addosso* (1963). *Album di ricordi* (1964). *Allegro con disperazione* (1965). *Ritratto in piedi* (1971). *Sulla soglia* (1974).

Bibliography

Bigongiari, P., *Prosa per il Novecento* (Florence, 1970), pp. 85–93. Bo, C., *Nuovi studi* (Florence, 1946), pp. 77–92. Cecchi, E., *Di giorno in giorno* (Milan, 1954), pp. 177–180. Contini, G., "G.M." *Schedario di scrittori italiani moderni e contemporanei* (Florence, 1978), pp. 118–119. Montale, E., "Il libro di cui si parla." *La fiera letteraria* (August 5, 1928). Panareo, E., *Invito alla lettura di Gianna Manzini* (Milan, 1977). Russo, L. *I narratori (1850–1957)* (Milan-Messina, 1958), pp. 362–363. Seroni, A., *Esperimenti critici sul Novecento letterario* (Milan, 1967), pp. 69–72. Sobrero, O., *I Contemporanei*, II (Milan, 1963). Tecchi, B., "Incontro col falco." *Solaria* IV, 6 (1929): 53–58. Varese, C., *Cultura letteraria contemporanea* (Pisa, 1951), pp. 243, 258, 267, 280.

Rinaldina Russell

Dacia Maraini

Born 1936, Florence, Italy
Genre(s): short story, novel, poetry,
*   journalism, drama*
Language(s): Italian

The daughter of a famous ethnologist (father) and painter (mother), Maraini spent the first several years of her life in Japan where, during World War II, she and her family were placed in a concentration camp for two years. She returned to Italy in 1946 and now lives in Rome. In the late fifties and early sixties, Maraini came into contact with several writers of the avant-garde group later known as "Gruppo 63." She published two short stories in the prestigious journal *Nuovi Argomenti*, directed by Alberto Moravia, before publishing, in 1962, her first novel, *La vacanza* (The Vacation). Her second novel, *L'età del malessere* (The Age of Uneasiness), was published in 1963 and won the prestigious Formentor prize. Her first collection of poetry, *Crudeltà all'aria aperta* (Cruelty in the Open), which appeared in 1966, reflects her involvement with the avant-garde. During the sixties, Maraini became active in theater; in 1969 she founded the Theater of Centocelle, an activist, populist group dedicated to presenting theatrical works to the working classes of Rome's poor neighborhoods. Her interest in feminism led to the founding, in 1973, of the feminist theatrical association, La Maddalena. Throughout the seventies Maraini's work reflected her continuing commitment to feminism; *Donne mie* (My Women), a collection of poetry published in 1974, and *Donna in guerra* (Woman at War), a novel of 1975, both center on such feminist issues as women's education, sexuality, and abortion. Both these works and her most recent ones are highly autobiographical and reveal Maraini's belief in the usefulness of self-analysis to the development and liberation of women.

Maraini's early novels are realistic portrayals of a young girl's sexual and moral evolution. Her poetry, prose, and theatrical works all reveal her dedication to the issues of female self-awareness and artistic expression. Maraini's writings are essentially anti-literary; instead of beautiful form and elegant language, they rely on the colloquial style of diaries and letters. This preference is ideologically motivated; in the poem "Le poesie delle donne" (Women's Poetry) she declares: "A woman who writes poetry and knows that /she is a woman can only make herself stick /closely to the subject because sophistication /of form is something that goes with power /and the power a woman has is always a /non-power, a burning inheritance never wholly hers." The confessional quality of her recent books (as in *Storia di Piera* [1980; Piera's Story] and *Lettere a Marina* [1981; Letters to Marina]) has moved her writing even closer to non-fictional *reportage*, in which "sophistication of form" is almost entirely sacrificed to "sticking to the subject." Maraini's writing overall can be seen, then, more as an instrument of investigation and existential liberation than as an aesthetic re-working of experience.

Works

Narrative: *La vacanza* [The Vacation] (1962). *L'età del malessere* [The Age of Uneasiness] (1963). *A memoria* (1967). *Mio marito* (1968). *Memorie di una ladra* (1973). *Donna in guerra* [Woman at War] (1975). [With Piera Degli Esposti], *Storia di Piera* [Piera's Story] (1980). *Lettere a Marina* [Letters to Marina] (1981). *Isolina* (1985).

Poetry: *Crudeltà all'aria aperta* [Cruelty in the Open] (1966). *Donne mie* [My Women] (1974). *Mangiami pure* (1978). *Dimenticare di dimenticare* (1982).

Theater: *Il ricatto a teatro e altre commedie* (1970). *Viva l'Italia* (1973). *Fare teatro* (1974). *La donna perfetta* (1975). *Il cuore di una vergine* (1975). *Don Juan* (1976). *I sogni di Clitennestra e altre commedie* (1981). *Lezioni d'amore e altre commedie* (1982).

Translations: *The Age of Malaise*, tr. Frances Frenaye (1963). *The Holiday*, tr. Stuart Hood (1966). *Memoirs of a Female Thief*, tr. Nina Rootes (1973). Anthologized in *The Defiant Muse: Italian Feminist Poems from the Middle Ages to the Present*, Beverly Allen, Muriel Kittel, Keala Jane Jewell, eds. (1986). *Woman at War*, tr. Mara Benetti and Elspeth Spottiswood (1989).

Bibliography

Nozzoli, A., *Tabù e coscienza. La condizione femminile nella letteratura italiana del Novecento* (Florence, 1978). Zagarrio, G., *Febbre, furore e fiele* (Milan, 1983).

General references: *Dizionario della letteratura italiana contemporanea* (Florence, 1973). Luti,

Giorgio, ed., *Narratori italiani del secondo Novecento: La vita, le opere, la critica* (Rome, 1985).

Rebecca West

Susana March

Born 1918, Barcelona, Spain
Genre(s): novel, short story, poetry
Language(s): Spanish

As a novelist and poet, March is bitterly critical of oppressive social conventions related to class and gender. Although the writer describes her style as *intimista*, the personal almost invariably signals the political in her work. The focus of her first novel, *Algo muere cada día* (1955; Something Dies Every Day) portrays the gradual destruction of a relationship by social forces. In *Cosas que pasan* (1983; Things That Happen), March presents a series of situations in which personal relationships are either stifled or destroyed by society. Although the man is damaged by social requirements and restraints, it is the woman who is ultimately the victim— occasionally of violence—in these short stories. Failed communication between the sexes is a frequent theme in March's poetry that has not gone unnoticed in Spain. The author of *Rutas* (1938; Routes), *Poemas de la plazuela* (1948; Poems from the Little Plaza), *Ardiente voz* (1946; The Burning Voice), *El viento* (1951; The Wind), March was awarded the prestigious Premio Adonais in 1953 for *La tristeza* (Sadness). A personal vision of time, aging, and mortality is articulated with strength and lyric grace in March's poetry. *Poemas (1938–1966)* (1966) includes selections from the poet's previous collections. March is also the co-author (with her husband Ricardo Fernández de la Reguera) of a series of historical novels entitled *Episodios nacionales contemporáneos* (Contemporary National Episodes).

Works

Algo muere cada día (1955). *Ardiente voz* (1946). *Cosas que pasan* (1983). *El viento* (1951). *La tristeza* (1953). *Poemas (1938–1966)* (1966). *Poemas de la plazuela* (1948). *Rutas* (1938).

Bibliography

Flores, A. and K., *Poesía feminista del mundo hispánico* (1984). Galerstein, C., ed., *Women Writers of Spain* (1986). Manrique de Lara, J.G., *Poetas sociales españoles* (1974).

Barbara Dale May

Concha de Marco

Born 1916, Soria, Spain
Genre(s): poetry, short story, essay,
guidebook, translation
Language(s): Spanish

This writer, educated in the natural sciences, has been hailed as the "most important feminine voice to emerge in the 1960s," according to Emilio Miró in an article published in the *Revista de la Universidad Complutense*. Marco was awarded the Juan Ramón Jiménez critical prize for the collection of poems entitled *Tarot* in 1973. Her poetry expresses a deep understanding of the depths of human suffering as well as the heights of human dignity and aspiration. Her poetic vision encompasses a broad historical and cultural perspective, yet her unique personal warmth is always present. Overall, her work is intelligent, sensitive, and imaginative. Marco has travelled extensively and was a Visiting Professor at the University of Puerto Rico. She has published articles in the journal *Insula* and collaborated with her husband on travel guidebooks.

Works

Poetry: *Hora 0,5* [Zero Hour, Thirty Minutes] (1966). *Diario de la mañana* [Morning Edition] (1967). *Acta de identificación* [Certificate of Identification] (1969). *Congreso en Maldoror* [Convention in Maldoror] (1970). *Tarot* [Tarot] (1972, 1973?). *Las Hilanderas* [The Spinners] (1973). *Una noche de invierno* [A Winter's Night] (1974). *Cantos del compañero muerto* [Songs of a Dead Comrade] (n.d.). Essays: *Veinticinco años de poesía femenina española* [Twenty-Five Years of Spanish Poetry by Women] (1969). *La mujer española del Romanticismo, estudios biográficos* [The Spanish Woman in Romanticism, Biographical Studies] (1969). Guidebooks: *Guía de Soria* [Guide to Soria] (1971, 1976, 1978, 1980, 1981).

Bibliography

Miró, E., "Poetisas españolas contemporáneas." *Revista de la Universidad Complutense* XXIV, No. 95 (enero-febrero 1975): 271–310. *Women Writers of Spain*, ed. C. Galerstein (1986).

Paula T. Irvin

Margaret of Austria

Born January 10, 1480, Brussels, Belgium;
*   died December 1, 1530, Malines*
Genre(s): letters, poetry
Language(s): French

Although this daughter of an Austrian prince, Maximilian, and a Burgundian duchess, Mary, seemed destined for a brilliant future, the misfortunes of her early life would have ruined a less sturdy character. These led her to adopt the motto *Fortune Infortune Fort Une*, which may be understood to mean that the variations of Fortune can torment sorely.

Married at the age of two to the French dauphin, the future Charles VIII, she was rejected when a marriage with Anne of Brittany seemed to have more to offer France. This rejection inspired in her a life-long hatred of France. A subsequent marriage to the heir to the Spanish throne, Juan of Castille, was cut short by the prince's premature death, but in Spain she learned her first lessons in diplomacy. A third marriage, to Philibert of Savoy, was arranged for her in 1501, but this, too, was ended by the prince's unexpected death three years later. Thereafter she refused all further suggestions of marriage and turned her attention to other ways of serving her family and their interests. In addition, she became a patroness of the arts, musician and builder, as well as the guardian and educator of several royal children, her nieces and nephew, whose destinies were important.

The center of these activities was the court she established in Malines, midway between Brussels and Antwerp. There she assembled an art collection and a library and surrounded herself with artists and men of letters. With her courtiers she made music and wrote poetry as a respite from the political administration that dominated her life. Her public life is recorded in the letters which she exchanged, first of all with her father,

by now the Holy Roman Emperor, and later with her ambassadors, her political rivals and, eventually, with her nephew Charles, King of Spain and, in his turn, Holy Roman Emperor. Many of these letters have been published, though others remain in manuscript. Their number is impressive and their contents reveal their writer's vitality, industry, adaptability and practicality. From 1507 until her death, she governed what is now Belgium, northern France, and Holland.

Margaret's albums of poetry and many of her books still exist, along with inventories of her art collection. Two of the albums include musical scores and painted decorations as well as poetry. She was the patroness of such painters as Baren Van Orly, Jacopo de Barberi and Jean Gossaert; she admired Erasmus, lending him one of her most precious manuscripts for his translation of the New Testament. In view of such tastes, it is curious that she preferred medieval poetic forms and the sort of poetic contests that were popular in a much earlier day.

Margaret's greatest diplomatic triumph was undoubtedly the Treaty of Cambrai in 1529, also known as the Ladies' Peace, which she negotiated for Charles V with her former sister-in-law, Louise of Savoy, who was representing her son, the French King Francis I. The animosity between the two rulers had been great, sharpened by competition for the Imperial crown and, even more, because of Francis I's capture by the imperial troops in Pavia in 1525 and subsequent imprisonment by the Emperor Charles in Madrid. Although released by the Treaty of Madrid in January 1526, the French King violated his part of the agreement, so it was expedient for the two ladies to try to arrange something better. Through Margaret's skill and intelligence, the new treaty, signed on August 3, 1529, was almost entirely favorable to her nephew, Charles.

The years of struggles to support his ambition had, however, taken their toll on Margaret. Although only fifty, her health declined so greatly that she died on the first day of December 1530. Her final letter to her nephew, dictated the day before, is a model of devotion and sorrowful leavetaking.

It was two more years before the memorial church she had been building for her husband at Brou was finished and she could finally be taken there to join him. In that lovely church, she lies in a tomb on two levels where she is represented in her worldly robes of state, and beneath this there is a simply clad recumbent figure prepared to meet her Maker.

Works

Correspondance de Marguerite d'Autriche et de ses ambassadeurs à la cour de France concernant l'exécution du Traité de Cambrai [The Correspondence of Margaret of Austria and Her Ambassadors to the Court of France Concerning the Execution of the Treaty of Cambrai] (1935). Albums Poétiques de Marguerite d'Autriche [The Poetical Albums of Margaret of Austria] (1934). Correspondance de L'Empereur Maximilian Iᵉʳ et de Marguerite d'Autriche sa fille, gouvernante des Pays Bas [The Correspondence of the Emperor Maximilian I and Margaret of Austria, His Daughter, the Governor of the Low Countries] (1840). Gedichte Margarethes von Ossterreich [Poems of Margaret of Austria] (1954). Correspondance de Marguerite d'Autriche, gouvernante des Pays-Bas, avec ses amis sur les affaires des Pays-Bas de 1405 à 1528 [The Correspondence of Margaret of Austria, Governor of the Low Countries, with Her Friends on the Affairs of the Low Countries from 1405 to 1528] (1842–1847).

Bibliography

Bruchet, Max, Marguerite d'Autriche, Duchesse de Savoie (Lille, 1927). De Boom, Ghislaine, Marguerite d'Autriche-Savoie et la Pré-Renaissance (Brussels-Paris, 1935). De Iongh, Jane, Margaret of Austria, Regent of the Netherlands, tr. M.D. Herter Norton (New York, 1958). Strelka, Josef, Der Burgundische Renaissance Margarethes von Osterreich und seine Literarhistorische Bedeutung (Vienna, 1957). Tremayne, Eleanor, The First Governess of the Netherlands, Margaret of Austria (London, 1908).

Charity C. Willard

Leonhard Marholm

(see: Laura Marholm-Hansson)

Laura Marholm-Hansson

(a.k.a. Leonhard Marholm)

Born May 1, 1854, Riga, Latvia, the Soviet Union; died 1928, Riga
Genre(s): drama, novel, novella, feuilleton
Language(s): German

The works of Laura Marholm are strongly influenced by the interest in physiological determinism and the psychology of sex which flourished in the 1890s, culminating in the writings of Sigmund Freud. Marholm was not only influenced by these intellectual currents, but her writings also contributed considerable fuel for the continuing debates.

Marholm was born Laura Mohr to a Danish father and a German-speaking mother. During her youth in Riga, she wrote some historical dramas and novellas under the name Leonhard Marholm. In 1886, Marholm moved to Copenhagen to learn Danish and to study with Georg Brandes. Marholm was able to support herself in Copenhagen and also in subsequent years by writing feuilletons for German newspapers. In 1889, Marholm and her new husband, the Swedish author Ola Hansson, moved to Friedrichshagen outside of Berlin where they took active part in the Freie Bühne circle, whose ranks included Gerhard Hauptmann, Arno Holz, Johannes Schlaff, Bruno Wille, and Wilhelm Bölsche, among others.

In 1893, the Hanssons left Friedrichshagen and moved to Schliersee in Bavaria. The move to Schliersee initiated the most productive phase in Marholm's career. In three years, Marholm published six major works. The first of these, Das Buch der Frauen (1895; Modern Women, 1896), became a bestseller and was translated into six European languages. In Modern Women, Marholm studies the fates of six famous women and seeks to illustrate that women cannot find contentment solely through the pursuit of intellectual careers. Full utilization of "feminine nature" only occurs in the roles of wife and mother. Conservative critics found shocking Marholm's claim that women have a sex drive and feminist critics objected to what they perceived as Marholm's reduction of women to physical, not intellectual beings. Das Buch der

Frauen, as well as Marholm's subsequent writings, received considerable attention from prominent theorists on the psychology of sex, including Havelock Ellis and Iwan Bloch. Marholm's novella "Was war es?" (What Was It?) from Zwei Frauenerlebnisse (1895; The Experiences of Two Women) shows Marholm at her narrative best. Drawn from Marholm's own experiences during her Copenhagen years, the lengthy novella presents an even-handed portrait of a single, independent woman from the end of the nineteenth century. Critics praised the novella for its keen observations and "feminine realism."

In 1898, Marholm and her husband converted to Catholicism and moved to Munich. Her conversion strongly colors her writings in the immediate years to follow. Of these later writings, the novella "Im Bann" from Der Weg nach Altötting und andere Novellen (1900; The Path to Altötting and Other Stories) stands out for its psychological complexity. A young woman lays the imagined or perhaps real specter of her mother to rest by confessing her mother's sins to a stern Catholic priest.

For both of the Hanssons, the years after the turn of the century were marked by severe financial, legal, and physical hardships which resulted in Marholm's acute case of paranoia. In 1905, Marholm was arrested by the Munich police and committed to a mental hospital. After this ordeal, Marholm wrote very little until after WWI, when she began writing articles in favor of socialism. After the death of her husband in 1925, Marholm returned to her native Riga where she died in 1928.

Laura Marholm's works have subsequently fallen into obscurity, but she exerted a considerable influence on the authors and scientists of her day. Her life and her authorship provide revealing insights into the status of women at the end of the nineteenth century.

Works

Gertrud Lindenstern (1878). Patkuls Tod (1880). Frau Marianne (1882). Das Buch der Frauen (1895). Wir Frauen und unsere Dichter (1895). Karla Bühring (1895). Zwei Frauenerlebnisse (1895). Frau Lilly als Jungfrau, Gattin, und Mutter (1897). Zur Psychologie der Frau, Theil I (1897). Der Weg nach Altötting und andere Novellen (1900). Die Frauen in der socialen Bewegung (1900). Das Buch der Toten (1900). Zur Psychologie der Frau, Theil II (1903).

English Translations: Modern Women, tr. Hermione Ramsden (1896). We Women and our Authors, tr. Hermione Ramsden (1899). The Psychology of Women, tr. Georgia A. Etchinson (1899).

Bibliography

Brantly, Susan, "The Life and Writings of Laura Marholm: A Portrait from the Fin de Siècle in Northern Europe." Diss., Yale University, 1987. Holm, Ingvar, "Laura Marholm." Ola Hansson. En studie i åttitalsromantik (Malmö, 1957), pp. 209–222. Scott-Jones, Marilyn, "Laura Marholm and the Question of Female Nature," in Beyond the Eternal Feminine, eds. Susan L. Cocalis and Kay Goodman (Stuttgart, 1982).

Susan Brantley

Marie de France

Supposed period of literary activity: c. 1160–c.1215

Genre(s): the Breton lay (the narrative lay), fables, saint's life

Language(s): Old French (Anglo-Norman dialect)

Marie de France has long been recognized as the first woman writer in the French language. The details of her life are few and not clear: she is thought to have been born in France, yet lived in England, supposedly at the time of Henry II Plantagenet and of Aliénor d'Aquitaine, perhaps even at their court. From her works one learns that she knew English and Latin, and that she knew something of the geography of both England and Normandy. She also shows her concern to be known as a writer by those who follow her; indeed, she even mentions long evening hours spent in poetic composition.

For about two hundred years scholars have maintained that Marie de France (so named since the first publication of her Fables in 1581 by Claude Fauchet, in Paris) is the author of at least three works, each written in octosyllabic rimed couplets. In the order of composition indicated by Marie herself, these works are: a group of twelve narrative poems that editors have called

Lais, preceded by a general Prologue; a collection of one hundred and two fables, or an *Isopet*, translated from the English, whose author Marie mistakenly identifies as King Alfred; finally, an *Espurgatoire de Seint Patriz*, based upon a Latin text by the monk Henry of Saltrey. Such an ordering points to a transition from the secular to the religious, or as one recent editor has noted, there is "a progression from entertainment through moralization to edification" (Ewert, *Lais*, vii).

Marie de France's literary activity is generally thought to date from c. 1160 to c. 1215. It is remarkable that each one of the works, created when most literary productions remained anonymous, is signed by a "Marie." In the beginning lines of the *lai* of *Guigemar*, the first narrative in Harley ms. 978, the author refers to herself as "Marie, / Ki en sun tens pas ne s'oblie"; in the Epilogue to the *Fables* she speaks of herself as "Marie ai nun, si sui de France"; and in the *Espurgatoire*, she both names herself and declares her literary purpose: "Jo, Marie, ai mis en memoire, / Le livre de l'Espurgatoire: / En Romanz, qu'il seit entendables / A laie gent e covenables."

The process of attribution of the three works mentioned took place over the course of several hundred years. Today, in spite of several recent attempts to discredit her authorship of all the *lais* in Harley ms. 978 (the earliest ms. and the only one to contain all twelve narratives, plus the Prologue and the *Fables*), the majority of researchers believe Marie de France to be the sole author of the three works. Furthermore, in 1974, the scholar Emanuel Mickel, Jr., when referring to specific similarities between the attributed works and *la Vie Seinte Audree*, strongly suggested that Marie is also the translator of that particular saint's life (*Marie de France*, 16).

Attempts to identify Marie de France with a known historical person have led to such suggestions as the figures of Marie de Champagne; Marie de Compiègne; Marie, daughter of Count Galeran of Meulan and his wife, Agnès; Mary, the Abbess of Barking; Mary, the illegitimate daughter of Geoffrey of Anjou, and sister of Henry II, who became the Abbess of Shaftesbury; and Mary, Abbess of Reading. The most likely identification is that of the Abbess of Shaftesbury, given the knowledge of contemporary court and legal matters shown by the poet. Marie de France's identification with the Abbess of Reading is not to be discounted, however, for ms. H. was probably executed at that Abbey. As for the poet's birthplace, it is now accepted that the phrase "de France" refers not to the royal family of France, but to her country of origin. The exact region of her birth is unknown. Mickel, when summing up the localities possible, mentions the wide acceptance that Marie was "probably a native of the Ile-de-France area or of Norman territory in close proximity" (*Marie de France*, 17).

That the *Lais*, thought to be dedicated to either King Henry II or to his son Henry, the Young King, were known to and loved by Marie's courtly contemporaries is undisputable. In his work, *La Vie Seint Edmund le Rei*, Denis Piramus offers a detailed reference to a *Dame Marie* who composed *vers de lais*. Further attestations to Marie's popularity and to the popularity of the genre of the narrative *lai breton* are the translations of the *Lais*, made during the Middle Ages, into Old Norse, Middle English, and Middle High German. There were, moreover, adaptations, "imitations and exploitations" as well as "explicit references" to Marie that were written in Old French (Ewert, *Lais*, xviii).

The reasons for the popularity of the *Lais* are self-evident: the theme of these narrative poems is love, shown in multiple varieties. The stories contain penetrating psychological insights, sharply delineated character portraits, folkloric themes and motifs (e.g., the man with two wives), elements of the *matière de Bretagne* (e.g., King Arthur, his queen and court; Tristan and Iseut), fantasy, a discriminating use of place and description, adventure, and symbolism. A *lai* is often constructed around an image or a symbol which may, in the course of the narration, accrete unto itself more and more meanings. In addition, Marie uses certain narrative themes or motifs (e.g. the wife unhappily married to a jealous husband), either primary or secondary, within an individual plot. Within the group of twelve poems, the reader will discern repetition of the themes and motifs, sometimes multiple repetitions, yet each time with a significant variation. Marie's *Lais* appeal to those who appreciate the art of a highly self-conscious story-teller. Today, many translations in a number of modern languages are available, with new translations being published almost yearly.

Although a renewed scholarly attention to Marie de France's works, begun some twenty years ago, has focused principally upon the *Lais* (five extant manuscripts), the *Fables* (twenty-three extant manuscripts) are currently beginning to receive the attention they merit. It is hoped that the studies of the late Marjorie Malvern will, in published form, reach a wider audience. The *Espurgatoire de Seint Patriz* (one manuscript only) has received the least scrutiny, in spite of its relation of a descent into Hell antedating that of Dante the poet.

Whether or not Marie de France is the creator of the novelistic genre, as is claimed by some critics, most assuredly she belongs to that group of twelfth-century tellers of tales (Thomas d'Angleterre and Chrétien de Troyes) who gave impetus to the appearance of the genre. That her influence is still felt in the twentieth century is clear from the words of John Fowles, perhaps the most significant creative writer in England today. In his collection of tales, *The Ebony Tower*, where one also finds repetitions and variations of themes, Fowles poignantly acknowledges his debt to Marie de France, saying:

> One may smile condescendingly at the naïveties and primitive technique of stories such as *Eliduc*; but I do not think any writer of fiction can do so with decency—and for a very simple reason. He is watching his own birth.

Works

(Listed in chronological order, according to Marie's own words): *Lais*; *Fables*, or *Isopet* (translation from English); *Espurgatoire de Seint Patriz* (translation from Latin text written in England).

Bibliography

Burgess, Glyn S., and Keith Busby, eds., *The Lais of Marie de France* (New York, 1986). Ewert, Alfred, and Ronald C. Johnston, eds., *Fables* (Oxford [Blackwell's French Texts], 1942; rpt. Oxford, 1966). Ewert, Alfred, ed., *Lais* (Oxford [Blackwell's French Texts], 1944; rpt. Oxford, 1965). Fauchet, Claude, *Recueil de l'origine de la langue et poésie françoise: ryme et romans, plus les noms et sommaire des oeuvres de CXXVI poètes François vivans avant l'an M.CCC* (Paris, 1581, rpt. Geneva, 1972). Ferrante, Joan M., and Robert W. Hanning, eds., *The Lais of Marie de France*. Foreword by John Fowles (New York, 1978). Jenkins, Thomas A., *Marie de France: Espurgatoire Seint Patriz, an Old French Poem of the Twelfth Century Published with an Introduction and a Study of the Language of the Author* (Philadelphia, 1894, rpt. Geneva, 1974). Jonin, Pierre, ed., *Les Lais de Marie de France* (Paris, 1979). Martin, Marylou, ed., *The Fables of Marie de France: An English Translation* (Birmingham, Ala., 1984). Warnke, Karl, ed., *Das Buch vom Espurgatoire S. Patrice der Marie de France und seine Quelle* (Halle, 1938). Warnke, Karl, ed., *Die Fabeln der Marie de France* (Halle, 1898, rpt. Geneva, 1974). Warnke, Karl, ed., *Die Lais der Marie de France, mit vergleichenden Anmerkungen von Reinhold Köhler* (Halle, 1925, 3rd ed.; rpt. Geneva, 1974).

Secondary Sources: Ashby-Beech, Genette, "Les *Fables* de Marie de France: Essai de grammaire narrative," in *Épopée animale, fable, fabliau*, Bianciotto, Gabriel and Michel Salvat, eds. (Paris, 1984), pp. 13–29. Baum, Richard, *Recherches sur les oeuvres attribuées à Marie de France* (Heidelberg, 1968). Brightenback, Kristine, "Remarks on the *Prologue* to Marie de France's *Lais*." *Romance Philology* 30 (1976–1977): 168–177. Bruckner, Matilda Tomaryn, "Repetition and Variations in Twelfth-Century Romance," in *The Expansion and Transformations of Courtly Literature*, Nathaniel B. Smith and Joseph T. Snow, eds. (Athens, Ga., 1980), pp. 95–114. Burgess, Glyn S., Marie de France: *An Analytical Bibliography* (London, 1977). Burgess, Glyn S., *Marie de France: Bibliographical Supplement No. 1* (London, 1986). Damon, S. Foster, "Marie de France: Psychologist of Courtly Love." *Publications of the Modern Language Association of America* 44 (1929): 968–996. Donovan, Mortimer J., *The Breton Lay: A Guide to Varieties* (Notre Dame, Ind., 1969). Eberwein, Elena, "Die *Aventure* in der altfranzösischen *Lais*." *Zur Deutung mittelalterlichen Existenz* (Bonn and Cologne, 1933), pp. 27–53. Ferguson, Mary H., "Folklore in the *Lais* of Marie de France." *The Romanic Review* 57 (1966): 3–24. Ferrante, Joan M., *Woman as Image in Medieval Literature from the Twelfth Century to Dante* (New York and London, 1975). Foulet, Lucien, "Marie de France et les lais bretons." *Zeitschrift für romanische Philologie* 29 (1905):

293–322. Foulet, Lucien, "Marie de France et la légende du Purgatoire de Saint Patrice." *Romanische Forschungen* 22 (1908): 599–627. Freeman, Michelle A., "Marie de France's Poetics of Silence: The Implications for a Feminine *Translatio*." *Publications of the Modern Language Association of America* 99 (5) (Oct. 1984): 860–883. Frey, John A., "Linguistic and Psychological Couplings in the Lays of Marie de France." *Studies in Philology* 61 (1964): 3–18. Hieatt, Constance B., "*Eliduc* Revisited: John Fowles and Marie de France." *English Studies in Canada* 3: 351–358. Hunt, Tony, "Glossing Marie de France." *Romanische Forschungen* 86 (1974): 396–418. McCulloch, Florence, "Length, Recitation, and Meaning of the Lais of Marie de France." *Kentucky Romance Quarterly* 25 (1978): pp. 257–268. Ménard, Philippe, *Les Lais de Marie de France* (Paris, 1979). Mickel, Emanuel J., Jr., *Marie de France* (New York, 1974). Mickel, Emanuel J., Jr., "Marie de France's Use of Irony as a Stylistic and Narrative Device." *Studies in Philology* 71 (1974): 265–290. Mickel, Emanuel J., Jr., "A Reconsideration of the *Lais* of Marie de France." *Speculum* 66 (1971): 39–65. Mickel, Emanuel J., Jr., "The Unity and Significance of Marie's *Prologue*." *Romania* 96 (1975): 83–91. Morse, Ruth, "John Fowles, Marie de France, and the Man with Two Wives." *Philological Quarterly* 63 (1) (Winter 1984): 17–30. Owen, D.D.R., *The Vision of Hell: Infernal Journeys in Medieval French Literature* (Edinburgh and London, 1970). Ringger, Kurt, "Die altfranzösischen Verspurgatorien." *Zeitschrift für romanische Philologie* 88 (1972): 389–402. Ringger, Kurt, *Die Lais: zur Struktur der dichterischen Einbildungskraft der Marie de France* (Tübingen, 1973). Ringger, Kurt, "Marie de France und kein Ende." *Zeitschrift für romanische Philologie* 86 (1970): 40–48. Riquer, Martin de, "La *aventure*, el *lai* y el *conte* en María de Francia." *Filologia Romanza* 2 (1955): 1–19. Rothschild, Judith Rice, "John Fowles and *The Ebony Tower*. Marie de France in the Twentieth Century," in *Selected Proceedings of the Twenty-Seventh Annual Mountain Interstate Foreign Language Conference* (Johnson City, Tenn., 1978), pp. 129–135. Rothschild, Judith Rice, "Manipulative Gestures and Behaviors in the *Lais* of Marie de France," in *Spirit of the Court*, Glyn S. Burgess, and Robert A. Taylor, eds. (Selected Proceedings of the Fourth Congress of the International Courtly Literature Society, Toronto 1983) (Cambridge, 1985). Rothschild, Judith Rice, "Marie de France's *Equitan* and *Chaitivel: Fin'amors* or *fabliau*?" in *The Worlds of Medieval Women: Creativity, Influence, and Imagination*, Constance H. Berman, Charles W. Connell, and Judith Rice Rothschild, eds. (Morgantown, W. Va., 1985), pp. 113–121. Rothschild, Judith Rice, *Narrative Technique in the Lais of Marie de France: Themes and Variations*, Vol. I (Chapel Hill, N. C., 1974). Rothschild, Judith Rice, "A *Rapprochement* between *Bisclavret* and *Lanval*." *Speculum* 48 (1973): 78–88. Sienart, Edgard, *Les Lais de Marie de France: Du conte merveilleux à la nouvelle psychologique* (Paris, 1977). Spiegel, Harriet, *Marie de France: Fables* (Toronto, 1987). Spitzer, Leo, "Marie de France— Dichterin von Problem-Märchen." *Zeitschrift für romanische Philologie* 50 (1930): 29–67. Spitzer, Leo, "The Prologue to the *Lais* of Marie de France and Medieval Poetics." *Modern Philology* 41 (1943–1944): 96–102. Sturges, Robert, "Texts and Readers in Marie de France's *Lais*." *Romanic Review* 71 (1980): 244–264. Vitz, Evelyn Birge, "The *Lais* of Marie de France: 'Narrative Grammar' and the Literary Text." *Romantic Review* 74 (1983): 383–404. Watts, Thomas D., Jr., and Raymond J. Cormier, "Towards an Analysis of Certain *Lais* of Marie de France." *Lingua e Stile* 9 (1974): 249–256.

J.R. Rothschild

Marie de l'Incarnation

(see: Marie Guyart)

Marie de Romieu

Born 1556?, Viviers, France
Genre(s): poetry
Language(s): French

Daughter of Estienne Romieu; sister of Jacques de Romieu (1555–1632). Only four copies of Marie's *Les Premieres oeuvres poetiques* (1581), containing her celebrated *Discours que l'excellence de la femme surpasse celle de l'homme*, have survived. The little that is known of her must be cautiously gleaned from her writings, those of her brother Jacques, and from the definitive research of Le Sourd. On the basis of archival studies, the latter has corrected two long-standing attributions, namely that Marie's noble family was related to the Maison de Joyeuse and that she was married and had a son. It now appears that the Romieus—the "de" before the family name was later added on by Jacques—were "de petites gens" (Winandy, 1972), bakers of Vivier. No evidence, indeed Marie is not even mentioned in baptismal documents, points to her marital status. She herself merely refers, in her prefatory letter to her brother, to the cares of "their" household which prevent her from devoting herself fully to the Muses. Marie was probably educated by her brother, a lawyer and canon who became "secretaire de la chambre du Roi." Whether Marie also authored the salacious *Instruction pour les jeunes dames, par la mere et la fille d'alliance, par M.D.R.* (Lyon, 1573), a translation of a piece by A. Piccolomini, remains unsolved. The initials M.D.R. after the title have been variously interpreted as those of Marie, or of her contemporary Madeleine des Roches of Poitiers. It is uncertain whether Marie knew Italian or drew on contemporary translations of Italian authors. The latter is more likely and would indicate that she did not write the Instruction. Furthermore, this work's Ovidian pedagogy does little to anticipate the courtly Neoplatonism of Marie's *Oeuvres*. Marie's discourse on the excellence of women reveals, better than any document, her social and literary aspirations. Adapting a piece by the conservative humanist bookprinter Charles Estienne (1554)—itself a translation of an excerpt from Landi's *Paradossi* (1543)—Marie's contribution is twice removed from its original in detail and in spirit. Where Estienne acclaims woman's ability to manifest her virtues *in spite* of her natural weaknesses, Marie celebrates women's achievements *by virtue* of their sex. Whereas Estienne's heroine is the humble-minded *mulier economica*, Marie's heroines are the famed academiciennes of the Paris Academy, such as the Marechale de Retz and Marguerite de Valois, and members of the royal entourage, such as Catherine de Medicis and her attending ladies. Marie's works testify to the quest for courtly patronage of a lower class but highly learned woman writer. They were dedicated to Marguerite de Lorraine on the oc-casion of her wedding in 1581 to Duc Anne de Joyeuse whose political power extended to Marie's homeland, the Vivarais. Most of her poems are tributes either to court figures during the reign of Henri III, or to local patrons, male family members in positions of authority, and learned ladies. Her works include fifteen different poetic genres ranging from the sonnet to the eclogue, elegy, epitaph, enigma, and *hymne*.

Works

Les Premieres oeuvres poetiques de Ma Damoiselle Marie de Romieu Vivaroise, contenant un brief Discours, Que l'excellence de la femme surpasse celle de l'homme, autant recreatif que plein de beaux exemples (1581), ed. A. Winandy (1972); ed. P. Blanchemain (1878).

Translation: translation of the *Discours* in *The Defiant Muse. French Feminist Poems from the Middle Ages to the Present* (1986), ed. Domna Stanton.

Bibliography

Le Sourd, A., *Recherches sur J. et M. de Romieu* (1934). Feugère, L., *Les Femmes poètes au XVIe siècle* (1861). Raymond, M., *L'Influence de Ronsard sur la poésie française (1550–1585)* II (1927). Richardson, L., *The Forerunners of Feminism in the French Literature of the Renaissance* (1929).

Anne Larsen

Mat' (or Monakhinia) Mariia

(a.k.a. Elizabeta Iur'evna Skobtsova, née Pilenko)

Born 1891, Russia; died March 31, 1945, Ravensbrück, Germany
Genre(s): poetry, criticism
Language(s): Russian

Mat' Mariia was an émigré poet and a vivacious, socially involved woman. Before the Russian revolution in October 1917, she took an active role in the SR party. In 1919, she immigrated to France. Her ardent faith committed her to a life of active Christianity. She became a social worker in the émigré community. She travelled all over the country, visiting her Russian compatriots and giving lectures on literature, Christianity, and social matters.

Mat' Mariia had a tragic life. She was twice married and had children before she took holy orders in Paris. Her daughter left her for the Soviet Union where she soon died. After the Nazi occupation of France, Mat' Mariia did not disguise her anti-German sentiments and activities. She managed to hide and save the lives of many Jews. Her poem, "The Star of David," which was devoted to the persecuted people, circulated and enjoyed great popularity in the underground circles of the Resistance movement. Mat' Mariia was eventually arrested by the Gestapo and was murdered in a gas chamber in Germany at the very end of the war. Her seventeen-year-old son was also deported to a death camp.

Mat' Mariia launched herself as a poet while she was still living in Russia. She developed her style fully, however, in France. In spite of the "Parisian note" of some of her works, her poetry is of a pronouncedly religious nature. In 1927, she published her two-volume *Lives of the Saints*. Her works in the volume entitled *Poems* (1937) treat biblical themes, the question of death, and the figure of the devil. Like many other Russian writers, she regards boredom and indifference as among the greatest evils.

Many of her early poems, two of her mystery plays, and her writings about wartime experiences were published only after her death, in the edition of her former husband, D. E. Skobtsov. Her critical writings about Dostoevsky, V. Soloviev and Blok are also noteworthy. Her poetry is endowed with strong spirituality and is formally traditional. Her life and work exemplify her views and guiding principles.

Works

Ruf' (1916). *Zhatva dukha: Zhitiia sviatykh*, 2 vols. (1927). *Mirosozertsanie V. Solovieva* (1929). *A. Khomiakov* (1929). *Dostoevsky i sovramennost'* (1929). *Stikhi* (1932). "Vstrechi s Blokom." *Sovremennyie zapiski* 62 (1936): 211–228. *Stikhotvoreniia i poemy, misterii. Vospominaniia ob areste i lagere v Ravensbriuk* (1947). *Stikhi* (1949).

Bibliography

Manukhina, T., "Monakhinia Mariia." *Novyi zhurnal* 41 (1955): 137–157. Struve, Gleb, *Russkaia literatura v izgnanii*. (Paris, 1984), pp. 328–329. Velichkovskaia, Tamara, "O poezii Materi Marii." *La Renaissance* 205 (1969).

Peter I. Barta

Louise de Marillac

Born August 12, 1591, Ferrières-en-Brie, France; died March 15, 1660, Paris
Genre(s): letters, devotional writings
Language(s): French

This co-founder of the Filles de la Charité, who later became the patron saint of social workers, began life inauspiciously as the natural daughter of an unknown mother and Louis de Marillac, member of the powerful de Marillac family of France. While her father was alive, she received the basis of an excellent humanist education at the Royal Convent at Poissy where her great-aunt, also a Louise de Marillac and also highly educated, instructed her in theology, philology, Latin, possibly Greek, and oil painting. Upon her father's death, the thirteen-year-old girl was sent to board with a poor spinster in Paris who appears to have run what we would now call an orphanage for abandoned and illegitimate children of the wealthy. An introverted and melancholy child, Louise showed her administrative talents early by organizing an embroidery business to ease the straitened financial situation at her new home. She also continued her studies alone, poring over such books as the writings of Luis of Granada, the *Imitation of Christ*, *La Perle Evangélique*, and the Holy Scripture. This capacity for combining the inner, meditative life with the outer, active life anticipates a major pattern in her life to come.

Although she expressed a keen desire to be a nun, her family vetoed this aspiration on the grounds of her weak health, wedding her instead on February 5, 1613 to Antoine Le Gras, a bourgeois who had risen to the post of the Queen's secretary of the household. In October of the same year, she gave birth to her only son Michel. Her first religious crisis was precipitated in 1623 by the illness of her husband, which she felt to be God's punishment for her failure to become a nun. The crisis was resolved by her first mystical experience, a vision of the Holy Spirit, on Pentecost 1623, an event that helps to explain her later devotion to the Paraclete.

On her husband's death in 1625, she took a vow of perpetual widowhood. Somewhat earlier, she had met St. Vincent de Paul, who now became her spiritual director and who exerted an influence on her that changed the direction of her life. Long a victim of deep spells of depression and occasional attacks of neurasthenia, she desperately needed an outside focus of steady work. She returned to her earlier dream of religious service and expressed to St. Vincent a desire to serve the poor. In return, he sent her on an inspection tour of the Confraternities of Charities, which he had established around Paris to minister to the needs of the destitute. On these trips in the icy open air, the former invalid discovered in herself not only an unexpected physical resilience but also an unsuspected genius for practical administration and a gift for persuasive speaking that drew people naturally to her. Despite the occasional opposition from local clergy, her visits were notable successes. Now forty years old, she dropped her husband's name, formulated a daring plan, and gained Vincent's approval to establish a congregation of women, who would be attached permanently and by vocation to the Charité's goal of serving the poor.

In 1633, she assembled a few peasant girls in her own home to form the first congregation of the new order—the Filles de la Charité. These girls, to whom she gave religious instruction as well as lessons in reading and caring for the sick, were the working servants of the well-born Dames de la Charité. As the order evolved, these gray sisters utilized the donations of the wealthier Dames for a wide range of charitable works. Louise's tireless administration was responsible for the success of such projects as the home for the "Enfants Trouvées," one of the first orphanages and foster children programs to be run along modern lines, and the hospital for the ill in Nantes. In addition, she was deeply concerned with the problem of educating the poor and helped to initiate popular education for the poor girls of Paris. Able to speak to her beggar/pupils in their own language, she also authored her own catechism and prayers.

The work of the Filles did not go unrecognized in Louise's lifetime. There were houses established as far away as Austria and Poland. In 1650, she co-authored a rule for the organization with St. Vincent, and she worked with him to obtain the official approval given in 1655. As a religious society, the Filles were the first congregation of women who were not cloistered but rather instituted to live a secular life of service in the community.

In her declining years, Louise dedicated herself more and more to her inner meditations. An early and enthusiastic supporter of the doctrine of the Immaculate Conception, she consecrated the Filles to this doctrine, making it the first society to be so dedicated in the history of the Church. She died in Paris on March 15, 1660 and was buried under an altar in the motherhouse of the order she had helped establish. Beatified on May 9, 1920, she was canonized on March 11, 1934.

Louise's writings—including her letters, her meditations, and her prayers—reflect a characteristic blending of the active and meditative life. While her style is most adequately described as plain, her French is both correct and clear, and she was able to turn it to persuasive use when the occasion called for it. Her letters to her daughters, to St. Vincent de Paul, and to the Dames de la Charité are both sharp and tender, grittily detailed and full of common sense. Her earlier education and her own familiarity with Luis of Granada, Francis de Sales and other religious figures gave her language a robust precision it never lost, even when she was recording inspirations brought by her habit of meditation. She was also capable of a great range of tones, from the simplicity of her letters to her peasant girls, to the more dense and allusive style in her epistles to St. Vincent and the members of her powerful family.

Unfortunately, it is difficult to delineate a development in her thought because she dated her letters only rarely and her meditations and notes almost not at all. Additionally, editors and other Filles de la Charité have occasionally added passages to her compilations, complicating the picture and obscuring what was originally present. Within the context of Sales and Pascal, however, several significant factors can be identified. Her meditations in particular exhibit a particular devotion to the Resurrection, the Paraclete, and the Immaculate Conception. Likewise, the hidden life of Jesus in the womb exercised a special fascination to the woman who had once been a small orphan, hidden away in a Paris boarding house.

The works of Louise de Marillac attest to a strong and forceful personality that grew from troubled adolescence to a rich and fulfilling adult life. Like many women before her, she was able to overcome the very real limitations of her birth—her illegitimacy as well as her sex—only through the institution of the Church. In return, she devoted her life to that institution and gave to it its first religious society for women that did not necessitate the formal safeguards of convent, enclosure, and distinctive dress. Her words give us a compelling picture of the complex life, both outer and inner, of a woman whose work provided an important stabilizing force in the very society that had threatened to exclude her in her own lifetime.

Works

Histoire de Mademoiselle le Gras, fondatrice des filles de la Charité [The Story of Mademoiselle le Gras, the foundress of the Daughters of Charity] (1883). Conférences aux Filles de la Charité [Conferences with the Daughters of Charity by Vincent de Paul, extracts of her letters] (1902). Violets Culled from the Garden of the Writings of St. Louise (1934). Maximes de la véneration [Maxims of Veneration] (1901).

Bibliography

Calvet, J., Louise de Marillac: A Portrait, tr. G.F. Pullen (New York, 1959). Flinton, M., Sainte Louise de Marillac: l'Aspect social de son oeuvre (Tournai, 1957). Poinsenet, M.D., De l'anxieté à la santeté: Louise de Marillac (Paris, 1958). Richomme, Sainte Louise de Marillac (Paris, 1961). Uglow, Jennifer, The International Dictionary of Women's Biography (New York, 1982).

Glenda Wall

Cella Marin

(see: Cella Serghi)

Benedetta Cappa Marinetti

Born 1899, Rome, Italy; died 1980
Genre(s): novel, poetry
Language(s): Italian

As a young woman Benedetta became a member of the Futurist movement, bringing to it her own spiritual conceptions. In 1926 she published Le forze umane, an "abstract novel" with graphic images accompanying it, a work that bore no relation to the literary production then current among women, and in this manner, she displayed a desire to speak in a newer voice. In 1931 she published Viaggio di Garara, a novel for theater with musical accompaniment. In 1935 she published Astrea e il sottomarino. The wife of founding Futurist F.T. Marinetti, Benedetta also contributed poetry to Italian journals such as "Rassegna Nazionale." Benedetta, accompanied by the other few women writers of the Futurist movement—Rosa Rosa, Eva Kuhn, Enif Robert, Emma Malpillero, Maria Ginanni and Valentine de Saint Point (who penned the "Manifesto della Donna futurista" in 1912)—participated in the general Futurist rebellion against the artistic and literary institutions of their time and contributed to the polemical debate against the most extreme misogynist attitudes of the men in the movement.

Works

Le forze umane (1926). Viaggio di Garara (1931). Astrea e il sottomarino (1935).

Richard J. Pioli

Raïssa Oumansoff Maritain

Born September 12, 1883, Rostov on the Don,
Russia; died November 4, 1960, Paris,
France
Genre(s): poetry, memoirs, literary criticism,
and theological essay
Language(s): French

Raïssa Maritain was born in Russia of an Orthodox Jewish family. To escape persecution, the family immigrated to Paris in 1893. Raïssa was admitted to the Sorbonne at age 16, where she met Jacques Maritain, whom she married in 1904. She and her husband were baptized into the Catholic Church in 1906. They were influenced spiritually by the novelist and Old-Testament style eccentric Léon Bloy and philosophically by Bergson, then lecturer at the Collège de France. But they eventually rejected the anti-intellectual aspects of Bergsonian vitalism and became strong advocates of a return to Thomism. After the fall of France to Hitler, the Maritains moved to Greenwich Village in New York, where Raïssa began writing her memoirs, entitled *Les grandes amitiés* (We've Been Friends Together). They give a detailed, somewhat sentimental account of the Catholic intellectual milieu during the period between the two wars and of her meetings with Péguy, Psicari, Bloy, Rouault, Massis, G. Sorel, and Cocteau. She continued producing works on esthetics, spirituality in the Catholic tradition, translations from the Latin of Thomas Aquinas, and several anthologies of poems.

Raïssa Maritain was a religious poet and a thoughtful commentator on the nature of poetry. In the essay "Sense and Nonsense in Poetry" (in *The Situation of Poetry*), she explores various types of obscurity and clarity and attempts to elucidate the spiritual nature of poetry, rejecting Henri Bremond's assertion that the poet is a mystic *manqué* and allotting to each a distinct role: the poet is the imitator of God the Creator, while the mystic (or saint, or contemplative) passes from expression to formless union with God. Both in this essay and in "Magic, Poetry, and Mysticism," she engages in dialogue with such aesthetic theorists as Marcel Raymond, Albert Béguin, and Paul Valéry.

Though she has been somewhat overshadowed by the renown of her neo-Thomist husband, Jacques, Raïssa Maritain's keen interest in mysticism and poetry and the literary qualities of her writing make her of interest to Catholic and non-Catholic readers alike. Her tendency to associate spiritual and artistic excellence represents an important link between nineteenth-century romantic idealism and the aesthetics of the present-day Catholic left, as reflected, e.g. in the review *Esprit*.

Works

De la vie d'oraison (1922). *Le prince de ce monde* (1932). *L'ange de l'école* (1934). *La vie donnée* (1935). *Situation de la poésie* (1938). *Lettre de nuit.*

La vie donnée (1939). *Les grandes amitiés: Souvenirs* (1941). *La conscience morale et l'état de nature* (1942). *Marc Chagall* (1943). *Les grandes amitiés: Les aventures de la grâce* (944). *Histoire d'Abraham ou Les premiers âges de la conscience morale* (1947). *Léon Bloy, Pilgrim of the Absolute*, ed. Raïssa Maritain (1947). *Chagall, ou l'orage enchanté* (1948). *Portes de l'horizon*—Poèmes (1952). *Au creux du rocher*—Poèmes (1954). *Liturgie et contemplation* (1959). *La contemplation sur les chemins: Notes sur le Pater* (1961).

Parts of Books: "Jours de soleil en France." *Les Oeuvres Nouvelles* (1943). "Lettres." *Lettres Inédites sur l'inquiétude Moderne* (1951). "Abraham and the Ascent of Consciousness." *The Bridge* (1955).

Articles: "Du recueillement poétique." *Etudes Carmélitaines* (1937). "Sens et non sens en poésie." *Deuxième Congrès International d'Esthétique et de Science de l'Art* (1937). "Henri Bergson." *The Commonweal* (Jan. 17, 1941). "Henri Bergson." *La relève* (March 1941). "Concerning Henri Bergson. Mme. Maritain's Reply." *The Commonweal* (March 7, 1941). "Communication: Bergson." *The Commonweal* (August 29, 1941). "Notre Maître perdu et retrouvé." *Revue Dominicaine* (1941). "La poésie comme expérience spirituelle." *Fontaine* (March-April 1942). "Poetry as Spiritual experience." *Spirit* (January 1943). "Léon Bloy's Columbus." *The Commonweal* (October 16, 1942). "For the Feast of St. Thomas." *The Commonweal* (March 13, 1943). "Handful of Musicians." *The Commonweal* (October 29, 1943). "Deus excelsus terribilis." *The Commonweal* (September 29, 1944). *La Nouvelle Relève* (January 1945). "Lettre sur Saint-Denys Garneau." *La Nouvelle Relève* (December 1944). "Chagall." *L'Art Sacré* (July–August 1950). "Léon Bloy: Master of Paradox." *The Commonweal* (May 25, 1951). "Life of Jesus." *Books on Trial* (October 1951). "Ode aux morts confédérés." *The Sewanee Review* (January-March, 1953). *Le Figaro Littéraire* (May 24, 1952). "Noël, et le dogme de l'immaculée conception de Marie." *Marie* (November-December, 1957). "Liturgy and Contemplation." *Spiritual Life* (June 1959).

Translations by Raïssa Maritain: *Des moeurs divines: Opuscule LXII de St. Thomas d'Aquin* (1921). *Jean de Saint-Thomas: Les dons du Saint-Esprit* (1950).

Translations of Raïssa Maritain: *The Prince of This World* (1933). *St. Thomas Aquinas: The Angel of the Schools* (1935). *We Have Been Friends Together* (1942). *The Divine Ways: A Little Work of Saint Thomas Aquinas* (1942), tr. Raïssa Maritain and Margaret Sumner. *Adventures in Grace* (1945). *The Situation of Poetry* (1955). *We Have Been Friends Together and Adventures in Grace. The Memoirs of Raïssa Maritain* (1961).

Bibliography

Gallagher, D.A., and I.J., *The Achievement of Jacques and Raïssa Maritain: A Bibliography, 1906–1961* (Garden City, 1962).

Michael B. Smith

Eugenie Marlitt

(a.k.a. Friederike Christiane Henriette John)

Born December 5, 1825, Arnstadt, Germany;
died June 22, 1887, Arnstadt
Genre(s): novel
Language(s): German

One of Germany's most famous and most beloved authors of "women's novels," Eugenie Marlitt was born on December 5, 1825 into modest circumstances in Arnstadt in Thuringia. Her father, a man of artistic inclinations, was a not-too-successful businessman. An early talent for singing brought Marlitt the patronage of the ruling Princess Mathilde von Schwarzburg-Sondershausen, who supervised and financed her education. She sent her for professional training as a singer to Wien in 1844. Marlitt had her professional debut in Leipzig in 1846 and performed on a number of stages in Austria between 1846 and 1849. An illness affected her hearing, and her promising career ended prematurely. From 1853 to 1863 she was employed as a companion by the Princess of Schwarzburg-Sondershausen until reduced financial circumstances forced a separation.

Marlitt returned to Arnstadt and devoted herself to her writing. Her first novella, *Die zwölf Apostel* (The Twelve Apostles), was published in the family magazine *Die Gartenlaube* in 1865. This novella and the novel *Goldelse*, serialized in *Die Gartenlaube* in 1866, made her immediately

a popular favorite. All her subsequent works were published in *Die Gartenlaube* before being issued in book form. This contributed substantially to the amazing success of the magazine. Marlitt's works were incredibly popular and were translated into many languages.

She appealed directly to middle-class and lower-middle-class sensibilities; blending a moderate (for the times) nationalism with nineteenth-century liberalism, she castigated religious intolerance (both Catholic and Protestant), bourgeois ostentatiousness and narrow-mindedness, and the undeserved privileges of the nobility. *Die Reichsgräfin Gisela* contrasts the model of a truly "noble" young German woman with the degenerate, rapacious, and devious nobleman of French origin.

Her novels all are essentially reworkings of the Cinderella story: young, beautiful, modest maiden finally, after some trials and tribulations, gains the deserved husband and her proper station in life. Although written purely for entertainment, the novels do contain a certain moralizing and didactic element.

Marlitt's success lasted beyond her lifetime. Her name has all but become a synonym for this type of literature. She is still remembered as the most famous author of the *Gartenlaube*-type novels, which characterized and influenced popular tastes in the second half of the nineteenth century. Although her works brought pleasure to millions of readers in the past, they no longer appeal to the modern reader as they are very dated, both in content and style.

Works

Goldelse (1867). *Das Geheimnis der alten Mamsell* (1868). *Die Reichsgräfin Gisela* (1869). *Thüringer Erzählungen* (1869). *Das Haideprinzechen* (1872). *Die zweite Frau* (1874). *Im Hause des Kommerzienrates* (1877). *Im Schillingshof* (1879). *Amtmanns Magd* (1881). *Die Frau mit den Karfunkelsteinen* (1885). *Das Eulenhaus* (fragment, completed by W. Heimburg, 1888).

Translations: (Marlitt's works were widely translated and reprinted repeatedly; only the first American translation of each work is listed below). *The Old Mam'sell's Secret* (1868). *Gold Elsie* (1868). *Countess Gisela* (1869). *Over Yonder* (1869). *Magdalena* (1870). *The Little Moorland Princess*

(1872). *The Second Wife* (1874). *At the Councillor's; or, a Nameless History* (1876). *In the Schillingscourt* (1879). *The Bailiff's Maid* (1881). *The Lady with the Rubies* (1885). *The Owl's Nest* (1888). *A Brave Woman* (1891). *Schoolteacher's Mary* (1935).

Bibliography

Best, Otto F., *Das verbotene Glück. Kitsch und Freiheit in der deutschen Literatur* (Zürich and München, 1978). Heissenbuttel, H., "Nicht Marlitt oder 'Anna Blume' sondern Marlitt und 'Anna Blume.' Rekonstruktion der Tradition." *Deutsche Akademie für Sprache und Dichtung: Jahrbuch 1981* (Heidelberg, 1981). Horovitz, Ruth, *Vom Roman des Jungen Deutschland bis zum Roman der Gartenlaube. Ein Beitrag zur Geschichte des deutschen Liberalismus.* Diss., Basel, 1937. Kienzle, Michael, *Der Erfolgsroman. Zur Kritik seiner poetischen Oekonomie bei Gustav Freytag und Eugenie Marlitt* (Stuttgart, 1975). Kienzle, Michael, "Eugenie Marlitt: Reichsgräfin Gisela (1869). Zum Verhältnis zwischen Politik und Tagtraum," in *Romane und Erzählungen des bürgerlichen Realismus: Neue Interpretationen*, Horst Denkler, ed. (Stuttgart, 1980). Klein, Albert, *Die Krise des Unterhaltungsromans im 19. Jahrhundert. Ein Beitrag zur Theorie und Geschichte der ästhetisch geringwertigen Literatur* (Bonn, 1969). Langner, Ilse, "Deutsche Wahlverwandschaften. Goethe und der Balzac der Gründerjahre: Eugenie Marlitt." *Frankfurter Hefte* 36, 3 (1981): 53. Mosse, George L., "Was die Deutschen wirklich lesen. Marlitt, May, Ganghofer," in *Popularität und Trivialität*, Reinhold Grimm and Jost Hermand, eds. (Frankfurt, 1974). Potthast, Bertha, *Eugenie Marlitt.* Diss. Köln, 1926. Sichelschmidt, Gustav, *Liebe, Mord und Abenteuer. Eine Geschichte der deutschen Unterhaltungsliteratur* (Berlin, 1969). Tizzi, Alessandra Barbanti, "Marlitt: Goldelse: Un caso di contiguita fra 'Trivialliteratura' e romanzo borghese." *Quaderni di Filologia Germanica della Facolta di Lettere e Filosofia dell'Universita di Bologna* 2 (1982): 97–113.
General references: *Allegemeine Deutsche Biographie (Leipzig, 1906), 52, p. 213.*

Hortense Bates

Monika Maron

Born 1941, East Berlin, East Germany
Genre(s): novel, short story
Language(s): German

After the *Abitur*, Monika Maron first learned in typical East German fashion a practical trade, then worked for two years as an assistant producer for East German television. She began after that to study theater and fine arts, became for three years an assistant at the *Schauspielschule* in Berlin and finally switched jobs once more to be a reporter for the journal *Wochenpost*. In 1976 she decided on a career as a writer, only to find all her work disapproved for publication in East Germany. Thus all her productions have appeared in West Germany. She now also lives there.

In 1981 her first novel *Flugasche* (Flight of Ashes) was published in West Germany. It is the story of a woman reporter, whose investigative journalism is rejected as too critical. Her assignment to visit and write about the industrial town of B. plunges her into the professional and personal battle of her life. What she found was "the filthiest town in Europe" with its dreadful load of soot emptied every day by the smokestacks on all the people of the town, an absolute disregard of life by the East German government. But the paper rejects her account, forcing her to choose between the exposure of truth and self-censorship. She sides with truth, uncompromised truth, and quits her job. Maron's next novel *Die Überläuferin* (1986) poignantly called the traitor, the transgressor, shows a woman protagonist already in the state of refusal. Maron continues taking issue with the deplorable conditions and rigid mechanisms of socialist politics, framing them, however, even more into terms of gender. The central character has fallen victim not only to the instrumental ratio of a phallocratic society, she is ultimately oppressed by the total turmoil of the male-female conflict. This produces a state of paralysis in which the character moves only in hallucinations, a human being is reduced to a hermetically internalized self. Maron's short stories *Das Mißverständnis* (1982) reiterate and reinforce the author's dismal experience of false hopes.

Works

Flugasche, novel (1981). Das Mißverständnis, short stories (1982). Die Überläuferin, novel (1986). Translations: Flight of Ashes, tr. David Marienelli (1986).

Margaret Eifler

Elena Maróthy-Šoltésová

Born January 6, 1855, Krupina, then in Austro-Hungary; died February 11, 1939, Martin, both towns now in Czechoslovakia

Genre(s): short story, novel, autobiography
Language(s): Slovak

Elena Maróthy-Šoltésová's several short stories, one novel, and novelistic autobiography represent early realistic Slovak prose fiction conceived as part of the battle of the smaller Slavic nationalities against their political repression in the Austro-Hungarian Empire before it fell apart with its defeat in World War I.

Born in 1855 into the nationalistic family of a rural Protestant clergyman, Daniel Maróthy, who was also a minor Slovak poet, she was educated at a girls' school until age twelve. In 1875 she married an older merchant, L'udovít Šoltés, apparently partly so that she could move to the small but nationally important town of Trenčiansky Svätý Martin. Her first story was published in 1881, and two years later she became vice-president, then president (1894–1927) of the only major women's organization, Živena. Simultaneously (1885–1922) she edited several periodicals directed against the Germanizing and Magyarizing tendencies in the old Empire. The deaths of both her children occasioned an autobiographical work in 1923–1924, which was her only critical and international success, though her fiction was always popular with the relatively few Slovak women readers. At Šoltésová's death in 1939 she was eulogized as much for her organizational and editorial work in encouraging and supporting other writers, both men and women, as for her own prose fiction.

Šoltésová's six short stories or novellas began and ended as descriptive, simply plotted, idealized accounts of small town love affairs, misunderstandings, and deaths. However, her one novel, Proti prúdu (Against the Current) in 1894, pictures a Magyarized nobleman of Slovak ancestry significantly named Šavelský who like Šavel (Saul) converts into Paul and becomes a Slovak nationalist at the instigation and love of his nationalistic wife, named Laskárová (loving woman). Šavelský then works against the social current of the Magyarized or Germanized Slovak gentry. This schematic, overidealistic presentation was condemned as inartistic as well as sociologically improbable, but Šoltésová defended it by the didactic function of literature. Her autobiographical accounts of her two children's development, illnesses, and deaths, collected together as Moje deti (My Children) in 1923–1924, were detailed and tender without sentimentalism.

Šoltésová's significance is more historical than aesthetic, not only as one of the two earliest Slovak women novelists and as the leader of the women's literary movement by her editorial activity but also as the creator of a new type of heroine that sees herself as a conscious, independent part of the national struggle.

Works

Stories and novellas: Na dedine [In the Village] (1881). Prípravy na svadbu [Wedding Preparations] (1882). V čiernickej Škole [In the Ciernicka School] (1891). Prvé previnenie [First Transgression] (1896). Popolka [Cinderella] (1898). Za letného večera [One Summer Evening] (1902).
Novel: Proti prúdux [Against the Current] (1894).
Autobiographical works: Umierajúce dieta [The Dying Child] (1885). Môj syn [My Son] (1913). Moje deti [My Children] (1923–1924). Sedemdesiat rokov 'ivota [Seventy Years of Living] (1925).
Collected articles (edited by others): Začatá cesta [The Way Begun (for Women)] (1934). Pohl'ady na literatúre [Literary Views] (1958).
Collected works: Zobrané spisy Eleny Maróthy-Šoltésovej (1921–1925).
Translations: Czech: Proti proudu (1897). French: Mes enfants du berceau à la tombe (1928, 1934). Czech: Moje deti (1957). Magyar: Gyermekeim (1958, 1977). Croatian: Moja djeca (1925). Slovenian: Moja otroka (no date).

Bibliography

Kern, Elga, Führende Frauen Europas (Munich, 1930). Kusý, Ivan, ed., Introduction to

Korešpondencia Timravy a Šoltésovej (Bratislava, 1952), pp. 5–35. Kusý, Ivan, ed., Introduction to *Pohl'ady na literatúre* (Bratislava, 1958), pp. 7–17. Mazák, Pavol, *Slovenský roman v období literárneho realizmu* (Bratislava, 1975): 57–68. Mráz, Andrej, "Elena Maróthy Šoltésová." *Slovenské pohl'ady* 51 (1955): 34–39. Mráz, Andrej, "Šoltésovej román Proti prúdu," *Slovenská literatúra* 2 (1955): 128–149. Rudinsky, Norma Leigh, *Incipient Feminists: Slovak Women Writers in the National Revival* (Columbus, 1990). Števček, Ján, *Esej o slovenskom románe* (Bratislava, 1979), pp. 163–182. Tkadlečková-Vantuchová, Jarmila, *Živena: Spolok slovenských 'ien* (Bratislava, 1969), pp. 41–48, 60–68, 103–110.

General references: *Dejiny slovenskej literatúry*, Vol. III (Bratislava, 1965), pp. 540–547. *Encyklopédia slovenských spisovatel'ov* I (Bratislava, 1984), 407–409. *Kindlers Literaturlexikon* (Zürich, 1964–1972).

Norma L. Rudinsky

Soeur Anne de Marquets

Born 1533, Marqués près d'Eu, France; died 1588, Poissy, France
Genre(s): poetry
Language(s): French

Little is known of the life of Anne de Marquets. She was born in Normandy of a noble family which she left at the age of nine or ten to enter the order of Saint Dominic at the royal monastery in Poissy. It is likely that she took the veil in 1548 or 1549 and remained cloistered until her death in May of 1588. At Poissy, Sister Anne's education would be a mixture of traditional church doctrine and the Humanist ideas espoused by her teacher Henri Estienne. She also met Dorat and, more importantly, Ronsard whose work would exercise a major influence on her own. She composed a number of religious poems, including prayers, hymns, meditations, and a large body of sonnets, many of which were published after her death. The conviction of Soeur Anne's faith pervades all her works and served as an inspiration for the members of her community and the Catholic populace as a whole during the troubled years of the Wars of Religion.

The *Sonnets, prières et devises* (Sonnets, Prayers and Sayings) written on the occasion of the "Colloque de Poissy" and circulated first in manuscript, criticized the Huguenots and placed her voice firmly in the Catholic camp. They portray, in allegorical form, the troubles of the Church and her eventual triumph. The pasquins, addressed to different Cardinals, are poetic biblical glosses that elicited a strong Protestant reaction, including criticism for having interpreted the Bible as favoring the Catholics. The *Response* (Reply) directed at Soeur Anne placed her in the limelight and prompted her to publish both the sonnets and the *pasquins* (libel-post poems) in 1562. To the *Divines poésies* (Divine Poems), a translation of the neo-Latin poet Flamino, she added a number of poems of her own, inspired mainly by the verse of Flamino. They are less inflammatory in subject but no less ardent in their faith. The *Sonnets spirituels* (Spiritual Sonnets) is her most important work, a collection of 180 devotional pieces that follow the church calendar. Here, Soeur Anne's originality lay less in her style, which while sure and with a certain flair for rhymes, is not unique, than in her artful union of the sonnet, perfected by Ronsard as the form *par excellence* of love poetry, with profoundly Christian themes. Her works are exemplary in the genre of religious poetry.

Works

Sonnets, prières et devises en forme de pasquins pour l'assemblée de messieurs les prélats et docteurs, tenue à Poissy (1562). *Les Divines poésies de Marc-Antoine Flaminius . . . avec plusieurs Sonnets & Cantiques ou Chansons spirituelles pour louer Dieu* (1568). *Sonnets spirituels de feue très-vertueuse et très docte Dame Sr. Anne de Marquets, religieuse à Poissy, sur les dimanches et principales solennites de l'annéee* (posthumous, 1605).

Bibliography

Seiler, Sister Mary Hilarine, *Anne de Marquets, poètesse religieuse du XVIe* (Washington, D.C., 1931).

Edith J. Benkov

Emil Marriot

(see: Emilie Mataja)

Colette Mart

Born 1955, Esch-sur-Alzette, Luxembourg
Genre(s): poetry, short story, journalism
Language(s): French, German

When she finished her secondary school studies in Luxembourg Colette Mart went to Brussels where she registered at the Université Libre, department of journalism and social communication. She studied in Brussels from 1974 to 1978 and left the university with a first in her degree. She worked in Belgium as a journalist, then in Germany; at present she is a journalist in Luxembourg.

She writes with ease in both French and German, using French for journalism and German for her own creative work. In her poetry and in her narratives, Colette Mart devotes her attention and sensibility to the position of woman in the contemporary world, to love, children, solitude; she is worried about the great problems of our age and conscious of her responsibility as a writer, mother, and citizen. She aspires to harmony, expressing in a discreet yet warm voice thoughts shared by many people.

Works

Der Tag am Meer und andere Erzählungen [The Day at the Seaside and Other Stories] (1983). *La Peau/Die Haut* [The Skin] (1986), collection of poems, bilingual edition.

Rosemarie Kieffer and Liliane Stomp-Erpelding

Elisabeth Martens

(see: Louise Cathrine Elisabeth Bjørnsen)

Carmen Martín-Gaite

Born December 8, 1925, Salamanca, Spain
Genre(s): short story, novel, children's
* literature, essay*
Language(s): Spanish

Carmen Martín-Gaite was born in Salamanca. She received a degree in Romance Philology from the University of Salamanca and Madrid and her doctorate in history from the latter. When she moved from her native Salamanca to the capital, she associated with a group of young writers who would soon become famous as social realists, among them her future husband Rafael Sánchez Ferlosio.

Martín-Gaite's fiction reflects literary and social changes spanning a thirty-year period in Spain. The monotony of Franco's oppressive regime is depicted in her early work. A second and third novel bear witness to her progressively more subtle psychological studies as well as more imaginative and experimental fiction. She has not only employed a wide range of fictional styles, including the social novel, the fantastic, metafiction and children's fairy tales but has also written essays and historical works, and has participated in various television productions.

Martín-Gaite's fiction has received an enthusiastic response from the Spanish public and critics. She was awarded the Premio Gijón in 1954 for *El balneario*, the Premio Eugenio Nadal in 1957 for her first novel *Entre visillos*, and more recently, *El cuarto de atrás* received the coveted Premio Nacional de Literatura 1978. The latter work, translated into English, has attracted a great deal of attention from critics in the United States as evidenced by three book-length studies and frequent invitations from American universities.

Several thematic concerns appear throughout her work, unifying literary and historical interests: the restriction of women's (and men's) role in society and the contradictions that arise when women attempt to change their status; the general conformity and tedium of life under the Franco dictatorship; the problematic of communication; and language and dialogue as an affirmation of life and love.

With the exception of the early novella *El balneario*, reminiscent of Kafka and a precursor of *El cuarto de atrás*, Martín-Gaite's first two novels and short stories have been considered social realist works. *El balneario* intermingles the protagonist's real life and her dream life, daily frustrations translating into nightmarish obsessions. The fragmentation of the two narrative levels and the surrealistic spatial configuration of this work sharply contrast with the author's straightforward first novel, *Entre visillos*. Although provincial life in all its dreary oppression is well drawn, the novel's conventionality and nearly documentary realism limit its appeal. The narrative centers upon the anguish of a few individuals struggling between rebellion and withdrawal within an overwhelmingly conformist society. As in her next novel, *Ritmo lento*, the rare characters who refuse to acquiesce to the social restrictions are condemned to loneliness.

Ritmo lento, along with Luis Martín-Santos' *Tiempo de silencio*, initiates a new social novel in Spain by eschewing the collective study of society for a focus upon a single extraordinary individual. While recalling the generation of 98's irresolute and weak heroes, the psychological portrait is more carefully described in Martín-Gaite's existentialist novel. The less "objective" and non-chronological style of *Ritmo lento* presages the author's next two novels. In *Retahílas* she finds her own voice, which can be noted in the experimental style, treatment of characters, and linguistic play. Here language becomes the very purpose of the narration, and the self defines itself and gains freedom through the word. The framing prelude and epilogue provide a literary pastiche of the nineteenth-century novel, counterpointed by the long central dialogue between two characters. The orality of this "dialogue" is undermined insofar as the simply communicative illusion of the novel is necessarily and self-consciously effaced by its written and literary quality, while the dialogues themselves are indeed more like monologues.

Martín-Gaite's most recent novel, *El cuarto de atrás*, continues in the self-reflexive and nostalgic vein of *Retahílas*, but its playfulness, humor and technical virtuosity make it the author's most intriguing and open work to date. The claustrophobic and apparently insoluble dilemmas of an era when women are either subservient to men or utterly alone are no longer the focus of her narratives. In this regard, it is not insignificant that Martín-Gaite began writing the novel the day Franco died. *The Back Room* is a world where the disparate co-exists: the sublime and the corny; romantic excess and the strength to write and invent as a woman; male and female; the conscious and unconscious; history, realism, fantasy and dreams combining into the fragmentary unity that is the unending process of living and writing. The novel is comprised of at least two stories: an encounter between the narrator and a man wearing a black hat, and the story of the novel's own generation: an emblematic pile of pages mysteriously accumulates parallel to the dialogue about writing which is the novel.

Many of Martín-Gaite's concerns in the novel are present in her non-fiction. Just as *El cuarto* exhibits an essay-like quality, so too her recent work, *El cuento de nunca acabar*, is an investigation of narrative in a style that combines both story telling and the essay. In her historical studies of the eighteenth century, *El proceso de Macanaz* (1970) and *Usos amorosos del siglo dieciocho en España* (1972), as well as her essays in *La búsqueda del interlocutor y otras búsquedas* (1982), essential themes converge and are explored as historical investigation, philosophical musing, or linguistic play. These include the problematic of the lack of communication and its opposite—the word as salvation from oblivion and from a hostile world. The issues of solitude, freedom, emotional ties, and identity are intimately connected to Martín-Gaite's formal experiments with dialogue and literature. According to her, literature is a place where the pleasure of life, love, and writing is grasped in its necessarily ephemeral and interconnected nature. Martín-Gaite's wide range of topics and modes aesthetically and intelligently manipulated in these works makes her one of the most important writers of contemporary Spain.

Works

Short Stories: *El balneario* (1955). *Las ataduras* (1960).

Novels: *Ritmo lento* (1963). *Retahílas* (1974). *Fragmentos de interior* (1976). *El cuarto de atrás* (1978).

Fairy tales: *El castillo de las tres murallas* (1981). Essays: *La búsqueda de interlocutor y otras búsquedas* (1973).

Combination of essays and fiction: *El cuento de nunca acabar* (1983).

Historical works: *El proceso de Macanaz* (1970). *Usos amorosos del dieciocho en España* (1972). Poetry: *A rachas* (1976).

Translations into English: Fiction: *The Spa. The Bonds. From Behind the Curtains. Conversational Stream. Interior Fragments. The Back Room. Never-Ending Tale.* Essays: *The Quest for an Interlocutor and Other Quests.* Historical works: *The*

Trial of Macanaz. Romantic Customs of the Eighteenth Century in Spain. Poetry: *By Fits and Starts.*

Bibliography

Boring, Phyllis Zatlin, "Carmen Martín-Gaite, Feminist Author." *Revista de Estudios Hispánicos* (1977): 11. Brown, Joan Lipman, *Carmen Martín-Gaite* and *Secrets From the Book Room: The Fiction of Carmen Martín-Gaite* (Boston, 1983). Brown, Joan Lipman, "'El balneario' by Carmen Martín-Gaite: Conceptual Aesthetics and 'l'etrange pur.'" *Journal of Spanish Studies: Twentieth Century* (1978): 6. Brown, Joan Lipman, "*Tiempo de silencio* and *Ritmo lento*: Pioneers of the New Social Novel in Spain." *Hispanic Review* 50 (1) (1982). Durán, Manuel, "Carmen Martín-Gaite: *Retahílas, El cuarto de atrás* y el diálogo sin fin." *Revista Iberoamericana* (1981): 47. El Saffar, Ruth, "Shaping the Chaos: Carmen Martín-Gaite and the Never-Ending Tale." *International Fiction Review* 11 (1) (1984). Matamoro, Blas, "Carmen Martín-Gaite: El viaje al cuarto de atrás." *Cuadernos Hispanoamericanos* (1979): 351. Navajas, Gonzalo, "El diálogo y el yo en *Retahílas* de Carmen Martín-Gaite." *Hispanic Review* 53 (1) (1985). Ordóñez, Elizabeth, "The Decoding and Encoding of Sex Roles in Carmen Martín-Gaite's *Retahílas*." *Kentucky Romance Quarterly* (1980): 27. Servodidio, Mirella, and Marcia L. Welles, eds., *From Fiction to Metafiction: Essays in Honor of Carmen Martín-Gaite* (Lincoln, 1983). Spires, Robert C., "The Metafictional Codes of *Don Julián* versus the Metafictional Mode of *El cuarto de atrás*." *Revista Canadiense de Estudios Hispánicos* 7 (2) (1983). Villanueva, Dario, "La novela irónica de Carmen Martín-Gaite." *Camp de l'Arpa: Revista de Literatura* (1975): 23–24.

General References: Sobejano, Gonzalo, *Novela española de nuestro tiempo* (Madrid, 1975).

Marie Murphy

Elisavet Moutzan Martinengou

(see: Elisavet Moutzan-Martinengou)

María Martínez Sierra

(a.k.a. María de la O Lejárraga, Gregorio Martínez Sierra [her husband's name])

Born December 28, 1874, San Millán de la Cogolla, Spain; died June 28, 1974, Buenos Aires, Argentina
Genre(s): drama, novel, essay, libretto, translation, autobiography
Language(s): Spanish

María Martínez Sierra, one of Spain's most popular playwrights in the early twentieth-century, did not sign her literary texts and essays with her name. Instead, she used her husband's name, Gregorio Martínez Sierra, until his death in 1947. This self-effacing gesture has set up a situation where most contemporary scholarship either erases her authorship altogether or grudgingly accepts it but only as joint authorship. Yet recent research, based on legal documents signed by Gregorio Martínez Sierra and testimonies of their contemporaries, confirms not only her contribution to their literary production but substantiates the hypothesis that María Martínez Sierra was, in many cases, the sole author of countless plays, poems, novels and essays on the "woman question."

Born in a small town in northern Spain, she moved to Madrid with her family when she was a small girl. She attended the Normal School of Madrid and became an elementary school language teacher. In 1899, she began her literary collaboration with Gregorio Martínez Sierra, seven years her junior, and married him one year later. Beyond writing, their projects were to include the creation of two literary journals: *Helios* (Sun) (a Modernist journal founded jointly with Juan Ramón Jiménez) and *Renacimiento* (Renaissance). Because their early years were economically difficult, María continued to teach and to do pedagogical research until their literary career could support them. In these years she did a great deal of translating, wrote travel books, and collaborated with Manuel de Falla as librettist of his ballets *El sombrero de tres picos* (The Three-Cornered Hat) and *El amor brujo* (Love's Sorcery).

Until Gregorio's death in 1947, all of María's considerable work was credited to him, for such was their joint decision; it was not until after Gregorio's death that María published under her own name. *El poema del trabajo* (Labor's Poem), the first project on which the couple collaborated, are allegorical prose poems in praise of work and published in 1898, two years before their marriage. Other early works, written in the Modernistic style, included *Diálogos fantásticos* (Fantastic Dialogues), *Flores de escarcha* (Frost Flowers), and *Teatro de ensueño* (Dream Theater). These were followed by more realistic narrations, *Tú eres la paz* (You Are Peace) and *La humilde verdad* (The Humble Truth). The early works, pantheistic in tone, are set most often in rural Spain. They demonstrate strong admiration for the simple, natural life and tend to present moral lessons through parables.

In approximately 1910, María and Gregorio, realizing that their interest lay more in people than in nature, began writing for theater and eventually produced over fifty plays, most of which featured strong, practical, maternal women characters. Most of the plays, unlike the preceding narrative works, were set in Madrid. Among the best known are: *Canción de cuna* (1911; Cradle Song, 1923), *Primavera en otoño* (1911; Autumn Spring), *El reino de Dios* (1915; The Kingdom of God, 1929), *Sueño de una noche de agosto* (1918; The Romantic Young Lady, 1929), *Seamos felices* (1929; Let's Be Happy), *Triángulo* (1930; Take Two from One, 1931). The best-known play, *Canción de cuna* (Cradle Song), translated into many languages and performed all over the world, concerns a group of cloistered nuns who adopt an infant girl abandoned to them. In the first act, the women find fulfillment in maternity. The second act takes place eighteen years later and shows the wedding day of the young girl and the farewell to her mothers. Several films and television plays have also been made of this work in various countries.

In 1931, Gregorio went to Hollywood to supervise filming of some of his plays and to write movie scripts for MGM and Paramount Pictures. María remained in Spain and was elected Socialist *diputada* (representative) to the Cortes (Parliament) during the Republic. With the outbreak of the Spanish Civil War (1936), María and Gregorio separated definitively: he went to Argentina with actress Catalina Bárcena, the mother of his child. María remained in Nice (France) during and after the war. After Gregorio's death in 1947, María moved to Buenos Aires, where she remained until her death just six months short of her one hundredth birthday.

As was the case with other women writers of this period, María Martínez Sierra was interested in feminist issues and became a feminist activist in the international women's movements. In 1914, Chrystal Macmillan, the British delegate to the International Women's Suffrage Alliance (IWSA), went to Spain and named her the Spanish Secretary of this organization. Between 1916 and 1932 she also wrote five series of essays on the "woman question." Four of which were, again, published with her husband's name. In the aftermath of the debacle of the international women's movement during World War I, she continued her feminist activities. In the early 1930s, she founded the Asociación Femenina de Educación Cívica (The Women's Association for Civic Education). Yet, her concern for social issues was not restricted to the problems of women. She joined the Socialist Worker's Party of Spain (PSOE) and in the 1933 Parliamentary elections was elected to represent the city of Granada. When the Civil War broke out in 1936 the Republican government assigned her to the Spanish embassy in Switzerland as the commercial attaché. She left for Switzerland in 1936 and never again returned to Spain. Between 1938 and 1952 she lived in the south of France. In 1953, María settled in Buenos Aires where she lived until her death in 1974. In exile, she made her living by translating and writing short stories, principally for the Buenos Aires daily, *La Prensa*. She also wrote two autobiographies.

Whereas the Martínez Sierra plays were extremely popular in their time (several generations of North American high school and college students have learned Spanish reading *The Cradle Song*), they are no longer read or performed. This could possibly be attributed to their sentimental themes and style. According to Patricia W. O'Connor, the leading authority on the Martínez Sierra, the most successful aspect of their literary production was the creation of strong and independent women as the central figures for their plays and novels. In these texts the author/s advocated careers for women particularly in the areas of medicine, education, social services, and literature.

María Martínez Sierra's feminist essays contributed to the feminist polemic in Spain. She was interested not only in the role and education of women in society but was also preoccupied with the question of sexual difference. In her early essays she depicted sexual difference as stemming from a "natural essence" that made women peaceful in opposition to men who were "naturally" violent. In 1932, no longer content with this explanation, she proposed that sexual difference had been constructed socially and culturally by men through their representation of women in literature. She suggested that male writers had created an image of women and that women, in turn, had internalized and imitated this masculine construction. Her cultural analysis is possibly the first of its kind in Spain and shows both her lucidity and commitment to the "woman question."

Her autobiographies, *Una mujer por los caminos de España* (A Woman on the Roads of Spain) and *Gregorio y yo* (Gregorio and I), are splendid. In them she chronicles her life as a writer and as an activist. They capture the literary and political atmosphere of her time and reveal a unique and gifted mind.

Works

Signed by Gregorio Martínez Sierra: *El poema del trabajo* (1898). *Diálogos fantásticos* (1899). *Flores de escarcha* (1900). *Almas ausentes* (1900). *Horas de sol* (1901). *Pascua florida* (1903). *Sol de tarde* (1904). *La humilde verdad* (1905). *La tristeza del Quixote* (1905). *Teatro de ensueño* (1905). *Motivos* (1905). *Tú eres la paz* (1906). *La feria de Neuilly* (1907). *Aldea ilusoria* (1907). *La casa de la primavera* (1907). *Aventura* (1907). *Aventura* and *Beata primavera* (1908). *El peregrino ilusionada* (1908). *Torre de marfil* (1908). *Juventud, divino tesoro* (1908). *Hechizo de amor* (1908). *La selva muda* (1909). *El agua dormida* (1909). *La sombra del padre* (1909). *El ama de casa* (1910). *El amor catedrático* (1910). *Todo es uno y lo mismo* (1910). *Primavera en otoño* (1911). *Canción de cuna* (1910). *El palacio triste* (1911). *La suerte de Isabelita* (1911). *Lirio entre espinas* (1911). *El pobrecito Juan* (1912). *Madam Pepita* (1912). *El enamorado* (1913). *Mamá* (1913). *Sólo para mujeres* (1913). *Madrigal* (1913). *Los pastores* (1913). *La vida inquieta* (1913). *La tirana* (1913). *Margot* (1913). *Las golondrinas* (1914). *La mujer del héroe* (1914). *La pasión* (1914). *El amor brujo* (1915). *Amanecer* (1915). *El reino de Dios* (1916). *El diable se rié* (1916). *Abril melancólico* (1916). *Cartas a mujeres de España* (1916). *Esperanza nuestra* (1917). *Navidad* (1916). *Feminismo, feminidad, españolismo* (1917). *La adúltera penitente* (1917). *Calendario espiritual* (1918). *Cristo niño* (1918). *Sueño de una noche de agosto* (1918). *Rosina es frágil* (1918). *Cada uno y su vida* (1919). *El corazón ciego* (1919). *Fuente serena* (1919). *La mujer moderna* (1920). *Vida y dulzura* (1920). *Granada* (1920). *Kodak Romántico* (1921). *El ideal* (1921). *Don Juan de España* (1921). *Torre de marfil* (1924). *Cada uno y su vida* (1924). *Mujer* (1925). *Rosas mustias* (1926). *Seamos felices* (1929). *Triángulo* (1930). *La hora del diablo* (1930). *Eva curiosa* (1930). *Nuevas cartas a las mujeres* (1932). *Cartas a las mujeres de América* (1941).

Signed by María Martínez Sierra: *Cuentos breves* (1899). *La mujer española ante la república* (1931). *Una mujer por los caminos de España* (1952). *Gregorio y yo* (1953). *Viajes de una gota de agua* (1954). *Fiesta en el Olimpo* (1960).

Translations: *Ana María*, tr. Mrs. Emmon Crocker (1921). *The Cradle Song*, tr. John Garrett Underhill (1917), pp. 625–679. *The Cradle Song*, tr. John Garrett Underhill (1917). *The Cradle Song and Other Plays*, tr. John Garrett Underhill (c.1922). *Holy Night: A Miracle Play in Three Scenes*, tr. Philip Hereford (1928). *Idyll*, tr. Charlotte Marie Lorenz. *Poet Lore* 37 (1926). *The Kingdom of God: A Play in Three Acts*, tr. Helen and Harley Granville-Barker (1927). *Let Us Be Happy*, tr. T.S. Richter (n.d.). *A Lily Among Thorns*, tr. Helen and Harley Granville-Barker. *Chief Contemporary Dramatists. Third Series*, ed. T.H. Dickinson (1930), pp. 457–471. *Love Magic*, tr. John Garrett Underhill. *Drama Chicago* 25 (1917): 40–61. *The Lover*, tr. John Garrett Underhill. *Stratford Journal* (1919): 33–44. *Plays of Gregorio Martínez Sierra*, tr. John Garrett Underhill. *Poor John*, tr. John Garrett Underhill. *Drama* 10 (1920): 172–180. *Reborn*, tr. Nena Belmonte (n.d.). *The Romantic Young Lady*, tr. Helen and Harley Granville-Barker (1923). *Take Two from One*, tr. Helen and Harley Granville-

Barker (1925). *The Two Shepards*, tr. Helen and Harley Granville-Barker, in *Plays for the College Theatre*, ed. G.H. Leverton (1932). *The Two Shepards*, tr. Helen and Harley Granville-Barker (1935).

Bibliography

Campo Alange, Condesa de, *La mujer española. Cien años de su historia, 1860–1960* (Madrid, 1964). Blanco, Alda, Introduction to *Una mujer por caminos de España* by María Martínez Sierra (Madrid, 1989), pp. 7–46. Cansinos Assens, Rafael, *La nueva literatura* (Madrid, 1925). Cejador y Frauca, Julio, *Historia de la lengua y literatura castellanas* (Madrid, 1919). Douglas, Frances, "Gregorio Martínez Sierra." *Hispania* V, 5 (April 1922): 267–369 and VI, 1 (February 1923): 1–13. Goldsborough Serrat, Andrés, *Imagen humana y literaria de Gregorio Martínez Sierra* (Madrid, 1965). Goldsborough Serrat, Andrés, *Imagen humana y literaria de Gregorio Martínez Sierra* (Madrid, 1965). Gullón, Ricardo, *Relaciones amistosas y literarias entre Juan Ramón Jiménez y los Martínez Sierra* (Rio Piedras, 1961). Massa, Pedro, "Los cien felices años de María Sierra." *Los domingos del ABC* (March 3, 1974): 22–25. O'Connor, Patricia W., "A Spanish Precursor to Women's Lib: The Heroine in Gregorio Martínez Sierra's Theatre." *Hispania* 55 (December 1962): 865–872. O'Connor Patricia W., "Death of Gregorio Martínez Sierra's Co-author." *Hispania* 58: 210–211. O'Connor, Patricia W., "Gregorio Martínez Sierra's Maternal Nuns in Dramas of Renunciation and Revolution." *The American Hispanist* 2 (1976): 8–12. O'Connor, Patricia W., "La madre español en el teatro de Gregorio Martínez Sierra." *Duquesne Hispanic Review* IV, I (1967): 17–24. O'Connor, Patricia W., *Gregorio and María Martínez Sierra* (Boston: Twayne, 1977). O'Connor, Patricia W., *Gregorio y María Martínez Sierra, crónica de una colaboración* (Madrid: La Avispa, 1987). O'Connor, Patricia W., *Women in the Theater of Gregorio Martínez Sierra* (New York, 1966). Owen, Arthur L., Introduction to *El ama de casa* (Chicago, 1927), pp. xi–xlv.

Alda Blanco and Patricia W. O'Connor

Helga Maria (Moa) Martinson, nee Swartz

Born 1890, Vårdnäs (Östergötland Province), Sweden; died 1964
Genre(s): novel, essay
Language(s): Swedish

Moa Martinson was one of those self-educated Swedish "proletarian writers" who came to prominence during the thirties. The only woman among them, she pleaded the cause of the tenant farmer's wife and the life of the working poor as she came to know it in her native province. Thanks to her the needy received lasting attention in Swedish literature, and as one of the writers who worked tirelessly in the fight against a social evil, she was, along with her colleagues Ivar-Lo Johansson, Wilhelm Moberg, and others, responsible for the abolishment of the statare-system (in which farmhands receive their wages in produce) in 1945.

After a childhood spent constantly moving with her mother and stepfather, Moa left home at the age of thirteen to become first a maidservant and later a waitress in a fast-food restaurant. In 1910 she got married and began to take care of her steadily growing family. In 1920 she began to write for the workers' press on social and political issues under the signature "Helga," which she changed to Moa in 1926. Her work brought her into contact with the labor movements, the syndicate, and various other social/political organizations which she actively joined. Poorly educated, she read voraciously whatever she could get—Zola, Dostoyevsky, Gorky, but most of all Martin Andersen Nexö. Despite her shortcomings, she began to write. Her first novel *Pigmamma*, was serialized in the labor movement's newspaper *Brand* in 1929. After her husband's death she remarried the much younger Harry Martinson, who also made his literary debut during the same year. Without doubt this marriage stimulated and developed her literary talent even further. In 1933 she published her first novel *Kvinnor och äppleträd* (Women and Appletrees). With this novel she started her portrayal of a long line of various women characters, each one patiently and stubbornly creating for herself and her children a tolerable environment that is constantly threatened by men's uncaring negligence and drinking. Rooted less in hate between the genders, but rather in social indignation, this attitude recurs time and again in Moa Martinson's work, especially in her autobiographical novels. The same feeling was also at the bottom of Moa Martinson's concern with social injustice: the difference between the lives of the protected wealthy and the insecure existence of the poor. *Sallys söner* (1934; Sally's Sons) is a continuation of her first novel—both later collected in *Boken om Sally. Rågvakt* (1935) and *Drottning Grågyllen* (1937; The Book About Sally, Rye-Watch, Queen Grey-Gold) show an epic tendency in depicting the historical development of the *statare*-system during the last century and an interest in popular legends and tradition.

Next came her autobiographical trilogy: *Mor gifter sig* (1936), followed by *Kyrkbröllop* (1938) and *Kungens rosor* (1939; Mother is Getting Married, Church Wedding, The King's Roses). Beginning with her insecure childhood in which her mother occupies a solid, brightening spot in her continuous effort to provide order and stability to an otherwise harsh existence, the author gives a realistic portrait of life in the Swedish countryside during the early part of the twentieth century. With their detailed description and width of conception, these novels are unique in Swedish autobiographical literature. In their portrayal of characters they remind strongly of Dostoyevsky and Maxim Gorky, though the emphasis is on the characterization of women.

Though many of them are autobiographical, Moa Martinson's next novels build on the historical background of her native district. *Vägen under stjärnorna* (1940; The Road Under the Stars), *Brandliljor* (1941; Firelilies), *Armén vid horisonten* (1942; The Army On the Horizon), *Den osynlige älskaren* (1943; The Invisible Lover), *Bakom svenskvallen* (1944; Behind the Swedish Rampart), *Kärlek mellan krigen* (1974; Love Between Wars, short stories and sketches), *Fem berättare* (1948; Five Tellers of Tales, short stories), *Livets fest* (1949), *Jag mötte en diktare* (1950; I Met a Poet), *Du är den enda* (1952; You Are the Only One), *Kvionnorna på Kummelsjö* (1955; The Women at Cairn Sea), *Klockor vid sidenvägen* (1957; Bells on the Path), and *Hemligheten* (1959; The Secret) followed in quick and steady succession.

Mostly known for her novels and essays, Moa Martinson also published a collection of poems, *Motsols* (1937; Opposite the Sun, extended edition 1954).

With her natural and original talent, Moa Martinson's work shows a wealth of compassion and an unrestrained delight in narrative detail. But these are also her shortcomings as a writer. Her stories often become a motley tangle of lively, impressionistic details with sketchy descriptions of milieu and character portrayals that lack coherence and concentration. In her novels and short stories she describes the proletarian daily life in the Swedish countryside as she had experienced it, becoming an outspoken champion for unconventional social and political views both as a writer and in personal public debate. Though lacking in formal training, but having years of daily toil and drudgery as a poor housewife behind her, she was able to describe this life of poverty and continuous strife in minute detail, amazingly enough without losing her humor, wit, and strong will to live. It is this which gives her work its enduring quality.

Works

Essays: "Att vara ateist." *Bonniers Litterära Magasin* (1957): 524–525. "Min debut." *All världens berättare* (1954): 1060–1067. "Min syn på bokhandeln." *Organ för svenska bokhandelsmedhjälpareföreningen* (1953): 4–5. "Minnen." *Folket i Bild* (1950): 37. "När jag debuterade." *Folket i Bild* (1955): 3. "Udda kamrater i Klara." *Folket i Bild* (1951): 50. "Sagan jag minns." *Hörde Ni?* (1954): 949–952. " . . . oreserverade synpunkter på edert författarskap . . ." *Horisont* (Spring 1942): 14–28. "Hur jag blev författare." *Mitt möte med boken* (Stockholm, 1943): 121–128. "Som det var!" *Mot ljuset: Nordisk prosa, dikt och konst. Tillägnade Martin Andersen Nexö* (1944): 101–106. "Vad jag vill med mina böcker." *Avsikter* (Stockholm, 1945): 194–156. "Mor gifter sig." *Barndomshemmet* (1947): 103–121.

Moa Martinson's work has been translated into numerous languages and is especially popular in the eastern Europe countries.

Bibliography

Berggren, Kerstin, "Påminnelse om Moa." *Studiekamraten*(1973): 116–117. Björklund, C.J., "Moa Martinson. Kvinna med taggar." *Orädda riddare av pennan* (Stockholm, 1960): 247–254. Björkman, Maja, "Moa Martinson och hennes diktning." *Mål och medel* (1943): 294. Forssell, Lars, "Rosor till Moa." *En bok för alla människor.* (Stockholm, 1975): 62–64. Johansson, E., "Moa Martinson. Författarinnan som infört den svenska proletärflickan i litteraturen." *Lantarbetaren*(1944): 1. Lindgren, Rune M., "En kvinnlig Gorkij, statarfolkets Selma." *Statsanställd* (1974): 45. Lundkvist, Artur, "Jag minns mitt gröna 30-tal." *Folket i bild* 39 (1959): 3–7 and 70. Löfstedt, Annie, *Figurer mot mörk botten*(Stockholm, 1943): 155–175. Remens, E., "Moa Martinson." *Studiekamraten* (1940): 11–12. Runnqvist, Åke, *Arbetarskildrare från Hedenvind till Fridell* (Stockholm, 1952): 134–151. Runnqvist, Åke, "Debuter i skymundan: Jan Fridegård och Moa Martinson." *Bonniers Litterära Magasin* (1953): 197–203. Rying, Matts, "Moa i blåsippeblåsten." *Röster i Radio* 19 (1959): 11 and 41 (Interview). Selman, Barrie, "Moa." *Våra författare* 13 (no pag.); *Folket i bild* (1974): 6; reprinted under different title in *Våra författare*(1974): 154–160. Stiernstedt, Marika, *Marika Stiernstedt om Moa Martinson* (Stockholm, 1946). Strindberg, Axel, *Människor mellan krig* (Stockholm, 1941), pp. 295–298. Svanberg, Victor, "Moas rikedom." *Till nutidens lov* (Stockholm, 1956): 160–164. Öhman, Ivar, "Moa." *Folket i Bild*, 39 (1954): (no pag., sing. Öhn.)

Hanna Kalter Weiss

Liberata Masoliver

Born 1911, Barcelona, Spain
Genre(s): novel, romance, children's fiction
Language(s): Spanish, Catalan

Little information is available on the life of Masoliver, although from the attitudes expressed in her novels, it can be deduced that she was reared in a conventional, traditional and religious family of the Catalan bourgeoisie in Barcelona in the years between the wars. She is a writer of more than a dozen novels, published from the late 1950s through the early 1970s, most of them treating either the Spanish Civil War and its aftermath, religious themes, the life of the Catalan upper class in the postwar period, or adventures in the jungles of equatorial Africa. Although she repeatedly treats such problems as rape and adultery, she is not at all "feminist" in her perspective, which is conservative, conformist, and supportive of the patriarchal establishment. The conflict between religious faith or duty and the human heart or desires of the flesh is a favorite theme, as is the related "conversion," or repentance, of the erring wife or mother who returns to her husband or family after recognizing the evils of carnal love. Romantic illusion, when tested by reality, tends to fade; similarly, selfish or materialistic motivations and values are juxtaposed by Masoliver to spiritual principles and self-abnegation, with the former being exposed as shallow, trivial, or sinful. Certain themes that appear in Masoliver's narratives were potentially controversial: impotence, infidelity, divorce, homosexuality, rape, sterility, venereal disease, surrogate paternity. However, none is examined profoundly or treated as a social problem; rather, they become the reasons why characters must make moral or ethical decisions. A more serious analysis of these problems would likely have run afoul of the censors, but Masoliver, with her traditional resolutions, appears to have had no difficulty.

Los Galiano (1957; The Galiano Family), a novel of the contemporary upper class in Barcelona, presents the *dolce vita* of the young urban singles, with a picture of literary pastimes, fashions in music and amusements, and fads of the day. *Selva negra, selva verde* (1959; Black Jungle, Green Jungle) has as its protagonist an Italian adventurer who idealized Mussolini (a probable concession to the Fascist regime in Spain), but whose somewhat unlikely tale concerns his life among a tribe of cannibals. More significant is *Barcelona en llamas*(1961; Barcelona in Flames), a historical novel of the Civil War that traces the imprisonment of a nationalist (Franco) sympathizer by the republican militia and her subsequent release thanks to the intervention of a republican friend, her sentimental involvement with a mysterious fugitive, and the final discovery that this man was a priest in disguise. *La bruixa* (1961; The Witch) is a modern fairy tale in

Catalan verse that retells the fantastic adventures of two children kidnapped by a witch whose broom crashes in their garden. In *La mujer del colonial* (1962; The Colonist's Wife), Masoliver returns to the adventure romance set in the equatorial jungle, this time presenting the brief, tempestuous affair of a wife left behind to manage the ranch in the absence in Spain of her impotent husband. As in the following novel, *Maestro albañil* (1963; Master Bricklayer), frustrated maternity is a theme along with the child born of an adulterous relationship, but in the former case, the woman renounces her child to repent and return to her husband, while in the latter, the long-suffering wife adopts the baby fathered by her husband during his liaison with a scandalous adventuress. The theme reappears with slight variation in *Pecan los buenos* (1964; When the Good Sin), in which a model wife discovers that her inability to conceive is the result of her husband's premarital venereal infections that left him sterile. Obsessed with motherhood, she has an affair with her husband's partner but repents and is reunited with her husband.

Nieve y alquitrán (1965; Snow and Tar) is one of several novels set in or near wealthy resorts on the Costa Brava—likewise the scene of *Maestro albañil*, and of *Casino veraniego*. It is one of several works in which the theme of human needs for friendship and communication are stressed. In this case, the focus is upon the May and December relationship between two outcasts, an adolescent girl and a male recluse, who eventually hangs himself when she falls in love with someone her own age. *Un camino llega a la cumbre* (1966; One Path Leads to the Summit) implies by its title the treatment of a spiritual ascent, in this case, the problems faced by a devout girl who is raped and tempted by suicide upon realizing that she is pregnant. *La retirada* (1967; The Retreat) is supposedly a documentary of the final year and a half of the Spanish Civil War as experienced by two members of the republican or loyalist army, one a leftist disillusioned by party purges, the other actually conservative and potentially a nationalist (Franco) sympathizer unable to escape the draft. The latter's religious faith provides the opportunity for his friend's ultimate conversion, although the religious emphasis does not manage to displace the chronicle of the retreat. In *Casino veraniego* (1968; Vacation Casino), the summer resort setting is the backdrop for a wealthy young lady's romantic drama of selection between several suitors. *Hombre de paz* (1969; Man of Peace) returns to the Civil War to portray the moral dilemma of a doctor, courageously tending the sick and wounded of both sides, who must kill in order to save his sister's life and subsequently suffers pangs of conscience. His postwar confession, prior to his planned marriage to a woman of the opposing side, comes just before his death in an automobile accident. *Dios con nosotros* (1970; God With Us) is a novelistic interpretation of the life of Christ; *Estés donde estés* (1972; Wherever You May Be) harks back to the life of a nineteenth-century founder of a missionary order for advice and example proffered a young homosexual. By contrast with the exemplary motifs of these religious novels, *Los mini-amores de Angelines* (1972; Angela's Mini-Loves) depicts the disastrous consequences provoked by a selfish, sensual flirt whose adulterous affairs eventually lead to her death and that of her latest lover at the hands of a jealous lover discarded earlier. An abundance of stereotypes and somewhat predictable plots are among the more bothersome shortcomings of Masoliver's work, counterbalanced by usually well-handled dialogue, realistic descriptions, and a sustained level of narrative interest. Her popular success was considerable although enduring literary achievements are few.

Works

Barcelona en llamas (1961). *La bruixa* (1961). *Un camino llega a la cumbre* (1966). *Casino veraniego* (1968). *Dios con nosotros* (1970). *Efún* (1955). *Estés donde estés* (1972). *Los Galiano* (1957). *Hombre de paz* (1969). *Maestro albañil* (1963). *Los mini-amores de Angelines* (1972). *La mujer del colonial* (1962). *Nieve y alquitrán* (1965). *Pecan los buenos* (1964). *La retirada* (1967). *Selva negra, selva verde* (1959). *Telón* (1969).

Janet Perez

Appolline-Hélène Massalska, Princesse de Ligne

Born 1763, Poland; died October 30, 1815,
*   Paris, France*
Genre(s): memoir, letters
Language(s): French

Descended on her father's side from the Massalskis, on her mother's side from the Radziwills, two of the historically most influential families in Poland and Lithuania, Appolline-Hélène Massalska was brought as an orphan to Paris in 1773 by her uncle, the prince-bishop of Wilna, himself fleeing arrest in Poland. She was placed in the distinguished convent school of the Abbaye-aux-Bois, and at age ten, began to write her memoirs depicting life there. She ended them at age fourteen, on the eve of her first marriage, to the junior Prince de Ligne. Her memoirs paint an invaluable picture of the education of young noble girls during the late eighteenth century, demonstrating in particular how sharply class distinctions were inculcated in the minds of the young pupils. Given her family's properties, she was an attractive match. Extensive marriage negotiations were conducted with the senior Prince de Ligne. A marriage contract was drawn up and signed on May 25, 1779, at Versailles, in the presence of the assembled court of Louis XVI, with the marriage itself being celebrated four days later. Hélène Massalska had had only one previous interview with her future husband. One daughter, Sidonie, was born from this union in 1786. Not surprisingly, the couple grew apart. Immediately following her husband's death in battle in 1792, she hastened to marry Count Vincent Potocki, himself recently divorced. The couple had three children, all of whom died in infancy or childhood. After the death of the third child in 1799, it appears that Hélène and her second husband became alienated from one another. They later reconciled, in part at the urging of her first father-in-law, in order to provide for the children from their previous marriages. In fact, Hélène's daughter Sidonie ended up marrying Vincent's son from his second marriage, thus amicably and conveniently settling all inheritance problems. Hélène largely remained in Paris after this time and produced a large body of correspondence that has only been partially edited. Her letters document on the one hand the upheavals of the Napoleonic Wars and on the other the turmoil of her private life experienced by a noble family with connections to every court in Europe. She died October 30, 1815 and was buried in Père-Lachaise.

Works

Her memoirs are reprinted with commentary in: Perey, Lucien (Clara Herpin), *Histoire d'une grande dame au XVIIIᵉ siècle, la Princesse Hélène de Ligne* (1887–1888). Parts of her correspondence are printed in the follow-up volume: *Histoire d'une grande dame au XVIIIᵉ siècle, la Comtesse Hélène Potocka* (1888). Both volumes are available in English.

Bibliography

Collidge, Susan, "The Countess Potocka." *Atlantic Monthly* 76 (October, 1895): 458–476. Doumic, René, "La Comtesse Hélène Potocka." *Le Correspondant* 151 (n.s. 115) (1888) 177–184.

Earl Jeffrey Richards

Jenny Mastorakē

(see: Jenny Mastoraki)

Jenny Mastoraki

(a.k.a. Jenny Mastorakē)

Born 1949, Athens, Greece
Genre(s): poetry, translation
Language(s): Greek

Jenny Mastoraki (or Mastorakē) grew up in Athens. She graduated with high honors from the University of Athens, where she concentrated in Medieval and Byzantine studies. Shortly after graduation she published her first book of poetry, *Diodia* (Tolls). Six years later she published *To soi* (The Kin) and five years after that *Histories gia ta vathia* (Stories About the Deep). Her translations of English, German, and Italian works into modern Greek are considered excellent. Among others, she translated J.D. Salinger's *Catcher in the Rye*, Upton Sinclair's *The Jungle*, and works by Heinrich von Kleist. Her own poetry has been translated into English, French, German, Italian, Spanish, Swedish, Dutch, Russian, Bulgarian, and Romanian and has appeared in many anthologies and journals outside of Greece.

Mastoraki's poems created a furor in the Greek literary scene in the early 1970s. Perhaps more so than any other poetess she can claim to have made a difference in modern Greek poetry. In *Diodia* (Tolls), a collection of terse and succinct poems that are more precisely statements of experience, she took it upon herself to shake off poetic conventions and contemporary practices and write in a style that is original and refreshing. In these statements of experience that are her poems, we sense that the persona is not too far removed from the poet herself, and the voice is an authentic feminine voice struggling to be heard, and the frustration at the inability to make oneself heard, the inability to find the "right" words for communication, and the inability to express what has been repressed or suppressed. But the task of the poet is to keep trying, to keep "fastening hope with nails and teeth" as she stands on the scaffolds of existence (*Diodia*, p. 22).

To soi (The Kin) deals with the family and relatives with whom one grows up. It exposes the reality, the cruelty, and the selfishness that are hidden beneath the surface of "loving and proper families." The poems in this collection are short and to the point also, but here the element of "play" is much more obvious. With skillful use of irony, the establishment of kin comes tumbling down, but this is done not maliciously but playfully, and the destroyer is a persona (or a number of personae) who, like a mischievous child, has had a great deal of fun in the process.

Among women poets writing today, Mastoraki is one of the best-known outside of Greece. Putting emphasis on the quality of her work rather than on the quantity (in contrast to many Greek writers, who have an obsession with the number of published works), she has produced poetry that, stripped of all ornamentation, speaks to an international audience about essential matters, even though her topics are sometimes very specific. The specificity, however, is not so much "local" as personal, and the poems touch us personally and thus deeply.

Works

Diodia [Tolls] (1972, 1982). *To soi* [The Kin] (1978). *Histories gia ta vathia* [Stories about the Deep] (1983, 1986).

Translations: *Books of Women Poets from Antiquity to Now*, ed. Aliki Barnstone and Willis Barnstone (New York, 1980). *Contemporary Greek Poetry*, tr. Kimon Friar (Athens, 1985). *Contemporary Greek Women Poets*, tr. Eleni Fourtouni (New Haven, 1978). *Modern Poetry in Translation* a34 (Summer, 1978). *The Penguin Book of Women Poets*, ed. Carol Cosman, Joan Keefe, and Kathleen Weaver (New York, 1978). "Three Young Poets: Jenny Mastoraki, Haris Megalinos, and Lefteris Poulios." *Boundary 2: A Journal of Postmodern Literature* (Winter, 1973): 508–513. *Twenty Contemporary Greek Poets*, ed. Dinos Siotis and John Chioles (San Francisco, 1979).

Bibliography

Decavalles, Andonis, "Modernity: The Third Stage, the New Poets." *The Charioteer*, vol. 20 (New York, 1978). Kolias, Helen Dendrinou, "Greek Women Poets and the Language of Silence." *Translation Perspectives IV* (Binghamton, N.Y., 1988). Review by George Giannaris. *World Literature Today*. 53, 4 (1979).

Helen Dendrinou Kolias

Emilie Mataja

(a.k.a. Emil Marriot)

Born November 20, 1855, Vienna, Austria; died May 5, 1938, Vienna
Genre(s): novel, short story, journalism
Language(s): German

While still quite young, Marriot felt acute disappointment at having been born a girl and resolved to achieve something special rather than accept the traditional female role. In adolescence she came to feel that writing would bring her self-fulfillment and, despite the opposition of her middle-class parents, she determined to establish herself as a writer. With the help of Paul Heyse, Ludwig von Sacher-Masoch, Karl Emil Franzos, Maximilian Harden, and others she achieved her goal. Her writing remained the center of her life until she concluded her career in 1920. In her nonfiction in newspapers, she often argued for the improvement of the situation of women, and in her fiction she often portrayed the experiences of girls and women.

Marriot's fiction provoked various and often conflicting reactions among critics. She was considered by some to be second only to Maria von Ebner-Eschenbach among Austrian women writers at the turn of the century. Some critics consider her a tendentious critic of the family, society, and the Catholic Church, while others find her an objective chronicler of contemporary life. In spite of their widely differing opinions, Marriot's critics agree almost without exception that her works are not merely entertainment. Her most famous work, the novel *Der geistliche Tod* (1884; Clerical Death), portrays the struggles of a decent man, unsuited to celibacy, who has become a Catholic priest. In her novels, *Novellen*, and other short fiction Marriot shows considerable skill in the portrayal of her characters' psychology in a way that brings to mind her famous Austrian contemporary Arthur Schnitzler. Marriot's oeuvre, which is part of one of the richest periods of Austrian literature, deserves reading and further evaluation.

Bibliography

Byrnes, John, *Emil Marriot: A Reevaluation Based on Her Short Fiction* (Bern, Frankfurt am Main, New York, 1983). Byrnes, John, "Emil Marriot Bibliography." *Modern Austrian Literature* 12, 3/4 (1979): 59–76. A Complete list of Marriot's works as well as of the secondary literature through 1979. Byrnes, John, "An Introduction to Emil Marriot." *Modern Austrian Literature* 12, 3/4 (1979): 45–57.

John Byrnes

Chiara Matraini

Born June 4, 1515, Lucca, Italy; died ca. 1604
Genre(s): poetry, letters, translation
Language(s): Italian

The Matraini family, at the time Chiara was born, belonged to the ruling class of Lucca. Their standing, however, was undermined when in 1531–1532 they played a leading role in the unsuccessful insurrection of the Straccioni. They were exiled for a brief period, and when they returned to Lucca they failed to regain their former social position. The family died out altogether in 1615, shortly after Chiara's death. Chiara, too, had an ambiguous relationship with the city of her birth. She is presented in both a negative and a positive light in local history, and she herself complains in letters and verse of unfair treatment by her husband's family, her own son, the city, and society in general, which had not permitted her the education she desired.

At the age of fifteen Chiara was married to Vincenzo Cantarini. By 1542 she had been widowed, and it seems, from documentary evidence corroborated by biographical references in her writing, that between 1547 and 1555 she was linked romantically with Bartolomeo Graziani, a married man, whose wife at least one contemporary historian depicted as the suffering victim of Chiara's villainy. Graziani was murdered in 1555, and history's recording of this event together with the love triangle, until the recent work of Giovanna Rabitti, has always had the characteristics of a sixteenth-century tragic tale. Chiara lived in Genoa in 1560–1562, during which time she was close to the circle of the Doge. She was back in Lucca by 1576, when she had her portrait made by the painter Alessandro Ardenti in the guise of the Cumaean Sibyl, part of the decoration of an altar she also commissioned for the church of Santa Maria Forisportam, where she was eventually buried. Because she was seen as a sibyl and seductress, Chiara Matraini has been, by fanciful extension, called an enchantress and a witch; she is more often, however, deemed an important intellectual and poet, and the latter claim is borne out by her impressive verse and epistolary collections.

The biography of Chiara Matraini is inextricably linked to her most important writing. She was a Petrarchist, and her poetry collection, like those of her principal models, Petrarch, but also Vittoria Colonna and Pietro Bembo, tells an earthly love story that is at the same time the story of her poetry and her journey to God. The first edition of her *Rime*, published in 1555, follows the story of her affair with Graziani, and part one ends with references to his tragic death. The spiritual itinerary, not yet convincingly imposed on the love story in the first edition of the *Rime*, is carefully developed in the 1595 and especially in the 1597 edition after thorough revisions of many of the poems, the attenuation of biographical references not easily allegorized, a reorganization of the sequence, and the inclusion of new material. The final edition, which the author saw through publication, represents one of the highest achievements of sixteenth century Petrarchism. While the language, imagery, and the significant moments of the love story are dependent on the models, as is the division of the book into a part "in life" and another "in death" of the beloved, the particular configuration they take on in the final version of the *Rime* has an extraordinary coherence and originality of its own, rare in the annals of Petrarchist imitation. The cohesion of the book depends on the writer's technical expertise and especially on her masterful exploitation of the dominant images of the sun and moon, their respective realms of day and night, and of the many metaphorical possibilities of that semantic field. The lover is the moon to the beloved's sun, but only the hierarchy remains constant, and the relationship is explored through the use of classical mythology, the biblical tradition, and Petrarchan (and Petrarchist) conventions. Finally, the collection as a whole shows that the image of the sun, present from the first poems to the last in a myriad of forms, can and must be read spiritually and neoplatonically as the instrument of the lover's elevation and salvation, as Divine love, reflected in the world and leading beyond the world. Matraini's letters, many of which are published together with the final editions of the poetry, illuminate her life and her work, and her writing during the years that intervened between the first and final editions of her poetry, largely religious in nature, contributed importantly to the final form her major collection assumed.

Virtually forgotten for centuries—there is not as yet a complete modern edition of her *Rime*, and her other writing has not been reprinted since the seventeenth-century—Chiara Matraini's work has in recent times been enthusiastically reevaluated; critics compare her to Gaspara Stampa, and some name her among the most important writers of sixteenth-century Italy.

Works

Poetry and letters: *Rime e prose di Madonna Chiara Matraini Gentildonna Lucchese* (1555). *Rime di diversi signori napoletani e d'altri... Libro settimo*, Lodovico Dolce, ed. (1556), pp. 68–154. *Lettere della signora Chiara Matraini, Gentildonna luchese, con la prima e seconda parte delle sue Rime* (1595). *Lettere di Madonna Chiara Matraini Gentildonna Lucchese, con la prima e seconda parte della sue Rime [. . .]* (1597). *Inediti vaticani di Chiara Matraini*, in *Studi di filologia e critica offerti dagli allievi a Lanfranco Caretti*, I, Giovanna Rabitti, ed. (1985), pp. 225–250.

Modern anthology selections: Baldacci, Luigi, ed., *Lirici del Cinquecento* (1957), pp. 497–530. Costa-Zalessow, Natalia, ed., *Scrittrici italiane dal XIII al XX secolo. Testi e critica* (1982), pp. 93–98. Gamba, B., ed., *Lettere di donne italiane del secolo decimosesto* (1832), pp. 157–164. Ferroni, G., ed., *Poesia italiana. Il Cinquecento* (1978), pp. 244–248. Muscetta, C., and D. Ponchiroli, eds., *Poesia del Quattrocento e del Cinquecento (Parnaso italiano IV.)* (1959), pp. 1297–1300.

Other works: *Orazione d'Isocrate*, tr. from Latin (1556). *Meditazioni spirituali di Madonna Chiara Cantarini de' Matraini, Gentildonna lucchese* (1581). *Breve discorso sopra la vita della Beata Vergine* (1590). *Considerazioni sopra i sette salmi penitenziali del Gran Profeta Davitati [. . .]* (1586). *Dialoghi spirituali di Madonna Chiara Matraini, Gentildonna lucchese* (1602).

Bibliography

Baldacci, L., "Chiara Matraini poetessa lucchese del XVI sec." *Paragone* 42 (1953): 53–67. Bullock, A., and Palange, G., "Per una edizione critica delle opere di Chiara Matraini." *Studi in onore di Raffaele Spongano* (Bologna, 1980), pp. 235–262. Rabitti, G., "Linee per il ritratto di Chiara Matraini." *Studi e problemi di critica testuale* 22 (1981): 141–165. Rabitti, G., "La metafora e l'esistenza nella poesia di Chiara Matraini." *Studi e problemi di critica testuale* 27 (1983): 109–145.

Elissa B. Weaver

Vicenta Maturana de Guitiérrez

Born 1793, Cádiz, Spain; died 1857, Alcalá de Henares
Genre(s): novel, poetry, prose poetry
Language(s): Spanish

Vicenta Maturana was the most famous woman writer during Ferdinand VII's time. She was a close friend of Amalia, the king's wife, and remained loyal to him until his death in 1833, when she went into exile in France. Soon after, Joaquin María Gutiérrez, her husband since 1820, was killed fighting for the Carlist cause.

Having started writing at the age of nine, against her parents' wishes, she published her first novel, *Teodoro o El huérfano agradecido*, anonymously in 1825. In 1829, following the publication, under her own name, of her second and most famous novel, *Sofía y Enrique. Novela original*, one of the better examples of the sentimental Byzantine novel, she explained that "the fear of being singled out, and the probability of attracting the malicious attacks of envy and ignorance" were not only the reasons for her own decision to publish anonymously but also the reasons that most Spanish women did not write at all. Vicenta Maturana belonged to several literary salons which were also frequented by María Josefa Massanés, Robustinana Armiño, Gertrudis Gómez de Avellaneda, and Carolina Coronado. While she often voiced support for women's rights in her prologues, her works did not principally treat the role of women in early nineteenth century Spain.

Maturana is mainly remembered for her poetry collection, *Ensayos poéticos* (1828), which contained 28 pastoral odes, 20 sonnets, and an impressive variety of other verse forms, and *Poesías de la señora doña Vicenta Maturana de Gutiérrez* (1841), a two-part work that reprinted the poems from her first collection and also introduced new work, most of it humorous or satirical in nature; however, it also included a sonnet on the death of María Josefa Amalia, wife of Ferdinand VII. In 1838, her prose poem, *Himno a la luna. Poema en cuatro cantos*, thought to be one of the earliest manifestations of the genre in Spain, was published. Inspired by reading *Himno al Sol*, written in French by Abbé de Reyrac, Maturana compared, with impressionistic flair, sun/man with moon/woman.

Regarded as a precursor of the Romantic revolution in poetry, her novels were also pre-Romantic in tone; her characters were rich, and her plots not subordinated to a moral thesis. As the best known woman writer of her times, Vicenta Maturana played a unique role in early nineteenth-century Spanish literature.

Works

Teodoro o El huérfano agradecido (1825). *Ensayos poéticos* (1828). *Sofía y Enrique. Novela original.* 2 vols. (1929). *Himno a la luna. Poema en cuatro cantos.* (1838). *Poesías de la señora doña Vicenta Maturana de Gutiérrez* (1841; third ed., 1859).

Bibliography

Galerstein, Carolyn L., ed., *Women Writers of Spain* (Westport, Conn., 1986). Pedraza, Felipe and Milagros Rodríguez Cáceres, *Manual de literatura española*, VI, Epoca romántica (Navarra, 1982). Serrano y Sanz, Manuel, *Apuntes para una biblioteca de escritoras españolas.* Biblioteca de Autores Españoles, vol. 270 (1903; rpt. Madrid, 1975).

Rosetta Radtke

Julia Maura

Born 1910, Madrid, Spain; died 1970
Genre(s): drama
Language(s): Spanish

Julia Maura was born into a distinguished family: her grandfather, Antonio Maura, was Prime Minister to King Alfonso XII; her father, Gabriel, Duke of Maura, was elected to the National Academies of Language, History and the Sciences; her uncle, Honorio Maura, was a successful dramatist. Julia Maura is the best known of the women dramatists in the period 1944–1970, when approximately eighteen of her plays were performed commercially in Madrid. She wrote conservative, moralistic comedies and dramas in traditional style usually about the upper middle classes in Spain. She frequently showed the evils of hypocrisy and the false system of honor that cruelly victimized many women. Her last play, *Jaque a la juventud* (Warning to Youth), initiated a new direction:

depicting Spain's new materialism and rapidly changing morality, this work showed a much more contemporary focus in terms of situation, character, and language. Her plays were admired by spectator and critic alike. Characteristic of her plays are *La mentira del silencio* (The Lie of Silence), *Chocolate a la española* (Hot Chocolate, Spanish Style) and *La eterna doña Juana* (The Eternal Doña Juana).

Works

La mentira del silencio [The Lie of Silence] (1944). *Siempre* [Always] (1952). *Estos son mis artículos* [These are my Articles] (1953). *Chocolate a la española* [Hot Chocolate, Spanish Style] (1953). *La eterna doña Juana* [The Eternal Doña Juana] (1954). *La riada* [The Torrent] (1956). *Como la tierra y el mar* [Like the Earth and the Sea] (1957). *Ventolera* [Whim] (1957). *¡Quien supiera escribir!* [If Only I Could Write!] (1957). *Artículos de fe* [Articles of Faith] (1959). *Historias crueles* (1963). *Jaque a la juventud* [Warning to Youth] (1965).

Bibliography

O'Connor, Patricia W., "Julia Maura." *Spanish Women Writers: A Bio-Bibliographical Sourcebook* (New York, 1990).

Patricia W. O'Connor

Zenta Mauriņa

Born December 15, 1897, Lejasciems, Latvia; died April 25, 1978, Basel, Switzerland
Genre(s): essay, criticism, autobiography, novel, short story
Language(s): German, Latvian

Zenta Mauriņa is one of the most remarkable women of the twentieth century. She was not only an extraordinarily intelligent and perceptive commentator on almost any phase or phenomenon of European culture but was also an exemplary human being, admired and esteemed by everyone who met her.

At the age of five, Mauriņa was crippled by poliomyelitis. She spent the rest of her life in a wheelchair, and she was often in very poor health and much pain. Her childhood, however, was beneficially influenced by her warm and optimistic father, who was a physician. Her pianist mother was German. Mauriņa grew up trilin-

gual, fluent in Latvian, German, and Russian; her secondary education was at a Russian *gymnasium*, and her earliest published work is a translation from Latvian into German. In 1938, she received a doctorate, *summa cum laude*, in Baltic philology from the University of Riga, where she had been active as a researcher and teacher since 1924. For a time she also studied literature and philosophy at Heidelberg. She was one of the founders of the Latvian People's University, one of the principal collaborators on a definitive history of Latvian literature and on a complete German-Latvian and Latvian-German dictionary. Her public lectures at her own literary institute in Riga attracted huge audiences. In 1936, she lectured in Florence and Paris, in 1939 in Helsinki. For ideological reasons she had been publicly threatened with summary execution, and with the approach of the Soviet Army in 1944, she fled Latvia, accompanied and assisted by her constant companion, Konstantins Raudive (a disciple of Unamuno and Ortega y Gasset and an author in his own right). They barely escaped into Germany. After an odyssey through Germany, they settled in Sweden in 1946, where Mauriņa mastered Swedish and became a guest lecturer at the University of Uppsala. She was greatly honored in her adopted country, eminently so by King Gustaf VI who personally made arrangements for her to travel in Italy. From 1951 on, she went on yearly lecture tours through West Germany, where she met with notable success. Her success was enhanced by the fact that she published an increasing number of works in German. She received numerous literary awards and prizes in both countries. In 1965, she settled in Bad Krozingen, West Germany, where she continued her work, and where she is buried.

Almost single-handedly, Mauriņa introduced the essay into Latvian literature. Stylistically, she was influenced by Seneca, Montaigne, and Pascal; morally, by Dostoievsky and the Latvian folksong (the *daina*), with its emphasis on closeness to nature and to working on the land. Mauriņa was extraordinarily well-read, but her preferences in literature were dictated not by prevailing opinion but by her own deep humanism and love of freedom. Her interests and knowledge were far-ranging, and she had a talent for capturing the essence of a writer's, philosopher's, or artist's thought. Her slightly fictionalized autobiography *Die weite Fahrt* (1951; A Long Journey), *Denn das Wagnis ist schön* (1953; Fair is the Venture), and *Die eisernen Riegel zerbrechen* (1957; The Iron Bars are Breaking), and the collection of essays *Mosaik des Herzens* (1947; The Mosaic of the Heart) best reveal her personality. After 1945 Mauriņa frequently wrote her books in both Latvian and German. From the German, many were translated into Swedish. She was active as translator of English, French, Norwegian, and Russian works and as a contributor to Latvian, German, and Swedish periodicals.

Works

(The following list attempts to indicate each work by the title that first appeared in print, whether Latvian or German.) *Da'i pamata motīvi Raiņa mākslā* (1928). *Jānis Poruks un romantisms* (1929). *Dostojevskis* (1933). *Baltais ceļš* (1935). *Dzīves apliecinātāji* (1936). *Dante tagadnes cilvēka skatījumā* (1937). *Friča Bārdas pasaules uzskats* (1938). *Grāmata par cilvēkiem un lietām* (1938). *Saules meklētāji* (1938). *Ziemeļu tēmas un variācijas* (1939). *Dzīves vilcienā* (1941). *Prometēja gaismā* (1942). *Kulturās saknes* (1944). *Trīs brāļi* (1946). *Mosaik des Herzens* (1947). *Tilti* (1947). *Spīts* (1949). *Gestalten und Schicksale* (1949). *Uguns gari* (1951). *Die Weite Fahrt* (1951). *Frančesca* (1952). *Sāpju noslēpums* (1952). *Latviešu esejas* (1953). *Pilsētas un cilvēki* (1953). *Tragiskais skaistums* (1954). *Cilvēces sargi* (1955). *Um des Menschen willen* (1955). *Begegnung mit Elly Ney* (1956). *Die eisernen Riegel zerbrechen* (1957). *Auf der Schwelle zweier Welten* (1959). *Über Liebe und Tod* (1960). *Die Langeweile und der gehetzte Mensch* (1962). *Schwedische Tagebücher: Nord- und südliches Gelände* (1962). *Welteinheit und die Augfabe des Einzelnen* (1963). *Im Anfang war die Freude* (1964). *Die Aufgabe des Dichters in unserer Zeit* (1965). *Schwedische Tagebücher: Jahre der Befreiung* (1965). *Lebensmeisterung* (1966). *Verfremdung und Freundschaft* (1966). *Lebensmeisterung* (1966). *Verfremdung und Freundschaft* (1966). *Birkenborke, Benjamin* (1967). *Porträts russischer Schriftsteller* (1968). *Wege zur Genesung* (1968). *Abenteuer des Menschseins* (1970). *Um der Freude Willen* (1971). *Der Mensch das ewige Thema des Dichters* (1972).

Tod im Frühling (1972). *Dzīves jēgu meklējot* (1973). *Kleines Orchester der Hoffnung* (1974). *Der Weg vom Ich zum Du* (1974). *Warum Kontaktlosigkeit* (1975). *Dzintargraudi* (1976). *Mein Lied von der Erde* (1976). *Die Marmortreppe* (1977). *Meine Wurzeln sind im Himmel* (1979). *Briefe aus dem Exil*, 1945–1951 (1980). Numerous shorter pieces and translations.

Translations: *A Prophet of the Soul: Fyodor Dostoievksy*, tr. C.P. Finlayson (1939). "Homo Fugiens: Man of Our Time." *Mosaic: A Journal for the Comparative Study of Literature and Ideas* 9. 2 (1976): 69–72. *A Long Journey, Fair Is the Venture*, and *The Iron Bars Are Breaking*, tr. Zoja Pavlovskis (in progress).

Bibliography

Dietrich, Maximilian, ed., *Buch der Freundschaft: Zenta Mauriņa zum 70 Geburtstag* (Memmingen, 1967). Lippelt, Christoph, ed., *Zenta Maurina: bilder aus ihrem Leben.* Also see Benjamiņs Jēgers, *Latviešu trimdas izdevumu bibliografija-Bibliography of Latvian Publications Published Outside Latvia, 1940–1960* (Sundbyberg, 1972; *1961–1970*, Sundbyberg, 1977; *1971–1980*, Stockholm, 1988).

Zoja Pavlovskis

Lizzy Sara May

Born 1918
Genre(s): poetry, short story, novel,
    autobiography
Language(s): Dutch

Lizzy Sara May's poetry is close in style to that of the Vijftigers (the *"Fiftiers,"* a group of poets led by Lucebert) and achieves at times the serenity of poems like Van Ostaijen's "Melopee" of Lucebert's "Visser van ma Yuan" ("Fisher of Ma Yuan"). Yet her prose is considered better and more significant than her poetry.

Lizzy Sara May trained as a dancer, and the worlds of ballet and music play an important role in a number of her works. Her preoccupation with rhythm and dance steps is reflected in the title of her first collection: *Blues voor voetstappen* (1956; Blues for Foot Steps). Together with *Weerzien op een plastic huid* (1957; Encounter on a Plastic Skin), it contains her best poems.

They were re-published under the title *Gebruikspoezie* (1978; Poetry You Can Use). It is because of the repetitions and parallelisms she used that her poetry was so popular in the fifties.

She proved her strength as a prose writer in books like *Het lokaliseren van pijn* (1970; Localizing Pain), *De tennisspelers of de som der mogelijkheden* (1972; The Tennis Players or the Sum of Possibilities), *Mimicri* (1973), and *Vader en dochter* (1977; Father and Daughter) in which certain fragments of reality are convincingly brought to life. May is a committed writer, interested especially in the plights of women. In *Het lokaliseren van pijn*, composed of thirty-seven short prose sketches, the female characters attempt to be themselves against all pressure from the outside. The pain lives in the loneliness and the worn relationships between women and men, between several women, and between a woman and the people around her. The author attacks the false notions people have about the life of single women and chides mothers who educate their sons for war. Each sketch, composed with subtlety and insight, is an attempt to get closer to the other(s) in the relationship, to expose the wounds, and then to begin the process of recovery.

In her most recent books, Lizzy Sara May has been writing increasingly about her Jewish past and childhood experiences. *Vader en dochter* consists of two parts and describes the author's relationship with her artistic parents—the father given to megalomania and self-pity; the mother a child-woman ill equipped for the responsibilities of motherhood—and her adolescence and gradual insight into the character and life style of her father. Several of her books have been translated into German.

Works

Poetry: *Blues voor voetstappen* (1956). *Weerzien op een plastic huid* (1957). *Tijd voor magnetisch vuur* (1963). *Zingend als een zinkend schip* (1960). *Grim* (1969).

Prose: *De parels van het parlement* (1960). *Oom Soes heeft gehuild* (1962). *Dansen op het koord en andere verhalen* (1965). *Het dubbelspoor* (1966). *De Haaien* (1969). *De tennisspelers* (1972). *De belegering* (1975). *De blauwe plek* (1979). *Bewogen foto's* (1980). *Beminnen met verstand* (1981).

Waarom loopt de klok rond? (1983). *Binnenkort in dit theater* (1984).

Bibliography

Moerman, Josien, *Lexikon Nederlandstalige auteurs* (1984), p. 155. Moor, Wam De, "Lizzy Sara May," in *'Tis vol van schatten hier*, vol. 2 (Amsterdam, 1986), pp. 217–218.

Maya Bijvoet

Marina Mayoral

Born September 22, 1942, Mondoñedo (Lugo), Spain
Genre(s): novel, short story, literary criticism
Language(s): Spanish

Already well established as a professor of literature and literary critic, Mayoral did not publish her own first creative work until 1979. Her subsequent novels include two, *La única libertad* (The Only Freedom) and *Contra muerte y amor* (Against Death and Love), that have been published by one of Spain's major presses and hence have brought her to the forefront of promising younger novelists. She also writes short stories and has been awarded several prizes for them, including the Hucha de Oro for 1982.

Mayoral was educated in Lugo and Santiago in her native Galicia before receiving her doctorate in Romance philology from the Complutense University in Madrid. She also holds a diploma in psychology. She has been a professor of Spanish literature (eighteenth-twentieth centuries) at the Complutense since 1978. Her scholarly work includes several books and editions on major women writers of Galicia, Rosalía de Castro and Emilia Pardo Bazán. The mother of two children, Mayoral is married to the painter Jordi Teixidor.

Mayoral's four novels to date differ in the complexity of their narrative structures but all retain some elements of the detective novel. They share the same novelistic world; characters from one work reappear in the others. The scene of the action shifts from Galicia to Madrid, but most of the characters are of Galician origin. Always in the background of the novels is the question of class prejudice, stemming from the almost feudal divisions that still linger in Galician society. The novels also deal with the status of women in that society, ranging from exploited servants in the rural community to educated professional women, including doctors and lawyers, in an urban setting.

La única libertad, an innovative metanovel, juxtaposes past and present as the narrator-protagonist, at the behest of her three great aunts, attempts to reconstruct her family's history in Galicia while simultaneously seeking her own identity and that of her father. *Contra muerte y amor* is a multiple perspective novel that explores a variety of themes, including the violence that erupts from the continuing class struggles of the past and the political terrorism of the present.

All four of Mayoral's novels illustrate her talent for story telling, her ability to create a variety of interesting characters, and her knowledge of different subcultures and lifestyles, ranging from the fishing villages of Galicia to the world of boxing, from the gay community and artistic circles to the old aristocracy. She has a thorough familiarity with narrative technique and promises to be one of the important writers of her generation.

Works

Cándida, otra vez (1979). Al otro lado (1980). La única libertad (1982). Contra muerte y amor (1985).

Bibliography

Arnosi, Milagros Sanchez, Interview with Marina Mayoral. *Insula* 431 (1982): 4. García Rey, José M, "Marina Mayoral: La sociedad que se cuestiona en medio de una dudosa realidad." *Cuadernos Hispanoamericanos* 394 (1983): 214–221. Valencia, Antonio, Prologue to *Al otro lado*. By *Marina Mayoral* (Madrid, 1981), pp. 9–15. Zatlin, Phyllis, "Women Novelists in Democratic Spain: Freedom to Express the Female Perspective," *Anales de la Literatura Española Contemporánea* 12 (1987): 29–44.

General references: *Women Writers of Spain: An Annotated Bio-Bibliographical Guide*, ed. Carolyn L. Galerstein (Westport, Conn., 1986).

Phyllis Zatlin

Friederike Mayröcker

Born 1924, Vienna, Austria
Genre(s): poetry, poetic prose
Language(s): German

Friederike Mayröcker has published texts in avant-garde journals and presses since 1947, making a living teaching English language and literature at a Viennese secondary school between 1946 and 1969. Since the 1950s, she has been in contact with the writers of the Wiener Gruppe (Vienna Group), such as Artmann, Rühm, Jandl, and Bayer, whose aims she shared at the beginning and whose achievements she has by now outdone. With her companion Ernst Jandl, she has co-authored plays and prose texts. She has also provided whimsical drawings for some of her books.

Friederike Mayröcker is without doubt the most versatile and experimental of contemporary poets in the German language and also the most cosmopolitan. With her anti-sentimental but highly playful attitude toward language and the world—which in her compatriot Wittgenstein's seminal philosophy are all but a complex oneness—she seems as close to Brechtian estrangement and *maudit* or beat casualness as she is to the entire twentieth-century avant-garde tradition, regardless of national origin or language. While making ample use of the by-now-well-exploited iconic properties of concrete poetry, she rarely remains within their perimeter but instead combines them with other modernist techniques in order to achieve a powerful and supple language enriched with typographical devices. Thus she is capable of expressing simultaneously several countervailing voices in one and the same text without the whole appearing incoherent to the serious reader.

Friederike Mayröcker is her own severest critic, judging her poetic output according to the extent to which "I have succeeded in converting to the precisest language possible the traces imposed on me by life and the world" (*Magische Blätter*, p. 18). Like all poets, she remembers childhood well in her texts, and especially the moment when she started writing: "Emerging unawares from a hermetic childhood, . . . I discover one day, how inconceivable, how mysterious, how incredible: I am writing my own poetry." Here, the fractured syntax and choice of the present tense express with subtle cogency the moment of the child's hesitant but joyous realization (*Magische Blätter*, p. 2).

In 1966, her first major anthology, a retrospective, was published, through which she finally became known to a wider audience. Bold is the best description of her stance. She employs her vast and contemporary erudition not in a traditional way, like Kaschnitz, but ranges freely and purposefully in a kind of associative, illogical dream logic first analyzed by her compatriot Freud and pioneered in literature by the French surrealists. Sometimes her oneiric combinations are far-fetched and on the borderline of comprehensibility, a border which she has vowed to expand, but most of the time, her poetic exploits are nothing short of stunning. She by no means shuns reality and private life: her love poems to Jandl are among the most moving today. Moreover, there has been a perceptible development in her writing: while her early poetry shows an autobiographical strain and a separate line of the "experimental for the experimental's sake," as it were, her recent texts are a masterful, tight but nevertheless airy synthesis of both. Friederike Mayröcker's prizes are many, although she deserves still more. She has lectured widely abroad.

Works

Larifari (1956). Metaphorisches (1965). Tod durch Musen (1966). Sägespäne für mein Herzbluten (1967). Minimonsters Traumlexikon (1968). Fantom Fan (1971). [With Ernst Jandl], Fünf Mann Menschen. (1972). Arie auf tönernen Fuszen. je ein umwölkter gipfel (1973). in langsamen blitzen (1974). meine träume im flugelkleid (1974). Das Licht in der Landschaft (1975). Fast ein Frühling des Markus M. (1976). rot ist unten (1977). Heiligenanstalt (1978). Ausgewählte Gedichte 1944–1978 (1979). Ein Lesebuch (1979). Die Abschiede (1980).

Bibliography

Borchers, Elisabeth, and Hans-Ulrich Müller-Schwefe, *Im Jahrhundert der Frau* (Frankfurt, 1984). Brinker-Gabler, Gisela, *Deutsche Dichterinnen* (Frankfurt, 1986). Puknus, Heinz, ed., *Neue Literatur der Frauen* (Munich, 1980). Serke, Jürgen, *Frauen schreiben* (Frankfurt, 1982).

Ute Marie Saine

Zane Me'adūja

(see: Anna Sakse)

Catherine de Medicis

Born 1519, Florence, Italy; died 1589, Blois, France
Genre(s): poetry
Language(s): French

Daughter of Lawrence II of Medicis and of Madeleine de La Tour d'Auvergne, niece of Pope Clement VII, Catherine de Medicis married in 1533 Henri son of Francis I, King of France. She became queen in 1547, but as long as her husband lived, his mistress Diane de Poitiers was all powerful. During the very short reign of Francis II, Marie Stuart and her uncles (the Guise) were in power, and Catherine de Medicis was able to take in hand the matters of the kingdom of France only when her two younger sons, Charles IX and Henri III, became kings.

Her followers tried to exalt Catherine's knowledge, especially her expertise in the "mathematic sciences." She was in fact interested in astrology, and very superstitious. She probably received less education than all the ladies who surrounded her at the French court, but she was able to write poetry.

Bibliography

Chavannes, Frédéric, *Notice sur un manuscrit du XVIᵉ* (Lausanne, 1844). Frémy, Ed, "Les Poésies inédites de Catherine de Medicis." *Correspondant* (1883). Joly, Aristide, "Quelques poésies de Catherine de Medicis et de sa fille Elizabeth de France, reine d'Espagne," *Bull. Soc. Normandie* (1883). Laugel, A. "La Correspondance de Catherine de Medicis." *Revue des Deux Mondes* (1862).

Marie-France Hilgar

Dolores Medio

Born 1914, Oviedo, Spain
Genre(s): novel, short story, biography, journalism
Language(s): Spanish

Dolores Medio is part of an encouraging phenomenon of post-Civil War Spain: the emergence of a strong generation of women writers, especially novelists. Reared and educated in the northern province of Asturias, Dolores Medio suffered displacement, poverty, and death of family members during the war. Trained as a teacher, she was relieved of her post in 1936 when her innovative methods came under attack. Her interest in education and children as well as other social issues has been a distinguishing mark since the days of the war. In 1962, for example, she was jailed for one month for being present at a women's demonstration.

Given her concern for social problems, especially those of the middle class, the subject matter and technique of her fiction are not surprising. In her first novel, *Nosotros los Rivero*, for which she was awarded the esteemed Premio Nadal, she portrays in the realistic vein of the nineteenth century novel middle class life in Asturias. Her selection as recipient of the award met with disapproval from many critics who found her style old-fashioned, unsuitable for a prize which they thought should go to groundbreaking writers. She continued to insist on straightforward narrative, description of externals and a clean, direct style, all characteristics of the older realistic novel.

The autobiographical elements of the first novel surface in later fiction, notably *Diario de una maestra*, whose schoolteacher protagonist clearly is the author herself. Economic and psychological hardships of the middle class in Madrid are another favorite topic, seen first, and effectively, in *Funcionario público*.

Dolores Medio's writings include fiction for children, short stories, biography, a guidebook to her native region of Asturias, literary criticism and many journalistic pieces. Although she has not received the critical acclaim in recent years that other women writers of her generation have, Dolores Medio is nonetheless an important figure on the landscape of twentieth-century Spanish literature.

Works

El milagro de la Noche de Reyes (1948). *Nosotros los Rivero* (1953). *Compás de espera* (1954). *Mañana* (1954). *Funcionario público* (1956). *El pez sigue flotando* (1959). *Diario de una maestra* (1961). *Bibiana* (1963). *El señor García.* (1966). *Isabel II de España* (1966). *Andrés* (1967). *Asturias* (1971). *Selma Lagerlöf* (1971). *La otra circunstancia* (1972). *Farsa de verano* (1973). *El fabuloso imperio de Juan sin tierra* (1981). *Atrapados en la ratonera: memorias de una novelista* (1980). *El urogallo* (1982).

Bibliography

Chown, Linda E., "American Critics and Spanish Women Novelists, 1942–1980." *Signs* 9 (Autumn, 1983): 91–107. Díaz, Janet Winecoff, "Three New Works of Dolores Medio." *Romance Notes* XI, 2 (Winter, 1969): 244–250. Fox-Lockert, Lucia, *Women Novelists in Spain and Spanish America* (Metuchen, 1979). Gil Casado, Pablo, *La novela social española* (Barcelona, 1968). Hoyos, Antonio De, *Ocho escritores actuales* (Murcia, 1954). Hutman, Norma L., "Disproportionate Doom: Tragic Irony in the Spanish Post Civil War Novel." *Modern Fiction Studies* 18: 199–206. Jones, Margaret E.W., *Dolores Medio* (New York, 1974). Nora, Eugenio G. De, *La novela española contemporánea* (1927–1960) (Madrid, 1962). Schyfter, Sara E., "The Fragmented Family in the Novels of Contemporary Spanish Women." *Perspectives on Contemporary Literature* 3 (1977), pp. 23–29. Winecoff, Janet, "Fictionalized Autobiography in the Novels of Delores Medio." *Kentucky Foreign Language Quarterly* XIII, 3 (1966): 170–178.

Mary E. Giles

Doeschka Meijsing

Born October 21, 1947, Eindhoven, The Netherlands
Genre(s): novel
Language(s): Dutch

Doeschka Meijsing, a novelist and editor, studied Dutch and Comparative Literature at the University of Amsterdam. Before she became an editor for the newspaper *Vrij Nederland*, she taught several years in a high school and was connected with the Institute for Neerlandistiek in Amsterdam.

Meijsing made her debut with a collection of short stories *De Hanen en andere verhalen* (1974) which was well received by critics. The volume consists of seven short stories each time told by a different first person narrator: a theology student, a librarian, a painter, a hotel manager, an undefined woman, a model and a detective. These persons share a similar vision on life in that they all escape from its transitoriness in dream or fantasy.

Robinson (1976), a short novel told from the point of view of a seventeen year old girl, Robinson, is as far as composition is concerned carefully designed and well constructed. The narrative is told from the point of view of the girl Robinson. Water plays an important symbolic role in this novel. Robinson compares the simple tripartite structure of a water molecule, about which she learns in her chemistry class, as a model of her own life. Similar to the relationships between the various parts of a water molecule, Robinson has clearly defined relationships with her parents, her boyfriend and her favorite teacher at school. Just as a water molecule changes its simple structure to a highly complicated and chaotic one under different atmospheric conditions, Robinson experiences that as she grows up, the relationships to the people she is most confronted with become as confused and complicated. Critics have praised this work for its intricate structure, well developed intrigue and organic relationship between the sustained water symbolism and the actual story. However, Robinson suffers from lack of suspense and, occasionally, poor stylistics. In an interview, Meijsing herself stated that the sketchy character depiction in Robinson—with exception of the protagonist—is more suited for a short story than for a novel.

In *De kat achterna* (1977; Going After the Cat), Meijsing adopts a much looser composition than in her earlier prose work. In the first part of the novel, we meet the central character Eefje who returns to The Netherlands following a one year stay in Canada. She tries to confront her past, an undertaking in which she never succeeds. Eefje never manages to get her life together, she is lived rather than lives herself. Life passes while she does not even seem to notice it.

Although the meaning of Meijsing's work is rarely one-dimensional, her style—in her later work—has become more lucid and transparent. For her most recent novel *Tijger, Tijger!*, she was given the Multatuli Prize in 1981.

Works

De Hanen en andere Verhalen (1974). *Robinson* (1976). *De kat achterna* (1977). *Tijger, Tijger!* (1980).

Bibliography

Backx, Petra, "Doeschka Meijsing Proza van fascinatie." *Streven* 34: 59–66. Buuren, Hanneke van, "Het binnenwater van Robinson." *Ons Erfdeel* (1965): 13–17.

Dianne van Hoof

Ulrike Marie Meinhof

Born 1934, Oldenburg, Germany; died 1976, Stammheim
Genre(s): journalism, essay, drama
Language(s): German

Meinhof's father died in 1939, her mother, of cancer, in 1948. She was adopted into a professor's family and studied philosophy, pedagogy, and literature in Marburg, Munster, and Hamburg. She participated in demonstrations against nuclear arms in 1958–1959 and subsequently, from 1959–1969, wrote for the leftist news magazine *Konkret*, as whose chief editor she served in 1962–1964. From 1961–1968, she was married to Klaus-Rainer Rohl, also of *Konkret*, whom she bore two children. In 1968, she became lecturer at the Berlin Free University. During this time of violent demonstrations, e.g., against the right-wing Springer Press, which were brutally countered by the anti-leftist Grand Coalition government in Bonn, Meinhof's political ideology shifted from radical leftist to terrorist: she belongs to the generation who, more than by Vietnam, is upset that in Germany, the older generation that managed Auschwitz is occupying public offices and the courts.

Abandoning writing, she advocated action according to the Tupamara model of Latin American urban guerrillas. After participating in freeing Andreas Baader from prison in 1970, she lived underground, having become the most wanted German criminal, and supposed co-founder of the so-called Baader-Meinhof Gang. Although many writers and intellectuals warned against right-wing hysteria, she was brutally treated after her arrest in June 1972. Incarcerated before the trial began in May 1975, she supposedly committed suicide in her cell in May 1976. Circumstances of her death have still not been elucidated.

Meinhof has left a host of essays, articles, and polemics establishing her as a first-rate, well-read political thinker shaped by the Marxist and Freudian traditions of the Frankfurt School. Titles like "Napalm and Pudding" or "Faking Democracy" head texts that are well-researched, to the point, and poignant. These extraordinary documents of the age are even surpassed by the play *Bambule*, excoriating the prison-like treatment of institutionalized orphaned girls in Germany. Based on sociological interviews with the "victims," these scenes illuminate the connection between reactionary politics and repressive psychology, what Adorno and Horkheimer had already more impassively analyzed and termed "the authoritarian personality." Meinhof's terrorist entanglements have served as an excuse so far for contemporaries not to come to terms with her writing and the challenge it represents.

Works

Bambule. Fürsorge—Sorge für wen? (1983). Die Würde des Menschen ist antastbar (1986).

Bibliography

Aust, Stefan, *Der Baader Meinhof Komplex* (Cologne, 1985). Brückner, Peter, *Ulrike Marie Meinhof und die deutschen Verhältnisse* (Berlin, 1984).

Ute Marie Saine

Hannes Meinkema

(a.k.a. Hannemieke Stamperius)

Born 1943
Genre(s): novel, story, criticism
Language(s): Dutch

The author of *Vrouwen en Literatuur* (1979; Women and Literature), which she published under her own name, Stamperius, Hannes Meinkema has also published numerous articles, novellas and novels. She is one of the most academic feminist critics in the Netherlands and was co-editor of the feminist journals *Chrysallis* and *Opzij*.

The fact that she was an illegitimate child seems to have had a profound influence both on her personal development and on her creative work. She studied Dutch and general literature at the University of Utrecht and received her doctorate in 1974 with a dissertation on the poetry of Marsman.

The protagonists in her novels and stories are mostly women who are able to gain new insights in a time of women's emancipation. Their new awareness, however, rarely leads to changed behavior. This double action of realizing one thing and doing another takes place on the inside of the character and is frequently rendered in a free, indirect style. Hannes Meinkema uses either first-person narration, as in *De Maaneter* (1974; The Moon-Eater) and in many stories in *Het wil nog maar niet zomeren* (1976; Summer is Not Coming Yet), or the third person form, as in her second novel *En dan is er koffie* (1976; And Then We Have Coffee) and in most stories in the collection *De groene weduwe en andere grijze verhalen* (1977, The Green Widow and Other Grey Stories). There is always a conflict between the character's inside and outside, the outside forming the powerless side of the person.

En dan is er koffie was on the Dutch bestseller list for weeks. The novel depicts life in the sixties, when the younger generation tried to shake off the stultifying Dutch "cosiness" of their parents for whom the drinking of coffee constitutes an important domestic ritual. The main theme is the break with parental morality. The most important character, Rosa, an illegitimate child like the author herself, knows that she does not belong in her bourgeois family but lacks the courage to actually break with them. In *Trouwdag* (Wedding Day), first story in the collection *De groene weduwe* (The Green Widow), a girl is misled and raped and later manipulated into believing that she provoked it and is therefore responsible for the crime herself. Other situations encountered in her work include an abortion, a daughter-in-law in conflict with her husband's family, women living in conflict with themselves, subject to guilt and feelings of insecurity.

Hannes Meinkema's feminist writing is rooted in the conviction that too little is known of the woman's world and that hardly any attention has been paid to it in literature.

Works

Fiction: *De Maaneter* (1974). *Het wil nog maar niet zomeren* (1975). *En dan is er koffie* (1976). *De groene weduwe and andere grijze verhalen* (1977). *Het binnenste ei* (1978). *De naam van mijn moeder* (1980). *De driehoekige reis* (1981). *Op eigen tenen* (1982). *Verhalen* (1983). *Te kwader min* (1983). Poetry: *Het persoonlijke in poezie* (1979).

Bibliography

Buuren, Hanneke van, "Geluk is greep krijgen op." *Ons Erfdeel* 20: 461–463. Waal, Margot de, and Suzanne Piët, "Women of Letters." *Insight Holland* 15 (March 1980): 3.

Maya Bijvoet

María Luz Melcón

Born 1946, Spain
Genre(s): novel, poetry
Language(s): Spanish

José María Martínez Cachero (*Historia de la novela española entre 1936 y 1975*, 1979, p. 284) considers her to belong to the group of the "nueva ola" or "novísimos" according to José Domingo's definition. She has also published poetry. Since her novel *Celia muerde la manzana* (1972; Celia Bites the Apple), she seems to have ceased publishing.

Celia muerde la manzana was the finalist for the Barral prize of 1971 with the same number of votes as the winner Haroldo Conte. This novel deals with life in a women's residence displaying a broad spectrum of characters: Sela and Dorita, the lesbian lovers; Adela, the prankster; Celia, the rebel; Esperanza, her friend; and the nuns. The contrasts and similarities between the nuns and the students are interesting. It is divided into three parts: "Nochenegra" with an epigraph by Rimbaud, "Fangodía" with another epigraph by Heraclitus, and an epilogue, "Rojoepílogo," with a quote from San Juan. There is an excess of episodes and complications as if the author were trying to shock the reader. It could be compared to *Aguas muertas* by María Dolores Boixadós.

Works

Celia muerde la manzana (1972).

Bibliography

Martínez Cahero, José María, *Historia de la novela española entre 1936 y 1975* (Madrid, 1979), pp. 280, 284, 287 and 348.

Concha Alborg

Melinno

Born ca. second century B.C., Magna Graecia
(area of Italy)
Genre(s): poetry
Language(s): Greek

Melinno wrote a poem in five sapphic stanzas on the world power of Rome, "From Melinno of Lesbos to Rome," quoted by Joh. Stobaeus in his Eclogue (3.7), in a collection of passages about bravery. Through an absurd reading of a word, "Rome," Stobaeus read "physical strength" instead of "Rome." This misreading was first observed by H. Grotius (sixteenth century A.D.).

The poem, in fact, has nothing to do with "physical strength," nor is there any good reason to think that the poetess came from Lesbos, as Stobaeus did. Of Melinno herself we know nothing. The appearance of the name "Automelinna" in an epigram of Nossis may possibly suggest that the name Melinno comes from Epizephyrian Locri but not necessarily that it was confined to that region or that this reference has anything to do with the poetess. Though she uses the sapphic strophe, she does not use the Lesbian dialect, of which there are only faint echoes. The poem is written in the mixed, artificial language familiar from choral poetry together with a few aeolisms. It calls attention more for its character and date rather than for the main sense, which is clear enough. Between Sappho and Alcaeus in the sixth century B.C. and Melinno in the second century B.C., only one sapphic stanza exists, which suggests that after the death of Sappho and Alcaeus the sapphic stanza was not much used. Melinno's use of that type of stanza can be explained either by her admiration of the Lesbian poets or by a revival of this rhythm in her time or by the fact that, as a woman, she felt the urge to imitate Sappho. In any case, the poem is metrically a unique specimen for its date. The five stanzas of the poem are sharply separated from one another unlike the practice of her Lesbian models. Scholars thought that Melinno wrote in the period between Horace (first century B.C.) and Statius (first century A.D.) and was influenced by Roman metrical practice. This view has been opposed by a number of scholars on the ground that Greek poets took very little notice of Latin poetry at any time. C.M. Bowra showed that a more important indication that she did not write during the Imperial age but under the Republic, is the absence of any mention of a princeps, particularly in a poem where Rome is deified. So, the first part of the second century B.C. is an appropriate date since the cult of the goddess Rome was then lively in Greek cities and may well have inspired Melinno.

Melinno treats her subject with certain inventiveness, which is not surprising since that composition of a Greek hymn to Rome had very little tradition behind it. She innovates by making Rome a daughter of Mars, whose only known daughters were the Amazons. For Melinno Rome is first and foremost the conqueror and the ruler of the world. She expresses her belief in the unalterable destiny of Rome and finally, in the last stanza, she compares the never-failing generations of Romans to the fruits of the earth sent forth by Demeter. Melinno's innovations notwithstanding, the hymn is based on a traditional element of Greek poetry. Her manner, learned and rich in echoes and mythological references, is what is expected from the second century B.C. The poem is notably lacking in local or personal references, which may be due to Melinno's desire to write in a high and detached manner worthy of her subject. The poem, compared with the hymns of Sappho and Alcaeus from which it is remotely descended, looks stiff and stilted; it lacks their ease and grace of movement. But, though Melinno's poem is not distinguished, it has its own character and conviction, which shows, as C.M. Bowra says "what impression the emergence of a new world-power made on the awe-struck Greeks of the disintegrating Hellenistic world."

Works

The text, together with a commentary, is found in *Ioannis Stobaei Anthologii Libri Duo Posteriores*, recensuit O. Hense, vol. 1, p. 312 (1894). It is also found in E. Diehl, *Anthologia Lyrica Graeca*, vol. 2, p. 315 (1925).

Bibliography

Bechtel, F., *Die Historischen Personnennamen des Griechischen bis zur Kaiserzeit* (Halle, 1917), p. 304. Birt, Th., *De Romae urbis nomine deque robore romano commentariolum* (Marburg, 1888). Bowra, C.M., "Melinno's Hymn to Rome." *Journal of Roman Studies* (1957): 21–28. Husener, H., "Beiläufige Bemerkungen." *Rheinisches Museum für Philologie* 55 (1900): 290. Malzow, S., *De Erinnae Lesbiae vita et reliquiis* (Petersburg, 1836). *Paulys Real-Encyclopädie der Klassisches Altertumwissenschaft*, Vol. 15, pp. 522–523. Schmid W., and O. Stählin, *Geschichte der griechischen Literatur* (München, 1929). Schneidewin, F.W., *Zeitschrift für die Altertumswissenschaft* (1836): pp. 209–216. Susemihl, F.F.K.E., *Geschichte der griechischen Literatur*, vol. 2 (Leipzig, 1891–1892). West, M., "Die griechischen Dichterinnen der Kaiserzeit," in *Kyklos Griechisches und Byzantinisches*, ed. R. Keydell (Berlin, 1978), pp. 102–104.

Aristoula Georgiadou

Melissanthē

(a.k.a. Melissanthi, Ēvē Skandalakē)

Born April 8, 1910, Athens, Greece
Genre(s): poetry
Language(s): Greek

Melissanthē (née Ēvē Chougia) was born on April 8, 1910 in Athens. She studied music and drawing, ballet, and classical dance, and for a time she hoped to become a professional dancer. She spent the years 1923–1924 in sanatoriums in Switzerland recovering from tuberculosis. She knows English well, and is a graduate of the French Institute and the German Academy in Athens. At times she has taught French in public and private high schools in Athens and has also written critical essays for newspapers and journals. In 1932 she married the writer Giannēs Skandalakēs.

Her knowledge of languages made the literature of Western Europe and America accessible to her, and she found kindred spirits in such poets as Robert Frost, Emily Dickinson, Longfellow, Verlaine, Pierre Garnier, Baudelaire, T.S. Eliot, and Rilke, some of whom she translated into Greek.

Her contribution to Greek poetry has been significant. Her first collection of poems came out in 1930, and since then she has remained a major force in modern Greek literature, publishing ten poetry collections between 1930 and 1974. In 1938 she was awarded an Athens Academy Award; in 1945, a Palamas Honorable Mention; and, in 1965, a Second State Prize for Poetry and a Gold Cross of the Order of Deeds of Merit.

Sophia Andzaka in her *Ē pneumatikē kai kritikē poreia tēs Melissanthēs* divides Melissanthē's work into two stages: the religious or "confessional" stage and the existential stage. Although these two stages may not be clearly separated, Andzaka's classification is useful. In the "first stage" there is a preoccupation with sin and with the need for forgiveness and union with God. In some of the early poems the soul searching for God is depicted by the female figure or bride in search of the divine and elusive bridegroom. In the 1940s, Melissanthē and her fellow poets found themselves in an unfriendly and estranging world, as Andonis Decavalles points out in his "Modernity: The Third Stage, the New Poets," a world that shook their faith in God and in their fellow men. A skepticism pervaded their work as they turned themselves inward to a personal world. This inward journey was often accompanied by existential *Angst* and marked by encounters with Nothingness and the Void. However, Melissanthē's verse is not depressing for she never loses totally her belief in the goodness of man and the power of love. Her extensive study of Carl Jung may have helped her see her yearnings as archetypical and may have reinforced for her her place in the world.

Melissanthē has always thought of herself as a poet and worked hard at perfecting her poems. She is one of a few Greek poets who mastered the sonnet form. Even when she allowed herself to write in a looser style, we detect a painstaking attention to form. The lyricism of her early period becomes somewhat subdued in her later poetry, but her images remain sharp and concentrated and her symbolism potent and acute.

In addition to her poetry, Melissanthē wrote a play for children, *O Mikros adelphos* (The Little Brother), for which she received the Sikiaridio Prize.

Works

Phonēs entomou [Insect Voices] (1930). *Prophēteies* [Prophecies] (1931, 1940). *Phlegomenē vatos* [Flaming Bush] (1935). *O gyrismos tou asōtou* [Return of the Prodigal] (1935 [1936?], 1938). *Ōsanna* [Hosanna] (1939). *Lyrikē exomologēsē* [Lyrical Confession] (1945). *Ē epochē tou ypnou kai tēs agrypnias* [The Season of Sleep and Wakefulness] (1950). *Anthropinē morphē* [Human Shape] (1961). *Phragma tēs siōpēs* [Barrier of Silence] (1961). *Eklogē* (Selection), *1930–1950* (1965). *Nea Poiēmata* [New Poems] (1974). *Ta poiēmata tēs Melissanthēs 1930–1974* [The Poems of Melissanthē] (1976).

Anthologized translations: *Introduction to Modern Greek Literature*, ed. and tr. Mary Gianos. Poetry tr. Kimon Friar (1969). *Skylark, Number 25* (Special Greek poetry number), ed. Baldev Mirza. *Modern Greek Poetry. From Cavafis to Elytis*, tr. Kimon Friar (1973). *Modern Greek Poetry*, tr., intro., commentaries, and notes by Kimon Friar (1982). *Modern Poetry in Translation 34* (Summer, 1978). (Five poems by Melissanthē translated by Maria Kotzamanidou and Michael Heldman.) Translations of Melissanthē's poems have appeared in French, Italian, Polish, Russian, and Czechoslovakian anthologies also.

Bibliography

Antzaka, Sophia, *Ē pneumatikē kai politikē poreia tēs Melissanthēs* (Athens, 1974). Dacavalles, Andonis, Review *World Literature Today* 51, 3 (1977). Decavalles, Andonis, "Modernity: The Third Stage, the New Poets." *The Charioteer* 20 (New York, 1978). Friar, Kimon, *Modern Greek Poetry* (New York, 1973). Gianos, Mary P., *Introduction to Modern Greek Literature* (New York, 196). Mirasgezē, Maria, *Neoellēnikē Logotechnia*, 2nd vol. (Athens, 1982). Politēs, Linos, *Historia tēs Neoellenikēs Logotechnias*, 3rd ed. (Athens, 1980). Savvas, Minnas, Review. *Books Abroad*, 49, 3 (1975): 589–590.

General references: *Columbia Dictionary of Modern European Literature*, 2nd. ed., ed. Jean-Albert Bede and William B. Edgerton (New York, 1980).

Helen Dendrinou Kolias

Melissanthi

(see: Melissanthē)

Josepha Mendels

Born 1902
Genre(s): novel
Language(s): Dutch

Because of her timely, feminist themes most of Josepha Mendels' works have been republished in the 1970s.

She worked as a teacher and journalist until 1943, when she had to flee to England to escape Nazi persecution. After the war she resumed her work in Paris. Her first novel, *Rolien en Ralien* (1947), was written there.

It deals with the theme of androgyny and the tyranny of gender roles. In a story within the story entitled *De kinderen van Mevrouw Staphorst* (The Children of Mrs. Staphorst—Staphorst is also the name of a small, Calvinist town in the Netherlands), the father perishes already after a few pages, simply because he seems completely irrelevant to the storyteller, the little girl Rolien. In almost all of Josepha Mendels' novels, with the exception of *Je wist het toch* (1948; You Knew It, Didn't You), men are somewhat pitiful creatures to whom physical love means no more than a fleeting sensual pleasure, which is the source of the marital unhappiness in these books.

Josepha Mendels has an almost mythical relationship with language; her words have a magical function. To her, writing is "listening"; plot and style emerge almost beyond the author's own volition. Both in *Rolien en Ralien* and in *Als wind en rook* (1950; Like Wind and Smoke), she uses the ancient Alpha/Omega symbolism but with an inversion; Alpha means the end, Omega the beginning. This is characteristic of the author who would have preferred to have been born one hundred years old to finish her life in the womb.

Works

Rolien en Ralien (1947). *Je wist het toch . . .* (1948). *Als wind en rook* (1950). *Alles even gezond bij jou* (1953). *Bon appetit; Frans koken in de lage landen* (1954). *De vader van Robinson Crusoe* (1954). *Zoethout en etamien* (1956). *Heimwee naar Haarlem* (1958). *De speeltuin* (1970). *Welkom in dit leven* (1981).

Bibliography

Balk-Smit Duyzentkunst, F., "Josepha Mendels." *'Tis vol van schatten hier*, vol. 2 (Amsterdam, 1986), pp. 82–83. Stamperius, Hanneke, *Vrouwen en literatuur* (Amsterdam, 1980), pp. 126–127.

Maya Bijvoet

Dorothea Mendelssohn-Veit-Schlegel

Born 1763, Berlin, Germany; died August 1839, Frankfurt
Genre(s): novel, articles, translation
Language(s): German

The daughter of Moses Mendelssohn and wife of Romantic writer and philosopher Friedrich Schlegel, Dorothea Schlegel wrote fiction, journal articles, and worked as a translator. She was at the center of the Jena Romantic movement.

The eldest daughter of the orthodox Jew and Enlightenment philosopher Moses Mendelssohn, Dorothea was educated by her father. After a long engagement she was married to Simon Veit in 1778, a banker chosen for her by her father. She bore four children, two of whom survived, Johannes and Philipp. Unhappy in her marriage, she met Friedrich Schlegel (born 1772), at the home of her friend Henriette Herz. In 1799 she separated from Veit and that autumn moved with her son Philipp to Jena to live with Friedrich and his brother August Wilhelm, and August Wilhelm's wife Caroline. The relationship between Dorothea and Caroline remained cordial for only six months. In 1800, to help support Friedrich financially, she wrote the novel, *Florentin*, which was thought to have been written by Friedrich. The novel has a male hero and reflects the influence of contemporary novels by Goethe and Tieck. Dorothea moved with Schlegel to Dresden in 1803 and then in 1804 to Paris. She was baptized a Protestant and married Friedrich on April 6, 1804. In 1805 they moved to Cologne, but in 1806 Veit got custody of the children in order to raise them as Jews. In 1808 Friedrich and Dorothea converted to Catholicism and were remarried in the faith. That year Friedrich procured an appointment as an Austrian court secretary, and they settled in Vienna. Dorothea took a two-year trip to Rome in 1818 to visit her two sons, who had become ardent Catholics and painters of the Nazarene school. Simon Veit, who had continued to provide her with financial support even after the divorce, died in 1819. Friedrich Schlegel died suddenly of a stroke in 1823, and Dorothea moved to Frankfurt and lived with her son Philipp. Dorothea Schlegel died on August 3, 1839.

Dorothea belonged to the group of Jewish salonières from Berlin that included Henriette Herz and Rahel Varnhagen. She differed from these two in her literary productivity and her utter devotion to her husband. Because of Friedrich she worked hard as a writer and translator, never asking for personal recognition. In addition to her novel, *Florentin*, she contributed to Friedrich's journals. Her most important and lasting contributions are her translations, particularly of Madame de Staël's *Corinne*. She played a significant role in presenting contemporary French women writers to German readers through her translations and articles.

Although Dorothea is characterized as an independent woman in Friedrich Schlegel's novel, *Lucinde*, she was not pleased with the identification, and she should not be considered an early feminist solely on the basis of her romantic relationship. Intensely devoted to Friedrich and following him in his increasing conservatism, she contributed to the German Romantic movement only as long as financially necessary and always under her husband's name or anonymously.

Works

Literary works and letters: *Briefe von Dorothea und Friedrich Schlegel an die Familie Paulus* (1913). *Briefe von Dorothea Schlegel an Friedrich Schleiermacher* (1918). *Der Briefwechsel Friedrich und Dorothea Schlegels 1818–1820 während Dorotheas Aufenthalt in Rom*, ed. H. Finke (1923).

Die Brüder Schlegel: Briefe aus frühen und späten Tagen der deutschen Romantik, ed. J. Körner (1926). *Caroline und Dorothea Schlegel in Briefen*, ed. Ernst Wieneke (1914). *Dorothea von Schlegel, geb. Mendelssohn, und deren Söhne Johannes und Philipp Veit. Briefwechsel im Auftrage der Familie Veit*, ed. J.M. Raich (1881). *Florentin*, ed. Friedrich Schlegel (1801). *Florentin: Roman, Fragmente, Varianten*, ed. L. Weissberg (1986). "Dorothea Veit-Schlegel." *Frauenbriefe der Romantik*, ed. Katja Behrens (1981). "Die Mutter bei der Aussetzung Moses. Gemälde von P. Veit" (1835). *Poetisches Taschenbuch für das Jahr 1806* (1806). Two poems: "Der Stolze," "Mein Geliebter."

Contributions to journals edited by Friedrich Schlegel: In *Athenäum*: Reviews of Madame de Genlis' *Les voeux téméraires* and Ramdohr's *Moralische Erzählungen*. In *Europa*: Poems: "Zu einer Volksmelodie," "Bei der Erblickung der Handschrift eines verstorbenen Freundes" (to Novalis). Essay: "Gespräch über die neusten Romane der Französinnen," which includes critique of De Staël's *Delphine*. Also essays on Parisian life, "Pariser Neuigkeiten," including, "Ueber den Zustand der Musik in Paris," written with J. Fr. Reichardt. In *Deutsches Museum*: Review of performance of Handel's *Timotheus oder die Gewalt der Musik*.

Translations: *Corinna, oder Italien; aus dem Französischen der Madame de Staël übersetzt* (1807–1808). *Geschichte der Jungfrau von Orleans. Aus altfranzösischen Quellen, mit einem Anhange aus Hume's Geschichte von England*, ed. Friedrich Schlegel (1802). *Geschichte der Margaretha von Valois, Gemahlin Heinrich des Vierten von ihr selbst beschrieben. Nebst Zusätzen und Ergänzungen aus andern französischen Quellen*, ed. Friedrich Schlegel (1803). *Die Geschichte des Zauberers Merlin; aus dem Altfranzösischen. Sammlung romantischer Dichtungen des Mittelalters: aus gedruckten und handschriftlichen Quellen* (1804). *Lothar und Maller eine Rittergeschichte. Aus einer ungedruckten Handschrift*, ed. Friedrich Schlegel (1805). *Valerie*. By Juliane von Krüdener (1804). *Die verwegenen Gelübde, nach den Voeux téméraires der Gräfin Genlis*.

Bibliography

Behler, Ernst. *Die Zeitschriften der Brüder Schlegel* (Darmstadt, 1983). Deibel, Franz, *Dorothea Schlegel als Schriftstellerin im Zusammenhang mit der romantischen Schule* (Palaestra 40) (Berlin, 1905). Eichner, Hans, "*Camilla*, eine unbekannte Fortsetzung von Dorothea Schlegels Florentin." *Jahrbuch des freien deutschen Hochstifts* (1965): 314–368. Hibberd, John, "Dorothea Schlegel's *Florentin* and the Precarious Idyll." *German Life and Letters* 30 (1976–1977): 198–207. Kahn, Robert, "Fifteen Letters from Friedrich and Dorothea Schlegel to J.G. Schweighäuser, Paris, 1802–1804." *PMLA* 75: 197–215. Kupferberg, Herbert, *The Mendelssohns: Three Generations of Genius* (New York, 1972). Susman, Margarete, *Frauen der Romantik* (Köln, 1960), pp. 40–76. Thornton, Karin Stuebben, "Enlightenment and Romanticism in the Work of Dorothea Schlegel." *German Quarterly* 39 (1966): 162–172. Zipes, Jack, *The Great Refusal. Studies of the Romantic Hero in German and American Literature* (Bad Homburg, 1970). Zondek, Theodor, "Dorothea Schlegel und Simon Weit." *Bulletin des Leo Baeck Instituts* 5, no. 20 (1962): 302–304.

Marjanne E. Goozé

Concha Méndez Cuesta

Born 1898, Madrid, Spain; died 1986, Mexico
Genre(s): poetry, drama
Language(s): Spanish

Recognized and praised in the twenties and thirties by leading writers and critics, Concha Méndez has virtually been forgotten today. Rebellious from a very young age, Méndez broke away from the restrictions placed on women by her family and society in 1928, when, alone and without funds, she went first to England and later to Buenos Aires. In both places she found her way into the local literary circles, forming friendships and collaborating in journals. Shortly after her return to Spain, she married the poet Manuel Altolaguirre with whom she founded and printed some of the leading poetry magazines of the day. Méndez was a founding member of the Lyceum Club Femenino, she published poetry regularly, and contributed to a number of journals. During the Spanish Civil War, she left Spain with her two-year old daughter and went to Paris, where her husband joined them at the war's end. They immigrated to Cuba and then in 1946 to Mexico where she would later die.

Although Méndez published four plays, she was known primarily as a poet. She began her career by publishing poems of short meter and enthusiasm for the sea in the vein of Rafeal Alberti. *Surtidor* (Fountain) continues the *ultraísta* images of her first book with an added note of melancholy and clear evidence of a thirst for travel. *Canciones de mar y tierra* (Songs of the Sea and the Land), a product of her trip to Argentina, repeats her favorite maritime themes and her predominant features of light, expansiveness, and optimism.

Vida a vida (Lives Together) represents a change of direction in her poetic production. A more personal and mature book, this collection reflects the peace that love can bring as well as the desolation that life can provoke. The death of Méndez's firstborn inspired her next book, a short work full of pathos and despair. Never to recover fully the joyous, carefree spirit of her youth, she went into exile where she continued to write poetry, although at a slower rate. *Lluvias enlazadas* (Frequent Rains) records the feelings of grief, disorientation, and nostalgia that exile caused. *Poemas, sombras y sueños* (Poems, Shadows and Dreams), a set of deeply emotional poems, records the despair caused by a new loss—her abandonment by her husband. While this book discloses a new pain, it also reveals the compensatory comfort the poet finds in her daughter and the inner strength she discovers within herself. Poet, woman, and mother suffer but survive.

To celebrate her eightieth birthday, her 1932 volume was republished as part of a collection of the poems she had written since *Sombras y sueños*. Memories, dreams, and the past replace the strong impulse for life and adventure that characterized her early poetry. Those who knew her in her youth describe her as active, dynamic, and adventurous, but those who read her poetry can find a more complex spirit that incorporates a whole gamut of sentiments.

Works

Inquietudes (1926). *Surtidor* (1928). *Canciones de mar y tierra* (1930). *El ángel cartero y El personaje presentido* (1931). *Vida a vida* (1932. *Niño y sombras* (1936). *El carbón y la rosa* (1936). *Lluvias enlazadas* (1939). *El solitario* (1941). *Poemas, sombras y sueños* (1944). *Villancico de Navidad* (1944). *Vida a vida y Vida o rio* (1979).

Bibliography

Altolaguirre, Manuel, "Noche de Guerra (de mi diario)." *Hora de España* 4 (1937; rpt. Barcelona, 1977), pp. 305–318. Ayala, Francisco, "Concha Méndez Cuesta. *Surtidor.*" *La Gaceta Literaria* 2.29 (1928): 3. Bellver, Catherine G., "*El personaje presentido*: A Surrealist Play by Concha Méndez." *Estreno* (forthcoming). Jiménez, Juan Ramón, "Y Concha." *Españoles de tres mundos* (Buenos Aires, 1972), pp. 157–158. Miró, Emilio, "Dos poetas del destierro. Concha Méndez y Juan Rejano." *Insula* 378 (1978): 6. Miró, Emilio, Nota preliminar a Concha Méndez, *Vida a vida y Vida o rio* (Madrid, 1979), pp. 11–34. Resnick, Margery, "La inteligencia audaz: vida y poesía de Concha Méndez." *Papeles de Son Armadans* 263 (1978): 131–146.

Catherine G. Bellver

Trina Mercader

Born 1919, Alicante, Spain
Genre(s): poetry
Language(s): Spanish

Mercader lived for a period of 20 years in Morocco, where she founded and served as director of the journal *Al-Motamid*, as well as publishing a series of books on poetry called "Itimad." Her works are not widely available either in Spain or the United States.

Works

Tiempo a salvo [Time Safe from Danger] (1956).
Sonetos Ascéticos [Ascetic Sonnets] (1971).

Bibliography

Miró, E., "Poetisas españolas conntemporáneas." *Revista de la Universidad Complutense* XXIV, No. 95 (enero-febrero 1975): 271–310. *Women Writers of Spain*, ed. C. Galerstein (1986).

Paula T. Irvin

Marie Mercier

(see: Marie Nizet)

Marie Mercier-Nizet

(see: Marie Nizet)

Elisa Mercoeur

Born June 24, 1809, Nantes, France; died January 7, 1835, Paris
Genre(s): poetry, novel, drama
Language(s): French

A poet of the transitional period between classicism and romanticism in France, Mlle Mercoeur dedicated her first volume to Chateaubriand in 1827 and was elected into associate membership of the Académie de Lyon and the Société académique de la Loire-Inférieure.

Raised in Nantes by her mother and stepfather, Mercoeur began writing poems in her youth and was well received in her region. She moved to Paris in 1828 with her mother, was provided a royal pension, and was received in fashionable salons. Her first collection of poems, published in 1827, was followed by her second volume in 1829. She turned to prose to help support herself. Mercoeur wrote a short novel, *La Comtesse de Villequiers* (1833). She also tried her hand at drama, but her best-received efforts were her poems. In the last several months of her life her poetry reflected the *ennui* and *mal du siècle* of her generation. Always frail, she died young of a "maladie de poitrine." Her mother collected, edited, and published her daughter's complete works in three volumes in 1843.

The delicate nature of the author is reflected in her lyrical poems. In a frequently quoted poem, Mercoeur combines melancholy dreams of former secure, happy days with a slow, rich cadence of full lines and music:

> Songe un peu de saisons que j'ai pu voir encore,
> Et combien peu ma bouche a puisé d'existence
> Dans le vase rempli dont je presse le bord;

Tends une main propice à celui qui
chancelle.
J'ai besoin, faible enfant, qu'on veille à
mon berceau;
Et l'aigle peut de moins, a l'ombre de
son aile,
Protèger le timide oiseau.

Certainly, the image projected by Mercoeur's
chief publicist (her mother) was one of a "timid
bird" longing to return to her cradle.

Works

"Bisson" (1827). *Poésies de Mlle Elisa Mercoeur*
(1827). *Poesies* (2nd ed. 1829). "La Comtesse de
Villequier, Nouvelle du xvie siècle par Mlle. Elisa
Mercoeur," in *Heures du soir* (1833), pp. 265–407.
*Oeuvres complètes d'Elisa Mercoeur, de Nantes,
précédées de mémoires et notices sur la vie de
l'auteur, écrits par sa mère.* 3 vols. (1843).

Bibliography

*Fleurs sur une tombe, à Elisa Mercoeur, par M.
Alfred de Montferrand, directeur de la Biographie
de femmes (1836).* Wismes, G., *Le Centenaire de
la naissance d'Elisa Mercoeur* (1910).
General references: *Biographie universelle ancienne
et moderne*, vol. 28. *Dictionnaire des lettres*, vol. 2.
Oxford Companion to French Literature.

Marilynn J. Smith

Sophie Mereau

*Born March 28, 1770, Altenburg, Germany;
died October 31, 1806, Heidelberg
Genre(s): novel, short story, poetry, translation
Language(s): German*

Sophie Mereau wrote novels, stories and
poems, translated, and published several journals.
Often portrayed as a writer of German
Empfindsamkeit, she had strong contact with
Weimar Classicism and was a significant con-
tributor to the Heidelberg Romantic movement.

Born in 1770 in Altenburg, Sophie Mereau
received a traditional female education in the
usual subjects but also learned Spanish, French,
English, and Italian. Her mother died when she
was sixteen and her father when she was twenty-
one. She lived in Jena where she met Schiller,
who had a major influence on her work. On April
4, 1793 Sophie married Carl Mereau; he was

twenty-eight, a lawyer, librarian, and law professor, but within a year she regretted her marriage.
She took a lover in 1794 and the following year
traveled with another to Berlin. Sophie had two
children with Carl Mereau: Gustav, born in
January 1794, and Hulda, born in September
1797. After Gustav's death in 1800, Sophie
Mereau decided to divorce her husband. She met
Clemens Brentano in 1798; he fell in love with
her immediately. Although they had a romantic
relationship, Sophie severed her ties to Clemens
when she left her husband and went to stay in
Camburg with relatives in the summer of 1800.
The time in Camburg was very productive: she
edited three literary journals, published a col-
lection of her poetry, wrote several stories,
translated, and finished her novel *Amanda und
Eduard* (Amanda and Eduard), parts of which
Schiller published in *Die Horen* (The Hours). In
December 1802 she resumed her relationship
with Brentano. At first she wished to live with
Clemens in Marburg but would not marry him.
Sophie finally consented in November 1803
when she became pregnant with their son, Achim
Ariel, who was born in May 1804 and died six
weeks later. Their marriage was often troubled
and they spent much time apart. Her fourth child
was born in May 1805 and also lived only a few
weeks. Sophie then threw herself into her work.
In late fall she was expecting her fifth child, but
at the end of the year she suffered a miscarriage
and became very ill. Her miscarriage brought
about a reconciliation with Clemens, and at the
end of the year they both converted to Catholicism. The time between her conversion and her
death in October 1806 was her happiest. She
died at the age of thirty-six from a hemorrhage
after delivering her sixth child.

Mereau's first novel, *Das Blüthenalter der
Empfindung* (1794; The Blossoming Age of
Sentiment), is written in the first person with a
male narrator although the woman in this work
is clearly more active and decisive than the man.
It portrays eighteenth-century revolutionary
political events and was one of the first novels of
the period to depict an immigration to America
for personal freedom. *Blüthenalter* deals with the
conflict between society and the individual, advising individuals to be guided by their feelings.
Mereau does not set feelings in opposition to

reason but sees them in consort with it. Major themes in Mereau's writings are man's relationship to nature and the search for personal freedom and love. In her stories "Elise," "Julie von Arwain," and the important "Die Flucht nach der Hauptstadt" (The Flight to the Capital), Mereau advocates career choices for women and the development of one's own personality. In "Marie" (1798), Mereau is one of the first of the Romantics to support free love. Her poems reflect the same themes as her prose works. The second novel, *Amanda und Eduard* (Amanda and Eduard), was finished after the divorce and speaks against arranged marriages. Written in epistolary form, it follows the traditions of the genre in its emphasis on characters' feelings and reactions to experiences rather than plot development. Although Mereau believed that women should be allowed greater personal freedom, her female characters are motivated and guided by love since it is a woman's nature to love. Mereau points out the unjust conditions of women's lives, but she never calls for political equality.

She also worked as a translator and editor. Of greatest significance are her translations of the *Letters of Ninon de Lenclos*, Madame de Lafayette's *The Princess of Cleves*, and Boccacio's *Fiametta*. She also translated Montesquieu's *Persian Letters* and two volumes of Spanish novellas. Between 1799 and 1801 she edited three journals: *Göttinger Roman-Calender* (Göttinger Novel-Calendar), *Berlinischer Damen-Calender* (Berliner Ladies-Calender), and two volumes of *Kalathiskos*.

Works

Amanda und Eduard (1803). *Das Blüthenalter der Empfindung* (1982). *Gedichte*, 2 vols. (1800, 1802). *Kalathiskos*, ed. Peter Schmidt (1968). "*Lebe der Liebe und liebe das Leben.*" *Der Briefwechsel von Clemens Brentano und Sophie Mereau*, ed. Dagmar von Gersdorff (1981). "*Meine Seele ist bey euch geblieben.*" *Briefe Sophie Bentanos an Henriette von Arnstein*, ed. Karen Schenck zo Schweinsberg (1985).

Bibliography

Gersdorff, Dagmar von, "*Dich zu lieben kann ich nicht verlernen.*" *Das Leben der Sophie Brentano-Mereau* (Frankfurt, 1984). Includes a complete bibliography. Hang, Adelheid, "Sophie Mereau in ihren Beziehungen zur Romantik." Diss., Frankfurt am Main, 1934. Hofe, Harald von, "Sophie Mereau-Brentano and America." *Modern Language Notes* 75 (1960): 427–430. Riley, Helene M. Kastinger, "Saat und Ernte. Sophie Mereaus Forderung geschleehtlicher Gleichberechtigung." *Die Weibliche Muse. Sechs Essays über künstlerisch schaffende Frauen der Goethezeit* (Columbia, S.C., 1986), pp. 55–88. Touaillon, Christine, *Der deutsche Frauenroman des 18. Jahrhunderts* (Bern, 1980; rpt. 1911). Weigel, Sigrid, "Sophie Mereau." *Frauen: Porträts aus zwei Jahrhunderten*, ed. Hans-Jürgen Schultz (Stuttgart, 1981), pp. 20–32.

Marjanne E. Goozé

St. Angela Merici

Born c. 1470–1475, Desenzano del Garda,
*   Italy; died January 27, 1540, Brescia, Italy*
Genre(s): spiritual writing
Language(s): Italian

Daughter of a small land-holding farmer at Desenzano, Angela was orphaned during her adolescence and left her family's farm to live with the locally prominent family of her maternal uncle Biancosi at Salò. At age eighteen, she became a member of the lay Third Order of St. Francis at Salò/Isola del Garda. It seems that as an adult she returned to the Desenzano farm, and that it was as a Third Order duty that she accompanied Catherine Patengola back to Brescia (1516) to console her on the loss of her husband and sons during this period of the French invasions of North Italy. Aside from pilgrimages, including to the Holy Land, and a few periods of exile with friends at Mantua and Cremona because of the French invasions, Angela remained in Brescia the rest of her life, becoming renowned not only for her charity and contemplation, but also for her spiritual knowledge: the Nazari documents, collected soon after her death, state that theologians and preachers consulted her for her interpretations of both Old and New Testaments, including the Psalms, and of other spiritual works.

It is important for an understanding of Angela's writings to note the Catholic lay evangelism movements in Brescia in her lifetime and preceding it. Several members of the families with whom Angela first lived at Brescia were members of the Company of Divine Love for laymen, founded at Rome by Ettore Vernazza, the "spiritual son" of St. Catherine of Genoa. It was at a girls' orphanage affiliated with the Divine Love's Hospital of the Incurables at Brescia that Angela held the first meetings of her lay Company of St. Ursula, which she founded there in 1535, naming it after the lay martyr Ursula and her companions. Angela's Company was composed of consecrated laywomen from all classes of Brescian society who continued to live in their own homes and surroundings while meeting regularly according to her Primitive Rule, which urged them to set a good example everywhere. It was for this lay Company that Angela wrote her *Rule, Counsels,* and *Testament* (*Regola, Ricordi, Legati*), which for their times were revolutionary not only spiritually, but also in the economic and social spheres of women's history. In these years before the concept of paid employment and before the existence of formal education for women, Angela specified that her Company's "Daughters" were entitled to wages even if court cases were necessary (*Rule,* Chap. 12), and specified regular meetings for spiritual instruction. Other characteristics of her writings are psychological insight into treating individuals according to their differing personalities; emphasis upon women's dignity; mystical contemplation and interpretation based upon the traditional symbolic exegesis of the soul's espousals with God (*Canticle of Canticles*), with the spiritual maternity flowing from it; and the influence of Greek Patristics and of Ficinian Neoplatonism. The latter is not surprising since Brescia was then in the Province of Venice, Diocese of Verona, where Bishop Gian Matteo Giberti, friend of Reginald Pole, Erasmus, and Thomas More, was known for his printing of Greek Patristics and desire to return to the Primitive Church. Angela also is recognized as a Pre-Tridentine Reformer of the Church.

After her death, Angela was clothed in the Third Order of St. Francis habit usual at the time, as can be seen today; she is one of those of widely-recognized holiness whose bodies have remained intact, and she is enclosed in a publicly-displayed crystal coffin at the Church of St. Angela, Brescia. She was canonized at Rome in 1807. The lay Company she founded existed at Brescia until 1810, when dispersed by Napoleon. It was re-established in the 1860s by the Brescian noble-women Maddalena and Elisabetta Girelli, and gave rise later to two lay Companies existing today, one a Diocesan Company and the other an international Secular Institute of Pontifical Right (approved 1958). Throughout history, only the lay Companies were ecclesiastically permitted to have Angela's "Primitive Rule," and there was no filiation or formation between these Companies and the Convents of Ursulines that arose after Angela's death, inspired by the fame of her writings, life, and work. Arising after the Council of Trent (1545–1563), these convents had their Diocesan Rules modified by their local Bishops, and the canonical community life and enclosure as mandated by Trent. Nevertheless, they consciously followed those of Angela's writings possible of adaptation and recognized her as foundress. The Ursuline Religious became the first to be permitted an active work in convents after Trent's edicts: education in the private, parish, and other types of schools arising after Angela's lifetime, especially those for girls and women, in her spirit.

Works

S. Angela Merici: Regola, Ricordi, Legati, ed. Luciana Mariani, O.S.U., and Elisa Tarolli (Brescia, 1975). This edition gives copies of the original MSS on pages alternating with their translation into modern Italian from the original sixteenth-century Brescian-Italian. Introduction by Ansgar Faller.

Bibliography

Bouquier, Denise, "La Sécularité de Ste Angèle Mérici." *Vie Consacrée* 52, No. 55 (November 15, 1980): 360–362. Cistellini, Antonio, *Figure della Riforma Pretridentina* (Brescia, 1948). Guerrini, Paolo, *Miscellanea di Studi: S. Angela Merici e la Compagnia di S. Orsola . . . Memorie Storiche della Diocesa di Brescia,* VII (Brescia, 1936). Guerrini, Paolo, *Memorie Storiche della Diocesa di Brescia,* XII (Brescia, 1944). Guerrini, Paolo, *Chronache Bresciane Inedite dei Secoli XV–XIX,* Vol. II (Brescia, 1927). Latz, Dorothy L., *St. Angela Merici and the Spiritual Currents of the Italian Renaissance.* Doctoral thesis, University of Strasbourg, 1986, pub. A.N.R.T., University of Lille III, France (1987). Latz, Dorothy L., "The Writings of St. Angela

Merici in the Light of Bonaventuran Exemplarism: The Motherhood, Fatherhood and Transcendence of God." *Mystics Quarterly* X, 3 (October 1984). Latz, Dorothy L., ed. and tr., *The Writings of St. Angela Merici*, with introduction (Toronto: Peregrina Press Translation Series, 1989). Ledochowska, Teresa, O.S.U., *Angèle Mérici et la Compagnie de Ste Ursule*, 2 vols. (Rome and Milan, 1967; English ed. 1969). Ledochowska, Teresa, O.S.U., "Angela Merici and the Ursuline Mission: A Second Look." *Review for Religious* (Nov.–Dec. 1984): 849–857.

Dorothy Latz

Théroigne de Méricourt

Born August 13, 1762, Marcourt, Belgium; died June 9, 1817, Paris
Genre(s): political and feminist pamphlets, speeches, letters
Language(s): French

Théroigne de Méricourt (née Anne-Josèphe Terwagne) was one of the leading and most notorious feminists in the early years of the French Revolution. As a political activist she was a member of several revolutionary societies and took part in the violent and bloody clashes between rival factions. Born in Belgium, she left home at age fourteen and became a companion to a French woman living in London. Théroigne studied music and gave concerts for several years. In 1784 she went to Paris and lived under the name Mme de Campinados; she acquired a benefactor, the old marquis Ann-Nicolas de Persan, comte de Dun et de Pateau, from whom she received an annual pension of 5000 francs. However, she abandoned her "career" as courtesan and went to Italy in 1788 to pursue her musical training, hoping eventually to sing on stage in Genoa. The generous marquis de Persan continued to support her until she returned to Paris after hearing of the meeting of the Estates-General in 1789. She foresaw the possibility of major reforms to benefit mankind and immediately made contact with the early revolutionaries such as Brissot, Desmoulins, Barnave, St. Just, and Siéyès. Her passionate support of the revolution was genuine; it presaged the dawn of a new age when equality between men and women would create a true fraternity.

However, the "belle Liégeoise" was accused of being a paid agent for the political ambitions of the duc d'Orléans. This was unlikely for she hated the monarchy, especially Marie Antoinette, on whom she blamed all the ills of France. She was interested in achieving liberty for women; to this end, she advocated creating regiments of women warriors, a company of "Amazones," to fight alongside men in battle. Intelligent and committed to a cause, "l'Amazone de la Liberté" proposed using violence to achieve her goals. Dressed in bright trousers, armed with pistols and a dagger, she participated in the women's march on Versailles in early October 1789. She circulated among the marchers, urging them to stand firm in their demands for food for the capital and to remove the royal family from Versailles to Paris. Their success won her recognition among female activists and led to her founding the society of Friends of the Law (1790). This "man's woman," who did not especially like women, crusaded for women's rights and tried to inspire Frenchwomen to serve their country. Her attempt to establish a club for working-class women failed; her violent nature and masculine attire alienated the very people she hoped to help realize full citizenship in an imminent utopia.

Ignored by those she tried to inspire and threatened by the revolutionary authorities, she fled to Belgium in late 1790. Arrested by the Austrians in February 1791, Théroigne was imprisoned, then sent to Vienna where she met with the Emperor Leopold III. She was subsequently freed, given 600 francs, and returned to Paris. This whole episode remains a mystery. But she was greeted as a heroine in Paris and asked to speak to the Société Fraternelle des Minimes and the Society for Revolutionary Republican Women. In her famous pamphlet, "Aux 48 sections" (1792), she called on women to enter politics to ensure full citizenship. Following her convictions, she took part in the attack on the Tuileries Palace on August 10, 1792, which resulted in the overthrow of the monarchy. During the long, bloody assault, she killed a royal defender, Suleau, and was awarded a civic crown by the National Assembly. Unfortunately, Théroigne threw her support to the moderate Girondins, whose influence was waning. In May 1793 she spoke to the National Convention; she warned them about

Austrian spies working to undermine the revolution and called on members to confer political offices on women. That same month, the Montagnards set out to destroy the Girondins and intimidate their supporters. On May 15, Théroigne was assaulted, beaten, and stripped naked by a mob of radical women when she tried to enter the assembly.

Méricourt never recovered from the attack, and a year later her brother had her committed to an asylum. Théroigne was insane and died in the hospital of Salpetrière in Paris on June 9, 1817. Her efforts to encourage the development of women as equal partners in a utopian republic and to make fraternity a reality were not realized. But Théroigne de Méricourt had made women aware of female abilities and potential.

Works

Aux 48 sections (1792). *Discours, prononcé a la Société Fraternelle des Minimes, le 25 mars 179. . . . en presentant un drapeau aux citoyennes du Faubourg St. Antoine* (1792).

Bibliography

Bourgeois, A., *Théroigne de Méricourt et la marquis de Saint-Huruge* (1903). Demarteau, Joseph, *Théroigne de Méricourt: lettres inédites, prison et bijoux* (1882). Duval, Georges, *Précis histoire sur la vie de Mlle Théroigne de Méricourt* (1790). Ernest, Otto, *Théroigne de Méricourt. D'après des documents inédits* (1935). Fuss, Th., *Théroigne de Méricourt, dite la belle Liégeoise* (1854). Hamel, Frank, *A Woman of the Revolution: Théroigne de Méricourt* (1911). Hervieu, Paul E., *Théroigne de Méricourt, pièce historique, en six actes* (1902). Lacour, Leopold, *Trois femmes de la Révolution . . . Théroigne de Méricourt* (1900). Laporte, G., *La vie trépidante de Théroigne de Méricourt* (1931). Pellet, M., *Etude historique et biographique sur Théroigne de Méricourt* (1886). Strobl-Ravelsberg, F., *Les Confessions de Théroigne de Méricourt* (1892). *Théroigne et Populus, ou la triomphe de la démocratie drame national, en vers civiques. Corrigé et augmenté de deux actes, etc. (Précis . . . sur la vie de Mademoiselle Théroigne de Méricour [sic])* (1790). Vicomte de V . . . y (Lamothe-Langon), *Théroigne de Méricourt (Anne-Josèphe) la jolie Liégeoise, correspondance*, 2 vols. (1836).

Jeanne A. Ojala

Aila Meriluoto

Born January 10, 1924, Pieksämäki, Finland
Genre(s): poetry, novel, juvenile literature,
*   detective novel, literary biography*
Language(s): Finnish, Swedish

Aila Meriluoto is one of Finland's most important poets since the Second World War. She has also written books for young people and translated Rilke's poetry. Rilke has influenced her own work, especially in its early stages.

As a poet Meriluoto gradually, in her own way, has broken away from the traditional romantic tradition. Her first collection, *Lasimaalaus* (1946; Stained Glass), marked both the last culmination of traditional poetry and the heralding of the new, modern poetry in the history of Finnish poetry. It contains both sensitive, girlish melodiousness and rhetorical strength, massiveness; it is uncompromising and passionate. In it the voice of post-war youth could be heard ("without belief or mercy"), and it was a critical and popular success. Meriluoto did not shift to free verse until the late fifties, and even later she has followed her own line in relation to the general development of Finnish poetry. In her poetry of the 1960s Lapland signified a distance setting everything past into perspective, in *Asumattomiin* (1963; To the Uninhabited), and *Tuoddaris* (1965). She lived in Sweden from 1962 to 1974, and the language became a problem for her. She has also written in Swedish. In her poems of the 1970s there is a new, conversational, everyday tone and humor.

Central to her work is a personal, confessional approach to the roles of woman and artist and the nature of creative work. In her first collections her attitude is romantically uncompromising; later irony and humor give a sense of proportion. Her intense marriage with the writer Lauri Viita lasted from 1948 to 1956, and its traumatic quality is seen both in poems and in her biography *Lauri Viita, legenda jo eläessään* (1974; Lauri Viita, A Legend in his Lifetime).

The most revealing and distressed of her volumes of poetry is *Pahat unet* (1958; Bad Dreams), after which she becomes more objective, with imagery drawn from biology. Nature often gives an erotic coloring to Meriluoto's poems, and she has powerfully described woman's life in all its range in her poetry.

Works

Lasimaalaus [Stained Glass] (1946). *Sairas tyttö tanssii* [A Sick Girl Dances] (1952). *Pommorommo* (1956). *Pahat unet* [Bad Dreams] (1958). *Portaat* [Steps] (1961). *Asumattomiin* [To the Uninhabited] (1963). *Ateljee Katariina* [Atelier Katariina] (1965). *Tuoddaris* (1965). *Meidän linna* [Our Castle] (1968). *Silmämitta* [Eyeshot] (1969). *Peter-Peter* (1971). *Elämästä* [Of Life] (1972). *Lauri Viita, legenda jo eläessään* [Lauri Viita, A Legend in His Lifetime] (1974). *Kotimakuin mies* [Homeland like a Man] (1977). *Varokaa putoilevia enkeleitä* [Beware of Falling Angels] (1977). *Sisar vesi, veli tuli* [Sister Water, Brother Wind] (1979). *Talvikaupunki* [Winter City] (1980). *Vihreä tukka* [Green Hair] (1982). *Lasimaalauksen läpi. Lasimaalaus ja päiväkirja vuosilta 1944–1947* [Through Stained Glass. Stained Glass and a Diary 1944–1947] (1986).

Bibliography

Toivonen, Pirjo-Maija, "Aila Meriluodon varhaislyriikan modernismi ja sen tausta. Tekstianalyyttinen tutkimus modernismin estetiikasta ja historiasta." [Modernism and Its Background in Aila Meriluoto's Early Poetry] Diss., 1986. *Jyväskylä Studies in the Arts* 24 (Jyväskylä, 1986), 291 pp. Meriluoto, Aila, *A Poet's Perspective*, intro. Kai Laitinen. *Youth revisited: extracts from a diary (1944–1947)*, poems and extracts, tr. Herbert Lomas. *Books from Finland* 4(1986): 217–228.

Liisi Huhtala

Hortense Allart de Méritens

(a.k.a. Mme. Prudence de Saman l'Esbatx)

Born October 7, 1801, Milan, Italy; died February 28, 1879, Monthléry, France
Genre(s): novel, essay
Language(s): French

Remembered mainly for associations with famous nineteenth-century French writers and thinkers, Hortense Allart wrote a number of varied works—romantic novels, serious philosophical, historical, and political essays, and reflective letters.

Allart was born in Milan while her father, Nicolas-Jean-Gabriel Allart, was there on business; her mother, Marie-Françoise Gay Allart, famous for her literary salons, wrote a novel and translated two British novels, including Anne Radcliffe's *The Italian*. Forced by her father to read Voltaire when she was 12 or 13, Allart lost her faith, though throughout her adult life she combined her cynicism with an undogmatic, sentimental Christianity. In a letter to Sainte-Beuve explaining why she had not married the father of her second child, she noted, "I have put this attachment before God, and God hasn't intervened." Allart's father died in 1817, leaving the family without any fortune. In 1823, while serving as a governess, Allart met the Comte de Sampayo, who was to be the father of her first child, Marcus Napoleon Allart, born in 1826. In 1824 she moved to Paris, where she met Béranger, Thiers, and Mignet. The following year she moved to Italy, where she stayed for four years, living in Milan, Florence, and Rome. In Italy she met Stendhal and later Chateaubriand, with whom she began a liaison after her return to Paris in 1829. In 1830 Allart met the English novelist Henry Bulwer-Lytton, and they began living together intermittently for several years. Two years later she met and became friends with George Sand. Allart became involved in several feminist issues in 1836, publishing *La Femme et la démocratie de nos temps*, collaborating on the *Gazette des Femmes*, and working with the feminist Flora Tristan. She returned to Italy in 1838, shortly after publishing her history of Florence, and met Marie d'Agoult and Liszt. In 1839 in Florence she had her second son, Henri-Marcus Diodati Allart. The next year she returned to the village of Herblay in France, where she spent much of her time between 1833 and 1850. In 1841 she began her affair with the critic Sainte-Beuve, who was to use her memoirs in writing his history *Chateaubriand et son groupe literaire*. Allart married Napoleon-Louis-Frederic de Méritens in 1842 but left him the next year. Until 1879, when she moved to Paris, Allart lived in various villages in France, writing mainly political essays and then religious treatises. Her fictionalized memoirs, *Enchantements de Mme. Prudence de Saman l'Esbatx*, described her various adventures, barely disguising the identities of her acquaintances and lovers. Barbey d'Aurevily attacked these memoirs, particularly for revealing intimate details about the revered Chateaubriand. Allart continued the memoirs in two more works, *Les Nouveaux Enchantements* and *Derniers Enchantements*. Allart died in 1879 and was buried at Bourg-la-Reine.

Allart's novels or romances are not exceptional in form; in *La Revue des deux mondes*, Sainte-Beuve criticizes *Sextus* for being too simple in its exposition and for its hasty character sketches, while he praises the novel for being moral without declamatory lessons. The novel's plainness may be a deliberate strategy rather than an aesthetic deficiency, however, for Allart refers to *Sextus* as a "roman austere" (austere novel). Sainte-Beuve is much more favorably disposed to the later novel *Settimia*, the story of an Italian woman who falls in love with a young Frenchman visiting Rome with his family. The critic appreciates in particular the novelist's handling of the conflict between love and ambition (Settimia wants her lover Marcel to become esteemed and powerful, yet she also wishes to dominate him; Marcel refuses his family's demand to return to France, but eventually he yields when his future career is threatened). Sainte-Beuve also lauds the novel's serious tone and its eloquence, qualities he had found lacking in *Sextus*. Other writers of the period were sympathetic to Allart's works: Stendhal praised the romance *Gertrude* for its frank depiction of contemporary manners and society and George Sand admired the treatises *Lettres sur les ouvrages de Madame de Staël* and *Novum Organum*, as well as writing the preface to the second edition of *Les Enchantements de Prudence*. Allart's memoirs or "*Enchantements*" are more famous for their frankly unconventional moral views than for their literary innovation. Her letters, on the other hand, have received more attention, primarily for their sensitive observations of persons, places, and manners.

Perhaps, as modern critics have suggested, Allart's works have been ignored because of her daring life and her frank revelations. A reassessment of her place in nineteenth-century literature and social thought is now in order, however. Recent feminist criticism has shown how Allart breaks new ground not only in subject matter but

in narrative form as well, although her diction and syntax embody the clichés of the romance. Moreover, studies of nineteenth-century fiction by women have suggested that the critical devaluation of popular women's literature may actually reflect the tendency of a male-dominated critical system to valorize those literary forms with traditional assumptions about gender. Additionally, the historical importance of Allart's feminist, social, and political thought merits a detailed examination.

Works

La Conjuration d'Amboise [The Conjuration of Amboise] (1821). *Lettres sur les ouvrages de Madame de Staël* [Letters on the Works of Madame de Staël] (1825). *Gertrude* (1827). *Jérôme, ou le jeune prélat* [Jerome, or the Young Prelate] (1829). *Sextus ou le Romain des Maremmes* [Sextus, or the Roman of Maremma] (1832). *L'Indienne* [The Indian Woman] (1832). *La Femme et la démocratie de nos temps* [Woman and Democracy in Our Time] (1836). *Settimia* (1836). *Histoire de la République de Florence* [History of the Republic of Florence] (1837, 1843). *Lettre à Abdel-Kader* [Letter to Abdel-Kader] (1847). *Premier petit livre* [First Little Book] (1850). *Second petit livre* [Second Little Book] (1850). *Troisieme petit livre* [Third Little Book] (1851). *Essai sur l'histoire politique* [Essay on Political History] (1857). *Novum organum* (1857). *Extrait de mémoires inédites* [Extract of Unedited Memoirs] (1860). *Nouvelle concorde des quatre évangélistes abrégée* [New Abridged Concord of the Four Evangelists] (1862). *Essai sur la religion intérieure* [Essay on Inner Religion] (1864). *Lettres choisies de Béranger à Mme Hortense Allart de Méritens* [Selected Letters from Beranger to Mme. Hortense Allart de Meritens] (1864). *Premiere [-Troisieme] Lettre de Mme. Hortense Allart de Méritens au Lord Comte Henry W.* [First [-Third]] Letter from Mme. Hortense Allart de Meritens to Lord Henry W.] (1865). *Histoire de la République d'Athènes* [History of the Republic of Athens] (1866). *Lettres de Mme. Prudence de Saman et de Lord Walter North* [Letters of Mme. Prudence de Saman and Lord Walter North] (1870). *Enchantements de Mme. Prudence de Saman l'Esbatx* [Enchantments of Mme. Prudence de Saman l'Esbatx] (1872, rev. 1873 and 1877). *Les Nouveaux Enchantements* [The New Enchantments] (1873, rev. 1882). *Derniers Enchantementts* [Last Enchantments] (1874, rev. 1882). *Timide essai sur la correspondance sublime de Cicéron* [Timid Essay on the Sublime Correspondence of Cicero] (1876). *Lettres inédites à Sainte-Beuve* [Unpublished Letters to Sainte-Beuve] (1908). *Lettres inédite à Gino Capponi* [Unpublished Letters to Gino Capponi] (1961). *Nouvelles lettres à Sainte-Beuve (1832–1864)* [New Letters to Sainte-Beuve] (1965).

Bibliography

Beaunier, André, *Trois amies de Chateaubriand* (1910). Billy, André, *Hortense et ses amants: Chateaubriand, Sainte-Beuve, etc.* (1961). Decreus, Juliette, "Hortense Allart de Méritens. Opinions et Portraits." *Le Bayou* 80 (1960): 478–494. Giraud, Victor, *Passions et romans d'autrefois* (1925). Rabine, Leslie, "Feminist Writers in French Romanticism." *Studies in Romanticism* 16 (1977): 491–507. Sainte-Beuve, *Premiers lundis*. Sainte-Beuve, *Nouveaux lundis*, vol. 7. Séché, Léon, *Muses romantiques: Hortense Allart de Méritens dans ses rapports avec Chateaubriand, Béranger, Lammenais, Sainte-Beuve, G. Sand, Mme d'Agoult* (1908).

General references: Citoleux, M., "Allart de Méritens." *Dictionnaire de biographie française.* Ciureanu, Petre, "Hortense Allart de Méritens." *Dizionario critico della letteratura francese.*

Stephen Hale

Lucretia Wilhelmina van Merken

Born August 21, 1721, Amsterdam, The Netherlands; died October 23, 1789, Leiden
Genre(s): poetry, drama
Language(s): Dutch

Lucretia Wilhelmina van Merken married Nicolaas S. van Winter in 1768, and she changed her last name to van Winter-van Merken. She became famous for her didactic poem *Het nut der tegenspoeden* (1762; Adversity Doesn't Help), and her contemporaries considered her to be the greatest poet of Holland. Her earlier works include a number of plays that were written in a French classical style. These works are in a clear, cultivated language.

Works

Plays: *Artemines* (1745). *Toneelpoëzig* [Plays] (1774–1786).

Poems: *Het nut der tegenspoeden* [Adversity Doesn't Help] (1762). *David* (1767). *Germanicus* (1779).

Bibliography

Geysbeek, P.G. Witsen, *Biogr. Anthol. en Crit. Woordenboek* 4 (1823): 401–402. Höweler, H.A., "L.W. van Merken en George Washington." *Tijdschr voor Nederl. Taal—en Letterk*, 52 (1933): 70–77. Kloos, W., *Een daad van eenvoudige rechtvaardigheit* (1909), pp. 231–256. Smit, W.A.P., "La Vogue de l'épopée biblique dans les Pays-Bas au XVIIIe siècle." *Twaalf studies* (1968). van Schoonnenveldt, C., *Over de Navolging der Klassiek-Fransche tragedie* (1906). van den Toorn, M.C., "De Germaanse oudheid als inspiratiebron voor de Ned. romantiek." *De Nieuwe Taalgids* 59 (1966): 219–232. Verwey, A., *Nederlandsche dichters* (1894). de Vries, J., *Tijdschr. v. Nederl. Taal—en Letterk* XLIX (1930). Wille, J., "De Leerschool van Lucretia Wilhelmina." *Literair-histor. opstellen* (1963): 202–249.

Adolf von Württemberg

Maria Messina

Born 1887, Alimena, Palermo, Sicily; died 1944, Pistoia, Italy
Genre(s): novel, short story
Language(s): Italian

Biographical information on Maria Messina is scarce and somewhat contradictory. We can say safely that she was born sometime in 1887 in Alimena, a small town in the province of Palermo in northwestern Sicily, received little formal education, and was encouraged toward a literary career by her older brother. Due to the nature of her father's work, her family lived in various cities of central and southern Italy, including Naples, Trani (Puglie), Ascoli Piceno, Arezzo, and Pistoia, as we know from the dates of her letters to the well-known Sicilian author Giovanni Verga. It is almost exclusively by these letters that we can piece together the facts of the small-town novelist and short-story writer's biography, and, in fact, little is known of her whereabouts after the last letter of the collection, other than that the family left Sicily probably for a long period of time, if not permanently.

As a result of Verga's interest in and efforts toward advancing the young writer's career, the short story "Luciuzza" was published in the April 6, 1914, edition of the important Italian literary magazine *La Nuova Antologia*. Messina published a number of short stories in this period, including "Calabrò," also in *La Nuova Antologia* (March 1, 1915), and "La Merica," a story of the effect of immigration on one woman's life, in *Donna* (March 15, 1915), and received the Medaglia d'Oro literary prize from a judging committee of *Donna* headed by Antonio Fogazzaro and Giuseppe Antonio Borgese. According to Teodoro Rovito, author of a volume on Italian journalists and literary figures of the period, at least one of these stories was warmly received by critics and readers, and according to the encyclopedist Mario Gastaldi, the Sicilian-born authoress secured herself great renown in the ten years preceding the 1936 edition of Gastaldi's encyclopedia of women writers.

Her first two short story collections, *Pettini fini* (1911) and *Piccoli gorghi* (1913), were enthusiastically welcomed by critics and praised by Verga, in fact earning her the label "Verga scholar" from Giuseppe Antonio Borgese in 1913. Other principal short story collections include *Le briciole del destino* (1918) and *Il guinzaglio* (1920), although one should not overlook her longer works, such as *Le pause della vita* (1926), a highly autobiographical story of a young authoress who yearns to leave her small home town in Sicily to see the world, *Alla deriva* (1920), one of several Messina creations with a male protagonist, and *La casa nel vicolo* (1921), the story of a young boy who rebels against a cruel, overbearing father. *La casa nel vicolo* was the second work of Messina re-released by Leonardo Sciascia through the Sellerio publishing house in Palermo. In 1981, the year before the appearance of this novel, Sciascia had reintroduced Messina to the literary scene with a collection of three short stories under the title of *Casa paterna*, appending it with a brief critical essay of his own, in which he proposed Messina as a Sicilian Jane Mansfield.

The authoress also wrote, like many other women of her time, various books and short stories for children, some quite humorous, including "Pirichito," a fable of three brothers and a magic purse; *Storie di buoni zoccoli e di cattive scarpe* (1925), a collection of three stories of little girls; and *I figli dell'uomo sapiente* (1915), the story of four orphans, Dottorino, Sapientino, Erudito, and Perfezione, made unfit to live in the world by their closeted and studious upbringing at the hands of a distracted intellectual.

The stories and novels of Messina are invaluable as social testimony; as works of literature, they are moving yet intriguing. She for the most part describes the life of women in the rural south of Italy in the early twentieth century with a haunting precision hardened by first-hand experience. Messina cannot, as so many other authoresses of her time and region, be accused of wanting to draw tears of pity for her unfortunate protagonists such as Lucia in "Gli Ospiti," who must live within the exaggerated restrictions of an oppressive father, or Caterina in "Il telaio di Caterina," who refuses to get married out of respect for the departed souls of her mother and sister. The plight of these characters in the hands of Messina stirs the imagination without making us melancholy. The vivid images of Mariangelina in "Lo Scialle," a girl who is economically forced from her home town by the jealous envy of her female neighbors, of Vastiana in "Il Ricordo," a girl who is seduced by the *padrone* of a nearby farm and grows to accept the ignominious reputation the townspeople immediately assign her, or Ciancianedda, a deaf girl in the story of the same name, who observes her husband making advances to a neighbor woman, provide us with an otherwise rare testimony to the oppression undoubtedly experienced by the women of the south. It is the cool aggressivity with which Messina constructs her plots and analyzes her characters' inner motives that leads one to think neither of the short stories of Giovanni Verga nor of those of Matilde Serao, noted "veristi" of the period but of the female protagonists of certain tales found in the *Novelle per un Anno* of another Sicilian writer, Luigi Pirandello.

Works

Pettini fini e altre novelle (1909, 1911?). *I Racconti di Cismè* (1912, 1913). *Piccoli gorghi* (1911, 1913). *La fiamma del focolare* (1914). *I figli dell'uomo sapiente* (1915). *Le briciole del destino* (1918). *Primavera senza sole* (1920). *Alla deriva* (1920). *La casa nel vicolo* (1921, 1982). *Il guinzaglio* (1921). *Ragazze siciliane* (1921). *Un fiore che non fiorì* (1923). *I racconti dell'Avemaria* (1923). *Storie di buoni zoccoli e di cattive scarpe* (1925). *Le pause della vita* (1926). *L'amore negato* (1928). *Personcine* (1922). *Cenerella* (1919). *Giardino dei Grigoli* (1921). "Pirichito," *Favola per giovani*, in *Corriere dei Piccoli*. *Il galetto rosso e blù* (1922). *Partono i bastimenti* (1980). *Casa paterna* (1981). *La fiamma del focolare*. *La morte del patriarca*.

Bibliography

Borgese, Giuseppe Antonio, "Una Scolara di Verga." *La vita e il libro* (Torino, 1913). Lanza, Concetta Greco, intro. to *Un idillio letterario inedito verghiano* (Catania, 1979). Salerno, Mirella Maugeri, "Maria Messina," in *Letteratura siciliana al femminile*, Sarah Zappalla Muscara, ed. (Rome, 1984). Sciascia, Leonardo, Note to *Casa paterna* (Palermo, 1981).

General references: Buti, Maria Bandini, *Poetesse e scrittrici: enciclopedia biografica e bibliografica italiana* (Rome, 1941). Gastaldi, Mario, *Donne luce d'Italia: panorama della letteratura italiana contemporanea* (Milano, 1936), pp. 434–435. Rovito, Teodoro, *Letterati e giornalisti italiani contemporanei* (Naples, 1922). Villani, Carlo, *Stelle feminili: indice storico bio-bibliografica* (Naples, 1916), p. 146.

Maria Lombardo

Kōstoula Mētropoulou

Born 1920, Piraeus, Greece
Genre(s): novella, drama, short story, novel
Language(s): Greek

Kōstoula Mētropoulou is one of the most prolific writers in Greece today, having three novellas, two plays, six books of short stories, and thirteen novels to her credit.

Her early works deal with familiar themes. *Leōforos chōris horizonta* (Boulevard Without Horizon) deals with the restlessness and problems of youth. *O Enochos* (The Guilty One) focuses on the existential crisis of the main character and his strange guilt and trial.

Recently, however, she has also published some works that leave the reader wondering: Is she a major innovator in modern Greek letters to whom we have to give much attention, or is she an imitator of important European writers such as Samuel Beckett and Jean-Paul Sartre? It seems that she is the latter. Although she is clever and innovative in her approach and her works should be of interest to all who deal with fictional technique, her fiction lacks the necessary polish and she seems to have subordinated quality to quantity. Her works appear to be first drafts, except for individual sections, such as the last part of *Ē zoē me tous allous*, which seems to have gone through careful revision. More often than not, in attempting to create a confusing world, she depicts her own lack of focus and control of her subject.

George Giannaris, in writing about her *Ē zoē me tous allous (To album me tis photographies)*—My Life with Others: The Album with the Photographs—and *O vithos (ē prodosia), ē dolophonia (O mythos)*—The Bottom (the Treason), the Murder (the Myth)—has praise for her technique: "Despite all complexity, her narrative technique and dramatic intensity create a lasting impression because of her originality and skill."

Giannaris admits that in such a work as *Ē zoē me tous allous (To album me tis photographies)*, where there is no plot and no character development or depiction, the result is a misty atmosphere where characters both living and dead come and go. Giannaris writes that Mētropoulou's imagery, language and syntax constitute a liturgical ritual in which the dead are resurrected and glorified and the living are warned. It is not necessarily true, though, that Mētropoulou wrote this book as a warning. Her concerns are psychological and philosophical, as shown quite clearly in her play *Tesseris erēmies* (Four Wildernesses).

In this play there are only two characters, a man and a woman, both nameless, and a narrator. The play is divided into four scenes that do not appear to have anything in common. The first one deals with two adulterers fleeing from accusing remarks made offstage. The next two deal with the inability of human beings to communicate. The last one contrasts two stages in the life of an actress—her heyday and her "present" abandoned condition.

Clearly, Mētropoulou is aware of what is being written abroad. Her strengths lie not in the unoriginal design of her works but in her short, sometimes one-paragraph depictions of such concepts as "Hell is other people," the emptiness of words, the inadequacy of words, the living dead (living in the objects and the consciousness of the people they leave behind), the inability of the self to pull free from the oppression of both objects and words, the blessing and the tyranny of love. For depicting all of the above, *Ē zoē me tous allous (To album me tis photographies)* is probably one of her best works.

Works

Novels: *Ē Chora me tous hēlious* (1958). *Leōforos chōris horizonta* (1961). *Antistrophē metrēsē* (1980). *Alphabētario* (1971). *To Englēma ē 450 ēmeres* (1972, 1975, 1981). *Ē Ektelesē* (1973). *To chroniko tōn triōn ēmerōn* (1974, 1980). *Hēliophaneia 288 ōres* (1974). *Ē prodosia kai o mythos* (1976). *Zaar 19* (1978, 1980). *Ē zōē me tous allous (To album me tis photographies)* (1981). *Auto to theatro ētan ekeinos* (1982).

Short stories: "Dyo epoches" (1960). "Prosopa kai phigoures" (1963). "Politeia chōris hēroes" (1964). "Ta dyo prosōpa" (1972). "Politeies kai anthrōpoi" (1980). "Arthro No. 22" (1975). "Perithōriakē zōē" (1980, 1981).

Plays: *Mousike gia mia anachōresē* (1980). *Tesseris erēmies* (1981).

Translations: *Cronaca dei tre giorni*, tr. Vincenzo Rotolo (1976). *Kroniek van drie dagen*, tr. Anneke Visée (1976). *A ló ès a repülő* (1969). *Rasskazy grecheskikh pisatelei* (1979).

Bibliography

Bulletin analytique de bibliographie hellénique, 1971 (Athens, 1971). *Hellēnides Pezographoi*, ed. Ersē Langē (Athens, 1975). Mirasgezē, Maria, *Neoellēnikē Logotechnia*, Vol. 2. Giannaris, George, Review. *World Literature Today* 57, 1 (1983): 146. Giannaris, George, Review. *World Literature Today* 58, 4 (1984): 642. Gounelas, C.D., Review. *World Literature Today* 56, 4 (1982): 733. Karampetsos, E.D., Review. *World Literature To-*day 58, 1 (1984) p. 145. Raizis, M. Byron, Review. *World Literature Today* 58, 2 (1984): 306–307.

Helen Dendrinou Kolias

Anja Meulenbelt

Born 1945
Genre(s): novel, essay, literary criticism
Language(s): Dutch

Although both her grandmothers were writers, Anja Meulenbelt never considered taking up writing as a profession until she got involved in the Dutch women's movement. She has become one of its most widely read and most enthusiastic defenders, although a critical and far from doctrinary one. She studied social sciences and is a part-time teacher.

The *succès de scandal* of her first novel *De schaamte voorbij* (1976; No More Shame), which is autobiographical, feminist, sexually explicit, and among the first books in Dutch to deal with lesbianism, established her as a popular author. In her less sensational second novel *Alba* (1984; Alba) the number of male and female lovers has been drastically reduced.

Meulenbelt is a prolific writer who revises little and rewrites almost nothing. She has published some 150 articles and essays plus a number of book-length studies about the relation between feminism and socialism, women in the People's Republic of China (*Kleine voeten, grote voeten*, 1982; Small Feet, Big Feet), and about sexuality and the way men and women develop. Her books have been translated into nine languages.

Works

Feminisme en socialisme (1976). *De schaamte voorbij* (1976). *Voor onszelf, vanuit vrouwen bekeken: lijf en seksualiteit* (1979). *Wat is feminisme?* (1981). *Kleine voeten, grote voeten. Vrouwen in China* (1982). *Brood en rozen, artikelen 1975–1982* (1983). *De schillen van de ui: hoe zijn we vrouwen en mannen geworden* (1984). *Mannen, wat is er met jullie gebeurd?* (Interview, 1984). *Facetten van seksualiteit: Een inleiding tot the seksuologie* (1984). *Alba* (1984).

Bibliography

Meulenbelt, Anja, ed., *Wie weegt de woorden. De auteur en haar werk* (Amsterdam, 1985), pp. 7–37, 155–171, 229.

Maya Bijvoet

Malwida von Meysenbug

Born October 28, 1816, Kassel, Germany; died April 26, 1903, Rome, Italy
Genre(s): drama, novel, short story, poetry, essay, travelogue, memoirs
Language(s): German

Malwida von Meysenbug is best known for her *Memoirs of an Idealist* and for her extensive published correspondence with famous contemporaries. Among them are Richard Wagner, Friedrich Nietzsche, Romain Rolland, and others.

Malwida was the daughter of Philippe and Ernestine Rivalier de Meysenbug. The development of her own unconventional religious and political ideas soon estranged Malwida from her family, and the Revolution of 1848 found her sympathetic to the principles of democracy and to women's emancipation. In her *Memoirs of an Idealist* she writes: "For the first time the thought of the *necessity* of women's economic independence . . . took hold in me." She realized the need to disengage herself from her disapproving family after the dissolution of her relationship with the theologian and revolutionary Theodor Althaus, whom she had hoped to marry. From 1850 until its disbandment in 1852, Malwida attended the newly established and controversial college for women (Frauenhochschule) in Hamburg, then moved to Berlin where her continued contact with revolutionaries and her journalistic activities resulted in her arrest and interrogation by police.

In May of 1852 she fled from Berlin via Hamburg to London, where she remained in exile until 1859. These years mark the beginning of a shift in her interests from the social, religious, and political areas to the aesthetic realm (literature, philosophy, music). Contacts with other political refugees—among them the Germans Marx and Kinkel, the Italian Mazzini, and the Russian Herzen—led to an expansion of her journalistic activity in German, English, and Italian papers (*Hermann, Daily News, Dio e il Popolo*). From December 1853 to April 1856 she was governess in the house of the widower Alexander Herzen, whose daughter Olga she adopted and raised.

In 1859 Malwida went to Paris where she befriended Richard Wagner, whom she had met earlier in London. Malwida's idealistic veneration of brilliant male contemporaries and her pedagogic disposition shaped her interests and writing in the second half of her life, with frequent travels and changes of domicile from Paris to Italy (1862), Bayreuth (1873), and Rome (1877). The first volume of her *Memoirs* appeared anonymously and in French in 1869; the first edition of this work was published in 1876–77. It made her name more famous than that of Nietzsche, whom she met 1872 in Switzerland and with whom she shared many years of friendship that ended in bitterness. "You have deluded yourself about almost everyone throughout your life. . . . You have never understood a single word by me," he wrote her 15 years later. There is some truth to his angry and harsh criticism.

Malwida had already published her *Sketches* (*Stimmungsbilder*, 1879), her novel *Phädra*, and the novella *Saint Michael* when she met her last great friend, the 23-year-old Romain Rolland, in 1889. He had read her *Saint Michael*—the story of an idealistic dilettante-painter—and "had been moved to tears" (letter to Malwida of September 24, 1890). For two years she was his confidante, friend, and teacher in Rome, sharing ideas and a common idealism. Malwida remembered him in her *Last Years of an Idealist* (1898); he dedicated the chapter "Amore, Pace" of his *Voyage Intérieur* (1942) to her memory.

Works

Memoiren einer Idealistin (1876–77). *Stimmungsbilder* (1879). *Der heilige Michael* (1885). *Phädra*, 3 vols., novel (1885). *Erzählungen aus der Legende und Geschichte für die reifere Jugend* (1890). *Lebensabend einer Idealistin* (1898). *Individualitäten*, critical essays (1901). *Himmlische und irdische Liebe*, novel (1905). *Gesammelte Werke*, 5 vols. (1922).

Letter editions: Schleicher, B., ed., *Briefe von und an M.v.M.* (1920). Schleicher, B., ed., *M.v.M. Im Anfang war die Liebe.* Letters to Olga Herzen-Monod (1924). *M.v.M. Briefe an Johanna und Gottfried Kinkel 1849–1885* (1982). Förster-Nietzsche, E., and P. Gast, *Friedrich Nietzsche. Briefwechsel mit H.v. Bülow, H.v. Senger, M. v. Meysenbug* (1905). Schleicher, B., ed., *Märchenfrau und Malerdichter. M.v.M. und L.S. Ruhl. Ein Briefwechsel 1879–1896* (1929). Rolland, R., *M.v.M. Ein Briefwechsel* (1932; 1946). *Unveröffentlichte Briefe R. Wagners an die Baronin v. Meysenbug* (1981).

Bibliography

Meyer-Hepner, G., *M.v.M.* (Leipzig, 1948). Sandow, E., "M.v.M. Bibliographie." *Mittelungen aus der lippischen Geschichte und Landeskunde* 36 (1967): 53–64. Schleicher, B., *M.v.M. Ein Lebensbild einer Idealistin* (Berlin, 1915). Tietz, G., ed., *M.v.M. Ein Portrait,* essays (Frankfurt am Main; Wien, 1985).

Helene M. Kastinger Riley

Marie-Jeanne Laboras de Mezieres

(see: Madame Riccoboni)

Hanny Michaelis

Born 1922
Genre(s): poetry
Language(s): Dutch

Hanny Michaelis writes subtle, sober poems. Love is often the central theme and life and the world are presented as seen through the eyes of one who has witnessed the horrors of the Second World War.

Her Jewish parents were deported to Auschwitz and never returned. She herself went into hiding and lived under cover from 1942 to 1945. She remembers the helplessness of this existence in the collection *De rots van Gibraltar* (1969; The Rock of Gibraltar). Her war experiences are the source of the sadness and disillusionment that characterize her poems.

Instead of resigning herself to the impossibility of happiness and goodness, however, Hanny Michaelis remains willing to open the door to happiness again and again, even though she is aware that one must not have any illusions. *Wegdraven naar een nieuw Utopia* (1971; Running Off Toward a New Utopia) warns of the futility of this human tendency.

The idea of unhappy love dominates the collections *Water uit de rots* (1957; Water From the Rock), *Tegen de wind in* (1962; Against the Wind), and *Onvoorzien* (1966; Unforeseen). In *De rots van Gibraltar* the poetry is again more down to earth, and the poet makes fun of her romantic illusions. Throughout, Hanny Michaelis wants to give expression to controlled emotion. She does so in finely chiseled, concentrated lines with a preference for poetic "small talk" rather than hollow grandiloquence.

Works

Klein Voorspel (1949). *Water uit de rots* (1957). *Tegen de wind in* (1962). *Onvoorzien* (1966). *De rots van Gibraltar* (1969). *Wegdraven naar een nieuw Utopia* (1971).

Bibliography

Moerman, Josien, *Lexicon Nederlandstalige auteurs* (1984), p. 159. Vegt, Jan van der, "Hanny Michaelis." *'Tis vol van schatten hier,* vol. 1 (Amsterdam, 1986), 151–152.

Maya Bijvoet

Karin Michaëlis

Born March 20, 1872, Randers, Denmark; died January 11, 1950, Copenhagen
Genre(s): novel, short story, essay, drama, children's literature
Language(s): Danish, German, English

Karin Michaëlis devoted her impressive literary production to women's issues, with a strong emphasis on female sexuality. Focusing particularly on puberty and menopause, she questioned existing sexual and social mores and thus took her place among the Danish women writers of the 1910s who explored the conflicts between work, sexuality, motherhood, and independence.

In rebellion against the narrow, provincial milieu of her native Randers, the young Michaëlis moved to Copenhagen to seek a career as a pianist. Instead, she married in 1895 the poet Sophus Michaëlis and established herself as an internationally recognized writer. After her divorce in 1911 and a short marriage to the American diplomat Charles Stangeland, she continued her prolific writing of novels, short stories, and essays. A popular lecturer and activist, she traveled extensively, especially in the United States. Settled at Thurø in later life, she opened her home to refugees from Nazi Germany.

Michaëlis' first successes were *Barnet* (1902; The Child) and *Lillemor* (1902; Little Mother), both of which explore the problematic female initiation into sexual maturity.

Den Farlige Alder (1910; The Dangerous Age) focuses on female sexuality, this time from the mature woman's perspective. The forty-three-year-old protagonist leaves her husband because of an infatuation with a younger man. She records in diary form the violent sexual lust of "the dangerous age," as well as her disgust with her seemingly abnormal desires and her fear of sexual demise and aging. *Elsie Lindtner* (1912), the sequel, advocates the single woman's right to motherhood, while works such as *Munken Gaar i Enge* (1905; The Monk Walks the Meadows), *Over Al Forstand* (1907; Beyond Reason), and *Pigen, der Smilede* (1929; The Girl Who Smiled) are subtle studies of female masochism.

Michaëlis celebrated her mother in several novels, most notably in *Mor* (1935; Mother), but her major autobiographical accomplishment is the five-volume *Traet paa Godt og Ondt* (1924-30; The Tree of Good and Evil), a fictionalized autobiography later revised into Michaëlis' memoirs, *Vidunderlige Verden* I–III (1948–1950; Wonderful World). The successful portrayal of girlhood characteristic of these works recurs in the *Bibi* books (1929–1939) for children.

In her thematic preoccupation with the construction of femininity, as well as in her experiments with form and genre, Michaëlis points toward Danish women writers of the 1970s and 1980s, who more militantly challenge the sexual and social politics of their world.

Works

Højt Spil (1898). *Fattige i Aanden* (1901). *Birkedommeren* (1901). *Barnet* (1902). *Lillemor* (1902). *Sønnen* (1903). *Liebe* (1903). *Hellig Enfold* (1903). *Bachfische* (1904). *Gyda* (1904). *Munken Gaar i Enge* (1905). *De Smaa Mennesker* (1906). *Tommelise* (1906). *Ghettoens Blomst* (1907). *Kyllingesorger* (1907). *Over Al Forstand* (1907). *Betty Rosa* (1908). *Tro som Guld* (1909). *Den Farlige Alder* (1910). *Kvindehjerter* (with Betty Nansen, 1910). *Danske Foregangsmaend i Amerika* (1911). *Elsie Lindtner* (1912). [With Joost Dahlerup], *Bogen om Kaerlighed* (1912). *Jens Himmelreich und Andere Erzählungen* (1912). *Grev Sylvains Haevn* (1913). *Glaedens Skole* (1914). *Hjertets Drømme* (1915). *Weiter Leben! Kriegs-Schicksäle* (1915). *En Mo'rs øjne* (1915). *Krigens Ofre* (1916). *Die Neuen Weiber von Weinsberg* (1916). *Atter det Skilte—* (1918). *Die Grosse Beichte* (1919). *Don Juan—Efter Døden* (1919). *30 Dages Laan* (1920). *Lille Unge Kone* (1921). *Mette Trap og Hendes Unger* (1922). *Syv Søstre Sad—* (1923). *Traet paa Godt og Ondt* I-V (1924–1930). *Der Fall d'Annunzio* (1925). *Die Perlenkette* (1927). *Famile Worm* (1928). *Flammende Tage* (1929). *Pigen, der Smilede* (1929). *Das Heilige Feuer* (1930). *Hjertets Vagabond* (1930). *Justine* (1931). *Die Grüne Insel* (1933). *Mor* (1935). *Little Troll* (1946). *Vidunderlige Verden* I–III (1948–50) and various children's books, including the Bibi series (1929–1939).

Translations: *The Child: Andrea*, tr. John N. Laurvik (1904). *The Dangerous Age: Letters and Fragments from a Woman's Diary*, tr. Beatrice Marshall (1912). *Elsie Lindtner*, tr. Beatrice Marshall (1912). *The Governor*, tr. Amy Skovgaard Petersen (1913). *Bibi: A Little Danish Girl*, tr. Lida S. Hanson (1927). *Venture's End*, tr. Grace Isabel Colbron (1927). *Bibi*, tr. Rose Fyleman (1936). [With Leonore Solsky], *Little Troll* (1946). "The First Party," tr. Ann and Peter Thornton, in *Contemporary Danish Prose: An Anthology*, ed. Elias Bredsdorff (1958; Copenhagen, 1974).

Bibliography

Andersen, Tine, and Karen Klitgaard Poulsen, "Karin Michaëlis," in *Overgangskvinden*, ed. Mette Bryld et al. (Odense, 1982). Fabricius, Susanne, "Karin Michaëlis," in *Danske Digtere i det 20.*

Aarhundrede I, ed. Torben Brostrøm and Mette Winge (Copenhagen, 1980), pp. 343–352. Iversen, Mette, "Karin Michaëlis: 'Den Farlige Alder.'" *Litteratur og Samfund* 7 (1975): 11–53.

Clara Juncker

Louise Michel

Born 1830, Vroncourt, France; died 1905, Marseilles, France
Genre(s): poetry, novel, memoirs, political text, drama
Language(s): French

Louise Michel, whose participation in the Commune earned her the nickname the "Red Virgin," is one of the premier figures of the French Socialist and Anarchist movements of the nineteenth century. Although she was neither a theoretician nor an organizer, her speeches and writings, her highly visible participation in demonstrations, and her numerous imprisonments made her a legend in her own lifetime. The details of her life come from many sources, not the least of which are her own memoirs. It is here, however, that it is sometimes difficult to sort out facts, for Michel not only eschews a chronological account but also presents a romanticized vision of the world. Michel's memoirs, when read with other sources (e.g., police surveillance records), do allow for an accurate picture of her life.

Born in 1830 at Vroncourt, the illegitimate daughter of a servant woman, her childhood was a happy one, for she was raised by both her mother and paternal grandparents, who treated her as if she were legitimate. She received her early education from her grandfather, a rational thinker who had fought in the French Revolution. After the deaths of her grandparents, Louise was sent to school, where she was trained as a schoolmistress, a career to which she would return at different moments in her life. Her first post was at a village not far from Vroncourt, where her mother was living. Although Louise formed many strong friendships with women and had a close companion in Théophile Ferré, her devotion to her mother was the one lasting emotional relationship she experienced.

Louise's interest in the Républicain movement and her nascent revolutionary conscious-

ness drew her to Paris, where she took a teaching job in 1856. There her activities were many. Her inherent curiosity led her to study science; to expand her political interests, she joined various Republican and women's rights groups; to ease her poverty and help support her mother, she gave music and drawing lessons and throughout she was contributing articles to journals and writing poetry and novels. This period of her life was marked by two events that shook French society and thrust Louise onto the political center stage: the Franco-Prussian War and the Commune. In 1870, France's impending defeat at the hands of the Prussians polarized political sentiments. The Republican government doubted the loyalties of the Paris revolutionaries and feared the National Guard. After the fall of Paris in 1871, the Guard declared the Paris Commune and separated itself from the Versailles government. Although the Commune barely lasted two months, the memory of its bloody battles would be long and the Communards became instant heroes or instant enemies, depending on which camp one was in. Louise, who fought on the barricades, was condemned as one of the Commune leaders. She was sentenced to perpetual banishment in New Caledonia, where she remained until a general amnesty was granted to all Communards in 1881.

The years in New Caledonia were kinder to Louise than she had expected. She set up a school for the prisoners' children and later for the Kanakas. She studied their language, collected their legends, engaged in an active correspondence concerning their rights, and was staunchly pro-Kanaka during their 1878 revolt. Louise continued to write poetry during her exile, inspired by the beauty of the islands. When amnesty returned her to Paris, it was not long before she was again arrested for her participation in a demonstration. Another arrest in 1883, this time for joining an Anarchist march and allegedly inciting looting, resulted in a six-year prison sentence.

She was granted a pardon and released from prison in 1886, but the shock of her mother's death the year before and the internal divisions in the Socialist movement seemed to sap some of Louise's spirit. When she was arrested in 1890 and threatened with a trumped-up insanity charge, she left France for a self-imposed exile in England where she would spend many of her remaining years. In England she found a greater affinity with the Anarchists than the Marxists, with whom she broke in 1895. Until her death, Louise continued her heavy schedule of speaking tours. She died in Marseilles, where the line of mourners at her burial was over a kilometer long. Yet, this was not her final resting place. Her body was disinterred and returned to Paris to be buried with all the pomp and circumstance of a national heroine, a martyr of the revolution.

Louise Michel's writings are inseparable from her life. Her output was massive and constant. Articles she composed over a period of fifty years are scattered in over a hundred journals. Much of what she wrote is still in manuscript form and much has simply been lost. And, as in the case of any writer with an enormous oeuvre, not all is of equal value. Although she wrote and published in many genres including theatre, e.g., *Le Coq rouge* (1888; The Red Rooster) and political essays, e.g., "Le Rêve" (1898; The Dream), the majority of her works take the form of novels, poetry, or memoirs. Louise felt that art had a social impact and thus should reflect political action. Her novels, often written in collaboration, were intended as a form of engaged literature that would present a realistic vision of society and inspire social change. However, her imagination and her love of drama often got the best of her, and the novels are melodramatic to an excess and abound with sensationalistic murders, suicides, and the like.

The *Mémoires* (1886; Memoirs) and the *Souvenirs et aventures de ma vie* (1905–1908; Memories and Adventures of My Life) present an equally problematic side of the writer. As auto-biography they are not always trustworthy since she would on occasion "tamper" with the evidence to create a more politically consistent portrait of herself. However, they contain descriptive passages that are stylistically linked to her poetry and that form a thematic bridge between her life and her art. Louise's poetry itself was marked most profoundly by Romanticism. The early poems are marked by Christian imagery as well as by her admiration of Victor Hugo, a writer who would remain a strong influence in her works. Political themes, often rendered with compelling emotion as, for example, in her pieces inspired by the Commune, and utopian visions are frequent in her poems. Yet, it is the poems of the New Caledonian exile that blossom forth with the full force of her Romantic temperament faced with the natural beauty of the islands and are by far her most successful.

Works

Lueurs dans l'ombre. Plus d'idiots, plus de fous. L'Ame intelligente. L'Idée libre. L'Esprit lucide de la terre à Dieu (1861). *Le Livre du jour de l'an, historiettes, contes et légendes pour les enfants* (1872). *La Grève dernière* (1881). [With Jean Guétre], *La Misère* (1882). [With Jean Guétre], *Les Méprisées* (1882). *Le Gars Yvon, légende bretonne* (1882). [With Jean Winter], *Le Bâtard impérial* (1883) [With Adolphe Grippa], *La Fille du peuple* (1883). *Contes et légendes* (1884). *Légendes et chants de gestes des canaques* (1885). *Les Microbes humains* (1886). *Mémoires* (1886). *L'Ere nouvelle, Pensée dernière, souvenirs de Calédonie* (1887). *Le Coq rouge* (1888). *Lectures encyclopédiques par cycles attractifs* (1888). *Le Monde nouveau* (1888). *Les Crimes de l'époque* (1888). *Le Claque-dents* (1890). *Prise de possession* (1890). *A travers la vie, poésies* (1894). *Le Rêve* in *Inquisition et Antisémitisme* (1898). *La Commune* (1898). *Oeuvres posthumes, v. I. Avant la Commune* (1905). *Souvenirs et aventures de ma vie* (published in serial form in *La Vie populaire* 1905–1908). [With Emile Gautier], *Les Paysans* (n.d.). *La Chasse aux loups* (n.d.).

In addition, Michel contributed many articles to newspapers and journals, e.g., *L'Aurore, La Bataille, L'Echo de la Haute-Marne, L'Intransigeant, Le Libertaire, La Marseillaise, La Patrie en danger, Le Pays, La Révolution sociale,* etc.

Translation: *The Red Virgin—Memoirs of Louise Michel,* eds. B. Lowry and Elizabeth E. Gunter (University, Ala.: University of Alabama Press, 1981).

Bibliography

Desanti, Dominique, *Visages de femmes* (Paris, 1955). Goldsmith, Margaret Leland, *Seven Women Against the World* (London, 1935). Lejeune, Paule, *Louise Michel, l'indomptable* (Paris, 1978). Thomas, Edith, *Louise Michel ou La Velleda de l'anarchie* (Paris, 1971).

Edith J. Benkov

Marie Michon

(see: Gabrielle-Anne Du Poilloüe de Saint-Mars)

Veronica Micle

(a.k.a. Corina)

Born 1850, Năsăud, Romania; died 1889, Văratec
Genre(s): poetry, short story
Language(s): Romanian

Veronica Micle, whose real name was Ana Cîmpan, made her debut with two romantic short stories—"Rendez-vous" (1872; The Rendezvous) and "Plimbarea de mai în Iaşi" (1872; May Stroll in Iaşi)—published under the pseudonym Corina. She was a regular contributor to the most important literary journals of the time—*Columna lui Traian, Convorbiri literare, Familia, Revista nouă,* and *Revista literară.* She also published in *Revista politică.* Her poems, some of which were collected in the volume *Poezii* (1887; Poems), are Heinean songs of love and hate, of a wish for sentimental revenge, and melancholy.

Veronica Micle is considered to be the first and most important disciple of the great Romanian poet Mihai Eminescu. The two lived through an intense and painful love episode that ended with Eminescu's death. Micle committed suicide less than two months later at the monastery of Văratec where she had spent the last weeks of her life putting together in an album entitled *Dragoste şi Poezie* (Love and Poetry) the poetic exchange between her and Eminescu.

United to Eminescu through poetry, love, and an almost simultaneous life span, Micle became the involuntary heroine of a romantic literary myth that was at the core of an impressive number of novels, plays, and poems from the end of the nineteenth century until today.

Micle translated works by Lamartine and Th. Gautier into Romanian.

Works

"Rendez-vous" [The Rendezvous] (1872). "Plimbarea de mai în Iaşi" [May Stroll in Iaşi] (1872). *Poezii* [Poems] (1887). *Poezii* [Poems] (1909). *Poezii* [Poems] (1914). *Dragoste şi Poezie* [Love and Poetry] (1969).

Translations: Vainer, Nelson, ed. and tr., *Antólogia da poesia romena,* tr. into Portuguese of the poem "Lui"/"A éle" (Rio de Janeiro, 1966).

Bibliography

Baboeanu, Nic. V., *Iubire–durere. M. Eminescu–Veronica Micle* (Bucharest, 1905). Cioculescu, Şerban, Vladimir Streinu, and Tudor Vianu, "Veronica Micle." *Istoria literaturii române moderne* I (Bucharest, 1944), pp. 229–230. Lovinescu, E., *Bălăuca* (Bucharest, 1935). Mănucă, Dan, "Veronica Micle." *Dicţionarul literaturii române de la origini pînă la 1900* (Bucharest, 1979), p. 564. Minar, Octav, *Veronica Micle* (Bucharest, 1914). Morariu, Leca, *Eminescu şi Veronica Micle* (Cernăuţi, 1939). Pop, Augustin Z.N., *Mărturii. Eminescu–Veronica Micle* (Bucharest, 1967). Sanda, George, *Veronica Micle* (Bucharest, 1972). Smara, *Veronica Micle. Viaţa şi operile sale* (Bucharest, 1892).

Sanda Golopentia

Jóreiðr Hermundardóttir í Miðjumdal

Born c. 1239, Iceland
Genre(s): visionary poetry
Language(s): Old Norse

Jóreiðr í Miðjumdal is credited with eight stanzas of dream verse in *Íslendinga saga,* part of *Sturlunga saga,* an account of current events written by Jóreiðr's contemporary Sturla Þórðarson. In the sort of Icelandic visionary verse of which Jóreiðr's poetry is typical, the poet attributes the origin of the poetry to a figure seen and heard in a dream or vision. In Jóreiðr's case, the dream-figure is one of the grand heroines of pagan legend, Guðrún Gjúkadóttir (from the story of Sigurd the Volsung). The verses and the frame-story that goes with them involve Jóreiðr's visions on a number of summer nights in 1255 in which she sees Guðrún dressed in dark clothing (which is often symbolic in Icelandic tradition of violent death) and mounted on a large gray horse. Jóreiðr asks the dream-woman about the fate of various of her friends and kinsmen, who are tangled up in political feuds elsewhere in Iceland. The dream-woman provides her with suitably doom-filled answers, sometimes in prose, but mostly in verse, in archaic Eddic style. Jóreiðr's poetry and the frame-story surrounding it are an evocative mirror of the apprehension and political tension characteristic of her time, the decline of the Icelandic republic. They are also noteworthy for two other reasons: (1) they represent the largest corpus attributed to any single woman *skald* in the Old Norse period; and (2) they comprise the largest body of counterevidence to the prevailing modern belief that women composed but little poetry after Iceland's conversion to Christianity.

Works

Finnur Jónsson, ed., *Den norsk-islandske skjaldedigtning* IIB (1915), p. 158. Kock, Ernst Albin, ed., *Den norsk-isländska skaldedliktningen* II (1949), pp. 84–85.

Translations: *Sturlunga saga*, tr. Julia McGrew, I, (1971), pp. 431–434.

Bibliography

Helgadóttir, Gu<d/>run , *Skáldkonor fyrri alda* I (Akureyri, 1961), pp. 131–136.

Sandra Ballif Straubhaar

V. Mikovlich

(see: Lidia Ivanovna Veselitskaya)

Milena Milani

Born 1922, Savona, Italy
Genre(s): poetry, novel, journalism
Language(s): Italian

Milena Milani is known for being a controversial, unconventional, and passionate personality. After studying in her native Savona, she entered the University of Rome, where she received a doctorate in letters. During the last years of war in 1944–1945, she took refuge in Venice, which was safe from the air raids. There she wrote her second book of poems, *La raqazza di fronte* (The Girl in Front). Her short, graceful verses reveal the future talents of the author—intensity, sensitivity, intelligence, imagination, and a relentless yearning for freedom. ("Se apro la finestra / vola il colombo /che crede al pane. /

Molte volte per lui / lo preparo. / Altre, per gioco, scuoto uno straccio" [If I open the window / the pigeon flies by / believing it's bread. Many times for him / I prepare it. / Otherwise, in fun, / I shake a rag.] She did not dare to show her poems to her literary mentor, Vincenzo Cardarelli, who helped her and guided in her career. After the war, she moved to Milan, where she opened an art gallery. Her first novel, *Storia di Anna Drei*, is considered by critics her best work. It is a bitter story but not a sad or sentimental one. Set in an apartment in Rome, an account of the protagonist's happier days by the sea filled with the light and warmth of sun is told in the attempt to alleviate her tormented life. Then in 1954 came *Emilia sulla diga*. The theme of this book is a girl's discovery of womanhood. The novel tells in first person of Emilia, a young girl of today, who during a summer vacation by the sea learns about herself, men, and life. It is a vibrant and joyful book. It took more than a decade for the second novel to appear. *La raqazza di nome Giulio* came out in 1964, breaking her self-imposed literary silence. The book was attacked even before publication on the grounds of obscenity. Accused of pornography, Milani was sentenced to six months in jail, a sentence that was later suspended. The book indicates the author's desire to fight the society's bigotry and conventions by using sex as an ideological metaphor. The clear and dynamic prose is pervaded by a melodic grace. In 1972 followed *Io donna e qli altri*, a tale of life and death. It follows the wanderings of the woman protagonist from Milan to Venice and then back to Milan, to Savona, back up north into the mountains, and finally down to the shores of Liguria in the hopeless search for the man she loved. Milani brings her *joie de vivre* and originality to the canvases that she paints and has had several exhibitions. She has also received several literary prizes. Her works have been translated in many countries of Europe and the Americas, including the United States. She is also known as a translator (of W. Kandinski) and art critic.

Works

Poetry: *Ignoti furono i cieli* (1944). *La ragazza di fronte* (1953).

Fiction: *L'estate,* short stories (1946). *Storia di Anna Drei* (1947). *Emilia sulla diga* (1954). *La ragazza di nome Giulio* (1964). *A Girl Called Jules* (1967). *Italia sexy* (1967). *Io donna e gli altri* (1972). *Soltanto amore* (1976). *La rossa di Tadino* (1979). *Mi sono innamorata a Mosca* (1980). *Umori e amori* (1982).

Bibliography

Apice, Mario, "Milena Milani: Umori e amori di un personaggio del nostro tempo." *Silarus* 18 (1982): 37–41. Barberi-Squarotti, Giorgio, *Poesia e narrativa del secondo novecento* (Milano, 1978). Bocelli, Arnaldo, *Il mondo* (June 1, 1954). Cecchi, Emilio, *Di giorno in Giorno* (Milan, 1954). Ceratto, Marino, *Il "Chi è" delle donne italiane, 1945–1982* (Milan, 1982). Manacorda, Giuliano, *Vent'anni di pazienza* (Florence, 1972). Pacifici, Sergio, *A Guide to Contemporary Italian Literature* (Cleveland, 1962). Pacifici, Sergio, *The Modern Italian Novel*, 3 vols. 1967–1979 (Carbondale, Ill., 1979). Piccione, Leone, "Racconti di Milena Milani." *Approdo* (April–June 1954). Pullini, Giorgio, *Il romanzo del dopoguerra italiano* (Milan, 1961).

Giacomo Striuli

Pilar Millán Astray

Born 1879, La Coruña, Spain; died 1949, Madrid
Genre(s): drama
Language(s): Spanish, Galician

Pilar Millán Astray was the sister of José Millán Astray, founder of the Spanish Foreign Legion and devotée of General Francisco Franco, dictator of Spain between 1939 and 1975. Like her brother, Millán Astray exhibits a conservative orientation to theater, social customs, and politics. Her plays are in the folkloric and humorous *sainete* tradition of stock characters, who speak the colorful language of the working classes. Although she portrays submissive and devout women positively, these women could become extremely strong when confronted by a moral question or when called to defend a member of the family. Typical of her many plays that were extremely popular with the general public are: *El juramento de la Primorosa* (Primorosa's Vow), *El millonario y la bailarina* (The Millionaire and the Dancer), *Los amores de la Nati* (Nati's Loves), and

La mercería de la Dalia roja (The Red Dalia Dime Store).

Works

La llave de oro [The Golden Key] (1921). *Rhut la isrealita* [Ruth the Israelite] (1923). *Al rugir el león* [When the Lion Roars] (1924). *Las ilusiones de la Patro* [Patro's Dreams] (1925). *La tonta del bote* [The Silly Girl with the Bucket] (1925). *Magda la tirana* [Magda the Tyrant] (1926). *Pancho Robles* (1926). *La Galana* [Galana] (1928). *El juramento de la Primorosa* [Primorosa's Vow] (1928). *Mademoiselle Naná* (1928). *El millonario y la bailarina* [The Millionaire and the Dancer] (1930). *Los amores de la Nati* [Nati's Loves] (1931). *La mercería de la Dalia roja* [The Red Dalia Dime Store] (1932). *La casa de la bruja* [The Witch's House] (1932). *Las tres Marías* [The Three Marys] (1936). *Cautivas; 32 meses en las prisiones rojas* [Women Held Captive; 32 Months in Red Prisons] (1940). *La condesa Maribel* [Countess Maribel] (1942).

Patricia W. O'Connor

Margareta Miller-Verghi

(a.k.a. Mărgărita Miller-Verghy, Marg. M.-V., Ariel, Dionis, Mama Lola, Ilie Cambrea, Ion Pravilă)

Born 1864; died 1951, Bucharest, Romania
Genre(s): novel, essay, drama, literary criticism
Language(s): Romanian

Margareta Miller-Verghi was old and blind when she started a genre to be later successfully represented in Romanian literature by other women writers. Her "sensational mystery" *Prinţesa în crinolină* (1946; The Princess in Crinoline) was dedicated "to a friend forever hostile to detective novels." The novel recounts the discovery by three improvised detectives (a woman acrobat, Clelia, disguised as a bricklayer, and two young men, Diomed and Florin) of the killer of Princess Ralù Muzuridi from Iaşi. While searching for clues, the three indulge in Turkish coffee and delicate fruit preserves, visit the Moldavian monasteries and the city of Braşov, are more or less invited to aristocratic hunting parties, and leisurely debate with English journalists like Gordon Seymour.

Verghi had published before—under the pseudonym Dionis—the novel *Theano* (1910; Theano) and had written—under the pseudonym Ilie Cambrea—a play entitled *Pentru tine* (For You), among others. Most important, she had co-authored (with Ecaterine Săndulescu) a book entitled *Evoluţia scrisului feminin în România* (1935; The Evolution of Feminine Writing in Romania), which is one of the most important references for any study devoted to literature written by Romanian women.

Miller-Verghi was a regular contributor to *Sămănătorul, Revista scriitoarei, Dreptatea, Flacăra, La Patrie, La Roumanie, Viaţa românească,* etc.

Works

[Dionis, pseud.], *Theano* [Theano] (1910). *Prinţesa în crinolină* [The Princess in Crinoline] (1946). [With Ecaterina Săndulescu], *Evoluţia scrisului feminin în România* [The Evolution of Feminine Writing in Romania] (1935).

Bibliography

Piru, Al, *Panorama deceniului literar românesc 1940–1950* (Bucharest, 1968), pp. 281–283.

Sanda Golopentia

Mărgărita Miller-Verghy

(see: Margareta Miller-Verghi)

Claudia Millian

(a.k.a. Claudia Cridim, Claudia Millian-Cridim, Claudia Millian-Minulescu, Rozina, D. şerban)

Born 1887, Bucharest, Romania; died 1961, Bucharest
Genre(s): poetry, drama, memoirs, journalism, translation
Language(s): Romanian

Claudia Millian studied in Bucharest and Ploieşti, graduated at the Bucharest Conservatory of Art, lived and painted in Paris for a while, and functioned as a professor of drawing while regularly contributing to the symbolist literary journals *Versuri (Şi proză, Insula, Cetiţi-mă,* to the feminist literary journal *Revista Scriitoarei,* and, in the last part of her life, to *Viaţa românească, Contemporanul, Gazeta literară, Luceafărul, Viaţa militară* (where she published poems, essays, etc., many of which have not been gathered in a volume until now).

Her symbolist poetry, collected in the volumes *Garoafe roşii* (1914; Red Carnations) and *Cîntări pentru pasărea albastră* (1922; Songs for the Blue Bird), proposes a fatuous and exotic vision of the world in which colors, silks, and tapestries abound. The death of her father is at the center of the nostalgic poems published in a subsequent volume entitled *Întregire* (1936; Fulfillment). At the same time Millian had also written a number of poems which she planned to gather under the title *Poeme simple* (Simple Poems). These were not published, however, with the exception of the cycle "Oamenii umili" (1936; Humble People), which appeared in the journal *Cuvîntul liber.*

Under the (male) pseudonym D(imitrie) Şerban, Millian authored a considerable number of boulevard plays which were successfully represented in Bucharest between the two world wars. One can mention, among them, *Masca* (The Mask), *Roxina, Vreau să trăiesc* (I Want to Live), *După paravan* (Behind the Screen), or *Şapte gîşte potcovite* (Seven Shod Geese).

A play dedicated to the poetic couple Veronica Micle and Mihai Eminescu—*Eminescu şi Veronica* (Eminescu and Veronica)—was represented only after Millian's death.

In 1945, after the death of her second husband, symbolist poet Ion Minulescu, Claudia Millian co-founded (with writer Mihail Sadoveanu) the "Association of Friends of Ion Minulescu."

Millian wrote essays and memoirs on Ion Minulescu and, more generally, on Romanian literary life between the two world wars. These were gathered in two posthumous volumes entitled *Despre Ion Minulescu* (1968; About Ion Minulescu) and *Carea mea de aduceri aminte* (1973; My Book of Remembering).

Together with Demostene Botez and Constantin Argeşanu, Millian was editor and translator of the volume *Antologia poeţilor decembrişti* (1951; An Anthology of the Decembrist Poets). She also translated into Romanian a number of works by Russian and Soviet writers.

Works

Garoafe roşii [Red Carnations] (1914). Cîntări pentru pasărea albastră [Songs for the Blue Bird] (1922). Întregire [Fulfillment] (1936). Despre Ion Minulescu [About Ion Minulescu] (1968). Cartea mea de aduceri aminte [My Book of Remembering], ed. Mihai Gafiţa. Cartea a patra [The Fourth Book] (1974). Cîntări pentru pasărea albastră [Songs for the Blue Bird. Selected Poetry] (1975). [With Demostene Botez and Constantin Argeşanu], Antologia poeţilor decembrişti [An Anthology of the Decembrist Poets] (1951).

Bibliography

Călinescu, G., Istoria literaturii române. Compendiu (Bucharest, 1968), p. 326. Novicov, Mihai, "Claudia Millian," in Bucur, Marin, Literatura română contemporană I. Poezia (Bucharest, 1980), pp. 71–72. Popa, Marian, Dicţionar de literatură română contemporană, 2nd ed. (Bucharest, 1977), p. 254.

Sanda Golopentia

Claudia Millian-Cridim

(see: Claudia Millian)

Claudia Millian-Minulescu

(see: Claudia Millian)

Tatiana Gritsi Milliex

(see: Tatiana Gritsi-Milliex)

Marga Minco

Born March 31, 1920, Ginneken (North Brabant), The Netherlands
Genre(s): journalism, short story, novel, television drama, children's literature
Language(s): Netherlandic

Marga Minco was born Sara Menco in an orthodox Jewish family. She grew up in Breda, where her father occupied the distinguished position of "parnas" (prelate) in the Jewish community. In 1938, Minco started working as a journalist for the local city paper, De Bredasche Courant. Due to her Jewish background, she was forced to quit her job shortly after the German invasion in May 1940. Subsequently, Minco accepted a position as a teacher of drawing in a Jewish primary school until the institution was closed down in 1942 after most of the children had been carried off to concentration camps. The following year, she saw her parents being transported to the German annihilation camp, Sobitur. Minco escaped because she went into hiding in Haarlemmermeer, where she worked as a housekeeper in a Dutch farmer's family. Under the pseudonym Fimkje Kooi and with her dyed blond hair, nobody suspected this blue-eyed girl of being Jewish. All of Minco's literary work is heavily colored by her Jewish origin and experiences in German-occupied Holland. In 1945, Minco married the Dutch poet Bert Voeten, who encouraged her in her literary ambitions. She made her debut with short stories in the journal Mandril and in the newspapers Het Parool and Het Haarlems Dagblad.

It took Minco two years to finish her first and best-known novel, Het Bittere Kruid (1957; Bitter Herbs). The subtitle "a little chronicle" is misleading, for the author does not merely relate events; she wants to emphasize that everything recounted is based on facts. The novel describes the persecution of a Dutch-Jewish family in the Netherlands during World War II as seen through the eyes of a twelve-year-old girl. The naivete and detachment the girl adopts toward these threatening, but for her incomprehensible, events turn this novel into a testimony of the vulnerability, anxiety and helplessness of the Jews. Minco adopts an objective, precise style, never using one word too many, a stylistic trait typical in her future work. One year after its publication, Het Bittere Kruid was given the Vijver Prize from the Jan Campert Association. To this day, the novel occupies an important place in the literature curriculum of high schools in Belgium and the Netherlands.

With De andere kant (1959), a collection of eight short stories with a powerful existentialist undertone, Minco wanted to prove she could handle a different subject matter than her war experiences and the Jewish question. Although the first story is entitled "Iets Anders," references to the war and antisemitism prove that *De andere kant* does not completely fulfill that promise. In almost every story we are confronted with a protagonist who is victimized, lonely, and doomed to remain an eternal outcast. One of the short stories, "Het adres," was rewarded the Mutator prize. In 1961, the author compiled *Moderne Joodse Verhalen*, an anthology of Jewish short stories to which—among others—Philip Roth, I.B. Singer, A. Wesker, and I. Shaw contributed.

By commission of the city of Amsterdam, Minco wrote the short story "Het huis hiernaast" (1965), which would turn into the first chapter of her second novel, *Een leeg huis* (1966). The empty house of the title refers to a residence on the Kloveniersburgwal in Amsterdam where Minco and other persons in hiding dwelled during the war. Here, she met Karel Appel, Corneille, Gerrit Kouwenaar and Lucebert, the core of the Vijftigers-movement. *Een leeg huis* is divided into three chapters that each deal with one day in the lives of Yona and Sepha, two Jewish girls who lived through the war. Unlike Sepha, Yona never managed to cut herself loose from those wartime experiences. Additional personal problems finally drive her toward suicide. Minco's frequent use of flashbacks and interior monologues show that her narrative techniques have become more daring.

An excellent and powerful storyteller, Minco uses a sober, almost cool, style that reveals her deep personal attachment. In an interview, she stated that she can only write well about things she intensely experienced; Minco writes from reality, not from fantasy. The suffering, disappointments, struggles and defenselessness of the Dutch Jews in WW II are the subjects that lie near to her heart. Even though her work consists of only a few novels and volumes of short stories, she is considered one of the Netherlands' major twentieth-century authors.

Works

De verdwenen ambtsketen, TV play (1955). *Het Bittere kruid* (1957). *De andere kant* (1959). *Kijk 'ns in de la*, children's book (1963). *Moderne Joodse Verhalen* (1964). *Het huis hiernaast* (1965). *Een*

leeg huis (1966). *Verzameld Proza* (1968). *Terugkeer* (1968). *De dag dat mijn zuster trouwde* (1970). *De hutkoffer*, TV play (1970). *Daniel de Barrios*, TV play (1975).

Translations: *Das bittere Kraut* (Hamburg, 1959). *Bitter Herbs* (London, 1960; New York, 1960). *Bitter var* (Oslo, 1961). *Bittra örter* (Stockholm, 1962). *Et tomt hus* (Stockholm, 1967). *Schau mal in die lade* (Switzerland, 1970).

Bibliography

Brokken, Jan, *Schrijven* (Amsterdam, 1980). Ferdinandusse, Rinus en Ros Martin, *Wat is het toppunt van ellende en 34 andere vragen aan Nederlandse auteurs (met dank aan Marcel Proust)* (Amsterdam, 1971). Meijer, Isha, *Interviews* (Den Haag, 1980). Middeldorp, A., *Over het proza van Marga Minco* (Amsterdam, 1981). Sanders van der Boede, C., *Marga Minco, series Ontmoetingen* (1970).

Dianne van Hoof

Minna

(see: Luise Maria Hensel)

Zelda Mishovsky

(a.k.a. Zelda)

Born 1914, Chernigov, Ukraine, the Soviet Union
Genre(s): poetry
Language(s): Hebrew

Zelda was born in Russia in 1914, the daughter of a hasidic rabbi, Shalom Solomon Schneurson. She moved with her family to Palestine in 1926 and eventually settled in Jerusalem, where she taught at a religious academy for women. Zelda's first volume of poetry, *Penai* (Time), did not appear until 1967.

The poetry of Zelda embraces reality with a traditional, orthodox religiosity. She does not fear to face whatever challenge reality may bring, for she possesses the spiritual security of a Lord who is on her side. The way she professes to cling to such security is through her devotions to the rituals of Jewish life. Three poems in *Penai* are devoted to the Sabbath. Sacred to her also is devotion to family. She worships the faith of her grandfather, as she likens him to Abraham, whose faith was strong enough to sacrifice his son Isaac.

Nature is also a sacred reality to Zelda. Occasionally the insignificant, such as a rose, takes on a metamorphosis to symbolize the messianic era. More often, though, Zelda celebrates the sky and the sea, and the plants and animals within, as giving pleasure to the lives of hard-working human beings.

Zelda writes of both the visible and invisible in her collection *Ha-Carmel ha-I-Nireh* (The Invisible Carmel). The visible (or the ordinary) can be claimed by everyone, but there also exists the invisible, that which can be experienced and known only by Zelda herself. The pleasures of life, those that both nature (from God) and humans provide, are, according to Zelda, a personal experience for each individual. Zelda then, leads her readers to this pleasure, but allows each of them their own experience, rather than sharing her own.

Works

Penai [Time] (1967). *Ha-Carmel ha-I-Nireh* [The Invisible Carmel] (1971). *Al Tarkak* [Don't Be Distant] (1974). *Haloh Har, Haloh Ash* [Surely a Hill, Surely a Fire] (1977). *Zelda shirim* [Verse of Zelda] (1979). *Shoni ha-mahiv* (1981) *She-nivdelu mi-kol merhak* [Those Separated from a Voice of a Distant Land] (1984). *Shire Zelda* [Poetry of Zelda] (1985).

Bibliography

Carmi, T., ed., *The Penguin Book of Hebrew Verse* (New York, 1981). Frank, Bernard, tr., *Modern Hebrew Poetry* (Iowa City, 1980). Glazer, Myra, ed., *Burning Air and a Clear Mind* (Athens, 1981). Silberschlag, Eisig, *From Renaissance to Renaissance II: Hebrew Literature in the Land of Israel: 1870–1970* (New York, 1977). Spicehandler, Ezra, and Curtis Arnson, eds., *New Writing in Israel* (New York, 1976).

JoAnne C. Juett

Janine Mitaud

Born 1921, Dordogne, France
Genre(s): poetry, translation
Language(s): French

Born in the Dordogne in southwest France, Janine Mitaud grew up in Bourdeilles. Of old peasant stock, her grandparents were craftspersons and her parents teachers—her father also was an unpublished poet. After studying at the Lycée de Périgueux and then at the Université de Bordeaux, she then taught in Bordeaux before moving to the Paris region, where she taught and still lives.

Although Janine Mitaud has translated the work of English and American writers—she is presently completing a translation of Ted Hughes' *Cavebirds*—and done occasional articles, the principal thrust of her literary activities has always been given to poetry. Her contemporary preferences go to Perse, Segalen, and Char, and her own work has been equally admired by her poetic peers. *L'Echange des Colères* (1965; The Exchange of Angers) may be said to represent a summit of her poetic endeavor to that date, her earliest publication going back to 1949 (*Hâte de vivre*). Prefaced by Char, *L'Echange des Colères* is a powerfully dense volume, full of ellipsis and parataxis, intense, even explosive, yet oddly serene and gentle at the same time. It speaks of the relationships between body, mind and language, and reveals a spiritual hunger working itself out through flesh, emotion and words. If the earth and its material reality play a central role in this poetry, so too do dream and a sense of implicit transcendence. Thus, themes such as death, memory, self and matter are offset by cosmic awareness, a search for meaning and truth, and the sense of love's overriding power. Janine Mitaud's "implacable passion for being" is conveyed in an often thickly metaphorical mode, beyond all gratuitousness. Unengaged she may be, but her combativity is everywhere.

Danger (1974; Danger) is prefaced by Seghers, who speaks of her "rugged controlled language." "Indomitable above all," he continues, "permanent combat, she is rigor and wheat, milk of life."

Janine Mitaud's most recent books are *De la rose à l'éros* (1983; From Rose to Eros), in which the futility of the "absurd," of derision, is exposed, and poetry is seen as movement toward some vaster interchange, indivision, initiation, and annunciation; and *Suite baroque* (1983; Baroque Suite), which is a more developed and complicated collection. Here the poet argues that written signs are the "nerve-ends of the torn soul of the gods."

Works

Hâte de vivre (1949). Bras étendus (1951). Silence fabuleux (1951). Rêverie (1953). Départs (1953). Armes fulgurantes (1955). Soleil de blé (1958). Le Futur et le fruit (1960). Le Visage (1961). L'Echange des colères, intro. René Char; design Casazza (1965). La Porte et la terre, illus. Rigal. (1969). La Parole Naturelle (1971). Danger (1974). Le Soleile sursoit, illus. Peyrolles (1974). Juillet plain-chant, illus. Staritsky (1977). Livre-poème (1979). Suite baroque (1983). De la rose à l'Eros (1983).

Bibliography

Bishop, Michael, "Contemporary Women Poets." *Contemporary French Poetry, Studies in Twentieth-Century Literature* (Fall 1988). Bosquet, Alain, "Trois poètes de l'évidence." *Le Monde*, 6582 (March, 1966): 15. Brindeau, Serge, "Janine Mitaud." *La Poésie contemporaine de langue française depuis 1945* (Paris, 1973), pp. 402–404. Char, René, Foreword to *L'Echange des colères* (Mortemart, 1965). Haiat, Pierre, *35 siècles de poésie amoureuse* (Paris, 1979). Mora, Edith, "Le chant de la nature." *Nouvelles Littéraires*, 2002 (jan. 1966): 4. Moulin, Jeanine, *Huits siècles de poésie féminine* (Paris, 1963). Rousselot, Jean, *Poètes français d'aujourd'hui* (Paris, 1965), p. 378. Seghers, Pierre, Preface to *Danger.* (Mortemart, 1974). Seghers, Pierre, *Le Livre d'or de la poésie française* (Paris, 1969).

Michael Bishop

Waltraud Anna Mitgutsch

Born 1948, Austria
Genre(s): novel
Language(s): German

Anna Mitgutsch, who studied German and English literature in Salzburg and at the Institute for American Studies in Innsbruck, Austria, now lives in Boston, where she teaches German literature. Her first novel, *Three Daughters*, was originally published in German as *Die Züchtigung* (1985) and was translated into English by Lisel Mueller. It won two prestigious awards, the Bruder-Grimm Preis and Die Goldene Claasen Rose.

Die Züchtigung means "punishment, flogging," and this bleak and disturbing novel is a study of child abuse, isolation, neglect, and torment. The ugliness and brutality that pervade these lives is underscored by the reader's awareness that it is an ongoing and frequent phenomenon.

Marie, the first daughter, is an ugly, unwanted, crippled child of a vicious father who "dragged (her) from the window by her thick red braids and came down on her with his fists and feet until blood ran from her nose and mouth. Then he went back to work. 'Wash your face,' her mother said; 'you look terrible.'" The other children look on with "a mixture of pleasure and horror as the leather strap whacks down on her bare thighs, calves, arms, again and again, until her head hits the edge of the stove and she falls down. Her mother grabs her by the arm and drags her off to the bedroom and into bed."

Marie gives birth to Vera, whom she beats systematically and maliciously with a carpet beater, "a fat, curved rubber sausage, wound around with an iron spiral, an instrument of torture." The third daughter of the title is the twelve-year-old child of Vera, who is spared the physical abuse. But she, too, is a victim of Marie, the grandmother, because as her mother, Vera, says, "she beat me to death thirty years ago, she took my body, appropriated my ideas, usurped my feelings . . . she always wins, in the name of obedience, reason and fear."

That abused children often become abusers is an ironic but well-documented phenomenon, and it is spelled out here in a series of graphic, repulsive images. The more subtle revelation goes beyond the power of all abusers to torment and cripple children emotionally and physically. Such children live forever in a nightmare world. They have no way to connect with society at large since their tormentors have replaced that world with a secret, unrelenting, and violent space that has become the child's only reality. There is a place to run from but no place to run to, and all routes lead to nowhere. Abused children are twisted and crippled at home, and they are thus perceived as twisted and crippled by outsiders. They function alone, however poorly, between those who abuse them and those who ignore them.

The novel describes not only what has already been lost, which is childhood, but makes agonizingly clear that when childhood is denied, only a stunted, pain-filled adult survives. Anna Mitgutsch's novel is powerful and passionate. Reading it is almost unbearably painful.

Works

Die Züchtigung (1985).
Translation: Three Daughters [Die Züchtigung], tr. Lisel Mueller (1987).

Bibliography

Chase, Elise, Library Journal vii, 2 (Feb. 15, 1987): 162 (1).

Mickey Pearlman

Margarete Mitscherlich (Mitscherlich-Nielsen)

Born 1917, Denmark
Genre(s): scholarly monographs
Language(s): German

The daughter of a Danish physician and a German schoolteacher, Margarete Mitscherlich-Nielsen lived a childhood and youth shaped by the experience of two nations, Denmark and Germany. She has stated that being confronted by two divergent ways of thinking has made her choose psychoanalysis as a field of inquiry. In Tübingen, Germany, she received her medical doctorate in 1951 and subsequently studied psychoanalysis in Stuttgart, London, and Heidelberg. In 1955, she married the well-known social psychologist and psychoanalyst Alexander Mitscherlich, with whom she closely collaborated for several years. The book Die Unfähigkeit zu trauern, republished several times, must be considered the main result of their shared research.

As results of her own investigations, several important books have appeared. Müssen wir hassen? of 1972 is an engrossing, clearly written introduction to psychoanalysis, which avoids the pitfalls of popularization. In the eight-essay volume Das Ende der Vorbilder, she discusses the pros and cons of idealization. Gender roles are the topic of her book Männer—zehn exemplarische Geschichten, co-authored in 1980 with Helga Dierichs. The particularly influential Die friedfertige Frau examines the cliché of women's traditional peaceful nature and its having prevented women from being successful in politics. Margarete Mitscherlich-Nielsen is a member of the German Association of Psychoanalysts (DPV—Deutsche Psychoanalytiker-Vereinigung) and of the International Psychoanalytical Association. Her importance beyond psychoanalysis as author is attested by her membership in the German PEN and the Hamburg Institute for Social Research. In 1982, she received the Wilhelm Leuschner Medal.

Works

[With Alexander Mitscherlich], Die Unfähigkeit zu trauern (1967). Müssen wir hassen? Über den Konflikt zwischen innerer und äusserer Realität (1972). Das Ende der Vorbilder. Vom Nutzen und Nachteil der Idealisierung (1978). [With Helga Dierichs], Männer. Zehn exemplarische Geschichten. (1980). Jugend braucht Vorbilder (1981). Die friedfertige Frau (1985).
Editions: Sigmund Freud, Briefe (1972).

Ingeborg Zeiträg

Erika Mitterer

Born March 30, 1906, Vienna, Austria
Genre(s): lyric, narrative prose, drama
Language(s): German

In May 1924 Mitterer sent the poem "Siehe, das Buch schlägt sich auf!" to Rilke at Muzot. From this initial paean arose the Briefwechsel in Gedichten (1950; Correspondence in Verse). Mitterer's side of the correspondence expresses not only her great devotion to the distant beloved and master but also a kindred sense of extreme loneliness and of the burden of being a poet. Her first published volumes of poetry, Dank des Lebens (1930; Thanks to Life) and Gesang der Wandernden (1935; Song of the Wanderer) retain the themes of solitude and longing while showing the development of a unique personal voice, one characterized by simultaneous celebration and questioning.

The strong sense of form and rhythm present in her early lyric production continued in Mitterer's postwar poetry. The interrogative approach is also maintained, but the themes have moved away from the personal sphere into problems of a social and religious nature. One theme common to the later works, *Klopfsignale* (1970; Someone's Knocking) and *Entsühnung des Kains* (1974; The Purification of Cain), is mourning of the loss of spirituality in the postwar world. Concomitant with this sense of spiritual impoverishment is a sharp critique of various aspects of materialist society.

Raised in a Protestant church, Mitterer converted to Catholicism late in life. However, her interest in the Catholic church began even before World War II. The novel *Der Fürst der Welt* (1940; The Prince of the World) shows the effect of corruption in the church on the machinations of the Inquisition as well as the danger inherent in the power exerted by the Inquisition on the secular realm. Mitterer's most recent work, the poetry collection *Das verhüllte Kreuz* (1985; The Covered Cross), is characterized by a critical religiosity on subjects ranging from the liturgy to the church's role in social reform.

Another important theme in Mitterer's early works is the classical world. Various Mediterranean landscapes are present in the early poetry, and a Greek island provides the setting for the story *Begegnung im Süden* (1941; Meeting in the South). Classical mythology is also a source for her poetry and for her retelling of the Cassandra story, *Die Seherin* (1942; The Prophetess).

For five years Mitterer worked as a social worker in the Austrian provinces of Tirol, Lower Austria, and Burgenland. Her experiences among the proletariat provided material for the novels *Hohensonne* (1933; Alpine Sun) and *Wir sind allein* (1945; We Are Alone). After the publication of *Dank des Lebens* Mitterer gave up social work and settled in Vienna as an independent writer. The city forms the background for the majority of her works, whether it is the Vienna of the early sixteenth century (*Der Fürst der Welt*), or the Vienna of postwar shortages.

The major theme of her postwar prose is the effects of the war. Her immediate experience of war is expressed in *Zwölf Gedichte. 1933–1945* (Twelve Poems). Mitterer spent the war near Vienna. *Die nackte Wahrheit* (1951; The Naked Truth) treats the desolation of the immediate postwar years from an adult vantage point, while *Kleine Damengröße* (1953; Misses Petite) deals with the same topic in relationship to a group of young women going through the traumas of adolescence. *Tauschzentrale* (1958; Central Exchange) also belongs in this group of works.

In her drama *Die Verdunkelung* (1958; The Eclipse) Mitterer confronts the Holocaust, telling the fate of a half-Jewish family in a small German university city from 1938–1941. *Alle unsere Spiele* (1977; All Our Games) offers a fictional exploration of the question of Austrian complicity in the Third Reich. It is a specifically Austrian contribution to the theme of "Vergangenheitsbewältigung," analogous in many ways to Christa Wolf's *Kindheitsmuster*.

One theme permeating all of Mitterer's works is that of the need for women to be strong and independent, to make their way in the world without relying on men. In her poetry, the beloved is inevitably distant. In her prose, the men are, more often than not, weak and liable to disappear when most needed (*Wir sind allein*, *Alle unsere Spiele*). If the man is strong, then he is manipulative, using the woman to further his own ambitions (*Der Fürst der Welt*). Although there is no outspoken feminism in her works, Mitterer does show a great awareness of the problems women face, both personally and socially.

For her accomplishments in literature Mitterer has been awarded the Julius-Reich Prize (1930), the Prize of the City of Vienna for Poetry (1948), the Enrica Handel Mazzetti Prize (1971), and the Cross of Honor for Science and Art (1975).

Works

Poetry: *Dank des Lebens* (1930). *Gesang der Wandernden* (1935). *Zwölf Gedichte. 1933–1945* (1946). *Gesammelte Gedichte* (1956). *Die Welt ist reich und voll Gefahr*, selected poems (1964). *Klopfsignale* (1970). *Entsühnung des Kain* (1974). *Das verhüllte Kreuz* (1985). *Briefwechsel in*

Gedichten mit Erika Mitterer. 1924–1926, correspondence with Rainer Maria Rilke (1950).

Novels: *Der Fürst der Welt* (1940). *Wir sind allein* (1945). *Die nackte Wahrheit* (1951). *Kleine Damengröe* (1953). *Wasser des Lebens* (1953). *Tauschzentrale* (1958). *Alle unsere Spiele* (1977).

Tales: *Hohensonne* (1933). *Begegnung im Süden* (1941). *Die Seherin* (1942).

Drama: *Charlotte Corday* (1931). *Die Verdunkelung* (1958).

Translation: Rainer Maria Rilke. *Correspondence in Verse with Erika Mitterer* (1953).

Bibliography

McViegh, Joseph, "Continuity as Problem and Promise: Erika Mitterer's Writings after 1945." *Modern Austrian Literature*, 3/4 (1979): 113–126.

Johns, Jorun B., "Erika Mitterer: Eine Bibliographie." *Modern Austrian Literature*, 19, 2 (1986): 77–95.

Katherine Quimby Johnson

Marina Mizzau

Born May 29, 1936
Genre(s): short story
Language(s): Italian

Terse, pointed, comic stories, many first published in periodicals like *Alfabeta, Nuovi argomenti, Parol, Linea d'ombra, Fluttuaria, Lapis,* and *il Manifesto* have been collected in *Come i delfini* (1988). Two of the 39 stories from this collection, "Salt for Boiling Water" and "Rita's Trip," are anthologized in translation in *New Italian Women* (1989). Quick, fluid expositions of protocol and nuance in daily life, the stories bring author and reader into shared recognitions and amused complicities.

Specializing in the psychology of communication, Marina Mizzau teaches on the Facoltà di Lettere e Filosofia of the University of Bologna. Her most important non-fiction works are *Techniche narrative e romanzo contemporaneo* (1965), *Prospettive della comunicazione interpersonale* (1974), *Eco e Narciso. Parole e silenzi nel conflitto uomo-donna* (1979), *Il caso Sofija Tolstoj* (1981, in collaboration with C. Cacciari and V. Cavicchiono), and *L'ironia. La contraddizione consentita* (1984). She has published dozens of articles on such subjects as stereotypes in daily thought, "Group Sensitivity Training," "Semantics and Psychoanalysis," personality tests, faking and lying, conversation compared with television dialogue, the doctor/patient interaction, silence as communication, irony and politeness, and agreeing and disagreeing. Writers whose work she has reviewed include Gregory Bateson, Erwin Goffman, Apollinaria Suslova, Thomas Szasz, Rudolf Arnheim, and Wolfgang Koehler.

Novelist-semiotician-critic Umberto Eco, distinguishing between two genres which may run together but which receive different kinds of credence from readers, factual report and fictional narrative, locates the "character sketch" midway between. This genre, traced back to the "Caratteri" of Theophrastus, comes up to date in scenes from daily life in works like Eric Berne's *Games People Play* and all the works of Erving Goffman. Encounters between Self and Other are symbolic interactions. Mizzau's subjects, as Eco writes in his column for *L'Espresso* (May 1, 1988), are disputes over whether a cactus needs water, at what moment to put salt into cooking water for pasta, who should take the last pear, and self-conscious anxieties about how to comport oneself in an elevator or whether and how to tell a joke. Mizzau's stories reveal that in conversation there are no innocent remarks; hence the most innocent speakers are those who lay themselves bare to others—who may respond just as innocently and inconsiderately.

Reviewer Chiara Zamboni, writing in *Il giornale di Vicenza* (August 11, 1988), cites Simone Weil's reflection that every person exerts a certain force that will expand like a gas to fill available space, in public or private life; and she says Mizzau's stories show how, consciously or not, such force is exerted in minute details of daily life. Even in banal talk, words can be used as knives or clubs. Most dramatic are conversations between a man and a woman; however trivial in detail, they seem to follow existential laws impossible to crack, but revealed in covert desires, secret insults, and withdrawal into incomprehension. Instead of allowing entrapment in "I think that you think that I think," Zamboni finds Mizzau proposing the game of aware, informed, ironic complicity that will lead to resolution rather than protract the one-upping in a contest for dominance. This strategy removes obstacles and irritations in favor of the liberating shared smile. The smile is the same, says Zamboni, between author and reader.

According to Renato Barilli, in *Corriere della Sera*, Mizzau's investigations of interpersonal communication and "Words and Silences in the Man/Woman Conflict" reinforced her storytelling impulse and led to direct creation. She shows how daily dilemmas expose conflicts between manners and impulse; characters similar to the reader would like to shake off social restraints but cannot or do not dare. The stories allow shared and amused recognition of this common plight.

Blossom S. Kirschenbaum

Paula Modersohn-Becker

Born 1876, Dresden, Germany; died 1907, Worpswede
Genre(s): journal, letters
Language(s): German

Paula Modersohn-Becker is today known best as one of the great women artists of this century, a radical and solitary innovator unaffiliated with any of the artistic movements or schools of her time (neo-Impressionism, Primitivism, Expressionism) whose work nevertheless both prefigured and influenced subsequent developments in twentieth-century art. Ironically, however, she first became known as a writer: when a selection of her letters and journals were published in 1919, the slim booklet became an immensely popular and often reprinted bestseller in the German-speaking world. However, it was not until six decades later, with the publication of the complete edition of her letters and journals, that her full range as a writer could be appreciated and assessed.

Born 1876 in Dresden to a family that prized gentility and decorum, Modersohn-Becker chose to pursue a career as an artist with only minimal familial support. She studied art in London, Bremen and at the Drawing and Painting School of the Society of Women Artists in Berlin; in 1901 she married the painter Otto Modersohn and settled with him in the artists' colony of Worpswede. Several extended visits to Paris (1900, 1903, 1905, 1906) acquainted her with what she enthusiastically described as the "most most modern painters" and confirmed her passion and commitment to the life and work of an artist. Nevertheless, she returned to Worpswede and her marriage in the spring of 1907. In November of that year she gave birth to a daughter; a few weeks later she died.

Covering the events of her life from 1892 to 1907, Modersohn-Becker's diary entries and letters to family, friends, and colleagues reflect a life-long tension between dutifulness ("I am trying very hard to learn a lot so I can be a good housekeeper . . . and so that you will feel comfortable and satisfied with me"—Letter to her parents, August 19, 1892) and a passionate ambition to be a good and serious artist ("Accomplish great things in your art; there is greater satisfaction in that than in anything else life can give you"—Letter to Otto Modersohn, Paris, April 25, 1906). Like her drawings and paintings, Modersohn-Becker's literary work can be described as an art of "monumental intimacy." The directness and unaffected honesty of her writing style reflects the same powerful, almost totemic simplicity of her figures, landscapes and still lives. In the intensity of her experience, the ordinary becomes monumental, significant beyond the immediacy of the particular moment portrayed. Whether she is describing a drawing instructor's antics, the ecstasy of life in Paris, a book she is reading or a young mother she is painting, her writing is marked not by a realism of representation (what something *is* like), but by a heightened psychological (Expressionist) "realism" (what something *feels* like). This quality of intense engagement and her fierce commitment to remain true to herself and to the path that she had chosen make her written work cohere beyond a mere collection of letters and journals. It has the grandeur and dramatic tension of a tragedy in prose.

Works

The Letters and Journals of Paula Modersohn-Becker, tr. J. Diane Radycki (1980). [Based mainly on *Die Briefe und Tagebuchblätter von Paula Modersohn-Becker*, ed. Sophie D. Gallwitz (1920)]. *Paula Modersohn-Becker in Briefen und Tagebüchern*, ed. Günter Busch and Liselotte von

Reinken (1979). *Paula Modersohn-Becker: The Letters and Journals, 1876–1907*, tr. Arthur Wensinger and Carole C. Hoey (1984).

Bibliography

Davidson, Martha, "Paula Modersohn-Becker: Struggle Between Life and Art." *The Feminist Art Journal* 11, 4 (Winter 1973–1974): 1, 3–5. Perry, Gillian, *Paula Modersohn-Becker: Her Life and Work* (New York, 1979). Rich, Adrienne, "Paula Becker to Clara Westhoff." *The Dream of a Common Language. Poems 1974–1977* (New York, 1978), pp. 42–45. Rilke, Rainer Maria, "[Requiem] Für eine Freundin." ["(Requiem) For a Friend."], tr. Lilly Engler and Adrienne Rich, in *The Letters and Journals of Paula Modersohn-Becker.*]

Angelika Bammer

Karin Moe

Born 1945, West Coast, Norway
Genre(s): criticism, novel, poetry, short story
Language(s): Norwegian

Karin Moe is an experimental writer whose literary voice has left its distinct mark on the contemporary Norwegian literary scene. She has worked in advertising, as a consultant to a publishing company, and as an instructor in French at the University of Oslo. Aside from working and writing she has been one of the organizers of a "stunt-poet" group the goal of which has been to raise the awareness of the media, the government, and the general public about the dismal situation of both literature and writers in Norway. In 1986 she staged her own mock burial from a hospital bed in Oslo. Before this rather untimely "death," Moe managed to publish five exciting, experimental, and unequivocally feminist texts.

Moe's overriding concern lies with her attempt to create a female specific *écriture norvégienne*. Language is the theme of her critical writing and her fiction. The influences are several, mainly poststructuralist French. She herself points to R. Barthes, Luce Irigaray, Hélène Cixous, Annie Leclerc, and Chantal Chawaf. Their suspicion of the referentiality of language is passed on to the Norwegian reader through Moe's texts. Entrenched conventional notions of "woman," "man," "sexuality," and "gender" are deconstructed and declared useless. Next to her interest in French matters, she admits that the oral traditions of the West Coast, in particular those passed on by women, are meaningful to her writing. Her playful manipulation of Norwegian persistently breaks with literary norms. Through her spiritedly satirical critique of phallologocentrism she seeks to offer the hope of a "counter"-language, where patriarchal constructs no longer can function.

She is much amused by male critics' open dismay and misunderstanding of what they call her "obsession" with sex and genitalia. It is her way of meeting the world head-on—writing about sex is simply to describe women's reality. She cannot, of course, do without common linguistic features, but she uses these to subvert the familiar, intent on making the reader cognizant of women's silence and marginal position. Philosophy, psychoanalysis, and the natural sciences are her tools.

Her language is not ordered and linear, it is chaotic, fluid, silent, listening, of/from the body. She writes with pleasure à la Barthes, and with a keen sense of layout, space, and rhythm. Her texts are sculpted, choreographed. By contextualizing language she produces new possibilities for naming that are non-universal, pluralistic, without control. Her language is thought-in-context/contact/body-for-others, providing the reader with a point of departure for further conceptualization. Hers is a *mis-en-scène* of language as the lack it is, and her writing contains women's traces within it. The major source of inspiration is the writings of Irigaray. Moe's linguistic maneuvers clearly have consequences for how the reader will perceive time, space, and human relations. Women writers who share her aesthetics are Christa Wolf, Alice Walker, Liv Költzow, Eldrid Lunden, and Chantal Chawaf.

Kyka/1984 (1984) represents an ambitious project in which not only the traditional meta-narrative is disrupted but the physical appearance of the book is part of the desire to make the reader aware of the appropriation process of "woman" into patriarchal structures, by man's lust for paradigms. *Kyka/1984* reveals the writer as a consummate literary concept-artist, an aspect of her work that is very much at play in *Mordatter* (1986) and *Sjanger*(1986). *Kyka/1984* refuses the reader the security-(ph)allacy of the macro-narrative, that Moe views as representative of the social realist and post-social realist novel writing in the 1970s and 1980s in Norway. The impossibility of hanging on to meaning, in the unfolding of the crime story (told via the "voice" of a six-year-old girl framed by a community gossip chorus, in small print in the margins of the pages, and a police report), is countered with the possibility of a new language, a different way of perceiving the "world." This (utopian) attempt is created in the writing books of the little girl, but the trust the reader puts in her story remains an illusion, as her familiar "I" vanishes. Her language however, is non-categorical and non-reflective, sharply contrastive of the Law of the Father.

Mordatter (1986) is a collection of poems in which Moe zeroes in on representations of motherhood, mother-daughter relations, and female socialization. Her veneration for the mother never becomes romantic abandonment, a belief in a given, natural identity. Not wanting the young daughter to become swallowed up by the mother's body and language, Moe prevents the daughter's initiation into patriarchal paradigms. Interestingly, the grandmother has survived the fate of her own daughter, perhaps because she is too deeply rooted in women's oral traditions. She remains harmonious, a sort of ur-mother. In describing their phases of womanhood, Moe appears to say that their relationship to language mirrors the relationship to the body, however different the result. Grandmother and granddaughter share a language that is open, multilayered, and unpredictable.

In *Sjanger* (1986), a collection of reviews, articles, fiction, short essays, poems, and fictional interviews with Irigaray and J. Derrida, written between 1980 and 1986, Moe contributes her sharply critical but humor-filled perspective to the post-modernist debate in Norway. The structure of the collection is characterized by an effective contrasting of "masculine," and "feminine," as well as by a variety of genres and styles. Her discussion centers on modernist and postmodernist views of art and literature, and the connection between these and French feminist theory and fiction.

The short texts chart Moe's travels through recent feminist perspectives, and in spite of feminism's outright philosophical and political questioning of the Great Narratives, she finds that her own feminist positioning has become ambivalent. All the same, *Sjanger* does show Moe's continual curiosity with masculine codes of signification, and she still insists on the importance of women's writing, past and present, and she certainly intends her own writing to subvert reading, writing, and meaning-producing structures. She wants the difference she represents to point to new strategies of female naming and speaking. In particular, she wants postmodernists to incorporate women's analyses, what masculine discourse is weary of, namely, the body, fluids, a different mother. The pluralism she offers, she writes, should replace postmodernism with the term "transmodernism."

Works

Kjønnskrift (1980). 37 Fyk (1983). Kvinne og kunstnar, ed. (1983). Kyka/1984 (1984). Mordatter (1986). Sjanger (1986).

Translations: "The Lady in the Coat," "Eagle Wings," from Kjønnskrift, in An Everyday Story: Norwegian Women's Writing, ed. Katherine Hanson (1984).

Bibliography

Eggen, Herdis, "Skriftens variasjoner," review of *Mordatter*. *Vinduet* 3 (1985): 63–64. Kjærstad, Jan, "Post Modernisme i norsk utakt." *Vinduet* 4 (1986): 48–57. Moe, Karin, "Homo preludens. Kvinna før leiken med mannen." *Basar* 2 (1981): 74–76. Ryall, Anka, "Å sprengja seg ut med gerilja gloser. Karin Moe: *Kjønnskrift. Skrifter fra 70-åra.*" *Vinduet* 4 (1980): 63–65. Tusvik, Sverre, "'Mitt kroppsspråk trugar konsulentens morsbilde': Karin Moe intervjua av Sverre Tusvik." *Vinduet* 2 (1981): 41–44.

Pål Bjørby

Moero

(a.k.a. Myro)

*Born approximately 320 B.C., Byzantium; exact
birth and death dates unknown*
Genre(s): epigram, epic poetry, lyric poetry
Language(s): Greek

Moero or Myro (the spelling of her name is
disputed) is closely linked to Anyte (see separate
entry) in the prologue to the *Garland*, an anthology of epigrams compiled by Meleager of
Gadara in the first century B.C. The two poets were
probably contemporaries and shared the same
artistic concerns; that they were personally acquainted is unlikely. In later antiquity, Moero is
remembered both for her own sake and as the
mother of the tragic poet Homerus (fl. 284–81
B.C.), on whose career she seems to have exercised
considerable influence.

One of the most highly regarded of ancient
women poets, Moero was also exceptionally
versatile. In addition to her epigrams and epic
poetry, samples of which survive, she is reported
to have composed lyrics, a hymn to Poseidon,
and a poem with the intriguing title *Arai*
("Curses"). Meleager claims to have included
many of her epigrams in his anthology, but only
two are preserved. The first (*AP* 6.119), a striking
variation upon the conventional dedicatory
epigram, speaks of a cluster of ripe grapes consecrated to Aphrodite in terms of a child parted
from its mother, the vine. The rich fusion of
epithalamic and funerary language, together with
the intense evocation of a sheltering maternal
presence, suggests that the quatrain may be read
as a symbolic statement about the sundering of
the mother-daughter bond on the occasion of the
daughter's marriage. The second (*AP* 6.189),
which owes much to Anyte 3 (*A.Pl.* 291), requests the Hamadryads, tree-spirits dwelling in a
grove of pines beside a river, to aid the dedicant.
These goddesses are pictured as nymphs tread-
ing the river-bottom with rosy feet—a vivid and
fanciful image for trees whose roots extend out of
the bank beneath the surface of the water. In both
epigrams, Moero's capacity to visualize nature in
human terms and invent daring anthropomorphic
metaphors is strongly felt.

Ten lines from her epic poem *Mnemosyne*
cited by Athenaeus (11.491B) expand Hesiod's
account of Zeus' infancy in Crete. Doves feed the
child-god on ambrosia, while an eagle brings
nectar in its beak; when, fully grown, Zeus
overthrows his father Cronus, he rewards his
nurses with unique privileges. In typical Hellenistic fashion, Moero flaunts her erudition by
neatly alluding to a long-disputed crux in Homer,
Od. 12.62, which could refer either to doves
(*peleiades*) or to the seven Pleiads, daughters of
Atlas. The title meanwhile implies that the epic
was primarily concerned with Zeus' encounter
with Mnemosyne ("Memory") and the subsequent
birth of their daughters, the nine Muses. Moero's
work may therefore have been a programmatic
or self-reflective pronouncement upon her own
poetic craft.

Works

Greek texts and German translations in Homeyer,
H., *Dichterinnen des Altertums und des frühen
Mittelalters* (Paderborn, 1979). Greek texts in
Collectanea Alexandrina, ed. J.U. Powell (Oxford,
1925). Commentary on epigrams in *The Greek
Anthology: Hellenistic Epigrams*, eds. A.S.F. Gow
and D.L. Page, II (Cambridge, 1965).

Translations: English translations of epigrams in
The Greek Anthology I, tr. W.R. Paton (Cam-
bridge, Mass.: Loeb Classical Library, 1916).
Translation of the *Mnemosyne* fragment in
Athenaeus, *The Deipnosophists* V, tr. C.B. Gulick.
(Cambridge, Mass.: Loeb Classical Library, 1955).

Bibliography

Baale, M.J., *Studia in Anytes poetriae vitam et
carminum reliquias* (Haarlem, 1903). Snyder, J.M.,
The Woman and the Lyre (Carbondale, Il., 1989).
Wilamowitz-Moellendorff, U. von, *Hellenistische
Dichtung in der Zeit des Kallimachos* I (Berlin,
1924).

General references: *Oxford Classical Dictionary*,
2nd ed. (Oxford, 1970), pp. 697. Pauly-Wissowa.
*Real-Encyclopädie der klassischen
Altertumswissenschaft* XV.2 (Stuttgart, 1932), pp.
2512–2513.

Other references: Luck, G., *Museum Helveticum*
11 (1954): 170–187.

Marilyn B. Skinner

Céleste Mogador

(a.k.a. Elisabeth-Céleste Vénard)

Born December 27, 1824, Paris, France; died
February 18, 1909, Paris
Genre(s): novel, drama, memoirs
Language(s): French

The best summary of Céleste Mogador's fairy-tale life is perhaps found in the subtitle chosen by her biographer, Françoise Moser: "Prostitute, Author and Countess." At the age of sixteen, in order to escape an intolerable family situation, Céleste Vénard had herself inscribed on the official list of prostitutes in Paris without knowing the social and legal consequences of such an act. Once set up in a bordello, she immediately regretted the decision she had made. As a dancer at the popular Bal Mabille, she was given the name Céleste Mogador in honor of the recently captured fort in Morocco. Her next professional venture was as a horseback rider in the Hippodrome. Through the parties she frequented, she met Count Lionel Moreton de Chabrillan, a nobleman who soon dissipated his fortune. After a stormy relationship and despite family opposition, he married Céleste in London in 1854, and they left for Australia where he had been named French consul.

While they were incommunicado during the long voyage, Céleste's memoirs, *Adieux au monde*, were published, revealing to the whole world her sordid past. In Australia, she composed *Les Voleurs d'or* (1857) and amassed much material for future writings. Her husband died in 1858, and Céleste returned to France, where she supported herself by writing novels, plays, and operettas. During the Franco-Prussian War she formed a nursing corps, Les Soeurs de France, and afterward created a home for war orphans. Her life shows that she was possessed of indomitable strength and determination but also of very good luck; she was always rescued from suicide or destitution by fortuitous interventions.

Céleste's memoirs provide chilling insights into the life of a working-class girl during the reign of Louis-Philippe, detailing wife-beating, insurrection, and conditions in women's prisons. The initial five volumes were followed in 1877 by *Un deuil au bout de monde*, an account of her marriage and life in Australia. *Les Voleurs d'or*, a novel much admired by Alexandre Dumas and well received by the critics, is a melodrama whose overly-complex plot is redeemed by its dialogue, characterizations, and evocation of Australian locales and mores. With the help of Dumas, the novel was later turned into a popular play in which she herself appeared. As the Comtesse Lionel de Chabrillan, Céleste published several other novels, the best known of which are *Miss Pewel* (1859), *Emigrantes et déportées* (1878), Australian works, and *Un amour terrible* (1896), also called *La Sapho*. Many of her thirty-odd plays and operettas were commercially successful.

An astonishing *personnage*, Céleste Mogador, Comtesse Lionel de Chabrillan, should be remembered less for her literary works than for her successful social ascent and the lasting impression she made on the French imagination of the mid-nineteenth century.

Works

As Céleste Mogador: *Adieux au monde*, 5 vols. (1854).

As Comtesse Lionel de Chabrillan: *L'Américaine* (1870). *La Duchesse de Mers* (1881). *Emigrantes et déportées*, or *Les Deux Soeurs* (1887). *En Australie* (1862). *En garde* (1864). *Est-il fou?* (1860). *Les Forçats de l'amour* (1881). *M'am Nicole* (1880). *Marie Baude* (1883). *Militairement* (1863). *Miss Pewell* (1859). *Nedel* (Musique de Marius Boullard) (1863). *Querelle d'Allemand* (1864). *Les Revers de l'amour* (1870). *Un amour terrible (La Sapho)* (1876). *Un deuil au bout du monde* (1877). *Un drame sur le Tage* (1885). *Un miracle à Vichy* (1860). *Les Voleurs d'or* (1857). *Les Voleurs d'or* (Play) (1867).

For further references, see Moser, pp. 345–347.

Delvau, Alfred (presumed author), *Mémoires d'une honnête fille* (1865). Céleste asserted she had written part of this volume.

Translations: *The Gold Robbers*, tr. Lucy and Caroline Moorehead (1970).

Bibliography

Haldane, Charlotte, *Daughter of Paris* (London, 1961). Moser, Françoise, *Vie et aventures de Céleste Mogador: Fille publique, femme de lettres et comtesse. (1824–1909)* (Paris, 1935).

Kathryn J. Crecelius

Ana María Moix Meseguer

Born April 12, 1947, Barcelona, Spain
Genre(s): novel, short story, poetry, children's
literature
Language(s): Spanish

Born in Barcelona into a conservative bourgeois family of Catalan origins, Moix spent an unhappy childhood within a highly restrictive and oppressive environment. At twelve she wrote her first book—"Todos eran unos marranos" (They Were All Pigs)—which has never been published. Even at that age she felt oddly defrauded, without knowing why, as she relates in some early autobiographical notes ("Poética," *Nueve novísimos poetas españoles*, ed. J.M. Castellet, 1970). That sensation has never left her, as her subsequent literary production, steeped in disillusionment and bitter regret, evidences. An early influence in her life was her brother Ramón, now Catalan novelist Terenci Moix, who, along with writer Pere Gimferrer, widened her circle of readings and literary relationships. Another brother, Miguel, left a deep impression upon her when he died at age seventeen. Although she attended classes at the University of Barcelona, she learned little there, she says, except for "a few names of authors and titles of books, what a strange and confusing thing my country is, and the teachings of two or three really good professors. . . ." (see Campbell). Today, she works professionally as a journalist, contributing articles, stories and interviews to a variety of publications in Madrid and Barcelona. She has published two books of non-fiction, *24 x 24 (Entrevistas)* (1972; Interviews) and, with J.M. Castellet, *Maria Girona. Una pintura en llibertat* (1977; Maria Girona. The Painting of Liberation). She has also done translations of such writers as Villiers de L'Isle Adam, Beckett, and Louis Aragon. And in 1976 she came out with a children's book, *La maravillosa colina de las edades primitivas* (The Marvelous Hill of Way Back When), in which she retells stories of ancient Egypt. Other books for children include: *Mi libro de . . . los robots* (1982; My Book of . . . Robots), an adaptation of the *Cantar de Mío Cid* (1984; Poem of the Cid), and *Miguelón* (1986; Dear Miguel).

Moix's work can be situated within two related contexts. One is the generation of young Spanish writers, like Pere Gimferrer, Félix Azúa, and Vicente Molina-Foix, who appeared in the late 1960s. Rebellious, heavily influenced by the popular culture of American movies and music then invading Spain, these were the "novísimos," the newest of a poetic vanguard referred to as "culturalistas" (culturalist) in intention and style and opposed to the earlier socially oriented poetry. Appropriately Moix appeared in an anthology of such poets, *Nueve novísimos poetas españoles* (1970; Nine of the Newest Spanish Poets), which excerpted some of her poetry from *Baladas del Dulce Jim* (1969; Ballad of Sweet Jim) and *No Time for Flowers* (1971). Both collections, written as prose poems, exploit late 1960s camp through sentimental surreality, in which the themes of death, love, and loneliness intertwine. Hermetic yet curiously shallow, Moix's poetry represents the best and the worst of an adolescent view of life. *No Time for Flowers* won the Vizcaya del Ateneo de Bilbao Prize; one section, "Call me Stone," originally appeared in a separate but limited edition. In 1983, Moix collected all her poetry published between 1969 and 1972 into one volume called *A imagen y semejanza* (Like the Spitting Image).

The second literary context for placing Moix's work is the resurgence of women's fiction in Spain's post-war period, particularly during the 1970s (for example, Esther Tusquets, Lourdes Ortiz, etc.). Many of these writers are markedly experimental in technique and style, with incursions into metafictionality and the surreal. Moix is no exception. Her first novel, *Julia* (1970), though narrated in the third person, is intensely subjective and intimate, drawing the reader immediately into the inner monologues of a tormented and self-destructive adolescent psyche. In exploring the dark world of a divided self, obsessed by a lost double from the past (the six-year-old Julia), Moix also delicately alludes to the problem of sexual identity as it takes shape in the form of unconscious lesbianism.

An apprentice novel, *Julia* also anticipates, at least thematically, her second full-length fiction, *Walter, ¿por qué te fuiste?* (1973; Walter, Why Did You Go Away?). A finalist for the Barral Prize for 1972, *Walter . . .* appeared in the much publicized "Hispánica Nova" series of Barral Publishers, which was intended to launch a "new wave" of Spanish novelists. A bizarre, even haunting display of recollection through dialogue, multiple points of view, metacritical commentary, and fantasy, Moix's novel is shaped by a mythic and hallucinatory vision of a social reality plunged into decay and incipient ruin. Simply put, it is the story of a group of cousins from a well-to-do Catalan family who spend their childhood and adolescent summers in a house that is only named "T." As in *Julia*, the obsessive pull of the past ultimately reveals the profound sense of loss and failure which infuses even the most sexually liberated of the characters. Indeed, sexual daring does not free Moix's characters, it enslaves them. (Nevertheless, Franco's censors made forty-five cuts in the manuscript.)

Moix's short stories continue to explore the same world of adolescent values, the feeling of having been cheated from the very start and the unremitting sense of alienation in an alien land. The ten narrations of *Ese chico pelirrojo a quien veo cada día* (1971; That Red-headed Boy I See Every Day) intriguingly blend the real and the surreal to suggest how ordinary reality disguises a yearning for the darker, Kafkaesque side of things. *Ese chico pelirrojo . . .* also contains one of the best and funniest vampire stories in a modern vein, "Yo soy tu extraña historia" (I Am Your Strange History).

Moix's most recent fiction, *Las virtudes peligrosas* (1985; Dangerous Virtues)—winner of the Ciudad de Barcelona de Narrativa Prize in Castilian—consists of five stories: the title story, which also appeared in *Doce relatos de mujeres*, ed. Y. Navajo (1982; Twelve Tales by Women), "Erase una vez" (Once upon a Time), "El inocente" (The Innocent), "El problema" (The Problem), and "Los muertos" (The Dead). The most suggestive and moving of these is "Las virtudes peligrosas," in which two women love one another unrequitedly from afar as they age. The remaining stories are too abstract in conception and execution, resulting in a form of reader alienation far more acute than the theme of alienation Moix set out to treat. Indeed, her considerable talent in capturing the elusive world of the marginal and the fragmented, especially the adolescent, also reveals ultimately the limitations of the autobiographical in fiction.

Works

Baladas del Dulce Jim (1969). *Call Me Stone* (1969). *Julia* (1970). *No Time for Flowers* (1971). *Ese chico pelirrojo a quien veo cada día* (1971). *24 x 24 (Entrevistas)* (1972). *Walter, ¿por qué te fuiste?* (1973). *La maravillosa colina de las edades primitivas* (1976). *Maria Girona. Una pintura en llibertat* (1977). *Mi libro de . . . los robots* (1982). *A imagen y semejanza* (1983). *Cantar de Mío Cid* (Adaptation) (1984). *Las virtudes peligrosas* (1985). *Miguelón* (1986). Unpublished Mss: *Todos eran unos marranos. El gran King*, Novela.

Bibliography

Campbell, F., *Infame turba* (1971). Jones, M.E.W., "Ana María Moix: Literary Structures and the Enigmatic Nature of Reality." *Journal of Spanish Studies: Twentieth Century* 4 (1976). Levine, L.G., "The Censored Sex: Woman as Author and Character in Franco's Spain," in *Women in Hispanic Literature*, ed. B. Miller (1983). Masoliver Ródenas, J. A., "La base sexta contra Ana María Moix." *Camp de l'arpa* (Jan. 1974). Ordóñez, E., "The Barcelona Group: The Fiction of Alós, Moix and Tusquets." *Letras Femeninas* (Spring 1980). Pérez, J.W., ed., *Novelistas femeninas de la postguerra española* (1983). Schyfter, S.E., "Rites Without Passage: The Adolescent World of Ana María Moix's *Julia*," in *The Analysis of Literary Texts*, ed. R.D. Pope (1980). Valis, N.M., "Reality and Language in Ana María Moix's *Walter, ¿por qué te fuiste?*" *Discurso Literario* (forthcoming).

General references: *Women Writers of Spain*, ed. C.L. Galerstein (1986).

Other references: *ABC* (Dec. 31, 1983). *La Estafeta Literaria* (Aug. 1, 1973). *El País* (Jan. 30, 1986).

Noël M. Valis

Herdis Møllehave

Born ca. 1945, Flensburg, Germany
Genre(s): novel, nonfiction
Language(s): Danish

Herdis Møllehave's books are a result of the many social changes and experiments with lifestyle that took place in the seventies in Europe, especially the women's movement and the peace movement. Like so many books written by women at that time, Møllehave's books are strongly autobiographical and try in a very direct way to address the problems being debated, emphasizing personal honesty rather than artistic and stylistic experiment.

Møllehave is a social worker, a recovering alcoholic who has gone public, and an outspoken partner in an open marriage with a writer/minister who is an extremely popular media personality. All of this she incorporates in her books in order to confront the readers with these options and deal with their own personal problems in an honest and untraditional way.

Le (1977), Møllehave's first book, describes the relationship between what she calls a "slip knot man," i.e., a macho man completely out of touch with his own feelings and unable to relate to women in any other way than a purely sexual relationship. This absolute lack of sensitivity makes all his relationships with women destructive and short-lived; in the book the protagonist commits suicide as a result of her affair with one such man. The book became a huge success, caused a fervent debate in the media, and made Møllehave the most sought-after lecturer in Denmark. Her next book, *Lene* (1980), posits open marriage as a viable and realistic solution, based on Møllehave's personal experience, and also caused a certain amount of debate in the papers.

Many critics have accused Møllehave's books of a lack of artistic merit. However, her success with the public speaks for itself, and as a social testimony of the seventies, her books do have a certain value.

Works

Le (1977). *Måske blir du gammel* (1979). *Lene* (1980). *Helene* (1983). *En bog uden navn-om det man ikke taler om* (1985).

Bibliography

Bryld, Mette, *Overgangskvinden* (1982). Clausen, Claus, ed., *Litteratur/80—en almanak* (1980). Tiderne, Skifter, Praest, Inger, et al., *Kaerlige kulinger. Analyser af romancer fra 70'erne* (1981).

Merite von Eyben

Erika Molny

Born June 28, 1932, Carinthia, Austria
Genre(s): journalism, filmscripts, radio drama, cabaret, satire, short story, poetry, ballad, novel, drama
Language(s): German

In her native Austria, Erika Molny is primarily known for the often provocative columns she wrote for many years in the country's most influential newsmagazine, *profil*. In addition to being a columnist, Molny has written for the cabaret (particularly for the "Lach- und Schießgesellschaft" in Munich), she has been a song writer and, together with her husband, Thomas Pluch, she has co-authored movie scripts and worked on a number of television productions. For many years, she has moved skillfully between journalism and literature. While not altogether abandoning her career as a journalist, in the eighties she has made a number of steps to also secure herself a position in the literary scene of Austria. In fact, a critic insists that her first novel, *Bruchstücke* (Fragments), published in 1984, places Molny among the important writers of Austria. Justifiably, the novel has been compared favorably with works by Peter Handke and Gernot Wolfgruber. Molny herself has confirmed her aspirations to devote more of her time pursuing a literary career and eventually be remembered as a writer.

In Molny's preoccupation with current issues such as corruption, consumerism, the lack of affection between humans, sexism, technology, militarism, and numerous excesses of modern society, her roles of journalist and writer frequently overlap. Not surprisingly, Molny, on many occasions, has taken up Austrian themes and has shown a penchant for destroying the country's image of an "Isle of the Blessed" as Pope Paul VI once called Austria. Above all, Molny has devoted much of her journalistic and literary career to women's issues. It would indeed be appropriate to call her a feminist writer although she herself prefers to be known as a humanist.

In her play, *Der Turm Davids* (The Tower of David), Molny introduces a couple whose life is destroyed by anonymous forces that are stronger than their love for each other. Both are celebrated architects but the wife is the more creative of the two and designs a beautiful cathedral. For reasons of convention and tradition, however, the husband gets all the credit, which, eventually, destroys the wife, who makes a suicide attempt. In this play, as in many other of her works, Molny wants to illustrate her conviction that women are not at all weak, neither in their creativity nor in their capability to suffer. They do, however, lack abilities to hold their own against forces of tradition.

Molny's novel, *Bruchstücke*, is the biography of an aging, impoverished woman, a borderline schizophrenic, who looks back at her ruined life. An illegitimate child, she is raised by foster parents and falls prey to a man who is only interested in himself and divorces her at his convenience. Her love for him, however, never ends, she accepts the blame for their failed marriage and continues to live a life of solitude and isolation. Molny's bleak, often satirical portrayals of women show affinities with contemporary Austrian woman writers such as Barbara Frischmuth, Brigitte Schwaiger, and Elfriede Jelinek.

Works

Mir san net aso, cabaret (1982). *Der Turm Davids oder Die befleckte Empfängnis* (1983). *Bruchstücke* (1984). *Was soll schon sein*, cabaret (1984). *Man müßte mit jemandem reden können* (1985). [With Thomas Pluch], *Der liebe Gott des Waldviertels: Waldviertler Geschichten* (1986). *Jetzt erst recht*, satirical play (1987). *Die Frau des Malers* (1988).

Jürgen Koppensteiner

Ilse Molzahn

Born 1895, Kowalewo, Province Posen; died 1981, West Berlin
Genre(s): novel, autobiography, poetry, essay
Language(s): German

Ilse Molzahn (née Schwollmann) was a professional dancer and married the painter Johannes Molzahn in 1919. Besides her childhood autobiography, she has published three novels, one volume of poetry and an essay, humorously, or perhaps sardonically, entitled "Do Women Have Humor?"

Works

Der schwarze Storch. Eine Kindheit in Ostpreussen (1936, rpt. 1980). *Nymphen und Hirten tanzen nicht mehr* (1938). *Haben Frauen Humor?* (1938). *Tochter der Erde* (1941). *Schnee liegt im Paradies* (1953).

Bibliography

Kürschners deutscher Literaturkalender, Nekrolog (1984).

Ute Marie Saine

Mathilde Monnier

(a.k.a. Thyde Monnier)

Born June 23, 1887, Marseilles, France; died 1967
Genre(s): poetry, novel, detective story, essay, children's literature
Language(s): French

Thyde Monnier spent her youth in Ardèche and in Southern France; she showed a vivid interest in literature early on. Her father, a great admirer of August Comte, Emile Zola and other intellectual figures, gave her access to his private library. She started to write poems at the age of twelve and was fascinated by the work of the poet Mistral. In 1909, she won a literary prize for the poem she wrote for the erection of the statue of Mistral in Arles. Her poem was read by Anna de Noailles.

Thyde Monnier continued to write poems, a few collections of which were published—*Cette vieille romance* (This Old Romance), *Or moi, bateau perdu* (Thus I, Lost Ship), *Amour de ma vie* (Love of my Life). She also wrote for various women's magazines such as *Femme de France*, *L'Art de la Mode*, *Les Dimanches de la Femme*, until the early forties. But she gained the attention of the public with the publication of *La Rue courte* (The Short Street), the first volume of her first serial novel, *Les Petites Destinées* (The Humble Destinies). The book seemed to promise an auspicious talent, showing Monnier's ability to render the life and way of thinking of rural people, but most of her other novels did not live up to *La Rue courte*. She mainly wrote in the *roman fleuve* style which had become very fashionable in the thirties in France, with four main serials: *Les Petites Destinées, Les Desmichels* (The Desmichels), *Franches-Montagnes* (The Franches-Montagnes), *Pierre Pacaud* (Pierre Pacaud). *Les Desmichels* was made into a series for television in the seventies, which rekindled some public interest in her work. Thyde Monnier also wrote in various genres: novels and tales for children, a detective story, and two essays.

Several of her works received literary prizes; *La Rue courte* received the Prix Cases, *Or moi, bateau perdu* received the Prix de la Proue, and *Nans le berger* (Nans the Shepherd) received the Prix de l'Académie française.

Although by far too melodramatic to be of significant literary value, Thyde Monnier's novels are of intrinsic interest because they were written by a woman, for women, in a genre which had been up to that point the exclusive domain of a group of men, known as *les écrivains du terroir* (writers of rural France) such as Jean Giono, François Mauriac, etc. Despite a style that is sometimes weak and precious, Thyde Monnier succeeded in portraying Southern France, in a vivid and "true to life" manner. In her memoirs, she admitted having used extensively members of her family as characters in her fiction. She seems at times to have been limited by them, lacking the imagination necessary to master her craft, lacking the technique to govern the profuseness of her writing.

Works

Collections of poems: *Cette vielle romance* (1923). *Or moi, bateau perdu* (1936). *Amour de la vie.*

Serials: *Les Petites Destinées*: I–"La Rue courte" (1937), II–"Annonciata" (1939), III–"Coeur" (1951). *Les Desmichels*: I–"Grand Cap" (1937), II–"Le pain de pauvres" (1938), III–"Nans le berger" (1940), IV–"La Demoiselle" (1943), V–"Travaux" (1944), VI–"Le Figuier stérile" (1946), VII–"Les forces vives" (1947). *Franches-Montagnes*: I–"La Combe" (1949), II–"Ingrattière" (1950), III–"Le grand Courbe" (1953), IV–"Image du parfait bonheur" (1954), V–"Eternellement." *Pierre Pacaud*: I–"Fleuve" (1942), II–"Barrage d'Arvillard" (1945), III–"Pourriture de l'homme" (1949), IV–"Largo" (1954). *Serial*: I–"L'Huile vierge" (1952), II–"Le Déjeuner sur l'herbe" (1954), III–"Retour aux îles" (1954).

Novels: *Permission d'être heureux* (1952). *Le Vin et le sang* (1946). *Ki Ki t'san fétiche* (1947). *La Désirade* (1956). *Madame Roman* (1957). *Je ne suis pas des vôtres* (1958). *Les Cinq Doigts de la main* (1959). *Le Jour vert* (1960). *La Graine* (1962). *J'ai joué le jeu* (1963).

Autobiographical writings: *Moi*, memoirs, in four volumes: I–"Faux Départ" (1949), II–"La Saison des Amours," III–"Sur la Corde raide," IV–"Jetée aux bêtes" (1955). *Entre Parenthèses: extraits de Journal* (1961).

Miscellaneous: *Brin d'Avoine*, novel for children (1945). *Histoires de Mamé*, tales for children (1945). *La Veuve aux yeux verts*, detective story (1945). *La Ferme des quatre reines*, historical novel (1963). *De l'Homme à la femme*, essay (1954). *La Dernière Esclave*, essay (19). *Il n'y a plus d'harmonicas*, short stories (1946).

Bibliography

Charpentier, John, "Les Romans." *Mercure de France* CCXVII, No. 996 (1ᵉʳ April, 1940): 129–135. Hertz, Henri, "Panorama des livres." *Europe* 44 (1937): 113–122. Magnan, Pierre. "Visage de Thyde Monnier." *Cahiers Parisiens*, 38: 3–9.

Valerie Lastinger

Sophie de Monnier

(see: Sophie de Ruffey, Marquise de Monnier)

Sophie de Ruffey, Marquise de Monnier

(a.k.a. Sophie de Monnier [posthumously])

Born 1754, Pontarlier (Doubs), France; died September 9, 1789, Paris
Genre(s): correspondence
Language(s): French

Sophie de Monnier is known for her liaison and correspondence with Mirabeau (1749–1791); the first part of this correspondence was published in 1792, shortly after Mirabeau's death, the second in 1903–1904. Born in Pontarlier (Doubs) to a wealthy noble family, and married at a young age to a man old enough to be her grandfather, Sophie de Monnier met Mirabeau, the celebrated orator of the French Revolution, during his confinement there in 1775. The couple ran off together, scandalizing their respective families, and finally taking refuge in Amsterdam, from where they were deported in May 1777, returned to France, and imprisoned separately. Sophie de Monnier, pregnant, was detained in a convent in Gien until 1783 but was allowed to correspond with Mirabeau, himself imprisoned in Vincennes, until December, 1780. Their exchanges consisted of an official correspondence, censored by the police, and a secret one, smuggled between the two by servants. The official correspondence is practical and matter-of-fact, containing advice to Sophie regarding the education of their daughter and other domestic matters. Its appearance in 1791 was tied to a personality cult of the late Mirabeau rather than any particular intrinsic merits. The secret correspondence is more emotional and subjective. Both sets of documents are important for the light they shed on Mirabeau's life. Sophie de Monnier had several lovers after Mirabeau and in 1789 committed suicide following the death of one of them.

Works

Lettres originales écrites du donjon de Vincennes, ed. Pierre Manuel, 4 vols. (1792). Lettres inédites de Sophie de Monnier à Mirabeau, 1775–1781, ed. Paul Cottin (1904). First appeared in serial form (and perhaps more accessible) in: La Nouvelle Revue rétrospective 19 (1903) and 20 (1904).

Bibliography

"Monnier, Sophie de Ruffey, marquise de," in Biographie universelle [Michaud], v. 28, p. 640; cf. also v. 12, p. 359.

Earl Jeffrey Richards

Thyde Monnier

(see: Mathilde Monnier)

Dolors Monserdà de Macía

Born 1845, Barcelona, Spain; died 1919, Barcelona
Genre(s): novel, poetry, journalism, drama
Language(s): Catalan, Spanish

Dolors Monserdà was born and raised in a cultured Barcelona home with an unusually well-read mother and bookbinder, bibliophile father. Her first works were written in Castilian, but by 1877, she had turned to Catalan, moving from poetry to novelettes, plays and novels produced as part of the Catalonian Renaixença (Revival). Monserdà's strong interest in social issues centered around problems of the working class and working women, concerns placing her well ahead of her time. Her depiction of contemporary social conditions, her consistently realistic approach to her material, were influential in bringing women fiction writers closer to realism and eliminating much of the moralizing sentimentalism found in earlier women novelists.

Ma corona (1877; My Crown), the writer's first collection of poetry in Catalan, was inspired by the death of her youngest daughter. Poesies catalanes (1888; Catalan Poems) treats patriotic, intimate, folkloric, and historic themes in addition to the maternal and religious of the first collection. Poesies (1911) repeats some earlier poems and adds new ones, but is not a complete compilation of all poetry published in the interim. In addition to these books of verse, Monserdà wrote lyric theater: Sembrad y cojeréis (1874; As You Sow, So Shall You Reap) and Teresa o un jorn de prova (1876; Teresa, or a Day of Trial). Amor mana (1930; Love Flows), Monserdà's only prose play, was written in 1913 but published posthumously.

La Montserrat (1893), Monserdà's first attempt at fiction in Catalan is a full-length novel whose female protagonist, Montserrat, is engaged to a young man whose father is obsessed with wealth and ambition. Eventually left a spinster by the would-be father-in-law's greed, Montserrat as jilted sweetheart proves much more practical than earlier stereotypes. By her example, she challenges the Spanish cultural archetype of the lonely, ridiculous, and embittered old maid, demonstrating through energetic pragmatism that a productive and reasonably happy life is still possible.

Monserdà's second novel, *La família Asparó* (1900; The Asparo Family), is experimental for its day, with an internal monologue by the male protagonist, perhaps adapted from the writer's apprenticeship in the theater. With its contemporary Barcelona setting and real characters drawn from the elegant bourgeoisie, *The Asparo Family* is a roman à clef, whose cast includes portraits of well-known society figures. Of a more moralizing bent than Monserdà's other fiction, this novel attempts an exposé of materialism and amorality among the fashionable upper-middle class.

La fabricanta: novela de costums barcelonines (1860–1875) (1904; The Factory Woman: Novel of Barcelona Customs) is deemed Monserdà's best and most powerful work. Notwithstanding its subtitle, concerns are more socioeconomic than *costumbrista* (a local-color genre painting regional customs). The ambient contrasts markedly with Monserdà's two earlier novels, depicting the world of cottage industries and shops of the urban lower class. The female protagonist, a weaver's daughter, sets up and operates her own loom after marrying a poor worker. Refusing to let marginalization and isolation overcome her resolve, she eventually manages to save her husband's workshop. The story line is innovative, as the "self-made woman" was rare in Barcelona at the end of the nineteenth century. The heroine's struggle is not a feminist search for autonomy, as she subordinates her interests to those of her husband and does not challenge the system. Nevertheless, with this depiction of the rise of small factories in Catalonia, Monserdà is more attuned to issues of class and gender than other women writers of her day.

In *La Quiteria* (1902), which traces the life of a foundling girl raised in a backward Catalan village, Monserdà contrasts rural and urban lifestyles. Quiteria's harsh, deprived upbringing and low self-esteem undergo modification when a city woman takes her to Barcelona as her maid. Eventually the heroine must choose between her new life with its relative self-determination and a more conventional existence as a village housewife. Perhaps predictably, Quiteria (with counseling from the local priest) chooses love and marriage.

María Gloria (1917) once again confronts problems of social class. Maria Gloria, the spoiled granddaughter of a formerly wealthy, newly impoverished family, indulges romantic fantasies and is pampered by her family until she is suddenly left a penniless orphan. Forced to confront stark reality, she finds her dream world replaced by working-class misery when she is taken in by her old wet-nurse. Monserdà paints in some detail the conditions under which working-class women maintained themselves by sewing and other ways of contributing to the domestic economy. Even though Maria Gloria marries a self-made member of the rising middle class, thereby obviating the problem of supporting herself, the novel exemplifies a heightened awareness of problems peculiar to class and gender.

In addition to these full-length fictions, Monserdà cultivated the short story, publishing a dozen tales in two slight volumes jointly entitled *Del Món* (1908; About the World). Nearly all have women as their focus, and many have first-person female narrators. The autobiographical presentation achieves optimum effects in treatment of marriage, feminine loneliness and isolation, the marginal existence of forgotten senior citizens, and the shallowness of materialism.

Monserdà focuses primarily on women, ranging from the young servant girl to the elderly middle-class widow, the self-made working woman and the amoral upper-class. She thus portrays a broad social spectrum, despite a preferential emphasis on middle- and working-class women, and recreates the several vital stages from adolescence to old age. Although most of her works are long out of print, Monserdà is unquestionably a key figure in early Catalan feminism, and her influence in moving women's fiction in the direction of realistic depiction of contemporary social conditions was decisive. Within the bounds of Catholic liberalism, she is a major realist, comparable in significance to better-known male writers such as Alarcón, Pereda, and Valera.

Works

Amor mana; comèdia en tres actes (1930). Buscant una ánima; novela de costums barcelonines (1919). Del Món, 2 vols. (1908). La fabricanta; novela de costums barcelonines (1860–1875) (1904). La família Asparó (1900). Ma corona (1877). María Gloria (1917). La Montserrat (1893). Poesies (1911). Poesies catalanes (1888). La Quiteria (1906). Sembrad y cojeréis (1874). Teresa o un jorn de prova (1876).

Bibliography

General references: Women Writers of Spain, ed. C.L. Galerstein (Westport, Conn., 1986).

Janet Perez

La Fille d'Alliance de Monsieur de Montaigne

(see: Marie le Jars de Gournay)

Georgette de Montenay

Born 1540, Toulouse, France; died 1581, Saint Germaine, near Toulouse
Genre(s): emblem
Language(s): French

Georgette de Montenay, the daughter of a well-to-do military family with property in Béarn, was taken into the court of Jeanne d'Albret, Queen of Navarre, when she was orphaned in early childhood. Serving successively as "fille d'honneur" and "dame d'honneur" to the Queen, she acquired both a solid education in the classics and a firm grounding in Evangelical principles. The twin influences are clearly reflected in her only published work, a suite of one hundred emblems, which is prefaced by epistles to Jeanne d'Albret and to the readers. Emblèmes, ou Devises chrestiennes was brought out by the Protestant printer Jean Marcorelle at Lyons in 1571. The "privilège" for the book, however, bears the date 1566, and internal evidence, such as fairly transparent references to Henri II, suggests that the composition of the emblems had commenced as early as 1558. To some extent the delay in publication may be accounted for by the fact that the engraver may have needed some time to complete the preparation of a hundred pictures, but the accomplished Pierre Woeiriot from Lorraine is unlikely to have taken such an unconscionably long time. It is more probable that

Georgette de Montenay was, like a number of other Protestant writers such as the tragedian Jean de la Taille, waiting for a favorable moment. That seemed to have arrived with the Peace of Saint-Germain August 8, 1570, though hopes were to be cruelly dashed by the Massacre of St. Bartholomew's Eve two years later.

Georgette de Montenay's medium is the emblem, the artful juxtaposition of a more or less obscure motto (often in Latin), a puzzling picture, and an explanatory verse which had become popular throughout Europe in the wake of Alciati's development of the genre. Theorists had attempted to maintain distinctions between the "device" (or "impresa") and the emblem, but Georgette de Montenay's juxtaposition of the two terms as alternatives shows that the words had already become virtually synonymous. Georgette de Montenay often picked mottoes with scriptural overtones, her verses can be a little pedestrian, and there is no doubt that the quality of the genre scenes and allegories engraved by Woeiriot contributes much to the overall impact of the book. Whilst earlier emblematists had been content to allow their collections to become miscellanies, sometimes with concentration on one theme for just a few items, Georgette de Montenay had the idea of using a suite of a century of emblems to illustrate one theme, namely the fundamental tenets of her Protestant faith and its consequent moral and political attitudes. This did not, however, mean that her book became narrowly sectarian, and it is particularly noteworthy that she avoided the abusive tone of so much religious polemic in the Reformation period.

Nothing is known about the immediate reception of the Emblèmes, but it seems likely it was not much appreciated when hostilities broke out again in 1572. The first writer who appears to have been influenced by her was Théodore de Bèze whose Icones date from 1580. Georgette de Montenay seems to have married Guyon de Goth some time in the 1570s; she died in 1581. Four years later an edition of her emblem book, with the French text and Latin translation, appeared in Zurich; it was reprinted in Heidelberg in 1602. Even more testimony to the abiding interest in Georgette de Montenay's work is the famous polyglot edition, which was published in Frankfurt am Main in 1619.

Works

Emblèmes ou Devises chrestiennes [Emblems, or Christian Icons] (1571); photofacsimile as Continental Emblem Books No. 15, intro. C.N. Smith (1974).

Bibliography

Beets, Nicolaas, "Polyglottische Uitgave van de Cent Emblemes van Georgette de Montenay." Verslagen en Medede lingen der K. Akad. van Wetenschappen, afd. Letterkunde 2ᵉ Reeks, 12 (1883): 189–194. Russell, Dennis S., The Emblem and Device in France (Lexington, 1985). Smith, C.N., "Georgette de Montenay's Christian Emblems." Journal of European Studies 4 (1974): 140–151. Zezula, Jindrich, and Clements, Robert J., "La Troisième Lyonnaise: Georgette de Montenay." L'Esprit créateur, 5 (1965): 90–101.

Christopher Smith

Rosa Montero

Born January 3, 1951, Madrid, Spain
Genre(s): novel, journalism, interview
Language(s): Spanish

Montero achieved national acclaim for her first novel, *Crónica del desamor* (1979; Chronicle of Indifference). Along with Montserrat Roig and Esther Tusquets, she stands at the forefront of the new women's narrative of democratic Spain.

While a student of journalism and psychology, Montero was involved briefly in independent theatre groups in Madrid and by 1969 began working for various newspapers and journals. Since the late 1970s she has been associated with *El País*, presently Spain's most important newspaper. In 1980–1981, she served as editor-in-chief of the Sunday supplement and has received major prizes for her interviews and newspaper articles.

Crónica del desamor, written partially in a documentary style, is an overtly feminist work that chronicles the female experience in contemporary Spain. The protagonist, Ana, is a journalist and single parent. Her daily struggle, both economic and emotional, is shown to be not only that of Ana but common to all her friends, who share the frustrations and problems faced by women in a male-dominated society.

Much more literary in structure, Montero's second novel, *La función delta* (The Delta Function), is written in the metanovelistic mode. Consisting of two narrative strands, it recounts in the first person the experiences of Lucía, a film director, during a week in 1980 and during her terminal illness in 2010. The narration from the past is in the form of a diary that Lucía is writing in the fictional present. Her friend Ricardo constantly critiques the diary, pointing out that Lucía has fictionalized her story. The diary in process evolves to reflect Ricardo's influence, including his own penchant for storytelling. Although the novel deals with a number of serious themes, the tone is often playful, particularly in its references to Lucía's one feature film: *Crónica del desamor*.

Te trataré como una reina (I'll Treat You Like a Queen) continues in the metanovelistic mode. It subverts the conventions of popular culture: Hollywood movies and romantic songs, like the bolero of the novel's title. The characters are from the outer fringes of society; much of the action is set in a sordid night club. But even the hardened singer and barmaid, Bella, is lured into accepting illusion as an escape from her reality. The frame of the novel is a magazine article that questions why Bella tried to murder a man. The extended flashback that forms the main novelistic text explores the lives of the various characters while defamiliarizing traditional sex roles.

Although Montero has published only three novels to date, she has already assumed a position of importance in contemporary Spanish narrative as a feminist writer and exponent of metafiction.

Works

España para ti . . . para siempre, interviews (1976). Crónica del desamor, novel (1979). La función delta, novel (1981). Cinco años de País (1982). Te trataré como una reina, novel (1983).

Bibliography

Gascón Vera, Elena, "Rosa Montero ante la Escritura Femenina." Anales de la Literatura Española Contemporánea 12 (1987): 59–77. Glenn, Kathleen M., "Victimized by Misreading: Rosa Montero's Te trataré como una reina." *Anales de la Literatura Española Contemporánea* 12 (1987): 191–202. Oyarzún, Luis A., "Eroticism and Feminism in Spanish Literature after Franco: *Los amores diurnos* de Francisco Umbral and *Crónica del desamor* de Rosa Montero." *Mid-Hudson Language Studies* 4 (1981): 135–144. Suñen, Luis, "La realidad y sus sombras: Rosa Montero y Cristina Fernández Cubas." *Insula* 446 (January 1984): 5. Zatlin, Phyllis, Rev. of *Crónica del desamor* and *La función delta*. *Hispanófila* 84 (1985): 121–123. Zatlin, Phyllis, "The Contemporary Spanish Metanovel." *Denver Quarterly* 17.3 (1982): 63–73.

General references: *A Dictionary of Literature of the Iberian Peninsula* (Westport, Conn., forthcoming.) *Women Writers of Spain: An Annotated Bio-Bibliographical Guide*, ed. Carolyn L. Galerstein (Westport, Conn., 1986).

Phyllis Zatlin

Élisabeth-Jeanne-Pauline Polier de Bottens (dite Isabelle), baronne de Montolieu

Born May 7, 1751, Lausanne, Switzerland; died December 28, 1832, Vennes
Genre(s): novel, translation/adaptation from English and German
Language(s): French

Best known as the French translator of J.D. Wyss' *Swiss Family Robinson* (published in 1813), Isabelle de Montolieu was one of the most prolific writers of her day. Her total corpus of original compositions and translations numbers at least 105 volumes. She was born in Lausanne, descended from a Huguenot family that had fled to Switzerland in the sixteenth century. She did not make her literary debut until she was thirty-five. By chance she happened to meet Madame de Genlis, tutor to the family of the duke of Orléans, during a voyage the latter made to Switzerland. In the course of their meeting, Isabelle de Montolieu apparently showed the famous French pedagogue the manuscript of her first novel, *Caroline de Lichtfield, ou Mémoires d'une famille prussienne* (Caroline of Lichtfield, or Memoirs of a Prussian Family), which Ma-

dame de Genlis subsequently claimed to have edited. The novel was an instant success; first published in Lausanne in 1786, it was reprinted that same year in both Paris and London, and quickly translated into English, Spanish and Portuguese. The first publisher of *Caroline de Lichtfield* was no less than the French translator of Goethe's *Werther*, Georges Deyverdunn. All of these facts surrounding the publication of *Caroline de Lichtfield* are pertinent in evaluating Isabelle de Montolieu's position within French Romanticism. One critic suggested that if she had spent her career in Paris rather than the Swiss countryside, she would have become one of the most distinguished novelists of her day. It is, however, more useful to see Isabelle de Montolieu as a cultural and literary intermediary between France and England and between France and Germany. The lion's share of her literary output consisted of translation—really, very free adaptations, since her mastery of English and German was imperfect—from English and German: besides *Swiss Family Robinson* (1813), she translated, among other works, Jane Austen's *Sense and Sensibility* (published in English in 1811; translated 1815) and *Persuasion* (published 1818; translated 1821; the *National Union Catalog, Pre-1956 Imprints* mistakenly lists both works as translations of *Sense and Sensibility*); Friedrich de Lamothe-Fouqué's *Undine* (published 1811; translated 1822); Schiller's *Geisterseher* (published 1787; translated 1810); Heinrich Zschokke's *Die Prinzessin von Wolfenbüttel* (published 1804; translated, 1820); and various works of Auguste Lafontaine. Her own original compositions often exhibit excessive pathos and imperfect rhetorical skills. All the same, they struck a responsive chord in a wide audience and, as such, attest to shifting literary tastes at the turn of the eighteenth century. The choice of the works she translated attests to her insights into the literary developments of her day.

Works

Caroline de Lichtfield, ou mémoires d'une famille prussienne [Caroline of Lichtfield, or Memoirs of a Prussian Family] (1786; English translation 1786, 1798). *Douze Nouvelles* [Twelve Novellas] (1812). *Le Châlet des Hautes-Alpes* [The Chalet of the Upper Alps] (1814). *Dix Nouvelles* [Ten Novellas] (1815).

Les Châteaux suisses [Swiss Castles] (1817). *Exaltation et piété, quatre nouvelles* [Exaltation and Piety, Four Novellas] (1818).

Bibliography

Anonymous, "Montolieu, Élisabeth-Jeanne-Pauline Polier de Bottens." *Biographie universelle* (Michaud), vol. 29. (Paris, 1854), pp. 186–188. Quérard, J.-M., *La France littéraire*, vol. 6 (Paris, 1834), pp. 269–270.

Earl Jeffrey Richards

Anne-Marie-Louise d'Orleans, Duchesse de Montpensier

Born May 29, 1627, Paris, France; died April 1693, Paris
Genre(s): novel, letters, memoirs
Language(s): French

Anne-Marie-Louise d'Orléans, la grande mademoiselle, was the daughter of Marie de Bourbon, duchesse de Montpensier, and Gaston d'Orléans, the younger brother of Louis XIII. She inherited her mother's immense fortune, which made her the richest woman in France, when Marie died a few days after giving birth. The inheritance proved a mixed blessing, however. Not only did it later present difficulties in finding an appropriate husband, but it also deprived her of her sole surviving parent during childhood. Gaston, a rebellious, discontented, fickle, and troublesome younger brother, was deeply distrusted by Cardinal Richelieu who separated father and daughter almost immediately after the mother's death. The young princess grew up alone in Paris.

She lived in apartments at Tuileries, cared for by her governess, Madame de St. George, and surrounded by a household staff numbering nearly sixty. It was not a childhood without joy. Anne-Marie was assured every physical comfort possible, and her childless aunt and uncle, the King and Queen, doted on her. As second in line to the throne of France, she grew up in more luxury than many heads of state.

When she was eleven years old several important changes took place. Queen Anne gave birth to an heir, the future Louis XIV, whose arrival placed Anne-Marie at a greater distance from the throne. Perhaps of more import personally, however, was her discovery of her father's untrustworthy nature. The executions of Cinq Mars and de Thous, whose rebellions her father had fostered and then abandoned, shocked her greatly.

In the years of her adolescence, following Louis XIII's death on May 14, 1643, more disappointments were in store. Renouncing love, she declared her interest in finding an "appropriate" establishment as the wife of a powerful European head of state. She was often proposed for several monarchs, including Frederick III, the Holy Roman Emperor; the future Charles II of England; and even Louis XIV himself. Her immense fortune, which the royal family was loath to lose, the disgraceful reputation of her father, and the political machinations of the Regent Anne and Cardinal Mazarin, blocked each and every union.

Deprived of an "establishment," she became embroiled in domestic politics and, partly from misplaced loyalty to her father, allied herself with the Prince de Condé and the Fronde in open rebellion against the King. The years of the Fronde were her years of glory. In 1652, she played a heroic role, helping to relieve the town of Orléans. Three months later she secured entry for Condé's troops into Paris, ordering the cannons of the Bastille to be turned on her cousin Louis and his royal forces.

Her decisiveness and bravery were much admired. But Louis inevitably won, and Anne-Marie's heroism, though gaining her the title of the Second Maid of Orléans, lost her the most brilliant prospect she would ever have—a place beside her cousin as queen and consort. Instead of a throne in Paris, her lot was self-exile to her estate in Saint-Fargeau. It was during this first four and a half year period of exile that she began her voluminous, fascinating, and, in Michelet's words, courageous memoirs, an undertaking inspired by her admiration for the memoirs of Marquerite de Valois, the divorced wife of Henri IV. This monumental task of authorship absorbed almost all of her energy. The rest of her exile was taken up in a series of degrading and distressing tangles with her father, who had been bleeding her estate to pay his gambling debts and to support his second wife and three daughters.

She was allowed to return to court in 1652, amid rumors of her impending wedding to Louis' younger brother, the Compte d'Anjou. She evaded such plans, however, as she also evaded the attempt in 1662 to marry her to mad King Alfonso VI of Portugal. Upon this second refusal, she was again banished from court, this time to Eu where she busied herself in establishing a school for the poor.

On her second return to Paris, she led the complex and highly codified life of a "petite fille de France." Her salon was frequented by such luminaries as the Marquis de Sévère, Madame de Lafayette, and the Marquis de la Rochefoucault. A great builder like her royal cousin, she was also one of the first patrons of Le Vau, the architect of Versailles. She dabbled in literature, writing two rather mediocre novels, *La Relation de l'île imaginaire* (The Story of an Imaginary Island) and *La Princesse de Paphlagonie* (Princess of Paphlagonie), which initially appeared under the name of her secretary, Segrais. She also patronized the arts. It was in her salon that the first complete public performance was given of Molière's *Tartuffe*.

Although in her youth she had been more interested in statecraft than in the "gallanterie" of her various marriage proposals, in middle age she fell victim to an unfortunate passion. At the age of forty, she fell in love with a Gascon captain in the King's bodyguard—Antoine Nompar du Caumont, the Compte de Lauzun. Lauzun, an adept social climber and a callous adventurer, seems to have returned her affection, at least initially, and after much subtle negotiation, Mlle obtained permission from Louis to wed. The marriage was delayed by a few days, however, and in that small space of time political pressures brought to bear on the King compelled him to withdraw his permission. Lauzun, his former favorite, was imprisoned in the Bastille.

Although Mlle worked frantically for his release, it was to take almost ten years to win his liberty. Even then, she obtained it only by giving part of her estate to Louis' illegitimate son, the Duc de Maine. It is possible that she married Lauzun shortly after he was granted a pardon in 1682, but her inability to procure additional favors at court, despite her numerous gifts of land and money, angered the Gascon lover. He turned on her, was cold, indifferent, and cruel, and they soon separated. The remainder of her life passed in charitable works, increased isolation, and the writing of her memoirs, which she began again in 1672, seventeen years after discarding them. She died of uremic poisoning at sixty-six years of age in April 1693 in her apartments in Paris. A grotesquely and undeservedly comic touch marred her state funeral when a jar containing her embalmed entrails exploded, bringing the ceremonies to a temporary halt.

It is difficult to categorize the works of Mlle de Montpensier. Even her novels are a strange melange of social history and fabulous story. *La Vie de Madame de Fouguerolles* (The Life of Madame de Fouguerolles), published in 1652 at Saint Fargeau, is the biography of one of her ladies-in-waiting. *La Relation de l'île imaginaire* (The Story of the Imaginary Island), written in two days in 1658 at Trévous, gives a utopian plan of government. *Histoire de la Princesse de Paphlagonie* (1659; The Story of the Princess of Paphlagonie) records her support of Mlle De Vandy in that lady's quarrel with the Comtesse de Fiesque. These, and the *Divers Portraits* (Several Portraits) published in 1659, are additionally difficult to evaluate because of their almost certain rewriting at the hands of Mlle.'s various secretaries. The *Relation* (The Story) and *Histoire de la Princesse* (The Story of the Princess) were published originally under Segrais' name.

Her letters and her memoirs, on the other hand, are just as certainly her own work but also just as certainly an odd mixture of fact and fiction. Her most celebrated correspondence, with Madame de Motteville, details a fictional utopian community where marriage is outlawed. Her reasons for this structuring not only reflect events in her own life but also prefigure many feminist arguments.

Recently her *Memoirs*, a vast collection numbering two thousand pages, have received renewed attention. In the past her lack of precision and her disregard for facts have been cited as flaws in the collection, as have Mlle's failings in grammar, spelling, factual dating, and construction. However, a new interest in her work, partly fueled by the publication of a more faithful text, has revealed some intriguing and little-anticipated aspects.

Mlle de Montpensier, despite her lack of a classical education, is a vivid observer. She stuffs her pages with minute descriptions of styles, dress, gestures, courtly functions, moonlight, and architecture. Her spontaneous and consciously uncorrected style, a decided contrast to the carefully written and rewritten memoirs of Madame de Motteville, has now been stripped of the regularization and polish of former editors. It can be seen as it once was—a remarkably effective document, recording the twists and turns of Mlle's often troubled mind. Her interesting use of direct as opposed to indirect style and a number of passages of self-reflection that had previously been cut are also exciting discoveries in the work of a feminine seventeenth-century memorialist.

Mademoiselle de Montpensier's *Mémoires*, if read in this recovered form, are the most personal and the most telling of their century. Their worth lies not so much in their illumination of great historical events as in their explorations of the pressures surrounding Anne-Marie. Written at four different intervals in her life, they are uniformly composed in places and times of exile or retreat. Their changing function makes a fascinating story in and of itself—from their first use, after the collapse of the Fronde, to affirm her individuality, to their later, Proustian utility, after her affair with Lauzun, to recapture a lost world. This changing purpose and many aspects for which they were once censured—a frequent melange of tones, a startling candidness, a lack of edifying sentiment, an occasional coexistence of contradictory codes, and an unsettling spontaneity and digressive structure—give us a unique insight not only into the court of Louis XIV but into the psyche and circumstances of a particularly difficult "fille de France." Ironically, those offenses against the classical style for which she was once censured are the very aspects that now permit us to detect wrenched and fascinating states of being in this text, states that can only be inferred from the silences and lacunae of other, more polished female memoirists of the same epoch.

Works

La Vie de Madame Fouquerolles [The Life of Madame Fouquerolles] (1652). *Relation de l'île imaginaire* [The Story of an Imaginary Island] (1658). *Histoire de la Princesse Paphlagonie* [The Story of Princess Paphlagonie] (1659). *Divers Portraits* [Different Portraits] (1659). *Lettres de Mademoiselle Montpensier* [The Letters of Mademoiselle Montpensier] (1806). *Mémoires de Mlle. Montpensier* [The Memoirs of Mademoiselle Montpensier](1858).

Bibliography

Bouyer, Christian, *La Grande Mademoiselle* (Paris, 1986). Doolittle, James, "A Royal Diversion: Mademoiselle and Lauzun." *Esprit Créature* 11 (1971): 123–140. Jal, Auguste, *Dictionnaire Critique de Biographie et d'Histoire* (Geneva, 1970), pp. 817–819. Lathuillère, Roger, *La Préciosité* (Geneva, 1966), pp. 61–65. Reid, Joyce, *The Concise Oxford Dictionary of French Literature* (Oxford, 1983), p. 425. Stegmuller, Francis, *La Grande Mademoiselle* (New York, 1956). Uglow, Jennifer, *The International Dictionary of Women's Biography* (New York, 1982), p. 138. Verdier, Gabrielle, "Mademoiselle de Montpensier et le plaisir du texte." *Papers on French Seventeenth Century Literature* (1983): 11–33. Watts, Derek, "Self-Portrayal in Seventeenth Century French Memoirs." *Australian Journal of French Studies* (1975): 263–285.

Glenda Wall

Johanna Moosdorf

Born 1911, Leipzig, Germany
Genre(s): poetry, prose, drama
Language(s): German

Johanna Moosdorf published her first book after the war, in 1946. She had been married to Peter Bernstein, who perished in Auschwitz in 1944. Since 1945, she has been living in Berlin. She has received the Thomas Mann Prize in 1950, the Zuckmayer Prize in 1952, and the Nelly Sachs Prize in 1963. Her first books consist of poetry, then she turned to the narrative genres, while her two last published volumes again are poems. No matter the genre Johanna Moosdorf writes in, her texts express the situation of human beings coming to terms with war and dictatorship.

Her visions refer to torture, imprisonment, and violent death, although at the end, she always expresses an unfounded hope. In her texts, the post-war world with its high rises, subways, and neon, far from representing a return to normalcy, seems to intensify the nightmares of the Holocaust and appears as a hollow ruin or a cancerous growth. Thus the atrocities of the war seamlessly blend into the post-war fears of nuclear annihilation.

Works

Brennendes Leben (1946). Zwischen zwei Welten (1947). Flucht nach Afrika (1952). Der Himmel brennt (1954). Schneesturm in Worotschau (1956). Nebenan (1961). Die lange Nacht (1963). Fahrt nach Matern (1964). Die Andermanns (1969). Die Freundinnen (1977). Sieben Jahr, sieben Tag (1979). Neue Gedichte (1983).

Bibliography

Kurschner, Josef, Deutscher Literatur-Kalender (1984). von Wilpert, Gero, Deutsches Literatur-Lexikon. 2nd edition (Stuttgart, 1975).

Ute Marie Saine

Fabiola de Mora y Aragon

Born June 11, 1928, Madrid, Spain
Genre(s): fairy tales
Language(s): Spanish

Privately educated in Madrid, Paris, and Rome, this daughter of an ancient Spanish noble family married Baudouin I, King of the Belgians, on 15 December 1960. Her languages are Spanish, French, Italian, English, German, and Dutch. She wrote, and partly illustrated, Los doce cuentos maravillosos (1955). The tales were translated into Dutch by Lia Timmermans (1961); into French by Marie Gevers (1961); and into German, by Renata Schimmöller (1961).

Works

Los doce cuentos maravillosos (1955).

Kristiaan P. Aercke

Giuliana Morandini

Born 1926, Udine, in the province of Friuli, Italy
Genre(s): novel, dramatic and literary criticism, journalism, children's literature
Language(s): Italian

Much has been written about Morandini's literary oeuvre, and virtually nothing about her life. Born in Udine, which she sometimes revisits, she used Friuli as background in her first novel, I cristalli di Vienna (Bloodstains), but in a stylized manner that does not reflect the contemporary reality. She has traveled extensively in Central and Northern Europe, and resides in Rome.

Long involved with theater, she has published an introduction to Samuel Beckett's Not I (in Carte Segrete, 1973, No. 22, 65–74); Le insensate (1975), a modern interpretation of Euripides' The Bacchantes; an introduction to the German edition of plays by Pasolini (1984); an introduction to Wedekind's Lulu; and newspaper and magazine reviews.

The crisis of psychiatric institutions during the 1960s and the evolving roles of women figure in . . . E allora mi hanno rinchiusa (1977, 1985; . . . And Then They Locked Me Up), introduced by an essay on the relationship between mental illness and the "woman question." The interviews with institutionalized women are prefaced by sensitive verbal portraits and bring to light the culturally distinct reality of women. Awarded the Viareggio Prize in 1977, this work has been partially translated into Finnish. The second edition contains a new essay evaluating relevant legal changes during the intervening decade.

She anthologized writings by obscure or forgotten Italian women, 1800–1900, in La voce che è in lei (1980; The Voice That Is in Her), which presents cultural themes and stylistic problems that generations of women have had to confront in order to express themselves. Used as a textbook in some schools, this work has also contributed to international feminist discourse. Morandini's collection of poetry by women is Poesie d'amore (1986; Love Poems). She has also published a children's book, Ricercare Carlotta (1979).

Each of her three novels to date lyrically explores the inner and outer worlds of its protagonist: the consciousness of a woman in crisis or quest reviewing and restructuring her past; and an environment that withholds secrets and presents threats as well as opportunities. In this sense each work is a "mystery": a spatial novel (though it has plot) that cannot be understood in linear progression but coheres through evocative language and recurrent imagery and is comprehended in its totality. Serious and psychological, the prose is not without humor—and not without awkward mannerisms. Morandini makes sensitive use of the child, or the recollected child, in these "spatial novels"—the vulnerable manipulative child who, often ignored, gains admission to situations from which adults are excluded; the child who experiences acutely, without adult comprehension but also without adult prejudice; the child whose motives, roles, and interpretations are too seldom reckoned with by others.

In her fiction Morandini has been moving eastward into Central Europe: from Friuli (1977, *I cristalli di Vienna*; Prato Prize, 1978), to Trieste (1983, *Caffè Specchi*; Viareggio Prize, 1983), to Berlin (1987, *Angelo a Berlino*; Campiello Prize, 1987). Her writing reflects a softening of either-or boundaries and a reappreciation of Central Europe. The female *bildungsroman* is recognized in its primacy and not merely as a variation on the male. Morandini's work is therefore considered not only important, but also timely.

I cristalli di Vienna is retrospective and lyrical, its plot thrusting toward new growth. It unfolds both how a girl grows up and how a soul emerges from estrangement into meaningfulness. Like novels by Curzio Malaparte (Italian) and John Horne Burns (American) set during the same period, it presents life under military occupation, showing the effect of both "enemy" and "friendly" troops on a civilian population. The orientation toward war is uncommonly maternal. (The main character sees the soldiers also as old babies.) The book implies no ultimate judgment or redemption but rather presents beleaguered people caught up in conflicts not of their own making. Recognizing a basic human attraction to both bestiality and elegance, the author seems to search out a kind of decency.

In *Caffè Specchi*, Katharina explores her inner life and the atmosphere of Trieste, finding correlations of feeling, memory, and recovered images. At stake at this point in her life is custody of her son, whom her husband, with hallucinatory rigidity, refuses to yield to her. With several languages at her command, she nevertheless remains inarticulate at critical moments. She encounters the conductor of a Berlin orchestra, a youth in a reddish-brown pullover, a Faustian old man; she walks randomly through the streets; her crisis is related to the malaise of the city and its culture, a murkiness of perception and paralysis of will. A ten-part adaptation of this novel for radio has been made by Massimo Franciosa and Luisa Montagnana.

Angelo a Berlino is set in Berlin divided by the wall, though Berlin also figures in historic dimensions and as dreamscape. The city, suspended between hostile governmental systems, threatens to overwhelm the main character with its noise, intensities, and diversity. Erika, the protagonist, is searching not only for traces of her personal aristocratic heritage (and traces of her dead sister), but also for a usable collective past. This double search, for the city's identity and her own, takes place amid American and Japanese tourists, Turkish emigrants, an African youth who smells of hibiscus. The panorama of Berlin appears more clearly as an analogue of her own inner dividedness. Just as the city must rebuild, Erika must reconstruct from a life rooted in disasters (the murdered sister, the firebombing of Dresden, the mad mother); and she must balance memory with a sense of future possibilities for love and creativity.

Involved at an international level in cultural debates, Morandini was a member of the Italian delegation at the Cultural Forum of Budapest in 1985 and participated at a conference in Bamburg in 1986.

Works

I cristalli di Vienna (1977). *Le insensate* (1975). . . . *E allora mi hanno rinchiusa* (1977). *La voce che è in lei* (1980). *Poesie d'amore* (1986). *Ricercare Carlotta* (1979). *Caffè Specchi* (1983). *Angelo a Berlino* (1987).

Translations: *Bloodstains*, tr. Blossom S. Kirschenbaum (St. Paul, 1987).

Bibliography

. . . E allora mi hanno rinchiusa: Lo Cascio, A., in *Rivista di psicologia analitica*, 16 (1977): 233–235. Cavani, L., "Grida dal manicomio." *Tuttolibri* (July 9, 1970). Chierici, M., "Ascoltando le donne sepolte." *Corriere della Sera* (May 29, 1977). Cuomo, F., "Manicomi: perchè la condizione della donna è diversa." *L'Avanti* (May 12, 1977). di Nola, A.M., "Per le donne oppresse la follia come rifugio." *La Repubblica* (May 28, 1977). Fusco, M., "Des femmes qui parlent." *Magazine littéraire*, 165 (Oct. 1980). Pautasso, S., *Anni di letteratura; guida all'attività letteraria in Italia dal 1968 al 1979*, p. 31, 132.

I cristalli di Vienna: Altomonte, A., "I cristalli di Vienna." *Il Tempo* (July 21, 1978). Bo, Carlo, "Fra i cristalli della memoria." *L'Europeo* (Oct. 6, 1978). Cattaneo, G., "Come in un sogno infantile." *La Repubblica* (June 30, 1978). Hinterhauser, H., "Ach so, Wien!" *Die Presse Wien* (Sept. 1981): 26–27. Memmo, F.P., "L'infanzia in frantumi." *Paese Sera* (July 16, 1978). Pautasso, S., *Anni di letteratura—guida all'attività letteraria in Italia dal 1968 al 1979*, p. 132. Tesio, G., "Vennero i nazisti, e finì l'infanzia." *Tuttolibri* (July 1, 1978). Westberg, A., "Förgörelsen och sexualitetens gåta." *Dagens Nyheter* (Stockholm, July 3, 1981).

La voce che è in lei: Cattaneo, G., "Ma la suora aspettava Garibaldi." *La Repubblica* (June 12, 1980). Cucchi, M., "Donne e romanzo un secolo fa." *l'Unità* (Aug. 14, 1980). De Rienzo, G., "Quella voce inascoltata." *Corriere della Sera* (Aug. 3, 1980). Ghidetti, E., "E altre ancora." *Rinascita* (Mar. 27, 1981). Maraini, D., "Scrittrici in rivolta." *La Stampa* (July 18, 1980).

Caffè Specchi: Ghidetti, E., "Lontane ormai le zingare slovene. . . ." *Rinascita* (Sept. 16, 1983). Giovanardi, S., "Un cadavere per Katharina." *La Repubblica* (Apr. 19, 1983). Manacorda, G., "Il fantasma si chiama Austria." *Il Tempo* (Apr. 8, 1983). Minore, R., "Katharina a Trieste s'aggira nel disagio." *Il Messaggero* (May 12, 1983). Pezzato, F., "Specchi inquietanti." *Il Resto del Carlino* (Apr. 28, 1983). Ronfani, U., "Una viaggiatrice senza bagagli all'interno della città labirinto." *Il Giorno* (May 29, 1983). Schwarz, K.P., "Katharina in der Kälte Mitteleuropas." *Die Prese* (Vienna, June 23–24, 1984).

The only known substantial review to date in English, by Giacomo Striuli, of *Bloodstains*, appeared in a Providence, R.I. newspaper, *The Echo*, Dec. 7, 1987.

Blossom S. Kirschenbaum

Elsa Morante

Born August 18, 1912, Rome, Italy; died November 26, 1986, Rome
Genre(s): novel, fairy tale, short story, essay, poetry, translation
Language(s): Italian

Elsa Morante started to write poems and fairy tales at a very early age. A self-educated student, she studied primarily at home for five years and then in Roman high schools. She was married for a number of years to one of Italy's most prolific and well-recognized writers, Alberto Moravia, an intellectually competitive relationship. Morante wrote slowly and painstakingly, often resorting to quasi-seclusion to better concentrate, her only company that of a cat. Her pronouncements on the literary and critical scene were rare, and as rare were her interviews. She wrote mostly novels although she also produced fairy tales, short stories and poems.

Morante is widely recognized as a major author in the literature of this century and her production continues to draw serious critical analysis. Her most successful novel was *La storia*, which came out in the Italy of the seventies, a time of political upheavals and tensions. It soon became a best-seller and was the most talked-about novel of the decade. It has since been fashionable for critics to debunk *La storia* and to read it as a pathetic tale of wartime slaughter. Morante's embrace of neo-realistic techniques was deemed anti-climatic and old-fashioned, her constructions too mystifying, her choice of down-to-earth characters to emblematize uncontrollable events too populistic. In a word, the writer was judged politically rather than artistically, a move she herself might have fostered by insisting on the publication of *La storia* at a down-to-earth price. When Marxist critics found they could not see in the novel what they thought should have been there, they put it down; critics from the right, on the other hand, did not seem satisfied with the presentation and treated it harshly.

Elsa Morante is most interesting when she relies on the power of memory to resurrect a world that no longer exists. Children are often her main characters. *Menzogna e sortilegio* is an epic of two generations doomed by impossible dreams. Elisa, the protagonist, knows that she has to remember her life with her parents if she wants to understand what attracted her to a reality that was magical in her childish eyes and yet proved destructive in her grown-up days. *L'isola di Arturo* broaches the issues of growing up and the failure of adults to satisfy children's dreams. The drama of exclusion is revisited in a mythic key, the beauty of a prelapsarian world is contrasted with the realization that the pleasure it gives is fleeting, that in order to grow the young must leave their nest. In *Aracoeli* memory brings back to life a story of defeat. Here the crisis of the family can no longer be mended, and the hope for regeneration is crushed time and again by a society that has become too violent and chaotic. As in the pessimistic *Menzogna e sortilegio*, the mother becomes the subject of conflicting allegiances, her very existence tied to a world forever lost and yet forever desired, albeit perhaps destructively. One can understand why Morante tried to commit suicide soon after its publication. She survived and spent two years confined to a hospital bed. She wrote no more.

Works

Le bellissime avventure di Cateri' dalla trecciolina [The Most Beautiful Adventures of Cateri with the Golden Braids] (1941). *Il gioco segreto* [The Secret Game] (1941). *Menzogna e sortilegio* [House of Liars] (1948). *L'isola di Arturo* [Arturo's Island] (1957). *Alibi* [Alibi] (1958). *Le straordinarie avventure di Caterina* [The Extraordinary Adventures of Caterina] (1959). *Lo scialle andaluso* [The Andalusian Shawl] (1963). *Il mondo salvato dai ragazzini* [The World Moved by Children] (1968). *La storia* [History. A Novel] (1974). *Aracoeli* [Aracoeli] (1982).

Bibliography

Camon, Ferdinando, "Il test della *Storia*." *Nuovi argomenti* NS 45–46 (1975): 186–239. Cases, Cesare, "Un confronto con *Menzogna e sortilegio*." *Quaderni piacentini* 13 (1974): 177–191. Debenedetti, Giacomo, "*L'isola di Arturo*." *Nuovi Argomenti* 26 (1957): 44–61. Dedola, Rossana, "Strutture narrative e ideologia nella *Storia* di Elsa Morante." *Studi novecenteschi* 5 (1976): 247–265. Evans, Annette, "The Fiction of Family: Ideology and Narrative in Elsa Morante," in *Theory and Practice of Feminist Literary Criticism*, eds. G. Mora and K.S. Van Hooft (Ypsilanti, 1962). pp. 131–137. Ferrucci, Franco, "Elsa Morante's Limbo Without Elysium." *Italian Quarterly* 7 (1963): 28–51. Finucci Valeria, "The Textualization of a Female 'I:' E. Morante's *Menzogna e sortilegio*." *Italica* 65 (1988): 308–328. McCormick, Allen, "Utopia and Point of View: Narrative Method in Morante's *L'isola di Arturo* and Keiserling's *Schwule Tage*." *Symposium* 15 (1963): 114–130. Nozzoli, Anna, *Tabu' e coscienza. La condizione femminile nella letteratura italiana del 900* (Firenze, 1978). Pupino, Angelo, *Struttura e stile della narrativa di Elsa Morante* (Ravenna, 1968). Ravanello, Donatella, *Scrittura e follia nei romanzi di Elsa Morante* (Venezia, 1980). Sgorlon, Carlo, *Invito alla lettura di Elsa Morante* (Milano, 1985). Sommavilla, Guido, "Anarchia e angelogia di Elsa Morante." *Letture* 29 (1974): 725–738. Stefani, Luigina, "Favola e ideologia in *Menzogna e sortilegio*." *Quaderno '70 sul Novecento*. Ed. A.A.V.V. (Padova, 1970). pp. 177–188. Venturi, Gianni, *Elsa Morante* (Firenze, 1977).

Valeria Finucci

Jana Moravcová

Born 1937, Černčice u Loun, Czechoslovakia
Genre(s): poetry, prose, translation
Language(s): Czech

Poet, prose writer, editor, and translator, Jana Moravcová graduated in Slavic philology from Charles University in Prague and lectured in her graduate field in Santa Clara and Havana, Cuba, from 1961 to 1963. Since 1975 she has been an editor at the Československý Spisovatel Publishing House. She began to write at an early age and published her first work while still a student. She is also a translator of poetry from Spanish and Russian. Moravcová's output is varied, including children's verse, mystery stories, fantastic prose, novels, psychological prose and poetry.

Works

O Zlobivém Delfínkovi [The Naughty Little Dolphin] (1969). Mořské Pohádky [Sea Fairy Tales] (1970). Veselý Rok [A Merry Year] (1970). Pohádky Stříbrného Delfína [Fairy Tales of the Silver Dolphin] (1973). Jak Se Strašák Bál [How the Scarecrow Was Scared] (1972). Klub Neomylných a Jiné Příběhy [The Infallibles' Club and Other Stories] (1973). Měsíc Krásného Zešílení [A Month of Beautiful Lunacy] (1975). Příběh Posvátného Jezera [Story of the Holy Lake] (1976). Zrození [Birth] (1976). Sněhokruh [Snow Ring] (1974). Zahrada z Kamene [The Stone Garden] (1977). Od Moře Přicházím [I Come from the Sea] (1977). Zátiší s Citadelou [Still Life with a Citadel] (1978). Archanděl Houbeles [The Archangel Houbeles] (1979). Tichý Kormorán [The Silent Cormorant] (1979). Dobrý Déšť [A Good Rain] (1981). Klub Omylnýck [The Fallibles' Club] (1983). Konec Vědeckého Sporu [End of a Scientific Dispute].

Warwick J. Rodden

Dea Trier Mørch

Born 1941, Copenhagen, Denmark
Genre(s): novel, nonfiction
Language(s): Danish

Like so many other women writers, Dea Trier Mørch's career really took off in the seventies. Before then she was a very productive graphic artist, and she still illustrates all her books. Mørch writes in the socialist-realist tradition, and until 1982 she was a prominent member of the Danish Communist Party. She was also a member of an artist's collective called Red Mama whose aim was to combine art and socialism.

Mørch's first work of fiction, *Vinterbørn* (1976), translated into English in 1986 as *Winter's Child*, was a huge success, lauded by critics, translated into thirteen languages, and filmed in 1978. It is about pregnancy and birth seen solely from the women's point of view. It covers exactly one month, the month in which the babies are born. The setting is a hospital ward for high-risk pregnancies, and the point Mørch wants to make is the discrepancy between the resources invested in the newborns and the lack of support from society as soon as they leave the hospital, making children the private responsibility of the parents.

Mørch's next book, *Kastaniealleen* (1978), focuses on childhood and the relationship between children and grandparents. *Den indre by* (1980) is a continuation of *Vinterbørn*, exploring the difficulties facing couples trying to juggle young children, work, political involvement and somehow finding time for themselves as well. *Aftenstjernen* (1982) describes the death of an aging parent and the confrontation with mortality that grown-up children are faced with in that situation. *Morgengaven* (1984) follows another character from *Vinterbørn* and again deals with marriage and young children. But unlike the protagonist in *Den indre by*, this one winds up divorced and disillusioned, though still a strong, positive role model.

Mørch's style is straightforward, down to earth, easy to read, and depicts recognizable people and problems that coupled with the topics she addresses, birth, relationships between men and women, children, have made her one of the most popular socialist writers in Denmark. Her early books adhere rather closely to the socialist literary doctrine demanding positive, strong role models and solutions within a socialist framework that disregard personal conflicts, but her recent books have been much bolder in their exploration of personal conflicts with no easy politically "correct" solutions and the depiction of troubled interpersonal relationships.

Mørch's treatment of children, the way she integrates them into her books, the believable way in which she describes them, and her solidarity with them without sacrificing her empathy for the parents is especially important. She may at times border on the overtly idyllic, suggesting too simple solutions, but her rendition of everyday existence in Denmark, her recognizable, low-key characters and her socialist-feminist perspective make her an important contemporary Danish writer.

Works

Sorgmunter socialisme (1968). Polen (1970). Vinterbørn (1979). Winter's Child (1986). En trekant (1977). Kastaniealleen (1978). Den indre by (1980). Aftenstjernen (1982). Morgengaven (1984).

Bibliography

Andersen, Bruun Michael, ed., *Dansk litteraturhistorie 8* (1985). Clausen Claus, ed., *Litteratur/80—en almanak* (1980). Kyndrup, Morten, *Dansk socialistisk litteratur i 70'erne* (1980).

Merite von Eyben

Maria Maddelena Morelli

(a.k.a. Corilla Olimpica)

Born 1727, Pistoia, Italy; died 1800 in Florence
Genre(s): poetry
Language(s): Italian

Maria Morelli was the most celebrated improvisationist of the seventeenth century. The seductions of poetry filled her youth, and her talents brought her to the gates of the academy of the Arcadians, where she took the name "Corilla Olimpica." For a decade, until 1775, she was poet to the Grand Ducal Court of Tuscany. With her poetic improvisations about Arcadia, she awakened such enthusiasm that in 1776 she was solemnly crowned in Campedoglio. She proved to have a remarkable flexibility of imagination when she proposed to treat a subject of poetry in public without preparation. Sometimes she spoke Italian with an ingenious liveliness, composing from inspiration considerable passages—almost entire scenes of tragedy. Her literary reputation brought her the triumph that had honored Petrarch but eluded Tasso: On August 31, 1766, at the Capitol, she received the crown of Laureate. Pasquin sarcastically protested against this homage, which the Abbot Pizzi, Director of the Arcadia and presider at the awards ceremony, repeated, laughingly saying that the crowning of Corilla had become for him the crowning of thorns.

Morelli's poetry bore the imprint of the Parmesan printer Bodoni, who published *Atti della incoronazione di Corilla Olimpica*, which is poetry of the same style and was written exclusively for the Easter occasion. Her poetry shared the defects of extemporaneous words and the characteristic emptiness of the school of Arcadia.

Separated from her husband, the Spanish dignitary F. Fernandez, Morelli traveled from court to court through many cities. She was loved by princes and abbots. At Florence, Rome, and Naples she hosted frequent evening parties. As she grew older, her gift for improvisation was replaced by one for sonnet-writing. She died in Florence from an attack of apoplexy on November 8, 1800.

Bibliography

Adelmollo, A., *Corilla Olimpica* (Florence, 1887). Tribolati, F., *Conversazione di G. Rosini* (Pisa, 1889), pp. 41–44. Vitagliano, A., *Storia di poesia estemporanea nella letterati italiani* (Rome, 1905).

Jean E. Jost

Morena

(see: Margita Figuli)

Ol'ga Morena

(see: Margita Figuli)

Beate Morgenstern

Born 1946, Cuxhaven, East Germany
Genre(s): short prose, radio drama
Language(s): German

The oldest of five children, Beate Morgenstern grew up in the Soviet Occupation Zone of Germany and in the German Democratic Republic. Her father was a Pietist minister, and Morgenstern spent formative years in Herrnhut, a historical center of Pietism. After completing her studies, in Berlin, of German literature and of art education, Morgenstern declined a teaching position to work as a salesperson, a postal employee, and as an office assistant. From 1970–1978 she was a picture editor for a magazine; after that, she was employed as a cultural liaison in a Berlin factory. In 1979, the publication year of *Jenseits der Allee* (Beyond the Avenue), her first and, to date, only collection of stories, she became a free-lance writer.

Morgenstern's stories depict brief but important moments in her protagonists' lives; her strength lies in her ability to evoke the milieu in which her characters move. She situates many of the stories in Berlin's Prenzlauer Berg area, along the Prenzlauer Avenue: " . . . two worlds: on this side and then beyond the avenue, which divided workers, delinquents, students, and artists from the bourgeoisie." None of her stories contains a first-person narrator. Sigrid Töpelmann sees the influence of Pietist tradition in that technique, noting that Pietism teaches concern for others and condemns self-celebration.

Several of Morgenstern's stories contain criticisms of GDR society. "Bruno" attacks sycophantism, while "Gemüse-Erna" (Erna the Vegetable Dealer) relates the story of a woman's vain effort to receive a widow's pension. In World War II, her husband had shot himself rather than fight the Soviets; hence, his widow is ineligible for a pension. However, widows of men who died fighting in the Soviet Union *do* receive pensions. "Glatteis" (Slippery Surface) discreetly mentions the Stalinist 1950s, and "Im Spreekahn" (In the Spree-Canoe) circumspectly discusses the Berlin Wall. These are balanced by "Von der anderen Seite" (From the Other Side), in which the protagonist is visited by her half-brother, who grew up in West Germany, and whose personality has been scarred by the competition of that society.

Morgenstern's texts are not unconcerned with feminist issues, though such issues are not their predominant themes, and are often approached indirectly. The protagonist of "Erna the Vegetable Dealer," for example, lives with a man 21 years younger than she, though that is not the point of the story. In "Der Anruf" (The Call), the protagonist is traveling to visit her sister, who cannot deal with her divorce and may have committed suicide; in transit, the protagonist encounters a rather pathetic acquaintance who, in order to fight her loneliness, has been married three times. Morgenstern's writing attracted attention in the GDR primarily due to its depiction of marginal figures: a vegetable dealer; the aged; an emotionally-disturbed Free German Youth leader; or a formerly alcoholic student who dreams of becoming an important artist. In *Herr in Blaßblau* (Gentleman in Light Blue), Morgenstern presents one of the very few portraits in GDR literature of a homosexual man.

Works

Jenseits der Allee (1979).

Bibliography

Hammer, Ingrid, "Beate Morgenstern." *Deutsch als Fremdsprache* 18 (1981). Sonderheft, pp. 69–72. Töpelmann, Sigrid, "Nachbemerkung: Beate Morgenstern." *Jenseits der Allee* (Berlin, 1979).

Thomas C. Fox

Irmtraud Morgner

Born August 22, 1933, Chemnitz (now Karl-Marx-Stadt), East Germany; died May 6, 1990
Genre(s): novel
Language(s): German

The novelist Morgner's intellect and erudition, her cultural insight, historical consciousness, and philosophical woman's perspective combined with her skill as a weaver of complex narrative tapestries make her one of the outstanding writers in German today. Morgner's subject is contemporary reality, its historical background and its possible future; her theme is ultimately the increasingly perilous state into which the dehumanizing obsession with technical specialization, hierarchy, conquest, and war inherent in the patriarchal value system have brought humankind. Refreshingly, she filters her concerns through imaginative language and metaphor pervaded with innate humor, and she shapes them into literature with protean fantasy.

The major formative influence on Morgner is the fact that she has lived in the socialist GDR since its inception (when she was sixteen). Born into a proletarian family, she was allowed to attend the University of Leipzig (1952–1956) where she majored in *Germanistik* and *Literaturwissenschaft*, studying under Hans Mayer. After university, she moved to East Berlin and worked as an editorial assistant for the official literary magazine, *Neue deutsche Blätter*, until 1958 when she began writing full-time. Her first two books (*Das Signal steht auf Fahrt*, 1959; *Ein Haus am Rand du Staddt*, 1962) were cast basically in the prevailing mold of socialist realism. *Ein Haus am Rand du Staddt*, in particular, shows promise of an independent, questing imagination, which refuses to avoid conflicts between socialist ideal and reality; thematically, her concern about women's limited, double-burdened role is already evident. Like her contemporaries, Christa Wolf, Sarah Kirsch and Günter de Bryn, Morgner's writing influenced GDR literature to become more subjective, less schematic, while remaining socialistically engaged.

Three works belong to what might be termed Morgner's second developmental phase, *Hochzeit in Konstantinopel* (1968), *Gauklerlegende* (1970), and *Die wundersamen Reisen Gustav des Weltfahrers* (published in 1972 but written before the former two). With *Hochzeit*—a work received with considerable enthusiasm, especially in the Federal Republic (1969)—Morgner had clearly begun to find her unique voice, the ability to sustain a critical dialectic between realism and fantasy. *Hochzeit*'s ever questioning heroine Bele H., a streetcar conductor in East Berlin, makes a prenuptial "honeymoon" trip to a resort somewhere on the Yugoslav Adriatic (Bele dubs it "Constantinople"). In the course of their three weeks there, Bele tries to help Paul, her physicist fiancé, gain touch with his own feeling, human side; Scheherazade-like, she tells him twenty-one allegorical tales based on fantasized interpretations of her own experiences, with the aim of opening new perspectives about human relationships to him. Blind to her deeper purpose, he remains the one-sided theoretician. When the trip is over, she bails out of the relationship, taking her future into her own hands.

The narrative voice of her next work, *Gauklerlegende*, is again a woman's; but here, too, it is her husband, the specialist male, who clearly has the socially more significant role; the subject of the wife's tales and active figure of the book, the Pied Piper/*Gaukler*, is obviously male as well. In *Die wundersamen Reisen*, Gustav, again a masculine title character, is both "amazing" traveler and narrative voice. The fictive "Vorwort der Verfasserin" and "Nachwort der Herausgeberin" (Preface and Afterword) added for the 1972 publication alter the perspective to that of Bele H., Gustav's granddaughter, who claims that, in a moment of inspiration, she learned to identify her own biography with his "prevaricated" adventures born of the "creativity of the powerless." Thus, in both *Gauklerlegende*

and *Die wundersamen Reisen* a further extension of Morgner's central themes emerges; the drawing together of past and present, seventeenth century *Gaukler* and modern woman, universe-traveling grandfather and granddaughter. The past, in each case, has "legendary" character and as such is used to point the way to a future in which those who are as yet powerless find the courage "to accomplish something greater" by leaps of the imagination that make it possible for them to step beyond the bounds of historical limitations.

Fantasy and humor, women's creativity, the concerns of everyday reality linked with legendary past, hope for the future; these factors come together in the third and ongoing phase of Morgner's writing, in which female figures assume the active, focal roles. With her 700-page montage/collage novel, *Leben und Abenteuer der Trobadora Beatriz nach Zeugnissen ihrer Spielfrau Laura* (1974), Morgner set a landmark of imaginative writing in German letters. Her nascent stylistic abilities based on surprising juxtapositions and funny contrasts had clearly matured and found their vehicle in conscious feminine perspectives. *Die Trobadora* combines elements as disparate as, for instance, an excerpt from an official GDR tract tabulating women's orgasms and an unpublished novel which Morgner had written in 1954 (it deals with tensions between pre- and postwar generations in the GDR, is inserted in seven *intermezzos*, and serves as background for numerous characters in *Die Trobadora*). We see the possibilities and shortcomings of the socialist state from the viewpoints of an historical twelfth century *troubadora* from Provençe, Beatriz de Dia, and her salaried minstrel Laura Salman, a contemporary, university educated streetcar driver and single mother in East Berlin. The reawakened Beatriz (she had made a deal with a fairy that she sleep until times were better for creative women) travels to the GDR of 1968, believing it to encompass the ideal realization of women's equality; Laura is still struggling with imperfect realities. Through these women, legendary and real, Morgner takes on her own times, ranging from the May 1968 Paris uprising through Chancellor Ulbricht's Bitterfelde decree that workers write and writers work, in a critical celebration of the socialist state for whose future she still had great hopes, based especially on the gradually improving position of women that the early 1970s seemed to promise. Various chapters in this nonlinear, open-formatted work further reflect the dynamics of the present by citing Morgner herself, Paul Wiens, editor of one of the GDR's most respected literary journals, *Sinn und Form*, and author Volker Braun, as well as other real personages. When *Die Trobadora* became available in the West in 1976, critics and the reading public made it a best-seller; feminists declared her a spokeswoman. Then almost a decade passed before Morgner published again.

Morgner's outspoken stance against capitalism notwithstanding, her open sexuality and criticism of the socialist system, particularly of its little-changed double sexual standard and commensurately unfair workplace/household load for women, made further publishing very difficult for her in the GDR. Her long-term personal relationship with Wiens, and the need to raise her young son, did not make writing easier. She, however, remained acutely aware of political developments in both her own country and Europe as a whole; these events, her continued reading in literature and philosophy, as well as her travels in Greece provided the basis for a continuation of the Beatriz/Laura story, *Amanda: Ein Hexenroman*, completed in 1982 and published a year later. *Amanda* is an even more complex melding of legendary past, present, and future than was *Die Trobadora*, an even more strongly contoured mosaic of the development of women's role in the world, one which stretches from pagan and Christian creation stories through the European peace movement of the late 1970s and early 1980s. Morgner's humor has darkened and tends to the grotesque, but it still pervades the structure of Amanda. Her fantasy continues to fly, not only in the guise of a mythological messenger for Beatriz but also within the world of a group of East Berlin women working for self-realization and centered around Laura. Beatriz is reincarnated as a siren, robbed of her tongue, and put in an owl's cage in the East Berlin Zoo; her role in *Amanda* is to record and interpret Laura's (i.e., ordinary women's) experience, purpose, and progress in the world. The group of women around Laura have help and positive examples from a symbolic world of activist

witches, themselves captives of patriarchal powers on the Brocken, the mountain of Walpurgis Night (April 30). Amanda, head of the androgynous witches and Laura's independent-minded other half, leads the witches and a select group of creative men (from Goethe through Marx) in a victorious rebellion against the arch-patriarchs, God and the Devil, who hold them in thrall. This fantastic coup embodies the hope that Morgner still has for the victory of peaceful forces—women and men—working together in the real world. She has found her example in Goethe's re-interpretation of the Pandora myth, where Pandora is the preserver of hope and symbol of humankind's ability to love instead of hate. *Amanda* thus offers a projection into a possible future. Morgner called it "only the first half of the victory" and promised, in her closing words in the book, to supply the rest in the yet-unnamed third volume of her Beatriz/Laura trilogy.

In 1984, as part of her only trip to the United States, Morgner read at the annual Women in German Conference and various universities from her working introduction to Book III and a pre-published trial chapter. That same year, at a literary conference in Solothurn, Switzerland, she presented the chapter which appeared, along with her own introductory works, excerpts from *Amanda*, and an interview, as *Die Hexe im Landhaus: Gespräch in Solothurn* (1984). The following year (1985) Morgner was the recipient of the Hroswitha von Gandersheim Literary Prize for outstanding women authors. In November 1989, the city of Kassel honored her as the first woman to receive their "Literary Prize for Grotesque Humor." These two symbols of literary recognition from the West, along with her Heinrich Mann Prize (1975) and GDR National Prize (1977), place Morgner among the most honored women writers of this century in both Germanies.

While writer in residence at the University of Zurich (1987–1988), Morgner underwent the first of four cancer operations. She lived to see the fall of the Berlin Wall. But in February 1990, she wrote of her frustration that illness had robbed her of the chance to participate actively in her country's peaceful revolution and of her unpreparedness for the extent of the "corruption" and "moral bankruptcy" come to light in the GDR. This, nevertheless, remained her "father-land" for whose "day after tomorrow" she had hoped and written since its inception in 1949 because, as she continued to believe, "capitalism was and is no alternative for me, or for any woman." she died just weeks after the land she would not leave and the Marxism she would not forsake were voted out of existence. As a writer, Morgner was an *agent provocateur*, whose still relevant goal was to "make not literature but a world" in which women "enter history," and whose unique humor was "a form of contending with life" that belonged to her "very being [and] therefore to [her] writing."

In his *laudatio* for Irmtraud Morgner in Kassel (1989), Walter Jens, honorary President of P.E.N. in Germany, author and professor, compares her to Joyce and Thomas Mann in her use of allusion and appeal to the intelligence of her readers. English writing has so far brought forth no authoress comparable to Morgner. The work of the sexually explicit Erica Jong, for example, shows nothing of Morgner's insights and writer's talent. The John Barth of *Giles Goatboy* and *Sotweed Factor* or the Thomas Pynchon of *Gravity's Rainbow* approach Morgner's ability to combine outrageous fantasy, the grotesque, hu-mor, and criticism, yet they, too, lack the scope of her vision and, more significantly, the revo-lutionary potential of her woman's perspective.

Works

Das Signal steht auf Fahrt. Erzählung (1959). *Ein Haus am Rand der Staddt. Roman* (1962). "Notturno. Erzählung" (1964). *Hochzeit in Konstantinopel. Roman* (1964). *Gauklerlegende. Eine Spielfraungeschichte* (1970). *Die wundersamen Reisen Gustav des Weltfahrers. Lügenhafter Roman mit Kommentaren* (1972). "Sündhafte Behauptungen [Annemarie Auer]," "Vexierbild [Günter Kunert]," "Bootskauf [Ludwig Turek]." Porträts (1972). "Das Seil. Erzählung" (1973). "Spielzeit. Erzählung" (1973). Diskussionsbeitrag zur Arbeitsgruppe II "Literatur und Geschichtsbewußtsein" (1974). "Bis man zu dem Kerne zu gelangen das Glück hat. Zufallsbegünstigte Aufzeichnungen über den Oberbauleiter vom Palast der Republik nebst Adjutanten und Ehefrau" (1974). *Leben und Abenteuer der Trobadora Beatriz nach Zeugnissen ihrer Spielfrau Laura. Roman in dreizehn Büchern und sieben Intermezzos* (1974). "Rede auf dem VII. Schriftstellerkongreß der DDR" (1978). [With Sarah Kirsch and Christa Wolf], *Geschlechtertausch* (1980). *Amanda. Ein Hexenroman* (1983). "Zeitgemäß unzeitgemäß: Hrostswith. Dankrede beim Empfang des 'Literaturpreises der Stadt Gandersheim zum Gedenken an die erste deutsche Dichterin, Hroswitha von Gandersheim, die vor 1000 Jahren ihr Lebenswerk vollendete'" (1986). "Nekromantie im Marx-Engels-Auditorium" (1984). "Die Schöne und das Tier" (1988), and "Guten Morgen, Du Schöner" (1990): Excerpts from the not yet published "Die Cherubinischen Wandersfrauen. Ein apokrypher Salmanroman" (Book III of Morgner's trilogy).

Translation: Achberger, Karen and Fritz, "The Twelfth Book of *Die Trobadora*, 'Gospel of Velaska, Which Laura Reads as a Revelation on the Day of the Trobadora Beatriz's Burial,' by Irmtraud Morgner." *New German Critique*, 15 (Fall, 1978): 121–146.

Bibliography

Berger, Doris, "Gespräch mit Irmtraud Morgner." *GDR Monitor* 12 (1984/1985). Herminghouse, Patricia A., "Die Frau und das Phantastische in der deuen DDR-Literatur: Der Fall Irmtraud Morgner," in *Die Frau als Heldlin und Autorin: neue kritische Ansätze zur deutschen Literatur* 10, ed. Wolfgang Paulsen (Bern: Amherster Kolluquium, 1977). "Irmtraud Morgner," in *Kritische Literaturlexikon*, ed. H-L. Arnold (Munich, ongoing) [secondary literature in German to August 1983]. Johnson, S.K., "A New Irmtraud Morgner: Humor, Fantasy, Structures, and Ideas in *Amanda. Ein Hexenroman*," in *Studies in GDR Culture and Society* 4, ed. M. Gerber (Lanham, New York, London, 1984). Gerhardt, Marlis, ed., *Irmtraud Morgner. Texte, Daten, Bilder* (Frankfurt a M.: Sammlung Luchterland, 1990). Kaufmann, Eva, "Interview mit Irmtraud Morgner," in *Weimarer Beiträge* 30 (1984). Martin, Biddy, "Irmtraud Morgner's *Leben und Abenteuer der Trobadora Beatriz*," in *Beyond the Eternal Feminine*, eds. S. Cocalis and K. Goodman (Stuttgart, 1982). Schwarzer, Alice, "Irmtraud Morgner. 'Jetzt oder niel Die Frauen sind die Hälfte des Volkes!'" (interview), *Emma* 2 (Feb. 1990): 32–38.

Sheila Johnson

Yunna Pinkhusovna (Petrovna) Morits

Born June 2, 1937, Kiev, The Soviet Union
Genre(s): poetry
Language(s): Russian

A contemporary Soviet poetess, Morits writes in a manner formally not dissimilar to Tsvetaeva's. Themes of fate and afterlife mingle with lyric symbolism in Morits' poetry. Her first collection of poetic works, *Razgovor o schast'e* (Conversation about Happiness), appeared in 1957 whereupon she enrolled in the literary institute named Maksim Gorky. She finished in 1961, the same year her second collection of verses appeared, *Mys zhelaniia* (Cape of Desire). Her creative oeuvre expanded in the seventies when two collections appeared, *Surovoi nit'iu: kniga stikhov* (1974; By a Coarse Thread) and *Pri svete zhizni* (1977; By the Light of Life). Most recently, a collection called *Na ètom berege vysokom* (1987; On this Tall Shore) has been published.

Morits is not well represented in translated literature, but not because of a lack of depth or power. Characteristically, each poem achieves an epiphany or exhibits an abrupt change of view or theme. Often, allegorical overtones are quite prominent. Formally, her poetry is quite interesting also, preserving as it does some of the elements of experimentation of Russian Modernism. Internal rhymes and symmetries tie her lines into psychological parallels. Clearly, she commands her images and while doing so renders them poetically.

Works

Razgovor o schast'e; stikhi (1957). *Mys zhelanii* (1961). *Surovoi nit'iu: kniga stikhov* (1974). *Pri svete zhizni* (1977).
Translations: *Three Russian Poets*, E. Feinstein, ed. (1979). *Russian Poetry: the Modern Period*, J. Glad and D. Weissbort, eds. (1974).

Bibliography

Lominadze, S., "Tvorchestkim vzgliadom?" *Nash sovremenik* (November 11, 1983): 188–191. Marchenko, A., "Kontury mechti." *Literaturnaia Gazeta* (November 13, 1962). Naumov, E., "Za poliarnom krugom." *Zvezda* 5 (1963). Rubin, B., "Poèziia vysokikh shirot." *Den' poèzii* (Moscow, 1962).

Chris Tomei

Isabella di Morra

Born ca. 1520, Favale, Italy; died ca. 1545,
Favale
Genre(s): poetry
Language(s): Italian

Very little is known about Isabella di Morra's life. Her writing has survived only because of the circumstances of her tragic death and the investigation which followed it. In *Familiae nobilissimae de Morra historia*, Marcantonio di Morra reconstructs her aunt Isabella's murder at twenty-five by her brothers. The Morra family was of noble origin. When Isabella's father, Giovan Michele, became a victim of shifting political winds and had to flee to France, the rest of the family took refuge in the rugged countryside of southern Italy. Isabella's education is attested to by the presence of a tutor in her castle at Favale. She was possibly known among acquaintances as a writer or, at least, as somebody who dabbled in poetry. If the information contained in one of her sonnets can be read as factual, she also entertained some kind of literary correspondence. We do not know when she started to write or whether she composed more poems than those that surfaced at her death. According to Marcantonio, sometime in 1544 a local nobleman and fellow dilettante poet, Diego Sandoval de Castro, started a correspondence with Isabella, possibly a literary one. They exchanged poems and letters, the tutor acting as an intermediary in what was intended to look like an exchange between Isabella and Diego's wife, Antonia Caracciolo. The brothers heard rumors of what was going on, judged it dishonorable to them, and killed first the tutor, then Isabella, and lastly Diego.

Totally unknown during her lifetime, Isabella's few sonnets and songs surfaced after they were made available to the prosecutors searching the Morra's property to investigate the murders. The poems are autobiographical in tone, Petrarchan in mood and format. The themes that Isabella almost obsessively reworks are her isolation and her frustration at not being able to see a way out of a life she thought was not worth living. Her poetry contains appeals to her father to free her from a *de facto* imprisonment, expressions of dislike for or fear of her brothers, moments of self-questioning, and passages of religious fervor. She insistently draws connections between the rugged nature outside and her seclusion or makes her desire for order through paternal care a reflection of her inability as a woman to improve her condition. One thinks of Tasso as well as Petrarch when reading her poetry.

It is difficult not to look at Isabella's sonnets retrospectively and not to see voiced in them what she eventually experienced tragically. Still her literary production stands on its own merits; the prosody shows a certain dexterity, and the poetic images seem carefully worked out. Although her recognition as a gifted writer came only in more recent times, Isabella was anthologized from the very beginning with the most interesting women writers of the Renaissance.

Works

"Rime." *Rime di diversi illustri signori napoletani e d'altri*, ed. Ludovico Dolce. Book 3 (Venezia: Giolito, 1552). Includes ten sonnets and a song. Rpt. 1555 (Book 5) and 1556 (Book 7), with two more sonnets and a song.

Bibliography

Baldacci, Luigi, ed., *Lirici del Cinquecento* (Firenze, 1957), pp. 628–635. Bulifon, Antonio, *Rime delle signore Lucrezia Marinella, Veronica Gambara et Isabella della Morra* (Napoli, 1693). Bronzini, D., *Isabella di Morra* (Matera, 1975). Caserta, G., *Isabella Morra e la societa' meridionale del Cinquecento* (Matera, 1976). Costa-Zalessow, Natalia, *Scrittrici italiane dal XIII al XX secolo* (Ravenna, 1982), pp. 68–72. Croce, Benedetto, *Isabella di Morra e Diego Sandoval de Castro* (Palermo, 1983). De Gubernatis, Angelo, *Isabella Morra. Le Rime* (Roma, 1907). De Villarino, Maria, *La vida tragica de Isabella Morra. Estudio y traduccion poetica* (Buenos Aires, 1943). Di Morra, Marcantonio, *Familiae nobilissimae de Morra historia* (Napoli, 1629). Domenichi, Ludovico, *Rime diverse d'alcune nobilissime et virtuosissime donne* (Lucca, 1559), pp. 86–99. Toffanin, G., *Le piu' belle pagine di Gaspara Stampa, Vittoria Colonna, Veronica Gambara e Isabella Morra* (Milano, 1935).

Valeria Finucci

Anna Mostowska

Born c. 1762, Lithuania; died before 1833, place uncertain
Genre(s): novel
Language(s): Polish

A daughter of the aristocratic Radziwiłł family, Mostowska traveled extensively throughout Europe where she became well acquainted with the works of Western European writers, among them Ossian, Anne Radcliffe, Horace Walpole, La Fontaine and Christoph Wieland, thus absorbing both Romantic and gothic trends in literature. Her own works are consequently strongly influenced by these writers and lack originality, some of them becoming outright adaptations. The Gothic influence of her novels is recognizable in such titles as *Strach w zameczku* (1806; Terror in a Small Castle) and *Zamek Koniecpolskich* (1806; The Koniecpolski Castle). Her best and most original novel is *Astolda, księżniczka ze krwi Palemona* (1807; Astolda, the Duchess of the Palemon Bloodline). She also wrote adaptations of novels by S.F. de Genlis and Wieland. Mostowska's works foreshadow Romanticism, but her most significant contribution is the fact that she introduced to Poland the historical and didactic-moralistic novel and that she modified the gothic elements into a more rational as well as sentimental mode. She was also the first to compose a Polish ballad, "Duma" (Pride), which appeared in *Astolda*.

Moreover, Mostowska was among the first literary figures to demand greater respect for women and recognition by society that the natures of men and women are of equal worth.

Works

Strach w zameczku [Terror in a Small Castle] (1806).
Nie zawsze tak się czyni, jak się mówi [Actions Do
Not Always Match Words] (1806). *Zamek
Koniecpolskich* [The Koniecpolski Castle] (1806).
Matylda i Danilo [Matilda and Danilo] (1806).
Astolda, księżniczka ze krwi Palemona [Astolda, the
Duchess of the Palemon Bloodline] (1807). *Zabawki
w spoczynku* [Games of Recreation] (1809).

Bibliography

"Mostowska Anna," in *Literatura polska;
Przewodnik encyklopedyczny*, ed. Julian
Krzyżanowski. Vol. 1 (Warsaw, 1984).
"Mostowska." *Polski Słownik Biograficzny*. Vol. 22
(Wrocław, 1977).

Irene Suboczewski

François Bertaut, Dame Langlois de Motteville

Born 1615 or 1621, France; died 1689, Paris
Genre(s): memoirs
Language(s): French

Confidant to a queen and one of the most
popular of the numerous memoirists of the French
seventeenth century, Françoise Bertaut was born
either in 1615 or 1621. Both dates are found in
her own accounts. She was the daughter of Pierre
Bertaut, the secretary to Henry IV and Louis XIII
and the nephew of French poet Jean Bertaut. Her
mother, Louise Bessin de Mathonville, spent her
youth with Spanish relatives in Spain and was
appointed to the service of the young Spanish
princess Anne of Austria when the latter wed
Louis XIII.

Louise was a loyal confidant to the queen.
She also gave her seven-year-old daughter
Françoise to the service, although soon after
mother and daughter were forced to retire to
their family estates in Normandy. Cardinal
Richelieu had exiled them to separate the Queen
from Mme Bertaut, who was thought to be sending
Anne's secret messages to Spain. There, from
1628–1639, Louise carefully groomed her
daughter for eventual royal service, fostering her
memory and love of Queen Anne and furnishing
a living example of the religious piety she felt
necessary for such service. In 1639, she wed

Françoise to an old, childless, but rich widower
of eighty, Nicholas Langlois, Seigneur de
Motteville, who conveniently died two years
later. His death left Françoise free to answer
Anne's recall to service, a call that followed
closely upon the death of Louis XIII and his
cardinal-minister.

From the moment of her reunion with Anne
in 1643, Madame de Motteville devoted herself
body and soul to the Queen Regent. Always
possessed of the Queen's confidence and favor,
she avowed her intention to write her memoirs
almost immediately after her return. She proceeded with the Queen's knowledge and approval,
recording court events and, in fact, the history of
the Queen's Regency, with a much admired
balance and a quiet self-effacement.

Soon after the Queen's death on January 20,
1666, Madame de Motteville retired from court
to a house in the Rue Saint-Dominique. Her visits
and sojourns at the Convent de Sainte-Marie de
Chaillet, where her sister was Mother Superior,
became more and more frequent as she grew
older. Ironically, the woman who had spent
much of her life recording her memories ended
her life without the ability to recall them.
Gradually lapsing into complete senility, she
died in Paris in 1689.

Madame de Motteville's memoirs have often
been justly admired. "Ce que j'ai mis sur le
papier," she wrote, "je l'ai vu et je l'ai ouï." She
emerges as an intelligent, indefatigable witness,
writing without passion but with great simplicity. The piety instilled in her by her mother not
only accounts for her balance but also for her love
of moralizing, which surfaces throughout the
book. In her distinctive, always lucid style, she
manages to capture the characters of those around
her with great immediacy and to fill her book
with vignettes of amazing power.

Never bitter, though often melancholy, the
memoirs may well have achieved their balanced
tone through careful rewriting. A partial copy of
what appears an early draft does exist. Here less
balanced judgments and a more spontaneous
flow of thoughts and reflections are to be had.
But whatever the circumstances of production,
the memoirs as they stand are a fascinating
record of their period. Their touching and faithful
portrayal of the Queen Regent, a portrait that is

always fair but also always sensitive to the pressures surrounding the Regency, give us a unique document—the story of a feminine regency as recorded by a feminine historian.

Works

Mémoires pour servir à l'histoire d'Anne d'Autriche [Memoirs to Serve as the History of Anne of Austria] (1878).

Bibliography

de Beaurepaire, Charles, *Recherches sur Madame de Motteville et sa Famille* (Paris, 1900). Dethan, Georges, "Madame de Motteville et Mazarine ou le Complexe d'Oenone," in *Les Valeurs chez les mémoralistes français du XVIIème siècle*, ed. Noemi Hepp and Jacques Hennequin (Strassbourg, 1979), pp. 103–109. Fumaroli, Marc, "La Confidente et la reine: Madame de Motteville et Anne d'Autriche." *Revue des Sciences Humaines* (July-September 1964): 265–278. Lalanne, Ludovic, *Dictionnaire Historique de la France*, Vol. II (rpt. New York: Franklin, 1967). Watts, Derek, "Self-Portrayal in Seventeenth-Century French Memoirs." *Australian Journal of French Studies* XIII, No. 3 (September–December 1975): 263–284.

Glenda Wall

Jeanine Moulin

Born 1912, Brussels, Belgium
Genre(s): poetry
Language(s): French

Having studied philosophy and letters at the Free University of Brussels, she devoted herself thereafter to poetry, literary criticism, and also to the organization of poetry readings that came to be known as *Midis de la Poésie* (Poetic Noondays) and provided a great variety of poets with the opportunity to read their works to a sympathetic audience.

She is, in her own poetry, an exponent of purity of expression. Her criticism as well as her poetry has shown a preference for feminine psychology, marked also by an attractive sense of humor even when it gives expression to what she calls "the politeness of despair." She has been at the forefront of the explosion of feminine poetry that has been a significant feature of Belgian literature since the Second World War.

Works

Les Chimères de Gérard de Nerval (1937). *Manuel Poétique d'Apollinaire* (1939). *Jeux et Tourment* (1947). *Gérard de Nerval. Les Chimères. Exégèses* (1949). *Guillaume Apollinaire ou la Querelle de l'Ordre et de l'Aventure* (1952). *Marceline Desbordes-Valmore* (1955). *Feux sans joie* (1961). *Christine de Pisan* (1962). *La Pierre à Feux* (1968). *Les Mains Nues* (1971).

Charity Cannon Willard

Elisavet Moutsa-Martinengou

(see: Elisavet Moutzan-Martinengou)

Elisavet Moutza-Martinengou

(see: Elisavet Moutzan-Martinengou)

Elisavet Moutzan-Martinengou

(a.k.a. Elisavet Moutza-Martinengou, Elisavet Moutsa-Martinengou, Elisavet Moutzan Martinengou)

Born 1801 on the island of Zakynthos (Zante); died 1832, Zakynthos
Genre(s): autobiography, poetry, drama, treatise, translation, letters
Language(s): Greek, Italian

Elisavet Moutzan-Martinengou was the daughter of Francisco Moutzan (or *Moutzas* or *Moutsas*) and Angelikē Sygourou. Both the Moutzan and the Sygourou families belonged to the aristocrats of Zakynthos, and Elisavet grew up secluded from the outside world, as was the custom for generations of upper-class girls of her time. Zakynthos belonged to the Napoleonic and British Empires during most of Elisavet's lifetime (and her father was governor under the British), but the civilization she was exposed to was essentially Venetian, for Zakynthos had for centuries been an important outpost of the Venetian Empire.

Her tutors were limited to respectable clergymen who were allowed to come to her home.

She began to consider herself a writer while in her teens. By the age of thirty-one, she had written twenty-two plays, eight in Greek and fourteen in Italian, poems in both Greek and Italian, modern Greek prose translations of Homer's *Odyssey* and Aeschylus' *Prometheus Bound*, two treatises in Greek ("On Economy" and "On the Art of Poetry"), letters in Greek, Italian, and French, and an autobiography (in Greek).

Her wish was to stay single and join a convent so she would be able to devote all her time to her studies and her writing. Her family, however, was opposed to such a plan and gave her no choice but to marry. In 1831 she succumbed to the wishes of her family and married Nicolas Martinengos. A year and a half later, sixteen days after giving birth to her son, she died.

None of her works was published until 1881 when her son, the poet Elisavetios Martinengos, published an edited version of her autobiography. He died four years later, and her work was more or less forgotten. It was rediscovered in 1947 by Dinos Konomos, who promised to publish it. Nothing was done until 1953, at which time a great fire following the major earthquakes of that year destroyed most of Elisavet's writings, which Konomos kept in his house. Her autobiography was reissued in 1956 by K. Porphyrēs and in 1965 by Ph. K. Boumpoulidēs.

Moutzan-Martinengou's autobiography is extremely important not in terms of artistic value but as a specimen of writing in an era and a place when writing by women was extremely rare. Hers is truly a feminist voice, and her feminism is derived from the prison-like atmosphere of her aristocratic home that hardly gave her room to breathe. Writing became her only escape from her oppressive surroundings. The autobiography ends before her marriage to Nicolas Martinengos, so we know nothing of her married life. The life she describes is a record of customs, attitudes, and practices of an age as they affect a bright and sensitive young woman.

Works

ē Mētēr mou: Autobiographia tēs kyrias Elisavet Moutzan-Martinengou, ekdidomenē hypo tou yiou autēs Elisavetiou Martinengou meta diaphorōn autou poiēseōn [My Mother: Autobiography of Mrs. Elisavet Moutzan-Martinengou]. Published by her son, Elisavetios Martinengos, along with several of his own poems (1881). "Ena Cheirographo pou glytose ston kairo" [A Hand-Written Paper That Survived]. *Heptanēsiaka Phylla* 10 (1947): 153. "Apo to theatriko ergo tēs Elisavet Moutsan: Ē Rodopē" [From Elisavet Moutsan's Theatrical Works: Ē Rodopē], *Heptanēsiaka Phylla* 10 (1947): 153. "Grammata tēs Elisavet Moutzan-Martinengou" [Letters]. *Heptanēsiaka Phylla* 10 (1947): 154–155. "Ena Apospasma," An excerpt from her translation of Aeschylus's *Prometheus Bound, Heptanēsiaka Phylla* 10 (1947): 155–156. *Autobiographia,* ed with intro. K. Porphyrēs (1954; reprint 1983). "Autobiographia," in *Elisavet Moutzan-Martinengou,* ed. Phaidōn K. Boumpoulidēs (1965), pp. 3–55. "O Philargyros" [The Avaricious Man], in *Elisavet Moutzan-Martinengou,* ed. Phaidōn K. Boumpoulidēs (1965). "Eis tēn Theotokon" [To the Mother of God], in *Elisavet Moutzan-Martinengou,* ed. Phaidōn K. Boumpoulidēs (1965). "Odē eis to pathos tou Iēsou Christou" [Ode on the Passion of Christ], in *Elisavet Moutza-Martinengou,* ed. Phaidōn K. Boumpoulidēs (1965). "Dialogos" [Dialogue], in *Elisavet Moutza-Martinengou,* ed. Phaidōn K. Boumpoulidēs (1965). "Apospasmata" [Fragments], in *Elisavet Moutza-Martinengou,* ed. Phaidōn K. Boumpoulidēs (1965). "Epistolai" [Letters], in *Elisavet Moutzan-Martinengou,* ed. Phaidōn K. Boumpoulidēs (1965), pp. 132–156. "Metaphraseis" [Translations], in *Elisavet Moutzan-Martinengou,* ed. Phaidōn K. Boumpoulidēs (1965), pp. 125–131. *My Story,* tr. Helen D. Kolias (1989).

Bibliography

Boumpoulidēs, Phaidōn K., *Elisavet Moutza-Martinengou* (Athens, 1965). Boumpoulidēs, Phaidōn K., *Neoellēnikai er eunai peri tous Zakynthious poiētas kai pezographous.* Dimaras, C. Th., *A History of Modern Greek Literature*, tr. Mary P. Gianos (Albany, 1972). Dimaras, K. Th., *Historia tēs Neollenikēs Logotechnias, apo tis prōtes rizes hōs tēn epochē mas.* 6th ed. (Athens, 1975). Kitromilides, Paschalis M., "The Enlightenment and Womanhood: Cultural Change and the Politics of Exclusion." *Journal of Modern Greek Studies* 1 (1983), pp. 39–61. Konomos, Dinos, "Elisavet Moutza-Martinengou." *Heptanēsiaka Phylla* 10

(1947): 141–56. Mirasgezē, Maria, *Neoellēnike Logotechnia*, vol. 1 (Athens, 1978). Vitti, Mario, *Storia della Letteratura Neogreca* (Torino, 1971).

Helen D. Kolias

Sanda Movilă

Born 1900, Cerbu (Argeş); died 1970, Bucharest, Romania
Genre(s): poetry, short story, novel
Language(s): Romanian

Sanda Movilă (née Maria Ionescu) moved from symbolist to militant poetry and from erotic to social novels.

After graduating in literature, she worked in Bucharest at the *Ministerul Învăţămîntului* (Ministry of Education) and became a regular contributor to a considerable number of prestigious literary journals of the time (*Adevărul literar şi artistic, Azi, Bilete de papagal, Caiet de poezie—*a poetry supplement issued by *Revista Fundaţiilor Regale, Cele trei Crişuri, Flacăra, Mişcarea literară*, Elena Farago's cultural journal *Năzuinţa, Sburătorul, Spre ziuă, Viaţa românească, Vremea*, etc.).

Movilă's debut volume of poetry—*Crinii roşii* (1925; Red Lilies)—with its celebrated cycle of "Japanese fans" attested already to a tension between the delicate fantastic imagery of porcelain princesses embroidering with precious stones, of pearls and mirrors, roads transmuting into red lilies, or silvery moons suspended over suicidal bourgs and the strong Sapphic accents of violent and cruel love. Twenty years later *Călătorii* (1946; Journeys) deepens the split by bringing together a cycle of exotic travels (to seas of sleep and fairytale landscapes, to imaginary coffee plantations vibrating in the sounds of the banjo, to Ohio or Leslie Howard's New York, to Cuba and China) with a cycle named "death years" in which the poet evokes the panic and suffering brought about by the Anglo-American aircraft raids over Romania towards the end of the Second World War. The volumes *Fruct nou* (1948; New Fruit) and *Poezii* (1967; Poems) are terminal points in the evolution of Sanda Movilă towards militant poetry.

The analytical novels *Desfiguraţii* (1935; The Disfigured) and especially *Marele ospăţ* (1947; The Grand Repast) as well as the volume of short stories *Nălucile* (1945; The Apparitions) concentrate upon inner experience. *Marele ospăţ* is a cosmopolitan novel whose characters evolve in Romania, Italy, Germany, and France, forever torn between the grand repast of physical love and the anguished quest for a twin soul. For Grigore Olmazu, who is the married protagonist of the novel, the twin soul will seem to be, in turn, the vaguely revolutionary Russian traveller Ludmila whom he met most briefly in a frontier railway station at Vincovici, Giulia Molaioli, the sensual Italian wife of his brother Ion, and French actress Josette Gabin who came to Bucharest to play in Racine's *Phèdre*. For Grigore's wife Lucia, it will appear to be represented by John Heward, whom she encounters in Paris. The erotic short stories contained in the volume *Nălucile* (1945; The Apparitions) are centered upon female characters whose inner states of jealousy (in a young girl against a newly born baby brother), envy (transmuted into lust in an adolescent woman), divided love (for male partners who do not deserve it or who are perceived as possible destroyers), hesitation (between female and male friendship) are explored in their newly discovered richness and complexity.

Two later novels—*Pe văile Argeşului* (1950; On the Valleys of the Argeş) and *O vară la Şipotul Fîntînilor* (1957; A Summer at Şipotul Fîntînilor)—show the orientation towards larger social contexts. In the first, the author depicts Romanian life during the period between 1912 and 1918. The second speaks about the peasant revolts that took place in Romania at the beginning of the twentieth century and especially after the great uprising of 1907.

Works

Crinii roşii [Red Lilies] (1925). *Desfiguraţii* [The Disfigured] (1935). *Nălucile* [The Apparitions] (1945). *Călătorii*, versuri [Journeys, Poems] (1946). *Marele ospăţ*, roman [The Grand Repast, a Novel] (1947). *Fruct Nou*, versuri [New Fruit, Poems] (1948). With a Preface by Octav Şuluţiu. *Pe văile Argeşului*, roman [On the Valleys of the Argeş, a Novel] (1950). *O vară la Şipotul Fîntînilor* [A Summer at 'Şipotul Fîntînilor] (1957). *Versuri* [Poetry] (1966). With a Preface by D. Micu. *Poezii* [Poems] (1967).

Bibliography

Piru, Al, *Panorama deceniului literar românesc 1940–1950*(Bucharest, 1968), pp. 61–67. Stancu, Zaharia, *Antologia poetilor tineri* (Bucharest, 1934), pp. 147–151. Şáineanu, Const., "Sanda Movilă, *Crinii roşii." Recenzii (1924–1926)*. (Bucharest [1926]), pp. 31–34.

Sanda Golopentia

Doris Mühringer

Born September 18, 1920, Graz, Austria
Genre(s): poetry, prose, children's literature
Language(s): German

Doris Mühringer is quintessentially a poet, although she also writes short prose pieces. Her earliest publications are in the tradition of postwar formalism, and from that background she developed a uniquely individual voice, often expressed in hermetic form. Her major themes are human existential concerns—loneliness, isolation, yearning for love, search for significance, and the meaning that death casts on it all. Mühringer's lifetime of literary creativity has come to fruition within the past two decades, which have seen the publication of her major works.

Mühringer was born in Graz in 1920, and the indelible impressions of the childhood years were decisive for her subsequent creative writing, according to her later testimony. At the age of eleven she moved with her parents to Vienna, where she finished high school and began a program of literary studies at the university, which was, however, interrupted by the war. From 1945 to 1950 she did secretarial work in Salzburg, which she then gave up to devote full time to writing. Upon return to Vienna in 1954 she was associated with the prominent circle of poets that gathered around Hans Weigel, and her work appeared in the now-legendary postwar anthologies *Stimmen der Gegenwart*. In 1969 she made a reading and lecture tour of the United States, and a trip to Romania in 1972 resulted in an important cycle of poems. Mühringer lives today as a free-lance writer in Vienna where she is a member of the PEN Club and associated with the "Podium" circle of poets. Mühringer's poems result from a long process of gestation, and thus although she does not publish prolifically, what she does submit to print is always substantial. She is widely respected in her native country for her high standards and discrete reserve.

Mühringer began writing in traditional forms, and the early poems often display rhyme and regular rhythm. The rhyme began to disappear in *Gedichte II* (1969; Poems II), and her third volume, *Staub öffnet das Auge* (1976; Dust Opens the Eye), explores the possibilities of unrhymed verse. That work represents the culmination of a development toward increasingly hermetic form, which is matched by a thematic and tone of existential crisis. Poetic expression is highly condensed, and the lines sometimes consist of a single word, which is then highly evocative in contrast to the surrounding silence. Compression of form is evident also in the fourth volume, *Vögel die ohne Schlaf sind* (1984; Birds Who Are Without Sleep), together with occasional rhymed verse and a more reconciliatory thematic after the critical period. A type of retrospective is offered by a volume of poetry and photography, *Mein Tag—mein Jahr* (1983; My Day—My Year), published together with Hannelore Valencak in a project of true teamwork. In 1985 a volume of short prose appeared, *Tanzen unter dem Netz* (Dancing under the Net), in which are collected prose pieces from the preceding fifteen years. A volume of humorous poetry, *Nicht stets ist ein Trampel ein Trampel* (A Hick is Not Always a Hick), appeared in 1988.

Mühringer takes an illusionless, unsentimental stance toward life, and if her poetry is ultimately reconciliatory, it is a fought-for and hard-won reconciliation. Although autobiographical elements appear only indirectly, as encoded in images and metaphors, her work may be seen as the quest of an individual to find meaning and authenticity in life. A sense of loneliness and isolation is all-pervasive as the self feels itself a stranger and outsider in search of shelter but finding no place of refuge. The yearning for union with someone or something outside the self is realized occasionally in moments of togetherness when the other is experienced as a true friend or "brother"; more frequent however is the conception of love as a fragile construct predicated in any case on distance. There is also a desire for communion and harmony with nature, as exemplified for example in the cycle "Conversations with Rumanian Gods." The world, however, often appears as empty and uncertain, and the doubt and despair are expressed in key metaphors of shadow, darkness, and night. Death is the unconditional central experience that casts a pall on all that precedes it.

The theme of death occurs in numerous variations, from the almost transfigurative death of the mother, as in "Between Organ and Ace of Diamonds" and "Plant Flowers," to the voluntary death of fellow poets in poems such as "Dying in Rome" (for Ingeborg Bachmann), "On the Death of Paul Celan," and "In Memory of Hertha Kräftner." The poet empathizes with the impulse to seek release from suffering in death, and the alternative of meaningless prolongation of existence is presented in the Hölderlin poem, "Tübingen, June 7, 1843. Clarity in the Tower." The poet's own death is metaphorically transacted in "Dies irae," and "Les enfants du paradis" presents a horror vision of the hereafter. Insight into the motives for death, however, leads the poet to acceptance of life with its burden of guilt and responsibility, as dialectically thematized in the important poem "To Sing in the Darkness." Just as pain gives rise to silence and awareness of the contingency of life, as in "Dust Opens the Eye," so also poetry originates where the pain had been an indication of change.

The development is not so schematic as presented here, and Mühringer, like all good poets, deals with contradictions. There are moments of almost perfect harmony, as in "Under the Clouds," and the continual renewal of life is enacted in "Everyone's Easter." Although there is no transcendence or hereafter in the traditional sense, there yet exists a metaphysical dimension to life in our quest for meaning beyond pure materiality, and however elusive the ideal may be, it serves as the motor behind the works. The vision manifests itself in strong images, as in "Lost Goldfish in Dream," and metaphor in many cases serves as the central structural principle. Fairy-tale motifs take the form of gnomic, almost magical sayings and serve to express archetypal human experiences such as sacrifice and mystic union. There is also a playful strain and a droll, comical tone reminiscent of Anglo-Saxon humor. The speaker throughout remains in the back-ground, and under elimination of all inessentials the poems work through the power of their language.

The short prose works display a highly rhythmical language and are so compact in form that they could more properly be designated prose poems. As in Mühringer's poetry, the human being stands at the center of the various modes of narration, which range from artist's biography to fairy tale, from children's story to legend, and from cultural criticism to archaic and archetypal images. The laws of gravity as well as of logic are suspended, and a magical element in nature is accompanied by an almost somnambulistically certain sensitivity to language as the poet carefully chooses each word and phrase to have exactly the intended weight. On the premise that consciousness is shaped by language, these finely-chiseled pieces explore further the central questions of Who am I? Where did I come from? Where am I going?

Mühringer's works speak first of all for a postwar generation keenly aware of the existential limitations of the human condition. Further they speak for an audience of all those who have lived and experienced much but are too honest to claim that one understands life. Her precise, lapidary language carries a challenge to live consciously and authentically, which entails also coming to terms with death. From that perspective the poet is able to win a place of stillness, and the inner balance expresses itself in joy, wonder, and amusement. The courage to live, despite the atrocities and sufferings of mankind, comes in and through the self and expresses itself most completely in the images and rhythms of Mühringer's strong poetic language.

Works

Gedichte I (1957). *Das Märchen von den Sandmännlein. Ein Kinderbilderbuch* (1961). *Gedichte II* (1969). *Staub öffnet das Auge. Gedichte III* (1976). *Ein Schwan auf dem See. Spielbilderbuch für Kinder* (1980). [With Hannelore Valencak] *Mein Tag—mein Jahr* (1983). *Vögel die ohne Schlaf sind. Gedichte IV* (1984). *Tanzen unter dem Netz. Kurzprosa* (1985). *Nicht stets ist ein Trampel ein Trampel* (1988).

Bibliography

Bjorklund, Beth, "Interview with Doris Mühringer." *The Literary Review* 25 (1982): 201–205. Koppensteiner, Jürgen, and Beth Bjorklund, "'Dunkel ist Licht genug': Zur Lyrik von Doris Mühringer." *Modern Austrian Literature* 12 (1979): 192–207. Loidl, Peter Christian, "Wege im Dunkel. Möglichkeiten zur Analyse von Doris Mühringers poetischem Werk." Dissertation, Vienna, 1983. Van D'Elden, Karl H., "Drei österreichische Lyrikerinnen—Versuch eines Vergleichs." *Podium* 22 (1976): 14–16.

Beth Bjorklund

Tiny Mulder

Born 1921, Beetsterzwaag, The Netherlands
Genre(s): poetry, journalism
Language(s): Fries

Married to Jilderd Zuidema. Fries poet and journalist. Editor of *Friesch Dagblad*. She has published poems for children, and she has translated the works of James Krüs and Lewis Carroll.

Works

It boek foar de Fryske bern (1954). *Juffer Kuorkebier* (1957). *Viadukt* (1965). *Hwer hast it wei?* (1971).

Mary Hatch

Elisabeth Mulder de Daumer

Born 1904, Barcelona, Spain
Genre(s): novel, short story, poetry
Language(s): Spanish

The daughter of a South American mother and Dutch-born father, Mulder enjoyed the benefits of a cosmopolitan, refined education. Her extensive travel experience is reflected in novels, frequently set in foreign lands or exotic places. Mulder's education included study of several languages, and she worked as a translator, rendering into Spanish works by Baudelaire, Duhamel, Shelley, Keats, Pearl Buck, and Pushkin, among others. Her early efforts at creative writing produced several collections of poetry, a genre in which she achieved a modest renown before the Spanish Civil War (1936–1939). Her more significant achievements, however, are in the narrative.

Una sombra entre los dos (1934; A Shadow Between the Two) is her first work of fiction and suffers the usual aesthetic limitations of the thesis novel. However, it has been considered an important feminist statement, by contrast with later works that have been labeled escapist. Most of Mulder's novels are subjective, sentimental, and introspective, emphasizing the emotions, and this—together with her usual upper-class focus—resulted in pejorative classification by post-war critics with a predilection for working-class "social" realism. *Crepúsculo de una ninfa* (1942; Twilight of a Nymph), Mulder's first post-war novel, typifies the rather tentative fiction of the period in its avoidance of problematic subject matter, presenting a lyrical and melancholy treatment of the pathetic rural idyll and self-destructive emotions of a woman enamored of a man suffering a terminal illness. Most of Mulder's fiction of the 1940s and 1950s reflects the period's strict censorship, eschewing political themes.

El hombre que acabó en las islas (1944; The Man Who Ended Up in the Islands) incorporates certain elements of psychological *tremendismo* (a post-war neo-naturalism), but also reflects Romantic and Gothic influences, so that the end product is something of a pastiche. The skeptical, hedonistic hero, Juan Miguel, renounces a past life of psychological turmoil and civilization's complexities for a simplistic earthly paradise in the perpetual inactivity of the Antilles.

One of Mulder's most valuable sociological studies is *Las hoqueras de otoño* (1945; Autumn Bonfires), which portrays a mid-life crisis in the relationship of a mature Spanish couple. In *Preludio a la muerte* (1946; Prelude to Death) the writer reconstructs the relationship of two women who meet while studying in Switzerland, becoming both friends and rivals. Here the use of a foreign setting may result from the potentially censurable suicide of the disillusioned protagonist at novel's end. With its sensitive insights into friendship and love, refined perceptions and sensations, profound and dramatic psychological analysis, this non-tendentious feminist novel has been seen as one of Mulder's best.

Alba Grey (1947) begins in the mansion of a dying marquis, proceeding to a tour of Egypt by way of Italy. More deserving of the escapist label than most of Mulder's works, this sentimental romance occasionally suffers from excess plot contrivance and, at its worst, exhibits stylized rhetoric and comes dangerously near the melodramatic. Alba, the heroine, struggles between the violent, absorbing passion inspired by Gian Carlo and a more serene, spiritual love offered by Lorenzo. Their passions are played out before a backdrop of heavily aristocratic decor with a cast of cosmopolitan Italian nobles. Relatively well received by conservative Spanish critics, the novel ends with a marriage of convenience.

In *El vendedor de vidas* (1953; The Seller of Lives), an astrologer who foresees his own death without realizing it becomes the center of a well-structured portrait of somber post-war Spain viewed from the perspective of lower-class Barcelona. The novel spans several years between the clairvoyant's vision of a fatal future incident and his own demise.

Although presentation of a pro-Republican perspective was impossible under the Franco regime, it slowly became feasible to move away from exaltation of the victors to general condemnation of warfare, the context in which Mulder's *Eran cuatro* (1954; There Were Four) should be placed. A mother whose four sons died in the Civil War undertakes a symbolic quest for reconciliation, visiting sites and persons important in the lives of her sons, three of whom served the victorious Nationalists (or Franco-led Fascists) as aviator, soldier, and spy, respectively, while the fourth was a Republican Anarchist. Failing in her desperate attempt to mediate a symbolic postmortem reduction of the conflict, the mother slips into madness and finally death. *Luna de las máscaras* (1958; Moon of the Masks), one of Mulder's best-executed novels, is of value as a contrasting, offsetting balance to contemporaneous products of novelistic *engagement*, which portrayed the wealthy almost exclusively as parasites. In *Moon of the Masks*, the writer recreates a love triangle, two of whose participants are a famous sculptor and a well-known actress. The characters' remembrances and introspective thoughts are precipitated by an automobile accident.

Mulder was highly regarded by Spanish critics and fellow practitioners of the narrative arts during the 1950s and 1960s, and Eugenio de Nora (the only professional scholar who has discussed this writer) judged Mulder a quarter century ago to be the only woman writer of the period potentially comparable to Pardo Bazán, a judgment that now appears out of phase. Some of Mulder's waning popularity in the past two decades may be due to her view of society as vitiated, characterized by depressing sterility, an apprehension producing bitter melancholy in her fiction. Her better qualities—exquisite sensibility, refinement of perceptions and sensations, the capturing of subtle nuances, and elegance of expression—recall the cult of "pure" prose among the "dehumanized" narrators of the Generation of 1925, likewise currently out of fashion.

Works

Alba Grey (1947; rpt. 1950). *La canción cristalina*, poems (1928). *Crepúsculo de una ninfa* (1942). *Los cuentos del viejo reloj*, children's stories (1941). *Una china en la casa y otras historias*, short stories (1941). *Día negro*, novelette (1953). *Embrujamiento*, poetry (1927). *Eran cuatro* (1954). *Flora*, novelette (1953). *La historia de Java*, children's story (1935; rpt. 1943, 1961). *Las hogueras de otoño* (1945). *La hora emocionada*, poems (1931). *El hombre que acabó en las islas* (1944; rpt. 1966). *Luna de las máscaras* (1958). *Las noches del qato verde*, children's story (1963). *Preludio a la muerte* (1946). *Sinfonía en rojo*, poetry (1929?). *Una sombra entre los dos* (1934). *El vendedor de vidas* (1953).

Bibliography

General references: Nora, Eugenio [García] de, *La novela española contemporánea*, II (2 ed. 1968). *Women Writers of Spain*, ed. C.L. Galerstein (Westport, CT, 1986).

Janet Perez

Christa Müller

Born March 8, 1936, Leipzig, Germany
Genre(s): short story, lyric poetry
Language(s): German

Christa Müller studied work psychology in Dresden and mass communications (film and television) in Babelsberg. Since 1962 she has worked as a dramatic advisor in the film industry. At present she resides in Potsdam (DDR). Her stories revolve around the feelings of children, the joys of child-raising, the burdens of women responsible for jobs and family. In the story "Flüge," the distinctly autobiographical ring to the sensitive description of growing up during World War II contrasts with its historical perspective.

Works

[Co-author] *Kieselsteine* [Pebbles], lyric poetry (1975). *Vertreibung aus dem Paradis* [Expulsion from Paradise], short stories (1979, 2nd ed. 1981). "Der Berg" rpt. in *Erzähler der DDR. Band 2* (1985). "Flüge" rpt. in *Gespräche hinterm Haus. Neue Prosa aus dem DDR* (1981).

Bibliography

DLL. Vol. 10, p. 1442. Hildebrandt, Christel, *Zwölf schreibende Frauen in der DDR. Zu den Schreibbedingungen von Schriftstellerinnen in der DDR in den 70er Jahren* (Hamburg, 1984), pp. 67–74. Schmitz, Dorothee, *Weibliche Selbstentwürfe und männliche Bilder. Zur Darstellung der Frau in DDR-Romanen der siebziger Jahre* (Frankfurt a.M., 1983).

Ann Marie Rasmussen

Clara Müller

Born February 5, 1861, Lenzen near Belgard/ Pomerania; died November 4, 1905, Wilhemshagen near Erkner
Genre(s): short story, essay, lyric poetry, autobiography
Language(s): German

Müller was the daughter of the minister Wilhelm Müller in Pomerania near the coast of the Baltic Sea. Until the age of twelve, her father, a strong admirer of the Social Democrats who consequently influenced his daughter in this direction, was her only teacher. After his death she continued studying by herself and passed the School of Commerce exam in 1877 in Berlin. Because of continuous sickness, she had to stay with her mother for many years, but she was able to home tutor students. In 1884 she moved to Kolberg and soon found employment with the *Zeitung für Pommern* (Pomeranian Newspaper). Clara Müller was one of the most outstanding socialist lyric poetesses in the nineteenth century and also published a number of remarkable short

stories and essays in various journals. She contributed to the journals *Neuland* (New Territory), *Deutsche Romanzeitung* (German Journal for Novels), *Monatsblätter* (Monthly Journal), the *Monatshefte für neue Litteratur und Kunst* (Monthly Journal for Literature and Art), and to the Social Democratic journals *Neue Welt* (New World) and *Gleichheit* (Equality) among others. Her poems contain strong images of social reality and describe man's desperate struggle against existential threats to his life. They also express Müller's fervent support of the Social Democratic movement. She married the painter Oskar Jahnke, who posthumously edited her poems in 1907.

Works

Mit roten Kressen [With Red Cresses], poems (1898; 2nd enlarged ed. 1900). *Sturmlieder vom Meer* [Storm Songs About the Sea], poems (1901). *Ich bekenne* [I Confess], autobiography (1904). *Gesammelte Gedichte* [Collected Poems], 2 vols. (1907). *Gesamtausgabe* [Collected Works] (1910).

Bibliography

Böttcher, Kurt, ed., *Lexikon deutschsprachiger Schriftsteller*, vol. 2 (Kronberg, 8. Ts. 1974), p. 112. *Kürschners Deutscher Literatur-Kalender, Nekrolog 1901–1935*, ed. G. Lüdtke, rpt. of the 1936 ed. (Berlin and New York, 1973), p. 479. Palaky, Sophie, ed., *Lexikon deutscher Frauen der Feder*, vol. 2 (Berlin, 1898).

Albrecht Classen

Herta Müller

Born August 17, 1953, Nitzkydorf, Romania
Genre(s): novel, short story
Language(s): German

Herta Müller grew up as a member of the dwindling German-speaking ethnic minority ("Siebenbürger Sachsen" and "Banater Schwaben") in Romania. From 1973 to 1976 she studied German and Romance literatures at the University of Temeswar (Temeschburg), Romania, where she later worked as a German teacher. Her first book, *Niederungen*, appeared in Romania in 1982. Its republication by the West Berlin publishing house Rotbuch in 1984 was a breakthrough, since the work of German-speaking Romanians rarely appears in the West.

After applying for permission to emigrate in 1985, Herta Müller, who is a committed socialist, was officially forbidden to travel and publish. Eventually, however, she and her husband, the poet Richard Wagner, received visas allowing them to leave. They arrived in West Germany in March 1987, where Herta Müller was awarded the Ricarda-Huch prize three months later.

Composed in acute, deceptively simple language, *Der Mensch ist ein grosser Fasan auf der Welt* (1986) follows the German-speaking miller Windisch, his life in a dying village in Romania whose occupants are leaving for the West, and his own preparations for emigration. The central presence in the work, however, is death—the passing of a language, a culture, a way of life—and the allusions to the work of Paul Celan are unmistakable. The depth and intensity of Müller's vision give her haunting story the force of contained passion.

Works

Niederungen [Lowlands], short stories (1982, 1984). *Der Mensch ist ein grosser Fasan auf der Welt* [Man Is a Great Pheasant in This World], story (1986). *Barfüssiger Februar* [Barefoot February], short prose (1987)

Bibliography

Delius, Friedrich Christian, "Jeden Monat einen neuen Besen." Rev. of *Niederungen* by Herta Müller. *Der Spiegel* 30 (July 1984). Hensel, Klaus, "Alles, was ich tat, das hiess jetzt: warten. Die ausgewanderte rumäniendeutsche Schriftstellerin Herta Müller im Gespräch mit Klaus Hensel." *Frankfurter Rundschau* 8 (August 1987); ZB 2 [interview]. "'Jetzt hoffen die Rumänen auf Gorbatschow.' Die Schriftsteller Herta Müller und Richard Wagner über die deutsche Minderheit im Ceausescu-Staat." *Der Spiegel* 4 (May 1987): 154–163 [interview]. Michaelis, Rolf, "Angst vor Freude. Herta Müllers fünfzehn Prosastücke *Niederungen*." *Die Zeit* 24 (August 1984). Michaelis, Rolf, "Angekommen wie nicht da." *Die Zeit* 20 (March 1987). Müller-Wieferig, Matthias, "Ein Fasan mit Ausreiseantrag. Die rumäniendeutsche Schriftstellerin Herta Müller über ihre Gründe im Lande Ceausescus." *Saarbrücker Zeitung* 7 (January 1987) [interview; partial reprint as "Kultur auf gepackten Koffern" in *TAZ* 24. March 1987]. Schneider, H., "Eine Apotheose des Hässlichen und Abstossenden. Anmerkungen zu Herta Müllers *Niederungen*." *Der Donauschwabe* (Weihnachten, 1984), p. 6. Wittstock, Uwe, "Hundert Beete voll Mohn im Gedächtnis. *Niederungen*—ein erstaunlicher Prosaband der deutsch schreibenden Rumänin Herta Müller." *Frankfurter Allgemeine Zeitung* 17 (April 1984). Reviews of *Der Mensch ist ein grosser Fasan auf der Welt: Neue Zürcher Zeitung* 10/11. (May 1986); *Süddeutsche Zeitung* 14./15. (June 1986).

Ann Marie Rasmussen

Elisabeth von Münden

(see: Elisabeth von Calenberg-Göttingen)

Anna von Munzingen

Born 1316, Adelhausen, Germany; died 1327, Adelhausen
Genre(s): Convent chronicle
Language(s): Latin

Anna von Munzingen, a nun and later prioress of the convent of Adelhausen near Freiburg (Black Forest) in the early fourteenth century, composed the convent chronicle of Adelhausen, *De sanctitate primarum sanctarum Sororum monasterii beatae virginis de annuntiatione in Adelhausen*, in 1318, presumably in Latin. While the original is not extant, the Freiburg city archive contains ms. 98, i.e., the German translation copied by Johannes Hull of Strasbourg in 1433. A later shortened version made for the purpose of monastic reform by Johannes Meyer in 1482 is extant in two identical versions (ms. 107, 268r–287v and ms. 108, 199r–212v). A further, more recent ms. may be seen in Einsiedeln (ms. 694, 133–215).

The convent of Adelhausen was founded in 1234, originally as a *samnunge* for beguines, and was transformed into a Dominican convent in 1245. It was reformed by Johannes Meyer in the late fifteenth century. The early members of Adelhausen took an active part in the mystical life common to many convents of Southern Germany and Switzerland—a woman's spiritual movement that preceded by about a century the much better-known masters of mysticism (Eckhart, Seuse, Tauler). The name of the convent of Adelhausen, which was dissolved in 1867, is familiar today mainly to art historians because of the famous sculpture in the convent, i.e., a statue of Christ with John resting against his chest—often considered the prototype of mystical art.

Anna von Munzingen's chronicle portrays the lives of thirty-four nuns, most of whom had died before she started to write. This collection of *vitae* of mystically gifted nuns is the earliest one in the tradition of contemporary convent chronicles written by women. [Others are Engelthal, Katharinenthal, Kirchberg, Oetenbach, Tö (see Elsbeth Stagel), Unterlinden (see Katharina von Gebersweiler) and Weiler.] *Schwesternbücher* (i.e. "Books of Sisters") are idealized descriptions of mystical experiences and special graces received by earlier members of the convents in question and of the nun's ascetic efforts. Rather than reacting to these *vitae* as sickening accounts of psychically overwrought nuns, as they have sometimes been labelled, the reader should understand them as inner biographies whose plots follow hagiographic patterns set by legends. The structural principle involved is that of an accounting of exemplary lives. Their authors (who are not considered mystics themselves) speak about the "special graces" as a desirable goal and compose the chronicles to provide edifying reading material in the convents.

The Adelhausen chronicle is not a mystical work as such. Anna von Munzingen merely intends to give a description of "*die gnade, die unser Herre hette getan semlichen swestern . . . ze Adelnhusen.*" The content of some of her accounts may equally be found in other chronicles and in various hagiographical writings of her time. Thus, for example, the story of the life and many visions of Else von der Nuwenstatt (Elisabeth of Neustadt) presumably existed in an earlier version and was used by several authors.

Judging (perhaps unfairly) by the German translation made ca. 1345–1350, the book is composed in a somewhat simple and repetitive style. But its writer, Anna von Munzingen, presumably was an educated woman and a capable author. She freely claims the authorship of her work whose intention, typical for writings of this kind, she states as: "*Wer das liset oder höret lesen, der sol Gott loben vnd ere sagen.*"

Works

Die Chronik der Anna von Munzingen, ed. J. König, in *Freiburger Diözesan Archiv* 13 (1880): 129–236.

Translation: "The *vita* of Elisabeth of Neustadt." *The Soul Afire*, ed. H.A. Reinhold (New York, 1944), pp. 83–86.

Bibliography

Blank, Walter, *Die Nonnenviten des 14. Jahrhunderts.* Diss., Freiburg, 1962. Kunze, Georg, *Studien zu den Nonnenviten des deutschen Mittelalters.* Diss., Hamburg, 1952. Krebs, Engelbert, "Die Mystik in Adelhausen," in *Festgabe Heinrich Finke* (Münster, 1904).

General references: *Verfasserlexikon*, 2nd ed. I (1978), p. 365f. (Walter Blank) and 1st ed. I (1933), p. 86f. (Engelbert Krebs). *Lexikon für Theologie und Kirche*, 2nd ed., 1 (1957), p. 141 (Wolfgang Müller). *Neue deutsche Biographie* I (1953), p. 303 (Friedrich Hefele). *Kirchliches Handlexikon* I (1907), p. 57 (Karl Bihlmeyer).

Other references: *Freiburger Diözesan Archiv* 69, n.s. 1 (1949–1950), pp. 132–148 (Heinrich Schneider).

Gertrud Jaron Lewis

Amélie Murat

Born 1882, Chamalieres, Puy de Dome,
    France; died 1940, Montferrand, France
Genre(s): poetry, novel
Language(s): French

What Amélie Murat wanted from life and what her life turned out to be were quite distinct. Although she loved, she never married nor did she ever seem content with her life as a single woman. She came to Paris in 1904, and the disappointments and frustrations she experienced there became the stuff of her poetry: *Le Sanglot d'Eve* (1923; Eve's Sobbing) is addressed to women who have suffered for love or *Passion* (1929) which includes her "Berceuse pour l'enfant qui n'existe pas" (Lullaby for the Child Who Does Not Exist). The recognition of her achievements brought Murat some satisfaction. In 1930, she received the Prix Jean-Moreas for her works and she was considered to be the greatest female poet from Auvergne. After her death she was not forgotten. In 1946, a posthumous collection of her poems, *Poésie, c'est délivrance* (Poetry—A Deliverance) was published. A few years later (1953), the Prix Amélie Murat was established in her honor to be given each year to female poets.

Murat's early works exhibit some infelicities of style and were not well received at their publication. They rely more upon their emotional force rather than their "poetry" to carry the reader along. As she developed both stylistically and thematically, she wrote with an increased sureness of rhythm and rhyme. Her recurrent themes are those of passion, sorrow, and loneliness, which she expresses in a mixture of Christian and nature imagery. Yet she is neither a religious poet nor a poet of nature, for neither role offers Murat the lasting comfort and solace she seeks. Her deliverance comes through poetry itself. *Vivre encore* (1937; Still Alive) celebrates life and is a fitting culmination to her career.

Works

D'un coeur fervent (1908). Le Livre de poésie (1912). Humblement sur l'autel (1919). Bucoliques d'été (1920). La Maison heureuse (1921). Le Rosier blanc (1923). Le Sanglot d'Eve (1923). Passion (1929). La Bête divine (1929). Solitude (1930). Le Rosaire de Jeanne (1933). Le Chant de la vie (1935). Vivre encore (1937). Poésie, c'est délivrance (posthumous, 1946).

Bibliography

Many reviews of her works can be found in the *Mercure de France*. Delzangles, F. ed., *Biographies et morceaux choisis d'écrivains d'Auvergne* (Tournemine, 1933). Dumas, André, *Poètes nouveau. Anthologie Delagrave* (Paris, 1939).

Edith Joyce Benkov

Anna Murià i Romani

Born 1904, Barcelona, Spain
Genre(s): novel, children's literature,
  journalism, criticism
Language(s): Catalan

Due in part to her growing up in Barcelona at a time when several popular movements were strong, Murià became involved in the women's movement at an early age. She studied at the Catalan Woman's Institute of Culture and Popular Library in 1927, the year which saw the beginning of her contributions to the daily press. She became a political activist shortly before the inception of the Republic in 1930 and was identified both with leftist groups and the Catalan regional independence movement. During the Civil War, she became a member of the Central Committee of the Estat Català, and as a result, was forced into exile in France when Barcelona fell to the Franco forces in 1939. That year, she met and married Agustí Bartra, a Catalan novelist and poet, sharing an odyssey of exile in the Dominican Republic, Cuba and Mexico, where they lived until 1970, when the pair returned to Catalonia after some three decades.

Distinguished for her critical studies of her husband's poetry and her works of children's fiction, Murià has also published a number of significant novels, little noticed by criticism within Spain (the usual fate of writers in exile during the Franco regime). *Joana Mas* (1933) is an ambitious portrait of two very different, contrasting female types. One, the protagonist and title character, realizes her life's ambition when she manages a marriage of convenience with a wealthy, older man. Representing an alternative lifestyle is a single and economically independent woman whose work constitutes a tenuous stability in her unsettled emotional life. Murià's apparent intention is to present opposed feminist models, alternative possibilities for women, but perhaps because of the dualistic conception, psychological profundity suffers.

La peixera (1938; The Fish-Bowl) may be viewed as a fable for the twentieth-century worker, in which the title image functions as a symbol for entrapment. Her protagonist, a young man, finds himself in an economic situation lacking all potential for advancement or self-improvement (circumstances perhaps still more applicable to the working woman). His job as a clerk in a dreary office (whose resemblance to a cell is enhanced by iron bars) permits him to glimpse the sky only via a tiny aperture in the ceiling, which suggests the limiting form of a fish-bowl with its open top. The extremes of boredom suffered by the young man, the unvarying monotony of his days, are unrelieved tedium, much like the existence of imprisoned fish.

Res no és veritat, Alícia (1984; Nothing Is True, Alicia) is a portrait of a potentially incestuous but unconfessed and unconsummated attraction between brother and sister. The female protagonist seeks out another man when a second woman becomes sentimentally linked to her brother, hoping to find in another the virtues perceived in her sibling. The novel ends somewhat inconclusively, its text followed by an authorial autobiography.

Murià's most ambitious narrative work is *Aquest serà el principi* (1985; This Will Be the Beginning), a complex narrative of some 500 pages spanning three historical epochs: (1) the period of the Second Republic 1931–1936; (2) the period of exile, 1939 to circa 1970; (3) the period of the exiles' return to Catalonia. The autobiographical basis is clear as well as the reflection of recent and contemporary Spanish history, but the work is not presented as an autobiography. There is no character representing the author; Murià's experiences are divided among several different characters, each corresponding to a specific aspect of her life. In addition to the absence of an authorial alter ego, there is an absent or missing narrator (or central narrative consciousness): all characters speak for themselves, with impressionistic perspectivism being the result.

Although Murià has received little attention from critics in Spain or elsewhere, this is the almost inevitable result of her writing in a minority language (Catalan) unknown to most of the reading public in her lands of exile, while her exile, until near the end of the Franco era, resulted in loss of contact with the cultural and intellectual in-groups within Spain. Her mature fiction is well-conceived and well-written and constitutes a significant contribution to the corpus of novels written by women in Catalonia.

Works

Aquest serà el principi (1985). Joana Mas (1933). La peixera (1938). Res no és veritat, Alícia (1984).

Bibliography

General references: *Women Writers of Spain*, ed. C.L. Galerstein (Westport, Conn., 1986).

Janet Perez

Marthe-Marguerite le Valois de Villette de Mursay, Comtesse de Caylus

(alphabetized as Caylus)

Vera Mutafčieva

Born March 28, 1929, Sofia, Bulgaria
Genre(s): novel, short story, criticism, film
*   script, scholarly monograph*
Language(s): Bulgarian

Mutafčieva became a novelist when she was a well-known scholar with more than fifty publications in Bulgarian and Ottoman history. The daughter of Petur Mutafčiev, one of Bulgaria's great historians, she is on her way to becoming one of Bulgaria's foremost novelists. Born, raised, and educated in Sofia, Mutafčieva graduated from the University of Sofia in 1951. She worked as a researcher at the Institute of History and the Institute of Balkan Studies of the Bulgarian Academy of Sciences and in 1978 received her doctorate in history. She has also served as director of the Center for Ancient Languages and of the Bulgarian Research Institute in Vienna. She is presently affiliated with the Institute of Literature in Sofia.

In 1960 her first popular historical works appeared, and in following years she published her first fiction with the series *Geroična letopis* (1961; Heroic Chronicle). *Letopis na smutnoto vreme* (1966–1967; Chronicle of the Time of Troubles) presents a vivid description of the Bulgarian-Ottoman time of troubles of the second half of the eighteenth century. The striking depiction of the forays, strife, and anarchy created by local freebooters is blended with the main trends of the sociopolitical struggles. Mutafčieva successfully integrates real historical events and personalities with imaginary episodes and figures to create authentic literary characters. *Slučajet D'em* (1967; The Dzem Case) is one of Mutafčieva's most successful novels. Praised by critics, it has been translated into many languages. It treats an East-West episode of the fifteenth century, the fate of an exile caught in "the great games" that states play in history.

Dzem becomes a pawn in the conflict between the Ottoman Empire and the Western powers, and the Balkans are caught in the middle. In *Ricarjat* (1970; The Knight), *Alkiviad Malki* (1975; Alcibiades the Little), *Alkiviad Veliki* (176; Alcibiades the Great), and other novels, Mutafčieva uses the past to make a point about the present. Mutafčieva evaluates each historical epoch, personality, or idea from an historical perspective.

Using her artistic skills and a psychohistorical approach, Mutafčieva analyzes each of her heroes/ villains in relations to both their time and ours. Being a scholarly novelist, Mutafčieva paints objective pictures of the past and discovers in events, personalities, and ideas many common elements throughout history.

Works

Goljamata borba (1961). Kŭrdzaliisko verme 91962). Povest za dobroto i zloto (1963). Da se znae (1964). Eseta (1969). I Klio e muza (1969). Poslednite Šišmanovci (1969, 1975). Geroika. Ocerci za Kozlodui (1972). Procesŭt. Povest (1972). Belot na dve rŭce (1973). Bogomili. Istoriceski razkaz za deca (1974; 1976). Železni stupki. Istoriceski razkaz za deca (1974). Povest s dvoino duno (1974). Kniga za Sofronii (1978). Bombite. Roman (1985). Sŭedinenieto pravi silata. Roman (1985).

Bibliography

Beljaeva, Sabina, "Istoriceskite romani na Vera Mutafcieva." *Plamŭk* 22 (1972): 62–68. Bŭčvarova, Svoboda, "S erudicija i darba." *Plamŭk* 7 (1968): 79–82. Davidov, Nešo, "Osmisljane no istorijata." *Literaturen front* 2 (January 2, 1968). Kolevski, V., T. Žecev, V. Bojad'ieva, *Ocerci po istorija na bŭlgarskata literatura sled deveti Septemvri 1944 godina. Pŭrva kniga. Teorija, roman, drama* (1979), pp. 255–272. Konstantinova, Elka, "Istorija i sŭvremennost." *Narodna kultura* 51 (December 23, 1967). Likova, Rozalija, "Čovekŭt i vremeto v edin istoričeski roman." *Narodna kultura* 33 (August 13, 1966). Nedelčev, Mihail, "Izmerenijata no 'Slučajat D'em." *Septemvri* 5 (1968): 235–238. Petrov, A., E. Konstantinov, Kr. Kuiumdziev, *Ocerci po istorija na bŭlgarskata literatura sled deveti Septemvri 1944 Vtora kniga: Poezija, Povest i razkaz* (1980), pp. 385–398.

Philip Shashko

Eva Mylona

Born 1938
Genre(s): poetry
Language(s): Greek

Eva Mylona's poetry is similar to Nana Isaia's in its preoccupation with the subjective self and feelings of emptiness and despair, but her style is significantly different. Her clean one-line strokes paint painstakingly accurate pictures that often bring to mind *The Waste Land*. At such times the poet exhibits extraordinary control over her material, which may mistakenly be interpreted as non-involvement or aloofness.

Her first book of poetry, *Taxidi* (Journey), published in 1972, deals with the journey within after all avenues for an outward journey have been cut off and all devices such as compasses and passports have been "scattered." William Spanos, in reviewing this book, observes that the best poems of this collection are not those that deal with the radically subjective interior journey, which border on solipsism, but rather those that depart from the journey within to encounter and address the admittedly deformed and limited world without.

In *Katharo Metallo* (Pure Metal), her second book of poems, Mylona pursues the theme of a beautiful world that has become a waste land more intensely, taking issue with the despoilers, and painting vivid pictures of lifelessness (people have become things) and death.

Works

Taxidi [Journey]. Bilingual edition (Greek-English), tr. Sylvia Mood (1972). *Katharo Metallo* [Pure Metal] (1975).

Anthologized translations: *Book of Women Poets from Antiquity to Now*, ed. Aliki Barnstone and Willis Barnstone (1980). *Contemporary Greek Poetry*, tr. Kimon Friar (1985).

Bibliography

Review by William Spanos. *Books Abroad*, 46, ä1 (1972): 158. *Bulletin analytique de bibliographie hellènique, 1970* (Athènes, 1973). Decavalles, Andonis, "Modernity: The Third Stage, the New Poets." *The Charioteer* 20 (New York, 1978).

Helen Dendrinou Kolias

Myro

(see: Moero)

Myrtiotissa

(see: Theone Drakopoulou)

Myrtis

Born date unknown, Anthedon, Boeotia
  (Greece)
Genre(s): lyric poetry
Language(s): Greek

Our most important information about Myrtis comes from a fragment (*PMG* 664a) attributed to a fellow Boeotian poet, the famous Corinna of Tanagra (q.v.). Corinna first describes Myrtis as "clear-voiced" (a conventional term for a lyric poet), then condemns her because "though a woman, she entered into contention with Pindar." What we know of Greek cultural realities points to the unlikelihood of mixed-sex singing contests actually taking place in fifth century B.C. Boeotia. Corinna must mean that Myrtis attempted to imitate Pindar's poetic manner. Her lines therefore serve as evidence for the existence of established Greek norms of "women's writing"—norms that Myrtis, in Corinna's view, expressly violated.

Since the link between Myrtis and Pindar is, consequently, a purely literary one, this fragment cannot be used to determine her date or that of Corinna although it gives the impression that Myrtis lived at a somewhat earlier period. Tales that Myrtis was Corinna's or Pindar's teacher are only biographical conjectures by much later commentators who knew no more than we do.

Plutarch (*Quaest. graec.* 40 Ć *PMG* 716) summarizes a myth recounted by Myrtis. Her story of Ochne's tragic passion for the Tanagrian hero Eunostos, similar in plot to the tale of Potiphar's wife, purported to explain why a grove sacred to him was forbidden to women. If this single sample is representative, Myrtis, like Corinna, was interested in preserving obscure local legends. Concern with the aetiology of a cult practice, though certainly not unheard of in earlier times, is especially characteristic of Hellenistic poets. Since modern scholarly opinion seems to be moving toward the acceptance of a late date for Corinna, that observation may also suggest an approximate date for Myrtis.

Works

Greek text in *Poetae Melici Graeci*, ed. D.L. Page (Oxford, 1962).

Translation: English translation in *Lyra Graeca* III, tr. J.M. Edmonds (Cambridge, Mass.: Loeb Classical Library, 1959).

Bibliography

Cupaiuolo, N., *Poetesse Greche: Corinna* (Naples, 1939). Kirkwood, G.M., *Early Greek Monody: The History of a Poetic Type* (Ithaca, 1974). Page, D.L., *Corinna* (Oxford, 1963). Snyder, J.M., *The Woman and the Lyre* (Carbondale, Il., 1989). Trypanis, C.A., *Greek Poetry from Homer to Seferis* (Chicago, 1981).

General references: *Cambridge History of Classical Literature I: Greek Literature*, eds. P.E. Easterling and B.M.W. Knox (Cambridge, 1985), p. 241. *Oxford Classical Dictionary* (Oxford, 1970), p. 716. Pauly-Wissowa, *Real-Encyclopädie der klassischen Altertumswissenschaft* XI.2 (Stuttgart, 1922), p. 1394.

Other references: Guillon, P., *Annales de la Faculté des Lettres et Sciences Humaines d'Aix* 33 (1959): 155–168. Skinner, M.B., *Tulsa Studies in Women's Literature* 2 (1983): 9–20.

Marilyn B. Skinner

N

Top Naeff

Born 1878; died 1953
Genre(s): criticism, drama, essay, poetry, novel
Language(s): Dutch

Top Naeff is mostly remembered for her girls' books, especially *Schoolidyllen* (1900), which brought her initial fame. The protagonists in these books come generally from more or less well-to-do middle class families, and they rebel against the hypocrisy, conventionalism, and authoritarianism of their virtuous parents. Later, however, they conform and resign themselves somewhat to their bourgeois fate.

Born into a well-to-do bourgeois family herself, the author was acutely aware of the limitations of her milieu and suffered from them but was emotionally too much rooted in her social environment to be able to detach herself from it completely. She never married and lived for most of her life in the house she owned in Dordrecht.

In her novels and novellas she depicts with irony and sometimes sarcasm the conventional bourgeois life that she experienced as stifling and hypocritical. Behind the "nice" marriages and the "nice" interactions of her characters she shows disillusionment, boredom, and suffering. Marriage as a comedy and empty duty is a stock element in her work. Most of her characters, as in the excellent novella collections *Voorbijgangers* (1925; Passers-By) and *Juffrouw Stolk en andere verhalen* (1936; Miss Stolk and Other Stories), are profoundly lonely and isolated people. Throughout her work one finds biting portrayals of the Dutch bourgeoisie as well as the author's own inescapable links with it.

Interestingly, the dark themes that pervade most of her fiction are practically absent from her witty autobiography *Zo was het ongeveer* (1950; That's More or Less the Way It Was).

Top Naeff worked for many years as theatre critic for *Elseviers Maanblad* and *De Groene Amsterdammer*, and wrote several plays herself. She also wrote a long study dedicated to a good friend, the actor Willem Royaards (1947).

Works

Verzameld Proza, 5 vols. (1953). *Dramatische Kronieken*, 4 vols. (1918–1923). *De genadeslag* (1899). *Aan flarden* (1901). *Het weerzien* (1905). *Zie de maan schijnt...* (1905). *Charlotte von Stein* (1921). *Twee toneelspeelsters: Sarah Bernhardt en Elenora Duse* (1934). *Schoolidyllen* (1900). *De tweelingen* (1901). *'t Veulen* (1903). *In den dop* (1906). *Zo was het ongeveer* (1950). *In mineur* (1902). *De dochter* (1905). *De glorie* (1906). *Oogst* (1908). *Vriendin* (1920). *Voorbijgangers* (1925). *Klein avontuur* (1928). *Offers* (1932). *Juffrouw Stolk en andere verhalen* (1936). *Mijn grootvader en ik en andere verhalen* (1966). *Tredmolen en andere verhalen* (1967). *De stille getuige* (1906). *Voor de poort* (1912). *Letje* (1926). *Een huis in de rij* (1935). *Klein witboek* (1947).

Bibliography

Bruning, Gerard, *Nagelaten Werk* (Nijmegen, 1950), pp. 194–201. Coster, Dirk, *Proza II*, pp. 99–108. Donker, Anthonie, *Critisch Bulletin* (Oct. 1949): 447–450. Knuvelder, Gerard, *Handboek tot de geschiedenis der Nederlandse letterkunde*, vol. 4, 2nd ed. (1961), pp. 204, 335, 336–338. Nijhoff,

Martinus, "Aagje Ammers en Top Deken," in *Gedachten of Dinsdag*, pp. 139–162. Romein-Verschoor, Annie, *De Nederlandse romanschrijfster na 1880* (Utrecht, 1935), pp. 82 ff. Vaartjes, Ge, "Top Naeff," in *'Tis vol van schatten hier*, vol. 1 (Amsterdam, 1986), pp. 210–211.

Maya Bijvoet

Ágnes Nemes Nagy

Born January 3, 1922, Budapest, Hungary
Genre(s): poetry, translation
Language(s): Hungarian

Nagy was educated in Budapest, also getting her teacher's diploma from the University of Budapest. Between 1945 and 1953 she worked for *Közneveles*, an education journal, and later taught in high school. Since 1957, she has supported herself with her writings. Her early poems in *Ujhold* and *Magyarok*, and her first volume of poetry, *Kettős világban* (1946; In a Double World), received favorable reviews. Two years later she won the Baumgarten Prize. During the repression of the 1950s, unable to publish her own works, she turned to translations. She is one of the most important translators of both poetry and drama, having translated Corneille, Racine, Molière, Berthold Brecht, etc. *Szárazvillám* (Heat Lightning), her second volume of poetry, was published in 1957, and in 1964 she published a collection of translations under the title *Vándorének* (Wandering Song). *Napforduló* (Solstice), a third volume of poetry, appeared in 1967, and in 1969 she published a selected volume as *Lovak és anyalok* (The Horses and the Angels). Her children's books, *Az arany ecset* (The Golden Brush) and *Lila fecske* (Purple Swallow) have the same fine feeling and intellectual approach as her other works. *64 hattyu* (64 Swans), a collection of essays on literature, appeared in 1975.

The early poems of Nagy reflect the horrors of war and the siege of Budapest, but her basic humanitarianism and her belief in her vocation triumph even here. She believed in the importance of poetry in human life, and this is evident in all of her work; in these early poems, tempering the horrors with detachment and perspective. Her poetry is intellectual and measured but not de-void of feeling. There is a balance and a wholeness in her verses, but her ideas are often expressed through abstractions. They are difficult, but their difficulty lies in the ideas they contain, not the style. "The modern poem," she has said, "is generally complicated because it wishes to elucidate complicated things. The obscurity of modern poetry is in reality the need for light" (Pomogáts, p. 416).

While far from an autobiographical author, certain aspects of her life find their way into her poetry. Nagy grew up equally at home in the city and in the country, for she spent her vacations with her relatives. An avid reader and a good student, she had the good fortune to have the poet Lajos Áprily as a teacher and as the principal of her school. An eccentric grandfather who was a great traveller gave her the image of the wise yet playful old man, and his book on ancient Egypt became the inspiration for one of her most important poem cycles. The Akhnathon poems carry some of her most complex ideas. She has said that "His mythically restless disposition—that of the perturber and the creator—is appropriate for me to attach to it the metaphysics of our age without metaphysics. Morality and death, materialism and resurrection—his figure can absorb all of these. . . . He lends us the countenance of the very first visionary man" (Tezla, p. 79). Her topic is existence, morality and ideas. Much less circumscribed by the Hungarian scene than most Hungarian poets, Nagy translates more easily. Her style and ideas, while deeply rooted in Hungarian culture, also transcend it. She avoids the expression of personal views to concentrate on universal solutions to human questions.

Works

Lila fecske (1965). *64 hattyu, tanulmányok* (1975). *Között, összegyüjtött versek* (1981). *Metszetek, esszék, tanúlmányok* (1982). *Selected poems*, tr. with an intro. and translator's preface by Bruce Berlind (1980). *Ocean at the Window, Hungarian Prose and Poetry since 1945*, Albert Tezla, ed. (1980).

Bibliography

"András Fodor, NNA—a költöi kép." *Kortárs*, no. 12 (1978), pp. 1992–1994. Berlind, Bruce, "ANN—poetry and translations." *New Hungarian Quarterly* 76 (1979): 153–160. Gálsai, Pongrác, "A lila *fecske." A besurranó szerkeszto* (Budapest, 1976), pp. 187–193. Gálsai, Pongrác, "NNA." *12 a 1 fo* (Budapest, 1978), pp. 134–148. "Iró szobám, Nemes Nagy Agnessel beszélget Mezei András." *Jelenkor*, no. 10 (1978), pp. 942–952. Lengyel, Balázs, "Között, NNA verseinek elemzése," in *Közelképek* (Budapest, 1979), pp. 326–349. Ottlik, Géza, "A Mondhatatlan és a nehezen mondható." *Kortárs* (1982): 130–133. Páskándi, Géza, "Nosztalgia Fenség és Rend utan." *Kortárs* (1982): 137–144. Pomogáts, Béla, *Az Ujabb magyar irodalom, 1945–1981* (Budapest, 1982). Pomogáts, Béla, "Rend és indulat, NNA." *Sorsát kereső irodalom* (Budapest, 1979), pp. 429–449. Szeles, Klára, "NNA liraja." *Kortárs* (1982): 1637–1641.

Enikő Molnár Basa

Zinaida Nagytė-Katiliškienė

(see: Liūnė Sutema)

Alice Nahon

Born August 16, 1896, Antwerp, Belgium;
    died May 21, 1933, Antwerp
Genre(s): poetry
Language(s): Dutch

In the wake of World War I and Flanders' devastation, Alice Nahon's poetry expressed the sense of loneliness, disillusion, and longing for happiness that most Belgians felt. Since then she has remained one of the most popular woman poets in Flanders, second only to the most widely-read poet, Guido Gezelle.

Her poems often speak of the misery she encounters in her short career as a nurse and of the powerlessness and pain she experienced as a tuberculosis patient in a sanatorium (1917–1923). Her early poems are overflowing with sentimentality, but the form is refreshingly simple. She has often been called "the poet of simplicity" because of the forthright stylistic grace with which she presents complex emotional experiences and longings. Nahon's work is clearly influenced by the poetry of Guido Gezelle, but her poems always strike a female sensitivity and a tone that we do not find in Gezelle's poetry. Her later work *Schaduw* (1928; Shadow), influenced

by the humanitarian expressionists, is less sentimental and embodies a more complex, richer use of language than her earlier poems.

Works
    Vondelingskens (1920). *Op Zachte Vooizekens* (1921). *Schaduw* (1928). *Gedichten* (1930). *Maart-April. Jeugdverzen en Nagelaten Gedichten, Verzameld en toegelicht door R. Korten* (1936). Translations: "Our Hands" (1928) from *Schaduw* (1928).

Bibliography
    A. Nahon Herdacht, with contributions by Marnix Gysen, Luc Indestege, Frans Smits, Urbain Van De Voorde, Gerard Walschap, and Lode Zielens (Brussels, 1934). Bossaert, H., *A. Nahon* (Antwerpen, 1974). Tazelaar, C., *Alice Nahon en haar Gedichten* (Leiden, 1926).

An Lammens

Marie von Najmájer

Born February 3, 1844, Budapest, Hungary;
    died August 25, 1904, Aussee, Austria
Genre(s): poetry, novel, drama, essay
Language(s): German, Hungarian

She was the daughter of the Royal-Hungarian court councillor Franz von Najmájer and experienced, as her parents' only child, a happy and carefree childhood. She learned her German only after her father was transferred to Vienna, where he died soon afterward in 1854. His death and her pain about it instigated her to begin writing lyric poetry although she had learned her German only recently. Since her mother had originally come from Vienna, they decided to stay in the Austrian capital. Through some friends Marie presented some of her works to the poet Franz Grillparzer, who encouraged the young poetess to publish her first lyric collection *Schneeglöckchen* (Snowdrops), which was warmly received by her reading audience. Marie was particularly concerned with the women's question and the position of the single working mother in her society, but she never joined the women's movement. She initiated the first scholarship for women students at the University of Vienna and financially supported the Association of Women Writers and Artists as well as a stipend for a girl at the Girls' High School in Vienna. She also published a number of articles on art and the women's movement in various journals.

Works

Schneeglöckchen [Snowdrops], poems (1868; 2nd ed. 1872). *Gedichte, neue Folge* [New Sequence], poems (1872). *Gurret-ül-Eyn, Bild aus Persiens Neuzeit in sechs Gesängen* [Gurret-ül-Eyn, a Picture from Persia's Modern History in Six Songs], epic poem (1874). *Gräfin Ebba* [Countess Ebba], epic poem (1877). *Schwedenkönigin* [Queen of Sweden], novel (1882, 2 vols.) *Johannisfeuer* [Midsummer Fire], play (1888). *Neue Gedichte* [New Poems] (1890). *Hildegun,* play (1899). *Der Stern von Navarra* [The Star of Navarra], 2 vols., novel (1900). *Die Göttin Eigentum* [The Goddess Materialism], poems (1900). *Kaiserin Julian* [Empress Julian], play (1903). *Nachgelassene Gedichte* [Posthumous Poems] (1905). *Dramatischer Nachla (Hildegund—Ännchen von Tharau—Der Goldschuh)* [Posthumous Plays—Hildegund—Ännchen von Tharau—The Golden Shoe] (1907).

Bibliography

Brümmer, Franz, "Marie von Najmájer." *Biographisches Jahrbuch* 9 (1906). Eisenberg, Ludwig, *Das geistige Wien*, vol. 1 (Vienna, 1893). Kosel, Hermann Clemens, ed., *Deutsch-Österreichisches Künstler-und Schriftsteller-Lexikon*, vol. 1 (Vienna, 1902). "Najmájer, Marie," in *Lexikon der deutschen Dichter und Prosaisten vom Beginn des 19. Jahrhunderts bis zur Gegenwart*, ed. Franz Brümmer, 6th rev. ed., vol. 5 (rpt. Nendeln/Liechtenstein, 1975), p. 99. Pataky, Sophie, ed., *Lexikon deutscher Frauen der Feder*, vol. 2 (Berlin, 1898).

Albrecht Classen

Lilika Nakou

Born 1903, Athens, Greece; died 1989
Genre(s): biography, novel, essay
Language(s): French, Greek

She is the daughter of the politician and sociologist L. Nakos. She studied piano and philosophy in Geneva and was a teacher of music for some time in Athens. Being fluent in French, she wrote in that language at the beginning of her literary career. While in Paris, she had the opportunity of meeting and interacting with such leading literary and scientific figures as R. Roland, Colette, Barbusse, A. Gide, Einstein, M. de Unamuno, and others. M. de Unamuno had a significant influence on her writings, and it is mainly thanks to him that Nakou started writing in Greek.

She worked for some time for the newspaper *Acropolis* to which she contributed popularized biographies such as *The Tragic Life of Molière, Dostoyevksi and His Age*, and others. She also created the first puppet theatre for children, for which she wrote the plays as well.

Her first collection of short stories, which appeared in 1931 under the title *I Xepartheni* (The Deflowered Maiden), caused a great stir when it was first published in 1933 (it appeared in French under the title *Alexandra*). It was a personal testimony and a confession given with rare realistic power and in a deeply pessimistic tone. On the other hand it was criticized for its rather careless style, which became more evident in her later work. During the Metaxa government in Greece, Nakou lived abroad contributing articles to Athenian newspapers. She returned to Greece when the Greek Italian war broke out in 1940, and soon after the liberation of Greece, she published *I Kolasi ton Paidion* (The Hell of Children); it is a series of short stories based on the wretchedness of the lives of children, who were gravely affected by the hunger, pain, despair and disaster caused by the war. This collection first appeared in Swiss newspapers due to the anti-government content and helped greatly the rise of the philohellenic spirit in Europe.

In 1951, she published in French the novel *I Gē tis Voiotias* (The Boeotian Land), which appeared simultaneously in Greek under the title *Ta Anthropina Pepromena* (The Human Fate). This novel, full of loving affection for her mother's birthplace, Levadia, presents some of the main traits of the Neohellenic personality and reveals indirectly the writer's humanistic and philosophic ideas. In 1954, she published first in French and then in Greek, the novel *Nausika*, and in 1956, *Yia Mia Kainouryia Zoē* (For a New Life), which is often regarded as a continuation of *The Boeotian Land*. In 1958, the novel *I Kyria Doremi* (Madame Doremi), which is considered as one of the products of the Greek "social" literature, appeared. The striking characteristics of this novel are its restrained sentimentality, the spontaneity of its humor and the lack of depression, elements that are so dominant in her other works.

What distinguishes her writings is her powerful narrative talent, which facilitates her confessional tendencies, her sensitivity to human suffering, her careless style, and the short-period structure that imitates conversational speech. Her characters are usually derived from the reality of her life; we recognize in them people we have already met in some way or another, such as Mr. Romas, the high-school master, or Miss Froso, the teacher of Greek in *Madame Doremi*, or Varvara and her grandfather in *The Boeotian Land*. Her characters are not complex, but usually fall within two distinct categories: the good, unselfish, educated, broad-minded, and understanding people and those who are the exact opposite—they are in a constant struggle with each other.

Nakou holds an important place among modern Greek writers and is one of the main figures to introduce "social realism" in Greek literature. She is widely read in French-speaking countries. She was awarded the International Prize of the Geneva Grande Revue for her narrative story *Maternité*.

Works

Novels: *The Lost* (1933). *The Boeotian Land* (1951). *Madame Doremi* (1953). *Nausika* (1954). *For a New Life* (1956).

Prose works: *Edgar Allan Poe's Life* (1963). *The Visualizers of Icaria* (1963). *Foteini* (in French). Short story collections: *The Deflowered Maiden* (1931). *The Hell of Children* (1944). Essay collections: *Personalities That I Met* (1965).

Bibliography

Biographical Encyclopaedia of Greek Writers, vol. 3, ed. Pagoulatos (1976), pp. 135–138. Ieronymidi, L., *Lilika Nakou* (Athens, 1974). Liatsos, D., *The Greek Women in Literature* (Athens, 1966), pp. 46–47. Patsis, C., *Great Encyclopedia of the Neohellenic Literature*, vol. 10 (Athens, 1968). Peranthis, M., *Greek Prose Writing*, vol. 4 (Athens, 1967), pp. 515–518.. Politis, L., *A History of Modern Greek Literature* (Oxford, 1973), p. 260. Rosenthal-Kamarinea, I., *Neugriechische Erzaehler* (1953), p. 414. Olten und Freiburg im Breisgau. Sachinis, A., *The Prose Writers of Our Times* (Athens, 1967), pp. 157–165. Vitti, M., *The Generation of the Thirties* (Athens, 1977), p. 269.

Aristoula Georgiadou

Nalęcz

(see: Maria Komornicka)

Zofia Nalkowska

Born 1884; died 1954
Genre(s): novel, drama
Language(s): Polish

The daughter of a well-known geographer and literary critic, Waclaw Nalkowski, Zofia made her literary debut with the early publication of poems in the periodical of the moderns, "Chimera," and during the next half century wrote over twenty volumes of prose, universally praised for their high quality. Nalkowska's early novels and short stories have been criticized for their "typically Young-Poland" over-refinement and the "sublime" unawareness of reality. They dealt with woman's psychology as a self-contained world, presented against the background of the life of the nineteenth-century intelligentsia. Later, the author herself stated that only with the advent of World War I did she come in contact with human suffering. In the reborn Polish state, Nalkowska became one of the most accomplished writers of psychological novels, preoccupied with the notion of evil and striving to represent in the most authentic way "the pressure of passions . . . in people and between people." Her focus was now the moral responsibility of the individual whose situation she presented as closely connected with public life and whose very self is predetermined by his or her place occupied in the network of interhuman relations. This notion appealed to critics attracted by Marxist-type social analysis. After the second world war, Nalkowska became active in political life as a member of parliament and the Commission for the Investigation of Nazi Crimes; she won public acclaim for her collection of short stories about life in concentration camps. Her two plays were staged and enjoyed popularity. Throughout her career, the author was celebrated not only for her simple, direct, and original writing, but also as a person of integrity and high moral standards.

Works

Kobiety [Women] (1906). Ksiaze [The Prince] (1907). Narcyza [Narcissa] (1911). Tajemnica krwi [Secret of Blood] (1917). Hrabia Emil [Count Emil] (1920). Romans Teresy Hennert [Teresa Hennert's Affair] (1923). Dom nad lakami [House by the Meadows] (1925). Choucas (1927). Niedobra milosc [The Wrong Kind of Love] (1928). Dom kobiet [Women's Home] (1930). Dzien jego powrotu [The Day of His Return] (1931). Sciany swiata [Walls of the World] (1931). Granica [Boundary Line] (1935). Medaliony [Medallions] (1946). Wezly zycia [Knots of Life] (1948). Moj ojciec [My Father] (1953).

Bibliography

Kridl, Manfred, An Anthology of Polish Literature (New York, 1957). Milosz, Czeslaw, The History of Polish Literature (California, 1969). Krzyzanowski, Julian, A History of Polish Literature (Warsaw, 1978).

Maya Peretz

Marie (Karoline Elisabeth Luise Von) Nathusius

Born March 10, 1817, Magdeburg, Germany;
    died December 22, 1857, Neinstedt
Genre(s): religious short story, novel, lyric
    poetry
Language(s): German

Marie Nathusius was born in Magdeburg in 1817, the daughter of Friedrich Scheele, a Protestant minister. While she was still very young, the family moved to Calbe. A sensitive, poetic, and understanding child, Nathusius had natural talent and self-developed abilities. When her brother became a pastor in Eichendorf in 1834, Nathusius spent some time traveling between Eichendorf and Calbe. Her experiences during these years provided the basis for her later Dorf und Stadtgeschichten (1858; Village and City Stories), ten short stories that give a realistic glimpse at everyday life in the village setting.

Nathusius was also musically gifted. She sang and played the harp, piano, organ, and guitar. In March of 1841, when she married the industrialist Philipp Nathusius, he was concerned that she further her musical abilities and encouraged her to write down her songs as well as the memories of her young years. Many songs were published posthumously in the collection, Hundert Lieder, geistlich und weltlich, ernsthaft und fröhlich, in Melodien von Marie Nathusius und mit Klavierbegleitung (1856; One Hundred Songs, Sacred and Secular, Serious and Humorous), which her husband published with Ludwig Erk.

The young couple traveled together throughout Europe before making their home in Althaldensleben. Their humanitarian endeavors helped improve the lives of those less fortunate in this factory area. They began a child-care institution, a women's group for the care of the poor, foster homes for boys and girls, and a young women's work school, at which Marie Nathusius herself taught sewing and knitting to the children of the neighborhood. As well as raising a family, she also wrote short stories for the children in her care and worked on a novel which was never published. In 1849 Philipp Nathusius gave up his business establishments in Althaldensleben, and after another trip, this time through France and England, the couple settled in Gute Neinstedt by Halle in the Harz Mountains. Here they founded a boys' foster home and a monastery.

Marie Nathusius began her career as a writer by publishing short stories for children in the Volksblätter für Stadt und Land (Newsletter for City and Country), which her husband edited beginning in 1849. Her stories embody her Christian ideals and, without sounding pedantic or pious, encourage young people to live good and upright lives. They are set in realistic, everyday situations, yet fantasy is never too far away. Her free-flowing prose is generously interspersed with lyric poems. Collections of her stories were later published as Die Geschichten von Christfried und Julchen (1859; The Stories of Christfried and Julchen) and Kleine Erzählungen (1859; Little Stories).

In some of her later works, Nathusius writes especially for young women. Langenstein und

Boblingen, published in 1855, presents the author herself as a young woman, and through a series of vignettes involving the same well-developed characters, emphasizes Christian morals. In *Tagebuch eines Armen Fräuleins* (1853; Diary of a Poor Young Woman), Nathusius employs the diary form, incorporating many poems and prayers that reveal the inner life of her character over the course of a year. In *Die Alte Jungfer* (1853; The Old Maid) Nathusius views daily events, friendship, love, and family life through the eyes of a single young woman. At the end of the short story, after a lapse of twelve years, the persona looks back and asks questions about the meaning of life, happiness, and singleness and finds comfort in God. Nathusius' last and most mature work is the novel *Elisabeth: Eine Geschichte, die nicht mit der Heirat schliet* (1858; Elizabeth: A Novel That Does Not End with Marriage). With her easy-going, humorous style, rich in detail and characterization, Nathusius portrays the joys and pains of a family covering the timespan of more than fifty years. The novel, which appeared after her death in 1857, achieved immediate success and was translated into many foreign languages. More works were published posthumously, including *Tagebuch einer Reise nach der Provence, Italien und der Schweiz* (Diary of a Trip to Provence, Italy, and Switzerland) and two *Jugendnovellen: Famillienskizzen* (Family Sketches), and *Herr und Kammerdiener* (1860; Lord and Servant).

Although the name of Marie Nathusius does not appear on the lists of widely-read women writers, she was enthusiastically received by her contemporaries.

Works

See Brummer, Franz, *Allgemeine Deutsche Biographie* (Leipzig, 1887); Pataky, Sophie, ed., *Lexikon deutscher Frauen der Feder* (Berlin, 1898). Translations: *Louise von Plettenhaus, or, The Journal of a Poor Young Lady* (1854). *Elizabeth: a Story Which Does Not End in Marriage*, tr. S.A. Smith (1860); M.A. Shryock (1891). *Above Her Station: The Story of a Young Woman's Life*, tr. H. Philip (1863). *Lowly Ways; or the Diary of a Poor Young Lady*, tr. F.E.B. (1871). *Katie von Walden; or Langenstein and Boblingen*, tr. M. Robinson (1891).

Bibliography

Grundler, Elise, *Marie Nathusius* (1909). *Lebensbild der Heimgegangenen Marie Nathusius*, 3 vols. (collected works vols. 13–15) (1867).

Ann Willison

Christiane Benedikte Eugenie Naubert

(a.k.a. Verfasser des Walther von Montbarry; Verfasser der Alme Verfasserin des Walther von Montbarry, Fontanges, et al.)

Born September 13, 1756, Leipzig, Germany; died January 12, 1819, Leipzig
Genre(s): novel, novella, fairy tale
Language(s): German

Christiane Benedikte Naubert was the most prolific German woman of her time and one of the earliest writers of historical novels and romances in German.

Naubert's father, Dr. Johann Ernst Hebenstreit, was a distinguished medical professor at the university in Leipzig, who died when his daughter was only a year old. Under the guidance of her stepbrother, also later a professor, she received an unusually good education for a woman of her day; she studied philosophy and history, learned Latin and Greek, and then taught herself Italian, English, and French. In her early twenties she wrote her first novel, the sentimental *Heerfort und Klärchen*, and published it—as she did all the rest until nearly the end of her life—anonymously. Her second book was devoted to a historical character, Emma, daughter of Charlemagne (1785). It was sufficiently successful to encourage her to publish more in this genre, for in the next year three new works appeared in six volumes. Naubert wrote rapidly, probably with no opportunity to revise. In 1788 she published five new titles in nine volumes, including three of her best known; *Geschichte der Gräfin Thekla von Thurn*, set during the Thirty Years War (2 v.), *Hermann von Unna*, about the secret tribunals of the fifteenth century (2 v., translated into French in 1801, English in 1794, and Dutch in 1802), and *Konradin von Schwaben* (2 v.), a story about the house of Hohenstaufen. In 1789 she began a five-volume series of "new fairy tales of the Germans" and came out with three new novels. This was her most prolific period; in the ten years from 1786 to 1795, starting when she was 30, she wrote 37 books in 52 volumes, mostly historical romances. Benedikte Naubert was one of Germany's earliest professional women writers.

But her name then was still Hebenstreit. Not until 1797, when she was 41 years old, did she marry for the first time. Her husband, Lorenz Holderieder, a merchant and estate owner in Naumburg, died after four years. She married again, another respected merchant, Johann Georg Naubert. The periods of her marriages are times of silence, with little or nothing published. As she aged, she suffered from weak eyes and deafness and thus wrote her last works by dictation.

Some of her books are among the best 18th-century novels by women. They demonstrate a good understanding of human nature, good use of language, and an unexpected sense of humor. Not surprisingly, they also show weaknesses that are common with rapid writing: repetition, diffuseness, overreliance on stock situations that are intended to thrill the readers. Still, Naubert attempted in her historical novels to use her sources fully; she even included footnotes to her texts. Most of the subjects are from German history, especially the Middle Ages, with occasional excursions into English history or other more exotic settings. Because all her abundant work until 1817 was published anonymously, readers were left to guess who this unusual author might be; they invariably mistook her gender.

Works

Heerfort und Klärchen; etwas für empfindsame Seelen, [Heerfort and Clara, Something for Sentimental Souls], 2 vols. (1779). Geschichte Emmas, Tochter Karls des Groen, und seines Geheimschreibers Eginhard [The Story of Emma, Daughter of Charlemagne, and His Scribe Eginhard], 2 vols. (1785). Die Ruinen [The Ruins], 3 vols. (1786). Amalgunde, Königin von Italien; oder Das Märchen von der Wunderquelle. Eine Sage aus den Zeiten Theodorichs des Groen [Amalgunde, Queen of Italy; or the Fairytale of the Miraculous Well. A Tale from the Time of Theoderich the Great], 2 vols. (1786). Walther von Montbarry, Gromeister des Tempelordens [Walter de Monbary, Grand Master of the Knights Templars], 2 vols. (1768; English tr. 1803). Die Amtmännin von Hohenweiler: eine wirkliche Geschichte aus Familienpapieren gezogen [The Magistrate's Wife at Hohenweiler, a True Story Drawn from Family Papers] (1787). Geschichte der Gräfin Thekla von Thurn; oder Scenen aus dem dreyssigjährigen Kriege [The Story of Countess Thekla von Thurn, or Scenes from the Thirty Years War] (1788). Hermann von Unna; eine Geschichte aus den Zeiten der Vehmgerichte [Hermann of Unna, a Series of Adventures of the Fifteenth Century, in Which the Proceedings of the Secret Tribunal . . . are delineated . . .] (1788; English tr. 1794). Konradin von Schwaben oder Geschichte des unglücklichen Enkels Kaiser Friedrichs des Zweiten [Conradin of Swabia, or the Story of the Unhappy Grandson of Emperor Friedrich II] (1788). Elfriede, oder Opfer väterlicher Vorurtheile [Elfriede, or the Victim of a Father's Prejudices] (1788). Pauline Frankini oder Täuschung der Leidenschaft und Freuden der Liebe [Pauline Frankini or Delusion of Passion and Joys of Love] (1788). Elisabeth, Erbin von Toggenburg: oder Geschichte der Frauen von Sargans in der Schweiz [Elisabeth, Heiress of Toggenburg, or the Story of the Women of Sargans in Switzerland] (1789). Emmy Reinolds; oder Thorheiten der Groen und Kleinen [Emmy Reinolds, or Follies of Great and Small] (1789). Hatto, Bischof von Mainz: eine Legende des zehnten Jahrhunderts [Hatto, Bishop of Mainz, a Legend of the Tenth Century] (1798). Neue Volksmärchen der Deutschen [New Fairy Tales of the Germans] (1789–1792). Alfons von Dülmen; oder Geschichte Kaiser Philipps und seiner Tochter. Aus den ersten Zeiten der heimlichen Gerichte [Alf von Duelmen, or the History of the Emperor Philip, and His Daughters] (1790; English tr., 1794). Barbara Blomberg, Vorgebliche Maitresse Kaiser Karls des fünften. Eine Originalgeschichte in zwei Theilen [Barbara Blomberg, Alleged Mistress of Emperor Charles IV, an Original Story in Two Parts] (1790). Brunilde. Eine Anekdote aus dem bürgerlichen Leben des dreizehnten Jahrhunderts [Brunilde, an Anecdote from Bourgeois Life of the 13th Century] (1790). Geschichte des Lord Fitzherbert und seiner Freunde, oder die verkannte Liebe [Story of Lord Fitzherbert and His

Friends, or Misunderstood Love] (1790). *Merkwürdige Begebenheiten der gräflichen Familie von Wallis* [Remarkable Events of the Family of the Count of Wallis] (1790). *Werner, Graf von Bernburg* [Werner, Count of Bernburg] (1790). *Gustav Adolf IV. aus Schauenburgischem Stamme* [Gustav Adolf IV of the Clan of Schauenburg] (1791). *Geschichte Heinrich Courtlands; oder, Selbstgeschafne Leiden* [History of Heinrich Courtland, or Selfmade Sorrows] (1791). *Edwy und Elgiva, oder die Wunder des heiligen Dunstan, eine altenglische geschichte* [Edwy and Elgiva, or the Miracle of Saint Dunstan, and Old English Story] (1791). *Gebhard Truchse von Waldburg, Churfürst von Cöln, oder die astrologischen Fürsten* [Gebhard Lord High Steward of Waldburg, Elector of Cologne, or the Astrological Princes] (1791). *Graf von Rosenberg, oder das enthüllte Verbrechen. Eine Geschichte aus der letzten Zeit des dreyssigjährigen Kriegs* [Count von Rosenberg, or the Discovered Crime, a Story from the Time of the Thirty Years War] (1791). *Lord Heinrich Holland, Herzog von Exeter; oder Irre geleitete Gromuth, eine Begebenheit aus dem Mittelalter von England* [Lord Henry Holland, Duke of Exeter, or Magnanimity Mislead, an Event from the English Middle Ages] (1791). *Marie Fürst, oder das Alpenmädchen* [Marie Fürst, or the Alps Girl] (1791). *Philippe von Geldern; oder Geschichte Selims, des Sohns Amurat* [Phillippe von Geldern, or the Story of Selim, Son of Amurat] (1792). *Konrad und Siegfried von Fehtwangen, Gromeister des deutschen Ordens* [Conrad and Siegfried von Fehtwangen, Grand Masters of the German Knights] (1792). *Miss Luise Fox, oder Reise einer jungen Englanderin durch einige Gegenden von Deutschland* [Miss Luise Fox, or Travels of a Young Englishwoman Through Some Parts of Germany] (1792). *Ulrich Holzer, Bürgermeister in Wien* [Ulrich Holzer, Mayor of Vienna] (1792). *Lucinde; oder, Herrn Simon Godwins medicinische Leiden. Nach dem Englischen* [Lucinde, or Mr. Simon Godwin's Medical Sufferings. From the English] (1793). *Heinrich von Plauen und seine Neffen, Ritter des deutschen Ordens. Der wahren Geschichte getreu bearbeitet* [Heinrich von Plauen and His Nephews, Knights of the German Order, Faithfully Told According to the True Story] (1793). *Alma; oder Ägyptische Mährchen* [Alma, or Egyptian Fairytales] (1793–1797). *Walther von Stadion; oder*

Geschichte Herzog Leopolds von Öesterreich und seiner Kriegsgefährten [Walter von Stadion, or the Story of Duke Leopold of Austria and His War Comrades] (1794). *Sitten und Launen der Groen, Ein Cabinet von Familienbildern* [Manners and Moods of the Great, a Cabinet of Family Scenes] (1794). *Der Bund des armen Konrads, Getreue Schilderung einiger merkwürdiger Auftritte aus den Zeiten der Bauernkriege des 16. Jahrhunderts* [Poor Conrad's Alliance, True Description of Some Remarkable Scenes from the Time of the 16th-century Peasant Wars] (1795). *Friedrich der Siegreiche, Churfürst von der Pfalz; der Marc Aurel des Mittelalters. Frey nach der Geschichte bearbeitet* [Friedrich the Victorious, Elector from the Pfalz, the Marcus Aurelius of the Middle Ages, Freely Told According to History] (1795). *Vellada; ein Zauberroman* [Vellada, a Novel of Magic] (1795). *Joseph Mendez Pinto. Eine jüdische Geschichte* [Joseph Mendez Pinto, a Jewish Story] (1802). *Cornelie, oder die Geheimnisse des Grabes* [Cornelie or the Secrets of the Grave] (1803). *Eudoxia, Gemahlin Theodosius der Zweiten. Eine Geschichte des 5. Jahrhunderts* [Eudoxia, Wife of Theodosius the Second, a Story from the Fifth Century] (1805). *Fontanges, oder das Schicksal der Mutter und Tochter, eine Geschichte aus den Zeiten Ludwigs XIV* [Fontanges, or the Fate of a Mother and Daughter, a Story from the Times of Louis XIV] (1805). *Die Gräfin von Frondsberg, aus dem Hause Löwenstein, eine vaterländische Geschichte aus den Zeiten des Mittelalters* [The Countess of Frondsberg, from the House of Löwenstein, a National Story from the Middle Ages] (1806). *Heitere Träume in kleinen Erzählungen* [Cheerful Dreams in Little Stories] (1806). *Lioba und Zilia* (1806). *Wanderungen der Phantasie in die Gebiete des Wahren* [Fantasy's Wanderings in the Territories of the True] (1806). *Attilas Schwert oder die Azimunterinnen* [Attila's Sword, or the Azimunter Women] (1808). *Die Irrungen* [The Errors] (1808). *Elisabeth Lezkau, oder die Bürgermeisterin* [Elisabeth Lezkau or the Mayor's Wife] (1808). *Azaria. Eine Dichtung der Vorwelt* [Azaria, a Story of the Past] (1814). *Rosalba* (1817). *Alexis und Luise. Eine Badegeschichte* [Alexis and Luise, a Story at a Bath] (1819). *Der kurze Mantel, und Ottilie; zwei Volksmärchen* [The Short Cloak, and Ottilia, Two Fairytales] (1819). *Turmalin und Lazerta* (1820).

Translation: Translation of "The Short Cloak" in *Bitter Healing: Anthology of German Women Authors from Pietism to Romanticism* (Lincoln, 1989).

Bibliography

Brinker-Gabler, Gisela, ed., *Deutsche Literatur von Frauen: Vom Mittelalter bis zum Ende des 18. Jahrhunderts* (München, 1988), pp. 450–452. Frederiksen, Elke, ed., *Women Writers of Germany, Austria, and Switzerland. An Annotated Bio-Bibliographical Guide* (New York, 1989), pp. 169–171. Friedrichs, Elisabeth, *Die deutschsprachigen Schriftstellerinnen des 18. und 19. Jahrhunderts. Ein Lexikon* (Stuttgart, 1981), p. 216. Schreinert, Kurt, *Benedikte Naubert. Ein Beitrag zur Entstehungsgeschichte des historischen Romans in Deutschland* (1941, rpt. Nendein, Lichtenstein, 1969). Hadley, Michael, *The German Novel in 1790. A Descriptive Account and Critical Bibliography* (Bern, 1973), pp. 110–114, 123–135 (Europäische Hochschulschriften). Schindel, Carl Wilhelm Otto August von, *Die deutschen Schriftstellerinnen des neunzehnten Jahrhunderts*. vol. 2 (Leipzig, 1825), pp. 32–47. Touaillon, Christine, *Der deutsche Frauenroman des 18. Jahrhunderts* (Wien und Leipzig, 1919).

Ruth P. Dawson

Ana María Navales

Born 1943 (?), Zaragoza, Spain
Genre(s): novel, poetry, essay, criticism
Language(s): Spanish

The scant information available on this writer comes from cover "blurbs," and thus is incomplete and perhaps not entirely authoritative. She was born in the provincial Aragonese capital of Zaragoza, probably to a family of the small middle-class intelligentsia. She studied at the University of Zaragoza, and received her doctorate in Romance Philology with a dissertation on the Spanish epistolary novel. Given her involvement with contemporary Aragonese literature (part of the post-Franco flowering of vernacular languages and literatures in the "autonomous" regions), it appears that she has continued to reside in Aragon, probably as a teacher at the secondary or university level. Her writings are more or less evenly divided between "creative" genres and the scholarly anthology or critical study.

Navales first became known as a poet, with several lyric collections appearing in the early 1970s: *En las palabras* (1970; In the Words), *Junto a la última piel* (1973; Next to the Last Skin), *Restos de lacre y cera de vigilias* (1975; Remains of Lacquer and Wax from the Midnight Candle). International recognition seems to have come before national notice: she was awarded gold medals in the international "Silarus" contest for poets in the Spanish language (held in Italy) and in another International Poetic Contest in Terni. Other books of poetry attributed to Navales (according to the covers of later books of fiction) include *Paternoy*, *Del fuego secreto* (Of the Secret Fire), *Mester de amor* (Medieval Love Lyric), *Los espías de Sísifo* (The Spies of Sisyphus) and *Neuva, vieja estancia* (Old, New Stay [or Room]), all undated, but presumably published during the late 1970s or in the 1980s. *Cuatro novelistas españoles* (1974; Four Spanish Novelists) contains studies of the contemporary novelists Miguel Delibes, Ignacio Aldecoa, Daniel Sueiro, and Francisco Umbral. Two anthologies, one of poets and the other of narrators, focus on contemporary writers in Aragon: *Antología de la poesía aragonesa contemporánea* and *Antología de narradores aragoneses contemporáneos*.

The first fiction by Navales is a short story collection, *Dos muchachos metidos en un sobre azul* (1976; Two Kids Inserted in a Blue Envelope). Twelve tales exhibit a good deal of stylistic versatility and thematic variation, ranging from the experimental mode to attenuated surrealist interior monologues and a more conventional neorealist mode. Distinctive features of the language include suppression of many verbs, telegraphic syntax, and unusually brief sentences. The next fiction of Navales located to date is a first or possibly second novel (as the cover of *El laberinto de Quetzal* identifies it as a third novel), *El regreso de Julieta Always* (1981; The Return of Juliet Always). The center of narrative interest is the mystery surrounding an aged, perhaps psychotic painter whose paintings were signed with the pseudonym Julieta Always. The author-narrator reads an obituary or notice of the painter's death, which sparks a variety of retrospective episodes providing separate perspectives of a somber country childhood, adolescence and young adulthood darkened by the Civil War and hardships as a refugee in France, followed by a Bohemian life in Paris, poverty and decadence, with ultimate confinement to an insane asylum. Navales employs a poetic style and open-ended structure to portray the tragic fate of a woman unaware of the exposition of her paintings and her tardy success. *El laberinto de Quetzal* (1985; The Labyrinth of Quetzal) is an experimental narrative that follows the vagaries of a labyrinthine narrative consciousness in mythical "excursion to distant times and places." The title evokes the pagan Mexican deity, Quetzal, symbolically associated with discovery, who serves to transmit a vision of life as a series of images whose superficial differences mask a fundamental sameness.

Works

Antología de la poesía aragonesa contemporánea. Antología de narradores aragoneses contemporáneos. Cuatro novelistas españoles (1974). Del fuego secreto. Dos muchachos metidos en un sobre azul (1976). En las palabras (1970). Los espías de Sísifo. Junto a la última piel (1973). El laberinto de Quetzal (1985). Mester de amor. Nueva, vieja estancia. Paternoy. El regreso de Julieta Always (1981). Restos de lacre y cera de vigilias (1975).

Janet Perez

Marguerite de Navarre (Marguerite d'Angoulême, Queen of Navarre)

Born April 11, 1492, Angoulême, France; died December 21, 1549, château d' Odos (Tarbes)
Genre(s): poetry, novellas and letters
Language(s): French

Daughter of Louise de Savoie and Charles d'Angoulême; married Charles d'Alençon, 1509; married Henri d'Albret, king of Navarre, 1527.

Imbued with the ideals of the Italian Renaissance, Louise de Savoie provided Marguerite with an excellent education, even allowing her to share some lessons with her brother Francis. Scholars disagree on the depth of her learning,

but it is clear that she had some knowledge of Latin and Italian, and at least began to study Hebrew. She was interested in philosophical and religious questions and dazzled contemporaries with her ability to discuss subjects ranging from Neoplatonism to contemporary Church reform. When Francis became king in 1515, Marguerite, who was more attractive and more animated than Queen Claude and who enjoyed her brother's confidence, helped set the intellectual tone of the French court. She protected gifted poets like Clément Marot and encouraged the translation of classical texts. François Rabelais, addressing her as "esprit ravy et ecstatique" dedicated to her the third volume of his adventures of Pantagruel. Although she never opposed royal policy and remained outwardly obedient to Rome, Marguerite supported reform of the Gallican Church, and Lefèvre d'Etaples, who translated the Bible into French, was one of her protégés.

When Francis I was held captive after the Battle of Pavia by Emperor Charles V, Marguerite went to visit her brother in prison and help negotiate his release. Upon Francis' safe return, she married Henri d'Albret, Charles d'Alençon having died after his return from the Battle of Pavia. The second marriage was to disturb the harmonious relationship between Marguerite and her brother. Fearing that Henri would arrange a political marriage with a Spanish prince, he took Marguerite's daughter Jeanne d'Albret out of her parents' custody and forced her into a marriage (later annulled) with the duke of Cleves. Marguerite was also distressed by the intermittent religious persecution that became a feature of her brother's reign. She remained devoted to Francis, but her influence at court gradually declined. After Francis' death in 1547 Marguerite withdrew to Navarre and devoted her final years to religious meditation and to writing.

Marguerite was a prolific poet. Her early works—allegories and meditations in *terza rima*, spiritual rondeaux, verse epistles to members of the royal family—remained in manuscript until they were rediscovered by scholars in the nineteenth and twentieth centuries. She began her public career in 1531 with the publication of *Le Miroir de l'âme pécheresse*, a controversial work that showed her adherence to the principles of *sola fides* and *sola scriptura*. The second edition of this work (1533) included the *Dialogue en forme de vision nocturne* in which Marguerite conversed with her late niece on a variety of topics including grace and free will. This edition of the *Miroir* was condemned as unorthodox by the Sorbonne, but the condemnation was retracted at the insistence of Francis I. In spite of the retraction Marguerite was regarded by many as a Lutheran sympathizer. Perhaps because of the controversy the Queen of Navarre waited until 1547 to publish a collection of her works, *Les Marguerites de la Marguerite des Princesses.* Many of the poems composed during the 1540s were omitted from the anthology, among them, *Les Prisons,* which is generally regarded as her most significant poems and *La Navire,* her final tribute to Francis. Marguerite was also interested in drama and wrote plays dealing with the birth of Christ, the visit of the three wisemen, the flight into Egypt and the massacre of the Holy Innocents. In addition she authored a series of symbolical "comédies profanes." The theatrical works, which may have been presented by ladies of the court, complement the poetry in conveying the principles of Marguerite's evangelical Christianity.

Critical response to Marguerite's poetry and drama has not always been enthusiastic. Her intellectual range, metrical versatility and importance as a religious poet have not been challenged, but she has been accused of lacking technical facility. While she admired Petrarch and Dante and was one of the first writers to use *terza rima,* she did not anticipate the Pléiade poets in cultivating classical genres and imitating classical authors.

Until recently, Marguerite's poetry has been overshadowed by her prose work, a collection of novellas inspired by the *Decameron.* Composed during the 1540s and incomplete at her death, the collection was first published in 1558 with the title *Histoires des amans fortunez.* A corrected and reorganized edition prepared by Claude Gruget and acknowledging Marguerite as author appeared in 1559 as the *Heptaméron des nouvelles de tres illustre et tres excellente Princesse Marguerite de Valois.* Imitating Boccaccio, Marguerite presents ten French aristocrats who are isolated by spring floods in the Pyrenees and spend their time in conversation and story-telling. Deviating from her Italian

model, she increases the number of women story tellers from three to five, gives much greater importance to the dialogue sequences that separate the various stories and cultivates a simpler narrative style. Because of its sympathetic yet subtle portrayal of women and severe criticism of masculine insensitivity, the *Heptaméron* can be regarded as a defense of feminine dignity. It is not, however, a feminist treatise. Marguerite's sophisticated manipulation of dialogue encourages multiple readings of the text. The *Heptaméron* reveals her interest in a variety of subjects from the *querelle des femmes* to courtly etiquette, from Neoplatonism to Scriptural exegesis and the validity of monastic life.

Works

Chansons spirituelles, ed. G. Dottin (1971). *La Coche,* ed. R. Marichal (1971). *Dernières poésies,* ed. A. Lefranc (1896). *Dialogue en forme de vision nocturne,* ed. P. Jourda (1926). *L'Heptaméron (Nouvelles),* ed. Y. Le Hir (1967). "Jugendgedichte Margaretes," ed. P.A. Becker, in *Archiv für das Studium der neuren Sprachen und Literaturen* (1913). *Lettres de Marguerite de Navarre,* ed. F. Génin (1841). *Nouvelles lettres de la reine de Navarre addreseés au roi François Ier,* ed. F. Génin (1842). *Les Prisons,* ed. S. Glasson (1978). *Les Marguerites de la Marguerite des Princesses,* ed. F. Frank, 4 vols. (1873). *Le Miroir de l'âme pécheresse,* ed. J. Allaire (1972); R. Salminen (1979). *La Navire,* ed. R. Marichal (1956). *Le Pater Noster,* ed. E. Parturier (1904); W.G. Moore (1930). *Petit oeuvre dévot et contemplatif,* ed. H. Sckommodau (1960). *Poésies inédites,* ed. P. Jourda (1930). *Théâtre profane,* ed. V.L. Saulnier (1946).

Translations: *The Heptameron,* tr. P.A. Chilton (1984). *Le Miroir de l'âme pécheresse, édition critique et commentaire suivis de la traduction faite par la princesse Elisabeth, future reine d'Angleterre,* in *The Glasse of the Synneful Soul,* ed. Renja Salminen (1979).

Bibliography

Cottrell, R., *The Grammar of Silence: a Reading of Marguerite de Navarre's Poetry* (1986). Davis, J., *The Storytellers in Marguerite de Navarre's Heptaméron* (1978). Febvre, L., *Autour de l'Heptaméron* (1944). Gelernt, J., *The World of Many Loves: The Heptaméron of Marguerite de Navarre* (1966). Jourda, P., *Marguerite d'Angoulême, duchesse d'Alençon, reine de Navarre:-étude biographique et littéraire*, 2 vols. (1930). Kraus, C., *Der religiöse Lyrismus Margaretes von Navarra* (1981). Sckommodau, H., *Die religiösen Dichtungen Margaretes von Navarra* (1955). Sommers, Paula, *Celestial Ladders: Readings in Marguerite de Navarre's Poetry of Spiritual Ascent* (1989). Tetel, M., *Marguerite de Naverre's Heptaméron: Themes, Language and Structure* (1973).

General references: *Dictionnaire des lettres françaises*, pp. 480–484. McFarlane, I.D., *A Literary History of France: Renaissance France*, pp. 61–63; 135–138; 243–248.

Paula Sommers

Beatrijs van Nazareth

Born 1200, Tienen, Belgium; died August 29, 1268, in the monastery of Nazareth near Lier
Genre(s): mystical treatise, autobiography
Language(s): Dutch

One of six children of Bartholomeus, an affluent citizen of Tienen who founded several monasteries in Flanders in the thirteenth century, Beatrijs received a solid education under the joint supervision of *magistri* in the *artes liberales* and the beguines at Zoutleeuw. At the age of sixteen, she entered the Cistercian monastery of Bloemendaal at Eerken, and in 1221 she moved to the monastery of Maagdendael at Oplinter. In 1236, she founded, with the help of her brother, the monastery of Our Lady of Nazareth near Lier, whose first prioress she was till her death in 1268. Soon after her death, an unknown cleric, presumably the confessor of Beatrijs, composed a *Vita B. Beatricis*, which—though largely suspect due to its hagiographic manipulations—remains our major source of information on Beatrijs' life and most of her *oeuvre*.

According to the *vita*, Beatrijs composed several mystical treatises and autobiographical texts. Of all her writings, only the tractate *Van seven manieren van heiliger minnen* (The Seven Manners of Holy Loving) has survived. This text, one of the earliest medieval Dutch prose documents, was published for the first time in 1926 and has since rightfully been hailed as "a great achievement" (Colledge, 8). The tractate describes the mystical searching of the soul for God and the progress in seven stages that man must pursue in order to reach unity with the divine. The early mysticism of this Flemish nun has often been compared with that of Hadewych of Antwerp. Yet, her simple, effective, and sometimes homely style and vocabulary—the result of an intensely ascetic and introspective life—is markedly different from that of her often ecstatic contemporary.

Works

Reypens, L. and J. van Mierlo, eds., *Seven manieren van minne* (1926). Vekeman, V. and J. Tersteeg, eds., *Beatrijs van Nazareth. Van seven manieren van heiliger minnen* (1971). English tr. in E. Colledge, *Medieval Netherlands Religious Literature* (1965).

Bibliography

de Laere, P., "Over de Vitae van Beatrijs van Nazareth." *Wetenschappelijke Tijdingen* 26 (1967). Heeroma, K., "Beatrijs van Tienen 1268—29 augustus 1968." *Spelend met de spelgenoten. Middelnederlandse leesavonturen* (1969). Hoste, A., "Beatrijs van Nazareth." *Twintig eeuwen Vlaanderen* 13 (1976). Ingels, F., "Beatrijs van Nazareth. Zeven manieren van minne." *De Brabantse Folklore* (1968). Reypens, L., ed., *Vita Beatricis. De autobiografie van de Z. Beatrijs van Tienen O. Cist. 1200–1268* (1964). Vekeman, H., "Minne in 'Seven manieren van minne' van Beatrijs van Nazareth." *Citeaux* 19 (1968). Vekeman, H., "Van seven manieren van heiliger minnen. Extase en traditie in een cultus van de minne." *Tijdschrift voor Nederlandse Taal-en Letterkunde* 88 (1972). General references: Knuvelder, G.P.M., *Handboek tot de geschiedenis van de Nederlandse letterkunde*, vol. 1 (1970), pp. 175–177. Meijer, Reinder P., *The Literature of the Low Countries* (1971), pp. 16–17. van Mierlo, Jozef, *Geschiedenis van de letterkunde der Nederlanden*, vol. 2 (1940).

Henk Vynckier

Suzanne Necker

*Born June 2, 1737, Crassier, Switzerland; died
     May 1794, Lausanne*
Genre(s): non-fiction
Language(s): French

The woman whom the history knows as
Mme Necker was born in 1737 in a little Swiss
village of Crassier as the only child of respected
and erudite, though poor, Protestant minister
Louis Antoine Curchod, who gave his talented
daughter as thorough an education as if she had
been a boy. Since Suzanne was beautiful and
lively as well as intelligent, in her youth she did
not lack admirers either in Crassier or Lausanne,
the city she frequently visited. During one of
those visits she organized a literary club called
"Académie des Eaux de la Poudrière." Its members were students of the Academy of Lausanne,
and Suzanne herself was elected its president
under the name of Thémire. Every member was
expected to send some literary work to the
"Académie des Eaux" once in a while.

In this circle Mlle Curchod reigned surrounded by many friends and admirers, the most
important being Edward Gibbon, destined to
become famous as the author of *The History of
the Decline and Fall of the Roman Empire*, who
was then undergoing a Protestant education in
Lausanne. In 1757 the two became engaged;
however, Gibbon was dependent on his father,
who did not approve the match. In 1758 the
young man returned to England, and four years
later he definitely broke off the engagement.

This was a heavy blow for Suzanne, and not
the only one. Her father died in 1760 and her
mother in 1763. M. Curchod's death left his
widow and daughter with nothing to live on
except his pension, so that from that time Suzanne
had to earn money by giving lessons—a bitter
ordeal for a woman of her pride. After her mother's
death Suzanne, subject to fits of melancholy and
bereft even of her father's pension, was worse off
than ever. Instead of escaping poverty by accepting one of the many proposals of marriage
she had received, she chose to go to Paris as the
companion of the rich young widow Mme. de
Vermenoux.

In Paris Suzanne soon met one of Mme de
Vermenoux' suitors, Jacques Necker, a thirty-
two-year-old financier from Geneva, already well
known in Paris for his ability. In the course of a
few months he transferred his affections to
Suzanne herself, and in 1764 they were married.
Although it was an excellent match for almost a
penniless woman, Suzanne undoubtedly married
for love, which was to last throughout the years
of her wedded life. In 1766 she gave birth to her
only child, Anne Louise Germaine, destined to
become even more famous than her mother as
Mme de Staël.

After her marriage Mme Necker decided to
form that typical institution of the eighteenth-
century Paris, a literary salon, in which she was
greatly assisted by Mme Geoffrin, herself the
mistress of one of the most renowned salons in
Paris. Helped by her husband's wealth, Mme
Necker soon completely realized her wish. To
her *réunions*, which took place on Fridays and
later also on Tuesdays, came the most famous
literary men of her time. The topics which they
discussed were at first mostly literary or philosophic, but in the later years, when the nation
was threatened by bankruptcy and revolution,
they lost the gay and carefree spirit that Mme
Necker enjoyed so much and became political as
well.

Probably the happiest years of Mme Necker's
life were those between her marriage and her
husband's first appointment by the French government in 1776, which, although it gave him a
most prominent position, brought many anxieties
and preoccupations to both. Mme Necker had no
interest in politics, except as it concerned her
husband; she was therefore most contented
discussing literary topics with her friends. She
lacked the gift of brilliant and witty repartee so
admired in the polite conversation of her time,
but she impressed by her intelligence, education,
and the sincerity of her convictions. In 1770 she,
who had visited Voltaire in Ferney in her youth,
proposed in her salon that a statue of the great
writer should be made. It was done, and six years
later the statue, sculpted by Pigalle, was erected
in Paris. Another of Mme Necker's undertakings,
and considered the most admirable by her contemporaries, was her founding of a hospital for
the poor in 1778. It was her idea to employ nuns
as nurses in it, a proceeding that later became

usual in France. This hospital bears her name even today.

The later years of Mme Necker's life were clouded by the threat of the revolution, the worries imposed by her husband's difficulties in his duties as the Minister of the Finances, and her own declining health. Germaine Necker, who was, as an extremely precocious child, very early introduced to the salon, became an important figure in it, finally to assume its leadership in her mother's stead, which she did not resign even after her marriage to the Baron de Staël in 1785.

The crucial role that M. Necker played in the French revolution is well known. After the failure of his attempts to save the finances of the nation, he and his wife in 1790 returned to their native country, to Coppet, the castle they had bought years earlier. Both were very depressed by the ruin of Necker's career and their imposed solitude. Besides, Mme Necker's health was completely broken. By 1793 her condition was so serious that her husband took her to Lausanne, where a famous doctor resided. In January 1794 she made her will, in which she laid down very precise instructions concerning her burial, the most important being that her husband upon his death should be laid at her side. In the last months of her life her sufferings were severe but alleviated by her husband's great affection and her religious convictions. She died in May 1794, and was buried in the tomb in the park at Coppet, the tomb which later received her husband and daughter.

Although Mme Necker wrote several non-fictional works, she is known in history not as a writer but as the mistress of a brilliant salon and one of the most remarkable women of the eighteenth century. Some of her acquaintances criticized what they considered her coldness, primness, and excessive ambition on her husband's behalf; however, the majority of her friends admired her for her intelligence, candor, generosity, and, most of all, great virtue in an age of rather loose morals.

Works

Les Inhumations précipités (1790). Réflexions sur le divorce (1794). Mélanges (1798). Nouveaux Mélanges (1802).

Bibliography

Gambier-Parry, Mark, *Madame Necker* (1913). Vicomte d'Haussonville, *Le Salon de Madame Necker* (1885). Madame la baronne de Staël, *Mémoires de la vie privée de mon père* (1818).

Neda Jeni

Torborg Nedreaas

Born 1906, Bergen, Norway; died June 30, 1987
Genre(s): novel, short story
Language(s): Norwegian

Torborg Nedreaas is generally regarded as one of the finest writers of prose fiction to emerge in post-World War II Norway. In 1945, the year of Norway's liberation from Nazi occupation, Nedreaas published two collections of short stories, of which one in particular won critical acclaim. *Bak skapet står öksen* (There Is an Axe Behind the Closet) was unique in that it did not play up to patriotic feelings with stories of heroic resistance fighters. Nedreaas chose instead to tell the story of ordinary Norwegians and the grey and dreary everyday existence that was their life for five long years. She also dared to depict, with sympathy and understanding, women and teenaged girls who associated with German soldiers. Sincerity—a need to tell the truth—and compassion with individuals whose social and economic situation puts them in a weak and vulnerable position are characteristic of everything Nedreaas has written.

Nedreaas' greatest contribution to Norwegian literature has been as the creator of Herdis, a character whose development we follow from the time she is a very little girl until she reaches the threshold of womanhood. Herdis appears in a series of stories and novels, spanning four books all together. The first of these, *Trylleglasset* (1950; The Magic Glass), is a short-story cycle set in Bergen during the early part of this century just prior to the outbreak of World War I. Herdis is a main figure in some of these stories, a secondary figure in others, but she is not the only link holding the stories together. They also share a common milieu and time frame. The former is a section of Bergen where families from both the working class and the lower middle class reside;

the latter is marked by economic and political unrest. Against a detailed and realistic depiction of neighborhood and neighbors, Nedreaas portrays, with great sensitivity and intuition, a little girl who feels she doesn't fit in at home or among her playmates.

In *Musikk fra en blå brönn* (1960; Music from a Blue Well) and *Ved neste nymåne* (1971; At the Next New Moon), the focus is more directly on Herdis and her family, although the depiction of milieu continues to be vivid and precise. Herdis' parents have divorced, and this both increases the gallery of family members and contributes to the emotional difficulties Herdis faces as she moves through childhood and into the turbulent years of puberty. She continues to feel like an outsider, and she seeks refuge and escape in her imagination and later, as she grows older, in music—Herdis is unquestionably an artistic personality.

Charting the course of female development has assumed a central place in the tradition of Norwegian women writers; both Sigrid Undset and Cora Sandel have composed outstanding trilogies in which they portray the development of female protagonists. With her books on Herdis, Nedreaas added a new dimension to this tradition, namely the psychological and emotional development of the female child.

Nedreaas has also drawn compassionate and insightful portrayals of adult women, in countless short stories as well as the novel *Av måneskinn gror det ingenting* (1947; Nothing Grows by Moonlight). This is the powerful story of lower-class women and the illegal abortions they are forced to submit themselves to because they lack the economic means to support a child. It is also the story of how the cruel exploitation of one woman's love gradually destroyed her personality. The narrator is this woman, and she tells her story to a stranger she meets in the street one night, just hours after learning she is terminally ill.

Torborg Nedreaas is a declared Communist; her political sympathies can sometimes be read between the lines in her fiction, but they are generally not intrusive. This is not the case, however, in *De varme hendene* (The Warm Hands), a novel from 1952 in which she attacks Norwegian membership in NATO. Her radical

opinions have also been expressed in numerous articles and radio causeries, which twice have been compiled and published in book form (1967 and 1982).

It is as a writer of short stories Torborg Nedreaas will best be remembered. While it is true that two of her books about Herdis are novels, the chapters in these books are so episodic in nature as to form independent segments, thereby actually contributing to Nedreaas' stature as master of the short story.

Works

Short stories: *För det ringer tredje gang* (1945). *Bak skapet står öksen* (1945). *Trylleglasset* (1950). *Stoppested* (1953). *Den siste polka* (1965).

Novels: *Av måneskinn gror det ingenting* (1947). *De varme hendene* (1952). *Musikk fra en blå brönn* (1960). *Ved neste nymåne* (1971).

Radio plays: *Det dumme hjertet* (1976).

Articles and radio talks: *Ytringer i det blå* (1967). *Vintervår* (1982).

Translations: *Nothing Grows by Moonlight*, tr. Bibbi Lee (1987). *Music from a Blue Well*, tr. Bibbi Lee (1988). *Slaves of Love and Other Norwegian Short Stories*, ed. James McFarland (1982). *An Everyday Story. Norwegian Women's Fiction*, ed. Katherine Hanson (1984). *Scandinavian Women Writers. An Anthology from the 1880s to the 1980s*, ed. Ingrid Claréus (1989).

Bibliography

Beyer, Edvard, ed., *Norges Litteratur Historie*, vol. 6 (Oslo, 1975). Bonnevie, Mai Bente et al., *Et annet språk. Analyser av norsk kvinnelitteratur* (Oslo, 1977). Longum, Leif, *Et speil for oss selv. Menneskesyn og virkelighetsoppfatning i norsk etterkrigsprosa* (Oslo, 1968). Nettum, Rolf Nyboe, ed. *I diktningens brennpunkt. Studier i norsk romankunst 1945–1980* (Oslo, 1982). *Nordens svale. Festskrift til Torborg Nedreaas på 70 årsdagen* (Oslo, 1976). Rasmussen, Janet E., "Dreams and Discontent: The Female Voice in Norwegian Literature." *Review of National Literatures. Norway*, vol. 12 (New York, 1983). Ökland, Einar, "Kunsten å sjå—og å skrive." *Samtiden* LXXV, 9 (Oslo, 1966).

Katherine Hanson

Neera

(a.k.a. Anna Radius Zuccari)

Born May 7, 1846, Milan, Italy; died July 19, 1918, Milan
Genre(s): narrative prose, lyric, essay
Language(s): Italian

Seen from the angle of her comfortable bourgeois life and serene marriage, Anna Radius Zuccari appears the epitome of conventional womanhood, devoted to husband, home, and children. Seen as Neera, however, her creative life was active, rich, and controversial. Writing in the last quarter of the nineteenth century, she was a familiar voice in the heated debates over the emancipation of women, on the side of traditional roles. Less polemical, her fiction is a subtle criticism of the treatment of women in society. In the naturalist vein, her stories and novels are directed primarily to a female reader, offering tales of abnegation, devotion, and sacrifice.

Having lost her mother at an early age, Anna Zuccari grew up reserved, isolated, sensitive, and misunderstood, finding escape in her books and imagination. After achieving balance in her marriage with Adolfo Radius, she began to give rein to her fantasies and express her ideas, protecting her privacy by publishing under a Horatian pseudonym.

From the start, Neera showed a marked predilection for the subtle psychological analysis of feminine states of mind. Her women are caught in the boundaries imposed by family, custom, and morality but long for spiritual fulfillment, emotional expression, and romantic love. In *Teresa* (1886), considered her best novel, the heroine is exploited by parents who use her as an unpaid housekeeper, babysitter, and nurse only to be denied her chance at love because no dowry is provided by her authoritarian father, who has channeled the family's funds and support to the unworthy male heir.

Neera's protagonists are always caught in limiting gender norms and are punished either socially or psychologically for any break with biologically determined behavior. Through her heroines, the writer addresses the injustice of such norms when they suppress the human spirit. Suffering from the corrosion of daily life, the inertia of subjugation, and self-defeatism, across class lines, these characters succumb or sublimate, seeking meaning in the traditional areas assigned women: marriage, service, and altruism.

Neera does not suggest that autonomy or political equality should be women's goals. Instead, she posits the spiritual value of sacrifice and loving within the family, seeing maternity—not passion—as woman's deepest and most natural attachment and suggesting the worthiness of platonic love, ideas that are clearly delineated in *Le idee di una donna* (1903; One Woman's Ideas).

Thus, there is an inherent dichotomy between the empathetic feminine portraits Neera paints and the author's personal stands against divorce and liberation. Yet, her concern with women's reality was deep-felt and even practical, leading her to compose educational tracts as well, including a dictionary of hygiene.

Conservative in both her politics and her style, Neera's fiction nevertheless appealed to major contemporary Italian critics, notably realist Luigi Capuana who defined her writing a "rêverie" and Benedetto Croce who appreciated her lyrical expressiveness and solid moral values. Today, Neera is perceived as an essentially feminist writer, if not a revolutionary one, who depicted the struggle between the individual and tradition in her heroines.

Works

Narrative: *Un romanzo* (1876). *Addio!* (1877). *Vecchie catene* (1878). *Novelle gaie* (1879). *Un nido* (1880). *Il castigo* (1881). *Iride* (1881). *La freccia del parto* (1883). *La Regaldina* (1883/1884). *Il marito dell'amica* (1885). *Fotografie matrimoniali* (1885–1898). *Teresa* (1886). *L'indomani* (1890). *Senio* (1891/1892). *Nel sogno* (1893). *Voci della notte* (1893). *Anima sola* (1894). *Lydia* (1894). *L'amuleto* (1897). *La vecchia casa* (1900). *La villa incantata* (1900/1901). *La freccia del parto e altre novelle* (1901). *Una passione* (1902/1903). *Conchiglie* (1905). *Il romanzo della fortuna* (1905/1906). *Crevalcore* (1907). *Duello d'anime* (1911). *La sottana del diavolo* (1912). *Rogo d'amore* (1913/1914). *Crepuscoli di libertà* (1916/1917). *Una giovinezza del XIX secolo* (1919, posthumous).

Profili, impressioni, ricordi (1920, posthumous). *Fiori* (1921, posthumous).

Lyric: *Poesie* (1898). *Il canzoniere della nonna* (1908). *Poesie* (1918, posthumous).

Essay: [With P. Mantegazza], *Dizionario d'igiene per la famiglia* (1881). *Il libro di mio figlio* (1891). *L'amore platonico* (1886/1897). *Battaglie per un'idea* (1898). *Il secolo galante* (1900). *Le idee di una donna* (1903). *La coscienza del fanciullo* (1908).

Translations: *The Amulet* [*L'Amuleto*] (serialized in *Living Age Magazine*, 1897). *The Old House* [*La vecchia casa*] (serialized in *Era Magazine*, 1901). *The Soul of an Artist* [*Anima sola*] (1905).

Bibliography

Baldacci, Luigi, "Introduzione," to *Teresa* (Turin, 1976). Costa-Zalessow, Natalia, "Anna Radius Zuccari (Neera)." *Scrittrici dal XIII al XX secolo* (Ravenna, 1982), pp. 240–247. Croce, Benedetto, ed., *Neera* (Milano, 1943). Kroha, Lucienne, "Neera: The Literary Career of a Woman of the Nineteenth Century." *Yearbook of Italian Studies*, n. 5 (1983): 77–101. Morandini, Giuliana, ed., *La voce che è in lei* (Milan, 1980). Pacifici, Sergio, "Women Writers: Neera and Aleramo." *The Modern Italian Novel From Capuana to Tozzi* (Carbondale, Ill., 1973). Pansa, Raimondo Collino, "Una femminista d'altri tempi: Neera," *Martinella* 31 (1977): 73–76.

Fiora A. Bassanese

Ada Negri

Born 1870, Lodi, Italy; died 1945, Milan
Genre(s): poetry, novel, short story, translation
Language(s): Italian

Negri was born in a working-class family: her mother labored in a textile factory 12 hours a day, her grandmother, who had once been a personal maid, worked as a doorkeeper in a rich family mansion. Negri studied to become a teacher in order to escape what she described as the humiliating condition of the serving class. From 1888, she taught at Motta Visconti, near Pavia, and began to publish poems in *Illustrazione popolare* of Milan. Her first collection of poetry, *Fatalità* (Fate), came out in 1892 and made her suddenly famous. From then until the end of the Second World War, she published many works of poetry, novels, and short stories. The Fascist Party tried to appropriate her fame by making her a member of the Italian Academy. She officially withdrew from the party at the beginning of the Second World War.

In *Fatalità*, Negri describes the fog-bound industrial centers of northern Italy, their industrial plants, their desolate workers' districts, the humble interiors of people leading repressed, hopeless lives. The volume appeared in a period of great social unrest, characterized by strikes, by demonstrations violently suppressed, and by the women's emancipation movement. In poems, such as "Fire in the Mine," "Strike," "Unemployed," "End of the Strike," which are contained in that volume as well as in the collections *Tempeste* (1886; Storms) and *Esilio* (1914; Exile), Negri spoke to her country with the voice of the oppressed working classes and told of their everyday feelings, their aspirations, their sufferings. That was also the age of Parnassian taste in literature; by contrast, Negri's descriptions were vigorous and straightforward, and they bore that unmistakable ring of authenticity that only personal experience can give.

Equally successful are the two volumes of short stores *Le solitarie* (1917; The Lonely Ones) and *Sorelle* (1929; Sisters). Here the lonely and drab existence of disadvantaged women are described with clear vision and in unimpeachable style. Many believe her best work to be *Stella mattutina* (1921; Morning Star), in which her own painful childhood and adolescence are recollected with great delicacy and lucidity. In some works, such as *Il libro di Mara* (1919; Mara's Book), *I canti dell'Isola* (1925; The Songs of the Island), *Vespertina* (1931; Evening Star), and *Il dono* (1936; The Gift), Negri makes concessions to the literary fashions of her day, to Giovanni Pascoli's sounding of rare inner experiences and to Gabriele D'Annunzio's energetic exaltation in the sunny Mediterranean landscape. Other works, published throughout the thirties and the early war years, show a progressive adherence to conventional middle-class values. Her new interest in religion and mysticism was manifest in her last volume, *Oltre* (Beyond), published posthumously in 1946, a hagiographic life of St. Catherine of Siena.

In retrospect, Negri's value can be clearly seen in her natural narrative vein and in her literary grace. Historically, she marks the first entrance of the working class into Italian letters.

Works

Fatalità [Fate and Other Poems] (1892; tr. A.M. Von Blomberg, 1898). *Tempeste*, from the Italian of Ada Negri (1896; tr. Isabella M. Debarbieri, 1905). *Maternità* (1904). *Dal profondo* (1910). *Esilio* (1914). *Le solitarie* (1917). *Orazioni* (1918). *Il libro di Mara* (1919). *Stella mattutina* [*Morning Star*] (1921; tr. Anne Day, 1930). *Finestre alte* (1923). *I canti dell'isola* (1925). *Le strade* (1929). *Sorelle* (1929). *Vespertina* (1930). *Di giorno in giorno* (1932). *Il dono* (1936). *Erba sul sagrato* (1939). *Fons amoris (1939-1943)* (1946). *Oltre* (1946).

Bibliography

Borgese, G.A., *La vita e il libro*. II (Milan-Rome, 1911), pp. 161–171. Caioli, F., *Ada Negri* (Catania, 1928). Casartelli, A., *Ada Negri nell'opera poetica* (Bergamo, 1956). Cecchi, E., *Libri nuovi e usati* (Naples, 1958), pp. 235–240. *Letteratura italiana del Novecento*. I (Milan, 1972), pp. 341–348. Croce, B., *La Lettertura della Nuova Italia*. IV (Bari, 1914), pp. 335–355. Fabbri, E., *Ada Negri* (Florence, 1921). Frattini, A., *Ada Negri* (Milan, 1921). Galati, V.G., *Ada Negri* (Florence, 1930). Levi, A., *Ada Negri e Paolina Ranieri* (Venice, 1900). Mannino, A., *Ada Negri e Paolina Ranieri* (Venice, 1900). Mannino, A., *Ada Negri nella letteratura contemporanea* (Rome, 1933). Mattalia, D., "Ada Negri." *I Contemporanei*, I (Milan, 1975), pp. 105–135. Padoan, L., *Ada Negri* (Piacenza, 1901). Podenzani, N., *Ada Negri nell'arte e nella vita* (Milan, 1930). Ronzy, P., *L'oeuvre poétique de Ada Negri* (Grenoble, 1931). Ravegnani, G., *I Contemporanei*. I (Milan, 1960), pp. 133–142. Russo, L., *I Narratori* (1950–1957) (Milan'Messina, 1958), pp. 219–221. Schilirò, V., *L'itinerario spirituale di Ada Negri* (Milan, 1938). Serra, R., *Le lettere* (Rome, 1920), pp. 223, 891–899.

Rinaldina Russell

Jo Nein

(see: Nini Roll Anker)

Margarita Nelken

Born July 5, 1896, Madrid, Spain; died March 9, 1968, Mexico City, Mexico
Genre(s): art criticism, literary criticism, essay
Language(s): Spanish, French

In 1931, Margarita Nelken was heralded on the pages of *El Socialista* (organ of the Socialist Workers' Party of Spain) as a representative of the new type of Spanish woman because, according to her interviewer, she combined her literary and artistic talent with political activism. Art critic, journalist, and feminist, Nelken was one of a handful of Spanish women elected to the Spanish Parliament during the Republic (1931–1936). A Socialist, she was the only woman elected in the three elections held during that period. Among her books and articles, her two most significant contributions to the "woman question" in Spain are: *La condición de la mujer en España* (1922; Women's Condition in Spain) and *Las escritoras españolas* (1930; Spanish Women Writers).

Margarita Nelken was born in Madrid in 1896 and from a very early age trained as a painter. She studied painting in Paris with Eduardo Chicharro and Maria Blanchard. In 1914 she participated in a collective show in Vienna, and in 1916 she had an individual show in the Sala Parés in Barcelona. Her paintings were also shown in Bilbao at the Sala de Artistas Vascos (the Basque Artists Gallery). By 1911, at the age of fifteen, she was already contributing articles on painting to *The Studio*, an English journal, and to the French *Le Mercure de France*. She had to give up painting for fear of going blind. Art, though, would always be her livelihood. Before the Civil War she was an art critic and professor at the Prado Museum. After the war, in her Mexican exile, she wrote many books on art criticism and was one of the art critics of the Mexico City daily, *El Excelsior*.

Deeply affected by the German Revolution, Nelken became interested in social issues and feminism. In 1922, she published *La condición de la mujer en España*, which, from the outset, was received as a revolutionary call for the development of feminism in Spain. In it she argued that women were exploited in every aspect of their lives: the work place, the home, their sexual relationships, the legal system, and their education. She extensively discusses comparable worth, the social ramifications of a negligible education for women, sexual hypocrisy, the Church's emotional exploitation of women, the lack of sexual education, the problem of illegitimate children, prostitution, single motherhood, and the need for divorce. This book was perceived to be groundbreaking because she did not isolate each problem and treat it as a single issue. Rather, she subsumed all of the different issues under the general category of exploitation. Her male contemporaries on the Right and the Left were shocked and upset by this book. The Right was scandalized by its tough anticlerical line. The Left was hurt because she did not exclude it from her critique. She often criticizes the Socialist Workers' Party for not paying attention to the woman question when, she argues, that women's oppression originates in the exploitation of women's labor. Her argument is that feminism can only be triumphant if the Left realizes that feminism is essential to its struggle and if the Spanish movement becomes cosmopolitan and links up with the women's movements in other countries. The importance of Margarita Nelken's position is that it proposes the unity of socialism and feminism in Spain.

Paradoxically, Margarita Nelken was against women's suffrage. Her analysis of the Spanish situation led her to conclude that women in Spain were not ready for political intervention. Already a deputy in the Parliament in 1931, she did not attend the session of the Cortes that was to vote on women's suffrage. Spanish women won the right to vote on that day.

Las escritoras españolas is a landmark book. Writing within a male-dominated literary tradition in which women writers were either considered exceptions to the rule or where copious lists of women writers were concocted in order to prove the existence of women writers, she chooses to establish the idea of a women's culture. For Nelken, there has always existed in Spain a tradition of women's writing and a strong participation of women in the world of culture. She argues that ecclesiastical censorship was always harder on women's writing than on men's, but that this censorship served as a stimulus for women writers. In fact, what she does in this book is establish a corpus and a tradition of women writers. She discovers that mysticism is the dominant theme of women's writing. In opposition to other contemporary women writers who spoke of the constraints placed on them by male writers, Nelken never mentions the difficulties of women writing within the male literary tradition. Rather, she chooses to set up an alternative and separate women's culture in opposition to the male literary tradition.

During the Civil War she was active in the defense of Madrid, participated in the International Congress of Antifascist Writers, was a reporter for several journals, and continued to lecture on art. She was first exiled in the Soviet Union, where her son Santiago died at the battle of Stalingrad, and then went on to Mexico where she died in 1968.

Works

Glosaario (Obras y artistas) (1917). *La condición social de la mujer en España* (1922). *La trampa del arenal* (1923). "La aventura de Roma" (1923). "Mi suicidio" (1924). "Una historia de adulterio" (1924). "Pitimini 'etoile'" (1924). "El viaje a Paris" (1925). *En torno a nosotras* (1927). *Tres tipos de vírgenes* (1929). *Las escritoras españolas* (1930). *La mujer ante las Cortes Constituyentes* (1931). *Ramon y Cajal. La mujer: conversaciones e idiario* (1933). *Por qué hicimos la Revolución* (1935). *Las torres del Kremlin* (1943). *Historia del hombre que tuvo el mundo en la mano. J. W. von Goethe* (1943). *Los judíos en la cultura hispánica* (194?). *Primer frente* (1944). *Carlos Orozco Romero* (1951). *Escultura Mexicana contemporanea* (1951). *Historia gráfica del arte occidental* (1953). *Ignacio Asúsolo* (1962). *El expresionismo en la plástica mexicana de hoy* (1964). *Un mundo etereo: la pintura de Lucinda Urrusti* (1976).

Bibliography

Capel, Rosa María, *El sufragio femenino en la 2ª república españa* (Granada, 1975). Kern, Robert, "Margarita Nelken," in *European Women on the Left*, ed. Jane Slaughter and Robert Kern (Westport, Conn., 1981). Rodrigo, Antonina, *Mujeres de España (Las silenciadas)* (Barcelona, 1979).

Alda Blanco

Bo'ena Němcová

Born February 4, 1820, Vienna, Austria; died
January 20, 1862, Prague
Genre(s): short stories and novels
Language(s): Czech

Němcová was a leading figure in late Czech romanticism and the first eminent Czech woman writer. She is still considered to be one of the most significant Czech prose writers, and her novel *Babička* (1855; Grandmother) is a classic of Czech literature and one of the most frequently translated works in Czech.

Her personal life was tragic. The illegitimate daughter of household servants to the nobility in Vienna, she spent her early childhood with her grandmother in the Czech village of Ratibořice, which later became the inspiration for her most famous novel. At the age of seventeen, she married Josef Němec, a Czech customs official, who was much older than she. Although the young and beautiful Němcová became involved in the intellectual life of Prague and counted among her friends Karel Havlíček, Josef Frič, J.E. Purkyně, Václav Nebeský, and many other literary and cultural leaders, her married life became increasingly chaotic and unhappy. Her husband was periodically accused of illegal political activities by the Austrian government, and this persecution led to frequent changes of residence and a low income for the family. After a hard life, Němcová died at the age of forty-two, poor, sick, and lonely. In contrast, her literary works convey a warm sympathy for humanity and faith in the goodness of Nature and God. As a disciple of Rousseau, Němcová sensed a natural harmony that transcends all social and economic distinctions.

Like her friend Karel Erben, an important Czech poet, Němcová began her literary career by collecting Czech folk tales and incorporating folk themes into her work, as in *Obrázek vesnický* (1847; Picture of the Village). Although her early stories are often sentimental and didactic, Němcová developed the narrative technique that she was to use in *Babička*.

Critics generally agree that the classic *Babička* transcends her other works. In this novel, Němcová combines autobiographical details from her childhood (the central character is obviously modeled on her own grandmother), with a sense of the universal. The figure of the grandmother is often associated with the Slavic ideal of motherhood, but in a larger sense, she represents a maternal, natural order of things, full of beauty and goodness.

Although Němcová continued to deal with similarly ethnographic materials, from *Pohorská vesnice* (1856; The Village in the Foothills) to her last tales, she was never able to repeat the artistic harmony she had achieved in *Babička*.

Němcová's literary accomplishment served as a model for future writers, and since her time, Czech women writers have exerted a strong influence on the development of the Czech novel, an influence that is notably lacking in other Czech literary genres.

Works

Národní báchorky a pověsti (1845–1846). *Domácí nemoc* (1846). *Dlouhá noc* (1846). *Obrázek vesnický* (1847). *Baruška* (1852). *Rozárka* (1854). *Babička* (1855). *Karla* (1855). *Divá Bará* (1855). *Pohorská vesnice* (1856). *V zámku a v podzámčí* (1856). *Chudí lidé* (1856). *Dobrý člověk* (1858). *Chy'e pod horami* (1858). *Slovenské pohádky a pověsti* (1857–1858).

Bibliography

Fučík, J., *Tři studie* (1947). Laiske, M., *Bibliografie Bo'eny Němcové* (1962). Nejedly, Z., *O literatuře* (1953). Otruba, M., *Bo'ena Němcová* (1962). Tille, V., *Bo'ena Němcová* (1911).

Reference works: *Čeští spisovatelé 19. a počátku 20. století*, eds. K. Homolová, M. Otruba, and Z. Pešat (1982). *Čeští spisovatelé deseti století*, ed. R. Š<t&r>astný (1974).

Clinton Machann

Nemophila

(see: Terézia Vansová)

Salomėja Nėris

(see: Salomėja Bčinskaitė-Bučienė)

Olga Nerská

(see: Marie Pujmanová)

Friedericke Caroline Neuber

(a.k.a. Die Neuberin)

Born March 9, 1697, Reichenbach, Vogtland;
   died November 30, 1760, Laubegast
Genre(s): drama
Language(s): German

The family of Weissenborn migrated from Stettin to Zwickau where Neuber was educated in the local girls' elementary school. At twenty-one she married the actor Johann Neuber and joined his troupe of strolling players. Friedericke Neuber became director of the troupe in 1720 and toured Germany until 1749.

Through collaboration with Johann Christian Gottsched, she introduced French classical drama to the German stage. After the production of Gottsched's *Der sterbende Cato*, the friendly collaboration came to an end. Neuber was one of the first producers to recognize Lessing's genius, and in 1748, she produced his drama, *Der Junge Gelehrte*.

Neuber played an important role in transforming the comic productions of the German stage into plays of artistic merit after the French model. Credited with banning the *Hanswurst* from the German stage, she arranged the script and composed prologues and epilogues of the plays that she produced. After 1748, the Neuber troupe suffered financial misfortune and was dissolved in 1749. She died in poverty one year after the death of her husband.

Works

Liebesbrief (1712). *Bey der hohen Vermählung Ihr. Königl. Hoheit Printz Friedrichs* (1733). *Bittgesuch an den Grafen Bruhl* (1734). *Ein deutsches Vorspiel* (1734). *Die Verehrung der Vollkommenheit durch die gebesserten deutschen Schauspiele* (1737). *Bittgedicht an den Graf von Hennicke* (1749). *Das Schäferfest oder die Herbstfreude. Ein deutsches Lustspiel in Versen an dem glorreichen Namensfeste Maria Theresia* (1753). *O: Künstler* (1756). *Geburtstagsgedicht* (1756).

Bibliography

Reden-Esbeck, Friedrich Johann Freiherr von, *Caroline Neuber und ihre Zeitgenossen* (Leipzig, 1881). Stümcke, H., *Die Frau als Schauspielerin* (Leipzig, 1905).

Mary Gies Hatch

Madeleine Neveu

(see: dames des Roches)

Giulia Niccolai

Born 1934, Milan, Italy
Genre(s): poetry, novel
Language(s): Italian, English

Giulia Niccolai's poetry is singular. It reflects her multilingual background and her particular sensibility, which is whimsical and yet sharply attuned to the intricacies of language. She is a master of rhetorical effects that emanate from her mastery of several languages; many of her poems are written in a punning mixture of Italian, English, French, and German. Born of an American mother and an Italian father, Niccolai has lived and worked as a photojournalist both in Italy and America; her novel *Il grande angolo* (1966) draws on her experience in that field. For several years she edited, with Adriano Spatola, the poetry review *Tam Tam*; she has traveled extensively and taken part in many readings and shows of visual poetry both in Italy and abroad.

Niccolai's poetry can be situated within the experimentalism of the Italian neo-avant garde of the 1960s when formal considerations came to the fore of poetic activity. However, she is finally more baroque than experimental in any ideological sense. Her verse is often "nonsensical" (à la Lewis Carroll), but the playful elements do not entirely hide the serious philosophical questions that nonsense subtly raises. In her concrete poetry, *Humpty Dumpty* (1969), she uses both Carroll and her beloved *Webster's Dictionary* to create visualizations of meanings and resonances inherent within language. Thus, one poem is the word "cheese" written in the shape of a broad smile; another consists of the word "impenetrability" printed so that the letters overlap to form an "impenetrable" mass. Her poetry is always about language itself: its visual, sonorous, and semantic potential. In *Greenwich* (1971) and *New Greenwich* (1975–1979), Niccolai writes poems made up entirely of place names. She explains in the preface to the collection that the poems are "a kind of voyage not in the territories of language but in the language of territories." They might first seem to be entirely nonsensical but her goal is "to evoke possible meanings relative to etymological roots" of the place names. Often the names are grammaticalized so that they serve as verbs or adjectives. The result is a nonsense verse that imitates the syntax and structure of "real" speech so that the poems create a teasing possibility of meaning while escaping from logic's typical lexical confines.

Some of Niccolai's most delightful poems are contained in her *Russky Salad Ballads* (1975–1977). Verses written to and for particular friends and acquaintances, they are, according to the poet, a "kind of ping-pong among Italian, English, French, and German" that serve in part to exorcise an obsession with inter-linguistic rhyming and semantic resonance. The poem *Harry's Bar Ballad* plays on the confusion of ordering dry martinis in various languages, for example; an American is in trouble if he asks for "nine dry martini" and the barman takes him for a German, for then he'll get no martini at all ("nein").

Prima e dopo la Stein (1978–1980) are poems that show a debt to Gertrude Stein's particular brand of linguistic play. They are more narrative and autobiographical than the earlier poems, but continue in the vein of multilingual play and illogic so dear to Niccolai. The poem *Bad Ragaz (quasi una lezione)* (Bad Ragaz [almost a lesson]) is built on the confusions created by the name "Ragaz" (a Swiss town) and the word "ragazzo" (Italian for "boy") which lead to other confusions (in Sydney "concrete poetry" became "concrete pottery" and in Melbourne "concert poetry"). The conversation of which the poem is made meanders from one subject to another in a comical "stream of consciousness" fashion until returning finally to the initial subject ("ragazzi") when the American interlocutor reveals that he teaches in a boys' ("ragazzi") school.

In her preface to *Greenwich*, Niccolai states that she used the World Atlas of the *Encyclopedia Britannica* as the primary source for the place names used in the poems because it has as its motto "All the World's Here—Unabridged." There is a sense in which Niccolai's poetry attempts to contain all of the world and more. Pushing against linguistic and semantic limits, she also pushes against the concrete limits of the world and our experience of it. By naming places, people, and things in new ways, her poetry creates new worlds; by daring to be nonsensical, it expands the limits of sense.

Works

Il grande angolo, a novel (1966). *Humpty Dumpty* (1969). *Greenwich* (1971). *Poema & Oggetto* (1974). *Substitution* (1975). *Russky Salad Ballads & Webster Poems* (1977). *Harry's Bar e altre poesie 1969–1980* (1981).

Poems anthologized in *Poesia degli anni settanta,* Antonio Porta, ed. (1979) and *Donne in poesia: antologia della poesia femminile in Italia dal dopoguerra ad oggi,* Biancamaria Frabotta, ed. (1977).

Poems translated and anthologized in *Italian Poetry 1960–1980: from Neo to Post Avant-garde,* Adriano Spatola and Paul Vangelisti, eds. (1982) and *The Defiant Muse: Italian Feminist Poems from the Middle Ages to the Present,* Beverly Allen, Muriel Kittel and Keala Jane Jewell, eds. (1986).

Bibliography

Del Giudice, Luisa; Verdicchio, Pasquale and Vangelisti, Paul, "Intervista con Giulia Niccolai: 'I think I'm becoming Japanese,'" in *Carte Italiane: A Journal of Italian Studies* 6 (1984–1985): 1–18. Manganelli, Giorgio, Preface to *Harry's Bar e altre poesie 1969–1980* (Milan, 1981), pp. 7–14.

Rebecca West

Marianne Niederweelen

(see: Marie Herzfeld)

Aīda Niedra

(a.k.a. Īda Niedra, Īda Salmiņa or
   Salmiņš [her married name], Aīda
   Nierda [a misprint])

Born March 23, 1899, in Vidzeme, Latvia; died
   November 23, 1972, Santa Monica,
   California
Genre(s): novel, short story, lyric poetry
Language(s): Latvian

Probably the most important Latvian woman
novelist after Anna Brigadere (q.v.), Aīda Niedra
was born and grew up in the country. Her given
name was originally Īda. Early childhood experiences and impressions created close ties and
love for the land, which is very evident in her
work. After secondary school she worked until
1932 as secretary to a Justice of the Peace in Riga.
She spent the years 1944 to 1949 as a war refugee
in Germany, and then immigrated to the United
States. Her novels are powerful studies of heroic,
archetypal figures, especially women, whose
primitive passions are purged by hard work,
motherhood, and suffering, and who exemplify
such national characteristics as *spīts* (stubborn
defiance). To achieve the idealization necessary
for her purposes, she frequently places her narratives in the nineteenth century and uses a
stylized, rhetorical mode of expression.

Works

Erōsa eleģias (1924). Sarkanā vāze (1927). Pie
Azandas upes(1933). Dziesminiece(1934). Ciema
spīgana(1935). Anna Dzilna(1936). Sieva(1938).
Rū'u Kristīne(1939). Ro'u pelni(1946). Kārdinātāja
(1949). Katrīne "bele (1950). Pasaules plauksta
(1952). Trīs Cannu sievietes (1954). Pilsēta pie
Daugavas(1955). Melnā magone(1956). Miera ielas
cepurniece (1957). Mū'lga Ieva (1958). Pērles
Majores draugs (1958). Ugunis pār Rata kalnu
(1959). Bulvāru čigāni(1960). Septītā clipa(1960).
Sieviete ar sarkaniem ērkšķiem(1961). Tas trakais
kavelieru gads (1962). Holivudas klauns (1963).
Melnas plūmes pie sarkanam lūpām, with Andrievs
Salmiņš(1964). Indrānes oši šalc(1965). Trīs laimes
meklētāji(1966). Sastapšanas pie operas kafejnīcas
(1967). Atkal Eiropā (1968). Grēka ābols (1968).
Varavīksnes pār Rīgu(1969). Rīga dienās, nedienās
(1970). "dams un Ieva (1971).

Bibliography

Andrups, Jānis and Vitauts Kalve, *Latvian Literature*, tr. Ruth Speirs (Stockholm, 1954), pp. 170–
172. Also see Benjamiņš Jēgers, *Latviešu trimdas
izdevumu bibliografija–Bibliography of Latvian
Publications Published Outside Latvia, 1940–1960*
(Sundbyberg, 1972); *1961–1970* (Sundbyberg,
1977); and *1971–1980* (Stockholm, 1988).

Zoja Pavlovskis

Īda Niedra

(see: Aīda Niedra)

Antonina Niemiryczowa

(a.k.a. A Polish Lady, A.Z.I.N.S.O.)

Born c. 1702; died c. 1760
Genre(s): poetry, translations
Language(s): Polish

Born in the eastern province of the Polish
kingdom, daughter of a landlord and regional
administrator, Niemiryczowa studied at the
monastery of Bernardine sisters in Lwow
(Lemberg). Having returned home upon graduation, she completed her education, studying
French, German, and Italian. At around twenty
years of age, she married Karol Niemirycz, a
Lithuanian dignitary, and moved to his property
in Czerniechow (Obrucki region). After her
husband's death in 1753, she lived first in her
village and then in Lwow, and later in Zolotyjow
near Rowne (presently Byelorussia). She died
before June 1760.

Works

Poetry: *Krotkie ze swiata zebranie roznych
koniektur odmienne alternaty przez piesni swieckie
wyrazajace, samej prawdzie nieskazitelnej Bogu,
przez krotkie aprobaty przyznawajace od jednej
polskiej damy, to jest: A.Z.I.N.S.O., komponowane
dla czestej refleksji Czlowiekowi roku* (1743).
Zebranie wierszow polskich, collected poems
(unpublished, written 1753).
Translations: J. de Prechac, *Feniz rzadki na swiecie,
to jest przyjaciel w roznych intrygach i awanturach
stateczny*. J.M. Pan, *Walewski na pamiatke i
pochwale kawalerow polskich wierszem polskim z
z franc. ... opisany*, French poems translated (1750).

Rady dane przyjaciolce przez P.P. *** *tlumaczone z franc* [Advice given by a lady to a friend] (tr. from French) (1755).

Sergiusz Piasecki

Aīda Nierda

(see: Aīda Niedra)

Galina Evgenievna Nikolaeva

(see: Galina Evgenievna Volianskaia)

Tove Nilsen

Born October 25, 1952, Oslo, Norway
Genre(s): novel, short story, youth and
children's literature
Language(s): Norwegian

Nilsen grew up in a working class neighborhood on the east side of Oslo. Both the area and the dialect spoken there have traditionally been considered by the establishment to be inferior. Having studied literature and worked as critic and freelance journalist, Nilsen has also been active in the Norwegian women's movement. In most of her books Nilsen has gleaned material—plot, theme, and language—from her home milieu. In addition she has taken up feminist issues as abortion, lesbianism, and the freedom of women as well as other issues of social justice, such as unemployment and juvenile delinquency. *Aldri la dem kle deg forsvarsløst naken* (1974; Never Let Them Dress You Defenselessly Naked), Nilsen's first novel, deals with the question of legalized abortion. The theme of *Fritt løp* (1980; Free Rein) is that of a woman leaving a dead-end relationship behind to break out of her passive female role and to seek love and life abroad. Together with two girlfriends, the protagonist, Mai, travels to Italy. There the women develop a relationship of sisterhood and fellowship, while maintaining a positive attitude toward men and sexuality. The author's point is not that women should be in opposition to men, but rather that they need to get the same freedom for themselves that men have always enjoyed. *Skyskraperengler*

(1982; Skyscraper Angels) portrays the lives of twelve-year-old girls growing up in a bedroom community on the east side of Oslo in the late 1950s. The title refers to their attempts at trying their wings before they are clipped. The protagonist of *I stedet for dinosaurer* (1987; Instead of Dinosaurs) is a middle-aged photographer named Kjell Østby, who is struggling to reconcile the conflict between the objective and the subjective in life.

Nilsen's books have been translated into Danish and Swedish (one short story has been translated into English), but otherwise she is little known abroad. A competent writer, committed to feminist issues, her books have sometimes been criticized for a lack of connectedness and for being somewhat predictable. Nilsen has been praised, however, for her entertaining style and for her efforts to legitimize the working class milieu and dialect.

Works

Aldri la dem kle deg forsvarsløst naken [Never Let Them Dress You Defenselessly Naked] (1974). *Helle og Vera* (1975). *Tonje–snart 11 år* [Tonje–Almost 11], children's book (1976). *Hendene opp fra fanget* [Hands Out of Your Lap] (1977). *De skulle bare visst* [If Only They'd Known], juvenile book (1977). *Gerhard* (1978). *Fritt løp* [Free Rein] (1980). *Skyskraperengler* [Skyscraper Angels] (1982). [With Trygve Bølstad], *Vi tier ikke!* [We Won't Keep Quiet!] (1983). *Den svarte gryte* [The Black Kettle] (1985). *I stedet for dinosaurer* [Instead of Dinosaurs] (1987).

Translations: "Scum," tr. Barbara Wilson, in *An Everyday Story*, ed. Katherine Hanson (Seattle, 1984), pp. 219–228.

Bibliography

Bramness, Hanne, and Anne Beate Tomterstad, "Tove Nilsen." *Profil* 1/2 (1981): 58–60 (Interview). Dahl, Willy, *Norges litteratur III: Tid og tekst 1935–1972* (Oslo, 1989), pp. 274, 295f. 314. Espejord, Anne Kristin, "Vi må komme videre . . ." *Sirene* 3 (1983): 30–31 (Interview). Rottem, Øystein, "Sympatisk, men opplagt: Tove Nilsen: *Fritt løp*." *Vinduet* 34.4 (1980): 56–58.

Margaret Hayford O'Leary

Clemenza Ninci

Lived early to mid-seventeenth century, Prato, Italy

Genre(s): drama

Language(s): Italian

Clemenza Ninci was a nun in the Benedictine convent of San Michele in Prato in the early to mid-seventeenth century. Cesare Guasti, a nineteenth-century specialist in the cultural history of Prato and the first scholar to study her writing, was unable to find mention of her either in documents from her convent or in those of the local bishopric. He knew only that she belonged to an upper-class family. He published her one known play, the *Sposalizio d'Iparchia filosofa* (The Marriage of Hipparchia, Lady Philosopher), in an almost, but not entirely complete edition, leaving out parts he found verbose and uninteresting.

Clemenza Ninci's play was written for convent performance, as is clear from the list alongside the names of the characters of the nuns who played the parts. Clemenza herself played one of the roles, that of a mad astrologer. The play follows the form of the typical convent genre, the spiritual comedy, though there is nothing spiritual about it except, perhaps, one message, not stressed but mentioned, that this life is a vale of tears. The play conserves, however, the structural and stylistic features of the genre: it is composed of interwoven plots, one of which is low comedy involving servants and peasants, the other, and in this play, the other two, of aristocratic heroes and heroines, participants in a serious and edifying story. The main plot is the story of Hipparchia, a noblewoman, urged to marry by her family, who will do so only on the condition that she be allowed to marry her teacher, the poor but virtuous philosopher Crates, who owns nothing but the humble clothes he wears. Obstacles to the marriage are introduced through misunderstanding and envy, and when they are overcome the play concludes happily with the couple's marriage. The second plot, completely unconnected in the story line to the first, is introduced after the other and concluded before it. It tells the story of Ardelone and Ermilla, the son and daughter of two royal families, whose marriage plans are disrupted by politics and war.

They flee to a pastoral setting, where with the magic of a sorceress and the intervention of Pluto all is resolved happily. There is yet a third, contrasting plot, a farcical subplot of the pastoral tale; it features peasants, a married couple, and a lecherous old man and is exploited for all of its comic possibilities.

Cesare Guasti read the combined message of the plots as a comparison of the mature love of philosophers with the tender love of princes and the ugly passion of an old man. If we add that there is also a clear contrast between the praiseworthy loves of nobles and the humorous and quaint love of peasants, this is probably a good reading of the intentions implied by the juxtaposition of plots. However, the play is more about marriage than about love and this is clear in all three plots, two of which conclude when appropriate marriages are arranged and the third, the comic subplot, overcomes threats to two marriages. There is also an interesting case of one female character, a sorceress, who was rejected by her husband and divorced by him. Although unable to help herself, she has magical powers she can use to help others, and indeed she is instrumental in uniting two young lovers. If the many marriages in the play entertained convent women by satisfying their curiosity about the secular world or by allowing them to enjoy that world vicariously, the story of the rejected woman whose life is dedicated to helping others looks as if it were intended as a paradigm for convent women.

Finally, the other important subject stressed by the play is the love of learning as embodied in Hipparchia, who above all wants to continue her studies. She will have her way and will have marriage as well, since she chooses to marry her teacher and to spend her life discussing philosophy with him. Orlando, the mad astrologer, who was played by the author herself, is an example of learning out of control. It is not clear whether this character is to serve as a warning or simply as an element of humor—perhaps both, and perhaps Orlando, Hipparchia's astrology teacher, is to be compared unfavorably with Crate, her philosophy teacher. Clearly, the protagonist, the lady philosopher, like the religious heroines of conventional convent theater, sets an example for the audience of a life devoted to learning, which sixteenth and seventeenth-century Tuscan convents afforded at least some of their women, certainly Clemenza Ninci. Her comedy is learned. The story of Hipparchia is taken from Diogenes Laertius' *Lives of the Philosophers*, the play is replete with stories from mythology, and there are allusions to Ovid, to Virgil, to Ariosto, perhaps, and almost certainly to Tasso and to the Italian pastoral tradition.

Works

Sposalizio di Ipparchia filosofa, ms., Riccardiana Library, Florence, cod. Ricc. 2974, vol. 3. Published, with some omissions, by Cesare Guasti in the *Calendario Pratese del 1850* (1849), pp. 53–101.

Bibliography

Introd. to *Calendario Pratese*, ed. Cesare Guarti, op. cit., pp. 53–63.

Elissa B. Weaver

Marie Nizet

(a.k.a. Marie Mercier-Nizet)

Born 1859, Brussels, Belgium; died 1922, Boisfort, Belgium
Genre(s): poetry, short story
Language(s): French

Marie Nizet was born to a family that was no stranger to literature. Her father François was not only a conservator at the Bibliothèque Royale in Brussels and a professor but also a poet. Her brother Henri became a naturalist novelist of some note in Belgian letters. Marie made her literary debut at eighteen with a series of works inspired by contact with her father's students of Slavic or Balkan origin. The struggle to free Romania from the oppressive regime of the tsars touched her political sensibilities, while the region's folklore and superstitions excited her imagination. Her career came to an abrupt halt with her marriage, an unhappy union that ended in divorce soon after the birth of a child. Marie spent the rest of her life in relative obscurity. It was only after her death and the publication of *Pour Axel* (1923; For Axel) that the extent of her talent was revealed.

The early works reflect the fascination with Romania during the reign of Napoleon III. *Le Capitaine vampire* (1877; The Vampire Cap-

tain), a typical tale of that country is one of the many vampire stories that proliferated during the period. Her poetry was often of a marked political tone. She pleads the Roumanian cause in *Moscou et Bucharest* (1877; Moscow and Bucharest) and *Pierre le Grand à Jassi* (1878; Peter the Great at Jassi). *Românîa* (1878), however, is a lyrical expression of the beauties of the land and its people, written with a sureness of tone and harmony rare in so young a writer. The posthumous publication of *Pour Axel* received much critical praise, and another side of the poet was brought to light. The poems are a lament for a dead beloved, a sailor claimed by the sea. The work displays a deft mixture of tone and themes. The sensualism and passion of a happy relationship give way to a Christian resignation and coming to terms with loss. The promise of Marie's first works is fully realized in *Pour Axel* and places her among Belgium's best poets.

Works

Le Capitaine vampire (1877). *Moscou et Bucarest* (1877). *Românîa (Chants de la Roumanie.)* (1878). *Pour Axel de Missie* (1923).

Edith J. Benkov

-nn-

(see: Wilhelmina "Minna" Ulrika [Johnson] Canth)

Anna-Elizabeth de Noailles (de Brancovan)

Born November 15, 1876, Paris, France; died April 30, 1933, Paris
Genre(s): poetry, novel, short story, memoirs
Language(s): French

The Countess of Noailles, author of twenty works that include poems, novels, short stories, and memoirs, was known and celebrated for a very brief time during her life before being condemned by the "intellectuals." She was much admired by Jean Cocteau, whose last work, *La Comtesse de Noailles: Oui et Non*, presents a fascinating picture of a woman both loved and despised. Her work was overtly sensual, in the tradition of Verlaine, which aroused both ire and fascination among her contemporaries; according to Cocteau, her real "fault" lay in the fact that her works did not include "un certain ennui," the sign of the serious and the privilege of a true masterpiece. Considered a "néo-romantic" by those who denigrated her work, she drew inspiration from "pagan" sources, and focused much of her attention on nature, the beautiful, and death which she referred to as "l'ombre" (shadow). Those who admired her did so with hyperbole: Joseph Reinach is reputed to have told her, "There exist three miracles in France: Joan of Arc, the Marne, and you," while Moréas nicknamed her the Hymettan Bee. She was touted by Maurice Barrés who marveled at her "obscured shivers, regal fevers," and presented her as a latter-day Sappho who—single-handedly, one surmises—revived the best of ancient Greek poetry. Colette also praised her, painting an unofficial portrait that celebrates her as poet first, beauty and aristocrat second, and includes two observations the Countess made about herself; the first, "I am wild, but without a trace of wickedness," the second, "I shall have been useless but irreplaceable." Interestingly, it was Gide and his circle of what Cocteau calls "encyclopedistes" at the *Nouvelle Revue Française* who treated Anna as a traitor to the cause.

The daughter of a Romanian father, Prince Gregory Bassaraba de Brancovan, and Greek mother, Ralouka Musurus, Anna-Elizabeth was born in Paris on November 15, 1876. Anna-Elizabeth had an older brother, Constantin, who, from 1903–1905, directed a journal called *La Renaissance Latine* for up-and-coming writers of the era; her younger sister, Hélène, the princess Alexandre de Caraman-Chimay by marriage, died in 1929.

Anna-Elizabeth spent her youth in Paris and Amphion, on the banks of Lake Léman, and in 1897, married Mathieu, Count of Noailles. From that time on she lived almost exclusively in Paris where she gave birth to a son, Anne-Jules, in 1908. She died in Paris on April 30, 1933, and was buried in the Père-Lachaise cemetery. Her heart, however, was taken to the cemetery of Publier in Haute-Savoie where it was buried separately beneath a steel inscribed with a line from one of her poems: "C'est là que dort mon coeur, vaste témoin du monde" (Here sleeps my heart, witness to the wide world).

Anna was made a member of the Académie Royale de Langue et de Littérature Françaises in Brussels in 1922—an honor in which she was followed by Colette—and was the first French woman to be promoted to commander in the Legion of Honor.

In 1938 a monument was erected in her honor in Amphion. The majority of her manuscripts belong to the Bibliothèque Nationale, which hosted an exhibition in her honor in 1953 on the twentieth anniversary of her death. There is some indication that her star is on the rise again.

Works

Le Coeur innombrable (1901). *L'ombre des jours* (1902). *La Nouvelle espérance* (1903). *Le visage emerveille* (1904). *La Domination* (1905). *Les Eblouissements* (1907). *De la Rive d'Europe à la Rive d'Asie* (1913). *Les Vivants et les morts* (1913). *Les forces eternelles* (1920). *Poésies* (1920). *Conte Triste avec une moralité* (1921). *Les innocentes ou la sagesse des femmes* (1923). *Les Climats* (1924). *Le poeme de l'Amour* (1924). *Passions et vanités* (1926). *L'honneur de souffrir* (1927). *Poèmes d'Enfances* (1929). *Exactitudes* (1930). *Le livre de ma vie* (1932). *Derniers vers* (1934, posthumous collection).

Bibliography

Perche, L., *Anna de Noailles* (1964). Tascu, Valentin, "Anna Brâncoveanu de Noailles." *Steava* 35 (1984): 31.

Sarah Spence

Marie Noël

Born February 16, 1883, Auxerre, France; died
December 23, 1967, Auxerre
Genre(s): poetry, prose texts, journal
Language(s): French

Noël lived the eighty-four years of her long life mostly in the ancient cathedral town of Auxerre, in Bourgogne, three hours south of Paris, on the river Yonne. Of poor health, she studied mostly at home but for the years 1897–1900 when she attended Lycée Paul Bert where her father (Louis Rouget, Philosophy Ph.D. and keen on handicraft) taught history of art. In 1900 she learned piano playing and discovered the old

French folk song, a main source of inspiration for her poetry. She had her first poetical attempts, first personal religious aspirations, and the torments that would evolve in her peculiar Catholicism. In Christmas, 1904, a love deception and the sudden death of a little brother inspired the choice of her pen name, *Noël*, the French word for Christmas, "my name of grace and, even more, my name of affliction." Both poetry and nervous disease arose from these trials. In 1908, she showed her poems to her godfather, Raphaël Périé, the first one who encouraged her and got her first poems published in *La Revue des deux mondes*, June 1910. In 1920, the encouragement of the head physician in the mental health clinic where she was treated got her to publish (on her own) her first collection of poems *Les chansons et les heures* (The Songs and the Hours). Songs had come to her through her childhood in the voices of her nanny, of her mother, of her grandmother, "my singer" as she called her; the sadness of an ancient folk song caused her to faint. Her poems are mostly song-structured with couplets and refrains: the word "song" comes sixty times in titles as well as "berceuse," "noël," "hymn," "dance," "canticle." She has written "I trusted the song, because it could hide me . . . I have never been a woman of letters; I'll ever be a wild girl singing for others their own loves and sorrows . . . I was possessed by a rhythm, a real devil: it was the rhythm which consumed my heart." Her "bouquets of poems" had three colors: Songs for myself, Songs for others, Songs of the Gospel on these themes: "*Love, or what took its place for me; warm tenderness, Compassion, Death, religious feeling, devotion to Mary. . . .*" The "songs for herself" were the most urgent ones: "dream-tenderness-prayer-imagination let free to spring." "Songs for others" are the expression of a cosmic joining in human affliction. She was appreciated and encouraged to develop her *genius* (as Montherlant called her talent) by two great priests of her times, Henri Bremond, S.J., French academic, a modernist and a writer, and Abbé Arthur Mugnier, much beloved in high society for his real charity, love of literature, and a wisdom full of kindness. In 1983, the centenary of her birth, Noël has been celebrated with a deeper sense of her complexity: a performance, a reading of her poems, and articles have attempted to enliven from inside the consecrated image of the laureate Catholic poet. For Noël a poet was "A blind messenger who . . . brings to the world . . . the unusual sound and the mysterious charm of what nobody knows from a reliable source."

Works

L'oeuvre poétique (1969). Oeuvres en prose (1977). Notes intimes (1959). Chants des quatre temps (1972). Records on her poems.
Translations: *Reflected Light, Poems of Marie Noël*, tr. Sara Woodruff (1964). *Notes for Myself* [*Notes intimes*], tr. Dr. Howard Sutton (1968).

Bibliography

Escholier, R., *La neige qui brûle* [Burning Snow] (Paris, 1967, last ed.). Gouhier, H., *Le Combat de Marie Noël* [The Struggle of Marie Noël] (Paris, 1971). For further information: Association Marie Noël—85, 2. Carnot, 92300 Levallois—France, publ. *Cahiers Marie Noël*.

Gabriella Fiori

Isotta Nogarola

Born c. 1416, Verona, Italy; died 1466
Genre(s): letters, oration, poetry
Language(s): Latin

Together with other women humanists of fifteenth-century Italy, Nogarola was the product of a new cultural revival, whereby the arts, the humanities, and other attainments of the human mind reached unprecedented popularity, and some of the educational advantages reserved for boys were extended to girls of the privileged classes. Born to Bianca Borromeo and Leonardo Nogarola, both of noble ancestry, Isotta found in her family an environment very favorable to learning. Her aunt, Angela Nogarola, was a poet; other members of the family had distinguished themselves in literature and in the sciences. Together with her sisters, Isotta studied Greek and Latin, first under Matteo Bosso, then under Martino Rizzoni, a favorite pupil of the celebrated teacher Guarino of Verona. In 1538, she moved to Venice in order to avoid the plague and the war between the Venetian Republic and Milan. After her return to Verona, in 1541, she made friends with Lodovico Foscarini, son of the Doge, who had become mayor of the city and kept a literary salon. Although she was sought after for her fame and beauty, Isotta declined marriage and pursued her studies in isolation. Sacred literature and theology became the exclusive subject of her study in the second part of her life. She was buried in the church of Santa Maria Antica in Verona.

Nogarola cultivated the genres popular with the literary elite of her times: the Latin epistle, Latin poetry, the oration, and the dialogue.

Her letters were addressed to literary men and to dignitaries of her region. In Verona, there is a letter in which Isotta congratulates the celebrated humanist Ermolao Barbaro on his election to prothonotary apostolic. In 1437, she worded an elegant and enthusiastic praise of Guarino of Verona, and sent it to him, hence a number of letters were exchanged between the Nogarola sisters, Guarino and his son, Girolamo. With Damiano del Borgo, she kept a lengthy correspondence, animated by reciprocal admiration and affection. To Foscarini she turned for advice and moral support. It is in disputation with Foscarini that Isotta wrote the dialogue on the relative culpability of Adam and Eve. Her letters were greatly admired in her times for their elegance and the frequent erudite citations and digressions. Their manuscripts were soon dispersed among various Italian towns and abroad. Arturo Pomello tells us that 564 of them could be found in the second half of the seventeenth century in one Parisian library alone.

One letter is written in the classical form of consolatoria and laments the death of J.A. Marcello's son. A second oration was written for the arrival of E. Barbaro, and a third one in praise of Saint Jerome. Isotta's best-known work, however, is the dialogue-disputation between herself and Foscarini about the relative culpability of Adam and Eve. Here Isotta finds herself in the position of defending Eve against the authority of the Bible and of Saint Augustine's commentary. Although she pleads for the weakness of the female sex, she holds Adam the guiltier of the two because of his greater knowledge and responsibility. She further argues in Eve's favor, in name of her compelling desire to acquire knowledge, a desire that is innate in humankind. The dialogue was published by the author's descendant, Count

Francesco Nogarola, in 1563, in a handsome Aldine edition. The text, however, was significantly altered and the liveliness of the original exchange between Isotta and Ludovico was lost in what became an erudite treatise, more subdued from a doctrinal point of view.

Nogarola is an important figure not only in the history of feminism, but for the sociological and anthropological study of western civilization. As an early bluestocking, she soon became aware of the structural obstacles encountered by women who, for the first time in history, received an education comparable to that of men. Recurrent in her letters is the complaint of being a woman and thus being subjected to "men's denigrations in words and fact." Her dialogue clearly attests to the distressing impasse of women who could not reject the cultural and religious traditions from which society drew the justification of an order strongly upheld.

Works

Isotae Nogarolae veroniensis dialogus quo utrum Adam vel Eva magis peccavit. Quaestio satis nota sed non adeo explicata, continetur (1563). *Isotae Nogarolae Veroniensis, opera quae supersunt omnia,* ed. E. Abel, 2 vols. (1886). Maria Ludovica Lenzi, *Donne e Madonne, L'educazione femminile nel primo Rinascimento italiano* (1982), pp. 209–216. "Of the Equal or Unequal Sin of Adam and Eve," in *Her Immaculate Hand. Selected Works by and About the Women Humanists of Quattrocento Italy,* eds. M.L. King and A. Rabil, Jr. (1983), pp. 57–69.

Bibliography

Bochi, G., ed., *L'educazione femminile dall'Umanesimo alla Controriforma* (Bologna, 1961), pp. 123–128. Cattelani, E. Levi, *Venezia e le sue letterate nei secoli XV e XVI* (Florence, 1879). Cosenza, M.E., *Biographical and Bibliographical Dictionary of the Italian Humanists and of the World of Classical Scholarship in Italy. 1300–1800,* 6 vols. (Boston, 1962), III, pp. 2484–2486. *Enciclopedia Biografica e bibliografica Italiana,* Ser. VI: *Poetesse e Scrittrici,* 2 vols., ed. Maria Bandini Buti (Rome, 1941), II, pp. 83–84. King, M.L., "Thwarted Ambitions: Six Learned Women of the Italian Renaissance." *Soundings* 59 (1976): 280–304. King, M.L., "The Religious Retreat of Isotta Nogarola (1418–1466): Sexism and Its Consequences in the Fifteenth Century." *Signs* 3 (1978): 807–822. King, M.L., "Book-lined Cells: Women and Humanism in the Early Italian Renaissance," in *Beyond Their Sex: Learned Women of the European Past*, ed. P.H. Labalme (New York, 1980), pp. 66–90. King, M.L. and A. Rabil, Jr., *Ibid.*, pp. 16–18, 57–59. Kristeller, P.O., "Learned Women of Early Modern Italy: Humanists and University Scholars." *Ibid.*, pp. 91–116. Lenzi, Maria Ludovica, *Ibid.*, pp. 20–23, 211–216. Pomello, A., *Le Nogarola* (Verona, 1908). Robathan, Dorothy M., "A Fifteenth-Century Bluestocking." *Medievalia et Humanistica* 2 (1944): 106–114. Sabbadini, R., "Notizie sulla vita e gli scritti di alcuni dotti umanisti del secolo XV raccolte da codici italiani. V: Isotta Nogarola." *Giornale storico della letteratura italiana* VI (1885), pp. 163–165. Sabbadini, R., *La scuola e gli studi di Gaurino Veronese* (Catania, 1896). Segarizzi, A., "Niccolò Barbo patrizio veneziano del secolo XV e le accuse contro Isotta Nogarola." *Giornale storico della letteratura italiana* 43 (104): 39–54. Woodward, W.H., *Vittorino da Feltre and Other Humanist Educators* (Cambridge, Mass., 1897).

Rinaldina Russell

Nel (Pieternella Margaretha) Noordzij

(a.k.a. P. Noorthey, Marie Claire Loupard)

Born October 17, 1923, Rotterdam, The Netherlands
Genre(s): poetry, novel, essay
Language(s): Dutch

Due to sporadic partial deafness and a predisposition to asthma, Nel Noordzij—the daughter of an industrial manager—spent a large part of her youth in children's homes (also in Switzerland) and in Catholic boarding schools. Illness interrupted her nurse's training, while her subsequent studies in education could not be completed as a result of war circumstances. In 1947 she attended a few courses of the Swiss psychoanalyst C.G. Jung. Around 1950, Nel Noordzij was working in a center for industrial psychology and in the Amsterdam Laboratory for Applied Psychology, while studying graphology in 's-Gravenhage. Her first story captured a prize in 1954, a year in which she also pub-

lished poetry—for the most part collected in *Leven zonder opperhuid* (1962; Living Without Scarfskin), introduced by Hella Haasse. By the end of the sixties—during her second marriage, and with the charge of three children—Noordzij started graduate studies in psychology, obtaining an American Ph.D. in 1972. Meanwhile her formerly intense literary activities had come to a standstill, but in 1975 she published a *Woordenboek van magie, okkultisme en parapsychologie* (Dictionary of Magic, Occultism, and Parapsychology) and a scientific study on graphology. Until 1978, she had a private practice as a behavior therapist.

In 1955, Noordzij's first two novels provoked a violent controversy in Dutch literary criticism, because of their frankness and "shocking" language. Even readers of her own sex were divided on the subject: Hella Haasse praised the author, while Renate Rubinstein pulled her to shreds. *Met de hand op een boomtak* (Hands on a Branch) deals with the imaginary disease of a woman with a pathological fear of sexuality, while *Het kan me niet schelen* (I Don't Care) presents a young female physician whose hatred-born promiscuity exceeds all bourgeois rules of life. In other works, too, Noordzij's characters suffer from autistic isolation and traumatic anxieties, obsessed as they are by a utopian longing for perfection. A recurrent underlying element is the (often incestuous) love-hate relationship between the female protagonist and her mother. The author's style is harsh, abrupt, fragmentary, "unliterary" by common standards: the emotional content—which is scarcely autobiographical—prevails in this sort of "existential naturalism."

Under the pseudonym of Marie Claire Loupard, Noordzij played a literary hoax upon her hostile critics with *Notities van een norse dame* (1959; Jottings of a Surly Lady): they all loved it. A year later, she wrote two essays on Rilke. Another favorite poet of hers is Emily Dickinson. Noordzij has made her appearance in several literary journals and has participated in radio and television programs. She has been a council member of the Dutch PEN club.

Works

Nederlandse dichteressen na 1900 [Dutch Poetesses After 1900] (2nd ed., 1957). *De schuldvraag* [The Question of Guilt], novel (1961).

Bibliography

Dubois, P.H., *Nieuw Vlaams Tijdschrift* (1956), pp. 440–442. Haasse, H., *Bladspiegel* (1985), pp. 84–85. Rubinstein, R., *Propria Cures* (December 23, 1955 and November 24, 1962). Veeger, P., *Kritisch lexicon van de Nederlandstalige literatuur na 1945* (1984).

Frank Joostens

P. Noorthey

(see: Nel [Pieternella Margaretha] Noordzij)

Hedvig Charlotta Nordenflycht

(a.k.a. En Herdinna i Norden [a shepherdess in the Northland])

Born November 28, 1718, Stockholm, Sweden; died June 29, 1763, Lugnet (near Stockholm)
Genre(s): lyric poetry, prose
Language(s): Swedish

Hedvig Charlotta Nordenflycht remains best known for the emotional intensity and candor of her poetry at a time when these elements were not yet commonly found in Swedish letters. Her lyrics combine a religious outlook with her thoughts on the philosophies of, among others, Voltaire and Rosseau. A literary figure of considerable importance during the middle of the eighteenth century, Nordenflycht, together with the poets Gustaf Creutz and Jacob Gyllenborg, established Sweden's first literary salon.

Nordenflycht was born to middle-class parents (though her father was ennobled for faithful government service in 1727) and led a life not unusual for middle-class girls of her day. She was taught to read Swedish by age five, but despite her literary bent she was given no formal education. Her brothers were allowed to tutor her in Latin and German, but this instruction was limited to their vacations from the university. She read avidly as a young girl, sometimes even while performing household chores. At age sixteen she was engaged to Johan Tideman at her dying father's request. The fiancé had inspired Nordenflycht's respect and friendship by means of his philosophical interests, but by her own reports he was physically repulsive to her. He died before they could marry, and in 1741 she married the more attractive Jacob Fabricius, a naval chaplain, with whom she enjoyed a short happy marriage. His death seven months later propelled Nordenflycht into her poetic career; her collection *Den Sörgande Turtur-Dufwan* (The Mourning Turtledove) of 1743 expresses the sorrow and despair she experienced at the death of her beloved husband. During the next six years she published four volumes of poems under the title *Qwinligit Tankespel* (Feminine Thought-Play), and in 1752 she was awarded a government pension for her literary contributions. Her poetry took on a Voltairean cast during the time of the *Tankebyggarorden* (Order of the Thought Builders), the literary salon of which she was the center. Toward the end of her life she met and fell in love with the much younger Johan Fischerström, and it is assumed that his inability to share her feelings resulted in a failed suicide attempt by drowning, during which she contracted a debilitating illness and died.

Nordenflycht's poetic production is a large one, as is the range of subject matter it encompasses. She grapples with different philosophical approaches and intense emotions, with occasional verse, women's rights and her own private passions. The quality fluctuates, and her rhymes and meter are at times uneven. She has been accused of lacking stylistic sensitivity and of not being capable of understanding the philosophical systems she explores. But a few of her poems (one in particular is "Min lefnadslust är skuren af . . ." [My Lust for Life Is Cut Asunder]) display a true poetic gift, especially those poems inspired by Nordenflycht's intense reactions to her personal misfortune. Her particular poetic essence can be characterized by a content that is ahead of its time (the reader is reminded of the "I"-centered emotional outbursts of Romanticism) encased in a rococo package.

Nordenflycht is considered Sweden's first career poet and one of its first feminists in her belief in women's right and duty to receive an education. Although her unfortunate love experiences have been cause for ridicule, her importance for Swedish letters and her considerable talent cannot be overlooked.

Works

Den Sörgande Turtur-Sufwan [The Mourning Turtledove] (1743). Qwinligit Tankespel (1–4) [Feminine Thought-Play] (1744–1750). Andeliga Skaldeqwäden [Spiritual Poems] (1758). Witterhetsarbeten [Literary Works] (1759, 1762). Utvalda Arbeten [Selected Works], collected by Fischerström (1774). Samlade Skrifter [Collected Works] (1852). Samlade Skrifter [Collected Works], collected by Hilma Borelius (1925–1938).

Bibliography

Axelsson, Sun, "Hedvig Charlotta Nordenflycht." Författarnas litteraturhistoria I (Stockholm, 1977). Bergom-Larsson, Maria, "En själ som ömt och häftigt känner." Kvinnornas litteraturhistoria (Stockholm, 1981). Borelius, Hilma, Hedvig Charlotta Nordenflycht (Uppsala, 1921). Heyman, Viveka, "Fru Nordenflycht, sökerskan." Kvinnornas litteraturhistoria (Stockholm, 1981). Kruse, John, Hedvig Charlotta Nordenflycht: Ett skaldinneporträtt från Sveriges rococo-tid (Lund, 1895). Kunitz, Stanley J., and Vineta Colby, eds., European Authors 1000–1900 (New York, 1967). Levertin, Oscar, "Fru Nordenflycht." Svenska gestalter (Stockholm, 1921). Nilsson, Albert, Fru Nordenflychts religiösa diktning (Lund, 1918). von Platen, Magnus, "Från fru Nordenflychts sista tid." 1700-tal: Studier i svensk litteratur (Stockholm, 1963).

Kathy Saranpa Anstine

Regine Normann

Born 1867, Vesterålen, Norway; died 1939, Norway
Genre(s): novel, short story, fairy tale
Language(s): Norwegian

Regine Normann wrote novels, stories, and tales imbued with the character and beliefs of the people of North Norway where she grew up. Normann's father died when she was four years old, and her mother sent her to live with relatives in Trondenes until she was eleven. At eighteen Normann was married to a teacher, but after ten brutal, unhappy years, she escaped to Oslo in 1894. Here she became a teacher in 1901.

Normann married the author Tryggve Andersen in 1908. They were divorced in 1913. In the summer of 1939, Normann retired to her old home in North Norway, where she died several months later.

Normann made her literary debut in 1905 with Krabvaag, Skildringer fra et lidet fiskevær. The book was well received by contemporary critics and is still considered to be a small masterpiece of realistic description, both sympathetic and objective. Bortsat followed in 1906 and Stængt in 1908. These three works reflect the tragic consequences of a narrow, pietistic Christianity in North Norwegian society, as young love and the opportunity for happiness are destroyed and women forced into oppressive marriages.

In the historical novel Dengang (1912) and its sequel Eiler Hundevart (1913), Normann turns again to the harsh, patriarchal society of North Norway in the difficult years just after 1800. In these novels, as in Krabvaag, the frame of the plot is a love story. But here the tone is milder, less bitter, and love conquers in the end.

Min hvite gut (1922) is a collection of stories from Normann's experiences as a much-loved teacher, marked by her pedagogical ideals and her opinions on religion and society. Stories and fairy tales she told to her students and friends are contained in the collections, Eventyr, Nye Eventyr, Nordlandsnat, Det gråner mot høst, and Usynlig selskap.

Although her work was of uneven quality, sometimes bordering on the sentimental, Normann captured the essence of the nature and milieu of North Norwegian life realistically and with great sensitivity. Regine Normann's greatest contribution to Norwegian literature was her ability to combine realistic description, human warmth, and a belief in the mystical—the underworld of trolls and fairies—in such a way that her readers also believe.

Works

Krabvaag, Skildringer fra et lidet fiskevær [Krabvaag, Sketches from a Little Fishing Village] (1905). Bortsat [Among Strangers] (1906). Stængt [Closed] (1908). Barnets tjenere [The Servant of the Child] (1910). Faafængt [Useless] (1911). Dengang [At That Time] (1912). Eiler Hundevart [Eiler

Hundewart] (1913). *Riket som kommer* [The Kingdom to Come] (1915). *Berit Ursin* [Berit Ursin] (1917). *Havørnens nabo* [The Sea Eagle's Neighbor] (1921). *Min hvite gt* [My White Boy] (1922). *Eventyr* [Tales] (1925). *Nye eventyr* [New Tales] (1926). *Nordlandsnat* [North Country Nights] (1927). *Det gråner mot høst* [Autumn Gray] (1930). *Usynlig selskap* [Invisible Company] (1934). *Ringelihorn og andre eventyr* [Ringelihorn and Other Tales] (1967).

Translations: "Love-Root," tr. Torild Homstad, in *An Everyday Story*, ed. Katherine Hanson (Seattle, 1984), pp. 46–50. "Dear Spring Sun," tr. Torild Homstad. *There Lies a Fair Land*, ed. John Solensten (St. Paul, 1985), pp. 79–81.

Torild Homstad

Nossis

Born Epizephyrian Locri, southern Italy; exact birth and death dates unknown; fl. approximately 275 B.C.
Genre(s): epigrams
Language(s): Greek

Nossis apparently belonged to one of the ranking families of Locri. In poem 3 (*AP* 6.265), our single source of biographical information, she terms herself "noble" (*agaua*), names her mother Theophilis and grandmother Cleocha, and commemorates Theophilis' presentation of an elaborately-worked robe to Hera Lacinia. Although we know nothing else about her private life, her epigrams indicate that she wrote exclusively for a circle of intimate women friends. At Locri, women may have enjoyed relatively high status. Archaeological evidence from an earlier period confirms the prominence of the joint cult of Persephone and Aphrodite, two fertility goddesses closely linked to the female sphere, and Persephone's supreme importance at Locri was certainly recognized in Hellenistic times. These cultural factors no doubt contributed to the intensely woman-identified nature of Nossis' poetry. It would be erroneous, however, to imagine her living in a quasi-matriarchal society, which would have been impossible in the Greek world at any time and place.

Nossis owes her limited survival to the first century B.C. anthologist Meleager of Gadara, who extracted representative pieces from her published book of verses for his epigram collection, the *Garland*. In his prologue, she is praised specifically as a love poet: Eros is said to have "melted the wax for her tablets." Furthermore, in poem 1 (*AP* 5.170), which must have originally introduced her own book, the author herself proclaims: "Nothing is sweeter than *eros*. All other delights are second. . . . This is what Nossis says." Love, then, was clearly a dominant theme of her poetry, but none of the eleven epigrams now preserved in the *Greek Anthology* (the authenticity of a twelfth, *AP* 6.273, is suspect) is overtly erotic. However, six of her quatrains ostensibly commemorating votive dedications by women discreetly evoke the sensual attractiveness of the dedicants as reflected in their statues and portraits. Meleager's capsule account of Nossis' poetry may imply that he himself sensed erotic undertones in those descriptive pieces, for "melting wax" could refer to the process of painting on wood in encaustic—a standard ancient medium for portraiture. Finally, Nossis confirms her artistic debt to Sappho both indirectly, through regular employment of Sapphic language (*aganos*, "gentle," which Nossis applies to three different women, was the earlier poet's term for her beloved Atthis), and explicitly in poem 11 (*AP* 7.718), the *envoi* to her collection. All this evidence indicates that Nossis' expressly erotic poems must have celebrated love between women. That hypothesis would also explain why her book was lost, and why only a few seemingly innocuous quatrains survived the centuries.

Among the multitude of Hellenistic and later epigrammatists, Nossis is an outstanding artist, even though she appears to have exercised little direct influence upon the mainstream tradition. Challenged by the strict limitations of the epigram form, she attempts, like the acknowledged master of the genre Callimachus, to fit searching pronouncements within its restrictive framework. In particular, she is fascinated by the connection between an aesthetic representation and its subject and employs the dedicatory epigram as a vehicle for probing the relationship of artistic product to model. Since the models she deals with are women, her epigrams necessarily touch on issues of female selfhood and individuation. For example, poem 8 (*AP* 6.353), which begins with the exclamation *automelinna tetuktai* ("Melinna's very being is fully wrought!") and lauds the verisimilitude of the portrait on display, goes on to observe how closely Melinna resembles her mother and concludes, "How good it is when children are like their parents." As the painter limns his model in pigments, so a mother, by analogy, replicates herself in her daughter's flesh: through her reproductive and nurturing efforts, she, too, acts as a creative artist and passes on to the next generation an image of herself. Yet the quatrain also depicts the tension between "Melinna herself," *automelinna*, and Melinna as the biological continuation of her mother: juxtaposing those two contradictory notions without reconciling them, it implicitly conveys the struggle over the daughter's autonomy inherent in the mother-daughter dyad. We may note further that this epigram appropriates the standard patriarchal sentiment that sons should resemble fathers, as evidence of their legitimacy, and transforms it into an affirmation of the exceptional biological bond between female parent and female child. In this and in several other epigrams (such as the programmatic 1 and 11, which proclaim a conscious choice of erotic themes and of Sappho as poetic model, and in 3, which examines the mother-daughter relationship autobiographically), it is clear that Nossis has assumed a firmly woman-centered stance in marked opposition to the attitudes of the dominant culture.

Nossis does try her hand at traditionally masculine themes. But even when she expresses patriotic feelings or admires the achievements of a male literary predecessor, she writes in a distinctly female voice. Thus her quatrain memorializing a Locrian victory over the indigenous Bruttians (poem 2, *AP* 6.132) voices that uncompromising hatred for a defeated enemy that women who had been confronted with the imminent possibility of rape and enslavement would understandably have felt. Similarly, her epitaph (poem 10, *AP* 7.414) for Rhinthon, author of tragic burlesques, staunchly proclaims the literary value of his supposedly slight productions and calls into question the conventional hierarchy of genres. This defense of Rhinthon is simultaneously a protest against the devaluation of women's writing, likewise confined to "lesser" poetic forms.

Living in an age when female homoeroticism was beginning to meet with strong cultural disapproval, Nossis risked much in choosing to write from a woman-identified perspective. That specimens of her poetry have survived at all is a testimony to the subtle ambiguities and delicate ironies she uses in order to convey her sensibility to an understanding reader.

Works

Greek texts and German translations in Homeyer, H., *Dichterinnen des Altertums und des frühen Mittelalters* (Paderborn, 1979). Commentary in *The Greek Anthology: Hellenistic Epigrams*, eds. A.S.F. Gow and D.L. Page, 2 vols. (Cambridge, 1965). English translations in *The Greek Anthology*, tr. W.R. Paton. 5 vols. (Cambridge, Mass., Loeb Classical Library, 1916).

Bibliography

Gigante, M., "La cultura a Locri," in *Locri Epizefirii: Atti del sedicesimo convengo di studi sulla Magna Grecia* (Naples, 1981). Reitzenstein, R., *Epigramm und Skolion* (Gissen, 1893). Skinner, M.B., "Nossis *thēlyglōssos*," in *Women's History and Ancient History*, ed. S.B. Pomeroy (Chapel Hill, 1990). Snyder, J.M., *The Woman and the Lyre* (Carbondale, Il., 1989). Trypanis, C.A., *Greek Poetry from Homer to Seferis* (Chicago, 1981). Webster, T.B.L., *Hellenistic Poetry and Art* (New York, 1964). Wilamowitz-Moellendorff, U. von., *Hellenistische Dichtung in der Zeit des Kallimachos*, I (Berlin, 1924).

General references: *Oxford Classical Dictionary* (Oxford, 1970), p. 738. Pauly-Wissowa, *Real-Encyclopädie der klassischen Altertumswissenschaft* XVII.1 (Stuttgart, 1936), pp. 1053–1054.

Other references: Barnard, S., *Classical Journal* 73 (1978): 204–213. Gigante, M., *Parola del Passato* 29 (1974): 22–39. Luck, G., *Museum Helveticum* 11 (1954): 170–187. Skinner, M.B., *Ancient History Bulletin* 1 (1987): 39–42. Idem. *Arethusa* 22 (1989): 5–18. Sourvinou-Inwood, C., *Journal of Hellenic Studies* 98 (1978): 101–121.

Marilyn B. Skinner

Christine Nöstlinger

Born October 13, 1936, Vienna, Austria
Genre(s): children's and youth literature,
   poetry
Language(s): German

Christine Nöstlinger is Austria's best-known, most productive, and most colorful author of books for children and adolescents. Following the publication of *Die feuerrote Friederike* in 1970, she has published at least one book per year and this does not take into account numerous reprints and translations into many languages. To date Nöstlinger has about seventy titles to her credit. *Wir pfeifen auf den Gurkenkönig* (1972; The Cucumber King), a humorous family novel about a twelve-year-old boy and his family who lead an uneventful life until the autocratic "Cucumber King" suddenly appears from the depths of their basement and, together with an equally autocratic father, conspires against the family, has reached an edition of well over 100,000 and has become a classic in its own right.

Nöstlinger, who grew up in a working-class district of Vienna and studied graphic arts at the Academy of Applied Arts in Vienna, started her writing career, rather inconspicuously, during a short and rather unhappy phase as a homemaker and the mother of two children in the sixties. Although she writes primarily for children, her books can be enjoyed by all age groups.

In her books, the typical Austrian setting, atmosphere, and language notwithstanding, Nöstlinger discusses topics and problems that affect children and adolescents worldwide. She writes about human shortcomings, typical family conflicts such as divorce, runaway children and restrictive grandmothers, prejudice and superstition, inhumanity, and war. Her pacifist attitude is best reflected in her popular autobiographical novel, *Maikäfer flieg!* (Fly Away Home), in which she recalls what life was like for her family in Vienna toward the end of World War II. Nöstlinger's primary goal as an author, however, is to entertain her readers. To accomplish this she wraps her social message in a cloak of magic, fantasy, and grotesqueness.

Nöstlinger's status as a preeminent writer of fiction for young people was confirmed in 1984 when she received the Hans Christian Andersen medal, the first Austrian writer to receive this coveted award, which has been called the Nobel Prize of children's literature. Currently, Nöstlinger spends most of her time in the Waldviertel region north of Vienna where, in addition to her book projects, she writes columns for various newspapers and magazines.

Works

Die feuerrote Friederike (1970). *Die drei Posträuber* (1971). *Die Kinder aus dem Kinderkeller* (1971). *Mr. Bats Meisterstück* (1971). *Wir pfeifen auf den Gurkenkönig* (1972). *Pit und Anja entdecken das Jahr* (1972). *Ein Mann für Mama* (1972). *Der schwarze Mann und der groe Hund* (1973). *Sim-Sala-Bim* (1973). *Maikäfer flieg! Mein Vater, das Kriegsende, Cohn und ich* (1973). *Der kleine Herr greift ein* (1973). *Iba de gaunz oaman Kinda* (1974). *Achtung! Vranek sieht ganz harmlos aus* (1974). *Gugurells Hund* (1974). *Ilse Janda, 14* (1974). *Der Spatz in der Hand . . . ist besser als die Taube auf dem Dach* (1974). *Konrad oder das Kind aus der Konservenbüchse* (1975). *Stundenplan* (1975). *Rüb-rüb-hurra!* (1975). *Der liebe Herr Teufel* (1975). *Winterzeit. Pit und Anja entdecken das Jahr* (1976). *Pelinka und Satlasch* (1976). *Das Leben der Tomanis* (1976). *Das will Jenny haben* (1977). *Lollipop* (1977). [With Bettina Anrich-Wölfel], *Der kleine Jo* (1977). *Luki-live* (1978). *Die Geschechte von der Geschichte vom Pinguin* (1978). *Andreas oder die unteren sieben Achtel des Eisbergs* (1978). *Rosa Riedl Schutzgespenst* (1979). *Dschi-Dsche-i Dschunior* (1980). *Gestapo ruft Moskau* (1980). *Einer* (1980). *Der Denker greift ein* (1981). *Rosalinde hat Gedanken im Kopf* (1981). *Gretchen Sackmeier* (1981). *Pfui Spinne* (1981). *Zwei Wochen im Mai. Mein Vater, der Rudi, der Hansi und ich* (1981). *Das Austauschkind* (1982). *Iba de gaunz oaman Fraun* (1982). *Ein Kater ist kein Sofakissen* (1982). *Das kleine Glück. Schrebergärten* (1982). *Anatol und die Wurstelfrau* (1983). *Gretchen hat Hänschen Kummer* (1983). *Otto Ratz und Nanni. Leseratten* (1983). *Hugo, das Kind in den besten Jahren* (1983). *Jockel, Jula und Jericho* (1983). *Am Montag ist alles ganz anders* (1984). *Geschichten vom Franz* (1984). *Liebe Susi, lieber Paul* (1984). *Olfi Obermeier und der Ödipus* (1984). *Die grüne Warzenbraut* (1984). *Prinz Ring* (1984). *Jakob auf der Bohnenleiter* (1984). *Vogelscheuchen* (1984). *Haushalts-schnecken* leben länger (1985). Liebe Oma, Deine Susi (1985). Neues vom Franz (1985). Der Wauga (1985). Der Bohnen-Jim (1986). Der geheime Grovater (1986). Geschichten für Kinder in den besten Jahren. 26 Erzählungen (1986). Man nennt mich Ameisenbär (1986). Oh, du Hölle! Julias Tagebuch (1986). Susis geheimes Tagebuch Pauls geheimes Tagebuch (1986). Iba de gaunz oaman Mauna (1987). Der Hund kommt (1987). Wetti und Babs (1987). Schulgeschichten vom Franz (1987). Der neve Pinocchio. Die Abenteuer des Pinocchio neu erzählt (1988). Neve Schulgeschichlen vom Franz (1988). Echt Susi (1988). Gretchen mein Mädchen (1988). Translations: Brainbox Sorts It Out [Der Denker greift ein], tr. Anthea Bell (1985). But Jasper Came Instead [Das Austauschkind], tr. Anthea Bell (1983). Conrad [Konrad], tr. Anthea Bell (1976). The Cucumber King [Wir pfeifen auf den Gurkenkönig], tr. Anthea Bell (1975). Fly Away Home [Maifäfer flieg!], tr. Anthea Bell (1975). Girl Missing [Ilse Janda, 14], tr. Anthea Bell (1976). Guardian Ghost [Rosa Riedl Schutzgespenst], tr. Anthea Bell (1986). Lollipop [Lollipop], tr. Anthea Bell (1982). Luke and Angela [Luki-Live], tr. Anthea Bell (1981). Marrying Off Mother [Ein Mann für Mama], tr. Anthea Bell (1978). Mr. Bat's Great Invention [Mr. Bats Meisterstück], tr. Anthea Bell (1978).

Bibliography

Czeitschner, Burgl, "Das andere Gesicht der Christine Nöstlinger." ORF-Nachlese 7 (1982): 22–26. Die Barke. Lehrer-Jahrbuch 1982. Ed. Österreichischer Buchklub der Jugend (N.p., n.d.), pp. 69–70. Schmölzer, Hilde, "Christine Nöstlinger: Kein bonbonfarbenes Kinderreich und keine Schwarzweimalerei." Schmölzer, Hilde, Frau sein und schreiben: Österreichische Schriftstellerinnen definieren sich selbst (Vienna, 1982), pp. 117–125.

Jürgen Koppensteiner

Helga Novak

Born 1935, Berlin-Kopenick, now East Berlin, Germany
Genre(s): novel, short story, lyric
Language(s): German

Helga Novak belongs to that generation of post-World War II poets who have been vehemently attacked for their attempts to reduce poetry to a Prosa der Fakten, a prose of the facts. Her work has been accredited and she has been awarded the Bremer Literaturpreis, the literary prize of the City of Bremen.

Helga Novak was born in Berlin-Köpenick, now East Berlin, in 1935; she left home at the age of eighteen against the will of her parents, and became an active member of the East German youth organization. From 1954–1957 she studied philosophy and journalism in Leipzig, married in 1961 and spent the following five years together with her husband in Iceland, where she worked in factories most of the time. In 1965 Novak returned to Leipzig, where she studied literature at the Johannes R. Becker Institute for Literature. In 1966 however she was exiled, and her East German citizenship was suspended. Novak left for Iceland a second time, moved to Frankfurt, West Germany, and chose this town as her permanent residence. In 1968, she received the Bremer Literaturpreis, in 1975, she spent several months with the members of a new cooperative in Portugal, Torrebela, and was honored with the honorary position of the town chronicler (Stadtschreiber) of Bergen-Enkheim, West Germany, in 1979–80.

Helga Novak's lyrics are representative of the Prosa der Fakten. It is a form of "chosisme," that had been employed by the post-war poets in the 1950s and 1960s as a response to their society and the environment. The major characteristic of these poems is a concentration on a small portion of reality and a laconic shortness. The tone of the poems is direct, the language cold, un-lyrical. Alltagsjargon, colloquialisms, and slang are introduced, and the geography of many of the poems is identical: kitchen, streets, gas stations. They expressed freely the personal feelings of the poets, their own inner selves; the poems and the techniques convey issues and "are written into the gap between the I and the object."

Geselliges Beisammensein (1980; Social Gathering) is a collection of short stories. The sentences are abrupt and not much more than a subject-verb-object construction without modifiers, relative clauses or compound sentences, which can create the impression that a child has written the text. "A group of elderly ladies enters the foyer. They chat. They nod at the manager." The stories open abruptly and end abruptly; there is no plot or development, but rather just a presentation of a short dialogue or a description of an isolated, trivial incident or issue. *Balladen vom kurzen Proze* (1975; Ballads of a Short Trial) is a collection of ballads. The title of the collection is ambiguous, as it can refer to a short court trial as much as it can be a play on a colloquialism, derived from the original meaning and conveying the idea of an almost unjustified abrupt handling of issues. As all the poems are short and the style abrupt, the "kurz" (short) is a reflection of the stylistic technique. Capital letters are used for nouns but not for the beginning of sentences; punctuation has been dropped in all poems. The lines are on-running; the stanzas consist of one sentence, arranged in stanza form. *Die Landnahme von Torrebela* (1976; The Taking of the Land of Torrebela) is a documentary on the experiences with and the development of the cooperative Torrebela. The individual sections read like a diary entry; the style is factual but flowing, not as abrupt as in the other stories unless Novak is describing objects and activities. "Entries" dealing with general issues, the history, the social and political background show the critical journalist. *Margarete mit dem Schrank* (1978; Margarete with the Closet) is another collection of poems that are less descriptive but show some affiliation with symbolism. The novel *Die Eisheiligen* (1979; The Ice Saints) mixes narrative and lyrical elements and gives the impression of a collage. Childhood memories of specific incidences and events form the main body of the novel, which is an autobiographical work about the years between 1939 and 1953, when the heroine has left her home against the will of her parents, and is written in the first person. Its style and atmosphere differ from those of Novak's short stories and poems.

Works

Novels, novellas: *Die Eisheiligen* (1979). *Bericht aus einer alten Stadt* (1972).

Stories: *Aufenthalt in einem irren Haus* (1971).

Nonfiction: *Geselliges Beisammensein* (1968). *Lesezeichen* (n.d.). *Reise einer Nihilistin nach Verona im späten Herbst* (1969). *Hauptpost* (1969). *Wohnhaft in Westend* (Protokolle) (1970). *Eines*

Tages hat sich die Sprechpuppe nicht mehr anziehen lassen. Texte zur Emanzipation. Lesebuch 3 (1972). *Winter in Residenz* (1973). *Die Landnahme von Torrebela* (1976).

Lyrics: *Die Ballade von der reisenden Anna* (1965). *Colloquium mit vier Häuten* (1967). *Balladen vom kurzen Proze* (1975). *Margarete mit dem Schrank* (1978).

Translations: *The Bookmark* (Lesezeichen, 1969). *Journey of a Woman Nihilist to Verona in Late Autumn* (Reise einer Nihilistin nach Verona im späten Herbst, 1969).

Jutta Hagedorn

Tereza Nováková

Born 1853, Prague, Czechoslovakia; died 1912, Prague
Genre(s): novel, short story
Language(s): Czech

Nováková is known not only for her fiction but also for her ethnographic studies, including *Kroj lidovy a národní vyšivání na Litomyšlsku* (1890; Folk Costume and Embroidery in Litomyšlsko) and *Z nejvýchodnějsích Čech* (1898; From Easternmost Bohemia). She had always spent a great deal of time in Eastern Bohemia on her researches. By 1908, her husband and four of her children had died, and she left Prague to retire to this region permanently. Nováková also wrote on women's history. From 1857 to 1908 she edited the journal *Ženský svět* (Woman's World). Her first published work was a lecture on the writer she was most inspired by, Karolina Světlá. One of her last works was *Z 'enského hnutí* (1912; From the Women's Movement).

Nováková's early urban works, *Z měst i ze samot* (1890; From the Cities and from Loneliness) and *Maloměstský román* (1890; Petit-Bourgeois Novel), are her weakest and least realistic. Much more accomplished are the stories set in Eastern Bohemia, in *Úlomky 'uly* (1902; Chunks of Granite). The five novels that followed are set in the same countryside and, like the stories, depict tenacious fighters and idealists. The novels are part of a "neo-Revivalist" movement in late nineteenth-century Czech literature, which looked back on the Czech National Revival movement of the earlier part of the century.

But first Nováková looked for the Czech national spirit even further back in history. The hero of *Jan Jílek* (1898), a member of the Protestant Czech Brethren, fights against Catholic persecution. A clear analogy is drawn between the ideals of the Czech Brethren and the socialist movement of the author's day. *Jiří Šmatlán* (1900) is the name of a poor weaver who becomes a fervent social-democrat although, by the novel's end, it seems his hopes for social justice are utterly unrealized. *Na Librově gruntě* (1901; On Libra Estate) presents conflict between peasants and landowners during the revolution of 1848 and the ensuing period of reaction. Once again, the hero is a simple man who fights oppression. In *Děti čistého 'ivého* (1907; The Children of the Pure Living One) the members of a religious sect, searching for the key to human happiness, adopt socialism. However, they are doomed to ineffectuality, as is the hero of *Drašar* (1910). This novel is based on the life of a minor figure of the mid-nineteenth century National Revival movement. The 1848 upheavals and their aftermath are shown again. Because of the moral flaws in himself and in his society, the hero, like so many of Nováková's heros, is unable to bring his ideals into practice.

Although Nováková's works tend to be overly polemical and didactic, they are noteworthy for her skillful use of ethnographic description and historical, documentary detail.

Works

Arne Novák, ed., *Sebrane spisy* [Collected Works], 17 vols. (1914–1930).

Bibliography

Chaloupka, Otakar, *Teréza Nováková a vychodní Čechy* (Havlíčkův Brod, Czechoslovakia, 1963). Nejedlý, Zdeněk, *Teréza Nováková* (Prague, 1958). Nejedlý, Zdeněk, *Osudová setkání* (Hradec, Czechoslovakia, 1978). Novotný, Jaroslav, *Kraj a dílo Terézy Nováková* (n.p.) (J.R. Vilimek, 1924).

Nancy Cooper

Émile Novis

(see: Simone Weil)

Helena Augusta Nyblom

(a.k.a. H., H.A.N.)

Born December 7, 1843, Copenhagen, Denmark; died October 9, 1926, Stockholm, Sweden
Genre(s): tales, poetry, novels, plays, autobiography
Language(s): Danish, Swedish

The daughter of the Danish painter and professor Jörgen Roed, Helena Roed was raised in the artistic circles of mid-nineteenth century Denmark. This was the society in which Hans Christian Andersen moved, and most of Helena Nyblom's literary endeavors seem to have been written in the spirit of this great countryman of hers. In 1864, Helena married Carl Rupert Nyblom, who eventually became a professor of aesthetics at Uppsala University. Their home became a centerpoint for the cultural life of Uppsala. Helena Nyblom was a woman of great energy and intellectual curiosity. After her marriage she wrote a multitude of poems, tales, and literary reviews, helped her husband edit a collection of Holberg plays, and at the same time, managed to raise six children. During the 1880s, she began to write in Swedish as well as Danish.

By and large, Helena Nyblom's work was unaffected by literary trends. She found herself at a loss during the wave of social realism in the 1880s, since her element was the realm of fantasy and the fairy tale. The 1890s, however, bought about a change in public taste. When Selma Lagerlöf published *Gösta Berlings saga* (1891; The Saga of Gösta Berling), Helena Nyblom was one of the first to defend the work against its detractors. Nyblom came into her own with her collection of tales, *Det var en gång. Sagor för små och stora* (1897–1898; Once Upon a Time: Tales for Young and Old). Ellen Key described these tales as "conceived of for adults, but told for children." The tales take place in a fantastic world filled with princesses and talking beasts, and most may be read as moral parables about growing up.

In 1900, Ellen Key announced that the "Century of the Child" had begun. The tenor of the time was such that Helena Nyblom's stories and plays for children were greatly appreciated, and she began to accrue distinctions. Nyblom received an award for her novel *Högvalla* (1907; Högvalla), and in 1908, she was presented a stipend from the state. In her later years, Nyblom also gained popularity as an author of one-act plays. The best known of these *Det ringer* (1910; It's Ringing) was, in her own words, "a parody of the meaningless telephone society." With considerable good humor, the play betrays a concern about the threat posed to old values by the hectic pace of modern society.

Against the background of World War I, the optimistic fantasy world of Nyblom's work became outdated. Helena Nyblom's tales have not been reprinted and her work has fallen into obscurity.

Works

Noveller af H. (1875–1881). *Digte* (1881–1894). *Under dansen* (1885). *Fortællinger og Skizzer* (1887). *Qvinnoöden* (1888). *Dikt och verklighet* (1890). *Till 'Orfei drèngar' den 9 april 1892* (1892). *Sveriges skans* (1893). *Fantasier* (1896). *Det var en gång* (1897–1898). *Det ringer!* (1904). *En sagokrans* (1903). *En trasslig härfva* (1904). *Hämnd* (1904). *Till kung Oscar efter hans trontal 1905* (1905). *Högvalla* (1907). *En gammal historia och andra noveller* (1908). *Ja och nej* (1908). *Finns det något bättre?* (1909). *I sista stund* (1910). *Kusinerna* (1910). *En musikkur* (1910). *Nye og gamle Digte och Dikter* (1910). *Porträttet* (1910). *Till fredens vänner* (1910). *Dollarprinsessan. En gammal violin* (1912). *Kusin Claudia och andra berättelser* (1912). *Sagospel tillägnade Sveriges barn* (1912). *Väninnorna* (1912). *Djur och människor* (1914). *Sju flickor* (1915). *Flickornas julbok* (1916). *Gamla violinen och annat ur dikt och verklighet* (1916). *Katten från Siena och andra fantastiska berättelser* (1917). *Håsjöstapeln* (1917). *En ostyring och andra berättelser för flickor* (1921). *Mina levnadsminnen* (1922). *Silvervit* (1931).

Translations: *Jolly Calle & Other Swedish Fairy Tales* (1912). *Top-of-the-World Stories for Boys & Girls*, ed. Emilie Poulssen (1916).

Bibliography

Åhlén, Bengt, *Svenskt författer Lexikon 1900–1940* (Stockholm, 1942). Nordlinder, Eva, "Konstnärskap och frihet. Två sagor av Helena Nyblom." *Tidskrift för litterturvetenskap* 14, no. 3 (1983), pp. 37–57.

Susan Brantley

O

Annalena Odaldi

Born April 28, 1572, Pistoia, Italy; died
December 1, 1638, Pistoia
Genre(s): drama
Language(s): Italian

Annalena Odaldi was born Lessandra Odaldi on April 28, 1572, the daughter of Camillo di Piero Odaldi and madonna Lucrezia Fioravanti. Her father was a merchant, part owner of a pharmacy and dry goods business. Her mother bore him fifteen children in the period of seventeen years from 1566 to 1583 (Lessandra was the sixth child, the third daughter). Camillo died in May or June of 1584, and shortly thereafter his widow saw to the marriage of her oldest daughter, Polita, and entered her second and third daughters, Laura and Lessandra, in important Pistoiese convents. In January of 1585, Lessandra entered the Franciscan convent of Santa Chiara taking the name of Sister Annalena. At least four of Annalena Odaldi's siblings, Laura, Mario, Bartolomeo, and Canida, also entered the religious life, four children died in infancy, and on the others the records are incomplete. Annalena held the convent offices of sacristan, bookkeeper (many times), and novice mistress. She died on December 1, 1638.

Annalena Odaldi was the author of five short farces. She wrote them between 1600 and 1604 when she was novice mistress for performance before an audience of nuns by the young women in her charge as part of the convent's Carnival festivities. The farces, known in a single, probably autograph manuscript in the Riccardiana Library in Florence (cod. Ricc. 2976, vol. 6), are in verse (seven-syllable lines, generally rhymed) and have no act or scene divisions; however, they amply use music and dance to suggest the passing of time and to allow for changes on stage.

The plays present traditional satires of physicians, lawyers, and old lechers, alongside those of plebeian characters. The subjects are entirely secular, but since they were intended for Carnival festivities they could be tolerated by convent authorities in the spirit of the "world upside down."

In the first of the farces, *Nannuccio e quindici figliastre* (1600; Nannuccio and fifteen stepdaughters), marriage is the explicit subject matter. The slim storyline is about Nannuccio di Pierone, a widower with fifteen unmarried and marriageable stepdaughters and one stepson, Beco Nero (reminiscent of Annalena's large family). Nannuccio wants to remarry before arranging matches and dowries for his children; but his son brings in a judge who rules against the irresponsible father. Nannuccio is Annalena's protagonist, but his lines are fewer, his part smaller that those of two women, Nencia and Pasquina, and their marriageable daughters, Fiorina and Nestasia, who argue and discuss dowries and rich prospects until the final scene of the play when Beco arrives with the judge.

Piero giuoca-asini (1600–1604; Piero Who'd Bet His Jackass) and *I tre lombardi* (1600–1604; The Three Lombards) stage marital squabbles, in the first case due to the husband's habit of gambling which is disastrous for the family finances. *I tre lombardi* opens with a husband's complaint that his wife has left him for a lover, but this is shown not to be true when the wife returns with a good excuse—motherly concern for their son. Most of the play, however, stages the humorous encounter of a lawyer from Bologna and a Tuscan physician whose dialects and predispositions prevent them from understanding one another until the subject raised by one—marriage arrangements—enormously interests the other, who happens to have a nubile daughter. *Mastro Pauoloccio medico* (1604; Master Pauoloccio, the Doctor) brings together a series of foolish characters. Mastro Pauoloccio is a physician who calls himself both surgeon and barber (and therefore dentist) and who kills (inadvertently, of course) rather than cures. *I tre malandrini* (1604; The Three Rogues) is about certain low-life characters intent on swindling some nuns; the play shows that nuns are too clever for that.

The plots of these farces are not always logical, and characters often introduce irrelevant issues, nevertheless, Annalena's writing does not fail from time to time to provide entertaining scenes, sketches, good lines, her dramatic skill to prompt a good laugh. The unevenness is characteristic of Tuscan convent theater as a whole, since the plays were often written by a teacher, such as Annalena Odaldi, who each year at Carnival time had to have a play ready for her students' performance. The strength and appeal of Annalena's work derive from cleverly devised and written farcical actions and linguistic play which presuppose a well-developed theater tradition in Santa Chiara and at least a few able performers. The comic devices, especially the use of dialect and rustic speech, show Annalena to be familiar with popular farce and a writer of considerable spirit and talent.

Works

Commedia di Nannuccio e quindici figliastre (1600). *Commedia di maestro Pauoloccio medico* (1604). *Commedia di tre malandrini* (1604). *Commedia di tre lombardi* (between 1600–1604). *Commedia di Piero giuoca-asini* (between 1600–1604). Early seventeenth century ms., probably autograph, Riccardiana Library, Florence, cod. Ricc. 2976, vol. 6.

Bibliography

Bandini Buti, Maria, ed., *Poetesse e scrittrici*, I (*Enciclopedia biografica e bibliografica italiana*,

Serie VI, Rome, Istituto Editoriale Italiano Bernardo Carlo Tosi, 1941), p. 40. Emanuele, Angelo, *Virtù d'amore di suor Beatrice del Sera* (Catania, 1903), pp. 44–46. Flamini, Francesco, *Il Cinquecento* (Milan, 1902), p. 299 (description of one of her farces in the Riccardiana Library, with no mention, however, of the name of the author). Weaver, Elissa, "Convent Comedy and the World: The Farces of Suor Annalena Odaldi (1572–1638)," in Dino S. Cervigni and Rebecca West, eds., *Women's Voices in Italian Literature*, Annali d'Italianistica, vol. 8 (1989).

Elissa Weaver

Irina Vladimirovna Odoevtseva

(see: Iraida Gustavovna Ivanoff [nee Heinecke])

Tami Oelfken

(a.k.a. Gina Teelen)

Born June 25, 1888, Blumenthal near Bremen, Germany; died April 7, 1957, Munich
Genre(s): novel, short story, poetry, translation, drama
Language(s): German

She was a teacher since 1908 and soon after joined the Worpswede art colony. In 1919 she became a delegate of the first revolutionary Reich school conference in Berlin. Together with the radical socialists (Spartakus) she fought in the barricade battles against the right wing military Kapp group in 1920. She founded her own school in Berlin in 1928, in which she tried to realize the socialist ideals of pedagogy. The Nazis, however, closed it in 1934. She immigrated to England in 1936, then to France, but in 1939 she returned to Germany although the Gestapo chased her as an opponent of the Nazi regime. She could hide, though, and stayed with friends in Überlingen near Lake Constance until the war was over. In her work she clearly condemns the barbarisms against humanity committed by the Nazis.

Works

Nickelmann, Roman für Eltern und Kinder [Nickelmann, Novel for Parents and Children], novel (1931). *Peter kann zaubern* [Peter Is a Magician], novel (1932). *Matten fängt Fisch* [Matten Is Catching Fish], play (1936). *Tine*, novel (1940). *Die Persianermütze* [The Cap out of Persian Lamb Skin], novel (1942). *Das Logbuch* [The Log Book], novel (1946). *Die Sonnenuhr* [The Sun Dial], short story (1946). *Madde Clüver*, novel (1948). *Zauber der Artemis* [Magic by Artemis], poems (1948). *Kuckucks-Spucke* [Cuckoo's Saliva], novel (1949). *Traum am Morgen* [Dream in the Morning], novel (1950). *Der wilde Engel* [Stine of the Läh], short story (1951). *Die Penaten* [The Penates], short story (1954). *Italienische Novellen* [Italian Short Stories], short stories (1956). *Eine Gröhlsche Hauspostille* [The Gröhl Home Prayer Book] (1957).

Oelfken co-edited *Junge Mädchen* [Young Girls], together with Axel Aggebrecht (1932). *Menschen im Spiegel* [People in the Mirror] (1950). *Pen-Almanach* (1954). She translated from French: *Mein Sohn der Herr Minister* [My Son the Minister] (1934).

Bibliography

Reisiger, Hans, "Tami Oelfken. Übereinstimmung von Persönlichkeit und Werk." *Literarische Revue* 4 (1949): 324–326. Rittinghaus, J., "Tami Oelfken: Das Logbuch." *Bibliothekar* 1 (1957). "Tami Oelfken. Befreiung aus dem Roten Plüsch." *Kiepenheuer Almanach* 10 (1950). "Tami Oelfken." *Börsenblatt* (Leipzig) 121 (1954): 879–880. "Tami Oelfken," in *Lexikon deutschsprachiger Schriftsteller*, vol. 2, G. Albrecht, K. Böttcher, et al., eds. (Kronberg/Ts., 1974), pp. 142f.

Albrecht Classen

Ofelia

(see: Otilia Cazimir)

Pino Ojeda

Born 1916, El Pakmar de Teror, Las Palmas, Spain
Genre(s): poetry; also unpublished drama, short story, novel
Language(s): Spanish

This lyric poet was awarded the second Adonais prize for poetry in 1953 for her collection *Como el fruto en el arbol* (Like the Fruit on the Tree). A proficient painter and author of plays and other prose works, her only published books are three volumes of sincere and powerfully expressive poetry.

Works

Niebla de sueño [Fog of Sleep] (1947). *Como el fruto en el arbol* [Like the Fruit on the Tree] (1954). *La piedra sobra la colina* [The Stone on the Hill] (1964).

Bibliography

Women Writers of Spain, ed. C. Galerstein (1986). Miró, E., "Poetisas españolas contemporáneas." *Revista de la Universidad Complutense* XXIV, No. 95 (enero-febrero 1975): 271–310.

Paula T. Irvin

Zoé Oldenbourg

Born 1916, St. Petersburg, Russia
Genre(s): novel, history, autobiography, drama
Language(s): French

The early years of Zoé Oldenbourg's life were marked by momentous historical events. World War I would end, and Lenin would come to power in her childhood. She was born in 1916 in St. Petersburg to a family of scholars. Her father, a White Russian, was a historian; her mother, a mathematician. Her earliest years were spent in Crimea with her mother and sister. After the Revolution, they returned to St. Petersburg to live with her grandfather, who was then the head of the Academy of Sciences. Life in the city was not without its hardships but the family managed. By this time, however, her father, who had fled the country for political reasons, had become established as a journalist in Paris. Her grandfather's remarriage and the difficulties of life in the first years of the Communist regime made France the logical next move, and in 1925, the family left Russia for Paris. There Oldenbourg would know a new set of hardships, those of the emigré.

The remainder of her youth would augment her Russian heritage with a foundation in French culture. She received her baccalauréat in 1934 at the Lycée Molière and attended the Sorbonne though she would never complete a degree. She then studied painting at the Académie Ranson, and throughout World War II would support herself and her family painting scarves. Indeed, at that point in her life her desire was to be a painter, not a writer. Encouraged by her father, however, she did write, and her first success came in 1946 with the novel *Argile et cendres* (The World Is Not Enough). Shortly thereafter she met Heinric Idalovici, whom she wed in 1948. Marriage and career were both successfully launched, and Oldenbourg's books would soon be seen proudly displayed in the windows of her husband's bookshop. She won the Prix Femina for her 1953 novel *La Pierre angulaire* (The Cornerstone) and has been a member of the jury for that prize since 1961.

While Oldenbourg has made relatively few forays into the genre of autobiography (*Visages d'un autoportrait* [1977; Faces of a Self-Portrait] and *Le Procès du rêve* [1982; The Dream Process]), the recurring themes of Russia and emigré life in many of her works are not unrelated to personal experience. She is best known, however, for her "historical" novels and, indeed, is considered one of the premier practitioners of that genre. Ironically, Oldenbourg objects to the epithet "historical" novelist. Novels, she maintains, are works of fiction whether they be set in the present or the past and should be judged by the same criteria. It is in those novels set in the past that she excels. The twelfth and thirteenth centuries come alive with her deft intermingling of accurate historical details and fiction. Her early works, *Argile et cendres* (The World Is Not Enough) and *La Pierre angulaire* (The Cornerstone), insured her fame and success as a popular writer.

Religion and the struggles it engenders are another theme in Oldenbourg's works. *La Joie des pauvres* (1970; The Heirs of the Kingdom) takes the reader to Jerusalem at the time of the Crusades. The Cathari heresy and the Albigensian Crusade have frequently been subjects of her fiction, e.g. *Les Cités charnelles* (1961; Cities of the Flesh) and *Les Brûlés* (1960; Destiny of Fire). She returned to that subject in her recent play *L'Evêque et la vieille dame ou la belle-mère de Paytavi Borsier* (1983; The Bishop and the Old Woman or Paytavi Borsier's Mother-in-Law), which is presented in a series of tableaux, not unlike medieval theatre. *Réveillés de la vie* (1956; The Awakened) and *Les Irréductibles* (1958; Chains of Love), treat the conflict between religions on a human scale through the story of Elie and Stéphanie, emigrés to Paris. Although this diptych was less well-received than first two novels, Oldenbourg did not abandon the theme of emigrés. *La Joie-souffrance* (1980; Joy-Suffering) is a more felicitous treatment of the theme and deals with a group of Russian emigrés living in the outskirts of Paris in the 1930s.

Oldenbourg's keen interest in history and religious conflicts is also apparent in her non-fiction writings. As with her fiction, the Middle Ages dominate her historical studies with *Le Bûcher de Montségur: 16 mars 1244* (1959; Massacre at Montsegur), *Essai historique sur les Croisades* (1963; The Crusades), *Saint Bernard* (1969). However, she has also written an insightful biography of *Catherine de Russie* (1965; Catherine the Great). An awareness of contemporary history and a deep-seated concern for humanity are the basis for her political essay, *Qui vous a donc fait Israël?* (1974; Who Made You Israel?), a historical indictment of antisemitism. *Qui nous est Hécube? ou un Plaidoyer pour l'humain* (1984; Who's Hecuba to Us, or a Plea for Humanness), her latest work, is an essay which treats questions of language and writing, of religion, of progress, and the importance of myth and imagination for human self-understanding. The confrontations of different cultures represented in all of her works find here an eloquent theoretical expression.

Works

Argile et cendres (1946). *La Pierre angulaire* (1953). "1214 A.D." *Colliers* 136 (Dec. 23, 1955): 35–36. *Réveillés de la vie* (1956). *Les Irréductibles* (1958). *Le Bûcher de Montségur: 16 mars 1244* (1959). *Les Brûlés* (1960). *Les Cités charnelles ou l'histoire de*

Roger de Montbrun (1961). *Essai historique sur les Croisades* (1963). *Catherine de Russie* (1965). *Saint Bernard* (1969). *La Joie des pauvres* (1970). *L'Epopée des cathédrales* (1972). *Qui vous a donc fait Israël?* (1974). *Visages d'un autoportrait* (1977). *La Joie-souffrance* (1980). *Le Procès du rêve* (1982). *L'Evèque et la vieille dame ou la Belle-mère de Peytavi Borsier* (1983). *Qui nous est Hécube? ou un Plaidoyer pour l'humain* (1984). *Les Amours égarés* (1987).

Translations: *The World Is Not Enough. The Cornerstone. The Awakened. The Chains of Love. Massacre at Montsegur; a History of the Albigensian Crusade. Destiny of Fire. Cities of the Flesh; or the Story of Roger de Montbrun. The Crusades. Catherine the Great. The Heirs of the Kingdom.*

Bibliography

Steinberg, Theodore L., "The Use and Abuse of Medieval History: Four Contemporary Novelists and the First Crusade." *Studies in Medievalism* 2(1) (Fall 1982): 77–93.

Edith J. Benkov

María de la O Lejárraga

(see: María Martínez Sierra)

Corilla Olimpica

(see: Maria Maddelena Morelli)

Antonia Hernanda de la Oliva

(see: Margarita Hickey-Pellizzoni)

Maria Antònia Oliver

Born 1946, Manacor (Majorca), Spain
Genre(s): *novel, short story, criticism, screenplay, travelogue, translation*
Language(s): *Spanish, Catalan*

Oliver has worked as a journalist and translator, as well as a television scriptwriter, in addition to writing long and short fiction. She is an assiduous proponent of Majorcan culture and an active feminist. A special concern in a number of her writings is the threat posed to traditional, oral, rural culture by rapid urbanization and development (resulting from booming tourism), as well as the ravages of the environment. As a translator, she renders works from both French and English into Catalan (including Catalan versions of several texts of Virginia Woolf, who has influenced Oliver's own fiction). She has also translated some of her own works composed in Catalan into Castilian. Oliver is well-read and well-educated, and frequently incorporates elements of myth, legend, folklore and various familiar literary topoi in her fiction.

Cròniques d'un mig estiu (1970; Chronicles of a Half Summer), a variation on the rites of passage theme, presents the sexual awakening of an adolescent boy. His loss of innocence constitutes the symbolic parallel for a symbolic loss of purity in somnolent, rural Majorca, threatened with environmental rape by commercial developers. *Cròniques de la molt anomenada ciutat de Montcarrà* (1972; Chronicles of the Oft-named City of Montcarra) treats a similar theme, the destruction of Majorca, but employs the family chronicle: three interconnected generations of related families are arranged in concentric circles which portray the changes over time in the proletarian emigrant sector. Fantastic Majorcan folktales ("rondalles"), popular sayings, and songs are incorporated in the fragmented narrative structure as a variety of fantastic creatures (fairies, giants, and other mythical beings from the "rondalles") intervene as agents of destruction in an apocalyptic ending which includes the island's symbolic disappearance.

Coordenades espai-temps per guardar-hi les ensaimades (1975; Space-Time Coordinates for Keeping "Ensaimadas" [Majorcan bread]), first printed separately, is actually a long short story, later incorporated in the collection *Figues d'un altre paner* (1979; A Horse of a Different Color). "Coordinates" recreates a dream of the author's returning to her childhood home in Manacor, while the subsequent collection features an important prologue in which Oliver explains aspects of her fictional development. Several stories contain the germs of later novels and screenplays. In *El vaixell d'iràs i no tornaràs*

(1976; The Ship That Never Returned), the magical heritage of Majorca again intrudes, producing magical adventures involving giants, rose-colored robots, and other fanciful creatures that invade the seemingly mundane ambience of an overnight ferry to Barcelona. Oliver employs the topos of the voyage as symbol for life and makes brief philosophical monologues a counterpoint for the narrative's absurdist episodes. A strong feminist subcurrent can be detected, especially in the attitudes of the crew toward females and the humorous role reversals in which women become the stronger sex. *Punt d'arròs* (1979; Knit-Purl) is still more feminist, from its initial quotation from Virginia Woolf to its emphasis upon the need for solitude in which a woman can find herself. The image of knitting is a significant structuring device, symbolizing the repetitive routines and monotony of domestic life.

Vegetal, i Muller qui cerca espill (1982; Vegetable, and Woman in Search of a Mirror), two television screenplays, present different approaches to the problems of woman's identity and self-realization. In the first, a middle-aged widow, previously dominated by her paternalistic tyrant of a husband, is unable to adjust to her own freedom beyond indulging herself through an orgy of buying plants previously forbidden by the deceased. Her final metamorphosis into a ficus symbolizes a life devoid of freedom of movement or function beyond looking decorative. *Muller qui cerca espill* depicts a bride-to-be whose dreams of stardom have been frustrated by conventional parents and a dull, solid suitor. The contrast between her fantasies of her triumph on the silver screen and the prosaic reality of her stodgy wedding, the death of future dreams, career, or self-realization, is underscored by her smashing of her mirror. *Crineres de foc* (1985; Manes of Fire) employs the contrapuntal technique favored by Oliver, interweaving parallel stories of the protagonist's growing up along with the development of her home town, combining environmental concerns with women's need for self-identification in a rapidly changing society. The narrative incorporates aspects of several sub-genres, including science fiction, fantasy, and the psychological novel, transcending traditional classifications. *Estudi in lila* (1987;

English trans., *Study in Lilac*) experiments with detective fiction as a vehicle for feminist concerns, especially the problem of rape and its aftermath as viewed in the fates of two very different victims, a vulnerable Majorcan adolescent and a wealthy antique dealer. Counterpoint reappears in the female detective's interrelating the victims (unknown to each other), who both struggle with similar feelings of shame, guilt, and outrage.

Works

Coordenades espai-temps per guardar-hi les ensaimades (1975). *Crineres de foc* (1985). *Cròniques de la molt anomenada ciutat de Montcarrà* (1972). *Cròniques d'un mig estiu* (1970). *Estudi en lila* (1985). *Figues d'un altre paner* (1979). *Punt d'arròs* (1979). *El vaixell d'iràs i no tornaràs* (1976). *Vegetal i Muller qui cerca espill* (1982).

Translation: *Study in Lilac*, tr. Kathleen McNerney (1987).

Janet Perez

Hagar Olsson

Born September 16, 1893, Gustavs, Sweden;
died February 27, 1978, Helsinki, Finland
Genre(s): novel, poetry, drama, short story
Language(s): Swedish, one work in Finnish

Hagar Olsson was the daughter of a clergyman. Born in the southwest part of the country, she grew up in Carelia and went to school in Viborg. She studied in Helsinki and worked at the same time as a journalist and writer. Hagar Olsson was the first critic to understand the new era that Edith Södergran was opening up in the country, and the two women became close friends. Unlike Edith Södergran, Hagar Olsson was given a long life, entirely devoted to writers and writing.

The dominant feature in her production is her deep conviction of a transcendent reality, and there are many mystical elements in her books. She is a visionary who always looks forward, beyond the immediate, with a certain impatience for the shortsighted.

In her first novel, *Lars Thorman och döden* (1916; Lars Thorman and Death), she allows the protagonist to find, through Buddhist mysticism, a freedom from self that releases in him a new insight into death. The same preoccupation with spiritual experience is included in *Själarnas ansikten* (1917; The Faces of the Souls), a collection of short stories.

Death and its innermost meaning is a problem she often reverts to; it is the chief theme of her prose poem *Kvinnan och nåden* (1919; Woman and Grace), and in *Mr. Jeremias söker en illusion* (1926; Mr. Jeremias Looks for an Illusion), she looks at death and beyond, into another world. Her early works are, however, chiefly exponents of her own search for a life philosophy, but her criticism of this early period is of greater importance as it helped open the gates for modernism and contemporary European poetry. In 1922, she became the leading figure for *Ultra*, the modernists' journal. In 1925 she published her best essays and reviews in a volume called *Ny generation* (New Generation).

She also wrote plays; the first one *Hjärtats pantomim* (The Pantomime of the Heart) was performed in 1928, but published only in the volume *Tidig dramatik* (Early Plays) in 1962. *S.O.S.*, published in 1928 and performed in 1929, envisages the problems nuclear weapons involve today although describing a chemist's reaction to poisonous gases.

Hagar Olsson is steadily moving towards the future, and the narrow perspectives at home are attacked in *Det blåser upp till storm* (1930; There Will Be a Gale). The criticism of prevailing attitudes and norms recurs in the play *Det blåa undret* (1932; The Blue Miracle). The novel *Chitambo* (1933) leaves the opposition and the revolutionary and focuses on a maturing process. Chitambo is the name of the place where David Livingstone died, and in a symbolic way the novel tries to open the road to the interior of man, as Livingstone did in Africa. *Chitambo* proved her creativeness; her next novel *Träsnidaren och döden* (1940; The Woodcarver and Death) exposes a similar intensity of style combined with mystic features.

Just before the Winter War of 1939–1940 she wrote a remarkable play, *Lumisota* (1939; The Snowball War), in Finnish. The play was immediately officially forbidden, since it queried the foreign policy of the country at the time. It was not performed until 1958, and a Swedish version did not occur until 1981. The play describes a Finnish Minister of Foreign Affairs and the events in his family that affect changes in beliefs and relations, also involving death and disaster. The intuitive sense of what was really happening around her, and her own reactions to it are also recorded in *Rövaren och jungfrun* (1944; The Robber and the Virgin), written near the end of World War II. In the play *Kärlekens död* (1952; The Death of Love), she let her fantasy loose and created a portrait gallery in a home for old people.

Her collections of essays are probably the truest expressions of her self. In *Arbetare i natten* (1935; Workers in the Night) she exposed her views on modernism in literature; *Jag lever* (1948; I Live) gives the keys to her own literary world where mysticism as she understands it is a central issue. Her finest work is probably the story *Kinesisk utflykt* (1949; Chinese Outing).

After a period devoted to short stories—*Hemkomst* (1961; Return Home), *Drömmar* (1966; Dreams), and *Ridturen* (1968; The Riding Tour)—she reverts to essays. *Möte med kära gestalter* (1968; Encountering Beloved Personalities) contains her evaluation of various personages. One volume of her reviews and essays published earlier on was edited by Olof Enckell in 1953 and given the title *Tidiga fanfarer* (Early Trumpets). Her own account of her friendship with Edith Södergran and of their correspondence was published in the volume *Ediths brev* (1955; Edith's Letters), a most valuable source of information about these two women who exerted such a deep influence on the literature in Finland in their day. Hagar Olsson's finest quality was her acute sense of the new trends and their best representatives, many of whom she both introduced and, if necessary, defended.

Works

Lars Thorman och döden [Lars Thorman and Death] (1916). *Själarnas ansikten* [The Faces of the Souls] (1917). *Kvinnan och nåden* [Woman and Grace] (1919). *Ny generation* [New Generation] (1925). *Mr. Jeremias söker en illusion* [Mr. Jeremias Looks for an Illusion] (1926). *Hjärtats pantomim* [The Pantomime of the Heart] (1928). *S.O.S.* (1928). *På Kanaanexpressen* [On the Kanaan-express] (1929). *Det blåser upp till storm* [There Will Be a Gale] (1930). *Det blå undret* [The Blue Miracle] (1932).

Chitambo (1933). *Arbetare i natten* [Workers in the Night] (1935). *Lumisota* [The Snowball War] (1939), written in Finnish. *Träsnidaren och döden* [The Woodcarver and Death] (1940). *Rövaren och jungfrun* [The Robber and the Virgin] (1944). *Jag lever* [I Live] (1948). *Kinesisk utflykt* [Chinese Outing] (1949). *Kärlekens död* [The Death of Love] (1952). *Tidiga fanfarer* [Early Trumpets, ed. Olof Enckell] (1953). *Ediths brev* [Edith's Letters] (1955). *Hemkomst* [Return Home] (1961). *Drömmar* [Dreams] (1966). *Ridturen* [The Riding Tour] (1968). *Möte med käre gestalter* [Encountering Beloved Personalities] (1963).

Bibliography

Åhlén, Bengt, *Svenskt författarlexikon 1900–1940* (Stockholm, 1942). Enckell, Olof, *Den unga Hagar Olsson* (Helsingfors, 1949). Linder, Erik, *Ny illustrerad svensk litteraturhistoria* V (Stockholm, 1965–1966). Warburton, Thomas, *Åttio år finlandssvensk litteratur* (Helsingfors, 1984).

Gunnel Cleve

Anna Maria Ortese

Born 1915, Rome, Italy
Genre(s): narrative prose, lyric poetry,
*   journalism*
Language(s): Italian

Anna Maria Ortese's first publication, *Angelici dolori* (1937; Angelic Sorrows) was a collection of well-received lyric prose pieces while her second volume, *Il mare non bagna Napoli* (1953; The Bay Is Not Naples), won her considerable critical acclaim, public attention, and the prestigious Viareggio Literary Prize. Stylistically dissimilar to her earlier fiction, this collection of five stories in the vein of Italian *verismo*, or regional realism, objectively depicted the human misery of life in the Neapolitan slums. Ortese's future works proceeded along these two stylistic and thematic lines: lyrical fantasy and naturalist representation.

Ortese's realistic fiction has an underlying sociopolitical agenda. By presenting a compassionate if controlled picture of poverty, human degradation, and social exploitation, Ortese suggests the need for change and reform. When the writer moved from sordid but sunny and lively Naples to the gray monotony of industrial Milan, she remained loyal to the plight of the downtrodden, changing her focus from the Southern Italian slumdweller to the Northern proletariat caught in a world of concrete and mechanization. The Milanese working class is the subject of both *Silenzio a Milano* (1958; Silence in Milan), a collection of short stories, and *Poveri e semplici* (1967; Poor and Simple), winner of the 1968 Strega Prize.

Ortese's lyrical side and love for the imaginative surface in her poetry and in works like *L'Iguana* (1965), the allegorical tale of an architect who falls in love with an enslaved iguana-girl on a fantastic island, only to die fighting for her freedom. Such works resound with echoes of Massimo Bontempelli's "magical realism" of the Twenties and Thirties and owe much to the Surrealist lesson.

After World War II, first in Milan and then in Rome, Ortese began a steady collaboration with some of Italy's major newspapers and magazines, often contributing to the women's pages of periodicals like *Oggi* and *L'Europeo*. Her piece on an Italian woman's view of Russia (1954), for the latter, won the Saint-Vincent prize for journalism.

The works for which Anna Maria Ortese is best remembered, however, are the realistic tales of human suffering and spirit, whether in the boisterous Neapolitan ghettos or in the dreary streets of Milan. In her rendition of Italy's poor, she joins a long tradition of sympathetic Italian narrators with roots in the nineteenth century novel.

Works

Angelici dolori (1937). *Il mare non bagna Napoli* (1953). *Silenzio a Milano* (1958). *L'iguana* (1965). *Poveri e semplici* (1967). *L'alone grigio* (1969). *Il porto di Toledo: Ricordi della vita irreale* (1975). *Poesie* (1939).
Translation: *The Bay is not Naples*, tr. F. Frenaye (1955).

Bibliography

Botta, G., *Narratori napoletani del secondo dopoguerra* (Naples, 1955). Casolari, Gabriele, "Anna Maria Ortese ovvero dell'amarezza." *Letture* 24 (1969): 844–853. Chiaromonte, N., "Ambiguities in Italian Literature." *The New Republic* 129 (October 5, 1953): 16–18. Farina, Lorenza, "Anna

Maria Ortese: Testimone del tempo." *Letture* 38 (December 1983): 891–900. Scaramucci, "Anna Maria Ortese." *I contemporanei* V (Milan, 1974), pp. 887–902. Stefanile, Mario, *Labirinto napoletano* (Naples, 1958).

Fiora A. Bassanese

Lourdes Ortiz Sánchez

Born 1943, Madrid, Spain
Genre(s): novel, essay, drama
Language(s): Spanish

Lourdes Ortiz studied liberal arts in Madrid where she still lives and teaches art history at the School of Dramatic Art. She writes often for newspapers and magazines on literature, sociology, and art. A prolific and diversified author, she is included in Ymelda Navajo's *Doce relatos de mujeres* (1982; Twelve Narratives by Women) as one of the new women writers who started to publish after 1970. She has also translated books from French and edited and provided an introduction for a collection of Mariano José de Larra's *Artículos políticos*.

Like other contemporary Spanish novelists— Ana María Matute, Jesús Fernández Santos— Lourdes Ortiz has written for children; her book *La caja de lo que pudo ser* (1981; The Box of What Could Have Been) dwells upon the theme of peace and history with originality and imagination. Her experimentations with the theatre have led her to write a farce in three acts and a prologue, *Las murallas de Jericó* (1980; Jericho's Walls), and *Penteo y Fedra* (Pentheus and Phaedra).

Each of Lourdes Ortiz's novels is totally different in theme and technique. Her first, *Luz de la memoria* (1976; Light of Memory), deals with the generation of the 1970s and its youth who cannot rid themselves of their bourgeois morals despite their experimentation with sex and drugs. At first, the protagonist is in a psychiatric hospital after having lost his voice in a violent crisis (which is ironic, since he never had a say). The rest of the novel consists of the futile attempts to assimilate him into society. The language has a strong, masculine tone with the use of some profanity and vulgar terms. The style is experimental; narrated in the second person, it can prove difficult to the reader.

Picadura mortal (1980; Deadly Bite) is a detective story or, as it is labeled on its jacket, a "novela negra." The female protagonist demythicizes the role of the typical detective by acting like a man. Her actions are those of a liberated woman who uses her gun, has casual encounters, and is self-sufficient. Having been called to investigate the disappearance of a businessman in the Canary Islands, she discovers the life of the very rich and their shady deals in drugs and sex. The use of suspense is effective in this light-hearted parody.

En días como éstos (1981; In Days Like These) is a dramatic and compact novel in which the action moves swiftly. Divided into three parts, it deals with the lives of some terrorists persecuted by the law as contrasted with the peaceful existence of the protagonist's family on their farm and the violent outcome. As in all of Lourdes Ortiz's novels, the predominant narrative technique is the interior monologue.

Ortiz's historical novel, *Urraca* (1982), is a serious attempt to recreate the life of Queen Urraca (1109–1126) of Castilla and León, the mother of Alfonso VII. The dialogue—which turns into monologue at times—that the imprisoned queen has with the monk who brings her food shapes the structure of the novel. Against the backdrop of the historical facts stands out the personality of the queen, her strength and ambition. The archaic language helps to recreate the medieval period. The novel was finished with a grant from the Fundación Juan March.

In her latest novel, *Arcángeles* (1986; Archangels), the author continues her experimentation. Gabriel, the protagonist, is presented in discontinued flashes—reminiscent of the video clip—in which he takes on the characteristics of different archetypal figures. In some very explicit scenes, emphasis is placed in the low-life characters of the drug culture in Madrid. Lourdes Ortiz has continued to prove her originality in themes and techniques in each of her five novels to date.

Works

Luz de la memoria (1976). *Comunicación crítica* (1977). *conocer Rimbaud y su obra* (1979). *Picadura mortal* (1979). *Las murallas de Jericó* (1980). *La caja de lo que pudo ser* (1981). *En días* como estos (1981). *Urraca* (1982). *Arcángeles* (1986).

Bibliography

Alborg, Concha, "Cuatro narradoras de la transición." *Anales de la Literatura Contemporánea* (1987). Morales Villena, Gregorio, "Entrevista con Lourdes Ortiz." *Insula* (Oct. 1986): 1, 10. Morales Villena, Gregorio, "Lourdes Ortiz y Alvaro Pombo: opera quinta." Insula (Nov. 1986): 13. Navajo, Ymelda, *Doce relatos de mujeres* (Madrid, 1982). Suñen, Luis, "Bajar a los infiernos. El análisis de lo real en Lourdes Ortiz." *El País* (27 Oct. 1986): 13.

Concha Alborg

Eliza Orzeszkowa

Born 1841, Grodno district; died 1910
Genre(s): novel
Language: Polish

Daughter of a landowning family, Orzeszkowa was born in the Grodno district, in the former Grand Duchy of Lithuania. She was taught at home at first and later sent to a Warsaw boarding school for girls. At sixteen she was married off to a man over thirty, the landowner Piotr Orzesko, with whom she became involved in the struggle against Russia's rule of Poland and with whom she played an active role in the 1863 national uprising. Unlike her husband, she was an ardent advocate of social equality and of rights for peasants and Jews and was concerned with the underprivileged position of women. When Piotr was deported to Siberia for his political activity, Eliza did not follow him, and upon his return initiated difficult and lengthy divorce proceedings. As both their estates were confiscated by the Tsar in the wave of retaliation against Polish insurgency, she had to earn her living and became the first Polish woman professional writer. In her later years, she married a life-long physician friend.

Though she was basically self-taught and spent most of her life in little provincial towns or in the country, Orzeszkowa was one of the leading intellectuals of her time, which, according to some critics, is more evident in her short stories and her correspondence with the elite minds of Poland and Europe than in her novels. Nevertheless, the latter were tremendously popular and influential in her time as well as in the years to come.

The problems of struggle for national independence and women's need for emancipation are the main focuses of her best known works. Often counted among positivist writers, she differed from the official doctrine of the positivists in her close emotional ties to the 1863 insurrection rejected by the positivists as "romantic folly," her preoccupation with ethical problems, and her often metaphysical perception of nature. Orzeszkowa's abundant literary output often has a didactic character, and her heroes are involved with the welfare of the community, rebelling against the superstitions of their ethnic group or social sphere. The characters and situations are drawn from her observations of Polish provincial life; peasants, Jews, and petty-gentry farmers with whose life she was best acquainted.

Works

Marta(1873). MeirEzofowicz(1877). Dziurdziowie (1884). Nad Niemnem (1886). Cham (1889). Bene Nati (1891).

Bibliography

Kryzanowski, Julian, *A History of Polish Literature* (Warsaw, 1978). Kridl, Manfred. *An Anthology of Polish Literature* (New York, 1957). Milosz, Czeslaw, *The History of Polish Literature* (1983).

Maya Peretz

Bronislawa Ostrowska

Born 1881, Warsaw, Poland; died 1928,
Warsaw
Genre(s): poetry, translation
Language(s): Polish

Ostrowska studied in a Warsaw high school for girls. In 1901 she married sculptor Stanislaw Ostrowski, who lived mostly in Paris, where a permanent colony of Polish writers and painters resided. A skillful translator of French poetry and prose, Ostrowska was highly impressed by Mallarme and Baudelaire whose daring eroticism encouraged imaginations of Polish women poets oppressed by a tradition of ascetic attitudes. The list of philosophers and writers who influenced Ostrowska in different periods of her life is long indeed and contains both her contemporaries and those long dead. Her artistic sensitivity and discrimination made her recognize early talents of some who were virtually unknown in her time (Milosz gives her special credit for having a good sense to appreciate the genius of his relative and namesake, the poet Oscar Milosz, nowadays ranked among the best French poets).

Ostrowska found her individual voice in poetry rather late in life; most of her early works appear epigonic to a modern reader. Witness her poem on the anguish and dreams of motherhood; it evokes a slightly patronizing smile nowadays with its imagery of "fairytales of sleepless nights / Which will reforge into the golden bell of might / My pain, and all my silence and my guilt." Yet even that poem is neither sentimental nor superficial. Ostrowska is a philosophical poet, though it took her a long time to overcome the tendency to imitate different influences. While most of the poetry of her period is unreadable today, some of Ostrowska's poems strike today's reader as quite modern in their simplicity and directness.

Recognized as one of the poets who formed themselves through their craft, she managed to achieve a kind of synthesis of "soul" and "body" as reflected in her direct and dynamic style. The condensation of symbolic meaning in the minimum of words in her religious poems reveals her skill. Critics maintain that Ostrowska eventually developed her poetry in the style of stoic "consolatio," though her stoicism is oftentimes colored by humor: she accepts life as it is, in all its everyday ordinariness. The stoic sense of oneness in Nature, of body and soul indivisible, pervades her work. Critics talk about her monistic philosophy, attributing its sources to the stoic doctrine of eternal return. All "bondage" here equals freedom.

Works

Opale(1902). Jesienne liscie(1905). Krysta, poemat dramatyczny (1910). Perscien zycia (1919). W starym lustrze (1928).

Bibliography

Biala godzina. Wybor poezji (Warsaw, 1969). Milosz, Czeslaw, The History of Polish Literature (California, 1969).

Maya Peretz

Elisabeth Oswald

(see: Bernhardine Schulze-Smidt)

Luise Otto

Born March 26, 1819, Meißen, Germany; died
    March 13, 1895, Leipzig, Germany
Genre(s): novel, poetry, essay, journalism,
    libretti
Language(s): German

Luise Otto, called by her contemporaries the "songbird (lark) of the German women's movement," was one of the most outspoken nineteenth century pioneers for social reform and women's rights. Her political consciousness, raised early through family discussions at home, was sharpened by witnessing the plight of workers in the mineral-rich region of Saxony's Erzgebirge during a visit there in 1840. Her first socio-political novel, *Louis the Waiter* appeared in 1843 and was quickly followed by others. *Palace and Factory* (1846–47), initially confiscated, roused considerable public attention. Her *Songs of a German Girl* (1847), a collection of poetry, focused attention on women's rights.

Luise Otto participated in the revolutionary uprisings in Dresden and Baden where she met the writer August Peters whom she married in 1858 after his release from prison. In 1849 she began publication of her journal *Frauenzeitung*, which was confiscated in 1852. She suffered repeated official reprimands and was banished from several cities. From 1855 to her death she was editor of the women's journal *Neue Bahnen*, which she had founded. In 1865 she participated in the first women's conference in Leipzig and founded the "Allgemeine deutsche Frauenverein" over which she presided beginning in 1875.

Luise Otto wrote more than 20 novels, also novellas, short stories, and opera-libretti besides her political and journalistic essays. Two years before her death a collection of her poems written over a span of 50 years was published under the title *My Life*.

Works

Novels: *Ludwig der Kellner*, 2 vols. (1843). *Kathinka*, 2 vols. (1844). *Die Freunde*, 3 vols.

(1845). *Schlo und Fabrik*, 4 vols. (1846–47). *Römisch und deutsch*, 4 vols. (1847). *Buchenheim*, 3 vols. (1851). *Jesuiten und Pietisten oder Cäcilie Telville*, 3 vols. (1852). *Zwei Generationen*, 3 vols. (1852). *Nürnberg*, 3 vols. (1858). *Die Schultheientochter von Nürnberg*, 3 vols. (1861). *Neue Bahnen*, 2 vols. (1864). *Die Idealisten*, 4 vols. (1867). *Die Stiftsherren von Straburg*, 2 vols. (1872). *Die Nachtigall von Werawag*, 4 vols. (1887).

Novellas and short stories: *Aus der neuen Zeit* (1845). *Aus der alten Zeit*, 2 vols. (1860). *Kunst und Künstlerleben* (1863). *Mädchenbilder aus der Gegenwart* (1864). *Musikerleiden und- freuden* (1871). *Zwischen den Bergen*, 2 vols. (1873). *Aus vier Jahrhunderten*, 2 vols. (1883).

Poems: *Lieder eines deutschen Mädchens* (1847). *Westwärts* (1849). *Gedichte* (1868). *Mein Lebensgang* (1893).

Other: *Adresse eines deutschen Mädchens* (1848). *Die Kunst und unsere Zeit* (1852). *Das Recht der Frauen auf Erwerb* (1866). *Privatgeschichten der Weltgeschichte*, 6 vols. (1868–72). *Frauenleben im Deutschen Reich* (1876). *Das erste Vierteljahrhundert des Allgemeinen Deutschen Frauenvereins* (1890).

Opera libretti: *Die Nibelungen* (1852). *Theodor Körner* (1867).

Editor or co-editor of journals: *Deutsche Frauenzeitung, Mitteldeutsche Volkszeitung, Neue Bahnen, Vaterlandsblätter* (contributor under the pseudonym Otto Stern).

Bibliography

Bäumer, G., *Gestalt und Wandel. Frauenbildnisse* (Berlin, 1939), pp. 312–348. Brinker-Gabler, G., *Deutsche Dichterinnen vom 16. Jahrhundert bis zur Gegenwart* (Frankfurt am Main, 1979), pp. 206–211 (incl. work selections). Joeres, R.-E.B., "L.O. and her Journals." *Internationales Archiv für Sozialgeschichte der deutschen Literatur* 4 (1979), 100–129. Mallachow, L., "Biographische Erläuterungen zu dem literarischen Werk von Louise Otto-Peters." *Weimarer Beiträge* 9, 1 (1963).

Helene M. Kastinger Riley

B. Oulet

(see: Berta von Suttner)

P

P.W.O.

(see: Maria Komornicka)

Henriette Paalzow

Born 1788, Berlin; died October 30, 1847
Genre(s): novel, drama, letters
Language(s): German

Henriette Paalzow was the youngest of three children. Her father, the war councillor Wach, had very conservative ideas about girls' education and did not allow her to expand her knowledge beyond the basic understanding necessary for the life of a woman in the household. Her brother Wilhelm Wach, however, was strongly supported by his parents and later became a famous painter. Since he had his own studio in their house in Berlin, Henriette met, among other influential and prominent personalities of society, Prince Wilhelm of Prussia, who became a very close friend. He died, however, in the Napoleonic wars in 1813. When Henriette was twenty-eight she married Major Paalzow upon her parents' recommendation, which resulted in five years of an unhappy life in Westphalia and on the Rhine and, finally, in a divorce. She moved back to Berlin to her now widowed mother and, after her death, into a house together with her brother Wilhelm. As both were gifted artists, they attracted a wide circle of well-known personalities such as Wilhelm von Humboldt and his family. In the early 1830s she began to write her first novel, *Godwie Castle. Aus den Papieren der Herzogin von Nottingham* (Godwie Castle. From the Pa-

pers of the Duchess of Nottingham), which was published in 1836. At the same time she moved to Cologne for almost a year for health reasons. There she wrote the play *Maria Nastasti*, which was published in 1846 against her own wishes. With her return to Berlin, her house became a center of cultural meetings. This again provided her with more material to write about. In 1839 followed the novel *Sainte-Rouche*, published in 1843, the novel *Thomas Thyrnau*, published in the same year, and, despite her many illnesses in the subsequent years, the novel *Jakob van der Nees* in 1845. After her brother died in 1845, she only survived him by two years. Her work has been both highly acclaimed and severely criticized, since the novels belong in the category of trivial, sentimental light fiction, but they were well-read, especially at the Royal Court in Berlin, and were very often reprinted due to their vast popularity until the end of the nineteenth century. They often deal with life in the world of aristocracy and glorify this lifestyle with its etiquette, virtues, and ideals. Her depiction of women characters and of various historical periods was a particularly strong aspect of her books.

Works

Godwie Castle. Aus den Papieren der Herzogin von Nottingham [Godwie Castle. From the Papers of the Duchess of Nottingham] (1836; 2nd ed. 1838; 9th ed. Stuttgart, 1892). *Maria Nastasi*, play (1845). *Sainte-Roche* (1839; 7th ed. Leipzig, 1894). *Thomas Thyrnau* (1842; 12th ed. Stuttgart, 1894). *Jakob van der Nees* (1844; 4th ed. 1895). *Sämmtliche Romane der Verfasserin von Godwie-Castle* [The Collected Novels of the Author of

Godwie-Castle] (1855; new eds. 1874–2975, 1884, 1892). *Ein Schriftstellerin-Leben: Briefe der Verfasserin von Godwie-Castle an ihren Verleger* [The Life of a Woman Writer: Letters of the Author to Her Publisher] (1855).

Bibliography

Brümmer, Franz, *Lexikon der deutschen Dichter und Prosaisten* (1884). Brümmer, Franz, "Paalzow, Henriette," *Allgemeine Deutsche Biographie*, vol. 25 (Leipzig, 1887), pp. 35–38. Pataky, Sophie, ed., *Lexikon deutscher Frauen der Feder*, vol. 2 (Berlin, 1898).

Albrecht Classen

Monika van Paemel

Born May 4, 1945, Poesele, Belgium
Genre(s): criticism, novel
Language(s): Flemish

The recipient of several literary prizes (for her first novel *Amazone met het blauwe voorhoofd* and the later novel *Marguerite*), Monika van Paemel is among the foremost women writers in modern Netherlandic literature.

Due to a severe illness she was bedridden from her ninth to her fifteenth year and spent most of this time reading. She decided very early on that she wanted to become a writer but first completed a course in commercial studies and entered the writing profession via journalism. She is married and has two daughters.

Her first three novels can be seen as a trilogy. In *Amazone met het blauwe voorhoofd* (1971; Amazon with the Blue Forehead), Monika van Paemel is on a search for her own identity. At the same time she brings the reader closer to his or her own identity through confrontations about country, blood relations, gender, and social prejudice. Her second book, *De confrontatie* (1974; The Confrontation), has a similar objective but proceeds in a more refined and complex manner; the central consciousness is split up into three first-person narrators with whom the reader can identify at will. *Marguerite* (1976) is again simpler and more controlled. The author places the protagonist opposite a dominant grandmother, who also appears in the earlier books, in an attempt to write the dominant woman out of her life so she can realize her autonomy and

reaffirm her own identity. At the end of the novel, when the grandmother has been dead for some time and the narrator roams through a museum in Arles and suddenly sees an old portrait with the exact likeness of her grandmother, the narrator knows that she will carry this Marguerite with her for the rest of her life. The book is composed of flashbacks and has a circular structure. The maturing granddaughter pushes further and draws ever wider circles around her subject, until Marguerite's death closes the circle. Dominant themes in these novels are the man-woman duality, the position of the modern woman in relation to previous generations, love and lovelessness, time and timelessness. *De vermaledijde vaders* (1985; The Cursed Fathers) is again set in rural Flanders, the land of the author's childhood, and deals with similar problems.

In addition to the novels, Monika van Paemel has written many novellas and critical essays. She often uses the collage and stream-of-consciousness technique and usually fuses fiction and autobiography while emphasizing in everything female characters and their perspectives as women. She has contributed to such prominent journals as *Nieuw Vlaams Tijdschrift*, *Dietsche Warande en Belfort*, and *De Vlaamse Gids*.

Works

Amazone met het blauwe voorhoofd (1971). *De confrontatie* (1974). *De kortste verhalen en gedichten* (1974). *Marguerite* (1976). "De stilte van de grote dagen" (1977). "Moeder waarom schrijven wij?" (1981). "Gebrek aan zolderkamers? Het Moment" (1982). "Het voorlaatste woord" (1983). "Het erotisch moment" (1983). "De westeuropese maagd," "Eerste liefde" (1983). *Zelfportret met juwelendoos. Vlaamse verhalen na 1965* (1984). *De vermaledijde vaders* (1985).

Bibliography

Buuren, Hanneke van, "Derde generatie." *Ons Erfdeel* 20 (1977): 317–318. Janssens, Marcel, "Strijd met grootmoeder." *Dietsche Warande en Belfort* 122: 204–206. Moerman, Josien, ed., *Ik ben een God in het diepst van mijn gedachten. Lexikon Nederlandstalige auteurs* (1984), p. 175. Stamperius, Hannemieke, *Vrouwen en Literatuur* (1980), pp. 131–134.

Maya Bijvoet

Paloma Palao

Born 1945, Madrid, Spain
Genre(s): poetry
Language(s): Spanish

Only a handful of indirect allusions provide clues to the life and literary career of Paloma Palao. One can deduce that she studied law, completed a degree, and devoted herself for at least a time to legal practice. Another somewhat hermetic reference links her to a diplomatic career (suggesting an upper-class background, as diplomatic posts have traditionally been reserved to the aristocracy in Spain). Although her family name is of Catalan derivation, there is no suggestion from the titles listed that she ever wrote in this language. Mention of her intense acquaintance with other cultures with affinities to Spanish implies that she may either have lived in an area of vernacular language (Catalan or Gallego) and culture within Spain, or have done diplomatic service in another country (France, Italy, Portugal) closely connected by similarities of language. She was a finalist for the important Adonais poetry prize in 1970 with a book entitled *El gato junto al agua* (The Cat Beside the Water), and was included in an anthology of poets in the Adonais collection (*Tercera antología de Adonais*, 1973). She either wrote or was included in a volume entitled *Del corazón de mi pueblo* (1977; From the Heart of My People), cited ambiguously as having brought her recognition. These bits are gleaned from the back cover of *Resurrección de la memoria* (1978; Resurrection of Memory), the only work by Palao which could be located.

Resurrección de la memoria is a slim collection of twenty poems, several of them inexplicably divided between two pages when the entire composition would have fit on a single side. Palao's verse is mildly experimental in such aspects as irregular, minimal, or missing punctuation and capitalization and extremely irregular line lengths (from one syllable to sixteen, with a few as long as nineteen). Polysyndeton is a frequent rhetorical device and several forms of repetition appear, but Palao's most important trope is the metaphor, often a visionary, somewhat surreal figure involving complex permutations of synaesthesia which deny the existence of limits between the several senses. Contrast, paradox, and oxymoron are favored by this poet, together with images of air and water, mirror and rock, light and darkness, desire and absence. In a general way, the poems of this collection are love poems, but they are also poems of an impossible encounter, of existential solitude and absurdity, the difficulties of communication and of authenticity, and the frustration of a woman trapped within the preordained roles and attitudes which a patriarchal society has defined for her.

Works

El gato junto al agua (1970). *Resurrección de la memoria* (1978).

Janet Perez

Isabel de Palencia

(a.k.a. Beatriz Galindo)

Born 1878, Málaga, Spain; died Mexico City, Mexico
Genre(s): journalism, novel, autobiography
Language(s): Spanish, English

Born into a prominent Malaga family in which the only career for a woman was marriage, Isabel de Palencia became one of Spain's leading female journalists. In 1907 she founded *La Dama* (The Lady), a magazine for women. According to Palencia in one of her two autobiographies, *I Must Have Liberty*, this journal was Spain's first journal for women whose object it was to familiarize women with the world of politics and news. The magazine lasted for two years, and de Palencia was its principal writer and organizer. She was also a daily correspondent for two important Madrid newspapers in the early twentieth century: *El Sol* and *La Voz*. Active in the Socialist Worker's Party of Spain (PSOE) and the women's movement, she was a delegate for the Association of Spanish Women at the Geneva Congress of the International Women's Suffrage Alliance. During the Republic (1931–1936) she was a delegate to the League of Nations' International Labor Conference as an expert of women and child labor. During the Civil War (1936–1939), she was the Republic's Ambassadress to Sweden. After the Civil War she was exiled in Mexico where she made her living from her writing, particularly children's stories.

In the period before the Civil War she combined her political activities with those as a translator and writer. Bilingual in English and Spanish, she translated British and American literature and was the translator of Havelock Ellis in the twenties. She wrote several novels, mostly autobiographical. After the Civil War, she wrote two autobiographies in English: *I Must Have Liberty* (1940) and *Smouldering Freedom* (1945).

Although in both of these autobiographical texts she concentrates on her political activities before and after the Civil War, her first autobiography is of particular interest to the student of Spanish literary women because, as one of the few women's autobiographies written during this period, it provides a good testimonial of the relationship between women and Spanish society. It not only focuses on the difficulties facing women but also depicts the ways in which women were able to break with a highly traditional society.

As is the case with many other women activists and writers before the Civil War, the life and work of Isabel de Palencia have not yet begun to be studied. Although she was neither a foremost writer nor an activist, she was one of many women who believed that women should participate in the political and literary arena and work toward the emancipation of women, in particular, and humanity, in general.

Works

El sembrador sembró su semilla (1923). *El alma del niño* (1923). *El traje regional de España* (1926). *The Regional Costumes of Spain* (1926). *The Regional Costumes of Spain* (1932). *Spain, Sweden and Mexico* (1939). *Saint Anthony's Pig* (1940). *I Must Have Liberty* (1940). *Juan, Son of the Fisherman* (1941). *Diálogos con el dolor: Ensayos dramáticos y un cuento* (1945). *Smouldering Freedom* (1945). *Día con el dolor* (1945). *Alexandra Kollontay, Ambassadress from Russia* (1947). *Del diario comer: cocina hogareña* (1951). *En mi hambre mando yo* (1959).

Alda Blanco

Pilar Pallarés

Born 1957, Culleredo (La Coruña, Galicia), Spain
Genre(s): poetry
Language(s): Spanish, Galician

Pallarés was born and reared in rural Galicia, in the village of Culleredo, a factor which favored her thorough grounding in the Gallego language (threatened with absorption by Castilian after centuries of discrimination which culminated with the Franco regime's outlawing of the vernacular languages for many years). Reaching university age at a time when the post-Franco movements for regional autonomy and cultural/linguistic independence were accelerating, she was drawn fully into the passionate commitment to Galician "nationalism," language, literature, and culture. She teaches Galician literature at the secondary-school level and has won several important prizes for poetry awarded by Galician cultural entities. Publishing poems in many Galician journals, she has not yet gathered all of them into book form.

Entre lusco e fusco, her first book, differs from most poetry written in Gallego during the postwar years (at least through the end of the Franco era) in that it is not motivated primarily and exclusively by social and political concerns as were a majority of poets of the previous generation. Their emphasis upon the poverty and backwardness of Galicia, the necessity for emigration and attendant separation and longing are themes almost totally lacking, displaced by a more personal, intimate love poetry. However, insofar as Pallarés is also passionately committed to her "country," expressing deep love for Galicia together with ties to linguistic, cultural, and legendary roots, there is some common ground which links her to Galician social poetry. *Entre lusco e fusco* (1980; Between Light and Shadow) illustrates the reverse of the process of poetry in Castilian, from the "I" to the "we" in the postwar "social" generation.

Séptima soledad (1984; Seventh Solitude) is Pallarés' second volume of love poetry, even more personal and private than the first, in which the emotions expressed are clearly not poetic protest but a reaction to the experience of love as marvelous and miraculous. Like many poets in

Castilian in the post-neorealist era, Pallarés envisions poetry as a means of epistemological discovery, and love specifically becomes a vehicle of encounter with surprising and unexpected realities and truths. Solitude, rather than an existential anguish, appears as another path to knowledge, self-discovery, and poetic realization. The surprising formal perfection and density of intertextual content indicate an author whose importance must be affirmed in future studies. Feminist poetry, as well as the influences of reading Portuguese, French, and German poets, are all identifiably present as part of the poet's world vision. Especially significant for the reader of Pallarés is awareness of the roles of silence and absence.

Works

Entre lusco e fusco (1980). Séptima soledad (1984). Also included in this anthology: *De Amor e Desamor*, I (89–103); *De Amor e Desamor*, II (89–92), ed. Sada (1984, 1985).

Janet Perez

Boris Palotai

Born May 23, 1907, Kassa, Hungary (today Kosice, Czechoslovakia); died 1984, Budapest, Hungary
Genre(s): novel, short story
Language(s): Hungarian

Palotai was a prolific writer with a keen interest in the life of women in the various political eras she witnessed in Hungary. She worked as a writer and journalist in Czechoslovakia until 1939. In many of the novels she wrote following the Communist takeover after World War II, she paid lip service to the "cultural authorities." *Puskásne* (1950; Mrs. Puskás) offers a highly schematic depiction of class conflicts and the life of the proletariat. In *Ünnepi vacsora* (1955; A Festive Dinner), she continues to explore social problems within the framework of the family. *A madarak elhallgattak* (1962; The Birds Will Be Quiet) and *A férfi* (1964; The Man) deal with the Nazi period in Hungary. Similarly historical is the outlook of *Keserű mandula* (1958; The Bitter Almond), which is about the Commu-

nist show trials at the end of the 1940s and in the early 1950s.

Palotai's more recent novels frequently deal with psychological and marital problems. *Zöld dió* (1968; The Green Walnut) discusses the emotional turmoils of a teenage girl. Several of the short stories in the collections *Pokroc az ablakon* (1970; Blanket Over the Window) and *Szerelmespar* (1973; The Loving Couple) uncover various emotional and social problems of unhappy and lonely women.

She is, undoubtedly, a good storyteller with a conventional style. The dogmatism and the predictability of conflicts in some of her more engagé pieces create an effect of unnaturalness. Yet her popularity results from her ability to render traumatic experiences accurately in her writings. Her quiet sense of humor is also a feature of some of her works.

Works

Isten öleben (1936). Hátsó lépcső (1941). Tűzhely (1949). *Puskásné* [Mrs. Puskas] (1950). Sztalinvárosi gyerekek (1953). Ünnepi vacsora [A Festive Dinner] (1955). Keserű mandula [The Bitter Almond] (1958). A madarak elhallgattak [The Birds Will Be Quiet] (1962). A férfi [The Man] (1964). Zöld dió [The Green Walnut] (1968). Pokróc az ablakon [Blanket Over the Window] (1970). Szerelmespár [The Loving Couple] (1973).

Bibliography

Magyar irodalmi lexikon (Budapest, 1976). Pomogáts, Béla, Az ujabb magyar irodalom története (Budapest, 1982).

Peter I. Barta

Digna Palou

Born 1940 (?), Tacoronte (Isle of Tenerife), Canary Islands
Genre(s): poetry
Language(s): Spanish

Palou was born and educated in the Canary Islands, studying law at the University of San Fernando in La Laguna. Subsequently she made a career change and obtained a degree in library science, specializing in children's literature. At present, she resides in Madrid. During the decade between 1967 and 1977, Palou published four books of poetry, creative activity which was followed by another decade of silence, although she wrote sporadically for various Spanish and foreign periodicals.

Information on this writer is scarce and brief, and only one book of poetry was available for examination. Its cover lists Palou's earlier publications as the following: *Árbol tendido* (1967; Stretched-out Tree); *Nudos* (1973; Knots); *Isótopo 56* (1974; Isotope 56); and *Isla de septiembre* (1977; Isle of September). *Rumor de límites* (1987; Sound of Limits) is a collection of fifty-two brief poems whose common denominator is love, a theme which the cover indicates had not previously been treated in Palou's poetry. Most of the poems employ either the first or second person singular and thus as a whole constitute a sort of implied dialogue with a mute interlocutor. Palou's free verse lyrics are deceptively simple, composed in a straightforward syntax, unrhymed, and without fixed or regular rhythms. Anaphora is a frequently used device, and Palou is also fond of parallel constructions, of repetition with slight ironic variation, and alliteration. Metaphors are the most important rhetorical figure, with similes being comparatively few. The frequent use of marine images and motifs, logical enough in a native of the islands, confers a characteristic indefiniteness and chastity on Palou's love poetry. Maritime and water imagery may be a metaphoric disguise for eroticism; Palou mentions separation and longing but not consummation, alludes to tenderness and desire but not to unleashed passion. It is in silences and in absence that her poetic content resides.

Works

Árbol tendido (1967). *Isla de septiembre* (1977). *Isótopo 56* (1974). *Nudos* (1973). *Rumor de límites* (1987).

Janet Perez

Inés Palou

Born 1923, Agramunt, Spain; died 1975, Gelida
Genre(s): novel
Language(s): Spanish

Inés Palou is one of a group of Spanish women novelists who wrote about social conditions during the Franco era. Palou distinguishes herself from her contemporaries by focusing on the world of the criminal. Her first novel deals with the experiences of women in prison; her second explores the causes and consequences of a particular criminal act.

Palou's interest in crime was not purely academic. Her first novel is based on her own experiences as a woman in jail. Palou was from a middle-class family and had received a good education. She was charged with manipulating the books of the firm where she worked and was sent to jail. This experience changed her completely. She became interested in women charged with civil, as opposed to political, crimes. She perceived crime as a hellish existence into which one might fall by accident. Ironically, one could never escape from this existence. This view may have led to Palou's death by suicide in 1975, the very year when both of her novels were published.

Carne apaleada (1975; Beaten Flesh) is the story of Berta, who appears to be a fictional representation of the novelist, and her experiences in prison, of the women she meets, and of Berta's discovery that she is a lesbian. Most importantly the novel deals with the transformation of the protagonist from a frightened and naive woman to one who is brave and compassionate.

Operación dulce (1975; Sweet Operation) tells the story of another criminal, Caridad, a minor character from Palou's first novel. Like Berta, Caridad grows and develops throughout the course of the novel. She learns to make positive, life-affirming choices and attempts to escape the life of crime into which she was drawn as an excitement-seeking girl. Despite her efforts, the novel ends with Caridad trapped in a hellish life.

Inés Palou is not widely known. Her scant production and brief life condemn her, even in death, to a marginal role in literary history. She is, nonetheless, an important figure. She deals with subjects too harsh for most of her contemporaries. The style and structure of her two novels reveal a careful, sensitive writer who developed rapidly in her craft. She left us a record of her life and the thoughts of a group that was singularly oppressed during the regime of Francisco Franco. Her skill as a writer enables us to feel and understand their pain; we do not merely observe it.

Works
Carne apaleada (1975). *Operación dulce* (1975).

Bibliography
Cárdenas, Karen Hardy, "Female Morality in the Novels of Inés Palou." *Selected Proceedings of the Third and Fourth Annual Wichita State University Conference on Continental, Latin American, and Francophone Women Writers* (Spring 1990).

Karen Hardy Oárdenas

Teresa Pàmies i Bertran

Born 1919, Balaguer (Lerida, Catalonia), Spain
Genre(s): novel, journalism, memoir,
*   autobiography, travel books*
Language(s): Spanish, Catalan

The daughter of a poor farmer who was a militant leftist, Pàmies began to work in a factory sweatshop at the age of eleven. As a self-educated teenager, she became a correspondent for the revolutionary press during the years of the Second Republic in Spain (1931–1936) and was active politically, presiding at meetings, delivering speeches, and later visiting the front and travelling for the republican government during the Civil War as part of a public relations and propaganda mission to obtain support from foreign governments. She and her family were exiled following the war, and she lived twelve years in France and twelve in Czechoslovakia, spending approximately eight in Mexico, where she studied journalism. She returned to Catalonia in 1971 during the liberalization which began in the twilight years of the Franco regime, and here she published most of her works. The rapidity with which she produced the first two dozen books indicates that many must have been written in exile at least in rough drafts. Most of her fiction is of the documentary type, often presented as

memoirs, autobiography, or epistolary narrative. She chronicles the Civil War, exile, clandestine political activity, and moments of recent international history (e.g., World War II), and much of her work qualifies as eyewitness accounts of contemporary social and political history.

La filla del pres (1967; The Prisoner's Daughter), apparently her first novel, is one of several reflecting experiences of imprisonment. *Testament a Praga* (1971; Testament in Prague) first called public attention to Pàmies shortly after her return to Spain. A controversial work, it was written in collaboration with her father, Tomás, and eloquently expresses the loneliness of the exile and homesickness for the distant homeland. The 1968 "Prague Springtime" political thaw, crushed by the Russian invasion of Czechoslovakia, provokes a reevaluation of socialism by the exiles, combined with fragments of the father's memories. *Va ploure tot el dia* (1974; It'll Rain All Day) continues the analysis of exilic experience via the thoughts of a Catalan woman bound for home after thirty years as a political exile. Police questioning sets off a chain of associations and flashbacks, while rain serves as a symbol of both passing time and of youth and other precious intangibles lost forever in exile. *Quan érem capitans* (1974; When We Were Captains), a memoir of the civil war, portrays important writers, artists, politicians, and other historic figures and expresses the anguish of defeat. *Quan érem refugiats* (1975; When We Were Refugees), equally autobiographical and dramatic, depicts the horrors and degradation of women in French refugee camps, little different than concentration camps. The five parts portray suffering in five different locations, with a particularly graphic section describing an abortion performed in a jail cell. *Gents del meu exili* (1975; People from My Exile) is essentially documentary. Its down-to-earth tone conveys the numbness of war's victims, real people whose pain and despair do not preclude the presence of a certain humor. *Records de querra i exili* (1976; Recollections of War and Exile) is a social document in much the same vein, as is *Cròniques de nàufrags* (1977; Chronicles of the Shipwrecked), comprising letters from forty allegorical survivors who describe their efforts to stay alive after the symbolic shipwreck (representing the war).

Pàmies recreates aspects of her years of clandestine revolutionary activity in *Romanticismo militante* (1976; Militant Romanticism) and *Amor clandestí* (1976; Clandestine Love) which contrasts a woman militant's true feelings with her external behavior. In *Dona de pres* (1975; The Prisoner's Woman), Pàmies sketches the brave, self-abnegating common-law wife, a symbolic "everywoman" representative of all women who have suffered physically and spiritually because of the politics of their husbands. While quite possibly based on a real-life model, this is one of the more "fictitious" of Pàmies works insofar as it has little in it that is autobiographical. *Una española llamada Dolores Ibárruri (La Pasionaria)* (1977; A Spanish Woman Called Dolores Ibarruri, The Passion Flower) is a tribute to the most famous woman leader of the Spanish Communist Party, the fiery orator known for her ability to inspire the troops.

A good many works by Pàmies belong to the category of travel narrative, although they too are often made vehicles for some sociopolitical message. *Vacances aragoneses* (1979; Vacation in Aragon) has as its starting point a summer in the mountain valleys of the Argonese Pyrenees, but it mainly concentrates on depicting the difficult lives and touching personal histories of humble residents of the area. *Busque-me a Granada* (1980; Seek Me in Granada) presents a Catalan woman's encounter with southern Spain, where unfamiliar history and ethnicity, new legends and landscapes are the catalyst for a journey back in time, with historical enigmas being intercalated in anecdotal form. In the summer of 1981, Pàmies traveled to Galicia, visiting places associated with the tragic life of the region's most famous woman poet and writing *Rosalia no hi era* (1982; Rosalia Wasn't There). More than a travel document, it becomes a sort of feminist biography which expresses Rosalia's suffering as a woman and mother and stresses her role as the voice of an oppressed minority culture (and one which came perilously closer to extinction than the Catalan minority culture represented by Pàmies). Also inspired by travels is *Matins de l'Aran* (1982; Mornings in Aran), the fruit of another vacation high in the Pyrenees,

but more frankly fictitious. Ten stories, linked by the common persona of the visiting author, recreate villages, landscapes, flora and fauna, and the lives of such inhabitants as farmers and woodsmen.

Several titles are motivated primarily by political considerations, including *Si vas a París, papá...* (1975; Daddy, If You Go to Paris), which analyzes the crisis of French ideals in May of 1968 and establishes parallels with events in Catalonia during the same months. History and fiction are blended, as are real and fictitious characters. *Crònica de la vetlla* (1976; Old Timer's Chronicle) harks back to years before the Republic, in the closing portion of the Primo de Rivera dictatorship, to recreate events in the writer's native city of Balaguer that lead up to the beginning of the Civil War. It thus antedates the historical chronology of almost all her other writings, although it also has an autobiographical substrata. Here, however, Pàmies goes beyond the memoir to attempt an analysis of the causes of the civil conflict in various social, economic, and ideological differences. *Aquell vellet gentil i pulcre* (1978; Those Nice, Clean People) develops its complex plot using several narrative perspectives and time-planes, moving from contemporary events to several earlier periods. The novelistic present portrays postwar Barcelona, contrasting the degradation of the vanquished with the arrogant power of Nazi refugees prospering in Spain. Also largely inspired by political concerns is *Cartes al fill recluta* (1984; Letters to My Son, the Recruit), an epistolary novel in which a woman writes her son in military service about the failed coup of February 23 which constitutes perhaps the most crucial moment in Spain's post-Franco transition to democracy. The writer's husband is situated at the crux of the action.

More personal, with definite aesthetic elements, is *Memòria dels morts* (1981; Memoir of the Dead), which begins with an encounter between the writer and her long-dead mother in the mist-shrouded, fantastic autumnal landscape of her native city Balaguer. This meeting with her mother's spirit allows Pàmies to put a final symbolic end to the war that had brought her mother's death and disrupted the family's life, both in reality and as portrayed in several earlier books. The truth spoken by the dead is contrasted with the "necessary" lies of the living, with emphasis on those lies whose victims are women. Somewhat unexpectedly, then, this personal catharsis becomes a feminist statement. *Massa tard per a Cèlia* (1984; Too Late for Celia) also deals with a dead woman, this time somewhat in the vein of the mystery novel, as the narrator searches for clues to Celia's suicide by interviews with her family, friends, and neighbors. Set in contemporary Slovakia, this is one of the most imaginative and most fully fictitious works by Pàmies to date, and one of the most accomplished in technique with its skillful use of interior monologue. Given the writer's obvious narrative facility and assuming that she has now exorcised many of the more personal demons of war and exile, she may well develop in more creative and imaginative directions.

Works

Amor clandestí (1976). *Aquell vellet qentil i pulcre* (1978). *Busque-me a Granada* (1980). *Cartes al fill recluta* (1984). *Crònica de la vetlla* (1976). *Cròniques de nàufrags* (1977). *Dona de pres* (1975). *Una española llamada Dolores Ibárruri [la Pasionaria]* (1977). *La filla del pres* (1967). *Gent del meu exili* (1975). *Maig de les dones* (1976). *Massa tard per a Cèlia* (1984). *Matins de l'Aran* (1982). *Memòria dels morts* (1981). *Opinió de dona* (1983). *Quan érem capitans* (1974). *Quan érem refugiats* (1975). *Records de querra i d'exili* (1976). *Romanticismo militante* (1976). *Rosalia no hi era* (1982). *Si vas a París, papà . . .* (1975). *Testament a Praga* (1971). *Va ploure tot el dia* (1974). *Vacances aragoneses* (1979).

Janet Perez

Pavlina Pampoudē

(a.k.a. Pavlina Pampoudi)

Born 1949
Genre(s): poetry
Language(s): Greek

Andonis Decavalles calls Pavlina Pampoudē (or Pampoudi) the most occult among Greek poets and finds "a touch of Blake" in her visions and concepts. Like Blake, she is a skillful artist,

and her India-ink drawings elaborate the themes of her poems.

Visionary, cryptic, and complex, Pampoudē is definitely different among Greek women poets. *Schedon chōris prooptikē dystychēmatos* (1971) deals with personal anguish that is couched in language that cannot easily be decoded. The anguish is real, but the reasons for it remain elusive, hidden behind the words. In *Autos egō* (He I) Pampoudē explores the relationship between male and female as they play against each other and yet appear to be part of each other. In *To mati tēs mygas* (1983), the poet looks at the world with the "eye of the fly" and the result is a surreal landscape—confusing and dream-like, peopled by humans devoid of humanity. Admittedly, Pampoudē is inventive and imaginative, and her poetry is thought-provoking and at times captivating. However, the reader may lose patience with individual poems and question the motives behind the poet's obscure style.

Some of Pampoudē's poems have been translated into English and Romanian.

Works

Schedon chōris prooptikē dystychēmatos [Almost Without Expectation of an Accident] (1971). *Ta mōra tōn angelōn aspra kai typhla* [The Babes of the Angels White and Blind] (1974). *Autos egō* [He I] (1977). *To mati tēs mygas* [The Eye of the Fly] (1983).

Anthologized translation: *Contemporary Greek Poetry*, tr. Kimon Friar (1985). *Twenty Contemporary Greek Poets*, ed. Dinos Siotis and John Chioles (1979).

Bibliography

Books Abroad 46, no. 4 (1972): 719. Decavalles, Andonis, "Modernity: The Third Stage, the New Poets." *The Charioteer* 20 (New York, 1978). Thaniel, G., Review. *World Literature Today* 52, no. 4 (1977): 675. Savvas, M., Review. *World Literature Today*, 58, no. 3 (1984): 453.

Helen Dendrinou Kolias

Pavlina Pampoudi

(see: Pavlina Pampoudē)

Avdot'ia Panaeva

(a.k.a. N. Stanitsky)

*Born 1819 or 1820; died March 30, 1893, St.
 Petersburg, Russia*
Genre(s): fiction, memoirs
Language(s): Russian

From the mid-1840s when Avdot'ia
Panaeva's husband, the writer Ivan Panaev (1812–
1862), and the poet Nikolai Nekrasov (1821–
1878) took over Russia's most famous literary
journal, *Sovremennik* (The Contemporary), she
had an unparalleled opportunity to observe
Russian radical circles for over fifteen years. In
about 1848 she became Nekrasov's lover, and
their *ménage à trois* offered the Petersburg *intelligentsia* much food for speculation. Panaeva
fed them literally as well, serving tea and meals at
one time or another to a roster of contributors
that included Aleksandr Herzen, Lev Tolstoy,
Ivan Goncharov, Vissarion Belinsky, and Nikolai
Chernyshevsky. During the critic Nikolai
Dobroliubov's final illness, Panaeva nursed him
and offered maternal support to his younger
brothers. Dostoyevsky, fresh from engineering
school, thought he was in love with Panaeva;
Turgenev loathed her and felt that this woman
from a clan of Petersburg actors had a degrading
influence on Nekrasov.

Panaeva was an unstinting contributor to
The Contemporary's literary and fashion pages.
She and Nekrasov produced two long novels
together, *Tri strany svetam* (1848–1849; Three
Parts of the World) and *Mertvoe ozero* (1851; The
Dead Lake), under her long-time pseudonym of
"N. Stanitsky." Nekrasov may have helped to
polish her most artful tale, *Semeistvo
Tal'nikovykh* (The Tal'nikov Family), but the
subject and voice are hers. With savage humor
and in grotesque detail, the narrator describes a
girlhood much like Panaeva's own in an "acci-
dental family" of performing artists where the
children languish in the nursery while the parents lead a raffish life in the drawing room. The
censor found the tale such a harsh attack on
family values and parental authority that the
almanac containing it, already in print, was
banned in 1848; it was not published until 1928.

A woman of no formal education, Panaeva
on her own produced stories that are almost
literally art-less. It is the sincerity and force of her
voice, thinly disguised as a man's, that give them
unity. Surrounded by radicals who preached the
doctrine of female liberation, Panaeva warned
women not to settle for a specious freedom that
depended on men's good faith:

> In a corrupt society, this emancipation
> will give you just enough freedom to
> serve a man's momentary lusts, without
> any sacrifice on his part, and then—also
> without any sacrifices—make it easy for
> him to part from you. Society is
> merciless to your children. . . . In the
> name of maternal love, let every decent
> woman renounce an emancipation like
> that. . . .

("Zhenskaia dolia" [1862; A Woman's Lot]). The
quotation undoubtedly reflects her bitterness
during the final days of her stormy relationship
with Nekrasov, but earlier works are equally
unsparing. "Bezobraznyi muzh" (1848; An Ugly
Husband) is a woman's epistolary account of
the folly of entering into a loveless marriage to
escape life as her father's housekeeper. "Zhena
chasovogo mastera" (1848; The Jeweler's Wife)
and "Neobdumannyi shag" (1850; A Heedless
Step) offer other variations on the theme of
unhappy marriage. Like other urban authors of
her time, Panaeva idealized the strong, independent country girl in "Stepnaia baryshnia"
(1855; A Young Lady of the Steppes).

In 1889 Panaeva published reminiscences
of her youth and her years with *The Contemporary*. Somewhat unreliable as to dates and
facts, they are nevertheless a valuable historical
document of the remarkable people and exciting
atmosphere she had known from the 1840s to
the 1860s. Panaeva's only surviving child, by her
marriage to Apollon Golovachev, was the writer
Evdokia Nagrodskaia (1866–1930), whose stories depict women's plight even more pessimis-
tically than those her mother wrote (*Ania*, 1911).

Works

Melochi zhizni (1854). *Roman v peterburgskom
polusvete* (1863). *Zhenskaia dolia* (1864).
Semeistvo Tal'nikovykh, intro. Kornei Chukovsky

(1928). *Vospominaniia*, intro. Kornei Chukovsky (1972).

Bibliography

Chukovsky, Kornei, *Zhena poeta* (Petrograd, 1922). Gregg, Richard, "A Brackish Hippocrene: Nekrasov, Panaeva, and the 'Prose in Love.'" *Slavic Review* (December 1975): 735–751. Iazykov, D.D., *Obzor zhizni i trudov pokoinykh russkikh pisatelei umershikh v 1893 godu* (Petrograd, 1916), pp. 71–73 [bibliography]. [Astman] Ledkovsky, Marina, "Avdotya Panaeva: Her Salon and Her Life." *Russian Literature Triquarterly* 9 (Ann Arbor: Ardis, 1974), pp. 423–432. Martsishevskaia, K., "Nekrasov i Avdot'ia Panaeva." *Literaturnoe nasledstvo*, vol. 53–54, pp. 118–130. Muratova, K.D., ed., *Istoriia russkoi literatury XIX v.: Bibliograficheskii slovar' russkikh pisatel'nits* (Moscow-Leningrad, 1962), pp. 538–539.

See also: *Kratkaia literaturnaia entsiklopediia*, vol. 5, col. 566 (F.M. Ioffe).

Mary F. Zirin

Sancho Pancha

(see: Alexandra Papadopoulou)

Vera Panova

(a.k.a. Vera Vel'tman, V. V-an, V.V., V. Starosel'skaja, V.S.)

Born March 20, 1905, Rostov-on-Don, Russia; died March 3, 1973, Leningrad
Genre(s): novel, short story, drama, film scenario, television adaptation, literary criticism, essay, children's literature, memoirs
Language(s): Russian

Vera Fëdorovna Panova is a highly talented and sensitive Soviet writer, whose work is noteworthy for its diversity of forms, wide choice of subject matter, and honest portrayal of ordinary people. She writes about war, work, human emotions, bringing up children, daily life, the art of writing, literature, history, and her own life. Though she has written much for the stage, screen, and television, Vera Panova is best known for her prose. Her war novel *Sputniki*, which presents some of the most memorable characters of Soviet literature, and *Serëzha*, a classic in the literature about children, have both been translated into many languages, including English.

Her personal life was very difficult. When she was five her father drowned in a boating accident. There was no money for formal schooling; she educated herself through reading. From age seventeen, she wrote sketches, feuilletons, articles, and stories for a number of Rostov newspapers and magazines, most often under the pen name Vera Vel'tman. She incorporated many of her experiences as a novice journalist during the turbulent twenties into her novel *Sentimental'nyj roman* (1958; A Sentimental Romance). Her years of practical work in journalism are reflected in her later prose style.

In 1925, Vera Panova married Arsenij Starosel'skij. The marriage ended in divorce two years later. Soon after, she married Boris Vakhtin, but this marriage did not last either. In 1937, Vakhtin was falsely denounced and arrested; he died in prison camp. Left alone to provide for her three children, she continued her journalism career and, influenced by Gorky's works, also began writing plays. Two of her dramatic works from this early period won prizes: *Il'ja Kosogor* (1939) and *V staroj Moskve* (1940; In Old Moscow). In 1941, the latter play had been staged successfully in Moscow and was already under rehearsal in Leningrad when World War II broke out. Panova, then living near Leningrad, soon was forced to flee German occupation. With her daughter she set out on foot to rejoin the rest of her family in the Poltava region. At Narva, she found shelter in a synagogue the Germans had turned into a barracks for refugees and Soviet prisoners of war. This wartime experience is the basis for her play *Metelitsa* (1942; The Snowstorm).

In 1943, Panova finally settled in Perm'. To support her family, which then included not only herself and her three children but also her mother and an orphan child, she worked long hours for the local radio and newspapers and also continued her creative writing. She began a novel, *Kruzhilikha*, about life at a large factory in the Urals. In 1944, she published her first long story, "Sem'ja Pirozhkovykh" (The Pirozhkov Family), later reworked and reprinted under the title "Evdokija" (1959). Exhausted by years of hard living and hard work, Panova accepted an unusual assignment: to write a brochure on the work aboard a military hospital train. She wrote the brochure and also the novel *Sputniki* (1946) The immediacy of the narrative, the intimacy she achieves with her characters, and its unusual perspective on the war earned for *Sputniki* a Stalin prize and assured her a prominent place in Soviet literature.

In 1945, Panova married David Jakovlevich Ryvkin, a writer who wrote under the pseudonym of David Dar. This marriage was to last almost twenty-five years. Together with her husband and his two children, Panova resettled herself and her own family in Leningrad.

In 1947, she published *Kruzhilikha*, and it, too, won a Stalin prize although it also sparked lively controversy. Soviet critics considered Listopad, the director of the factory and the main character of the novel, a "negative hero." Though Panova defended her right to create such heroes, she took no risks with her next work, *Jasnyj bereq* (1949; Bright Shore), about post-war life on a collective farm; it followed all the accepted precepts for a Socialist Realist novel. Though *Jasnyj bereq* also received a Stalin prize, Panova openly acknowledged that it was very weak. Nonetheless, the book contains some beautifully rich pages devoted to the five-year-old Serëzha and his world. In the post-Stalin era, she returned to this young hero and made him the central figure in her short novel, *Serëzha* (1955).

Just after Stalin's death in 1953, when the icy constraints on Russian literature were beginning to thaw, Vera Panova published her most daring novel, *Vremena goda* (Seasons of the Year). In this work she boldly exposes some of the Party bureaucracy and corruption; she also disproves the myth that good Communist families produce good children. The novel was immensely popular with the reading public, but Panova was harshly censured in the press for her "naturalism" and "objectivism."

Despite her critics, she maintained her place in the top ranks of Soviet writers. At the Writers Congresses in 1954 and 1959, she was elected a member of the Presidium of the Union of Soviet Writers; she was twice awarded the Order of the Red Banner of Labor (1955, 1965). Being an established writer, Panova was allowed to travel to England, Scotland, and Italy. In 1960, she toured the United States. Her published travel notes and articles, including an epilogue to the Russian translation of *The Catcher in the Rye*, attest to her affinity for Western life and culture.

In the sixties and seventies, Panova also wrote several original film scenarios and adapted many of her own prose works for the screen, the most successful being *Serëzha* (1960) and *Vstuplenie* (Entry into Life), based on her stories "Valja" and "Volodja." Both these films won international awards.

A number of the themes and character types found in Panova's prose works also are used in the plays that she wrote in the sixties. Though many of these plays were successful, she preferred to write prose, claiming that prose forms gave her greater artistic freedom. Toward the end of her life, she experimented with a variety of prose styles: historical tales, *Liki na zare* (1966; Faces at Dawn); a novel in rough form, *Konspekt romana* (1965; Synopsis of a Novel); essays, criticism and travel sketches, *Zametki literatora* (1972; Notes of a Writer); a book of personal reminiscences, *O moej zhizni, knigi i chitateljakh* (1975; About My Life, Books, and Readers); and the fairytale novel *Kotoryj chas?* (1981; What Time Is It?).

In 1967, Vera Panova suffered a stroke that left her partially paralyzed. Though incapacitated, she continued to work, with the help of her family and numerous secretaries, until the day of her death.

The scope of Panova's writing is most impressive, but she will be remembered best for the work devoted to children and young people. Being concerned more with portraying the public and private lives of ordinary individuals than with exploring major political and social themes, Panova often did not meet the demands of Socialist Realism. Her willingness to overstep boundaries and her sincere sentiment coupled with a genuine talent for writing, assure for her a well-deserved place in world literature, as well as in Soviet literature.

Works

Prose: *Sputniki* [The Train] (1946). *Kruzhilikha* [The Factory] (1947). *Looking Ahead* (1964). *Jasnyj bereq* [Bright Shore] (1949). *Vremena goda* [Seasons of the Year] (1953). *Serëzha* [Seryozha] (1955). *Time Walked* (1959). *A Summer to Remember* (1962). *On Faraway Street* (1968). *Sentimental'nyji roman* (1958). *Evdokija* [Jevdokia] (1944–1959). "Valja" (1959). "Volodja" (1959). "Troe mal'chisek u vorot" (1961). "Kotoryj chas?" (1941–1963). "Sëstry" [Sisters] (1965). *Konspekt romana* [Synopsis of a Novel] (1965).

Plays: *Il'ja Kosogor* (1939). *V staroj Moskve* (1940). *Metelitsa* (1957). *Devochki* (1945). *Provody belykh nochej* (1960). *Kak pozhivaesh' paren'?* (1962). *Skol'ko let, skol'ko zim!* [It's Been Ages!] (1966). *Nadezhda Milovanova*, also known as "Vernost'" and "Pogovorim o strannostjax ljubvi" (1967). *Eshchë ne vecher* (1968). *Tred'jakovskij i Volynskij* (1968).

Film and TV scenarios: *Serëzha* (1960). *Evdokija* (1961). *Visokosnyj god* (1962). *Vstuplenie* (1962). *Rano utrom* (1964). *Poezd miloserdija* (1964). *Rabochij posëlok* (1965). *Mal'chik i devochka* (1966). *Chetyre stranitsy odnoj molodoj zhizni* (1967). *Svad'ba kak svad'ba* (1974).

Collections: *Sobranie sochinenij v pjati tomakh* (1969–1970). *P'esy* (1985). *Selected Works* (1975). Translations: *The Train* [Sputniki] (1949). *The Factory* [Kruzhilikha] (1949). *Looking Ahead* [Kruzhilikha] (1964). *Bright Shore* [Jasnyj bereq] (1950). *Span of the Year* [Vremena goda] (1957). *Seryozha* [Serëzha] (1956). *Time Walked* [Serëzha] (1959). *A Summer to Remember* [Serëzha] (1962). *On Faraway Street* [Serëzha] (1968). *Jevdokia* [Evdokija] (1964). "Sisters" [Sëstry] (1971). "Notes for a Novel" [Konspekt romana] (1966). "It's been Ages!" [Skol'ko let, skol'ko zim!] (1968).

Bibliography

Alexandrova, V., *A History of Soviet Literature 1917–1962* (1963). Boguslavskaja, Z., *Vera Panova* (1963). Brown, E.J., *Russian Literature Since the Revolution* (1982). Fradkina, S., *V mire geroev Very Panovoj* (1961). Gasiorowska, Z., *Women in Soviet Fiction, 1917–1964* (1968). Gornitskaja, N., *Kinodramaturgija V.F. Panovoj* (1970). Kochetov, V., "Kakie éto vremena." *Pravda* (May 27, 1954). Kreuzer, R.L., "A New Bright Shore for Serë'a." *SEEJ* 27, No. 3 (Fall, 1983): 339–364. Moody, C., "Vera Panova," introductory essay to Panova's "Serëzha" and "Valya" (New York, 1964). Ninov, A., "Dramaturgija Very Panovoj." *Siberskie oqni* 9 (1963). Ninov, A., *Vera Panova: Ocherk tvorchestvo* (1964). Ninov, A., *Vera Panova: Zhizn'. Tvochestvo. Sovremenniki* (1980). Ninov, A. i dr., *Vospominanija o Vere Panovoj: Sbornik* (1988). Plotkin, L., *Tvorchestvo Very Panovoj* (1962). Tevekeljan, D.V., *Vera Panova* (1980).

General references: *Portraits of Prominent USSR Personalities*, eds. E.L. Crowley, A.I. Lebed, H.E. Schulz (1968). *Kratkaja Literaturnaja énciklopedija*, ed. A.A. Surkov (1968). *Modern Slavic Literature. A Library of Literary Criticism*. Vol.1, *Russian Literature*, ed. V.D. Mihailovich (1972). *Bolshaja sovetskaja énsiklopedija*, ed. A.M. Prokhorov, 3rd ed. (1975). *Handbook of Russian Literature*, ed. V. Terras (1985).

Ruth L. Kreuzer

Betty Paoli

(see: Babette Elisabeth Glück)

Katina Papa

Born 1903, Giannitsates, Epeiros, Greece; died 1959
Genre(s): short story, poetry
Language(s): Greek

Katina Papa studied literature at the University of Athens and taught in high schools in Corfu and Athens. Her writing is directly or indirectly associated with her experiences as a teacher. This is especially so in her last collection of short stories, *S'ena gymnasio thëleōn*, which was published after her death.

For her first book, *Stë sykamia apokatō*, she received an Academy of Athens Award. This book has been translated into German and Dutch. Some of her work has also appeared in a Romanian anthology.

Many of Papa's main characters are young girls. In "O Toichos" (The Wall)—in *An allazan ola*—dreams about the beautiful world beyond the wall are shattered when the wall comes tumbling down and the young girl is faced with the ugliness beyond. She is left to deal with her disappointment as the author makes her point about the world of dream and the world of reality. In another story in the same collection,

"Tasoula," a young servant-girl in Corfu dreams of going to live with her godfather in Athens and writes to him about her dreams. He answers, but she does not open his letter, afraid that his answer might be negative. Thus she continues living in her dreams and does not let the probable (or possible) contents of the letter shatter her dreams.

Works

St\u0113 sykamia apokat\u014d [Under the Mulberry Tree] (1935; 2nd ed. 1971). An allazan ola [If Everything Changed] (1948). S'ena gymnasio th\u0113le\u014dn [At a Girls' High School]. Poi\u0113mata [Poems] (1963).

Bibliography

Mirasges\u0113, Maria, Neoell\u0113nik\u0113 Logotechnia (Athens, 1982).

Helen Dendrinou Kolias

Hortensia Papadat-Bengescu

Born 1876, Ive\u015fti (Gala\u0163i), Romania; died 1955, Bucharest
Genre(s): novel, short story, drama, essay, poetry
Language(s): Romanian, French

Hortensia Papadat-Bengescu had an overprotected childhood with studies in a local "French pension" and a family that, out of the type of deforming love parents often dispense to daughters, barred her from going to study in Paris as she planned and did not encourage her to write although her interest in literature was quite explicit. To escape at least partially she married quite early and spent her life in many of the provincial towns of Romania (Turnu-M\u0103gurele, Buz\u0103u, Foc\u015fani, Constan\u0163a) before establishing in Bucharest. She came to public writing, first in French and then in Romanian, rather late in her life, due to the advice and action of a woman friend, Constan\u0163a Marino-Moscu, herself a writer.

Hortensia Papadat-Bengescu's first three volumes—Ape ad\u00eenci (1919; Deep Waters), Sfinxul (1921; The Sphinx) and Femeia \u00een fa\u0163a oglinzii (1921; The Woman in Front of the Mirror)—contained lyrical introspective short stories in which she approached the passionate "life without deeds" of urban female characters

that gathered, as in Duras' "Les Dames des Roches Noires," on the terrace of a summer spa hotel and exchanged unending convergent stories evolving around essential silence, noisy gestures, violent gaze, desire, refusal, and repulsion. No one until Hortensia Papadat-Bengescu had either shown with such lucid strength the value, vitality, and dynamism of the specifically female inner experience or had the capacity to bring to consciousness and illuminate, from an unyieldingly feminine point of view, the struggle of hate between women and men in love and life. Hortensia Papadat-Bengescu was acclaimed and attacked with passion from the very beginning as a strong and daring intellectual writer, evoking Proust but at the same time radically different from him due to her unorthodox preference for the unprejudiced exploration of female intersubjectivity.

Basically at the same time, in a "document novel" entitled Balaurul (1920; The Dragon), Hortensia Papadat-Bengescu was among the first in Europe to provide a critical account of the First World War the point of view of a female character. During the war, the writer had worked as a volunteer nurse for the Red Cross, and the volume is visibly written with an attention to the accurate reproduction of each and every detail. Pages like those devoted to the peasant soldier "whose heart was visible" as the result of a shell splinter wound were and remain powerful and paved the way for a rich series of Romanian novels dealing with World War I by Rebreanu, Sadoveanu, or Cezar Petrescu.

By combining the introspective and documentary writing hypostases Hortensia Papadat-Bengescu became the founder of the modern urban novel in Romanian literature. The most important of her novels—Fecioarele despletite (1926; The Dishevelled Maidens), Concert din muzic\u0103 de Bach (1927; Concert from Bach Music), Drumul ascuns (1932; The Hidden Way), R\u0103d\u0103cini (1938; Roots), and the unpublished Str\u0103ina (The Stranger Woman), which was mysteriously lost and did not resurface until now—build up a Proustian and Freudian "comédie humaine" centered upon the different generations of a pseudo-aristocratic Romanian family—the Hallipa's. Hortensia Papadat-Bengescu speaks about physical decay and moral aridity, about character mutations and annihilation, about sickness and death. Hers is an ample and ironic chronicle of Romanian urban and suburban life as well as a revealing and as yet unequalled analysis of the diversity of suffering—from the medically informed unforgettable pages about men and women surveying the progression and then gradually surrendering to tuberculosis, cancer, cardiac affections, neurosis, or ulcer to the incisive pages describing the annihilation of disarmed sick wives by cold professional husbands, of erratic aristocrats by vital upstart wives or the inexorable transformation of soft, peaceful, and devoted human beings into hateful, resentful ones due to their being systematically wronged and abused by indifferent and strong life partners. There is a wide diversity of characters, from the princes, pseudo-princes, established bourgeois, and nouveaux-riches to the suburban pimp, from the submissive wives and disoriented, almost animalist daughters, who work painfully to accumulate money for their husbands, lovers, or fathers, to the feminists, from bankers, business women and men, neurologists, obstetricians, to university professors and composers, from miserable servants or poor marginal members of well-to-do families to cold and authoritative women that distractedly subdue the whole community around them, including at times a shy, loving husband.

In 1946, with the occasion of her sixtieth birthday, Hortensia Papadat-Bengescu received the prestigious National Award for Prose Writing. Due to her a new and important avenue was opened to the Romanian modern novel. As far as feminist writing goes she has not yet been surpassed in Romanian literature and has to be considered, together with Virginia Woolf, Nathalie Sarraute, or Marguerite Duras, among the most important European women writers of our time.

Works

Ape adînci [Deep Waters] (1919). Bătrînul [The Old Man], play (1920–1921). Sfinxul [The Sphinx] (1921). Femeia în faţa oglinzii [The Woman in Front of the Mirror] (1921). Balaurul [The Dragon] (1923). Romanţă provincială [Provincial Romance], short stories (1925). Fecioarele despletite [The Dishevelled Maidens] (1926). Concert din muzică de Bach [Concert from Bach Music] (1927). Desenuri tragice [Tragic Drawings], short stories (1927). Drumul ascuns [The Hidden Way] (1932). Logodnicul [The Fiancé] (1935). Rădăcini [Roots], 2 vols. (1938). Străina [The Stranger Woman] (Lost while in press at Cioflec). Teatru [Plays], ed. Eugenia Tudor (1965). Opere [Works], 3 vols., ed. Eugenia Tudor (1972, 1975, 1979).

Bibliography

Călinescu, George, Ulysse (Bucharest, 1967), pp. 127–131, 257–260. Ciobanu, Valeriu, Hortensia Papadat-Bengescu (Bucharest, 1965). Ciopraga, Constantin, Hortensia Papadat-Bengescu (Bucharest, 1973). Iosifescu, Silvian, Proză şi luciditate (Bucharest, 1974). Mihăilescu, Florin, Introducere în opera Hortensiei Papadat-Bengescu (Bucharest, 1975). Protopopescu, Al, Romanul psihologic românesc (Bucharest, 1978). Tudor, Eugenia, Pretexte critice (Bucharest, 1973). Vianu, Tudor, Arta prozatorilor români (Bucharest, 1941), pp. 334–345. Zaciu, Mircea, Glose (Cluj, 1970).

Sanda Golopentia

Alexandra Papadopoulou

(a.k.a. A.P., Alexandra, Anatolitissa [Woman from the Orient], Vyzandis, Sataniski, Sancho Pancha, Thrakopoula [Thracian girl])

Born 1867, Constantinople; died 1906, Constantinople
Genre(s): short story, historical fiction, chronicle, critical essay, poetry
Language(s): Greek

Alexandra Papadopoulou was born in 1867 in a Greek suburb of Constantinople. She studied to become a teacher in Constantinople and later followed philosophy courses in the University of Bucharest. Having to support her family, she worked all her life as a teacher in various schools or for wealthy families of the Balkan Greek communities while, at the same time, she became deeply involved in the Greek irredentist cause and used both her position and her pen to promote national consciousness.

Papadopoulou started her literary career at the age of twenty-one, with the publication of the

Ladies' Almanac of Constantinople (1888–1889), which she co-edited with Ch. Corakidou. From 1889 on, she contributed to the most prestigious literary publications of Athens, where her talent was quickly recognized by the literary avant garde, known as the *generation of the 1880s*. Her writings were published in such publications as *Eklekta Mythistorimata* (Selected Novels), *Estia Hearth, Kiryx* (Messenger), *Pikili Stoa* (Miscellaneous Porticum), *Efimeris ton Kyrion* (The Ladies' Newspaper), *Panathinaia, Imeroloyion Const. Skokou* (Almanac of Const. Skokos). She took an active part in the passionate linguistic debates that divided Greek intellectuals into partisans of the purist, archaïc Greek (*katharévoussa*)—the officially recognized language—and partisans of the spoken, living, modern Greek (*dimotiki*) in which she wrote. Because of her positions, her writings were banished from more than one literary publication of Constantinople, which was the center of linguistic purism and intellectual conservatism. She belonged to the team that published *Filoyiki Icho* (Literary News), the first publication in favor of *dimotiki* in Constantinople, and became one of its two editors together with Gryparis (1896–1897).

Although Papadopoulou wrote chronicles, critical essays, and poems, she was first and foremost a short story writer. In fact, she was one of the first major representatives of this genre, which appeared in Greek literature in the late 1870s. She wrote more than 150 short stories, which mainly deal with the new urban society of Constantinople, its social relations, the tensions and dilemmas it created among the urban middle classes. With unique ironic lucidity, she carefully dissected the desperate pursuit of social success (*O thiefthindis tis trapezis*—1896; The Bank Director), the importance of appearances (*To skoundima*—1896; The Accident) and conspicuous consumption (*Yinekes tou Sirmou*—1897; Women of Fashion), the subordination of qualitative to quantitative values (*Ta chirografa tou Kostaki*—1895; Kostakis' Manuscripts), the double sexual morality and mercenary marriage arerwfiwa (*Ios ke Kori*—1894; Son and Daughter and *Patriki storyi-Mitriki Storyi*—1899; Father's Love–Mother's Love). Instead of the long and detailed descriptions of her contem-

porary realist prose, Papadopoulou skillfully sketched her characters through an almost theatrical use of dialogue and stream of consciousness. Her social critique is particularly sensitive to women's transformation into means of upward mobility by the urban middle-classes (*Alithis Fili*—1892; A Real Friend and *Kori Efpithis*—1893; A Dutiful Daughter) to the transformation of dowry into a central means of capital accumulation (*I epistoli tis enochou*—1908; The Letter of the Guilty Woman), to the humiliating position of the "old maid" and the miserable and degrading conditions of work open to women (*Peripetie mias thithaskalissis*—1891; Adventures of a School Mistress and *I Prika tis Annas*—1897; Anna's Dowry).

Alexandra Papadopoulou is the only woman included in the first anthology of Greek short stories (*Ellinika Diiyimata*—Greek Short Stories) published in 1895. Although there is no edition of her complete works, there are several anthologies of her short stories. She was highly respected by the most eminent intellectuals of her generation such as Psichari, Xenopoulos, and Gryparis, and her fiction was favorably reviewed during her lifetime. She died of cancer in 1906 at the age of thirty-nine.

Works

Thesmis Thiiyimaton [Selected Short Stories] (1889). *Thiiyimata. Meros A* [Short Stories, Part I] (1891). *Thiiyimata. Meros B* [Short Stories. Part II] (1891). *Peripetie mias thithaskalissis. Thiiyimata* [Adventures of a School Mistress. Short Stories] (1891). *Meta thekaetian* [Ten Years After] (1891). *Imeroloyion tis thespinithos Lesviou* [Diary of Miss Lesviou] (1894). *Thiiyimata* [Short Stories] (1929). *Thiiyimata* [Short Stories] (1954). *Apanda Neoellinon Klassikon. Jean Moréas. Stephanos Martzokis. Alexandra Papadopoullou* [The Complete Modern Greek Classics. Jean Moréas, Stephanos Martzokis. Alexandra Papadopoullou] (n.d.).

Bibliography

Papakostas, Yiannis, *I zoi ke to ergo tis Alexandras Papadopoulou* [The Life and Work of Alexandra Papadopoulou] (Athens, 1980). Spanouthi, Sofia, "Thyo Lismonimenes" [Two Forgotten Women]. *Eleftheron Vima* [Free Tribune] (January 19, 1939). Stavrou, Tatiana, "I *Philoyiki Icho*" [The Literary

News]. *New Estia* [New Hearth] 44 (1948): 1355–1358, 1419–1424, 1482–1497. Xenopoulos, Grigorios, "Alexandra Papadopoulou." *Panathinea* 11 (1905–1906). Xenopoulos, Grigorios, "Yinekia Portreta. I thespinis Alexandra Papadopoulou" [Female Portrais. Miss Alexandra Papadopoulou]. *To Periothikon mas* [Our Periodical] 1 (1900).

Eleni Varikas

Lena Pappa

Born 1932, Athens, Greece
Genre(s): poetry
Language(s): Greek

Lena Pappa studied archeology and French literature. Her early poems are lyrical and flowing with abundant pastoral elements. In her later poetry she depicts the elusiveness of happiness and the anxiety of existence, but even then the harshness is mellowed by the implication that this is part of the human condition, which we all share.

Some of Pappa's work has been translated into English, French, and Polish.

Works

Poiēmata [Poems] (1956). *Lampidōnes* [Radiations] (1960). *Autographa* [Autographs] (1967). *Kath'odon* [On the Way] (1973).

Bibliography

Books Abroad 45, no. 1: 178. *Modern Poetry in Translation* 34 (Summer 1978).

Helen Dendrinou Kolias

Bertha Pappenheim

Born 1849, Vienna, Austria; died 1938,
Frankfurt, Germany
Genre(s): children's literature, novella, drama,
travel diary, essay, poetry
Language(s): German

Renowned as a pioneer social worker, philanthropist, and Jewish feminist in central Europe, founder of the Juedischer Frauenbund, Bertha Pappenheim was identified in 1953 by Freud's biographer, Ernest Jones, as the Anna O. of Freud's *Studies in Hysteria*. In 1880, at the age of twenty-one, this scion of the wealthy bourgeoisie of Vienna, described by her physician, Josef Breuer, as a girl "bubbling over with intellectual vitality" and in tacit rebellion against the puritanical milieu of her family, began a two-year period of severe hysterical paralysis and deprivation of speech, marked by terrifying hallucinations. She was eventually cured of her hysterical symptoms by recounting memories and hallucinations to Breuer in a self-induced hypnotic trance, which she labeled the "talking cure." Freud thus considered her the actual founder of the psychoanalytic method. After a lengthy stay in the Swiss sanatorium Bellevue, Pappenheim moved to Frankfurt in 1890, taking up residence with maternal relatives. It was in Frankfurt that Pappenheim's identity as a strong and charismatic feminist leader emerged. She founded orphanages, homes for unwed mothers, venereal hospitals. She was an ardent and outspoken opponent of prostitution who travelled throughout the Middle East investigating conditions in brothels to which Jewish girls from Eastern European villages had been sold. Unfortunately, Bertha Pappenheim's reputation as a feminist has eclipsed her third identity as a serious author who self-consciously cultivated her craft from the 1880s until her death on the eve of the Nazi Holocaust in 1938.

Each decade of Pappenheim's life was marked by literary effort. Her *Kleine Geschichten fuer Kinder* (1888; Little Stories for Children), a collection of tales written in the tradition of the Romantic *Kunstmaerchen*, contains both foreboding stories of irremediable loneliness and exile, such as the "Weihernixe" (The Pond Sprite), an Ovidian tale of death and transfiguration, as well as the optimistic "Im Storchenland" (In the Land of the Storks), which foreshadows Pappenheim's vocation as surrogate mother for society's outcasts. *In der Troedelbude* (In the Junkshop), published pseudonymously in 1896, is Pappenheim's most masterful collection, marked both by *fin de siecle* pessimism and biting Yiddish humor. A junk shop serves as a metaphor for the world and outcast objects, animistic reifications of their owners' damaged lives, engage in a "talking cure," unburdening themselves of the weight of painful memories. In the collection of novelle, *Kaempfe* (1916; Struggles), Pappenheim turns to a more melodramatic mode of examination of Jewish village life in Eastern Europe. Themes of Jewish mysticism and of failed love affairs between Jews and Christians dominate. *Sisyphus-Arbeit* (Sisyphus Labour), published in 1924, a collection of open travel letters written in the course of Pappenheim's feminist work, 1911–1912, includes graphic descriptions of life in poor-houses and brothels. *Bertha Pappenheim: Leben und Schriften* (Bertha Pappenheim: Life and Writing), edited by Dora Edinger in 1963, includes the author's letters and travel diaries of the 1930s, detailing the rise of fascism. Included are Pappenheim's poems and prayers, ranging from the private and lyrical to incendiary diatribes against injustice.

Bertha Pappenheim's writing is significant as a revelation of the inner life of the first patient of psychoanalysis, who later led an energetic and engaged life of leadership, devotion, and service. Yet, the intrinsic merits of the work should not be dismissed. Throughout Pappenheim's *oeuvre*, trenchantly simple language serves as the vehicle for an outpouring of imagery that is either emotionally charged or hauntingly oneiric. Both fiction and non-fiction are powerful and evocative.

Works

Kleine Geschichten fuer Kinder (1888). *In der Troedelbude. Geschichten von P. Berthold* (1896). *Kaempfe* (1916). *Sisyphus-Arbeit* (1924). *Gebete* (1936). *Bertha Pappenheim: Leben und Schriften*, ed. Dora Edinger (1963).

Bibliography

Anna O. Fourteen Contemporary Reinterpretations, ed. Rosenbaum and Muroff (1984). Jensen, Ellen, *Anna O./Bertha Pappenheim. Ein Fall fuer die Psychiatrie, Ein Leben fuer die Philanthropie* (1985). Kaplan, Marian, *The Jewish Feminist Movement in Germany* (1979).

Donald Friedman

Larin Paraske

Born 1833, Lempaala, Finland; died 1904, Metsapirtti
Genre(s): rune songs
Language(s): Finnish

The names of thousands of rune singers are known from the Karelian cultural area on both sides of the border between Finland and Russia. At various stages of the Finnish national romantic movement, primarily during the nineteenth century, an abundance of archaic folksong, characterized by trochaic meter and alliteration, was collected from these singers. The most famous of them was Larin Paraske, an illiterate peasant woman who was Orthodox in religion.

Larin Paraske was born and raised as the daughter of a serf on the Russian side of the border. She was orphaned at a young age and, at the age of twenty, married forty-year-old Kaurila Teppananpoika from the Finnish side of the border. As his wife, she became known as Larin Paraske, named after his poverty-stricken farm. Nine children were born to them, and of these only three grew to maturity. Because her husband was sickly and the need was great, Paraske sought additional income in many ways: she pulled barges on the river, begged, and raised children from orphanages in St. Petersburg. Widowed in 1888, Paraske came upon a new source of income: the clergyman, Adolf Neovius, who was collecting folklore, noticed Paraske's talent and, paying her small sums, he began to write down the songs she had in her memory.

This was the beginning of a collaboration which lasted for many years. When he moved from Karelia to the environs of Helsinki, Neovius invited Paraske to come along as well. There he introduced the singer to numerous prominent artists of the time and continued recording her runes. It was during this time that Albert Edelfelt and Aksel Järnefelt painted their renowned portraits of Larin Paraske, and it was she who gave Jean Sibelius his most significant contact with folksong. The collection completed by Neovius contains one of the most extensive repertoires of folksong collected from a northern European woman.

Equally represented in Larin Paraske's repertoire of 1,500 folksongs were all the primary genres of southern Karelia, including epic, lyric, wedding and charm runes. Central to her repertoire and that of the entire poetry area, is an emphasis upon lyric verse and women's experience. It was women's song which reigned in these areas during the nineteenth century. Paraske sang an abundance of young women's songs concerned with the relationship between children and parents, particularly the mother. There are also many songs about helplessness at the death of parents. Larin Paraske's verse is rich in wedding songs concerned with the difficulties entailed in a bride's departure from her home. There are mother's songs and lullabies intuiting a child's future and sorrow at a child's death. There are some love songs as well, a great many songs about marriage and, in the final phase, widow's songs. There is also an abundance of songs about care, the theme of which is a nameless, undefined sorrow. In one way or another, of course, these relate to the experience of women as do her other songs.

Although the poetic subject matter in Paraske's songs relates to general human experience, her songs are also autobiographical. Larin Paraske's tendency to improvise, to join together traditional subject matter in a new way, to continuously return to a particular subject, to rearrange certain songs, is clearly unique to her singing. In examining these dimensions of her songs, one observes, for example, that the relationship between husband and wife takes on more prominence in Paraske's songs than is usual for rune singers, making her widow's songs uniquely forceful and piercing.

Primarily, however, Paraske addresses us as one who has powerfully expressed the rich women's culture typical of her particular background. Her repertoire, which is the truest and most complete example of southern Karelian folksong, demonstrates that, even when subordinated and under difficult circumstances, women have been able to create a culture out of their own experiences and, with its aid, come to master their own lives.

> Alahall on allin mieli
> uiess villuu vettä,
> alempaann on armottoman
> käyvess kylän vällii,
> syvän kylmä kyyhkysellä
> syyvess kylän kekkoo,
> vilu vatsa varpusella
> juuvess villuu vettä:
> kylmemp on miu poloisen
> kylmemp on miu mittäi.
> Low the long-tailed duck's spirits
> swimming in chilly water
> lower the orphan's

> walking about the village
> cold the pigeon's heart
> pecking the village haystack
> chilly the sparrow's belly
> drinking chilled water:
> colder mine, poor me
> colder than any.
> Translation: Keith Bosley

Bibliography

Köngäs-Maranda, Elli, "The Carriers of Folklore and the Careers in Folklore." *Folklore Women's Communication. Newsletter of the Women's Section of the American Folklore Society* 27–28 (Fall-Winter 1982). "Parasken runot ja loitsut." *Suomen Kansan Vanhat Runot* V_3, ed. Väinö Salminen (Helsinki, 1931). Rahm, Karl, "Ein neuer Beitrag zur Kalevala-literatur." *Globus. Illustrierte Zeitschrift für Länder-ind Völkerkunde.* LXIV (1893). Timonen, Senni, ed., *Näin lauloi Larin Paraske* (Pieksämäki, 1982).

Senni Timonen

Emilia Pardo Bazán

Born 1851, La Coruña, Spain; died 1921, Madrid, Spain
Genre(s): short story, novel, literary criticism
Language(s): Spanish

Emilia Pardo Bazán stands out in the history of Spanish literature as one of Spain's few recognized women writers before the twentieth century. She was famous in her own time not only as a novelist, short story writer, and literary critic and historian of the first order but also as a woman of amazing versatility and independence. In an age when women were advised to remain in the roles assigned by convention—wife, mother, nun—Pardo Bazán audaciously wrote feminist essays and introduced into Spain the shocking theories of French naturalism propounded by Émile Zola. Although she never subscribed to the determinist theories of Zola's naturalism, she did employ its techniques and themes. Pardo Bazán's literary interests, however, exceeded any one literary school or method, and during her long career she wrote in the traditional style of Spanish realism and the spiritual-mystical mode in fashion during the turn of the century. She also incorporated the dictates of naturalism, modifying them to suit the temper of her talent and times. Eclectic is the word that best applies to Pardo Bazán.

Emilia Pardo Bazán's intellectual curiosity and determination were manifested early; she virtually educated herself, reading avidly and widely in classical and modern literature, learning English so that she could read that literature, reading French and Italian literature in the original language, and delving into philosophical and aesthetic problems. She wrote essays and books on subjects as varied as St. Francis and Christian mysticism, modern French and Russian literature, and the Russian revolution. No subject seemed inappropriate to this energetic woman who even founded a literary magazine for which she herself wrote all the material for several years.

Although married and the mother of three children, she spent most of her time apart from her husband, maintaining a home in Madrid where she reigned over a literary salon. In recognition of her intellectual abilities and acute knowledge of modern literature, she was honored as the first woman to occupy a professorship at the University in Madrid.

Pardo Bazán was a controversial figure, inspiring both acclaim and disdain, but she was nonetheless accepted, even by those less than enthusiastic about her insistence on proving herself as a writer and intellectual, and becoming one of the most significant writers of her time. Her reputation has grown in the years since her death. Today Pardo Bazán is seen as a major writer and critic and as a pioneer in women's issues. She wrote twenty novels, several volumes of literary criticism and history, hundreds of short stories, and hundreds of essays.

Works

Obras completas. 44 vols. (1886–1926). *Obras completas*, ed. Federico Carlos Sainz de Robles. 2 vols. (1947).

Translations: *Short Stories by Emilia Pardo Bazán*, ed. Albert Shapiro and F.J. Hurley (1933). *The Son of the Bondwoman*, tr. Ethel Harriet Hearn (1976).

Bibliography

Baquero Goyannes, Mariano, *Emilia Pardo Bazán, Temas Españoles*, Num. 526 (Madrid, 1971). Barroso, Fernando José, *El Naturalismo en la Pardo Bazán* (Madrid, 1973). Bravo-Villasante, Carmen, *Vida y obra de Emilia Pardo Bazan* (Madrid, 1962). Bretz, Mary Lee, "Naturalismo y feminismo en Emilia Pardo Bazán." *Papeles de Son Armadans* 87 (Dec. 1977): 195–219. Brown, Donald Fowler, *The Catholic Naturalism of Pardo Bazán*. University of North Carolina Studies in the Romance Languages and Literatures, 28 (Chapel Hill, N.C., 1957). Clémessy, Nelly, *Emilia Pardo Bazán romancière. La critique, la théorie, la pratique. Thèses, Mémoires et Travaux*, 2 vols. (Paris, 1973). Davis, Gifford, "The Critical Reception of Naturalism in Spain before *La cuestion palpitante.*" *Hispanic Review* XXII, 2 (April 1954): 97–108. Eoff, Sherman H., *The Modern Spanish Novel. Comparative Essays Examining the Philosophical Impact of Science on Fiction* (New York, 1961). Giles, Mary E., "Impressionist Techniques in Descriptions by Emilia Pardo Bazan." *Hispanic Review* XXX, 4 (Oct. 1962): 304–316. Giles, Mary E., "Symbolic Imagery in *La sirena negra.*" *Papers on Language and Literature* 4 (1968): 182–191. Giles, Mary E., "Feminism and the Feminine in Emilia Pardo Bazan's Novels." *Hispania* 63, 2 (May 1980): 356–357. Glascock, Clyde C., "Two Modern Spanish Novelists: Emilia Pardo Bazán and Armando Palacio Valdés." *University of Texas Bulletin* 2625 (1926). González Lopez, Emilio, *Emilia Pardo Bazán, novelista de Galicia* (New York, 1944). Hilton, Ronald, "Doña Emilia Pardo Bazán and the Europeanization of Spain." *Symposium* 6–7 (1952–1953): 298–307. Hilton, Ronald, "Emilia Pardo Bazán et le mouvement féministe en Espagne." *Bulletin Hispanique* LIV (1952): 153–164. Lopez-Sanz, Mariano, *Naturalismo y espiritualismo en la novelística de Galdós y Pardo Bazán* (Madrid, 1985). Martín, Elvira, *Tres mujeres gallegas del siglo XIX: Concepción Arenal, Rosalía de Castro, Emilia Pardo Bazán* (Barcelona, 1962). Nelken, Margarita, *Las escritoras espanolas* (Barcelona-Buenos Aires, 1930). Osborne, Robert E., *Emilia Pardo Bazán, su vida y sus obras* (México, 1964). Pattison, Walter T., *Emilia Pardo Bazán* (New York, 1971). Pattison, Walter T., *El naturalismo español. Historia externa de un movimiento literario* (Madrid, 1965). Scari, Robert M., "Aspectos distinctivos del lenguaje de Morrina." *Cuadernos hispanoamericanos* CV, 313 (July 1976): 191–199. Varela Jácome, Benito, *Estructuras novelísticas de Emilia Pardo Bazán* (Santiago de Compostela: Anejo XXII, 1973).

Mary E. Giles

Sofiia Iakolevna Parnok

(a.k.a. A. Polianin)

Born 1885, Taganrog, Russia; died 1933,
  Karinskii
Genre(s): poetry, criticism, translation
Language(s): Russian

An Acmeist poet and a friend of Marina Tsvetaeva, Sofiia Parnok remains one of the most obscure literary figures of her period. She moved often and destroyed a great deal that might have served as biographical material. While in Moscow, she belonged to the "Lyric Circle," along with V. Khodasevich, G. Shengeli and L. Grossman, among others.

Parnok lost her mother shortly after her birth and remained with her father to whom she was never close. She began writing verse at a very young age and was first published in 1906. Perhaps her greatest love was for music. She went abroad to live in Geneva with the Plekhanov family and enrolled in the conservatory there. She did not finish the course, however, and returned to Russia. She was married briefly to another poet, V. M. Vol'kenstein, who had considerable influence on her literary production for a time.

From 1913 she was a regular contributor to Severnye zapiski (Northern Notes) and literary critic for Russkaia molva (Russian Rumor). In some ways, her most interesting achievements are her opera libretti for Veiberg's Rusalochka and Spendiarov's Almasti. These she wrote with a particular passion, either with or without the composer's supervision.

Parnok's poetry is formally classically oriented often reminiscent of the Greek Sapphic strophe with long lines (sometimes hexameter) of ternary meter. Her style is very clear, obviously related to the Acmeists although some Symbolist tendencies are displayed both in the sound patterning as well as the choice of motifs: ennui, remove, loneliness, etc. Parnok's work is not very well known, so it is difficult to judge its importance to Russian literature.

Works

Stikhotvorenia (1916). Loza (1922). Rozy Pierii (1922). Muzyka (1926). Vpolgolosa (1928). Sobranie stikhotvoreniia (1979).

Translations: Modern Russian Poetry, ed. V. Markov and M. Sparks (1967), pp. 368–371.

Bibliography

Kratkaia literaturnaia entsiklopediia, vol. 5, p. 603. Poliakova, S., Introductory article [Vstupitel'naia stat'ia] to Sobranie stikhotvoreniia (Ann Arbor, 1979), pp. 1–106. Poliakova, S., Zakatnye ony dni—Tsvetaeva i Parnok (Ann Arbor, 1983).

Christine Tomei

Callirhoe Parren

(a.k.a. Maïa)

Born 1861, Rethymno, Crete; died 1940,
  Athens, Greece
Genre(s): journalism, novel, short story,
  drama, essay, literary criticism
Language(s): Greek

Callirhoe Siganou was born in 1861 in a middle-class family of Crete. She studied in the best schools for girls in Athens and, in 1878, she graduated from the Arsakeion School for training teachers. After her graduation, she was invited to run the Greek community school for girls in Odessa, where she worked during two years. She also ran, for several years, the Zapeion School of the Greek community in Adrianople. In 1880 she was married to the French journalist Jean Parren, the founder of the Athens News Agency, and some years later she moved permanently to Athens.

Callirhoe Parren was the leading figure of late-nineteenth and early-twentieth century Greek feminism. In 1887 she started publishing the Efimeris ton Kyrion (1887–1918; Ladies' Newspaper), the first feminist publication in Greece, exclusively edited by women. Under her editorship, the Ladies' Newspaper became not only the organizational center for women's emancipation but also one of the best distributed weeklies in Greece and among the Greek diaspora (5000 copies). Its campaigns for women's rights had a big impact and resulted in the first successful protective legislation for women. Parren was closely connected to the European and American women's movement and represented the Ladies' Newspaper in several International Conferences (1888, 1889, 1896, and 1900 in Paris and 1893 in Chicago). In 1896, she founded the *Union of Greek Women*. She was also the founder of various welfare organizations for women (*Sunday School*, *Asylum of Sainte Catherine*, *The Soup Kitchen*, etc).

Besides her unremitting activity as a pedagogue, feminist, and social reformer, Parren was also one of the main intellectual figures of the late-nineteenth-century cultural life in Athens. She was the first professional woman journalist and worked for two of the biggest daily newspapers, *Acropolis* and *Asty* (City). She published her *Woman's History* in 1889. Her *salon*, known as the "literary Saturdays," attracted the most prominent representatives of the literary and artistic avant-garde of the end of the century. Her wide culture, her knowledge of foreign languages (she spoke English, French, Russian and Italian fluently), her travelling experience but most of all her strong personality, won her a wide recognition both in Greece and abroad. Among her friends were Jules Simon and Juliette Adam as well as some of the leading figures of the literary avant-garde of the 1880s like Gavriilidis, Xenopoulos, and the national poet Kostis Palamas, who wrote a famous poem for her. A skillful tactician, she used her own exceptional admission in this male milieu to build up a policy of alliances with the women's movement. But this did not prevent her from being a fearsome polemicist who could publicly attack the most respected male intellectuals if she considered women's interests were jeopardized. Her violent dispute with Roïdis, the father of Greek literary criticism, provoked the famous "*querelae* over women writers" (1893), which occupied the Athenian press for months.

For Parren writing was an invaluable arm in women's hands, a privileged means for self-assertion. As an editor of the *Ladies' Newspaper*, she did everything to promote women's literature, including the organization of literary competitions, and managed in a very short time to get contributions from nearly all the major women writers of the late nineteenth century, including those who did not consider themselves feminists. Women writers, she believed, should have a double goal: "free themselves from the implacable tyranny of public opinion which turns their writings into another evidence of their servile

submission" and, at the same time, "convince the multitude that the New Woman is the moral and intellectual equal of man and deserves total liberty." This double, and to a certain extent contradictory, function she attributed to women's literature marked her own fiction, which is characterized by a permanent tension between didactic intention and genuine literary ambition. Written at a time when realism and the "urban novel" were making their first appearance in Greek literature, her novels developed a virulent critique of existing gender relations in a developing society fascinated by the most superficial expressions of the bourgeois decency in the "civilized" West, and yet largely submitted to the most obscurantist social codes of the Mediterranean traditional culture. But while showing that women bear the brunt of this transitional social order, Parren is also working out the first articulate utopian visions of gender relations, putting forward alternative social values based on gender equality, women's autonomy and self-fulfillment, female friendship and solidarity.

Parren's novels were first published in the *Ladies' Newspaper* under the pen name *Maïa* and met with an enthusiastic response from the female readership of the journal. The first three novels were published subsequently in three volumes: *I Hirafetimeni* (1900; The Emancipated Woman), *I Mayissa* (1901; The Enchantress) and *To Neon Symvoleon* (1902; The New Contract) formed a trilogy (*Ta Vivlia tis Avyis*, The Books of Dawn) about the solitary and tormented odyssey of two generations of Greek women towards emancipation and self-accomplishment. The trilogy had a favorable reception from such critics as Grigorios Xenopoulos and Costis Palamas who underlined the "generous contribution of Parren in the development of Greek social novel." The trilogy also served as a basis for a play called *Nea Yineka*. (New Woman) put on in 1907 with the participation of Marika Cotopouli, the most popular dramatic actress of the 20th century, which contributed to the popularization of the work and ideas of its author. *The Emancipated Woman* was translated into French and published in *Journal des Débats* and *Revue Littéraire*. Her other novels, *To Maramenon Krinon* (The Faded Lily) and *Horis Onoma* (Without a Name), were also published, but they have been lost. We know them, however, from their initial publication in the *Ladies' Newspaper*.

Callirhoe Parren died in 1940, in Athens. Although she was one of the most controversial and influential figures of her time, she gradually sank into oblivion until the late 1970s, when she was rediscovered by the emerging feminist scholarship. Her writings have not yet been reprinted.

Works

Istoria tis Yinekos [Women's History] (1889). *Zoi Enos Etous* [One Year of Life] (1894). *Epistole Athineas is Parissinin* [Letters of an Athenian Woman to a Parisian] (1896–1897). *I Hirafetimeni* [The Emancipated Woman] (1900). *I Mayissa* [The Enchantress] (1901). *To Neon Symvolean* [The New Contract] (1902). *Nea Yineka* [New Woman] (1907). *To Maramenon Krinon* [The Faded Lily] (1909). *Horis Onoma* [Without a Name] (n.d.). Ta Taxithia Mou [My Trips] (n.d.).

Translations

"*L'Emancipée*," *Journal des Débats* (February 4 to March 18, 1907).

Bibliography

Karavia, Emilia, "Parren Callirhoe." *Megali Helliniki Egkyklopedia* [Great Greek Encyclopedia], vol. 9, p. 746–747. Michaïlithou, Soultana, *Callirhoe Parren* (Samos, 1940). Palamas, Kostis, "Yinekos Mythistorima" [A Woman's Novel] (1900), in *Apanda* [Complete Works], vol. 2 (Athens, 1960), p. 200. Varikas, Eleni, *I Exeyersi ton Kyrion: yenessi mias feministikis synithissis stin Hellatha, 1833–1908* [The Revolt of the Ladies: The Formation of a Feminist Consciousness in Greece, 1833–1908] (Athens, 1987).

Elini Varikas

Vesna Parun

Born April 10, 1922, on the Dalmatian island Zlarin in Croatia, Yugoslavia
Genre(s): poetry, drama, essay, children's literature, journalism
Language(s): Serbo-Croatian

Vesna Parun went to high school in Split, a large coastal town that still bears powerful marks of the Roman Empire, and then she studied at the Philosophical Faculty of the University of Zagreb. She has written for many literary periodicals in Yugoslavia, and in addition to the poetry that has been collected in book form, she has written drama, film scripts, critical essays, children's poetry, and journalistic feature articles.

Parun's first published collection of lyrics, *Zore i vihori* (1947; Dawns and Whirlwinds), was a great event in literary circles. She was hailed as a new voice, youthful, sincere and heartfelt, expressing sentiments that had not surfaced previously in the Yugoslav literary tradition. She wrote of intimate emotions at a time when most poetry was programmatically concerned with the rebuilding of a shattered country and the building of socialism. Parun was sharply and repeatedly taken to task by the establishment for the personal tone of her work, even when she was writing of the sorrows of war. And yet, what she was doing was the all-important task of healing. Her second collection, *Pjesme* (1949; Poems), expressed her great dedication to the rebuilding of her country. She was, in fact, a member of the loosely-knit group of poets called Prugaši (Rail-layers). Her hopes for the very difficult period in which she was living were expressed in the same attractive, nonformulaic way that is characteristic of her poetry of love and emotions. One critic points out dismissively that she soon dropped her "vital, virile, revolutionary voice" and relapsed into love lyrics and then into virtual silence. Few mention her further growth, perhaps by way of journalism, into an able satirist, as in *Apokaliptičke basne* (1976; Apocalyptic Fables).

Vesna Parun's lyricism is erotic. Poetry and love are one, and the love is of the earth, of country, and of man. Nature, desire, joy, sorrow, love of homeland, all are perceived through the body, and this perception is transmitted in a startlingly communicative way. Her vocabulary is rich and unexpected; the Adriatic coast is vividly brought to the page amid a treasury of plant and animal names.

Parun has been called, by admiring critics, inventive rather than innovative. She has not created new language but has found her own way to use her own literature and history as well as modern French poetry. Her great contribution has been to lead the way to a lyricism that seemed miraculously new until large numbers of contemporaries had followed in her footsteps.

Works

Zore i vihori (1947). Pjesme (1949). Crna maslina (1955). Vidrama vjerna (1957). Ropstvo (1957). Pusti da otpočinem (1958). Koralj vraćen na moru (1959). Ti i nikad (1959). Bila sam dječak (1963). Jao jutro (1963). Vijetar Trakije (1964). Pjesme (1964). Ukleti da'd (1969). Apokaliptičke basne (1976).

Translations: Translations of articles on individual works in Modern Slavic Literatures, Vol. II, pp. 652–654.

Bibliography

Eekman, T., Thirty Years of Yugoslav Literature (1945–1975) (1978), pp. 2–4. Krmpotić, V., Afterword to Pjesme (1964).

Gertrud Champa

Pilar Paz Pasamar

Born 1933, Jerez de la Frontera (Andalusia), Spain
Genre(s): poetry
Language(s): Spanish

Pasamar's family moved to Madrid at the close of the Civil War (1939), and there she received her education. In her university days she was especially drawn to the theater. Mara (1951), her first poetry collection, appeared when she was only eighteen and was highly praised by Juan Ramón Jiménez, Spain's senior poet in exile and one of the century's most demanding critics. The major concern of the book is metaphysical, a search for God, completely unrelated to her immediate cultural context and surroundings, disconnected from the poetic currents of the day and the social preoccupations of the post-war poets. Pasamar's poetic universe is one of pantheistic quietude, solitude, and existential doubt in which she initiates a dialogue with the deity and with poetry itself. Los buenos días (1954; The Good Days) was the runner-up for the 1953 Adonais Prize for Poetry, awarded to Claudio Rodríguez (curiously, both books coincided in the metaphysical quest for ultrasensorial essences). In this, as in Pasamar's earlier work, observers have detected a coincidence with the mature poetry of Juan Ramón Jiménez in Dios deseado y deseante. She also follows fully in the Spanish mystic tradition, in the vein of St. John of the Cross and St. Teresa. Minute things or those often overlooked—taken for granted, such as the light, and the morrow—are seen as revealing the divine essence.

Ablativo Amor (1956; Ablative Love), and Del abreviado mar (1957; Of the Abbreviated Sea) exhibit the same poetic inspiration in their intrinsic conception of poetic language, but their styles differ. Sonnets predominate in the first, while in the second, form is much freer, approaching free verse and evoking the interior monologue with its syncopated expression. In Ablativo Amor, the inspiration is existential, an ever more urgent search for a silent God, in which the love for the things of nature and fellow humans forms the backdrop for struggle with loneliness and silent emptiness. Del abreviado mar recounts impressions and meditations upon God and life in the maritime language well known to the poet, who since her marriage while still a university student has lived in Cadiz, a few yards from the Atlantic. La soledad, contigo (1960; Solitude, With You) continues the quest for God in the little things of daily life, of the poet's domestic world, now melancholic and sentimental, as she seeks the Holy Spirit in the laurel, parsley, and saffron whose fragrances fill her kitchen. While still pantheistic in spirit, this book is more "human" in its language; it is also unmistakably feminine. It is a book that could only have been written by a woman, permeated by maternal and domestic tasks and duties, satisfactions and frustrations. In 1964, Pasamar published an essay (apparently book-length) entitled Poesía femenina de lo cotidiano (Feminine Poetry of Everyday Things), which should be of great interest if available.

Violencia inmóvil (1967; The Motionless Violence) is the most disquieting collection of Pasamar's production. The subject is life's mysteries, and especially Mystery, life's ultimate meaning. Daily or quotidian perceptions of the world are deliberately contrasted with "intellectual" vision, and the text moves between concreteness and ambiguity, the clarity of names and the indefiniteness inherent in poetry. Images are no longer drawn from the poet's domestic world and maternal experience, as in the previous work, but from a more literary and contemporary series of intertexts. Rather than individual poems, this book is a single, uninterrupted discourse.

Pasamar belongs chronologically and by reason of her origins and subsequent residence to a group of Andalusian poets known as "Platero," who represent the southern wing of the "mid-century generation" or generation of the 1950s, including Caballero Bonald, Fernando Quiñones, Julio Mariscal, José Luis Tejada, and others, and with them she participated in literary *tertulias*, and the publishing of a literary review. Her poetic concerns were always personal, however, differing from the sociopolitical poetry of most others of the "Platero" cohort. With marriage (in 1957) and numerous children, she was forced to renounce her writing for a time, and a fifteen-year hiatus intervenes between *Violencia inmóvil* and her next collection, *La torre de Babel y otros asuntos* (1982; The Tower of Babel and Other Matters). This collection is a compilation of largely unrelated poems not previously published rather than a thematic whole of a unitary discourse, as was the case with earlier collections. *La alacena* (1985; The Kitchen Cabinet) is an anthology containing excerpts from all of Pasamar's published books as well as an excerpt from *Orario* (a play on homophones, one meaning timetable, the other prayer schedule).

Works

Ablativo amor (1956). *La alacena* (1985). *Los buenos días* (1954). *Del abreviado mar* (1957). *Mara* (1951). *Orario* (1986). *La soledad, contigo* (1960). *La torre de Babel y otros asuntos* (1982). *Violencia inmóvil* (1967).

Janet Perez

Claude Pascal

(see: Monica Lovinescu)

Françoise Pascal

Born February 1632, Lyon, France; died ca. 1698, Paris
Genre(s): drama, verse
Language(s): French

Born in the bourgeoisie, Françoise Pascal received somehow a much better education than most girls of her social class. She had the opportunity to see dramatic performances in her native Lyons, and she soon tried to write plays. In 1655, her *Agathonphile martyr* was published in Lyons. It is taken from Camus' novel *Agathonphile* which had already served as a source for Marthe Cosnard's *Chastes Martirs*, but Françoise Pascal probably did not know the latter's play. She did not follow the rules of classical theater; scenes are not linked, the action is not unified, it does not take place only within Rome, and it requires at least two days.

Two years later, her second play, *L'Endymion*, was published again in Lyons. It is more satisfactorily constructed; it also requires an elaborate setting, with a chariot for Diane, forest, trees, flowers, an altar, etc. That same year in her *Diverses Poésies* appeared two one-act farces, *L'Amoureuse Vaine et ridicule* (The Vain and Ridiculous Amorous Woman) and *L'Amoureux extravagant* (The Extravagant Amorous Man). In the first one, the central figure, though old and ugly, is convinced that all men who see her fall in love with her. The other farce shows a ridiculous poet who is deprived of his money by a clever valet.

In 1681, Françoise Pascal went back to a five-act play with *Sésostris*. She still paid little attention to the classical unities, but the characters are moved by genuine emotion and the story is well told. This play shows considerable progress over her earlier works.

For her last play, Françoise Pascal returned to the farce. *Le Vieillard amoureux* (The Amorous Old Man) uses eight-syllable verse. The plot is made of tricks played by a girl and her helpers to overcome her father's opposition to her marriage. The miserly father falls in love with his daughter's lover who has disguised himself as a young woman.

Françoise Pascal also loved music and painting. In the latter part of her life she published several collections of pious verse. She was the first woman dramatist of the seventeenth century who wrote more than a single play.

Works

> *Agathonphile martyr* (1655). *La mort du grand et véritable Cyrus* (1655). *L'Amoureuse vaine et ridicule* (1657). *L'Amoureux extravagant* (1657). *L'Endymion* (1657). *Sésostris* (1661). *Le vieillard amoureux* (1664). *Le commerce du Parnasse* (1669). *Cantiques spirituels ou noëls nouveaux* (1670). *Les réflexions de la Magdelène dans le temps de sa pénitence* (1674). *Les entretiens de la Vierge et de S. Jean l'Evangeliste* (1680).

Bibliography

Baldensperger, F., "Françoise Pascal, 'fille lyonnaise.'" *Etudes d'Histoire Littéraire* (1939).

Marie-France Hilgar

Jacqueline Pascal

Born October 4, 1625, Clermont-Ferrand,
France; died October 4, 1661, Port-Royal
Genre(s): poetry
Language(s): French

Jacqueline Pascal, the third and youngest child of Etienne Pascal, was born two years after her famous brother, the philosopher Blaise Pascal. They were welcome in literary salons at an early age because of their intelligence and their precocity. Jacqueline was thirteen years old when she sent to the Queen a sonnet to congratulate her on her pregnancy. She played a part in *l'Amour tyrannique* by Scudéry when she was fourteen years old, and at age fifteen wrote *Stances contre l'amour* (Stanzas Against Love).

Under the influence of Jansenist friends, she entered the convent of Port-Royal in 1652, where she died in 1661.

Bibliography

Cousin, Victor, *Jacqueline Pascal* (Paris, 1856).

Marie France Hilgar

Pasionaria

(see: Dolores Ibarruri)

Heidi Pataki

Born November 2, 1940, Vienna, Austria
Genre(s): journalist, poetry, prose, essay
Language(s): German

Heidi Pataki is one of the keenest observers and sharpest critics of contemporary society. She is well known for her satirical, provocative poetry which unites language experimentation with social criticism. She is also known as an essayist and film critic, and she was one of the earliest activists in the Austrian women's movement.

Pataki was born in 1940 in Vienna, where she attended school and studied at the university with a concentration in journalism and art history. Since 1970 she has worked as editor of the journal *Neues Forum* and in the early 1980s also as editor of *Filmschrift*. She lives today as a freelance writer and journalist in Vienna, where she is a frequent contributor to newspapers and radio stations. She is a member of the Graz Authors' Association and also of various women's groups.

How does one write a poem today? Is poetry even possible any more? That is the question Pataki poses, and she answers it in the negative, as paradoxically exemplified in two outstanding volumes of poetry: *schlagzeilen* (1968; headlines) and *stille post* (1978; rumor). Poetry today is seen not as a moral or political problem nor even as a psychological or aesthetic one but solely as a problem of language. Is our language still usable; or has it not rather exhausted itself? Anything we say has been said a thousand times before, and this use and abuse of language has rendered it vacuous. What was once metaphor is now commonplace, profundities have become trivialities, and meaningful expression has degenerated to hackneyed phrases.

Pataki confronts the situation with clear-eyed and cold-blooded radicalism, as expressed in a theoretical statement accompanying *schlagzeilen* entitled "Eleven Theses about Poetry": "Originality is nonsense," and "anyone who still tries to write a new poem is anachronistic." She draws the conclusions for her own poetry by picking up the "headlines"—clichés, banalities, and slogans—from ordinary discourse and arranging them in a montage-like construction. Paying more attention to the sound and rhythm than to the meaning (which is in any case absent), she establishes unexpected connections and invents unusual meanings, and the pawn-shop-particles of language are powerfully evocative in their new associative context. Although she treats poetry as if it were a game, a certain sadness is also present, as exemplified in the programmatic poem, "you have taken my language away." One is driven to despair at the realization that one's language has been so co-opted by advertising, politics, and all sorts of misuse that the words no longer mean anything. Despair, however, manifests itself in irony and parody rather than sentiment or nostalgia, and the apparent debunking of language only bears witness to its vital importance for our well-being.

Stille post takes its title from the party game in which a sentence is whispered around a circle only to come out at the end in drastically muti-lated form. The poetry demonstrates this crisis of language by a plundering of the literary tradition in true postmodernist fashion. Lines and frag-ments from the "sacred" canon of *Minnesang* and folksong, from Goethe, Eichendorff, Heine, Rilke, Trakl, and many more appear in this montage—recognizable, but radically altered by the context. "hosanna," for example, presents a collection of famous "whoever" and "whenever" lines without, however, any result clauses. The irony is global, but the parody is not of the tradition but of contemporary society. The philosophical and linguistic presuppositions are reflected upon in a series of poems with the illustrative titles "metaph./ysics" and "semant./ical & c.," in which unreadability itself becomes thematic.

Some of the same snippets from the tradition are taken up for further variation in "metaphor./ics & c." and intertwined with banal slogans, whereby the metaphors are phonetic and syntactic rather than semantic and thus untranslatable. In this cliché-ridden world where individuality and authenticity are mere anachronisms, the title poem ironically opens with the admonition: "mister meier, get real!" and concludes as anonymously with a "place for mister maier! / (mayer?) / meier." The crass juxtaposition of disparate elements reveals the paradox of poetry in present-day society and questions the possi-bility of speaking at all. The montage stands, as the author states in her "epilogue" to *stille post*,

as "a museum displaying the dried-up trophies of the indestructible tradition. To destroy the in-destructible—that is the paradox of the poem."

The apparently disrespectful parody and play with language are not so much a critique of the tradition as they are a questioning of its meaning for us, given the collective, mechanized, consumer-oriented society in which we live. The aggressive act of deformation can only be un-derstood as a result of passionate attachment. Pataki knows the literary tradition extremely well, and she demonstrates the thesis that any poem quotes its predecessors. But what happens to art that undergoes reproduction ad nauseam? Pataki possesses an extraordinary lyrical, rhyth-mic talent, and one has the feeling she could write any number of poems in the conventional manner. By taking, however, the poem itself as her topic she has created a type of metalinguistic commentary in which the poem turns back on itself to investigate the conditions of its own existence.

Pataki is obviously not the first to cry "rot-ten!" to "2000 years of Western culture." A Nietzschean influence is evident in her radical critique of language and culture as well as in her vitalistic affirmation of life; Nietzschean is also the maddening disparity between social con-vention and utopian vision, which elicits a strong emotional reaction. With wit, humor, and irony Pataki demonstrates the "pastness" of the past, and she demands a language and art commen-surate with the present. The provocative nature of the undertaking is visually represented by photographs of the author linking the spiritual striptease with a physical one. Given the excess baggage with which we are all encumbered, according to Pataki's perspective, one cannot be radical enough.

Works

schlagzeilen. gedichte (1968). fluchtmodelle. zur emanzipation der frau. politisch-soziologische satiren (1972). stille post. gedichte (1978).

Beth Bjorklund

Jean Paulhan

(see: Pauline Réage)

Hertha Pauli

Born 1909, Vienna, Austria; died 1972, New
York, U. S. A.
Genre(s): novel, radio drama, short story,
children's literature, biography
Language(s): German, English

Pauli studied drama at the Academy of
Dramatic Arts in Vienna and began her career as
an actress in Germany. She began her literary
career by writing stories and radio plays. In 1933
she moved to France, and in 1941 she came to
the United States. She wrote both in German and
English. In 1967 Pauli received the Silver Medal
of Honor from the Austrian government for her
contribution to the understanding of Austrian
culture.

Works

Toni, ein Frauenleben, novel about Ferdinand
Raimund (1936). Nur eine Frau (1937). Alfred
Nobel Dynamite King, Architect of Peace (1942).
Silent Night, children's book (German tr. Ein Lied
vom Himmel, Die Geschichte von Stille Nacht
1943, 1954). [With A.B. Ashton], I Lift My Lamp
(1948). Das Genie eines liebenden Herzes, ein
Bertha v. Suttner Roman (English tr. Cry of the Heart
1955, 1957). Jugend Nachher (1959). Jugend vor
Gericht (1962). The Secret of Sarajevo (German tr.
Das Geheimnis von Sarajevo 1967). Der erste
Christbaum, children's book (1967). Handel and
the Foundlings (1968). Der Riss der Zeit geht durch
mein Herz, ein Erlebnisbuch, biographical (French
tr. Dominique as Le Déchichure de Temps; English
tr. as The Break of Time 1970; 1973).

Bibliography

Austrian Writers in the U.S. 1938–1968. An exhibition of the Austrian Institute and the Austrian
Forum (New York, 1968). Stern, Desider, Werke
von Autoren jüdischer Herkunft in deutscher
Sprache, 3rd ed. (Vienna, 1970) pp. 286, 289,
345, 1137–1139.

M.A. Reiss

Pauline

(see: Kathinka [Katharina] Rosa
Pauline Modesta Zitz-Halein)

Karolina Pavlova

Born July 22, 1807, Iaroslav, Russia; died
1893, Dresden, Germany
Genre(s): poetry, translation
Language(s): Russian, French, German

Karolina Karlovna Pavlova (née Jaenisch),
generally considered Russia's major nineteenth-
century woman poet, was born in Iaroslav, north
of Moscow, into a family that was German on her
father's side and French and English on her
mother's. Her father, Karl Ivanovich Jaenisch,
studied medicine at Leipzig University. He then
returned to Russia, married Karolina Karlovna's
mother, Elisaveta, and received an appointment
as professor of physics and chemistry in the
Moscow Medical-Surgical Academy after Karolina
Karlovna's birth.

Pavlova had an eventful and stormy life. Her
earliest memory as a five-year-old, she wrote in a
memoir, was fleeing Moscow with her family in
1812 at the approach of Napoleon's army. In the
same memoir she recounted that in 1816, when
she was nine, her seven-year-old sister died.
Perhaps because Karolina Karlovna thus became
an only child, she received an unusually good
education for a woman of her time through
private tutors. She showed an early gift for languages and by the time she was eighteen knew
French, English, German, Italian, and of course
Russian, as well as some Spanish and Polish. In
the course of her career Pavlova would write in
and translate to and from a variety of languages.
Although best known as a Russian poet, she also
wrote poetry in French and German, and translated others' poetry from German, French, English, Polish, and Greek into Russian; from
Russian, Polish, English, and French into German;
and from Russian into French.

By 1825 when she was eighteen, Pavlova
had begun to attend the literary salon of Princess
Zinaida Volkonskaia, a salon that attracted leading
literary and philosophical lights of the day, including Aleksandr Pushkin. Here Karolina
Karlovna met Adam Mickiewicz, the exiled Polish
revolutionary and poet. Mickiewicz, who was
impoverished, started giving her Polish lessons,
and in November 1827 he proposed to her.
When a rich uncle who disapproved of the match
threatened to disinherit Karolina Karolovna and

her entire family, Mickiewicz quickly lost interest and moved to St. Petersburg. He did not, however, bother to break the engagement until 1829 when Karolina Karolovna asked him to clarify their relationship and he was about to leave Russia. Although Pavlova never saw him again, this experience appears to have affected her deeply; over the course of her life not only did she translate several of Mickiewicz's works into French, but she also wrote several poems about him, two entitled "November 10," the date of his proposal to her.

In 1833 Karolina Karlovna made her literary debut with *Das Nordlich* (Northern Lights). The book consisted of her translations into German of works by Russia's most famous poets (Aleksandr Pushkin, Vasily Zhukovksy, Nikolai Iazykov, Evgeny Baratnsky, Anton Delvig, Dmitry Venevitinov) as well as her own German poetry. *Das Nordlich*, which was published in Dresden, received excellent reviews, both in Russia and Germany, including praise from Goethe himself.

In 1836 the Jaenischs' rich uncle finally died, thus at the age of twenty-nine Karolina Karlovna suddenly found herself an heiress surrounded by eager suitors. Her choice was unfortunate. In 1837 she married Nikolai Filippovich Pavlov (1805–1864), a promising writer enjoying great success at literary salons at the time thanks to his *Tri povesti* (1835; Three Tales) which attacked the institution of serfdom. Pavlov later told his friends that he had married his wife for her money.

During the 1840s the Pavlovs ran a distinguished literary salon where Westernizers (those who believed Russia should become part of Europe), hotly debated the Slavophiles (those who rejected Western European values), and where such writers as the Aksakovs, Evgeny Baratynsky, Afanasy Fet, Nikolai Gogol, Timofei Granovsky, and Alexander Herzen read their latest works.

In 1839 Ippolit, the Pavlovs' only child, was born, and Pavlova published two new works. *Les Preludes* consisted of Pavlova's translations, into French this time, of English, German, Polish and Russian poetry, as well as some of her own French poetry. Pavlova's translation into French of Schiller's play, *Joan of Arc*, also appeared during this year. She had already started writing

poetry in Russian, much of which began to appear in various Russian literary journals.

Meanwhile Nikolai Pavlov's literary career was not keeping pace. Reviewers expressed disappointment that his second collection of stories (1839) did not live up to the promise of the first. He stopped writing, and increasingly spent his time (and Pavlova's fortune, which he controlled) playing and losing at cards.

It was during this period that Pavlova wrote and published her best known work, *Dvoinaia Zhizn'* (1848; A Double Life). The work, which was very well received, recounts in alternating prose and poetry sections the daytime life and nighttime visions of Cecilia, an eighteen-year-old member of Moscow society. Although the prose section seems to end happily, with Cecilia marrying the man she loves, in the poetry sections Pavlova suggests that this marriage will bring Cecilia only pain, disillusionment, and the loss of her true self.

Pavlova's own marital situation grew worse. In 1849 she invited a relative, Evgeniia Aleksandrovna Tannenberg, to live with her. Pavlov fell in love with Tannenberg, moved her into a separate apartment, and had three children by her. In the meantime he continued to gamble with and lose tremendous amounts of his wife's money. In 1852 Pavlova's parents complained to the Moscow military governor about Pavlov, who had tried to mortgage his wife's estate without telling her. The governor, reportedly angry on his own account because of an epigram Pavlov had written about him, took the occasion to have Pavlov's library searched. When the search revealed forbidden books critical of the government, Pavlov was arrested and exiled to Perm for a year. Pavlov suddenly became a martyr for the liberal cause and Pavlova the object of ridicule and condemnation for causing his imprisonment.

To escape this social obloquy Pavlova and her parents moved from Moscow to St. Petersburg where misfortune quickly followed; her father died of cholera in 1853. When Pavlova did not go to the funeral, supposedly because of fear of infection, a new scandal erupted, and Pavlova and her mother moved to Dorpat (Tartu), Estonia.

During this time "Razgovor v Kremle" (1854; Conversation in the Kremlin) appeared, a narrative poem perceived at the time as expressing Slavophile views. Consequently, Pavlova was once again attacked by the liberal press.

In Dorpat Pavlova became acquainted with Boris Utin, a law student 25 years her junior at the University of Dorpat, who between 1853 and 1855 became her last and most intense love, and the inspiration for a cycle of love poetry. Pavlova made a few short visits back to Russia in 1855 and 1857 and traveled through Europe and to the Middle East. In 1858 she settled in Dresden where, because her husband had squandered her estate, she would live in poverty until her death in 1893.

In 1859 she published *Quadrille*, a narrative poem in which four women who meet at a ball try to determine if they or society are to blame for their unhappy marriages. In 1861 the politically controversial narrative poem, *Conversation in Trianon*, was published in London. The poem, which Pavlova had written in 1848 in reaction to the French revolution of that year, expressed her idea that revolutions were both inevitable and ultimately futile since new dictators would simply replace the old. The work could not be published in Russia because the censorship forbade any reference to revolutions.

In 1863 Pavlova had her collected works published in Russia where they were not well received. The literary climate had changed in twenty years and now the most influential Russian literary critics found Pavlova's elegiac, romantic, beautifully crafted poetry old-fashioned and frivolous.

Pavlova's last important friendship was with A.K. Tolstoy, a playwright (and distant relative of Leo Tolstoy) whom she met in Dresden in 1861 and who visited her there frequently until his death in 1875. Tolstoy managed to arrange a small pension for Pavlova, perhaps in gratitude for her very popular translations of his plays into German.

Pavlova died in 1893 having outlived Mickiewicz, her husband, her son, and A.K. Tolstoy. Some of the obituaries mentioned that she left a trunk of unpublished manuscripts, others mentioned a draft for an expanded version of her complete works which she had entrusted to her grandson. Nothing further was heard of either.

Scholarship about Pavlova, as often happens with woman writers, has focused disproportionately on her relations with the various men in her life; her father, the men she loved, the men who loved her, her husband, and male critics' reactions to her work (the most famous, Vassirion Belinsky, praised her for her "muzhestvennyi energiia," her "masculine energy"). There is, however, ample evidence that women and women's experience played an important role in Pavlova's work. She wrote several works concerned with women's position in society (*A Double Life*, *Quadrille*, "Jeanne d'Arc") and two poems about women poets ("Three Souls" [1845] and "On Reading the Poetry of a Young Woman" [1846]). Twentieth-century Russian women poets in their turn have honored Pavlova in their work. Sofiia Parnok (1885–1933) dedicated a poem to her and Marina Tsvetaeva (1892–1941) named one of her poetry collections *Remeslo* (Craft) after one of Pavlova's most famous poems in which she describes poetry as her "sacred craft."

Works

Polnoe sobranie stikhotvorenii. Vstupitel'naia stat'ia P.P. Gromova (Moscow, Leningrad, 1964).
Translation: *A Double Life*, tr. Barbara Heldt (1986).

Bibliography

Briggs, Anthony, "'Twofold Life': A Mirror of Karolina Pavlova's Shortcomings and Achievement." *Slavonic and East European Review* XLIX, 114 (1971): 1–17. Greene, Diana, "Karolina Pavlova's 'Tri dushi': The Transfiguration of Biography," *Proceedings of the Kentucky Foreign Language Conference 1984: Slavic Section.*, pp. 15–24. Lettmann-Sadony, Barbara, *Karolina Karlovna Pavlova: Eine Dichterin Russisch-Deutscher Wechselseitigkeit* (Munchen, 1971). Monter, Barbara Heldt, "Introduction." *A Double Life* (Oakland, Calif., 1986). Sendich, Munir, "Karolina Janisch Pavlova and Adam Mickiewicz." *The Polish Review* XIV, 3 (1969): 68–78. Sendich, Munir, "Evenings at Karolina Pavlova's." *Die Welt due Slaven* XVI:1 (1971), 58–69. Sendich, Munir, "Karolina Pavlova and Boris Utin." *Russian Language Journal* (Spring 1974): 63–88. Sendich, Munir, "Twelve Unpublished Letters of Karolina Pavlova to Aleksey Tolstoy." *Russian Literature Triquarterly* 9 (1974): 541–558. Zontikov, V.K, "'Pishu ne smelo ia, ne chasto . . .' (Stikhotvorenie

Karoliny Pavlovoi)." *Vstrechi s proshlym: sbornik materialov.* TsGALI (Moscow, 1982), pp. 35–39.

Diane Greene

Maria Pawlikowska-Jasnorzewska

Born November 24, 1891, Cracow, Poland;
died July 9, 1945, Manchester, England
Genre(s): poetry, drama
Language(s): Polish

As the daughter of the artist (painter) Wojciech Kossak, Pawlikowska grew up in a privileged and artistic environment, being tutored at home, educating herself by extensive reading, but receiving no formal education. Her work can be divided into three phases. During the 1920s and early 1930s, her poems and plays were lighthearted and playful, often reflecting the frivolity of some in her circle. But the poems demonstrate an original style in love poetry and are distinguished by the chiseled perfection of a miniaturist. They are economical, concise, almost aphoristic but gem-like and sparkling. Titles such as *Różowa magia* (1924; Pink Magic), *Pocałunki* (1926; Kisses), and *Wachlarz* (1927; The Fan) testify to the joyfulness of the content. However, after 1927 the tone of her work changes to a serious contemplation of nature, its unpredictable and often cruel ways, the ephemerality of life, the inevitability of death. Having fled Poland at the start of the Second World War, first to Paris and then to England, Pawlikowska's pessimism turns to pacifism, fueled by the loss of loved ones and nostalgia for the homeland. These sentiments are expressed in *Róża i lasy płonące* (1940; The Rose and Forests in Flames) and *Gołąb Ofiarny* (1941; Sacrificial Dove).

Only four of Pawlikowska's plays have appeared in print, two of them as fragments. The others were only performed.

Works

Poems: *Niebieskie migdały* [Woolgathering] (1922). *Różowa magia* [Pink Magic] (1924). *Pocałunki* [Kisses] (1926). Dancing (1927). *Wachlarz* [The Fan] (1927). *Cisza leśna* [Sylvan Silence] (1928). *Paryż* [Paris] (1928). *Profil białej damy* [Profile of a White Lady] (1930). *Surowy jedwab* [Raw Silk] (1932). *Śpiąca załoga* [The Sleeping Crew] (1933). *Balet powojów* [Ballet of Creepers] (1935). *Krystalizacje* [Crystallizations] (1937). *Szkicownik poetycki* [Sketchbook of Poetry] (1938). *Róża i lasy płonące* [The Rose and Forests in Flames] (1940). *Gołąb ofiarny* [Sacrificial Dove] (1941).

Plays: *Szofer Archibald* [Driver Archibald] (1924). *Kochanek Sybilli Thompson* [Sybil Thompson's Lover] (1926). *Bracia sjamscy* [Siamese Brothers] (1932). *Egipska pszenica* [Egyptian Wheat] (1932). *Powrót mamy* [Mother's Return] (1935). *Zalotnicy niebiescy* [Heavenly Wooers] (1936). *Dowód osobisty* [Proof of Identity] (1936). *Mrówki* [The Ants] (1937). *Nagroda literacka* [The Literary Prize] (1937). *Baba-Dziwo* [The Wondrous Hag] (1938). *Dewaluacja Klary* [The Devaluation of Klara] (1939). *Popielaty welon* [The Gray Veil] (1939). Translations of Pawlikowska's poetry are included in the following anthologies: Gillon, Adam and Ludwik Krzyzanowski, eds., *Introduction to Modern Polish Literature; An Anthology of Fiction and Poetry.* 2nd ed. with a New Poetry Sec. ed. by Adam Gillon and Krystyna Olszer (New York, 1982), pp. 405–409. Filip, T.M., comp., *A Polish Anthology*, tr. M.A. Michael (London, 1944), p. 229. Kirkconnell, Watson, tr., *A Golden Treasury of Polish Lyrics* (Winnipeg, 1936). Notley, Frances, tr., *The Years of Exile; Selections from Polish Poets Now in Britain* (London, 1943). Peterkiewicz, Jerzy and Burns Singer, eds., *Five Centuries of Polish Poetry; 1450–1970.* 2nd ed. with new poems trans. in collab. with Jon Stallworthy (London, 1970), p. 92.

Bibliography

Buczkówna, Mieczysława, "Maya w ogrodzie słów." *Poezja* 6.7 (1970): 9–22. Dzieniszewska, Anna, "Zielnik poetycki Marii Pawlikowskiej-Jasnorzewskiej: Przegląd motywów kwiatowych w twórczości obejmującej lata 1904–1928." *Poezja* 15.5 (1980): 56–69. Józefacka, Maria, "Krystalizacje dramatyczne (komedie Marii Pawlikowskiej-Jasnorzewskiej)." *Roczniki Humanistyczne* 13.1 (1966): 68–97. Korzeniewska, Ewa, ed., *Słownik współczesnych pisarzy polskich*, Vol. 2 (Warsaw, 1964; 4 vols. 1963–1966). Kwiatkowski, Jerzy, "Pawlikowska-Jasnorzewska Maria," in *Literatura polska; Przewodnik encyklopedyczny*, ed. Julian Krzyżanowski. Vol. 2 (Warsaw, 1985; 2 vols. 1984–

1995). Pruska-Carroll, Małgorzata, "Poetry of Maria Pawlikowska-Jasnorzewska." *The Polish Review* 26.2 (1981): 35–50. Siomkajłówna, Alina. "Kilka uwag o wierszach Marii Pawlikowskiej." *Roczniki Humanistyczne* 19.1 (1971): 183–188.

Irene Suboczewski

Maria Maddalena de' Pazzi

Born April 2, 1566, Florence, Italy; died May 25, 1607, Florence
Genre(s): mystical revelation
Language(s): Italian

Caterina de' Pazzi, born of a noble Florentine family, is a typical representative of the Baroque spirituality oriented toward a theatrical sense of the holy. Despite her privileged upbringing, she was skilled in every branch of housework, and, at the same time, eager to meditate upon theological mysteries and interested in painting and music.

The main peculiarities for which Santa Maddalena became famous are her mystical raptures defined, by early commentators (V. Puccini and V. Cepari, to whom we owe the first biographies of the saint) as "excesses of love" which, in some cases, lasted up to forty days with minimal intervals necessary for the corporal needs. While in ecstasy, Santa Maria Maddalena used to reenact the Passion of Christ by playing the roles not only of the main figures involved (the judges, Judas, Pontius Pilate, etc.), but also of a spectator of the scene by means of unaccountable alterations in the tone of her voice, which has suggested the hypothesis that the mystic suffered from a form of characteriopathology (c.f. Ancona). Thus her voice turned grave and austere when she was impersonating Christ; she burst out crying when reverting to the part of the observer; or the distorted inflection of her speech suggested wickedness when the enemies of Christ were imitated. Such effects of the Passion were accompanied at times by the position of Christ on the cross.

Most of the saint's "excesses of love" took place when she handled or touched water: she would fall into a rapture when washing her hands, doing the laundry (as in the episode of her hands freezing in the tub while washing clothes in the wintertime), or even eating, with her glass full of water raised to drink, or while making bread.

Directly connected with her ecstatic states are Santa Maria Maddalena's writings, divided according to subject matter and circumstances of dictation. Agostino Campi, confessor of the Carmelite convent of Santa Maria degli Angeli at Borgo San Frediano (Florence) where the saint took the habit and chose the name of the Magdalene, ordered her fellow nuns to write down the saint's utterances during her mystical raptures. Thus most works of the Carmelite mystic belong to the category of automatic writing, when the author is unaware of dictating or composing. The only major exception is represented by *Avvertimenti* (Admonitions), a collection, preserved by her disciples, of sayings and teachings of the mystic when she was an instructor of the novices. The question of Santa Maria Maddalena's literacy is still open: Puccini does not hesitate to emphasize the miraculous occurrence of the learning of Latin by the Florentine saint described by him as a functional illiterate. However, recent studies (Larkin) have indicated that the mystic must have attended, as a student, the monastery of St. Giovanni dei Cavalieri for at least six years between 1574 and 1581; this would explain the fact that some of the saint's letters seem to have been written by her own hand.

Santa Maria Maddalena de' Pazzi was canonized by Clement IX on April 28, 1669. Her revelations generated a remarkable amount of devotional literature until the late eighteenth century, although her renown has somewhat faded away in our times. However, the recent publication of the original text of her works in 1960 created the premises for a scientific investigation concerning her writings and the events of her life. Santa Maria Maddalena's typically Baroque style is prolix, repetitious, and often excessively adorned with metaphors and allegories. The major themes of the Saint's works are the Eucharist, Christ, the Trinity, and, almost omnipresent in her pages, love as the medium through which communication is established between man and God.

Works

Libro de' quaranta giorni [Book of the Forty Days] (ca. 1584). *Libro dei colloqui* [Book of the Colloquies] (ca. 1585). *Libro delle revelatione e intelligentie* [Book of Revelations and Intelligences] (ca. 1585). *Libro della renovatione della Chiesa* [Book of the Renovation of the Church] (1586). *Libro della probatione* [Book of the Probation] (1590). *Avvertimenti et avvisi della Madre Beata Maria Maddalena* [Admonitions] (1589–1604). *Tutte le opere di Santa Maria Maddalena de' Pazzi dai manoscritti originali* (1960).

Bibliography

Ancona, Leonardo, "S. Maria Maddalena de' Pazzi alla luce della psicologia." *Carmelus* XIII (1966): 3–20. Antoni, Claudio G., *Sistemi stilistici ed espressione mistica: saggi sulla tradizione cateriniana* (Pisa, 1985). Dingwell, Eric, *Very Peculiar People* (New York, 1962). Ermanno dell SSmo. Sacramento, P., "Los éxtasis de Santa María Magdalena de' Pazzi." *Revista de Espiritualidad* LIX (1956): 184–200. Ermanno del SSmo. Sacramento, P., "I manoscritti originali di S. Maria Maddalena de' Pazzi." *Ephermides Carmeliticae* VII (1956): 323–400. Larkin, E.E., "Pazzi, Mary Magdalene de', St." *New Catholic Encyclopedia* (Washington D.C., 1981), Vol. XI, pp. 36–37. Petrocchi, Massimo, *L'estasi nelle mistiche italiane della Riforma cattolica* (Napoli, 1958). Vaussard, Maurice, *Santa Maria Maddalena de' Pazzi: estasi e lettere* (Firenze, 1924).

C.G. Antoni

Olena Pcilka

(see: Ol'ha Petrivna Kosaceva)

Auteur du Péché de Madeleine

(see: Pauline Caro [Mme. Elme])

Al'běta Pechová

(see: Eliška Krásnohorská)

Pecka

(see: Katri Vala)

Marija Pečkauskaitė

(see: Šatrijos Ragana)

Paloma Pedrero Diez-Caneja

Born 1957, Madrid, Spain
Genre(s): drama
Language(s): Spanish

Pedrero studied sociology at the University of Madrid and dramatic arts at the Royal Academy. She is an actress, and one of the most respected of the new Spanish dramatists. Her *La llamada de Lauren* (Lauren's Call), concerning a married couple who exchange clothing and gender roles, was performed in Madrid in 1985 with Pedrero in a leading role. *Invierno de luna alegre* (Happy Winter Moon) won the prestigious Tirso de Molina Prize in 1987.

Works

La llamada de Lauren [Lauren's Call] (1985). *Besos de lobo* [Wolf Kisses] (1987). *Invierno de luna alegre* [Happy Winter Moon] (1987). *El color de agosto* [The Color of August] (1988). *Resguardo personal* [The Receipt] (1989). *Esta noche en el parque* [Tonight in the Park] (1990).

Bibliography

Galán Font, Eduardo, "Paloma Pedrero, una joven dramaturga que necesita expresar sus vivencias," interview. *Estreno* 16.1 (Spring 1990). O'Connor, Patricia W., *Dramaturgas españolas de hoy* (Madrid, 1989). O'Connor, Patricia W., "Women Playwrights in Contemporary Spain and the Male-Dominated Canon." *Signs: Journal of Women in Culture and Society* 15.2 (Winter 1990). Zatlin, Phyllis, "Paloma Pedrero and the Search for Identity." *Estreno* 16.1 (Spring 1990).

Patricia W. O'Connor

Erica Pedretti

*Born February 25, 1930, Steinberg (Moravia),
Czechoslovakia*

Genre(s): novel, short story, radio drama
Language(s): German

Erica Pedretti, whose mother tongue is German, was born Erica Schefter in Northern Moravia, a province of Czechoslovakia. Her father, whose mother was a Swiss Jewess, was a silk manufacturer in Hohenstadt/Zabreh until he was conscripted for factory work by the invading Germans. After Liberation the family, as German-speakers and capitalists, lost all their property. In December 1945, a Red Cross transport brought Pedretti to an aunt in Switzerland, where she studied applied arts in Zurich. Her family slowly reassembled in Switzerland, but, unable to obtain permanent residence, they immigrated to the United States in 1950. Pedretti worked for two years as a silver- and goldsmith in New York before returning alone to Switzerland in 1952 to marry the painter and sculptor Gian Pedretti, with whom she has five children. Having lived in the Alpine canton of Graubünden for many years, she and her husband now live in La Neuveville in canton Berne. In 1984 Erica Pedretti won the Ingeborg Bachmann prize for literature.

Though Pedretti wrote as a child, she did not take up writing as an adult until after the birth of her last child in 1965. Her first books work and rework the traumas of the war years and the loss of her childhood home into complex, original forms, in which reality is deliberately abbreviated into contiguous fragments of memories, dreams, and quotations. Any tendency towards abstraction is counteracted by her powerful evocations of vulnerability, fear, and peril and by the vigor of her dense, sensual language. Her latest novel *Valerie oder das unerzogene Auge* (1986) is a "tour-de-force" of simultaneity between past and present, between imagined history and fiction. In it the painter Franz obsessively draws his model and mistress Valerie, a cancer victim living under the shadow of death. Their story parallels, repeats, and quotes that of the Swiss painter Ferdinand Hodler (1853–1918) and his paintings and drawings of his dying lover Valentine Godé-Darel (painted between February 1914 and January 1915). By choosing the perspective of the dying woman, however, Pedretti's work meditates on the integrity of art's object, in this case the mortal model, and on the relationship between art and life.

Works

Harmloses, bitte [Harmless, Please] (1970, 1974, 1979). *Il trais sudos/Die drei Soldaten* [The Three Soldiers], children's story illustrated by author (1971). *Catch as Katz Can* [rpt. in *Was geschah, nachdem Nora ihren Mann verlassen hatte? Acht Hörspiele* (1982)], radio play (1972). *Heiliger Sebastian* [Saint Sebastian], novel (1973, 1981). *Badekur* [Taking the Waters], radio play (1974). *Veränderung oder die Zertrümmerung von dem Kind Karl und anderen Personen* [rpt. as *Die Zertrümmerung von dem Kind Karl und anderen Personen: Veränderung*, 1985], novel (1977) [The Destruction of the Child Karl and Other Characters: Change]. *Sonnenaufgänge, Sonnenuntergänge* [Sunrises, Sunsets], short stories (1984). *Mal laut und falsch singen. Eine Geschichte* [To Once Sing Loud and False. A Story], children's story illustrated by author (1986). *Valerie oder das unerzogene Auge* [Valerie or the Uncultivated Eye], novel (1986).

Translations: *Stones, or the Destruction of the Child Karl and Other Characters* [*Veränderung*], tr. Judith L. Black (London, New York, 1982).

Bibliography

Klagenfurter Texte zum Ingeborg-Bachmann-Preis 1984 ed. Humbert Fink and Marcel Reich-Ranicki (München, 1984) [Press reviews and reactions to the 1984 competition]. Matt, Beatrice von, "Vom Unterwandern der Katagorien. Zur Schreibart in Erica Pedretti's Erzählungen *Sonnenaufgänge, Sonnenuntergänge.*" *Lesarten. Zur Schweizer Literatur von Walser bis Muschg* (Zurich, 1985), pp. 203–208 [First published 1984]. Pulver, Elsbeth, "Erica Pedretti." *Kindlers Literaturgeschichte der Gegenwart. Die zeitgenössischen Literaturen der Schweiz,* ed. Manfred Gsteiger (München, 1974), pp. 299–301. Pulver, Elsbeth, "Erica Pedretti." *Kritisches Lexikon zur deutschsprachigen Gegenwartsliteratur,* ed. Heinz Ludwig Arnold (München, 1978ff) [good bibliography]. Pulver, Elsbeth, "Erica Pedretti." *Neue Literatur der Frauen. Deutschsprachige Autorinnen der Gegenwart,* ed. Heinz Puknus (München, 1980), pp.138–143. Rohr, Esther,

"Schreiben als Herausforderung. Das Prosawerk von Erica Pedretti." Lizentiatsarbeit. Master's Thesis, U. of Berne, 1982. Serke, Jürgen, "Erica Pedretti. 'Wenn man schreiben könnte, ohne den Mann, die Kinder oder sonst jemanden zu verletzen!'" *Frauen schreiben. Ein neues Kapitel deutschsprachiger Literatur* (Hamburg, 1979), pp. 226–241. Zeltner, Gerda, "Erica Pedretti." *Das Ich ohne Gewähr. Gegenwartsautoren aus der Schweiz. Essays* (Frankfurt a.M., 1980), pp. 101–123.

Ann Marie Rasmussen

Yolanda Peglē
(a.k.a. Yolanda Pegli)

Born 1934, Athens, Greece
Genre(s): poetry, translation
Language(s): Greek

Yolanda Peglē (or Pegli) is one of the most prolific of Greek women poets. In addition to writing poetry she has translated literary works by various writers, including Jules Verne.

Many of Peglē's poems add up to a sustained criticism of a society that calls itself Christian but is in fact far from practicing Christianity, i.e., a society of Pharisees. The central figure in many of her poems is Christ himself, either as the one speaking, the one addressed, or as understood to be in the background. The individual poems are not overtly didactic but miniature dramatizations rich in religious imagery and religious overtones and set against surreal landscapes of the imagination. The tone is sad and melancholy.

Peglē's later poetry is more secular, more personal (*Fevruarios*: February), and more concerned with social problems (*Omorphos Kosmos*: Beautiful World). The title of this last work is ironic, for she does not think there is anything beautiful about a world where technology has taken over and has made man its subject and its slave.

Some of Peglē's poems have been translated into Polish. Translations by Helen D. Kolias of "Between Dream and Reality" and "Premonitions" (from *Pros Phariseous*) appeared in *Doubles/ Dialogs: A Folio of Poetry Translations* (Binghamton, N.Y. 1980).

Works
Lazaroi en aposynthesē [Lazaroi in Decomposition] (1964). *Anthrōpos paschōn* [Man Suffering] (1965). *Ē Thaumasia peripeteia* [The Wonderful Adventure] (1966). *Akouste* [Listen] (1970). *Pros Pharisaious* [To the Pharisees] (1971). *Angathi to amaranto* [Thorn Unwithering] (1972). *Fevruarios* [February] (1978). *Mēn patate stēn chloē* [Don't Step on the Grass] (1981). *Omorphos kosmos* [Beautiful World] (1984).

Helen Dendrinou Kolias

Yolanda Pegli
(see: Yolanda Peglē)

Lazdynu Pelėda
(see: Sofija Pšibiliauskienė-Ivanauskaitė)

Stanka Pencheva

Born 1929, Sliven, Bulgaria
Genre(s): poetry, prose
Language(s): Bulgarian

Stanka Pencheva attended secondary school in Sliven, later graduating from the Kliment of Ohrid Sofia University in Russian philology. She has worked as an editor in Radio Sofia, for Narodna Mladezh Publishers and the *Septemvri Review*. She has also been a correspondent for the newspaper *Narodna Kultura* and currently is deputy editor-in-chief for the *Otechestvo Review*. Stanka Pencheva has been awarded the title "Cultural Figure of Merit." Her poetry has been translated extensively into Russian, Polish, Czech, Romanian, Slovak, Serbo-Croatian, Slovenian, German, Arabic, French, English, Spanish, Italian, and Hindi.

Works
Coming of Age (1952). A Stretched Cord (1957). The Well of Birds (1960). Universe (1964). Land of Fires (1965). The Bitter Herb (1966). The Apple-tree Orchard (1967). Autumnal Lights (1968). My Power (1970). The Sand Lily (1972). Bread and Salt (1973). A Planet for Two (1977). A Man for

Man (1976). *Izbranna Lirika* [Selected Lyrics] (1979). *Slivenski Okrug* (1979). No Witnesses (1980). Unfinished World (1982). A Slender Fir-Tree Between Them (1982). Excavations (1984).

Warwick J. Rodden

Caterina Percoto

Born 1812, Udine, Italy; died 1887, Udine
Genre(s): short story
Language(s): Italian

Born to a noble family of Friuli, which was then under Austrian occupation, Percoto spent seven years of her adolescence in a boarding school. Her decision to live a celibate life came as a consequence of her family's opposition to her marrying the man she loved, a stand she saw as a proof of prejudice and as an act of violence. She spent her life on her farms, sharing the laborer's work, totally dedicated to her writing and to charitable works.

When her writing came to the attention of F. Dall'Ongaro, she began to publish some of her stories in the Trieste magazine, *Favilla*. Her subsequent publications—*Racconti* (1858; Short Stories), *Novelle vecchie e nuove* (1861; New and Old Tales), *Novelle scelte* (1880; Chosen Tales), *Novelle popolari edite and inedite* (1883; Popular Tales, Published and Unpublished)—are all stories and sketches of events and life conditions of the poor people she observed around her. They give a compassionate view of the hardships and the abuses suffered by farmers and village population under the Austrian rule, by their wives and children, by curates and parish priests. Especially moving are the portraits of enduring and sacrificing women, described by her as "women of courage," whose condition she articulated in a speech as the "heavier burden befallen on that half of humanity."

Percoto's place in Italian literary history is with a group of novelists, such as Giulio Carcano, Ippolito Nievo and Luigia Codemo, who described and denounced the condition of poverty in the forgotten countryside and thus came to represent what was called the "rustic" narrative genre. Unlike theirs, Percoto's stories are free from the easy idealism of romantic writers and from the paternalistic attitudes usually found in populist literature. Her sober and simple prose is due to her unrelenting loyalty to true stories and characters and to her refusal to change her spoken language and the Friuli dialect into Tuscanized Italian. She is seen now as the first realist writer of Italian literature, and, as such, she enjoyed a considerable revival during postwar neo-realism.

Works

Racconti (1858). *Novelle vecchie e nuove* (1861). *Novelle scelte*, II (1880). *Novelle popolari edite e inedite* (1883). *Gli ultimi anni di Caterina Percoto* (*Lettere all'ab. F. Bernardi*), ed. N. Minghetti (1915). *Scritti friulani*, ed. B. Chiurlo (1929). *Sotto l'Austria nel Friuli 1847–1865*, ed. E. Levi (1918). "Lettere inedite al Dott. G. Pompili." *Bollettino della Società filologica friulana* (1938). *"L'anno della fame" e altri racconti*, ed. A. Spaini (1945). *L'album della suocera e altri racconti*, ed. A. Gatto (1945).

Bibliography

Barbiera, R., "Figure delle terre dolorose: C.P." *Nuova antologia* CXCVI (1918): 22–30. Bonini, P., *Le prose friulane di C.P. Versi friulani* (Udine, 1898). Branca, V., "Per Caterina Percoto." *Lettere italiane* XI (1959): 249–253. Brognoligo, P., "Caterina Percoto." *Rassegna nazionale* XXIII (1 ott. 1919). Chiurlo, B., *Antologia della letteratura friulana* (Udine, 1927), pp. 294–306. "C.P." *Nuova antologia di letteratura friulana* (Udine, 1960). D'Aronco, G., "Contributo a una bibliografia ragionata di C.P." *Aevum* XXI (1947), pp. 26–61. De Tommaso, P., "Caterina Percoto." *Studi in memoria di Luigi Russo* (Pisa, 1974), pp. 295–318. Fracassetti, L., *Per il centenario di un'accademica: C.P.* (Udine, 1912). Mariani, G., *Ottocento romantico e verista* (Naples, 1972), pp. 304–306. Petronio, G., "Nievo e la letteratura popolare." *Società* XXI (1956), pp. 1094–1103. Russo, L., *I narratori* (Milan-Messina, 1958), pp. 64–66. Spaini, A., *Introduzione a C.P. L'anno della fame, ed altri racconti* (Turin, 1945).

Rinaldina Russell

La Peregrina

(see: María Gertrudis Gómez de Avellaneda)

Perilla

Flourished early 1st c. A.D., Rome
Genre(s): lyric poetry
Language(s): Latin

The writings of Perilla (evidently a pseudonym) are not preserved, and she is known only from a beautiful and tantalizing poem addressed to her by Ovid (*Tristia* III.7). This is one of Ovid's poems of lament, mostly in the form of poetic letters, that he wrote from exile in Tomis (now Constanza, in Rumania on the Black Sea). Ovid had been condemned to this exile by the Emperor Augustus, on unknown grounds that have been the subject of much speculation. It has been conjectured that Perilla was Ovid's stepdaughter. While there are many references in the poem that lend plausibility to this conjecture, there can be no certainty. Ovid speaks of Perilla as his poetic protegee from her early youth. He describes in detail her reading her poems to him and his reciprocating by reading his own poems to her; his being both her critic and her teacher; and his chiding her when she was unproductive. An interesting picture emerges of some aspects of Roman education, in this case of a woman. Ovid urges Perilla not to give up writing poetry because of his misfortunes and assures her that if she perseveres, she will be surpassed only by Sappho. Whether Perilla took Ovid's advice and whether her poems were ever published are equally unknown.

Bibliography

Luck, George, ed, Commentary on *Tristia* IV.7 (Heidelberg, 1967), vol. 2, pp. 199–204. Nagle, Betty Rose, "The Poetics of Exile." *Collection Latomus* CLXX (Brussels, 1980). Schanz, M., and C. Hosius, *Geschichte der römischen Literatur* (Munich, 1935), vol. 2, p. 273.

Paul Pascal

Vibia Perpetua

Born ca. A.D. 181; died A.D. March 7, 203,
Carthage
Genre(s): autobiography, dream vision
Language(s): Latin

Early in A.D. 203, Perpetua and her companions were arrested for refusing to sacrifice to Emperor Septimius Severus on his birthday. At the time of her arrest, Perpetua was a catechumen, a candidate for baptism (she was baptized while in prison). One of her brothers was also a catechumen; her father was a pagan; and the rest of her family seem to have been Christian sympathizers though probably not Christians. Perpetua was nursing her infant son at the time of her arrest and imprisonment. Her narrative describes the discomforts of prison, her trial before the tribunal, her concern for her baby, and her father's repeated attempts to beg or bully her into recanting her faith. In addition to these events, she also describes four visions she had while in prison. These visions deal with her approaching death, the painful friction between her and her father, and her fears for the soul of her brother Dinocrates, who had died at the age of seven. In the visions, Perpetua deals forcefully and creatively with each of these problems and awakens strengthened and revitalized to continue her struggle. Her narrative ends: "This is what I have done till the day before the contest; if anyone wants to write of its outcome, let them do so." The day after she wrote this, according to the *Passio*, Perpetua was gored to death by a wild cow in the arena, and her companions were also killed by various beasts.

All that we have of Perpetua's work is contained in the (3rd century?) *Passio SS. Perpetuae et Felicitatis*. The author of the *Passio* claims to have preserved Perpetua's work "as it was set down by her own hand" (*Passio* II,3), and the flavor of the passage (*Passio* III-X) seems to support his claim. Perpetua's style is immediate, colloquial, and direct. Her visions have a strikingly authentic and original quality; they do not seem to have been altered to conform to any theological or stylistic norm. Moreover, Perpetua very rarely attempts to interpret the visions or to assign allegorical meanings to them; she vividly describes what she has seen and lets it stand for itself. Her simplicity lends still more power to events and images that are striking enough in themselves. Her vision of the upcoming gladiatorial combat is riveting: she sees herself stripped naked and anointed by her supporters and transformed into a man; she defeats a huge Egyptian in hand-to-hand combat and is awarded the prize by her kind, fatherly fencing-master.

She awakens realizing that she will be condemned to death and that she will win the true contest, which she will fight against the powers of evil.

Although we have only a few pages of Perpetua's work, there can be little doubt that she holds a unique place in the literary canon, both for her unaffected yet skillful literary style and for her brilliant psychological and spiritual insights. Both her life and her writing reveal a uniquely courageous and perceptive woman whom readers of any age can admire.

Works

Acta Sanctorum collecta digesta illustrata (1643), vol. VII, pp. 629–637. Van Beek, C.I.M.I., ed., *Passio Sanctarum Perpetuae et Felicitatis* (1936). Van Beek, C.I.M.I., ed. *Passio Sanctarum Perpetuae et Felicitatis, Latine et Graece* (1938).

Translations: Dronke, Peter, *Women Writers of the Middle Ages: A Critical Study of Texts from Perpetua (a203) to Marguerite Porete (a1310)* (1984, rpt. 1985), pp. 2–4. Musurillo, H.R., tr., "The Passion of Ss. Perpetua and Felicitas" in Elizabeth Alvilda Petroff, ed., *Medieval Women's Visionary Literature* (1986). Ower, E.C.E. *Some Authentic Acts of the Early Martyrs* (1927).

Bibliography

Augustine, *Sermo CCLXXX*, in *Sancti Aurelii Augustini Hipponensis Episcopi opera omnia* (Paris, 1841), vol. V, part 1, col. 1281. Tertullian, *DeAnima*, c. 55, in *Corpus Christianorum Series Latina* (Turnolti, 1954), vol. II, pp. 862–863. Von Franz, M.-L., in C.G. Jung, *Aion* (Zurich, 1951), pp. 389–496.

Lila F. Ralston

Maria Petijt

Born January, 1623, Hazebroek; died November, 1677, Mechelen, The Netherlands
Genre(s): spiritual autobiography, confessional letters
Language(s): Dutch

Born in the wealthy, commercial Flemish middle class, Maria Petijt was educated in a boarding school before she began her noviciate with the Augustinian Canonnesses in Ghent in 1642. She had to give up her intention of be-coming a regular canonness because of a lingering eye disease. Very eager nevertheless to live devoutly in sincere contemplation, Petijt submitted herself to the spiritual guidance of several Carmelite friars—at first alone, in Ghent, and from 1657 until her death, with a few other women in Mechelen (Malines). The most influential of these friars was Michael a Sancto Augustino; he became Petijt's Father Confessor and would also become directly responsible for her spiritual and literary fame. It was Michael a Sancto Augustino who initiated Petijt into the techniques of contemplative meditation. She was never a nun, but she and her companions took the vows of chastity and poverty and of obedience (i.e., to the spiritual director, Michael). It is most likely that Maria Petijt wrote her many letters to Michael, on his request; the letters show her development in the practice of meditation and her spiritual growth. Probably she began writing her spiritual autobiography for the same reason. It must be assumed that she never had purely literary or artistic intentions.

Perhaps precisely for this very reason, Petijt's prose is still eminently readable today. Her style impresses through its vivacity, its directness, and personal feeling. With a single detail she can sketch an entire situation; her self-confidence in writing reminds the reader of the powerful sparseness of her great English contemporary, John Bunyan. For instance, a practical description of what "to withdraw one's self from the world" concretely means in daily life, is contained in the following anecdote: the young woman is still living with her parents but has decided to deny herself the joys of companionship at the table, as a spiritual exercise:

> As soon as I was through with my meal, I would take my plate from the table, greet those present, and then I would leave the table without saying one more word. And so I went up then to my room. (my translation of Petijt's words in Deblaere, o.c., 27).

After her death, Michael a Sancto Augustino edited her manuscripts and translated a selection into Latin (Ghent, 1683). The autobiography "Leven van de weerdighe Moeder Maria a Sta Teresia (alias) Petijt" (The Life of the Worthy Mother . . .) appeared as volume I of the four-volume edition. Remarkable is the analytical instead of chronological organization that Michael imposed upon the texts. It is generally assumed that he had in mind a possible beatification process of Petijt, for which the spiritual writings would have to serve as evidence—hence the Latin translation of key passages. The other three volumes of the edition contain the spiritual letters that she had directed to Michael in his role of Father Confessor.

From these letters and her autobiography, Petijt emerges as an exceptionally intelligent, sensitive mystic with a good feeling for original imagery. The development of her searching soul follows a purifying pattern from repentance, despair, and consolatory grace to exquisite mystical experiences. Merciless in her self-criticism, and preceding the intense cult of the Holy Heart (especially in France), Petijt achieved an altogether unique, Baroque symbiosis of the authentic Flemish mysticism and the Spanish type. The former emphasizes the total immersion of the soul in God (the image "as a drop of water in the sea" recurs time and time again), the latter records more ecstatic experiences. A. Deblaere writes that "because of the careful observation and the differentiated representation of the psychological effects of the mystical experiences on her spirit and her soul, her testimony is altogether unequalled in continental mystical literature" (my translation o.c., 684). Maria Petijt has been put forward as the equal in thought and expression of the great Saint Teresa of Avila.

Works

Michael a Sancto Augustino, ed., *Het leven van de weerdighe moeder Maria a Sta Theresia (alias) Petijt* (1683), 4 vols. Michael a Sancto Augustino, tr., *Vita venerabilis matris Mariae a Sta Teresia* (ms., Collegio S. Alberto, Rome, Post. III). Fragments of this text have been translated into French by L. Van Den Bossche, "De la vie 'Marie-forme' au mariage mystique," in *Et. Carmél.*, 16 (1931), pp. 236–250 and 17 (1932), pp. 279–294. In English translation: MacGinnis, Th., *Union With Our Lady. Marian Writings of Ven. Maria Petyt of St. Teresa* (1954).

Bibliography

Deblaere, Alb., *De mystieke schrijfster Maria Petijt (1623–1677)* (Ghent, 1963) (contains a rich anthology).

Kristiaan P. Aercke

Vanya Petkova

Born 1942, Sofia, Bulgaria
Genre(s): poetry, prose, translation
Language(s): Bulgarian

Vanya Petkova graduated in Slavic philology from Sofia University, then went to Havana to specialize in Spanish at the José Marti Institute for Foreign Languages. After working as editor for the journal *Slaveiché* and the newspaper *Literatouren Front*, she became the editor of the journal *Suvremenik*. She has to her credit seventeen publications, both poetry and prose, and is a translator from Spanish and Arabic. Her poetry has been translated into Russian, Spanish, French, Greek, English, Armenian, Polish, Czech, Arabic, and Hindi.

Works

Salt Winds (1965). Attraction (1967). The Sinner (1968). Prophecy (1970). The Black Dove (1972). The Counter-River (1976). A Vow for Silence (1979). A Triptych (1980).

Warwick J. Rodden

Kata Szidónia Petróczi

Born 1662, Kaszavára, Hungary; died October 21, 1708, Beregszentmiklós, Hungary
Genre(s): poetry, translations
Language(s): Hungarian

Petróczi lost her mother early in life, possibly when she was born, as one of her poems suggests; shortly afterward, she was made a ward of the Jakussith family as her father was indicted in the Wesselényi Conspiracy, an attempt by the leading nobles of the country to resist Habsburg absolutism. She was eventually sent to safety in Poland, where she was brought up. Deeply religious, and influenced by Pietism, she turned to writing for consolation. In the troubled times of late seventeenth- and early eighteenth-century

Hungary, with her family's military and political obligations, as well as the ambitions of her husband, Lőrincz Pekry, she had few peaceful years. In 1690 she published a translation from Friedrich Johannes Mayer entitled *A Pápista vallásra hajlott lutheránusok lelkek ísmeretének kínja* (The Agony of the Acquaintances of Those Lutheran Souls Who Have Converted to Catholicism), undertaken because her husband had, at least outwardly, changed his religion to assure himself advancement in the Habsburg-ruled Hungary. Characteristically, neither this nor other translations were purely for her own use: she published her translations, unlike her poems, during her own lifetime. During her imprisonment by the Austrian forces in the fortress of Szeben, she again turned to a German pietist, Johannes Arndt, and translated a selection of his poems and prayers under the title *A kereszt nekéz terhe alatt elbágyadt szíveket élesztő jóillatí XII liliom* (Twelve Fragrant Lillies That Revive the Hearts Wearied under the Weight of the Cross). In the lengthy title she also indicates the occasion: "translated into Hungarian while suffering unjust imprisonment for her dear husband in Szeben: and now freed by the grace of God, in eternally thankful memory of which, and for the spiritual benefit of the saints bearing the burden of the cross, printed at her own expense by Countess Kata Szidónia Petrőczi." A similar explanation accompanies her third volume of translations, again from Arndt, which she had printed in 1708, *Jó illattal füstölgő igaz szív* (The True Heart Smoking with Good Fragrance); she wrote it for the spiritual welfare of Christians while suffering exile for the fourth time, in Huszt. Petrőczi's tribulations of these years were the result of her husband's having again changed his allegiance in 1702, when he offered his services to Prince Francis Rákoczi II, who led an almost successful revolt against the Habsburgs. Thus, while the ideological and spiritual estrangement that called forth the first work was lauded, the fortunes of war took a physical and spiritual toll on her.

These poems are free translations and adaptations, for she did not follow her sources closely. It was the ideas that she sought to convey, and for this she paraphrased some passages and even supplied some new material. Her original poems, written purely for herself and not published in her lifetime, follow the same concerns but also reflect the wealth of Hungarian oral song-literature of the late Middle Ages and Renaissance. They were probably circulated in manuscript, particularly between 1690 and 1694 when she was living in Trencsén. Here, several aristocratic ladies wrote poetry, and she undoubtedly exchanged verses with them: her vocabulary and store of images expand at this time as evidence that she belonged to an active literary circle.

The poems deal with her sorrows and her country's troubles—the same motives that led to her translations. They are religious, some being prayers or meditations, but all of them infused with religious feeling and trust in God's mercy. The strong faith that illumines them keeps them from being depressing.

As in her topics, so also in her style, she reflected Hungarian literary traditions of the seventeenth century, except that there is a freshness and originality not found in some of her more learned male contemporaries. While she uses the classical pantheon and the machinery of Protestant religious poetry, she also takes images from nature or echoes the language and meters of the rich store of songs, only a fraction of which has been preserved.

Some personal details also emerge from her poems, and these are possibly the most interesting. "My Poor Head" reflects on her isolation when, as a young woman, she lived in Transylvania and her husband was under suspicion of treason by the Chancellor Mihály Teleki; he was imprisoned, and much of both his and her property was confiscated. She also refers to her mother's early death, the unkind guardians, and particularly the troubles since her marriage, in which she had sought happiness. Her ill health and the loss of her properties, but more especially her feeling of isolation and abandonment are mentioned. Similarly, "The Injured One" refers to her husband's imprisonment and the danger that threatens him, as well as the loss of her properties and security. But "When Will My Sorrows Cease" asserts her faith in God's power: he can protect her and even turn her sorrow to joy. "Dear Violet" is a long poem in which she reacts to her husband's infidelity: she proudly asserts her own greater worth and refuses to let herself be the object of pity and gossip.

The religious and political troubles of her homeland also form one of her themes, one she turns to with increasing frequency in her later years. "Oh Merciful God" is a prayer for help against the forcible re-Catholicization of Upper Hungary when it came under Habsburg rule, while "Light of Our Souls" seeks succor against political oppression.

Works

Translations from German: *A Pápista vallásra hajlott lutheránusok lelkek isméretének kínja* (1690). *A Kereszt néhez terhe alatt elbágyadt szíveket élesztő, jóillatú XII liliom* (1705). *Jó illattal füstölgő igaz szív* (1708).

Manuscript book: *Petrőczi Kata Szidonia tulajdon kezével irt énekei* (1915).

Bibliography

Antalffy, Endre, *Petróczy Kata Szidonia élete és munkái, 1664–1704* (Budapest, 1903). Harsányi, Ilona, *A XVII. és XVIII. század magyar költőnői* (Budapest, 1976). Rimeg, Ödön, *Gróf Pekry Lőrincné báró P.K. Sz. élete és költészete* (Marosvásárhely, 1905). S. Sárdi, Margit, "Baroque et piété dans l'ouevre de deux femmes de letters hongroises." *Baroque* 8: 95–104. S. Sárdi, Margit, *Petróczy Kata Szidonia Költészete* (Budapest, 1976).

Enikő Molnár Basa

Maria Petrovykh

Born 1908; died 1979
Genre(s): poetry, translation
Language(s): Russian

Despite high praise from her contemporaries such as Anna Akhmatova, Osip Mandelstam and Boris Pasternak, Maria Petrovykh and her work have remained in relative obscurity and only a fraction of her original lyric poetry has been published. Her published poetry did not appear separately but instead appeared along with her translation work in Erevan, not Moscow, in her book entitled *Dalnee Derevo* (A Distant Tree) in 1968.

Mandelstam dedicated to Petrovykh his well-known poem "Masteritsa Vinovatykh Vzorov" (Mistress of Guilty Glances). Akhmatova con-

sidered her "Naznach Mne Svidanie Na Etom Svete" (Make Me a Date on This Earth) one of the masterpieces of twentieth-century Russian lyric poetry.

Petrovykh is also known for her fine translations of the prominent Jewish poets S. Galkin and P. Markish. Although she translated from Serbo-Croatian and Bulgarian, her main work was from Armenian and Polish. She translated the poetry of Ovanes Tumanian, Avetik Isaakian, Atanas Dalchev, Bolieslav Lesmian, Julian Tuvim, Vladislav Bronevskii, Ildefons Galchinskii, and many others. Petrovykh also worked frequently as editor for editions of foreign translations; in 1977 in Erevan she edited *Armianskaia Klassicheskaia Lirika* (Classical Armenian Lyric Poetry) and with the collaboration of I. Karymian brought out *Kniga Skorbi* (The Book of Sorrow), a collection of works by the poet-monk Grigor Narekats. From 1959 to 1964 Maria Petrovykh conducted an ongoing seminar for young translators with the assistance of D.S. Samoilov. Petrovykh's association with Akhmatova lasted from the fall of 1933 to her death in 1965 and was most fruitful for both poets who valued each other's work. Akhmatova showed all her poems, translations, and articles on Pushkin to Petrovykh whose judgment as a poet and literary expert she held in high esteem. Petrovykh assisted Akhmatova in compiling a volume of her poetry which appeared in 1961.

Works

Dalnee Derevo [A Distant Tree] (1968).

Warwick J. Rodden

Lovisa Petterkvist

(see: Alfhild Agrell)

Lisalotte von der Pfalz

(see: Elisabeth Charlotte Pfalzgräfin, Herzogin von Orléans)

Elisabeth Charlotte Pfalzgräfin, Herzogin von Orléans

(a.k.a. Lisalotte von der Pfalz)

*Born May 27, 1652, Heidelberg, Germany;
died August 12, 1722, Saint-Cloud
Genre(s): letters, correspondence, memoirs
Language(s): German, French*

Elisabeth Charlotte, Countess and Duchess of Orléans, was the daughter of the Elector Karl Ludwig of the Palatine and of Charlotte, Princess of Hessen. Her parents' marriage was not a very happy one and they were divorced; her father remarried a chambermaid by whom he had many children and to whom Elisabeth Charlotte became very attached.

In the year 1671 she was married to Philipp, the Duke of Orléans, who was recently widowed by the death of his first wife, Henrietta of England. A condition of her marriage to this wealthy and influential personage was her conversion to Catholicism. It was a political marriage, by which the Elector of the Palatine hoped to gain friendship and peace with France. However, it was not a very happy marriage; Elisabeth Charlotte never really felt at home in the French court. However, she did love the theatre and often read and attended the plays of Molière; she met, was acquainted with and highly respected the works of Corneille and Racine. Elisabeth Charlotte had three children. The first died in early childhood, and her eldest son was betrothed to the bastard daughter of the King of France, Louis XIV. Her relationship to the French court and its courtesans became so unbearable that she eventually withdrew from them altogether and retreated to her own garden, devoting herself to the study of gems and precious stones, art and engraving, and, above all else, cultivating an extensive correspondence with her stepsisters, with her aunt in Hannover, and with friends and relatives. Her correspondence was a source of joy to her friends in Germany; Liebnitz, the famous philosopher, who apparently read some of her letters, is said to have marvelled at her rich language and her unique expressions and considered her epistles more than mere letters; he called them works of art. She wrote over four thousand letters.

The letters provide us with a rich source of the cultural life of that time, especially of German and French cultural expressions. Life at court, bourgeois traditions, religious practices, work habits and entertainment, music, theatre, medicine, and health care are discussed in detail. Elisabeth Charlotte never recovered from her homesickness for Germany. In the year 1701 her husband, Philipp of Orléans, died, and Elisabeth Charlotte experienced feelings of reconciliation for her husband and for his country.

Works

Anekdoten vom Französichen Hofe vorzuglich den Zeiten Ludwigs XIV und des Duc Regent aus Briefen der Madame d'Orléans . . . Herzog Philipp I von Orléans Witwe, herausgegeben von A.F. Veltheim [Anecdotes from the French Court Particularly of the Time of Louis XIV and of the Duke Regent Taken from the Letters of Madame of Orléans, the Widow of Duke Philipp I] (1789). *Bekenntnisse der Prinzessin Elisabeth Charlotte von Orléans. Aus ihren Originalbriefen* [Confessions of the Princess Elisabeth Charlotte of Orléans from the Original Letters] (1791). *Memoires sur la court de Louis XIV et de la Regence* [Memoirs of the Court of Louis XIV and of the Regency] (1823). *Memoires, fragments, historiques et correspondance* [Memoirs, Fragments, Histories and Correspondance] (1832). *Briefe an die Raugräfin Louise 1676–1722* [Letters to the Countess Louise 1676–1722; letters to her stepmother] (1843). *Die Briefe der Herzogin Elisabeth Charlotte von Orléans aus den Jahren 1676–1722* [Letters of the Duchess Elisabeth Charlotte of Orléans from the years 1676–1722] (1867–1881). *Briefe an Leibnitz herausgegeben von Zeitschrift des historischen Vereins für Niedersachsen* [Letters to Leibnitz edited by the Journal of the Historical Society of Neidersachsen] (1884). *Aus den Briefen der Herzogin Elisabeth Charlotte von Orléans an Kurfürstin Sophie von Hannover herausgegeben von E. Bodemann, 2 Bande* [Letters from the Duchess Elisabeth Charlotte of Orléans to the Princess Sophie of Hannover, edited by E. Bodemann, 2 volumes] (1891). *Briefe über die Zustände am französischen Hofe unter Ludwig XIV. Ausgewählt aus den Jahren 1672–1720, herausgegeben von R. Friedmann* [Letters about the Conditions of the French Court under Louis

XIV. Selections from the years 1672–1720, edited by R. Friedmann] (1903).

Bibliography

Allgemeine Deutsche Biographie. Hrsg. von der Historischen Kommission bei der Bayer. Akademie der Wissenschaften. red. R. von Liliencron und F.X. von Wegele. Vol. 6 (1884; rpt. Berlin, 1967). Kosch, Wilhelm, *Deutsches Literatur-Lexikon. Biographisches und bibliographisches Handbuch* (Bern, 1949). *Neue Deutsche Biographie*, ed. the Historical Committee of the Bavarian Academy of Sciences (Berlin, 1960).

Brigitte Edith Zapp Archibald

Athēna D. Phanariotou-Philippou

Born 1912, on the island of Nisiros; died 1935, Athens
Genre(s): poetry
Language(s): Greek

The daughter of Georgios and Eirēnē Philippou, Athēna showed at an early age an inclination and love for poetry. After finishing school in Nisiros, she went to Athens, where in 1933 she married Dēmētrios Phanariotēs. Her early death two years later put an end to a promising future in modern Greek poetry. Her poems were posthumously published in New York in 1945 as a result of the diligent efforts of her countryman, George Casavis.

Most of her poems may be called "love poems," but within this general category she draws fine delineations: The fear of rejection, the need to forget, the hope for a brighter tomorrow, the consolation found in the loved one, and the pain of disillusionment are some of the themes with which she deals.

Her poetry lacks sophistication, but it reads smoothly and effortlessly. This effortlessness, however, is the result of painstaking care to achieve the rhymes and rhythms that give her poems their song-like quality and of her ability to focus on something specific in each one of them. Thus she achieves a unity and coherence that is uncommon in the poetry written by the women of her generation. Many of her poems may be called lyrical gems and earn for her a place she rightfully deserves next to better-known figures in modern Greek poetry.

Works

Phanariotou-Philippou, Athēna D., *Lyrika Tragoudia*, ed. and intro. George Casavis (1945).

Helen Dendrinou Kolias

Anne Philipe

Born June 20, 1917, Brussels, Belgium
Genre(s): novel, poetry, essay, travel diary
Language(s): French

The Belgian-born author came to France at the age of twenty-one, in 1939. In 1951, she married Gérard Philipe, a well-known actor and movie star. Anne Philipe started a career as a writer by publishing *Caravanes d'Asie* (Caravans of Asia) the diary that she kept during her exceptional stay in China in 1948. She had decided to come back from China through India, by the Silk Route, traveling with a group of merchants on their way to Kashmire. She was the first woman to cross the Sin-Kiang.

Anne Philipe continued her work as a reporter, publishing her articles in prestigious newspapers, such as *Le Monde, Libération*. She was in charge of the book reviews for *Les Lettres Françaises*. She also made several documentary movies on Asia and Africa. She collaborated with the French cinematographer Jean Rouch in order to organize the Comité du film ethnographique.

In 1959, her husband died of cancer, and this event prompted her to write her first novel, *The Temps d'un soupir* (The Length of a Sigh), published in 1963. This dialogue between Anne Philipe and her dead husband about life, death, and love sets the tone of other novels. Her subsequent books have all be very well received by the critics.

It is difficult to classify Anne Philipe as a novelist, because if she does indeed write in prose, the importance of the images over the narrative in her writings forces the reader to associate her more with poets. Philipe herself has explained that she does want to achieve a blend of the three genres that she has used so far: diary, novel and poetry.

Her love for her husband, his death, her struggle for survival after his death are the central themes of her books. She evokes these themes through a set of images closely related to nature, particularly of the sea. She has been praised for the serenity of her tone, for the delicacy of her expression, and the celebration of life in her books, which are so closely concerned with death.

Works

Caravanes d'Asie (1955). Le Temps d'un soupir (1963). Les Rendez-vous de la colline (1966). Atome, le petit singe de la lune (1970). Spirale (1971). Un été près de la mer (1977). Promenades à Xian (1980). Les Résonnances de l'amour (1982). Je t'écoute respirer (1984).

English translations: No Longer Than a Sigh (1964). Wait for Dawn (1968). Atom, the Little Moon Monkey (1970).

Bibliography

Baroche, Christiane, "Une Saison dans la vie d'une femme." La Quinzaine Littéraire 272 (February 1, 1978): 7. Brochier, Jean-Jacques, "Le Bruit du liquide aspiré dans la seringue." Le Magazine Littéraire 189 (November 1982): 65. Garcin, Jérôme, "Un Eté près de la mer." Les Nouvelles Littéraires 2604 (September 29, 1977): 23. Pudlowski, Gilles, "Anne Philipe. Petite sonate en mort mineur." Les Nouvelles Littéraires 2856 (October 7, 1982): 38. Trèves, Nicole, "Un Eté près de la mer." World Literature Today LIII (1979): 72–73. Vandenschrick, Jacques, "Ici, là-bas, ailleurs." Revue Nouvelle LX (July-December 1974): 577–578. Wright, Barbara, "A Woman's Lives." The Times Literary Supplement LXXIV (1975).

Valerie Lastinger

Marianne Philips

(a.k.a. M. Goudeket-Philips)

Born March 18, 1886, Amsterdam; died May 13, 1951, Naarden
Genre(s): novel, short story
Language: Dutch

Marianne Philips was an activist in the women's liberation movement. She won the CPNB Book Award for her novella De zaak Beukennoot (1950; The Beukennoot Affair). After her death her family established the M. Philips Prize for outstanding authors.

Works

Novels: De wonderbare genezing [The Wonderful Recovery] (1929). De biecht [The Confession] (1930). Bruiloft in Europa [Marriage in Europe] (1934). Henri van de overkant (1936). De Doolhof [The Labyrinth] (1940).

Novellas: De jacht op de vlinder [The Butterfly Hunt] (1932). Het ogenblik [The Moment] (1935). De zaak Beukennoot [The Beukennoot Affair] (1950.

Bibliography

Romein-Verschoor, A., Vrouwenspiegel (1936).

Adolf von Württenberg

Verfasserin der Philosophie eines Weibes

(see: Marianne Ehrmann)

Karoline Pichler

Born September 7, 1769, Vienna, Austria; died July 9, 1843, Vienna, Austria
Genre(s): poetry, novel, novella, drama, memoirs
Language(s): German

Karoline Pichler is best known today for the literary salon she maintained in Vienna. She was also a talented, prolific, and successful writer. The house of her father, Hofrat Greiner, was the center of literary life in Vienna and Karoline had the opportunity in her early youth to meet the most outstanding contemporary poets. Together with her brother she received an excellent education and was taught Latin, French, Italian, and English. Under the tutelage of individuals from among Vienna's literary and scholarly elite she read carefully selected works by classical and modern poets in the original languages. At age twelve she published her first poem—"On the Death of a Playmate"—in the Wiener Musenalmanach für 1782. Her early taste favored the idyllic poetry of Voss and Gessner, and several of her own works, such as Idyllen (1803), Ruth (1805), and Bibliscne Idyllen (1812), also belong to that genre. In 1796 she married Andreas Pichler and continued the literary salon in her own house. Visitors from abroad and Vienna's intellectuals, writers, and musicians frequented her home. Among them were the historian Hormayr and the writers Grillparzer, Luise Brachmann, the brothers Schlegel, Zacharias Werner, Tieck, Brentano, and Mme de Staël.

Pichler published several novels and dramatic works, of which some have patriotic, others historical subjects in the manner of Walter Scott. *Lenore* (1804), a novella in two parts, as well as the tendentious letter-novel *Agathokles* (1808) established her fame as a writer. *Agathokles*, set in the time of early Christianity, was translated into several languages and enjoyed considerable popularity. Shortly before her death she wrote her *Memorabilia from My Life*, published in four volumes after her death, which are the best source of biographical information, include specifics about her works from their inception to their conclusion, and provide a richly detailed description of Vienna's intellectual and cultural life of the time.

Works

Collections: Sämmtliche Werke, 53 vols. (1820–1844). Sämmtliche Werke, 60 vols. (1828–1844). **Major works:** *Gleichnisse* (1800). *Idyllen* (1803). *Lenore*, 2 parts (1804). *Ruth* (1805). *Agathokles* (1808). *Die Grafen von Hohenberg*, 2 vols. (1811). *Biblische Idyllen* (1812). *Frauenwürde*, 4 vols. (1818). *Gedichte* (1822). *Die Belagerung Wiens*, 3 vols. (1824). *Die Schweden in Prag* (1827). *Die Wiedereroberung von Ofen*, 2 vols. (1829). *Friedrich der Streitbare*, 4 vols. (1831). *Elisabeth von Guttenstein* (1835). *Denkwürdigkeiten aus meinem Leben*, 4 vols. (1844).
Drama: *Ferdinand II* (1816). *Amalie von Mansfeld*. **Libretti:** *Mathilde, Rudolf von Habsburg*.
Also numerous short stories, essays, travel reports. Many of these shorter works were also translated into various languages and appeared in contemporary journals.

Bibliography

Bittrich, B., "Österreichische Züge am Beispiel der C.P.," in Polheim, K.K., *Literatur aus Österreich—österreichische Literatur* (Bonn, 1981), pp. 167–189. Hoffmeister, G., "Der literarische Frauensalon." *Deutsche und europäische Romantik* (Stuttgart, 1978), pp. 180–183. Schlossar, A., "K.P.," *Allgemeine Deutsche Biographie* 26 (1888), pp. 106–108.

Helene M. Kastinger Riley

Vera Piller

Born December 31, 1949, Wiesbaden, West Germany; died May 15/16, 1983, Zurich, Switzerland
Genre(s): poetry, short prose
Language(s): German

Vera Piller's oeuvre is tiny—it consists of some one hundred poems and a handful of short prose pieces—and it has awkened little critical resonance. Nevertheless, her work not only typifies the artistic scene in Zurich during the late 1970s and early 1980s but also bears witness to the powerful voice of a self-taught writer whose vision of life was naked, intense, and utterly without illusions.

Born and raised in West Germany, where she completed her formal education with training as a sales clerk, Piller came to Zurich in 1968 after marrying the Swiss artist Dominique Piller. Her various odd jobs (waitress, sales clerk, etc.) were their primary financial support. She began writing during the breakdown of her marriage in 1977, making contacts with other writers and artists in Zurich and collaborating on theater productions and a radio play. The identity crisis and depressions that followed Piller's divorce in 1978 were rapidly worsened by her deteriorating health: chronic migraine headaches, a heart attack in 1980, and a series of strokes eventually debilitated her entirely. Sometime during the night of May 15, 1983, Piller suffered a stroke while showering and drowned. Her body was discovered 30 hours later, when the water flooded the apartment below.

Though at times awkward, the authenticity of Piller's poetry is convincing—her race with death left her no time for sentimentality. Her stripped-down, plain language and simple, everyday imagery contrast with the brutal intensity of her themes—pain, terror, sleeplessness, death. By turns composed, ironic, desperate, angry, or witty, her voice is unmistakable, and though the body that produced it was frail, the spirit was not.

Works

Kaputtmacher AG Söhne & Co. [Kaputtmacher Inc. Sons & Co.], poetry (1979). Kinderlieder. Aus meinen grossen Schmerzen mach ich kleine Lieder [Children's Songs. From My Great Sorrow and Pain I Make Little Songs], poetry (1980). Macht damit was ihr wollt. Lyrik und Prosa [Do What You Will With It. Poetry and Prose] (1984).

Bibliography

Orte. Schweizer Literaturzeitschrift 44 (1983). Entire issue devoted to Piller.

Ann Marie Rasmussen

Constance Pipelet

(see: Constance-Marie de Théis, princesse de Salm-Reifferscheid-Dyck)

Christine de Pizan

Born ca. 1365, Venice, Italy; died ca. 1430, Poissy, France
Genre(s): poetry, history, literary criticism, autobiography, essay, letters, narrative
Language(s): French

Although born in Italy into a family which originated in Pizzano, near Bologna from whose celebrated university both her father and grandfather held degrees, she moved at an early age to Paris, where her father was appointed medical advisor and astrologer to the French king, Charles V (1365–1380). Nevertheless, her origin undoubtedly influenced her ideas so that she combined her Italian heritage with her observations on French life and thought.

From her early years she apparently showed signs of unusual intellectual curiosity that were encouraged by her father, although her opportunities for formal education were limited because of contemporary attitudes towards the education of women and because at fifteen she was married to Etienne du Castel, a young Picard notary who, the year of the marriage (1380) was given a promising appointment as secretary in the royal chancellory.

The marriage was a happy one, producing two sons and a daughter, but after ten years Etienne died suddenly and unexpectedly, the victim of an epidemic. Thus Christine, aged twenty-five, was left a widow with young children and an elderly mother in her care. Her sorrow was profound and her lack of preparation to cope with her new responsibilities almost complete, but out of these misfortunes her career as a writer developed.

At the beginning she wrote poetry to express her grief and to find comfort for it in the popular forms of her day: balades, rondeaux and virelais. It is also possible that she served a sort of apprenticeship copying manuscripts for the blossoming Parisian book-trade. At the same time, she started on a program of self-education through reading, beginning with a translation of Boethius' Consolation of Philosophy and the medieval Ovide Moralisé (Ovid Moralized). This led to her first long allegorical, mythological work, L'Epître d'Othéa (The Letter of Othea), which took the form of a letter from the goddess of wisdom (Othéa) to a young man who had reached the age of knighthood concerning the proper moral and spiritual education for a young knight. The education of the young would be a favorite concern throughout her career, and her ideas on the subject were well in advance of her times.

Her writing gained increased attention through her part in a literary debate concerning the merits of Jean de Meun's continuation of the Romance of the Rose. This pitted her wits against those of several members of the royal chancellery, her husband's former colleagues, but she was supported in her protestations against the misogyny and exaggerated popularity of the poem by the Chancellor of the University of Paris, Jean Gerson. The discussion inspired her to write two further works in defense of women: La Cité des Dames (The City of Ladies), intended to correct Boccaccio's ironical view of women in the De Claris Mulieribus (Of Famous Women), and the Livre des Trois Vertus (The Book of the Three Virtues), a guide to enable women to enjoy a more respected place in society.

These works and a biography of Charles V, the Fais et Bonnes Meurs du Sage Roi Charles V (The Deeds and Good Character of the Wise King Charles V), commissioned by the late king's younger brother, the Duke of Burgundy, turned Christine from writing poetry to prose, usually didactic in inspiration. Before this, however, she had composed a long allegorical and historical poem entitled *La Mutacion de Fortune* (The Changes of Fortune). Her subsequent writing included a semi-autobiographical *Avision-Christine* (Christine's Vision) and more educational treatises, notably the *Livre du Corps de Policie* (The Book of the Body Politic), the *Faits d'Armes et de Chevalerie* (Deeds of Arms and of Chivalry) on preparation for warfare and knighthood, and the *Livre de la Paix* (The Book of Peace), addressed to the French dauphin Louis de Guyenne concerning his duties to his country. She demonstrated increasing concern for the state of France, threatened by both internal conflict and a renewal of war with England. She appealed in turn to those she thought had a responsibility to try to save the country, to Isabeau de Bavière in her "Epître à la Reine" ("Letter to the Queen") and to the elderly Duke de Berry, the king's uncle, in her "Lamentacions sur le Maux de la Guerre Civile" ("Lamentations on the Evil of Civil War") as well as to Louis de Guyenne. But no amount of goodwill could stem the misfortunes that soon overtook France, the Cabochian revolt in 1413, a veritable reign of terror, and the French defeat by the English at Agincourt two years later. This was soon followed by the death of Louis de Guyenne, the prince on whom Christine had pinned so many hopes. Soon after writing a letter to console the widows and other relatives of the victims of Agincourt, the "Epître sur la Prison de Vie Humaine" ("Letter on the Prisonhouse of Human Life"), Christine retired to the Dominican Abbey in Poissy, where her daughter had been a nun for many years. Her voice was heard only one more time when she hailed the victory of Joan of Arc at Orleans and the coronation of Charles VII at Reims. Her "Dittié sur Jeanne d'Arc" ("Song on Joan of Arc"), dated July 31, 1429, was the first poem to celebrate these events which were bringing about a change in France's fortunes. This was the last that was heard from her, but her works were copied, printed and read well into the sixteenth century.

Works

First poetry (1392–1402). *Epître au Dieu d'Amour* [Letter of the God of Love] (1399). *Le Débat de Deux Amants* [The Debate of the Two Lovers] (ca. 1400). *Le Livre des Trois Jugements* [The Book of the Three Judgments]. *Le Dit de Poissy* [The Tale of Poissy]. *L'Epître d'Othéa* [The Letter of Othéa]. *Les Epistres sur le Roman de la Rose* [The Letters on the Romance of the Rose] (1401–1402). *Le Dit de la Rose* [The Tale of the Rose] (1402). *Le Chemin de Long Estude* [The Long Road of Learning] (1403). *La Mutacion de Fortune* [The Mutations of Fortune] (1404). *Le Livre des Faits et Bonnes Meurs du Sage Roy Charles V* [The Book of the Deeds and Good Character of Wise King Charles V] (1404). *Le Livre de la Cité des Dames* [The Book of the City of Ladies] (1405). *Le Livre des Trois Vertus ou le Trésor de la Cité des Dames* [The Book of the Three Virtues or the Treasure of the City of Ladies] (1405). *L'Epistre à la Reine de France* [The Letter to the Queen of France] (1405). *L'Avision-Christine* [Christine's Vision] (1404). *Le Livre de la Prod'homie de l'Homme* [The Book of Man's Prudence. Also called *Le Livre de Prudence*] (1406). *Le Livre du Corps de Policie* [The Book of the Body Politic] (1407). *Sept Psaumes Allegorisés* [Seven Psalms Allegorized] (1409). *Le Livre des Faits d'Armes de le Chevalerie* [The Book of the Deeds of Arms and of Chivalry] (1410). *La Lamentacion sur les Maux de la Guerre Civile* [Lamentation on the Ills of Civil War] (1410). *Le Livre de la Paix* [The Book of Peace] (1412–1413). *L'Epistre de la Prison de Vie Humaine* [The Letter of the Prisonhouse of Human Life] (1418). *Les Heures de Contemplacion sur la Passion de Nostre Seigneur* [The Hours of Contemplation on the Passion of Our Lord] (1422–1424). *Dittié de Jeanne d'Arc* [The Song of Joan of Arc] (1429).

Translations: *The Book of the City of Ladies* [*Le Livre de la Cité des Dames*], tr. Earl Richards (1981). *La Cité des Dames* [*Le Livre de la Cité des Dames*], tr. Thérèse Moreau and Eric Hicks (1986 in modern French). *The Book of Fayttes of Armes and of Chyvalerie* [*Le Livre des Faits d'Armes de le Chevalerie*], tr. William Caxton, ed. A.T.P. Byles (1931). *A Medieval Woman's Mirror of Honor* [*Le Livre des Trois Vertus*], tr. Charity Cannon Willard (1989).

Bibliography

Cerquilini, Jacqueline, ed., *Cent Ballades d'Amant et de Dame* [A Hundred Ballads of the Lover and His Lady] (Paris, 1982). Hicks, Eric, *Le Débat sur le Roman de la Rose* (Paris, 1977). Kennedy, Angus J., and Kenneth Varty, eds., *Dittié de Jeanne d'Arc* (Oxford, 1977). Kennedy, Angus J., *Christine de Pizan: A Bibliographical Guide* (London, 1984). Kennedy, Angus J., *Epistre de la Prison de Vie Humaine* (Glasgow, 1984). Lucas, Robert, ed., *Le Livre du Corps de Policie* (Geneva, 1967). McLeod, Enid, *The Order of the Rose: The Life and Ideas of Christine de Pizan* (London, 1967). Rains, Ruth Ringland, ed., *Sept Psaumes Allégorisés.* (Washington, D.C., 1965). Solente, Suzanne, ed., *Le Livre des Faits et Bonnes Meurs du Sage Roy Charles V*, 2 vols. (Paris, 1936–1941). Solente, Suzanne, ed., *Le Livre de la Mutacion de Fortune*, 4 vols. (Paris, 1959–1966). Varty, Kenneth, ed., *Christine de Pisan: Balades, Rondeaux and Virelais* (Leicester, 1965). Willard, Charity Cannon, ed., *Le Livre de la Paix* (The Hague, 1958). Willard, Charity Cannon, ed., *Le Livre des Trois Vertus* (Geneva, 1989). Willard, Charity Cannon, *Christine de Pizan: Her Life and Works* (New York, 1985).

Charity C. Willard

Elisabeth Gräfin Plessen

Born March 15, 1944, Neustadt/Holstein,
West Germany
Genre(s): novel, essay, lyric
Language(s): German

Elisabeth Plessen belongs to the young generation of West German writers trying to address new topics in contemporary literature. Her personal experiences and general philosophical problems are the main subjects of her works. She came from an old aristocratic family in Holstein, West Germany, and studied philosophy, literature and history in Paris and Berlin. Extensive travels took her to the West Indies, South America and the Soviet Union. She spent many years in Berlin, but she has moved to Munich in the recent past. She became first known with her famous edition (together with Michael Mann) of Katia Mann's memoirs (Thomas Mann's widow), *Ungeschriebene Memoiren* (1974; Unwritten Memoirs). Her novel *Mitteilungen an den Adel* (1976; Information for the Aristocracy), reprinted in 1979, was widely received and acknowledged as a remarkable literary landmark. Plessen created an autobiography-novel, in which her own life is the basis for her fictional text, highlighting the tensions between father and daughter that lead to a bitter generation conflict. Her experiences in the student movement in the 1960s in Berlin and her resistance and revolt against the aristocracy in the form of her own father, hence between two different classes (in philosophical terms), are extensively analyzed and critically depicted. Plessen documented therein the trend of *New Subjectivity*, since individual views and concerns are confronted with social-historical aspects. Her second novel *Kohlhaas*, 1979, reprinted in 1982, however, represented her turn to the past. Although Heinrich Kleist's short story (novella) "Kohlhaas" had inspired her to rewrite this topic, Plessen insisted on her own investigations into the historical circumstances of this peasant-revolutionary seeking personal justice in the eighteenth century. Just as Dieter Kühn did in famous "historical" investigation-novels on medieval poets, she presents her own research efforts and historical analyses. Yet the recreation of the historical novel left many critics disappointed, and this criticism increased when her *Zu machen, da ein gebraten Huhn aus der Schüssel laufe* (1981; To Make a Fried Chicken Run Out of the Bowl), reprinted in 1984, appeared. It consists of an amorphous collection of travel impressions, dreams and short prose texts, which quickly refute Plessen's own claim to have written short stories. This decline in her creativity became also noticeable in her latest novel *Stella Polaris* (1984; North Star), where the amorphous character, the obsession with details, the lack of innovation, and the kaleidoscopic appearance throughout the book documented the author's problems with ideological orientation and social identification. A few poems appeared in *Literaturmagazin* 9, Reinbeck 1978, p. 278ff, whereas a number of scholarly articles on writing fiction, women figures in literature, historical female personalities and contemporary prose literature were published in various West German journals.

Works

Ungeschriebene Memoiren [Unwritten Memoirs, ed.] (1974). *Mitteilungen an den Adel* [Information for the Aristocracy] (1976, 1979). *Kohlhaas* (1979). *Zu machen, da ein gebraten Huhn aus der Schüssel laufe* [To Make a Fried Chicken Run Out of the Bowl] (1981). *Stella Polaris* [North Star] (1984). "Spannungen oder die Fächer in munem Kopf," in *Bausteine zu einer Poetik der Modeone* (Munich, 1987).

Bibliography

Frieden, S., "'Selbstgespräche': Elisabeth Plessens *Mitteilungen an den Adel.*" *Seminar* 18 (1982): 271–286. Frieden, S., *Autobiography: Self Into Form. German-Language Autobiographical Writings of the 1970s* (Frankfurt, Bern, New York, 1983). Helbling, R.E., "Kohlhaas—Metamorphosen," *Sprache und Literatur*, FS für Arval L. Streadbeck zum 65. Geb. e. G.P. Knapp, Wolff A. von Schmidt, H.-F. Rahde. Utah Studies in Literature and Linguistics 20 (Bern, Frankfurt, Las Vegas, 1981), pp. 65–74. Kraft, H.W. and H. Marshall, "Elisabeth Plessen's Discourse with the Past: Two Historical Novels from the 1970s." *Monatshefte* 77 (1985), pp. 157–170.

Albrecht Classen

Luise von Plönnies

Born November 7, 1803, Hanau, Germany;
   died January 22, 1872, Darmstadt
Genre(s): lyric, romance, drama, translation
Language(s): German

Luisa von Plönnies was a highly acclaimed writer during her lifetime; she was acquainted with such poets as Freiligrath and Uhling and was respected by Annette von Droste-Hülshoff. Her work fell into oblivion after her death. The range of her writing is enormous: translations from English, Dutch, and French; children's literature; biblical poetry and drama; and original verse. Raised in her maternal grandfather's home in Darmstadt after being orphaned at an early age, the young girl received comprehensive instruction in foreign languages, which led to her extensive career in translating, particularly of English lyric. In Darmstadt she was connected to Eduard Duller and his literary circle, which was militantly Catholic in orientation. This religious inclination is reflected in her enormous output of religious works. But Luisa von Plönnies was more than just a religious poet. Like the poetry of Blake, her lyrics reflect an interest in social issues. One early poem, "Glas" (Glass), is a sharp protest against child labor in glass factories of the day. Her poetry is well crafted and rhetorically powerful. Her interest in Flemish culture, reflected in *Die Sagen Belgiens* (The Sagas of Belgium), led to her being named a member of the Royal Academy in Brussels and of the literary academies of Ghent and Antwerp. Her version of *Maryken von Nymegen* is the history of an alliance with the devil in which Maryken becomes a female Faust figure.

Works

Die Kinder im Walde, nach dem Englischen frei bearbeitet (1838). *Britannia, Eine Auswahl englischer Dichtungen alter und neuer Zeit* (1843). *Reise-Erinnerungen aus Belgien* (1845). *Die Sagen Belgiens* (1846). *Gedichte* (1844). *Abälard und Heloise, Ein Sonettenkranz* (1849). *Oskar und Gianetta* (1850). *Neue Gedichte* (1851). *Maryken von Nymwegen* (1853). *Die sieben Raben* (1862). *Sawitri* (1862). *Lilien auf dem Felde* (1864). *Ruth, Biblische Dichtung* (1864). *Joseph und seine Brüder, Epische Dichtung* (1866). *Maria von Bethanien, Neutestamentliches Gedicht* (1867). *Englische Lyriker des 19. Jahrhunderts* (1867). *Die heilige Elizabeth* (1870). *Maria Magdalena, Ein geistliches Drama in fünf Aufzügen* (1871). *Sagen und Legenden nebst einem Anhang vermischter Gedichte* (1874).

The only modern edition of any of her works is a selection of three poems in: Gisela Brinker-Gabler, ed., *Deutsche Dichterinnen vom 16. Jahrhundert bis zur Gegenwart* (Munich, 1978), pp. 185–193. The only translations of her work are a French translation of her work on Belgian legends: *Légendes et traditions de la Belgique, traduit librement du text allemand par Louis Piré* (Cologne, 1848), and an English translation of one of her short prose works: *Princess Ilse, A Story of the Harz Mountain* (Boston, 1867).

Bibliography

Brinker-Gabler, Gisela, Karola Ludwig and Angela Wöffen, "Plönnies, Luisa von." *Lexikon deutschsprachiger Schriftstellerinnen, 1800–1945*

(Munich, 1986), p. 32. Brümmer, Franz, "Plönnies, Luisa von." *Allgemeine Deutsche Biographie*, 26 (1888): 309–310. Kraus, Otto, *Geistliche Lieder im 19. Jahrhundert* (Gütersloh, 1879), p. 385.

Earl Jeffrey Richards

L'udmila Podjavorinská

(see: L'udmila Riznerová)

Jeanne-Marie-Fabienne Poinsard, Mme. Marie

(see: Jenny P. d'Héricourt)

Dianne de Poitiers

Born 1499(?), St. Vallier, France; died 1566, Anet
Genre(s): poetry, epistle
Language(s): French

Dianne de Poitiers' life spanned the first sixty-six years of the sixteenth century, when festive pageantry and lyric poetry flourished at the French royal court. As the intimate confidante of King Henry II, Dianne penned love poems to him while inspiring other poets to dedicate their own works to her. The French translation of the *Amadis of Gaul* was dedicated to Dianne, as well as books of poetry by Pierre de Ronsard, Joachim Du Bellay, and Olivier de Magny. Dianne also wrote numerous letters concerning court politics and management of the royal household.

This talented member of the French aristocracy was born at St. Vallier on the Rhone at the close of the fifteenth century. Through her father she was related by marriage to the Dauphin Louis (later King Louis XII). Dianne's maternal grandfather was a close friend of Anne of France, the powerful daughter of King Louis XI. At the age of fifteen Dianne was married to Louis de Brézé (age fifty-six at the time), a grandson of King Charles VII and his mistress Agnes Sorel. The marriage evidently was a happy one and produced two daughters. In 1521 when Dianne became a wealthy widow, she focused her energies on managing her substantial estates. During the

1530s she returned to court where she became the mistress of Prince Henry, by whom she probably had a daughter in 1537 (Diane of France). Dianne was one of the most influential women in France while Henry reigned as king, 1547–1559. After his untimely death, she retired to her estates in Normandy, where she died peacefully in 1566.

Dianne requested that Henry destroy her letters to him and he apparently acquiesced. None of her letters to him has ever appeared. For the same reason, only two of Dianne's poems to Henry are extant. There are, however, more than one hundred extant letters to other correspondents from Dianne, written mostly during the last twenty years of her life.

Her two extant poems demonstrate that the mythological imagery of pageantry did not inspire her private lyrics. The simple charm of her poetic style recalls the *chansons* of the latter fifteenth century. The same directness and delightful simplicity clearly speak to the modern reader through Dianne's letters, a model of French epistolary style from the mid-sixteenth century.

To our knowledge, none of Dianne's work was published during her lifetime. Her love poem to Henry II was printed in Ernest Quentin Bauchart, *Les femmes bibliophiles de France*, vol. I (1886), pp. 63–64, where he noted that the manuscript of the poem was in the Bibliothèque Nationale. Dianne's farewell poem to Henry was first printed in Georges Guiffrey, *Lettres inédites de Dianne de Poytiers*, 1866, which contains her known letters. The farewell poem was also printed in Grace Hart Seely, *Diane the Huntress: The Life and Times of Diane de Poitiers*, 1936, p. 203.

Dianne's farewell poem was translated by Grace Hart Seely, p. 204. Both the farewell poem and the love poem are translated in my "Dianne de Poitiers: The Woman Behind the Legend" in *Renaissance Women Writers*, 1987, pp. 158–176, in which sixteen of her letters written between 1545 and 1562 are translated on pp. 165–172.

Bibliography

Bardon, Françoise, *Diane de Poitiers et le mythe de Diane* (Paris, 1963). Bushnell, George, "Diane de Poitiers and Her Books." *The Library*, 4th series, 7 (1927): 283–302. Chastel, André, "Diane de

Poitiers: L'éros de la beauté froide." *Fables, Formes, Figures*, vol. I (Paris, 1978), pp. 263–272. Courde de Montaiglon, Anatole de, *Diane de Poitiers et son goût dans les arts* (Paris, 1879). Erlanger, Philippe, *Diane de Poitiers* (Paris, 1955). Guiffrey, Georges, *Lettres inédites de Dianne de Poytiers* (Paris, 1866). Henderson, Helen Watson, *The Enchantress: Dianne de Poytiers* (London, 1928). Maulde La Clavière, René de, *Les femmes de la Renaissance*, tr. George Herbery Ely (London, 1905). Porcher, Jean, "Les livres de Diane de Poitiers." *Les Trésors des Bibliothèques de France* 26 (Paris, 1942), pp. 78–89. Quentin Bauchart, Ernest, *Les femmes bibliophiles de France*, vol. I (Paris, 1886). Seely, Grace Hart, *Diane the Huntress: The Life and Times of Diane de Poitiers* (New York and London, 1936). Sider, Sandra, "Dianne de Poitiers: The Woman Behind the Legend." *Renaissance Women Writers* (Athens, Ga., 1987), pp. 158–176. Thierry, Adrien, *Diane de Poitiers* (Paris and Geneva, 1955).

Sandra Sider

A. Polianin

(see: Sofiia Iakolevna Parnok)

A Polish Lady

(see: Antonina Niemiryczowa)

Evelyne Pollet

Born August 12, 1905, Antwerp, Belgium
Genre(s): novel
Language(s): French

Only recently, since 1830, has the Flemish language assumed an important independence in Belgium's culture. It has since become a focal point for artists, writers, and politicians seeking to promote and unify a Flemish cultural identity.

Within this language-cultural division (Flanders-Flemish, Wallonia-French) the writings of the Flemish Pollet, a few novels written in French between 1924 and 1950, hold a very minor place in the literature due in part perhaps because they were aimed at a limited audience of non-Flemish speakers in a Flemish culture.

Pollet's novels are reminiscent of "commuter train" literature: captivating romances with happy endings for the major, that is "good," characters. Pollet surpasses this categorization though only because of her open-mindedness. In *La Maison Carrée* (1941; The Square House) for example, she introduces premarital sex, which immediately put the book on the critics' "black list." Even though her novels were translated into Flemish, Pollet remains a very minor, isolated figure.

Works

La Bouée (1924). *Primevères* (1940). *La Maison Carrée* (1941). *Grandes Vacances en Angleterre* (1945).

An Lammens

Elizavéta Grigór'evna Polónskaia

Born June 14 (26), 1890, Warsaw, Poland;
died 1969, Leningrad, The Soviet Union
Genre(s): poetry, children's literature,
memoirs, translation
Language(s): Russian

Polónskaia wrote a great number of politically inspired revolutionary verses and generally belongs to the group of Soviet socialist-realist authors.

From 1906 through 1908 she wrote agitation propaganda in Petersburg. She left for Paris where she studied in the medical school at the Sorbonne from 1907–1914 to avoid possible arrest for her activities. She began to write poetry after her return to Moscow in 1915. Her first book of poems, *Znamen'ia* (1921), reflects the events of the revolution and the civil war as does her second book, *Pod kamennym dozhdem* (1923; Under a Rain of Stones). She also began writing children's poetry, which appeared in the books *Zaichata* (1923; Baby Rabbits), *Gosti* (1924; The Guests), *Chasy* (1925; The Hours) and others. Her book *Upriamyi kalendar'* (1929; The Stubborn Calendar) is a self-styled verse diary of the twenties.

In her capacity of a correspondent of "Leningradskaia pravda," Polónskaia traveled quite bit, her works relative to her travels collected in the book *Liudi sovetskix budnei* (1934;

Workaday Soviet People). Other memoirs of more note include her remembrance of M. Zoshchenko in *Trudy po russkoj i slavianskoi filologii*, Tartu, 1963, and articles in the journals *Zvezda*, etc.

Polónskaia was a prolific translator, rendering into Russian the works of Hugo, Molière, Shakespeare, Calderon, Kipling, Garcia Lorca and others.

Works

Znamen'ia (1921). *Pod kamennym dozhdem* (1923). *Zaichata* (1923). *Gosti* (1924). *Chasy* (1925). *Upriamyi kalendar'* (1929). *Goda, izbrannye stikhi* (1935). *Stikhotvoreniia i poèma* (1960). *Izbrannoe* (1966).

Chris Tomei

Maria Polydourē

(a.k.a. Maria Polydouri)

*Born 1902, Kalamata, Greece; died 1930,
    Athens*
Genre(s): poetry, novella, journal, novel
Language(s): Greek

Maria Polydourē was the daughter of Eugenios Polydourēs and Kyriakē Markatou. Her father was a high school teacher of literature and her mother was very much interested in women's issues. She attended the public schools of Gythion, Philiatra, and Kalamata. Upon graduation from high school she became a government clerk. After the death of her father and mother in 1920, she left Kalamata for Athens where she continued as a government clerk and registered in the Nomikē Scholē (Law School) of the University of Athens. Shortly afterwards she met the poet Kōstas Karyotakēs, the most important love of her life and the main subject of her poetry and the journal she was keeping at that time. In 1925, after Karyotakēs refused her proposal of marriage and after she broke off her engagement to another young man, she quit her studies at the university and spent a summer vacation near Aigion. At this time she probably wrote her novella, entitled simply *Mythistorēma* (Novel). Later that year she studied drama and appeared in dramatic performances. In 1926 she traveled to Paris and attended sewing classes at the Ecole Pigier, from which she received a diploma. Before the end of 1926, however, she learned that she had tuberculosis and was hospitalized. In 1928 she returned to Athens and entered Sotēria, a hospital for tuberculosis victims. During this year also she published her first collection of poetry and learned of the suicide of Karyotakēs. The following year she published her second poetry collection. She died on April 29, 1930.

Polydourē's life has drawn more attention than her work, probably because her work is simply an extension of her life. She was not an artist in the usual sense of the word. Her poems are cries of frustration, rejection, nostalgia, hope, despair. They create the impression that she is overtaken by an inner emotion, and, as Lilē Zographou suggests in her introduction to Polydourē's collected works, she is in a hurry to get rid of a weight bearing down on her and has no time for fine details.

Kōstas Karyotakēs was already an established poet when she met him, and, as her journals and poems testify, she felt an immediate attachment to him. Much of her poetry is a celebration of eros, the physical attraction, the embraces and kisses she longs for, the heart that beats loudly for him. Even though many of her poems appear to be unrefined emotional outbursts, they communicate a dynamism that is Polydourē herself, making a definite imprint on her age.

As she approached the end of her life, and learned of Karyotakēs' death, her poems became more reflective and melancholy, but even then we detect the energy that informed her earlier work.

Her novella and journal, both published in Takēs Mendrakos' edition of *Ta apanta* (Complete Works), are important not so much as works of art but as documents of a historical period and as depictions of the climate in Athens in the 1920s.

Polydourē's thirst for life, depicted throughout her writing but especially in her poems, kept her in the midst of a circle of friends with literary and intellectual interests and talents. These friends were with her even at the end. There is no doubt that she left her mark on them.

Works

Oi trillies pou svinoun [Trills That Are Fading] (1928). *Echō sto chaos* [Echo in Chaos] (1929).

Mythistorēma [Novel], *Ta apanta*, ed. Takēs Mendrakos (1982). "To hēmerologio" [Journal], *Ta apanta*, ed. Takēs Mendrakos (1982). "Anekdota poiēmata" [Unpublished Poems], *Ta apanta*, ed. Takēs Mendrakos (1982).

Translations: Maria Polydourē translated Jean Moreas' "L'insidieuse nuit..." and "Belle source ...," Henry Bataille's "Souvenirs," and Leconte de Lisle's "A un poete mort" into modern Greek. Her translations are published in Takēs Mendrakos' edition of her collected works (*Ta apanta*—see above).

Anthologized translations: Anagnostopoulos, Athan, "The Poetry of Maria Polydourē: A Selection." *Journal of the Hellenic Diaspora* 5, 1 (1978): 41–67. *The Penguin Book of Greek Verse*, intro. and ed. Constantine A. Trypanis, with plain prose translations of each poem (Great Britain, 1971). *A travers le Parnasse néo-grec*, tr. Marie-Louise Asserin, translations of six women writers (Athens, 1934). *Grèce. Poètes contemporains*, tr. Dimitri Yanoulakis (Athens, 1959). *37 poètes Grecs de L'Indépendance à nos jours*, tr. Dominique Grandmont (Hornfleur, 1972). *Arodafnusa. 32 poeti Neogreci (1880–1940)*, tr. Bruno Lavagnini (Atene, 1957). *Poesia greca del '900*, introduzione e traduzione di Mario Vitti (Parma, 1957). *Az újgörög irodalom kistükre* (Budapest, 1971). *Nowe przestrzenie Ikara. Antologia poezij greckiej XX wieku*, tr. Nikos Chadzinikolau (Warsaw, 1972).

Bibliography

Dimaras, C.Th., *A History of Modern Greek Literature*, tr. Mary P. Gianos (Albany, N.Y., 1972). *Encyclopedia Hēlios*, Vol. 16. Hondrogiannēs, Giannēs, *Ē Maria Polydourē meta ton Karyotakē* (Athens, 1975). Kokkinēs, Spiros, *Anthologia Neoellenikēs Poiēseos 1708–1977* (Athens, 1977). "Kritiko Anthologio" [Critical Anthology], in Takēs Mendrakos' *Ta apanta*. Includes short articles (some untitled) by Kleon Paraschos, Tasinopoulos, Tellos Agras, Kostas Stergiogoulos, Angelos Sikelianos, Lilē Zographou, Angelos Terzakēs, and Giannēs Chatzinēs, previously published as follows: Paraschos—*Nea Estia* (Mar. 15, 1930); Tasinopoulos—*Nea Estia* (Jan. 1, 1929); Stergiopoulos—*Ē Hellēnikē Poiēsē* (Athens, 1980); Sikelianos—*Hellēenikon Hēmerologion Orizontes*, vol. B (1945); Agras—*Periodiko Pnoē* (1930), Chronos B, Phyllo 16–17; Zographou—from her intro. to *Ta apanta tēs M. Polydourē* (Athens, 1961);

Terzakēs—"O matōmenos lyrismos," *To Vēma* (April 19, 1961); Chatzinēs—"Ē zoē kai ē poiēsē tēs Marias Polydourē," *E Kathēmerine* (Sept. 22, 1954). Mirasgezē, Maria, *Neoellēnikē Logotechnia*, vol. 2 (Athens, 1982). Pappageotes, George, *The Story of Modern Greek Literature* (New York, 1972). Politis, Linos, *A History of Modern Greek Literature* (Oxford, 1973). Politis, Linos, *Historia tēs Neoellēnikes Logotechnias* (Athens, 1980). Sakellariadēs, Ch.G., *Ē pragmatikē Polydourē kai ē ekdoseē tōn apantōn tēs* (Athens, 1969). Stamelos, Dēmētrēs, *Neoellēnes: Pneumatikes kai kallitechnikes physiognomies tou 19ou kai 20ou aiōna* (Athens, 1968). Zōgraphou, Lilē, *Biographia—Apanta M. Polydourē* (Athens, 1961). Zōgraphou, Lilē, *Karyotakes, Polydourē—E Archē tēs amphisvētēsēs*. 2nd ed (Athens, 1980).

Helen Dendrinou Kolias

Maria Polydouri

(see: Maria Polydourē)

Nùria Pompeia

Born 1938, Barcelona, Spain
Genre(s): cartoon, short story, journalism
Language(s): Spanish, Catalan

Nùria Pompeia (the pseudonym of a cultured woman of refined background who has not publicly revealed her real name) was born to an upper-class family in Barcelona in 1938 and was reared during the Franco regime. A product of postwar oppressiveness, she has reacted against the narrow Victorian morality and conventional, patriarchal mores of her upbringing in a series of cartoon books lampooning the stereotypes and fallacies of education for females in Spain. She has the somewhat unusual distinction of being the only woman to make a name for herself as a cartoonist, and she has created a character (Palmira) similar to Lucy of the "Peanuts" comic strip, an irrepressibly unpleasant brat known to newspaper readers not only in Spain but throughout the Spanish-speaking world. As a journalistic cartoonist, she was a regular collaborator for the Barcelona weekly, *Triunfo*, and subsequently became managing editor of another weekly, *Por Favor*. She writes both in Castilian and Catalan, with her most characteristic works being of a hybrid nature, between literary and graphic, a blend of cartoons and texts. Her themes are predominantly, and indeed almost exclusively, feminist; her style is satiric and frequently hilarious, but with a profound underlying seriousness.

Y fueron felices comiendo perdices (1970; And They Lived Happily Ever After Eating Partridges) alludes to a popular saying while undercutting the myth of the woman whose problems in life end happily at the altar. *Pels segles dels segles* (1971; For Centuries and Centuries) continues in much the same vein, deflating the stereotypes of romantic love. Another collection of cartoons and texts featuring Palmira, this one contrasts masculine and feminine views of woman's lot and implicitly combats the view of marriage as the logical goal of feminine existence. In *La educación de Palmira* (1972; Educating Palmira), Pompeia tackles the traditional premises of Spanish education as simplistic, erroneous deformations of the female's natural intelligence and creativity, the underlying causes of future existential alienation and frustration. *Mujercitas* (1975; Little Women), a compendium of themes found in the preceding collections of cartoons and text, combines side-splitting humor with incisive satire to indict societal attitudes that transform the active, creative, spontaneous girl-child into a passive, inhibited, and boring adult. Traditional stereotypes, the cliches of sexist role-typing, the idealization of marriage and motherhood, as well as biblical justifications of male domination are juxtaposed with contemporary feminine reality. *Maternasis* (1967; The Disease of Maternity), an early collection that links most clearly with *Mujercitas*, insofar as neither depends on Palmira, relies heavily on visual effects to communicate the changes in a woman's body and lifestyle that come with motherhood.

Cinc cèntims (1981; Five Cents), Pompeia's first exclusively verbal work, is a collection of twelve short stories with predominantly feminist themes, composed in precise, vivid, and colloquial Catalan. A secondary thematic nucleus emerges in several tales: an incisive critique of the bourgeois lifestyle and values as seen in a drunken dinner party, ritual weekend outings, a variety of pseudo-intellectual pursuits, and pseudo-artistic collections. Sexist education, matrimony as a form of patriarchal despotism, sexual politics, and the frustration of women's aspirations toward liberation by one regime after another are other subjects treated.

Works

Cinc cèntims (1981). *La educación de Palmira* (1972). *Maternasis* (1967). *Mujercitas* (1975). *Pels segles dels segles* (1971). *Y fueron felices comiendo perdices* (1970).

Janet Perez

Fani Popova-Mutafova

Born October 16, 1902, Sevlievo, Bulgaria; died July 9, 1977, Sofia
Genre(s): short story, novel, children's literature
Language(s): Bulgarian

Popova-Mutafova completed her elementary schooling in her native town and graduated from a high school in Sofia. Then she went to Germany where she studied music (1922–1925). She married Cavdar Mutafov, a representative of the formalist and expressionist trends in Bulgarian literature. Her first publications appeared in *Vestnik na Ženata* (Journal for Women) in 1924. Popova-Mutafova contributed also to *Bŭlgarska misŭl* (Bulgarian Thought) and *Zlatorog* (Golden Horn). Besides her stories for children Popova-Mutafova's works deal with two major themes, the fate of women in contemporary society and the struggles of Bulgarian historical personalities of the past.

In her short stories of the 1920s *Ženi* (Women), *Ženata s nebesnata roklja* (The Woman in the Blue Dress), *Srebrena svatba* (Silver Wedding), and *Ženata na prijatelja mi* (My Friend's Wife), Popova-Mutafova presents a woman's point of view of life. Some of the stories reveal in great detail the daily life of women in various domestic and social situations. Love, the relationship between mother and children, family problems, the fate of aging women, the difficulties and vicissitudes of village girls in the city, the role of career women, and other aspects of women's existence are portrayed in her works. Popova-Mutafova knew the psychology of women well, especially urban women. Without being a feminist in the present meaning of the term, Popova-Mutafova fought for the recognition of the moral and social worth and role of women and for their full equality as human beings.

Popova-Mutafova is remembered today mostly for her historical novels. In such works as *Solunskijat čudotvorec* (1929–1930; 1942, 2nd ed; 1969), *Dŭsterjata na Kalojana* (1936; Kalojan's Daughter), *Car Ivan Asen II* (1936), *Hristo Botev* (1937), *Angel Kŭncev* (1938), and *Doktor Petŭr Beron* (1972), the author evokes the heroism of Bulgaria's medieval past and the national renaissance period. Her novels depict the psychological make-up of individual heroes rather than the panorama of historical events and scenes.

Works

Momina skala. Legendi (1930). *Nedjalka Stamatova. Povest* (1933). *Junoši* (1934). *Ogledalo, nimbi i cvetja. Razkazi* (1934). *Car Kalojan. Istoriceska kartina* (1934). *Veliki senki. Razkazi* (1935, 1940, 1967, 1970). *Edna 'ena. Razkazi* (1936). *Na Krŭstopŭt. Povest* (1937, 1942). *Prikazki za Krali Marko* (1937, 1940). *Bojanskijat maistor* (1938). *Ioan Asen. Roman* (1938, 1940). *Poslednijat Asenovec. Roman* (1939, 1947). *Červeneta mantija* (1939, 1943). *Legendi* (1941). *Razkazi I–II* (1941–1943). *Kogato bjahme malki. Razakazi* (1979).

Bibliography

Dinekov, P., "Razkazite na Fani Popova-Mutafova." *Bŭlgarska misŭl* 16, 10 (1941): 543–551. Iliev, A., "Razkazite na Fani Popova-Mutafova." *Bŭlgarska misŭl* 5, 11 (1930): 163–168. Moser, Charles, *A History of Bulgarian Literature, 1865–1944* (1972), pp. 206–207. Nedjalkov, H. "Črez primera na beszmŭrtieto (Veliki senki)." *Literaturen Front,* 52 (March 21, 1967).

Philip Shashko

Adelheid Popp

Born 1869, near Vienna, Austria; died 1939
Genre(s): autobiography
Language(s): German

Adelheid Popp's autobiography *Die Jugendgeschichte einer Arbeiterin* (1910; The Autobiography of a Working Woman) and its sequel *Erinnerungen. Aus meinen Kindheits- und Mädchenjahren. Aus der Agitation und anderes* (1915; Memoirs. Childhood and Young Womanhood. Times of Struggle and Other Things) is important not only as one of the first proletarian autobiographies published in Europe around this time, it is also one of the most powerful and eloquently written of these texts. In addition, it is one of the relatively few books written by a woman about the particular lot of proletarian women, who were not only exploited as workers but sexually harassed, abused, and exploited as women. *Die Jugendgeschichte einer Arbeiterin* describes the social upheaval and class conflict in Austria during the years of the author's childhood and young womanhood, years of industrialization and capitalist expansion. It is a model of a socialist success story, charting a working-class child's rise out of poverty and oppression into the pride and dignity of a class-conscious struggle for rights and social change.

Born outside of Vienna, Adelheid Dworak was the fifteenth child of a weaver family. Her father, an alcoholic who frequently beat and abused his wife and children, died when she was six. After a mere three years of schooling, she was sent to work: domestic work in Viennese bourgeois households, piecework as a seamstress, and factory work in a variety of different establishments. Hospitalized for exhaustion as a result of overwork and inadequate physical care at age thirteen, she was able for the first time to rest, read, and think about life, work, and the options awaiting her in the future. Finding her own thoughts and experience reflected in contemporary socialist ideas, she involved herself in the Austrian socialist movement. From that time on nothing—not even marriage, two children and the need to continue wage labor—detracted her from the political path she chose: to organize and agitate for socialism and the emancipation of women and men of the working class. As an organizer, co-founder, and editor of a newspaper for women workers and the author of numerous treatises on women, politics, and work, Popp became internationally known as one of the leaders of the socialist women's movement in Austria.

Her *Jugendegeschichte*, which was first published through the support and under the auspices of the International Socialist movement (August Bebel wrote the foreword), was an immense popular success, especially among working-class women, the very audience Popp had most urgently wanted to reach. Within the first year of its publication, it had already gone through three editions; it was translated into English, French, Italian, Polish, Romanian, Swedish, Czech and Hungarian. Beginning with her childhood and ending in the present with the death of her husband and her commitment to a life of service in the socialist cause, *Jugendgeschichte* reads as the proletarian version of the bourgeois *Bildungsroman*, detailing her ascent out of the darkness of oppression into the light of working-class consciousness. Popp describes the bleakness of a joyless childhood: the scarcity of material things, the lack of education, the fear and helpless anger that turn into familial violence. She then describes the process of reading her way up and out: beginning with the escapist fiction (romantic tales of love and adventure) produced for a poorly-educated mass audience, she moves on to the classics of bourgeois high culture until she finally discovers the literature of socialist theory and analysis. This trajectory also marks the position from which she writes. Popp's narration of the experiences of her childhood and youth is informed by her present socialist-feminist consciousness. The "philanthropy" of a factory owner at Christmas thus, in retrospect, throws into even starker relief the fundamental brutality of the relationship between the haves and have-nots in a capitalist economy. Popp tells her story in a simple and straightforward way, without embellishments or sentimentality.

Popp's narrative focus and persona stand in marked contrast to the conventional bourgeois model of autobiographical writing. Her focus is not so much on the process of self-individuation as on the relationship between individual lives and the larger structures of class and social power relations within which they are embedded. In *Erinnerungen*, a text in which the autobiographical elements are consciously backgrounded to a much more programmatic emphasis on socialist and feminist analyses, personal stories (her own and those of people she has known or heard about) serve mainly to illustrate and anchor her political theses. The personal is of interest insofar as it is exemplary and can shed light on the larger, i.e., collective, social issues. Popp makes no effort to disguise her didactic intent: "If I felt the need to write about how I became a Socialist, it was solely out of the desire to encourage those countless women workers who yearn for fulfillment with a heart full of longing, but always draw back because they have no faith in their ability to achieve anything" (*Jugenderinnerungen*). For Popp, speaking as a woman worker for and to others like herself, writing is itself a politically emancipatory act.

Works

Autobiography: *Die Jugendgeschichte einer Arbeiterin* [The Autobiography of a Working Woman] (1910; tr. E.C. Harvey 1912; rpt. 1983). Note: The first, significantly edited, version of Popp's autobiography was published anonymously in 1909 as *Lebensgeschichte einer Arbeiterin von ihr selbst erzählt* [Life Story of a Working Woman as Told by Herself], in a series of working-class autobiographies published by E. Reinhardt. A late version was entitled simply *Jugend einer Arbeiterin* [Youth of a Working Woman] (1915; rpt., 1977). *Erinnerungen. aus meinen Kindheits- und Mädchenjahren. aus der Agitation und anderes* [Memoirs. Childhood and Young Womanhood. Times of Struggle and Other Things] (1915).

Political treatises: *Die Arbeiterin im Kampf ums Dasein* [The Working Woman in the Struggle for Survival] (1911). *Frauenarbeit in der kapitalistischen Gesellschaft* [Women's Work in Capitalist Society] (1922).

Bibliography

Emmerich, Wolfgang, ed., *Proletarische Lebensläufe. Autobiographische Dokumente zur Entstehung der Zweiten Kultur in Deutschland* (Reinbek bei Hamburg, 1974).

Angelika Bammer

V. Porechnikov

(see: Nadezhda Khvoshchinskaia)

Ethel Portnoy

Born March 8, 1927, Philadelphia,
*   Pennsylvania, U.S.A*
Genre(s): essay, short story, travel literature,
*   journalism*
Language(s): Dutch

Ethel Portnoy studied English literature in Wisconsin and New York and ethnology in Paris where she took classes with Lévi-Strauss, Leroi-Gouhan, and Roland Barthes. In 1961 she gave up a successful career at the International Theater Institute of UNESCO to devote all her time to writing. Since 1970 she has lived in The Hague, the Netherlands, with her husband, the Dutch writer and journalist Rudy Kousbroek. She states that she writes in English; her husband and friends help with the translation into Dutch.

Most of Ethel Portnoy's writing—whether "short stories," "sketches," or "travel stories"—is thinly veiled nonfiction, a successful amalgam of diary notes, cosmopolitan journalism and, above all, nimble-witted cultural reflection. The resulting genre, more American than Dutch and undoubtedly appropriate for *The New Yorker*, is an original contribution to a literature that has only very few practitioners of the cultural-historical essay in general.

Some of the pieces in *Steen en been* (1971; Stone and Bone), Portnoy's first collection of so-called short stories, have already become classics of contemporary Dutch letters. "Melk" (Milk) is both the emotional account of the writer's own (failed) attempt at breastfeeding her son and the cool intellectual observation of modern attitudes or "myths" about the issue. Memories of her childhood and youth among the Jewish immigrant community in Bronx Park East are recorded in "Een krans voor Sylvia" (A Wreath for Sylvia) and "Rosebud." Portnoy's own behavior and that of her friends during and after May 1968 in Paris are the topic of "I Dreamed I Went to the Revolution in My Maidenform Bra," which carries, between the lines, the sobering message that the "revolution" has not made much difference. In the

characteristic "Mijn bijdrage aan de Amerikaanse oorlogsinspanning" (My Contribution to the American War Effort) the author—as an artistically-minded young girl—meets her returned pen pal soldier but spoils the rendezvous by asking him what he would have done if he had been forced to make a choice between saving a human life and saving the Uffizi.

The relentless juxtaposition of different norms, customs, and behavior is not unrelated to the author's training in cultural and social anthropology. So is her careful and seemingly impassionate observation (marked by precise word choice), her capacity for wonder, and her interest in a wide range of topics. In "In memoriam Roland Barthes" (in Vliegende vellen), Portnoy observes that she was particularly struck by Barthes' curiosity about, if not love for, even the most trivial things. Like her admired teacher, she tries to read and understand the "signs" of our culture. *De geklede mens* (1986; Clothed Man) is a study on clothing seen as a reflection of sociological processes. The anthropologist Portnoy is most clearly at work in *Broodje aap* (1978; Monkey Sandwich), a slim volume subtitled "the folklore of post-industrial society." It is a curious collection of half-page reports—carefully numbered and annotated (sources, variants, significance . . .)—each one recording some (often well-known) instance of folk belief, such as the presence of monkey meat in hot dogs or the existence of revolving mirrors in fitting rooms for the purposes of white slavers.

Since *Steen en been*, Portnoy has contributed regularly to various literary journals and papers and collected her essays and stories on contemporary life and manners in a number of well-received volumes. Some very perceptive sketches on modern America, written from the vantage point of the informed outsider who occasionally returns to observe, record, and expose, are included in *Vliegende vellen* (1983; Flying Sheets) and *Vluchten* (1984; Flights). Portnoy also co-founded *Chrysallis* (1978–1981), a semi-annual journal published in book format aimed at promoting women authors and artists, and she edited a series of women authors in Dutch translation.

Though Ethel Portnoy is undoubtedly a refreshing and stimulating presence in Dutch literature, her elegant style, erudition, and ironic distance have occasionally been mistaken by critics unfamiliar with the genre for intellectual posing and lack of commitment. The choice of her topics, however, and the turn her observations take (she professes to try to achieve some sort of catharsis within the reader) betray great concern for mankind (as well as great fear of what is happening to it). In *Vliegende vellen* Portnoy characterizes modern Western consciousness as "enlightened cynicism." The term could easily be applied to her own sketches—with the emphasis on "enlightened" rather than "cynicism."

Works

Steen en been (1971). *De brandende bruid* (1973). *Belle van Zuylen ontmoet Cagliostro: een toneelstuk in twee bedrijvan* (1978). *Broodje aap* (1978). *Het ontwaken van de zee* (1981). *Vliegende vellen* (1983). *Vluchten* (1984). *Amourettes en andere verhalen* (1984). *Een hondeleven* (1984–1985). *De geklede mens* (1986).

Bibliography

Brunt E., interview "De angst om levend begraven te worden." *Haagse Post* (January 6, 1979). *Ethel Portnoy, Informatie* (Literair Moment) (1984). Spoor, C., Interview, *De Tijd* (March 23, 1984). Van der Veken, I., "Ethel Portnoy over Chrysallis." *De Vlaamse Gids* 62, No. 4 (1978). Vogelaar, J.F., *Konfrontaties: kritieken en commentaren* (1974). General references: *De Nederlandse en Vlaamse auteurs van middeleeuwen tot heden* (1985). *Kritisch Lexicon van de Nederlandstalige Literatuur na 1945* (article on Portnoy by D. Schouten, 1980). *Winkler Prins Lexicon der Nederlandse letterkunde* (1986).

Ria Vanderauwera

Veronica Porumbacu

(a.k.a. Maria Radu)

Born 1921, Bucharest, Romania; died 1977, Bucharest
Genre(s): poetry, memoirs, short story, translation
Language(s): Romanian

Veronica Porumbacu's poetic debut—*Visele Babei Dochia* (1947; The Dreams of Baba Dochia)—was promising and acclaimed. Hers

seemed to be a poetry of organic life and serene lyrical wandering and meditation. Then came twenty years of sad confusion between poetry and politics. Veronica Porumbacu turned into "Comrade Veronica," a member of the cultural *nomenklatura*, and her poetry, crushed by ideological disponibility and dominated by such conventional themes of the Romanian fifties as the glorification of the Communist Party, of life in the Soviet Union, of the electrification and industrialization, of the Revolution, of Marxist-Leninist aesthetics—this was the substance of the volumes *Anii aceştia* (1950; These Years), *Mărturii* (1951; Testimonies), *Ilie Pintilie* (1953), *Generaţia mea* (1955; My Generation), *Lirice* (1957; Lyrical Poems)—simply ceased to matter. In 1971 Porumbacu gathered in a volume entitled *Cerc* (Circle) fifty poems which represented all that could be redeemed from an overproductive and self-destructive poetic career. This sober autocritical gesture made public an implicit and tenacious process of personal and poetic recovery initiated in the volumes *Dimineţile simple* (1961; Simple Mornings), *Memoria cuvintelor* (1963; The Memory of the Words), *Intoarcerea din Cytera* (1966; The Return from Cythera), *Histriana* (1968) and brought to relevant fruition in the authentic and personal *Mineralia* (1970) or *Voce* (1971; Voice). The last two volumes spoke simply and strongly about duty and guilt, deserved abandonment, the fear of words, the loss of identity, and spiritual death. It was late though, Porumbacu's contact with the public had been irremediably harmed, and her new poems were neither read by ordinary readers nor taken into consideration by the literary critics of the seventies. The years between 1970 and 1977 (when Veronica Porumbacu died in the great Bucharest earthquake of March 3) were years of silent, solitary, and unacknowledged expiation.

Besides poetry, Veronica Porumbacu wrote several volumes of short stories and memories— *La capătul lui 38* (1947; At the End of 38), *Bilet în circuit* (1965; Circuit Ticket), *Porţile* (1968; The Gates), *Drumuri şi zile* (1969; Journeys and Days), *Voce şi val* (1976; Voice and Wave)—as well as a dramatic poem—*Fata apelor* (1954; The Maid of the Waters). Her numerous poems for children were gathered in *Ilinca pleacă la ţară* (1956; Ilinca Leaves for the Countryside), *Din lumea noastră* (1960; From Our World), *Lung e drumul Dunării* (1964; The Way of the Danube Is Long), *Ferestre deschise* (1971; Open Windows), *Cercul și Anamaria* (1974; The Circle and Anamaria).

Veronica Porumbacu was an inspired translator into Romanian of Rafael Alberti, Mariana Alcoforado, Max Frisch, St. Hermlin, N. Hikmet, József Attila, Kiss Jenó, Fr. Schiller, W. Raabe, Szemler Ferenc, Emily Dickinson (among others) as well as the dynamic editor of an anthology of feminine lyricism (1960). Her subtle study of Romanian writers in *Legende la niște portrete* (1974; Legends for Some Portraits) attest to another facet of her artistic personality and show her generous openness to beauty in others' work and expression.

Works

La capătul lui 38 [At the End of 38] (1947). *Visele Babei Dochia* [The Dreams of Baba Dochia. Poetry] (1947). *Anii aceștia.* Versuri [These Years. Poetry] (1950). *Mărturii.* Versuri [Testimonies. Poetry] (1951). *Femeia în Republica Populară Română, constructor activ al socialismului* [The Woman in the Popular Republic of Romania, An Active Builder of Socialism] (1952). *Ilie Pintilie.* Versuri [Ilie Pintilie. Poetry] (1953). *Prietenii mei.* Versuri [My Friends. Poetry] (1953). *Fata apelor.* Poem dramatic [The Maid of the Waters. A Dramatic Poem] (1954). *Generația mea.* Versuri [My Generation. Poetry] (1955). *Ilinca pleacă la țară* [Ilinca Leaves for the Countryside] (1957). *Lirice* [Lyrical Poems] (1957). *Întreg și parte.* Versuri [The Whole and the Part. Poetry] (1959). *Din lumea noastră.* Versuri pentru copii [From Our World. Poetry for Children] (1960). *Pagini din Coreea* [Pages from Korea] (1960). *Diminețile simple.* Versuri [Simple Mornings. Poetry] (1961). *Memoria cuvintelor.* Versuri [The Memory of the Words. Poetry] (1963). *Lung e drumul Dunării.* Versuri pentru copii [The Way of the Danube Is Long. Poetry for Children] (1964). *Bilet în circuit.* Proză [Circuit Ticket. Prose] (1965). *Întoarcerea din Cytera.* Versuri [The Return from Cythera. Poetry] (1966). *Histriana.* Versuri [Histriana. Poetry] (1968). *Porțile.* Proză [The Gates. Prose] (1968). *Drumuri și zile.* Proză memorialistică [Journeys and Days. Memoralistic Prose] (1969). *Mineralia.* Versuri [Mineralia. Poetry] (1970). *Cerc* [Circle] (1971). *Ferestre deschise.* Versuri pentru copii [Open Windows. Poetry for Children] (1971). *Legende la niște portrete. Desene* [Legends for Some Portraits. Drawings] (1974). *Voce.* Versuri [Voice. Poems] (1974). *Cercul și Anamaria.* Versuri pentru copii (1974) [The Circle and Anamaria. Poetry for Children]. *Voce și val.* Proză [Voice and Wave. Prose] (1976).

Translations: Emery, George, ed., *Contemporary East European Poetry*, tr. Marguerite Dorian and Elliott Urdang (Ann Arbor, 1983), pp. 314–315. *Mondus Artium*, tr. Marguerite Dorian and Elliott Urdang, The Journal of International Literature and the Arts VII, 2 (1974): 112.

Bibliography

Caraion, Ion, *Duelul cu crini* (Bucharest, 1972), pp. 123–125. Caraion, Ion, *Jurnal I.* Literatură și contraliteratură (Bucharest, 1980), pp. 149–160. Călinescu, G., *Literatura nouă* (Craiova, 1972), pp. 106–113, 204–208. Georgescu, Paul, "Evocare," in Veronica Porumbacu, *Versuri.* Antologie întocmită de Paul Georgescu (Bucharest, 1978), pp. 15–18. Popa, Marian, *Dicționar de literatură română contemporană.* 2nd ed. (Bucharest, 1977), pp. 451–452.

Sanda Golopentia

L. Post-Beukens

(a.k.a. Ypk van der Fear, Ella Wassenaar)

Born 1908, Sondel, The Netherlands
Genre(s): novel
Language(s): Dutch

She writes serious novels on themes chosen from church history. She has also written love lyrics under her pseudonym Ella Wassenaar.

Works

Utskot (1943). *De deade by de libbene* (1959). *Reade runen* (1959, 1974). *Eilân fan de silligen* (1966).

Bibliography

Tiny Mulder in Hwer hast' it wei (1971).

Mary Hatch

Jan Powalski

(see: Aniela Gruszecka)

Antonia Pozzi

Born February 13, 1912, Milan, Italy; died
December 8, 1938, Milan
Genre(s): poetry, literary criticism
Language(s): Italian

A suicide at age twenty-six, Antonia Pozzi died unpublished, having shared her poetry with few privileged friends. The posthumous publication of her only collection, privately funded by her family, received critical plaudits both in Italy and abroad, including translations into French, German, and Romanian. Although quite individual, Pozzi's lyrics mirror poetic trends of the Italian 1930s, notably Hermeticism's symbolic use of imagery and emphasis on the word and a lingering crepuscular melancholy and weariness.

Pozzi demonstrated an innate talent for literature both as a poet and as a budding critic. Her doctoral thesis on French literature at the University of Milan, *Flaubert. La formazione letteraria* (Flaubert's Literary Formation), was also privately published after her death and exhibits a keen critical sensitivity although not yet fully developed.

Her major work, *Parole 1930–1938* (1939; Words 1930–1938), underwent three editions in ten years, each adding to Pozzi's published output. The last (1948) includes a significant preface by Nobel laureate Eugenio Montale, who discusses Pozzi's lack of sentimentality and her poetic vigor. In fact, her verse is a frank and often pessimistic expression of emotion, depicted through a series of natural images (such as ice, frozen waters, darkness, and birds) that recall the analogical play of Hermetic poetry. Its themes of death, separation, and hopelessness are moderated by *Parole*'s religious overtones and certain feminine nuances.

Having rejected the rhetorical eloquence of much conventional Italian verse, Pozzi's prosody is reductive. *Parole* emphasizes the essentialism of the single, pure word—understood as sound as well as image—in its relationship to the object signified, in the manner of such great masters of Hermeticism as Giuseppe Ungaretti and Salvatore Quasimodo.

Works

Poems: *Parole 1930–1938* (1937, 1943, 1948).
Criticism: *Flaubert: La formazione letteraria* (1940).

Bibliography

Amelotti, L., *Antonia Pozzi nella sua poesia* (Genova, 1953). Annoni, Carlo, "*Parole* di Antonia Pozzi: Lettura tematica." *Saga og sprak: Studies in Language and Literature*, ed. John M. Weinstock (Austin, 1972), II, pp. 242–259. Montale, Eugenio, "La poesia di Antonia Pozzi." *Fiera letteraria* (November 21, 1948). Solfrizzi, Ada, "Antonia Pozzi." *Iride* 9 (1969): 94–98. Spagnoletti, Giacinto, *Antologia della poesia italiana (1909–1949)* (Parma, 1950).

Fiora A. Bassanese

Catherine Pozzi

Born July 13, 1882; died 1934, Paris
Genre(s): poetry, essay
Language(s): French

Catherine Pozzi was blessed with many talents: she handled equally easily music, poetry, physics, and mathematics. Her poetry, similar in spirit to that of Louise Labe in its focus on inner transformation, is deeply inspirational and elaborate. Gerard d'Houville named her "one of the rarest feminine minds that we knew."

Works

"Poemes." In *Mesures*. Published posthumously, with introduction by J. Benda (1936). *Peau d'ame*, philosophical and scientific essays with introduction by G. d'Houville (1937).

Bibliography

Lexicon der Frau. Encyclios verlag, Vol. 2 (Zurich, 1954).

Jean E. Jost

Modesta Pozzo

(a.k.a. Moderata Fonte)

Born 1555, Venice, Italy; died November 2,
1592, Venice
Genre(s): treatise, madrigal, sonnet
Language(s): Italian

Modesta Pozzo de' Zorzi, the second child of Cicilia and Hieronimo Pozzo, was born in Venice. Both her parents died in her infancy, and she was raised by relatives. As customary for girls at the time, she was sent to a convent until she reached the age of nine. Back home, her relatives noticed her eagerness to learn and allowed her to start serious study of Latin, painting, music, and math. Soon Modesta came to be known as a child prodigy and was even asked by the Venetian oligarchy to recite her poems in their presence. She married Filippo de'Zorzi and had four children.

In 1581 some of Modesta Pozzo's madrigals and sonnets were published under the title *Tredici canti del Floridoro*. But Pozzo's fame rests on *Il merito della donne*, a posthumous treatise which appeared under the pseudonym Moderata Fonte. According to her daughter Cicilia, who was responsible for the publication together with Pozzo's other son, Pietro, Modesta was still working on *Il merito* the day she died.

Pozzo's treatise was one of tens published during the Renaissance. Most were printed in Venice, a city famous both for the quantity and quality of its publication. Several works on women's worth are justifiably famous, such as Book 3 of B. Castiglione's *Il libro del cortegiano* (1528; The Book of the Courtier) and G.F. Capella's *Della eccellenza et degnita' delle donne* (1529; Of the Excellence and Worth of Women). But no treatise by a woman had ever been published before Pozzo's *Il merito delle donne*.

Pozzo's structure is dialogic with an even number of discussants, pro and con, facing each other. In *Il merito* there are six debaters: three argue in favor of women's need for recognition, education and independence; and three argue for maintaining the *status quo*. The conversation occurs in a garden, a place more accessible to "honest" women than either the streets or salons of earlier, male-authored treatises on women. Remarkable in Pozzo's work is the authority with which women talk about politics, medicine and philosophy, and the familiarity they display with past and contemporary literature. Statements and verses by famous authors are occasionally quoted almost *verbatim*, but the effect is different.

What makes the difference is that women do the talking in *Il merito* and the result is startlingly original. By comparison, Castiglione had the most influential male discussants in his group take the defense of women, praise them and talk on their behalf. But they talked as men, thus enforcing, propagandizing and legitimizing men's opinions about women's identity and proper sphere of action. Were they interested in knowing what women think and how they value themselves, they would have asked the court ladies to join in their discussion. Instead they used women's presence to universalize their ideological assumptions; since women could not speak, let alone protest, they assumed that they approved what they heard about themselves.

In this context Pozzo's treatise is strikingly revisionary. She questions and challenges history because it excludes women. She expounds at length on herbal medicine because customarily women have known much about herbs. She praises famous antique women, but not for the conventional virtue of chastity. Her tone can be vituperative, calm or philosophical. Whatever the scene, she is conscious of her rhetorical power and uses logic to her advantage. Today she will be remembered, together with Lucrezia Marinella and Arcangela Tarabotti, as one of the three most gifted women writers of the 17th century.

Works

Tredici canti del Floridoro (1581). *Le feste. Rappresentazione* (1581). *La Passione di Christo* (1582). *La Resurrettione di Giesu Christo Nostro Signore* (1592). *Il merito della donne* (1600, rpt. 1979, 1988).

Bibliography

Chemello, Adriana, "Gioco e dissimulazione in Moderata Fonte," in Moderata Fonte, *Il merito delle donne*, ed. Adriana Chemello (Venezia, 1988). Chemello, Adriana, "Donna di palazzo, moglie, cortigiana: ruoli e funzioni sociali della donna in alcuni trattati del Cinquecento," in *La corte e il cortegiano* II. *Un modello europeo*, ed. Adriano Prosperi (Roma, 1980). Chemello, Adriana, "La donna, il modello, l'immaginario: Moderata Fonte e Lucrezia Marinella," in *Nel cerchio della luna. Figure di donna in alcuni testi del XVI secolo*, ed. Marina Zancan (Venezia, 1983). Chemello, Adriana, "Giochi ingegnosi e citazioni dotte: immagini del 'femminile'." *Nuova dwf* 25/26 (1985): 39–55. Conti-Odorisio, Ginevra, "Moderata Fonte. *Il merito delle donne*," in *Donna e societa' nel Seicento* (Roma, 1979). Zanette, Emilio, "Bianca Capello e la sua poetessa." *Nuova Antologia* 88 (1953): 455–468.

Valeria Finucci

Ion Pravilă

(see: Margareta Miller-Verghi)

Praxilla

Born Sicyon, Greece; fl. about 451 B.C.
Genre(s): poetry
Language(s): Greek

Nothing is known of Praxilla's life, and only a few lines of her poetry are preserved. The most notorious come, apparently, from a hymn to Aphrodite in hexameter verse (*PMG* 747). Adonis, the youth beloved by the goddess and slain by a boar, is asked by the inhabitants of the underworld to name the most beautiful thing he has left behind, and naively responds: "Most beautiful is the light of the sun; second, the shining stars and the moon's face; and also ripe cucumbers and apples and pears." As the cult of Adonis was linked to the cycle of vegetation, the dead boy's nostalgia for fruits in season is ritually appropriate. But the abrupt juxtaposition of celestial bodies and cucumbers, poignant to the modern reader, was too bizarre for ancient critics; "sillier than Praxilla's Adonis" became proverbial.

A second fragment (*PMG* 754) is enigmatic. A female addressee "looking beautifully through the windows" is termed "as to your head, unwedded; bride beneath." This is, according to the standard explanation, a riddling description of Selene, the moon: shining high in the night sky, she appears coldly virginal, but, sinking beneath the horizon, she enters the bed of Endymion. Recent guesswork associates the lines with the iconography of a Near Eastern fertility goddess portrayed as sitting at a window.

Praxilla also wrote a dithyramb entitled "Achilles." The single surviving line tells of the hero's refusal to yield to persuasion—probably an allusion to the unsuccessful Greek embassy in the ninth book of the *Iliad*. She gave novel treatment to other mythic themes, making Dionysus the child of Aphrodite and having Chrysippus, the son of Pelops, carried off by Zeus. Two pieces of proverbial wisdom attributed to her were encapsulated in *paroinia*, short drinking-songs sung at symposia; both reflect a conventionally aristocratic, male-ordered view of experience.

Works

Greek texts and German translations in Homeyer, H., *Dichterinnen des Altertums und des frühen Mittelalters* (Paderborn, 1979). Greek texts in *Poetae Melici Graeci*, ed. D.L. Page (Oxford, 1962). English translations in *Lyra Graeca* III, tr. J.M. Edmonds. Loeb Classical Library (Cambridge, Mass., 1959).

Bibliography

Kirkwood, G.M., *Early Greek Monody: The History of a Poetic Type* (Ithaca, 1974). Snyder, J.M., *The Woman and the Lyre* (Carbondale, Il., 1989). Trypanis, C.A., *Greek Poetry from Homer to Seferis* (Chicago, 1981).

General references: *Cambridge History of Classical Literature I: Greek Literature*, eds. P.E. Easterling and B.M.W. Knox (Cambridge, 1985), p. 241. *Oxford Classical Dictionary* (Oxford, 1970), p. 874. Pauly-Wissowa, *Real-Encyclopädie der klassischen Altertumswissenschaft* XXII.2 (Stuttgart, 1954), pp. 1762–1768.

Marilyn B. Skinner

Gabriela Preissová

Born 1862, Kutná Hora, Czechoslovakia; died 1946, Prague
Genre(s): short story, drama
Language(s): Czech

Although Preissová (born Ro'ena Sekerová) wrote numerous short stories and plays up until the 1930s, her most important work dates from the 1880s. Her works almost always describe the everyday life of country folk with much local color. Against this background, the focus is typically on a young heroine, an innocent victim of ill-fated love and of social prejudices. Preissová's interest in peasant life and folk traditions was influenced by the example of Bozena Nemcova, Carolina Svetla, and other Czech writers. Jan Herben was a precursor in the depiction of

Slovak life. Preissová also drew on her life and travels in Bohemia, Moravia, Slovakia, and Austrian border areas.

Preissová's best-known works are the three-volume short-story collection *Obrázky ze Slovácka* (1886–1889; Pictures from Slovakia) and two plays, *Gazdina roba* (premiere, 1889) and *Její pastorkyňa* (premiere, 1890; Her Ward). These plays premiered at Prague's Národní Divadlo (National Theater), at that time one of the most important centers of the Czech national revival movement. Preissová's plays were among the very first Realist plays depicting country life performed at the National Theater. As such, they influenced later plays in this genre. *Gazdina roba* was used by J.B. Foerster as the basis of his opera *Eva* (1899); *Její pastorkyňa* was reworked by Leos Janáček for his opera *Jenůfa* (1904). Preissová's works are in the mainstream of Czech "ethnographic" literature. They are important as a part of the cultural renaissance of the second half of the nineteenth century.

Works

Preissová, Gabriela, *Spisy sebrane* [Collected Works] (Prague, 1910–1915), in 18 vols. For a complete list of works, see Závodský, below, pp. 269–279.

Bibliography

Homolová, Květa, and Mojmír Otruba, Zdeňka Pešsta, eds., *Čeští spisovatelé 19. a počátku 20. stoletî: Slovníková přiručka* (Prague, 1982), pp. 219–220. Závodský, Arthur, *Gabriela Preissová* [Spisy University J.E. Purkyně v Brně. Filosofická fakulta, vol. 88] (Prague, 1962).

English translations: Roskicky, Rose, tr., "Immortal," "Just before Sunset," "The Whistle," in *Českobratrský věstník* (1927). Tr. of "Nesmrtělný," "Před západem slunce," "Máma píst'alka."

Nancy Cooper

Paula von Preradović

Born October 12, 1887, Vienna; died May 25, 1951, Vienna, Austria
Genre(s): poetry, novella, novel, wrote the national anthem of Austria
Language(s): German

Paula von Preradović may be considered a connecting link between the two Austrias, the supranational, multicultural monarchy and the small German-speaking republic that replaced it in 1918. Born in Vienna in 1887, she spent her childhood in Pola (now Pula, Yugoslavia), Austria's main naval port, where her father, Du'an, served in the imperial navy. Her grandfather was Petar von Preradović, a general and the most important Croatian writer of the nineteenth century. Her mother was the daughter of a German aristocrat.

The duality that is characteristic for the poet's biography is reflected in her oeuvre. When, after the collapse of the empire, Preradović began to write, she elevated that part of Austria that had been lost politically into the sphere of literature. As reflected in the titles of her poetry collections, *Südlicher Sommer* (Southern Summer) and *Dalmatinische Sonette* (Dalmatian Sonnets), her poetic world encompasses the Adriatic coast with cities such as Trieste, Pola, and Ragusa (now Dubrovnik), the peninsula of Istria with its Italian population amidst a Croatian environment and, above all, the Adriatic Sea, that common bond between the various nationalities of the region.

However, just as Preradović did not succumb to a futile yearning for something that could not be regained and adjusted to the new realities, she includes her more limited Northern homeland with its mountains, its glaciers, and its waterfalls in her poetry. As the title of her poetry collection *Lob Gottes im Gebirge* (Praising God in the Mountains) suggests, many of her poems have a religious overtone that critics, applying today's standards, have labeled naive and old fashioned. Preradović had attended a prestigious Catholic school in St. Pölten and, consequently, Catholicism became a constituent element of her entire life and work.

Between the wars Preradović lived in Vienna as the wife of a prominent journalist and newspaper editor, Ernst Molden. Both of them were

Austrian patriots, and the events of 1938 did not bend their spirits. In spite of interrogations and imprisonment, Preradović's love for Austria prevailed. It is reflected, albeit cautiously, in *Pave und Pero*, a novel set in Vienna and Dalmatia and based on the correspondence between her grandfather and his first wife. It is the story of a young woman who does not have the courage to confess to her husband the death of her child. She gets caught in a web of lies and finally commits suicide. In her novel Preradović also conjures up the spirit of Austria, something not to be taken for granted in 1940. A second edition of the novel was not approved.

Paula von Preradović closed the link between the two Austrias when, after World War II, she wrote the lyrics for the country's new national anthem (based on a melody by Mozart), a work for which she is probably best known in contemporary Austria.

The publication of *Pave und Pero* in a new edition in 1987 is an indication that, after many years of neglect, there is renewed interest in the work of Paula von Preradović.

Works

Poetry: *Südlicher Sommer* (1929). *Dalmatinische Sonette* (1933). *Lob Gottes im Gebirge* (1936). *Ritter, Tod und Teufel* (1947).
Novel: *Pave und Pero* (1940).
Novellas: *Nach dem Tode* (1949). *Königslegende* (1950). *Die Versuchung des Columba* (1951).
Collections: *Meerferne Heimat*, ed. Werner Röttinger (1961). *Gesammelte Werke*, ed. Kurt Eigl (1967).

Bibliography

Eigl, Kurt, "Einleitung. Paula von Preradović," in *Gesammelte Werke*, ed. Kurt Eigl (Vienna, 1967), pp. 7–16. Röttinger, Werner, Foreword, "Paula von Preradović," in *Meerferne Heimat*, ed. Werner Röttinger (Graz, Vienna, 1961), pp. 5–23. Rovan, Joseph, "Paula von Preradović." *Autonomie und Kontrolle: Steuerungskrisen der modernen Welt: Europäisches Forum Alpbach 1986*, ed. Otto Molden (Vienna, n.d.), pp. 485–497. Vospernik, Reginald, "Paula von Preradović: Leben und Werk." Diss., University of Vienna, 1960.

Jürgen Koppensteiner

Madame de Pringy

Born probably second part of XVIIth century; died first part of XVIIIth century
Genre(s): novel
Language(s): French

Very little is known about the life of Mme de Pringy except that she was the daughter of M. de Marenville. She married the Count of Pringy, and after his death she married M. d'Aura, lord of Entragues, in 1709 but kept writing under the name of Pringy.

Her works are characterized by a tone of severe and high morality and by the somewhat haughty elegance of her style. The success of La Bruyère's *Characters* incited many authors to follow his example. Her *Diverse Characteristics of the Ladies of the Century* describes successively a coquette, a religious bigot, a miserly woman, a gambler, and a litigious one, to chastise them and to advise them on how to improve.

Madame de Pringy also wrote discourses praising Louis XIV and a book on the life of Father Bourdaloue, a Jesuit famous for the quality of his sermons. This particular work, though incomplete, and in spite of its eulogistic tone, is factually exact and has been one of the most important sources of information on Bourdaloue's life.

Works

Les différents caractères de l'amour [The Diverse Characteristics of Love] (1685). *Les différents caractères des femmes du siècle, avec la description de l'amour propre, contenant six caractères et six perfections* [The Diverse Characteristics of the Ladies of the Century, with the Description of Self Esteem, Including Six Characteristics and Six Ways to Improve] (1694). *Junie ou les sentiments romains* [Junie or Roman Feelings] (1695). *L'amour à la mode, satire historique* [Fashionable Love, a Historical Satire] (1695). *Critique contre la prévention* [Criticism Against Prevention] (1702). *La vie de P. Bourdaloue, de la C.J.* [Father Bourdaloue's Life] (1705). *Traité des vrais malheurs de l'homme* [Essay on True Human Misfortune] (1707).

Marie-France Hilgar

Aulikki Prinkki

(see: Elvi Sinervo)

Anna Prismanova

Born 1898, Russia; died 1960, Paris, France
Genre(s): poetry
Language(s): Russian

Anna Prismanova was part of the "first wave" of emigrants to depart Russia after the Revolution of 1917 and the ensuing Civil War. Unlike the emigrants of the "older" generation (V. Khodasevich, G. Adamovich), she and other young poets developed their craft only during life in exile. Her poetry was not in keeping with the "Parisian note," a term defined in large part by Adamovich. This mood or taste in poetry was characterized by a dislike for aestheticism, *épatage*, and experimentation and instead inclined towards the direct expression of emotion and simplicity. Prismanova's poetry is not easily accessible and requires very careful reading.

It is unfortunate that Anna Prismanova's work is not well known in the West, for her poetry is remarkably original and innovative. Her versification is quite simple and conventional (the iamb is her favorite meter), but strong concrete images seemingly unrelated to one another are juxtaposed, which lends to her work a strong grotesque element. This effect is heightened by her experiments with the rules of grammar and logic. It is necessary to "read her poems carefully, they are purposely made difficult, in them is almost always a second plane [of meaning]" (Gleb Struve).

Works

Ten' i telo (1937). Bliznetsy: Vtoraya kniga stikhov (1946). Sol': tretya kniga stikhov (1949). Vera: liricheskaya povest' (1960).
Translations: "Blood and Bone" (1946), in *Modern Russian Poetry*, ed. Vladimir Markov and Merrill Sparks (1967), pp. 476–477. Selected poems, in *A Russian Cultural Revival*, ed. and tr. Temira Pachmuss (1981), pp. 396–399.

Bibliography

Ivask, Yurii, "Poeziya staroi emigratsii," in *Russkaya literatura v emigratsii: Sbornik statei*, ed. N.P. Poltoratskii (Pittsburgh, 1972), p. 65. Pachmuss, Temira, ed. and tr., *A Russian Cultural Revival* (Knoxville, 1981), pp. 396–397. Struve, Gleb, *Russkaya literatura v izgnanii* (New York, 1956), pp. 336–337.

Laura Jo Turner McCullough

Proba

(a.k.a. Faltonia Proba, Falconia Proba, Betitia Proba, Betitia)

Flourished c. A.D. 350 Italy
Genre(s): poetry
Language(s): Latin

Proba belonged to the Anicii family, whose members held high office in the Late Empire. There were several women named "Proba" in the family, however, and which one composed the cento is not entirely certain. The most likely candidates are Falconia Proba, who was the wife of the proconsul Clodius Celsinus Adelphius, and her granddaughter, Faltonia Proba, with the former enjoying slightly more favor among scholars. At some stage, Proba converted to Christianity but rejected asceticism. She probably wrote her cento in response to Julian the Apostate's edict forbidding Christians to teach rhetoric in the schools. Her work also represents an act of self-assertion in a community which, in the tradition of Paul, excluded women from engaging in theology. Nevertheless, in her religious views Proba follows the orthodox line, including the doctrine that woman was the original cause of evil in the world.

The cento is prefaced by an introduction in which Proba says that before her conversion to Christianity she had written of "civil wars": this has given rise to speculation that she tried her hand at epic poetry. The cento proper is about 700 lines in length and begins with the Creation, the Fall, and the Flood. After the story of the Exodus and the Giving of the Laws, Proba leaves the Old Testament, with the comment that everyone knows it anyway, and moves on to tell a highly abbreviated version of the life and death of Jesus Christ.

Virgil's lines are adapted to their new Christian purpose with varying degrees of success.

The Creation, for example, is a happy patchwork of appropriate lines from the *Eclogues*, the *Aeneid*, and especially the *Georgics*. In the Exodus and the Last Supper, however, the language is frequently strained, almost to the point of incomprehensibility. Several words and phrases ring somewhat strangely in the ears of a reader familiar with the original Virgilian context; in addition, spellings are changed, syllables are lengthened, and metrical rules are disregarded. Equally, the impossibility of finding enough Virgilian lines to retell all the biblical stories in detail sometimes results in drastic cuts or obscurity. It may have been for this reason that Jerome condemned the cento, which was relegated to the list of Apocryphal writings by Pope Gelasius in 496.

In spite of its faults, Proba's cento was immediately popular and remained so, particularly, it may be assumed, among educated Romans who found the language and style of most Christian writers disagreeably primitive. The cento also testifies to the great influence of Virgil on later Latin poetry and to Proba's remarkably thorough knowledge of his works.

Bibliography

A critical text of the cento is found in *Poetae Christiani: Minores, Pars I: Probae Cento*, ed. C. Schenkl, in *Corpus Scriptorum Ecclesiasticorum Latinorum*, vol. 16 (Vienna, 1890), pp. 511–609. A text, translation, and comprehensive bibliography are provided in E.A. Clark and D.F. Hatch, *The Golden Bough, The Oaken Cross. The Virgilian Cento of Faltonia Betitia Proba (American Academy of Religion, Texts and Translations 5)* (Chico, CA, 1981). von Aschback, J.R., *Die Anicier und die Romische Dichterin Proba* (Wien, 1870). *A Lost Tradition. Women Writers of the Early Church*, ed. P. Wilson-Kastner (Washington, 1981), pp. 33–69.

David H.J. Larmour

Betitia Proba

(see: Proba)

Falconia Proba

(see: Proba)

Faltonia Proba

(see: Proba)

Alvilde Prydz

Born August 5, 1846, Berg i Østfeld, Norway;
died September 5, 1922, Christiania
Genre(s): novel, novella, drama
Language(s): Norwegian

Alvilde Prydz' authorship has its roots in the idealistic individualism of Kierkegaard and Ibsen. A central theme in her works is that self-realization without the interference of societal pressure and conventions is a basic right and duty for all mankind.

As a young woman, Alvilde Prydz worked as a governess until she had a breakdown in 1870 from overwork. Thereafter, she kept house for her father for many years. Alvilde Prydz was an avid reader and felt a calling to write fiction. She had difficulties finding a publisher and had to pay for the publication of her first work, *Agn og Agnar* (1880; Agn and Agnar), herself.

In 1884, at the age of thirty-eight, she travelled to Copenhagen, which was her first foray outside of Norway. In Copenhagen, she was influenced by her personal acquaintances with Erik Skram and Camilla Collette. Alvilde Prydz achieved most of her literary successes in the 1890s. Her novel *Lykke* (1890; Happiness) tells the story of a woman wasting away in a marriage, even though her circumstances conform to society's formula for happiness. Her best novel is generally considered to be *Gunvor Thorsdatter til Hæro* (1896; The Heart of the Northern Sea, 1907), in which Alvilde Prydz presents in the title character her image of ideal womanhood: free, strong, independent and loyal. Bjørnstjerne Bjørnson described *Gunvor Thorsdatter til Hæro* as one of the best novels of the year.

Alvilde Prydz continued to write throughout her life, but she was never able to match her attainments of the 1890s. Some feel that the topical concerns of her novels have not worn well through time. Alvilde Prydz' life was fraught with personal hardship and financial worries. She is perhaps best remembered for her lament to Bjørnson: "What an unspeakable torment it is in this country to be a woman and a writer!"

Works

Agn og Agnar (1880). *I Moll* (1885). *Undervejs* (1889). *Lykke* (1890). *Paa Fuglvik* (1891). *Arnak* (1892). *Mennesker* (1892). *Drøm* (1893). *Bellis* (1895). *Gunvor Thorsdatter til Hærø* (1896). *Smaastel*(1896). *Blade* (1898). *Sylvia* (1899). *Aino* (1900). *Det Lovede Land* (1902). *Undine* (1904). *Barnene paa Hæro Gaard* (1906). *I Ulvedalen* (1909). *Fortællinger* (1910). *Mens det var sommer* (1911). *To enaktere: Han kommer; I Fortrolighet* (1911). *Torbjørn Vik* (1913). *Paa Granem Gaard* (1915). *Digte* (1916). *De dage og de aar* (1918). Translations: *The Heart of the Northern Sea*, tr. Tyra Engdahl and Jessie Row (1907). *Sanpriel. The Promised Land*, tr. Hester Coddington (1914). "He Is Coming, A Play in One Act," tr. Hester Coddington, in *Poet Lore* XXV, No. 3 (1914): 230–244. "In Confidence, A One-Act Play," tr. Arvid Paulson (1923).

Bibliography

Brochmann, Georg, "Striden om statsstøtte og stipendier. Sivlesaken og Alvilde Prydzsaken." *Den norske forfatterforening* (1952). Dahl, Willy, *Nytt norsk forfatterleksikon* (Oslo, 1971). Halvorsen, J.B., *Norsk Forfatter-Lexikon 1814–1880* (Christiania, 1896). Heber, Lilly, *Kvindeskikkelser i norsk aandslivs historia* (Oslo, 1925). Thesen, Rolv, *Mennesket i oss* (1951). Tunold, Solveig, "Alvilde Prydz." *Norsk Biografisk Leksikon* (Oslo, 1952).

Susan Brantley

Dagny Juel Przybyszewska

Born June 8, 1867, Kongsvinger, Norway; died
June 5, 1901, Tblisi, Caucasus, Georgia
(USSR)
Genre(s): drama, poetry, sketches
Language(s): Norwegian

Among the bohemian circle of Scandinavian writers and artists who gathered at *Zum schwarzen Ferkel*, The Black Piglet Pub of 1890s Berlin, was the Norwegian author, playwright, poet, and *femme fatale*, Dagny Juel. Juel acted as a catalyst, "the inspiration (for Scandinavian) geniuses" active in Berlin (*Norges Litteratur Historie*, 4, 57), August Strindberg and Edvard Munch among them (*Aschehoug og Gyldendals Store Norske Leksikon*, 6, 560). To the acclaimed grand old man of the Scandinavian bohemians, August Strindberg, Dagny Juel became "the incarnation of the vampire ideal" (*NLH*, 4, 57); Strindberg referred to Juel as "Aspasia and Laï . . . as a sort of demonic, symbolic figure (who) lived on in his fantasy for a long time" (Gunner Brandell, *Strindberg—ett författarliv*, p. 309). As a writer and playwright, "a woman in storm . . . (and) a new feminist before new feminism" (Martin Nag, "Dagny Juel-norsk lyrikks Camilla Collett?," 1975, 512, 521), Dagny Juel and her literary *oeuvre* deserve considerable attention, at least as much attention as her turbulent, "vagabond life" (*Aschehoug*, 6, 560); and her four plays, which "deal with women in a desperate struggle" (Martin Nag, "Dagny Juel-en norsk Tsjekhov?," 1976, 61), merit performance: "(Juel) deserves mention in the great (company of Ibsen, Hamsun, Strindberg . . .). In her own way, she was a pioneer for new drama. She deserves a place—and by no means an insignificant one—in Norwegian, Scandinavian, and international drama. Whether she gets the place, only the future will show" (Nag, "Dagny Juel . . .," 1976, 61).

Dagny Juel was born to a "good family" (Brandell, p. 309), on June 8, 1867, in Kongsvinger, Norway; her thoroughly respectable parents were Minda Blehr and the Kongsvinger district doctor, Hans Lemmich Juel (Nag, "Dagny Juel . . . ," 1975, 521). At the age of eighteen (1885), Juel left Kongsvinger to study in Christiania (Oslo). She and her sister Ragnhild met the famous expressionist painter, Edvard Munch, during the summer of 1892; Munch painted both Dagny and the four-years-younger Ragnhild (Nag, "Dagny Juel . . . ," 1975, 521). During the autumn of 1892, Dagny Juel left Norway for Berlin, in order to study music. In Berlin, Juel renewed her contacts with Munch, who painted his famous portrait of Dagny and she became acquainted with Strindberg and the Polish author Stanislaw Przybyszewski, eventually her husband (Nag, "Dagny Juel . . . ," "1975, 521). Juel's affair with August Strindberg, a fleeting episode in Strindberg's life, began congenially, "but quickly became intense and intimate . . . [for] a few weeks" (Brandell, p. 309). In early March 1893, Juel, sexually liberated by the 1880s bohemian movement and demand for sexual freedom (Brandell, p. 309; *NLH*, 4, 57), joined the circle of Scandinavians at *Zum Schwarzen Ferkel*: "Dagny Juel appeared with her inexplicable erotic charm in the circle of Nordic artists . . . (she) got them to kneel before her, to hate and love her. Among the victims were Strindberg and Munch. In her footsteps jealousy grew like a poisonous plant" (*NLH*, 4, 57). At the end of March, 1893, Juel broke with Strindberg, and deepened her relationship with Przybyszewski, much to the bitter ire of Strindberg, who "saw his worst suspicions about women confirmed in (Dagny)" (*NLH*, 4, 56). Juel returned to Kongsvinger and became engaged to Przybyszewski; on August 18, 1893, the couple married in Berlin (Nag, "Dagny Juel . . . ," 1975, 523). There now followed a dizzying succession of travels, stays, new moves and visits, and new domiciles, for the Przybyszewskis as a married couple and for Dagny Juel Przybyszewska alone (Nag, "Dagny Juel . . . ," 1975, 523). In 1895, Przybyszewska returned to Kongsvinger where her son Zenon was born on September 28; she then spent the remainder of the year in Stockholm, and, in January 1896, she travelled with her husband to Copenhagen, where she sought unsuccessfully to win performance to her first play, "Den sterkere: (1895–1896; The Stronger; Nag, "Dagny Juel . . . ," 1975, 523). Przybyszewska returned home to Kongsvinger briefly but rejoined her husband in Copenhagen, where the couple learned of the suicide of Przybyszewski's lover (and the mother of his child), Marta Foerder, before returning to Berlin (Nag, "Dagny Juel . . . ," 1975, 523). Przybyszewska's second child, Iwi, was born on September 5, 1897, in Kongsvinger. A new period of travel, together and alone, to Paris, Spain, and Poland, ensued. In September 1899, Stanislaw Przybyszewski and his wife agreed to a divorce (Nag, "Dagny Juel . . . ," 1975, 523). Przybyszewska continued an almost frenetic vagabond existence, punctuated by trips to Krakow and Lwow, to Berlin, Prague, Paris, and

to Kongsvinger, and by her efforts to renew contact with Munch (1900). In the spring of 1901, Przybyszewska travelled to Warsaw with her son Zenon (Nag, "Dagny Juel . . . ," 1975, 523); on invitation from her last lover, a young Polish student (*NLH*, 4, 58), Wladyslaw Emeryk, Dagny Juel Przybyszewska and her son travelled on to Tblisi in the Caucasus Mountains of Georgia. Emeryk decided to take Przybyszewska's life on May 29, 1901, and his plan, including his own suicide, was carried out on June 5, 1901 (Nag, "Dagny Juel . . . ," 1975, 524), "without meaning or motive" (Brandell, P. 309). Dagny Juel Przybyszewska was buried in Tblisi on June 8, 1901; her hectic life quickly became a legend (*NLH*, 4, 58), a drama as intriguing, mysterious, and strange as her own plays and poems: "Behind the laconic data (of Dagny Juel's life) is a drama of fate, almost with the dimensions of a Greek tragedy—a drama filled with riddles and secrets, with double depth, with mysteries" (Nag, "Dagny Juel . . . ," 1975, 524).

Despite the sudden, dramatic close to her thirty-four turbulent, frenetic, agitative years, Dagny Juel Przybyszewska contributed significantly to Scandinavian literature and the literary scene; Przybyszewska wrote all of her thirteen poems, four dramas, and several prose fragments at the turn of the century, within a five or six year period (Nag, "Dagny Juel . . . ," 1975, 521). Dagny Juel Przybyszewska was also "a poetic personality, a fighting, strong woman, a new feminist pioneer in life and literature" (Nag, "Dagny Juel . . . ," 1976, 64), and her entire *oeuvre* reflected a life of strife, of conflict, and of strength and strong will. Dagny Juel Przybyszewska's first drama, "Den sterkere," was published in the journal *Samtiden* in 1896, after her unsuccessful attempt to introduce the play to the Copenhagen theatre. In the play, Siri, the female protagonist, is torn between two men, Knut Tonder, her proper partner-tormentor-husband, and Tor Rabbe, an "adventurer . . . (who appeals) to her demonic nature, her evil side" (Nag, "Dagny Juel . . . ," 1976, 57). Siri chooses Tor, which seems to suggest that he is the stronger of the title, but "Knut—the thought of him—will perhaps continue to haunt and pursue her" (Nag, "Dagny Juel . . . ," 1976, 57). Przybyszewski gives us a clear picture of a desperate, fighting woman who tries to free herself from the manipulation of male society—and both succeeds and does not (Nag, "Dagny Juel . . . ," 1976, 58). Siri manages to wrest herself free (or does she, really and completely?) from Knut, but she chooses her new life and her new path "on Tor's—not her own—premises" (Nag, "Dagny Juel . . . ," 1976, 58), and she remains tormented by Knut; if Siri is the stronger, she is only partially so. Siri is a representative of all Przybyszewska's characters, of the playwright herself, and of the author's conclusion that "it is difficult, if not impossible, for a woman to free herself from male society, for both written and . . . unwritten laws paralyze her" (Nag, "Dagny Juel . . . ," 1876, 62). Przybyszewska's next play, "Ravnegård" (Ravnegård), presents another conflict and choice situation: Thor is torn between two sisters, Gunhild, his vindictive, evil former lover who rules at Ravnegård (Nag, "Dagny Juel . . . ," 1976, 59), and Sigrid, the wife he married to spite Gunhild. A visit to Ravnegård by the married couple causes old fires to flame, with disastrous consequences for Sigrid and for Gunhild, whose revolt, whose efforts to break free lead on to a blind track (or dead end) and only have destructive power. Gunhild and Thor are "the strongest" in the strife, but "shadows . . . (remain) over Ravnegård" (Nag, "Dagny Juel . . . ," 1976, 59), haunting shadows of the past and of a negative struggle and choice. The third play, "Synden" (The Sin), again casts a woman, Hasada, between two men, Miriam (her husband) and Leon. Leon seduces her and then Hasada poisons her husband "who would choose [his own] death over infidelity" (Nag, "Dagny Juel . . . ," 1976, 60): Hasada's deed is a form of "unarticulated protest against male society's hypocritical moral code" (Nag, "Dagny Juel . . . ," 1976, 60), and a revolt which goes awry. In Przybyszewska's final play, "Når solen går ned (When the Sun Goes Down), Fin drives his wife to death to make room for his lover, Ivi, only to discover that his murdered wife "haunts and pursues the living . . . that perhaps she is the stronger after all" (Nag, "Dagny Juel . . . ," 1976, 60). Przybyszewska's four plays concentrate on scenic vibrations, on demi-tones, suggestions, on the unseen play behind the play, on the secret of hidden meaning" (Nag, "Dagny Juel . . . ," 1976, 61). Her characters speak past each other, "distractedly . . . on their own world, in their own world" (Nag, "Dagny Juel . . . ," 1976, 61).

Dagny Juel Przybyszewska's four untitled prose sketches were published in *Samtiden* in the spring of 1900; her four fragments repeat the central theme or motif of her plays: "the dead manipulate the living, the past controls (and destroys) the present" (Nag, "Dagny Juel . . . ," 1976, 62). The prose fragments also depict women striving to break free, to throw off the shackles of male dominance, and only partially succeeding. Przybyszewska also contrasts man and woman, depicting the gulf between opposing psyches. The author's fourth fragment describes a woman's search for an answer to her own desperate situation, to life's perplexities; her own efforts lead irrevocably to death (Nag, "Dagny Juel . . . ," 1976, 63). Dagny Juel Przybyszewska also wrote thirteen poems between 1895 and 1900, poems of a "more continental orientation" (Nag, "Dagny Juel . . . ," 1975, 521), as suggested by the subtitle taken from Verlaine, "De la musique avant toute chose" (Music Above All Else; Nag, "Dagny Juel . . . ," 1975, 521). Przybyszewska's poems have a "rhythmical-musical quality, both on their own and mutually . . . (as) a sort of poetic cycle . . . they have an inner import, a tension, a poignant expressive power . . . an artistic quality" (Nag, "Dagny Juel . . . ," 1975, 512). Like many of her plays and prose sketches, Dagny Juel Przybyszewska's poems describe "a desperate, terrified woman, fighting in vain, a female victim" (Nag, "Dagny Juel . . . ," 1975, 513), never able to break free of the conventions of the past and the present male-dominated society. In her plays, her poems and her prose fragments, the controversial, exciting, enchanting, and mysterious Dagny Juel Przybyszewska chose to depict women governed by male interests, male competition, and the ponderous conventions of past and present.

Works

"Den sterkere." *Samtiden* (1896). "Ravnegård," "Synden," "Når solen går ned" (1896–1900). "Prosaskissene." *Samtiden* (1900). *Digte* (1895–1900).

Bibliography

Aschehoug og Gyldendals Store Norske Leksikon 6 (1983). Brandell, Gunnar, *Strindberg—ett författarliv. Andra delen. Borta och hemma 1883–1894* (Stockholm, 1983). Hagemann, Sonja, "Dagny Juel." *Samtiden:* (1963). Kossak, Ewa K., *Dagny Przybyszewska: En vandrestjerne* [Dagny Przybyszewska, A Wandering Star]. (Warszawa, 1973). Nag, Martin, "Dagny Juel–en norsk Tsjekhov?" *Samtiden* (1976): 57–64. Nag, Martin, "Dagny Juel–norsk lyrikks Camilla Collett?" *Samtiden* (1975): 512–524. *Norges Litteratur Historie, 4, Fra Hamsun til Falkberget*, pp. 56–58. Sandøy, Haakon, *Dagny*, film (1977).

Lanae Hjortsvang Isaacson

Stanisława Przybyszewska

(a.k.a. Andrée Lynne)

Born October 1, 1901, Cracow, then in
   Austro-Hungary; died August 14, 1935,
   Danzig (Gdańsk), then a free city
Genre(s): historical drama, short story,
   novella, letters
Language(s): Polish, German, French, English

One of the most remarkable twentieth-century Polish writers, Przybyszewska was almost totally forgotten until the late 1960s when the unpublished manuscripts of her plays were unearthed, staged, and eventually published. Her masterpiece, *The Danton Case*, probably the best drama about the French Revolution since Georg Büchner's *Danton's Death*, is now firmly established in the repertory of the Polish theatre and known throughout the world in Andrzej Wajda's 1983 film version, *Danton*, a French-Polish production starring Gerard Depardieu.

The illegitimate daughter of the then-celebrated modernist playwright and novelist Stanisław Przybyszewski and Aniela Pająk, an impressionist painter, Przybyszewska was educated in Western Europe (Austria, Switzerland, France), where she lived first with her mother, then with her maternal aunt after her mother's death. Upon her return home in 1916, Przybyszewska attended teachers college in Cracow, from which she graduated in 1919, briefly enrolled at the university in Poznań, studied piano and violin, and came into contact with the literary and artistic avant-garde. Suffering from nervous exhaustion brought on in large part by her close and tragic relationship with her father, Przybyszewska moved to Warsaw in 1922, where she worked in a left-wing bookstore and was arrested and for a short time imprisoned for her alleged involvement in the socialist movement. In 1923 she married Jan Panieński, a young artist, and moved to Danzig when her husband obtained a teaching position at the Polish Gymnasium. After Panieński's sudden death in 1926, Przybyszewska chose to remain in Danzig where she spent the last ten years of her life in almost total isolation and growing misery and ill health, brought on by morphine addiction—both her father and husband abused the drug—which led to her death in 1935 at the age of thirty-four.

Determined at all costs to be a writer, Przybyszewska clung stubbornly to her sense of calling and substituted literary creativity for life, convinced of her own genius and ultimate vindication at the hands of posterity. Systematic work, careful revision, and endless polishing were the foundations of her artistic method for dealing with the public issues—revolution, social justice, the role of exceptional individuals in history—that dominated her thinking. During the composition of her trilogy—*Thermidor* (1925, in German), *'93* (completed in 1928), and *Sprawa Dantona* (The Danton Case, completed in 1929)—Przybyszewska adopted the revolutionary calendar devised by Fabre d'Eglantine and began dating her correspondence according to it and talking of Danton and Robespierre as though they were her contemporaries. Living on the margin of her own age, she found herself on happier ground with the heroic figures of 1789.

Because of her deep immersion in the tumultuous world of revolutionary Paris, Przybyszewska is able to create masterful psychological portraits of the venal sentimental idealist, Danton, and the incorruptible Robespierre, genius of the revolution, who knows that by institutionalizing the Terror so that the government may survive he is bringing about his own downfall and sowing the seeds of dictatorship that will be reaped by Bonaparte. Although documentary in spirit and based on extensive research, *The Danton Case* is a contemporary reading of the past, based on the parallel that the author perceives between the events in France at the end of the eighteenth century and those taking place in Russia in the twentieth century. Przybyszewska's finest play is a brilliant study of the mechanisms of power and the inevitable drift of revolution towards totalitarianism by a writer committed to the cause of radical social change—and, in fact, by her own account, in love with Robespierre for many years.

It is in her letters that Przybyszewska most fully reveals herself and describes the discovery of her vocation as an artist, the nature of her creative struggles, and the ceaseless battle for material survival. Her correspondence (published in three volumes, 1978–1985) offers a remarkable biography of a mind confronting itself in all the anguish of loneliness and despair, while at the same time proudly asserting the cultivation of one's own consciousness to be the highest duty. Written in four languages, sometimes addressed to famous writers such as Mann, Bernanos, and Cocteau, and often unfinished and unsent, Przybyszewska's letters were her only means of communicating with those mental peers that she felt must exist somewhere and that she has finally found in future generations.

Works

Dramaty [Dramas], ed. and introd. Roman Taborski, afterword by Jerzy Krasowski (1975). *Listy* [Letters], ed. Tomasz Lewandowski, volumes 1–3 (1978–1985). *Ostatnie noce Ventôse's* [The Last Nights of Ventôse], ed. Stanisław Helsztyński (1958). Translations of *Sprawa Dantona*: English—*The Danton Case* and *The Danton Affairs* (adapted by Pam Gems). French—*L'Affaire Danton* (1982). Swedish—*Affären Danton* (1985). German—*Sache Danton* (1930). *The Danton Case Thermidor*, Two Plays, tr. Bolesław Taborski (Evanston, Illinois, 1989).

Bibliography

Beauvois, Daniel, "Chronique: *L'Affaire Danton* de Stanisława Przybyszewska." *Annales Historiques de la Revolution Française* 240 (April-June, 1980): 294–305. "Biografia i egzystencja: Stanisław Przybyszewska." *Osoby: transgresje 3*, ed. Maria Janion and Stanisława Rosiek (1984), pp. 98–186, 471–490. Bojarska, Anna, "Andrée Lynne: Proze Stanisławy Przybyszewskiej." Przegląd Humanistyczny 11 (1978). Helsztyński, Stanisław, "Cityoenne Przybyszewska." *Meteory Młodej Polski* (Cracow, 1969), pp. 134–150. Kolińska, Krystyna, *Stachu, jego kobiety, jego dzieci* (Cracow, 1978). Kosicka, Jadwiga, and Daniel Gerould, *A Life of Solitude: Stanisława Przybyszewska. A Biographical Study with Selected Letters* (London, 1986, Evanston, Illinois, 1989). Lewandowski, Tomasz, *Dramat intelektu. Biografia literacka Stanisławy Przybyszewskiej* (Gdańsk, 1982). General references: *Encyclopedia of World Drama*, Vol. IV. 2nd ed. (New York, 1984), p. 171. *Literatura Polska. Przewodnik encyklopedyczny*, Vol. II (Warsaw, 1985), p. 255.

Jadwiga Kosicka and Daniel Gerould

Petroula Psiloreiti

(see: Galatea Kazantzaki)

Soledad Puértolas Villanueva

Born 1947, Zaragoza, Spain
Genre(s): novel, short story
Language(s): Spanish

She was born in Zaragoza and studied journalism; in 1971 she grew disillusioned with the political situation in Spain and lived in Norway for a short while. From there she went to California where she received an M.A. in Spanish Literature at the University of California in Santa Barbara, returning to Spain in 1975. Presently she lives in Madrid and has had an official job with the Socialist government of Felip González as Asesora del Ministro de Cultura (Adviser in the Ministry of Cultural Affairs).

She is considered to be one of the most promising new women novelists of the writers included in *Doce relatos de mujeres* (1982; Twelve Narrations by Women), edited by Ymelda Navajo. Her first published novel, *El bandido doblemente armado* (1980; The Double Armed Bandit), is a beautiful book which won the "Premio Sésamo" in 1979 and is divided into ten chapters individually titled so that each could almost be read independently as a short story. Its originality is due, in part, to the well-defined foreign characters who are portrayed. The key element of the novel is the narrator, a young man who tells candidly of his relationship with the Lennox family. The theme is friendship and trust, the title is symbolic.

Her next book is a collection of short stories, *Una enfermedad moral* (1982; A Moral Sickness), which according to the author's preface, all have in common a moral problem. Although this book was not as highly praised by the critics as her first novel, it nevertheless contains very appealing narratives set in different times and places. Some of these are: "Un país extranjero" (A Foreign Country), the story of the estrangement of an older lady; "La indiferencia de Eva" (Eva's Indifference), the amusing tale of a novelist—not the author, by her own admission—who flirts with the radio announcer who interviews her and "El origen del deseo" (The Origin of Desire), the only one that is autobiographical.

Burdeos (1986), her latest novel to date, has earned her wide acclaim. Puértolas continues to show the preference for foreign settings and characters, which was evident in her two earlier works, since the French city that titles the book unites the three narratives. Its actual genre has been questioned because they could also be read as independent stories despite their loose connections. (This style is reminiscent of Pío Baroja on whom she wrote a literary essay: *El Madrid de La lucha por la vida*, 1971). The three main characters of *Burdeos*, an old spinster, a bourgeois young man, and an American divorcee, are sensitively and suggestively drawn in their loneliness.

Soledad Puértolas has achieved her well-deserved recognition despite the fact that she has not followed the mainstream trends in Spanish literature today. Her work shows her ability to draw unique characters in original settings with a style that is personal and unaffected. Her themes of alienation and loneliness demonstrate a concern for human nature even if it does not reflect the situation of her native country.

Works

El Madrid de La lucha por la vida (Madrid, 1971). *El bandido doblemente armado* (Madrid, 1980). *Una enfermedad moral* (Madrid, 1982). *Burdeos* (Barcelona, 1986).

Bibliography

Alborg, Concha, "Cuatro narradoras de la transición." *Anales de la Literatura Contemporánea*, f1987. Conte, Rafael, "La feria de los discretos." *El País* (Aug. 21 1986): 2–3. Goñi, Javier, "Entrevista con Soledad Puértolas." *Cambio 16* (Aug. 11 1986): 96. Navajo, Ymelda, *Doce relatos de mujeres* (Madrid, 1982).

Concha Alborg

Marie Madeleine d'Arsant de Puisieux

Born 1720, Paris, France; died 1798
Genre(s): drama, novel, moral philosophy, feminist tracts
Language(s): French

Marie Madeleine d'Arsant was two years old when her father died, and was at age twelve sent to boarding school at the Paris Port-Royal, which advocated similar education principles to those of Port-Royal des Champs. She seems to have benefited from a good education for the times, although this also meant that she was deprived from maternal affection, for her mother was seldom allowed to visit her.

Married in 1739 to Philippe-Florent de Puisieux, an attorney to the French Parliament, Mme de Puisieux gave birth to her first child in 1739. In 1746, she met the famous encyclopedist, Denis Diderot. Their friendship lasted until 1755. Her first story, "Céphise," was published the following year. A. Laborde reports that her collaboration with Diderot begins at that time, first on *L'oiseau Blanc*, a moral tale, and then on *Les Bijoux Indiscrets* published by Diderot in 1748. In 1761 appears the *Réflexions et Avis sur les Défauts et les Ridicules à la Mode, pour Servir de Suite aux Conseils à Une Amie*. This work is filled with autobiographical details and anecdotes concerning her contemporaries as well as judgments on the works of several well-known authors including Jean-Jacques Rousseau. According to Laborde, eight works had already been published by that time: *Conseils à Une Amie* (1749); *Les Caractères I* (1750); *Les Caractères II* (1751); *La Femme n'est pas Inférieure à L'homme* (1750); *Le Plaisir et la Volupté* (1752); *Les Mémoires de* la *Comtesse de Zurlac* (1753); *Zamor et Almanzine* (1755); *L'histoire de la Marquise de Terville* (1756).

It seems that Diderot's influence is felt throughout her work. In particular, she apparently exploited Diderot's scientific knowledge, his philosophical ideas, even his atheism in her feminist tract, *La Femme n'est pas Inférieure à L'homme*, a very important Enlightenment text.

On September 4, 1795, Madame de Puisieux received two thousand pounds from the Convention. This sum was given to her in consideration for her literary production. Laborde reports the government's generosity was probably due to a publication on the education of Third Estate children: *Prospectus Relatif à L'éducation des Enfants du Peuple*.

Works

Poésie Diverses (1746–1747?). "Céphise" (1747?). Conseils à Une Amie (1749). Les Caractères (1750). Les Caractères II (1751). La Femme n'est pas Inférieure à L'homme (1750). Le Triomphe des Dames (1751). Le Plaisir et la Volupté (1752). L'éducation du Marquis de ***ou Mémoires de la Comtesse de Zurlac (1753). Zamor et Almanzine ou L'inutilité de L'esprit et du Bon Sens (1755). Histoire de la Marquise de Terville (1756). Reflexions et Avis sur les Défauts et les Ridicules à la Mode (1761). Alzarac ou la Nécessité d'Etre Inconstant (1762). La Marquis à la Mode (1763). Histoire de Mademoiselle de Terville (1768). Les Mémoires d'un Homme de Bien (1768). Prospectus sur un Ouvrage Important (1772). L'histoire du Règne de Charles VII (1775).

Bibliography

Garnier, Camille, *Madame de Puisieux: Moraliste et Romancière*. Laborde, Alice, *Diderot et Madame de Puisieux* (Saratoga, Ca., 1984). Laborde, Alice, *Diderot et L'amour* (Saratoga, Ca., 1979). Mylne, Vivienne, and Janet Osborne, "Diderot's Early Fiction, *Les Bijoux Indiscrets et L'oiseau Blanc.*" *Diderot Studies* 14 (1971). Pellisson, Maurice, "Une femme moraliste au XVIIIème siècle." *La Revue Pédagogique* (September 15, 1910).

Colette Michael

Marie Pujmanová

(a.k.a. Olga Nerská, Marie Hennerová)

Born 1893, Prague, Czechoslovakia; died 1958, Prague
Genre(s): novel, short story, poetry
Language(s): Czech

Pujmanová was a liberal from a well-to-do background who steadily moved closer to Communism. During the 1920s and 30s, she contributed journalistic pieces, theater and literary criticism and poetry to many publications. (Some of the early works are signed "Olga Nerská.") Her literary reputation was established by the late 1930s, and grew immensely after 1948 when she was celebrated as an exemplary Communist writer.

Pujmanová's first novel, *Pod křidlem* (1919; Under the Wing, published under her maiden name, Hennerová) is a fictionalized recasting of her own happy if overprotected childhood. The works that followed shared the same upper-middle-class urban setting. In *Povídky z městkého sadu* (1920; Stories from a City Garden), this society is shown as beginning to fall apart. *Pacientka doktora Hegelu* (1931; Doctor Hegel's Patient) portrays a young woman's rebellion from the middle-class world. Pujmanová set out to broaden her picture of Czech society in *Lidé na kři'ovatce* (1937; People at the Crossroads), by juxtaposing life in a bourgeois family with the lives of the workers in a textile factory from the end of World War I to the economic crisis of the 1930s. The factory in the novel is closely based on a real factory. Pujmanová here intended to delineate the history of entire social classes rather than individual characters.

During the Nazi occupation, Pujmanová of necessity abandoned political fiction. She wrote one novella, *Předtucha* (1942; Premonition), as well as poetry centered on intimate themes.

The novel *Hra s ohněm* (1948; Playing with Fire) was meant to be second part of a trilogy that began with *Lidé na kři'ovatce*. (The third part was never written.) The history of the Czech Communist movement is brought up to the beginning of the Nazi occupation. The novel features a prototypical socialist-realist hero. *Svítání* (1949; The Dawn) is a hybrid collection of prose pieces (both fiction and nonfiction) incorporating much autobiographical material. Pujmanová compares her children's world with the world of her own childhood and contrasts the horrors of the Nazi period with the new Communist regime. In the final parts of this work Pujmanová glorifies collective labor, as she does in *Život proti smrti* (1952; Life against Death). The collective itself, rather than any individual, is the hero of the latter novel.

In her early works, Pujmanová used the techniques of traditional realism. Beginning especially with *Lidé na křižovatce*, Pujmanová strove to capture "the typical" and dispense with the idiosyncratic. But, as happens to many writers of her generation, the principles of socialist realism only vitiated her creative talent.

Works

Pujmanová, Marie, *Dílo* [Works], in 10 vols. (1953–1959).

English translations: F. Long, tr., "The Journey to Prague," in *Hundred Towers: A Czechoslovak Anthology of Creative Writing*, Franz C. Weiskopf, ed. (1945), pp. 119–132 Vilimova, E. tr., "Jarmila's Pilgrimage" [Excerpt from *Předtucha*], in *The Linden Tree: An Anthology of Czech and Slovak Literature 1890–1960*, ed. Mojmír Otruba and Zdeněk Pešat (c. 1962), pp. 228–232. "Sova's Sister," in *Czech and Slovak Short Stories* , Jeanne W. Němcová, ed. and tr. (1967), pp. 130–135.

Bibliography

Blahynka, Milan, *Marie Pujmanová* (Prague, 1961). Hrzalova, Hana, "Marie Pujmanová, basnířka moderního člověka." *Literární měsíčník* 2; 4 (1973): 237–246. Součková, Milada, *A Literature in Crisis: Czech Literature 1938–1950* (New York, 1954), pp. 103–106.

Nancy Cooper

Antonia Pulci

Born c. 1452, Florence, Italy
Genre(s): religious drama, poetry (?)
Language(s): Italian

Little is known about Antonia Pulci: she was the daughter of Francesco Giannotti; she married Bernardo Pulci in 1470 and was childless. From letters of her family members, we learn that from 1473 her health deteriorated and that, in 1488, when her husband died, she withdrew into a convent. The date of her death is unknown.

The Pulci were a noble Florentine family of reduced circumstances and the three Pulci brothers, Bernardo, Luigi, and Luca, were encouraged in their literary activities and helped financially by Lorenzo de' Medici and by his mother, Lucrezia Tornabuoni, who was a poet in her own right. Antonia's output, like theirs, was consistent with Lorenzo's cultural plan to promote the Italian language and to upgrade such popular genres as the medieval religious drama, whose productions were presided over by lay-guilds and still enjoyed great popular favor. In Florence, the literary level of the miracle plays rose, thanks to authors such as Antonia, her husband Bernardo, the well-known Feo Belcari and Lorenzo the Magnificent himself.

As far as we know, Antonia wrote four plays: *Figlio prodigo* (The Prodigal Son), *Santa Guglielma* (Saint Guglielma), *Santa Domitilla* (Saint Domitilla) and *San Francesco* (Saint Francis). Judging from the many copies found in Tuscan libraries, the plays were popular and repeatedly staged in the fifteenth and the sixteenth century. As it was customary for the genre, Antonia drew her plots from the Old Testament and from hagiography. As in all medieval religious drama, narrative interest prevails over character depiction and dramatic conflict. Topical flavor is given by lively dialogues describing contemporary types and scenes. What distinguishes Antonia's treatment of the traditional subject matter is her tendency to humanize divine intervention and to stress points of morality, whose rewards are to be found in life, not exclusively in heaven.

Her most successful play was *Santa Guglielma*. It can be described as a dramatized narrative in octaves, and it shows the influence of the picaresque *novella* as well as of the secularized lives of Saints. These popular genres often dealt with beautiful and virtuous girls, vilified and tortured by sadistic men but in the end prodigiously rescued and rewarded. The Guglielma of Pulci's play is the dutiful daughter of the English king, who marries the king of Hungary in obedience to her parents. During her husband's absence, she rejects the advances of her brother-in-law and is accused to the king of adultery. Condemned to death, she is spared by his executioner and escapes into the wilderness. The happy solution is brought about by divine intervention. Guglielma has acquired the capacity of curing the sick who have repented of their sins, and, when summoned to the sick bed of her brother-in-law, she restores him to health and herself to her husband's love. The success of the play was due to the adventure story, the changing exotic landscape, and to the gratification deriving from just retribution. Antonia's style is graceful, her drawing of situations is clear, and the dramatic suspense evenly distributed.

According to F.S. Quadrio, Antonia is the author of an epic poem in four cantos known by the title of *La Regina d'Oriente* (The Queen of the Orient).

Works

Colomb de Batines, *Bibliografia delle antiche rappresentazioni italiane sacre e profane stampate nei secoli XV e XVI* (1852), pp. 15–18. *La rappresentazione del Figliuol prodigo* (1825). *Santa Guglielma. Sacre rappresentazioni dei secoli XIV, XV e XVI*, ed. A. D'Ancona (1872) III, pp. 199–234. *San Francesco. L'antico dramma sacro italiano*, ed. P. Torchi (1927) II, pp. 654–696. *Santa Guglielma. Sacre rappresentazioni del Quattrocento*, ed. L. Banfi (1958), pp. 537–558.

Bibliography

Apollonio, M., *Storia del teatro italiano* (Florence, 1943), p. 242. Costa-Zalessow, N., *Scrittrici italiane dal XIII al XXX secolo* (Ravenna, 1982), pp. 49–53. D'Ancona, A., *Origini del teatro italiano* (Turin, 1891), I, pp. 268–269. *Enciclopedia Biografica e Bibliografica Italiana*, Serie VI: *Poetesse e Scrittrici* (Rome, 1941), II, 154–155.

Rinaldina Russell

Q

Elena Quiroga

Born October 26, 1921, Santander, Spain
Genre(s): novel
Language(s): Spanish

Upon receiving the Nadal prize of 1950 for *Viento del norte* (Northwind), Quiroga became one of several women novelists of her generation to achieve national recognition. In the years that followed, however, her work did not receive the critical attention it deserved, perhaps in part because she was writing stream of consciousness, while the dominant novelistic current in Spain was social realism. In 1983 she became the second woman elected to the Spanish Royal Academy, thereby securing her status as a major author.

Although Quiroga was born in Santander, where her mother's family lived, and attended boarding school there, she considers herself Galician. Much of her childhood and her early adult years were spent in that region, at her father's home in the province of Orense. Her mother died when Quiroga was only two years old. The absence of the mother, like the landscape of Galicia, forms an important theme in Quiroga's works. Largely self-educated, Quiroga had access to her paternal grandfather's extensive library and later to the library of La Coruña, when her father moved to that coastal city. In 1950 she married historian Dalmiro de la Válgoma and moved to Madrid. Since 1968, when her husband was named permanent secretary of the Royal Academy of History, they have lived in the building that houses the Academy.

Viento del norte, still Quiroga's most popular novel, is written in a linear structure and traditional narrative form. It presents a penetrating psychological study of authentic Galician characters during the pre-Civil War period and is related to Quiroga's later novels by the introduction of such themes as orphanhood, loneliness, and social class distinctions. The beginning of Quiroga's mature writing, however, is marked by the publication of *Algo pasa en la calle* (Something's Happening in the Street) in 1954. Its analysis of the psychological effects of divorce was particularly daring in Franco Spain, where the model divorce law of the Second Republic had been abolished retroactively. Far removed from the traditional structure of *Viento del norte*, *Algo pasa en la calle* introduced such Faulknerian techniques as multiple perspectives and stream of consciousness.

Quiroga's second major novel of the 1950s was *La careta* (1955; The Mask). Her most developed use of stream of consciousness, it also reflects her interest in existentialist philosophy. Moisés, the alienated protagonist, has never overcome the psychological damage caused by his parents' death in the Civil War. Like *Algo pasa en la calle*, it is a daring novel for its introduction of taboo topics, including sexuality and a criticism of the Catholic Church.

Tristura (1960; Sadness) and *Escribo tu nombre* (1965; I Write Your Name) are interrelated works dealing with the childhood and adolescence of a protagonist whose life experiences are in some ways similar to the author's. Like Quiroga, Tadea is a motherless child who is sent from Galicia to live with her mother's family in Santander and attend boarding school there. *Tristura*, winner of the Critics Prize, is told from the perspective of the young child. It develops themes of absence and silence while also presenting a strong criticism of the social and religious hypocrisy of middle-class defenders of the status quo. The criticism becomes stronger in the sequel novel, where the convent school Tadea attends is treated as a microcosm of society. The repression of freedom within the school is paralleled by the backlash against the reforms of the Second Republic that gave rise to the Civil War.

Quiroga's last published novel, *Presente profundo* (1973; Profound Present), like *Algo pasa en la calle*, presents multiple perspectives and a shifting narrative point of view. It juxtaposes the stories of two suicides, that of an older Galician woman who feels herself no longer needed by her husband and children, and that of a cosmopolitan young divorcee who, separated from the child she loves, drifts into the drug culture. The link between these narrative strands is a doctor who seeks a better understanding of himself as he reconstructs the lives of the two women.

Quiroga's use of innovative novelistic structures, her willingness to deal with topics considered taboo in Franco Spain, and her sensitive treatment of social and psychological problems, particularly those of women, have established her as a major author of postwar Spain.

Works

La soledad sonora (1949). *Viento del Norte* (1951). *La sangre* (1952). *Algo pasa en la calle* (1954). *La enferma* (1955). *La careta* (1955). *Plácida, la joven y otras narraciones* (1956). (Includes three short novels: the title novel and two works originally published in 1953, *Trayecto uno* and *La otra ciudad*.) *La última corrida* (1958). *Tristura* (1960). *Escribo tu nombre* (1965). *Presente profundo* (1973).

Bibliography

Brent, Albert, "The Novels of Elena Quiroga." *Hispania* 42 (1959): 210–213. Marks, Martha Alford, "Elena Quiroga's Yo Voice and the Schism between Reality and Illusion." *Anales de la Novela de Posguerra* 5 (1980): 39–55; "La perspectiva plural en dos novelas de Elena Quiroga." *Cuadernos Hispanoamericanos* 359 (1980): 428–433; "Time in the Novels of Elena Quiroga." *Hispania* 64 (1981): 376–381. Villegas, Juan, "Los motivos estructurantes de *La careta*, de Elena Quiroga." *Cuadernos Hispanoamericanos* 75 (1968): 638–648. Zatlin-Boring, Phyllis, *Elena Quiroga.* Twayne World Authors Series 459 (Boston, 1977). "Faulkner in Spain: The Case of Elena Quiroga." *Comparative Literature Studies* 14 (1977): 166–176. "Divorce in Franco Spain: Elena Quiroga's *Algo pasa en la calle.*" *Mosaic* 17.1 (1984): 129–138.

General references: *Dictionary of Literature of the Iberian Peninsula* (New York; Westport, Conn.; London, in press). *Las mejores novelas contemporáneas*, ed. Joaquin de Entrambasaguas, vol. 12 (Barcelona, 1971), pp. 1281–1307. *Women Writers of Spain: An Annotated Bio-Bibliographical Guide*, ed. Carolyn L. Galerstein (New York; Westport, Connecticut; London, 1986).

Phyllis Zatlin

Françoise Quoirez

(a.k.a. Françoise Sagan)

Born June 21, 1935, Cajare (Lot), France
Genre(s): novel, drama, short story,
    screenplay, song, reminiscence
Language(s): French

It sounds almost like a fairy-tale. Once upon a time a girl by the name of Françoise, having failed her exams at the Sorbonne, sat down and wrote a little book called *Bonjour tristesse* and sent it off to a big Paris publisher. No one expected very much of the little book, not even Françoise herself; her father wouldn't even let her put the family name on it, so she borrowed the name of a princess from Proust: Sagan.

Then the miracle happened. Not only was her little book published, but it won the Prix des Critiques for 1954 and within a year had sold a million copies in France alone and made its teenage author rich and famous.

In retrospect, it is easy to see why *Bonjour tristesse* was a success. It had something for everybody. For the critics there was its style: cool, analytical, lucid, understated, and yet full of unsuspected nuances. It was prose in the grand tradition of *La Princesse de Clèves* and *Adolphe* and seemed to confirm what they had always been saying about the classic style, that it could be mastered by any bright French schoolgirl. For the young there was the book's heroine, Cécile, a cool, laid-back teenager whose indifference thinly veils a naively egocentric, sentimental view of life. At her most introspective, Cécile reveals a vague sense of unease at having driven her father's fiancée to suicide. Take these ingredients, add a dash of false candor, a suggestion of incest, a hint of Raymond Radiguet, the *enfant terrible* of the 1920s, and *voilà! un best-seller!*

Elizabeth Janeway comes quickly to the heart of the work: *Bonjour tristesse* was a precocious book. It stamped a pattern of impossible, though amusing events upon reality in a teen-age dream of wickedness, seduction, sophistication and power—for Cécile controlled and manipulated the adults about her at will. Her story was pure wish-fulfillment, carried off by the intensity and immediacy with which it was told but inclined, whenever the author's concentration faltered, to turn absurd.

First novels being what they are, it was inevitable that the author should be identified with her heroine. Thanks to François Mauriac, among others, Sagan soon became in the public eye the incarnation of the Beat Generation in France. A near fatal automobile crash that led to a dependency on morphine, two unsuccessful marriages, and a chronic weakness for gambling and whisky and fast cars would seem to suggest she did her best to live up to her reputation.

In fact the image of the "charming amoral little monster" with the Jaguar and the leopard-skin coat has held up somewhat better than that of the writer. As most critics have observed over the years, Sagan's subsequent novels remain essentially what *Bonjour tristesse* was, highly stylized arrangements of idle pseudo-sophisticates seeking to manipulate one another's lives in order to find momentary relief from boredom. It is sadly ironic that when she finally did try to escape the world of *Bonjour tristesse* and wrote a novel about working-class people in a mining district of northern France (*Le Chien couchant*, 1980), she was taken to court on a charge of having plagiarized it.

Little is to be gained by an itemized survey of her work, for there is little change from book to book. Nora Rosen takes a charitable view, seeing Sagan as a sort of modern-day Gautier "who has refined her material down to its essence." The trouble is that beneath the brilliantly hard, crystalline surface there is nothing worth concealing. There are only the usual love-triangles enacted in fashionable apartments and five-star hotels and beach houses, the Ferraris and the Chanel suits and the Creed jackets, the father-figures, the generation-gap, and throughout it all, apt and epigrammatic observations about people in love.

There is throughout Sagan's work a certain exquisite quality one ordinarily associates with the craft of the miniaturist. The language of the critics is revealing here: she is "a player of boudoir chess" (Stanley Kaufmann); her stories are "fragile sand dollars—elegant, delicate designs" (*Time*); her characters "more caryatids than people" (Brigid Brophy) who "drift like those toy boats with camphor tied behind them" (Ronald Bryden) and comprise "a pricey collection of tiny figurines and minute porcelains" (Valentine Cunningham). Perhaps the best analogy is that of Anatole Broyard, who likens her characters to "exotic fish, drawn forward or sideways by whatever or whoever happens to be suspended nearest."

As one might suspect, this sort of writing comes very close to soap opera, and is saved from this fate only by Sagan's pellucid style and occasional flashes of ironic humor. It cannot approach serious literature, though, because in the final analysis the reader doesn't care what happens to her people because they don't care themselves. A novel need not be profound, nor even be about interesting people. But it has to be about things that matter, or at least about people who think they do.

The underlying mood of emptiness, far from echoing the *grito* of the Existentialist, becomes self-indulgent parody, and love is reduced to a state of being just a little less bored than usual. In *Des yeux de soie*, a woman who has just been abandoned by her lover seeks solace dancing with a stranger in a night club:

He: "Life goes on, I'm still here,
you're still here. We're dancing."

She: "We'll dance for the rest of our lives. We're the sort of people who dance . . . ."
Then later, in bed:
"You know," she said in a calm voice, "it's a funny thing, life, all that . . ."
"What?" he said.
"I don't know,"—and turning toward him, she fell asleep on her side.

Works

Novels: *Bonjour tristesse* (1954). *Un certain sourire* (1956). *Dans un mois, dans un an* (1957). *Aimez-vous Brahms?* (1959). *Les merveilleux nuages* (1961). *La chamade* (1965). *Le garde du coeur* (1968). *Un peu de soleil dans l'eau froide* (1969). *Des bleus à l'âme* (1972). *Un profil perdu* (1974). *Le lit défait* (1977). *Le chien couchant* (1980). *La femme fardée* (1983). *Un orage immobile* (1983). *De guerre lasse* (1985).

Shorter fiction: *Des yeux de soie* (1976). *Musiques de scènes* (1982).

Plays: *Château en Suède* (1960). *Les violons, parfois* (1962). *La robe mauve de Valentine* (1963). *Bonheur, impair et passe* (1964). *Un jardin sur la mer* (1964). *Le cheval évanoui, suivi de l'Écharde* (1966). *Un piano dans l'herbe* (1970). *Il fait beau jour et nuit* (1979).

Other: *Toxique*, autobiographical fragments (1964). *Réponses*, interviews (1974). *Avec mon meilleur souvenir*, biography (1984). *Sand et Musset: Lettres d'amour*, correspondence (1985). Also numerous screenplays, texts for collections of photographs and tableaux vivants, scenarios, and lyrics for the singer Juliette Greco.

Robert Harrison

R

Rachilde

(a.k.a. Marguerite Valette)

Born February 11, 1860, Château-l'Évêque,
France; died April 4, 1953, Paris
Genre(s): novels, short story, drama, essay,
criticism
Language(s): French

Born in 1860 in the Périgord as the daughter of Joseph Eymery, a colonel in the French army and Gabrielle Feytaud, the only daughter of a wealthy publisher, Marguerite Eymery cultivated her literary ambitions at an early age when, barely sixteen years of age, she published her first novels, a number of *romans-feuilleton*, in the local Périgord press. At the age of eighteen, she moved to Paris where she embarked on a prolific career as a novelist, playwright, essayist, and *grande dame* of French literature that would continue deep into the twentieth century. Together with her husband Alfred Vallette whom she married in 1889, she participated in the founding of the *Mercure de France* in 1890—a journal that soon became the leading French literary journal and that especially championed the cause of the new symbolist and decadent authors. Rachilde was also famous for her *mardis*, a prestigious weekly salon for the Parisian writers and intellectuals associated with the *Mercure de France*. One of the most visible figures of French literature during the *fin de siècle* and the *belle époque*, Rachilde outlived the age which had brought her fame by many decades. In her later years, she fervently resisted new generations of avant-gardists. Especially dadaists and surrealists found no favor in her eyes because of their contemptuous attitude towards nineteenth century élitist doctrines concerning art and society. This inability of Rachilde to admit new developments in art and literature no doubt contributed to the sheer anonymity of her death on April 4, 1953.

Rachilde's *oeuvre* is vast. She published at least one volume every year throughout most of her long life, and her talents and interests led her to compose novels, short stories, plays, essays, and short criticism. Among her early novels, especially *Madame de Sans-Dieu* (1878; Madam Without-God), a *roman-feuilleton* often erroneously identified as *Madame de Sangdieu*, and *Monsieur de la nouveauté* (1880; Mister Novelty), the first major novel published by Rachilde following her arrival in Paris, are memorable. Yet, it is probably *Monsieur Vénus. Roman matérialiste* (1884; Mister Venus. A Materialist Novel) which is chiefly responsible for the literary notoriety Rachilde achieved early in her career. This "materialist novel," which was published the same year as J.-K. Huysmans' *A Rebours*, was banned immediately following its publication on a charge of pornography, and its female protagonist, Raoule de Vénérande, is to be ranked with Huysmans' Des Esseintes as one of the most bizarre figures in French *fin-de-siècle* fiction. Yet, Rachilde refused to be intimidated by the furor surrounding the publication of her novel and published during the next two decades no less frenetic novels such as *Nono. Roman de moeurs contemporaines* (1885; Nono. Novel of Contemporary Manners), *La Marquise de Sade* (1887; The Marquise de Sade), *Madame Adonis* (1888) and *Les Hors-nature. Moeurs contemporaines* (1897; The Unnaturals. Contemporary Manners). In fact, she continued to write this type of novel several decades into the twentieth century: e.g. *La Tour d'amour* (1914; The Tower of Love), *Au seuil de l'enfer* (1924; On the Threshold of Hell), and *Madame de Lydone, assassin* (1929; Madam of Lydone, Assassin).

Among Rachilde's plays, *La Voix du sang* (1890; The Voice of the Blood) and the psychological *Madame la Mort* (1891; Madam Death) deserve mention. She also wrote some significant literary criticism and was one of the early admirers of Alfred Jarry whom she studied in her *Alfred Jarry ou le Surmâle des lettres* (1928; Alfred Jarry or the Superman of Literature). Her *Portraits d'hommes* (1930; Portraits of Men) consists of a series of literary portraits.

Rachilde, who identified herself as "Rachilde homme de lettres" on her name-cards, was highly estimated during her life by such luminaries of French literature as Maurice Barrès, Arsène Housaye, Marcel Schwob, Camille Lemoinier, Jean Moréas, Jean Lorrain, and Guillaume Apollinaire—many of whom wrote prefaces to various publications of hers. Similarly, academic scholar Mario Praz identified her in his *The Romantic Agony* of 1930 as one of the professionals of the French decadent and "sensualist" school. Rachilde's writings, indeed, typically introduce the reader to a distinctively decadent cast of characters. Dandies, sadists, androgynes, transvestites, effeminate men, Amazon women, vampires, madmen, and necrophiles proliferate—especially in her novels and short stories. Yet, it would be incorrect to completely divorce the sexual confusion, the artifice, the frenetic furor, and demented phantasmagoria that typify Rachilde's fictional universe from its deliberately pseudo-scientific, anti-naturalist mockery. As the subtitles of some of her studies of "contemporary manners" indicate, much of Rachilde's decadent fiction, like Huysmans', involves a frontal attack on the claim to social seriousness and mimetic accuracy of much of French nineteenth century bourgeois literature. As such, her *oeuvre* deserves as much renewed attention as some other exponents of decadent fiction such as J.-K. Huysmans, Jean Lorrain, or P. H. Villiers de l'Isle-Adam have recently enjoyed.

Works

A complete Rachilde bibliography does not exist and, in fact, is not attempted by her most recent biographer Claude Dauphiné, in his *Rachilde, femme de lettres 1900* (1985). The following is therefore a limited survey of some of Rachilde's most important writings. *Madame de Sans-Dieu* (1878). *L'étoile filante* (1879). *Monsieur de la Nouveauté* (1880). *La Mort d'une petite fille de marbre; la Petite Vierge de plâtre* (1880). *Monsieur Vénus. Roman matérialiste* (1884). *Nono. Roman de moeurs contemporaines* (1885). *La Virginité de Diane* (1886). *A Mort* (1886). *La Marquise de Sade* (1887). *Madame Adonis* (1888). *Théâtre: Madame la Mort, Le Vendeur de Soleil, La Voix du sang* (1891). *La Sanglante Ironie* (1891). *L'Animale* (1893). *Le Démon de l'absurde* (1894). *L'Heure sexuelle* (1893). *Les Hors-nature. Moeurs contemporaines* (1897). *La Jongleuse* (1900). *Le Meneur de louves* (1905). *La Tour d'amour* (1914). *Le Grand Saigneur* (1922). *La Haine amoureuse* (1924). *Au seuil de l'enfer* (1924). *Alfred Jarry ou le Surmâle des lettres* (1928). *Refaire l'amour* (1928). *Madame de Lydone, assassin* (1929). *Portraits d'hommes* (1930). *Notre-Dame des rats* (1931). *Jeux d'artifices* (1932). *Mon étrange plaisir* (1934). *Les Accords perdus* (1937). *Face à la peur* (1942).

Bibliography

The only recent comprehensive biography of Rachilde is Dauphiné, Claude, *Rachilde, femme de lettres 1900* (1985). See also David, André, *Rachilde, homme de lettres, son oeuvre* (1924) and Gaubert, Ernest, *Rachilde* (1907). Few critical articles have been devoted to Rachilde in recent years: see Bakker, Rodolf, "De heer Venus en mevrouw de Sade, of: Het dubbelleven van Rachilde." *Maatstaf* 26 (1978): 23–75; and Besnard-Coursodon, Micheline, "Monsieur Vénus, Madame Adonis: sexe et discours." *Littérature* 54 (1984): 121–127.

Henk Vynckier

Radegunde

Born A.D. 520, Thuringia; died 587, Poitiers
Genre(s): episcopal correspondence
Language(s): Medieval Latin

Radegunde (A.D. 520–587) is the subject of three narrative sources written before 610 by contemporaries who knew Radegunde as a Merovingian queen, as the founder and a nun of the St. Croix nunnery in Poitiers, and as the patron saint for a new kind of cult worship during the period of the Catholic Christianization of barbarian Europe. The dramatic events of Radegunde's life attracted moral interpretation by the Gallo-Roman historian Bishop Gregory of Tours; the Italian poet-priest Fortunatus; and the humble Frankish nun Baudonivia.

Radegunde was born into one of the three ruling families in Thuringia, a tribal territory bordering Frankish Gaul. In early childhood, Radegunde's parents were assassinated by her uncles, and when she was ten years old, one uncle allied with the neighboring Franks to make war on the other uncle. One of the Frankish kings captured Radegunde and her younger brother in this war as his victory prizes. Catholic bishops arbitrated a judgment about Radegunde, and she was taken to a Gallo-Roman villa to work and to be educated until the time of her forced marriage to Clothar I, son of Clovis I and Clothilde. At the Merovingian court in Soissons, Radegunde lived as a Catholic queen among concubines until her husband murdered her brother. Following this murder, Radegunde fled to the shrine of St. Martin in Tours. At the altar, she exchanged her jewels for the intercession of powerful churchmen against Clothar. Negotiations between several bishops and Clothar eventually enabled Radegunde to establish St. Croix, an independent nunnery for more than 200 women in Poitiers, a frontier area of Frankish conquest and Christian conversion. The nuns lived immured under the Rule of Caesarius of Arles, communicating with the outside kingdom largely through the diplomacy of Bishop Gregory and through the pen of Fortunatus.

As both a barbarian queen and a Catholic saint, Radegunde lived on the crux of cultural assimilation for the Christianization of Merovingian Gaul. The story of Queen-Saint Radegunde is one of the earliest examples of the cultural and religious accommodation accomplished in barbarian Europe by means of a woman's example in life and in literature.

Works

Epistula ad episcopus (written before the Council of Tours, 587) in *Historia Francorum*, Bk. IX, Gregory of Tours, *Monumenta Germanica Historia Script. rer. mer.* 1–450. Internal evidence in primary sources for other correspondence, but manuscripts are not identified by scholarship to date.

Bibliography

Aigrain, Rene, *Sainte Radegonde* (Paris, 1953). Baudonivia, *De Vita Sanctae Radegundis Liber II*, ed. B. Krusch, *MGH Script. rer. mer.* 2, pp. 377–395. Briand, Emile, *Sainte Radegonde, Reine de France* (Paris, 1908). Brion, M., *Fredegonde et Brunehaut* (Paris, 1935). Fortunatus, Venantius, *De Vita Sanctae Radegundis Liber I*, ed. B. Krusch, *MGH Script. rer. mer.* 2, pp. 364–377. Gregory of Tours, *Historia Francorum*, ed. B. Krusch and W. Levinson, *MGH Script. rer. mer.* pp. 1–450. Thorpe, Lewis, tr. *The History of the Franks* (Harmondsworth, England, 1974). McNamara, Jo Ann, and Suzanne Wemple, "Sanctity and Power: the Dual Pursuits of Medieval Women" in *Becoming Visible: Women in European History*, eds. Renate Bridenthal and Claudia Koontz (Boston, 1977) pp. 91–118.. Schulenburg, Jane Tibbetts, "Sexism and the Celestial Gynaeceum from 500–1200" *Journal of Medieval History* 4 (1978): 117–133.

Duey White

Maria Radu

(see: Veronica Porumbacu)

Eva Raedt-De Canter

Born January 2, 1900, Breda, The Netherlands;
died February 27, 1975, Edam
Genre(s): novel
Language(s): Dutch

Eva Raedt-De Canter (née Anna Elisabeth Johanna de Mooy) is in the first place a translator who also wrote one collection of poems and eight novels for which she was never widely known.

She was also editorial secretary for *Groot Nederland.*

Eva Raedt-De Canter's novels pay particular attention to the subject of women and the institutions that enslave them, such as marriage (1932; *Huwelijk*) and women's prisons (1935; *Vrouwengevangenis*). A forerunner of the Dutch feminist writers, Raedt-De Canter explores the psychological complexion of young women trapped in institutional confines.

Without being moralistic, she manages to incorporate in her work her unconventional ideas about the function and role of the woman as an independent person, equal to her male partner. Her last novel, *Engelen en Dieven* (1962; Angels and Thieves) is purely entertainment, a light adventure story that is at the same time a travel (trip to Italy) and a detective story.

In the strictly male-oriented literary world between the two world wars, Eva Raedt-De Canter did not manage to let her voice be heard; she continues to be virtually unknown.

Works

Geboorte. *Roman van een jong Leven* (1931). *Huwelijk* (1932). *Boheme* (1933). *Ons Anneke* (1934). *Vrouwengevangenis* (1935). *De Vreemdeling in uw Poorten* (1938). *Wankele Waarheid* (1941). *Engelen en Dieven* (1962). Poetry: *Internaat* (1930).

Bibliography

Kelk, C.J., *Rondom Tien Gestalten* (Utrecht, 1938). Romein-Verschoor, A.H.M., *Vrouwenspiegel* (Nymegen, 1936, 1977). Van Vriesland, V.E., in *Onderzoek en Vertoog*, Vol.1 (Amsterdam, 1958).

An Lammens

Sarolta Raffai

Born 1930, Hungary
Genre(s): poetry, novel, drama, short story
Language(s): Hungarian

Raffai began her career as a schoolteacher near Kalocsa; later she worked as a librarian. She became director of the Petőfi Irodalmi Muzeum (Petőfi Museum of Literature), and a representative in Parliament. Indigenous Hungarian literary traditions inform her poetry. Her fiction addresses the conflicts that arise from the post-World War II changes in the social order in Hungary.

Works

Poetry: *Részeg Virágzás* (1966). *Ne Félts, Ne Félj* (1975).
Novels: *Egyszál Magam* (1967). *Morzsahegyek* (1974). *Jöhetsz Holnap Is* (1978). *Egyszeri Kaland*, short stories (1975).
Plays: *Diplomások* (1969). *Utolsó tét* (1972). *Vasderes*, collection of plays (1977).

Bibliography

Pomogats, Béla, *Az Újabb Magyar Irodalom: 1945–1981* (Budapest, 1982).

Gyorgyi Voros

Šatrijos Ragana

(a.k.a. Marija Pečkauskaitė)

Born March 8, 1877, Medingėnai, Lithuania;
died July 24, 1930, Židikai, Lithuania
Genre(s): novella, short story, sketch
Language: Lithuanian

Writing in the early decades of the twentieth century, Marija Pečkauskaitė was one of the first Lithuanian authors to emphasize subjective moods and psychological analysis in her novellas, short stories, and sketches. Lyrical, romantic descriptions of nature and of the "noble soul" are combined with a strong ethical, pedagogical intent rooted in religious faith and in idealistic philosophy. Her works portray the national cultural revival and a humanitarian concern with rural misery and with the need for mass education. Spiritual dilemmas, such as conflicts between altruistic duties and personal inclinations, are frequent themes in her work. In addition to fiction, she wrote and translated treatises on the education of young people.

Born into a family of impoverished rural gentry, Marija Pečkauskaitė was raised in social circles in which Polish language and culture predominated. Through the patriotic zeal of her tutor, Povilas Višinskis, she became aware of Lithuanian culture and of the needs of the Lithuanian-speaking peasantry. Her first narratives in Lithuanian (1895) were written with his encouragement and help. After completing her secondary education with private tutors, she received a scholarship in 1905 that enabled her to study pedagogy, psychology, and literature in Switzerland. There she was influenced by the philosophy of Friedrich Wilhelm Foerster and later translated a number of his works on education into Lithuanian. After returning to Lithuania, from 1909 to 1915 she taught and served as director of a secondary school for girls in Mariampolė. From 1915 to her death in 1930 she lived in the village of Židikai, where, in spite of her failing health, she continued to write and to devote herself to educational and charitable work among the rural population.

Her most important literary works are the novellas *Viktutė* (1903), *Vincas Stonis* (1906), and *Sename dvare* (1922; On an Old Estate). Outstanding among her many shorter prose narratives is the story "Irkos Tragedija" (Irka's Tragedy). *Viktutė*, written in diary form, traces the spiritual-ethical maturation of a young, upper-class woman who sacrifices her own professional ambitions to the needs of her family and who discovers a personal mission in Lithuania's cultural awakening. The author's sensitive characterization of children is evident in *Vincas Stonis*, which traces a talented boy's intellectual and moral development under the guidance of a humanistic and patriotic teacher. "Irka's Tragedy," told from the perspective of a young girl, reveals the suffering of a child who feels unloved and neglected by her parents. The longest and best-known narrative by Šatrijos Ragana, *On an Old Estate*, is a nostalgic description of family life among the rural gentry prior to the first World War, as seen through the eyes of an eight-year-old girl. Correcting and balancing the girl's view are passages from her mother's diary, which reveal some darker sides of this patriarchal order. The idyllic descriptions of nature and the lyrical, melancholy mood have led critics to characterize this work as the "swan song" of the Lithuanian gentry.

Her interest in depicting the inner life of characters led Marija Pečkauskaitė to introduce subjective modes of narration into Lithuanian literature, such as interior monologue, narrated monologue, and the diary form. However, the emphasis on feelings created at times an excess of sentimentality. Her graceful, musical prose style served to express the neo-romantic view of art and literature, that art seeks to reveal the spiritual world beyond the material one. Her concern with ethical and religious issues, with spiritual growth and individual responsibility, tends to make some of her works overtly pedagogical or didactic.

Works

Raštai, collected works, Vols. 1–6 (1928), Vol. 7 (1939). *Irkos Tragedija* and *Sename dvare*, selected works, 2 vols., ed. A. Zalatorius (1969). *Laiškai* [Letters], ed. J. Žėkaitė (1986).

Bibliography

Cibiras, K., *Gyvenimo menininkė—Marija Pečkauskaitė* (Marijampolė, 1937). Cipliauskaitė, B., "Šatrijos Ragana lietuvių pasakojimo raidos perspektyvoje." *Lituanistikos Instituto darbai* (Chicago, 1977), pp. 107–118. Gulbinas, K., *Das pädagogische Lebenswerk der litauischen Dichterin Marija Pečkauskaitė* (Paterborn, 1971). Kelertienė, V., "Moteris moterų prozoje." *Metmenys* 50 (1985): 68–93. Zalatorius, A., *Lietuvių apsakymo raida ir poetika* (Vilnius, 1971), pp. 272–286. Žėkaitė, J., *Šatrijos Ragana* (Vilnius, 1984).

Audronė B. Willeke

Karen Margrethe Rahbek

Born October 19, 1775, Copenhagen, Denmark; died January 21, 1829, Frederiksberg
Genre(s): letters, autobiography
Language(s): Danish

In the unpretentious atmosphere of "Bakkehuset," Kamma Rahbek was the focal point for two generations of Danish writers, among them P.A. Heiberg, Jens Baggesen, N.F.S. Grundtvig, Adam Oehlenschläger, Poul Martin Møller, B.S. Ingemann, Thomasine Gyllembourg, and Hans Christian Andersen. Married to Knud Lyhne Rahbek in 1798, Kamma Rahbek entertained in her famous *salon* a gallery of literary luminaries, who were drawn to "Bakkehuset" not least because of the hostess' wit, intelligence, and diplomacy.

While Kamma Rahbek's social talents have a long-standing place in Danish literary history, contemporary critics increasingly judge her extensive correspondence with guests and friends as valuable literature in its own right. In letters to

I.P. Mynster and Christian Molbelch, for example, she discusses in a modern, original language a wide range of topics, including the bombardment of Copenhagen, the literature and *literati* of her circle, and her own private thoughts and emotions. Particularly in her correspondence with Molbelch, Kamma Rahbek reached for the intimacy and confidence that nineteenth-century social conventions did not provide.

Besides her uncontested importance in creating a productive literary exchange among Danish writers in the first decades of the nineteenth century, Kamma Rahbek established with her correspondence a bridge between Charlotte Dorothea Biehl's autobiography (1787) and Mathilde Fibiger's *Clara Raphael* (1851) through a shared belief in—and demonstration of—female individuality and strength.

Works

Erindringer af Mit Liv (1824–1829). *Om Karen Margrethe Rahbeks Brevvexling og Hendes Correspondenter: Meddelelser af Efterladte Breve,* ed. P.H. Boye (1881). *Breve fra I.P. Mynster,* ed. I.P. Mynster; includes K.M. Rahbek's letters (1866). *Christian Molbelch og Karen Margrethe Rahbek,* ed. Christian K.F. Molbelch (1883).

Bibliography

Brandes, Georg, "Kamma Rahbek." (1865). *Samlede Skrifter* I (Copenhagen, 1899). Dalager, Stig, and Anne-Marie Mai, *Danske Kvindelige Forfattere* I (Copenhagen, 1982), pp. 130–138. Jensen, Anne E., *Kamma Rahbek 1775–1829. Frederiksberg Gennem Tiderne* 15 (Copenhagen, 1975). Kyrre, Hans, *Knud Lyhne Rahbek, Kamma Rahbek og Livet paa Bakkehuset* (1914; rpt. Copenhagen, 1929).

Clara Juncker

Rahel Bluwstein

(a.k.a. Rahel)

Born 1890, Russia; died 1931, Tel Aviv, Israel
Genre(s): poetry
Language(s): Hebrew

The woman who was destined to pave the way for "Miriam's Daughters," Rahel Bluwstein, was born in Russia in 1890. She attended a Hebrew public school in Poltava and graduated from a Russian gymnasium. She began her studies at Kiev Art School, but she could no longer hold back her deep yearnings for the Promised Land. In 1909 she left Kiev and went to Palestine.

Rahel arrived in Jaffa and found work as an *Haluzah* (agricultural worker), first in Rehovot, then on the banks of the Sea of Galilee in the cooperative colony of Kinneret. Although she deeply loved the land and people, Rahel was not destined to remain in Palestine long. In 1913 her interest in agronomy took her to Toulouse, France, where she could receive the best training in that subject. Again, her studies were cut short, this time due to the outbreak of World War II, and Rahel was forced to return to Russia, where she taught in a school for refugee children.

In 1919, Rahel returned to Palestine. However, a lingering illness, tuberculosis, prevented her from doing any physical labor, and over the next ten years this fatal disease took its toll. The effects of the disease, however, cast a splendid aura of tragedy over the poetry of Rahel. The greatest part of her poetic work was accomplished during the last ten years of her life, as she seemingly strove to leave the world a record of her love for the Promised Land and her yearning to experience a longer life in it.

She strove to resign herself to her fate, but she could not conceal the sorrow and grief of renunciating much of what she deemed important for her life. Rahel accepted her loss of opportunity for love and motherhood, yet she still regarded this loss as a curse. In her poem *Akarah* (Childless), she writes wistfully of her desire to have a child (the subject of the poem, Uri, is the name later given to her nephew). Another poem expresses the deep pathos Rahel experienced as she pleads to a friend to name her daughter Rahel. There is no tone of bitterness in the poetry of Rahel, but rather there is a sense of mourning as she struggles to accept her death and reach a peace in her soul. She wants to experience the joy life offers in the present, and she strives not to succumb to wrath and anger.

Rahel successfully found comfort for her tragic present in looking to the brighter moments of her past. She reaches for her memories of the beauty of the Promised Land, and she recreates her deep feeling of love for the land. Rahel reveals tender feelings for Palestinian soil, as she reflects on what she gave to this land. There is a sense of pride in the tree that she planted by the Jordan or the paths she trod through the fields in *El Arzi* (The Fields). Rahel writes in quiet celebration in *Temurah* (Transformation) of the elements of her body disintegrating to mingle with the grass and soil, so as to enrich her sacred land.

Rahel also consoles herself by reflecting upon her life as an *Haluzah*. *'Al ha-Goren* (At the Barn) and *Halibat Lailah* (Milking at Night) represent the very soul of Rahel: for her the ordinary and mundane events of life are the extraordinary gifts some receive with which they may live out their lives, returning to the soil an insignificant part of what they have received. There is an intense desire to labor on the land, which is best described by Rahel's poem *Zaw ha Goral* (The Decree of Destiny). She seems to resign herself to her tragic fate, yet she refuses to retire her desires as she requests burial at the Kinneret, the beginnings of her labor in the Promised Land. Where her work began, so there would it also end. Her grave at this site has been immortalized in a poem by Levi ben Amittai, *Mazzevet Rahel* (Memorial of Rahel).

Poetry was not the only literary contribution of Rahel. She also felt that she had to repay a debt to her native Russia. Therefore, she translated the works of Pushkin, Yesenin, Moravskaya, and Akhmatova from her native language of Russian to Hebrew.

There is an idealism in Rahel's poetry that celebrates life and warns us not to overlook the seemingly insignificant. Her work pushes us to find nobility in the *Haluzah*, the one who is devoted and self-sacrificing for the rehabilitation of Palestine. Rahel's poetry is not that of tragic individualism, but rather it is a true and sincere example of the generous spirit that creates a great land.

Works

Safiah [Aftergrowth] (1927). *Mineged* [From the Opposite] (1930). *Nevo* [Mt. Nebo] (1949). *Shirat Rahel* [The Poetry of Rahel] (1949).

Bibliography

Halkin, Simon, *Modern Hebrew Literature* (New York, 1950). Mintz, Ruth F., ed., *Modern Hebrew Poetry* (Berkeley, 1966). Penueli, S.Y., and A. Ukhmani, eds., *Anthology of Modern Hebrew Poetry, Vol. 1* (Jerusalem, 1966). Silberschlag, Eisig, *From Renaissance to Renaissance II: Hebrew Literature in the Land of Israel: 1870–1970* (New York, 1977). Waxman, Meyer, *A History of Jewish Literature, Vol. 4* (Cranbury, N.J., 1960).

JoAnne C. Juett

M. Francisco Ramírez de Madrid

(see: Beatriz Galindo)

Ranina

(see: Dora Petrova Gabe)

Clara Raphael

(see: Mathilde Lucie Fibiger)

Lea Ráskai

Born fifteenth century; died sixteenth century
Genre(s): translation, copyist of ecclesiastical works
Language(s): Hungarian, Latin

Very little is known of the life of Lea Ráskai. She was a Dominican nun in the cloister on the Nyulak Szigete (Island of the Hares), known today as St. Margaret's Island, and was most likely of aristocratic birth. Her cloister had been founded by King Béla IV for his daughter, Margaret. Ráskai copied the legend of St. Margaret (*Margit legenda*), probably also translating it from the Latin. This would indicate a high degree of education, as indeed is also suggested by the reforms that were being carried out at this time: the rules call for extensive readings in liturgical works as well as the Bible, and most of this was still in Latin. The *Margit legenda* (Margaret Legend) was done in 1510. Ráskai's literary talent is demonstrated in the care she took to make each detail of her subject's life come alive by minute references to the cloister; such passages might even be embellishments of the Latin original. The Margaret legend is important as a record of the life of a princess of the House of Árpád, but Ráskai's contribution extended beyond this one work.

The Cornides-codex is perhaps her most important work. This was copied between 1514–1519 and consists of fourteen sermons and eleven legends. The source of the sermons is a fifteenth-century collection by an unknown compiler who calls himself Paratus. These are full of parables and many similes from nature. The Easter sermon serves almost as a reply to the lament of Mary, setting forth how Jesus appears to Mary while she was still at home and how the angels, Adam and Eve and the prophets, the patriarchs, and saints glorified her. The one for All Saints Day recounts the dedication of the Pantheon in 605 to the Blessed Virgin and all the saints. For Trinity Sunday, one of the great mysteries of faith is explained in the best tradition of medieval philosophy. Most of the legends in this work are based on the *Legenda Aurea*, but the *Catalogus Sanctorum* is the source of the legend of St. Potenciana and the legend of St. Dorothy comes from the *De Sanctis* of the popular Hungarian preacher, Plébart of Temesvár. Most of the saints are virgins and martyrs from the early days of the Church, though St. Helena is included as an example of chaste widowhood. While following her sources fairly closely, Ráskai nevertheless shows some passages of rare poetic beauty, particularly in the legend of St. Dorothy. She also copied about half of the *Példák könyve* (The Book of Examples) in 1510, in 1517 the legend of life of St. Dominic, and in 1522 the Horváth-codex. Her contribution to Hungarian literature has provided a rich source of earlier traditions.

Sister Lea belonged to the new generation of nuns to whom Hungarian literature owes a great debt, for they preserved earlier legends through their copying. Though somewhat anachronistic in their dedication to the ideals of the Middle Ages on the threshold of the Renaissance, they were not untouched by the spirit of Humanism. Better educated than their predecessors, they were freer in spirit and more in touch with the world: the mother of King Matthias took an active interest in the major monasteries and had free access to the one on St. Margaret's island also. Familiar with Latin, the sisters also used Hungarian to transmit the teachings and the legends of the Church to those unschooled in the Church's language. Ráskai speaks with feeling of the peace to be found in the cells: "outside the cells there is nothing but warfare. . . . In the cells we pray, write, study, . . . read Holy Writ, or serve God." Ironically, though we do not know when Ráskai died, the disintegration of the Hungarian kingdom was sealed with the defeat at Mohács in 1526 when the young king was killed. The monasteries of Buda were no longer the refuges they had been earlier, and in 1541, when the city fell to the Turks, all of them were closed and the inhabitants were forced to flee.

Works

Margit legenda (1510). *Példák könyve*, first part (1510). *Cornides-codex* (1514–1519). *Domonkos-legenda* [Legend of St. Dominic] (1517). *Horváth-codex*.

Bibliography

Horger, Antal, *Magyar nyelvőr* (1897). Horváth, János, *A Magyar irodalmi műveltség kezdetei, Szent Istvántól Mohácsig* (Budapest, 1944). *A Magyar irodalom története 1600-ig*, vol. 1, Tibor Klaniczay, ed., in *Magyar Tudományos Adadémia Irodalomtörténeti Intézete, A Magyar irodalom története* (Budapest, 1964). Szerb, Antal, *Magyar irodalomtörténet* (Budapest, 1939).

Enikő Molnár Basa

Irina Ratushinskaia

Born March 4, 1954, Odessa, The Soviet Union
Genre(s): poetry, short story
Language(s): Russian

A descendant of Russianized Polish nobility, a physicist and mathematician by training, Irina Ratushinskaia has been writing poetry since childhood. She realized her true vocation as a poet when at the age of twenty-five, she read Pasternak, Mandelshtam, and Tsvetaeva. She describes it in her brief autobiographical sketch "My Homeland" as a sudden encounter with the eternal light of truth, making her aware of the inhumanity of existence under the Soviet regime. The result was a profound spiritual awakening, which released an avalanche of poetic creativity.

Since that revelation she has committed herself to speak out in protest against the Soviet disrespect of basic human rights and, by that same token, become a dissident poet. Her courageous poetic attack on injustice, obviously, could not be published in the USSR; instead her poetry was spread unofficially by *samizdat*, and some of it reached the West where three collections of her work were published: one in 1984, two in 1986.

Ratushinskaia's poetic activity resulted in her arrest in September 1982 and subsequent sentence to seven years' hard labor and five years' exile in March 1983. On October 10, 1986, Ratushinskaia was released before completing her term and even allowed to leave the Soviet Union with her husband (she married Igor Gerashchenko in 1979) to go to England for medical treatment. For the time being she decided to stay in the West.

During the three and a half years in jail in incredible, inhuman conditions, suffering physical and mental torture, Ratushinskaia has composed more than two hundred poems writing them down with a burnt match on a piece of soap and committing them to memory until retainment. To avoid additional punishment, she washed off the lines when she knew them by heart.

Frequently, her lyric voice assumes the power of a modern Cassandra foreseeing her confinement and martyrdom. The sublimation of her own pain channels her creative impulse towards compassion for her fellow-inmates, her abandoned husband: "Lord, how is life for him? Keep a watchful eye, / Lest that bare cubbyhole apartment drive him to madness!" (April, 1983). The motif of bitter denunciation of the Soviet system's brutality is overcome by the constantly recurring theme of trust in Divine Grace and a sense of mission to bring truth to the world. Her moral anguish is fleeting and mild, she likens it to a tiny tame animal: "As a domesticated cub, my anguish / Lives in tranquillity, responds to "shoo"! / She needs so little: Some attentive scratching." (October, 1982).

Ratushinskaia also has written short stories, one of which ("The Debt" [October 5, 1986]) has appeared in the Russian emigre daily *Novoye Russkoe Slovo* (The New Russian Word). A collection of Ratushinskaia's short stories, *The Tale of Three Heads*, came out in Russian and English at the very end of 1986.

Ratushinskaia's lyrics range from classical meters and rhyme schemes to various modes of modern versification. Most of her poetic output, as a genuine lyrical testimony to the cruel persecution of human dignity, belongs to the, alas, well-established genre of "prison-diary."

Works

Poems, text in Russian, English, and French, tr. Meery Devergnas (French) and Philip Balla, Pamela White Hadas, Susan Layton, Ilya Nykin (English) (1984). *Vne limita* [Beyond the Limit], selected poetry (1986). *Ia dozhivu* [I'll Survive], poems (1986). *Skazka o trekh golovakh* [The Tale of Three Heads], tr. Diane Nemec Ignashev (1986).

Marina Astman

Adda Ravnkilde

Born July 30, 1862, Sakskøbing, Denmark;
died November 30, 1883, Copenhagen
Genre(s): tale, poetry
Language(s): Danish

Adele Marie Ravnkilde was born in Sakskøbing, Denmark, daughter of a government official who later became mayor of Saeby. She began to write poetry at an early age and from twelve to fourteen attended school in Copenhagen. Her literary and intellectual interests were further stimulated by a close female friend, an influence which displeased Ravnkilde's father. In 1880 he sent her to Snoldelev's parsonage to work as a governess. A year later she returned to her parents' home in Saeby. There she wrote three tales: "en Pyrrhussejr" (A Pyrrhic Victory), "Judith Fürste" (Judith Fürste), and "Tantaluskvaler" (Tantalus-Torments). In 1883 she went to Copenhagen to prepare herself for a teaching career. Literary life in the Danish capital at that time was dominated by the famous critic and professor of literature Georg Brandes, an outspoken champion of women's liberation and free love. At Brandes' advice, Ravnkilde abandoned her plans to become a teacher and began to study for a degree in the arts. She expressed the desire to make her own name famous in literature instead of publishing anonymously or under a pseudonym. A short while later, after attending one of Brandes' lectures, she committed suicide.

Judith Fürste, a novel-length psychological tale that shows the influence of Charlotte Brontë's *Jane Eyre*, was published in 1884 with a foreword by Brandes. The heroine of this work suffers in marriage because of her "Artemis-nature." Ravnkilde's two other tales were edited and brought out in 1884 by the Norwegian novelist Amalie Skram and her husband Erik Skram, as *To fortaellinger* (Two Tales). The first of these, "En Pyrrhussejr," is a plea for female independence and equality. Ravnkilde's best work, "Tantaluskvaler," portrays the passion and suffering of a love affair between two exceptional individuals.

Adda Ravnkilde was a talented and tragic peripheral figure in the cultural ferment and debate of the 1880s surrounding the woman question. She can be considered a forerunner of modern feminist literature in Denmark. Though posthumously, she was one of the first Danish women to publish under her own name.

Works

Judith Fürste (1884). *To fortaellinger* (1884; includes "en Pyrrhussejr" and "Tantaluskvaler"). *Digte*, poems (n.d.).

Bibliography

Brandes, Georg, *Samlede Skrifter* (1919). *Illustreret Dansk Litteraturhistorie*, Carl Petersen and Vilhelm Andersen, eds. (1924–1925). Løn, Anne Marie, *Adda Ravnkilde* (1978) (Danish). Pearson, Jean, "Adele Marie Ravnkilde." *Kvindelige forfattere* (1985).

Jean Pearson

Pauline Réage

Genre(s): erotic novel
Language(s): French

Pauline Réage is one of the rare female pseudonyms assumed by a male writer and is commonly thought to be the pen name for Dominique Avry or for Jean Paulhan, who both worked at *La Nouvelle Revue Française*. Even though no positive identification has been made, Pauline Réage's two books, *Histoire d'O* (The Story of O) and its sequel, *Retour à Roissy* (Return to Roissy), have never been attributed to a woman.

Jean Paulhan's preface to *Histoire d'O*, "Du Bonheur dans l'esclavage" (Of Happiness in Slavery), has a revengeful tone toward women, thanking Réage for at last having a woman confess her desire to be mastered and dominated by a man. *Histoire d'O* tells the story of a young woman who willingly agrees to be the slave of a man, complying with all his sexual desires and letting him prostitute her for his own sexual pleasure as well as his financial benefit. The greater part of the story takes place in a castle in Roissy, in the Paris suburbs. The overriding theme of Réage's book is the absolute compliance and acceptance by O of her condition. She finds happiness in wearing irons and chains, in being whipped, and ultimately in being branded with her master's initials.

Histoire d'O was a subject of scandal at the time of its original publication, but most of the interest in Pauline Réage and O had vanished by the time of the publication of the sequel, *Retour à Roissy*.

Works

Histoire d'O (1954). *Retour à Roissy: Une Fille amoureuse* (1975).
Translations: *The Story of O* (London, 1976). *Return to the Chateau: Story of O: A Girl in Love* (New York, 1980).

Bibliography

Brown, Nathaniel, and Rebecca Faery, "The Total 'O.' Dream or Nightmare?" *Mosaic* XVII (1984): 189–206. Desforges, Régine, *O m'a dit: Entretiens avec Pauline Réage* (Paris, 1975). Pallister, Janis. "The Anti-Castle in the Works of 'Pauline Réage,'" *The Journal of Midwest Modern Languages Association* XVIII, 2 (Fall 1985): 3–13.

Valerie Lastinger

Elisabeth (Elisa) Charlotte Konstantia von der Recke

(a.k.a. Elisa, Elise)

Born June 1, 1754, Schönberg, Courland; died April 13, 1833, Dresden, Germany
Genre(s): poetry, exposé, drama, diaries
Language(s): German

Elisa von der Recke was known in her own time primarily for her exposé of the great swindler Cagliostro, but she is also important for her posthumously published diaries and letters, less so for her poetry.

The daughter of Johann Friedrich von Medem (1722–1785) and Luise Dorothea von Korff (d. 1758) was born into an aristocratic German family of estate owners in the far northeastern region of Courland (now forming parts of Latvia and Lithuania), Elisa was sent after the death of her mother to be raised by her harsh and domineering grandmother, Constantia Ursula von Korff (1698–1790), who tried (unsuccessfully) to raise the child to endure without complaint the cultural aridity and boredom of an aristocratic woman's life in Courland. At age seventeen the girl, who nurtured her aethereal feelings and sensitivity in accordance with the sentimental literature of her time, was married against her will to a respectable but prosaic aristocrat, Baron Georg Peter Magnus von der Recke, who was interested primarily in managing his estate and having healthy heirs. Five years after the marriage they separated. (Wilhelm von Humboldt wrote that after finding Elisa building a memorial to Young, author of the melancholy and sentimental *Night Thoughts*, the furious husband banished his wife from his property.) With her she took their child, who was, to the disappointment of the father, a girl. Elisa refused all later opportunities to remarry.

The next three years brought a series of additional traumas. In 1777 the three-year-old daughter died. In 1778 von der Recke's beloved brother died. And in 1779 Cagliostro came to Mitau, the capital of Courland. He was a necromancer and alchemist, and the enthusiastic, battered von der Recke was a highly vulnerable target for him. For a year she was under his influence. What the erotic components and consequences of this experience were is not known. Unmistakable, however, is the decisive turn toward rationalism that she took after her disillusionment (1780) with the Italian imposter.

Meanwhile her attention and energy were directed increasingly toward the welfare of her half-sister, Dorothea. She made sure that Dorothea's marriage to the divorced Duke of Courland was properly recognized and then spent years lobbying in Warsaw and Berlin to ensure the continued independence of the territory, to no avail. In 1796 Courland became a province of Russia under Catherine the Great.

By then Elisa von der Recke was officially divorced (1781). Her father and both stepmothers were dead. She was frequently estranged from her sister, whose frivolity she thought had contributed to the downfall of her cause. She was no longer the citizen of a free state and in fact had no home to which she could return. Now she became a familiar visitor in the cultural centers of Central Europe. She met (and to some extent influenced), virtually all the important German writers of her time, especially becoming a close friend of the influential but argumentative Enlightenment publisher and editor, Nicolai, in Berlin. To be recognized, she needed only to sign herself "Elisa." Friends were of utmost importance to Elisa von der Recke. She had several intense friendships with women, most notably with Sophie Becker, later Schwarz, but also with 13 young women whom she considered her informal foster daughters (Pflegetöchter). From 1804 on, von der Recke's friend and companion was a man, the sentimental and unworldly poet and aesthete Christoph August Tiedge. They are buried together.

Her fame was derived first from her brief book about Cagliostro. In it Elisa tried to do two things, describe and explain Cagliostro's techniques, and describe and explain her own vulnerability. With the help of hindsight and faith in rationalist argument, she believed these tasks could be easily and completely accomplished. Thus to some extent she failed to capture the power of Cagliostro. Nonetheless, she gave a revealing and brave account of her experience and published it under her own name, explaining that only in this way did she think the truth of her account could be fully credited. The form of her study is innovative and effective, giving inside and outside views of the events simultaneously by printing diary excerpts on one page and, facing them, her later comments and explanations.

Recke's poetry is impersonal, aiming for sublimity and purity, but without distinctive tone or subject matter. The travel books are better anchored in concrete reality and of interest in part for the sheer uncommonness of travel literature by women in that time. Inspired by her friendship with the great actor and director Schröder in Hamburg, she also wrote at least two plays. One of them Schiller considered revising; the other, "Family Scenes, or Developments at a Masked Ball," Recke herself later published. It is about marital problems, all of which revolve around character and morality, with resignation and accommodation recommended as women's best response to adversity. Finally, she wrote two biographical sketches of two men she had known and honored, describing them as she personally knew them and stressing wherever possible how they met her ideal of selfless gentility. Her posthumously published diaries offer fascinating insights into the life of an eighteenth-century aristocratic woman.

Works

Geistliche Lieder einer vornehmen kurlandischen Dame mit Melodien von Hiller [Spiritual Songs of an Aristocratic Lady with Melodies by Hiller] (1780). *Elisens Geistliche Gedichte, nebst einem Oratorium und einer Hymne von C.F. Neander* [Elisa's Spiritual Poems, Along with an Oratorio and Hymn by C.F. Neander] (1783). *Nachricht von des berüchtigten Cagliostro Aufenthalt in Mitau 1779 und von dessen dortigen Operationen* [News of the Stay of the Notorious Cagliostro in Mitau in 1779 and of His Dealings There] (1787). *Elisens und Sophiens Gedichte* [Elisa's and Sophia's Poems] (1790). *Über C.F. Neanders Leben und Schriften. Eine Skizze* [C.F. Neander's Life and Writings, a Sketch] (1801). *Gedichte* [Poems] (1806). Supplement: *Anhang zu den Gedichten* (1816). Second Edition: *Gedichte* (1816). *Tagebuch einer Reise durch einen Teil Deutschlands und durch Italien in den Jahren 1804–1806* [Journal of a Trip Through Part of Germany and Through Italy in the Years 1804–1806] (1815–1817). *Gebete und religiöse Betrachtungen* [Prayers and Meditations] (1826). *Familien-Scenen oder Entwickelungen auf dem Masquenballe. Schauspiel in vier Aufzügen* [Family Scenes or Developments at a Masked Ball, Play in 4 Acts] (1827). *Geistliche Lieder, Gebete und religiöse Betrachtungen* [Spiritual Songs, Prayers, and Religious Meditations] (1833). *Elisa von der Recke. Aufzeichnungen und Briefe aus ihren Jugendtagen* [Journals], ed. Paul Rachel (1902). *1927 Mein Journal. Elisas neu aufgefundene Tagebücher aus den Jahren 1791 und 1793/95*, ed.

Johannes Werner [My Journal, Elisa's Recently Discovered Diaries from the Years 1791 and 1793–1795] (1927).

Bibliography

Frederiksen, Elke, ed., *Women Writers of Germany, Austria, and Switzerland. An Annotated Bio-Bibliographical Guide* (New York, 1989), pp. 184–185. Friedrichs, Elisabeth, *Die deutschsprachigen Schriftstellerinnen des 18. und 19. Jahrhunderts. Ein Lexikon* (Stuttgart, 1981), p. 244. Schulz, Günter, "Elisa v.d. Recke, die Freundin Friedrich Nicolais." *Wolfenbütteler Studien zur Aufklärung* 3 (1976): 159–173. Träger, Christine, *Elisa von Der Recke. Tagebücher und Selbstzeugnisse* (München, 1984). Schindel, Carl Wilhelm Otto August von, *Die deutschen Schriftstellerinnen des neunzehnten Jahrhunderts*, vol. 2 (Leipzig, 1825), pp. 126ff.

Ruth P. Dawson

Ruth Rehmann

Born June 1, 1922, Siegburg, Germany
Genre(s): radio play, short story, song, novel
Language(s): German

Ruth Rehmann was born on June 1, 1922. Her father was a pastor in Siegburg, an outlying area of Bonn, where Rehmann grew up. After she completed her gymnasium education, she went to Hamburg where she studied to be a translator. Later she studied art history and archaeology in Berlin and Cologne, but she eventually concentrated on German literature and music, in which she received a diploma in music performance, i.e., violin. In the following months Rehmann led a nomadic existence, wandering from France to Italy, Africa, and Greece, earning her livelihood by composing songs after lyrics by Brecht, Villon, and Lorca and performing them in different bars. She also worked at the American and Indian embassy in Bonn as a press secretary. Already in the early 1950s, Rehmann started to publish short stories in literary magazines such as *Akzente* and *Story*. In 1959 the publication of her first novel, *Illusionen* (Illusions), and her reading at the Gruppe 47 Conference the previous year combined to catapult her into the public eye. In 1964, she was awarded the Niedersachsischer

Forderungspreis, and in 1967, her second novel, *Die Leute im Tal* (The People in the Valley), won first prize for the literature contest: "Der Bauer in der Industriegesellschaft." After living in Bonn and Düsseldorf, she then moved to Altenmarkt, a small town in Bavaria, in 1958. She is married and has three children. Ruth Rehmann is a member of the Gruppe 47 and the PEN club.

In her first novel, *Illusionen* (1959), she describes the hopeless situation of four employees during a weekend, during which they cannot escape from their artificial office world, neither in hope nor in dreams. She reveals the illusions through which they try to create a personality different from what they actually are. This text is mainly based upon her perception and experience of society in the area around Bonn during the time of Konrad Adenauer.

The setting of her second novel, *Die Leute im Tal* (1968), is a very rural area. Here Rehmann describes the encounter between the traditional world of an old peasant and the progressive world of his son, which is influenced by modern technology. Rehmann enlarges the topic of the generation conflict to the extent of the discrepancy between the older peasant tradition on the one side, and the development of high technology on the other. Eventually she returns to the conflict between father and son, in which the old peasant refuses to hand over his farm to his son.

Rehmann's later novel, *Der Mann auf der Kanzel, Fragen an einen Vater* (1979; The Man in the Pulpit, Questions Addressed to a Father), can be seen as the attempt of a woman to find her true self by writing about her own childhood. She concentrates particularly on the relationship with her father who now, from an adult's point of view, appears to be a strict and authoritarian patriarch. She also tries to reveal his social and political life, i.e., as a protestant pastor he refused to participate in the resistance against the Nazi regime.

Inspired by questions from her son, Rehmann reflects on the private life and the political opinion of her father, who died in 1941 at the age of sixty-six.

The problem of biographical writing is also treated in her two most recent novels, *Abschied von der Meister Klasse* (1985; Farewell from the Master-class) and *Die Schwaiger in* (1987; The

Woman from Schwaig Farm). In these instances, however, biography is handled from a woman's point of view. In *Abschied von der Meister Klasse*, Rehmann describes the difficulties a young journalist encounters in writing a biography about an old but famous violinist; problems which turn out to be personal and closely connected with the journalist's own past. Having failed to succeed in her once ambitious design to become a violinist, the journalist is deeply unsettled by the fact that the celebrated maestra about whom she is to write was her former violin teacher. Set in the morbid ambience of a sanitarium, Rehmann depicts the escalating quarrels between the two women about careers and the price one has to pay for success.

In her most recent work, *Die Schwaigerin*, Rehmann descibes the life of the peasant woman Anna. The story is narrated in the first person by a female friend of Anna who moved from the same farm in the city. Similar to her second novel, *Die Leute im Tal*, Rehmann focuses on the discrepancy between rural life in the country and urban life in the city. The novel can also be read as a chronicle depicting the hardship of rural people migrating to the city. In *Die Schwaigerin*, however, this transition is reflected in the unusual friendship between two women, where Anna's urban friend puts into words what Anna can only experience directly about country life.

In conclusion, it may be said that Ruth Rehmann's work—her novels, short stories, and radio plays, considered as a whole—presents a very sensitive, lively description of society and of the average person, in particular. She has a supreme talent for articulating common situations and impressions from her personal point of view in such a way that hidden implications are conveyed to the reader.

Works

Novels: *Illusionen* (1959). *Die Leute im Tal* (1968). *Der Mann auf der Kanzel, Fragen an einen Vater* (1979). *Abscheid von der Meister Klasse* (1985). *Die Schwaiger in* (1987).

Stories: *Paare* (1978). *Der Abstieg* (1987).

Radio plays: *Ein ruhiges Haus* (1960). *Flieder aux Malchien* (1964). *Drei Gespräche über einen Mann* (1966). *Ich mag Deine Freunde* (1970). *Frau Violets Haus* (1974). *Gehörbildung oder Ein exemplarischer Reinfall* (1974). *Herr Seliger geht zu weit* (1977).

Bibliography

Beer, Johannes, ed., *Der Romanführer*, Vol. XIII (Stuttgart, 1964), p. 304f. Kröll, Friedheim, *Die Gruppe 47* (Stuttgart, 1977), p. 128. Lattmann, Dieter, ed., *Kindlers Literaturgeschichte der Gegenwart* (Zurich/Munich, 1973), p. 250, 254, 765. Lennarz, Franz, *Deutsche Schriftsteller des 20. Jahrhunderts im Spiegel der Kritik*, Vol. III (Stuttgart, 1984), p. 1383f.

Friederike Emonds

Brigitte Reimann

Born July 21, 1933, Burg, near Magdeburg, East Germany; died February 20, 1973
Genre(s): radio and television scripts, prose, novel
Language(s): German

Brigitte Reimann's father was a journalist, and he instilled in his daughter a love for writing. After completing her high school education, she was engaged as a teacher for two years. Thereafter she was employed in various professions until she joined the brigade of the "Schwarze Pumpe" in Hoyerswerda, a literary group. She collaborated with her husband, Siegfried Pretschmann, from whom she later separated. In 1965 she received the Heinrich Mann Prize for Literature. Just before she turned forty she developed the cancer that caused her death.

In all her works, Brigitte Reimann extols socialism. Her novel, *Ankunft im Alltag* coined the term for a new type of DDR-Literature: "Ankunftsliteratur" (arrival literature). It is the literature about homelessness and about those driven from their homes during World War II, who have finally arrived at home, a new home. They have come back to a new society and a new social order: the socialist state in which they find confidence and which they can trust. Reimann's characters demonstrate how to fit into the new order and how to be happy by means of re-education and indoctrination into the socialist state.

Works

Die Frau am Pranger [The Woman in the Pillory] (1956). *Das Geständniss* [The Confession] (1960). *Sieben Scheffel Salz. Ein Hörspiel* [Seven Bushels of Salt. A Radio-drama] (1960). [With Siegfried Pretschmann], *Ankunft im Alltag* [Arrival in the Workday] (1961). *Geschwister. Eine Erzählung* [Brothers and Sisters. A Story] (1963). *Das Grüne Licht der Steppen. Tagebuch einer Sibirienreise* [Green Light of the Steppes. A Diary of a Trip to Siberia] (1965). *Franziska Linkerhand. Roman* [Franziska Linkerhand. A Novel] (1974; published posthumously).

Bibliography

Emmerich, Wolfgang, *Kleine Literaturgeschichte der DDR* (Darmstadt, 1981). Franke, Konrad, *Die Literatur der Deutschen Demokratischen Republik* (Zürich and München, 1974). *Neue Literatur der Frauen*. Herausgegeben von Heinz Pukins (München, 1980).

Brigitte Edith Archibald

Ida von Reinsberg-Düringsfeld

(a.k.a. Thekla)

Born November 12, 1815, Militsch, Silesia; died October 25, 1876, Stuttgart, Germany
Genre(s): poetry, novel, novella, short story, travelogue, fairy tale, translation, scientific work
Language(s): German

Ida von Düringsfeld received an early and intensive training in Romance and Slavic languages, English, music, and literature. Her family encouraged her talents, and particularly her aunt (Frau von Wurmb) and her aunt's brother (Lt. Col. von Platen) directed her literary education. As early as 1830, her first poems appeared in Theodor Hell's *Abendzeitung*, and in 1835 she published a collection of them under the pseudonym "Thekla." Her studies of Spanish literature influenced her romances *Der Stern von Andalusien* (1838), a cyclical work with Spanish-Arabian historical themes.

The first novel to establish her literary fame was *Schloß Goczin* (1841, 1845), which was quickly followed by various other novels and novellas between 1842 and 1845. Among them are *Marie, In der Heimat, Haraldsburg, Magdalene, Hugo, Graf Chala,* and *Hedwig.* On October 20, 1845 Düringsfeld married the Swiss Baron Otto von Reinsberg with whom she travelled extensively to Italy, Dalmatia, Belgium, and Switzerland. Impressions from these travels were partly incorporated in her fictional work, partly used for cultural and historical studies which she produced prolifically. The first of these works was *Margarete von Valois* (1847), which was based on a careful study of French memoirs. Others resulting from travel impressions were: (Italian) *Antonio Foscarini* (1850), *Am Canal Grande* (1848), *Aus Italien* (1851); (Swiss) *Aus der Schweiz* (1850), *Eine Pension am Genfer See* (1851), *Esther* (1852), *Clotilde* (1855); (Netherlands) *Nico Veliki* (1856–1864), *Norbert Dujardin* (1861), *Von der Schelde bis zur Maas* (1861), *Hendrik* (1862), and the short story "Der Bildhauer von Mecheln," which was published in her collection of novellas *Prismen* (1873). Dalmatia serves as background to the novellas "Die rote Mütze" and "Milena" (1863), and to the study *Aus Dalmatien* (1857). Bohemian and Austrian life is reflected in the novellas "Ignota" and "Auf Goyen" (both published in *Prismen,* 1873) and in the short story "Der Stroblwirth" (*Westermann's Monatshefte*). She also wrote several cultural studies in collaboration with her husband (*Aus Kärnten,* 1857; *Aus Meran,* 1868; *Culturgeschichtliche Skizzen aus Meran,* 1874).

Besides translations of Slavic and Italian folksongs, fairy tales, and collections of her own poetry, Reinsberg-Düringsfeld also wrote some critical, biographical, and scientific tomes. Among them are *Byrons Frauen* (1845), a translation of the Königinhof-Manuscripts (1858), and the *Buch denkwürdiger Frauen* (1863), which went through five editions in quick succession. With her husband she collaborated on a lexicon of 2000 proverbs in 230 dialects titled *Sprichwörter der Germanischen und Romanischen Sprachen* (1872–1875, reprint 1973).

In her later years she suffered from asthma and a heart ailment and unsuccessfully sought relief at various health resorts. She died suddenly on October 25, 1876, while in Stuttgart and was followed by her husband, who took his own life the next day.

Works

["Thekla," pseud.], *Gedichte* (1835). *Der Stern von Adalusien,* cycle of romances (1838). *Schriften,* 9 vols. (1845). *Für Dich,* collection of lyric poetry (1851, 1865). *Amimone, ein Alpenmärchen vom Genfersee,* fairy tale (1852). *Böhmische Rosen* (1851) and *Lieder aus der Toskana,* translations of Slavic and Italian folk songs (1854–1859). *Die Literaten,* novel (1863). A three-volume work on proverbs: vol. 1, *Das Sprichwort als Philosoph* (1863); vol. 2, *Das Sprichwort als Praktikus* (1863); vol. 3, *Das Sprichwort als Humorist* (1863); also published as *Das Sprichwort als Kosmopolit,* 3 vols. (1863, 1866). *Brauch und Glaube der Hochzeit bei den christlichen Völkern Europas* (1871). *Prismen,* collection of novellas (1873). *Lieben und Freien in Piemont* (1875). *Forzino* (1877). *Ethnographische Curiositäten* (posth., 1879).

Bibliography

Brinker-Gabler, G., *Lexikon deutschsprachiger Schriftstellerinnen 1800–1945* (Munich, 1986), pp. 76–77. Pyl, T., "Ida von Reinsberg-Düringsfeld." *Allgemeine Deutsche Biographie* 28 (1889), pp. 102–104, lists entries in various literary histories, including one with Reinsberg-Düringsfeld's portrait (Kurz, *Deutsche Litteratur* IV, pp. 101, 796). Warner, C.D., *Biographical Dictionary and Synopsis of Books* (1965), p. 158. Brinker-Gabler, G., *Lexikon deutschsprachiger Schriftstellerinnen 1800–1945* (Munich, 1986), pp. 76–77.

Helene M. Kastinger Riley

Gerlind Reinshagen

Born 1926, Königsberg, Germany
Genre(s): drama, radio play, novel
Language(s): German

Although Gerlind Reinshagen has published works of narrative prose in recent years, she is above all a playwright, one of the few women dramatists in Germany today. She began her career in the 1960s as the writer of radio plays, adapting many for stage production. Her professional success was firmly established in the early and mid-1970s when her plays *Himmel und*

Erde (1974; Heaven and Earth) and *Sonntagskinder* (1976; Sunday's Children) found frequent production on the major stages of West Germany. In 1974 Reinshagen received the Schiller-Förderpreis, and the Mülheimer *Dramatikerpreis* in 1977. Despite their success, these plays were not published until 1981. Since that time Reinshagen's popularity as a female dramatist and prose writer has grown, as the 1986 edition of her collected plays attests.

Reinshagen was born in Königsberg in 1926 and studied first in Braunschweig and then West Berlin, where she currently lives. Her first play to draw critical attention was the adapted radio play *Leben und Tod der Marilyn Monroe* (1971; Life and Death of Marilyn Monroe) in which she portrays the stellar rise and ultimate destruction of a female celluloid "myth." In this myth, created in the image abstracted and desired by secularized modern society, the creator seeks affirmation of its impoverished existence.

All of Reinshagen's plays are characterized by experimentation with and explosion of traditional dramatic structure. The plays are written in scenes, with only occasional act or part designations (e.g., nineteen scenes in *Tod und Leben der Marilyn Monroe*, and four stations in *Himmel und Erde*). Reinshagen frequently employs *Verfremdungseffekte* (distancing effects) such as the projection of expository titles at the start of each scene, frequent use of songs juxtaposed with eloquent dialogue, and occasional direct address of the audience by the actors. The author also suggests innovation in acting and production style. In the list of characters in *Tod und Leben der Marilyn Monroe*, Reinshagen requests that each character be played by several actors and actresses in the course of one production.

Reinshagen's plays treat a variety of themes and problems that other post-war German literary artists have also examined. The complex issue of the Third Reich, and specifically the civilian relationship to Naziism and provincial fascism, is the focus of the play *Sonntagskinder*. Here, the Nazi past is mediated through the perspective of the fourteen-year-old main character, Elsie. Reinshagen shows how through fascism and adult domination the moral and personal development of a child is slowed, arrested, and regresses. This play, with its presentation of the destruction of the child's instinctive innocence by the ruling provincial and fascist adult world, demonstrates an affinity with the works of the German playwright and novelist Marieluise Fleißer (1901–1974).

Reinshagen also employs the narrative perspective of the child in the short prose diary "Elsas Nachtbuch" (1980; Elsa's Diary) and in the accompanying play *Das Frühlingsfest* (1980; The Springtime Celebration). Herein she addresses the economic and moral restoration of post-war Germany. Economic rehabilitation and the modern business world are introduced in Reinshagen's early play *Doppelkopf* (1971; Twohead), in which the young aspiring protagonist climbs the corporate ladder only to become sickened and repulsed by the inhumanity at the managerial pinnacle. This contemporary theme is delivered through an expressionistic play structure. The story of the ambitious but unsuccessful apprentice, who strives to enter the managerial ranks, is also told in Reinshagen's humorous first novel *Rovinato oder die Seele des Geschäfts* (1982; Rovinato or the Soul of the Company).

In her plays Reinshagen portrays predominantly female main characters without adopting a strong feminist viewpoint; however, in her latest works Reinshagen specifically addresses a feminist literary issue. In the novel *Die flüchtige Braut* (1984; The Fleeting Bride) and the play *Die Clownin* (1985; The Clown Woman) Reinshagen seeks to uncover and establish a female literary tradition through the anachronistic introduction of nineteenth-century literary figures into the twentieth-century stories. In the novel Reinshagen transposes a Romantic intellectual circle in present-day West Berlin. The characters, of which the majority are writers, scholars, and artists, adopt the characteristics of a past literary author or figure. Significantly, the main character, Dora, selects Emily Brontë as her alter ego. Both Dora and Emily reappear in *Die Clownin*.

Although hardly known outside of West Germany, Gerlind Reinshagen has become Germany's first successful contemporary female playwright. Her works offer representations of contemporary social and political issues while clearly addressing the urgent question of the importance of literary tradition for the modern writer.

Works

Plays: *Doppelkopf* (1971). *Leben und Tod der Marilyn Monroe* (1971). *Himmel und Erde* (1974). *Sonntagskinder* (1976). *Das Frühlingsfest* (1980). *Die Clownin* (1985).

Prose: *Elsas Nachtbuch* (1980). *Rovinato oder die Seele des Geschäfts* (1982). *Die flüchtige Braut* (1984).

Bibliography

Andres, Mury, "Dramaturgie des Eigensinnes. Zu den Theaterstücken von Gerlind Reinshagen." *Spectaculum* 36 (1982): 277–279. Bossinade, Johanna, "Haus und Front. Bilder der Faschismun in der Literatur von Exil- und Gegenwartsautorinnen. Am Beispiel Anna Seghers, Imrgard Keun, Christa Wolf und Gerlind Reinshagen." *Neophilologus* 70 (1986): 92–118.

Stephanie B. Paßenberg

Mirkka Rekola

Born 1931, Tampere, Finland
Genre(s): poetry, aphorism
Language(s): Finnish

Rekola is a poet and aphorist who seldom appears in public or literary discussions. Her writing, begun in 1954, had steadily though slowly accumulated to 13 collections by 1984. She started when the crisis in poetry was at its fiercest and wrote poems, like Helvi Juvonen and Eila Kivikkaho, both in the old and new style. Rekola quickly developed a strongly individual style, moving apparently outside the world of common speech. Her poetry is demanding, but the general experience that it is "difficult" is partly due to false expectations. Her expression is sparsely elliptical, suggestive; precise in language although deliberately ambiguous in thought. In her beliefs she is a mystic, influenced by both Christian and Eastern religions and philosophies. She wages a quiet but persistent war against dualisms of thought and experience. She aims at refuting and overcoming the basic distinctions of Western thought between past and future time, the self and others, time and place, etc. Her final goal is the experience of a great harmony, the oneness of the world. Rekola's 1969 collection brought an aphoristic dimen-

sion to her work. In her three aphoristic works, laconic prose poems and aphorisms both alternate and are mixed with one another. Rekola's reputation among literary scholars is high, but she is not popular with the wider reading public.

Works

Runot, poems, 1954–1978 (1979). *Kuutamourakka* [Moonlighting] (1981). *Puun syleilemällä* [The Tree-embraced] (1983). *Silmänkantama* [Eyeshot] (1984). *Tuoreessa muistissa kevät* [In Fresh Memory Spring], the aphoristic collections (1987).

Bibliography

Liukkonen, Tero, "Maiseman mieli" [Landscape Mind]. *Parnasso* 6 (1986).

Markku Envall

Caroline Rémy

(see: Séverine)

Reseda

(see: Terézia Vansová)

Carmen Resino

Born 1941, Madrid, Spain
Genre(s): drama
Language(s): Spanish

Resino holds a degree in history from the University of Madrid and began writing stories, novels, poetry, and plays quite early in life. Constants in her many works are history in combination with certain human themes like alienation, frustration, cruelty, non-communication, pain, loneliness, etc. Some of her plays are naturalistic while others are in the tradition of the Theater of the Absurd. In the latter vein is the short piece *Ultimar Detalles* (To Wind Things Up), in which a pretentious young man rejects an aging and overweight woman.

Works

El presidente [The President] (1968). *La sed* [The Hunger] (1972). *¿Mamá, el niño no llora!* [Mama, the Child Doesn't Cry!] (1982). *Ulises no vuelve*

[Ulises Isn't Coming Back] (1983). *Ultimar detalles* [To Finish Things Up] (1984). *Personal e intransferible* [Personal Property Not Transferable] (1989). *Nueva historia de la princesa y el dragón* [The New Story of the Princess and the Dragon] (1989).

Bibliography

Sueiras, Daniel, "Aproximación a la obra de Carmen Resino." *Estreno* 10.2 (Fall 1984): 31–34. Lamartina-Lens, Iride, "Myth of Penelope and Ulysses in *La tejedora de sueños, ¿Por qué corres Ulises?* and *Ulises no vuelve.*" *Estreno* 12.2 (Fall 1986): 31–34.

Patricia W. O'Connor

Josine Reuling

Born September 29, 1899, Amsterdam, The Netherlands; died October 21, 1961, Amsterdam
Genre(s): novel, youth literature
Language(s): Dutch

Josine (Gerardina Anna) Reuling was two years old when her parents, both opera singers, began a roving life in eastern Europe (Russia and Latvia). The family returned to Holland in 1914. The author's first novel, the girl's book *Siempie* (1927), was written when she was twenty-two and working as a clerk for an Amsterdam paper wholesaler. She left the job for reasons of health in 1931 and migrated, via Switzerland, to France, where she lived—with an interruption between 1940 and 1942—till 1945. In 1949 she was engaged by the Amsterdam public library, first as a typist, then as a teacher and as a supervisor of reading groups. During her stay in Paris she had a love affair with a *couturière* of Russian origin; *De verwachting* (1948; The Expectation) was inspired by this period in the author's life. As a matter of fact, her whole work—consisting of some juvenile literature and of realistic psychological novels—has an autobiographical base.

Works

Siempie (1927). *Sara Vierhout* (1932). *Intermezzo met Ernst* [Intermezzo with Earnest] (1934). *Het vreemde vaderland* [The Foreign Homeland] (1939). *De verwachting* (1948). *Poeders en parels* [Powders and Pearls] (1953).

Bibliography

van Riemsdijk, G.A., *Jaarboek van de Maatschappij der Nederlandse letteren 1971–1972* (1973). Schuyf, J., *Homojaarboek* (1981).

Frank Joostens

Franziska Gräfin von Reventlow

Born May 18, 1871, Husum, Frisia; died July 27, 1918, Muralto, Tessin
Genre(s): short story, essay, poetry, translation, diary, letters, novel
Language(s): German

In 1899 Fanny Liane Sophie Auguste Wilhelmine Adrienne Gräfin zu Reventlow left her parents and the world of aristocracy and changed her name to "Franziska," under which she was to become famous as a literary figure. She grew up in Lübeck (since 1889) and Hamburg, lived in Munich from 1892 to 1909, and then in Ancona, southern Switzerland. During her years in Munich she led a life free from all social conventions and tried to become a painter. Financial troubles, however, forced her to turn to writing. All her novels reflect her own life during those years. The crucial autobiographical novel *Herrn Dames Aufzeichnungen* (Notes of Mr. Dames) caused a storm of public outcry by those who were depicted in it. Her correspondence with Emanuel Febling, a schoolmate of Heinrich and Thomas Mann, dates back to 1890, her diary to 1895. She was a fervent admirer of Friedrich Nietzsche and strongly advocated the philosophy of *Life as Art* and *To Live Only For Art*. This interest is particularly reflected in her first novel *Ellen Olestjerne* (1903), which mirrors many modern trends in literature and art of the turn of the century. Henrik Ibsen also deeply influenced her, which resulted in Fanny's extreme and absolute form of subjectivism and in a dominant quest for independence in her life. Thus her works include women figures of strong personality who decide on their own what to do with their life.

She concluded a brief marriage with the court assistant Walter Lübke from Hamburg on May 23, 1894, but she became pregnant by the painter Henryk Walkow and gave birth to her son Rudolf on September 1, 1897, in Munich. Her decision to raise him alone came close to a scandal in Schwabing/Munich and was another act of her self-determination. In 1912 she wrote *Von Paul zu Pedro* (From Paul to Pedro). In 1916 appeared *Der Geldkomplex* (The Money Complex) and in 1916–18 *Der Selbstmordverein* (The Club of Suicidals), which was to be published only in her complete works in 1925. All these novels reveal Franziska von Reventlow to be master of a literary style influenced by French authors such as Marcel Prévost, Anatole France, and Guy de Maupassant, whose works she extensively translated for the Albert Langen publishing house. In her novels she excelled in humor, graciousness, and a very light conversational tone that often hides tragedy and suffering. Even though she had many literary contacts with R.M. Rilke, Emnil Ludwig, and Klabund, she followed her French amorous models of the nineteenth century (*Von Paul zu Pedro*). In *Der Geldkomplex* she satirized the bohemian lifestyle and talked openly about the misery and economic plight of the class of artists.

Works

[With Eugen Thosson], *Klosterjungen* [Monastery Boys], collection of humorous sketches (1897). *Ellen Olestjerne. Eine Lebensgeschichte* [Ellen Olestjerne. A Story of a Life] (1903). *Von Paul zu Pedro. Amouresken* [From Paul to Pedro. Amorous Stories] (1912). *Herrn Dames Aufzeichnungen oder Begebenheiten aus einem merkwürdigen Stadtteil* [Notes of Mr. Dames or Events in a Strange City Neighborhood] (1913). *Der Geldkomplex oder von der Kunst, Schulden mit Charme zu ertragen* [The Money Complex or of the Art of Coping with Debts in a Gracious Way] (1916). *Das Logierhaus zur schwankenden Weltkugel und andere Novellen* [The Pension of the Staggering Globe and Other Short Stories] (1917). *Gesammelte Werke* [Collected Works] (1926). *Briefe* [Letters] (1929). *Tagebuch* [Diary], printed in 1971] (1895–1910).

Bibliography

Angermann, Franz, "Franziska Gräfin zu Reventlow." *Kritische Rundschau* 2 (1919–20): 64–66. Budzinski, Klaus, "Einsamkeit und dazwischen ein schöner Rausch. Leben und Lieben der Franziska zu Reventlow," in *Die schöne Münchnerin*, ed. Hanns Arens (Munich, 1969), pp. 112–123. Gerhardt, Marlis, "Franziska zu Reventlow. 1871–1918," in *Frauen, Portraits aus 2 Jahrhunderten*, ed. H. J. Schultz (Stuttgart, 1981), pp. 226–243. Graetzer, Franz, "Die Humoristin." *Literarisches Echo* 20 (1917–18), cols. 837–841. Green, Martin, *The von Richthofen Sisters. The Triumphant and the Tragic Modes of Love*, many entries (New York, 1974). Kerényi, Karl, *Auf den Spuren des Mythos*, ed. K. K., many entries (Munich-Vienna, 1967). Obermüller, Klara, "Das literarische München um die Jahrhundertwende," in *München um 1900*, ed. M. Gasser, many entries (Bern-Stuttgart, 1977). Schröder, Hans Eggert, *Ludwig Klages, Die Geschichte seines Lebens*, part 1, many entries (Bonn, 1966). Sékely, Johannes, *Franziska Gräfin zu Reventlow. Leben und Werk. Mit einer Bibliographie* (Bonn, 1979). von Rantzau, Johann Albrecht, "Zur Geschichte der sexuellen Revolution. Die Gräfin Franziska zu Reventlow und die Münchener Kosmiker" *Archiv für Kulturgeschichte* 56, 2 (1974): 394–446.

Albrecht Classen

Jacques Reynaud

(see: Gabrielle-Anne Du Poilloüe de Saint-Mars)

Caterina de'Ricci

Born April 23, 1522, Florence, Italy; died February 2, 1590, Prato
Genre(s): letters, spirituality
Language(s): Italian

Sprung from a noble Florentine family, Caterina entered the convent of S. Vicenzio in Prato at the age of thirteen. Significantly, this convent had been founded early in the century in the reforming spirit of Savonarola. She would always have a special devotion to the Florentine reformer, who like her had been a Dominican. She would even compose a lauda in his honor.

For twelve years, beginning with Holy Week, 1542, Caterina would weekly relive the Passion of Christ from noon on Thursday to four in the afternoon on Friday. She had the special power of visiting people she had never met, e.g., St.

Philip Neri in Rome and St. M.M. de' Pazzi in Florence. She was also reputed to have received the stigmata.

She came to be regarded as a woman of great good sense and served as the spiritual adviser of many of her contemporaries. Within her own convent she was prioress from 1560 to 1590. Her greatest monument is her collected letters, now available in a recent edition.

Works

Epistolario [Correspondence], ed. G. Di Agresti, 5 vols. (Florence, 1973–1975).

Joseph Berrigan

Madame Riccoboni

(a.k.a. Marie-Jeanne Laboras de Mezieres)

Born 1714, Paris, France
Genre(s): novel, letters, translation, drama
Language(s): French

Marie-Jeanne Laboras de Mézières was born in Paris in 1714. She married Francesco Antonio Riccoboni (1707–1772), an Italian playwright. Madame Riccoboni wrote sentimental novels showing the influence of Richardson and Stern. Yet, one denotes in these works a special brand of feminism: women reign supreme in the domain of emotion and feelings; only they can truly understand the power of love; only they can develop unusual sensitivity, a realm more or less closed to men, unless a rare one among them exhibits "feminine" attributes.

Madame Riccoboni is credited with authorship of the twelfth part of *La Vie de Marianne* (the famous novel of Marivaux). The latter actually saw this "Suite" and was extremely flattered by the superb imitation of his style. Grimm, in the *Correspondance Littéraire*, commented favorably on her style which, while confined by a poor model, he stated, was "very superior to that of Marivaux."

She entertained epistolary relations with numerous contemporaries. Her letters to Choderlos de Laclos after the publication in 1772 of *Les Liaisons Dangereuses* have become a classic: "Tout Paris s'empresse de vous lire, tout Paris s'entretient de vous."

Not only was Madame Riccoboni well read, but she also spoke several languages, translating, among others, a novel by Fielding, *Amelie*; several English plays by Moore, *L'Enfant Trouvé*; by Murphy, *La Façon de le Fixer*, by H. Kelly, *La Fausse Délicatesse*; by G. Colman, *La Femme Jalouse*. She also wrote several comedies in the style of Goldoni. *Les Caquets*, for instance, is a clear imitation of "I Pettegolezzi." Her contemporaries showed admiration for her works. *L'Aveugle de Palmyre*, a comedy by M. Desfontaines (March 5, 1767) was a stage adaptation of one of her novels: *L'Aveugle*. Another comedy, *L'Amant Bourru*, by M. de Monvel, follows the outline of the *Lettres d'Adélaide de Dammartin, Comtesse de Sancerre*.

La Harpe, Grimm, Diderot, and numerous other authors have written comments on her writings. The complete edition of her works published in seven volumes in 1780 by the Imprimerie de la Société typographique includes *Lettres de Fanny Butler*, *Histoire du Marquis de Cressy*; *Suite de Marianne de Marivaux*; *Letters de Milady Juliette Catesby*; *Lettres d'Adélaide de Dammartin*; *Rencontre dans les Ardennes*; *Extrait des Amours de Gertrude et de Roger*; *Lettres de Mylord Rivers*; *Histoire d'Ernestine*; *L'Abeille*; *Histoire d'Aloise de Livarot*.

Works

Oeuvres Completes (1786): *Les Amours de Roger et de Gertrude*; *Les Caquets*; *Histoire de Miss Jenny*; *Ernestine*; *Caliste*; *Ourika*.

Bibliography

Crosby, Emily, *Une Romancière Oubliée, Mme. Riccoboni. Sa Vie, Ses Oeuvres, Sa Place dans la Littérature Anglaise et Française du XVIII* Siècle* (Paris, 1924). Steward, J. H., *The Novels of Madame Riccoboni* (Chapel Hill, 1976). Picard, Raymond, "Notes sur le portrait en littérature de 1720 à 1760." *De Racine au Parthénon. Essais sur la littérature et l'art à l'age classique* (Paris, 1977). Demay, Andrée, *Marie-Jeanne Riccoboni ou de la Pensée Féministe Chez une Romancière du XVIII* siècle* (Paris, 1978). Abensour, Léon, *Histoire Générale du Féminisme* (Paris, 1921). Mme. Riccoboni's Letters to David Hume, David Garrick, and Sir Robert Liston, 1764–1783, ed. James C. Nicholls in *Studies on Voltaire and the Eighteenth Century*, Vol. 149 (1976).

Colette Michael

Carme Riera Guilera

Born 1948, Palma de Mallorca
Genre(s): essay, journalism, novel, short story, drama
Language(s): Catalan, Spanish

Carme Riera was born on the island of Majorca, where she spent her childhood. She moved to Barcelona to attend the university, where she studied romance philology, specializing in the literature of the Spanish Golden Age. Riera's literary career was launched when she won the 1974 Recull prize for her short story "Te deix, amor, la mar com a penyora." This story served as the title work to her first collection of stories, published in 1977, which has love as its main theme, mostly seen through the eyes of women. Her second collection, *Jo pos per testimoni les gavines*, published in 1977, is similar in theme and tone, recalling the author's childhood in Majorca and stressing the theme of women's feelings. Both collections have had more than twenty editions in the original Catalan version. The Spanish adaptation of these two books, entitled *Palabra de mujer*, has had the same enormous success, with several editions since 1980. In this same year Riera wrote a report for a Barcelona newspaper entitled "Els cementeris de Barcelona," combining the insight of a reporter with the creativity of a fiction writer to produce a mood piece about the cemeteries in that city. The study *Quasi be un conte, la vida de Ramon Llull*, also appeared in 1980, a retelling for young audiences of the life of the Majorcan mystic. The literary essays published as *La escuela de Barcelona* won the 1988 Anagrama Essay prize.

In 1981 Riera published her first novel, *Una primavera per a Domenico Guarini*, which won the Prudenci Bertrana literary prize, and in which a woman wrestles with the connections between personal and public actions. Her 1988 epistolary novel, *Cuestión de amor propio*, deals with the themes of love and deceit. The short story collection *Epitelis tendrissims* (1981) is quite different from Riera's usual themes. Here she presents an erotic collection of tales infused with humor and lightness. Riera's literary work extends to the theater. Her drama *Senhora, ha vist el mes fills?*, dealing with war and the solitude and desperation of women as victims of the conflict, was presented at the Second International Theater Encounter in Greece, in 1982, receiving favorable reviews from the critics. Her short stories and articles appear in many journals and anthologies, and her position as an influential member of the group of women writers who are changing the map of contemporary literature of Spain is undeniable.

Works

Novels: *Una primavera per a Domenico Guarini*. [A Spring for Domenico Guarini] (1981). *Cuestión de amor propio* [A Matter of Self Respect] (1988).

Short stories: *Epitelis Tendrissims* [Tenderest Epistles] (1981). *Palabra de mujer* [Words of Women] (1980). *Jo pos per testimoni les gavines* [I Bring the Seagulls as Witnesses] (1977). *Te deix, amor, la mar com a penyora* [I Leave You, My Love, the Sea as a Remembrance] (1975). Theater: "Senhora, ha vist els meus fills?" [Lady, Have You Seen My Children?] (1982).

Essays: *Quasi be un conte: la vida de Ramon Llull* [Almost Like a Story: The Life of Ramon Llull] (1980). *La escuela de Barcelona* [The School of Barcelona] (1988).

Bibliography

Galerstein, Carolyn L., ed., *Women Writers of Spain* (Westport, Conn., 1986). Molas, Joaquim, and Josep Masot i Muntaner, *Diccionari de la literatura Catalana* [Dictionary of Catalan Literature] 62 (Barcelona, 1979). Ordoñez, Elizabeth, "Beginning to Speak: Carme Riera's *Una primavera para Domenico Guarini*," *La Chispa '85*, in Paolini, Gilbert, ed. (New Orleans, 1985). Pérez, Janet, *Contemporary Women Writers of Spain* (Boston, 1988).

Lina L. Cofresí

A.E. Ries or Reiss

(see: Anna Elisabet Weirauch)

Madam Rigal

Born circa 1750, France
Genre(s): revolutionary rhetoric
Language(s): French

Not much is known about Madame Rigal who distinguished herself with one of the most elegant gestures in history: she is credited with a movement and a speech that gave the impetus to women to donate their jewels to the French impoverished General Assembly. The speech presented on September 20, 1789 in front of the women jewelers and artists is a special call to duty: "Let us sanctify our frivolous attires and our *mondaine* displays by sacrificing them to the public good; . . . that luxury become a virtue." The gifts were presented to the General Assembly, and the speech that accompanied them was published in 1789.

Works

Michael, Colette, ed., *Les Tracts Féministes au XVIIIᵉ Siècle* (1986). Levy, Applewhite, and Johnson, *Women in Revolutionary Paris, 1789–1795* (1979).

Bibliography

Sullerot, Evelyne, *Histoire de la Presse Féminine en France des Origines à 1848* (Paris, 1966).

Colette Michael

Catherine Rihoit

Born 1946, Caen, France
Genre(s): novel
Language(s): French

Rihoit was born in Normandy. She was very young when she passed her "agrégation" in English. She then started teaching at the University of Paris-Sorbonne while working on a dissertation on Henry James. She still teaches at the Sorbonne and writes for the woman's magazine *Marie-Claire*.

Much of her work seems to be inspired by her own experience as a brilliant young graduate student, more used to the isolation of study than to the reality of living. *Le bal des débutantes* (Debutantes' Ball) is the story of a young "agrégée" in Italian, who has been assigned to her first teaching job in a small school and has to move to the north of France for her work. Six years of college studies have not prepared her for real life, its boredom and loneliness, nor for a freedom she does not know how to handle. She becomes manipulated by her married lover and her strange roommate. But during a student demonstration, she meets a prostitute/painter and her boyfriend, a political activist, who show her a different lifestyle. She discovers then that her life is her own and that she should not allow parents, friends, or men to treat her as a puppet.

In *Les abîmes du coeur* (The Abyss of the Heart), which is set in the beginning of the century, Rihoit depicts a similar fight: a young girl, who has been raised in a convent, has to struggle for her psychological, emotional, sexual, and social independence.

The theme of a woman striving for her independence appears in all her novels and is presented in a suspenseful way. One identifies very quickly with the woman narrator and wonders whether she will free herself from a web of sexual and social prejudices, in a world where a woman is still defined in terms of her relationship with a man. Rihoit's style is both refined and humorous. Her knowledge of English and American literature is quite evident in the subtle literary and structural references that can be found in her stories.

Works

Portrait de Gabriel (1977). *Le bal des débutantes* (1978). *Histoire de Jeanne transsexuelle* (1980). *Les abîmes du coeur* (1980). *Nocturne* (1980). *Les petites annonces* (1981). *La Favorite* (1982). *La nuit de Varennes, ou, L'impossible n'est pas français* (1982). *Regards de Femmes* (1983). *Tentation* (1983). *Triomphe de l'amour* (1983). *Kidnapping*, play in three acts (1984). *Soleil* (1985). *Brigitte Bardot, un mythe français* (1986).
Translations: *Le bal des débutantes—La puesta de largo*, tr. Ana Marbia Moix, film adaptation of *La nuit de Varennes* by Ettore Scola (1980).

Bibliography

Le Monde (Jan. 27, 1980; June 13, 1980). *Le Nouvel Observateur* (Mar. 31, 1980). *Le Point* (May 19, 1980).

Michèle M. Magill

Luise Rinser

Born March 30, 1911, Pitzling, Bavaria, Germany
Genre(s): short story, essay, autobiography, drama, novel
Language(s): German

Luise Rinser's work shows a mixture of conservativism and *Neue Sachlichkeit*, of the real and the fictitious. Her novels, short stories, and essays are attempts to deal with the past and the present; they are personal and critical and show the ability to analyze and penetrate the surface. Her work made her a dangerous enemy of the Third Reich.

Luise Rinser's life until after the war was a constant odyssey and not always a voluntary one. Each step of this odyssey was faithfully recorded and reflected in her work. 1915–1917 she spent in a monastery, near Weilheim; from 1916–1918 she visited the *Volksschule* (elementary school) in Ettlingen, and from 1918–1924 a school overseas, where her father was the head teacher. From 1924–1930, Luise attended the *Lehrerinnenbildungsanstalt* (seminary for female teachers) in Munich, in 1928 already, with special permission, she was a guest-student for pedagogic psychology at the University of Munich. In 1932, Luise worked temporarily for her father as his substitute, in 1933 she was selected to build a *Landschulheim* (summer camp for students) for the *Freiwilligen Arbeitsdienst* (voluntary work duty). In 1934 she passed the *Staatsexamen* (state exam) for female teachers and taught in a school for difficult children until 1937. Her original design to study psychology and to write on Freud and Adler had to be given up due to the political climate. Luise continued to work as a teacher until 1939. Threatened with dismissal from school duty if she did not enter the party, she left and married Horst G. Schnell, a distinguished musician. In May of 1939, she started her literary career with a collection of twelve short stories *Gläserne Ringe* (1940; Rings of Glass). Both she and Schnell were vehement opponents of Hitler and his regime, with the result that in 1941 Luise was prohibited to write and expelled from the *Schriftstellerverband* (Organization of Writers). From that moment on the persecution by the regime did not stop for her or for her husband. In 1941 the family (with sons Christopher, 1940, and Stephan, 1941) moved to Rostock where Schnell became music director. In September of 1942, Schnell was drafted for "political unreliability," sent to the Eastern Front, where he died shortly afterwards. In April of 1942, Luise and her sons had left Rostock for Silesia as Rostock had been bombed, and in June she returned to Bavaria, where she lived under deplorable conditions; the last narration of *Weihnachts-Triptychon* (Christmas-Triptychon) describes her experiences during that time. On October 12, 1944, a former friend and colleague denounced her, and she was arrested by the *Gestapo*, the secret police. The accusations were high treason and disruption of the military (*Wehrkraftzersetzung*). Luise spent the rest of the war in prison, from where she was freed because her documents and the evidence against her were burnt; *Gefängnistagebuch* (Prison Diary) is a documentary of that time. Through recommendations of Erich Kästner, Luise became a staff member of the American newspaper *Neue Zeitung*. The years until 1950 were hard, and she owed her survival mostly to friends and strangers. In 1953 she married Carl Orff but was separated from him in 1959; she moved to Rome where she bought a house.

Rinser's work is to a large extent autobiographical, and after 1950, critics do not praise it unanimously any more. The change in style and atmosphere may be the result of her more harmonious life after 1950 without pressure and fear. Her first publication, *Gläserne Ringe*, portrays in twelve stories the life of the five- and six-year-old Luise. In *Gefängnistagebuch* (1946), she compiled the notes she took during her prison days in 1944–45, and in its edition of 1963, she added the facts about her liberation. In the preface to the first edition she claimed that in spite of the personal statements and experiences conveyed, she wanted to put the emphasis on the political reality of the days. In almost brutally realistic manner the inmates, the hunger, the dirt, the maltreatment of the prison camp were described. The book deserves attention for its deep psychological insight and analysis and its concern for the fate of the prisoners. The documentary closes with a letter of apology from the denouncer. *Die Stärkeren* (1948; The Stronger), which dealt with the fate of two children who grew up between 1914 and 1945, is another deep psychological study of the consequence of war and the subsequent insecurities it causes. *Jan Lobel aus Warschau* (1948; Jan Lobel from Warshaw) belongs in the same category. Completely different is *Martins Reise* (1949; Martin's Journey). A concoction of fairy-tales, history, dream, and reality, this book shows the pedagogical side of Rinser: directed towards young people, *Martins Reise* is entertaining and didactic. *Mitte des Lebens* (1950; The Middle of Life) was eventually combined with its independent continuation *Abenteuer der Tugend* (1957; Adventure of Virtue) under the title *Nina* (1961). *Mitte des Lebens* received both positive and negative criticism as did all Rinser's work from then on. The novel is an attempt to reconstruct the desperate and fruitless love affair between Nina and Dr. Alexander Stein. Diary notes written by Stein and sent to Nina after his death reveal her life between 1922 and 1948—the indecisiveness, the despair, the hopes and disillusions of both lives. The novel also presents a sister-sister relationship that is rediscovered after many years. Guilt, pain, regret, and hope are the keywords of this novel; partly epistolary, partly narrative, it is written in the first person, told from the perspective of the sister Margaret. The roughness of Nina's character and the lack of emotion in the lives of the characters are reflected in the cold and abrupt style, the short sentences, and the brutal language. *Abenteuer der Tugend* (1957) is an epistolary novel describing Nina's struggle to find herself after she had fled Germany to denounce her own past. The letters reflect her attempts to understand the attitude of the Catholic church toward marriage, the sacrifices of a wife and mother, and the saving belief in God. The style of the letters is complex due to the lack of dialogue partners, whose reactions and responses had to be incorporated into Nina's own letters, which slows down the pace greatly. *Der Schwerpunkt* (1960; The Emphasis) is a collection of essays on five contemporary writers. *Vom Sinn der Traurigkeit* (1962; On the Meaning of Sadness) is a treatise on the origin of melancholy. *Weihnachts-Triptychon* (1963) is comprised of three autobiographical stories about Christmas. Luise Rinser's work reflects her life, her ability to observe critically but passionately, her urge for freedom, justice, and truth. Her style is generally clear and simple as befits a representative of *Neue Sachlichkeit*.

Works

Novels: *Hochebene* (1948). *Die Stärkeren* (1948). *Mitte des Lebens* (1950). *Daniela* (1953). *Der Sündenbock* (1955). *Abenteuer der Tugend* (1957; with *Mitte des Lebens* and *Nina*, 1961). *Die vollkommene Freude* (1962). *Ich bin Tobias* (1966). *Der schwarze Esel* (1974). *Bruder Feuer* (1975). *Mirjam* (1983).

Short stories: *Die gläsernen Ringe* (1940). *Erste Liebe* (1946). *Jan Lobel aus Warschau* (1948). *Martins Reise* (1949). *Sie zogen mit dem Stern* (1952). *Eine Weihnachtsgeschichte* (1953). *Ein Bündel weier Narzissen* (1956). *Geh fort, wenn du kannst* (1959). *Weihnachts-Triptychon* (1963). *Septembertag* (1964). *Das Geheimnis des Brunnens* (1979).

Drama: *Das Ohstädter Kinder-Weihnachtsspiel* (1949).

Autobiography: *Gefängnistagebuch* (1946). *Baustelle* (1970). *Grenzübergänge* (1972). *Kriegsspielzeug* (1972–1978). *Den Wolf umarmen* (1981). *Nordkoreanisches Reisetagebuch* (1981).

Essays, other prose: *Pestalozzi und wir* (1947). *Die Wahrheit über Konnersreuth* (1954). *Fülle der Zeit. Carl Zuckmayer und sein Werk* (1956). *Der Schwerpunkt* (1960). *Vom Sinn der Traurigkeit* (1962). *Ich wei deinen Namen* (1962). *Über die Hoffnung* (1964). *Gespräche über Lebensfragen* (1966). *Hat Beten einen Sinn?* (1966). *Jugend unserer Zeit* (1967). *Gespräche von Mensch zu Mensch* (1967). *Zölibat und Frau* (1967). *Laie nicht ferngesteuert* (1967). *Fragen und Antworten* (1968). *Von der Unmöglichkeit und der Möglichkeit heute Priester zu sein* (1968). *Unterentwickeltes Land Frau* (1970). *Hochzeit der Widersprüche* (1973). *Dem Tode geweiht?* (1974). *Wie, wenn wir ärmer würden?* (1974). *Hallo Partner* (1975). *Leiden, sterben, auferstehen* (1975). *Wenn die Wale kämpfen* (1976). *Der verwundete Drache. Dialog über Leben und Werk des Komponisten I. Yun.* (1977). *Khomeini und der islamische Gottesstaat* (1979). *Mit wem reden?* (1980).

Anthology: *Mein Lesebuch* (1979).

Translation: *Nina* (1956). *Rings of Glass* [*Gläserne Ringe*] (1958).

Jutta Hagedorn

Adine Riom

(a.k.a. Louise d'Isole, Comte de Saint-Jean)

Born 1818, Le Pellerin (Loire-Atlantique),
    France; died August 28, 1899, Nantes
Genre(s): poetry, novel, drama
Language(s): French

Adine (Madame Eugène) Riom, née Broband or Brobant, was primarily a literary representative of the Breton regional revival, through her volumes of lyric poetry, her poetic retellings of Breton legends, and her novels. Her work is marked by appeals to personal, religious, and patriotic sentiment, as well as by its evocation of Brittany and its legends.

A grand-niece of Joseph Fouché (1754–1820), Napoleon's Minister of Police, she married a notary from Nantes, where she seems to have spent the rest of her life. Her salon was a meeting place for many writers of the region; José-Maria de Heredia, the Parnassian poet, and other well-known writers appeared there occasionally. Though essentially a regional writer, she had a number of her books brought out by leading Parisian publishers, notably Alphonse Lemerre. Drama was a minor aspect of her work, but Vapereau states that one of her two comedies, *Les Oiseaux des Tournelles* (The Birds in the Turrets) was performed in Paris at the "Troisième Théâtre Français" (the Châtelet?). She contributed to periodicals both regional and Parisian, including the *Revue de Bretagne et de Vendée*, *Revue de Paris*, *Revue Contemporaine*, and *Revue Française*. She collaborated in the publication of an *Anthologie des poètes bretons du XVIIᵉ siècle* (1884).

Despite a modestly successful literary career, Madame Riom did not win a permanent place in French literary history.

Works

Poetry: *Oscar* (1847). *Reflets de la lumière* (1857). *Flux et reflux* (1859). *Passion* (1864). *Après l'amour* (1867). *Merlin* (1872, repub. 1887). *Histoires et légendes bretonnes* (1873). *Salomon et la reine de Saba* (1874). *Fleurs du passé* (1880). *Légendes bibliques et orientales* (1882). *Légendes bretonnes* (1887). *Les Adieux, poésies bretonnes* (1895). *Oeuvres poétiques* (1897).

Novels: *Le Serment, ou La Chapelle de Bethléem* (1854). *Mobiles et zouaves bretons* (1871). *Michel Marion, épisode de la guerre d'indépendance bretonne* (1879, repub. 1882, 1884). *Les Routes croisées* (1894).

Drama: *Les Oiseaux des Tournelles* (1877). *Les Préjugés* (1898).

Bibliography

Le Mercier d'Erm, Camille, *Les Bardes et poètes nationaux de la Bretagne armoricaine. Anthologie contemporaine des XIXᵉ-XXᵉ siècles* (Rennes and Paris, 1918). Rousse, Joseph, *La Poésie bretonne au XIXᵉ siècle* (Paris, 1895). Séché, Alphonse, *Muses romantiques. Anthologie des femmes poètes (1800 à 1891)*, vol. 1, portrait photograph (Paris, 1908). Vapereau, G., *Dictionnaire universel des contemporains*, 6th ed. (Paris, 1893).

James S. Patty

Alice Rivaz

(see: Marthe-Marguerite le Valois de Villette de Mursay, Comtesse de Caylus)

Christine de Rivoyre

Born November 29, 1921, Tarbes, France
Genre(s): novel
Language(s): French

Christine de Rivoyre was born in the south of France. She always has felt a special love for the region of Landes which appears in many of her novels. She earned a B.A. in English at La Sorbonne, and was a student at the journalism school of Syracuse University in New York (1948–1950). She began her journalistic career in 1950 with the newspaper *Le Monde* (her first interview was with William Faulkner). In 1955, she became the literary director of the woman's magazine *Marie-Claire*. Since 1966, she has dedicated herself exclusively to writing novels and articles. In 1956 she received the "Prix Quatre-Jurys" for her first book, in 1968 the Interallié prize for her novel entitled *Le Petit Matin*, and in 1984, The Académie Française awarded her the Paul Morand prize for the body of her works. She is a member of the jury for the "Prix Médicis" and the "Comité Supérieur des Lettres."

Many have compared her to Colette, for whom she readily admits her "adoration." She indeed shares Colette's love for nature and her great talent for describing the simple pleasures of life. Although her first novels have a certain sophisticated outlook, in *Le Petit Matin* (Early Morning), a beautiful tale of war and love, full of aggressive sensuality and bittersweet memories, she returns to a simple and poetic style. In all her later works, the themes of friendship, love, solitude, and the past are evoked with tenderness and sarcasm, warmth and taste, and rendered in a polished and concise style.

Works

L'Alouette au Miroir (1955). *La Mandarine* (1957). *La Glace à l'Ananas* (1962). *Les Sultans* (1964). *Le Petit Matin* (1968). [With Alexandre Kalda], *Le seigneur des Chevaux* (1969). *Fleur d'Agonie* (1970). *Boy* (1975). *Le voyage à l'Envers* (1977). *Belle Alliance* (1982). *Reine-Mère* (1985).

Bibliography

Le Figaro (April 16, 1968; December 3, 1968). *Le Figaro Littéraire* (December 9, 1968). *Le Monde* (February 3, 1968); March 19, 1982). *L'Express* (April 15, 1968; March 26, 1973; July 13, 1977; March 19, 1982). *Le Nouvel Observateur* (April 21, 1973; July 20, 1977; April 9, 1982). *Le Magazine Littéraire* (June 1982). *Le Monde des Livres* (June 26, 1977).

Michèle M. Magill

L'udmila Riznerová

(a.k.a. L'udmila Podjavorinská)

Born April 26, 1872, Horné Bzince, then in Austria-Hungary, now called Bzince pod Javorinou in Czechoslovakia; died March 2, 1951, Nove Mesto nad Váhom, Czechoslovakia
Genre(s): short story, poetry, children's literature
Language(s): Slovak

Podjavorinská simultaneously and alternatively wrote both prose and poetry for both adults and children and produced enough work to modestly support herself. Somewhat of an antifeminist, she was not close to the other Slovak women writers of her time despite the nationalist efforts she shared with them. She received the title "National Artist" in 1947.

She was born L'udmila Riznerová and grew up in a small-town Protestant teacher's family of Slovak nationalists like the families of her older associates Elena Maróthy-Šoltésová, Terézia Vansová, and Timrava. Never marrying, she lived in the same town until 1910 when she moved with her parents to the nearby small city of Nové Mesto nad Váhom; she remained there until her death. She began publishing at age fifteen, and her first book of verse appeared when she was twenty-three. She was the first Slovak woman to collect her verses into book form. Her last book appeared when she was seventy-four years old.

Podjavorinská's early, conventionally romantic verses were amateurish, but her prose pieces in the tradition of Slovak realism were based on her social observation and on autobiographical elements of her own loneliness and financial insecurity. In some stories she continued the nationalist heroine typical of Šoltésová, such as *Ideál* in 1896 and *Z domova* (Away from Home) in 1898. Her early humorous pieces such as *Kmotrovia figliari* (Mischief-making Godparents) in 1892 are attractive, but the best works are three novellas. The first, *V otroctve* (In Slavery) in 1905, sharply condemns social and economic exploitation; her antisemitism (a constant in most literature of this time) is confined to economic problems without the superstition and malice apparent in the earlier tragic story of a young Jewish girl in love with a Christian village boy in *Protivy* (Opposites) in 1893. The second novella, *Blud* (Error) in 1906, also condemns exploitation, but here the characters' fate is explained in Christian terms. The third novella, *Žena* (Wife) in 1910, has a penetrating portrait of a peasant woman as the positive heroine who resists the evil influences of the city while holding to the rural virtues Podjavorinská advocated. Interestingly, moving to the city stopped Podjavorinská's realistic work, and she began experimenting with a versified novella in imitation of Alexander Pushkin's *Eugene Onegin* but without the passion and intellectual strength of Pushkin's novel. *Po balé* (After the Ball) in

1903, *Na balé* (At the Ball) in 1905, and *Prelud* in 1915 show satirically the effect of mammon in smothering all human feeling, but they remain incomplete experiments. Throughout her career, Podjavorinská wrote verses and stories for children, and in one such story she reached the peak of her adult prose. *Baránok bo'í* (The Lamb of God) in 1932 tells of an orphaned village boy sent to a city foundling home and shows again the dichotomy of city evils against rural virtues. But here Podjavorinská utilizes the free shepherd/mountaineer symbol against the destructive force of a class-divided city and effectively personalizes the dichotomy within the lonely boy. The style of the story is close to that of "lyrical prose" or the Slovak expressionism of the time. Podjavorinská's poetic experiments included the art ballad, following the earlier Štúr movement imitating the folk ballad, and she published the results in *Balady* in 1930. Some have lasting value, especially the humorous cycle with the bagpiper Filúz. Finally, Podjavorinská's last major work was again lyrical poetry, a half century after her first lyrics, and these *Piesne samoty* (Songs of Solitude) in 1942 are an economical, unaffected, unsentimental reflection of her Christian humanism.

Characterized by a large variety of genres and unsteady quality, Podjavorinská's work is in great part important only historically, but her best prose and her intimate lyrics that anticipated the "Slovak Modern" movement have earned her a permanent place in Slovak literature.

Works

Poetry: *Z vesny Života* [From the Springtime of Life] (1895). *Balady* [Ballads] (1930). *Výber z balád* [Selected Ballads] (1936). *Piesne samoty* [Songs of Solitude] (1942). *Balady a povesti* [Ballads and Tales] (1946).

Collected stories and novellas: *Protivy* [Opposites] (1893). *V otroctve* [In Slavery] (1905). *Kde sa vzal?* [Where Did He Go?] (1906). *Dvaja bratia a Nešt'astie pôvodcom št'astia* [Two Brothers and Unhappiness That Brings Happiness] (1909). *Žena* [Wife] (1910). *Otrok* [Slave] (1914). *Postavy a figúrky* [Characters and Figures] (1942).

Collected works: *Zobrané spisy*, 3 vols. (1925–1926, 1929).

Translations: Her children's books.

Bibliography

Gáfrik, Michal, ed., "Basnické dielo L'udmily Podjavorinskej." *Pret'atý 'ivot cez poly* (Bratislava, 1970), pp. 201–212. Klátik, Zlatko, ed., Afterword to *Balady a povesti* (Bratislava, 1965), pp. 71–75. Kusý, Ivan, "Podjavorinská—prozaička." *Romboid* 7 (1972): 48–52. Šimkovič, Alexander, ed., "Poznámky o próze L'udmily Podjavorinskej." *Z domova* (Bratislava, 1970), pp. 409–417. Šmatlák, Stanislav, *Znie hudbou ka'dý verš* (Bratislava, 1971), pp. 5–19, 33–37. Tomčík, Miloš, "Postavenie L'udmily Podjavorinskej v slovenskej literatúre." *Slovenské pohl'ady* 67 (1951): 254–256. Tomčík, Miloš, ed., Introduction to *V otroctve* (Bratislava, 1954), pp. 9–24.

General references: *Dejiny slovenskej literatúry* IV (Bratislava, 1975), pp. 156–173, 327–334. *Encyklopédia slovenských spisovatel'ov* II (Bratislava, 1984), pp. 41–44.

Norma L. Rudinsky

Christiane Rochefort

Born July 17, 1917, Paris, France
Genre(s): novel
Language(s): French

Born into a family of modest means and reared in one of the poorer sections of Paris, Rochefort worked as press secretary for the Cannes Film Festival for some twenty years. She resigned in the late 1960s to devote herself full time to writing.

In her novels, the values of modern bourgeois society are presented as repressive and life-inhibiting. They come into conflict with the natural and life-enhancing values of children and adults who, in one way or another, live outside the bounds set by society. The language is colloquial, occasionally vulgar, and the tone is often ironic and comic. The heroine of her first widely-read work, *Le repos du guerrier* (1958), "keeps" a man (he spends his days in bed drinking whiskey) because he enables her to enjoy sex fully. In this book, Rochefort parodies the conventions of the love novel. *Les petits enfants du siècle* (1961) is the satiric tale of a young girl whose family lives on welfare subsidies. *Les stances à Sophie* (1963) is about a lower-class girl who marries into a bourgeois family. *Printemps au parking* (1969) is the account of an adolescent boy who runs away from his bourgeois home and lives with Parisian beatniks for several days before returning to his parents. Several later novels also deal with children or young people. Rochefort's longest novel, *Archaos, ou le jardin étincelant* (1972), is set in an imaginary country during a period somewhat like that of the Middle Ages. The citizens overthrow their repressive king and establish a golden age.

Rochefort has said that in spirit she is close to the German romantics. "I seek harmony with the world, not its conquest." Displaying a remarkable talent for linguistic inventiveness, she has created works that are at times extravagant but always exuberantly alive.

Works

"Le démon des pinceaux" [The Demon of Paintbrushes] (1953). "Le fauve et le rouge-gorge" [The Wild Beast and the Robin] (1955). *Le repos du guerrier* [Warrior's Rest] (1958). *Les petits enfants du siècle* [Children of Heaven] (1961). *Les stances à Sophie* [Cats Don't Care for Money] (1963). *Une rose pour Morrison* [A Rose for Morrison] (1966). *Printemps au parking* [Springtime in the Parking Lot] (1969). *C'est bizarre l'écriture* [It's Strange, Writing] (1970). *Archaos, ou le jardin étincelant* [Archchaos, or the Sparkling Garden] (1972). *Encore heureux qu'on va vers l'été* [Still Happy That We Are Going Towards Summer] (1975). *Les enfants d'abord* [Children First] (1976). *Ma vie revue et corrigé par l'auteur* [My Life Reviewed and Corrected By the Author] (1978). *Quand tu vas chez les femmes* [When You Go Visiting Women] (1982). *Le monde est comme deux chevaux* [The World Is Like Two Horses] (1984).

Bibliography

Biblio, Special Rochefort issue (Nov. 1965): 2–15. Cluny, Claude Michel, "Entretien avec Rochefort." *Les lettres françaises* 21 (May 1969): 3–4. Herz, Micheline, "Le groupe et l'amour dans l'oeuvre de Rochefort." *Perspectives on Contemporary Literature* 3 (Nov. 1977): 52–57. LeClec'h, Guy, "Rochefort: entre le réalisme et l'utopie, la liberté." *Nouvelles Littéraires* (Oct. 30, 1972). McMahon, Joseph H., "What Rest for the Weary." *Yale French Studies* 27 (1961): 131–139.

Robert D. Cottrell

Dames des Roches: Madeleine Neveu and Catherine Fradonnet

Madeleine Neveu, born c. 1520, Poitiers, France; died 1587, Poitiers. Catherine Fradonnet, born 1542, Poitiers; died 1587, Poitiers
Genre(s): poetry, prose dialogue, tragicomedy, letters, translation
Language(s): French

The Dames des Roches lived their entire lives in and around Poitiers. Madeleine married in 1539 the lawyer André Fradonnet who died eight years later. Catherine was their sole surviving child. Madeleine was remarried in 1550 to Francois Eboissard, Seigneur de la Villée et des Roches, a lawyer active in local politics. Madeleine probably frequented humanist circles during Poitiers's first period of literary fame (1545–1555) that included the poets J. Pelletier, J. Tahureau, and J.-A. de Baïf. Her primary concern was Catherine's education. Madeleine and Catherine's co-authored works and partnership over their *salon* testify to a close relationship founded on esteem and a lively exchange of ideas. Their mutual devotion was so great that contemporary *elogia* attribute Catherine's refusal of matrimony to her desire to remain with her mother. An unstated corollary is that Catherine's marriage would doubtless have terminated her venture in cooperative scholarship. Their publications first appeared in the 1570s when they were establishing a *salon*. In 1577, the court's three-month residence in Poitiers prompted them to write poems honoring members of the royal family. These were published the following year in a first volume of works, followed in 1579 by an expanded second edition. By then, their fame attracted to their *salon* Parisian lawyers present at the 1579 assizes or "grands jours" of Poitiers. Among them was E. Pasquier who, chancing to see a flea on Catherine's bosom, suggested a contest of versified wit. This was the start of *La Puce de Madame des Roches*, a ninety-three folio collection containing numerous *blasons* by the habitues of the *salon*. Madeleine and Catherine published two further volumes of works before their death of the plague in 1587. The publications of the Dames des Roches, which include a wide variety of poetic genres, prose dialogues, a tragicomedy, letters, and first translations of Latin works, constitute an impressively extensive and diversified body of writings. Madeleine's contribution, entirely in verse with the exception of her *missives*, dwells on largely personal topics such as matters of health, a thirteen-year lawsuit, her ambitions for her daughter, the role of women, the religious wars and misfortunes of Poitiers, marital love, and epitaphs to deceased public figures. Although her work is more limited in length and scope than her daughter's—she published only late in life when she became a widow—Madeleine's presence figures prominently throughout the *oeuvres*. The valorization of the Mother is perhaps the most striking feature of these works. Madeleine and Catherine wrote for and of each other. Catherine frequently dedicates individual poems to her mother whom she calls "the life of my life." The daughter's appeal to maternal discourse is further embodied in her mythical heroines Agnodice, Pasithee, Charite, the Amazons, Proserpina, Pallas Athena, the "Femme forte" of Proverbs, Phyllis, who constitute so many legitimizing "foremothers" in her quest for poetic origins. Also integral to Catherine's feminine economy is her praise of the distaff in her often cited "A ma Quenoille" (1579). Catherine is the first woman writer to challenge humanist norms that either considered women's education as secondary to household duties (Erasmus, More, Vives), or treated learned women as exceptional "honorary males" unfit for, and alienated from, the traditional occupations of their sex.

The Dames des Roches's unique social and familial situation enabled them to combine harmoniously the duties of a household, *salon*, and dual writing careers. They were fully integrated in a community of humanist legists and scholars whose conservative royalist, nationalistic, and gallican views they shared. Their works provide a fascinating glimpse into the vitality of humanist learning among the provincial upper bourgeoisie and *noblesse de robe*.

Works

Les Missives de Mes Dames des Roches de Poitiers, mere et fille, avec le Ravissement de Proserpine

prins du Latin de Clodian. Et autres imitations et meslanges poetiques (1586). *Les Oeuvres de Mes Dames des Roches de Poitiers, mere et fille* (1578). *Les Oeuvres . . . seconde edition, corrigee et augmentee de la Tragicomedie de Tobie et autres oeuvres poetiques* (1579). *Les Premieres Oeuvres . . . Les Secondes Oeuvres . . . troisieme edition* (1604). *La Puce de Madame des Roches*, ed. D. Jouaust (1582, 1583, 1610; rpt., 1868). *Les Secondes Oeuvres de Mes Dames des Roches de Poitiers, mere et fille* (1583).

Bibliography

Diller, George, *Les Dames des Roches. Etude sur la vie littératire à Poitiers dans la deuxième moitié du XVIe siècle* (1936). Pasquier, E., *Les Recherches de France* I (1723; rpt. 1968), p. 703; and *Choix de Lettres sur la littérature, la langue, et la traduction*, ed. D. Thickett (1966).

General references: Perouse, G., *Les nouvelles françaises du seizième siecle. Images de la vie du temps* (1976). Rose, M. B., ed., *Women in the Middle Ages and the Renaissance* (1986). Wilson, K., ed., *Women Writers of the Renaissance and Reformation* (1987).

Other references: *Allegorica* 7 (1982). *PMLA* 48 (1933).

Anne Larsen

Edith Rode

Born February 23, 1879, Copenhagen, Denmark; died September 3, 1956, Frederiksberg, Denmark
Genre(s): novel, memoirs, poetry, drama, journalism
Language(s): Danish

Edith Rode came of age at the turn of the century and published her first two novels in 1901 during a period in Danish literary history when writers from previously silent or overlooked social milieus, including women, began to make themselves heard. Although Rode wrote successfully in all genres, she excelled in the short story.

As the daughter of C.H.H. Nebelong, a physician to the court of King Christian IX, Rode grew up among conservative aristocrats. Nevertheless she received a fairly broad liberal education and attended Erna Juel Hansen's experimental school. After a brief early marriage which ended in divorce, she married the mystical symbolist poet Helge Rode, who was a major figure in Danish literary circles. She travelled widely, living for periods of time in France and Italy. Her resulting exposure to different walks of life served her well; an insight into late-nineteenth-century female childhood can be gleaned from the autobiographical *De Tre smaa Piger* (1948); and her volumes of memoirs, *Der var engang* (1951), *Paa togt i Erindringen* (1953) and *Paa rejse i Livet* (1957), contain interesting portraits of her friendships with famous artists and poets like Edvard Munch, Sophus Claussen, and Rainer Maria Rilke. In 1913, she began writing for the Copenhagen daily newspaper, *Berlingske Tidende*. Her subsequent long career in journalism not only gave her the opportunity to develop her talent for the short story but produced two travel books, a series of cookbooks, an advice book titled *Livskunst uden Filosofi* (1948), and an invaluable contribution to Danish women's history, *Den Gyldne Bog om Dansker Kvinder* (1941), which she edited. As a dramatist, she wrote two plays, *Sejren* (1913) and *Det evige Glæder* (1920), a series of radio plays, and two screenplays. Three collections of Rode's poetry were also published, in 1920, 1933, and 1950.

Rode's earliest novels, *Misse Wichmann* (1901), *Maja Engell* (1901) and *Gold* (1902) drew on her own experiences in their portrayal of young bourgeois heroines venturing among bohemian artists. One of their main themes is the incompatibility of men's expectations with women's own needs for both love and liberation. They treat a number of moral and sexual topics, such as frigidity, with a frankness that was surprising in a young woman at the time. Similar themes were also featured in her following novels, *Tilfredse Hjerter* (1905) and *Grazias Kærlighed* (1909), which both take place in Italy, thereby contrasting the mores, including sex role expectations, of the South with those of the North.

Rode had already produced two volumes of short stories, *Kvinde* (1908) and *Af Kundskabens Træ* (1912), before she began writing for the *Berlingske Tidende*, but at that point her talent for the genre really began to blossom. Her stories were reprinted in a succession of collections of

which *I tidens Klo* (1949) is a distillation of the best. Many of her stories have erotic themes, treating feminine psychology with insight and irony. For example, "Den evige tilbeder" (The Eternal Adorer), her only story to have been translated into English twice, is written from the point of view of a sophisticated woman who receives a young man bearing a note from one of her female friends, advising her to kill him immediately. After several weeks of the boring young man's importunate devotion, the narrator understands her friend's note and sends him on to another friend with a note of her own. Such stories led one of her admirers to compare Rode to Guy de Maupassant.

Although at her death Tom Kristensen praised Rode's poetry for its lyrical quality and considered her a pioneer among twentieth-century Danish women poets, her insight into feminine perspectives and conflicts was most fully developed in her fiction. Susanne Fabricius considers Rode's skill with the Danish language superior to that of most writers of entertainments despite certain cloying overtones in her style. Rode perhaps deserves more attention than she has received for her understanding of sexual politics and her examination of the underlying social and psychological motives that hindered many women from participating in their own liberation.

Works

Af kundskabens Træ [From the Tree of Knowledge] (1912). *Afrodite smiler* [Aphrodite Smiles] (1920). *Det bittersode æble* [The Bittersweet Apple] (1920). *Digte* [Poems] (1920). *Digte* [Poems] (1933). *Digte* [Poems] (1952). *Gold* [Barren] (1902). *Grazias Kærlighed* [Grazia's Love] (1909). *I tidens Klo; atten noveller, gamle og nye* [In the Claw of Time: Eighteen Short Stories, Old and New] (1949). *John Piccolo arver 60 millioner dollar* [John Piccolo Inherits 60 Million Dollars] (1932). *Idyllen, vaudeville uden sang* [Idyll: Vaudeville Without Blood] (1932). *Livets Ekko, 10 noveller* [Life's Echo: Ten Short Stories] (1932). *Livskunst uden filosofi* [The Art of Life Without Philosophy] (1948). *Maja Engell* (1901). *Mennesker i mondo* (1935) [People in the World]. *Misse Wichmann. Ogsaa i de andre huse* (1927) [Also in the Other Houses] (1901). *Paris i en nøddeskal* [Paris in a

Nutshell] (1927). *Pige* [Girls] (1914). *Sejren; skuespil i fire akter* [Victory: A Play in Four Acts] (1913). *Smaa børn og store* [Little Children and Big] (1950). *Tilfredse Hjerter* [Contented Hearts] (1905). *De tre smaa piger* [Three Little Girls] (1948). *Den tunge dør* [The Heavy Door] (1922). *Der var engang, et kig tilbage* [Once Upon a Time: A Glance Back] (1951).

Translations: "The Eternal Adorer," tr. Evelyn Heepe, in *Modern Danish Authors* (1946, 1974). "The Eternal Adorer." *The Norseman* 8, no. 5 (Sept.-Oct. 1950): 344–346. "Illusion," trs. Ann and Peter Thornton, in *Contemporary Danish Prose. Mieze Wichmann* (n.d.). *The Three Little Girls* (extracts), tr. Evelyn Heepe, in *Modern Danish Authors* (1946, 1974). *Unfruchtbar*, tr. Helene Klepetar (1908).

Bibliography

Fabricius, Susanne, "Edith Rode." *Dansk biografisk leksikon* (Copenhagen, 1982), vol. 12, pp. 258–259. Knudsen, Mogens, "Edith Rode," in *Danske digtere i det 20 århundrede*, ed. Frederik Nielsen and Ole Restrup (Copenhagen, 1965–1966), vol. 1, pp. 235–244. Kristensen, Tom, "Ved Edith Rodes død." *Oplevelser med lyrik* (Copenhagen, 1957), pp. 128–130.

Kristine Anderson

Mercè Rodoreda i Gurgui

Born 1909, Barcelona; died 1983, Barcelona
Genre(s): short story, novel
Language(s): Catalan

The recent translation of Rodoreda's works into Spanish and English is one indication of the increasing recognition of this writer's tremendous contribution to modern literature. Long considered one of Catalonia's most gifted writers, Rodoreda began her career as a journalist in Barcelona during the period preceding the Spanish Civil War. In 1933 she wrote her first novel, *Sóc una dona honrada* (An Honorable Woman). Four years later in the midst of the chaos of the Civil War she completed a draft of what most critics consider her first outstanding novel, *Aloma*, which was not published until 1969. It was during Rodoreda's long years in exile in Switzerland that she dedicated herself primarily to the writing of novels. Like *Aloma*, *El carrer de les Camèlies* (1966; Camelia Street) is a novel with a sensitive female protagonist in a brutally indifferent society. *Jordi vora el mar* (1967; The Garden by the Sea), although unlike both previous novels in that it revolves around an elderly male protagonist, is typical of Rodoreda's work in that the language is simple and lyrical. *Mirall trencat* (1974), a gloomy, powerful examination of a family over a period of many years, is, along with *Quanta, quanta guerra* (1980; So Much War) one of Rodoreda's most complex works dealing with the war. Very skillfully translated into Spanish by Enrique Sordo and more recently into English by David Rosenthal, *La Plaça del Diamant* (1962; Diamond Square) is considered by many critics to be Rodoreda's finest work. Returning to a female protagonist, the author examines from a young woman's point of view the chaos and violence of the Civil War as well as the disorder and destruction inherent in her marriage. Rodoreda's short stories, characterized by a richness of technique and an impeccably lyrical language, are collected in *Vint-i-dos contes* (1957; Twenty-two Stories), *La meva Cristina i altres contes* (1967; My Cristina and Other Stories), *Semblava de seda i altres contes* (1978; As If of Silk and Other Stories), and *Viatges i flors* (1980; Travels and Flowers).

Works

Aloma (1969). *El carrer de les Camèlies* (1966). *Jordi vora el mar* (1967). *La meva Cristina i altres contes* (1967). *La Plaça del Diamant* (1962). *Mirall trencat* (1974). *Obres Completes* [Complete Works] (1979). *Quanta, quanta guerra* (1980). *Semblava de seda i altres contes* (1978). *Sóc una dona honrada* (1933). *Viatges i flors* (1980). *Vint-i-dos contes* (1957).

English translations: *La meva Cristina i altres contes: My Christina and Other Stories*, tr. David Rosenthal (1984). *La Plaça del Diamant: The Pigeon Girl*, tr. Eda O'Shield (1967). *The Time of the Doves*, tr. David Rosenthal (1983).

Bibliography

Letras Femeninas II, números 1–3 (primavera otoño 1986). *Novelistas femeninas de la Postguerra española*, ed. Janet W. Pérez (1983). *Women Writers of Spain*, ed. C. Galerstein (Westport, Conn., 1986).

Barbara Dale May

Astrid Roemer

(a.k.a. Zamani)

Born April 27, 1947, Paramaribo, Surinam
Genre(s): novel, poetry
Language(s): Dutch, Sranan Tongo

"I am married to Surinam, I am in love with Holland, I have a homosexual relationship with Africa, and I am likely to have an affair with any other country." Like so many Caribbean writers, the Surinam author Astrid Roemer has a complex relationship with the country of her birth, the old mother country, the continent of her roots, and the world at large. Her life and work, largely dedicated to the fight against racism and sexism, bear witness to that complexity.

She was trained as a teacher in the Surinam capital Paramaribo, but lived and worked alternately in Holland and Surinam before definitively settling in Holland after Surinam became independent in 1975. At age twenty-two, she published her first collection of poetry, *Sasa* (1970; Swahili for "spirit of the time"), under the pseudonym Zamani (Swahili for "wherefrom I sprang and wherein I shall return") setting both the theme of identity that runs through much of her work and the visionary awareness characteristic of her best fiction.

The novel *Over de gekte van een vrouw* (1982; On a Woman's Madness), brought out by a Dutch publisher, marked Roemer's breakthrough. The story, set in Surinam, is the protagonist's search for her identity as a woman, a black, and a lesbian, which proves a difficult task in a multiracial and macho environment. Sexually disgusted, Noenka runs away from her husband of nine days, has an affair with a man who teaches her the pleasures of the senses, and discovers her lesbian passion for an older woman in the end. Roemer's originality lies in the effective combination of a plot typical of the feminist novel of the seventies with the hallucinatory prose and magic realism of contemporary South American fiction. Similar to the poetry in *Sasa*, Roemer's narrative in *Over de gekte van een vrouw* is more evocative than explicit and sometimes deliberately confusing. The characters and their motivations are not always easy to fathom, but the book never fails to suggest that

Noenka's search has a deeper spiritual meaning involving History, Ancestry, Womanhood, and Love. The novel was nominated one of the best books written by a woman in 1982 and 1983 by the feminist periodical *Opzij* and has been reprinted various times.

Nergens, Ergens (1983; Nowhere, Somewhere), a rewrite of the earlier *Neem mij terug Suriname* (1974; Take Me Back, Surinam), is a more traditional Caribbean novel of exile. It portrays the pain and loneliness of Surinamese émigrés trying to adapt to Dutch society. Roemer collected more poetry under the subtitle "liederatuur" (a pun on "lied"—"song"—and "literatuur") in *En wat dan nog* (1985; So What) and *Noordzee Blues* (1985; North Sea Blues). Compared to *Sasa*, this later poetry is somewhat mannered and artificial.

Roemer insists on seeing her work as part of the ongoing struggle against misogyny and negrophobia. She wants to show her mainly European readership a reality that is more complex than the generally perceived distinctions between men and women, black and white, and rich and poor. She includes, for example, poems in Sranan in her poetry collections to confront her readers with the multilingualism of Surinam society (Sranan is an English-based Creole that is widely spoken in Surinam). Roemer is also very much aware of the special position of the black woman, her divided loyalty between her race and her sex, and the different nature of her emancipation in the developing Third World compared to that of the white woman, who is "merely" fighting for personal improvement and a career.

Astrid Roemer has also published literary and journalistic work in various periodicals. She has written theater and radio plays and worked for film and television. She is a popular lecturer, and she has conducted writing workshops for women. Belonging to a new generation of Surinam writers living in exile, she has become a leading voice in the Netherlands, doggedly explaining the position of the modern black woman. So far she has, however, not matched the literary achievement, the intensity, and gripping quality of her successful novel *Over de gekte van een vrouw*.

Works

[Zamani, pseud.], *Sasa. Mijn actuele zijn* (1970). *Neem mij terug Suriname* (1974). *De wereld heeft gezicht verloren* (1975). *Waarom zou je huilen mijn lieve lieve* (1976). *Over de gekte van een vrouw* (1982). *Nergens ergens* (1983). *Een vrouw van een man* (1985). *En wat dan nog* (1985). *Noordzee Blues* (1985).

Bibliography

Timmers, R.-M., "Wat bindt meer: Ras of sexe? Een interpretatie van Astrid Roemers *Over de gekte van een vrouw*." Diss., University of Nijmegen, 1984. **General references:** *Caribbean Writers. A Bio-Bibliographical-Critical Encyclopedia*, ed. D.E. Herdeck (1979).

Other references: Engels, H., "'Taal is mijn medium,' In gesprek met Astrid Roemer" (interview). *Bzzletin*, 143 (February 1987). Phaf., I., "Interview met Astrid Roemer." *Ongehoorde Woorden*, ed. M. Schipper (1984).

Ria Vanderauwera

Alma Rogge

Born 1894, Brunswarden, Oldenburg, Germany; died 1969, Bremen
Genre(s): poetry, short story, drama
Language(s): German, Low German

Alma Rogge was born into an old peasant family. She studied literature and art history in Gottingen, Berlin, and Munich before obtaining her doctorate in Hamburg. Throughout her life, she worked as editor of various periodicals in Lower Saxony and Bremen. She first established herself with novellas, naturalist dramas, and popular comedies as a regional and dialect author of Germany's north sea coast. Much later, in the 1950s, she also published narratives and poetry in standard High German.

Works

Up de Freete (1918). *De Straf* (1924). *Hochzeit ohne Bräutigam* (1952). *Seid lustig im Leben* (1953). *An Deich und Strom* (Selections) (1958). *Land aus dem ich geboren bin* (1970).

Bibliography

von Wilpert, Gero, *Deutsches Literatur-Lexikon*, 2nd ed. (Stuttgart, 1975).

Ute Marie Saine

Anne de Rohan-Soubise

Born May 19, 1584, Le Parc-Soubise, France;
died September 20, 1646, Paris
Genre(s): poetry
Language(s): French

The daughter of René de Rohan and Catherine de Parthenay, Anne de Rohan-Soubise was famous for her piety and for her knowledge: she knew how to read Hebrew. She wrote numerous poems dealing, most of the time, with someone's death: that of Henri IV in 1610, of the duchess of Nevers in 1618, of her sister in 1624, and of her mother in 1632.

Works

Poésies d'A. de R. Soubise (1962).

Bibliography

Marcheray, Paul, *Recherches sur les poésies de Mlle de Rohan-Soubise* (La Roche-sur-yon, 1874).

Marie-France Hilgar

Roig I Fransitorra Montserrat

Born June 13, 1946, Barcelona, Spain
Genre(s): novel, short story, essay, newspaper articles, interviews
Language(s): Catalan, Spanish

Roig gained recognition in Catalonia as a promising young author when her first book of stories, *Molta roba i poc sabó . . . i tan neta que la volen* (Lots of Clothes and Little Soap . . . and So Clean They Love It) won the Victor Català prize for 1970. In 1980, with the translation to Castilian Spanish of her subsequent trilogy of novels, *Ramona, adéu* (Goodbye, Ramona), *El temps de les cireres* (Cherry Time), and *L'hora violeta* (The Violet Hour), she achieved national acclaim as one of the major women writers to emerge in democratic Spain.

During her early years, Roig was educated in Catholic schools. She then attended a school of theatre arts and entered the University of Barcelona, where she received her degree in Hispanic literature in 1968. As a student, she participated in an anti-Franco demonstration and became associated with the movement for Catalan nationalism. She has referred to Castilian Spanish as a "borrowed" language in which she sometimes writes because of historical circumstance.

Roig is well known for several series of television interviews and for her frequent collaboration in newspapers and magazines. Her books include collections of interviews and newspaper articles as well as documentary essays.

To date, Roig has published five novels. Although these vary in narrative structure and style, they all take place in the author's native city and tend to repeat characters from the same novelistic world.

In the initial trilogy, which presents a sweeping vision of Barcelona from the turn of the century through the decade of the 1970s, Roig focuses on the women members of two families related by marriage, the Miralpeix and the Ventura-Claret. *Ramona, adéu* (1972) juxtaposes the daily lives and frustrated loves of three generations in the latter family. The experiences of grandmother, mother, and daughter are variously presented in first- and third-person narrations and are played against significant historical moments, including the Spanish Civil War in the 1930s and the student revolts of the 1960s.

El temps de les cireres (1977) shifts to the Miralpeix family and concentrates more on the present, although the memories of some of the characters extend back in time. The central figure is Natàlia, a nonconformist, professional woman, who returns to Spain after twelve years of exile in England. The social and political commentary in this second novel is more overt, as Roig brings to the foreground her criticism of moral hypocrisy, cultural decay, and materialism. At times the satire verges on the grotesque: a Tupperware party that degenerates into an orgy, or Aunt Patricia Miralpeix's discovery that the man she secretly loves is her husband's lover.

The satirical tone and, to some extent, the political thrust of *El temps de les cireres* disappears in *L'hora violeta* (1980), a complex metanovel that openly reflects a number of feminist issues. Central to the experiences of the principal characters—Natàlia, her rival Agnès, and their mutual friend, the writer Norma—are their relationships with men. Although, of the three, Agnès is initially the most traditional, ultimately it is she who achieves independence, rejecting both her errant husband and her role as

"Odysseus's Penelope." Juxtaposed with the stories of these women in the present are the diary and letters of Natàlia's mother, potential basis for a novel Norma plans to write.

As the title indicates, there is also a strong metafictional current in *L'òpera quotidiana* (1982; The Daily Opera). The interwoven narrative strands reveal the lives of several characters on the fringes of society who escape from their realities through fantasy. One of them, the elderly Patricia Miralpeix, astutely observes that insane asylums are filled with those who have tried to live out the conventions of popular culture, whether in the form of the operas and romantic novels of the past or of the television series and rock music of the present.

La veu melodiosa (1987; The Melodious Voice) likewise reflects musical structures in its narration and continues, at least partially, in the vein of theatricalized life. The protagonist is a monstrously ugly young man. Since birth, he has been sheltered from reality by a wealthy grandfather who banishes mirrors from their apartment and provides him with an education based on an idealized world. The young man's inevitable initiation to reality makes him confront social injustice and his own weakness. Under torture, he betrays his comrades in a clandestine student movement that he does not fully understand.

While the style of *La veu melodiosa* is much more poetic than Roig's earlier narrative works, she has returned to the situation of the 1960s and to characters introduced in her first novel. She has created a rich novelistic world that should provide the basis for future probings of the human heart and the ills of contemporary society.

Works

Molta roba i poc sabó . . . i tan neta que la volen, short stories (1971). *Ramona, adéu* (1972). *Los hechiceros de la palabra*, essay (Col. Perfiles Ibéricos, 1975). *Rafael Vidiella, l'aventura de la revolució*, essay (Col. les Eines, 1976). *Retrats parellels* I, II, III, interviews (Col. Biblioteca Serra d'Or, 1975–1978). *El temps de les cireres*, novel (1977). *Els catalans als camps nazis*, essay (Col. Cultura Catalana Contemporánea, 1977). *Noche y niebla: los catalanes en los campos nazis* (1979). *Personatges*, interviews (1978). *Personatges, segona sèrie*, interviews (1980). *I Tiempo de mujer?*, essays and interviews (1980). *L'hora violeta*, novel. *Mujeres en busca de un nuevo humanismo*, interviews (1981). *L'òpera quotidiana*, novel (1982). *Carnet de mujer* (1984). *L'aqulla daurada [La aquja dorada]*, essay (1985). *El femenismo*, essay (Colección Salvat Temas Clave, 1986). *La veu melodiosa [La voz melodiosa]*, novel (1987).

Translations: *Carnet de mujer*, tr. Enrique Sordo. *La hora violeta [L'hora violeta]*, tr. Enrique Sorto (1980). *Ramona, adiós [Ramona, adéu]*, tr. Joaquim Sempere (1980). *Tiempo de cerezas [El temps de les cireres]*, tr. Enrique Sordo (1980). *Aprendizaje sentimental [Molta roba i poc sabó . . . i tan neta que la volen]*, tr. Mercedes Nogués (1981). *La òpera cotidiana [L'òpera quotidiana]*, tr. Enrique Sordo (1983). *La voz melodiosa [La veu melodiosa]*, tr. José Agustín Goytisolo (1987).

Bibliography

Bellver, Catherine G., "Montserrat Roig and the Penelope Syndrome." *Anales de la Literatura Española Contemporánea* 12.1–2 (1987): 111–121. Gerling, David Ross, Review of *La hora violeta*. *Anales de la Literatura Española Contemporánea* 8 (1983): 243–245. Gilabert, Joan J., Review of *La veu melodiosa*. *España Contemporánea* 2.3 (1989): 146–148. Nichols, Geraldine C., "Mitja poma, mitja taronja: Génesis y destino literarios de la catalana contemporánea." *Anthropos* 60–61 (1986): 118–123. Pérez, Janet, *Contemporary Women Writers of Spain*. Twayne's World Author Series 798 (Boston, 1988), pp. 189–192. Rogers, Elizabeth S., "Montserrat Roig's *Ramona, adiós*: A Novel of Suppression and Disclosure." *Revista de Estudios Hispánicos* 20.1 (1986): 103–121. Sánchez Arnosi, Milagros, Review of *La òpera cotidiana*. *Insula* 468 (Nov. 1985): 19. Zatlin, Phyllis, Review of *Ramona, adiós, Tiempo de cerezas*, and *La hora violeta*. *Hispanófila* 84 (1985): 117–120.

General references: Galerstein, Carolyn L., ed., *Women Writers of Spain: An Annotated Bio-Bibliographical Guide* (New York, 1986).

Phyllis Zatlin

P. Rokytovsky

(see: Terézia Vansová)

Jeanne-Marie (called Manon) Phlipon Roland

Born March 17, 1754, Paris, France; died
November 9, 1793, Paris
Genre(s): memoirs, discourse
Language(s): French

Mme Roland is above all famous for the utterance "O Liberty, what crimes are committed in thy name!" as she mounted the steps of the guillotine in the Place de la Révolution in Paris, a victim of the anti-Girondin movement. Her life is, however, hardly less interesting than her death. The daughter of a highly skilled goldsmith who, at least during her childhood, was quite well off, Jeanne-Marie Phlipon was a precocious child with an inordinate love of reading, so she was able to profit to an extraordinary degree from the excellent private education that she was given. At an early age she enjoyed Tasso's *Jerusalem Set Free*, Fénelon's *Adventures of Telemaque* and Plutarch's *Lives*, which inspired her with heroic ideals. At the time of her preparation for First Communion, she read the works of Bossuet and other classic religious apologists. For a while their arguments convinced her, but then she was more attracted to the doctrines of the Deists. Finally she discovered the ideas of Jean-Jacques Rousseau, which brought her reading, experiences, and ideas into focus. Among her early works was a discourse on the theme "How the education of women could serve to make men better"; submitted for a competition organized by the Academy of Besançon, it owed a good deal to Rousseau's *Discourse on the Origins of Inequality*.

In 1780 she married Jean Roland de La Platière, a younger son of a minor noble family from Burgundy who had entered the public service as an inspector of manufactures and was charged with helping French trade and industry to adopt new methods. Though their relationship was, according to Mme Roland, more that of father and daughter than of husband and wife, the couple got on well, and in October 1781 a daughter, Eudora, was born. Mme Roland did much to help her husband further his career; she assisted him in couching his treatises on advancing technology in readable French, she negotiated with publishers, and, with some success, pleaded his cause in government ministries. In 1784 they went to England together; for her it was the fulfillment of a dream for not only had she learned to read English, but she also, like many of her compatriots at the time, saw in England an example in politics and toleration that France would do well to follow. The Rolands returned to live for a time in the relative quiet of the area around Lyons. Then the Revolution gave them, as they thought, the opportunity they were looking for. Mme Roland had been disgusted by the snobbishness of the *Ancien Régime*, and her reading had prepared her for change. After her husband had attracted some attention by his contributions to the Revolutionary press in Lyons, the couple moved to Paris. M. Roland was, perhaps a little unexpectedly, appointed Minister of the Interior in the Girondin cabinet, and Mme Roland became a leading light of the Girondin party. She knew everybody and, it was said by many, she knew too much; her support of her husband at every turn was taken by some as petticoat influence. When the Girondin party fell from favor, she was arrested. While in prison she composed her *Memoirs*; in them, inspired by Rousseau, she gave a remarkably frank account of her early life as well as a sturdy defense of her subsequent actions. She also wrote many letters, some of them to François Buzot, a Girondin deputy with whom she had fallen in love in her late thirties. She bore her captivity and execution with Stoic imperturbability worthy of the Plutarchan heroes she had admired in the days of her youth. Her husband committed suicide on hearing of her fate. Nineteenth-century historians such as Lamartine and Michelet made much of Mme Roland as an example of female heroism in the face of the cruel tyranny of the French Revolution.

Works

Oeuvres, 3 vols. (1800). *Mémoires particuliers*, preface by G. Huisman (1929; tr. as *The Private Memoirs*, ed. E.G. Johnson, 1901). *Une éducation bourgeoise au XVIIIᵉ siècle, suivi du Discours de Besançon*, ed. Charles Lalloue (10/18, 1964).

Bibliography

de Sainte-Beuve, Charles-Augustin, "Madame Roland." *Portraits de femmes. Oeuvres*, ed. Maxime Leroy, "Bibliothèque de la Plèiade." (Paris, 1960). May, Gita, *Madame Roland and the Age of Revolution* (New York, 1970).

Christopher Smith

Dominique Rolin

Born 1913, Brussels, Belgium
Genre(s): novel, drama, short story, children's literature
Language(s): French

Rolin's Belgian heritage—from Breughel's earthy colors to the gray Northern seascape—vividly informs her work, yet she is no more representative of "Belgian literature" than she is of the postwar literary scene in Paris, where she has spent over half of her life. In general, her career has evolved outside the literary movements and schools of either place. The question of Rolin's cultural identity is, as with many writers of Belgian origin, a complex one. A resident of France since the age of thirty-three, she chose French nationality in 1955, but Belgium continued to form the backdrop for many of her novels, contributing as well to her heterodox humor and unique aesthetic sensibility.

Primarily a novelist, Rolin has also published drama, short stories, and works for children; in addition, she is a published illustrator of children's books. Her mother—a deaf teacher of elocution—and her father, a librarian, instilled in her a passion for language at an early age. Rolin, the oldest of three children, studied fine arts as well as training for a library career herself; she worked in that capacity at the Université Libre de Bruxelles from 1933–1936. Her literary career has been the opposite of meteoric. Rather, it is characterized by a gradual, rich evolution of a very personal narrative style through two dozen novels, most of which allude to the drama of her own family life, with recurrent figures of a tyrannical father, a self-effacing mother, and precociously lucid children. While certain details corresponding to her actual life have emerged more clearly in her work, Rolin's style cannot be said to have become more realistic. In her work at least three major phases may be identified, ranging from the romantic-gothic (1942–1944), through the realistic (1946–1958) and, after an important transitional period (1960–1965), evolving into insistent introspective fabulation, the paradox of expansive introversion (1967–1985).

In 1936, Rolin's novella *La Peur* was awarded the Prix de la Nouvelle by the international review *Mesure* (directed by Paulhan, Ungaretti, and Groethuysen). Six years later her first novel, *Les Marais*, appeared and was hailed as a success by Jean Cocteau and Max Jacob; this recognition was among the factors motivating her move to Paris in 1946, after the dissolution of a first marriage in Belgium that had resulted in the birth of a daughter (1938). Rolin's arrival in Paris coincided with the publication of her third novel, *Les Deux soeurs*. Soon after, she met the sculptor Bernard Milleret, to whom she was married in 1955; she transposed many of the elements of their life together in the first-person narration of her novel *Moi qui ne suis qu'amour* (1948), which was followed in 1950 by *L'Ombre suit le corps*. Four years later, her career gained momentum with the publication in 1952 of a collection of short stories, *Les Enfants perdus*, and a sixth novel, *Le Souffle*, which was awarded the Prix Fémina and was both a critical and commercial success (enabling Rolin to move with Milleret to a house in Villers-sur-Morin, at 40 kilometers from Paris); this novel also marked the climax of her most traditional period, which saw the publication of three more books: *Les Quatre coins* (1954), *Le Gardien* (1955), and *Artémis* (1958). Both *Le Souffle* and *Les Quatre coins* were soon published in English.

A turning point in Rolin's life as well as in her literary career came in the wake of her husband's untimely death from cancer in 1957. Returning to Paris in 1959 to begin work as a reader for at least two large French publishing companies, she continued to write. Late in 1958, Rolin met the "Jim" of her later works who became her longtime companion. *Le Lit* (1960), a soberly written fictionalized journal of her dying husband's last days, inaugurated a departure from her previous writing; this stylistic transformation became even more dramatic in *Le For intérieur* (1962), with its economical style, its departure from narrative linearity, and its focus, which later dominated Rolin's writing, on the first-person narrator's introspection. The first of these transitional novels was adapted for the screen by the Belgian director Marion Hänsel (1982). Before plunging wholeheartedly into a series of introspective autobiographical novels, Rolin was to publish a third transitional novel, *La Maison la forêt*. Unique among Rolin's works in its virtually "nouveau roman" architecture, the novel explores two domains and two rhythms in the alternating monologues of her aged reminiscing father (forêt) and mother (maison).

Maintenant (1967) can be seen as the first full-fledged novel of Rolin's third phase, made up of a series of ten novels in which the narrator's interior monologues take up progressively more space, and which, though readable as individual works, benefit from strong intertextual resonances within the series. *Les Eclairs* (1971) relies on two elements of increasing importance in Rolin's work: use of words as metamorphic treasure-objects, and "speculative memories" of the marriage that resulted in her own birth. The latter theme inspired the *Lettre au vieil homme* (1973) to her father. *Deux* (1975) dramatized the interaction of the writer Dominique Rolin and her alter ego in "the real world"; its fine-grained evocation of muffled interactions between the real and the imaginary spheres has occasioned comparisons with Sarraute's *tropismes*. Refining this technique of psychical microspeculation, Rolin continued her "self-exorcism" in *Dulle Griet* (1977), named after the Breughel painting. The theme of Breughel is also brought forth *L'Enragé* (1978; awarded the Prix Frans Hellens), an apocryphal "biography" of the painter that, apart from its recognizable style, represents a radical, if temporary, divergence from the series of autobiographical novels begun with *Maintenant*. Rolin then resumed the style of her series, which culminated in a trilogy whose narrative begins before the narrator is born—*L'Infini chez soi* (1980; awarded the Prix Kleber Haedens)—and ends with the post-mortem voyage described in *La Voyageuse* (1984). In between these extremes of existence is Rolin's exuberant, phantasmagorical autothanatography, *Le Gâteau des morts* (1982). This fugue-like *ars moriendi* in which the author-narrator wrestles with angels of language, of family, and of memory, is widely regarded as her best novel. The trilogy seems to have closed Rolin's period of "auto-science-fiction"; her next novel, *L'Enfant-Roi* (1985), while not wholly abandoning the preoccupation with autobiographical fantasy and the mysteries of reproduction, explores the mind and body of a remarkable boy-child, sending Rolin's still-evolving work in new directions.

Through all its phases, Rolin's work has shown a unique coherence in its relentless probing beneath the surface of family relationships and in its mix of almost visionary mysticism with fleshly mischief. Her idiosyncratic passion, lyrical perseverance, humor, and acute awareness throughout the never-finished process of writing are appreciated by faithful readers and a broad spectrum of critics. This steady and prolific writer continues to find a steady readership.

Works

Novels: *Les Marais* [The Marshes, translated into Dutch] (1942). *Anne la bien-aimée* [Anne the Beloved, translated into Dutch] (1944). *Les Deux soeurs* [The Two Sisters, translated into Serbo-Croatian] (1946). *Moi qui ne suis qu'amour* [I Who Am All Love, translated into Dutch] (1948). *L'ombre suit le corps* [The Shadow Follows the Body] (1950). *Le Souffle* [The Pulse of Life, Prix Fémina) [translated into English and Italian] (1952). *Les Quatre coins* [The Girl Who Ran Away, translated into English] (1954). *Le Gardien* [The Guardian] (1955). *Artémis* (1958). *Le Lit* [The Bed, translated into Dutch, English, German, Greek, and Spanish] (1960). *Le For intérieur* [Deep Down, translated into German] (1963). *La Maison la forêt* [House and Woods] (1965). *Maintenant* [Now] (1967). *Le Corps* [The Body] (1969). *Les Eclairs* [Lightning] (1971). *Lettre au vieil homme* [Letter to the Old Man] (1973). *Deux* [Two] (1975). *Dulle Griet* (1977). *L'Enragé* [The Enraged One] (1978). *L'Infini chez soi* [The Infinite Within] (1980). *Le Gâteau des morts* [The Deathday Cake] (1982). *La Voyageuse* [The Voyager] (1984). *L'Enfant-Roi* [The Child King] (1985).

Short stories: "Les Enfants perdus" [The Lost Children] (1951).

Drama: *L'Epouvantail* [The Scarecrow] (1957).

Children's literature: *Casquette ou les tribulations d'un chien* [Casquette, or The Trials of a Dog] (1975).

Translations: *The Pulse of Life* [*Le Souffle*], tr. D. Moore (1954). *The Girl Who Ran Away* [*Les Quatre Coins*], tr. J. Emerson (1956). *The Deathday Cake* [*Le Gâteau des morts*], tr. J. Gage (1987). *The Bed* [*Le Lit*], tr. Selma Teich.

Bibliography

Assier, Annick, *Dominique Rolin: Un Livre: "L'Enragé." Une Oeuvre* (1986). De Haes, Frans, "'Une espèce de coma frais': *L'Infini chez Soi* de Dominique Rolin." *Ecritures de l'imaginaire: Dix études sur neuf ecrivains belges* (1985). De Haes, Frans, "Le Péche oublié." *Mille et un soirs au Théâtre-Poème* (1983). Dufourrier, Paul, "Dominique Rolin romancière." *Quintessences* 3. Linze, Jacques-Gérard, "Dominique Rolin et l'exigence grandissante." *Revue générale* 3 (March 1970). Mora, Edith, "Dominique Rolin." *La Revue des Deux Mondes* (Nov. 15, 1969).

Jennifer C. Gage

Lalla Romano

Born 1909, Demonte, Cuneo, Italy
Genre(s): poetry, novel, journalism, translation
Language(s): Italian

Lalla Romano was born in Demonte, near Cuneo, in 1909, the daughter of a well-to-do family. She spent a happy childhood in Demonte. In her writings she will always return to this time of innocence and beauty; so much so that critics consider her literature exemplary of what is called a *letteratura della memoria*, a literature of remembrance. At twelve she moved to Cuneo with her family to study at the local high school. There she began to write her first poems and to develop her interests in literature and painting. She entered the University of Turin, where she met Cesare Pavese and other intellectuals who encouraged her in pursuing her cultural and artistic aspirations. Two of her professors deeply influenced her. Ferdinando Neri fostered Romano's interest in literature (Baudelaire and French Symbolists) and Lionello Venturi her passion for painting (she then studied for several years with Felice Casorati). After graduating summa cum laude in 1928, she moved back to Cuneo where she worked as a librarian and as a high school teacher. She married, had a son, and decided to return to Turin where she could teach and, at the same time, maintain direct contact with other writers and intellectuals. In 1935 after Eugenio Montale expressed his favorable criticism, Romano collected and published a volume of verse called *Fiore* (1941), which was critically praised for the evocative and lyrical quality of her poems. The themes are clearly inspired by the poets she admired, the *stilnovisti* (subject of her doctoral dissertation) and the French symbolists: love, the romanticized landscape, all sounds and colors of nature: ("simile a un fiore il cielo / dagli orli vermigli posa / lieve sulla terra oscura / . . ."— like a flower the sky / with crimson edges rests / lightly on the obscure earth).

Italy was by 1942 in its second year of war. Romano flew to Cuneo to escape the heavy bombings of Turin. There she translated—at Cesare Pavese's request—Flaubert's *Tre Racconti* (Three Tales) and edited an anthology of Delacroix's writings. She also actively collaborated with partisan groups.

At the end of the war, she joined her husband who had gone to Milan to work. She resumed her teaching and began writing her first novel, *Maria*. These were crucial years for Romano. Fighting against dire financial conditions, she realized that she had to choose between painting and a literary career. Having resolved to give up painting, she concentrated on a second work *Le metamorfosi*, a collection of prose writings published in 1951. Well liked by critics, this work marks Romano's beginning as a creditable writer. The book is structured in fourteen chapters, which are thematically grouped into the tales of five narrators. Each story, told in first person, is a tale of a dream. These dreams give one insight into the author's mind, her concerns for her familial world, her ideas on her art—as she describes it: "un cammino dalla poesia alla prosa." *Maria* was completed the same year and after being approved by Pavese, Ginzburg, and Vittorini, was published by Einaudi. The book was coolly received by critics, but after Montale's review it became a success and was awarded the Veillon prize. The book is a first-person account of the life of a country girl who leaves the fields to go to work as a maid. It is a delicate tale of sacrifice and honesty, a chronicle of domestic values and simple virtues.

In 1955, Romano published a small collection of poems *L'autunno*, written in her charac-

teristic terse and rigorous style. She was already working on *Tetto murato*, published in 1956 (Pavese Prize). By now the name Romano was associated with that of other important women writers, such as Banti, Manzini and Ginzburg. Her recollections of her travels as to Greece are contained in *Diario di Grecia* (1960). In 1961, she returned to fiction with *L'uomo che parlava solo* (The Man Who Spoke to Himself). The lack of a sense of autobiographical intimacy sets this work itself aside from Romano's production.

Her mother's death that same year caused a severe trauma in Romano's life. In order to gain a sense of equilibrium, the author returned to the places of her childhood, to Demonte. The fourth novel, *La penombra che abbiamo traversato* (The Dimness That We Have Gone Across), which was published four years later, in 1964, dealt with her recent experience of grief and death. The book records the spiritual agony of the protagonist as a result of her mother's death. In a spiritual, often magical, journey to a recollected childhood, the protagonist rediscovers a sense of self. The book was exalted by some and attacked by others. In 1969 Romano received the Soromprist prize in recognition of her artistic career.

The novel that followed *Parole tra noi leggere* took four long years of work but was rewarded with critical and commercial success. Published in 1969, it received the Strega prize and was a best-seller. The novel is once again autobiographical and has as its theme the relationship between mother and son. The success of the novel can be attributed to the public general response to Romano's ability to deal lyrically and intelligently, without false sentiments, with a topic of great actuality and to the reader's identification with the vicissitudes of the story. After *L'ospite* (1973; The Guest) follow novels like *La villeggiante* (The Lady on Vacation) that reveal a new and lighter side of Romano. *Una giovinezza inventata* (1979; A Fabricated Youth) is based once again on personal memories. Romano describes the social conventions by which she was brought up in Turin during the 1920s. Presently, she lives a very private life with her husband. Writing is still her most important occupation, as she continues to produce novels and critical works.

Works

Poetry: *Fiore* (1941). *L'autunno* (1955).

Fiction: *Le metamorfosi* (1951, 1967). *Maria* (1953, 1973). *Tetto murato* (1957, 1971). *L'uomo che parlava solo* (1961). *La penombra che abbiamo traversato* (1964, 1972). *Le parole tra noi leggere* (1969 and 1972). *L'ospite* (1973). *La villeggiante* (1975). *Pralève* (1978). *Una giovinezza inventata* (1979). *Lo stregone* (1979). *Inseparabile* (1981).

Travel book: *Diario di Grecia* (1960, 1974).

Translations: *Tre racconti*, by G. Flaubert (1944, 1956). *Diario 1822–1863*, by E. Delacroix (1945). *Leone Morin, prete*, by B. Beck (1974).

Critical work: *Lettura di una immagine* (1975).

Bibliography

Barberi-Squarotti, Giorgio, *Poesia e narrativa del secondo novecento* (Milano, 1978). Bo, Carlo, *Fiera letteraria* (Sept. 20, 1953). Ceratto, Marino, *Il "Chi è" delle donne italiane, 1945–1982* (Milano, 1982). De Robertis, Giuseppe, "Ritratto di una serva." *Tempo* 7 (1954). Manacorda, Giuliano, *Vent'anni di pazienza* (Firenze, 1972). Petrignani, Sandra, *Le signore della scrittura* (Milano, 1984). Pullini, Giorgio, *Il romanzo del dopoguerra italiano* (Milano, 1961). Vincenti, Fiora, *Lalla Romano* (Firenze, 1974).

Giacomo Striuli

Bieiris de Romans

Flourished first half of the thirteenth century [?], Romans (Drôme), Southern France
Genre(s): canso
Language(s): Occitan

The Occitan *canso* (or love song) "Na Maria, pretz e fina valors" (PC 93, 1) is ascribed by a rubric in the single fourteenth- or fifteenth-century manuscript that preserves it (MS. T, Paris, B.N. fr. 15211, fo. 208b) to the otherwise unknown *trobairitz* (or woman troubadour) Na (or Lady) Bieiris de Romans, who is presumed to have flourished in the first half of the thirteenth century. It is probable that *Romans* refers to the cantonal seat of that name in the *arrondissement* of Valence (Drôme) in the Rhône valley of the Dauphiné. The *canso*, a hymn of erotic love addressed to a "Lady Maria," raises difficult questions of attribution and intention. The poem is composed of two *coblas* (or strophes) and two *tornadas* (or envoys). It opens with an apostrophe to the Lady Maria and a list of the qualities possessed by her: worth, wit, beauty, cultivated speech, charm, lack of guile, etc. The speaker then begs for her love, asserting that in her lies all hope for joy and urging her not to give her love to a false (male) lover.

In the medieval Occitan *canso*, where conventionally the author is identified with the speaking voice of his text, an erotic apostrophe by the author's persona to a member of the same sex would imply a homosexual relationship. If its author is a woman, "Na Maria" is "the sole extant example of medieval love poetry written in a vernacular language by one woman to another" (Boswell 265). Critical opinion is divided on the questions of the gender of *Bieiris* and the proper context in which to place "Na Maria." Some scholars argue that its author is not a woman because of the rarity of celebrations of homosexual and particularly of lesbian love in the medieval lyric, their virtual non-existence in Occitan poetry, and the improbability that a male troubadour should have chosen to adopt a feminine persona. It has been asserted that the rubric is a mistranscription of *N'Alberis de Roman* or Alberico da Romano, a thirteenth-century Italian nobleman, patron, and occasional troubadour (Schultz, "Nabieiris"); for *En* ("Lord"), the masculine counterpart of *Na*, contracts to *N'* before a vowel. The possibility that the rubric contains a copyist's error is strengthened by the fact that the song contains no internal markers identifying the speaking voice as that of a woman. On the contrary, it conforms in every respect to the conventions of the troubadour song with a masculine poetic voice.

In favor of the opposing view, it has been proposed that the song is a devotional work, a literary exercise, a piece of innocent flattery, a joke, or half of a *tenso atypique* (or dialogue poem alternating not by strophes, as is normal, but by halves) between a male and a female voice, only the first half of which has survived (Huchet 64). This latter suggestion does not resolve the problem of the name given by the rubric, for even if, as often happens with *tensos*, the name of only one interlocutor is given, *Bieiris* would have to refer to the male, the female necessarily being named

Maria. While the hypothesis that it is a paean to the Virgin is rendered implausible by its erotic character (esp. v. 16), the suggestions that it is facetious (Bec 198), ironic, or fragmentary are not so easily dismissed.

Bibliography

Bec, Pierre, *Burlesque et obscénité chez les troubadours. Pour une approche du contre-texte médiéval* (Paris, 1984), pp. 197–200. Bogin, Meg, *The Women Troubadours* (New York and London, 1976), pp. 176–177. Boswell, John, *Christianity, Social Tolerance, and Homosexuality. Gay People in Western Europe from the Beginning of the Christian Era to the Fourteenth Century* (Chicago and London, 1980). Dronke, Peter, *Women Writers of the Middle Ages. A Critical Study of Texts from Perpetua (d. 203) to Marguerite Porete (d. 1310)* (Cambridge, 1984), p. 98. Huchet, Jean-Charles, "Les Femmes troubadours ou la voix critique." *Littérature* 51 (October 1983): 59–90. Schultz, Oscar, *Die Provenzalischen Dichterinnen. Biographien und Texte nebst Anmerkungen und einer Einleitung* (Leipzig, 1888, Geneva, 1975), pp. 16, 28. Schultz, Oscar, "Nabieiris de roman." *Zeitschrift für romanische Philologie* 15 (1891): 234–235.

Merritt R. Blakeslee

Annie Romein-Verschoor

Born February 4, 1895, Hatert, The
    Netherlands; died February 5, 1978,
    Amsterdam
Genre(s): literary, cultural, and historical essay
Language(s): Dutch

The writer of many sociologically oriented essays and articles on literature and other topics, Annie Romein-Verschoor led an intellectually and socially very active life spanning a period beginning with the European left of the twenties and thirties and ending with the feminism of the seventies.

Part of her formative teenage years were spent in the Dutch East Indies where she developed a strong antipathy to colonialism. The experience served as a background for her first book, *Aan de Oedjoeng* (1928; On the Ujung), a story for girls. She studied Dutch literature and history in Leyden, where she also became acquainted with leftist student groups. Throughout her life she remained a confirmed believer in the political left and a fervent critic of the right and its policies. Always sensitive and self-opinionated, she was never a staunch dogmatist or theoretician. (As a matter of fact, she was expelled from the Dutch Communist Party in 1927.)

In 1920 she married the "bolsjewist" and later historian Jan Romein. The couple had three children in quick succession. While Jan devoted his time and energy to study and research, Annie took care of home and family. Later she wrote that she thought of herself as "a part-time maid," and that she might have become a journalist if she had not been married or had been married to someone else.

She turned out to be a prolific writer, nevertheless. Her book reviews for the *Algemeen Handelsblad* became the basis for her doctoral thesis on Dutch women novelists after 1880—in its second edition published as *Vrouwenspiegel* (1936; Mirror of Women). A highly idiosyncratic version of historical materialism (influenced by the Marxist historian Franz Mehring), *Vrouwenspiegel* combined Romein's literary sensitivity with historical and sociological insights. She also wrote an introduction to new Dutch literature for foreigners, *Slib en Wolken* (1947) (published in English as *Silt and Sky*) and *De vruchtbare muse* (1949; The Fertile Muse) on *littérature engagée*. She received the prize for prose of the city of Amsterdam for *Vaderland in de verte* (1948; The Fatherland in the Distance), a historical novel set in the seventeenth century, based on the tragic life of the Dutch statesman-in-exile Hugo de Groot and his courageous wife Maria van Reigersberch. It showed Maria's development from blind admiration for her husband's wisdom to growing irritation with his otherworldliness.

Jan and Annie Romein worked together on *De lage landen bij de zee* (1934; The Low Countries by the Sea), a popularizing history of the Netherlands, which became a bestseller in the pre-war years of Dutch national awareness, and *Erflaters van onze beschaving* (1938–1940; Testators of Our Civilization), short biographies of major figures in Dutch history (note that only one woman figured in the four-volume book).

After her husband's death in 1962, Annie Romein-Verschoor completed his work on the last turn of the century—*Op het breukvlak van twee eeuwen* (1967; On the Fault Line of Two Centuries)—and until her own death in 1978, she contributed a substantial number of essays on a wide variety of topics to various journals, including the feminist *Opzij*. *Drielandenpunt* (1975; Three Countries Touching) and *Vrouwenwijsheid*(1981; Women's Wisdom) are collections of this later work. She spent the last years of her life in a nursing home for artists and intellectuals. She remained critical and active, voicing the problems of the elderly and denouncing the authoritative and patronizing manner of her caretakers.

Annie Romein-Verschoor emerges from her writing as an erudite and discerning woman with a strongly developed sense of justice. She made use of the essay, a little-practiced genre in the Low Countries, and developed a style that was opinionated, complex, and disgressional. Distancing herself from mainstream leftism and feminism, she advocated a third way, her own. Her most interesting works are undoubtedly her memoirs *Omzien in verwondering* (1970–1971; Looking Back in Wonder—the pun is deliberate), which include a perceptive portrayal of the leftist milieu of the first half of the century and of life during the war years. They are the testimony of a woman who, with great perseverance and love, balanced raising children and caring for an admittedly difficult husband with valuable intellectual and social work. Annie Romein-Verschoor was awarded the 1970 Constantijn Huygens Prize for her entire literary oeuvre. The feminist seventies marked a new interest in her life and work. Since then, much of her earlier writing has been reissued.

Works

Aan de Oedjoeng (1928). [With Jan Romein], *De lage landen bij de zee* (1934). *Vrouwenspiegel* (1936). [With Jan Romein], *Erflaters van onze beschaving*, 4 vols. (1938–1940). *Slib en wolken* (1947). *P.C. Hooft, 1581–1647*(1947). *Vaderland in de verte*(1948). *De vruchtbare muze*(1949). *Man en vrouw* (1951). *Met eigen ogen* (1953). *Spelen met de tijd*(1957). *Zedelijkheid en schijnheiligheid* (1962). *Omzien in verwondering*, 2 vols. (1970–1971). *Ja vader, nee vader*(1974). *Drielandenpunt* (1975). *Vrouwenwijsheid*, ed. C. Rappange (1981). **Translations:** *Alluvions et Nuages* [*Slib en wolken*] (1947); *Silt and Sky* [*Slib en wolken*] (1950).

Bibliography

Auwera, F., *Geen daden maar woorden* (1970). Bibeb. *Veertien vrouwen. Interviews* (1974). *Bzzletin* 81, special issue on Romein-Verschoor (Dec. 1980). Florquin, J., *Ten huize van . . .*, 11 (1975). Romein, J., *Zesentwintig biografieën* (1949). **General references:** *De Nederlandse en Vlaamse auteurs van middeleeuwen tot heden* (1985). *Moderne encyclopedie van de wereldliteratuur* (1980–1984). *Winkler Prins Lexicon der Nederlandse letterkunde* (1986).

Ria Vanderauwera

Concha Romero

Born 1945, Cordoba, Spain
Genre(s): drama
Language(s): Spanish

Concha Romero collaborated with Cecilia Bartolomé on several film scripts before turning to theater. *Un olor a ámbar* (A Scent of Amber) concerns a power struggle in the Church for the politically-advantageous remains of St. Teresa. In addition to its historical accuracy and possible feminist reading, the play contains lively dialogue and some splendid moments of grotesque humor.

Works

Un olor a ámbar [A Scent of Amber] (1983). *Las bodas de una princesa* [The Wedding of a Princess] (1988).

Bibliography

"Encuesta: ¿Por qué no estrenan las mujeres en España?" *Estreno* 10.2 (1984): 22–23. Pérez-Stansfield, María del Pilar, "La desacrilización del mito y de la historia: texto y subtexto en dos nuevas dramaturgas españolas." *Gestos* 2.4 (1987): 83–99.

Patricia W. O'Connor

Marina Romero Serrano

Born February 5, 1908, Madrid, Spain
Genre(s): poetry
Language(s): Spanish

Born in Madrid, Marina Romero was a pupil from age four to ten at the International Institute for Girls in Spain. Later she attended the Instituto Escuela, an offshoot of the famed Institución Libre de Enseñanza. She also taught there for a number of years, from 1929 to 1935. Her guardian was *institucionista* Luis Simarro, to whom she dedicated the first poem of *Nostalgia de mañana* (1943). In 1935, armed with a degree from the Escuela Normal de Maestros and grants from the Spanish Republic and Smith College, she went to the United States, where she earned an M.A. at Mills College and taught Spanish literature at Douglass College (New Brunswick, N.J.) from 1938 to 1970. She now resides in Madrid.

Undoubtedly her early training in the liberal and open atmosphere created by the Institución Libre de Enseñanza and her contact with such *institucionistas* as Luis Simarro and others would remain a strong influence in her life and writings. Her love for Spanish literature and culture spilled over not only into her teaching, where for decades she instilled that love in her young American students, but in texts such as *Paisaje y literatura de España. Antología de los escritores del 98* (1957; Landscape and Literature of Spain. An Anthology of the Generation of 1898), where she attempted to fuse literature and accompanying color photographs into a single aesthetic experience.

But it is her poetry that captures best the intimate, moving spirit of Marina Romero. Her early books, *Poemas "A"* (1935) and *Nostalgia de mañana* (1943), reflect the influence of the poetic generation of 1927, especially Pedro Salinas. *Poemas "A"* (Poems "To"), for example, was written at the height of the *poesía pura* of Jorge Guillén and other Spanish poets of the vanguard period. Romero's pleasure in word play and verbal virtuosity is offset by the exploitation of the simple rhythms and imagery of popular poetry. This tendency to merge refined and popular strains of writing into one is highly characteristic not only of the period but of much of Spanish literature in general. *Nostalgia de*

mañana (Nostalgia for Tomorrow) incorporates some of these earlier poems written between 1930 and 1935 but also anticipates in the second group of poems (1938–1943) a deepening of tone and feeling that is more fully realized in her later poetry from the 1950s and 1960s. The theme of love and its absence is revealed through a desire to write "un presente / que no existe" ("a present / that does not exist") and a future "con fuerza de presente" ("with the force of the present"), lines which may very well reflect the bitter experience of exile and the melancholy of personal loss. The book was published in Mexico under the "Rueca" impress, which was closely associated with the contingent of exiled Spanish republicans.

Her next three books of poetry, *Presencia del recuerdo* (1952), *Midas* (1954), and *Sin agua, el mar* (1961), were published, though not conceived, in Spain. Luminosity of style and intimacy of tone mark all three volumes. *Presencia del recuerdo* (Presence of Memory) is dedicated to the memory of the great love poet, Pedro Salinas, who had died the year before. Deceptively simple and clear in language, the poems are often constructed through a series of paradoxes, such as "mi querer no queriendo" ("my loving not loving"), "y tú no estás, estando" ("being there, you're not there"), and "la muerte / te hace más presente" ("death makes you more present"). The themes of time and death, the memory of lost love, and the poet's solitude will reappear in *Midas. Poema de amor* (Midas. A Love Poem). The fifty-three separate poems may be read as a single long poem, and the sequence runs from the fullness of possession to the emptiness of loss. Romero's loss of love is closely identified with the seeming loss of language and reality itself, in lines like "Ya no sé qué decir" ("I no longer know what to say") and "Ya no sabré las calles / sin tu andar" ("I will no longer know the streets / without your step"). But paradoxically, she concludes *Midas* by affirming the self and its experience through language as a form of verbal imprisonment: "Ya quedas para siempre / creado en mi palabra, / y no habrá lenta gota / que logre emanciparte" ("Now you are forever / created in my words, / and no slow drop / can free you").

Her next book, *Sin agua, el mar* (Without Water, the Sea), consists of thirty-three poems numbered backwards, a device reflecting an inner process of self-diminishment that culminates in an intense vision of nothingness in lines such as these: "Sin agua, / el mar. / Sin tiempo / el reloj. / Sin aire / el suspiro. / Sin calor / este frío, / este vacío / sin mar, / sin tiempo, / sin aire, / este vacío" ("Without water, / the sea. / Without time, / the clock. / Without air / the sigh. / Without heat / this cold, / this emptiness / without sea, / without time, / without air, / this emptiness"). The preposition "sin" (without) functions anaphorically as a consistent leitmotif, suggesting desolation and deprivation so extreme that words and sentence structure are reduced to their minimum expressivity. It should also be noted that *Sin agua, el mar* evidences a greater social awareness than Romero's earlier poetry.

Romero's last books have been written for children. In *Alegrías* (1972; Happiness), *Campanillas del aire* (1981; Little Bells in the Air), *Churrupete va a la luna en busca de la fortuna* (1985; Churrupete Goes to the Moon in Search of Fortune), and *Disparatillos con Masacha* (1986; Nonsense with Masacha), all written in verse, she returns to that light-hearted spirit and sense of playfulness evident in her early poetry. She creates a childlike language, using techniques of repetition, alliteration, and similar sounding phonemes unconnected semantically, to suggest the delightfully irrational and imaginative world of childhood. In this sense, her work, which has gone from the joyous sense of plenitude to despair and anguish, has also come full circle, allowing Romero to recapture that feeling of wonder and discovery all writers experience. Thus she dedicates these last poems to all children, "Para vosotros todos, chicas y chicos, y hasta para los grandes, la alegría y el gozo de estos poemas para que sigáis soñando" ("For all of you, boys and girls, and even big children, the happiness and pleasure of these poems so you may keep on dreaming").

Works

Poemas "A" (1935). *Nostalgia de mañana* (1943). *Presencia del recuerdo* (1952). *Midas. Poema de amor* (1954). *Paisaje y literatura de España* (1957). *Sin agua, el mar* (1961). *Alegrías. Poemas para niños* (1972). *Campanillas del aire* (1981). *Churrupete va a la luna en busca de la fortuna* (1985).

Disparatillos con Masacha (1986). *Poemas a doña Chavala y don Chaval* (1987). *Cuentos rompecabezas* (1988).

Unpublished manuscripts: *Arte, historia y literatura de Toledo (siglos XI al XX)*, Antología. *Honda raíz*, Sonetos. *Poemas de ida y vuelta. Viento en contra. Lyric Anthology of the Young Galician Generation. Las cuatro estaciones*, Pieza teatral para niños.

Translation: *Touchstone* 10 (1985).

Bibliography

Doreste, V., "A propósito de Marina Romero." *Insula* (Aug. 15, 1953). Valis, N.M., "The Language of Treasure: Carolina Coronado, Casta Esteban, and Marina Romero," in *In the Feminine Mode*, eds. C. Maier and N. Valis (forthcoming).

General references: *Women Writers of Spain*, ed. C.L. Galerstein (1986).

Other references: *Insula* (April 15, 1955). *Insula* (April 15, 1958). *Insula* (June 1962). *Poesía Española* (August 1953). *Poesía Española* (June 1954). *Poesía Española* (October 1961). *Revista Hispánica Moderna* 22 (1956).

Noël M. Valis

Margherita Ronaca

Born c. 1600, Rome, Italy; died c. 1657
Genre(s): poetry, letters, opera, drama
Language(s): Italian

Poetess and courtesan of wide renown, Margherita Costa Ronaca was born in Rome around the year 1600 of a lower-class family. During the third decade of the *Seicento*, she moved to Florence where she began to write poetry in the hope of securing the protection of a maecenas. The period 1638–1641 was one of great activity for Margherita, marked by the appearance in 1638 of *Le ottave per l'incendio dei Pitti* and by the publication, the same year, in Germany, of her first volume of poetry: *La chitarra*. In 1639 appeared *Lo stipo* and a prose work in the form of an amorous correspondence, *Lettere amorose*. The year 1640 marked the publication, in Florence, of *Flora feconda*, a drama in ten cantos and a work in ottava rima, *La selva dei cipressi*, which was written on the occasion of the death of the duke of Gioiosa and of the prince of Granville. A verse comedy in three acts, *Li buffoni*, appeared in Florence in 1641, and in 1645 she published in Rome *Cecilia martire*, a religious-allegorical poem in four cantos. It was in this year that Margherita moved from Florence to the court of Torino as a chamber singer and, after a brief stay there, established herself in Rome where she found a position as a singer with a group of musicians at the service of the cardinals Antonio and Francesco Barberini. At the request of Cardinal Mazarin, in 1646 Margherita left for Paris with the same group of musicians, and it was here that, a year later, she published two volumes of poetry: *La tromba di Parnaso* and *Selva di Diana*, and the *Festa reale er balletto a cavallo*, an allegorical and theatrical composition in verse form that made use of musical accompaniment, mythological figures, and effective staging techniques. Her last literary creation was a dramatic opera in three acts and in verse form which appeared in 1654 in Venice. Margherita died about the year 1657. Although she tried her hand at several forms of literature—dramas, prose compositions, narrative poems and lyrical poetry—her entire production suffers from structural imperfections.

Works

Le ottave per l'incendio dei Pitti (1638). La chitarra (1638). Lo stipo (1639). Lettere amorose (1639). Flora feconda (1640). Li buffoni (1641). Cecilia martire (1645). La tromba di Parnaso (1646). Festa reale per balletto a cavallo (1646).

Bibliography

Bianchi, D., "Una cortigiana rimatrice del Seicento: Margherita Costa." *Rassegna della letteratura italiana* XXIX, Nos. 1–6 (1927), pp. 1–31; XXX, Nos. 7–12 (1925), pp. 187–203. Costa-Zalessow, Natalia, *Scrittrici italiane dal XIII al XX secolo* (Ravenna, 1982), pp. 146–152.

Sandro Sticca

Rosalbe

(see: Kathinka [Katharina] Rosa
  Pauline Modesta Zitz-Halein)

Rosalie

(see: Magdalene Philippine Engelhard)

Ana Rosetti

Born 1950, San Fernando, Cádiz, Spain
Genre(s): poetry, novel
Language(s): Spanish

Of a well-to-do traditional family, Rosetti was convent-educated and as an adolescent was attracted by mystics and martyrs to consider the religious life; however, the discovery of art and beauty in multiple forms (from religious statuary to silks, from the music of Mozart or Handel to poetry) exercised a powerful influence on her sensuality and aesthetic sensibilities. She was able to travel considerably in Europe and Africa, and evolved somewhat like others of her generation—rebels of the late sixties, attracted by peace movements and free love (not only "make love, not war," but a philosophic exaltation of eroticism as the only truth, one of life's few realities). Rosetti's formation is to a considerable extent autodidactic, including extensive reading and a "bohemian" period with several temporary jobs, notably (because of literary echoes) one in a cabaret or music-hall. She is an exceptionally erotic poet, noteworthy not merely because she is a woman but because Spain lacks a tradition of erotic poetry.

Her first book of poems, *Los devaneos de Erato* (1980; The Frenzies of Erato [muse of lyric poetry]) has an acknowledged autobiographical basis, with insistent evocations of the past. The writer indicates that it was not written as a related entity but is a selection of poems previously composed; however, *Dióscuros* (1982; Dioscuri [allusion to Castor and Pollux]) was conceived as an integrated volume. Published in a limited edition for bibliophiles, it contains nine poems and evinces increased concern with form and language. *Indicios vehementes* (1985; Vehement Signs) contains Rosetti's poetry written from 1979 to 1984, including the two titles mentioned above and previously unpublished pieces. *Devocionario* (1985; Devotionary) was awarded the King Juan Carlos International Prize for Poetry in 1985, the most significant recognition accorded Rosetti to date. *Devocionario* evokes the language of the most impassioned mysticism with the difference that the object of mystic contemplation is not God but Eros. Rosetti's "mysticism" is not metaphysical but palpably physical, a corporeal mysticism of the senses expressed in language which is violent, sometimes extreme, with occasionally brilliant metaphors, incorporating ingredients of Catholic liturgy.

In 1988, Rosetti published her first novel, *Plumas de España* (Plumes of Spain), a modern variant of the picaresque tradition in which the characters are homosexuals, music-hall dancers, variety show artists and eccentrics (although the writer—or her persona—functions as the first-person narrator, a well-known woman poet who is thinking of writing a novel). With a good deal of humor and irony and vivacious, colorful language, Rosetti playfully toys with the contemporary vogue for metafiction. *Yesterday* (1988), her latest collection of poetry, contains a good deal of intertextuality and allusions to other cultures, from classical mythology to contemporary advertisements (for blue jeans and undergarments), titles or phrases drawn from other languages—English, Latin, French, Italian—Spanish and Latin American poets and novelists, popular songs, movies, and the mass media. Fusing her appreciation for beauty with a mistico-profane world view and unabashed eroticism, Rosetti offers in *Yesterday* a selection from *Los devaneos de Erato*, *Indicios vehementes*, and *Devocionario*, together with other poems either unpublished or not previously issued in book form.

Works

Aquellos duros antiguos (1987). *Los devaneos de Erato* (1980). *Devocionario* (1985). *Dióscuros* (1982). *Indicios vehementes* (1985). *Plumas de España* (1988). *Yesterday* (1988).

Janet Perez

Maria Rosseels

(a.k.a. E.M. Vervliet)

Born October 23, 1916, Borgerhout-Antwerp, Belgium
Genre(s): film criticism, essay, novel
Language(s): Dutch

For many years after World War II, Maria Rosseels contributed journalistic essays and film reviews to *De Standaard*, the voice of the Flemish Catholic intelligentsia in Belgium. Rosseels emphasized the role and value of cinematography as an art form in her columns and in a long, separately published essay, *Kunst van schaduwen en dromen* (1954; Art of Shadows and Dreams). She also wrote two long essays against sexism and the discrimination of women, of which *Het Woord te voeren past den man* (1957; To Talk Is the Man's Task) is the better known.

The theme of womanhood was obviously Rosseels' primary concern in her initial efforts as a novelist. Her real literary debut—after a novel for youthful readers, *Sterren in de Poolnacht* (1947; Stars in the Polar Night)—was *Spieghelke* (1952), a novel presented in the form of a young girl's diary. The following, voluminous trilogy *Elisabeth* (1953), *Ic segh adieu* (1954; I Bid Thee Farewell) and *Het derde land* (1954; The Third Land), is again an elaboration upon the theme of a young girl's growth into a fascinating, intellectual woman. Especially *Elisabeth* is still among Rosseels' most widely read novels; many of the scenes presented through the child's consciousness are drawn with an impressive tenderness that lacks all affectation.

In her second thematic period, Rosseels examines closely the position and problems of the practicing, self-conscious Christian in the modern world. "Christian" for Rosseels obviously means "Catholic." Of these "novels of ideas," *Ik was een Kristen* (1957; I Was a Christian) and *Wacht niet op de Morgen* (1969; Don't Wait for Morning) are the best known. These two novels, both with a historical setting, and the intervening *Dood van een Non* (1961; Death of a Nun) confirmed Rosseels' reputation as one of the major conservative novelists in Dutch of the 1950s and 60s. *Dood van een Non* was successfully made into a movie picture by P. Collet and P. Drouot (1975). For *Wacht niet op de Morgen* Rosseels received the prestigious Scriptores Catholici prize in 1970. In 1984 she was awarded the highest official recognition, the State Prize, for her entire *oeuvre*.

Rosseels is not an innovator; her existential themes are obviously more important to her than experiments with form and technique.

Works

Numerous contributions to *De Standaard*.

Essays: *Kunst van schaduwen en dromen* (1954). *Het woord te voeren past den man* (1957). *Oosters cocktail* (1960). *Vrouwen in Licht en Schaduw* (1963). *Liefde is een zeldzaam kruid* (1966). *Onze tijd in de spiegel van de film* (1966). *Gesprekken met gelovigen en ongelovigen* (1967).

Fiction: [E.M. Vervliet, pseud.], *Sterren in de Poolnacht* (1947). *Spieghelke* (1952). *Nieuw Dagboek van Spieghelke* (1953). *Elisabeth* (1953). *Ic segh adieu* (1954). *Het derde land* (1954). *Ik was een Kristen* (1957). *Dood van een Non* (1961). *Wacht niet op de morgen* (1969). *Het Oordeel, of vrijdag zingt de nachtegaal* (1975).

Bibliography

Durnez, Gaston, *Maria Rosseels* (Beveren, 1981).

Kristiaan P. Aercke

Amelia Rosselli

Born 1930, Paris, France
Genre(s): poetry, translation
Language(s): Italian

Daughter of the well-known antifascist Carlo Rosselli who, along with his brother Nello, was assassinated in 1937, and an English mother, Amelia Rosselli lived in France, England, Switzerland, and the United States before settling in Rome where she lives today. She is a theoretician and composer of music as well as a translator and poet. Her official debut as a poet took place in 1963 when Pier Paolo Pasolini presented a group of her poems in the journal *Menabò*. Her first book of verse, *Variazioni belliche* (Martial Variations) appeared in 1964. Since then she has published several collections of poetry, and in 1981 she received the Pasolini Prize for her entire body of work.

Rosselli's poetry is recondite, demanding, and often maddeningly private. Her manipulation of rhythms and images is reminiscent of musical variations on a main melodic theme, the sense of which is created primarily through sonority and resonance. Shunning logical syntactic or narrative development, Rosselli instead creates an aura of great emotive force that is almost mystical and yet quite sensual. She is typically associated with the neo- and post-avant-garde tendencies of much recent Italian poetry because of her rejection of traditional models and her willful obscurity. Rosselli is clearly influenced by Freudian and Jungian concepts in her search for a language that might go beyond the conscious mind into the depths of less accessible experience. Her poems, often written in the first person, are elaborate surrealistic parables of desire, pain, and loss.

In the 1976 collection *Documento* (Document), which contains poems written between 1966 and 1973, Rosselli at times moves beyond the intense privacy of her earlier verse into the external world, as in "General Strike 1969" but the majority of the poems are evocative of subjective states and intimate concerns: love, aging, solitude. There is great sonorous beauty in Rosselli's verse, however; even the most impenetrable poems finally capture the ear and, often, the heart with their resonances and rhythms.

Works

Variazioni belliche [Martial Variations] (1964). *Serie ospedaliera* (1969). *Documento* [Document] (1976).

Anthologized in *Poesia femminista italiana*, ed. Laura Di Nola (1978), and *Donne in poesia: antologia della poesia femminile in Italia dal dopoguerra ad oggi*, ed., Biancamaria Frabotta (1977).

Anthologized and translated in *The New Italian Poetry: 1945 to the Present*, Lawrence R. Smith, ed. and trans. (1981); *Italian Poetry, 1960–1980: From Neo to Post Avant-garde*, Adriano Spatola and Paul Vangelisti, eds. (1982); *The Defiant Muse: Italian Feminist Poems from the Middle Ages to the Present*, Beverly Allen, Muriel Kittel, Keala Jane Jewell, eds. (1986).

Bibliography

Mengaldo, Pier Vincenzo, in *Poeti italiani del Novecento* (Milan, 1978). Papa, Marco, "Gli Appunti di Amelia Rosselli." *Il Lettore di Provincia* 16 (1985): 46–48.

General references: *Dizionario della poesia italiana* (Milan, 1983). Luti Giorgio, ed., *Poeti italiani del Novecento: La vita, le opere, la critica* (Rome, 1985).

Rebecca West

Evdokiia Rostopchina

Born December 23, 1811, Moscow, Russia;
died December 3, 1858, Moscow
Genre(s): poetry, drama, short story, novel
Language(s): Russian

At the height of her renown in the 1830s, Rostopchina was one of the most copiously published, extravagantly praised, and assiduously courted Russian poets. Although her reputation subsequently plummeted, her popularity, while it lasted, was staggering.

A native Muscovite, Rostopchina came from an affluent family with literary aspirations, especially on her father's side. When Rostopchina was not yet six, her mother (Dar'ia Pashkova) died of tuberculosis. Shortly after, the government office for which her father, Petr Sushkov, worked transferred him to Petersburg. Deprived of both parents, Rostopchina and her two younger brothers remained in Moscow under the indifferent care of their maternal grandparents. Only a modicum of adult attention and guidance shaped the children's early development, however, for their grandfather secluded himself in his study, emerging only for meals, while their grandmother's waking hours revolved around social occasions, her toilette, and the hordes of guests who daily swarmed to the house.

Tutors and governesses of dubious qualifications assumed responsibility for the children's upbringing and for their irregular education. Like most young girls of the era, Rostopchina studied the Bible, Russian, French, and German, a smattering of arithmetic, and a negligible dose of history and geography in addition to the mandatory drawing, piano, and dance. Blessed with a lively intelligence, a retentive memory, and an inquiring mind, the young girl successfully filled the vast lacunae in her education on her own initiative. Later she acquired a working knowledge of both Italian and English.

In the heat of her enthusiasm for Schiller, Byron, Pushkin, and Zhukovskii Rostopchina began scribbling verses that in 1830 caught the notice of a discriminating visitor to the Pashkov house: the poet and critic Petr A. Viazemskii. Without her knowledge he published one of her lyrics, "Talisman," in a Petersburg almanac in 1831, thereby launching her literary career. Instead of instant fame, Rostopchina's reward was a sharp rebuke from her scandalized grandparents, who deemed "versifying" an unseemly pastime for a decent unmarried young lady. That bewildering reaction effectively prevented Rostopchina from trying to publish her poetry until after she was married.

Rostopchina's marriage, paradoxically, both eased and complicated her circumstances. Her spouse, Count Andrei Rostopchin, the son of the famous governor-general of Moscow during Napoleon's invasion, was younger than Rostopchina, not of age when the couple married in 1833 and utterly incapable of fulfilling any of the customary marital obligations. Although her family and acquaintances saw the match as a brilliant coup, Rostopchina, who accepted the offer with reluctance, had profound qualms about the union. They soon proved to be justified.

However mismatched the couple was, Rostopchina nonetheless now had entree to the best society and felt free to pursue openly her literary inclinations. Published cryptically at first under the name "Countess R – – na" and then under her full name, Rostopchina's lyrics caused a near sensation. Such an exaggerated response to poems that are charming, sometimes good, very occasionally excellent, but generally unremarkable, now seems puzzling. But the author's gender—and her identity as a young woman from high society, with beauty, personal style, and grace in addition to talent—doubtless stirred the public imagination. Furthermore, Rostopchina had had solid personal ties with members of the literary circles from her childhood days at the Pashkov residence and had known the unequalled poet Pushkin from the age of eighteen. So she was no stranger to literary salons, and when she arrived in Petersburg with her husband in 1836, she had no difficulty renewing friendships or striking up new ones with the foremost representatives of Russian letters of the time. The list of cosmopolitan guests regularly gracing the soirées at the resplendent Rostopchina house included some of the most famous contemporary writers, artists, music critics, and thinkers.

Rostopchina's poetry, frequently written between social engagements and quite often recording her impressions of or emotional reactions to events transpiring during these gatherings, was published in a separate volume in 1841. It treated the conventional Romantic themes of love, disillusionment, solitude, and yearning in a manner that clearly reflected sundry West European and Russian influences. Composition came easily to her, and the rapidity and casualness with which she was able to dash off one stanza after another inevitably resulted in some rather facile images, phrases, and formulations.

Encouraged by her success in lyric poetry, Rostopchina in 1838 experimented in prose. Her two tales, "Chiny i den'gi" (Rank and Money) and "Poedinok" (The Duel), appeared above the somewhat presumptuous signature of "Iasnovidiashchaia" (Clairvoyant), and came out the following year in a book bearing the title *Ocherki bol'shogo sveta* (Sketches of Grand Society). In the preface the author expressed her views on society, which she castigated for prizing only position and wealth instead of inherent virtues. Whereas the critical reception of Rostopchina's poetry had been consistently laudatory, her prose passed practically unnoticed. Only a few spoke favorably of the tales, among them an editor who compared Rostopchina to George Sand, then the most generous of compliments. The tales, like all of Rostopchina's fiction, suffer from insignificant content, unconvincing characterization, and protracted gushes of emotional intensity couched in metaphors and similes punctuated by sighs and gasps. Drenched in the bathos for which Romanticism at its most immature had an inexplicable weakness, they have a historical and sociological value that cannot compensate for their lack of literary merit.

Between 1837 and 1839 Rostopchina had two daughters and a son, and traveled south, presumably for reasons of health. In 1840 she returned to Petersburg without her husband, and resumed the whirl of social activities that she criticizes so vehemently in her prose. In 1845 the entire Rostopchina household went abroad for two years. From Italy Rostopchina sent her ballad "Nasil'nyi brak" (The Forced Marriage), which appeared in a conservative Petersburg daily in 1846. It caused a scandal. While some read the ballad as Rostopchina's indiscreet exposé of her marital woes, many interpreted it as an allegory decrying Russia's subjugation of Poland. In any event, Rostopchina fell into disgrace at court, and the general attitude toward her cooled, steadily worsening over the next twelve years.

When Rostopchina returned to Russia in 1847 and settled down in Moscow for good, her creativity sought new and not entirely felicitous modes of expression. Instead of lyrics, she began writing prose novels and large-scale works in blank verse. In the last decade of her life, she was unusually and indiscriminately prolific, turning her hand to a wide variety of genres, including several five-act dramas in blank verse, novels (*Schastlivaia zhenshchina* [1851–1852; A Fortunate Woman], *Palazzo Forli* [1854], *U pristani* [1857; At the Pier/At a Refuge]), comedies, and a one-act verse drama called "Vozvrat Chatskogo v Moskvu" (1856; Chatsky's Return to Moscow). These were all received with repeated indifference and occasional abuse.

In 1858 Rostopchina took to her bed, fully aware that she had little time left. Her last extant written communication was in French to Alexandre Dumas, to whom she sent a letter and a note containing information about the biography of the Russian poet Mikhail Lermontov. By the end of the year Rostopchina was dead.

Rostopchina was in several significant ways a typical product of the aristocratic milieu in which she moved during her adulthood. Personally and ideologically conservative, she was cushioned from countless hardships by her social standing and her financial security. Writing for her was neither an irresistible inner impulse nor a professional necessity for the sake of earning a livelihood; it had the appeal of an agreeable hobby, a pleasurable means of whiling away the hours, even though negative reviews wounded her pride deeply. A percentage of her poems reveal a generous lyric talent, an ear for pleasing rhymes, and an instinct for poignant images and delicate effects. Some of them wonderfully capture moods of melancholy, resignation, and despair in the face of love's expectations, of disappointments, and of loss. Several evidence the poet's responsiveness to nature's beauty and her strong religious feeling. Only a handful of her poems, however, bear an individual stamp and make a lasting impression, for the rest tend to be generalized, almost anonymous. Her output as a whole smacks of the "dear diary" school of writing.

Not only the "lightness" of Rostopchina's poetry but also the privileged conditions in which she lived led the socially committed critics of the 1860s and 1870s to disparage her contribution to Russian poetry in immoderate and rather vulgar attacks on her works and her way of life. Nor was their evaluation of her prose more generous, even though they must have found much to sympathize with in her repeated diatribes against the emptiness of the *beau monde*, with its constant parties, gossip, materialism, pettiness, and insignificance. But her criticism came from within, since she was, at least for a while, one of the most prominent celebrities within that glittering set that the later generations of utilitarian critics despised. Literary criticism of the twentieth century has treated Rostopchina even more cruelly, in a sense, for its indifference has practically relegated her to the ranks of the forgotten.

Works

Collections and more significant publications: *Ocherki bol'shogo sveta: sochineniia Iasnovidiashchei* (1839). *Stikhotvoreniia* (1841). *Neliudimka: drama v 5-i deistviiakh* (1850). *U pristani: roman v pis'makh*, 4 vols. (1857). *Stikhotvoreniia*, izd. 2 (1857–1860). *Vozvrat Chatskogo v Moskvu: prodolzhenie komedii Griboedova "Gore ot uma"* (1965). *Dnevnik devushki: roman [v stikhakh]* (1866). *Sochineniia graf. E.P. Rostopchinoi*, 2 vols. (1890). *Sobranie sochinenii* (1910). *Dom sumasshedshidh v Moskve v 1858 godu* (1911).

Translations: "Nasil'nyi brak" [The Forced Marriage], tr. Louis Pedrotti, *op. cit.*, p. 202. "Chiny i den'gi" [Rank and Money], tr. Helena Goscilo. *Russian and Polish Women's Fiction* (Knoxville, 1985), pp. 50–84.

Bibliography

Bykov, Petr, "Russkiia zhenshchiny-pisatel'nitsy, IV. Grafinia E.P. Rostopchina." *Drevniaia i novaia Rossiia* 7 (1878), pp. 238–243. Ernst, S., "Karolina Pavlova i gr. Evdokiia Rostopchina." *Russkii bibliofil* 6 (Petrograd, June 1916), pp. 5–35. Khodasevich, Vladislav, "Grafina E.P. Rostopchina: Ee zhizn' i lirika." *Stat'i o russkoi poezii* (Petrograd, 1922), pp. 7–42. Nekrasova, E., "Grafinia E.P. Rostopchina, 1811–1858." *Vestnik Evropy* III (March 1885), pp. 42–81. Pedrotti, Louis, "The Scandal of Countess Rostopchina's Polish-Russian Allegory." *Slavic and East European Journal* 30, No. 2 (Summer 1986), pp. 196–214. Rostopchina, I.A., *Semeinaia khronika* (Moscow, n.d.). Rostopchine, Lydie, *Les Rostopchine (Chronique de famille)* (Paris, 1909; tr. of above work). Sushkov, D.P., "K biografii E.P. Rostopchinoi." *Istoricheskii vestnik* VI (June 1881), pp. 300–305. Sushkov, S., "Vozrazhenie na stat'iu E.S. Nekrasovoi." *Vestnik Evropy* III. (February 1888), pp. 388–437. Sushkov, S., "Biograficheskii ocherk." E.P. Rostopchina, *Sochineniia graf. E.P. Rostopchinoi*, Vol. I (Petrograd, 1890), pp. 3–48. Tsebrikova, M., "Russkie zhenshchiny-pisatel'nitsky." *Nedelia*, 13–14, pp. 438–440. Veselovskii, Turii, "Poeziia gr. E. Rostopchinoi." *Etiudy po russkoi i inostrannoi literature*, Vol. I (Moscow, 1913), pp. 5–22.

Other references: Golitsyn, N.N., *Bibliograficheskii slovar' russkikh pisatelnits* (Petrograd, 1889), pp. 209–216. Lerner, N., *Russkii biograficheskii slovar'*, pp. 220–229. Muratova, K.D., *Istoriia russkoi literatury XIX v. Bibliograficheskii ukazatel'*. (Moscow/London, 1962), pp. 615–617.

Helena Goscilo

Roswitha

(see: Hrotsvit of Gandersheim)

Stella Rotenberg

Born March 27, 1916, Vienna, Austria
Genre(s): poetry
Language(s): German

Stella Rotenberg, one of the many German-speaking Jewish writers who settled in England, has published but two collections of poetry. In her verse she reflects in an almost prototypical manner the traumas of European Jews who escaped the death camps but who can never escape their many lingering effects.

Rotenberg is the daughter of Bernhard Siegmann, a merchant, and his wife, Regine. The German annexation of Austria in 1938 signaled the end of her study of medicine at Vienna. In 1939 she fled to Holland and then, shortly before the outbreak of the war, to England. In 1939 she married Juda Wolf Rotenberg, a physician. Until the birth of her son, Adrian, in 1951, she worked as a medical orderly and bookkeeper. The Rotenbergs have lived in Leeds since 1948.

Like Hilde Domin and several other exiles, Rotenberg turned to poetry relatively late in life. Her first book, *Gedichte* (1972; Poems), reflects the temporal distance from the events that shaped—and continue to dominate—her life: memories of the Holocaust, of the Jewish dead, of the apathy of so many people. Time has filtered the perspectives and emotions: there is little rancor in her commemorations of the victims or reflections on those who incurred guilt by acts of omission or commission. But neither is there any indication that the terrible events have been forgotten. Her second book, *Die wir übrig sind* (1978; We Who Remain), is artistically more polished; rhyme and traditional forms are still present in most of the poems, although some are now written in a free verse reminiscent of Brecht. In general the themes are similar: the Jewish dead, the problems of the survivors (especially those living abroad in continuing exile), and language.

As Rotenberg observes (in an image) in one poem, she does not aspire to poetic greatness but hopes to be able to make a modest contribution to posterity by means of her verse. A writer who refuses to conform to the latest trends in form or content, preferring rather to address universal issues (if, often, in relation to the Holocaust), she may well continue to be read long after poets who are now much more popular have been forgotten.

Works

Gedichte (1972). *Die wir übrig sind* (1978).

Jerry Glenn

Rotsuith

(see: Hrotsvit of Gandersheim)

Nelly Roussel

Born January 5, 1878, Paris, France; died
*   December 18, 1922*
Genre(s): essay, poetry, journalism
Language(s): French

Nelly Roussel remains one of the most incisive French writers on the woman question. Born to a Parisian bourgeois family, her formal education was limited to the elementary level, where she earned her *brevet* (diploma). But she had access to her grandfather's library and spent many hours reading there. She also developed a strong interest in the theatre. When she was twenty, she married the thirty-five-year-old sculptor Henri Godet; three children were born within the next six years. The pair were active in the popular university movement, and through a family marriage alliance Nelly Roussel met Paul Robin, who had become the leader of French efforts to spread contraceptive information to the working class.

In 1903 Nelly Roussel appeared as a speaker for Robin's *Ligue pour la régénération humaine* (League for Human Regeneration) and began writing for the all-women's newspaper, *La Fronde*. From that time forth she became an active lecturer and writer on women's rights, particularly women's right to control their own bodies, and she toured throughout France and in Europe. One of her most frequently-delivered addresses was *L'Eternelle sacrifiée* (She who is eternally sacrificed) which has recently been republished. At the conclusion of her lectures, she often performed a theatrical scene, "Par la Révolte," which she had composed.

Nelly Roussel resisted alliance with political parties, considering herself an independent, though her sympathies clearly lay on the socialist left. Most of her publications took the form of newspaper editorials and periodical pieces, many of which were republished in collections following her untimely death. These collections include *Quelques lances rompues pour nos libertés* (Some Lances Broken in Pursuit of Our Liberties), *Paroles de combat et d'espoir* (Words of Hope and Combat), and *Derniers combats* (Final Battles).

Works

Par la révolte, theatrical scene. *La Fronde* (May 1903). *Quelques discours* (1907). *Pourquoi elles vont à l'église* (1910). *Quelques lances rompues pour nos libertés* (1910). *Paroles de combat et d'espoir: discours choisis* (1919). *Ma Forêt*, poems (1920). *Trois conférences de Nelly Roussel* (1930). *Derniers combats; recueil d'articles et de discours* (1932). *Nelly Roussel: l'Eternelle sacrifiée*, préface, notes et commentaires par Daniel Armogathe et Maïté Albistur (1979). Published articles in *L'Action*, *Régénération, La Fronde, L'Almanach féministe, La Voix des femmes* (1917–1922). Forthcoming collection of her works, edited by M. Albistur and D. Armogathe.

Translations: A number of her speeches published in English in *The Malthusian* (London, 1903–1907). Two texts from *La Fronde* in *Women, the Family, and Freedom: The Debate in Documents*, ed. S.G. Bell and K. Offen (1983).

Bibliography

Dossier, Bibliothèque Marguerite Durand, Paris. Albistur, Maïté, and Daniel Armogathe, *Histoire du féminisme français* (Paris, 1978). Albistur, Maïté, and Daniel Armogathe, *Le Grief des femmes*. (Paris, 1978). Albistur, Maïté, and Daniel Armogathe, "Introduction" to *Nelly Roussel: l'éternelle sacrifiée* (Paris, 1979). *Centenaire Nelly Roussel. A l'avant-garde des combats actuels (1878–1922). Catalogue . . . Exposition tenue à la Bibliothèque Marguerite Durand du 5 janvier au 4 mars 1978* (Paris, 1978). Ronsin, Francis, *La Grève des ventres* (Paris, 1980).

Karen Offen

Léonie Rouzade

Born September 6, 1839, Paris, France; died mid-October, 1916
Genre(s): novel, journalism, lecturer
Language(s): French

Léonie Camusat grew up in a Parisian Republican family. Nothing is known of her education. An embroideress until, at twenty-one, she married Auguste Rouzade, she devoted herself to writing and social reform. She and her husband lived a comfortable existence in Meudon, where he was the municipal accountant.

Rouzade's first published works (*Connais-toi toi-même* and *Ci et çà, çà et là*) were metaphysical speculations. In 1872 she published three utopian feminist novels, *Le Monde renversé*, *Le Roi Johanne*, and *Voyage de Théodose à l'île d'Utopie*. These three novels, while not literary landmarks, are extremely interesting as critical reflections on the situation of women in French society. They deserve further attention as manifestations of nineteenth-century feminist thought.

After attending the 1878 International Congress on Women's Rights in Paris, Léonie Rouzade, then approaching her fortieth birthday, became increasingly active in political life, and particularly in socialist politics, winning a solid reputation as an orator for the *Parti ouvrier* from 1879 on.

In 1880 Rouzade and several other women founded the *Union des femmes*, a group designed to give women representation within the *Parti ouvrier*. She was elected to the first national committee of the *Parti ouvrier*, 1881, and that same year became a socialist candidate for the Paris Municipal Council. Among other controversial issues, she argued firmly for state subsidies for mothers. Her candidacy (the votes were actually counted) brought to a climax the disagreement over the role of women among the socialists and precipitated a twenty-year long split between the Broussist and Guesdist factions of the emergent French socialist party.

Léonie Rouzade was anticlerical and a staunch advocate of collectivism. She devoted her remaining years to promoting these causes, emphasizing the affinity between the situation of women and the proletariat. In contrast to the

Marxist socialists, she refused to let the woman question drop until after the revolution.

Works

Connais-toi toi-même (1871). Ci et çà, çà et là (1872). Le Monde renversé (1872). Le Roi Johanne (1872). Voyage de Théodose à l'île d'Utopie (1872). Les classes dirigeantes et les travailleurs jugés par une femme (n.d.). Développement du programme de la Société "l'Union des femmes" (1880). Articles in Le Prolétaire, 1879 to 1883. "Le socialisme," La Revue socialiste (1885). "Les femmes devant la démocratie," La Revue socialiste (1887). Discours de Mme Léonie Rouzade [sur le rôle social de la femme] à l'occasion du Congrès de la libre-pensée de la région de l'Est du 13 août 1893, à Chalon-sur-Saône (1893). Petit catéchisme de morale laïque et socialiste (1895; rpt. 1903, 1904, 1906). La Femme et le peuple, organisation sociale de demain (1896; rpt. 1905, 1906).

Translations: The Feminist Catechism. The Social Organization of Tomorrow, Being the Concluding Chapter of "La Femme et le peuple" (1911).

Bibliography

Boxer, Marilyn J., "Socialism Faces Feminism in France, 1879–1913." Ph.D. diss., University of California at Riverside, 1975. Dossier "Rouzade." Bibliothèque Marguerite Durand, Paris. "Louise-Léonie Rouzade." Equité (May 1914). Sowerwine, Charles, "Women and the Origins of the French Socialist Party: A Neglected Contribution." Third Republic/Troisième République 3–4 (1977). Sowerwine, Charles, Sisters or Citizens? Women and Socialism in France since 1876 (1982).

Karen Offen

Clémence Augustine Audouard Royer

Born April 21, 1830, Nantes, France; died February 6, 1902, Neuilly-sur-Seine, France
Genre(s): essay, journalism, philosophical and scientific commentary, translation
Language(s): French

Clémence Royer was known to contemporaries as a remarkable femme de lettres. Instructed by her parents and schooled briefly at a convent in Le Mans, she was largely self-taught. Her intellectual convictions were far removed from the Legitimist politics of her royalist father, once a naval officer, and the Catholicism of her mother. Among her wide ranging interests were economics, science, anthropology, philosophy, pacifism, and feminism. By translating Charles Darwin's Origin of Species into French in 1862 and also adding a lengthy and controversial preface to that translation, Royer attracted the attention of intellectuals in France and elsewhere in Europe. In three editions of her translation, her commentaries on biological evolution and her analogies between the Darwinian "struggle for existence" in nature and competition and conflict in human society caused Darwin to regard her as "one of the cleverest and oddest women in Europe" and also prompted him to seek another French translator for later editions of the Origin of Species.

Royer's subsequent commentary on parallels between the natural and social sciences appeared in Origine de l'homme et des sociétés (1869), Le Bien et la loi morale (1881), articles in such periodicals as the Journal des économistes and La Philosophie positive, and presentations to the Society of Anthropology of Paris, of which she was the first female member. Her defense of laissez-faire economics with references to biological and social evolution were early examples of "social" Darwinism in France. Such argumentation also prompted comparisons of her thought with that of Herbert Spencer, the English philosopher, although she protested that her ideas were original. Ernest Renan praised her as "almost a man of genius."

In addition to writing theoretical works and commentary on social and economic questions, Royer embraced republican politics and anticlericalism. She also supported the causes of pacifism and feminism. She sympathized with the French republicans in exile during the Second Empire, who supported the Ligue de la paix et de la liberté (League of Peace and Liberty), founded in Geneva in 1867. In 1889 she joined the male feminist Léon Richer as an honorary president of the second International Congress for Women's Rights, held in France. From 1897 until her death she contributed to La Fronde, a feminist newspaper.

Impoverished after the death in 1885 of Pascal Duprat, the republican politician who was her longtime companion and father of her son René, Royer eventually received a small annual pension from the Ministry of Public Instruction. In 1900 she published *La Constitution du monde,* an ambitious monist combination of science and philosophy that she regarded as her magnum opus. Republican politicians and Royer's feminist friends cooperated to sponsor a large banquet in her honor in 1897, and several politicians secured the Legion of Honor for her in 1900. During the last years of her life and after her death, the feminist press celebrated her as an outstanding female intellectual whose life work was proof that a woman could master the hitherto all-male spheres of science and philosophy.

Works

Novel: *Les Jumeaux d'Hellas* [The Twins of Hellas] (1864).

Philosophical and scientific commentary: *Théorie de l'impôt ou la dîme sociale* [Theory of Tax or the Social Tithe] (1862). *Origine de l'homme et des sociétés* (1869) [Origin of Man and Societies]. *Le Bien et la loi morale: éthique et téléologie* [The Good and the Moral Law: Ethics and Teleology] (1881). *Natura rerum: La Constitution du monde, dynamique des atomes, nouveaux principes de philosophie naturelle* [The Constitution of the World, Dynamics of Atoms, New Principles of Natural Philosophy] (1900). *Histoire du ciel* [History of the Heavens] (1901).

Translations: Charles Darwin, *De l'Origine des espèces, ou des lois du progrès chez les êtres organisés* [On the Origin of Species by Means of Natural Selection; or, The Preservation of Favored Races in the Struggle for Life] (1862, 1st French ed.). *De l'Origine des espèces par sélection naturelle, ou des lois de transformation des êtres organisés* (1866, 2d French ed.; 1879, 3d French ed.; 1883; 1918).

Bibliography

Clark, Linda L., *Social Darwinism in France* (University, Alabama, 1984), pp. 12–16, 24–28, 34–37, 56–59. Fraisse, Geneviève, *Clémence Royer, Philosophe et femme de sciences* (Paris, 1985). Milice, Albert, *Clémence Royer, sa doctrine de la vie.* (Paris, 1926). Moufflet, André, "L'Oeuvre de Clémence Royer." *Revue internationale de sociologie* 18 (1910): 658–693.

Linda L. Clark

Rozina

(see: Claudia Millian)

Maria Veronika Rubatscher

Born 1900, Hall near Innsbruck, Austria
Genre(s): novel, short story, biography, poetry
Language(s): German

Born into an old Tyrolean peasant family, Rubatscher spent her youth in Brixen, South Tyrol (today Bressanone, Alto Adige, Italy). After studies at the teacher seminary in Pölten, Austria, she taught in Merano, Udine, Rome, and Gröden, Tyrol. Her works reflect her interest in Tyrolean folk culture excluding neither of the ethnic groups, despite the fact that elements thereof were at each others' throats during her lifetime (e.g., *Alrgrödner Geschichten, Luzio und Zingarella*). Although herself a Catholic, she has written a biography of Protestant theologian and humanitarian Bodelschwingh. The city of Bressanone has awarded her an honorary diploma, and in 1982, she received a medal from the Accademia degli Agiati in Rovereto.

Works

Maria Ward (1927). *Sonnwend* (1932). *Luzio und Zingarella* (1934). *Altgrödner Geschichten* (1935). *Genie der Liebe—Bodelschwingh* (1954). *Es war einmal ein Schützenfest* (1958).

Bibliography

Kosch, August, *Deutsches Literatur-Lexikon in einem Band* (Munich, 1963). von Wilpert, Gero, *Deutsches Literatur-Lexikon*, 2nd ed. (Stuttgart, 1975).

Ute Marie Saine

Renate Rubinstein

(a.k.a. Tamar)

Born November 11, 1929, Berlin, Germany
Genre(s): journalism, essay
Language(s): Dutch

Renate Rubinstein studied social and political sciences at the University of Amsterdam. She was editor of the journal *Propria Cures* but is best known for her travel reports in the magazine *Avenue* and especially her short polemical essays written under the pseudonym Tamar in the newspaper *Vrij Nederland*. The latter consist of reflections on contemporary political and social events written with a sharp, lucid pen. Many of these essays were published in book form in *Namens Tamar* (1964), *Met verschuldigde hoogachting* (1966), *Tamarkolommen en andere berichten* (1973) and *Was getekend Tamar* (1977). In *Hedendaags Feminime* (1979) Tamar formulates her views on feminism and attacks the jargon that prevails in feminist writings. *Niets te verliezen en toch bang* (1978) is an autobiographical account in which the author describes her emotions, anger and fear after she divorced her husband of eleven years. In *Klein Chinees Woordenboek* (1975), which was written in consequence of Rubinstein's visit to Peking as a member of the Dutch delegation, she expresses her disgust for communism. *Met gepast wantrouwen. Notities over de Hollandse ziekte* (1982) was written as a reaction to the antinuclear movement.

Works

Namens Tamar (1964). *Met verschuldigde hoogachting* (1966). *Jood in Arabie-Goi in Israel* (1967). *Sta ik toevallig stil* (1970). *Tamarkolommen en andere berichten* (1973). *Klein Chinees Woordenboek* (1975). *Was getekend Tamar* (1977). *Niets te verliezen en toch bang* (1978). *Hedendaags Feminime* (1979). *Een man uit Singapore* (1979). *Het woelt hier om verandering*, prose (1979). *Twee eendjes en wat brood* (1981). *Met gepast wantrouwen. Notities over de Hollands ziekte* (1982). *Liefst verliefd* (1983).

Translations: *Niets te verliezen en toch bang* has been translated into German.

Bibliography

Auwera, F., in *Geen daden, maar woorden* (1970). Dalen (Van) R., in *Harlekijn* 10 (1980). Pen., J., in *Hollands Maandblad* 15 (1974).

Dianne van Hoof

Fredrika Charlotta (Tengström) Runeberg

(a.k.a. "-a-g")

Born September 2, 1807, Jakobstad, Finland;
died May 27, 1879, Borgå, Finland
Genre(s): novel, short story, poetry, and
journalism
Language(s): Swedish

Fredrika Runeberg's primary claim to fame is that she married Finland's great national *skald*, Johan Ludvig Runeberg. Although she directed most of her talents and energy to caring for him and their eight children, she spent her spare moments on the "joy" of writing. Her works generally portray nurturing, submissive women like herself. However, in settings removed in time and place from nineteenth-century Finland, she was able to explore issues of women's emancipation more freely than her domestic situation would permit. Her characters swallow the bitterness of male oppression, often looking to themselves for the cause of their unhappiness; they see their greatest hope in the harmonious sisterhood of all women.

Fredrika Tengström was born into an educated and cultured family; her paternal uncle became Finland's first archbishop. Her father encouraged her love of reading, and she received as much education as possible for a girl, learning French, German, and English in addition to other subjects. Because of her enthusiasm for scholarship, she was treated as an oddity by most of her cousins, save one: J.L. Runeberg. They married in 1831; at this time she seems to have given up her writing for a time, having either burned most of her literary attempts herself (something she regularly did) or lost them in 1827 in the great fire of Turku, the city in which the Tengströms had lived since 1809.

Her husband became editor of the newspaper *Helsingfors Morgonblad*; Fredrika Runeberg assisted him in this task and eventually took it over in all but name. Her first prose sketches were published in 1844, and she continued to publish smaller items in periodicals throughout her life, making her Finland's first female journalist. Her first novel was published in 1858, 15 years after its completion (she had kept it hidden): *Fru Catharina Boije och hennes döttrar*. This historical novel deals with the question of arranged marriage and its consequences. Her other historical novel, *Sigrid Liljeholm* (1862), was somewhat misunderstood and received lukewarm reviews. Here the idea of an *independent* life for a woman is discussed in the setting of the Finnish Club War. Fredrika Runeberg will remain best known, however, for the great service she has done Runeberg scholarship in the reminiscences about her life with him in *Anteckningar om Runeberg*, published in the same volume as *Min pennas saga*, where she discusses her own "authorship." For as much as she loved to write, she always questioned her right, as a woman, to do so. She felt her greatest duty was to assist and to care for her husband, a "national treasure," in all ways; this she did faithfully, even after a stroke in 1863 left him virtually helpless for the remaining thirteen and one-half years of his life.

Fredrika Runeberg is viewed as Finland's first champion of women's rights; she, among other things, began a women's association in Borgå as well as a school for poor girls. Had she remained unmarried and out of the immense shadow of her husband, perhaps her literary talent could have become of greater consequence. However, her ideas, if not their specific formulation, remain inspirational to Finnish and Swedish audiences.

Works

Novels: *Fru Catharina Boije och hennes döttrar* (1858). *Sigrid Liljeholm* (1862).

Letters: *Brev till sonen Walter* (1971). *Intima interiörer: hundra brev från Fredrika Runeberg och Johan Ludvig Runeberg samt andra vänner till Emilie Björkstén* (1938).

Other prose: *Anteckningar om Runeberg. Min pennas saga* (1946) [the notes were actually completed in 1869]. *Teckningar och drömmar* [collected sketches and narrations from Finnish periodicals] (1861).

Bibliography

Allardt-Ekelund, Karin, *Fredrika Runeberg* (Helsinki, 1942). Ekelund, Erik, *Finlands svenska litteratur 2: Från Åbo brand till sekelskiftet* (Helsinki, 1969). Mazzarella, Merete, *Från Fredrika Runeberg till Märta Tikkanen* (Helsinki, 1985). Stenwall, Åsa, *Den frivilligt ödmjuka kvinnan. En bok om Fredrika Runebergs verklighet och diktning* (Helsinki, 1979). Tikkanen, Märta, "Fredrika Runeberg—författaren, människan." *Kvinnornas litteraturhistoria* (Lund, 1981). Tuulio, Tyyne, *Fredrikan Suomi* (Helsinki, 1979). Westermarck, Helena, *Fredrika Runeberg* (Helsinki, 1904). von Willebrand, Reinhold Felix, *Fredrika Runeberg* (Helsinki, 1904).

Kathy Saranpa Anstine

Erika, Maria Runge

Born January 22, 1939, Halle, East Germany
Genre(s): novel, documentary
Language(s): German

Runge was born in 1939 in Halle, GDR, the daughter of a judge. During her childhood she experienced the bombing raids, the hunger and misery of the war and post-war period in Germany. After finishing high school she studied various liberal art subjects in Saarbrücken, Berlin, München, and Paris. She received her Ph.D. degree in 1962. Since then she has worked as a writer and film director and has received several prizes for her films and books.

As a writer Runge finds her subject matter among those people who usually have no voice in the bourgeois literature. Her first publication *Bottroper Protokolle* (1968), is one of the most important contributions to German documentary literature. It is a collection of reports and conversations compiled on the basis of tape-recorded interviews. Workers and their families describe their lives and especially voice their fears about the foreclosure of their workplace, a coalmine. Runge's subsequent publications are characterized by the same documentary approach. In *Frauen: Versuche zur Emanzipation* (1969) she lets seventeen women of different ages, socioeconomic backgrounds and professions narrate their lives. Their reports span seventy years of German history, emphasizing the lack of opportunities for the emancipation of women. In *Reise nach Rostock, DDR* (1971) Runge interviewed people of various professional and social backgrounds living in the district of Rostock, in the German Democratic Republic. Her reports provide an extensive, informative picture of the district, geared at filling an information gap in West Germany about life in the GDR. They lack, however, a critical attitude and sometimes present propaganda. In *Südafrika-Rassendiktatur zwischen Elend und Widerstand: Protokolle und Dokumente zur Apartheid* (1974), Runge combines the reports of victims and opponents of apartheid with documentary and historical material. The book entails a comprehensive and critical presentation of the South African regime. Runge has been criticized at times for not disclosing her interview strategies, thus concealing her authorship in the various documentations. Runge reflects on this issue in the essay "Überlegungen beim Abschied von der Dokumentarliteratur" (1976). She admits her own contributions in selecting and arranging the material. Her preference for this form of literature indicated her own lack of imagination for which she compensated by listening and recording the problems of other people. Runge now rejects documentary literature as too narrow a framework and advocates the presentation of individual subjectivity. Runge is currently working on a novel.

Runge's importance lies primarily in her contributions to documentary literature. Her books preserve the authenticity and subjectivity of the individual's voice. At the same time they present a general picture of the consciousness and living conditions of various social groups.

Works

Bottroper Protokolle (1968). *Frauen: Versuche zur Emanzipation* (1969). *Zum Beispiel Bottrop . . . Szenische Dokumentation* (1971). *Reise nach Rostock* (1971). "Parteilichkeit und Zensur im Fernsehn." *kürbiskern* 3 (1971). *Südafrika–Rassendiktatur zwischen Elend und Widerstand: Protokolle und Dokumente zur Apartheid* (1974). "Sich der Wehrlosigkeit widersetzen." *Kürbiskern* 4 (1975). "Überlegungen beim Abschied von der Dokumentarliteratur." *Kontext I." Literatur und Wirklicheitkeit*, ed. U. Timm (1976). "Die betonierte Phantasie." *Literatur konkret* 3 (1978). "Kindheit." *Stichworte zur "Geistigen Situation der Zeit,"* ed. J. Habermas (1982).

Bibliography

General references: *Neue Literatur der Frauen: Deutschsprachige Autorinnen der Gegenwart*, ed. H. Puknus (1980). *Kritisches Lexikon zur deutschsprachigen Gegenwartsliteratur*, ed. H.L. Arnold (1978).

Monica Shafi

Maria Clemente Ruoti

Born ca. 1619, near Florence, Italy; died
January 11, 1690, Florence
Genre(s): drama
Language(s): Italian

Maria Clemente Ruoti, the daughter of Prospero Ruoti, was born in the Mugello valley north of Florence. She was baptized Ottavia in the church of San Cresci. First a boarder (from 1619) at the Franciscan convent of San Girolamo (called San Giorgio because of its location on the Costa di San Giorgio in Florence), in 1621, together with her sister Margherita, she entered the house as a novice, taking the name of Sister Maria Clemente. In the convent she became a writer. She wrote religious plays for her convent's production which for their merit came to the attention of the city's literati. *Giacob patriarca* (1637; Jacob the Patriarch), dedicated to the Grand Duchess of Tuscany, Vittoria della Rovere, was published in Pisa in 1537. A poem in praise of her literary talent, written by Carlo Dati, was published with the play, and in 1549 she numbered among the members of a Florentine literary academy to which Dati also belonged, the Accademia Apatista. Maria Clemente's other surviving play, *Il Natal di Cristo* (ca. 1657; The Birth of Christ), may have been published since the surviving manuscript in the Riccardiana Library in Florence contains a publishing privilege, granted to the author in January 1558 by local Franciscan authorities. From the few existing biographical documents that regard her we learn that in 1671 Maria Clemente was deputy prioress (*vicaria*) of San Girolamo and that in 1680 she commissioned three large religious paintings to be made for the convent's choir of Saint Bonaventure paid for with interest revenues from her dowry: one depicted Jesus, Mary and Joseph, one St. Nicholas of Bari, and the third St. Bonaventure. She died at San Girolamo on January 11, 1690.

Giacob patriarca is based on the biblical story of the return of Jacob and his family to Canaan from Mesopotamia, the homeland of his wives Leah and Rachel (*Genesis* 31:17–34:31). The conflicts with Laban and Esau constitute the main plot, while two love stories provide subplot interest. The story of the rape of Dinah, Jacob's daughter, is given a happy matrimonial ending, dramatically different from the biblical tale, and the love of Jacob's son Reuben for a Mesopotamian shepherdess, Norminda, would seem to be entirely invented. The themes of faith in God, obedience, the destiny of Jacob's descendants, and God's justice are stressed. There is a strong misogynistic message portrayed through the recurrent disobedience and foolishness of the women, and the jealousy of Leah for which women are shown to need the guidance of men; at the same time there is a *leit motif* of complaint by the women for their subjection. Indeed, quite unlike the biblical account, it is the female characters who dominate the action of this play.

Il Natal di Cristo, a play written for performance during Christmas festivities, has a double plot. The first is the story of a lecherous and hypocritical Pharisee and his chaste, widowed sister-in-law. She would marry him, but he'd prefer to have her illicitly. Two virtues, Charity and Truth, disguised as beautiful women together with Alburnea, the Tibertine Sibyl, try to reform the evil man and his cohorts, but they fail, have the Pharisee swallowed up by the earth, and save the good women from unjust punishment. Meanwhile, Joseph and Mary find shelter for the night and Christ is born. The efforts of the Virtues and the Sibyl are not lost on other Pharisees, however, and they are allowed to witness and participate in the adoration of the Christ child. One of the converts marries the good widow in a finale of choruses of shepherds, angels and heavenly virtues.

The earlier play is in verse, the second in prose, while both have interact choruses. They are both well constructed and entertaining. There are humorous scenes based on linguistic play and on the alternation of exalted and humble actions: for example, in the *Natal di Cristo* the terrible plot against the chaste widow shares the stage with a card game in which the Virtues defeat two cheating Pharisees. Both plays have an author's preface in which Maria Clemente discusses her art and especially the problems specific to a convent playwright, whose work necessarily suffers because of convent restrictions on her reading and experience and from the convent's small financial resources. She writes: "The way to Parnassus . . . for a simple virgin enclosed within four walls is not just difficult, it is virtually unknown" (*Giacob patriarca*, c. 2r). And again the image of the four enclosing walls is invoked when she explains: ". . . I have no knowledge of a world other than that within the tight quarters of these four walls, where I shut myself up at nine years of age; I have no experience of [stage] machines, nor the ability to put them to work so that I have had to adapt my poetry to my possibilities and not someone else's purse to my inventions as poets do" (*Il Natal di Cristo*, c. 1v). Her accomplishments were significant and were noticed in her time, as her academy membership attests, and she is mentioned in at least one, Giulio Negri's eighteenth-century history of Florentine writers.

Works

Giacob patriarca (1637). *Il Natal di Cristo* (ca. 1657). cod. Ricc. 2783, vol. 7, ms., probably autograph, contains publishing privilege dated January 1658.

Bibliography

Negri, Giulio, *Istoria degli scrittori fiorentini* (Bologna, 1973; rpt. of Ferrara, 1722), p. 395. Weaver, Elissa, Introduction to edition of Beatrice del Sera, *Amor di virtù* (Ravenna, forthcoming 1989), p. 33.

Elissa Weaver

An Rutgers van der Loeff-Basenau

(a.k.a. Rutger Bas)

Born March 15, 1910, Amsterdam, The
*   Netherlands*
Genre(s): children's books
Language(s): Dutch

It was under the impulse of her mother, a born story-teller, that An Rutgers van der Loeff made her first steps in translation and writing. She studied classical literature and started publishing shortly after the second World War. Her books have had a worldwide impact on the development of juvenile literature since 1950: she introduced a sincere taboo-breaking realism in the genre, with a sharp eye for (sometimes too exhaustive) details, relying on scrupulous preliminary documentation. Central to each of her plots is a concrete conflict between the protagonist and his/her surroundings. The author has been awarded the Dutch National Prize for Children's Books in 1968 and different prizes in—among other countries—Germany, Austria, Italy, and the United States.

Works

De kinderkaravaan [The Children's Caravan] (1949). *Mens of wolf* [Man or Wolf] (1951). *Je bent te goed, Giacomo* [You're Too Good, Giacomo] (1957). *Gideons reizen* [Gideon's Travels] (1960). *Als je zou durven* [If You Would Dare] (1965).

Bibliography

Gosselink, H., *Lexicon van de jeugdliteratuur* (1982). Gosselink-van Hagen, L.J.M., and H. Gosselink, *An Rutgers van der Loeff.* 2nd ed. (1977). Sutherland, Z. e.a., *Children and Books* (1981), p. 365. de Swert, F., *Over jeugdliteratuur* (1977), passim.

Frank Joostens

Zenaida R-va

(see: Elena Gan [Hahn])

Ulla Ryum

Born May 4, 1937, Frederiksberg,
*   Copenhagen, Denmark*
Genre(s): novel, short story, drama, poetry
Language(s): Danish

Ulla Ryum's literary *oeuvre* is an intriguing, intricate blend of imagery, flights of fantasy, realistic and surrealistic scenes of modern life, and keen criticism of an urban society that favors competition, mutual indifference, and hostile aggression at the expense of humanity and mutual caring. Ulla Ryum's strong Catholic upbringing is evident in her mystical view and portrayals of the city. Ulla Ryum's plays and novels challenge her readers and the audience of her plays to the full. The central theme of Ulla Ryum's plays and prose works concerns the essence of Christian love. Her protagonists are invariably women who emulate Christ by sacrificing self, by considering others first, by giving physical love and emotional affection with no qualification or reservation. For Ryum, we often fail to know ourselves, hence, we never really come to know each other; we "miss each other" in a very hostile metropolis governed solely by competition, self-concern, and total disregard for others. In her works, Ryum suggests that there may be an answer to our common search for identity in the unconditional love of women now depicted as Christ-like figures (*DLH*: 8, 526–527). Ulla Ryum uses surrealistic scenes, fantastic images and events, deep Catholic mysticism, and a medieval search for allegory, myth, and a faith for *Enhver* ("Everyman," *DLH*: 8, 526), to reveal new perspectives on reality (Dalager 2, p. 130).

Ulla Ryum was born in the Frederiksberg area of Copenhagen on May 4, 1937; her parents are Sten Ryum (born 1910), a lawyer and commission/secretariat director, and Elise Kirstine Hammer (born 1908, *DbL*: 12, 502). Ulla Ryum began her literary career, she claims, while working in an Østerbro, Copenhagen, restaurant kitchen, as part of her training in hotel operations (*DbL*: 12, 502). (Her early practical work provided the realistic ballast for a literary *oeuvre* of imagination, Catholic symbolism, myth, and rare fantasy.) Ulla Ryum's début as a writer came in 1962, with the novel *Spejl* (Mirror); *Spejl* concerns a modern individual's efforts to realize an identity (*DLH*: 8, 303) within the frightening setting of an impersonal city. The scenes of modern life in *Spejl* are terrifying, often grotesque, for individuals communicate and often act at cross-purposes. Yet, Ulla Ryum holds out a ray of hope for a solution, for a way out of the modern maze. In *Spejl*, one woman at least points the way out of the negative, counterproductive mælstrom of modern city life.

Ulla Ryum's next novel was *Natsangersken* (1963; The Night Singer). In this novel, Ulla Ryum's Christian/Catholic message of love and sacrifice comes to the fore. The alcoholic little songstress of *Natsangersken* sacrifices for others and chooses to die in reconciliation with herself and other even weaker, flawed individuals. The songstress' life has been one of diminished, reduced possibilities, of great, enclosing barriers and limits for her as *le deuxième sexe, den anden* (the second sex); her own father and all the men she has ever known have only denied and degraded her, depriving her of worth and identity.

Limits and barriers established for the songstress have also diminished the *men* who have known and used her. In denying her essential humanity, they have also clearly denied their own. In the end, the songstress dies as a Christ figure who reconciles those around her.

The novel *Latterfuglen* (The Bird of Laughter) followed *Natsangersken* in 1965. The protagonist of *Latterfuglen* is a humble dancer in a chorus line, Hortenzia, pursued and possessed by an egg merchant, Ludvig Mandelin, whose own maze of schedules and systems deprive him of love and emotion. The fearful—and fearfully insecure and immature—Mandelin simultaneously seeks to protect himself from human contact and to denigrate Hortenzia. Mandelin's efforts result in Hortenzia's suicide and, then, in a symbolic journey to find the girl—and himself—in the realm of death; Mandelin's search parodies the Orpheus Myth (*DLH*: 8, 526). In the case of *Latterfuglen*, the journey to the other world fails completely, for Mandelin is unwilling to reach Hortenzia, incapable of recognizing the needs of others and loving himself. Ulla Ryum ends her novel with a comical, fantastic, yet grotesque scene, a parody-scene "punning" the deadly serious Mandelin: Ludvig Mandelin visits a bath in a symbolic effort to cleanse, find forgiveness and a new life, but he is so scoured and rinsed by the women attendants (that) "when they are finished, there is nothing left of him" (Dalager, 2, p. 130).

Ulla Ryum followed *Latterfuglen* with *Jakelnatten* (1967; The Night of Punch-and-Judy) and *Byen K* (1967; The City K), and, then, with two collections of short stories: *Tusindskove: Hændelser og Historier* (1969; Thousand Woods: Events and Stories), and *Noter om idag og igår. Nye og gamle Historier* (1971; Notes on Today and Yesterday: New and Old Stories). From 1968 on, her literary career took on dramatic—and political—dimensions, as Ryum began to write plays, screen-plays, TV and radio dramas. Her plays have followed in fairly rapid succession: "Den bedrøvede bugtaler" (1971; The Grief-Stricken Ventriloquist, Radioteatret); "Myterne" (1975; The Myths, Comediehuset); "Krigen" (1975; The War, Det kongelige Teater); "Cirkus" (1975; Circus, Fiolteatret); "Faster er død" (1975; Aunt has Died, TV); "Jægerens ansigter" (1978; Faces of the Hunter, Comediehuset); "Rummene" (1979; The Rooms, Århus); "Og Fuglene synger igen" (1980; And the Birds are Singing Again, Radio); "Digt om et Døgn" is a fantastic, lively play, in which Ryum has given free rein to her considerable talents for the bizarre, the imaginary, *la farce noire*, and the humorous. In "Digt om et Døgn," the poet, Johan Herman Wessel, an historical figure from "the Spring 1783—but probably (from) today" (p. 2), finally awakens from alcohol-induced slumber to encounter Trude Mansdatter, the proprietress of a tavern; her son Ludvig Morten List; and the waitress, Alberte. The characters engage in continuous, fantastic discourse, approaching each other and stepping away, contacting and failing to communicate, engaging and insulting each other. After Ludvig and Alberte retreat from the scene together, in love or ready for love, Wessel pursues an implausible, curious dialogue with "the mute *Pifteren*, a tongue-less oboe and mouth-organ player" (p. 2), frequenting the tavern and providing music for entertainment. The dialogues of the play create an aura of absurdity and madcap happenstance, as Trude and Wessel, Ludvig and Alberte, speak and act past one another. The fate of the players on the scene is the fate of Everyman (or *Mansdatter*, Man's Daughter), a tragic-comic destiny which Ulla Ryum aptly describes in the subtitle to "Digt om et Døgn:" "a merry tragedy for four speakers and one player" (p. 1).

Ulla Ryum has also written a drama for radio, "Denne ene Dag" (1976; That One Day) as well as a long prose-poem soliloquy, *Natten* (1975; The Night), for the actress Berthe Qvistgaard (*DbL*: 12, 503). In *Natten*, Ryum has again emphasized an essential message of love, responsibility, and service. The idea of Christian love and sacrifice is a constant in Ulla Ryum's work to date. Ryum's most recent work is yet another novel, *Baglands Tekster* (1985; Texts from Hinterland), representing a return to the genre (Wamberg, *Out of Denmark*, p. 169).

Ulla Ryum has also been active politically and on behalf of Danish authors, playwrights, the theatre and film. From 1973 to 1976, Ryum served as a director of the Association of Danish Authors; she has also been a chair of the Danish Democratic Women's Association (1975) and a directing associate of the National Art Endowment's Board for Literature (1977–1980). Ryum has also taught at the National Drama School and the Film School of Denmark. She has been a member of the Commission for the National Drama School (1978) and of the Directorate for the Royal Theatre (1979). Ryum has also been most active as an adviser for Bagsværd Amateur Theatre; Radio Theatre; and the Royal Theatre's *Comediehus* (Comedy Scene), which has presented her plays "Denne ene Dag," "Jægerens ansigter," and "Rejse gennem dagen" (*DbL*: 12, 502). Ulla Ryum has received additional recognition in the form of a National Art Endowment Fellowship (1965–1968); an honorary award from Danish Dramatists (1975); and, in 1981, a Travel Grant from the Tagea Brandt Foundation (*DbL*: 12, 503).

Ulla Ryum's *oeuvre* is rich, diverse, and complex. Her novels introduce us to fantastic characters and events while depicting the loneliness and the lack of love and self-knowledge which seem the plight of the modern individual. Ryum's plays are strangely engaging, filled with the improbable, the absurd, the poetically beautiful, the curious and bizarre. Through the course of her work, Ulla Ryum has stressed essential themes: service and greater self-realization through the quintessential gift of unconditional, Christian love.

Works

Spejl [Mirror] (1962). *Natsangersken* (1963). *Latterfuglen* (1965). *Jakelnatten* (1967). *Byen K* (1967). *Tusindskove: Hændelser og Historier* (1969). *Noter om idag og igår. Nye og gamle Historier* (1971). "Den bedrøvede bugtaler" (1971). "Myterne" (1973). "Krigen" (1975). "Cirkus" (1975). *Natten* (1975). "Denne ene Dag" (1976). "Faster er død" (1978). "Jægerens ansigter" (1978). "Rummene" (1979). "Og Fuglene synger igen" (1980). "Digt om et Døgn" (1980). "Rejse gennem dagen" (1980). "En kærlighedshistorie" (1981). *Baglandstekster* (1983).

Bibliography

Dalager, Stig and Anne-Marie Mai, *Danske kvindelige forfattere. Bind 2. Fra Adda Ravnkilde til Kirsten Thorup. Udvikling og perspektiv* (København, 1982). *Dansk biografisk Leksikon 12* (1979), pp. 502–503. *Dansk Litteratur Historie: 8. Velfærdsstat og Kulturkritik, 1945–1980* (København, 1985). Ryum, Ulla, "Digt om et Døgn," København: Folketeatret/Thaning og Appels Forlag (Folketeatrets repertoire nr. 3, Saisonen 1980–1981) (1981). Wamberg, Bodil, ed., *Out of Denmark: Isak Dinesen/Karen Blixen 1885–1985, and Danish Women Writers Today* (Copenhagen, 1985).

Lanae Hjortsvang Isaacson

S

Milka S.

(see: Terézia Vansová)

Madeleine de Sablé

Born probably 1598 or 1599, Touraine,
France; died January 16, 1678, Paris
Genre(s): maxim
Language(s): French

Madame de Sablé is chiefly remembered for
the important literary salon which she presided
over for several years and for the influence she
had on La Rochefoucauld. She was the daughter
of the Marquis de Souvré, a soldier who rose to
the distinction of Marshal of France and whose
qualities were such that he was appointed
guardian of Louis XIII during his minority. After
serving as a maid of honor to Queen Marie de
Medicis, she was married at the age of fourteen to
the Marquis de Sablé. Nine children were born to
the couple, but the marriage was an unhappy
one: the Marquis was unfaithful and ruinously
extravagant, running through his own fortune
and his wife's, and when in 1619 she returned to
Paris from the family estates at Sablé, she, too,
had a number of affairs that were the object of
much gossip. Like Madame de Rambouillet, she
instituted a salon where the aristocracy met with
leading writers of the day for polite and witty
conversation and to indulge in literary pastimes
and which many of the leading Jansenists were
pleased to frequent; Molière's *Les Précieuses
Ridicules* of 1659 gives only a warped and comic
impression of what took place, for in the refinement of language, in finesse of psychological
penetration and, particularly at the salon of Mme
de Sablé, in the ever-increasing awareness of the
potential complexities of love, major contributions were made to the development of French
literature, above all in the sphere of the analysis
of the human condition. Mme de Sablé was the
target of many jokes on account of her extreme
hypochondria, and she was also famous for her
addiction to good food, yet there was a serious
side to her. In earlier years she took a great
interest in political affairs, and it seems likely that
her "conversion" to Jansenism in about 1640,
around the time of her husband's death, had had
a long preparation. Debts obliged her to sell her
property at Sablé in 1648, and she was to have
financial difficulties intermittently for the rest of
her life. For a while she resided with a friend, the
Countess de Maure, in *appartements* in the Place
Royale, Paris. Then she moved, in 1655, into a
house specially built to be near to the Jansenist
stronghold of Port-Royal. When she died, she
was noted in the Port-Royal necrology for her
support and generosity.

The most notable aspect of the influence of
Mme de Sablé's salon on the development of
French literature is seen in the emergence of the
maxime as a prose form encapsulating a view of
human life and aspirations which was often
deeply pessimistic within a single concise and
mordant sentence enlivened on occasion with a
vivid image. The collection of ancient aphorisms
and the coining of new ones was, of course, a
passion of the Renaissance, but the revived genre
was deeply marked by the Jansenist pessimism
that permeated Mme de Sablé's salon. To abase

human pride and, in particular, to show the hollowness of the aristocratic values of honor and chivalry, became major objectives. François, Duke de La Rochefoucauld (1613–1680), wrote the most accomplished volume of *maximes*, the first edition appearing in 1664, and there can be no doubt that Mme de Sablé played an important role in both its composition and its revision. She, too, wrote *maximes*, a collection appearing shortly after her death. They lack the verbal brilliance of La Rochefoucauld's, and the Christian inspiration is allowed to be rather more obvious.

Works

Maximes (1678).

Bibliography

Grandseignes d'Hauterive, R., *Le Pessimisme de La Rochefoucauld* (Paris, 1914). Ivanov, N., *La marquise de Sablé et son salon* (Paris, 1927). Lafond, Jean, "Madame de Sablé et son salon." *Images de La Rochefoucauld: Actes du tricentenaire*, ed. J. Lafond et J. Mesnard (Paris, 1984).

Christopher Smith

Marguerite Hessein de la Sablière

Born 1640, Paris, France; died January 6, 1693, Paris
Genre(s): letters, maxims
Language(s): French

Marguerite Hessein de la Sablière is remembered today as much for her intelligence and erudition as for her brilliant salon and her long-term patronage of the French fabulist La Fontaine. She was born in 1640 into a Huguenot family most probably originating in the Low Countries. Her education was remarkably thorough for her day. She was one of the few women of her time to be able to read Greek as well as Latin, she displayed an early talent for mathematics and in later life could recall numerous verses of Virgil and Horace by heart. The influence of her uncle, Antone Menjot, a friend of Pascal, brought her to blossom in many fields.

Like all young women of her class and fortune, she was destined to marry. She wed her cousin Antoine de Rambouillet, the seigneur de la Sablière, on February 20, 1654. The couple were members of the same social milieu and class, and both were noted for their intelligence and talent. Antoine, in fact, was the author of a number of French madrigals. Initially they were happy, and the union produced three children— Anne (1655), Nicholas (1656), and a bit later Marguerite.

When Marguerite's father died, misfortune struck. Antoine discovered that the Hessein fortune had been considerably eroded by speculation. Problems developed immediately. Madame de la Sablière was obliged to move to the Convent of Charonne in 1667 and, because of continuous pressure from her husband, she sought and obtained a final, formal separation. The notice was issued on May 30, 1668. From that time on, she lived apart from both husband and children.

Her life was not totally empty, however. From 1669–1680 her apartments in the Rue Neuve de Petits-Champs were the setting for one of Paris' most interesting salons. Although not yet published, she had already acquired a degree of notoriety and was able to attract such guests as Sobiesky, Brancas, Charleval, Pellisson, Mme Scarron, les Marquises de Lambert et de Sévigné, Queen Christina of Sweden, and even Mlle de Lenclos, the former lover of Antoine. Her desire for learning was insatiable. Her library of seventy-five volumes includes works by the saints Augustine, Bernard, Cyprian, Frances Xavier, John Chrysostom, and Teresa of Avila, as well as books by Epictetus and Marcus Aurelius. Her *Traité de l'Equilibrium des liquids* (A Treatise on the Equilibrium of Liquids) and a personal telescope testify to her scientific interests. In addition, she took lessons from some of France's most illustrious savants. François Bernier taught her natural history, anatomy, and astronomy; Roberval and Sauveur, geometry and mathematics. The philosophical speculations of Gassendi and Descartes were common topics of conversation at her home.

From 1673–1680, she provided La Fontaine with a refuge and a home. His *Fables* may well have grown from her discussions of Descartes and his speculations about the souls of animals. Certainly "La Fable des deux rats du Renard et de l'oeuf (Discours à Madame de la Sablière)" (The Fable of the Two Rats of Renard and the Egg [Discourse to Madame de la Sablière]), and his fables of the crow, the gazelle, the tortoise, and the rat directly reflect her influence and milieu. Although his patroness did not love flattery, La Fontaine was not ungrateful and gave voice to his appreciation several times.

Indeed, most of the literary men of her day enjoyed and valued Madame de la Sablière's companionship. Although Boileau, perhaps stinging from her correction of his science in the "Fifth Epistle," attacked her learning in his "Satire sur les Femmes" (Satire on Women), Perrault answered it in his "Appreciation des Femmes" (Appreciation of Women). La Fontaine, among numerous other compliments, once wrote that she had "beauté d'homme avec grace de femme." Additionally, her studies were recognized by the king, who awarded her a pension of 2000 livres a year.

She was less happy in her private affairs, however. An unfortunate interlude with Charles de la Fare led her to embrace religion. In the 1680s she converted to Catholicism. The same year she retired to the Hôpital des Incurables. At this time, in a fervent search for solitude and with a growing distaste for worldly concerns, she penned her *Les Maximes Chrétiennes* (Christian Maxims) and her letters to Père Rancé. At the hôpital, she helped to tend the sick. She observed all the duties of cloistered life, and, in declining health, battled her way through to a fervent reconciliation with her God. She died at the hôpital on January 6, 1693.

The writings of Madame de Sablière reveal her erudition and her elegance, her talent for a precise use of the French language, and her later religious fervor. The *Maximes*, first published in 1705, are so good that they have been attributed at times to that master of the aphorism, La Rochefoucault. Her letters let her mystical temperament, her energetic and decisive character, and her fervent sense of repentance unfold. The style, though tranquil, is no less passionate. In both the maxims and the letters, Madame de Sablière's learning is everywhere apparent. Although her subject matter in both is religious, one can clearly detect the personality who first brought together the French aristocracies of blood and letters. Madame de la Sablière rests today in Saint-Sulpice in Paris.

Works

Les Maximes Chrétiennes [Christian Maxims] (1705). *Pensées Chrétiennes* [Christian Thoughts] (1923).

Bibliography

Busson, H., "Commentaire," in *Discours à Madame la Sablière* by La Fontaine (Paris, 1938). d'Elbenne, Menjot, *Madame de la Sablière, ses pensées Chrétiennes et ses lettres à l'abbé de Rancé* (Paris, 1923). Hallays, André, *Les Grandes Salons Littéraires* (Paris, 1928), pp. 49–78. Jal, Auguste, *Dictionnaire Critique de Biographie et d'Histoire* (rpt. New York, 1970), p. 741. Uglow, Jennifer, *International Dictionary of Women* (New York, 1982), p. 135.

Glenda Wall

Oliva Sabuco de Nantes Barrera

Born 1562, Alcaraz (Albacete), Spain; died 1622?, Alcaraz
Genre(s): psychological treatises
Language(s): Spanish

For over three hundred years, Oliva Sabuco de Nantes Barrera was supposed to be the author, as the title page claimed, of *Nueva filosofía de la naturaleza del hombre* (1587), a collection of psychological and medical treatises whose form and style classify them as belles lettres. In 1900 her biographer José Marco Hidalgo published her life. Shortly afterward he discovered notarial documents in her home town in which her father Miguel Sabuco y Alvarez (?–1588) clearly stated that he wrote the book and put his daughter's name on it "to honor her." Marco Hidalgo published the documents in the journal of Spain's national society of archivists (1903), and librarians around the world lost no time in despoiling Doña Oliva, as she was commonly and affectionately known, of her authorship.

Still, nagging questions remain which, if answered, would tend both to support and to undermine Marco Hidalgo's claims and would also tarnish the reputation of a father who seemingly attributed the book to his daughter out of pride and affection. Why did he publish *Nueva filosofía* under her name in 1587 and then in that same year reclaim it for his own? Were the treatises on "Vera medicina" written by him, by a friendly physician named Alonso de Heredia who honored his godchild Doña Oliva, or are all the treatises really by her as the title page states? Did Miguel Sabuco reclaim the *Nueva filosofía* because it was selling well and he wanted to turn over the Portuguese rights to his son? Did he put Doña Oliva's name on the title page in the first place because he feared Inquisitorial censorship (which did occur), and he thought a young woman would be less vulnerable to reprisal? Did a fellow townsman named Juan de Sotomayor praise Doña Oliva in two sonnets as a part of a conspiracy or because he admired the young woman whom he knew to be the author? Did the father go so far in the deception as to introduce the *Nueva filosofía* with a dedicatory letter to King Philip II ostensibly written by Doña Oliva in which she repeatedly alludes to herself as a woman? Florentino Torner, writing about 1936, raised such questions, but otherwise scholarship since 1903 has not occupied itself with the despoliation that Oliva Sabuco suffered at the hands of her father and her twentieth-century biographer.

Be the author Doña Oliva or her father, the treatises in the book have been recognized as pioneering efforts in the field of experimental sensualism along with the better known *Examen de ingenios para las ciencias* (1575) by Juan Huarte de San Juan (1530?–1591?). The most substantial part of *Nueva filosofía*, consisting of seventy "Titles" (short chapters), is the treatise "Un coloquio del conocimiento de sí mismo." Sabuco explores the relationship between human emotions and the body's physiology. "Believe in experience and not in philosophy," admonishes the author in the prologue to what Menéndez y Pelayo describes as a treatise on experimental psychology (59:371). While placing the origin of ideas in the senses, Sabuco (daughter or father) advanced the theory that the central nervous system is bathed in fluid, a discovery that has been compared to Miguel Servet's observation of the circulation of the blood. Menéndez y Pelayo (58:315) comments that the analysis of the

emotions in *Nueva filosofía* resembles that in certain chapters of Juan Luis Vives' psychological treatise *De Anima et Vita* (1538).

Nueva filosofía may be categorized as belonging to humane literature because of the style in which it is written. In the "Coloquio del conocimiento de sí mismo," for example, the ideas are advanced through graceful dialogues among three shepherds, Antonio, Velonio, and Rodonio. The most loquacious, to whom the others address questions, is the wise and sensible Antonio. In "Vera medicina" a traditional doctor defends the classical medicine of Hippocrates and Galen while the wise shepherd Antonio advances ideas on "keeping health" that are derived as a necessary consequence of man's nature (Torner 31).

It is worth observing that *Nueva filosofía* was written in the region of La Mancha about the time that Cervantes imagined that his knight errant Don Quixote was travelling there for the purpose of righting wrongs committed against people, especially ladies, who could not defend themselves; but the situation of Doña Oliva's deprivation did not come to the knight's attention.

Works

Nueva filosofía de la naturaleza del hombre, no conocida ni alcanzada de los grandes filósofos antiguos, la cual mejora la vida y salud humana (1587). *Obras*, ed. Octavio Cuartero (1888). "Coloquio del conocimiento de sí mismo" and "Coloquio de ls cosas que mejoran este mundo." *Obras escogidas de filósofos*, ed. Adolfo de Castro (1873).

Bibliography

Marco Hidalgo, José, *Biografía de doña Oliva de Sabuco* (Madrid, 1900). Marco Hidalgo, José, "Doña Oliva de Sabuco no fue escritora." *Revista de Archivos, Bibliotecas y Museos* 7 (1903): 1–13. Menéndez y Pelayo, Marcelino, *La ciencia española*, ed. Enrique Sánchez Reyes. Edición Nacional de las Obras Completas, vols. 58–60 (Santander, 1943), passim. Sánchez Ruano, José, *Doña Oliva Sabuco de Nantes (escritora ilustre del siglo décimosexto)* (Salamanca, 1867). Torner, Florentino M., *Doña Oliva Sabuco de Nantes, siglo XVI* (Madrid, 1936).

John Dowling

Nelly Sachs

*Born December 10, 1891, Berlin, Germany;
    died May 12, 1970, Stockholm
Genre(s): poetry, drama, translation
Language(s): German*

Nelly (Leonie) Sachs was the only child of Margarethe (nee Karger) and William Sachs, a Berlin businessman. Although she eventually became best known as "the poetess of Jewish destiny," her upbringing, like that of many cultured and wealthy assimilated German Jews, did not stress religious training, and she herself never learned either Hebrew or Yiddish. In her early youth, Sachs was interested in the dance, only turning to writing in her teenage years. This interest in theater would reemerge in later years in the form of her dramatic works. Her early writings included puppet plays (none published) and poems, many of which appeared in newspapers. Her first published book, *Legenden und Erzählungen* (Legends and Tales), was a collection of short stories, many set in the Middle Ages, and dedicated to her early literary heroine and mentor, the Swedish novelist Selma Lagerlöf, with whom she was in correspondence since the age of sixteen. These early works showing the influence of nineteenth-century German Romanticism and nature poetry, did not gain much critical attention. They also did not show any traces of the influence of the avant-garde artists active in Berlin between the wars. Later in life, Sachs would distance herself from these early works, omitting them from the collections and anthologies, all published after the War.

The turning point in Sachs's life and works came with the ascent to power of the National Socialist party in 1933, with its overtly antisemitic policies. No longer allowed to publish except in Jewish journals, she began her unsystematic study of Hasidic literature and the mystical tradition of the Kaballah. Hearing of the fate of deported Jews, friends of the family worked desperately to get exit visas for Nelly Sachs and her widowed mother. Through the tireless efforts of various friends, the help of Prince Eugene of Sweden and the intercession of Selma Lagerlöf, they were finally able to get permission to immigrate to the United States, which in turn enabled them to obtain the desired letters of transit through to neutral Sweden, their intended goal. They arrived in Sweden in 1940. Mother and daughter managed to escape Germany just in time, thanks to the advice of an official who recommended to the naive Sachs that she ignore the deportation notice and board the earliest flight out of Germany. A short time later, all exit visas out of Germany were cancelled. All her Jewish friends and members of her family who remained behind perished in the ensuing Holocaust. Sachs spent the rest of her life in Sweden, eventually became a Swedish citizen, and refused all suggestions and offers to return to Germany, even though she was granted honorary Berlin citizenship in 1967.

Both in her personal life and in her work, these experiences exerted an immense effect on the poet. Her new life as a 50-year-old impoverished exile marked a complete break from the earlier comfortable bourgeois existence. This break also marked the beginning of her mature poetry, a poetry completely free of any metric conventions and stanzaic breaks, driven on solely by force of themes and images, and arranged in cycles. The narrow escape from death haunts all her poetry, as she herself said in a letter: "The terrible experiences which brought me personally to the brink of death and darkness became my tutors. Had I been unable to write, I would not have survived. Death was my tutor. How could I have occupied myself with anything else? My metaphors are my wounds. Only through them is my work to be understood." Indeed, shortly after her arrival in Sweden, she tried to write a continuation of *Legenden und Erzählungen* but never finished the project. She was to publish no more creative prose the rest of her life.

Both of her early postwar collections, *In den Wohnungen des Todes* (In the Habitations of Death) and *Sternverdunkelung* (Eclipse of the Stars), as well as the play *Eli* were direct results of her attempts to come to terms with those "terrible experiences" through their disturbing images of life, death, and suffering in the concentration camps. These works, with their strong themes of pain, loss, separation, and disappointment in love, are the ones which brought her international attention.

A reclusive person, Sachs seldom gave interviews, and was reluctant to reveal any details about her personal life, either past or present. She was hardly known, even in the German-speaking world, until she was awarded the Nobel Prize for Literature in 1966, which she shared with the Israeli writer S.Y. Agnon. In part, her secretiveness was due to ill health suffered after the death of her mother in 1950. Two heart attacks and a series of nervous breakdowns kept her in hospitals or sanitoriums for long periods of time.

While even in the earlier mature poetry, Sachs's works evinced a trace of hermeticism, but it is the later poetry, such as the *Glühende Rätsel* (Glowing Enigmas) which has been most problematic to literary critics. Many have asserted that Sachs's works cannot be read apart from her later works. Their increasingly mystical and enigmatic language was interpreted by some to signify reconciliation and even forgiveness through quietism and acceptance. However, such a simplistic interpretation of the later works was one that she herself went out of the way to deny. It is obvious that these later pieces show her being increasingly influenced by her readings of cabalistic literature, especially through Gershom Scholem's (1897–1982) German translation of the Book of Sohar. But the move towards mysticism was not only through Jewish lines; other, including Eastern, mystical traditions can be evinced in these works as well. In time, the ashes of the crematoria became the dust of ages, and themes of metamorphosis and the sands of time grew more significant than the fate of the Jewish people and the sorrows of the Holocaust.

As the language of her poetry became more mystic, the poems also became more universal. Writing in German, she rejected the literary and cultural traditions associated with that language. She was a poet who managed to forge a language of her own—an ahistorical German. Exiled from her native land, she created a unique place for herself: a purely linguistic existence in response to both the Nazi dictum that "when a Jew writes in German, he lies," and the Zionist statement that the concepts of writing in German and being Jewish were mutually incompatible. She became a writer with no linguistic homeland, writing poetry which many German postwar critics had

difficulty assimilating into literary history. At first, Sachs was classified, along with Paul Celan, under the rubric of "exile poet." Later on, the label of "poetess of Jewish destiny" would be used. However, neither of these characterizations adequately accounts for the movement towards mysticism in her later works, and much remains to be done before any study or assessment of her works can claim to be in any way definitive. There has, for example, been very little critical attention paid to her fourteen dramatic pieces, even though some have been performed as radio plays, and the Swedish composer Moses Pergament even set *Eli* to music.

While Sachs was awarded many prizes and awards (the city of Dortmund, which houses the Nelly Sachs archives, presented her with the first Nelly Sachs Prize in 1961), the slow recognition by some critics of her poetry could be ascribed to the publication of her early collections in East Berlin and in Amsterdam, as well as the attitude of many German critics towards German exile writers. However, the continued lack of critical attention must be ascribed to the general difficulty of her works and her refusal to include biographical details in her poetry, preferring instead to mysticize her experiences, or universalize them through such themes as exile, loneliness, or metamorphosis. To this day she remains, unfortunately, better known by reputation than by personal acquaintanceship with her works.

One important facet of Sachs's work which has been neglected is her role as translator. She was the person most responsible for introducing postwar Swedish poetry to the German-language audience, championing the works of Edfelt, Ekelof, Lindegren, and others. For this work, she was awarded a number of Swedish literary prizes.

Works

Legenden und Erzählungen [Legends and Tales] (1921). *Fahrt ins Staublose: Die Gedichte der Nelly Sachs 1* [Journey into the Dustless Realm: The Poetry of Nelly Sachs, 1] (1961). This anthology and the following one include all of her mature poetry, including posthumous works. *Suche nach Lebenden: Die Gedichte der Nelly Sachs 2* [Search for the Living: The Poetry of Nelly Sachs, 2] (1971), ed. Margarethe Holmqvist and Bengt Holmqvist.

Zeichen im Sand [Markings in the Sand] (1962). Includes all fourteen dramatic works.

Letters: *Briefe der Nelly Sachs* [Letters of Nelly Sachs] ed. Ruth Dinesen and Helmut Müssener (1984). Includes bibliography of Sachs' translations from Swedish as well as translations of Sachs' own works into other languages.

Translations: *O the Chimneys: Selected Poems, Including the Verse Play, Eli,* tr. Michael Hamburger et al. (1967). Published in the U.K. as *Selected Poems: Including the Verse Play "Eli"* (1968). *The Seeker and Other Poems,* tr. Ruth Mead, Matthew Mead, and Michael Hamburger (1970). *Contemporary German Poetry,* selections, ed. and tr. Gertrude C. Schwebell (1964).

Bibliography

Bahr, Ehrhard, *Nelly Sachs* (1980). Berendsohn, Walter A., *Nelly Sachs. Einführung in das Werk der Dichterin jüdishen Schicksals* [Nelly Sachs. Introduction to the Work of the Poetess of Jewish Destiny] (1974). Bezzel-Dischner, Gisela, *Poetik des modernen Gedichtes: zur Lyrik von Nelly Sachs* [Poetics of Modern Verse: Towards the Lyric Verse of Nelly Sachs] (1970). Blomster, W.V., "A Theosophy of the Creative Word: The Zohar-Cycle of Nelly Sachs." *The Germanic Review* 44 (1969): 211–227. Falkenstein, Henning, *Nelly Sachs* (1984). Holmqvist, Bengt, ed., *Das Buch der Nelly Sachs* (1968). Kersten, Paul, *Nelly Sachs*, bibliography (1969). Kersten, Paul, *Die Metaphorik in der Lyrik von Nelly Sachs* [The Metaphoric in the Lyric Verse of Nelly Sachs] (1970). *Nelly Sachs zu Ehren,* Festschrift upon her 70th birthday, 1961. *Nelly Sachs zu Ehren II,* Festschrift upon her 75th birthday, 1966. Rosenfeld, Alvin H., "The Poetry of Nelly Sachs." *Judaism* 20, 3 (Summer 1971): 356–364. Slater, Joseph, "From Death to Rebirth." *Saturday Review* 50, 4 (Nov. 4, 1967). Spender, Stephen, "Catastrophe and Redemption." *New York Times Book Review* (Oct. 8, 1967).

Oscar Lee

Barbara Sadowska

Born February 24, 1940; died October 1986
Genre(s): poetry
Language(s): Polish

During her funeral at the Warsaw Powazki cemetery on October 6, 1986, in the presence of thousands, poet Wiktor Woroszylski spoke about Sadowska, calling her "the Polish Mater Dolorosa, a sister to all mothers of murdered sons. . . ." Sadowska's son, nineteen-year-old Grzegorz, was dragged from the street into the police station and beaten to death in May 1983. Several weeks earlier, Sadowska herself was hit on the head by "unknown thugs" who broke into St. Martin's church in Warsaw, where she was sorting out medication packages to be delivered to people arrested under the "martial law." As a consequence of that attack, the poet underwent two serious skull operations. She had been in trouble with the regime since the fifties when, as a teenager, she frequented the unofficial stage performances; she was often called for investigation, and later the police tried to link her case to the murder of a son of a well-known Catholic publications' editor committed at that time. In 1968, she supported the student revolt against the regime, and in 1976 she joined the KOR, Committee for Workers' Defense, organized by prominent intellectuals to help the jailed factory employees and their families. She joined the "Solidarity" movement at its outset, working all the time with the Archbishop's Air Committee at St. Martin's.

She made her debut as a seventeen-year-old with the poem "Mama" in issue no.10 of the journal *Nowa Kultura.* Her first volume of poetry was warmly received by both literary critics and the wider audience. Her second volume, however, met with accusations of being "uncommunicative," "dark," and "obscure." She had to wait for almost ten years to see her next book in print. She never belonged to any literary groups and did not seek support from influential people. Her fourth volume was severely abbreviated by the censors. She published nothing through official channels for the last twelve years of her life. Her poetry was printed by underground publications.

> She wrote in 1983:
> on scraps of paper
> I insult the Department of Justice
> the court of law
> and the government
> with the child
> whom you will not manage
> to kill

Works

Zerwane druty [Torn Wires] (1959). *Nad ogniem* [Over the Fire] (1963). *Nie mozesz na mnie liczyc, nie bede sie bronic* [Don't Count on Me, I Will Not Defend Myself] (1972). *Moje* [Mine] (1974). *Tumor*(1981). *Slodko byc dzieckiem Boga* [It's Sweet to Be a Child of God] (1985).

Bibliography

Kurecka, Maria, "Barbara." *Kultura* 12/471 (Paris, 1986): 107–108.

Maya Peretz

Françoise Sagan

(see: Françoise Quoirez)

Saint Teresa of Jesus

Born March 28, 1515, Avila, Spain
Genre(s): mystical treatise
Language(s): Spanish

Saint Teresa of Jesus was born in Avila, as the daughter of Alonso Sánchez de Cepeda, the son of a converted Jew from Toledo. Alonso Sánchez married for the first time in 1505; his wife, Catalina del Peso, died two years later, leaving him two children. In 1509 Alonso married Beatriz de Ahumada, Teresa's mother. The couple had ten children. Beatriz had a fondness for romances of chivalry, which she had to read with her children unbeknownst to her husband. Teresa was captivated by the romances. At the age of five she persuaded one of her brothers to flee the paternal house and go with her to "the land of the Moors" to seek martyrdom.

Teresa wrote four long works: *The Book of Life* (1562), *The Way of Perfection* (1564), *Book of the Foundations* (1573), and *The Dwelling Places of the Interior Castle* (1577). All except the second one begin with an assertion of the advantages of good lineage as an omen of future accomplishments. The first chapter of *The Life* is titled: "To have had virtuous and God-fearing parents along with the graces the Lord granted me should have been enough for me to have led a good life, if I had not been so wretched."

Teresa wrote the first draft of her *Life* in 1562. Although the book went through several revisions and was not published until 1588, we know that it was scrutinized by theologians and inquisitors for several years since the book, which narrated extraordinary experiences, was written by an "idiot"—a person who did not know Latin—and a woman.

The first ten chapters tell of her life up to the moment of the conversion, when she began to receive the mystical experiences. Chapter eleven is devoted to a description of the degrees of prayer or mercies that she had received up to the moment of drafting the book. This chapter is emblematic of Teresa's mystic writing. She avoids abstract doctrine in favor of events; she avoids concepts and tries to be understood through images. The way of perfection is compared in this chapter to the irrigation of a garden, and the different stages along the way are four different modes of irrigation. The resort to images accounts for Teresa's literary mastery. At some points the images are so deep and sublime that the reader cannot anticipate the possibility of surpassing them. And yet, he is always surprised by Teresa's genius in finding new comparisons that convey ever greater intensity and beauty.

Four degrees of prayer are described in *The Life*: recollection, quiet, sleep of the faculties, and union. Recollection can be attained through human effort. It is not a struggle with the human faculties as it was in the Franciscan school; it is simply a decision to renounce worldly values and attitudes. The other three degrees are all "supernatural," that is, unattainable by natural means; they are mercies from God.

The Way of Perfection was written for the nuns of the reformed monastery of Avila in 1564. The book consists of two parts: chapters 1–42 contain the basis of spiritual perfection for the nuns. Humility is posited as the foundation of the spiritual edifice. All values of the world, especially honor in the sense of lineage, must be renounced. The second part (chapters 43–73) is a commentary on the *Pater noster*.

Her last and most acclaimed book, *The Dwelling Places of the Interior Castle* (1577), describes the way of perfection as a quest for the center. The soul is portrayed as a castle with different mansions. In the innermost mansion or center of the soul God dwells with his infinite majesty, love, and light. Messages and inspirations radiate from that center to the faculties, inviting them to flee from the dangerous outskirts of the castle (sin) and from the exterior chambers (dispersion), and reach to God and themselves. For Teresa, the conquest of God is the conquest of our personal identity.

The Dwelling Places of the Interior Castle is divided into seven sections of different lengths, each one devoted to a set of dwelling places or mansions. The division of the book into seven sections may have been inspired by the popular septenaries of the Catholic Church: seven virtues, seven deadly sins, or seven sacraments. But the book is not an allegory based on numerical symbolism; in it Teresa narrates her own life, the nuances of her experiences being more important than the external frame of the book.

In order to appreciate Teresa's cultural and literary originality, one must measure her accomplishments against the handicaps she had to overcome: she was a woman in sixteenth-century Spain, of Jewish descent, a nun in a monastery of closure, and severely ill since the age of twenty-two. Settled in God as her center, she had a clear hierarchy of values, was able to appreciate or deride social and religious institutions, had an exemplary sense of freedom, gave a new impulse to religious life and mystical literature, and through her insistence on courage, provides us with a formula that is still valid to banish the ghost of alienation.

Works

Obras completas de Santa Teresa, ed. Efrén de la Madre de Dios and Otger Steggink (1967).
Translations: *The Collected Works of St. Teresa of Avila*;, tr. Kieran Kavanaugh and Otilio Rodríguez, 2 vols. (1976–1980). *The Complete Works of St. Teresa of Jesus*, tr. E. Allison Peers. (1946)

Bibliography

Auclair, Marcelle, *Teresa of Avila*, tr. Kathleen Pond (New York, 1953). Clissold, Stephen, *St. Teresa of Avila* (New York, 1982). de la Madre de Dios, Efrén, and Otger Steggink, *Tiempo y vida de Santa Teresa* (Madrid, 1977). Egido, Teófanes, "The Historical Setting of St. Teresa's Life." *Carmelite Studies* 1 (1980): 122–182. Gabriel de Santa María Magdalena, *Saint Teresa of Jesus: Mistress of Spiritual Life*, tr. a Benedictine of Stanbrook Abbey (Cork, 1949). García de la Concha, Victor, *El arte literario de Santa Teresa* (Barcelona, 1978). Hatzfeld, Helmut, *Santa Teresa de Avila* (New York, 1969). Lincoln, Victoria, *Teresa: A Woman*, ed., and intro. Elias Rivers and Antonio T. de Nicolás (Albany, N.Y., 1984). Llamas Martínez, Enrique, *Santa Teresa de Jesús y la Inquisición española* (Madrid, 1972). Papasogli, Giorgio, *St. Teresa of Avila*, tr. G. Anzilotti (New York, 1958). Peers, E. Allison, *Handbook of the Life and Times of St. Teresa and St. John of the Cross* (London, 1954). Ramge, Sebastian, *An Introduction to the Writings of St. Teresa* (Chicago, 1963). Sullivan, John, ed., "Centenary of Saint Teresa." *Carmelite Studies* 4 (1984). Trueman Dicken, E.W., *The Crucible of Love* (New York, 1963). Walsh, William Thomas, *Saint Teresa of Avila* (Milwaukee, 1943).

C.M. Arroyo

Monique Saint-Côme

(see: Monica Lovinescu)

Comte de Saint-Jean

(see: Adine Riom)

Laure Saint-Martin Perman Junot d'Abrantes

Born November 6, 1784, Montpellier, France; died June 7, 1838, Paris
Genre(s): novel, memoir
Language(s): French

Descendant of the family Des Commene, Laure Saint-Martin was also distantly related to Napoleon Bonaparte, who, as a general, was a frequent visitor to her mother's fashionable salon. At age sixteen, Laure married General Junot, an aide to Napoleon, who made him duc d'Abrantes in 1808. During the Consulate and the Empire, she was well known in Court circles. Imperial society met in her salon. Her husband encountered some disfavor and eventually committed suicide in 1813. After the fall of Napoleon, she had to deal with penury and decided to provide for her needs with her writings. Her novels are all but forgotten, but her *Memoires ou Souvenir Historiques sur Napoleon, la Revolution, le Directoire, le Consulat, L'Empire et la Restauration (1831–1835)*, in eighteen volumes, show insight in the mores of the time and a first-rate, if somewhat biased, documentary on the life of the Emperor. She painted a vivid—and rather valuable—picture of the period. Part of these memoirs are in fact a biography of the Des Commene, an ancient Greek imperial family who immigrated to Corsica when the Byzantine empire was invaded by the Turks. Her fate was closely linked to that of Napoleon. She was bitterly disappointed when his friends abandoned him, and she lived in retirement. Encouraged by the success of her first *Memoires*, she wrote a sequel covering the Restoration, the July Revolution and the first year of the reign of Louis-Philippe, but this fell short of the mark.

Works

Memoires de Mme la Duchesse d'Abrante, ou Souvenirs Historiques sur Napoleon, la Revolution, le Directoire, le Consulat, l'Empire et la Restauration (1831–1835, 18 vols. Catherine II (1834). [With Joseph Straszewiez], Les Femmes Celebres de Tous les Pays (1834). Histoires Contemporaines (1835). Louise, 2 vols. (1839). La Duchesse de Vallombray (1838). Les Deux Soeurs, Scenes de la Vie d'Interieur (1840). Etienne Saulnier (1838). Memoires sur la Restauration ou Souvenirs Historiques sur Cette Epoque, la Revolution de Juillet et les Premieres Annees du Regne de Louis-Philippe, 6 vols. (1835–1836). Choix de Memoires et Ecrits des Femmes Françaises aux XVIIe, XVIIIe, XIXe Siècles (1892). Scenes de la Vie Espagnole (1836). Souvenirs d'une Ambassade et d'un Sejour en Espagne et au Portugal de 1808 à 1811, 2 vols. (1837).

Bibliography

Malo, Henri, *La Duchesse d'Abrantes au Temps des Amours* (1972). Malo, Henri, *Les Annees de Boheme de la Duchesse d'Abrantes* (1927).

Colette Michael

Anna Sakse

(a.k.a. Trīne Grēciņa, Zane Me'adūja, Austra Sēja, Smīns)

Born January 16, 1905, Vidzeme, Latvia; died March 2, 1981, Riga, Latvia
Genre(s): novel, short story, fairy tale, children's literature
Language(s): Latvian

Critical opinion about Anna Sakse is sharply divided between Western Europe, which either ignores or condemns her for her cooperation with the Soviet régime, and Eastern Europe, which praises her as one of the greatest writers in the history of Latvian literature.

Sakse was born into the family of a poor farmer. For a while she studied pedagogy and Baltic philology at the University of Riga, but she left soon disillusioned with the prevailing conservatism. She then worked as translator and proofreader for various periodicals and publishers. In 1934, with the help of her future husband, Edgars Abzalons, she joined the then-illegal Communist party. At the outbreak of World War II she fled to Russia, where she spent the war years as one of the editors of the Latvian Communist periodical *Cīņa*. In 1944 she returned to Latvia with the Soviet army. Active in Latvian politics, especially in undertakings to further peace, she was repeatedly rewarded by the Soviets for her political as well as literary achievements. Her prizes for the latter include the title of a People's Writer of the Latvian SSR (1965).

Most of Sakse's work exemplifies the tendencies of "socialist realism." In her fairytales, however, she manifests a charming gift for fantasy, notably in *Pasakas par ziediem* (1966; Tales About Flowers). Her works have been translated into numerous Eastern European and Asiatic languages. Several of Sakse's books were published in Russian translation prior to their appearance in Latvian.

Works

(Several of Sakse's books were published in Russian translation prior to their appearance in Latvian.)
Darba cilts (1941). *Mierīgs iedzīvotājs*, in Russian (1943). *Atgriešanās dzīvē* (1945). *Skarbais piesitiens* (1946). *Pasakas* (1946). *Jaunā maiņa*

(1947). *Pret kalnu* (1948). *Lūzums* (1949). *Pēdējais divnieks* (1950). *Dzirksteles naktī* (1957). *Lidojums uz mēnesi* (1958). *Laimes kalējs* (1960). *Tēva dāvana* (1961). *Pīka kunga stāsts* (1962). *Pasakas par ziediem* (1966). *Nokaltis zars* (1968). Numerous shorter pieces, especially for children, and translations from Russian into Latvian.

Translations: "The Return to Life" (a portion of *Atgriešanās dzīvē*), tr. Eve Manning, *Soviet Literature* 12 (1944), 2–14. An English translation of *Pasakas par ziediem* (Riga, 1978) has not been available to the present writer.

Bibliography
Bērsons, Ilgonis, *Padomju Latvijas rakstnieki* (Riga, 1976). Ekmanis, Rolfs, *Latvian Literature Under the Soviets: 1940–1975* (Belmont, Mass., 1978). Also see: "Writers discuss their work: Anna Sakse." *Soviet Literature* 6 (1952), pp. 161–164.

Zoja Pavlovskis

Concha de Salamanca

(see: Concha Zardoya)

Elizaveta Salhias de Tournemir

(a.k.a. Evgeniia Tur)

Born August 12, 1815, Moscow, Russia; died March 15, 1892, Warsaw, Poland
Genre(s): short story, novel, literary criticism, children's literature
Language(s): Russian

"Evgeniia Tur" was a famous name in Russian literature for over forty years. Salhias's career falls into three distinct periods: she wrote light prose fiction from 1849–1856; she was an editor and critic from 1856 to the mid-1860s; and in later years she won a secure reputation as the author of lively and edifying books for children and youth.

Salhias's parents gave their daughters an excellent private education by hiring Moscow's leading professors and intellectuals to tutor them. Her sister Sofia (1825–1867) became a landscape painter, and her brother Aleksandr Sukhovo-Kobylin (1817–1903) was the author of a famous

trilogy of harsh satiric comedies. Salhias herself began to publish fiction after her husband, a French count, squandered her large dowry on a venture to produce champagne in Russia. Her stories and two novels, *Plemiannitsa* (1850; The Niece) and *Tri pory zhizni* (1854; Three Stages of Life), were elegantly polished productions reminiscent of the "society tales" of the late years of Russian Romanticism. In the epoch of social conscience that began with Alexander II's accession to the throne in 1855, the public and critics soon tired of her slight romantic plots and exalted rhetoric.

From 1856 to 1860 Salhias served as literary editor of *Russkii vestnik* (The Russian Herald). The magazine was particularly hospitable to Russian women writers during her tenure; among others, Karolina Pavlova, Maria Markovich ("Marko Vovchok"), Iulia Zhadovskaia, Nadezhda Sokhanskaia ("Kokhanovskaia"), and Nadezhda Khvoshchinskaia ("V. Krestovsky") published in its pages. In 1861 Salhias founded her own semi-weekly newspaper, *Russkaia rech'* (Russian Discourse), with the ambitious program of reviewing "literature, history, art and society in the West and in Russia." After it failed, she continued to write wide-ranging cultural criticism for a variety of journals until the mid-1860s. As a critic, she put her fine education to the service of bringing major figures and currents of Western, and particularly French, literatures to the attention of the Russian reader. Among others, she wrote articles about Michelet, Mme Récamier, Béranger, Victor Hugo, Charlotte Brontë, Horace Walpole and the American preacher William Channing. She reviewed George Sand's *L'histoire de ma Vie* and Flaubert's *Madame Bovary* shortly after their appearance in France.

From the mid-1860s to her death, Salhias translated and wrote impeccably conservative stories for children, many of them drawn from Roman and church history. Her historical novels about Russia, *Kniazhna Dubrovina* (1887; Princess Dubrovina) and *Serezha Bor-Ramensky* (1888), were among her most popular original works for young people. *Semeistvo Shalonskikh* (1880; The Shalonsky Family), written as a young girl's reminiscences of her childhood during the Napoleonic wars, still makes enjoyable light reading. Salhias's memoirs, published in

Poliarnaia zvezda (The Pole Star, 3, pp. 9–59) in 1881, were apparently never finished. Her son, Evgenii Salhias de Tournemir (1841–1908), followed the family's lettered tradition by becoming a prolific historical novelist.

Works

Povesti i rasskazy, 4 ch. (1859).

Bibliography

Feoktistov, E.M., *Za kulisami politiki i literatury. 1848–1896. Vospominaniia* (Leningrad), pp. 362–372, 398–399. *Handbook of Russian Literature*, Victor Terras, ed. (New Haven, 1985), pp. 487–488 (*Christine Tomei*). Iazykov, D.D., *Obzor zhizni i trudov pokoinykh russkikh pisatelei i pisatel'nits umershikh v 1892* (St. Petersburg, 1912), pp. 164–175 [bio-bibliography]. *Istoriia russkoi literatury XIX v.: Bibliograficheskii slovar' russkikh pisatel'nits*, K.D. Muratova, ed. (Moscow-Leningrad, 1962), pp. 709–711. *Kratkaia literaturnaia entsiklopediia*, vol. 7 (Moscow, 1972), cols. 655–656 (L.I. Men'shutina).

Mary F. Zirin

Mercedes Salisachs

(a.k.a. A. Dan, María Ecín)

Born September 18, 1916, Barcelona, Spain
Genre(s): novel, short story
Language(s): Spanish

One of contemporary Spain's most commercially successful authors, Salisachs has won major novel prizes, such as the City of Barcelona (1956) and the Planeta (1975). Her works have been translated to various languages, including English, French, German, Italian, Portuguese, Swedish, and Finnish.

Following her early education in a Catholic school, Salisachs studied business at the School of Commerce in Barcelona. She married in 1935 and had five children, one of whom died in an automobile accident in 1958. In addition to her extensive literary career, she has been a partner in an interior decorating firm and has also written on that subject. She has traveled widely in many regions of the world.

Salisachs' first prize-winning novel, *Una mujer llega al pueblo* (1960; The Eyes of the Proud), deals with the death of a young woman who returns to her Catalonian fishing village to give birth to her illegitimate baby. Faulknerian in technique, the work gives a grotesque image of both a frivolous upper class and a hypocritical middle class. Only a few characters, including the protagonist and the village priest, escape the author's stinging satire.

La gangrena (Gangrene), Salisach's other major prize-winning novel, is less innovative in structural terms than some of her earlier works but continues a scathing attack on postwar Barcelona society. It represents the culmination of the social criticism found in *Primera mañana, última mañana* (First Morning, Last Morning)—a work featuring an alternate-chapter structure also reminiscent of Faulkner—and *La estación de las hojas amarillas* (The Season of the Yellow Leaves). She deals repeatedly with adultery, homosexuality, alcoholism, and drug addiction against the background of a materialistic society that has lost all moral values.

In recent years Salisachs has fallen into a formula with the result that her novels, while still attracting a large reading audience, have been of little interest to scholars. Her early works, however, are varied in style, structure and content—including an exploration of the fantastic mode—and deserve far more critical attention than they have received.

Works

Primera mañana, última mañana (1955). *Carretera intermedia* (1956). *Más allá de los raíles* (1957). *Adán Helicóptero* (1957). *Una mujer llega al pueblo* (1957). *Pasos conocidos* (1958). *Vendimia interrumpida* (1960). *El declive y la cuesta* (1962). *La estación de las hojas amarillas* (1963). *La última aventura* (1967). *Adagio confidencial* (1973). *La gangrena* (1975). *Viaje a Sodoma* (1977). *El proyecto y otros relatos* (1978). *La presencia* (1979). *Derribos* (1981). *La sinfonía y las moscas* (1982). *El volumen de la ausencia* (1983).

Bibliography

Alborg, Juan Luis, *Hora actual de la novela española*, Vol. 2 (Madrid, Taurus, 1962), pp. 383–404. Conte, Rafael, "Novela y burguesía: Mercedes Salisachs y Lorenzo Villalonga." *Insula* 353 (1976): 5. Huertas, Ricardo, "El escritor al día: Mercedes

Salisachs." *La Estafeta Literaria* 530 (1973): 16–18. Lado, María Dolores, "Mercedes Salisachs y la novela católica." *Letra Femeninas* 12 (1986): 114–120. Zatlin Boring, Phyllis, "Mercedes Salisachs, novelista de su época." *Novelistas femeninas de la postguerra española*, ed. Janet W. Pérez (Madrid, José Porrúa Turranzas, 1983), pp. 7–17.

General references: *A Dictionary of Literature of the Iberian Peninsula* (New York; Westport, Connecticut; London: Greenwood Press, forthcoming). *Quien es quien en las letras españolas*. 3rd ed. (Madrid: Instituto Nacional del Libro Español, 1979). *Women Writers of Spain: An Annotated Bio-Bibliographical Guide*, ed. Carolyn L. Galerstein (New York; Westport, Connecticut; London: Greenwood Press, 1986).

Phyllis Zatlin

Madame la princesse Constance de Salm

(see: Constance-Marie de Théis, princesse de Salm-Reifferscheid-Dyck)

La comtesse de Salm-Dyck, Madame la princesse Constance de Salm

(see: Constance-Marie de Théis, princesse de Salm-Reifferscheid-Dyck)

Īda Salmiņa or Salmiņš

(see: Aīda Niedra)

Sally Alina Ingeborg Dührkop-Salminen

Born April 25, 1906, Vårdö, Åland, Finland; died July 18, 1976, Copenhagen, Denmark
Genre(s): novel, short story
Language(s): Swedish

Sally Salminen (she wrote under her maiden name even after her marriage to Danish artist Johannes Dührkop in 1940) entered the literary spotlight as a Cinderella: her first novel, *Katrina*, won first prize in a writing contest in Scandinavia in 1936, and she was propelled to instant fame.

Born in the Swedish-speaking Åland Islands, Salminen was the seventh of twelve children. Her father worked as a logger and farmer; her mother, also from a farming family, was a professional tailor. When Salminen was seven, her father drowned. Despite the difficult times the family experienced (or perhaps because of them), five of the eleven children who reached adulthood became writers. In 1930, after working in Sweden for a few years in shops and as a bookkeeper, Salminen went to New York to work as a maid for a wealthy family. In her spare time, she wrote her first novel, perhaps motivated by homesickness to describe on paper the Åland she had left.

Katrina became an immediate international success and was translated into over twenty languages. It presents the story of a Finnish girl who falls in love with a sailor, a good-natured but undependable fellow, who paints a larger-than-life picture of his circumstances in his native Åland. She marries him and leaves her home and family, only to find that in reality her new abode is much humbler than portrayed, her new life will be quite difficult, and her husband will leave the next day for the sea. The novel is the story of the brave and strong-willed woman's fight against poverty and sometimes against the upper-class "barons" of the island, a fight which she wins without sacrificing either her keen sense of honor or her enduring love for her husband. Although some critics see a political (socialist) side to *Katrina*, the author is even more concerned with psychological portraiture and extremely detailed physical descriptions.

Unfortunately, Salminen felt that critics were her enemies. An autodidact, she felt inferior to the "learned," and it has been theorized that this was the reason she could not reproduce the success of *Katrina*. The natural, attractively naive style of her first book is not to be found elsewhere in her production though the novels *Barndomens land* (My Childhood's Country) of 1948 and *Prins Efflam* (Prince Efflam) of 1953 as well as the autobiographical sketch *Upptäcktsresan* (Voyage of Discovery) of 1966 have received a good deal of praise.

Salminen returned to Åland in 1936; after her marriage, she moved to Denmark where she lived until her death in 1976. She continued to travel throughout her life, and her later works are often moulded out of impressions from foreign countries (for example Israel) and other autobiographical materials.

Works

Novels: *Katrina* (1936). *Den långa våren* [The Long Spring] (1939). *På lös sand* [On Loose Sand] (1941). *Lars Laurila* (1943). *Nya land* [New Lands] (1945). *Barndomens land* [My Childhood's Country] (1948). *Små världar* [Small Worlds] (1949). *Klyftan och stjärnan* [The Abyss and the Star] (1951). *Prins Efflam* [Prince Efflam] (1953). *Spår på jorden* [Tracks on the Earth] (1961). *Vid havet* [By the Sea] (1963).

Autobiographical prose: *Upptäcktsresan* [Voyage of Discovery] (1966). *Min amerikanska saga* [My American Saga] (1968). *I Danmark* [In Denmark] (1972). *Världen öppnar sig* [The World Opens] (1974).

Travel description: *Jerusalem* (1969). *På färder I Israel* [On the Road in Israel] (1971).

Translations: *Katrina*, tr. Naomi Walford (1937). *Mariana* [*Den långa våren*], tr. Barrows Mussey (1940). *The Prince from the Sea* [*Prins Efflam*], tr. Evelyn Ramsden (1954).

Bibliography

Bäckman, Anna-Lisa, "Upptäcktsresan: om Sally Salminen," in *Kvinnornas litteraturhistoria*, Marie Louise Ramnefalk and Anna Westberg, eds. (Lund, Sweden, 1981). Bukdahl, Jørgen, "Romanens kunst: Sally Salminen." *Mellemkrigstid 1935–1940* (Copenhagen, 1945). Engman, Bo, and Månsson, Lilian, eds., *Litteraturlexikon* (Stockholm, 1974). Sjöstrand, Martin, *Bonden i svensk litteratur* (Stockholm, 1948). Sjöström, Gunnar, ed., *Vem är ven i Norden* (Stockholm, 1941). *Uppslagsverket Finland* (Helsinki, 1985). Warburton, Thomas, *Åttio år finlandssvensk litteratur* (Helsinki, 1984).

Kathy Saranpa Anstine

Annie Salomons

(a.k.a. Ada Gerlo)

Born 1885; died 1980
Genre(s): poetry, novel
Language(s): Dutch

The subject matter of Annie Salomons' novels, the problems of intelligent, well-educated young women living in a society that recognized only marriage as woman's proper destiny, made her very popular with her contemporaries. Her poetry, on the other hand, four collections in all, did less well. She also wrote "Indian" (i.e, Indonesia) stories about the Dutch in Indonesia, as for example in *Heilige stenen* (1957; Sacred Stones), and achieved enormous popular success with her *Herinneringen uit den ouden tijd aan schrijvers die ik persoonlijk gekend heb* (1957 and 1960; Memories from the Old Days of Writers I Have Known Personally) in which she discussed Boutens, Couperus, Leopold, De Meester, Top Naeff, Querido, Van de Woestijne, Geerten Gossaert, A. Roland Holst, Dirk Coster and others, all of them authors of importance.

Works

Poetry: *Verzen*, 4 vols. (1905). *De ongerepte droom* (1950).

Prose: *Een Meisjesstudentje* (1907). *Herinneringen van een onafhankelijke vrouw* (1915). *De oude schuld* (1922). *Het huis in de hitte* (1933). *Een meisje en een jongetje* (1933). *Heilige stenen* (1957). *Herinneringen uit den ouden tijd aan schrijvers die ik persoonlijk gekend heb* (1957, 1960). *Nog meer herinneringen uit de oude tijd* (1962).

Bibliography

Donker, Anthonie, *Critisch Bulletin* (June 1950): 241–250. Donker, Anthonie, *Critisch Bulletin* (Dec. 1950): 595. Jacobs, M.A., *Dietsche Warande en Belfort* (Oct. 1955): 484–489. Knuvelder, Gerard, *Handboek tot de geschiedenis der Nederlandse letterkunde*, Vol. 4, 2nd ed. (1961): 339–340. *Maatstaf* (June 1960) issue entirely devoted to Annie Salomons.

Maya Bijvoet

Diodata Saluzzo-Roero

(a.k.a. Glacilla Eurotea)

Born 1775, Turin, Italy; died 1849, Turin
Genre(s): poetry, prose novels, verse romance
Language(s): Italian

Diodata Saluzzo-Roero was an Arcadian poet born in Turin July 31, 1775, the first born of Count G.A. Saluzzo di Monesiglio, descendent of the Marquises of Saluzzo. This old illustrious line began in 1142 with Manfred, son of Boniface, marquis of Savona, and continued until 1548, when the city and territory were seized by the French. In 1799, Diodata married Count M. Roero di Revello, but was widowed three years later. She lived a poor life, influenced only by her family, her land of Piedmont, her king, and her faith. These sources inspired her poetry, which recalls the work of Parini, Alfieri, and Manzoni and elicited the admiration and respect of her contemporaries. In her poetic works, she reconciled the effects of formal decorum, not congenial to the syntax of the educated classes (which she learned through her teacher, the Abbot of Caluso and Prospero Balbo), and the themes and tastes of romanticism. Especially noteworthy are her stories, which she derived from domestic traditions as well as the vigor of the times, and those inspired from the famous ode "Le Rovine," called an example of the perfect romantic lyric by L. Di Breme.

The versatile Madame Saluzzo-Roero composed tragedy (the melodramatic *Erminia* and the Alfieri-like *Tullia*), comedy (which she wished to be burned after her death), novels and witty stories (including the biblical *Morte di Eva*), and the poem "Ippazia ovvero delle filosofie." But her most successful lyrics, many composed from earliest youth until her final years, have austere and delicate moral overtones.

Works

Ippazia (1827; revised and corrected, 1834). *Novelle*, eight prose romances with verses interspersed within them (1830). *Poesie Postume* (1853). *Versi* (1796; reprinted complete in four volumes, 1816–1817).

Bibliography

Bagnolo, C. di, "Elogio storico." *Poesie postume* (Torino, 1853). Collino, L., *Diodata Saluzzo-Roero* (Torino, 1925). Croce, B., In *Critica* 25 (1927): 255–262. Romani, R., *Critica letteraria* (Milano, 1883). I, p. 381 ff.; II, p. 73 ff.

Jean E. Jost

Mme. Prudence de Saman l'Esbatx

(see: Méritens Hortense Allart de)

Teresa Barbero Sanchez

(a.k.a. Teresa Barbero)

Born 1934, Avila, Spain
Genre(s): novel
Language(s): Spanish

Barbero was one of the originators of the "El Cobaya" literary group in 1953. In 1959 she moved to Madrid, began publishing poetry, and then established her reputation as a novelist. She is also known for her study of Gabriel Miró, a novelist of the previous generation. Her novels are notable for their psychological insight and use of interior monologue and memory, and for their depiction of the limitations Spanish society places on the lives of women. *Una manera de vivir* (1965; A Way of Life), which won the Premio Sésamo, is a condemnation of a society that does not prepare women to face reality and features a twenty-year-old woman whose family believes women should marry early and never work. Unable to finance her university studies or find a job, she descends into anguished emptiness and slashes her wrists. In *El último verano en el espejo* (1967; The Last Summer in the Mirror), an indictment of the education of Spanish girls, the protagonist recalls her childhood and adolescence in a small town. The repression, prejudices, and frustrations of that life have reduced her to a shadow, a victim of mid-twentieth-century malaise, dominated by men, revealed as a person only within the narrow focus of her mirror. *Un tiempo irremediablemente falso* (1973; An Irremediably False Time) portrays a loveless marriage. The wife, drowning in domesticity, has no idea that women can enjoy sex until she leaves her husband and children for a lover. After the death of her husband and lover she develops a career and rebuilds her relationship with her daughters. The protagonist of *La larga noche de un aniversario* (1982; The Long Night of an Anniversary) feels fossilized at age nineteen and has no interest in life, which to her seems incomprehensible. Victim of the typical upbringing of Spanish females, she leaves the university to work at a series of dull jobs. *Y no serás juzgado* (1985; And You Will Not Be Judged), winner of the Premio Asturias de Novela 1982, depicts the crisis in the marriage of a teacher and a woman executive as representative of the crisis of the entire Spanish post-war generation, a truly "lost generation" whose anguish lies in the inability to feel part of the society. The fearful husband resents his wife's business success and sexual frigidity. She is the prototype of women who grew up in dictatorial families within a dictatorial society, and neither love, work nor material possessions can fill the emptiness of her life.

Works

Muchacha en el exilio poetry (1959). *Apenas llegue el buen tiempo* (1964). *Una manera de vivir* (1965). *El último verano en el espejo* (1967). *Un tiempo irremediablemente falso* (1973). *Gabriel Miró* (1974). *Las larga noche de un aniversario* (1982). *En las manos de Albertina* (1984). *Y no serás juzgado* (1985).

Carolyn Galerstein

George Sand

(see: Amandine-Aurore-Lucie Dupin, Baronne Dudevant)

Jules Sand

(see: Amandine-Aurore-Lucie Dupin, Baronne Dudevant)

Cora Sandel

Born 1880, Kristiania (Oslo), Norway; died 1974, Uppsala, Sweden
Genre(s): novel, short story
Language(s): Norwegian

Cora Sandel has the distinction of having had more of her works translated into English than any other Norwegian woman writer, with the exception of Nobel Prize recipient Sigrid Undset. Sandel is best known in the English speaking world for her *Alberta* trilogy, now widely recognized as a feminist classic. Few English readers, however, realize that Sandel published five collections of short stories, and that, possibly, she achieves her greatest artistic success in this literary genre.

Cora Sandel is actually a pseudonym chosen by Sara Fabricius when, at forty-two years of age, she submitted her first story for publication in a literary magazine. She was born in 1880 in Kristiania (present-day Oslo) to middle-class parents of good standing. While their situation was not without economic difficulties, Sara's parents did manage to maintain a home based on traditional bourgeois norms and values. In 1892 the family moved to Tromsö, far above the Arctic Circle in the north of Norway, at that time a small, provincial town.

Sara Fabricius aspired to become a painter, and in 1899 she went to Kristiania to study painting with Harriet Backer. Unable to get a stipend, she had to curtail her study after one year and return to Tromsö. Finally, in 1905, she was able to leave Tromsö and resume her painting; she spent one year in Kristiania and in 1906 went to Paris. She had funds enough to keep her in Paris for only six months, but she stayed on, often living from hand to mouth, and did not return to Scandinavia until 1921. Her art studies brought her into contact with other expatriate artists, and they became her circle of friends. In 1913 she married the Swedish sculptor Anders Jönsson. The couple continued to live on the Continent throughout the war years, spending time in Florence, Paris, and Brittany. By the time they were ready to move home, Sara had abandoned painting in favor of writing; in her suitcase were notes intended for a novel based on her childhood.

They had had a child, born in Paris in 1917, and the three of them settled in Sweden, outside of Stockholm. The marriage was disintegrating, however; in 1922 she separated from her husband, and four years later they were divorced. Cora Sandel chose to make her home in Sweden and she died in Uppsala in 1974, ninety-four years old. She always wrote in Norwegian though and continued to regard herself as a Norwegian author.

Cora Sandel was very protective about her private life; she felt that an author owed no more to her public than the books she wrote, and this attitude explains much of the reason she opted to use a pseudonym. There can be no doubt that much of what she experienced went into her writing. Impulses received from living many years in France, for example, are evident in her art. Sandel's depictions of life in a northern Norwegian town, in *Alberte og Jakob* (Alberta and Jacob), *Kranes konditori* (Krane's Café) and several stories, are drawn from personal experience. Her own unhappy marriage ending in divorce and a custody battle over her only child is echoed in novels and stories. And finally, Sandel's struggle to become an artist, to overcome the external and internal barriers specific to her as a woman, inspired her to write the novels depicting Alberta's development as a woman and an artist.

In the first book of the trilogy, *Alberta and Jacob* (1926), Alberta is a teenager living with her family in a middle-class home. Because of their strained economic circumstances, her parents are eager to marry their daughter off to the first eligible suitor. Unhappily, Alberta fails to meet her parents' expectations; she is plain looking and timid and not the least bit interested in learning domestic skills. She longs to continue her schooling, but since her parents can barely afford to keep her brother in school, she is forced to stay home and help her mother mend clothes and keep house. In spite of her isolation and seemingly hopeless situation, Alberta manages to keep alive her dream for a future where she will be free to learn and to realize her talents. There is a defiant spirit behind the shy and insecure exterior.

Alberta does succeed in escaping small-town existence, and when *Alberte og friheten*

(1931; Alberta and Freedom) opens, she has arrived in Paris. She is now independent and can pursue her art studies, but she finds that freedom can be a hard reality for a single woman who has neither money nor saleable skills. And she discovers that neither she nor her female companions receive much support in their work from their male friends even though they, too, are struggling artists and should be sympathetic. When the relationship becomes steady, these same men seem to expect that both partners should concentrate on his career and that she should keep his house and raise his children.

In the third book, *Bare Alberte* (1939; Alberta Alone), Alberta has a husband and child. She is no longer painting—for one thing, art supplies are an expensive outlay for a poor artist couple. Instead she has started to write; notes and fragments on scraps of paper are as much as she can manage in between answering the demands made on her time and energy by child and husband. But by the end of the book, she has completed a manuscript, and she has won the self-assurance and conviction that enable her to leave her child and husband and, manuscript in hand, set out on her search for a publisher.

Thirteen years passed between the publication of the first and last books of the trilogy. Alberta underwent a long maturation process. Cora Sandel is a careful writer—her prose is perfectly shaped, and there are no superfluous or poorly chosen words. She is also a writer who is not satisfied until she has understood her characters thoroughly; consequently her portrayals demonstrate remarkable psychological depth and insight. This is not only evidenced in her Alberta trilogy but in her novel *Krane's Café* and in her many and exquisitely crafted stories as well.

Works

Novels: *Alberte og Jakob* (1926). *Alberte og friheten* (1931). *Bare Alberte* (1939). *Kranes konditori* (1945). *Kjøp ikke Dondi* (1958).

Short stories: *En blå sofa* (1927). *Carmen og Maja* (1932). *Mange takk, doktor* (1935). *Dyr jeg har kjent* (1945). *Figurer på mörk bunn* (1949). *Barnet som elsket veier* (1973).

Translations: *Alberta and Jacob*, tr. Elizabeth Rokkan (1962, U.S. edition 1984). *Alberta and Freedom*, tr. Elizabeth Rokkan (1963, U.S. edition

1984). *Alberta Alone*, tr. Elizabeth Rokkan (1965, U.S. edition 1984). *Krane's Café: An Interior with Figures*, tr. Elizabeth Rokkan (1968, U.S. edition 1986). *The Leech*, tr. Elizabeth Rokkan (1960, U.S. edition 1986). *Cora Sandel: Selected Short Stories*, tr. Barbara Wilson (1985). *The Silken Thread. Stories and Sketches*, tr. Elizabeth Rokkan (1986, U.S. edition 1987). *Slaves of Love and Other Norwegian Short Stories*, ed. James McFarlane (1982). *An Everyday Story. Norwegian Women's Fiction*, ed. Katherine Hanson (1984). *Scandinavian Women Writers. An Anthology from the 1880s to the 1980s*, ed. Ingrid Claréus (1989).

Bibliography

Beyer, Edvard, ed., *Norges Litteratur Historie*, vol. 5 (Oslo, 1975). Bonnevie, Mai Bente et al., *Et annet språk. Analyser av norsk kvinnelitteratur* (Oslo, 1977). Bretteville-Jensen, Sigurd, "Beretterteknikken i *Kranes konditori*." *Norsk Litterær Årbok* (Oslo, 1969). Engelstad, Irene, and Överland, Janneken, *Friheten til å skrive. Artikler om kvinnelitteratur fra Amalie Skram til Cecilie Löveid* (Oslo, 1981). Gimnes, Steinar, "'Tilværelsen kleber.' Om kvinner og frigjering i nokre Cora Sandel-noveller." *Norsk Litterær Årbok* (Oslo, 1976). Lervik, Åse Hiorth, *Menneske og miljö i Cora Sandels diktning. En studie over stil og motiv* (Oslo, 1977). Mangset, Berit Ryen, *Alberte–fra et kvinnesynspunkt* (Oslo, 1977). Överland, Janneken, *Cora Sandel om seg selv* (Oslo, 1983). Rasmussen, Janet E., "Dreams and Discontent: The Female Voice in Norwegian Literature." *Review of National Literatures. Norway*, vol. 12 (New York, 1983). Solumsmoen, Odd, *Cora Sandel. En dikter i ånd og sannhet* (Oslo, 1957). Zuck, Virpi, "Cora Sandel, a Norwegian Feminist." *Edda* (Oslo, 1982), pp. 23–33.

Katherine Hanson

Rosa de Sant Jordi

(see: Rosa María Arquimbau)

Ilia di Sant'Ismael

(see: Grazia Deledda)

Francesca Sanvitale

Born May 17, 1928, Milan, Italy
Genre(s): novel, criticism, journalism
Language(s): Italian

Born in Milan, Francesca Sanvitale lived for a while in Florence, then settled down in Rome. Beside being an accomplished novelist, Sanvitale writes for some of the most influential Italian newspapers and journals (her pronouncements on Tozzi and Neera are often quoted), and is a skillful interviewer (her interviews of French Academician Yourcenar were made for the Italian RAI-TV).

We can reconstruct Sanvitale's youth from the lines of her quasi-autobiographical novel *Madre e figlia*. The work is a reevocation, sometimes in a mythical key, often in a realistic mood, of a love-hate relationship between a mother who cannot grow and a daughter who needs assertive role models because she wants to grow. The narrative is in the third person, the point of view that of the daughter, although at times an "I" intervenes in the presentation. The tale moves between the two poles of total subjugation and sudden revolt, and between intervals of bewilderment and moments of clarity. *Madre e figlia* is the book of an impossible rebellion which is nevertheless attempted; the story of the threat that claustrophobic relationships inevitably foster and of the release that only death can bring about.

Il cuore borghese was composed early in the writer's career but published only in 1972. Like *Madre e figlia*, it is a Bildungsroman, but one in which the self-questioning of the intellectual leads only to failure. Salvation for the bourgeoisie is shown to be possible only when one chooses a life that is a non-life, or opts for the void which comes when indifference has thoroughly paralyzed the will. Yet this pessimistic outlook is not overriding. The action progresses by scenes rather than through an old-fashioned plot to better depict the stasis that wraps the middle class society analyzed.

L'uomo del parco is another unusually structured novel. A sequence of micro-narratives tells the story of a woman's rebirth. The slow-moving action and the magical landscape function as the background for a tale of inward search. Giulia, the main character, knows that in order to be cured she must lucidly diagnose her disease. Only then can she—and will she—find a way out of her predicament.

Sanvitale has progressively gained recognition as one of the most promising writers of this generation, and her books have enjoyed both critical and popular success.

Works

Il cuore borghese [The Bourgeois Heart] (1972). *Madre e figlia* [Mother and Daughter] (1980). *L'uomo del parco* [The Man in the Park] (1984).

Bibliography

Baldacci, Luigi, Introduction to *Il cuore borghese* (Milano, 1986), pp. 5–15. Biellock, Paola, "Studio tematico delle scrittrici italiane contemporanee." Diss., Rutgers U., 1982. Pampaloni, Geno, Introduction to *Madre e figlia* (Milano, 1986), pp. V–IX. Toscani, Claudio, "Romanzo: femminile plurale." *Il lettore di provincia* 45–46 (1981): 61–70.

Valeria Finucci

Agnes Sapper

Born April 12, 1852, Munich, Germany; died March 19, 1929, Würzburg
Genre(s): novel, children's literature
Language(s): German

Agnes Sapper was born in Munich in 1852, the daughter of the Bavarian jurist and politician Karl Brater and his wife Pauline. Raised in financially modest but intellectually stimulating circumstances, Sapper spent her youth in Munich and in Erlangen. In 1875 she married the magistrate Eduard Sapper; they lived first in Blaubeuren (Württemberg) and later in Calw. After his death in 1898, she moved to Würzburg, where she remained for the rest of her life.

Sapper's writing career began at the suggestion of her own children. Her writings, generally for children, have remained a popular mainstay of German children's literature. They praise the virtues of modesty, charity, doing one's duty, moderation, and obedience, strongly influenced by Protestant ethics and patriotic sentiments. Sapper attempted to deal with contemporary social issues but did so in a fairly ineffective manner. Her strongest attempt, the story *Im Thüringer Wald*, deals with the exploitation of homeworkers in the toy industry, but offers only a semi-miraculous cure for one family's problems; no suggestion for a possible solution to the area-wide problems is even hinted at. Nevertheless, thousands of children and adults alike enjoyed her stories of the Pfäffling family, a caring portrayal of a modest middle-class family in Germany at the turn of the century.

Works

Für kleine Mädchen (1892). *Die Mutter unter ihren Kindern* (1895). *Das erste Schuljahr* (1895). *Kuoni. Eine Geschichte aus dem 30 jährigen Krieg* (1896). *Gru von Rigi den Kindern daheim. Erzählungen für die Jugend* (1896). *Gretchen Reinwalds letztes Schuljahr* (1901). *Das kleine Dummerle, und andere Erzählungen zum Vorlesen im Familienkreise* (1904). *Die Familie Pfäffling* (1906). *Lieschens Streiche, und andere Erzählungen* (1907). *Frau Pauline Brater. Lebensbild einer deutschen Frau* (1908). *Werden und Wachsen: Erlebnisse der grossen Pfäfflingskinder* (1910). *Märchen. Für die Jugend ausgewählt von Agnes Sapper* (1911). *In der Adlerapotheke* (1911). *Mutter und Tochter* (1912). *Erziehen oder Werdenlassen* (1912). *Das Dienstmädchen* (1913). *Im Thüringerwald* (1914). *Kriegsbüchlein für unsere Kinder* (1914). *Ohne den Vater. Erzählung aus dem Krieg* (1915). *Ein geplagter Mann* (1916). *Urschele hoch. Ein Lustspiel für das Haustheater* (1916). *Das Enkelhaus* (1917). *Frieder: Die Geschichte vom kleinen Dummerle* (1920). *Valentin Andrea und sein Patenkind* (1922). *Der junge Gärtner* (1922). *Nach Hamburg* (1922). *In Not bewährt. Fünf neue Erzählungen* (1922). *Ein Gru an die Freunde meiner Bücher* (1922). *Der Vikar vom Heiligengrund* (1922). *In Wasserfluten* (1922). *Die Weihnachtskiste* (1924). *Regine Lenz. Ein geplagter Mann. Hoch droben: Drei Erzählungen aus Das kleine Dummerle* (1924). *Lilli. Erzählung aus dem Leben eines mutterlosen Kindes* (1924). *Johannes Ruhn. Feuerschau. Adlerapotheke: Drei Erzählungen aus Das kleine Dummerle* (1924). *Im Familienkreis. Kleine Lustspiele für die Jugend* (1926). *Ein Wunderkind und andere Erzählungen* (1926). *Die Heimkehr und andere Erzählungen aus Krieg und Frieden* (1938). Translations: *The First School Year* (1899).

Bibliography

Festschrift zum 70. Geburtstag (1922). Herding-Sapper, Agnes, *Agnes Sapper. Ihr Weg und ihr Wirken* (1931).

Hortense Bates

Sappho

Born c. 620 B.C., Eresus on Lesbos
Genre(s): poetry
Language(s): Greek

Although we possess a relatively large amount of biographical data about the supreme woman poet of antiquity, much of it may not be historically valid. Attic vase-paintings show that within a century of her lifetime Sappho had already become a figure of romantic legend; thus on a *kratēr* by the Brygos Painter she is shown rejecting the amorous lyric advances of her contemporary and fellow countryman Alcaeus. Fourth-century B.C. comic writers invented satiric details about her life that were incorporated into later biographies, such as the allegation that she was married to a wealthy trader from Andros called Cercylas (the name puns on *kerkis*, designating both the *plectrum* employed to strike the lyre strings and, on a subliterary level, the male sexual organ). They may also have manufactured the tale of her suicidal plunge from the cliff of Leucas prompted by unrequited love for the boatman Phaon—a story clearly occasioned by a lost Sapphic poem recounting Aphrodite's doomed passion for a mortal lover, either Phaon or his equally mythic counterpart Adonis (see fr. 211a-c Campbell).

Other biographical details, however, appear to be culled directly from Sappho's poetry. We are told that her mother's name was Cleis, and that she had one daughter, named after her grandmother (*POxy* 1800.1). In the surviving fragments the poet does mention her mother once (fr. 98a) and speaks of her daughter Cleis repeatedly (frr. 98b and 132; cf. 150 and 213A); as subject and addressee, the latter apparently played a prominent role in Sappho's compositions. A mutilated papyrus scrap (no. 14 in Campbell's collection of testimonia) informs us that Sappho wrote a poem about her brothers; their names, known from other sources, were Charaxus, Larichus, and Erigyius. As a youth,

Larichus performed the important function of pouring wine for the assembled committeemen in the town hall, an office held only by boys of high birth, and his sister commemorated this honor in her verse (fr. 203). The sensational story that she publicly castigated Charaxus for his affair with a courtesan is borne out by frr. 5 and 15, where she welcomes her brother home, laments his past errors, and wishes ill upon his mistress Doricha. It has been suggested, however, that the "errant brother" motif is an archaic Greek literary convention employed as a point of departure for moralizing blame poetry; this would explain why the poet is not ashamed to expose a family scandal.

Sappho composes for her female companions (fr. 160); some, like Atthis, are expressly singled out as addressees. The nature and purpose of this circle of listeners and her exact relationship to its members are subjects that have generated much controversy. Later antiquity imagined her a teacher of well-born young women, but Wilamowitz' chivalrous idea of Sappho as prim mistress of a girls' finishing school is an amusing anachronism. The current popular notion of her as leader of an organized female separatist group also conflicts with all we know of the behavior of women in the archaic Greek world. In reality, nothing in the fragments implies that Sappho's poetic activities or social situation were unusual for a woman of her rank. The Greek concept of song as quintessentially feminine, incarnated in such mythic emblems as sirens, sphinxes, and the nine Muses, permitted women to express themselves in choral dance and solo lyric performance and so prepared Sappho's male contemporaries to recognize and cherish a female poetic genius. Likewise, the evidence of social history suggests that at all temporal periods Greek women, though restricted in their dealings with men not blood relatives, freely interacted with other women in broadly-based same-sex networks and derived prestige and satisfaction from their position within such networks.

Sappho's lesbian thematics—her eloquent appreciations of female beauty and intense evocations of homosexual desire—can also be situated within her own social and historical context. Hallett correctly observes that her verse, like all archaic lyric, must have been intended as a public rather than a personal statement. It does not automatically follow, however, that the quasi-autobiographical confessions of passion in Sappho's poetry are wholly conventional, divorced from any private feeling. With its marked separation between men's and women's cultures, the society of archaic and classical Greece, while strongly patriarchal, seems to have been remarkably tolerant of deep emotional bonding and actual homoerotic relationships between women. Certainly Sappho's poetry would not have attained a widespread popularity throughout Greece or been collected and preserved by Alexandrian scholars had it expressed sentiments repugnant to Greek men. Thus, while this body of verse affords a distinctly female perspective upon reality and reflects a woman-identified consciousness, its presentation of women's experience must have conformed, at least in broad outline, to the expectations prevailing within the dominant culture.

The poems of Sappho are monodies, solo songs performed to the accompaniment of the lyre. Several characteristics set her work apart from that of male lyric poets: a preoccupation with intimate relationships and with the subjective emotional state of the speaker or her addressee; direct and familiar encounters with the divine world; personalized treatment of myth; and the subtle employment of sensual imagery, especially that of sight, sound, and touch. In particular, Sappho's concept of the erotic relationship is clearly distinguished from attitudes toward love found elsewhere in archaic Greek poetry. Male poets treat sexual activity as agonistic, fitting it to a pattern of dominance and submission in which the lover takes his keenest pleasure from the difficult pursuit and mastery of the unwilling beloved, whether boy or woman. Sappho depicts the ideal sexual encounter as egalitarian and reciprocal, with the participants displaying a like measure of desire and need for each other. She is fond of appropriating the language and conventions of Homeric combat scenes to portray the psychological tensions of the erotic situation, but her erotic wars are always struggles between equally matched combatants, and for her the female sphere of love and desire is as charged with the potential for sublime heroism as is the male sphere of military conflict. Many of the surviving fragments are imbued with an atmosphere of romantic yearning for a lost companion. In fr. 94, for example, the speaker urges remembrance of past happiness as a partial anodyne for the grief of separation. The girls who leave go unwillingly and long for their friends left behind (fr. 96). The circumstance behind these shattering departures was evidently an arranged marriage, the young woman being given no choice in the matter. Implicitly, then, Sappho depicts women's homoerotic love as precarious and fragile, readily sacrificed to patriarchal and heterosexual convenience: female lives are adequately lived only in the interstices of the public social structure.

Yet her poetry is not always romantically despondent; the fragments reveal that she devoted her creative energies to a remarkable variety of themes. Many of Sappho's songs invoke Aphrodite, sometimes in company with the Muses, and her single surviving complete text, the so-called "Ode to Aphrodite" (fr. 1), is a profound realization of the compelling personality of that goddess; similarly, fr. 2 summons Aphrodite to an imagined garden of sensual enchantment to join the speaker and her companions in feasting. Several citations make it clear that Sappho attacked other women in verse. While her targets are generally assumed to be sexual rivals, it appears that some polemics had political overtones (e.g., fr. 71), and the tradition of her exile in Sicily may have been prompted by outspoken denunciations of the female members of families hostile to her own. Finally, several short quotations from her *epithalamia* and the broken text of a lengthy description of the wedding procession of Hector and Andromache (fr. 44) indicate that she could represent marriage as a joyful occasion and write of heterosexual love with no less delicacy of feeling.

Works

Greek texts in *Poetarum Lesbiorum Fragmenta*, eds. E. Lobel and D.L. Page (Oxford, 1955). *Sappho et Alcaeus*, ed. E.-M. Voigt (Amsterdam, 1971). Texts, testimonia, and English translations in *Greek Lyric I*, tr. D.A. Campbell, Loeb Classical Library (Cambridge, Mass., and London, 1982).

Bibliography

Bowra, C.M., *Greek Lyric Poetry from Alcman to Simonides* (Oxford, 1961). Burnett, A.P., *Three Archaic Poets: Archilochus, Alcaeus, Sappho* (Cambridge, Mass., 1983). Dover, K.J., *Greek Homosexuality* (London, 1978). Page, D.L., *Sappho and Alcaeus* (Oxford, 1955). Snyder, J.M., *The Woman and the Lyre: Women Writers in Classical Greece and Rome* (Carbondale and Edwardsville, 1989). Wilamowitz-Moellendorff, U. von, *Sappho und Simonides* (Berlin, 1913).

General references: *Oxford Classical Dictionary* (Oxford, 1970), pp. 950–951. Pauly-Wissowa, *Real Encyclopädie der klassischen Altertumswissenschaft*, Ser. 2, I.2. (Stuttgart, 1920), pp. 2357–2385 and Supp. XI (Stuttgart, 1968), pp. 1222–1239.

Other references: Hallett, J., *Signs* 4 (1979): 447–464. Lefkowitz, M.R., *Greek, Roman and Byzantine Studies* 14 (1973): 113–123. Marry, J.D., *Arethusa* 12 (1979): 71–92. Merkelbach, R., *Philologus* 101 (1957): 1–29. Stehle, E.S., *Women's Studies* 8 (1981): 47–63. Winkler, J., *Women's Studies* 8 (1981): 65–91.

Marilyn B. Skinner

Manuela Saraiva de Azevedo

Born 1911, Lisbon, Portugal
Genre(s): poetry, short story, drama, essay
Language(s): Portuguese

Studied journalism. Her poetry expresses religious sentiment and her short stories deal with everyday themes. Her theatrical piece is rather melodramatic.

Works

Poetry: *Claridad* [Clarity] (1936). *Um Anjo Quase Demonio* [A Nearly Demonic Angel] (1945).

Short story: *Filhos do Diablo* [Children of the Devil] (1954). *Filhos de Deus* [Children of God] (n.d.).

Theater: *Camilo e Fanny* [Camilo and Fanny] (1957).

Essay: *"Amor de Perdiçao,"* a novela camiliana [Love of Perdition, the Camilian Novel], on Portuguese author Camilo Castelo Branco (1955).

Bibliography

Literatura Portuguesa Moderna, ed. M. Moisés (1973).

Paula T. Irvin

Galateia Sarantē

(a.k.a. Galateia Saranti)

Born 1920(?), Patras, Greece
Genre(s): novel, novella, short story, children's literature
Language(s): Greek

Galateia Sarantē studied law at the University of Athens but gave that up to devote her time to writing. She has written five novels, three novellas, three volumes of short stories, and several children's books. She has been recognized as an important figure in modern Greek literature and has received several awards for her work.

Her first book, *To vivlio tēs charas* (The Book of Joy), published in 1947, includes two short works, both of which deal with the theme of breaking up and going apart in male-female relationships. The potential union in each case is not quite achieved.

Her second published work, *To vivilio tou Giochanes kai tēs Marias* (The Book of Johannes and Maria), which was published in 1952 but first appeared in 1947 in *Nea Estia*, takes place during the Nazi occupation of Greece: A physician and his daughter take into their home a Jewish family. The young man, Johannes, falls in love with the physician's daughter, Maria, but his love remains pure and unrequited, for her heart is already given to another. In all three of these early works we find the seeds of what will mark her later writing: the delicate sensibility of the author reflected in the insightful portrayal of her characters; the lyrical flow of her prose; the nostalgia for family traditions and customs, her preoccupation with relationships. Her major characters are good people, above malice, hatred, and selfish interest, and many of her young people are idealists and dreamers with intellectual and spiritual yearnings.

In her *Paschalies* (Lilacs), *Epistrophē* (Return), and *To palio mas spiti* (Our Old Home), Sarantē lingers in the security of familiar surroundings seen against the background of World War II. *Paschalies* contrasts conditions in Greece before the war and afterwards as they affect one closely-knit family and their *patriko* home in the country where the lilacs bloom (or bloomed before they and the house were burned). It is a tale of love and war told from a female point of view. The main character is the youngest girl in the family, Lina, who has inclinations towards writing and in this most autobiographical of Sarantē's novels is probably a spokesman for the author herself.

The main character of *Epistrophē*, Anna Xerou, returns home after ten years of studying abroad and has to deal with problems of readjusting to conditions and situations in Greece after the war among physical, financial, and human ruins.

To palio mas spiti (Our Old Home) deals with two people, a brother and a sister, who try to keep their dignity and that of their family, despite the financial ruin of their father and many other misfortunes, including a broken engagement, a necessary end to the brother's studies, a broken heart, and the death of a loved one. They find strength and comfort in each other, and, although saddened, they are not completely defeated. The brother, a war veteran with a slight limp, finds peace in his books.

Her best-known novel, *Ta oria* (The Boundaries), published in 1966, deals with a woman who is rejected by a lover and, being the mother of a child and lacking the protection of a husband, becomes gradually estranged from society and eventually feels completely alienated.

In her short story "Elenē," published in her 1982 collection of short stories by the same title, Sarantē depicts a situation where the break-up of a "perfect" marriage is inevitable because of the childish concepts the marriage was based on.

Sarantē's strength and emphasis lie not in plot development but in the fine shadings of feeling. Her subtle portrayal of character, especially of the women characters, gives the reader a deep insight into human relationships. The world she describes is an inner world of thought and emotion. Unfortunately, sometimes this inner world becomes too abstract, her characters too good to be true, and their thoughts too indefinite and unspecific to be convincing. But, neverthe-less, her creations are memorable and sometimes disturbing, especially when she depicts the outsider within the group, the one who does not quite fit in. As the supportive family of her early period gives way to the alienating tendencies of modern society in her later work, one cannot help but notice the writer's personal development from "the way we would like things to be" to acceptance of "the way things are."

Works

Novels: *To vivlio tēs charas* [The Book of Joy] (1947). *Paschalies* [Lilacs] (1949, 1973). *To vivlio tou Giochanes kai tēs Marias* [The Book of Johannes and Maria] (1952). *Epistrophē* [Return] (1953). *To palio mas spiti* [Our Old Home] (1959). *Ta oria* [The Boundaries] (1966). *Rōgmes* (Cracks).

Short stories: *Chrōmata empistosynēs* [Colors of Trust] (1962). *Na Thymasai tē Vilna* [Remember Vilna] (1972). *Elenē: Diēgēmata* [Helenē: Short Stories] (1982).

Children's literature: *Sta chronia tou Pavlou Mela: To liontari kai to phidi* [In the Time of Pavlos Melas: The Lion and the Snake] (1962). *Charazei ē lephteria: Oi mparoutomyloi tēs Dēmētsanas* [Freedom Is Breaking: The Gunpowder Mills of Demetsana] (1971).

Translations: *Hilmu fataten*, Tr. Naiim Atia (1978). *Polawiacze Gabek. Antologia greckich opowiadań morskich.* Wybor, przekład, wstęp i aneks biograficzny Nikos Chadzinikolaou (1981). *Nygrekiska berättare.* Sammanställningoch översättning Senta Hadjópoulos Slöör (1964).

Bibliography

Manning, Clarence, Review. *Books Abroad* 28, 4 (1954): 493. *Bulletin analytique de bibliographie hellènique, 1972* (Athens, 1978). Mirasgezē, Maria, *Neoellenikē Logotechnia*, vol. 2 (Athens, 1982). Politis, Linos, *A History of Modern Greek Literature* (Oxford, 1973). Politis, Linos, *Historia tēs Neoellēnikēs Logotechnias*, 3rd ed. (Athens, 1978). Sachinēs, Apostolos, *Neoi Pezographoi* (Athens, 1965). Thrillos, Alkis, *Morfes tēs Hellēnikēs Pezographias* (Athens, 1970). Vitti, Mario, *Storia della Letteratura Neogreca* (Torino, 1971). Holton, David, Review,. *World Literature Today* 57, 4 (1983): 671.

Helen Dendrinou Kolias

Galateia Saranti

(see: Galateia Sarantē)

Margherita Sarfatti

*Born 1883, Venice, Italy; died 1961,
    Cavallasca near Como*
*Genre(s): journalism, essay, art criticism and
    theory, novel*
Language(s): Italian

Margherita Sarfatti's meteoric rise to the supreme arbiter of artistic taste during the first fifteen years of the Fascist regime in Italy and her abrupt fall from her powerful role illustrate the mercurial fortunes of talented individuals who choose to collaborate with dictatorships. Born to a Venetian Jewish family of distinguished lineage, she early became involved with her husband Cesare in the Socialist movement and joined the staff of that party's newspaper *Avanti!* as one of its art critics. But in 1915 Sarfatti grew disgusted with the pacifism of the Italian Socialist Party and broke with it to agitate for Italy's entry into the First World War on the side of the Allies against the Central Powers. Ironically she was to lose her son Roberto (1900–1918) in that very war. In turning against the Socialists and supporting participation in the war, Sarfatti was actively working with Benito Mussolini as he established his bellicose newspaper *Il Popolo d'Italia*, in 1915. Serving as the art critic for *Il Popolo d'Italia*, Margherita Sarfatti entered into a romantic liaison with the future dictator. After Mussolini founded the Fascist Party in 1919 to counter the threat of a Socialist revolution in Italy following the general disillusionment of World War One, Sarfatti joined the Fascist ranks that by the Fall of 1922 took control of the nation with the march on Rome.

Along with Mussolini himself, Margherita Sarfatti co-directed the Fascist Party's official monthly journal *Gerarchia*. Her journalistic pursuits led her to write the book *Tunisiaca* in 1924 on the conditions of Italians living in Tunisia, a region whose political control Italy had disputed with France since the late nineteenth century. Even after her romantic involvement with the womanizing dictator had ended, Sarfatti remained one of the Fascist Party's foremost spokespersons, especially through the officially sanctioned biography of the ruler that first appeared in English in 1925 as *The Life of Mussolini* and later in Italian as *Dux*. But her most important role was as art critic, aesthetic theorist, and organizer of major exhibitions. Although the Fascists came to power with the enthusiastic support of the ultra-modernistic Futurists like Tommaso Filippo Marinetti who longed to demolish the out-moded monuments of Italy's past to construct a dynamic new art, by the mid-1920s the Duce's desire to regain for the country the greatness of the ancient Roman Empire resulted in a conservative fashion in art that led to a taste in sculpture for muscular heroic statuary, to a severe imperial Roman style in architecture, and a revived classicism in painting. Unlike the Nazis who in the 1930s would violently suppress all adherents of Modernism as decadentists, the Italian Fascist art critics generally tolerated non-rhetorical and Modernist artists so long as they never openly defied the regime. As the most prominent art theorist of the period, Margherita Sarfatti in texts like *Segni, colori e luci* (1925) and *Storia della pittura moderna* (1930) cultivated the idea of "the Italian tradition in art": centuries-held practices of rendering tone, relief, and chiaroscuro together with a Mediterranean feeling for composition and placing in space. Sarfatti in particular emphasized the importance of the human figure in art as being sacred to the Italian tradition. But Sarfatti was willing to acknowledge, if only in a cursory manner, the work of one of the most unrhetorical of painters and etchers: the Bolognese recluse Giorgio Morandi (1890–1964), whom she invited to take part in the first exhibition of the Novecento Group (Twentieth-Century Artists) in 1926 and then again in 1929 even though the human figure was not one of his preoccupations as an artist. Above all, Sarfatti sought to awaken Italians to a pride in the country's cultural heritage.

Beginning in 1936 Mussolini came to identify the aims of his regime with those of Italy's military ally Nazi Germany. An ideological *rapprochement* with Nazi racial policies led to the passage by the Fascist Grand Council in autumn 1938 of anti-Semitic laws defining Jews as "Italian citizens of the Hebrew race." Banished from the

Fascist Party and removed from all her official posts, Margherita Sarfatti took exile in the United States. Her autobiographical text *Acqua Passata* of 1955 attempts to survey the era of her youth and the individuals who played major roles during that period.

Works

La fiaccola accessa (1917). *Tunisiaca* (1924). *The Life of Mussolini* (1925) (*Dux*, Milan, 1926). *Segni, colori e luci* (1925). *Il palazzone* (1929). *Storia della pittura moderna* (1930). *Segni del meridiano* (1931). *Daniele Ranzone* (1935). *Casanova contro Don Giovanni* (1950). *Acqua passata* (1955).

Bibliography

Giorgio Morandi, ed. James Demetrion (Des Moines, 1981). Picchio, C., *Il Mattino* (March 27, 1956). Villaroel, G., *Giornale d'Italia* (March 10, 1950).

Douglas Radcliff-Umstead

Nathalie Sarraute

Born 1900, Ivanovo-Voznessensk, Russia
Genre(s): novel, essay, drama
Language(s): French

Nathalie Sarraute was born in Ivanovo-Voznessensk, Russia, in 1900. She grew up in a milieu of Russian intellectuals: her mother published numerous novels under a masculine pseudonym, and her father, an industrialist, encouraged her interest in scholarly achievements. Her parents divorced when Nathalie was just two. She spent her early childhood with her mother in France and spent vacations with her father in Russia and Switzerland. When she was eight, she moved to Paris with her father and lived with him and her stepmother permanently.

Nathalie Sarraute was a brilliant student at the Sorbonne (B.A. in English), at Oxford (where she started a B.A. in history), and Berlin (where she studied sociology), and was fluent in Russian, French, German, and English. In 1922 she entered the University of Paris Law School, where she met Raymond Sarraute, whom she married three years later. She was a member of the Paris bar from 1925 to 1941, and had three daughters.

In 1932 she wrote a few texts which she published in 1939 as *Tropismes* (Tropisms). Her work had a favorable welcome from Jean-Paul

Sartre and Max Jacob but otherwise was unnoticed. During the Second World War, she hid from the Germans in a little town near Paris. She took the name of Nicole Sauvage, and posed as her own daughters' governess. During the war she met Jean-Paul Sartre, who wrote the preface for her second novel, *Portrait d'un Inconnu* (Portrait of a Man Unknown), finished in 1946.

Although she refuses this label to her work (or any other label), Nathalie Sarraute is considered a pioneer of the "New Novel" school. Like the other writers of this school, she demands an active collaboration from the reader, reflects on the creative act that produces the work within the work itself, and uses new methods aimed at renewal of the genre of the novel. Her many theoretical essays present literature as a search for new ways of perceiving reality and insist that form cannot be separated from content. She sees the work of art as an entity in itself, and creating constitutes an end in itself. Thus she does not believe in any didactic use of literature, even for worthwhile causes (this disinvolvement among the New Novelists has caused the most passionate objections from their critics).

Sarraute's work is based on human sensations and relationships although she offers no moral lessons. The reader has to perceive reality through the anonymous "characters'" consciousness, rearrange a fragmented reality, and supply the missing elements of the text (missing words, unfinished sentences, mixture of "real" and imaginary scenes, repetition of the same scenes through different points of view). The suppression of plot and chronology, the disappearance of narrative discourse gives way to immediate, spontaneous, and ordinary dialogues (conversations and "subconversations") between undefined, interchangeable characters presented as "she," "he," "I" or "we."

Whereas the New Novelists have an obsession with objective description (in which the critics see an aim to the "reification" of the external world), Sarraute's work is centered on what Robbe-Grillet has called a "psychology of the depth," or interior movements and changes. Her earliest novels presented the tensions and conflicts threatening family members. Her later works unmask the danger of social fear, ignorance, and intolerance for individuals. In her latest novel, *Enfance* (Childhood), for the first time in eighty-three years, she explores her own "tropisms," her own contradictory feelings, by writing about her childhood and her personal relationships with her father, mother, and stepmother. As in her other works (and this has been a reproach often made to her) she talks only about herself, but more openly, and even more deeply. She unveils what hides human anxiety (certitudes, hopes, traditions, dogma), and speaks to and about every human being. According to Claude Mauriac, she, "of all living writers, is the one who has most profoundly and fundamentally renewed our knowledge of mankind." Her works have been translated into 23 languages.

Works

Tropismes (1939). *Portrait d'un Inconnu* (1948). *Martereau* (1953). *Le Planetarium* (1959). *Les Fruits d'or* (1963). *Le silence*, suivi de *Le Mensonge* (1967). *Entre la vie et la mort* (1968). *Isma*, suivi de *Le Silence et Le Mensonge* (1970). *Vous les entendez* (1972). *C'est beau* (1973). *Disent les imbéciles* (1976). *Elle est là* (1978). *Enfance* (1983).

Bibliography

Allemand, André, *L'Oeuvre romanesque de Nathalie Sarraute* (Neuchâtel, 1980). Besser, Gretchen Rous, *Nathalie Sarraute* (Boston, 1979). Blot, Jean, *Nathalie Sarraute. Une fine buée* (Paris, 1968). Bory, Jean-Louis, "Le Sapeur Sarraute." *Le Nouvel Observateur* (December 6, 1976). Bouraoui, Henri A., "Sarraute's Narrative Portraiture: The Artist in Search of a Voice." *Critique* XIV (1972–1973). Bouraoui, Henri A., "Silence ou Mensonge: Dilemme du nouveau romancier dans le théâtre de Nathalie Sarraute." *French Review* XLV, Special issue No. 4 (1972). Butor, Michel, "*Le Planétarium*: le jeu compliqué des paroles et des silences." *Arts* (June 3–9, 1959). Cagnon, Maurice, "*Le Planetarium*, quelques aspects stylistiques." *French Review* XL (1967). Calin, Françoise, *La Vie retrouvée, étude de l'oeuvre romanesque de Nathalie Sarraute* (Paris, 1976). Cohn, Ruby, "Nathalie Sarraute's Sub-*consciouversations*." *Modern Language Notes* LXXVIII (1963). Contesse, André, "L'imagination chez Nathalie Sarraute. La dialectique du fluide et du solide." *Etude de lettres* NS 6 (1963). Cranski, Mimica, and Belaval, Yvon, *Nathalie Sarraute* (Paris, 1965). Eliez-Rüegg, Elisabeth, *La Conscience d'autrui et la conscience des objets dans l'oeuvre de Nathalie Sarraute* (Berne, 1972). Finas, Lucette, "Nathalie Sarraute ou les métamorphoses du verbe." *Tel Quel* 20 (1965). Galey, Matthieu, "Sarraute spéléologue." *L'Express* (October 4–10, 1976). Goldman, Lucien, *Pour une sociologie du roman* (Paris, 1964). Grobe, Edwin P., "Symbolic Sound Patterns in Nathalie Sarraute's *Martereau*." *French Review* XL (1967). Jaccard, Jean-Luc, *Nathalie Sarraute*, thesis (Zurich, 1967). Janvier, Ludovic, *Une Parole exigeante: Le nouveau roman* (Paris, 1964). Knapp, Bettina L., "Interview avec Nathalie Sarraute." *Kentucky Romance Quarterly* XIV (1967). Magny, Claude-Edmonde, "Retour au paganisme." *Littérature et Critique* (Paris, 1971). Mauriac, Claude, "Nathalie Sarraute." *L'Allittérature contemporaine* (Paris, 1969). Micha, René, *Nathalie Sarraute* (Paris, 1966). Minogue, Valérie, "Nathalie Sarraute's *Le Planétarium*. The Narrator Narrated." *Forum for Modern Language Studies* IX (1973). Minor, Anne, "Nathalie Sarraute. *Le Planétarium*." *Yale French Studies* 14 (1959). Newman, A.S., *Une Poésie des discours. Essai sur les romans de Nathalie Sarraute* (Genève, 1976). Nourissier, François, "*Vous les entendez?* par Nathalie Sarraute." *Les Nouvelles Littéraires* (March 6–12, 1972). Picon, Gaetan, "*Le Planétarium*." *Mercure de France* 1151 (July 1959). Pingaud, Bernard, "Le Personnage dans l'oeuvre de Nathalie Sarraute." *Preuves* 154 (1963). Poirot-Delpech, Bertrand, "*Disent les imbéciles*, de Nathalie Sarraute." *Le Monde* (September 24, 1976). Racevskis, Karlis, "Irony as a Creative and Critical Force in Three Novels of Nathalie Sarraute." *The French Review* LI, No. 1 (October 1977). Raillard, Georges, "Nathalie Sarraute et la violence du texte." *Littérature* 2 (1971). Suzuki, Shingeo, "L'art de la composition dans les oeuvres de Nathalie Sarraute." *Etudes de Langue et de Littérature Française* XII (1968). Temple, Ruth Z., *Nathalie Sarraute* (New York, London, 1968). Tison Braun, Micheline, "L'Art de la stylisation chez Sarraute." *Nouveau Roman: Hier, Aujourd'hui* (Paris, 1972), vol. 2. Tison Braun, Micheline, *Nathalie Sarraute ou La Recherche de l'Authenticité.* (Paris, 1971). Whiting, Charles G., "Nathalie Sarraute moraliste." *French Review* XLIII (1970). Wunderli-Mueller, Christine B., *Le Thème du masque et les Banalités dans l'oeuvre de Nathalie Sarraute*, thesis (Zurich, 1970) Zeitner, Gerda, "Nathalie Sarraute et l'impossible réalisme." *Mercure de France* 1188

(1962). Zeitner, Gerda, "Quelques phrases au narrateur du *Portrait d'un Inconnu* de Sarraute." *Les Cahiers du Chemin* XIII (1971).

Michèle M. Magill

Albertine Sarrazin

Born 1937, Algiers; died 1967
Genre(s): novel
Language(s): French

In September 1937, a newborn baby was abandoned at the "Bureau d'Assistance Publique" in Algiers. She was named Albertine Damien. At age two she was adopted by a middle-aged couple. As an adolescent, she was a brilliant student, but undisciplined, and her adoptive parents decided to place her at *Le Bon Pasteur*. She escaped from this school of correction and hitch-hiked to Paris, where she became a prostitute. Hoping to give up that kind of life, she attempted a hold-up that failed, and was condemned to seven years in prison. She escaped by jumping over a wall, and broke the bone called "l'astragale" (astragalus), which is the title of her most famous work. A passer-by, Julien Sarrazin, helped her, hid and nursed her: two years later they got married. They both spent much of their time in prison, and though their life together was brief, their love has become legendary.

While in jail, Albertine wrote two novels, *La Cavale* (On the Run), and *L'Astragale*, which instantly became best-sellers in the fall of 1965. In 1966, she received the Prix des Quatre-Jurys in Tunis. Her works are mainly autobiographical: they evoke her life in jail and its boredom, and her thirst and passion for life when she is free. The themes of love, desire, and death are dominant in all of them. Though writing was always a passion for her, it became her way of escaping beyond the bars, if only in her mind, and gave her a sense of freedom she may not have found otherwise.

Her happiness, money and fame were short-lived: on July 10th, 1967, she died during surgery in Montpellier. She was not yet thirty. Her husband sued the doctors, who were found guilty of grave negligence. With the money, he opened a publishing house for the unedited texts left by Albertine.

Since her death, her work has inspired many critical studies and dissertations, in France and abroad. Albertine the novelist, the poet, the moralist might even be surpassed by the epistolarian. Her letters to Julien and her friends, written quickly and spontaneously, reveal a style as refined as in her other texts. The abandoned child of Algiers is now considered a true classical writer, whose liveliness, originality, humor and courage are widely admired.

Works

Journal de Prison (1959). *La Cavale* (1965). *L'Astragale* (1965). *La Traversière* (1966). *Oeuvres* (novels, letters, poems) (1967). *Poèmes* (1969). *Lettres à Julien 1958–1960* (1971). *Lettres de la Vie Littéraire* (1974). *Bibiche* (short story). *Le Passe-Peine* (diary) 1949–1967 (1976). *Biftons de Prison* (1977).
Articles: *Les Lettres Françaises* (Jan. 1967; July 1967; July 1969; June 1972). *Le Figaro Littéraire* (Nov. 11, 1965; Dec. 1, 1966; July 17, 1967; May 20, 1972). *Le Magazine Littéraire* (Dec. 1972; March 1972). *Les Nouvelles Littéraires* (March 1966; July 1967). *L'Express* (Jan. 2–8, 1967; December 18–22, 1968). Revue des *Deux-Mondes* (Jan. 1966; Jan. 1969). The *Times Literary Supplement* (Feb. 3, 1966; Jan. 12, 1967). The New York *Times Book Review* (June 9, 1968, Jan. 1966). *Esprit* (Jan. 1966). *Réalités* (Nov. 1965). Le *Monde* (Jan. 13, 1967). Elle (Feb. 7, 1972.)
Translations in almost twenty languages. L'Astragale was adapted for cinema by G. Casaril in 1968 and *La Cavale* by M. Mitroni in 1971.

Bibliography

Duranteau J., *Albertine Sarrazin* (Paris). Meyer, Ursula, *Albertine Sarrazin: pathetische und ironische Elemente im Gesellschaftsbild der Autorin und in ihrer Selbstdarstellung* (Konstanz, 1984).

Michèle M. Magill

Sataniski

(see: Alexandra Papadopoulou)

Victoria Sau Sánchez

Born 1930, Barcelona, Spain
Genre(s): essay, sociopolitical treatise,
    children's fiction
Language(s): Spanish

A professor of psychology at the Central University in Barcelona, Sau has an active career as a writer, public speaker, and feminist (who acknowledges the influence of Simone de Beauvoir and Betty Friedan). She is also a practicing psychologist in Barcelona and founder of a group with the somewhat inscrutable title of "Permanent Investigative Seminar for New Women's Psychology." She has done little "creative" writing beyond her children's books (and several of these appear to be adaptations of Russian and Yugoslav legends). Other titles unrelated to her profession include what appear to be domestic manuals: La decoración del holgar (1967; Home Decoration) and Aprende a cocinar sin errores (1977, Learn to Cook Without Mistakes). Other miscellaneous volumes treat such themes as religion, popular songs, and Catalan separatism: Sectas cristianas (1971; Christian Sects), Historia antropológica de la canción (1972; Anthropological History of Song), El catalán, un bandolerismo español (1973; Catalanism as Spanish Banditry).

Manifiesto para la liberación de la mujer (1975; Manifesto for Womens' Liberation) includes an extensive background study of women's issues and feminine types, examining such themes as marriage, adultery, incest, prostitution, and virginity and analyzing various archetypes including the witch, the old maid, the priestess/prophet, the devourer of men, and the frigid woman. Mujer: matrimonio y esclavitud (1976; Woman: Marriage and Slavery) criticizes marriage as an institution—social, economic, and sexual—in which woman is an unequal and disenfranchised partner, lacking freedom for personal realization. La suegra (1976; The Mother-in-Law) is an extension of Sau's analysis of types, although she begins at the commencement of the life cycle (each mother-in-law was once a naive, romantic bride, then a young mother and perhaps a disillusioned wife, often making of her children her major reason for living, only to find that if she succeeds in raising her charges, they marry and leave, making her a suegra). And as a mother-in-law, she has become a negative stereotype, feared and unloved, traditional rival of the bride, in a self-renewing cycle with each generation. Mujeres lesbianas (1979; Lesbians) provides a historical overview of lesbianism, especially insofar as it is also a political phenomenon, studies ideological differences between lesbians and gays, and identifies relationships between feminism and lesbianism. Un diccionario ideológico feminista (1981; A Feminist Ideological Dictionary) attempts to provide feminist definitions of significant terms related to family relationships, sexuality, sexual politics, and other concepts necessary for the analysis or understanding of male-female relationships, of dominance and exploitation, and the scientific explanation of these.

Works

Aprede a cocinar sin errores (1977). El baúl viajero (1973). El catalán, un bandolerismo español (1973). La decoración del hogar (1967). Un diccionario ideológico feminista (1981). La duquesa resfriada. Leyenda rusa (1973). El globo (1973). Historia antropológica de la canción (1972). Manifiesto para la liberación de la mujer (1975). Mujer: matrimonio y esclavitud (1976). Mujeres lesbianas (1979). El secreto del emperador, adaptación de una leyenda yugoslava (1973). Sectas cristianas (1971). La suegra (1976).

Janet Perez

Louise de Savoie

Born 1476, Pont-d'Ain, France; died 1531,
    Grez, France
Genre(s): journal, poetry
Language(s): French

Louise de Savoie is one of the premier figures of the French Renaissance and of the royal family. She was the daughter of Philip, Duke of Savoy and of Marguerite of Bourbon. She was married to Charles of Orleans, Duke of Angoûleme and was the mother of Francis I (born 1494) as well as Marguerite de Navarre (1492). Charles died in 1496, leaving Louise a widow at the age of nineteen. When she was left alone with her children, strong bonds of affection and loyalty developed, and they were later to be known as the "Trinity." She twice served as Regent of France during Francis' Italian campaign in 1515 and again beginning in 1525. Throughout her life she exercised considerable political power. In 1529, she spoke for Francis in peace negotiations with Marguerite of Austria, who was representing the Emperor Charles V. The Treaty of Cambray is still known as the "Peace of the Ladies."

In many ways Louise de Savoie is nearly eclipsed by her children. The scope of her literary contributions and their merit do not match those of her daughter, nor even those of her son. Yet it is surely she who provided the model for their development. Her interest in the arts and in letters as a patron was well known. She would often commission works, including the reproduction of manuscripts for her private library. The *Chants royaux* (Royal Songs) reproduced at her request in 1517 is typical. Louise composed works of her own as well. While her poetry is conventional, it is a precious testimony of the spirit of the Renaissance when an exchange of poems was as common as an exchange of letters, and an educated woman could express herself in verse with ease and grace. Louise's *Journal*, a brief account in an almost telegraphic style records some of the major events in her life, testifies to her devotion to her son (the majority of the entries concern him), and is an invaluable source of historic information.

Works

Journal de Louise de Savoie in Histoire généologique de la royale maison de Savoie (1660). *Poésies du roi François I, de Louise de Savoie, duchesse d'Angoûlème, de Marguerite de Navarre* (1847).

Bibliography

Jacqueton, Gilbert, *La Politique extérieure de Louise de Savoie; relations diplomatiques de la France et l'Angleterre pendant la captivité de François I (1525–1526)* (Paris: E. Bouillon, 1899). Maulde de la Clavière, Marie Alphonse René de, *Louise de Savoie et François Ier, trente ans de jeunesse (1485–1515)* (Paris, 1895).

Edith J. Benkov

Marguerite de Savoy

Born June 5, 1523, Saint-Germain-de-Laye, France; died 1574?
Genre(s): poetry, letters
Language(s): French

Born at Saint-Germain-de-Laye on June 5, 1523, Marguerite was the daughter of the French king Francis I (1494–1547) and of Claude (1499–1524). Even before Claude's death the year after Marguerite was born, Francis had been strongly influenced by his sister Marguerite of Angoulême, who admired Petrarch and Erasmus and who became a patron of various contemporary writers, including Rabelais. Accordingly, Francis entrusted Marguerite's upbringing to his sister, whose intelligence and broad-mindedness made a great impression on her young niece.

Marguerite was four years younger than her brother Henry II (1519–1559). Henry succeeded their father Francis on the throne in 1547 but was killed twelve years later in a tournament accident during a celebration of the Treaty of Cateau-Cambrésis. Marguerite was thirty-six at the time of her brother's death, the same year that she married the Duke of Savoy, Emmanuel-Philibert. Her marrying for the first time at this age was the occasion of pointed remarks at the court but, ironically, the marriage was a condition of the Treaty of Cateau-Cambrésis signed by her brother Henry and Philip II of Spain. A further irony is that, although by marrying Emmanuel-Philibert Marguerite became the Duchesse of Savoy, the Treaty whose celebration occasioned Henry's death caused France to renounce its claim to Savoy, thus considerably reducing Marguerite's new land holdings. She was also known as Marguerite of France.

Influenced by her celebrated aunt, Marguerite developed an early love of learning and art. At the court of her brother she supported the incipient efforts of the Pléiades, the progressive "Brigade" of seven poets headed by Pierre de Ronsard (1524–1585). Committed to renewing the language through the introduction of Greek and Latin vocabulary, the Pléiades found in Marguerite an influential patron who could shelter them from the assaults of reactionary critics. Similarly, at the court of Turin, she fostered the endeavors of many literary figures, extending her patronage to poets who demonstrated innovative uses of language. She was thus an instrumental figure in a limited but important linguistic revolution. She also wrote poetry, but her primary personal contribution is her letters, which first drew editorial interest in the nineteenth century.

Bibliography

Loutchisky, Jean, and Jacque-Philippe Tamizey de Larroque, *Marguerite de France: Lettres inédits* (Rev. hist., 1881), vol. 16, p. 304; vol. 17, p. 89.

Cory L. Wade

Alessandra Scala

Born 1475, Florence, Italy; died 1506,
   Florence
Genre(s): poetry
Language(s): classical Greek

As the fifth and youngest daughter of Bartolomeo Scala, author and prominent chancellor in the government of Lorenzo de' Medici, Alessandra Scala grew up in daily contact with the literati and the influential of Florentine society. She was educated at the Studio Fiorentino under the tutelage of Giano Lascari, Demetrio Calcondila, and Angelo Poliziano, from whom she gained an excellent knowledge of Greek and Latin. She became celebrated for her charm and beauty as well as for her knowledge and intelligence. In 1493, at the age of eighteen, she earned high praise for her outstanding performance in the title role of Sophocles' *Electra* in the original Greek. Both Lascari and Poliziano courted her avidly. Poliziano wrote several Greek epigrams in praise of her beauty, grace, and intellect, incorporating no small number of double entendres, his compliments hiding other meanings. Poliziano offered his courtship and praise despite his age, his vow of celibacy as a priest, and his animosity toward Scala's father. She responded with epigrams of her own, one of which is still highly regarded for its graciousness. Poliziano probably introduced Scala and her father to the Venetian humanist Cassandra Fedele, with whom she conducted a long correspondence. Ultimately, she married the roving Greek soldier-poet Michele Marullo Tarcaniota. Through him, she encountered other poets and humanists and traveled to other principalities in Italy. When, in 1500, her husband drowned while attempting to ford the Cecina River near Volterra, Scala retired to the convent at San Pier Maggiore in Florence, where she died six years later.

Works

"Epigramma greco," in Poliziano, Angelo, *Prose volgari inedite e poesie latine e greche.*, ed. Isodoro del Lungo (1867).

Bibliography

Bignone, A., "A Proposito di alcuni epigrammi greci di Poliziano." *Studi italiani di folologia classica* IV (1927), pp. 392–397. Brown, Alison, *Bartolomeo Scale, 1430–1497; Chancellor of Florence* (Princeton, N.J., 1979), pp. 210–212, 246–247. Del Longo, Isidoro, *La Donna fiorentina del buon tempo antico* (Florence, 1906), pp. 187–190. Pesenti, Giovanni, "Alessandra Scala: una figurina di rinascenza fiorentina." *Giornale storico della letteratura italiana* LXXXV (1925), pp. 241–264.

Stanley Longman

Nine van der Schaaf

Born 1882, Friesland; died 1973
Genre(s): poetry, novel
Language(s): Dutch

An important yet somewhat neglected representative of Dutch Neo-Romanticism and Symbolism. Her later work is more realistic in vision.

Having earned her living first as a maid servant and then as a primary school teacher, Nine van der Schaaf later devoted herself entirely to literature, producing poetry and prose that was greatly admired by the foremost critics of her day, P.N. van Eyck and Albert Verwey, though not by a wide readership.

Her first collection of poems, *Gedichten* (1917; Poems), drew the attention of van Eyck who hailed van der Schaaf as one of the finest and most original poets in modern Holland. In *Gedichten* she gives expression to her dreams of a new, happy world saturated with and animated by eternity, an eternity that is complete in the human moment, in our humanity, which blooms forth out of eternity. Love is the inspiring force of life, the universe, the individual, and of humanity as a whole, which has not yet attained the fullness of love. The lengthy rhymeless lines of these verses lack poetic force, however. The second collection, *Naar het onzichtbare* (1929; Toward the Invisible) is equally pure in inspiration but technically weak.

The characters of her novels *Santos en Cypra* (1906) and *Amanie en Brodo* (1908) move in a realm of almost unlimited imagination in which the author introduces sporadically some facts that refer to a reality familiar to the reader. Yet many associations are deeply personal and difficult to decode.

In her later work this exalted imagination makes place for a more realistic vision (as in her memories of village life in Friesland: *Friesch dorpsleven*, 1921) or for stories in which fantasy and historical fact are fused into a fictional whole, as in *Het leven van Karel de Stoute* (1938; The Life of Charles the Bold).

Works

Poetry: *Gedichten* (1917). *Naar het onzichtbare* (1929).

Prose: *Santos en Cypra* (1906). *Amanie en Brodo* (1908). *Friesch dorpsleven* (1921; rpt as *Heerk Walling*, 1936). *De uitvinder* (1932). *De liefde van een dwaas* (1937). *Het leven van Karel de Stoute* (1938). *Een vrouw van de Vlecke* (1947). *In de stroom* (1956). *De tovenaar* (1957).

Bibliography

Eyck, P.N. van, *De Beweging* II (1917): 294–298; 342–351. Donker, Anthonie, *Critisch Bulletin* (Sept. 1932). Knuvelder, Gerard, *Handboek tot de geschiedenis der Nederlandse letterkunde*, 2nd ed., vol. 4 (Amsterdam, 1961), pp. 332–334. Romein-Verschoor, Annie, *De Nederlandse romanschrijfster na 1880* (Utrecht, 1935), p. 102. Uyldert, Maurits, *De Beweging* III (1907), p. 86. Verwey, Albert, *Proza* I, pp. 132–150; *Proza* III, pp. 151–172.

Maya Bijvoet

Renate Schaider

Born 1943, Graz, Austria
Genre(s): short story, journalism, translation
Language(s): German

Renate Schaider, an aspiring and versatile author of short prose, is a native of Graz, a city considered by many critics to be the "literature capital" of the German-speaking countries. After completing a Ph.D. and teaching in Turkey for six years, Schaider currently is a university instructor and a freelance journalist as well as a writer and translator.

Schaider has written mostly short stories, many of which were broadcast on Austrian national radio and have appeared in various anthologies. Schaider's prose shows affinities with authors as diverse as Joseph Roth, Franz Kafka, Ernest Hemingway, and Gabriel García Márquez. Rooted in an Austrian tradition, Schaider, in her work, combines fantastic, grotesque, even macabre elements with a social message and a touch of feminism.

Works

"Der Garten" (1984). "Mord nicht ausgeschlossen" (1985). "Die Tür" (1986). "Melchisedich" (1986). "Der Mayr mu weg" (1987).

Jürgen Koppensteiner

Jeanne Gabrielle van Schaik-Willing

(a.k.a. Gabrielle van Loenen)

Born October 8, 1885, Amsterdam, The
Netherlands; died October 1, 1984
Genre(s): drama, novel
Language(s): Dutch

Using the pseudonym Gabrielle van Loenen, J.G. van Schaik-Willing was a drama critic for the *Mosgroene*; later she wrote under her own name for *De Groene Amsterdanner* (1952–1966). She published a collection of her critical articles in *Na afloop* (1959; For the Outcome) for which she received Amsterdam's essay prize in 1959. The city awarded her another essay prize in 1966 for *Uit de stalles* (1966; Out of the Stables). Her novels, stories, and plays have strong visual effects. She has a creative imagination and a fatalistic outlook on life.

Works

De sloof [The Apron] (1924). *Appassionata* (1926). *Mannequin* (1927). *Een verloren vrouwe* [A Lost Lady] (1927). *De jeugd van president Schuyler* [A President is Born] (1927). *Parachute* (1929). *De roman van een Amerikaansch meisje* [Stardust] (1929). *Millioenen* [Five and Ten] (1930). *De vrouw in de schaduw* [Backstreet] (1932). *Uitstel van executie* [Delay of Execution] (1932). *Langs het leven* [Imitation of Life] (1933). *Sofie Blank* (1934). *Anitra's dans* [Anitra's Dance] (1935). *Nachtvorst* [Groundfrost] (1936). *Hun toevlucht* [Great Laughter] (1937). *Uitgestelde vlucht* [Postponed Getaway] (1938). *De zondaar en het meisje* [The Sinner and the Girl] (1938). *Vier dochters* [Sister Act] (1939). *Free People* (1945). *Er wordt geklopt* [Someone Knocked] (1947). *Leerschool* [Training College] (1947). *De Overnachting* [Overnight Stay] (1947). *Het Portret* [The Portrait] (1948). *Marmer en abrikosen* [Marble and Apricots] (1949). *Een reis naar Roussillon* [A Trip to Rossillon] (1949). *De witte veren* [The White Feather] (1949). *Odysseus weent* [Odysseus Weeps] (1953). *De feesten van Josien* [The Feasts of Josien] (1953). *Ondanks alles* [In Spite of Everything] (1955).

Bibliography

Kelk, C.J., *Rondom tien gestalten* (1938). Romein-Verschoor, A., *Vrouwenspiegel* (1935).

Adolf von Württemberg

Zinaïda Schakovskoy

(a.k.a. Jacques Croisé)

Born 1906, Moscow, Russia
Genre(s): history, novel, lyric poetry, literary criticism, journalism
Language(s): Russian, French

The epic nature of her life story puts Zinaïda Schakovsky into that rare category of writers who feel equally at ease in two languages for their creative medium. As a descendant of an ancient Russian aristocratic family she became a fugitive from her home country after the 1917 revolution. Princess Zinaïda Schakovsky completed her studies in Belgium and France, half starving and supporting herself by working at odd jobs. Simultaneously, she participated vigorously in French and Russian émigré literary circles contributing regularly, since the mid-twenties, to major French, Belgian and Russian émigré literary journals. With her husband Sviatoslav de Malévsky-Malévitch, painter and diplomat, Zinaïda Schakovsky has lived in most European countries, in North Africa, North America and the USSR, while making her permanent home in Paris. During World War II Schakovskoy worked in the *Service de Santé de l'Armée française* but went underground in 1941, and became a war correspondent in London. For her services in the underground movement she has been decorated with the *Croix des Évadés* (Belgium); she has been elected *Officier de la Légion d'honneur* and *Officier des Arts et Lettres*. Since 1956 in charge of cultural programs at the *Radio-Télévision Française* Schakovskoy also became editor-in-chief of the weekly *Russian Thought*, 1968–1978, and raised this journal to its former first-rate standards. In 1981, she started the new literary *Russian Almanac* in Paris in collaboration with émigré fellow writers. She is a member of the *Institut des Hautes Études Slaves* at the Sorbonne, of the *Société des Écrivains Français*, the PEN Club, the Syndicate of French critics.

Her subtle lyric voice made itself heard both in Russian and in French. Three collections of poetry in Russian appeared in, respectively, 1934, 1935, and 1970; her French volume of poetry, *Insommies*, was published in 1937.

Between 1937–1967 four novels and several volumes of memoirs and historical works were published in French. In 1949 she was awarded the Writer's Premium of Paris and was twice prize winner of the *Académie Française* for her historical works. Many of the books written originally in French were translated into several languages including Chinese. Three volumes of literary memoirs and criticisms appeared in Russian 1978–1979.

Schakovskoy is most representative of those many gifted émigré women writers who defied the odds of fate at a time when, in her own words, "the Russian muse was destitute and abandoned as never before in history." Like some of her fellow female poets and writers, she made it a point to join in the culture of her new surroundings and to familiarize the West with the Russian cultural and spiritual heritage and make it part of world civilization.

Works

In Russian: *Ukhod* [Farewell], poems (1934). *Doroga* [The Road], poems (1935). *Pered snom* [Before Sleep], poems (1970). *Otrazhenia* [Reflections]. literary memoirs (1978). *Rasskazy, stat'i, stikhi* [Stories, Articles, Poems] (1978). *V poiskakh Nabokova* [In Search of Nabokov] (1979).

Novels: [Jacques Croisé, pseud.], *Europe et Valérius* (1949). *Sortie de Secours* (1952). *La parole devient Sang* (1955). *Jeu de Massacres* (1956).

Poetry: *Insomnies*, poèmes (1937, rpt. 1939).

Memoirs and historical works: *Une Enfance* (1939). *Vie d'Alexandre Pouchkine* (1937). *Ma Russie habillée en U.S.S.R.* (1958). *La Vie quotidienne à Moscou au XVIIe siecle* (1963). *La Vie quotidienne à St. Petersbourg à l'époque romantique* (1967). *Tel est mon siècle* (memoirs): I. *Lumières et Ombres* (1964). II. *Une Manière de vivre* (1965). III. *La Folle Clio* (1966). *La Drole de Paix* (1967).

Translation: *The Precursors of Peter the Great* (1964). *The Fall of Eagles* (1964).

Bibliography

Poltoratzky, Nikolai P., *Russian Émigré Literature* (Pittsburgh, 1972). Struve, Gleb, *Russian Literature in Exile* (New York, 1956).

Marina Astman

Margot Scharpenberg

Born December 18, 1924, Cologne, West Germany
Genre(s): narrative prose, lyric
Language(s): German, English

Born and raised in Cologne, Margot Scharpenberg also worked there as a scientific librarian for the central catalogue of Nordrhein-Westfalen until her immigration to the United States. In 1957 she came to America for the first time. The experiences she had in the United States inspired her to start writing, and the first collection of her poems was published in the same year. Back in Germany, Margot Scharpenberg decided to accept a job as instructor in the language laboratory of Carleton University in Ottawa, Canada, where she stayed from 1960 to 1962. After her marriage to Dr. Klaus Wellmann, a professor of pathology, in 1962 she moved to Brooklyn, New York, where her husband was working. In 1978 they both moved to Manhattan where she still lives following the death of her husband.

Margot Scharpenberg and her husband both shared the same interest in nature and local peoples, which motivated them to go on long trips throughout the United States. They also travelled to Mexico and South America.

Although Margot Scharpenberg has been living in North America for 25 years now, she still maintains German as her primary language. Therefore, all her publications are in German and appear in West Germany before she eventually translates some of her works into English. To keep in touch with her native language Margot Scharpenberg usually returns to Cologne—her second residence—twice a year. And it is in Germany where most of her readings take place. However, she also has been invited to Amsterdam, London, Quito, Atlanta and to other places throughout Canada and the United States. Her work has been published in newspapers, magazines, and anthologies. Since 1957 Margot Scharpenberg has published eighteen lyric and three narrative prose volumes. In 1968 she received the George-Mackensen award for the best short story, and in 1975 she won the Ida-Dehmel literature prize for her complete poetry. She is now a member of the P.E.N. club.

Margot Scharpenberg's strongest gift lies in the lyric genre on which she has been concentrated almost exclusively. She has especially focused on the *Bildgeschichte*, an old literary concept which combines poetry with the visual arts, paintings in particular, to the extent that the poem is the direct description of the painting. In her six lyric volumes in which she deals with this concept, she has achieved a congenial sensitivity and mastery in transforming the content and form of the fine arts into the media of language. Her poems reflect complex experiences of time resulting from the multiplicity of aspects from the realms of theology, philosophy, psychology, anthropology, and history that are interwoven in her literary work. These different aspects all contribute to an authentic portrait of the art epoch from which the painting she is writing on is taken. Her writings do not attempt mere descriptions or interpretations of the work of art but emphasize the multiplicity and richness of its meaning and bring it to new life.

Works

Poems: *Gefährliche Übung* (1957). *Spiegelschriften* (1961). *Brandbaum* (1965). *Schwarzweiss* (1966). *Vermeintliche Windstille* (1968). *Mit Sprach–und Fingerspitzen* (1970). *Spielraum* (1972). *Spuren* (1973). *Bildgespräche mit Zillis* (1974). *Neue Spuren* (1975). *Veränderung eines Auftrags* (1976). *Fundfigur* (1977). *Bildespräche in Aachen* (1978). *Fundort Köln* (1979). *Domgespräch* (1980). *Moderne Kunst im Bildgespräch* (1982). *Fallende Farben* (1983). *Windbruch* (1985). *Verlegte Zeiten* (1988).

Prose: *Ein Todeskandidat und andere Erzählungen* (1970). *Einladung nach New York* (1972). *Fröhliche Weihnachten und andere Lebensläufe* (1974).

Friederike Emonds

Margo Sybranda Everdina Scharten-Antink

Born 1869, Zutfen, The Netherlands; died 1957, Florence, Italy
Genre(s): journalism, novel
Language(s): Dutch

Margo Scharten-Antink was one of the first women writers of quality in Dutch literature. Her trilogy *Sprotje* (1905–1910), about the life of the poor servant girl Sprotje, is considered the first truly worthwhile novel by a woman after the famous *Sara Burgerhardt* (1782) of Betje Wolff and Aagje Deken.

She was a French teacher in the provincial town of Zutfen until she married the poet and critic Carel Th. Scharten (1878–1950). They moved to Paris where they both worked as journalists and co-authored a number of novels which are, however, inferior to the ones Margo Antink wrote by herself. After 1924, they lived in Florence, Italy.

Her debut, the long novella *Catharina*, published in 1899, is entirely in the impressionistic style of the *Beweging van Tachtig* (a literary movement of the 1880s in Holland and Flanders) and is the expression of a strong, unique personality. The novella drew the attention of the critic Lodewijk van Deyssel, who praised the author and wrote extensively about the piece.

He took it for granted that it had been written by a man. Margo Antink did not continue in the style of this first success but instead turned toward the naturalistic themes of the brothers de Goncourt. Like *Germinie Lacerteux*, *Sprotje* is written in the kind of 'natural' language that marked the realism of the turn of the century. In her later works, Margo Antink maintained the psychological realism of *Sprotje* and tried to make psychological situations tangible in concrete aspects of people and things. She did this very successfully in the novella *Angelina's huwelijk* (1918; Angelina's Marriage).

Works

Catharina (1899). *Van scheiding en dood* (1900). *Sprotje*, 3 vols. (1905–1910). *Angelina's huwelijk* (1918). *In den vrije Amerikaan* (1921).

With Carel Scharten: *Een huis vol mensen* (1908). *De vreemde heerschers* (1911). *Julie Simon* (1914). *'t Geluk hangt als een druiventros* (1919).

Bibliography

Deyssel, Lodewijk van, *Verzamelde Opstellen* V, pp. 89–95. Kloos, Willem, *Nieuwere Literatuur* III, pp. 182–183. Knuvelder, Gerard, *Handboek tot de geschiedenis der Nederlandse letterkunde* 2nd ed., vol. 4 (1961), pp. 201–204. Moerman, Josien, *Lexicon Nederlandstalige auteurs* (1984), p. 205. Pienaar, Elize, "De jeugd van Fransesco Campana: C. en M. Scharten-Antink." *Klasgids* 14, ii (1979): 22–26. Romein-Verschoor, Annie, *De Nederlandse romanschrijfster na 1880* (Utrecht, 1935), pp. 41–51.

Maya Bijvoet

Rosalie Scherzer

(see: Rose Ausländer)

Anna Schieber

Born December 12, 1867, Eßlingen, Germany; died August 7, 1945, Tübingen
Genre(s): novel, children's literature
Language(s): German

The daughter of an old business family, Anna Schieber began writing stories for children in 1897. Later she also wrote novellas and novels for adults. In all her works she depicts with love and a sense of humor her part of Germany: Schwaben and the Black Forest.

Her books are populated with realistic characters, and the author's affection for them, and mankind, in general, can be felt throughout. This concern for mankind, as well as her religious faith, led her to work as a nurse during World War I and guided her in her political activities.

Although considered a "regional" author (thus implying a limitation to her appeal), Schieber has written works that reflect time and place so well, they have become part of the cultural tradition of her region. The books, written with lasting values and relating timeless tales, are still appealing.

Works

Sonnenhunger. Geschichten von der Schattenseite (1903). *Im Schlo Hausbaden. Die kaiserliche Familie in der Sommerfrische* (1903). *Sonnenstrahlen* (1903). *Ninetta* (1904). *Einen Sommer lang* (1904). *Was Annegret zu helfen fand* (1905). *Eine Geschichte vom Heimkommen* (1906). *Alle guten Geister* (1907). *Röschen, Jaköble und andere kleine Leute* (1907). *Gesammelte Immergrün Geschichten* (1910). *Allerlei Kraut und Unkraut. Gesammelte Bilder und Geschichten für große und kleine Leute* (1910). *Wanderschuhe und andere Erzählungen* (1911). *Sum, sum, sum. Ein Liederbüchlein für die Mutter und ihre Kinder* (1912). *Aus Kindertagen* (1912). *Fröhlich, fröhlich, Weihnacht überall. Drei kleine Weihnachtsspiele für Kinder* (1912). *Der Glückstag der Haderkornin* (1912). *Und hätte der Liebe nicht. Weihnachtliche Geschichten* (1912). *In der Klemmbachmühle* (1912). *Jungfer Salomes Verwandtschaft* (1913). *Wie die Kinder* (1913). *Amaryllis und andere Geschichten* (1914). *Guckkastenbilder. Kindern und Kinderfreunden gezeichnet* (1915). *Heimat* (1915). *Zugvögel und andere Geschichten* (1915). *Ein Vater* (1916). *Die neue Zeit* (1916). *Das Kind* (1916). *Kriegssommer. Lose Blätter aus den Heimatberichten des Johannes Weinland, pensionierten Schullehrers in Rommelsbach, an seinen Sohn im Feld* (1916). *Der Unnutz* (1916). *Geschichte, von einer, die tat, was sie wollte* (1916). *Unterwegs. Tagebuchblätter einer Verstorbenen* (1916). *Der fromme Maier* (1916). *Kameraden*

(1917). *In der Sagmühle* (1917). *Dreizehn aus Schwaben. Fröhliche Geschichten schwäbischer Erzähler* (1917). *Ludwig Fugeler* (1918). *Die Familienbuche* (1919). *Zwei Kino-Konferenzen* (1919). *Alte Geschichten* (1919). *Der Lebens–und der Liebesgarten* (1919). *Warme Herzen* (1919). *Des Reiches Sonnenwende. Ein Mahnruf schwäbischer Dichter* (1919). *Unser Bekenntnis zur neuen Zeit* (1919). *Das Opfer und andere Erzählungen* (1920). *Drei Weihnachtsgeschichten* (1921) (with Elisabeth Halden). *Was des anderen ist* (1921). *Weihnachtsgeister. Gedanken und Erzählungen* (1922). *Annegret. Eine Kindergeschichte* (1922). *Die Erfüllung und andere Erzählungen* (1924). *Rosel* (1924). *Der Narr Gottes* (1924). *Das Hemd des Glücklichen* (1924). *Zur Genesung* (1924). *Vom Innesein* (1925). *Lebenshöhe* (1925). *Johann Peter Hebel: Biblische Geschichten aus dem alten Testament. Mit einem Brief an junge, jung gebliebene und wieder jung gewordene Menschen von Anna Schieber* (1926). *Bille Hasenfu. Wie er sich und den Gänserich bezwang* (1926). *Echte Menschen* (1926). *Aber nicht weitersagen. Ein Märchenbuch* (1926). *Die sieben Schwaben* (1926). *Aus Gesprächen mit Martina* (1926). *Drei Ranken* (1926). *Balladen und Lieder* (1927). *Bruder Tod. Ein Lied vom lebendigen Leben* (1927). *Eh'ne wott mei Kend verkaufa. Schwäbisches Volksstück* (1927). *Der Zeitungsbub* (1928). *Zurückgesetzt?* (1928). *Geschichten von gestern und heute, von mir und dir* (1930). *Ein Tag aus Bimberlins Leben* (1930). *Das große Ich* (1930). *Im Banne des Unbedingten. Christoph Schrempf zugeeignet von Hermann Hesse, Otto Engel, Anna Schieber, u. a.* (1930). *Die Herzblüte und andere Weihnachtsgeschichten* (1931). *Doch immer behalten die Quellen das Wort. Erinnerungen aus einem ersten Jahrsiebent* (1932). *Aus dem Weihnachtsbilderbuch* (1934). *Die Laute* (1934). *Der Bandelmann* (1934). *Aus Zeit und Überzeit. Lose Blätter* (1934). *Wachstum und Wandlung. Ein Lebensbuch* (1935). *Veronika und ihr Bruder* (1936). *Der Weinberg* (1937). *Der Unzerbrechliche* (1937). *Das große Angesicht. Ein Lebensbericht* (1938). *Notpfennig* (1940). *Vetter Engelbrecht* (1947). *Das Kind im Schnee* (1947). *Das Schmiedefeuer* (1948). *Macht der Güte* (1951). *Wie der Großvater das Lachen gelernt hat* (1951). *Der Königsadler* (1952). *Aller Menschen Tag und Stunde* (1958). *Heimkehr zum Vater* (1961).

Bibliography

Kürschners Deutscher Literatur-Kalendar: Nekrolog 1936–1970 (Berlin, 1973), p. 587.

Hortense Bates

Dorothea Caroline Albertine Michaelis Böhmer Schlegel Schelling

Born 1763, Göttingen, Germany; died 1809, Maulbronn
Genre(s): letters
Language(s): German

Caroline Michaelis, born on September 2, 1763, was the daughter of Johann David Michaelis, a Göttingen University Professor of Oriental Studies. Her educated, comfortably-situated, and respected family gave her access to learning, to local and international leaders, artists, writers, and to the university community (including Benjamin Franklin, Alexander von Humboldt, Johann Wolfgang von Goethe, Novalis, Friedrich Schiller, and Gotthold Ephraim Lessing), with the result that she mastered English and French and was exposed to the theater at an early age. At nineteen, she married Johann Franz Wilhelm Böhmer, a young doctor who had lived nearby since her childhood, even though she expressed reservations abut marrying at all. Her move to Clausthal removed her from the previous life of the mind that she had so enjoyed in Göttingen. She bore two daughters, Auguste and Therese, and was pregnant with her third child when Böhmer died in 1789 after a sudden illness. This child, Wilhelm, did not live long, and Caroline, having moved back to Göttingen, found solace in the homes of her friends, where she became acquainted with August Wilhelm Schlegel. She later moved to Marburg, where Therese died, and then to Mainz. Arrested for revolutionary sympathies during the turmoil surrounding the French Revolution, and pregnant with a child who died two years later, she turned to Schlegel for aid, and moved to Braunschweig to be nearer to her mother. Her marriage to Schlegel took place in 1796, with a common agreement for each partner to respect the other's freedom. The household moved to Jena, where Schlegel was a professor. Her daughter Auguste died at fifteen; her marriage did not turn out to be an equal partnership, and she turned for solace to a newly hired professor, Friedrich Wilhelm Joseph Schelling, whom she married in 1803 after her divorce from Schlegel.

Much of her literary achievement is lost, as her collaborative aid to her husbands and to her circle, if passed on, was not signed. However, her many lively and well-written letters tell of strong ties to her stepbrother Fritz, who fought for the Hessians in the American Revolution, Luise Stieler (who later married Wilhelm Gotter, in Goethe's circle at Weimar), Therese Heyne (who married the world-traveller Georg Forster), and the Göttingen librarian Meyer. She consistently expressed pro-feminist, emancipatory, and revolutionary sympathies in these letters, which are uniformly insightful, observant, and crowded with observations about the intelligentsia of late eighteenth- and early nineteenth-century Germany. Her fascinating life inspired literary works, among them *Lucinde*, and various twentieth-century versions of her life, and her epistolary legacy testifies to the obstacles surmounted and rewards gained by an extraordinary woman whose strong personality, humor, and intelligence gained her access to the literary-philosophical circles of her time.

Works

Caroline: Briefe aus der Frühromantik, ed. Erich Schmidt (Leipzig, 1913). *Unruhvolles Herz: Briefe der Caroline Schelling*, ed. Willi A. Koch (Munich, 1951). *Lieber Freund, ich komme weit her schon an diesem frühen Morgen: Caroline Schlegel-Schelling in ihren Briefen*, ed. and intro. Sigrid Damm (Darmstadt, 1980).

Bibliography

Klessmann, Eckart, *Caroline: Das Leben der Caroline Michaelis-Böhmer-Schlegel-Schelling 1763–1809* (Munich, 1975). Mangold, Elisabeth, *Caroline: Ihr Leben, Ihre Zeit, Ihre Briefe* (Kassel, 1973). Murtfeld, Rudolf, *Caroline Schlege-Schelling: Moderne Frau in revolutionärer Zeit* (Bonn, 1973). Ritchie, Gisela F., *Caroline Schlegel-Schelling in Wahrheit und Dichtung* (Bonn, 1968).

Susan L. Clark

Paula Schlier

Born 1899, Neuburg/Donau, Austria
Genre(s): poetry, prose
Language(s): German

Schlier began work as a political journalist, but soon her prose and poetry emphasized religious themes. In 1932 she became a devout Catholic, which is reflected in all her subsequent work. Her first poems were published in *Der Brenner*, in which she had an active role and where she worked closely with Ludwig Ficker. She was under arrest by the Gestapo from 1942 to 1945.

Works

Konzept einer Jugend (1926). *Chorónoz* (1926). *Der Kommende Tag* (1948). *Die Mystische Rose; eine Dichtung* (1949). *Legende zur Apokalypse* (1949). *Das Menschenherz; Traumbilder des Lebens* (1953).

Bibliography

Das Groessere Österreich, ed. Kristian Sotriffer (Wien, 1982), p. 152.

Mary Ann Reiss

Dr. Schmid

(see: Kathinka [Katharina] Rosa
    Pauline Modesta Zitz-Halein)

Annie M.G. Schmidt

Born 1911
Genre(s): children's literature, radio,
    television, theatre
Language(s): Dutch

Holland's foremost author of light verse and entertaining texts, admired by all segments of the Dutch population, Annie M.G. Schmidt has delighted several generations with her verbal virtuosity and great sense of humor.

She was the daughter of a minister, born in the Protestant province of Zeeland, and wrote poetry even as a child but worked for many years (1932–1946) as a library assistant and librarian before taking up writing as a full-time occupation. This happened after she joined the newspaper *Het Parool* as a documentation specialist and wrote the text for a show presented at a personnel party, which brought her into contact with Wim Kan and Wim Sonneveld, the leading comics on the Dutch stage. Her first poem for children appeared in *Het Parool* in May 1947. Her first column followed soon thereafter. Three years later she published the collection *En wat dan nog?* (1950; So What?) and *Het fluitketelje* (1950; The Little Water Kettle), light verse and poetry for children. These two little books instantly established her popularity both with children and adults. *Jip en Janneke*, her stories for children also first published in *Het Parool*, reached eight volumes (1953–1960). Then she produced the radio series *In Holland staat een huis* (Somewhere in Holland there is a house . . ., the first line of an old Dutch children's song), which appeared in book and record form under the title *De familie Doorsnee* (1952–1958; The Averages).

From the fifties onward, she has written without interruption, producing highly successful comedies for television and the theatre, the series *Pension Hommeles* (1957–1959; Boarding House Hommeles) and *Ja zuster, nee zuster* (1966–1968; Yes Sister, No Sister), and her musicals *Heerlijk duurt het langst* (1965; Delicious is Forever), *En nu naar bed* (1971; And Now Off to Bed), and others.

She has kept writing light verse for children throughout the years and was awarded, in 1964, the Dutch National Prize for Children's Literature. Research has indicated that her work contains all the thematic elements and linguistic characteristics considered essential in children's literature.

Works

En wat dan nog (1950). *Het fluitketelje* (1950). *Brood en mangelpers* (1950). *Dit is de spin Sebastiaan* (1951). *Het schaap Veronika*, 2 vols. (1951–1953). *Impressies van een simpele ziel* (Columns), 3 vols. (1951–1953). *Cabaretliedjes* (1952). *Veertien uilen* (1952). *In Holland staat een huis* (1952–1958; De Familie Doorsnee). *Jip en Janneke*, 8 vols. (1953–1960). *Abeltje* (1953). *De Toren van Bemmelekom* (1953). *De lapjeskat* (1954). *Weer of geen weer* (1954). *De A van Abeltje* (1955). *Ik ben lekker stout* (1955). *In Holland staat mijn huis* (1955). *De vrouw zo, de man zus* (1955). *Op visite bij de reus* (1956). *Huishoudpoezie*

(1957). *Pension Hommeles* (1957–1958). *Wiplala* (1957–1962). *Het beertje pippeloentje* (1958). *Drie stouterdjes* (1958; series). *Prelientje* (1958; series). *Iedereen heeft een staart* (1959). *Dag meneer de kruidenier* (1960). *Woelewippie onderweg* (1960). *Dikkertje Dap* (1961). *De Wim Wam reus en andere liedjes voor de jeugd* (1961). *Troost voor dames* (1962). *Pluis en Poezeltje* (1963; series). *Mevrouw averecht, meneer recht* (1963). *Vingertje Lik en een heleboel andere versjes* (1964). *Heksen en zo*, fairy tales (1964). Heerlijk duurt *het langst* (1965). *Het gedeukte fluitketelje* (1966). *Het beest met de achternaam* (1968). *En ik dan?* (1969). *Minoes* (1970). *Pluk van de Petteflet* (1971). *Floddertje* (1973). *Water bij de wijn* (1973). *Het fornuis moet weg!* (1974). *Tom Tippelaar* (1977). *Waaidorp*, 2 vols. (1979–1981). *Otje* (1980). *Er valt een traan op de tompoes* (1980). *Een visje bij de thee* (1983). *Oja . . .* (1984). *Ping Ping* (1984).

Bibliography

Harmsel, Henrietta Tten, "Annie M.G. Schmidt: Dutch Children's Poet." *Children's Literature* 11 (1983): 135–144. Kuipers, Reinold, "Annie M.G. Schmidt." *'Tis vol van schatten hier*, vol. 2 (Amsterdam, 1986), pp. 68–69. Moerman, Josien, *Lexikon Nederlandstalige auteurs* (1964), p. 207.

Maya Bijvoet

Alexandrine Martina Augusta Schnabl

(a.k.a. Martina Wied)

Born December 10, 1882, Vienna, Austria; died January 25, 1957, Vienna
Genre(s): narrative prose, poetry, essay, drama
Language(s): German

Born into a musical and art-loving family, Schnabl had already published some poems when she was still in school. For that purpose she assumed the pseudonym Martina Wied, which she used for all her subsequent writings. Her earliest publications reveal naturalistic tendencies, but more enduring were her affinities with Expressionism, to which her contributions to Ludwig von Ficker's *Der Brenner* (from 1912 onwards) testify.

Wied studied history, art history, and philosophy at the University of Vienna. She also had a deep interest in psychology and in foreign literature (English, French, and East European). This, coupled with her innate moral seriousness, infuses her major works (as well as her essays and reviews scattered in many newspapers and magazines) with a high cultural and ethical content.

Wied converted to Catholicism from Judaism and is regarded by some as a Catholic writer. Rather surprisingly, she does not treat Jewish problems in her works. From 1939 to 1947 she lived in exile in England, Wales, and Scotland, which influenced her novel *Das Einhorn* (1948; The Unicorn) based on the later life of Charles Edward Stuart (Bonnie Prince Charlie) in Florence.

An important theme in Wied's writings is *exile*; the theme is especially important in the novels *Das Einhorn* and *Kellingrath* (1950) and links her with many other German and Austrian writers of the period 1938–1945. However, since the theme of exile occurs in works written also before her own exile from Austria—in the dramas *Der Spielberg* (1924) and *Besuch aus Spanien* (1925)—it may be considered to possess the broader meaning of existential homelessness. Existentialism occurs most explicitly in *Kellingrath*, whose title figure is based on Sören Kierkegaard.

Another central theme in Wied's works, the relationship between life and art, is treated in *Das Einhorn* and in *Rauch über Sanct Florian* (1937). The main figure in the latter novel is modeled on the poet Paul Ernst, a personal friend of Wied's.

Wied's writings generally depict a struggle to find meaning amidst the chaos and suffering of the modern age or of historical periods that mirror the present day. They are always written from the point of view of a male protagonist.

Wied wrote sensitive, highly personal, musical, and yet disciplined lyrics her life long. They are collected in *Brücken ins Sichtbare* (1952).

In 1953, on the occasion of her seventieth birthday, she was awarded the Austrian State Prize for Literature.

Works

Novels: *Rauch über Sanct Florian* [Smoke over St. Florian] (1937). *Das Einhorn* [The Unicorn] (1948). *Kellingrath* [Kellingrath] (1950). *Das Krähennest* [The Crow's Nest] (1951). *Die Geschichte des reichen Jünglings* [The Story of the Rich Youth] (1952). *Der Ehering* [The Wedding Ring] (1954). *Das unvollendete Abenteuer* [The Unfinished Adventure] (1955).

Poems: *Bewegung* [Movement] (1919). *Brücken ins Sichtbare* [Bridges to the Visible] (1952).

Plays: *Der Spielberg* [The Play-Mountain] (1924). *Besuch aus Spanien* [Visitors from Spain] (1925).

Bibliography

Berry, Jesse, *Martina Wied. Austrian novelist. 1882–1957*. Ph.D. Diss., Vanderbilt, 1966. Braun, Felix, "Nachruf auf Martina Wied." *Wort in der Zeit* 3 (1957): 262–263. Brunmayr, Hans, "Les romans de Martina Wied." *Austriaca* 3 (1977): 45–54. Langer, Norbert, *Dichter aus Österreich*, 1. Folge (Vienna, 1956), pp. 127–131. Langer, Norbert, Intro. to *Das Einhorn* (Vienna, 1964), pp. 5–29. Mornin, Edward, "'Bonnie Charlie's now awa' . . .'. Charles Edward Stuart after the '45. On the uses of history in fiction" (On *Das Einhorn*). *Forum for Modern Language Studies* 26 (1988): 97–110. Winter, Hanns, "Martina Wied." *Wort in der Zeit* 3 (1957): 257–262.

Edward Mornin

Adalbert von Schonen

(see: Amalie [Emma Sophie Katharine] Schoppe)

Amalie (Emma Sophie Katharine) Schoppe

(a.k.a. Adalbert von Schonen)

Born October 9, 1791, Burg, Insel Fehmarn, Germany; died September 25, 1858, Schenectady, New York
Genre(s): poetry, historical novel, short story, youth literature
Language(s): German

Amalie Schoppe completed her education in Hamburg after her father, the medical doctor Friedrich Wilhelm Weise, died when she was very young. At the age of twenty, she married Friedrich Heinrich Schoppe, a lawyer. In 1829, after eighteen years of marriage, Amalie Schoppe was widowed.

Schoppe's poems were first published in the almanac of her friend, Justinus Kerner. Later, she turned to prose, writing primarily for young people. *Erzahlungen und Novellen* (1827–1836; Stories and Novella) and *Die Frühlingsgabe* (1827; The Gift of Spring) are collections of stories for young people involving romance, mystery, and adventure. In *Die Helden und Götter des Nordens* (1832; The Heroes and Gods of the North) Schoppe retells the stories of the Germanic legends. *Robinson in Australien* (1843; Robinson in Australia) follows the adventures of a young boy alone in a new world. In addition to her books for young people, Schoppe also published *Iduna*, a children's newspaper (from 1831) and founded a girls' grammar school. She authored several historical and biographical novels, including *König Erich XIV und die Seinen* (1830; King Eric XIV and His People), *Tycho de Brahe* (1839), *Die Schlacht bei Hemmingstedt* (1840; The Battle by Hemmingstedt), and *Maria Stuart* (1841).

Schoppe played an important role as the encourager and supporter of the young dramatist Franz Hebbel. She published his early poems and stories in the *Pariser Mödeblatter*, of which she was editor. Her interest in the advancement of Hebbel's education enabled him to move to Hamburg although her influence on his later career was short-lived.

In 1838 Schoppe's two-volume autobiography, *Erinnerungen aus meinem Leben* (Memories from My Life) appeared. In this work, Schoppe presents brief descriptive portraits of the colorful people with whom she was associated.

In 1851 Amalie Schoppe moved to Schenectady, New York, to be with her one remaining son. She died in Schenectady in 1858. Her literary contributions number 130 volumes. Her stories and novels were somewhat popular during her lifetime, while the interest she showed in the young Hebbel has had more of an historical impact.

Works

See Goedeke, Kosch, ADB. *Gesammelte Erzählungen und Novellen* (3 vols.; 1827–1836).

Bibliography

Schindel, Carl von, *Die deutschen Schriftstellerinen der neunzehnten Jahrhunderts* (1823–1825) (Hildesheim and New York, 1978). *Oxford Companion to German Literature*. ADB.

Ann Willison

Solveig Margareta von Schoultz

Born August 5, 1907, Borgå, Sweden
Genre(s): *children's literature, poetry, short story, drama, autobiography*
Language(s): *Swedish*

Solveig von Schoultz is a very sensitive writer, whose imagination derives from lyricism, but she transfers her keen application of associative language to her prose works as well. She is an untiring observer of human relationships, above all relationships between women and between mother and child. Her descriptions of relations between men and women are acutely seen from the woman's point of view.

Her very first book was a book for children, *Petra och silverapan* (1932; Petra and the Silver Monkey); it was followed by *December* (1937).

Her first three volumes of poetry, *Min timme* (1940; My Hour), *Den bortvända glädjem* (1943; The Froward Joy) and *Eko av ett rop* (1945; Echo of a Cry) are filled with a warm feeling for life. In these works, her poems still have rhymes; perhaps she needed them at the time to harness her fountainlike fantasy. But from *Nattlig äng* on (1949; Night Meadow), her language is more serene and controlled, and the rhymes have disappeared.

In her first collection of short stories, her psychological approach and fine sense of shades in people's reactions already establish themselves; they are later on to become the hallmark of her prose. *Ingenting ovanligt* (1947; Nothing Special) was followed by short stories in which the tone is more experimental, as, e.g., in *Närmare någon* (1951; Closer to Someone), but in *Den blomstertid* (1958; The Time of Summer Flow-

ers) she reverts to a style that comes naturally to her, exact and penetrating, but womanly and warm. She decidedly concentrates on what she knows best: the feelings, reactions and moods of women, their tensions and reflections. Women are constantly in focus: she studies children, young girls and maturing women, middle-aged women, and old women. She has also written a study of her two daughters, called *De sju dagarna* (1942; The Seven Days), referring to the seven days of creation in which a human being matures. This book is one of the most intriguing and most informative books in Swedish literature on the relation between parents and child.

In the series of related short stories, *Ansa och samvetet* (1954; Ansa and Conscience), she uses material from her own childhood and from that of her girls. Ansa is finding her feet in the incomprehensible world of adults; the stories cover a child's experience of guilt and remorse, of anxiety, and need to be cared for.

Twenty years later Solveig von Schoultz reverted to autobiographical material in *Där står du* (1973; There You Stand), and in *Porträtt av Hanna* (1978; Portrait of Hanna); the latter covers a liberation process from her mother, Hanna.

In *Allt sker nu* (1952; All Happens Now) a new independence asserts itself; this book is more concerned with clarifying her own stands, as a woman, than the earlier ones. It uses more stringent language, a feature that becomes fully apparent in *Nätet* (1956; The Net), her lyric masterpiece. *Terrassen* (1959; The Terrace) is an experiment in dense Japanese form, and in the subsequent *De fyra flöjtspelarna* (1975; The Four Fluteplayers) and *Bortom träden hörs havet* (1980; Beyond the Trees, Hark—the Sea) all irrelevant items have vanished, and the language carries weight in every word.

Solveig von Schoultz has also written plays, especially for radio and television, but the short stories and sometimes almost novella-like stories and lyrics are her proper media.

Her more recent short stories cover *Även dina kameler* (1970; Your Camels, Too), *Rymdbruden* (1970; Space Bride), *Somliga mornar* (1976; Certain Mornings) and *Kolteckning, ofullbordad* (1983; Charcoal Drawing, Unfinished). Personal relations, a wide variety of them, remain her focal interest. The relationships are looked at from the woman's point of view: the wife's perspective, the mother's perspective.

Solveig von Schoultz wrote as she did long before the feminist movement came to the fore, and by its representatives she was at first criticized for conservatism. Now winds have changed, and she is recognized for the strength her female characters expose, admittedly a maternal kind of strength, as she looks upon women as "mother-gods," encompassing everything in their strength. There seems to be a constantly ongoing debate about women and their relations to the surrounding human beings in all her works. In that sense, she is one of the first "feminist" writers in this country. She herself declares that lyricism is her mother tongue, a statement that holds good for her prose style as well.

Works

Prose: *Petra och silverapan* [Petra and the Silver Monkey] (1932). *December* (1937). *De sju dagarna* [The Seven Days] (1942). *Nalleresan* [The Bear Journey, A Children's Story] (1944). *Ingenting ovanligt* [Nothing Special] (1947). *Närmare någon* [Closer to Someone] (1951). *Ansa och samvetet* [Ansa and Conscience] (1954). *Den blomstertid* [The Time of Summer Flowers] (1958). *Millaskolan* [The Milla School, A Children's Book] (1960). *Även dina kameler* [Your Camels, Too] (1965). *Rymdbruden* [Space Bride] (1979). *Där står du* [There You Stand] (1973). *Somliga mornar* [Certain Mornings] (1976). *Porträtt av Hanna* [Portrait of Hanna] (1978). *Kolteckning, ofullbordad* [Charcoal Drawing, Unfinished] (1983). *Ingen dag förgäves* [No Day in Vain] (1984).

Poetry: *Min timme* [My Hour] (1940). *Den bortvända glädjen* [The Froward Joy] (1943). *Eko av ett rop* [Echo of a Cry] (1945). *Nattlig äng* [Night Meadow] (1949). *Allt sker nu* [All Happens Now] (1952). *Nätet* [The Net] (1956). *Terrassen* [The Terrace] (1959). *Sänk ditt ljus* [Lower Your Light] (1963). *Klippbok* [Cuttings] (1968). *De fyra flöjtspelarna* [The Four Fluteplayers] (1975). *Bortom träden hörs havet* [Beyond the Trees, Hark—the Sea] (1980). *En enda minut* [One Single Minute] (1981). A number of short plays for radio performance.

Bibliography

Forsström, Zaida, "En kvinna om kvinnor." *Studk* (1952): 65–66. Mazzarella, Merete, *Från Fredrika Runeberg till Märta Tikkanen* (Helsingfors, 1985). Müller, Erik, "Från Hedda till Hanni." *Perspektiv* (1956): 226. Warburton, Thomas, *Åttio år finlandssvensk litteratur* (Helsingfors, 1984). Numerous reviews in newspapers and periodicals.

Gunnel Cleve

Margrit Schriber

Born June 4, 1939, Lucerne, Switzerland
Genre(s): novel, short story, radio play
Language(s): German

Margrit Schriber's origins are modest: her mother was a hairdresser and her father a faith-healer. The novel *Kartenhaus* (1978) is a memoir of her childhood. She trained as a commercial clerk and worked as a bank clerk, secretary, and model before devoting herself full-time to writing. Divorced after fourteen years of marriage, she now lives in the canton of Aargau.

Precise language and short, paratactic sentences are the hallmarks of Schriber's style. Her protagonists, usually women narrating in the first person, are observers, intelligent but passive, yearning but contained. It is no accident that the imagery of watching, of windows, and framed views pervades her fiction. Action is rare, though her novels are carefully and realistically plotted. Her work contemplates the repetition, revival, and extinction of emotion, very often in terms of the conflict between the traditional expectations of women and their own desires. An example is her latest novel, in which the liaisons between secretaries and managers in a city bank are observed by the *Tresorschatten* (vault shadow), a forty-year-old woman who has retreated to this protected and isolated position after an unhappy love affair twenty years earlier. Is it uniquely Swiss that in these works security is the consummate good, and that safety lies in maintaining a carefully constructed, well-lit, and surveyable distance between oneself and life?

Works

Aussicht gerahmt [Framed View], novel (1976, 1981). *Ausser Saison* [No Longer in Season], short stories (1977). *Kartenhaus* [Cardhouse], novel (1978). *Ein Platz am Seitenpodest* [A Seat on the Sidepedestal], radio play (1978). "Dazwischen: ein monologischer Dialog." "Ein wenig Lärm im Keller: Monodrama." "Montag." *Texte für die Theaterwerkstatt*, Vol. 4 [In Between: A Monologistic Dialogue. A Little Noise in the Cellar: Monodrama. Monday] (1979). *Vogelflieg* [Fly Away Bird], novel (1980, 1983). *Luftwurzeln* [Aerial Roots], short stories (1981, 1985). *Muschelgarten* [Mussel Garden], novel (1984). *Tresorschatten* [Vault Shadow], novel (1987).

Translations: "At the First Opportunity," tr. Bianca Rosenthal. *Dimension* 10 [translation of short story "Bei Zeit und Gelegenheit" from Ausser *Saison*] (1977).

Bibliography

Cantieni, Benita, "M.S." *Schweizer Schriftsteller persönlich* (Frauenfeld, 1983), pp. 77–95. Krättli, Anton, "M.S." *Kritisches Lexikon zur deutschsprachiger Gegenwartsliteratur*, ed. Heinz Ludwig Arnold (München: edition text ą kritik, 1978ff) [bibliography]. Rasmussen, Ann Marie, "Women and Literature in Switzerland: Tendencies in the 1980s." *Deutsche Frauenliteratur seit 1945*. *Amsterdamer Beiträge zur neuer Germanistik* (1989).

Ann Marie Rasmussen

Helga Schubert

Born 1940, Berlin, Germany
Genre(s): short story, film script
Language(s): German

Born in wartime Berlin, Schubert never knew her father, who died as a German soldier on the Russian front. Schubert was raised by her mother in Berlin. She received her *Abitur* and, after a year of factory work, studied psychology at East Berlin's Humboldt University. Finishing her studies in 1963, she began work as a psychotherapist. In 1977 she became a free-lance writer though she continued working once a week at a marriage and sexual counseling clinic in East Berlin.

Schubert began writing for newspapers, journals, and anthologies in 1973. Encouraged and supported by Sarah Kirsch, she published her first anthology of stories, *Lauter Leben* (True Life), with the East German publishing house, Aufbau, in 1975. Her second collection appeared as *Das verbotene Zimmer* (The Forbidden Room)

in 1982 with the West German Luchterhand press. It was then printed as *Blickwinkel* (Point of View) in 1984 with Aufbau, without three stories: "Frühere Standpunkte" (Earlier Standpoints), "Ansichtskarten" (Postcards), and "Mildernder Umstand" (Mitigating Circumstance). The first deals with changes in the East German party line, the second with postcards sent to East Germany from former citizens, and the third with the problem of writing.

Helga Schubert writes short, declarative, nonpathetic sentences about the difficulties of quotidian life. Detailed observation and psychological verisimilitude—coming no doubt from her work as a psychologist—characterize her stories. Many of her figures suffer in a society where attitudes have not changed as quickly as laws. One of her most famous stories, "Meine alleinstehenden Freundinnen" (My Unmarried Female Friends), employs an increasingly relentless narrator who unmasks the assertions of independence and happiness professed by her single female friends. Women comprise the majority of Schubert's protagonists and narrators, though she is not exclusively, or even primarily, concerned with a feminist agenda, and her works do not evidence the more militant feminism of, for example, Irmtraud Morgner. She does, however, often describe interpersonal relationships, which are generally depicted as unhappy ("Die Ausnahme" [The Exception] features one of her few happy couples), lacking communication, and defined by feelings of entrapment.

Schubert's stories are strongly autobiographical, and many evince a documentary quality. In "Mein Vater" (My Father), for example, she tells the story of her own father, and she often treats the difficulties of single women with children, difficulties experienced by her mother and, for many years, by the author herself. Schubert was diagnosed as having cancer in 1975, and she examines that subject in "Knoten" (Knots) and in her film script *Beunruhigung* (Unease). In a self-statement for the volume *Point of View*, Schubert notes that, for her, writing constitutes self-therapy. However, in an interview with Ariane Thomalla, she also asserted that she writes with didactic intent, in the hope that readers may learn to master their problems. Her works combine declarations of loyalty to socialism with cautious criticism, especially regarding restrictions on travel or on writing. In 1986 Helga Schubert was awarded the prestigious East German Heinrich Mann Prize.

Works

Lauter Leben (1975). *Das verbotene Zimmer* (1982). *Blickwinkel* (1984).

Bibliography

Graut, Alyth F., "Allein zwischen Anspruch und Wirklichkeit: Helga Schubert's 'Lauter Leben.'" *Seminar* 22 (1986): 71–87. Grohnert, Dietrich, Helga *Schubert, Deutsch als Fremdsprache* 18 (Sonderheft, 1981): 38–43. Thomalla, Ariane, "Schriftstellerin und Psychotherapeutin in der DDR. Gespräch mit Helga Schubert." *Deutschland Archiv* 10 (1986): 1104–1110.

Thomas C. Fox

Bernhardine Schulze-Smidt

(a.k.a. Elisabeth Oswald)

Born August 19, 1846, Bremen, Germany;
died (unknown) probably after 1911
Genre(s): novels, novellen
Language(s): German

Bernhardine was the eldest daughter of an old established family in Bremen: her father was a senator and her grandfather the mayor of Bremen and the founder of Bremerhaven. She had a happy childhood among many brothers and sisters. Her father encouraged her in her literary endeavors which she began in 1874. In 1869 Bernhardine married the privy councillor, Schulze, who died in 1886. As a widow, she moved to Munich for several years and then returned again in the late 1890s to her native Bremen.

Her novels and short stories display a delicate psychology and a gentle Christian attitude. In all her works the theme of conciliation and reconciliation is evident. Mental suffering and the inner spiritual life are topics of the novels, *Er lebt* (He Lives) and *Wenn man liebt* (If One Loves). Her best known work, *In Moor und Marsh* (In the Moorland and Fenland), poetically treats the perilous era of the Napoleonic repression and of the year of 1812. It is an impressive, emotional picture of the people living on the island of St. Jürgen in northern Germany. Bernhardine realistically and faithfully reproduces the local color and customs of simple people; it is the story of the hero Leberecht Klaudius, associate pastor of the old town church, his struggles, his successes and his faith.

Bernhardine also writes about foreign peoples. She wrote novels about the Turks, the Russians, and the Dalmatians.

Works

Fern von der Weltgetriebe [Far from the World's Bustle] (1874). *Heimat und Fremde* [Homeland and Foreign Parts] (1875). *Im Aquarium* [In the Aquarium] (1876). *Ritta Gerrets* [Ritta Gerrets] (1878). *Inge von Rantum* [Inge of Rantum] (1880). *Tote Kohlen* [Dead Coals] (1882). *Er Lebt* [He Lives] (1883). *Pfadfinder* [Pathfinder] (1890). *Wenn man Liebt* [If One Loves] (1891). *In Moor und Marsch* [In the Moorland and Fenland] (1892). *Mellas Studentenjahr* [The Student Years of Mella] (1892). *Holde Siebzehn* [Sweet Sixteen] (1893). *Rosenblätter* [Rose Leaves: Turkish Poems] (1893). *Mit dem Glückschiff* [With the Ship of Happiness] (1895). *So wachsen deiner Seele Flügel* [Thus Grow the Wings of the Soul] (1896). *Pave der Sünder* [Pave the Sinner] (1896). *Weltkind* [Child of the World] (1896–1898). *Kein Gitter hindert Cupido* [No Fence Impedes Cupid] (1897). *Franzosengeschichten* [Stories of the French] (1898). *Die Drei* [The Three] (1899). *Akadien* [Acadia] (1900). *Leiden* [Suffering] (1901). *Schattenblümchen* [Little Flowers in the Shadow] (1901). *Ein Bruder und eine Schwester* [A Brother and a Sister] (1902). *Aus dem goldenen Buche* [From the Golden Book] (1903). *Drei Freundinnen* [Three Girl Friends] (1904). *Kinderherz* [Heart of the Children] (1905). *Fliebendes Wasser* [Flowing Water] (1908). *Die Tat* [The Deed] (1909). *Allerlei Volk* [All Kinds of People] (1910). *Die Engelswiege* [The Cradle of the Angels] (1911).

Bibliography

Koenig, Robert, *Deutsche Literaturgeschichte*, Vol. 2 (Leipzig, 1910). Kruger, Anders Hermann, *Deutsches Literatur-Lexikon* (Munich, 1914). *Lexikon Deutscher Frauen der Feder*, ed. Sophie Pataky (Bern, 1971).

Brigitte Edith Zapp Archibald

Anna-Maria van Schurman

Born 1607, Cologne, Germany; died 1678,
*   Wieuwerd (Dutch Frisia)*
Genre(s): translation, poetry, treatise
Language(s): Dutch, Latin, French, others

Called a "marvel" and the "star of Utrecht," Anna-Maria van Schurman was considered the most learned woman of her age. She was highly accomplished both in the arts and in a great number of scientific disciplines. The living proof of women's intellectual capacities, she supported the idea of education and scholarship for women yet held a conservative view of the feminine role in society.

The daughter of staunchly Reformed parents, Anna-Maria grew up in an orthodox Calvinist milieu. Her exceptional artistic talents and intellectual abilities manifested themselves very early. She was given the same education as her brothers, and under the tutelage of her father she learned quickly and eagerly a wide variety of subjects: arithmetic, geography, astronomy, music, Latin, Greek, Hebrew, and a large number of Oriental and modern languages as well as theology, which became increasingly important for her. To avoid persecution, the family moved from Cologne to Utrecht in 1615. They moved to Franeker in 1623, so that Anna-Maria's brothers could attend the university there, but went back to Utrecht when her father died shortly thereafter. When the new university of Utrecht opened its doors, rector Voetius arranged for Anna-Maria to attend the lectures unseen by the other (male) students. Under Voetius, she studied languages and theology and began gradually to drop art and poetry as frivolous pursuits. The death of her mother in 1637 left her with the care of two blind and old aunts, who demanded her full attention. Though she was by now known all over Europe and great thinkers like Descartes made a point of looking her up when in Utrecht, she turned away from her scholarship to devote herself to her family and became increasingly involved with the saintly Pietist, Labadie, whose community she joined and followed, from Amsterdam to Herford and Altona in Germany to Wieuwerd in Friesland, where she died completely detached from Europe's intellectual scene.

Despite her glorious accomplishments as an artist and a scholar, Anna-Maria van Schurman remained modest and reluctant to display her gifts. She would not have published anything were it not for the insistence and pressure of her friends. Her *Amica Dissertatio . . .* (1638; Friendly Dissertation) is written in scholastic format and debates the question whether the study of letters befits a Christian woman. A careful and conservative defender of the feminist cause in the early seventeenth century, van Schurman advocates education and knowledge mostly for those women whose hands are free of household tasks, and warns that learning should never become the basis for claiming one's superiority. Moreover, the desire to glorify God should always be in the student's mind. In *Eucleria* (1673–1675), her autobiography written during her stay with the Labadist community in Altona and Wieuwerd, she explains her reasons for joining Labadie's group, a sort of commune, thus answering her contemporaries' objections to this step. *Over de Paelsteen onzes Levens* (1639; About the End of Our Life) is a theological treatise which attempts to answer the question of whether divine decisions about the end of our life are changeable. The author shows that everything depends on God's unchangeable decision and that the term of our life is fixed. In *Mysterium Magnum* (1699), she contemplates the future of the divine kingdom.

Though Anna-Maria van Schurman renounced in her old age most of what she had achieved and promoted earlier on, she made a permanent contribution to the cause of female education.

Works

Amica Dissertatio inter Annam Mariam Schurmanniam et Andr. Rivetum de capacitate ingenii muliebris ad scientias (1638; 1641). *Paelsteen van den Tijt onzes Levens* (1639). *Opuscula Hebraea, Graeca, Latina, Gallica, Prosaica et Metrica* (1648). *Eucleria seu melioris partis electio* (1675). *Mysterium Magnum* (1699). *Uitbreiding over de drie eerste Capittels van Genesis and Vertoog van het Geestelijk huwelijk van Christus met de Geloovigen* (1732).

Translations: *Question Célèbre*, s'il est nécessaire, ou non, que les filles soient sçavantes [*Amica*

Dissertatio], tr. G. Colletet (1646). *De Vitae Termino* [*Paelsteen van den Tijt onzes Levens*] (1639). *Eucleria of Uitkiezing van het Beste Deel* [*Eucleria seu melioris partis electio*] (1684).

Bibliography

Birch, Una, *Anna van Schuurman: Artist, Scholar, Saint* (London, 1909). Douma, Anna M.H., *Anna Maria van Schurman en de studie der vrouw* (Amsterdam, 1924). Irwin, Joyce, *Womanhood in Radical Protestantism: 1525–1675* (New York, 1979), pp. 145–156. Irwin, Joyce, "Anna Maria van Schurman: The Star of Utrecht," in *Female Scholars: A Tradition of Learned Women before 1800*, ed. J.R. Brink (Montreal, 1980), pp. 68–80. Irwin, Joyce, "Anna Maria van Schurman," in *Women Writers of the 17th Century*, ed. Katharina M. Wilson (Athens, 1988). Schotel, G.D.J., *A.M. van Schurman* (1853). Yvon, Pierre, "Abrégé sincère de la vie et de la Conduite et des vraies sentiments de feu Mr. De Labadie," in Gottfrid Arnold *Unparteyische Kirchen und Ketzerhistorie* (1715), II, pp. 1264ff.

Maya Bijvoet

Jutta Schutting

Born 1937, Lower Austria
Genre(s): poetry, prose, drama
Language(s): German

Both in prose and poetry, Jutta Schutting is concerned with evoking elusive and equivocal states, *Halbschlafbilder*, images of waking dream in progress. For Schutting, art is the act of creation, rather than the finished artifact. In the manner of Marguerite Duras and other French practitioners of the *nouveau roman*, she accentuates the *process* of writing the text by positioning and abandoning and taking up again various possibilities of plot. Jutta Schutting's world is one of fluctuating representation in which reality is infinitely malleable and fluid. Her writing is governed by the subjunctive and conditional modes, expressing wishful possibility rather than certitude. Schutting conceives of her art as a series of *Lichtungen* or clearings. A poem is "an undiscovered island to be drawn on an imaginary map," "a window open upon a foreign reality," and "something which reminds us of something of which there is no memory." The poetic moment is essentially that of ambiguous metamorphosis in which an object remains the same and simultaneously is something else. In works such as *Am Morgen vor der Reise* and *Der Wasserbueffel*, she explores the freshness of vision of the child, master of metamorphosis. Schutting is fascinated by the child's penchant for ritual, game-playing, and the riddle. Her children-artists play *Privatgalerie*, thinking up titles for paintings and then conjuring suitable images. They imagine the sounds of falling chestnuts as pistol shots beneath their window. They engage in oneiric searches for non-existent addresses. Distinction between the natural and supernatural, the concrete and symbolic is typically blurred in Schutting's writing, particularly in *Der Vater* and *Salzburg Retour*. In these texts, death of a loved one motivates a series of intertwined memories. The world of *Salzburg Retour* is literally ominous, replete with omens, objects, and experiences that bespeak the writer's inner state. A romanticism of subject matter (recurrent imagery of angels, perfume, swans, and honey) is nonetheless explored in a prose which is detached, controlled, and sometimes clinical in tone. Intense emotion, dissection of emotion, and ironical distancing from emotion are dominants in an *oeuvre* dedicated to questioning the fixity of reality. Schutting's settings are most often Austrian, and she is rooted in the Austrian tradition of Grillparzer, Schnitzler, and Hofmannsthal, writers fascinated with the threshold between waking and dream, attempting to capture elusive experience of that threshold in language.

Works

Poetry: *In der Sprache der Inseln* (1973). *Lichtungen* (1976).

Prose: *Hundesgeschicte* (1986). *Das Herz eines Loewen: Betrachtungen* (1985). *Der Wasserbueffel: Geschichten aus der Provinz* (1981). *Der Vater* (1980). *Stechenpferde* (1977). *Salzburg Retour: Trauermusik* (1977). *Parkmord: Erzaehlungen* (1975).

Donald Friedman

Helga Schütz

Born October 2, 1937, Probsthain/Falkenstein
(now Zlotoryja, Poland)
Genre(s): film script, television script,
documentary, prose
Language(s): German

Helga Schütz was born in Falkenstein, which today is a part of Poland. Her father was a metalsheet worker. In 1944 the family moved from the countryside to live in the city of Dresden. In 1955 Helga, after having studied horticulture, again moved, this time to Potsdam. In Potsdam Helga completed her secondary school education, then worked and studied at the College of Potsdam-Babelsberg. At Potsdam she studied the art of the film, film-producing, and writing. Schütz has received much recognition for her work on the film.

The writings of Helga Schütz demonstrate an originality springing from her own experiences. She is noted for the creation of a village called "Probstein" (a compilation of her early memories of Probstein and Falkenstein in Silesia), which she cyclically portrays in all her works.

In 1973 she was awarded the honored DDR Heinrich Mann prize for literature and was praised as a writer of "grace" and "modesty." The same character, a woman named Juliette, or Jette, appears in almost all of her works. Jette is a product of World War II: A foundling after Dresden had been leveled by the bombs, she lives with grandparents in the DDR and visits both East and West Germany. Her theme is the routine of daily life in a socialist society.

Works

Lots Weib [Lots' Wife] (1966). *Vorgeschichte oder Schöne Gegend Probstein* [Pre-history or the Beautiful Area of Probstein] (1971). *Das Erdbeben bei Sangerhausen* [The Earthquake at Sangerhausen] (1972). *Die Schlüssel* [The Keys] (1974). *Festbeleuchtung* [Festival Lighting] (1974). *Lotte in Weimar* [Lotte in Weimar] (1975). Based on Goethe's work. *Die Leiden des jungen Werther* [The Sorrows of Young Werther] (1976). Based on Goethe's work. *Mädchenrätsel* [The Mystery of a Young Girl] (1977). Ursula (1978). Based on Gottfried Keller's work. *Erziehung zum Chorgesang* [Training for Choral Singing] (1981).

Bibliography

Franke, Konrad, *Die Literatur der Deutschen Demokratischen Republik* (Zurich and Munich, 1974). Lennartz, Franz, *Deutsche Schriftsteller des 20. Jahrhunderts im Spiegel der Kritik*, Vol. 3 (Stuttgart, 1984). *Neue Literatur der Frauen.* Herausgegeben von Heinz Puknus (Munich, 1980). Serke, Jürgen, *Frauen Schreiben* (Frankfurt, 1982).

Brigitte Edith Archibald

Brigitte Schwaiger

Born April 6, 1949, Freistadt, Upper Austria
Genre(s): novel, short story, drama, radio
drama
Language(s): German

Brigitte Schwaiger created a sensation when, in 1977, she published her first novel, *Wie kommt das Salz ins Meer* (How Does the Salt Get into the Ocean). Praised lavishly by critics and authors as diverse as Johannes Mario Simmel, Friedrich Torberg, and Peter Turrini, this novel by the then twenty-seven-year-old former actress, sculptor, housewife, secretary and schoolteacher from a small town in Northern Austria became an instant bestseller and was translated into many languages. The reason for Schwaiger's initial success is her ability to create characters that readers worldwide could easily identify with. The novel's protagonist is a young woman who gets married without really knowing why and, after a divorce, a love affair and an abortion wants to retreat into her childhood. Parallels with Madame Bovary come to mind, whose little sister she has in fact been called. She loves her indecisiveness and thrives on self-pity.

All of Schwaiger's fiction is autobiographical in nature. However, in *Wie kommt das Salz ins Meer* (as in her other books) the author never reflects about herself but merely confronts the reader, in a style combining self-irony and naiveté, with events of her life. The unnamed heroine of the novel, mirroring the author's own situation, wants to liberate herself from the bourgeois trappings of family and home town. In doing so, however, she is incapable of analyzing her problems. She remains passive and blames her environment for her misery. No wonder critics have called Schwaiger's techniques a therapy without analysis.

Unfortunately, Schwaiger could not rise to the expectations generated by her first novel. Pressed by publishers and a voracious reading public, she allowed herself to imitate herself in subsequent books. *Mein spanisches Dorf* (My Spanish Village) is a collection of monologues, diaries, letters, and episodes revolving around herself and her home town of Freistadt with which she seems to have a love-hatred relationship. Similarly, in *Lange Abwesenheit* (A Long Absence), Schwaiger discusses her relationship with her father, a powerful and despotic figure portrayed earlier in *Wie kommt das Salz ins Meer*. *Malstunde* (Painting Hour) is a series of interviews with the Austrain painter, Arnulf Rainer. Attacked by critics as masochistic self-annihilation of an author and the epitome of banality, the book seems to indicate a drying-up of Schwaiger's poetic abilities. *Die Galizierin* (The Galitian) is the story of a Jewish woman's life and suffering. Eva Deutsch, listed as the co-author of the book, narrates her life to Schwaiger, who, in turn, records it as a monologue using the narrator's authentic language, High German combined with Polish and Yiddish elements.

Her latest book to date, *Der Himmel ist sü* (Heaven is Sweet), a childhood memoir, again reveals Schwaiger's limits as a writer of fiction and confirms her reputation as an author of confessions as the subtitle of her book suggests.

Works

Wie kommt das Salz ins Meer (1977). *Mein spanisches Dorf* (1978). *Lange Abwesenheit* (1980). [With Arnulf Rainer], *Malstunde* (1980). [With Eva Deutsch], *Die Galizianerin* (1982). *Der Himmel ist sü* (1984).

Translation: *Why is There Salt in the Sea?*, tr. Sieglinde Lus (1988).

Bibliography

Lederer, Herbert, "Von Arthur Schnitzler bis Brigitte Schwaiger–Der weite Weg ins einsame Land." *Modern Austrian Literature* 13.1 (1980): 47–62. Schmölzer, Hilde, "Brigitte Schwaiger: Halb Kindfrau, halb emanzipiert." Hilde Schmölzer. *Frau sein & schreiben: Österreichische Schriftstellerinnen definieren sich selbst* (Vienna, 1982), pp. 135–144. Wolfschütz, Hans, "Brigitte Schwaiger." in *Kritisches Lexikon zur Gegenwartsliteratur*, Heinz Ludwig Arnold, ed. (Munich: [edition text a kritik]), p. 8, Nlg. 1–6.

Jürgen Koppensteiner

Alice Schwartzer

Born 1942, Wuppertal, West Germany
Genre(s): essay, documentary
Language(s): German

Alice Schwartzer has become known in the German-speaking countries and France in particular since the 1960s through her almost radical feminism and her provocative attitude towards everything "male."

Born in 1942 in Wuppertal, Alice Schwartzer worked as a journalist and publicist, in Paris as much as in Germany. The major aim of her work is the analysis of the female position in modern postwar Germany, especially in areas where women obviously have never enjoyed an equal opportunity, such as in the professional life. In her opinion, women are exploited by employers, husbands, children, the law, and thus, by society in general. Women, the larger part of society, have been made its slaves and outsiders. Schwartzer tries to analyze the reasons for the underprivileged situation of women and sees men not only as woman's counterpart but as woman's arch-enemy. Most of her works are based on interviews and personal statements of women on working conditions, on abortion, or on love.

Her radical attitude provoked Ester Vilar to establish a different perspective; trying to analyze man's behavior, she came to the conclusion that man is woman's victim, calling her most famous book: *Der dressierte Mann* (The Trained Man). In a famous television discussion in Paris in the 1960s Ester Vilar and Alice Schwartzer had the opportunity to present and exchange their opinions, but the discussion culminated in mutual insults, misunderstanding, and intolerance.

In *Frauen gegen den Paragraphen zweihunderachtzehn* (Women Against I 218), Schwartzer collected opinions and statements of women on the abortion paragraph in the German criminal code: combining individual viewpoints with short personal comments, Alice Schwartzer tries to establish that women have a right to decide what happens to their own bodies and are unwilling to let man tell them what to do. Schwartzer sees the abortion paragraph as an unjustified intervention from the part of man. *Frauenarbeit-Frauenbefreiung* (Women's Labor-Women's Liberation) analyzes the exploitation women experience on the job with documents and personal statements of working women.

The book that established her fame, *Der "kleine" Unterschied und seine großen Folgen* (The "Little" Difference and Its Big Consequences), marks the beginning of the women's liberation discussion in Germany in a more radical vein. It discusses, like almost all of her works, the "little" biological difference that supposedly justifies the tremendous exploitation of women. *Simone de Beauvoir heute–Gespräch aus zehn Jahren* (Simone de Beauvoir Today) introduced this French feminist and companion of Sartre to the German audience.

Alice Schwartzer is provocative in style, expression, and opinion. Even though her opinions are hardly ever objective, she achieves credibility by giving women the chance of expressing their own opinions and using their statements and these documentary materials to prove her own point and to establish credibility.

Works

Der "kleine" Unterschied und seine großen Folgen. Frauen über sich-Beginn einer Befreiung, Frauen gegen den Paragraphen zweihundert-achtzehn; Frauenarbeit-Frauenbefreiung. Praxis Beispiele und Analysen (1973). *Simone de Beauvoir heute—Gespräche aus zehn Jahren; Durch dick und dünn. Mit Leidenschaft: Text 1968–1982* (1982). *So fing es an! Die neue Frauenbewegung* (1983). *Lohn: Liebe. Zum Wert der Frauenbefreiung* (1986). Translations: *Simone de Beauvoir Today.*

Jutta Hagedorn

Sibylle Schwarz

Born February 14, 1621, Greifswald,
Germany; died July 31, 1638
Genre(s): poetry drama, novella, letters
Language(s): German

Sibylle Schwarz was born on February 14, 1621, and died seventeen years later of dysentery on July 31, 1638. A native of the northern German city of Greifswald, she was the youngest child of upper-class parents, which accounted for her formal education in reading, catechism, music, mathematics, and the memorization of psalms. Schwarz's letters, written in a time when few women read, wrote, or passed on thoughts in print, document additional independent study, tutoring, and exchange of books with her university-educated brothers and mentors, among whom were Greifswald University's mathematics and medicine professor Johann Schöner, logic and metaphysics professor Alexander Christian, and theology professor Barthold Krakewitz. Her work, which includes sonnets, numerous "occasional" poems, a Susanna-drama, a tragedy commemorating the burning of the family's country estate at Fretow, a bucolic novelette, and a number of letters, demonstrates that she could read and write German and translate from Dutch and Latin, and was familiar not only with contemporary German Baroque poetry but also with figures and myths from classical antiquity. Schwarz's father's various civil service positions also brought the family into contact with royalty and nobility, and several of Schwarz's "occasional" poems accordingly celebrate events in their lives, for example, the matriculation of the Duke Ernst von Croy at the University of Greifswald.

Just as social status offered Schwarz an education and powerful connections, so did the family's comfortable economic situation provide a buffer against extreme hardship in the Thirty Years War. When first imperial troops and then Swedish forces descended on Greifswald, Schwarz and other young children were sent to safety at Fretow, which is idealized and eulogized in several of her poems, letters, and dramas as the most beautiful place on earth, a symbol of friendship and the virtuous life. The burning of Fretow was as traumatic for Schwarz as the sudden death of her mother on January 25,

1630. Her father was posted in Stettin from 1629–1631, and the Schwarz children, left in Greifswald, were effectively orphans. Care of the household was first turned over to the eldest daughter, widowed Regina, and then, upon her remarriage, to Emerentia, whose nuptials occurred the day Schwarz died from a sudden illness.

Not only a prodigy in producing verse, but also a phenomenon in the sense that she was a female writer and a prolific one at that, Schwarz left as her written legacy two substantial volumes of verse and prose, which total over one hundred and fifty pages. Routinely her efforts go beyond predictable rhyme schemes and themes and exhibit metrical skill, intense communication of feelings, a variety of poetic voices, and mastery of current poetic techniques. On the one hand, Schwarz worked to join the literary establishment, often praising Opitz and consciously emulating him or at the very least drawing from his models. On the other hand, she was very aware that she wrote "in a different voice" in her age, as the German Baroque was a time of ornamentation that did not take kindly to women who wanted to be more than ornaments. Schwarz's consciousness of being female in a male literary community gave her an unusual status, as well as access to a group of writers who, critics themselves, were in the position to make judgments about what constituted good and publishable material, yet the little girl dubbed "the Pommeranian Sappho" was viewed by many in somewhat the same manner as Samuel Johnson's walking dog.

In short, Schwarz chronicled marker events in the lives of many females around her but did not participate in their rites of passage.

In the final analysis, Schwarz offers a unique window into female experience in the Baroque era. While her work expresses the conventional Baroque sentiments that echo in the works of her male contemporaries—life's transitoriness, pacifistic beliefs, awareness of God's destructive and restorative aspects, the pains and pleasures of love, and the pleasant existence of shepherd and shepherdesses, for example—as well as adheres to the formal elements that prescribed and described German Baroque prose and verse, the additional dimensions to Schwarz's writings came about because she grew up female and died tragically young in an age not noted for an enlightened attitude toward women and in a country devastated by war.

Works

Deutsche Poetische Gedichte, Nuhn Zum ersten mahl au jhren eignen Handschrifften, heraugegeben und verleget Durch M. Samuel Gerlach, au dem Hertzogtuhm Würtemberg. und in Danzig Gedrukt, bey seel. Georg Rheten Witwen, im M.D.C.L. Jahr. *Ander Teil Deutscher Poëtischer Gedichten*, Nuhn zuhm ersten mahl Au jhren eignen Handschriften heraugegeben und verleget von M. Samuel Gerlach, au dem Hertzogtuhm Würtemberg. und zu Danzig Gedrukt, bey seel. Georg Rheten Witwen, im M.D.C.L. Jahr.

The above are accessible in Curt von Faber du Faur, *German Baroque Literature: A Catalogue of the Collection in the Yale University Library* (New Haven, 1958–1969). The Faber du Faur collection is available on microfilm at most major research libraries. Schwarz's work comprises Volumes 271 and 272 of this collection.

Bibliography

Clark, Susan L., "Sibylle Schwarz," in *17th-Century Women Writers*, ed. Katharina M. Wilson. Garland, Henry, and Mary, *The Oxford Companion to German Literature* (Oxford, 1976). Morhof, Daniel Georg, *Unterricht von der teutschen Sprache und Poesie* (Kiel, 1682). Newald, Richard, *Die deutsche Literatur: Vom Späthumanismus zur Empfindsamkeit 1570–1750* (Munich, 1965). Schoolfield, George C., *German Baroque Lyric*, University of North Carolina Studies in the Germanic Languages and Literatures, 29 (Chapel Hill, 1961; rpt. New York, 1966). Szyrocki, Marian, *Die deutsche Literatur des Barock* (Stuttgart). Ziefle, Helmut W., *Sibylle Schwarz, Leben und Werk*. Studien zur Germanistik, Anglistik, und Komparatistik, 35, ed. Armin Arnold and Alois M. Haas (Bonn, 1975).

Susan L. Clark

Ludamilia Elisabeth, Countess of Schwarzburg-Hohnstein

Born April 7, 1640, Schwarzburg-Rudolstadt;
died March 12, 1672, Rudolstadt
Genre(s): Baroque religious hymns, poetry
Language(s): German

Ludamilia Elisabeth grew up at the court of the Count of Schwarzburg-Rudolstadt, one of four children along with an adopted cousin, a distinguished and noble family. Her parents, Ludwig Gunther and Emilie Antonie, were well educated and widely travelled. It is reported that their family life was a very happy one but that Ludwig Gunther died when Ludamilia was only six years old. Emilie Antonie saw to it that her daughter, Ludamilia, received the best possible education. It was through their tutor, Ahasverus Fritsch, a poet himself, that Ludamilia was inspired to write her poems and hymns.

On December 20, 1671, Ludamilia was formally betrothed to Count Christian Wilhelm of Schwarzburg-Sonderhausen. Just about that time measles was raging in the district and the whole house of Rudolstadt became infected and one after another the sisters died, until Ludamilia also contracted the disease and died in her thirty-second year. Her poetry was published posthumously by her adopted sister.

Ludamilia's poems display aspects of her mental and spiritual life in all her poems. Her poems consist of prayers, praise, thanksgiving, meditation and edification of the believer. There is a noticeable lack of attention given to the physical aspects of life: the pleasure derived from the senses of touch, sight, smell, taste, hearing, the wonder and beauty of the natural world and the joys of human relationships. The poetry concentrates predominantly on spiritual existence and spiritual life.

Works

Die Stimme der Freundin, d.i. Geistliche Lieder,
welche aus brünstiger und bis ans Ende Begarrender
Jesus-Liebe verfertiget und gebrauchet Weiland
die hochgeborne Gräfin und Fräulein, Frl.
Ludamilia Elisabeth, Gräfin und Fräulein zu
Schwarzburg und Hohnsein, usw. Christseligen
Angedenkens [The Voice of the Friend, That Is, Spiritual Songs Which Have Been Prepared and Used from an Ardent and Eternal Love of Jesus by the Noble Countess and Young Lady, Miss Ludamilia Elisabeth, Countess of Schwarzburg and Hohnstein, etc. Blessed Christian Remembrance] (1687).

Bibliography

Allgemeine Deutsche Biographie. Hrsg. von der Historischen Kommission bei der Bayer. Akademie der Wissenschaften, red. R. von Liliencron und F.X. von Wegele, Vol. 1, 8, 19, 22 (1884 rpt; Berlin, 1967). Archibald, Brigitte Edith Zapp, *Ludamilia Elisabeth, Gräfin von Schwarzburg-Hohnstein and Aemilia Juliane, Gräfin von Schwarzburg-Rudolstadt: Two Poets of the Seventeenth Century.* Ph.D. diss., Knoxville, 1975. Faber du Faur, Curt von, *German Baroque Literature. A Catalogue of the Collection in the Yale University Library* (New Haven, 1958). Frommel, Emil, *Ludamilie von Schwarzburg-Rudolstadt und Marie von Lippe Schaumberg. Zwei Stilleben aus dem 17. und 18. Jahrhundert* (Berlin, 1874). Kosch, Wilhelm, *Deutsches Literatur-Lexikon* (Bern, 1949).

Brigitte Edith Zapp Archibald

Annemarie Schwarzenbach

(a.k.a. Clarac, Clark, Clark-Schwarzenbach)

Born May 23, 1908, Zurich, Switzerland;
November 15, 1942, Sils, Switzerland
Genre(s): prose fiction, poetry, biography,
travel literature, journalism, photography
Language(s): German

It is an irony of sorts that the wealthy, powerful, and privileged family of beautiful, talented Annemarie Schwarzenbach was in many ways a destiny she could not transcend. Her father's wealth derived from the textile industry; her maternal grandfather was the influential Swiss General Ulrich Wille, and her maternal grandmother was born a von Bismarck, third cousin of the chancellor Otto von Bismarck. Schwarzenbach, neither robust nor self-confident, was never able to extricate herself from the destructive love-hate bond that tied her to her strong-minded, traditionalist, and politically conservative mother.

Schwarzenbach's profound rebellion against everything her family stood for broke out in 1931, during an eighteen-month stay in Berlin. Its forms remained constants in her life: anti-fascist politics, intimate friendship with Erika and Klaus Mann (the eldest children of Thomas Mann), the overweening drive to write, lesbianism, morphine addiction. After 1933 her life was one of restless, unceasing travel, punctuated by the cycle of hospitalization for drug withdrawal in Switzerland and relapses into drug abuse. Her whereabouts changed with a rapidity that suggests desperation as Schwarzenbach unsuccessfully sought to find peace within herself: 1934, Moscow and Central Asia; 1935, after a suicide attempt, Persia, where she suddenly married a French diplomat; 1936 to 1938, the United States, Danzig, Moscow, Vienna, and Prague; 1939, Afghanistan (with Ella Maillart); 1940, a return trip to America that included a love affair with Carson McCullers and ended as a nightmare voyage through the insane asylums of New York; 1941, the Belgian Congo; 1942, the final return to Switzerland, where she died as the result of head injuries sustained in a cycling accident.

Schwarzenbach lived to suffer, and she lived to write. She completed a Ph.D. in history at the University of Zürich, and her numerous magazine and newspaper articles reveal a practiced, critical eye for the political and social complexities of the many lands she visited. Her photography, mostly unpublished, is often brilliant. Her fictional work, on the other hand, can overwhelm the reader with an unrelenting, static subjectivity that is often frozen in its obsession with the extremes of fear, despair, and loneliness. Where she retains control of her text, however, Schwarzenbach convincingly depicts the torments of her hauntingly inconsolable characters, and produces lyric moments of great beauty. The paradoxes of her work surely reflect her own inner contradictions. Unfortunately, some of Schwarzenbach's papers (including diaries and correspondence) seem to have disappeared after her death, and many of the remaining works are either out of print or unpublished. At present Lenos Verlag, Basel, is reissuing her work.

Works

Beiträge zur Geschichte des Oberengadins im Mittelalter und zu Beginn der Neuzeit [Contributions to the History of Upper Engadin in the Middle Ages and in the Early Modern Era], Diss. U. of Zürich (1931). *Freunde um Bernhard* [Friends of Bernhard], short story (1931). [With Hans Rudolf Schmid], *Das Buch der Schweiz. Ost und Süd* [The Book About Switzerland. East and South], journalism (1932). [With Hans Rudolf Schmid], *Das Buch der Schweiz. Nord und West.* [The Book About Switzerland, North and West], journalism (1933). *Lyrische Novelle* [Lyrical Novella], short story (1933). *Winter in Vorderasien. Tagebuch einer Reise* [Winter in the Near East. A Travel Journal], travel literature (1934). *Lorenz Saladin. Ein Leben für die Berge* [Lorenz Saladin. A Life Lived for the Mountains], biography (1938). *Das glückliche Tal* [The Fortunate Valley], novel (1940, 1987). "Die Schweiz—Das Land, das nicht zum Schuss kam." *Der Alltag* 2 (1987): 17–22 (written 1940). "Das Wunder des Baums," excerpt from unpublished novel of same title, completed 1942, *Der Alltag* 2 (1987): 23–33.

Bibliography

Landshoff-Yorck, Ruth, *Klatsch, Ruhm und kleine Feuer. Biographische Impressionen* (Köln, 1963), pp. 172–188 (memoirs and impressions of Annemarie Schwarzenbach). Linsmayer, Charles, "Leben und Werk Annemarie Schwarzenbachs. Ein tragisches Kapitel Schweizer Literaturgeschichte." Afterword to *Das glückliche Tal.* (Frauenfeld, 1987), pp. 160–223 (includes numerous photographs). Maillart, Ella, *The Cruel Way* (London, 1986) (memoir of trip with Annemarie Schwarzenbach). Meienberg, Niklaus, *Die Welt als Wille und Wahn. Elemente zur Naturgeschichte eines Clans* (Zürich, 1987), pp. 109–125. Perret, Roger, "Annemarie Schwarzenbach." *Der Alltag* 2 (1987): 7–16. Shortened version appeared in the *Neue Zürcher Zeitung* 7/8 (March 1987): 81–84; rpt. as afterword to Ella Maillart, *Flüchtige Idylle. Zwei Frauen unterwegs nach Afganistan* (1988).

Ann Marie Rasmussen

Madeleine de Scudery

Born 1607, Le Havre, France; died June 2, 1701, Paris
Genre(s): novel
Language(s): French

Better educated than most of the women of the period, Madeleine de Scudery had learned several foreign languages and read extensively when she joined her brother in Paris in 1639. She quickly became a social feature in the salon of Catherine de Vivonne, Marquise de Rambouillet. *La chambre bleue d'Arthénice* (Arthenice's Blue Bedroom) was then a renowned meeting place for intellectuals and fashionable society. It is there that was first developed a movement later known as *preciosité*—overly stressing refinement of language and manners. The glory of the Hotel de Rambouillet declined after the death of Vincent Voiture and of the Marquis de Rambouillet, and interest shifted to the salon, in the Marais in Paris, of Mademoiselle de Scudery. She invited well-known *gens de lettres* (men of letters) such as Conrart, Pellisson, Ménage, Godeau, Chapelain, and d'Aubignac. Each year, Mlle de Scudery published one or more volumes of her serial novels—*roman fleuve*. The first edition of *Le Grand Cyrus*—the exact title is *Artamène ou le Grand Cyrus*—was published between 1649 and 1653 (10 vol.) under her brother Georges de Scudery's name. It was followed (1654–1661) by *Clélie*, also in 10 volumes.

Although Mlle de Scudery's novels are situated in ancient times and in faraway places (*Ibrahim ou L'illustre Bassa* [1641] in Turkey, *Le Grand Cyrus*, in ancient Persia, *Clélie* in Rome), her guests are recognizable in her heroes. Mlle de Scudery herself is Sappho; Pellison is Acante; Godeau is Mage de Sidon; la Marquise de Rambouillet, Cléomire; Voiture, Callicrate; Jullie d'Angennes, Philonide, etc. In his study of seventeenth-century society, Victor Cousin has identified many of the author's contemporaries. The heroes act and talk in measured and polite terms; their conversations are witty and learned, setting the tone for polite conversations of polite society. In this sense, Mlle de Scudery had a great influence on the mores of her time, but her novels no longer have much appeal. They are endless stories of adventures with no apparent plot. Yet, her novels were translated in many languages, including German, English, Italian, Spanish and Arabic. The *carte du tendre* in *Clélie* was much admired as the map to the roads of true love. The receptions in Mlle de Scudery's salon no doubt had a great influence on the literary personalities of the time such as La Rochefoucauld, Mme de La Fayette, and Madame de Sévigné.

Works

Almaiide ou L'esclave Reine (1660–1663). Artamène ou le Grand Cyrus (1649–1653). Clélie, Histoire Romaine (1654–1660). Ibrahim ou L'illustre Bassa (1641). Conversations sur Divers Sujets (1680). Conversations Nouvelles sur Divers Sujets (1684). Conversations Morales (1686). Nouvelles Conversations Morales (1688).

Bibliography

Aragonnes, Claude, *Madeleine de Scudery*. Bray, R., *La Préciosité et les Précieux* (1948). Cousin, Victor, *Mademoiselle de Scudery, Sa Vie et Sa Correspondance* (1934).

Colette Michael

Dora Sedano

Born 1902, Madrid, Spain
Genre(s): drama, novel
Language(s): Spanish

Dora Sedano was born into a very conservative upper middle-class family. Although groomed by her family to be a concert pianist, she always wanted to write. In her childhood, so many of her short novels and stories were published in a magazine of children's literature, *Pulgarcito* (Tom Thumb), that her picture was on the cover when she was thirteen. Because she had no family connections in theater, as an adult she often wrote in collaboration with two established dramatists, Luis Fernández de Sevilla and Luis Tejada. Many of her plays, principally domestic comedies and political melodramas reflecting a conservative political and social orientation, were performed in the period 1940–1960. Her major work, *La diosa de arena* (The Sand Goddess) won a prestigious Pujol prize in 1952. In this political melodrama set just prior to the Spanish Civil War, a young woman brainwashed by the evils of communism eventually sees the light after her marriage into a pious Catholic family.

Works

Mercaderes de sangre [Merchants of Blood] (1945). La diosa de arena [The Sand Goddess] (1952). Nuestras chachas [Our Maids] (1953).

Bibliography

O'Connor, Patricia W., "ZQuiénes son las dramaturgas españolas, y qué han escrito?" Estreno

10.2 (1984): 9–12. "Encuesta: ¿Por qué no estrenan las mujeres en España?" *Estreno* 10.2 (1984): 24–25.

Patricia W. O'Connor

Anna Seghers

Born November 19, 1900, Mainz, Germany;
died June 1, 1983
Genre(s): novel, short story
Language(s): German

Anna Seghers studied Art History and Sinology at Heidelberg University, finishing in 1924 with a doctoral thesis on the Jewish tradition in the work of Rembrandt. In 1925 she married the sociologist and writer Lászlo Radvanyi and decided in 1928 to join the communist party; both were to be life-long affiliations. In 1933 she immigrated to France; her books were banned by the National Socialist Regime. In the Spanish Civil War she was an active supporter of the Republicans. In 1941 she escaped to exile in Mexico, returning to East Germany in 1947, where she became prominent as an author and participant in cultural politics, unswervingly, though at times critically, supporting the official organs of the GDR, receiving many high awards and presiding from 1952–1978 over the Deutsche Schriftstellerverband der DDR. Seghers' literary work has become internationally acclaimed in eastern as well as in western critical circles. The general esteem for her work rests on her concern for humanity, altruism, social justice, solidarity, and personal responsibility as well as on her progressive art consideration, which often defied conformist cultural politics. She must have appreciated Christa Wolf's reverence for her and been proud to see her leading the next generation. Anna Seghers' style of prose writing was formed by the French and Russian realists of the nineteenth century, and her topics are all narrative commentaries of epochal social experiences. Her very first short story, *Grubetsch* (for which she used the name Seghers), was a milieu study, the next, *Aufstand der Fischer von St. Barbara*, in 1928 (filmed by Piscator in the Soviet Union, 1934) a piece about striking fishermen and their plight of poverty and exploitation. *Auf dem Wege zur amerikanischen Botschaft* (1930) deals with the execution of Sacco and Vanzetti. Her first novel, *Die Gefährten* (1932), describes the defeat of revolutionary movements after World War I; *Der Kopflohn* (1933) confronts the thought processes of a SA-man and an antifascist worker; and *Der Weg durch den Februar* (1935) depicts the failure of resisting Vienna workers, explaining that a revolutionary ideology without power is doomed. Her most famous novel *Das siebte Kreuz* appeared in 1942 (filmed in the United States in 1944), a moving epic about the terrors of concentration camp and exile life. It was followed by *Transit* (1944), a further aspect on emigration, the anguish of uprootedness, being reduced to the uncertainty of chance and helpless moments of waiting before passage into exile. After *Der Ausflug der toten Mädchen* (1946), which begins a process of recapitulation by fusing present, dream, and memory, Seghers produced a new novel, *Die Toten bleiben jung* (1949, filmed in 1968, for which Christa Wolf wrote the film script), in which the authoress tried to summarize her view of events from 1918 to 1945. The historical structures of continuation from 1947 to 1953, which reflect Seghers' personal conviction for a new German state with Marxist social behavior, are portrayed in the novel *Die Entscheidung* (1959), followed by the sequel *Das Vertrauen* (1968). The titles indicate that decision and trust are necessary to build this new world, signified by the literary composite of dialectical opposition, the fight of western against eastern, reactionary versus progressive, capitalist versus socialist, bourgeois versus marxist forces. Her many anthologies of short stories round out her positions on the political and social experiences of her time.

Works

Jude und Judentum im Werke Rembrandts, Diss. (1924). *Grubetsch*, short story (1927). *Aufstand der Fischer von Santa Barbara*, short story (1928). *Auf dem Wege zur amerikanischen Botschaft*, anthology (1930). *Die Gefährten*, novel (1932). *Der Kopflohn*, novel (1933). *Die Stoppuhr*, short story (1933). *Ernst Thälmann. What He Stands For* (1934). *Der Weg durch den Februar*, novel (1935). *Der letzte Weg des Koloman Wallisch* short story (1936). *Die Rettung*, novel (1937). *Die schönsten Sagen vom Räuber Woynok, Sagen von Artemis*

(1940). *Das siebte Kreuz*, novel (1942). *Transit*, novel (1944). *Der Ausflug der toten Mädchen*, anthology (1946). *Das Ende*, short story (1948). *Die Toten bleiben jung*, novel (1949). *Die Hochzeit von Haiti*, anthology (1949). *Die Linie*, anthology (1950). *Crisanta*, short story (1951). *Die Kinder*, short stories (1951). *Der Mann und sein Name*, short story (1952). *Der erste Schritt*, short story (1953). *Frieden der Welt*, collection of speeches (1947–1953). *Die groe Veränderung in unserer Literatur*, speech (1956). *Brot und Salz*, short story (1958). *Die Kraft des Friedens*, speech (1959). *Die Entscheidung*, novel (1959). *Karibische Geschichten*, anthology (1962). *Über Tolstoi. Über Dostojewski*, essays (1963). *Die Kraft der Schwachen*, anthology (1965). *Das wirkliche Blau. Eine Geschichte aus Mexiko* (1967). *Vietnam in dieser Stunde* (1968). *Das Vertrauen*, novel (1968). *Briefe an Leser* (1970). *Über Kunstwerk und Wirklichkeit*, essays (1970–1971). *Überfahrt. Eine Liebesgeschichte* (1971). *Sonderbare Begegnungen*, anthology (1973).

Translations: *The Dead Stay Young* (1950). *Revolt of the Fisherman of Santa Barbara. A Prize on His Head* (1960). *The Seventh Cross* (1968).

Bibliography

Roos, Peter, and Friedericke Hassauer-Roos, eds., *Anna Seghers-Materialienbuch* (Darmstadt and Neuwied, 1977). Sauer, Klaus, *Anna Seghers* (Munich, 1978).

Margaret Eifler

Sophie de Ségur

(a.k.a. La Comtesse de Ségur, née Rostopchine)

Born July 19, 1799, St. Petersburg; died January 31, 1874, Paris
Genre(s): children's literature
Language(s): French

The daughter of the Count Rostopchine, minister of Tzar Paul I, and of Anna Protassov, the countess lived either at Woronowo, her father's feudal domain, or at the court of Alexander I until the age of seventeen. Her education was very closely supervised by her mother, who, strongly influenced by the French philosophers of the eighteenth century, imposed on her children the most ascetic regimen. Anna Protassov, who suddenly converted to Catholicism against the will of the count, battled relentlessly to win their children over to the Catholic faith. Sophie eventually followed her mother over to the Catholic side of the family. In 1816, the count, feeling in political disfavor, decided to exile his family to Paris, where the young Sophie was very soon married, in 1819, to the Count Eugène de Ségur. The Count Rostopchine presented the young couple with a chateau in Normandy, Les Nouettes, where Sophie de Ségur was to spend the major part of her life. The marriage was not a very happy one, and she decided to live in Normandy with her eight children. Though she had always been a good story teller, it is only when her grandchildren moved away to England that she started to write, mailing them the stories they had enjoyed so much at home.

Upon the insistence of Louis Veuillot, director of the ultramontane newspaper *L'Univers*, she decided to publish her work. In 1856, Louis Hachette published *Les Nouveaux contes de Fées* (New Fairy Tales), with illustrations by Gustave Doré. The book was an instant success and during the next thirteen years the countess wrote about twenty novels for children, the best known of which are *Les Malheurs de Sophie* (Sophie's Misfortunes), *Les Petites Filles Modèles* (Exemplary Little Girls), *Les Mémoires d'un Ane* (Memoirs of a Donkey). She also wrote more didactic books, such as *l'Evangile d'une grand-mère* (A Grandmother's Gospel), *La Bible d'une grand-mère* (A Grandmother's Bible), *Les Actes des Apôtres* (The Acts of the Apostles) and *La Santé des enfants* (Children's Health), an essay on childcare. Her novels and fairy tales are still widely read and studied today despite some harsh criticism.

Her literary style contributes much to her success. She succeeds in mixing the theatrical genre, by using the direct style extensively, with the narrative, providing the very young reader with a novel that is easy to read and interesting. However, it is probably her approach to children's literature that best explains her popularity: in her works, the didactic intentions, which weighed so heavily in the books of her predecessors, become secondary. She presents the reader with heros who are on a more human scale. Good does not always prevail, instincts are always taken into account.

Some critics have made psychoanalytical readings of the countess and have strongly expressed their concern about her sado-masochistic tendencies and the dangers that she represented to society as a whole.

These characteristics of her work are still very passionately discussed in France, some critics going so far as to ask that her books be banned from young children's libraries or that they be heavily censored. The main points of controversy in her work are related to her depictions of nineteenth-century French society from an aristocratic perspective, according to which there is little hope for the members of the lower classes. However, her writings are of considerable interest to historians, who have been able to reconstitute from her descriptions the day-to-day life of a wide range of the society of the Second Empire.

The most interesting aspect of the countess' work is her relentless effort to express her understanding of childhood and, to a lesser extent, of adulthood. Throughout her writing there emerges a genuine concern for children and the role of parenting at all levels.

Probably influenced by the teaching of her mother, who was a great admirer of Rousseau, the countess advocates a simple lifestyle: clothing is to be comfortable and practical, allowing the young child to get physical exercise through play. Food is to be natural and abundant: she severely condemns both gluttony and the starvation of children by parents as a means of punishment. Skills taught to children—even those of aristocratic families—must be of a practical nature as well as of an intellectual one. Parents must provide children with a basic healthy routine that forbids late nights, mundane amusement, and luxury, but which must fulfill the children's need for sleep, food, and physical exercise. Her conception of childhood is original for the nineteenth century in the sense that it recognizes the child as a person having legitimate needs different of those from his parents.

The countess also spoke about adulthood. She did it primarily in the name of women, showing many a woman as head of a household, successfully managing important domains without the help of a husband, a brother, or any kind of male support. Even more daringly, she depicted mothers totally in charge of the spiritual fate of their children, excluding the intervention of priests. She imprinted in her readers' mind the portrait of women as potentially the total equals of men, as self-reliant human beings. In her later works, intended for teenage readers, she tried to fight on more specific grounds, such as the right for girls to choose their husbands, the necessity of a marital relationship based on love, respect, and understanding on the part of both the husband and the wife. She even revealed to her readers how sexual power could be used by women in order to change a relationship, also advocating that women have a right to see their sexual desire adequately fulfilled by their husbands. Her young heroines show a very positive understanding of sexual feelings, taking the leadership role in the couple's private life.

However, the countess also showed that men were unjustly treated by society: she therefore tried to see that her male characters be treated sensibly. She demanded that men be nurturing to their children, affectionate, and even tender.

The variety of themes and problems expressed in the works therefore justifies her place of honor among nineteenth-century French writers. In the past few years, the process towards her canonization has begun, with the inclusion of some of her works in high school curricula.

Works

Nouveaux Contes de Fées (1856). *La Santé des Enfants* (1857 and 1862). *Les Petites Filles Modèles* (1857). *Les Vacances* (1859). *Les Malheurs de Sophie* (1859). *Les Mémoires d'un Ane* (1860). *Pauvre Blaise* (1860). *La Soeur de Gribouille* (1861). *Les Bons Enfants* (1862). *L'Auberge de l'Ange-Gardien* (1862). *Les Deux Nigauds* (1862). *François le Bossu* (1863). *Un Bon Petit Diable* (1865). *Jean qui grogne et Jean qui rit* (1865). *La Fortune de Gaspard* (1866). *Le Général Dourakine* (1866). *Le Mauvais Génie* (1866). *Evangile d'une Grand-Mère* (1866). *Comédies et Proverbes* (1866). *Diloy le Chemineau* (1867). *Quel Amour d'Enfant* (1868). *Après la Pluie le Beau Temps* (1871). *Actes des Apôtres* (1866). *Bible d'une Grand-Mère* (1870). English translations: *The Misfortunes of Sophie* (1936). *The Wise Little Donkey* (1931). *The Angel Inn* (1976). *Old French Fairy Tales* (1920). *The Acts of the Apostles for Children* (1912). *A Life of Christ for Children* (1909).

Bibliography

Audiberti, Marie-Louise, *Sophie de Ségur, l'inoubliable comtesse: ses anges, ses dîmens* (Paris, 1981). Beaussant, Claudine, *La Comtesse de Ségun ou l'enfance de l'art* (Paris, 1988). Bléton, Paul, *La Vie Sociale sous le Second Empire* (Paris, 1963). Doray, Marie-France, "Cleanliness and Class in the Countess de Ségur's Novels." *Children's Literature* 17 (1989): 64–80. Hédouville, Marthe de, *La Comtesse de Ségur et les siens* (Paris, 1953). Herz, Micheline, "The Angelism of Mme de Ségur." *Yale French Studies* 27 (Spring-Summer 1961): 12–21. Kreyder, Laura, *L'Enfance des saints et des autres. Essai sur la Comtesse de Ségur* (Fasano, Italy, 1987). Laden, Richard A., "Terror, Nature dans le Sacrifice in the Comtesse de Ségur's *Les Petites Filles Modèles.*" *Modern Language Notes* 94 (1979): 742–756. Laurent, Jacques, "Etrennes Noires." *La Table Ronde* 13 (1949): 157–167. Soriano, Marc, *Guide de Littérature pour la Jeunesse* (Paris, 1975). Soriano, Marc, Préface à *La Fortune de Gaspard* (Paris, 1972). Vinson, Marie Christine, *L'Education des petites filles dez la Comtesse de Ségur* (Lyon, 1987).

Valerie Lastinger

La Comtesse de Ségur, née Rostopchine

(see: Sophie de Ségur)

Ina Seidel

Born September 15, 1885, Halle, Germany;
died October 2, 1974, Munich
Genre(s): novel, short story, poetry
Language(s): German

Seidel was a prolific writer of novels, short stories, and poems. She figures with the expressionists and writers of the Weimar Republic.

Ina Seidel was the daughter of a surgeon in Halle and came from a family of writers. She grew up in Munich and Braunschweig. In 1907 she married her cousin Heinrich Wolfgang Seidel, who was a pastor in Eberswalde and Berlin and who in 1934 gave up his pastorate to devote himself full time to writing.

Due to a childhood illness she suffered from lameness throughout her life. This fact undoubtedly fostered her great interest in writing and in pursuing a writing career. Her successful novels and short stories enabled her to become popular during her lifetime among the middle classes.

Ina Seidel shows her indebtedness to Romanticism in poetry and in her short portraits of Bettina and Clemens Brentano. The values that made the middle class great are extolled in her novels. Her earlier novels stand out because of their careful and insistent handling of woman's importance in family life; her specialty is the relationship of brothers and sisters. Ina Seidel's masterpiece is *Das Wunschkind* (The Wish Child). The hero's mother is the daughter of a patrician family in Mainz; she is married to a Prussian officer, whose child, the Wish Child, she conceives the night before his departure to fight the French revolutionaries. He is killed. As the boy grows up the mother's situation is that of Parzival's mother: the boy belongs to a Prussian family of officers. He must fight. He is as dedicated to death as his father was. The mother's sister marries a French officer who has risen from the ranks, and the child of this union, a daughter, is brought up with the old grandfather, a man of heroic mold, on the Prussian estate. The boy falls in love with his cousin though the French blood in her veins makes her flighty and unfit for a Prussian hero. He is more than Prussian: the great collective ideal for the future is the fusing, say, of a kind of state chemistry, of German provincial characteristics into a perfect character who will stand for ideal and Supreme Germany. Thus, in the young lad, the artistic qualities of the Rhineland are blended with the hard metal of military Prussia.

Perhaps a more insistent burden of the tale is the absolute and statesmanlike necessity of the Prussian military machine and its essential humanity—in the sense that the man is served by the machine, which must no more be questioned than the machines in a factory. The doctrine of categorical imperative is developed at immense length in this novel and is also found in her other works.

In her last book, *Michaela* (1959), she presents the blindness and helplessness of the middle-class society in the face of the Hitler terror. In the novel *Lennacker* (1938), Seidel portrays a young man who returns from the war and experiences in dream visions the history of his family from the time of Luther to the end of the typically bourgeois civilization. Her style displays a Christian-Humanistic ethic; it is cultivated and psychological and always places the protagonists in a spiritual, individual, moral foundation.

Works

Gedichte [Poetry] (1919). *Das Labyrinth* [The Labyrinth] (1922). *Sterne der Heimkehr* [Stars of Homecoming] (1923). *Neue Gedichte* [New Poetry] (1927). *Der volle Kranz* [The Complete Garland] (1929). *Das Wunschkind* [The Wish Child] (1930). *Meine Kindheit und Jugend* [My Childhood and Youth] (1935). *Gesammelte Gedichte* [Collected Poems] (1937). *Lennacker* [Lennacker] (1938). *Unser Freund Peregrin* [Our Friend Peregrin] (1940). *Das Unerwesliche Erbe* [The Incorruptible Inheritance] (1954). *Michaela* [Michaela] (1959).

Bibliography

Annalen der deutschen Literatur, ed. Heinz Otto Burger (Stuttgart, 1952). *Autorenlexikon deiutschsprachiger Literatur des 20. Jahrhunderts*, ed. Manfred Brauneck (Hamburg, 1984). Bithell, Hethro, *Modern German Literature* (London, 1939). *Deutsche Schriftsteller im Portrait*, ed. Karl-Heinz Habersetzer, vol. VI (Munich, 1984). Horst, K.A., *Ina Seidel. Wesen und Werk* (1956).

Brigitte Archibald

Maria Seidemann

Born 1944, Engelsdorf bei Leipzig, East
Germany
Genre(s): poetry, novel, film, television
Language(s): German

Marie Seidemann went to school in Leipzig and later in Dresden, where she completed her high school education. She studied from 1964 to 1967 at the Fachschule für Archivwesen in Potsdam, where she was later employed as a teacher of German history. She also studied history at the Humboldt University in Berlin. It is believed she started writing around 1971. In 1972–1973 Maria attended the Johannes R. Becher Institut for Literature in Leipzig. Since 1974 she has been a free-lance writer.

Maria Seidemann's themes in poetry and in prose deal with societal problems: mental retardation, the influence of living conditions on human behavior, professions, jobs and education, the experience of art and its influence on society. Her style is terse, demanding, and exacting. She does not minimize the deficiencies and imperfections of her own society; she expostulates the weakness of every society.

Works

Fünf geben Auskunft: Porträts über Zeitgenossen, contemporary portraits (1974). *Letzter Aufenhalt* [The Last Abode], story for film (1974). *Kieselsteine* [Pebbles], poetry (1975). *Der Tag an dem Sir Henry Starb* [The Day on Which Sir Henry Died], collection of prose (1975).

Bibliography

Kritik 81: Rezensionen der DDR-Literatur, ed. Eberhard Gunther, Werner Liersch, and Klaus Water (Leipzig: Halle, 1981).

Brigitte Edith Archibald

Lidia Seifullina

Born March 22, 1889, Orenburg province,
Russia; died April 25, 1954, Moscow
Genre(s): short story, novella, journalism
Language(s): Russian

Lidia Seifullina is remembered with great affection by a generation of younger Soviet authors whom she encouraged at the beginning of their careers. She was also one of the most remarkable regionalists of Soviet literature who produced, in the 1920s, a small body of fine tales from the life of her native Orenburg province south of the Ural mountains.

Seifullina was the daughter of an Orthodox priest of Tatar stock and a Russian peasant woman, who was taught to read and write by her husband. The mother died before her two daughters were of school age, and, brought up by her maternal grandmother, Seifullina was long ashamed of her dark, Asian looks and heritage. It was from her Tatar father, however, that she got her abiding love of Russian literature. After graduation from secondary school in Omsk, Seifullina tried teaching and acting, travelling the country from Lithuania to Central Asia and the Caucasus with a theatrical troupe. Back in the Orenburg region, she worked in bookstores and village libraries and tried her hand occasionally at writing. From 1917 to 1919 she was a member of the social-revolutionary party and then a committed Soviet citizen. In 1920 she was admitted to a pedagogical institute in Moscow.

From 1921 to 1923, Seifullina and her husband (the critic and writer V.P. Pravdukhin, who was purged in 1937 and died in 1939) were commanded to Novosibirsk (then Novonikolaevsk). There they and a small band of enthusiastic colleagues founded the first serious literary and sociopolitical journal in Siberia, *Sibirskie ogni* (Siberian Fires). The still fresh excitement of this venture is recorded in Seifullina's "A Memorable Five Years" (1927). She began writing fiction for the early issues of the new magazine. Her first story, "Four Chapters: A Tale in Fragments" (1922), is the depiction of a woman's progress from actress to mine-owner's mistress to schoolteacher and Soviet citizen. It is marred by a staccato telegraphic style, in which seven-word sentences stand out as long. Her next story, "Lawbreakers," written in a less terse and more effective idiom, relates the history of a colony dedicated to rehabilitating the street-wise orphans left as debris from the civil war.

Among Seifullina's finest works, all in an increasingly ornamental *skaz* diction, are: "Peregnoi" (1922; Humus), "Virinea" (1924), and "Kain-kabak" (1926; a Turkic title that Seifullina translates as "birch ravine"). All three of these long tales (*povesti*) depict the turbulent early years of the Soviet state and vital protagonists destroyed by counter-revolutionary forces or by their own internal contradictions. They are well observed, non-tendentious, and permeated with the dialect, *mores*, and lore of the Orenburg region. Seifullina and Pravdukhin adapted "Virinea" for the theater in 1925. It is not surprising that the play became very popular: Virinea, a rootless farm-laborer and day-worker, easy in morals and independent in ideas, is one of the most attractive heroines of Soviet literature.

While much of Seifullina's later prose has the same vivid language and settings, it suffers from the facile didacticism of social realism at its least effective. "Pevets" (1940; The Singer), for instance, depicts as given the transformation of a primitive village into a cultured *kolkhoz*, but it offers no insight into the magic formula. Other strong-minded and attractive heroines appear in stories like "Na svoei zemle" (In One's Own Land) and "Sasha," written during and about World War II, but "Virinea" and Seifullina's other tales of the 1920s are acknowledged in the Soviet Union as her lasting legacy.

Works

Pisateli: Avtobiografii i portrety sovremennykh russkikh prozaikov, Vl. Lidin, ed. (1928), pp. 290–292. *Sovetskie pisateli, Avtobiografii,* Ia. Brainina and E.F. Nikitina, comp. (1959), vol. 2, pp. 320–331. *Sobranie sochinenii,* 4 vols. (1968–1969).

Bibliography

Galmanova, M.A., "Master narodnoi rechi," *Russkaia rech'* 2 (1979): 57–62. *Handbook of Russian Literature,* Victor Terras, ed. (New Haven, 1985), p. 394 (Victor Terras). Ianovskii, N., *Lidia Seifullina: Kritiko-biograficheskii ocherk* (Moscow, 1959). Ianovskii, N., "Lidia Seifullina: K 90-letiiu so dnia rozhdeniia," *Moskva* 4 (1979): 208–210. Kardin, V., *Dve sud'by: Lidiia Seifullina i ee povest' "Virineia."* (Moscow, 1975). *Kratkaia literaturnaia entsiklopediia,* vol. 6 (Moscow, 1971), cols. 729-730 (N.N. Ianovskii).

Mary F. Zirin

Austra Sēja

(see: Anna Sakse)

Fehime Selimi

Born 1954, Preshevě, Yugoslavia
Genre(s): poetry
Language(s): Albanian

Selimi went to school in Skopje and Prishtinë, Kosově (the predominantly Albanian-populated area of Yugoslavia). Later she studied at the Faculty of Arts in the University of Prishtinë.

Works

Fjala ime ka etje [My Word Is Thirsty] (1980). *Lule në ethe* [Feverish Flowers] (1982).

Philip Shashko

Anna September

(see: Eeva-Liisa Manner)

Beatrice del Sera

*Born April 3, 1515, Florence, Italy; died
    January 27, 1585, Prato*
Genre(s): drama, lyric poetry
Language(s): Italian

Beatrice del Sera, the daughter of a Florentine merchant, was taken at two years of age to the Domenican convent of San Niccolò in Prato where she lived until her death at the age of sixty-nine. It is not known when she took her vows, but she was a professed nun by the age of fourteen and became prioress of the convent in 1562. She seems to have left the convent only once, in 1530, when she and 29 other nuns of her convent took refuge in a Domenican house in Pistola out of fear of a sack of Prato by Imperial troops of Charles V. In Pistoia she had access to books which she read avidly, and from which the rest of her life took direction. She became a writer, a dramatist, and lyric poet, but all that has survived of her production is one five-act play in verse, the *Amor di virtù* (Love of Virtue), written between 1548 and 1555, and two sonnets written in the margins of her edition of Petrarch's poetry.

Beatrice's only surviving play, the *Amor di virtù*, is a spiritual comedy, a genre combining sacred and profane elements in the plot. In the sixteenth century this new genre, which owed its structure and many of its characteristics to the revival of classical theater, replaced the one-act *sacra rappresentazione* (mystery play) in popularity in Tuscan convents. Beatrice's play is a "spiritualizaion" of the love story Giovanni Boccaccio narrates in his early romance the *Filocolo*. The story of the love, separation, trials, reunion, and conversion of the young couple (from Longus's *Daphnis and Chloe* via the French Floire and Blancheflor tradition) is read as an allegory for the love story of the soul for God following the age-old tradition of mystical religious literature. Boccaccio's story is maintained in its general lines, though erotic elements not functional in the allegory are eliminated or attenuated. There is a second allegory also inspired by Boccaccio's example but very different from it. The story of the vicissitudes of the heroine, whose name is changed to Aurabeatrice, is read autobiographically and her tower prison represents the author's enclosure in the convent, allowing the introduction into the play of a feminist polemic, an indictment of men for locking women up against their will. "They are women," one character says, "not pictures to hang on the wall."

The play is very well written, especially in its lyric passages (lovers' laments, letters, songs, *intermezzi*) and its imagery, and it displays a sophisticated handling of allegory. The production, judging from references to the set and music in the stage directions, must have been quite elaborate. Beatrice's other works, to which she refers in a prose epilogue to *Amor di virtù*, have been lost. Her two lyric poems written in the margins of her copy of Petrarch, are spiritualizations of Petrarchan language and themes.

The play exists in a single, sixteenth-century manuscript belonging to the Riccardiana Library in Florence. The text seems to have been used for a performance, since scene divisions have been added in a later hand, but the manuscript is a formal copy, beautifully executed by a copyist and opening with an accomplished pen and ink drawing painted over in watercolors. There are corrections in the manuscript, some accessory poetry, and a prose epilogue which seem to be autograph.

Works

Amor di virtù, ms., Riccardiana Library, Florence, cod. Ricc. 2932 (fall 1989, by Elissa Weaver, Ravenna, Longo Editore). "Alma, a che più nelli caduchi e frali," and "Il senso il mondo e l'oziose piume," two sonnets, are published in Ageno article (see bibliography). Selections from *Amor di virtù* (part of the sonnet "Al discreto lettore" and the intermezzo "Alma gentil che siete . . .") in Trucchi, Francesco, ed., *Poesie italiane inedite di dugento dall'origine della lingua*, III, pp. 305–311.

Bibliography

Ageno, Federico, "Rime autografe di Suor Beatrice del Sera in un rarum della biblioteca universitaria di Pavia, *Bolletino della Società Pavese di Storia Patria* 19 (1919): 1–21. Bandini Buti, Maria, ed., *Poetesse e scrittrici* I (*Enciclopedia biografica e bibliografica italiana*, Serie VI) (Rome, 1941), p. 221. Emanuele, Angelo, *Virtù d'amore di Suor Beatrice del Sera* (Catania, 1903). Meucci, Felice, *Il ruolo delle religiose del monastero di S. Niccolao*, ms. dated 1750, Archives of San Niccolò, A-2, p. 130. Weaver, Elissa, "*Amor di virtù*: il *Filocolo* spirituale di suor Beatrice del Sera," *Studi sul Boccaccio* 15 (1986): 265–286. Weaver, Elissa, "Spiritual Fun: A Study of Sixteenth-Century Tuscan Convent Theater," in Mary Beth Rose, ed., *Women in the Middle Ages and Renaissance: Literary and Historical Perspectives* (Syracuse, N.Y., 1986), pp. 187–197.

Elissa B. Weaver

Matilde Serao

Born 1856, Patras, Greece; died 1927, Naples, Italy
Genre(s): short story, novella, journalism
Language(s): Italian

Born in Greece, to which in 1848 her father had fled in order to avoid Bourbonic repression, Matilde Serao returned to Italy with her family in 1860. Her early years were heavily influenced by her Greek mother, less so by her often absent journalist father. Although her early education was haphazard, she eventually trained to be a teacher; her experiences in school formed the basis for her very successful autobiographical short story *Scuola normale femminile* (Women's Teachers College) published first in the Milanese journal *La Farfalla* and later as a book with two other stories in 1886. Rather than taking up a career in teaching, however, Serao worked from 1876 to 1878 for the State Telegraph Office and began her journalistic activities with articles for a number of newspapers and periodicals. In 1881 she was made an editor for the Roman *Capitan Fracassa* and moved to Rome where she became involved in the fervent political and literary atmosphere that surrounded the journal. Directed by the brilliant "Gandolin" (Luigi Vassallo) and edited by the young Scarfoglio and D'Annunzio, *Capitan Fracassa* was an organ of the new and polemical both in politics and in literature. The young Neopolitan Serao soon became one of the most popular representatives of the paper's vivacious modernity, writing under various pseudonyms on topics as diverse as literature and fashion. Her first novel, *Cuore infermo* (Infirm Heart), was published in 1881, followed in 1883 by *Fantasia* (Fantasy). The latter was reviewed positively by all of the most important literary journals, and what would be Serao's life-long career as journalist and narrator was definitively underway. In 1883 Serao wrote two of her most important works: the novella *La virtù di Checchina* (Checchina's Virtue) and the long report on Naples for *Capitan di Fracassa* entitled *Il ventre di Napoli* (Naples' Belly). The first is the story of a young bourgeois housewife who dreams of escaping the dreary confines of her meaningless domestic life yet fails to act. The two definitions of "virtù" (both "chaste morality" and "potential") ironically highlight Checchina's essence: she is "virtuous" precisely because she does not realize her potential as a thinking and feeling individual. The second piece is an astoundingly penetrating portrait of Naples' underside or "belly," which was the result of Serao's investigations of the working-class neighborhoods of cholera-devastated Naples. Far from being a Socialist sympathizer, Serao nonetheless succeeded in understanding and empathizing with the lowest levels of human corruption and suffering and in infusing her prose with a sort of objective passion.

When, in 1885, she married her colleague Edoardo Scarfoglio, Serao was already a celebrated writer, known and admired by other equally famous figures such as D'Annunzio, Verga, and the actress Eleanora Duse. She and her husband continued to be active on the journalistic and literary scenes; they founded their own newspaper, *Il Corriere di Roma*, to which Serao contributed under the pen name of Gibus; in 1886 a collection of her stories entitled *Il romanzo della fanciulla* (The Young Girl's Novel) appeared; in 1887 they moved to Naples where both Scarfoglio and Serao took up leading positions in the world of journalism. In 1892 Scarfoglio founded *Il Mattino*, in which were reflected his rightist political views. In addition to her journalistic collaboration, Serao continued publishing fiction; in 1887 *Vita e avventure di Riccardo Joanna* (The Life and Adventures of Riccardo Joanna) recreates Scarfoglio's difficulties in founding his own newspaper; in 1891 *Il Paese di Cuccagna* (Land of Plenty) returns to an analysis of Neopolitan society reminiscent of the earlier *Ventre di Napoli*. Between 1894 and 1900 Serao published several other pieces of fiction that enjoyed popular success.

The last period of Serao's life, from 1901 to her death, is marked by her estrangement from her husband and children (the latter born in the 1880s). She wrote her last article for *Il Mattino* in 1901 (a piece against divorce); in 1904 the first issue of *Il Giorno* appeared. Although not its official editor, the newspaper was in fact Serao's and in it appeared a series of articles that were direct polemics against Scarfoglio's stands. By 1922 Serao showed certain sympathies with the Socialists and in that year (Scarfoglio had died in 1917) Serao published pieces against her late husband's pro-fascist newspaper. With her anti-war novel of 1926, *Mors tua . . .* (Your Death), and the anti-fascist stand of her newspaper, Serao provoked the anger of Mussolini who intervened against the assignation of the Nobel Prize to her. The prize went instead to Grazia Deledda. Serao died at her desk in 1927.

Although often accused of sentimentalism and/or imitative naturalism, Serao's work deserves serious critical attention. The autobiographical and documentary elements of many of her books reveal a great sensitivity to the details of everyday life as well as strong insight into the psychological and social realities of early modern Italian society. Her feminine characters do not often reflect Serao's own ability to attain success in a "man's world," yet it is precisely that success—and the intelligence and strength that made it possible—to which contemporary students of literature and culture could profitably devote their efforts toward understanding both the limitations and the achievements of pre-liberation women.

Works

Cuore infermo [Infirm Heart] (1881). *Fantasia* (1883). *Il ventre di Napoli* [Naples' Belly] (1883). *La virtù di Checchina* [Checchina's Virtue] (1884).

Il romanzo della fanciulla [The Young Girl's Novel] (1886). *Vita e avventure di Riccardo Joanna* [The Life and Adventures of Riccardo Joanna] (1887). *Il paese di Cuccagna* [Land of Plenty] (1891). *Castigo* (1893). *Donna Paola* (1897). *La ballerina* (1899). *Suor Giovanna della croce* (1900). *La leggenda di Napoli* (1906). *Parla una donna* (1916). *Mors tua . . .* [Your Death] (1926). *La mano tagliata* (1979). Collections: Banti, Anna, ed., *L'occhio di Napoli* (1962). Pancrazi, Pietro, ed., *Romanzi e racconti italiani dell'Ottocento: Serao* (1944). Translations: *The Ballet Dancer and On Guard* (1901). *The Essential Matilde Serao*, tr. Anthony M. Gisolfi (1968).

Bibliography

Banti, Anna, *Matilde Serao* (Turin, 1965). Buzzi, Giancarlo, *Matilde Serao*. (Milan, 1981). Harrowitz, Nancy, "Figuring the Material in Mystery: Matilde Serao's *La mano tagliata*," in *Stanford Italian Review* VII, 1–2 (1987): 191–204. Infusino, Gianni, ed., *Matilde Serao tra giornalismo e letteratura* (Naples, 1981). Olken, Irene T., "*La virtù di Checchina*: Anachronism and Resolution," in *Kentucky Romance Quarterly* 29 (1982–1983): 45–59. General references: *Dizionario degli autori italiani* (Messina-Florence, 1973). *Dizionario della letteratura italiana contemporanea* (Florence, 1973). Caccia, E., ed., *I minori* (Milan, 1962). Croce, Benedetto, *Letteratura della nuova Italia* (Bari, 1915). Luti, Giorgio, ed., *Narratori italiani del primo Novecento: La vita, le opere, la critica* (Rome, 1985).

Rebecca West

D. Şerban

(see: Claudia Millian)

Cella Serghi

(a.k.a. Cella Marin)

Born 1907, Constanţa, Romania
Genre(s): novel, short story, memoirs,
journalism, translation
Language(s): Romanian

Cella Serghi studied law, worked as a lawyer and journalist, and made her debut in 1938 with the novel *Pînza de păianjen* (Cobweb). Written in the Proustian tradition of affective memory, the novel has as narrator-protagonist a poor young woman, Diana Slavu, who struggles to evade a stifling universe and sentimental failure by orienting herself towards collective endeavors. The novel was revised in 1946, when it appeared in the prestigious collection *Romanul românesc* (The Romanian Novel) and then was reprinted with modifications in 1962 and 1971. Like Gide, Cella Serghi told the story of how she wrote her first novel in the volume of confessions *Pe firul de păianjen al memoriei* (1978; On Memory's Spider Thread).

Serghi is a Durassian type of novelist who keeps rewriting and reorienting her novels. A second cycle of transformations includes *Cad zidurile* (1950; Walls Are Falling), which she remade in 1967 into *Cartea Mironei* (Mirona's Book) and finally converted into *Mirona* (1972; Mirona). The novels meander around and throughout the life of Mirona Runcu, a rich intellectual who, again, fails in love, meets with the international communist circles, and becomes vitally involved in political action.

The female character who cannot grow except by sacrificing love will occur again in the Bildungsroman *Genţiane* (1970; Gentians) where the young heroine aims this time not at immersing herself into anonymous political or social efforts but at becoming a play director and evolving into a strong, independent creator.

Fetele lui Barotă (1958; Barota's Daughters), which later shifted into *Iubiri paralele* (1974; Parallel Loves) as well as the "official" *Cîntecul uzinei* (1950; Song of the Factory) and *S-a dumirit şi moş Ilie* (1950; Old Ilie Finally Understood) are novels devoted to the presentation of the social and economic changes brought about by the installation of the communist regime in Romania. The plot of the first is structured around two days in the lives of the bourgeois and worker tenants of the same urban building at the beginning of the Republic years. The second and third speak about nationalization, socialist industry, and changes in mentality which correspond to wishful ideological thinking rather than to significant existential reality.

Cella Serghi translated into Romanian works by F. Mallet-Joris.

Works

Pînza de păianjen, novel [Cobweb] (1938). *Cad zidurile*, novel [Walls Are Falling] (1950). *Cîntecul uzinei*, novel [Song of the Factory] (1950). *S-a dumirit şi moş Ilie* [Old Ilie Finally Understood] (1950). *Surorile* [The Sisters] (1951). *Cantemiriştii* [The Cantemir People] (1954). *Fetele lui Barotă* [Barota's Daughters] (1958). *Cartea Mironei* [Mirona's Book] (1967). *Genţiane* [Gentians] (1970). *Iubiri paralele* [Parallel Loves] (1974). *Mirona* [Mirona] (1975). *Pe firul de păianjen al memoriei* [On Memory's Spider Thread] (1978).

Bibliography

Piru, Al, *Panorama deceniului literar românesc 1940–1950* (Bucharest, 1968), pp. 356–359. Popa, Marian, *Dicţionar de literatură română contemporană*, 2nd ed. (Bucharest, 1977), pp. 502–503.

Translations: Maurer, Georg, ed. and tr., *Rumänien erzählt* (Berlin, Volkseigener Verlag, 1955) ("Die Jugendbrigade," from *Cîntecul uzinei*).

Sanda Golopentia

Raffaella de' Sernigi

Born 1472 or 1473, Florence, Italy; died December 13, 1557, Florence
Genre(s): drama
Language(s): Italian

All that is known of the life of Raffaella de' Sernigi, the author of *Moise* (Moses), a mid-sixteenth century *sacra rappresentazione* (mystery play), is that she was a nun and the prioress of the Augustinian convent of Santa Maria della Disciplina just south of Florence. The necrology of the convent (*Obitorio del monastero*, Florentine State Archives), in the report of her death on December 13, 1557, states that Raffaella de' Sernigi died at the age of 84 and that she was the venerable and exemplary prioress of the convent and had been for 35 years.

The first edition of her play, entitled *Rappresentazione di Moise quando Idio gli dette le leggie in sul monte Sinai* (The Play of Moses When God Gave Him the Law on Mount Sinai), was published in Florence, it seems, between 1550 and 1557. The edition bears no date nor mention of the publishing house, though its publication was sponsored by Giuseppe di Pietro da Treviso. The title page mentions that the author is the prioress of her monastery, so it was certainly published before her death in 1557; bibliographers place it after 1550. A second edition, also without date or publisher, came out ten to twenty years later.

The play, like most Florentine mystery plays, is written in verse, in narrative octaves, with some slight variation of the form, and it ends with a ballad. It dramatizes the biblical story beginning as Moses leaves for the mountain. It narrates Moses' return, his wrath for the idolatry of the Israelites, and ends as he forgives and reads the commandments to them. As was conventional, realistic elements were added to the biblical account; there is, in this play, some discussion of the qualities of the wine that will help the people on their journey to the mountain.

Works

La rappresentazione di Moise quando Idio gli dette le leggie in sul monte Sinai (ca. 1550–1557 and Florence 1578? ca. 1600?).

Bibliography

Cioni, Alfredo, *Bibliografia delle sacre rappresentaziomi*, Parte II LXXI (Florence, 1961), p. 59. *Obitorio del monastero* [of Santa Maria della Disciplina a Portico]. Florentine State Archives. *Conventi Soppressi*, 207, f. 109, c. 35v.

Elissa B. Weaver

Isabella van Tuyll van Serooskerken

(see: Belle de Charrière)

Nùria Serrahima

Born 1937, Barcelona, Spain
Genre(s): novel, journalism, painting
Language(s): Catalan

Born to a bourgeois Barcelona family, Serrahima began life under traditional auspices in an atmosphere of conservatism. Up to age fourteen, she was educated in a private convent school, which she abandoned to devote herself intensively to the study of painting under master Ramon Rogent. Following some five years of apprenticeship (1952–1957), she turned to literature, shortly before her father's death in 1958. This second apprenticeship, largely in journalism, eventually produced her first novel, *Mala quilla* (1973; The Bad Sprout), written in Catalan during the last years of Franco when the "boom" in vernacular literatures had not yet gathered impetus.

Autobiographical content in *The Bad Sprout* is evident in paralleling of the novelist's and protagonist's experience. The adolescent's maturation is portrayed in the context of postwar readjustment under Franco, a formative period filled with attempts to repress and restrict female students, aborting artistic or literary interests, limiting independence and self-expression, with continual insistence on sin and confession punctuated by distant echoes of World War II. Against the fear aroused by her totalitarian grandparents, the girl's relationship with her late father emerges as especially significant.

L'olor dels nostres cossos (1982; The Odor of Our Bodies), a collection of three novellas, is united by common feminist thematics, the use in all of a first-person narrative perspective and a female protagonist. Gloria, in the title novella, spends a sleepless night beside her snoring husband, anguished by her low self-esteem, disillusionment with romantic love, and her economic dependence. She reflects upon married life, Rafael's paternalistic tyranny, and her love for their children, which is the major impediment to separation or her choice of suicide as the only solution. Their relationship, characterized by numerous affairs for both partners, is strictly a matter of maintaining appearances. The matter-of-fact style contrasts with the lyrical, almost surrealistic effects of the second tale, "Negres moments d'Emma" (Emma's Black Moments). Emma's disordered memories constitute many brief "moments," significant incidents recollected without regard to chronology. Emma is brilliant but neurotic, insecure, alcoholic and suicidal, claustrophobic, asthmatic, hysterical, and utterly alone in a hallucinatory world. Dissatisfied despite many affairs, she longs to escape responsibility while suffering homicidal urges. Separation of reality from fantasy and hallucination is extremely difficult. "Amants" (Lovers) presents another collection of memories, this time in a lighter vein: the narrative consciousness, who has assigned a letter of the Spanish alphabet to each of her thirty former lovers, recalls them in alphabetical order in brief, nostalgic fragments resembling prose poems.

Works

Mala quill (1973). L'olor dels nostres cossos (1982).

Bibliography

General references: *Women Writers of Spain*, ed. C.L. Galerstein (Westport, CT, 1986).

Janet Perez

Séverine

(a.k.a. Caroline Rémy, Mme Adrien Guebhard)

Born April 27, 1855, Paris, France; died April 23, 1929, Pierrefonds
Genre(s): journalism, essay, drama, autobiography, lecturer
Language(s): French

Séverine ranks as a major French journalist of the late nineteenth and early twentieth centuries; certainly she was the stellar woman journalist of her era. Trained on the job by a talented mentor, Jules Vallès, for whom she worked as a copyist, Séverine assumed the editorship of *Le Cri du peuple* following Vallès' death in 1885. She and her husband, Adrian Guebhard, later sold the paper. She subsequently made a good living as a free-lance journalist, publishing in a wide spectrum of Parisian newspapers. These included the all-woman daily *La Fronde* (1897–1903), edited by her old friend Marguerite Durand, for which she covered the Dreyfus Affair.

Séverine's career as a journalist was far from preordained. She was the only child of a petit-bourgeois municipal employee and his wife, who raised their daughter by very strict disciplinary standards designed to break her spirit. They did not succeed. She fled into marriage at the age of seventeen. By the time she began working for Vallès in the 1880s she had been separated for many years from her first husband, Henri Montrobert, from whom she had run away fol-lowing the birth of their son. In the interim she had been living with Adrien Guebhard, whom she met while employed as a reader for his mother. She bore a son by him and married him after the 1884 divorce law allowed her to terminate her marriage to Montrobert. Meanwhile she had met Vallès in Brussels. After his return to Paris she went to work for him and soon became Vallès' spiritual daughter. Her two sons were sent out to nurse and then away to school.

Through the press and her flair for self-dramatization, Séverine became a Parisian ce-lebrity. She pioneered first-hand investigative reportage and interviews in the French press. After 1900 she embarked on a new career as a speaker, generally for advanced political causes. Always an enemy of authoritarianism, whether on the political right or the left, and insistent on maintaining her liberty of ideas and action in the face of pressures to affiliate with parties, causes, etc., Séverine surprised many in 1921 by joining the emergent French Communist Party. Several years later, however, she was purged for refusing to abandon her concurrent support for the League of Rights of Man. She was particularly noted for her support of anarchism, women's rights, and pacifism.

Séverine's book-length publications include five volumes of her articles, culled from the six thousand and more she published, a play, and *Line*, an autobiography covering her early years. Her correspondence with Vallès found later publication in his collected works. Séverine also composed many prefaces for books by colleagues, a number of speeches, and published longer essays in various publications such as the *Revue philanthropique*. There is no complete critical edition of her works.

Works

Ed., *Le Cri du peuple* (1885–1888). *Pages rouges* (1893). *Notes d'une Frondeuse (de la Boulange au Panama)* (1894). *Pages mystiques* (1895). *En marche* (1896). *Affaire Dreyfus—Vers la lumière—Impressions vécues* (1900). *A Sainte-Hélène, pièce en 2 actes, en prose* (1904). *Sac-à-tout* (1906). *Line (1855–1867)* (1921). *Correspondance entre Séverine et Jules Vallès*, in Vallès, *Oeuvres complètes* (1972). *Séverine: Choix de papiers, du Cri du peuple à la Fronde*, annotés par E. Le Garrec (1982).

Bibliography

Braude, B., "Séverine, ambivalent feminist." *The Feminist Art Journal* (1973). Braude, B., "Séverine, écrivain de combat" (in English). *Nineteenth Century French Studies* (1976). Braude, Beatrice, "Séverine, the Independent." Ph.D. dissertation, City University of New York, 1971. University Microfilms 72–5069. Lecache, Bernard, *Séverine* (Paris, 1930). Le Garrec, Evelyne, *Séverine, une rebelle (1855–1929)* (Paris, 1982). Rafferty, Frances, "Madame Séverine (1855–1929)." Ph.D. dissertation, University of Notre Dame, 1974. University Microfilms 75–01866. Rafferty, Frances, "Madame Séverine: Crusading Journalist of the Third Republic." *Contemporary French Civilization* (1977).

General references: *Dictionary of Modern Peace Leaders* (Albert S. Hill). *Historical Dictionary of the Third Republic* (L. Leclair).

Karen Offen

Sibylle Severus

Born 1937, Oberbayern, Germany
Genre(s): prose, novel, short story
Language(s): German

Prior to her marriage Sibylle Severus worked as a violin maker in both Amsterdam and Zürich. During her writing career she has published countless stories in various newspapers and journals. Her first novel, *Zum Mond Laufen* (Running to the Moon), appeared in 1981. *Seiltanz* (High-wire Act) was published by Benziger Verlag in 1984 and centers on the duration of love and its various possible forms in the lives of four people caught up in conflict between reason and feeling, thought and action. Today Sibylle Severus works and writes in Zürich.

Works

Zum Mond Laufen (1981). *Seiltanz* (1984).

Warwick J. Rodden

Marie de Rabutin-Chantal, Marquise de Sévigné

Born February 5, 1626, Paris, France; died
April 15, 1696, Grignan
Genre(s): letters
Language(s): French

Marie de Rabutin-Chantal was born in the fashionable Marais quartier of Paris in 1626. Her father, from an old and illustrious aristocratic Burgundian family, married the wealthy daughter of a recently ennobled Parisian tax-farmer. Orphaned at the age of seven, Marie was raised by maternal relatives, the de Coulanges, in a warm, loving atmosphere. She was well educated for a girl and was allowed a great deal of freedom; she knew Latin and Spanish and was fluent in Italian. History, literature, and writing, along with religious instruction, riding and dancing lessons produced the well-rounded, independent, self-confident woman who became the most famous *epistolière* of the seventeenth century. At age eighteen, the beautiful, wealthy heiress married Henri de Sévigné, a charming but extravagant and faithless Breton nobleman. They were members of the Parisian *beau monde*, habituées of the famous salons of the capital, where they mingled with writers and ministers, courtesans, and courtiers. In 1651 de Sévigné was killed in a duel, leaving his wife with two young children. Choosing not to remarry (to take another "master" as she put it), the twenty-five year old widow embarked on a full and independent life. She never regretted this decision; "the state of matrimony is a dangerous disease," she could write after 38 years of widowhood. Mme de Sévigné continued to spend most of her time in Paris, but she also lived for long periods at her château of Les Rochers in Brittany and at her uncle's Abbey of Livry outside of Paris; her lyrical descriptions of these rural retreats clearly reveal a love of nature and the countryside that was unusual among her contemporaries. Numerous estates provided the financial security Mme de Sévigné needed to live well and to ensure her children's future. Her son, Charles, had an unsatisfying military career before he took up the life of a country gentleman at his mother's favorite estate of Les Rochers. Witty, intelligent, and charming,

Charles never received the passionate devotion that Mme de Sévigné lavished on her daughter, Francoise-Marguerite, "the prettiest girl in France." Two years after marrying the comte de Grignan, this beloved daughter moved to Provence where her husband was the Lieutenant-General (Governor), and the famous correspondence between mother and daughter commenced.

Over 1500 of Mme de Sévigné's letters are extant; unfortunately those of her daughter were destroyed by her granddaughter, Pauline de Simiane, who had intended to burn the entire correspondence. Mme de Sévigné's letters are unmatched in style and tone. They provide a vivid and immediate account of aristocratic life during the reign of Louis XIV. She wrote in a natural, conversational style, moving easily from subject to subject, infusing life into people and events of the time. There is a sense of immediacy in her writing that holds the reader's interest and transports him or her into her world. Mme de Sévigné was an intelligent, keen observer with a realistic view of life. Without moralizing or merely gossiping, she gave character and depth to the men and women of her acquaintance. She described life at court, lavish fêtes and gruesome executions, wars and love affairs, dreaded illnesses, horrendous medical practices, the dread of growing old, and the agonies of dying. One of the most interesting people found in this vast correspondence is Mme de Sévigné herself. Few historical figures are as well-known as she—her daily routine, her health (very robust), her diet, her friends, her frequent travels, her moods and character, her fears and joys are all revealed in her incomparable style. Her love of reading, her periodic need for solitude, and her appreciation of nature were unusual for women of her class and time. Cultured, witty, friendly, and cheerful, Mme de Sévigné displayed a *joie de vivre* that was only occasionally tinged with melancholy. Her attractive personality is one of the reasons for the appeal of her letters. Although she was not a professional writer, she was an accomplished stylist and knew the importance of writing well. She could make anything interesting, even the weather or a walk in her woods. In her letters Mme de Sévigné bequeathed an eternal vitality and vivacity to the momentous and trivial aspects of the Splendid Century.

Works

The Letters of Madame de Sévigné, 7 vols. (1927). Duchêne, Roger, ed., Madame de Sévigné: Correspondance, 3 vols. (1972–1978).

Bibliography

Aldis, Janet, The Queen of Letter Writers: Marquise de Sévigné (1907). Allentuch, Harriet R., Madame de Sévigné: A Portrait in Letters (1963). Aubenas, J. A., Histoire de Madame de Sévigné, de sa famille, et de ses amis (1842). Backer, Dorothy A. L., Precious Women (1974). Bailly, Auguste, Madame de Sévigné (1955). Barbier, A. A., Recueil des lettres de Mme de Sévigné (1801). Barthélemy, E. M. de, La Marquise d'Huxelles et ses amis, Mme de Sévigné, etc. (1881). Béziers, A., Les lectures de Madame de Sévigné, etc. (1863). Boissier, Gaston, Madame de Sévigné (1901). Brunet, G. Evocations littéraires. Madame de Sévigné, Bossuet, etc. (1930). Buffenoir, Hippolyte, "Les résidences de Madame de Sévigné," in La Nouvelle revue CXVII (March 1899): 299–321. Burill, I. M., La Marquise de Sévigné, docteur en médicine, honoris causa, etc. (1932). Bussy-Rabutin, Roger, Histoire amoureuse des Gaules par le Cte de Bussy-Rabutin suivie de la France galante: Romans satiriques du six-septième siècle attrybues au comte de Bussy, edition nouvelle avec des notes et une introduction by J. Auguste Poitevin, 2 vols. (1857). Combes, F., Madame de Sévigné historien: le siècle et la cour de Louis XIV (1885). DuBois, Louis F., Madame de Sévigné et sa correspondance relative à Vitré et aux Rochers (1838). Duchêne, Roger, Madame de Sévigné ou la chance d'être femme (1982). Esprit de Mmes de Sévigné et de Maintenon, ou choix de ce qu'il y a de plus piquant dans leurs lettres, 2 vols. (1824). Faguet, E., "Madame de Sévigné," in Les Femmes Illustres (1910). Fitzgerald, Edward, Dictionary of Madame de Sévigné, 2 vols. (1971). Hall, Evelyn B., The Women of the Salons and other French Portraits (1969). Hallays, André, "Madame de Sévigné," in Essais sur le XVIIe siècle (1921). Hammersley, Violet, Letters from Madame la Marquise de Sévigné (1956). Hyatt, Alfred H., ed., "Madame Sevigne: Whimsicalities, Witticisms and Reflections from Her Letters," in Maxims of Life, 2 (1911). Jouhandeau, Marcel, "La vraie Sévigné," in Écrits de Paris (Sept. 1959): 76–84. LaBrière, L. de, Madame de Sévigné en Bretagne (1882). Lamartine de Prat, M.L.A. de, Madame de Sévigné (1864).

Lemoine, Jean M.P.J., *Madame de Sévigné, sa famille et ses amis, etc.* (1926). *Lettres choisies de Mesdames de Sévigné et de Maintenon* (1800). *Lettres de Madame de Sévigné, de sa famille et de ses amis,* 10 vols. (1820). *Madame de Sévigné and her contemporaries,* 2 vols. (1841). Malherbe, E., *La jeunesse de Madame de Sévigné* (1904). Marcu, Eva, "Madame de Sévigné and Her Daughter," in *Romanic Review* LI (Oct. 1960): 182–191 Mavic, E., *Madame de Sévigné et la médicine de son temps* (1932). Noyes, Alfred, "The Enigma of Madame de Sévigné," in *Contemporary Review* CLXXXIX (March 1956): 149–153. *Pensées, traits brillans, anecdotes, bons-mots, et judemens littéraires, extraits des lettres de Madame de Sévigné . . .* (1810). Pradel, G., *Madame de Sévigné en Bourbonnais* (1926). Puliga, la comtesse de, *Madame de Sévigné: Her Correspondents and Contemporaries* (1873). Richie, Anne Isabella (Thackeray), *Madame de Sévigné* (1881). Saint-René Taillandier, M., *Madame de Sévigné et sa fille* (1938). Sonnié-Moret, P., *La marquise de Sévigné. Une amie de la médicine, ennemie des médecins* (1926). Stanley, Arthur, *Madame de Sévigné: Her Letters and Her World* (1946). Tilly, Arthur A., *Madame de Sévigné. Some Aspects of Her Life and Character* (1936). Walckenaer, C. A., *Memoires touchant la vie et les écrits de Marie de Rabutin-Chantal, dame de Bourbilly, marquise de Sévigné,* 5 vols. (1843–1856). Williams, Charles G. S., *Madame de Sévigné* (1981).

Jeanne A. Ojala

William T. Ojala

Ippolita Sforza

Born 1445, Milan, Italy; died 1488, Capua
Genre(s): oratory
Language(s): Latin

Sprung from a union of the two Milanese dynasties (the daughter of Francesco Sforza and Bianca Maria Visconti), Ippolita became a famous patron of the arts in her own right in the Kingdom of Naples. As a child, she had been the student of Guiniforte Barzizza and Costantino Lascaris. She was married in 1465 to Alfonso, Duke of Calabria. Two of her orations have been made available in *Her Immaculate Hand.*

Works

Cosenza 4, 3261, *Her Immaculate Hand,* 44–50. "Oration in Honor of Her Mother." "Oration to Pius II and His Cardinals."

Joseph Berrigan

Marietta Shaginian

(a.k.a. Jim Dollar)

Born March 21, 1888, Moscow, Russia; died March 1982
Genre(s): journalism, history, literary criticism, poetry, fiction
Language(s): Russian

Marietta Shaginian's career spanned seventy-five years, from her first poem, published in a provincial newspaper in 1903, to the final pages of *Chelovek i vremia* (Man and Time), which she signed as finished at age "ninety years and four months" in 1978. After a brief flirtation with modernism and the "decadent" ideals of the first decade of the twentieth century, Shaginian put her considerable talents, intellect, and wide-ranging interests (among others, philosophy, music, psychology, and textiles) to the service of the new revolutionary Soviet society, both propagating and exemplifying the tenets of a committed literature faithfully and ingeniously.

Shaginian was born into a family of Russified Armenians. Her father was a hard-working medical doctor, a lecturer at Moscow University, a convinced atheist, and an admirer of Goethe; his daughter inherited much of his intellect and ideals. Left unprovided for by his early death in 1902, Shaginian's mother returned to her family in Nakhichevan' near Rostov on the Don. Despite worsening otosclerosis, young Marietta returned to Moscow and began earning her living at fifteen. She tutored and published poetry, prose fiction, and literary and art criticism for provincial journals in order to complete her education at the pre-revolutionary equivalent of a women's college. For several years Shaginian's work reflected the Symbolism and apocalyptic philosophy ("revolution with the cross") of the Petersburg circle, which revolved around the historical novelist Dmitry Merezhkovsky and his wife, the writer Zinaida Gippius. She broke with the

Merezhkovskys in 1912. As she pointed out, life with her younger sister in one windowless room and constant financial struggle "created a healthy antidote to any refined decadence" (*Sovietskie pisateli*, 646). Her first novel, *Svoia sud'ba* (1916; One's Own Fate, first published in full in 1923), is already programmatic, outlining an anti-Freudian method of treating psychological disfunction that, rather than burrowing into the "negative" past, reinforces positive social behavior.

Shaginian spent the years of the 1917 revolution and succeeding civil war in Nakhichevan', where she founded a textile school. The reversals and chaotic situation in the Don region over that period are synthesized in her kaleidoscopic short novel *Peremena* (1923; Change). From 1920 to 1927 she lived in Petrograd-Leningrad where, under the sponsorship of Maxim Gorky, she began her "participation in the great and difficult process of creating a Soviet literature. . . . I suddenly felt a need to write for newspapers as a lyric necessity. . . . And this sensation of a lyric, vital need for the newspaper word remained with me for the rest of my life" (650).

Responding to the call for popular, ideologically correct reading for the masses, Shaginian, under the pseudonym "Jim Dollar," produced *Mess Mend* (1923), a fantastic spy novel devoted to the adventures in New York and the Soviet Union of a band of American radical superheroes working to counter an evil capitalist plot. The work, issued as a serial in ten parts, was wildly successful, but even Shaginian herself found it difficult to develop much enthusiasm for its two sequels. "*Kik*" (the title is an acronym for the Russian words for Witch and Communist), a tale that treats the mysterious disappearance of a Soviet official, is Shaginian's idiosyncratic protest against specialization by genre in literature. The story is developed through newspaper accounts and by four witnesses who put their testimony in the form of a poem, a novella, a melodrama in verse, and the outline for a documentary film.

Shaginian's most popular pre-revolutionary book of poetry, *Orientalia* (five editions between 1913 and 1922), is based on Armenian themes. Her marriage in 1917 to the philologist Ia. S. Khachatrianets sealed her return to her roots. During the 1920s she made frequent journalistic forays to study the transformation of her homeland under the Soviets, and she describes herself from 1927 as "no longer a guest in the republic, but a constant dweller in Armenia" (654). There she closely followed the construction of a hydroelectric dam and described it in a novel of industrialization, *Gidrotsentral'* (1929; Hydroelectric Plant). *Journey through Soviet Armenia* (1950) is a summary of her many studies of her homeland.

The 1930s to the mid-1950s were marked by intensive journalistic forays all over the Soviet Union and Western Europe. After spending World War II writing propagandistic literature in the Urals, Shaginian displayed her erudition in major studies of literary figures as diverse as Goethe, the twelfth century Persian writer Nizami Ganjawi, and the nineteenth century Ukrainian poet Taras Shevchenko. The 1957 edition of a tetralogy (two "chronicle" novels and two sets of sketches) devoted to Lenin and his family, on which Shaginian worked for over thirty years, was awarded the Lenin Prize in 1972. She was admitted to the Communist Party in July 1942, and in 1950 she was named a corresponding member of the Armenian Academy of Sciences. Her philosophical memoir of Russia in the last years before the revolution, *Man and Time*, brought her long, active career to a triumphant end.

Works

Sovetskie pisateli: Avtobiografii, Ia. Brainina i E.F. Nikitina, comp. (Moscow, 1959), vol. 2, pp. 640–660. *Sobranie sochinenii*, 9 vols. (Moscow, 1971–1975). *Chelovek i vremia: Istoriia chelovecheskogo stanovleniia* (Moscow, 1980).

Translations: "Man and Time" [excerpt], tr. Helen Tate. *Soviet Literature*, 9 (1980): 33–107. *Mess Mend: The Yankees in Petrograd*, tr. S.D. Cioran (Ann Arbor, Mich., 1987).

Bibliography

Kosachov, Natalie, *Literary and Related Arts: Biography by Marietta Shaginian*, thesis, Ottawa, 1973. Muratova, K.D., ed., *Istoriia russkoi literatury kontsa XIX—nachala XX veka: Bibliograficheskii ukazatel'* (Moscow-Leningrad, 1963), pp. 432–433. Serebriakov, Konstantin, "*The Truth of Time: A New Book. . . .*" *Soviet Literature* 9 (1980): 107–113. Skorino, L., *Marietta Shaginian—khudozhnik:*

Zhizn' i tvorchestvo (2nd ed., rev. Moscow, 1981). Terras, Victor, ed., *Handbook of Russian Literature* (New Haven, 1985), pp. 400–401 (Sonia Ketchian). See also: *Kratkaia Literaturnaia entsiklopediia*, vol. 8 (Moscow, 1975), cols. 575–576 (L.N. Chertkov).

Mary F. Zirin

Galina Shcherbakova

Born 1930s?
Genre(s): short story, novella, drama
Language(s): Russian

A journalist by profession, Shcherbakova took up fiction in the 1970s. Her comparatively modest output, consisting of two prose collections plus a few individually published stories and novellas, deals with a generation indelibly marked by the impact of the second World War. Her narratives examine the psychology of love and the effects of time's passage on the post-war generation in a modern setting. One of her better-known novellas, *Vam i ne snilos'* (You Wouldn't Dream of It), adapted into a popular film by the same name and a play entitled *Roman i Iul'ka* (Roman and Julie), portrays the self-sacrificing love of two tenth-graders. Other pieces, such as "Stena" (The Wall) and "Sluchai s Kuzmen'ko" (The Incident with Kuz'menko), explore the dynamics of marriage, tracing the disillusionments, betrayals, and dissatisfactions that accrue over the years. *Stena* also confronts the issue of vulgar materialism and the price paid in human values by those self-deluded careerists who operate according to purely pragmatic considerations.

Like most contemporary women writers in Russia, Shcherbakova has the habit of retrospection, seeking clues to characters' current dilemmas in experiences and decisions made in the past. As part of that movement backward, she allows her characters to reveal themselves in interior monologues and mental free associations that provide highly suggestive links and explanations.

Possibly because of her training as a journalist, Shcherbakova's writing has the concise, unadorned preciseness of reportage. It also reflects a keen eye for the eloquent gesture and an ear sensitive to individual speech patterns.

Works
Sprava ostavalsia gorodok. Povesti (1979). *Vam i ne snilos'* (1983).
Translations: "Stena" [The Wall], tr. Helena Goscilo, in HERitage and HEResy: Recent Fiction by Russian Women (1988).
Play: *Roman i Iul'ka. P'esa-razmyshlenie* (1982).

Helena Goscilo

Mariya Shkapskaya

Born 1891, St. Petersburg, Russia; died 1952, Moscow
Genre(s): poetry, prose poem, feuilleton, essay
Language(s): Russian

Mariya Shkapskaya (née Andreevskaya) was born in St. Petersburg into a highly cultured family. She was expelled from secondary school for participation in revolutionary activities and eventually graduated from the emigre gymnasium in Paris. Later she also graduated from the faculty of letters of Toulouse University in 1914.

Her first volume of poetry, *Mater Dolorosa*, came out in 1920. The most characteristic traits of Shkapskaya's poetry are present in this collection: formal simplicity, short, compressed verses. More important to contemporary critics and modern readers are the recurring themes of her poetry, which were quite novel at the time. Marriage and the birth of her children played a central role in the development of Shkapskaya's thematics, which are concerned with "a woman's Golgotha," and matters of the flesh, including conception, abortion, and the death of a child. The experience of a woman as procreator is poignantly expressed without relying on the usual metaphysical trappings. Boris Filippov has called her the "Vasilisa Rozanova of Russian poetry, for, like Vasily Rozanov, she restored in her lyrics the sacred rights of the flesh. Also, the high tragedy of a woman's lot." Other literary publications of Shkapskaya's include *Chas vechernii* (1921), *Baraban strogogo gospodina* (1922), *Krov'-ruda* (1923), *Zemnye remesla* (1925), *Tsa-tsa-tsa* (1923). Unfortunately, Mariya Shkapskaya's poetry has not been published in the Soviet Union after 1925, and she is now remembered in her own country primarily as a feuilletonist, an essayist for various newspapers and periodicals.

Works

Mater Dolorosa (1920). Chas vechernii (1921). Baraban strogogo gospodina (1922). Krov'-ruda (1923). Yav': poema (1923). Kniga o Lukavom Seyatele (1923). Zemnye remesla (1925). Stikhi, with introd. essays by B. Filippov and E. Zhiglevich (1979). Sama po sebe (1930). Voda i veter (1931). Pyatnadtsat' i odin (1931). Chelovek rabotaet khorosho (1932). Eto bylo na samom dele (1942). Puti i poiski (1968).

Bibliography

General references: Terras, Victor ed., Handbook of Russian Literature (New Haven, 1985).

Laura Jo Turner McCullough

Sabine Sicaud

Born 1913, Villeneuve-sur-Lot, France; died 1928, Paris, France
Genre(s): poetry
Language(s): French

Sabine Sicaud's poetic gift showed itself at an early age; by the time she was six, she was already scribbling her observations of nature on old publicity flyers she found about her house. Her interest in poetry was encouraged by her parents, both liberal thinkers, who engaged private tutors for their son and daughter rather then sending them away to school. Isolated from the outside world at her family home quite aptly named La Solitude, Sabine's education emphasized letters, music and drawing; word games, not dolls, were her favorite form of amusement. This sort of life nurtured her talents; from the ages of ten to thirteen she produced a major part of her works. The Poèmes d'enfant (A Child's Poems), published by Anna de Noailles, in 1926 revealed the girl's genius to the world. Before she had a chance to develop and mature both as a poet and a person, Sabine fell ill and died two years later at the age of fifteen. So short a life was not forgotten: a full thirty years after her death, a new edition of her works came out, which collected a number of unpublished works.

Sabine's premature death put an end to a career that had barely begun. Her output is small,

yet even in the few poems she wrote, one can discern her gifts. In her early works, there is the naivete and spontaneity of youth. The hours she spent roaming the family gardens were not an idle pastime; images of nature dominate these poems that reveal the world in which she lived. A series of poems entitled "Chemins" (Roads) leads the poet down many paths: to imaginary voyages, to garden walks, to metaphysical questions. Her last poems, written while she was slowly dying, are (quite understandably) uneven. Yet at their best, e.g. "Laissez-moi crier" (Let Me Cry Out), they show what she could have achieved had she the chance.

Works

Poèmes d'enfant (1926). Les Poèmes de Sabine Sicaud (1958).

Bibliography

Clouard, Henri, "Une oeuvre unique." Journal des Beaux Arts (Brussels, March 27, 1959). Miguel, André, "Morte de quinze ans." Journal des Poètes (Brussels, March 1959).

Edith Joyce Benkov

Gregorio Martínez Sierra

(see: María Martínez Sierra)

Ieva Simonaitytė

Born 1897, Vanagai, Lithuania Minor, the Klaipėda (Memel) district; died 1978, Vilnius
Genre(s): novel
Language(s): Lithuanian

Because of poor health, Simonaitytė did not attend regular schools and became a self-educated person. In early youth, Simonaitytė worked as an itinerant seamstress. In 1921, she came to Klaipėda, learned typing and stenography, and worked in various offices. The first longer piece, a story called "Tu am'inai mane minėsi" (You Will Remember Me Forever) was published in 1933. In 1935 Simonaitytė published her first novel-length story, Aukštujų Šimonių likimas (The Fate of the Šimonys of Aukštujai), which received the Lithuanian State Prize for Literature and is indeed the best work of her career. The novel deals with the decline and eventual obliteration of an ancient family of Lithuanian nobles living in the territory that was known previously (before the Russians settled there in 1944) as "Lithuania Minor"—actually, East Prussia. The territory was long occupied and colonized by the Germans, but the Lithuanian element did nevertheless remain quite strong into the nineteenth century. We first see this family, the Šimonys, in the Middle Ages, resisting the onslaughts of the German Teutonic order with great determination but ultimately without effect. The main part of the novel, however, deals with the period of established German rule in the eighteenth and nineteenth centuries. The family begins gradually to assimilate; its members lose their sterling old-time Lithuanian moral qualities and enter a decline both spiritually and in social status. Worst of all, they lose their national identity, blend in with the Germans, and ultimately become just another ordinary family of German burgers and farmers—a pitiful condition indeed, because Simonaitytė, in her personal and historical anti-German indignation, paints them all, without exception, in the blackest hues of her palette. As an artistic chronicle of this long decline, the story reaches an epic quality and remains unique to this day as the only large-scale artistic commentary upon the destiny of the Lithuanian nation, or at least this particular "Prussian" part of it, from which so many of the best scholars and artists had come in those centuries when the main body of Lithuania was kept in darkness and stagnation by the Russian Tsars.

When Hitler took the Klaipėda district in 1939, Simonaitytė came to live in Lithuania itself. There she met the Soviet occupation and the Second World War, during which she remained in the country and was harassed by the German occupiers. When the Soviets came to power, Simonaitytė entered with great dedication into post-war reconstruction work, most particularly as an artist, producing a great number of large prose works, inevitably in the spirit of "Socialist realism"—a strangely convoluted esthetic predicated upon its function as a tool of the totalitarian Soviet dictatorship. The story "Pikčiurnienė" (1953; Pikčiurnienė) portrays the long life of a well-to-do peasant woman, a "kulak";

this designation was invented by Stalin to mark people that were to be destroyed as "class enemies." Naturally, Pikčiurnienė lives up to her name (which translates approximately as "the nasty hag") and cheats, scolds, persecutes others all her life, only to say on her deathbed that she thought she'd lived honestly and for the good of others. Aside from the political idiocies of Socialist realism, there is also an impersonal, dark spirit in the novel. There is the presence of a relentless force of evil, very much like that of the Germans in the Šimonys novel, who, like Pikčiurnienė, were not only evil persons but also somehow the embodiment of a destiny of almost Shakespearean darkness. The main hero of the novel *Vilius Karalius* (Vilius the King, first part published in 1939, others in later years, under the Soviet regime) is again a similar figure of decay and evil, again a representative of the exploiting classes, a "kulak." Other heroes are portrayed as positive, painfully searching and eventually finding ideals worthy of commitment, those of the Soviet society. In this novel, however, Simonaitytė does demand personal responsibility (and implicitly recognizes the personal power) of each individual for his own destiny, whatever the dark force over everybody's heads. *Vilius Karalius* is written in conventional third-person narrative, without any attempts at modernistic style, or even without any of the grand, solemnly poetic, rhetorical cadences that can be found in *Aukštujų Šimonių likimas.*

Simonaitytė has written three more novels, *Pavasariu audroj* (1938; In the Storm of Springtime), *Be tėvo* (1941; Without Father), *Pakutinė Kūnelio kelionė* (1971; The Last Journey of Kūnelis), and a number of short stories and tales, some autobiographical.

Some critics have considered Simonaitytė, not altogether without reason, to be herself a harsh, hard-bitten person, self-righteous, graceless, tyrannical, and a believer in the prevalence of evil over good. Nevertheless, there is genuine power in her prose, and a grim honesty straight into the face of any evil force, be it the Germans, the kulaks, Socialist realism, or even she herself. Hers were the habits and bearing of an imperious literary figure, which, in Lithuania, she has indeed remained, standing there as a pillar of strength and forging a link between the older and the younger generations in Lithuanian prose.

Works

Aukštųjų Šimonių likimas, novel (1st ed. 1939). Pavasarių audroj, novel (1938). Vilius Karalius, novel (1st ed. 1939). Be tėvo, novel (1941). "Pikčiurnienė," story (1953). Collected Works, 6 vols. (1957–1958). O buvo taip . . . , Ne ta pastogė (1963), and Nebaigta knyga (1965), both autobiographical tales. "Meilutis ir Gu'iukas," a story for children (1967). Gretimos istorijėlės, autobiographical tales. Kūnelio kelionė, novel (1968).

Bibliography

Dambrauskaitė, R., Ieva Simonaitytė. A monograph (Vilnius, 1968). Dambrauskaitė, R., Ievos Simonaitytės kūryba (Vilnius, 1958). Kostkevičiūtė, I., "Ieva Simonaitytė." Literatūros dienovid'iai. (Vilnius, 1964). Kubilius, V., Ievos Simonaitytės kūryba (Vilnius, 1987). Kubilius, V., "Skaitant Vilių Karalių." V. Kubilius Naujų kelių ieškant (Vilnius, 1964). Sluckis, M., "Takas, atvedęs <ai> vieškel<ai>." Sunkiausias menas (Vilnius, 1960).

R. Šilbajoris

Elvi Sinervo

(a.k.a. Aulikki Prinkki)

Born May 4, 1912, Helsinki, Finland; died
    August 28, 1986, Helsinki
Genre(s): poetry, short story, novel, drama,
    journalism, translation
Language(s): Finnish

Elvi Sinervo (Elvi Aulikki Sinervo-Ryömä) was one of the founders of Kiila, a left-wing group of artists and writers that influenced in particular the development of Finnish-language poetry. Her work as a writer was closely linked with the aims and fortunes of Kiila. In the thirties Sinervo was—by her own definition—"a professional revolutionary." In 1941 she was sentenced to four years penal servitude for political reasons—her husband was in prison, too, and her child in the care of others. Some of her poems have been popular poetry of the class struggle, and of her short stories, those that portray the lives of working-class children are particularly esteemed. Her prison experiences are reflected in the short novel Toveri, älä petä (1947; Don't Let Us Down, Comrade) and the volume of poetry Pilvet (1944; Clouds), which was written in prison. The central themes of this collection are love and motherhood, which are also emphasized in her later poetry. In the 1950s the mysterious Mother Poem-Maker appears—a kind of Urmother and woman, who urges the young to live for the future and to love.

Two of Elvi Sinervo's sisters became writers and influential in politics. The family is described, lightly disguised, in a novel, Palavankylän seppä (1939; The Smith of Burning Village). Sinervo's major work, the novel Viljami Vaihdokas (1946; William the Changeling) reflects the postwar optimism of the Communists in Finland. The principal character dies after torture by the state police during the war, but the novel ends with the belief that "life is coming near." In this novel, myth, fairy tale and realistic social description are combined in a special way. Sinervo wrote the beginning of the novel, about William's childhood, while she was in prison, and here the fairy-tale quality is most marked. The theme of the novel is from Maxim Gorky: the tale of Danko, who tears out his burning heart to be a torch and thus leads his people out of darkness. The same kind of belief in the future is suggested in the title of Sinervo's play Maailma on vasta nuori (premiere 1952, published 1980; The World Is Only Young). From the mid-1950s Sinervo was silent as a writer but translated into Finnish much Finland-Swedish literature, etc. There was renewed interest in her works in the 1970s.

Works

Runo Söörnäisistä [Poem of Söörnäis] (1937). Palavankylän seppä [The Smith of Burning Village] (1939). Onnenmaan kuninkaantytär ja ihmislapset [The King's Daughter of the Land of Happiness and the Mortals] (1944). Pilvet [Clouds] (1944). Desantti [Parachute Spy] (1945). Viljami Vaihdokas [William the Changeling] (1946). Toveri, älä petä [Don't Let Us Down, Comrade] (1947). Vuorelle nousu [Up the Mountain] (1948). Neidonkaivo [Maiden's Well] (1956). Runot [Poems 1931–1956] (1977). Novellit [Short Stories] (1978). Maailma on vasta nuori [The World Is Only Young. The Plays of Elvi Sinervo] (1980).

Bibliography

Karhu, Eino, "Literatura aktivnogo dejstvijak 70-letiju Elvi Sinervo." *Sever* 4 (Petroz): 113–120. Palmgren, Raoul, "Elvi Sinervo, kiilalaisen realismin klassikko" [Elvi Sinervo, Classic of Kiila Realism]. *Kirjallisuudentutkijain Seuran vuosikirja* 34 (1982): 9–32. Summary.

Liisi Huhtala (Translated by Philip Binham)

Pilar de Sinués de Marco

Born 1835, Zaragoza, Spain; died 1893, Madrid
Genre(s): novel, conduct book, translation
Language(s): Spanish

María del Pilar de Sinués is one of a group of professional women writers who, in the second half of the nineteenth century, wrote women's fiction and conduct books advocating the cult of domesticity. She also directed a magazine for women, *El ángel del hogar* (1864–1869; The Angel of the House). Although she published some one hundred extremely popular novels and conduct books, her name is mostly absent for literary histories. When included, her critics describe her writing as "costume jewelry prose" and belittle it for being liked by the "simple classes of Spain." Yet, Sinués is an important writer worthy of study for several reasons. From a sociological perspective, her prolific and successful literary career suggest the existence of a substantial female audience, which can begin to explain the emergence of professional women novelists during this period. Also, if one reads her domestic fiction as narratives about female subjectivity rather than as, simply, badly fictionalized conduct books for women, Sinués becomes a key figure in the creation of the discourse of Spanish womanhood.

What little is known about her life seems to be very contradictory. She married the playwright José Marco y Sanchís sight unseen and their marriage ended in a separation. Because of this she was forced to support herself by writing. In contrast to her novels where romantic love triumphs in the face of adversity and her women characters—given their domestic talents of frugality and selflessness—live happily ever after, she died alone and in poverty having squandered a great deal of money.

In her conduct books and novels, she advocated the virtuous woman, bourgeois domesticity and Christian motherhood. But it is also common to find in her works negative portrayal of the aristocratic lady, the woman of letters, and women who favor women's education. She argued that women should only be educated and write if they were willing to give priority to their domestic duties and behave like "angels in the house." Sinués' contemporaries noted her habit of receiving visitors while immersed in her needlework, thereby proving her own domesticity. They also remembered that she never seemed to finish her pieces.

Sinués argued that women should not write novels given their tendency to write romantic fiction. She believed that the writing of this type of narrative unleashed the writer's passion, which for her was associated with a form of illicit sexual activity antithetical to the notion of "the virtuous woman." In spite of this admonition, she herself wrote passionate and romantic novels. In her two-volume conduct book, *El ángel del hogar* (The Angel in the House), this contradiction can clearly be seen. She does not limit herself to an analysis of the different types of women in society and the behavior appropriate to their position (as does Mrs. Ellis, her English equivalent). She intercalates several novellas to explain and exemplify her analysis and advice. Yet, these short narratives are not presented as fiction. Rather, they are narrated as "real life" stories seen or heard by the narrator. Clearly, though, given the symmetry of characters and plot, these narratives are fiction. This paradox underscores the ambivalence felt by Pilar de Sinués, and many other women writers of her period, about writing in a society with a very weak women's novelistic tradition and where women writers were thought to be committing, in her own words, a grave sin.

The importance of a writer such as Pilar de Sinués is not only her astounding productivity but also her articulation of the contradictions facing women writers at this historical moment in Spain. On the one hand, she exalts the woman as the angel of the house with all of its constraining implications for the woman of letters and, on the other, she cannot control her need to write. She conforms and, in her own way, rebels. María del Carmen Simón Palmer, one of the few critics to address this question, has argued that many of the women writers of this period became spokeswomen for the angel in the house because this way they could be forgiven for the "offense" of writing.

Works

Mis poesías (1855). La diadema de perlas (1857). Amor y llanto. Colección de leyendas (1857). Margarita (1857). Premio y castigo (1857). Rosa (1857). La ley de Dios (1858). El ángel del hogar. Obra recreativa dedicada a la mujer (1859). El ángel del hogar. Estudios morales acerca de la mujer (1862). Flores del alma (1860). Un nido de palomas (1861). Fausta Sorel (1861). A la sombra de un tilo (1861). A la luz de la lámpara (1862). La rama del sándalo (1862). Narraciones del hogar. Primera serie (1862). Memorias de una joven de la clase media (1862). El lazo de flores (1862). Hija, esposa y madre (1863). Celeste (1863). Dos venganzas (1863). La virgen de las lilas (1863). La senda de la gloria (1863). El sol de invierno (1863). El almohadón de rosas (1864). El cetro de flores (1865). Sueños y Realidades. Memorias de una madre para su hija (1865). No hay culpa sin pena (1864). Galería de mujeres célebres (1864–1869). El alma enferma (1864). El ángel de la tristeza (1865). Querer es poder (1865). A río revuelto (1866). Cuentos de color de cielo (1867). El camino de la dicha. Cartas a dos hermanos sobre la educación (1868). Veladas del Invierno en torno de una mesa de labor (1866). Volver bien por mal (1872). Las alas de Ícaro (1872). Una hija del siglo (1873). Un libro para damas (1875). El becerro de oro (1875). La vida íntima, en la culpa va el castigo (1876). Combates de la vida. Cuadros sociales (1876). Plácida (1877). Un libro para las madres (1877). La mujer en nuestros días (1878). Las mártires del amor (1878). Palmas y flores (1878). Cortesanas ilustres (1878). Damas elegantes (1878). Las esclavas del deber (1878). La gitana (1878). Reinas mártires (1878). Glorias de la mujer (1878). La abuela (1878). Tres genios femeninos (1879). Luz y sombra (1879). La primera falta . . . (1879). Un libro para jóvenes (1879). La Dama elegante. Manual práctico y completísimo del buen tono y del buen orden doméstico (1880). Armas galantes (c. 1880). Una herencia trágica . . . (1882). Verdades dulces y amargas. Páginas para la mujer (1882). Dramas de familia . . . (1883–1885). La vida real (1884). Leyendas morales (1884). Mujeres ilustres (1884). Una historia sencilla (1886). La misión de la mujer (1886). La expiación (1886). Páginas del corazón (1887). Isabel. Estudio del natural . . . (1888). Cómo aman las mujeres . . . (c. 1889?). Novelas cortas (1890). Morir sola (1890). Los ángeles de la tierra (1891). Cuentos de niños (1897).

Bibliography

Aldaraca, Bridget, "El ángel del hogar: The Cult of Domesticity in Nineteenth-Century Spain," in Theory and Practice of Feminist Literary Criticism, ed. Gabriela Mora and Karen S. Van Hoofk (Michigan, 1982). Andreu, Alicia G., Galdós y la literatura popular (Madrid, 1982). Simón Palmer, María del Carmen, "Escritoras españolas del siglo XIX o el miedo a la marginalización." Anales de la literatura española 2 (1983): 477–490.

Alda Blanco

Jórunn Skáldmær

Flourished ca. 910, Norway
Genre(s): skaldic poetry
Language(s): Old Norse

Of the early Scandinavian women skalds (skáldkonur) composing in Court Meter (Dróttkætt), Jórunn Skáldmær ("Jórunn the Poet-Maiden") is the likeliest to have enjoyed professional status as a court skald in the employ of a king—most probably Harald Fairhair of Norway, or his son Hálfdan the Black. Unfortunately, all that remains of Jórunn's life's work are five scattered fragments (two full eight-line stanzas and three half-stanzas), cited in various contests by Snorri Sturluson, all seeming to belong to one long poem called Sendibit ("Sent Biter," or "Biting Message"). She refers in the poem to the court skald Gutþormr sindri (early tenth century) as a colleague; she also seems to have been familiar with the work of Gutþormr's contemporary Þorbjorn hornklofi, since her poetry exhibits similar diction to his (common kenningar and heite, and one common line). Sendibit was written in near-flawless dróttkvætt, presumably as a praise-poem lauding the role of Gutþormr sindri in reconciling Hálfdan the Black with his father Harald Fairhair. Since court skalds were often involved in many other aspects of court life—up to and including the defense of their patron kings in battle—it should perhaps also be noted that Jórunn is called "*skjaldmær*" ("shield-maiden"), instead of *skáldmær* ("post-maiden"), in a variant reading in one manuscript of Snorri's *Ólafs saga helga* (Flateyjarbók MS.). It is an intriguing speculation that perhaps, in addition to the service of skaldship, she rendered to her king a swordswoman's service as well.

Works

Jónsson, Finnur, ed. *Den norsk-islandske skjaldedigtning* (1915), IB, pp. 53–54. Kock, Ernst Albin, ed., *Den norsk-islándska skaldedigtningen* (1949), I, pp. 33–34. Sturluson, Snorri, *Heimskringla* II, ed. Bjarni Aðalbjarnarson, *Íslenzk fornrit* XXVII (1941), pp. 426–427.

Translations: Vigfússon, Guðbrandur, and F. York Powell, *Corpvs poeticvm boreale* (1883), II, pp. 321–322. Sturluson, Snorri, *Heimskringla*, tr. Lee Milton Hollander (1964), p. 91

Bibliography

Kreutzer, Gert, "Jórunn skáldmær." *Skandinavistik* 2 (1971): 89–98.

Sandra Ballif Straubhaar

Ēvē Skandalakē

(see: Melissanthē)

Elizabeta Iur'evna Skobtsova

(see: Mat' [or Monakhinia] Mariia)

Amalie Skram

Born 1846, Bergen, Norway; died 1905,
    Copenhagen, Denmark
Genre(s): novel, short story, drama
Language(s): Norwegian

With the publication of *Constance Ring* in 1885, Amalie Skram broke taboos that had silenced generations of women. Like her predecessor Camilla Collett, whom she greatly admired, Skram attacked the institution of marriage. But where Collett had leveled her criticism at the way in which marriage was arranged, Skram denounced the double standard and deplored the sexual ignorance of young women at the time they entered marriage. Never before had there been such a frank discussion of woman's sexuality in a Norwegian book—by a female author, no less—and public and critics alike were scandalized.

Amalie Alver was born in 1846 in Bergen. Her father was a merchant, though not a terribly successful one, and the family's economic situation was never secure. In 1863 her father went bankrupt, and he left for America to try his luck there. Later that same year Amalie, an extraordinarily beautiful seventeen-year-old, was engaged to marry a man nine years her senior. Her fiancé was the captain of a merchant ship and after they were married, the Müllers sailed together for a number of years, visiting distant ports all over the world.

Amalie showed herself to be a good sailor; she was never seasick and obviously enjoyed being on deck when the ship was under sail. These experiences were to inspire some of the best depictions of life at sea in Norwegian literature, in *Forrådt* (1892; Betrayed) and the second volume of her tetralogy *Hellemyrsfolket* (1887–1898; The People of Hellemyr). But even though she took well to the sea voyages, her marriage with Müller proved to be difficult and unhappy. Initial attempts to break away from the marriage were frustrated by her family, who sought to discourage her because of the scandal associated with divorce. This plus the resistance she encountered in trying to obtain custody of her two sons created a tremendous emotional strain, and in 1877 she suffered a nervous breakdown and had to be admitted to Gaustad mental hospital in Kristiania (present-day Oslo).

She was released after three months and at that time (1878) was granted her divorce and took up residence with her brothers together with her sons. Needing an income, Amalie Müller turned to writing. Her first published pieces were reviews of works by Ibsen, the Danish author J.P. Jacobsen, Camilla Collett, to mention a few. She was exposed to radical ideas and attitudes both through her reading and her social interactions, and book reviews written during this period reveal a growing receptivity to a naturalistic philosophy.

In 1884 Amalie Müller married the Danish writer Erik Skram, and she went to live with him in Copenhagen where she remained for the rest of her life. From the time of their first meeting, Erik Skram had encouraged Amalie to write fiction, and the first ten years of their marriage marked a period of intense creative productivity. But the stress of trying to fulfill three demanding roles—as wife, mother and writer—took its toll, and in 1894 Amalie Skram once again had a nervous breakdown. She was committed first to a psychiatric ward and then, much against her will, was transferred to a mental hospital. Fortunately, she succeeded in convincing a doctor that she was not mentally ill, and he arranged her release. This traumatic experience resulted in two books, *Professor Hieronimus* and *På St. Jörgen* (At St. Jörgen's), both published in 1895. Through a fictitious character, Skram tells of the treatment she received at mental institutions, and her descriptions gave rise to a heated debate in Copenhagen and actually resulted in improved conditions for psychiatric patients.

Skram's condition had hardly improved, however. Her health had suffered considerably as had her nerves, and in 1899 her marriage with Erik Skram ended in divorce. She continued to write, albeit sporadically due to her broken health, until she died in 1905.

Marriage and the problematic relationship between the sexes were issues that occupied Skram throughout her life, and she wrote four novels and several short stories on this subject. After *Constance Ring*, Skram went on to write *Lucie* (1888), *Fru Inés* (1891) and *Betrayed* (1892), all novels dealing with women who experience unhappy marriages. Skram was intent on exposing marriage as a hypocritical institution. Her heroine Constance Ring grows up believing that marriage is sacred, instituted by God. But when, having learned that her husband has made the servant girl pregnant, she goes to her mother and aunt and finally her pastor for help in obtaining a divorce, she is rebuffed by all. They explain to her that men are by nature promiscuous and that this, contrary to what they had taught her earlier, is the reality of married life. Fur-

thermore, it was her Christian duty to stay with her husband and to wield a positive influence over him. Although Constance does agree to abandon her divorce suit, she is not able to reconcile herself with a life she perceives to be built on lies and deceit. Some years after this crisis, her husband dies in a sailing accident, and Constance, initially overcome by guilt and depression, finally does open herself to new relationships with men. But the double standard is ever-present and, as Constance is unable to cope with disillusionment, each new attempt to find love founders.

Women would be much better equipped to deal with marriage, even the double standard, Skram argued, if they were given a proper education in their youth. Mothers avoided all discussion of sexuality. Teenaged brides were given in marriage to older, established men without ever being told that they would share the same bed on their wedding night. This obviously hindered women from developing a natural and healthy attitude toward their own sexuality and the sexual desires of their husbands, to the ultimate unhappiness of both partners. Ory, the young bride in *Betrayed*, responds with fear and shock to her husband's sexual overtures on their first night together. She comes to regard sex as something ugly and repulsive, and though she longs to be a good wife and to love her husband, she remains cold to all his attempts at intimacy. Her own sexuality having been thwarted, she takes a perverse interest in hearing about her husband's earlier sexual encounters. This becomes an obsession that eventually causes him to lose his mind.

Amalie Skram was driven by a need to tell the truth and depict life as she saw it in everything she wrote. That she was influenced by the French naturalists can be seen in her earliest stories, and concerning her novel *Constance Ring*, she asked that it be regarded as a *document humain*. The determining influence of heredity and environment is most fully developed in her four volume work *The People of Hellemyr*, the story of a family through several generations. This tetralogy is considered to be the finest example of a naturalistic work in Norwegian literature. For many years Amalie Skram's place in literary history rested on her reputation as one of Norway's foremost representatives of naturalism. Recent scholarship, however, has focused on her "marriage" novels, pointing out her important contribution as an outspoken feminist author.

Works

Novels: *Constance Ring* (1885). *Hellemyrsfolket* (tetralogy): *Sjur Gabriel* (1887). *To venner* (1887). *S.G. Myre* (1890). *Afkom* (1898). *Lucie* (1888). *Fru Inés* (1891). *Forraadt* (1892). *Professor Hieronimus* (1895). *Paa St. Jörgen* (1895). *Julehelg* (1900). *Mennesker* (1902–1905).

Short stories: *Börnefortællinger* (1890). *Kjærlighed i nord og syd* (1891). *Sommer* (1899).

Drama: [With Erik Skram], *Fjældmennesker* (1889). *Agnete* (1893).

Letters: *Mellom slagene*, ed. Eugenia Kielland (1955).

Criticism: *Optimistisk Læsemaade. Amalie Skrams litteraturkritikk*, ed. Irene Engelstad (1987).

Translations: *Betrayed*, tr. Aileen Hennes (1986). *Constance Ring*, tr. Judith Messick with Katherine Hanson (1988). *Norway's Best Stories*, ed. Hanna Astrup Larsen (1927). *Slaves of Love and Other Norwegian Short Stories*, ed. James McFarlane (1982). *An Everyday Story. Norwegian Women's Fiction*, ed. Katherine Hanson (1984).

Bibliography

Amadou, Anne-Lise, "Madame Bovary i *Constance Ring.*" *Fransk i Norge* (Oslo, 1975), pp. 87–105. Beyer, Edvard, ed., *Norges Litteratur Historie*, vol. 3 (Oslo, 1975). Bjerkelund, Ragni, *Amalie Skram. Dansk borger, norsk forgatter* (Oslo, 1988). Bonnevie, Mai Bente, et al., *Et annet språk. Analyser av norsk kvinnelitteratur* (Oslo, 1977). Dalerup, Pil, "Den kvindelige naturalist." *Vinduet*, vol. 2 (Oslo, 1975), pp. 30–37. Engelstad, Irene, *Amalie Skram. Kjærlighet og kvinneundertrykking* (Oslo, 1978). Engelstad, Irene, *Amalie Skram om seg selv* (Oslo, 1981). Engelstad, Irene, and Överland, Janneken, *Friheten til å skrive. Artikler om kvinnelitteratur fra Amalie Skram til Cecilie Löveid* (Oslo, 1981). Engelstad, Irene, *Sammenbrudd og gjennombrudd. Amalie Skrams romaner om ekteskap og sinnssykdom* (Oslo, 1984). Engelstad, Irene et al., *Norsk kvinnelitteraturhistorie* (Oslo, 1988). Krane, Borghild, *Amalie Skram og kvinnens problem* (Oslo, 1951). Krane, Borghild, *Amalie Skrams diktning. Tema og variasjoner* (Oslo, 1961). Rasmussen, Janet E., "Amalie Skram as Literary Critic." *Edda* (Oslo, 1981). pp. 1–11. Rasmussen, Janet E., "Dreams and Discontent: The Female Voice in Norwegian Literature." *Review of National Literatures. Norway* 12 (New York, 1983). Tiberg, Antonie, *Amalie Skram som kunstner og menneske* (Kristiania [Oslo], 1910).

Katherine Hanson

Bo'ena Slančíková

(a.k.a. Timrava)

Born October 2, 1867, Polichno, then in Austro-Hungary; died November 27, 1951, Lucenec, both towns now in Czechoslovakia
Genre(s): short story, novella, poetry, drama
Language(s): Slovak

Arguably the best Slovak woman writer to date, Timrava has been categorized as a "critical realist" by Marxist scholars for her condemnation of the materialistic and hypocritical small-town society she portrayed. She received the title of "National Artist" in 1947.

Born into the family of Protestant minister Pavol Slančík in southern Slovakia, Timrava was educated at home except for one year in a girls' school at age fourteen. She spent four unhappy months as companion to a rich widow in 1900 but otherwise lived all her creative life in the village where she was born and in a neighboring village. Unmarried, she lived with her family and worked as a nursery school teacher to supplement her royalties, which were meager for most of her life. The financial instability of a single woman increased Timrava's insight into current women's issues, and she portrayed many female characters whose rebellion against their position usually remained internal and only half-understood. Less nationalistic than her older sister writers Elena Maróthy-Šoltésová and Terézia Vansová, Timrava did not see the solution of the national problem as the solution to women's inequities.

Timrava's fifty-odd stories and novellas are primarily autobiographical or based on close observation of the village society she lived in. Her early slightly satiric verses about her family and friends were never published, but she developed them into ironic stories of courtship leading to marriage as a financial bargain that remind one of Jane Austen's novels written over a half-century earlier. Among the best of them are *Bez hrdosti* (No Self-Respect) in 1905, *Veľké šťastie* (Her Great Good Fortune) in 1906, and *Strašný koniec* (An Awful Ending) in 1912—all showing rebellious females who despise their position as pawns but who resign themselves to a loveless "prudent" marriage or to a lonely single life. During the same period Timrava was also writing a separate series of powerful, often tragic stories about the second village caste, the peasants. *Tá zem vábna* (That Alluring Land) in 1907 showed the problem of massive emigration from the point of view of those left behind. The longest and best of these peasant stories, *Ťapákovci* (The Ťapák Clan) in 1914, was immediately acclaimed by critics as an epiphany of the backward extended family so downtrodden they no longer wanted to improve their lives. The clear dramatic and philosophical contrast between a sister who loves the old ways and a young wife who demands progress is characteristically complicated by the tragic element of the sister's crippled legs that embittered her life. In a masterpiece of irony, the pacifist novella *Hrdinovia* (Great War Heroes) in 1918, Timrava showed both the rich and the poor and how differently the Great War affected them. Two stories present an interesting though incomplete autobiographical picture of a woman writer in the national movement: *Skúsenosť* (Experience) in 1902 and *Všetko za národ* (Give Your All for the Nation) in 1926.

Timrava is unique among Slovak writers (men as well as women) for the perceptive, realistic clarity of her characters and the bitter terseness of her satire. Much praised by Marxist critics for her early recognition of many of the contradictions of capitalism, she is also striking for her early perception that women were at least inwardly rebelling against their limitations, that some ordinary young girls were already incipient feminists.

Works

Tá zem vábna [That Alluring Land] (1907). *Márnosť všetko* [The Vanity of It All] (1908). *Dedinské povesti* [Village Tales] (1920). *Hrdinovia* [Great War Heroes] (1928). *Všetko za národ* [Give Your All for the Nation] (1930). *Dve doby* [Two Epochs] (1937). *Novohradská dedina* [A Novohrad Village] (1937). *Výber z diela* [Selected Works] (1937). *Výber z rozprávok* [Selected Tales] (1937). *Prvé kroky* [First Steps] (1938). *Zobrané spisy* [Collected Works] (1921–1945).

Translations: Czech: *Zkušenost* (1958). Russian: *Bez radosti* (1960). Magyar: *Hözök* (1960, 1975). English: "The Ťapák Family" (excerpt) (1962). Polish: *Za kogo wyjść* (1984). English: "The Assistant Teacher," "That Alluring Land," "No Joy at All," "An Awful Ending," "The Ťapák Clan," "Great War Heroes" (1990).

Bibliography

Gáfrik, Michal, "Timrava a slovenská moderna." *Slovenská literatúra,* 15 (1968): 174–179. Kusý, Ivan, et al., *Timrava v kritike a spomienkach* (Bratislava, 1958). Miko, František, "Aktuálnosť výrazu v próze literárneho realizmu." *Litteraria 7* (1964): 81–115. Rudinsky, Norma Leigh, *Incipient Feminists: Slovak Women Writers in the National Revival* (Columbus, 1990). Števček, Ján, *Esej o slovenskom románe* (Bratislava, 1979), pp. 224–242.

General references: *Dejiny slovenskej literatúry,* Vol. IV (Bratislava, 1975), pp. 135–151 and 225–232. *Encyklopédia slovenských spisovateľov* (Bratislava, 1984), II, pp. 193–197. *Kindlers Literaturlexikon* (Zürich, 1964–1972). *Le Muse: Enciclopedia di tutte le arti* (Novara, 1964–1968).

Norma L. Rudinsky

Helena Šmahelová

Born 1910, Restoky near Chrudim,
*   Czechoslovakia*
Genre(s): prose
Language(s): Czech

On leaving grammar school Helena Šmahelová worked as a health-insurance clerk, graduating in 1952 from the philosophical faculty of Palacký University in Olomouc. Since 1956 she has devoted herself to full-time writing and currently lives and works in Prague. Šmahelová's writing is mainly for young people, although she has also written biographical works. Her novels for young people have been translated into English, German, Hungarian, Polish, Russian and Serbo-Croatian.

Works

Sedmý Den Odpočívej [Rest on the Seventh Day] (1940). *Pelantovi* [The Pelants] (1944). *Mládí na Křídlech* [Youth on the Wing] (1956). *Velké Trápeni* [Great Suffering] (1957). *Planá Ru'e, Ru'ička Šípková* [Wild Rose, Little Briar Rose] (1958). *Magda* (1959). *Dva Týdny Prázdnin* [Two-week Vacation] (1960). *Cesta ze Zármutku* [The Way out of Grief] (1961). *Kárlinská Číslo 5* [Kárlinská Street No. 5] (1961). *Devět Tisíc Dnů* [Nine Thousand Days] (1963). *Jsem u' Valká Divka* [I'm a Grown Girl Now] (1963). *Dobrá Mysl* [Good Mood] (1964). *Chrabrovka* (1965). *Dora a Medvěd* [Dora and the Bear] (1968). *Sobvectví* [Egoism] (1969). *Mu'a Žena* [Man and Woman] (1972). *Bratra Sestra* [Brother and Sister] (1973). *Dědicové Snu* [Heirs to Dreams] (1974). *Žárlivost* [Jealousy] (1975). *Dora na Cestách* [Dora Abroad] (1979). *Vzpomínky na Jaromíra Johna* [In Memory of Jaromír John] (1979). *Vůně Letních Jablek*, biography (1980). *Dum Radosti* [House of Joy] (1982).

Warwick J. Rodden

Smara

(a.k.a. Smara Gîrbea, Smaranda Garbini[u], Frusinica, Baba Vişa)

Born 1857, Tîrgovişte, Romania; died 1944, Bucharest

Genre(s): novel, short story, drama, poetry, essay, children's literature, journalism, memoirs, translation

Language(s): Romanian

Smara (Smaranda Gheorghiu, née Andronescu) combined in one person and under a variety of pseudonyms a determined feminist, an enlightened and dynamic cultural entrepreneur, and a vigorous militant writer.

She travelled widely in Romania, Italy, Belgium, France, Sweden, Denmark, Greece, etc., lecturing on education and women's emancipation, was among the organizers of the Universal Union of Women's Congress for Peace, and represented Romania repeatedly at international congresses such as the Orientalists' Congress (1889), the Latin Congress (1902), etc. Smara founded a literary circle which was attended by the superlative Romanian poet Eminescu among other prestigious writers of the time. In 1890, one year after the tragic death of Veronica Micle, she published a monograph acknowledging the romantic woman poet's contribution to Romanian literature. In 1893, Smara issued a literary journal—*Altiţe şi bibiluri* (Lace and Frills). The name of the journal was meant to draw the attention of the cultivated public to women's folk art of needlework and, more generally, of folk costume sewing as a legitimate constituent of Romanian culture. In books like *Feciorii şi fetele noastre* (1896; Our Sons and Daughters) and *Inteligenţa femeii* (1896; Women's Intelligence), Smara advocated equal education for girls and boys while opposing male chauvinistic cultural policies and ideologies of the time. After years of tenacious campaigning Smara managed to introduce and popularize the idea of outdoor schools.

A regular contributor to *Convorbiri literare, Fîntîna Blanduziei, Revista literară, Literatorul, Revista poporului, Romînul literar, Tribuna literară, Universul, Adevărul, Şcoala romînă*, etc., Smara published several novels among which *Fata tatii* (1912; Daddy's Girl), *Băiatul mamii* (Mom's Boy), and *Domnul Bădină* (Mr. Bădină) are best known. In the second, the principal character, an unhappily married woman, becomes a feminist and, subsequently, depressed by the baseness of her lover, commits suicide. In the other novels, the female characters are also weakened and humiliated by selfish, despotic, and opportunistic husbands/lovers.

Her short stories—some of which were collected in the volumes *Novele* (1890; Short Stories) and *Dumitriţe brumate* (1937; Hoarfrosted Marigolds)—are either nostalgic evocations of rural life or compassionate depictions of the life of the poor, of recruits, convicts, etc.

Smara's long plays focus upon incest (*Mîrza* 1904) or plead for legalizing men's paternal responsibilities (*Ispăşire* 1905; Expiation). Smara's short plays are circumstantial celebrations of the Union of the Romanian principalities (*La 24 ianuarie* 1905; On January 24th), of patriotism (*Dorul de ţară* 1905; Homesickness), or of human work (*Meseriaşii* 1905; The Craftsmen).

Her volumes of erotic, contemplative, or patriotic poetry—such as *Ţara mea* (1905; My

Country) and *Spade strămoşeşti* (Ancestors' Swords)—are rather conventional.

Smara's numerous lecture trips provided the material for rich and vivid travel recollections such as *Schiţe şi amintiri din Italia* (1900; Sketches and Memories from Italy), *Schiţe şi amintiri din Cehoslovacia* (1925; Sketches and Memories from Czechoslovakia), and especially *O româncă spre polul Nord* (1932; A Romanian Woman towards the North Pole) in which Smara recounts Denmark, Sweden, Finland, and her encounter with Ibsen.

Smara translated works by E.A. Poe and James Fenimore Cooper into Romanian.

Works

Din pana suferinţei [Suffering's Pen] (1888). *Novele* [Short Stories] (1890). *Veronica Micle. Viaţa şi operile sale* [Veronica Micle. Her Life and Works] (1892). *Feciorii şi fiicele noastre* [Our Sons and Daughters] (1896). *Inteligenţa femeii* [Women's Intelligence] (1896). *Mozaicuri* [Inlays] (1897). *Schiţe din Tîrgovişte* [Sketches from Tîrgovişte] (1898). *Schiţe şi amintiri din Italia* [Sketches and Memories from Italy] (1900). *Calvar* [Calvary] (1901). *Mîrza* [Mîrza] (1904). *Dorul de ţară. Meseriaşii. La 24 Ianuarie. Ispăşire* [Homesickness. The Craftsmen. On January 24th. Expiation] (1905). *Ţara mea* [My Country] (1905). *Conferinţe şi discursuri* [Speeches and Addresses] (1905). *Stîlpi de pază* [Watch Studs] (1906). *Fata tatii* [Daddy's Girl] (1912). *Băiatul mamii* [Mom's Boy] (n.d.). *Spade strămoşeşti* [Ancestors' Swords] (n.d.). *Schiţe şi amintiri din Cehoslovacia* [Sketches and Memories from Czechoslovakia] (1925). *Simfonii din trecut* [Symphonies from the Past] (1927). *O româncă spre Polul Nord* [A Romanian Woman towards the North Pole] (1932). *Domnul Bădină* [Mr. Bădină] (n.d.). *Corbul cu pene de aur* [The Raven with Golden Feathers] (1925). *Dumitriţe brumate* [Hoarfrosted Marigolds] (1937). *Cîntă Dorna* [Dorna Is Singing] (1939).

Bibliography

Creţu, Stănuţa, In *Dicţionarul literaturii române de la origini pînă la 1900* (Bucharest, 1979), pp. 793–794. *Jubileul de 75 de ani al scriitoarei Smara* (Bucharest, 1932). Miller-Verghi, Margareta, and Ecaterina Săndulescu, *Evoluţia scrisului feminin în România* (Bucharest, 1935), pp. 197–205.

Sanda Golopentia

Alie Van Wijhe-Smeding

Born 1890; died 1938
Genre(s): novel
Language(s): Dutch

Alie Smeding wrote in a strongly naturalistic manner which was thought of as scandalous and shocking, especially since she was the daughter and the wife of a minister.

Her novels *De zondaar* (1927; The Sinner) and *De naakte waarheid* (1932; The Naked Truth) caused an outrage because of their allegedly pornographic character. The author later turned to religious and moral themes and wrote in a more subdued, sentimental vein.

Works

Menschen uit een stil stadje (1920). *Duivels naaigaren* (1926). *De zondaar* (1927). *De domineevrouw van Blankenheim* (1930). *De naakte waarheid* (1932). *Hunkering* (1934). *Bruggenbouwers* (1938).

Bibliography

Knuvelder, Gerard, *Handboek tot de geschiedenis der Nederlandse letterkunde*, vol. 4 (2nd ed. Amsterdam, 1961), p. 340. Moerman, Josien, *Lexicon Nederlandstalige auteurs* (1964), p. 214. Waal, Margot de, and Suzanne Piët, "Women of Letters." *Insight Holland* 15 (1980): 2.

Maya Bijvoet

Smīns

(see: Anna Sakse)

Andrée Sodenkamp

Born June 18, 1906, Brussels, Belgium
Genre(s): poetry
Language(s): French

Andrée Sodenkamp married Camille Libotte on February 12, 1938. Much of her poetry deals with daily life: her husband, cat, dog, the seasons, and human relations. She believes that the end of life is nothing more than a long sleep. She won the Prix Renée Vivien for her second volume of poetry, *Sainte Terre* (1954); the Prix de la province de Brabant for *Les Dieux obscurs* (1959);

three prizes, the Prix triennal de littérature (1968), Prix Desbordes-Valmore (1970), and the Prix Van Lerberghe (1976) for her fourth book, *Femmes des longs matins*; and the Prix Louise Labé for La Fête débout.

Works

Des Oiseaux à tes lèvres [The Birds at Your Lips] (1950). *Sainte Terre* [Saint Earth] (1954). *Les Dieux obscurs* [The Obscure Gods] (1959). *Femmes des longs matins* [Women of Long Mornings] (1965). *La Fête débout* [The Feast] (1973). *Autour de moi-même* [Around Myself] (1976).

Adolf von Württemberg

Edith Irene Södergran

Born April 4, 1892, St. Petersburg, Russia; died June 24, 1923, Raivola (now Rosjtjino), Finland
Genre(s): lyric poetry
Language(s): German and Swedish

Edith Södergran occupies a unique place among Swedish writers in Finland, in that she opened the gates to European and modernist influence on a type of poetry that had lived a rather secluded life of its own. Educated at the German Girls School in St. Petersburg (now Leningrad), she grew up in a cosmopolitan atmosphere and even in Raivola, the village on the Carelian isthmus, where her family lived, the mixture of Finnish and Russian culture was clearly present. The specific nature of her home village, the cosmopolitan atmosphere of St. Petersburg, and a certain eccentric preoccupation with her "self," peculiar to the only child type of writer, color her poetry, which is new in form, fresh in expression, and bears the clear signature of its author. Much of it can only be understood against these three background factors: Raivola, St. Petersburg, and the fact that she was her mother's only child and was brought up almost entirely by her mother, who always stayed with her during terms in St. Petersburg. Her father died of consumption in 1907, an illness that was to end his daughter's life as well less than twenty years after his death. In 1909 it was discovered that she had the contamination, and the rest of her life was a constant fight against the illness.

It is important to notice that her switch from German to Swedish, which was her mother tongue, coincides with this crisis in her life. From 1909 on, her poetry becomes all her own with the typical Södergran-features of free form, no rhymes, "catalogue" poems that resemble some of Walt Whitman's poetry, and the intensely feminine use of language that is one of her chief characteristics. At this time her mother was still wealthy, and she tried to find a cure for her daughter in Switzerland. The years 1911–1913 were spent on the Continent, and when Edith returned home early in 1914, she was filled with dreams of a literary future. She visited several people in 1915, asking them for an evaluation of her poems. She published her first volume, *Dikter* (Poems), in 1916. She could hardly foresee the reaction. Stylistic features that she was familiar with from the Continent—rhymelessness and a dashing swiftness of associations—were so new to the Swedish reading public that people were shocked, and this harsh reaction seems to have taken Edith Södergran entirely by surprise. All her desperate attempts to establish contacts with what she terms "literary personalities" were refuted, and she returned to Raivola in 1917 to remain there for the rest of her life. In November, the Russian Revolution deprived Edith and her mother of all their property, except the house in Raivola, and in the spring of 1918, the war spread to the village and was followed by famine in the summer. But at that time Nietzsche had become the source of inspiration for Edith, and there is a deep contrast between her creative heights and the poverty and illness she is living in. Her second book, *Septemberlyran* (1918; The September Lyre) reflects both the first beginnings and her almost ecstatic final embracement of Nietzsche's teachings. In them she finds the strength to cope with her illness and poverty, facts that are not tolerated in the sublime world of her poetry. Critical appraisal moved from chilly to cold, but one person, Hagar Olsson, herself a critic and writer, appreciated Edith's poems and entered upon a correspondence with Edith that led to a lifelong friendship. Södergran's visionary poetry is maintained in *Rosenaltaret* (1919; The Rose Altar) but there are also specimens of her early lyric poems. *Framtidens skugga* (1920; The Shadow of Future) is the summit of her lyric achievement: prophetic, visionary and Södergranian. She has now made acquaintance with Steiner's religious views and is about to give up writing all together.

By 1920 other modernists had established themselves, and they looked to Edith Södergran as their idol. But her physical strength was now broken, and though she now gained the friendship of people who appreciated her, and even occasionally resumed writing herself, she was unable to fight her illness much longer. She died on Midsummer Day, 1923.

Hagar Olsson published posthumously a collection of late poems called *Landet som icke är* (1925; The Country That Is Not). In a volume called *Edith's Letters* (1955), she published their correspondence, a fascinating portrait of two friends and two important women writers.

Edith Södergran opened a new era of poetry in Finland and reached out across the language barrier to Sweden. She has been rated as the most important Swedish lyric writer in Finland in the twentieth century.

Works

Dikter [Poems] (1916). *Septemberlyran* [The September Lyre] (1918). *Rosenaltaret* [The Rose Altar] (1919). *Brokiga iakttagelser* [Gaudy Observations] (1919). *Framtidens skugga* [The Shadow of Future] (1920). *Landet som icke är* [The Country That Is Not] (1925).

Bibliography

Olsson, Hagar, *Ediths brev* (Helsingfors, 1955). Tideström, Gunnar, *Edith Södergran* (Helsingfors, 1949).

Gunnel Cleve

Nadezhda Sokhanskaia

(a.k.a. Kokhanovskaia)

Born February 17, 1823, near Korocha, Russia; died December 3, 1884, "Makarovka" (manor), Kharkov province
Genre(s): short story, autobiography, publicity, ethnography-history
Language(s): Russian

If Nadezhda Sokhanskaia ("Kokhanovskaia") had been born fifteen years earlier and begun publishing as a contemporary of Nikolai Gogol, she would have had a better chance to be recognized as one of the great regionalists of Russian literature. In the post-emancipation era of the 1860s and 1870s, however, she was clearly out of step: sympathetic to the Slavophiles, she published most of her works in Ivan Aksakov's newspapers and other conservative forums. Deeply religious, she supported the Cyril and Methodius societies created to protect Orthodox Ukrainians in the western borderlands. Her journalism displayed antisemitic bias, and her contentious character made the protest letter one of her most practiced *genres*. Prescriptive critics failed to appreciate the internal logic of Sokhanskaia's fiction. Because she described her simple protagonists' adventures from their own viewpoint in a stylized voice that drew heavily on oral tradition, she was accused of approving their *mores* and casting a rosy glow over the harsh realities of rural life under serfdom. The Soviets seem content to let this reputation stand, and Western scholars have yet to evaluate Sokhanskaia's original talent.

Born into near poverty, Sokhanskaia was educated as a scholarship student at the Kharkov Institute, one of the infamous "closed" boarding schools for girls. After she returned at seventeen to "Makarovka," the humble family manor in the eastern Ukraine, she made the interpretation of the history and contemporary life of the area her life work. She published several articles of collected popular songs, and her fiction is steeped in folklore. The protagonists of her stories were drawn from the impoverished gentry, Cossack, and merchant classes; she reported on peasant attitudes in brief reports to newspapers (under rubrics like "S khutora" [From the Farm]), but the peasantry plays only a subordinate role in her fiction. Her most admired work, "Starina" (1861; Olden Times), was a set of sketches of her ancestors, including a woman who turned her hand to banditry. This historical compilation was complemented by several fictional tales set in the eighteenth century: "Iz provintsial'noi gallerei portretov" (1859; From a Provincial Portrait Gallery), "Roi Feodosii Savvich na pokoe" (1864; Swarm—the hero's nickname, because he was born in an apiary—Feodosii Savvich at Rest), and "Krokha slovesnogo khleba (1874; [A

Literary Breadcrumb]—so called because the story appeared in a book published for charity; Sokhanskaia usually referred to it as "Prus" after the nickname of her hero, a veteran of the Prussian wars who travels to Petersburg to seek justice in a land dispute).

Sokhanskaia's weakest story is the most realistic and autobiographical ("Gaika" [1856–1860; meaning "nut" or "screw" but in context best translated as "The Linchpin"]). She was clearly fascinated by the challenge of depicting larger-than-life characters like Swarm and all three heroes—father, daughter and suitor—of "From a Provincial Portrait Gallery." For virtually the first time, and very nearly the last, in Russian literature, Sokhanskaia depicts the entrepreneur as a positive type ("Gaika"; "Kirilla Petrov i Nastas'ia Dmitrova," 1861). Despite her affectionate tone and the exuberant language and glittering stylization in which she describes her protagonists' flamboyant ways, Sokhanskaia never loses sight of the despotism and patriarchal *mores* that rule their world. In this rigid society her female characters suffer most. In "Posle obeda v gost'iakh" (1858; An After-Dinner Visit), Liubov' Arkhipovna tells the frame narrator how she learned to cherish the clumsy, kind merchant her mother forced her to marry. It takes a single question from her listener to reveal the full extent of the girl's tragic loss of a chance for happiness with a lover whose quicksilver character and talents matched her own.

When Sokhanskaia sent her first efforts at fiction to the Petersburg editor Petr Pletnev in 1846, he suggested that the neophyte hone her craft by writing the history of her own life. This remarkable autobiography, written before she was twenty-five, was published posthumously in *Russkoe obozrenie* (The Russian Review, 1896, 6–9). It evokes still fresh memories of Sokhanskaia's carefree childhood, unhappy years at school, and the shock of her return to an earth-floored house in a region composed largely of women living alone on isolated farms and estates. Much of her later life is covered in correspondence with Ivan Aksakov and his wife (Russian Review, 1897, 2–12). A long article she wrote in answer to criticism of "From a Provincial Portrait Gallery" offers valuable information about her creative priorities (*Russkaia Beseda* [Russian Colloquy],

1859, 6, crit., pp. 123–152). While her widowed mother and spinster aunt were still vigorous, Sokhanskaia had time to write; from the late 1860s, she had to devote most of her energies to caring for them and the farm they had struggled to build. At her death she left unpublished only a fragment of reminiscence from her aunt's life, "Sumerechnye rasskazy" (Twilight Tales), and the historical introduction to a projected novel, "Stepnaia baryshnia sorokovykh godov" (A Young Lady of the Steppes of the '40s).

Works

Povesti, 2 vols. (1863).

Translation: "Les Ames du bon Dieu," N.A. Kolbert, tr., *Barines et moujiks* (1887).

Bibliography

Heldt, Barbara, *A Terrible Perfection: Women and Russian Literature* (Bloomington, Ind., 1987). *Istoriia russkoi literatury XIX v.: Bibliograficheskii ukazatel'*, K.D. Muratova, ed. (Moscow-Leningrad, 1962), pp. 378–380. *Kratkaia literaturnaia entsiklopediia*, vol. 3 (Moscow, 1966), cols. 779–780 [I.T. Trofimov]. Platonova, N.N., *Kokhanovskaia (N. S. Sokhanskaia) 1823–1884: Biograficheskii ocherk* (St. Petersburg, 1909). Ponomarev, S.D., "Opis' bumag ostavshikhsia posle N.S. Sokhanskoi (Kokhanovskoi)," *Russkoe obozrenie* (1898), 1, pp. 277–312 [bibliography].

Mary F. Zirin

Dona Sol

(see: Otilia Cazimir)

Amalia Solla Nizzoli

Born circa 1806, Tuscany, Italy; died circa 1845, Greece
Genre(s): memoirs
Language(s): Italian

Solla was born and lived in Tuscany until she was about thirteen years old. At the time, her family was called to Egypt by a maternal uncle, who was the doctor of the Defterdar-Bey, Finance Minister of the Ottoman Viceroy. The young girl soon learned Arabic and was able to move freely in the female society of Cairo's upper class. When she was about twenty years old, she married Giuseppe Nizzoli and went to the Greek island of Zante, where he had been made the Austrian vice-consul (at the time, part of northern Italy was included in the Austrian-Hungarian Empire). The exact date of her death is unknown.

Solla's claim to fame are her memoirs of Egypt: *Memorie sull'Eqitto e specialmente sui costumi delle donne e gli harem, scritte durante il suo soggiorno in quel paese, 1819–1828* (1941; Memories of Egypt and Especially of Women's Customs and of Harems, Written during her Sojourn in that Country, 1819–1828). Gracefulness of style and a lively storytelling ability characterize this work, but its main interest lies in the unusual subject matter. We are told of shipboard life, of the customs and regulations at sea, of the uncommon set of people who plied the Mediterranean waters at the beginning of the 1800s. During one of her journeys, Solla's elder daughter dies and is buried at sea. During another trip, her husband, who was a dedicated archaeologist, tries to hide from the superstitious crew the existence on board of some mummies destined for European museums. The author is able to offer an inside view of the Arabic-Turkish society, its customs and ways of thinking, the coming together of different cultures, the segregated world in which the women lived. Solla's graceful and generally unbiased attitude has created a very pleasant and, one may argue, a more truthful record of that world than the strongly accusatory description that Cristina di Belgioioso gave of her travels through Turkey a few years later.

Works

Memorie sull'Egitto e specialmente sui costumi delle donne e degli harem, scritte durante il suo soggiorno in quel paese, 1819–1828 (1841).

Bibliography

Cappuccio, C., ed., *Memorialisti dell'Ottocento*, III (Milan-Naples, 1958), pp. 53–122. Costa-Zalessow, N., *Scrittrici italiane dal XIII al XX secolo, Testi e critica* (Ravenna, 1982), pp. 216–223. *Enciclopedia biografica e bibliografica italiana* (Rome, 1941–1942), Serie VI: *Poetesse e scrittrici*, ed. Baldini-Buti, II, p. 79.

Rinaldina Russell

Poliksena Sergeevna Soloviëva

(a.k.a. Allegro)

Born March 20, 1867, Moscow, Russia; died August 16, 1924, Moscow
Genre(s): poetry
Language(s): Russian

Writing during the period of Symbolism, Soloviëva reflects not so much her contemporaries Blok or Merezhkovskij, as Fet. Her poems sigh in lyric contemplation, abandoning the Symbolist pose of the artist-as-prophet or "chosen one" (izbrannik). As a poet-artist, though, she is well-suited to her artistic time.

Soloviëva grew up in an illustrious family, her father Sergei a famous historian and brother Vladimir a philosopher-poet. As a young woman, she studied painting in Moscow for several years. Her first published poems began to appear in 1895, primarily in Symbolist journals. Soon afterward, her first collection, *Stikhotvoreniia* (1899; Poems), was published with her own illustrations. She wrote in a male voice (Ja ukhodil . . . Ty ne mogla togda menia poniat') to a female figure. Her poems center on motifs of grief and loneliness and frequently involve an invocation of nature.

In addition to her poetic oeuvre, Soloviëva wrote versified stories in a collection called *Perekrestok* (1913; Crossroad) and children's stories, *Tainaia pravda* (1912; The Secret Truth). Her principal work, though, continued to be poetry with many of her published books accompanied by her own illustrations.

Works

Stikhotvoreniia (1899). *Inei, risunki i stikhi* (1905). *Elka* (1907). *Plakun-trava* (1909). *Svad'ba Solntsa i Vesny* (1912). *Vecher* (1914). *Poslednie stikhi* (1923).

Chris Tomei

Elsa Sophia, baroness von Kamphoevener

(alphabetized as Kamphoevener)

Sophie A.

(see: Mathilde Lucie Fibiger)

Mireille Sorgue

Born March 19, 1944; died August 1967
Genre(s): poetry, correspondence
Language(s): French

In her volume of poems *L'Amant* (The Lover) and the related *Lettres à l'amant* (Letters to the Lover), Mireille Sorgue gives frank, vivid expression to the sexual feelings of a high-spirited and independent-minded young woman. It appears that her lover was an older man, one François Solesmes, who presented his side of the relationship, as seen from the standpoint of the survivor, in *L'Amante* (The Lover), brought out at the same time (1968) and by the same publisher as *L'Amant*. Both works were published by Robert Mael.

Mireille Sorgue died in an accident at the age of twenty-three before her manuscript was published. In his review of *L'Amant*, Pierre-Henri Simon voiced the suspicion that its "dazzling" style really belongs to an established author using the pen name of Mireille Sorgue. *L'Amant* won its author the Prix Hermès in 1969.

Works

L'Amant (1968; rpt. 1985). Lettres à l'amant (1985).

Bibliography

Brisac, Geneviève, "La soif exigeante de Mireille Sorgue." *Le Monde (des Livres)* (March 8, 1985): 23. Carrell, Susan L., "La lettre d'amour aujourd'hui: Mireille Sorgue." *Cahiers de l'Association Internationale des Etudes Françaises* 39 (May 1987): 205–218. Lalou, Etienne, "La voix des éternels amants." *L'Express* (November 4–10, 1968): 50. Simon, Pierre-Henri, "Review of L'Amant, Lettres à l'amant, and L'Amante." *Le Mondes (des Livres)* (September 6, 1985): 1.

James S. Patty

Elena Soriano Jara

Born 1917, Fuentidueña de Tajo (Madrid),
Spain
Genre(s): novel, essay
Language(s): Spanish

Elena Soriano is a contemporary of Carmen Laforet and Camilo José Cela, belonging to the first generation of novelists immediately after the Spanish Civil War. She studied humanities planning to be a teacher, but her studies were interrupted by the war. She directed the literary magazine *El Urugallo* from 1969 to 1976 and often writes essays for Spanish journals. Her first novel, *Caza menor* (1951; Small Game), shows some traditional characteristics of a nineteenth-century novel, such as the depiction of customs and an interest in local color. Unlike the rest of her novels, the three major characters are men; three brothers who fight for the same woman and their inheritance until the Civil War breaks out and each of them is left to his own devices.

Her trilogy *Mujer y hombre* (1955; Woman and Man) is formed by three independent novels that have a relationship between the sexes in common. The first one, *La playa de los locos* (Crazy People's Beach) was censored in Franco's time and therefore was not widely read. The other two, *Espejismos* (Mirages) and *Medea*, received favorable reviews by the critics.

La playa de los locos is the story of a woman who relives her only love affair twenty years after it occurred by returning to the seaside town where it took place, but it is too late to recapture her lost lover and her lost youth. *Espejismos* treats a similar theme in the life of a couple who has been married a long time and their marriage has grown stale. *Medea* is a contemporary version of the classical tale. Daniela, the wife scorned, sets out to destroy the love of the husband for a younger woman. All three novels make an effective use of interior monologues, flashbacks, and rich language. Elena Soriano's introspection into the female psyche, if somewhat dated, is of interest to the feminist reader. The trilogy has just been published in its entirety for the first time (Barcelona, 1986).

In 1985 Elena Soriano published an auto-biographical account of the life and death of her only son, Juan José. *Testimonio materno* (A

Mother's Testimony) is a chilling commentary on the sixties generation and their experimentation with drugs and alternative life styles.

Works

Caza menor (1951). La playa de los locos (1955). Espejismos (1955). Medea (1955). Testimonio materno (1985).

Bibliography

Alborg, Juan Luis, Hora actual de la novela española (Madrid, 1962), pp. 349–372. Fox-Lockert, Lucía, Women Novelists in Spain and Spanish America (New Jersey, 1979), pp. 94–106. Núñez, Antonio, "Encuentro con Elena Soriano." Insula (Junio 1986): 1 and 12. Suñén, Luis, "Elena Soriano y Enrique Murillo: volver y empezar." Insula (Marzo 1985): 5. Winecoff, Janet, "Existentialism in the Novels of Elena Soriano." Hispania XLVII: 309–315.

Concha Alborg

Marie de Sormiou

(see: Marie-Thérèse-Charlotte Buret)

Didō Sōtēriou

Born 1913 (1914?), Smyrna, Turkey
Genre(s): novel, journalism
Language(s): Greek

In her first two works (published in 1959 and 1962), Didō Sōtēriou deals with the land she was born and spent her childhood in, Asia Minor, and contrasts the days of peace before the 1922 disaster to the days of persecution, inhuman treatment, and flight. In writing these works Sōtēriou gives expression to the pain of separation from one's homeland and the nostalgia felt by all those who have been uprooted. Her Matōmena Chōmata (Bloodied Earth) is probably one of the best historical novels that have emerged out of the events of 1922 and their aftermath.

In her Entolē (Commandment), Sōtēriou turns to the Greek Civil War, which she experienced later, and writes a novel using the figure of the resistance fighter Nikos Beloyannis as the major character. Soteriou's aim, as she herself states, is not to arouse old passions but to seek catharsis. Dealing with a sensitive and contro-

versial subject which split Greece in two, she attempts to be honest and compassionate, to heal rather than to open old wounds. Kostas Myrsiades calls this book the major prose work of the Left and one of contemporary Greece's major novels.

Sōtēriou's work has been translated into German, Russian, Bulgarian, French, Hungarian, Romanian, and Turkish.

Works

Oi nekroi perimenoun [The Dead Await] (1959, 1976). Matōmena chōmata [Bloodied Earth] (1962, 1977). Entolē [Commandment] (1978). Katedaphizometha [We Are Being Razed to the Ground] (1982).

Bibliography

Langē, Ersē, Hellēnides pezographoi (Athens, 1975). Mirasgezē, Maria, Neoellēnike Logotechnia, Vol. 2 (Athens, 1982). Politēs, Linos, Historia tēs Neoellēnikēs Logotechnias (Athens, 1980). Review by Kostas Myrsiades, World Literature Today 54, No. 1 (Winter, 1980): 148.

Helen Dendrinou Kolias

Ersē Sotēropoulou

Born 1953, Patras, Greece
Genre(s): poetry, novel, novella
Language(s): Greek

Ersē Sotēropoulou lived several years in Italy and studied cultural anthropology in Florence. In the fall of 1981 she took part in an international seminar on writing at the University of Iowa. She has published a collection of poems entitled Melo a Thanatos a ... a ... (Apple a Death a ... a ...), two novels, Diakopes chōris ptōma (Vacation Without a Corpse) and Ē Pharsa (The Farce), and a novella, Eortastiko Triēmero sta Giannena (Three-Day Holiday in Giannena).

Her last work, Ē Pharsa, deals with two young women who close themselves up in a depressing city apartment and make disturbing telephone calls to unsuspecting males of some social importance. The calls are hardly more than word games accompanied by preposterous propositions that subject the listeners to ridicule and entertain the reader. But this is not a book for light reading. Beyond this farcical atmosphere is another farce: the farce of life, the illusions set up by institutions and individuals in their attempt to live in dignified seriousness. Lastly, there is the farce of the meaningful novel: The structure and style of the work expose the fact that meaning is a superimposed activity and writing is a play with words. Sotēropoulou uses language to expose the tyranny of language and the blind conservatism of Greek society. The net result is a powerful disturbance of the average reader's apathetic state of being.

In his informative introduction that places this novel in a Lacanian context, Nanos Valaorites writes that *Ē Pharsa* is the first Greek work that makes us consciously aware that oppression starts with language, both ideological and emotional (p. 8).

Works

Mēlo ạ Thanatos ạ . . . ạ . . . (1980). *Diakopes chōris ptōma* (1980). *Eortastiko triēmero sta Giannena* (1982). *Ē Pharsa* (1982).

Bibliography

Sotēropoulou, Ersē, *Ē Pharsa.* Introduction by Nanos Valaorites (Athens, 1982). Review by Liana Sakelliou, *World Literature Today,* 57, No. 3 (1983): 493.

Helen Dendrinou Kolias

Sopia de Mello Breyner Andresen de Sousa Tavares

Born 1922, Oporto, Portugal
Genre(s): poetry, short story, children's
    literature, literary criticism
Language(s): Portuguese

Andresen studied classical philology at the University of Lisbon and is the mother of five children. She has collaborated on various journals including *Cadernos de Poesia, Tavola Redonda, Unicórnio, Arvore,* and *Diario Popular.* She has translated Shakespeare and other poets and written critical essays, including one on the Brazilian poet she is said to resemble, Cecilia Meireles.

Andresen cannot be easily classified as a member of any specific literary group of her time although she is known as a postsymbolist, and her early poetry shows the influence of the sixteenth-century Portuguese lyricists, especially Fernando Pessoa. Her verse is characterized by its mastery of structure and seriousness of tone. Her intuition mediates between intellect and emotion, but this balance unfortunately gives way to the dominance of the intellect in her later poetry, diminishing its quality. Her abstract lyrics make use of symbols from nature, and her favorite metaphors utilize the sea, the wind, the air, the night, the garden, and distant horizons. Her poetry frequently expresses her deeply felt indignation at humankind's callousness and the injustices of society. Other themes are the essential loneliness of human existence and the transitory nature of human relations and affections. Her use of marine and aerial symbols expresses her quest for communion with nature, for liberation from earthly limitations, and for contact with a spiritual realm. Andresen writes both free and traditional verse forms, and her language, simple and direct, has become increasingly succinct in her later works. Her children's stories and essays do not achieve the same level of quality as her poetry. She is an authentic contemporary poet whose verse gives voice to the tragic sentiment of modern life.

Works

Poetry: *Poesia* [Poetry] (1944). *Dia do mar* [Ocean Day] (1947). *Coral* [Coral] (1950). *No tempo dividido* [In Divided Time] (1954). *Mar Novo* [New Ocean] (1958). *Poesia* [Poetry] (1959). *O Cristo Cigano* [The Gypsy Christ] (1961). *Livro Sexto* [Sixth Book] (1962). *Antologia* [Anthology] (1968). *Dual* [Dual] (1972).

Short stories: *Contos exemplares* [Exemplary Tales] (1962).

Children's literature: *A menina do mar* [The Maiden of the Sea] (1958). *A Fada Oriana* [The Fairy Oriana] (1958).

Bibliography

Columbia Dictionary of Modern European Literature, ed. J.A. Bédé and W.B. Edgerton (1980). *Encyclopedia of World Literature in the 20th Century,* ed. L. Klein (1981). Guimaraes, F., "A Poesia de Ruy Cinatti, Jorge de Sena, Sophia Andresen, e Eugenio de Andrade," *Estrada larga,* vol. 3 (1962). Mourao-Ferreira, D., *Vinte poetas contemporáneos* (1960). *Literatura Portuguesa Moderna,* ed. M. Moisés (1973). Sena, J., "Sophis de Mello Breyner Andresen." *Grande dicionário de literatura portuguesa*, pt. 6 (n.d., ca. 1973).

Paula T. Irvin

Adélaïde-Marie-Emilie Filleul de Flahaut de Souza

Born May 14, 1761, Paris, France; died April 16, 1836, Paris
Genre(s): novel, drama
Language(s): French

Adélaïde de Souza is one of a number of French women writers of the turn of the eighteenth century. Most of them are forgotten today, and their works unread, but in their time they were popular and successful. They form the transition from eighteenth-century literature to the new Romantic esthetic.

Adélaïde Filleul was orphaned early and educated in a convent. At the age of eighteen, she married the Count de Flahaut, who was fifty-seven. He was the superintendent of King Louis XVI's gardens. Her marriage placed her in the highest social and political circles; her salon was frequented by Talleyrand, Laclos, the Countess d'Albany and the American political figure Gouverneur Morris. Her husband was guillotined during the French Revolution, and she fled with her son to England, Holland, Switzerland and Germany, where she met the future Louis-Philippe. Her first novel, *Adèle de Sénange*, was published by subscription in England in 1793 and netted her 40,000 francs, which she badly needed to support herself and her son in exile. In 1802, she married José-Maria de Souza, a Portuguese nobleman who was himself a writer; he translated Guilleragues' *Lettres portugaises* in Portuguese, and edited Damoes' *Lusiads*. As the minister plenipotentiary to the First Consul (Napoleon Bonaparte), M. de Souza brought his wife back to Paris, where she continued to write and publish under her new name.

Adélaïde de Souza published seven novels and one play; she was best known for her first novel, *Adèle de Sénange*, composed around 1788 but published in 1793, and for *Eugène de Rothelin* (1808). Both deal with women married to men they do not love; these unions are unconsummated, in *Adèle de Sénange* because the husband is much older, really a father figure to his wife, and in *Eugène de Rothelin* because the husband leaves immediately after the wedding. The women fall in love with younger, more suitable partners and eventually marry them. She drew on her life in England for *Charles et Marie* (1801), while *Eugénie et Mathilde* (1811) depicts a noble family's experiences during the Revolution. Souza excels at portraying young lovers and the birth of passion. Character is her forte, but her plots are creaky. Her portraits of older, worldly characters are especially well-drawn. Among her themes is the depiction of happy convent education, which is in contrast to the dismal and terrifying portrait of convent life found in the works of eighteenth-century male authors. She also deals with motherhood and maternal feelings in her novels. Souza's attempts at historical fiction, in *Mademoiselle de Tournon* (1820) and *La Duchesse de Guise* (1832, a play), were not as well received as her other works.

Souza's esthetic is very much that of the eighteenth century. She deals with nobles and with the social conventions of the aristocracy. Her best work utilizes her background and depicts in a delicate and precise way a society that was forever banished by the Revolution; it has the charm of an eighteenth-century miniature. Those later works that show the trace of the pre-romantic influence are her weakest. While Adélaïde de Souza is not a "lost" woman novelist whose works should be part of a newly constituted canon, she is important both for what her works teach us about women's fiction between two great literary periods and for the strong influence she had on readers, especially women readers, of the first third of the nineteenth century.

Works

Oeuvres complètes, 6 vols. (1821–1823). *Adèle de Sénange*, vol. I. *Eugénie et Mathilde*, vol. II. *Eugène de Rothelin*, vol. III. *La Comtesse de Fargy*, vol. IV. *Emilie et Alphonse*, vol. V. *Mademoiselle de Tournon*, vol. VI. *La Duchesse de Guise, ou intérieur d'une famille illustre dans le temps de la Ligue* (1832).

Bibliography

Bearne, Catherine Mary, *Four Fascinating French Women* (London, 1910). Decreus-Van Liefland, Juliette, *Sainte-Beuve et la critique des auteurs féminins* (Paris, 1949), pp. 108–121. Le Breton, André, *Le Roman français au XIXᵉ siècle avant Balzac* (Paris, 1901), pp. 52–68. Maricourt, André, baron de, *Madame de Souza et sa famille: les Maigny-les Flahaut-Auguste de Morny (1761–1836)* (2nd ed. Paris, 1907). Sainte-Beuve, Charles-Augustin, *Portraits de femmes*, nouvelle édition (Paris, 1876), pp. 42–61.

Kathryn J. Crecelius

Irini Spanidou

Born May 27, 1946, Trikala, Greece
Genre(s): novel
Language(s): English

Irini Spanidou, who was born in the northern mountainous Greek province of Thessaly and attended high school in Athens, moved to the United States in 1964. She received a B.A. from Sarah Lawrence College and an M.F.A. from Columbia University.

Although she has lived in New York City for the past twenty-one years and has been a United States citizen for eight years, her first novel, *God's Snake* (1986) is rooted in her own experience. She and the character, Anna, are "Army children," who moved around the country with their military families, destined to be "outsiders in a small village or town, new kids in school who have to claim and defend their ground, then abandon it and move on." As Spanidou has said, such children "have a stiffness in their bearing," but they also have a "submerged melancholy." It is just this paradoxical sense of opportunity and loss, of adventure and solitude, that marks this novel as distinctly Greek and universally accessible. *God's Snake* is the story of a little girl caught between the dictatorial, repressive cruelty of her authoritarian father and the indifference and fragility of her beautiful but emotionally crippled mother. She is an innocent encapsulated in a world of people who believe devoutly in evil. According to Spanidou "the characters are very Greek—[in] their pride, sense of fate, the way they go to extremes, their articulateness" and

Doris Lessing has noted that the novel has "the hard simplicity of a Greek myth . . . a very old story, as much as it is a new one."

Anna's world, like the novel, is an interweaving of the destructiveness and regenerative qualities of people and animals. There are chapters individually dominated by a snake, crow, wolf, deer, and a dog, who replicate or suggest the savage potential of the child molesters and the child beaters and also the sadness and sensitivity of the orphans, lonely women, tuberculars, and Anna's grandmother—"melancholic, enigmatic . . . a young woman thwarted by destiny from her dreams." The sense here is of outraged emotions. The women—Anna, her mother, grandmother and unmarried aunts—hunger after love, and the men—Anna's father, uncles, grandfather—gorge themselves with a sense of maleness that feeds on anger, control, and mastery.

Spanidou has said that it was her intention to "show how a child comes to terms with hurt [when] . . . it is born with expectations of love and not with knowledge of evil." But she has done far more than explore a child's emotions. She has written a splendid first novel about the agony and passion of being alive.

Works

God's Snake (1986).

Bibliography

Mitgang, Herbert, *The New York Times* (September 18, 1986). Pearlman, Mickey, "An Interview with Irini Spanidou," in *Inter/view: Talks with America's Writing Women*, by Mickey Pearlman and Katherine Usher Henderson (forthcoming).

Mickey Pearlman

Maria Luisa Spaziani

Born 1924, Turin, Italy
Genre(s): poetry, journalism, translation, scholarship
Language(s): Italian

Spaziani began her journalistic activities at a young age; she founded the review *Il Dado* as a student, and contributed to it and other reviews in the early forties. In 1948 she received her college degree with a thesis on Marcel Proust.

Her first collection of poetry, *Le acque del Sabato* (The Sabbath's Waters) was published by Mondadori in 1954. After several years of extensive travels from England to the Soviet Union, from Belgium to Greece, and after stays in Milan and Paris, she moved to Rome where she lives today. Since 1964 Spaziani has taught French language and literature at the University of Messina. She has written many collections of poetry, several of which have won literary prizes; she has also published numerous translations from French and German as well as scholarly studies on French topics. Spaziani is currently president of the "Centro Internazionale Eugenio Montale," a center for the dissemination and study of poetry that awards the "Eugenio Montale International Prize" for translations and publications of Italian verse.

Spaziani's early poetry was greatly influenced by the hermetic tendencies of the thirties and forties and, more specifically, by certain formal and thematic aspects of Ungaretti's and Montale's verse. Highly literary and technically controlled, the poems of *Le acque del sabato*, for example, reveal her debt not only to the hermetic influence but also to the Italian high lyric tradition from Leopardi through the early twentieth century. In that first volume, Spaziani succeeded in forging a genuine voice, however, that far surpasses mere imitation or technical excellence. Memory and an acute sensitivity to the natural world inform her well-wrought poems; the voice is at once highly subjective and distanced by the elegant formal control. There is nothing confessional or easily melodic about these poems, yet they have the emotive and musical intensity of authentic song.

Her succeeding volumes (*Il gong*, 1962; *Utilità della memoria*, 1966; *L'occhio del ciclone*, 1970; *Geometria del disordine*, 1981; *La stella del libero arbitrio*, 1986) remain true to her vocation as a highly literary, essentially anti-romantic poet. There is always present a strong and immediate sense of the natural lived world, but equally powerful is the debt to poetry as tradition and inherited richness. Spaziani's sense of culture, especially Italian and French, permeates even her most autobiographical verse. The poems reverberate with echoes of other poets, yet the heritage is consistently transformed by Spaziani's sensibility and intelligence.

Although indebted to many poets of many times and places, Spaziani is particularly close to Eugenio Montale both in technical excellence and in her refusal to use poetry as an instrument of self-display. She was, in fact, the source of inspiration for Montale's poetic woman, known as "Vixen" and immortalized in a series of poems called "Madrigali privati" (Private Madrigals) included in his 1956 volume *La bufera e altro*. There, she is portrayed as an intensely earthy and sensual presence by whom the poet is overwhelmed. One poem in the series, "Da un lago svizzero" (From a Swiss Lake), contains an acrostic of Spaziani's name, the only example of such word play in all of Montale's verse.

In a series of responses to questions pertaining to feminist poetry published in the anthology *Donne in poesia* (Women in Poetry), Spaziani makes clear her implicit refusal of such a label. She is sympathetic to the feminist movement but characterizes it as simply another step "in the transformation of Ptolemaic man into Copernican man." Her debt to other women writers is not greater than her debt to other writers in general, given that "the unique voice of a woman poet has worth in and of itself, for its emotive and moral singularity, the same singularity that differentiates important books written by men." Her own contribution to poetry proves, in its consistent excellence, that important books can and should be gender-free.

Works

Poetry: *Le acque del Sabato* [The Sabbath's Waters] (1954). *Primavera a Parigi. Luna lombarda* (1959). *Il Gong* (1962). *Utilità della memoria* (1966). *L'occhio del ciclone* (1970). *Ultrasuoni* (1976). *Transito con catene* (1977). *Geometria del disordine* (1981). *La stella del libero arbitrio* (1986).
Poems anthologized in *Donne in poesia: Antologia della poesia femminile in Italia dal dopoguerra ad oggi*, ed. Biancamaria Frabotta (1976).
Poems anthologized and translated in *The Defiant Muse: Italian Feminist Poems from the Middle Ages to the Present*, Beverly Allen, Muriel Kittel, Keala Jane Jewell, eds. (1986).
Scholarly works: *Ronsard fra gli astri della Pléiade* (1972). *Il teatro francese del Settecento* (1974). *Il*

teatro francese dell'Ottocento (1975). *Il teatro francese del Novecento* (1976). *Alessandrino e altri versi fra Ottocento e Novecento* (1978).

Bibliography

Forti, Marco, *Le proposte della poesia e nuove proposte* (Milan, 1971). Petrucciani, Mario, *Segnali e archetipi della poesia* (Milan, 1974). Ramat, Silvio, *Storia della poesia italiana del dopoguerra* (Milan, 1976). Wedel, Giovanna, "La memoria divinatoria di Maria Luisa Spaziani." *Italian Quarterly* (Fall 1986): 45–49.

General references: *Dizionario della letteratura italiana contemporanea* (Florence, 1973). Luti, Giorgio, ed., *Poeti italiani del Novecento: La vita, le opere, la critica* (Rome, 1985).

Rebecca West

Adrienne von Speyr

Born September 20, 1902, La-Chaux-de-Fonds (Swiss Jura); died September 17, 1967, Basel
Genre(s): essay, memoirs
Language(s): German

Von Speyr's life is marked by two features: the wish to become a medical doctor and supernatural signs (the first being the meeting with Ignatius de Loyola when she was six, on Christmas 1908) that led her to the conversion from Protestantism to Catholicism (meaning for her "unity and wholeness of faith") on All Saint's Day, 1940, under the spiritual leading of Hans Urs von Balthasar, S.J., the well-known theological writer. Their cooperation continues until von Speyr's death (Balthasar is still leading both the St. John's Community they founded together in 1945 and the publishing house Johannesverlag-Einsiedeln, which he founded in 1946 to print von Speyr's writings). From 1941 to her death, in the full activity of a physician visiting from 60 to 80 patients a day offering them free treatment if necessary with an ever present consideration of their family, religious and economic problems, every year she experienced a series of "Passions" (sympathy with Jesus' inner pains) and descents to "Infernos." In 1942, she received visible stigmata that she begged in her constant state of prayer to be made invisible. Besides, she was sent on "journeys" nightly, out of her body, wherever need be of help in war concentration camps, seminaries, confessionals, Roman curia, totally neglected churches. The main features of her character were *happiness*—joyfulness, humor, zest for surprise amidst incomprehensions, tortures of physical diseases—and *courage*. She worked as a physician from 1931 to 1954 when her illness (diabetes, arthrosis, heart disease) obliged her to stop. She enjoyed reading especially French literature and women's writings (Colette was her favorite); among her greatest friends were the essayist Albert Béguin, Henri de Lubac, Gabriel Marcel, Romano Guardini, Hugo Rahner. She mostly dictated her many writings for twenty to thirty minutes a day; Balthasar wrote them in shorthand. He decided to stop this real flood of inspired texts ca. 1950, for they had reached the sixty volumes and he thought "a limit of readableness had been attained." Her first book, *Magd des Herrn* (Lord's Maid), written from the end of January to the beginning of February 1946 and published 1948, gives the basic meaning of her mysticism. The first chapter is entitled "The light of consent." Mary's life is concentrated in her consent: it is faith, hope and charity all in one. She becomes pure space made free for the incarnation of the Word. From Mary all can take a form: the soul opens to the dimension of the Church consent (which is Marian) and is plastic in the hands of God. Von Speyr's mysticism is "radically anti-psychologic, theologic and historic-eschatological" (Balthasar). She meant it as a service to the whole of the Church in order not to develop dogma, but to deepen and enliven the center of the universal Church. Through the mystery of the Trinity life of charity, a mystery which we enter through the Christ and His obedience as a Son, we utter and live *the original prayer*, i.e., the root of our service.

Works

(Among her many works, on the Holy Scriptures, on different single subjects, death, medical profession, prayer, Christian state, on herself, published and unpublished, I give a few titles, with their English editions.) *Das Johannesevangelium—Das Wert wird Fleisch [Meditations on the Gospel of St. John 1, 19-5, 47 (1959)]*, pp. 191, abridged (1949). *The Word. A Meditation on the Prologue to St.*

John's Gospel 1, 1–19 (1953) pp. 159. *Magd des Herrn*(1948; *The Handmaid of the Lord*, 1956, pp. 174). *The Handmaid of the Lord* (1985; new translation), pp. 178. *Die Welt des Gebetes*(1951; pp. 288, *The World of Prayer*, 1985, pp. 311).

Bibliography

von Balthasar, Hans Urs, *Erster Blick auf Adrienne von Speyr* (3rd ed., Einsiedeln, 1979), pp. 288. First glance at Adrienne von Speyr (San Francisco, 1981), pp. 249. For further information: Amitié A.V.S. 61, r. de Bruxelles, 5000 Namur, Belgium.

Gabriella Fiori

Hilde Spiel

Born October 19, 1911, Vienna, Austria
Genre(s): novel, short story, biography,
editions of historical documents
Language(s): German

Hilde Spiel is one of the highly recognized contemporary Austrian writers. She was born on October 19, 1911, in Vienna. She studied philosophy under M. Schlick and K. Bühler in Vienna and received her Ph.D. in 1936. In the same year she moved to London with her husband Peter de Mendelssohn, where she worked for the *New Statesman*. In her position as correspondent, the same journal sent her back to Vienna in 1946. She also worked as a theater critic for the *Welt* in Berlin from the end of 1946 to 1948. When she again returned to England, she wrote numerous reports on cultural events for many German and Austrian journals and radio stations. In 1963 she finally settled in Vienna and continued her work as a journalist and writer. In her work she focuses on historical situations, particularly of Germany and Austria after World War II, and on man's individual and psychological situation in our modern times.

She received the following literary awards: Member of PEN, 1937, Austrian Association of Poets, Vienna, Julius-Reich Award in 1934, Salzburg Prize of Critics in 1970, Cross of Honor for Arts and Sciences in 1972, Award from the German Academy for Language and Sciences in 1972, Prize of the City of Vienna in 1976, Johann Heinrich Merck Award in 1981, Roswitha von Gandersheim Award in 1981, Danauland Award in 1981.

Works

Novels: *Kati auf der Brücke* [Kati on the Bridge] (1933). *Verwirrungen am Wolfgangee* [Confusions at the Wolfangsee] (1935; rpt. 1961 as *Sommer am Wolfgangsee* [One Summer at the Wolfgangsee]). *Flöte und Trommeln* [Flute and Drums] (1948). *Lisas Zimmer* [Lisa's Room] (1965). *Die Früchte des Wohlstands* [The Fruit of Prosperity] (1981). *Mirko und Franca* [Mirko and Franca] (1982).

Essay collections: *Der Park und die Wildnis* [Park and Wilderness] (1953). *Welt im Widerschein* [World Reflected] (1960). *Fanny von Arnstein oder Die Emanzipation einer Frau an der Zeitwende 1758–1818* [Fanny von Arnstein or The Emancipation of a Woman at the Turn of the Century 1758–1818] (1962). *In meinem Garten schlendernd* [Strolling in My Garden] (1982).

Diary: *Rückkehr nach Wien* [Return to Vienna] (1968).

With Elisabeth Niggemeyer: *London: Stadt, Menschen, Augenblicke* [London: The City, Its People and Impressions] (1956).

With Franz Vogler: *Verliebt in Döbling, die Dörfer unter dem Himmel* [In Love with Döbling, Villages under the Stars] (1965).

Editions: *Wien. Spektrum einer Stadt* [Vienna, Spectrum of a City] (1971). *Die zeitgenössische Literatur Österreichs* [The Contemporary Austrian Literature] (1976). *Der Wiener Kongress in Augenzeugenberichten* [The Viennese Congress In Eyewitness Accounts] (1965). *Englische Ansichten: Berichte aus Kultur, Geschichte und Politik* (1984) [English Views: Reports about Culture, History and Politics].

Stories: *Der Mann mit der Pelerine und andere Geschichten* [The Man with the Cape, and Other Stories], illus. Georg Eisler (1985).

Spiel also translated a large number of British novels into German and extensively published scholarly articles on contemporary Austrian and German poets and on exile literature.

Translation: *The Congress of Vienna, an Eyewitness Account*, tr. R.H. Weber (1968).

Bibliography

Kunisch, H., ed., *Handbuch der deutschen Gegenwartsliteratur*, vol. 2 (2nd ed., Munich, 1970), p. 219f. Lennartz, F., *Deutsche Schriftsteller der Gegenwart* (11th ed., Stuttgart, 1978), pp. 696–698. Pabisch, P., "Hilde Spiels Rückkehr nach Wien—eine besondere Thematik der Exilliteratur," *Exil: Wirkung und Wertung*, ausgewählte Beiträge zum 5. Symposium über deutsche und österreichische Exilliteratur, ed. D.G. Daviau and L.M. Fischer (Columbia, SC, 1985), pp. 173–183. Zeller, E., "Nicht Figur geworden. Laudatio für Hilde Spiel," *Deutsche Akademie für Sprache und Dichtung, Darmstadt, Jahrbuch* 1981, 2 (1982): 63–66.

Albrecht Classen

Johanna Spyri

Born June 12, 1827, Hirzel, Switzerland; died July 7, 1901
Genre(s): short story, novel
Language(s): German

Johanna Spyri, née Heusser, is best remembered—if she is remembered in literary circles at all—as the Swiss author of the children's novel *Heidi*. Although her international reputation is limited to this book, Spyri wrote and published fifteen other books (novels and short-story collections), most of which have been translated into English. Her classical children's stories are entertaining, but her didactic themes reveal deeper social criticism as well. Although celebrated primarily as an author of children's entertainment, Spyri also aimed to teach adults how to educate youngsters. She has been compared to Hans Christian Andersen for her interest in the young and for her simplicity of style. Both authors shared a fundamental Christian belief in "God's plan" and wrote their social criticism through the perspective of innocent children.

Spyri spent her entire life within a twelve-mile radius between Hirzel, Switzerland, the village of her birth, and the city of Zurich where she lived after her marriage at age twenty-five to Bernard Spyri, a lawyer and town clerk. Daughter of a physician (Johann Jakob Heusser, after whom she was named), and a mother (Meta Schweitzer Heusser) who wrote poetry and songs, Spyri enjoyed a good education and moderate financial security. The fourth of six children, she had abundant companionship and social stimulation from family members, family friends, and her

father's patients. Spyri's only child, a son, died of tuberculosis at the age of twenty-nine.

Spyri wrote from her own life experiences. Her works, set between mountain peaks and city walls, seek a compromise between the extreme cultural backwardness of the isolated alpine hut and the unhealthy surfeit of a congested urban environment. Her solution is the enlightened highland village, half-way up the mountain. Here the urban sophisticate and the alpine hermit meet, brought together by their common recognition of the detrimental effects of both extremes, especially on the physical and emotional well-being of children.

Spyri's first book of short stories, published anonymously in 1871 when she was forty-three years old, was motivated by her desire to contribute money to the refugees of the Franco-Prussian war. *Heidi* was published in 1880–1881, also anonymously, and translated into English in 1884. It is Spyri's best-known work and first novel, and it has been widely translated (over 30 languages), extensively illustrated, and variously adapted for stage and screen.

A classic of juvenile fiction, *Heidi* is a female *Bildungsroman*. The full German title, *Heidis Lehr- und Wanderjahre* (Heidi's Years of Apprenticeship and Travels), reveals a kinship to Goethe's novel of Wilhelm Meister's apprenticeship and travels. Heidi, like Goethe's Mignon, is of Italian heritage; her curly black hair and black eyes resemble those of her Neopolitan grandmother.

In the novel the orphaned Heidi is brought to a state of anorexia nervosa and sleep-walking when she is taken from the free environment of her able grandfather's alpine hut to the confines of the Sesemann's heavily curtained home in Frankfurt. Mr. Sesemann's stern housekeeper, Miss Rottenmeier, expects in Heidi a Swiss angel as companion to Mr. Sesemann's only child, Clara, but Rottenmeier sees in Heidi only "an utter little barbarian." The pale and delicate Clara has been crippled by the atmosphere in the household; her foot never touches earth but moves from footstool to wheelchair. After a few weeks in the Frankfurt household even Heidi's light step begins to drag. In the end, Heidi reunites happily with her grandfather, recovers fully, and eventually brings her grandfather out of his mountain hermitage to a reconciliation with the villagers. When Clara visits Heidi on the mountainside she undergoes an awakening, prompted by a goat's affection, and begins to walk again.

Other works by Spyri, most of which have been ignored, include *Arthur and Squirrel*, *Chel*, *Cornelli*, *Dora*, *Gritli's Children*, *Joerli*, *Maezli*, *Maxa's Children*, *Moni the Goat-Boy*, *The Rose Child*, *Uncle Titus*, and many other stories of varying length. Some of these works have been cannibalized for sequels to *Heidi*, such as Charles Tritten's *Heidi Grows Up*, 1938, and *Heidi's Children*, 1939.

Works

For a list of the various editions of Spyri's works in English, including different translations and featuring different illustrators, consult *Something About the Author: Facts and Pictures about Authors and Illustrators of Books for Young People*, ed. Anne Commire (Detroit, 1980), Vol. 19, pp. 232–244; *Briefwechsel 1877–1897 mit einem Anhang: Briefe der Johanna Spyri an die Mutter und die Schwester C.F. Meyer 1853–1897*, Hans and Rosmarie Zeller, eds. Intro. Rosemarie Zeller (1977).

Bibliography

"Heidi—or the Story of a Juvenile Best Seller." *Publishers Weekly* (July 25, 1953). Ulrich, Anna, *Recollections of Johanna Spyri's Childhood*, tr. Helen B. Dole (New York, 1925). For more information: Johanna Spyri Foundation, Zeltweg 13, 8032 Zurich, Switzerland.

Lisa Ohm

Marguerite-Jeanne Cordier de Launay, Baronne de Staal

Born August 30, 1684, Paris, France; died July 15, 1750, Gennevilliers
Genre(s): memoirs, comedy, lyric poetry, letters
Language(s): French

Born to an impoverished mother, who had left her émigré husband in England, Rose Delauney was given her mother's name and retained it. She had no subsequent knowledge of her father. Charmed by her precocious intelligence and good manners, the prioress of Saint-Louis (Rouen) took charge of the child. She was given a solid education, which she continued on her own, and treated with a distinction that later conflicted with the subservience demanded by the "in service" positions she needed for a livelihood. From a premature attraction to the religious life, Staal passed briefly through enthusiasm for novels to a more lasting apprenticeship in philosophy. A short treatise has survived from this period. It more significantly marks both her letters and memoirs. It was through her letters, first collected for publication at the request of the duc de Choiseul, that she first began a disillusioning ascent in the world guided by Fontenelle and the scholar-poet Nicolas Malézieu. Her conversational letters like those to Mme du Deffand show both the philosophical control exerted to master that disillusion and the consolation of the friendship she enjoyed, especially in the salon of Mme de Lambert with Chaulieu and Voltaire, with Valincour and Dacier (who courted her).

For the duchesse du Maine's pleasures, in the "*Divertissements de Sceaux*" and its *Grandes Nuits* (1713–1714), Staal produced verse, wrote and sang songs (sometimes to music by Campra), planned fireworks, and composed two three-act comedies in prose: *L'Engouement* and *La Mode*. Eschewing Molière's broader farce, which was severely criticized in the Hôtel de Lambert, Staal's light-handed comedy of manners continues in both plays to treat concerns for women's education discussed there. Both are character studies of women with sole responsibility for a family but without the education to manage it properly. Both absence of education and the society that fosters frivolity in its place are satirized.

The journey from downstairs to upstairs splendors at Sceaux narrated in Staal's *Mémoires* meant more than participation in the team of retainers supplying the duchesse's pleasures and patience in serving the often imperious and capricious granddaughter of the Great Condé. At the cost of a year's imprisonment in the Bastille (from December 1718), Staal learned the dangers of political intrigue. Loyalty to her mistress, if nothing more, implicated her in the abortive Cellamare conspiracy, by which the duchesse had hoped to further the political fortunes of her husband. The unexpected boon in the Bastille was a lasting friendship with another prisoner, the chevalier de Ménil, and a rallying of old friends. But imprisonment became philosophically emblematic to the writer of the *Mémoires* and deepened her experience of writing itself, which becomes an intellectually sustained effort to balance past promises against present failures, the constraining forces of others in her life against a freedom of self-definition in writing. Account-settling with Mme du Maine is left for other occasions. The *Mémoires* end with the death of the duc du Maine and seemingly were not written after 1741 and her marriage to the obscure baron de Staal arranged by Mme du Maine. After being delivered to the altar, "bound and decorated," Staal wrote, no more was to be said. Nothing of a personal nature is known of the last years of Staal's life.

Although Staal offers her views of historical events from her privileged point of view, the history she makes is her own. By discreet and subtle turns of narrative, juxtapositions, and ellipses that betray her introspective quest for self-definition, Staal moves the historically-oriented seventeenth-century genre of memoirs fully into autobiography. As Grimm wrote when they first appeared (1755), they "enriched our literature by a work unique in its genre."

Works

Abréqé de métaphysique, ed. Léa Gilon (posth., 1978). *Mémoires* (posth., 1755). *L'Engouement* (posth., 1755). *La Mode* (posth., 1755). *Lettres*, ed. abbé Barthélemy (posth., 1801). "Portrait de Mme la duchesse du Maine," ed. La Harpe (posth., 1801).

Translations: *Memoirs of Madame de Staal-De Launay*, tr. Cora Bell (1892).

Bibliography

Buchanan, Michelle, "The French Editions and English Translations of the Mémoires of Madame de Staal." *Eighteenth-Century Studies* 6 (1972–1973): 322–333. Buchanan, Michelle, "Une Ombre à la fête de Sceaux: Madame de Staal." *French Review* 51 (1977–1978): 353–360. Curtis, Judith, "The Epistolières," in Samia I. Spencer, *French Women in the Age of Enlightenment* (1985), pp. 226–241. Doscot, Gérard, ed., *Mémoires de Madame de Staal-Delauney* (1970). Gilon, Léa, *Mme de Staal-de Launay, femme de théâtre* (1978). Contains the *Abrégé de métaphysique*. See *DAI* 39, 309A. "Mme. de Staal-Delauney, dramaturge sous la Régence." *Studies on Voltaire and the Eighteenth Century* 192 (1980): 1506–1513. Kinsey, Susan R., "The Memorialists," in *French Women and the Age of Enlightenment* (1985): 212–225. Lewis, W.H., *The Sunset of the Splendid Century. The Life and Times of Louis-Auguste de Bourbon, duc du Maine, 1670–1736* (1955).

Charles G.S. Williams

Ilse von Stach

Born February 17, 1879, Haus Pröbsting bei Borken (Westfalia); died September (Nov.) 1941, Münster, Germany
Genre(s): novel, short story, drama, poetry
Language(s): German

The daughter of a baron, Ilse von Stach converted to Catholicism in 1908 and married the art historian Martin Wackernagel in 1911. Her works develop Christian themes and religious moods: the novel *Haus Elderfing* (1915), for example, varies a traditional romantic tale of love triumphant (in this case across confessional lines) by showing how marital love is slowly transformed into obedience to a more exalted love of God.

Works

Wer kann dafür, dass seines Frühlings Lüfte weh'n! [No One Is to Blame for His Springtime Breezes], poetry (1898). *Das Christ-Elflein. Weihnachtsmärchen.* Musik von H. Pfitzner [The Christchild Elf. A Christmas Fairy Tale] (1906). *Der heilige Nepomuk. Dramatische Dichtung* [Saint Nepomuk, A Dramatic Poem] (1909). *Die Sendlinge von Voghera* [The Emissaries from Voghera], novel (1910). *Missa poetica. Religiöse Dichtung* [Missa Poetica, Religious Poetry] (1912). *Die Beichte* [The Confession], novel (1913). *Haus Elderfing* [House Elderfing], novel (1915). *Requiem. Religiöse Dichtung* [Requiem, Religious Poetry] (1918). *Genesius. Eine christliche Tragödie* [Genesius, A Christian Tragedy] (1919). *Griseldis. Dramatische Dichtung in einem Vorspiel und drei Akten* [Griseldis, A Dramatic Poem with a Prologue and

Three Acts] (1921). *Tharsicius. Ein Festspiel aus der Katakombenzeit* [Tharsicius, A Festival Play from the Time of the Catacombs], excerpted as *Maranatha. Ein Bild aus dem Weihespiel.*Tharsicius [Maranatha, A Scene from the Devotional Play Tharsicius] (1948). *Wehe dem, der keine Heimat hat* [Woe to Him Who Has No Home] (Rpt. as *Non serviam* [1931], novel (1921). *Melusine. Schauspiel in drei Akten* [Melusine, A Play in Three Acts] (1922). *Petrus. Eine göttliche Komödie* [Peter, A Divine Comedy] (1924). *Die Frauen von Korinth. Dialoge* [The Women of Corinth, Dialogues] (1929). *Der Rosenkranz. Meditationen und Gedichte* [The Rosary, Meditations and Poems] (1929). *Der Petrus-Segen. Erinnerungen und Bekenntnisse* [Peter's Blessing, Memories and Confessions] (1940). *Wie Sturmwind fährt die Zeit. Gedichte aus drei Jahrzehnten* [Time Passes Like a Stormwind, Poems from Three Decades] (1948).

Bibliography

LdS. 296–297 [includes bibliography].

Ann Marie Rasmussen

Angela Stachova

Born twentieth century
Genre(s): novel
Language(s): German

Angela Stachova's *Kleine Verführung* treats the problem of noble single women in an immoral evil world. In each of the three stories within the volume, the author presents the figure of a young, single woman as the heroine. Each woman is sensitive and experiences injustice, maltreatment and oppression from a lover or a loved one. The common thread in each of the three stories is that the heroine, who seeks a pure, unselfish and true love, cannot find it in a lover. Instead she encounters coldness, dishonesty, and exploitation. Stachova treats the age-old themes of the double standard and the battle between the sexes. The seduction of an innocent as a theme coalesces with the problem of a just and moral society.

Works

Kleine Verführung [A Small Seduction] (1983).

Bibliography

Kritik 83. Rezensionen zur DDR-Literatur. Herausgegeben von Eberhard Günther, Werner Liersch und Klaus Walter (Halle, Leipzig, 1981).

Brigitte Edith Archibald

Germaine Necker, Baronne de Staël-Holstein

Born April 22, 1766, Paris, France; died July 14, 1817, Paris
Genre(s): novel, essay, literary criticism, tales, drama, letters
Language(s): French

Mme de Staël was one of the major precursors of Romanticism and modern criticism whose writings reflected the liberal Republican spirit of the late eighteenth century. An avid supporter of the revolutionary ideals of 1789, she became disenchanted with the radicals who instituted the Terror. Similarly, she admired Napoleon until he shattered her hope for a liberal republic in France.

Her father, Jacques Necker, whom she idolized, was a wealthy Swiss Protestant financier; he was appointed Controller-General of Finance in 1777 by Louis XVI. Germaine's youth was spent among the great figures of the Enlightenment (Buffon, Diderot, Grimm, Talleyrand) who frequented her mother's salon in Paris. She was a precocious child; at age twelve, she wrote a comedy, and at twenty-two, a work on Rousseau. In 1785 she made an unhappy marriage with Baron de Staël-Holstein, Swedish ambassador to France. Three children were born before the couple separated in 1798.

In 1789 Mme de Staël welcomed the Revolution, predicting that it would inaugurate a new age of liberty and justice. Disillusioned with the bloodshed and quarrelsome political factions, she left France for England in early 1793, finally settling at her family's estate of Coppet, near Geneva, during the Terror. She began a long, stormy liaison with the politician and writer Benjamin Constant and continued her writing. She returned to Paris in 1795 but was forced to leave by the Directory government. Two years later she was back in Paris and reopened her salon. Her liberal sentiments and open criticism of Napoleon forced her into exile several times during his fifteen-year rule. Undaunted by the emperor's antipathy toward her, Mme de Staël travelled widely in Europe, where she won sympathy as a victim of Napoleon's tyranny. During her travels she met with European intellectuals and rulers and gathered materials for her writings. She was convinced that she had a mission to acquaint the parochial French with cultures beyond the Rhine. For many years she lived at Coppet, which became a lively center of cosmopolitan culture and of open resistance to Napoleon. Only after the Emperor's abdication in 1814 was she able to return to Paris.

Mme de Staël represented the cosmopolitan spirit of the eighteenth century in the best sense of the term: a product of aristocratic Parisian society, liberal, free-thinking, imbued with ideas of progress, liberty, and the natural goodness of humanity. She favored the enlightened political and moral ideas of Montesquieu and Rousseau, from which she never wavered. She had a passion for "polite society" and the good taste it embodied. The solitude of her country house at Coppet did not appeal to her; Mme de Staël was a social being and longed for the urbane, brilliant society of Paris. Her intelligence, wealth, and position were not sufficient for her. She wanted to be accepted as an intellectual equal by her male contemporaries. Consequently, she felt a deep sense of the isolation of genius, especially of a woman of genius. Her dynamic (at times strident) and domineering personality and her strong will often alienated people, which caused her suffering and increased her feelings of isolation and loneliness. She had a quick and penetrating mind and did not hesitate to make value judgments on people, events, or cultures. Her writings were extremely subjective; her verbose and colorless style was overcome only when a character or experience was close to her own.

In her writings she strove to show the linkage between political ideas, ethics, literature, and cultural differences. Her "L'Essai sur les Fictions" (Essay on Fiction) concerned the role of writers as moral guides, a popular theme among later Romantic writers. Another moral essay, "De l'influence des passions sur le bonheur des individus et des nations" (The Influence of Passions on the Happiness of Individuals and Nations), is devoted to passions, such as love, that cause unhappiness and how to combat them. The object of her famous work *De la littérature considerée dans ses rapports avec les institutions sociales* (Literature Considered in Relation to Social Institutions), was, in her words, "to examine the influence of religion, customs, and laws on literature, and the influence of literature on religion, customs, and laws," an ambitious project for which she lacked the depth or breadth of knowledge necessary to handle these subjects. However, she was one of the first to study literature as a reflection of national mentality, growing out of a particular society. The book lacks synthesis, but it demonstrates her analytical abilities. Another influential work, *De l'Allemagne* (On Germany), attempts to acquaint the French with Germany and its culture which she admired. Actually she had little more than a superficial knowledge of her subject and did not fully understand the brand of German nationalism she so ardently admired. It is, however, a good illustration of her romantic attitudes and spiritual concepts.

The heroines of Mme de Staël's two novels, *Delphine* and *Corinne*, are well-drawn self-portraits; the other characters are, however, rather one-dimensional. *Dix années d'exil* (Ten Years of Exile) is a fragmentary autobiography describing her experiences as she travelled in Austria, Poland, and Russia in 1812. Finally, Mme de Staël returned to Paris in 1814, via Stockholm and England, after Napoleon's downfall, but she was forced to seek refuge at Coppet again during the Hundred Days. She had ambiguous feelings about Napoleon's return; she mistrusted his liberal pronouncements, but she feared that France would be crushed and punished by the Allies if Napoleon were defeated again.

In her last three years, she secretly married Albert Rocca, a young Swiss officer, and wrote a book on the Revolution that clearly reveals her liberal idealism and her dislike of Napoleon. His major flaw (as she saw it) was his lack of respect for humankind. She died in Paris at age fifty-one. Mme de Staël's reputation rests primarily on *De la littérature* and *De l'Allemagne*, and not on her novels. Although her scholarship was often inadequate, her critical analyses of a variety of subjects were often insightful and original.

Works

Considérations sur les principaux événements de la Révolution française (1818). *Correspondance générale,* ed. B. Jasinski, 6 vols. (1960-). *Corrine* (1807). *De l'Allemagne* [On Germany] (1810). *Du charactère de M Necker et de sa vie privée* (1804). "De l'influence des passions sur le bonheur des individus et des nations" [The Influence of Passions on Individuals and Nations] (1796). *De la littérature considerée dans ses rapports avec les institutions sociales* [Literature Considered in Relation to Social Institutions] (1800). *Delphine* (1802). *Dix années d'exil* [Ten Years of Exile] (1821). "Essai sur les fictions" [Essay on Fiction] (1795). *Lettres sur les ouvrages et le caractère de J.-J. Rousseau* (1788). *Reflexions sur le suicide* [Reflections on Suicide] (1813).

Bibliography

Balayé, S., *Mme. de Staël, Lumières et Liberté* (1979). Berger, Monroe, ed., *Madame de Staël on Politics, Literature and National Character* (1964). Blennerhasset, Lady, *Mme. de Staël et son temps* (1890). Charvet, P. E., *A Literary History of France.* Vol. IV, *The Nineteenth Century, 1789-1870* (1967). Clarke, Isabel C., *Six Portraits* (1967). Diesbach, Ghislain de, *Madame de Staël* (1983). Forsberg, Roberta J., *Madame de Staël and Freedom Today* (1964). Gautier, P., "Un grand roman oublié: Corinne." *Revue des Deux Mondes,* III (1927): 435–451. Gibelin, J., *L'esthétique de Schelling et l'Allemagne de Madame de Staël* (1934). Gwynne, G.E., *Madame de Staël et la Révolution francaise, politique, philosophie, littérature* (1969). Haggard, Andrew C.P., *Madame de Staël, Her Trials and Triumphs* (1922). Haussonville, comte de, *Madame de Staël et l'Allemagne* (1928). Herold, J.C., *Mistress to an Age. A Life of Madame de Staël* (1959). Larg, D.G., *Madame de Staël, la Vie dans l'Oeuvre, 1766-1800* (1924). Larg, D.G., *Madame de Staël: la seconde Vie, 1800-1807* (1928). Levaillant, Maurice, *The Passionate Exiles. Madame de Staël and Madame Récamier* (1958). Pange, Pauline L. M., *Auguste-Guillaume Schlegel et Madame de Staël* (1938). Posgate, Helen Belle, *Madame de Staël* (1968). Souriau, M., *Les Idées morales de Madame de Staël* (1910). West, Anthony, *Mortal Wounds* (1975). Whitford, Robert C., *Madame de Staël's Literary Reputation in England* (1918). Winegarten, Renée, *Madame de Staël* (1985).

Jeanne A. Ojala

William T. Ojala

Elsbeth Stagel

Born beginning of fourteenth century; died ca. 1360, Töß, Switzerland
Genre(s): convent chronicle
Language(s): Middle High German

Elsbeth Stagel (Stagelin, Stägelin), daughter (presumably) of Senator Rudolf Stagel, was a nun and later a prioress in the Dominican convent of Töß, in Winterthur near Zürich. Töß was founded in 1233 and placed under the spiritual direction of the Dominicans of Zürich. By 1350 the convent had ca. 100 members. The convent of Töß became famous for its scriptorium, its convent school, and a library (whose catalogue is not extant). Töß was dissolved in 1525.

Elsbeth Stagel is perhaps best known for her association with the mystic Heinrich Seuse (Suso), whom she met ca. 1336. Their twenty-five year long relationship, documented by their correspondence, is one of the famous spiritual friendships of the Middle Ages. Seuse, also known as "Amandus," is often seen as the *minnesinger* among the German mystics.

It is under Seuse's influence that Elsbeth Stagel began to study and to copy writings of the mystics. Eventually she translated a number of works in prose and even rendered some of Seuse's Latin material into German verse. Seuse calls Elsbeth Stagel his "spiritual daughter." Their friendship is responsible for Seuse's *vita* (1365) which is written for edification and based on material (sermons, letters, conversations) secretly collected by Elsbeth Stagel. The second part of this *vita* is a description of Elsbeth Stagel's own life.

Elsbeth Stagel also began to write herself. She is the author of several of the *vitae* of the *Tösser Schwesternbuch,* i.e., the convent chronicle of Töß (see Anna von Munzingen for convent chronicles). This chronicle of Töß contains a nucleus, i.e., two lives that had been written earlier, that of Sophia von Klingnau and of Mechthilt von Stans, around which some thirty-six lives of members of the convent from its beginning until ca. 1340 are gathered.

The Töß chronicle is perhaps the most famous one of its genre. Its date is ca. 1340, its language is Middle High German. The text is extant in three fifteenth-century manuscripts, the best of which is cod. 603 (Stiftsbibliothek St. Gallen).

The *Tösser Schwesternbuch* concentrates on the ascetic striving (*ir hailig ubung*) and the signs of grace (*die usgenomnen gnaden und wunder*) apparent in the lives of mystically inclined nuns of the convent. It was written with the intent of spiritually revitalizing convent life. Among the noteworthy *vitae* are those of Anna von Klingnau (*ain luchtendes liecht an hochem leben*), Mezzi von Klingenberg, who donated paintings and German books to the convent, Margret Finkin (of whom it is said that *die gnad hat sie usgenomenlich, das sy als luttseliklich von Got rett*); and especially that of Jützi Schulthasin, in whose *vita* the intellectual insights (*erkantnus*) this sister gained during seven years of visions are emphasized.

The *Tösser Schwesternbuch* is the first known attempt of biographical writing in German. While abounding in clichés and repetitions, the work contains some notable passages, and its author(s) coined a number of powerful new terms, such as the various compounds for love: *minnebewegung, minwund, minzaichen,* etc.

Works

La Vie mystique d'un monastère de Dominicaines au Moyen-Age d'après la Chronique de Töss, ed. Jeanne Ancelet-Hustache (Paris, 1928). *Deutsches Nonnenlegen: Das Leben der Schwestern zu Töß.* . . . ed. Margarete Weinhandle (München, 1921). *Das Leben der Schwestern zu Töß beschrieben von Elsbeth Stagel, samt der Vorrede von Johannes Meyer*, ed. Ferdinand Vetter (Berlin, 1906). Pez, Bernardus, *Bibliotheca ascetica antiquo-nova* (Regensburg, 1725; rpt. 1967), pp. 448–452. Murer, Henricus, ed., *Helvetia Sancta* (1643, 2nd ed. Luzern, 1648), pp. 358–369.

Bibliography

Blank, Walter, "Umsetzung der Mystik in den Frauenklöstern," in *Augustinermuseum*, ed. Hans H. Hofstätter (Freiburg, 1978). Zeller, Winfried, *Deutsche Mystik* (Düsseldorf, 1967), pp. 7–151. Pleuser, Christine, In *Heinrich Seuse*, ed. Ephrem M. Filthaut (Köln, 1966), pp. 135–170. Ancelet-Hustache, Jeanne, "Le Problème de l'authenticité de la vie de Suso," in *La Mystique rhénane* (Colloque du Strasbourg) (Paris, 1963), pp. 193–205. Blank, Walter, *Die Nonnenviten des 14. Jahrhunderts*. Diss., Freiburg, 1962. Suso, Heinrich, *The Exemplar*, tr. A. Edward Dubuque (1962), 2 vols. Dänicker-Gysin, Marie-Claire, *Geschichte des Dominikanerinnenklosters Töß* (Winterthur, 1958). *The Letters of Henry Suso to His Spiritual Daughter*, tr. Kathleen Goldmann (London, 1955). Kunze, Georg, *Studien zu den Nonnenviten des deutschen Mittelalters*. Diss., Hamburg, 1952. Loewe, Otto, *Das Tösser Schwesternbuch*. Diss., Münster, 1921. Schiller, Ernst, *Das mystische Leben der Ordensschwestern zu Töß bei Winterthur*. Diss., Bern, 1902. Vetter, Ferdinand, *Ein Mystikerpaar des 14. Jahrhunderts.* (Vortrag) (Basel, 1882). Preger, Wilhelm, *Geschichte der deutschen Mystik im Mittelalter*, Vol. 2 (München, 1881 rpt. Aalen, 1962), pp. 257–269. "Sor. Elisabetha Staglin," in Quétif, Jacobus and Jacobus Echard, *Scriptores ordinis praedicatorum*, Vol. 2 (Paris, 1721), 831f. Zittard, Conrad, *Das Lebel der Heiligen vnd seligen Junckfrawn vnd Schwestern Prediger Ordens* (Dillingen, 1596), pp. 166–168.

General references: *EDR* (*Encyclopedic Dictionary of Religion*), III (1979), p. 3377 (Tracy Early). *NCE* (*New Catholic Encyclopedia*), 13 (1067), pp. 627f. (C. Hahn). *LThK* (*Lexikon für Theologie und Kirche*), 2nd ed., 9 (1964), p. 1006 (Hilda C. Graef) and 10 (1965) 261 (Josef Siegwart). *DSp.* (*Dictionnaire de Spiritualité*) 4 (1960), pp. 588f (Jeanne Ancelet-Hustache). *Lexikon der Frau* 2 (1954), p. 1337. *Verfasserlexikon*, 1st ed., 4 (1953), pp. 256–258 (Engelbert Krebs).

Other references: *ZfdA* (*Zeitschrift für deutsches Altertum*) 98 (1969), pp. 171–204 (Klaus Grubmüller).

Gertrud Jaron Lewis

Henriette Yvonne Stahl

Born 1900, St. Avald, France
Genre(s): novel, short story, poetry, translation
Language(s): Romanian, French

While studying at the Conservatory of Dramatic Arts in Bucharest (1922–1925), Henriette Yvonne Stahl published in *Viaţa românească* her first novel, *Voica* (1924; Voica), which was subsequently reprinted as a volume first in 1929 and later in 1972. This lucid rural novel focussed upon the violent and modern confrontation between Dumitru who plans to bring home a child he had with another woman and his wife Voica who reacts to this by trying to force her husband to put their land in her name.

Stahl's subsequent novels were all located in urban and at times cosmopolitan environments. In *Steaua robilor* (1934; Milky Way) the author presents female desire and women's deep urge for sexual freedom. Male critics were shocked, and one may read with profit the unhappy comments by G. Călinescu or Al. Piru. *Între zi şi noapte* (1941; Between Day and Night), translated into French by the author in 1969, tackled an even more unorthodox theme in presenting Ana Stavri's love "beyond facts or explanations" for a woman, Marta Vrînceanu, who, frigid because of a traumatic childhood experience inflicted upon her by her father, tries to calm her sexual neurosis by taking drugs. Ana purveys Marta with the drugs she needs and devotedly struggles to bring her friend back to some form of livable life in the setting of a labyrinthine, dark, and oppressive Bucharest. *Marea bucurie* (1947; Great Joy) is a lyrical novel about exile, bigamy, and spiritual love. Intertextually related to Dostoievski and Weininger, it reminds mostly of Charles Morgan in its depiction of Polish actor-director Ossendowski's life and love in Berlin as a political exile. The problem of moral responsibility in the social setting of interwar Romanian bourgeoisie is central to the novel *Fratele meu, omul* (1965; My Brother, Man). Finally *Pontiful* (1972; The Pontiff) depicts, in what could be a partially autobiographic vein, a woman writer's para-doxical love for the unbearable environment which feeds her creativity while emptying her life.

Henriette Yvonne Stahl's short stories have at times the lucid and sober lyricism of her novels—such is the case with the volume *Mătuşa Matilda* (1931; Aunt Matilda) which depicts the poetry of things that get out of use, out of fashion, out of touch with real, dynamic lives. Other times they are full of humorous fantasy and Onofrei, the forever available, infinitely pliable and protean story-teller in *Nu mă călca pe umbră* (1969; Don't Step on My Shadow), who cannot conceive of using anything but the third person to speak about himself, might well be a previously hidden playful alter ego of the austere novelist.

Between 1940–1967 Stahl was also the author of a number of elegiac erotic poems, which were collected in the lyrical anthology *Orizont, linie severă* (1970; Horizon, Line Severe).

She translated into Romanian works by John Galsworthy.

Works

Voica [Voica] (1929). *Mătuşa Matilda, nuvele* [Aunt Matilda], short stories (1931). *Steaua robilor, roman* [Star of Slaves [Milky Way], a novel](1934). *Între zi şi noapte* [Between Day and Night] (1941; rpt. 1971). *Marea bucurie* [The Great Joy] (1947). *Fratele meu, omul* [My Brother, Man] (1965). *Nu mă călca pe umbră* [Don't Step on My Shadow](1969). *Entre le jour et la nuit* (1969). Traduit du roumain par l'auteur. *Orizont, linie severă* [Horizon, Line Severe] (1970). *Pontiful* [The Pontiff] (1972).

Translations: *S"vremenni rum"nski raskazi* ["Table d'hôte]," tr. Spaska Kanurkova (1972). "*Kwitnacy bez" i inne opowiadania rumúnskie*(1959) ["Ciotka Matylda"/"Mătuşa Matilda"], tr. D. Czara-Stec and A. Stojowski.

Bibliography

Călinescu, G., *Istoria literaturii române* (Compendiu, Bucharest, 1968), pp. 289–290. Piru, Al, *Panorama deceniului literar românesc 1940–1950* (Bucharest, 1968), pp. 310–313. Popa, Marian, *Dicţionar de literatură română contemporană*(2nd ed. Bucharest, 1977), pp. 517–518.

Sanda Golopentia

Gaspara Stampa

Born ca. 1524, Padua, Italy; died 1554, Venice
Genre(s): lyric poetry
Language(s): Italian

Gaspara Stampa occupies a distinctive and distinguished place among Italian lyric poets of the sixteenth century. Born in Padua of a bourgeois family, she moved to Venice while still a girl and seems, with her siblings Cassandra and Baldassare, to have become a member of the brilliant demi-monde of that city—then at the zenith of its political and cultural power. In all probability, Gaspara was a *cortigiana onesta*, or "honest courtesan," in no simple sense a prostitute but a member of a social class that enjoyed, in Renaissance Venice, not only admiration but indeed respect. The *cortigiana onesta*, who did not bestow her favors lightly or promiscuously, normally had a liaison with only one man—at least during the period of the liaison—and her "protectors" often included great nobles, princes of the Church, and famous writers, artists, and intellectuals.

Gaspara's protector was the young Count Collaltino di Collalto, and her passionate love for him, both before and after his abandonment of her, is the source of her art, virtually her sole theme. Like all sixteenth-century love poets, she is an imitator of Petrarch, but her sexual identity enforces certain adaptations of Petrarchan conventions—adaptations that the Venetian poet effects with imagination, ingenuity, and brilliance. Not distant and unattainable, like Petrarch's Laura, Collaltino has been her lover, albeit a faithless one. Despite her reiterated assertions of his superiority to her, it becomes clear in her sequence of sonnets and songs that Gaspara's fidelity and intensity of passion have made her in fact the superior one, and that the validation of that superiority is her art—an art that, despite its severely limited subject matter, continues to sound across the centuries its notes of erotic joy, hopeless desire, and pain. Dramatic vigor and inventive imagery are among the hallmarks of her poetry.

Gaspara Stampa's poems were collected and published after her death by her sister. In the course of the nineteenth century her greatness was recognized, and she is now seen to be a very important figure in Italian poetry.

Works

Rime, ed. Abdelkader Salza (1913). Translations: *Three Women Poets; Renaissance and Baroque*, ed. Frank J. Warnke (1986). *Women Writers of the Renaissance and Reformation*, ed. Katharina M. Wilson (1987).

Bibliography

Bassanese, Fiora A., *Gaspara Stampa* (Boston, 1982). Croce, Benedetto, *Conversazioni critiche* (2nd ed., Bari, 1924), pp. 223–233. Donadonio, Eugenio, *Gaspara Stampa* (Messina, 1919). Guernelli, Giovanni, *Gaspara Stampa, Louise Labé y Sor Juana Inés de la Cruz: Triptico Renacentista-Barroco* (San Juan, 1972). Vitiello, Justin, "Gaspara Stampa: The Ambiguities of Martyrdom." *Modern Language Notes* 90 (January 1975): 58–71.

Frank Warnke

Hannemieke Stamperius

(see: Hannes Meinkema)

Anna Stanislawska

Born between 1651 and 1654; died between
October 14, 1700 and June 2, 1701
Genre(s): poetry
Language(s): Polish

Called a "rhymemaker" by historians of literature, Stanislawska was the first woman poet who wrote in Polish in the seventeenth century, when the majority of Polish poets still used Latin. Born in an aristocratic family with lands in the east of Poland and the Ukraine, she was a daughter of a high provincial dignitary and administrator. Her mother died when Anna was very young, and she was raised at a monastery and in 1668 forced by father and stepmother to marry a degenerate son of a wealthy governor, J.K. Warszycki; the marriage was annulled a year later by King John III (Sobieski), her protector after her father's death. At the end of 1669, she married Cpt. Jan Z. Olesnicki who was killed in 1675 during the war with Turkey, and in the summer of 1677, Chamberlain Jan B. Zbaski, who died during the siege of Vienna in November 1683. Widowed, she managed all her property and finances and represented herself in court in her effort to regain the lands she inherited from her father, which were newly liberated from the Turks. She established several charitable foundations, which was probably the reason why she was shunned by her family and left to die alone. The exact dates of her birth and death are not known.

Works

An autobiographic poem, *Transakcja albo opisanie calego zycia jednej sieroty przez zalosne treny od tejze samej pisane roku 1685*. Publ. A. Brueckner: *Wiersze zbieranej druzyny. Pierwsza autorka polska i jej autobiografia wierszem* (Biblioteka Warszawska, 1893), vol. 4, pp. 424–429.

Maya Peretz

N. Stanitsky

(see: Avdot'ia Panaeva)

V. Starosel'skaja

(see: Vera Panova)

Tatiana Stavrou

Born 1898, Constantinople (Istanbul)
Genre(s): novel, short story
Language(s): Greek

Tatiana Stavrou (née Adamantiadou) was born and grew up in Constantinople. She immigrated to Greece after the Greek-Turkish conflicts that forced many Greeks of Asia Minor and the area of Constantinople to leave their homelands. She married Dēmētrios Stavrou, a scholar and translator.

She wrote two novels and three books of short stories. For her *Ekeinoi pou emeinan* she won a commendation from the Academy of Athens, and for her *Mystikes pēges* she won the first prize of the Ministry of Education.

Stavrou's writings are autobiographical, reflecting the historical conditions of her lifetime: uprootedness from one's homeland; adaptation to new surroundings; the oppression of the war years; dealing with hunger and cold during the Nazi occupation. She is one of many Greek writers of Anatolian descent who brought new perspectives to modern Greek literature.

Some of her work has been translated into French, German, and Russian.

Works

Ekeinoi pou emeinan [Those Who Were Left Behind], short stories (1934). Deals with the years of WWI. *Oi prōtes rizes* [The First Roots], a novel. *Mystikes pēges* [Mystical Springs], short stories. *To kalokairi perase* [Summer Went By], short stories (1943). *To allo prosōpo tou anthropou* [Man's Other Face], short stories (1958). *Monomachia* [Duel], a novel. *O en Konstantioupolē hellēnikos philologikos syllogos* [The Greek Literary Organization of Constantinople, 1861–1922].

Bibliography

Hellēnides pezographoi, ed. Erse Lange (Athens, 1975). Mirasgezē, Maria, *Neoellenikē Logotechnia* (Athens, 1982). *Neoteron Engyklopaidikon Lexikon Hēliou*, Vol. 17 (Athens). Pattichē, Maria. "Ē Logotechnia stē zoē mas: Mia syzētēsē me tēn Tatiana Stavrou." *Pnevmatikē Kypros* (Nicosia, Cyprus, 1966). Sachinēs, Apostolos, *Neoi Pezographoi* (Athens, 1965). Vitti, Mario, *Storia della letteratura neogreca* (Torino, 1971).

Helen Dendrinou Kolias

Maria van der Steen

Born 1906
Genre(s): poetry, novel
Language(s): Dutch

Anger and bitterness about social inequities and a deep sympathy for all victims of exploitation, be they housewives or industrial workers, have inspired all of Maria van der Steen's work.

She was born into a large, poor Catholic worker's family. Though she proved a quick and gifted learner in the village primary school, she was sent to work in a factory at the age of eleven. She continued to educate herself, however, and became a secretary, an assistant librarian, then a social worker, before choosing to become a full-time writer later in life. She is divorced, has a son, and lives in The Hague.

Maria van der Steen's difficulties in getting published, especially at first, can be attributed to the fact that she is not an academic writer and writes better social commentary about lower-class characters whose psychological and emotional problems are compounded by material difficulties.

Works

Prose: *Totale uitverkoop* (1956) and *Balans* (1956) (both revised and reprinted with the new titles *Vechten tegen de bierkaai* and *Wel bij brood alleen*, 1979). *Die Annie ben ik* (1977). *Hazelegger* (1982). Poetry: *Sintels rapen* (1970). *Laat maar* (1971). *Geen Paniek* (1974). *Twistgesprekken van een huisvrouw met God* (1975). *Zeg het stamelend* (1975). *De onderste steen* (1976). *Altijd onderweg* (1976). *Wakker worden* (1978). *Een zaadbal in majn hand* (1980). *Huiver* (1983).

Bibliography

Meulenbelt, Anja, ed., *Wie weegt de woorden. De auteur en haar werk* (Amsterdam, 1985), pp. 127–137, 227–228.

Maya Bijvoet

Verena Stefan

Born 1947, Switzerland
Genre(s): prose, lyric poetry
Language(s): German

In 1968 Verena Stefan went to Berlin, the avant-garde center for feminist thought and activity, to become a physical therapist, to study sociology at the Freie Universität, but foremost, to rise to fame as the first radical feminist on the German literary scene. Her small book *Häutungen* of 1975, published under tremendous financial difficulties, had sold by 1980 over 200,000 copies. It is a very carefully crafted prose piece, set in the immediacy of the autobiographical style of writing but based on the sober analyses of language use and sexual mores. She makes the female body the focal point of all her discussion, exposes it as the political center of male domination and exploitation, which has turned woman into an object of self-estrangement. Particularly interesting is Stefan's investigation into existing language, which she sees as perpetuating phallocratic norms by misogynic usage. Solutions she offers

are the recapture of female authenticity, the right of naming that which has been speechless female essence and the rupture with heterosexual compliance. The title of her book, *Shedding*, wants to hint at the mythological beast, that has decided to shed its skin as an act of getting rid of all that hinders growth. In 1980 she published her second book, a collection of poems, entitled *mit Füssen mit Flügeln*, thematically arguing for an archaic remembrance of femininity as the departure point toward a genuine women's future.

Works

Häutungen (1975). "Klytemnestra wohnt nebenan," review of Christa Reinig's *Entmannung. Die Zeit* (6 Aug. 76). *mit Füssen mit Flügeln*, poems (1980).

Bibliography

Classen, Brigitte, and Gabriele Goettle, "'Häutungen' eine Verwechslung von Anemone und Amazone." *Courage* 1 (Sept. 76). "Körperbewu tsein und Sprachbewu tsein: Verena Stefans *Häutungen*." Ricarda Schmidt, *Westdeutsche Frauenliteratur in den 70er Jahren* (Frankfurt, 1982).

Margaret Eifler

Charlotte Albertine Ernestine von Stein

Born December 25, 1742, Eisenach, Germany;
died January 6, 1827, Weimar, Germany
Genre(s): drama, poetry
Language(s): German

Charlotte von Stein became famous as the friend, confidante, and advisor of Germany's foremost poet, Johann Wolfgang von Goethe. It is practically unknown that she also wrote plays and poems, and only her tragedy *Dido* (written in 1794) gained some notoriety because the male lead role (the poet Ogon) was said to resemble Goethe in speech and mannerisms.

Charlotte von Stein was the youngest daughter of Johann Wilhelm Christian and Concordia Elisabeth von Schardt. At age eighteen, Charlotte, who was bright, witty, and gifted, became lady-in-waiting to duchess Anna Amalia, herself a composer and patron of the arts who drew the most gifted poets and composers to the court of Weimar and made it a cultural center of Germany. In 1764 Charlotte married G.E.J. von Stein (1735–1793) and had seven children in the first eleven years of marriage. All of these children died at an early age, except her first-born, Karl, and her youngest, Friedrich. A strong sense of duty and dependability carried her through this adversity, of which she confessed: "Exhausted from crying, I fell asleep and on awakening dragged myself through another day, and the question weighed heavily upon me why nature determined half her creatures to bear this pain."

A sense of duty and loyalty to her husband also characterized her relationship with Johann Wolfgang von Goethe, whom she met in 1775. Goethe found in her a woman of brilliant wit, empathy, charm, social grace, and reason who did not succumb to his amorous fervor and his ardent declarations of love. A long-lasting friendship developed between them that was to become proverbial and accorded Charlotte von Stein immortality in German literature. Goethe addressed numerous letters and poems to her, and their friendship cooled only in 1788 after his return from a lengthy Italian sojourn and his establishment of a common-law marriage with Christiane Vulpius (later legalized). The formal dissolution of their friendship occurred in the summer of 1789 and their later reconciliation (see letters between 1796 and 1826) never reached the original measure of trust and warmth. Before her death von Stein asked for the return of letters she had written Goethe and destroyed most of them. She gave specific instructions that her funeral procession was not to pass by Goethe's house on the "Frauenplan"—a wish that curiously was not heeded. Goethe did not pay her his last respects and was represented at her funeral by his son.

The extent of von Stein's literary efforts is not known because she apparently placed little value on the publication of her work, and no systematic search or research has shed light on her literary bequest. In 1803 her tragedy in four acts was published anonymously under the title *The Two Emilies* (Stuttgart: Cotta), and the reprint in *Neueste deutsche Schaubühne für 1805* erroneously named Friedrich von Schiller (another of Germany's literary giants) as its author.

Her other known works remained unpublished or were published only long after her death.

Her first comedy, *New System of Freedom, or The Conspiracy Against Love*, was written in 1799 and earned Schiller's acclaim. Despite its rich humor it was never published—probably because some of her famous friends thought their foibles portrayed in it. Only a much distorted version of it—"revised for the modern stage"— appeared in 1948 in Braunschweig under the editorship of F. Ulbrich. A similar fate almost befell her tragedy *Dido*. The first public notice of it occurred in an anonymous essay in the *Allgemeine Zeitung* (September 3, 1863), and H. Düntzer published the manuscript in 1867. A new edition of 150 copies appeared in 1920. Although Schiller had accorded it the highest praise, it was almost immediately denounced as the vengeful work of a woman spurned. This misrepresentation of the play (which contains no objectionable or even discernible references to persons of note) has been repeated indiscriminately in bibliographies to date. Of her poems and minor works, the playlet "Rino" (written in 1776) was first published by H. Düntzer in *Deutsche Vierteljahrsschrift* 33 (1870) and later by A. Schöll, editor of *Goethe's Letters to Frau von Stein*, vol. 1 (1899), pp. 471–474. Two of von Stein's poems of 1786, "Flee me, contemplative thoughts" and "To the moon (according to my style)" are reprinted in J. Fränkel's edition of *Goethe's Letters to Charlotte von Stein*, vol. 3 (1960), pp. 483–485. Fränkel also reprints "Rino" in volume one of his edition (pp. 505–511). The poems appeared first in volume one of H. Düntzer's biography of Charlotte von Stein (pp. 267–268), which also contains excerpts from and references to other works by von Stein. Unfortunately, a lack of documentation (and sometimes even of the titles of these works) limits the usefulness of this work.

Works

"Rino" (1776). *Dido* (1794). *Neues Freiheitssystem oder die Verschwörung gegen die Liebe* (1799). *Die zwey Emilien*, poems (1803).

Bibliography

Allgemeine Deutsche Biographie, vol. 35 (1893). Düntzer, H., *Charlotte von Stein. Goethes Freundin*

(1874). Exhibition catalog, *Weimar zur Goethezeit* (1961). Fränkel, J., ed., *Goethes Briefe an Charlotte von Stein* (1960, 1962). Gleichenrusswurm, A. von, *Charlotte von Stein. Dido* (1920). Nicolai, H., *Zeittafel zu Goethes Leben und Werk* (1977). Taxis-Bordogna, countess O., *Frauen von Weimar* (1948).

Helene M. Kastinger Riley

Edith Stein

(a.k.a. Teresia Benedicta a Cruce)

Born October 12, 1891, Breslaw, now Wroclaw; died August 9 (presumably), 1942, Auschwitz
Genre(s): autobiography, philosophy, social and theological essay
Language(s): German

Deeply rooted in a Jewish family, the last and most cherished of eleven children, Stein was brought up with love, strength, and respect for her great intelligence by her mother Augusta Courant who, a widow as early as 1893, conducted with courage and strong religious ethics both her numerous family (seven living children) and the business her husband had left in debt. She supported university studies for all her children who wanted them. Although she was fond of school since age six, out of an existential crisis at puberty, Stein quit the gymnasium to live for a time with her married sister Elsa in Hamburg. Voluntarily abandoning Jewish religious practice, she resumed studies in the Lyceum 1908–1911 and, declaring herself an atheist, became intensely involved in women's problems and a Prussian group for "votes for women" during her university years in Breslaw. Here (1911–1913) Stein studied German philology (out of her love for languages), history (as an instrument for facing the present "with a sense of social responsibility") and psychology (to understand the "*person* problem").

After deciding she had been deceived by the positivistic psychological view of Hönigswald and Stern, Stein went to Göttingen University to attend Edmund Husserl's (1859–1938) lectures. Through the revelation of Husserl's *Logical Researches*, Stein saw phenomenology as the way to prepare "the conceptual instruments" psychology needed to acquire as its basical "clear principles." In Göttingen (1913–1915) where, though an atheist, she felt a continuous "thirst for truth," which was also a form of "endless prayer," her friendship with A. Reinach, Max Scheler and others of Husserl's disciples who valued the religious phenomenon as well as a return to her mother's faith led Stein toward Catholicism. She was convinced all of a sudden, after reading in one night St. Teresa of Avila's *Autobiography* and was christened in January of 1922.

After a period of nursing work in World War I, Stein became assistant to Husserl in Freiburg University and worked on a thesis on *empathy* (1916). Stein's academic career was interrupted, first because of her Catholicism (Heidegger, Husserl's successor in Freiburg, rejected her in 1931 although Stein was already a well-known essayist and lecturer), and then by Nazi anti-Semitic decrees which prevented her appointment at the German Institute of Scientific Pedagogy (Münster, 1932). At last, with peaceful certainty, Stein saw her way: Carmel. There were obstacles: age (42), poverty, her mother's sorrow, even greater at Stein's conversion.

After acceptance from Köln Carmel, Stein took the veil in 1934, received an order to complete a theoretical work on Aquinas' thought, and afterward wrote her metaphysical text *Eternal Being and Limited Being*. As the Transcendent Being is also "He who mercifully turns down to his creature," the Eternal Being is in fact the foundation and support of the limited one. The contemplation of Christ is Stein's strength. After the notorious anti-Semitic *Kristallnacht* (November 9, 1938), Stein asked to join the Echt Community in Holland in order to be safer and was joined by her sister Rosa. In Echt Stein wrote *Ways to the Intuition of God* under the inspiration of Pseudo-Dyonisius, *Treatises*, and *Letters*. The *Ways* are the signs and calls of nature, which send us back to the One who mysteriously reveals Himself so. We can experience "a person-to-person encounter with God." Stein begins to write *Scientia crucis* (unfinished because of her imprisonment), a study on St John of the Cross, and reached the conclusion that "the nuptial union of the soul with God—the aim of its creation—has been obtained through the Cross, consummated on the Cross and sealed with the Cross for all eternity. On March 26, 1939 (Passion Sunday) in a message to her prioress, Stein asked for permission to offer herself to Jesus' Heart on behalf of Jews, to hinder the coming war. On August 2, 1942, the SS came and took Stein with Rosa to Westerbork camp; on August 7 they were taken to Auschwitz.

Works

Autobiography: *Aus dem Leben einer jüdischen Familie—Kindheit und Jugend* [Life of a Jewish Family—Childhood and Youth] (1933). *Wie ich in dem Kölner Karmel Kamzx* [How I Came to Köln Carmel], Christmas gift to her prioress and first biographer, Mother Teresia Renata de Spiritu Sancto (1938). *E.S.* (1952; transl.). Teresia Matre a Dei, *E.S.* (1971; transl.). Elisabeth de Miribel, *E.S.* (Paris, 1954 and 1984).
Complete Works, ed. Lucy Gerber (1950) (some vols. also in French). *Zum problem der Einfühlung*, Ph.D. thesis, 1917 (English tr. *On the problem of Empathy,* 1970). "Jarbuch für Philosophie und Phänemenologische Forschung." *Psychische Kausalität* [Psychic Casualty] (1922). *Eine Untersuchung über den Staat* [A Research on the State] (1925). *Husserl's Phänomenologie und die Philosophie des hl. Thomas van Aquino* [Husserl's Phenomenology and Aquinas' philosophy] (1929). Several writings on women, mostly from her Austria, Germany, and Switzerland lectures.

Bibliography

Articles by E. Przyvara, S.J., A. Koyré, H. Conrad-Martius. In Italy, a specialist on Stein, Carla Bettinelli, wrote *Il pensiero di Edith Stein Dalla fenomenologia all scienta della croce* [E.S.'s Thought from Phenomenology to the Science of the Cross] (Milano, 1976).

Gabriella Fiori

Marius Stein

(see: Maria Janitschek)

Steinunn Refsdóttir Skáldkona

Flourished ca. 999, Hofgarðr, Snæfellsnes, Iceland
Genre(s): skaldic poetry
Language(s): Old Norse

Steinunn Refsdóttir is cited in two later prose accounts (*Njáls saga* and *Kristni saga*) as having composed two oral stanzas in the classic skaldic meter *dróttkvætt* (court meter). These were *níðvísur* (lampooning stanzas) addressed by Steinunn, an adherent of the old pagan religion, to Þangbrandr, an early Christian missionary in Iceland. The *Njáls saga* account of the poem's delivery places it in the context of a debate between the missionary and the skald. As a conclusion to her argument, Steinunn refers to Þangbrandr's recent shipwreck and recites her two *níðvísur,* in which she claims that it was Þórr who smashed Þangbrandr's ship while the White Christ stood by, unable to save it. Whether Þangbrandr was impressed with this argument or not is not recorded, but his mission to Iceland can be counted successful, since the entire country became Christian by an act of Parliament the following year. Steinunn's two stanzas are structurally near perfect, according to the rules of *dróttkvætt* governing alliteration and internal rhyme; in addition, they exhibit a rollicking rhythm appropriate to the sea-going topic. Little background information is known about Steinunn, other than the location of her family farm and that her son, Hofgarða-Refr, was also a skald. (A dozen or so stanzas by Refr have been preserved.)

Works

Jónsson, Finnur, ed., *Den norsk-islandske skjaldedigtning* (1915), IB, pp. 127–128. Kock, Ernst Albin, ed., *Den norsk-isländska skaldediktningen* (1949), I, p. 71. *Brennu-Njáls saga,* ed. Einar Ólafur Sveinsson, *Íslenzk fornrit* XII (1954), pp. 265–267. *Kristini saga,* ed. Bernhard Kahle, *Altnordische Saga-Bibliothek* 11 (1905), pp. 27–28.
Translations: *Njal's Saga,* tr. Magnus Magnusson and Hermann Palsson (1960), p. 222.

Bibliography

Guðrún Helgadóttir, *Skáldkonur fyrri alda* (Akureyri, 1961), I, pp. 119–122. Ohlmarks, Åke, *Tors skalder och Vite-Krists: trosskiftetidens isländske furstelovskalder: 980–1013* (Stockholm, 1957), pp. 36–37, 306–307.

Sandra Ballif Straubhaar

Stephanie

(see: Kathinka [Katharina] Rosa Pauline Modesta Zitz-Halein)

Lydia Stephanou

Born 1927
Genre(s): poetry, translation, literary criticism
Language(s): Greek

Lydia Stephanou has written at least four books of poetry and a book on the study of poetry. She has also translated Dylan Thomas into modern Greek.

Works

Exi epeisodia apo ton kyklo tōn teratōn [Six Episodes from the Cycle of the Beasts] (1971). *To provlēma tēs methodou stē meletē tēs poiēsēs* [The Problem of Method in the Study of Poetry] (1972). *Ta megaphona* [The Loudspeakers] (1973). *Oi Lexeis kai ta pragmata* (1983) [Words and Things]. Anthologized translations: *The Charioteer: An Annual Review of Modern Greek Culture* 15 (1974). *The Chicago Review* (August, 1969). *Contemporary Greek Poetry*, tr., intro., and notes by Kimon Friar (1985).

Bibliography

Friar, Kimon, Review. *Books Abroad* 49, 2: 372.

Helen Dendrinou Kolias

Lilyana Stephanova

Born 1929, Sofia
Genre(s): poetry, prose
Language(s): Bulgarian

Lilyana Stephanova graduated from the Maxim Gorky Institute of Literature in Moscow and has since then been involved in literature as a writer and editor. She has edited the poetry section of the newspaper *Literatouren Front*, been the deputy editor-in-chief of the journal *Septemvri* and served as president of the Sofia Council of Culture. Currently she is editor of *Obzor*, a journal devoted to Bulgarian arts and letters, and is also president of the Bulgarian PEN-Club.

Stephanova has more than twenty publications to her credit, including poetry and nonfiction. She is a recipient of the Dimitrov Prize and is the Deputy Minister of Education. Her work has been translated extensively into English, French, Spanish, German, Italian, Hindi, Hungarian, Polish, Arabic, Mongolian, and all Soviet languages.

Works

Poetry: In Moscow (1952). When We Are Twenty (1956). The World I Love (1958). Marching With You (1961). Day, Don't Go Away (1965). Love and Sorrow (1967). A Voice from the Future (1969). The Sun Kissed Me (1970). Password (1973). Fiery Orbit (1974). Beyond the Speed Limit (1976). Magnetic Field (1978). Lyrics (1979).

Nonfiction: Autumn in America. The Volcanoes of Mexico Are Smoking. Japan Without Kimono or Fan. I Write So I Love. Not a Duel, but a Single Combat.

Warwick J. Rodden

Margareta Sterian

Born 1897, Buzău, Romania
Genre(s): poetry, novel, journalism, translation
Language(s): Romanian

Margareta Sterian is a well-known Romanian painter who also wrote poems, which were mainly collected in the volume *Soare difuz* (1974; Diffuse Sun), an autobiographical novel entitled *Castelul de apă* (1972; Water Tower), as well as a number of essays (published in *Contimporanul*, *Azi*, etc. beginning in 1930). Her lyricism, which has been aptly defined by the literary critic Lucian Raicu as a form of "tender cognition," stems from a cultivated spirit and a vital though reserved personality.

Sterian translated into Romanian works by Whitman, O'Neill, Faulkner, and Aldridge as well as a number of old Irish poems. Part of her translations were collected in an anthology of American lyricism entitled *Aud cîntînd America* (1947; I Hear America Sing), which was republished in 1973.

Works

Castelul de apă [Water Tower] (1972). *Soare difuz* [Diffuse Sun](1974). *Aud cîntînd America* [I Hear America Sing] (1947; 2nd ed., 1973).

Bibliography

Popa, Marian, *Dicționar de literatură romănă contemporană* (Bucharest, 1977), p. 528. Raicu, Lucian, "Margareta Sterian—cunoaștere tandră." In *Critica—formă de viață* (Bucharest, 1976), pp. 215–217.

Sanda Golopentia

Daniel Stern

(see: Marie [-Catherine-Sophie de Flavigny], countess d'Ágoult)

Maria Anna Antonia Sternheim

(see: Marianne Ehrmann)

Stig Stigson

(see: Alfhild Agrell)

Vigdis Stokkelien

Born March 11, 1934, Kristiansand, Norway
Genre(s): novel, short story, journalism, drama
Language(s): Norwegian (bokmål)

Since her literary debut in 1967, Vigdis Stokkelien has written a number of novels and short stories about life at sea, many of which are critical of modern society. She also has written suspense stories, as well as a children's book and plays for both radio and television theater.

Educated as a radio operator, Stokkelien has used her experiences sailing in the Norwegian merchant marine in her writing, such as in *Den* *siste prøven*(1968; The Last Trial), and *Granaten* (1969; The Grenade), which are both set on ships carrying war materials to Vietnam. In both Stokkelien depicts the moral dilemma of the protagonists and the consequences of their decisions on their later lives. *Lille-Gibraltar*(1972; Little Gibraltar) tells about young people growing up in the occupation during World War II, and criticizes the self-righteous attitude many Norwegians had toward collaborators and their children. The sequel to *Lille-Gibraltar* is *Båten under solseilet*(1982; Boat Beneath the Awning), where Gro, now a grown woman, takes a job as a radio operator on a tanker sailing to India, Indonesia and Singapore. Still haunted by her memories of the occupation, she grapples with the question of what constitutes treason. If several of her loved ones had been traitors, what did that make her? Other themes are hypocrisy and discrimination against both women and minorities. *I speilet* (1973; In the Mirror) is a collection of short stories about the oppression of women.

Vigdis Stokkelien's experiences working in the male dominated shipping milieu combined with her strong political consciousness have given her a unique perspective on problems of modern society.

Works

Dragsug [Undertow] (1967). *Den siste prøven* [The Last Trial] (1968). *Granaten* [The Grenade] (1969). *Sommeren på heden* [Summer on the Heath] (1970). *Lille-Gibraltar* [Little-Gibraltar] (1972). *I speilet* [In the Mirror] (1973). *Gru & Grøss* [Shivers and Shudders] (1976). *Vi* [We] (1976). *TV-heksen* [The TV-Witch] (1977). *Alle de som lengter* [All Those Who Long] (1978). *Strega og andre svarte historier* [Strega and Other Black Stories] (1981). *Grensefolket* [Living at the Border] (1981). *Båten under solseilet* [Boat Beneath the Awning] (1982). *Måkeslipp* [Seagull Release] (1983). *Stjerneleden* [The Star Course] (1984).

Translations: "A Vietnamese Doll," tr. Barbara Wilson, in *An Everyday Story*, ed. Katherine Hanson (Seattle, 1984), pp. 187–191.

Bibliography

Beyer, Harald and Edvard, *Norsk litteraturhistorie* (Oslo, 1978), pp. 424–425. Dahl, Willy, *Fra 40-tall til 70-tall* (Oslo, 1977), p. 156. Dahl, Willy,

Norges litteratur III: Tid og tekst 1935–1972 (Oslo, 1989), p. 313. Kristensen, Tom, "Vigdis Stokkelien–en presentasjon," in Vigdis Stokkelien, *Granaten og andre tekster* (Oslo, 1976), pp. 7–10. Øverland, Janneken, "Kvinneroller–tilpasning eller opprør? Om Vigdis Stokkeliens og Bjørg Viks forfatterskap," in *Linjer i norsk prosa 1965–1975*, ed. Helge Rønning (Oslo, 1977), pp. 241–80. Rosenberg, Brita, "Oppgjør fra skogene . . ." *A-Magasinet* 41 (1983): 12–14, 16.

Margaret Hayford O'Leary

Verena Stössinger

Born 1951, Lucerne, Switzerland
Genre(s): novel
Language(s): German

On leaving secondary school Verena Stössinger attended drama school, then worked variously as a drama assistant and an assistant film director in Berlin. Prior to her marriage in 1978, she worked for a publisher in Basel. Since 1982 she has engrossed herself in Nordic and Germanic studies and sociology, while writing occasionally for newspapers and radio. Her first publication, *Muttertage: Leben mit Mann, Kindern und Beruf* (1980; Mother Days: Life with Husband, Children and Career), was written in collaboration with Beatrice Leuthold and Franziska Mattmann. This work is about divorced mothers and mother and child case studies in Switzerland. Stössinger's second publication, a novel entitled *Fallen* (Traps) that appeared in 1984, focuses on a young, independent woman living alone in a remote, old house, who experiences the process of self-realization. Verena Stössinger now lives and writes in Binningen.

Works

Muttertage: Leben mit Mann, Kindern und Beruf (1980). *Fallen* (1984).

Warwick J. Rodden

Charlotte Strandgaard

Born 1943, Brørup, Denmark
Genre(s): poetry, novel
Language(s): Danish

Charlotte Strandgaard is one of the few younger writers who made the transition from modernism in the 1960s to the subjective realism of the 1970s and 1980s. She has a degree in library science and published her first collection of poetry, *Katalog*, in 1965. It was different from most of the poetry published at that time because of its feminist perspective, describing women as sex objects and victims of a male-dominated society. Strandgaard continued to address women's issues but until her first novel, *Når vi alle bliver mødre* (1981) still utilized a modernist framework.

All Strandgaard's later works are about women's issues in a mostly realistic, straightforward style that emphasizes the physical aspects of being a woman, menstruation, pregnancy, infertility, childbirth, soiled diapers, all the "unpleasant" everyday elements of women's lives that men don't often address in a recognizable way in their writings. *Når vi alle bliver mødre* is about different aspects of motherhood, a teenage boy's possible suicide, his mother's feeling of complete failure, and her difficult pregnancy that is to replace her lost child and enable her to continue her life. The book is also about women mothering each other, helping each other live through crises, of coming to terms with their aging bodies and the terrible loss of a child. *Lille menneske* (1982) deals with a different aspect of womanhood, of not wanting to grow up and meet the challenges of being an adult. Again the central character is a mother and her relationship with her threatened child, this time an anorexic teenage girl, and the effect the girl's refusal to become a woman like her mother has on the protagonist. Again Strandgaard explores the relationships between women, the kind of sisterhood and support necessary to endure as a woman in a capitalist, male-dominated society that is not sensitive to the needs of women and children. *En flug foruden vinger* (1985) takes that theme even further and examines the impact of modern reproductive technology, which is controlled by men, on women's lives. It is a story of the relationship that develops between a childless woman and the surrogate mother of her child, of how alienating such high-tech procedures can be to women, their beneficial outcome notwithstanding, and how one woman's caring and untraditional attitude towards another woman in need can make surrogate motherhood an ultimately beautiful experience for both of them, so long as they do not let the technology control them as well.

Strandgaard's books are important aspects of women's demands for equality and equal opportunity in their sensitive and realistic depictions of what it is like to be a woman in a patriarchal, technologically advanced capitalist society, which considers reproduction and the upbringing of children women's responsibility only. Strandgaard's message is that women are indeed different, that they should not try to emulate men but teach them and society, the value of their kind of life without having their right to equality jeopardized.

Works

Katalog (1963). Afstande (1966). Uafgjort (1967). Det var en lørdag aften (1968). Herinde (1969). Gade op og gade ned (1973). Naesten kun om kaerlighed (1977). Braendte børn (1979). Når vi alle bliver mødre (1981). Lille menneske (1982). En fugl foruden vinger (1985). Lille dråbe (1986).

Bibliography

Andersen, Bruun Michael, ed., *Dansk litteraturhistorie 8* (1985). Bang, Bodil, *Analyser af moderne dansk lyrik II* (1976). Brostrøm, Torben, ed., *Danske digtere i det 20 århundrede* (1982). Clausen, Claus, ed., *Litteratur/80—en almanak* (1980). Levy, Jette, *De knuste spejle* (1976). Marcus, Maria, *Kvinde i dag. Samtaler med elleve danske dvinder* (1973).

Merite von Eyben

Lulu von Strauss und Torney

Born September 20, 1873, Buckeburg, Germany; died June 19, 1956, Jena
Genre(s): lyric poetry, ballad, novel, short story, drama, history
Language(s): German

In Lulu von Strauss und Torney's lyric poetry the people and the region of Lower Saxony in Germany found their perhaps most elaborate expression. She was born on September 20, 1873, in Bückeburg as the daughter of a General Major and Adjunct of the Duke of Schaumburg-Lippe. After her high school years in Bückeburg she continued her study by herself in the princely Library. Since 1900 she had contacts with the literary circle around Börries von Münchhausen and began to publish her first ballads in the *Göttinger Musenalmanach* in 1901. In these years she also travelled extensively and was introduced to the literary world of Berlin, where she became friends with the poet Agnes Miegel and the later West German president Theodor Heuss. She married the publisher Eugen Diederichs in 1916 and lived with him in Jena, where she started her career as lector for his publishing house. Thus she was in a position decisively to influence the company's literary program. Her lyrics have never been highly acclaimed because of their naive and stereotyped imagery of the peasant figure, harvest, the year's seasons, generations and traditions, which was to become so popular under the Nazis. Her ballads, however, demonstrated her talents as a naturalistic poet in the tradition of the nineteenth century, depicting man's fight against nature in extreme situations. She drew her material particularly from the time of the Reformation, the Peasant War, and the French Revolution and glorified the triumph of a nobly spirited mind over fate and human failures. Next to Agnes Miegel and Börries von Münchhausen she is considered as the leading ballad poet in the first half of this century because of the especially successful dramatic structures in her ballads. Her narrative texts similarly focus on the history of her homeland and its people. Her characters are stereotypes—rural, heroic, and unspoiled by civilization and critical thought. In contrast, her presentations of the anonymous masses of people ruled by such basic emotions as hatred, fanaticism, and cowardice are valuable literary achievements. The Frisian and North German characters and her enthusiasm for history and the heroic figure dominate her work. Some of these ideals and values expressed in her poetry, ballads and prose texts were also expounded and then perverted by the Nazis in their admiration for the heroism and leadership of the Aryan race. In consequence, Lulu von Strauss und Torney's poetry is less popular today and little read.

Works

Poetry: *Balladen und Lieder* [Ballads and Songs] (1902). *Neue Balladen und Lieder* [New Ballads and Songs] (1907). *Reif steht die Saat* [The Crop is Ripe, under the same title she edited a complete collection of her poems in 1926 and 1929] (1919). *Erde der Väter* [Our Forefathers' Soil] (1936).

Novels: *Aus Bauernstamm* [Made out of Peasant Wood] (1902). *Ihres Vaters Tochter* [Her Father's Daughter] (1905). *Luzifer, Roman aus der Stedingerzeit* [Luzifer, a Novel from the Time of the Stedinger] (1907). *Judas* (1911). *Der jüngste Tag* [The Day of Judgement] (1922).

Short stories: *Bauernstolz* [Peasant's Pride] (1901). *Eines Lebens Sühne* [Lifelong Atonement] (1904). *Das Erbe* [The Inheritance] (1905). *Der Hof am Brink* [The Farm at the Brink] (1906). *Das Meerminneke* [The Sea Maid] (1906). *Sieger und Besiegte* [The Winner and the Defeated] (1909). *Die Legende der Felsenstadt* [The Legend of the City of Rock] (1911). *Das Fenster* [The Window] (1926; rpt. as *Das Kind am Fenster* [The Child at the Window], 1938). *Auge um Auge* [Eye for Eye] (1933).

Drama: *Der Tempel* [The Temple] (1921).

History and literary criticism: *Die Dorfgeschichte in der modernen Literatur* [The Village Story in Modern Literature] (1901). *Aus der Chronik niederdeutscher Städte* [From City Chronicles in North Germany] (1912). *Mitteilungen aus den Akten betreffend den Zigeunern Tuvia Panti aus Ungarn und Anderes* [Informations from the Files Concerning the Hungarian Gypsies Tuvia Panti and Other Stories] (1912). *Totenklage* [Death Mourning] (1919). *Das Leben der Heiligen Elisabeth* [Life of the Saint Elisabeth] (1926). *Deutsches Frauenleben zur Zeit der Sachsenkaiser und Hohenstaufer* [Life of Women at the Time of the Saxonian and Hohenstaufer Emperors] (1927). *Vom Biedermeier zur Bismarckzeit, Aus dem Leben eines Neunzigjährigen* [From Biedermeier to the Bismarck Period, From the Life of a 90-Year Old-Man], a study about her grandfather Viktor von Strauss und Torney (1932). *Eugen Diederichs, Leben und Werk* [Eugen Diederichs, Life and Work] (1936). *Angelus Silesius: Blüh auf, gefrorner Christ!* [Angelus Silesius: Bloom, You Frozen Christ!] (1938). *Annette von Droste-Hülshoff: Einsamkeit und Helle, Ihr Leben in Briefen* [Annette von Droste-Hülshoff: Solitude and Clarity, Her Life in Letters] (1938).

Memoirs: *Das verborgene Angesicht, Erinnerungen* [The Veiled Face, Memories] (1943).

Essay: *Schuld* [Guilt] (1940).

Correspondence: *Theodor Heuss: Theodor Heuss und Lulu von Strauss und Torney, Ein Briefwechsel* [Theodor Heuss and Lulu von Strauss von Torney, A Correspondence] (1965).

Ballads and short stories: *Tulipan* (1966).

She also translated a number of French and American novels into German.

Translation: *The Seafarer* (poem), tr. M. Münsterberg, in *The German Classics in the 19th and 20th centuries*, vol. 18 (New York, 1914), pp. 314–317.

Bibliography

Fechter, P., "Lulu von Strauss und Torney," *Die Neue Literatur* 34 (1932). Hamann, R. and J. Hermand, *Epochen deutscher Kultur von 1870 bis zur Gegenwart*, vol. 4 (Munich, 1973). Köpf, G., *Die Balladen* (Kronberg i. Ts., 1976). "Lulu von Strauss und Torney," in W. Duwe, *Deutsche Dichtung des 20. Jahrhunderts*, vol. 1 (2nd ed., Zurich, 1969), pp. 69–73. Oschilewski, G., *Über Lulu von Strauss und Torney* (1944). Zander, L., *Die Balladen der Lulu von Strauss und Torney, Eine Würdigung nach Gehalt und Gestalt*. Diss., 1951.

Albrecht Classen

Veronika Strēlerte

Born October 10, 1912, Dobele, Latvia
Genre(s): lyric poetry, short story;
Language(s): Latvian

Veronika Strēlerte is the most outstanding modern Latvian woman poet. Originally her first name was Rudīte. As daughter of the editor of a periodical, she was born into an intellectual family; her interest in literature led her to study Romance philology in Riga and to translate (mainly while in exile) numerous Italian and French classics into Latvian. Her poetry is highly sophisticated; her early works showing a strong influence of the Italian Renaissance. At the approach of the Soviet forces in 1945 she, like many other Latvians, especially intellectuals, went into voluntary exile in Sweden, where she has been active since then not only as poet and translator but also as editor of the literary periodical *Daugava* and of a selection of Latvian folksongs (*dainas*). She is married to the Latvian essayist and critic Andrejs Johansons; previously she was married to the Latvian historian and poet Arvēds Švābe.

Strēlerte's poetry is characterized by perfection of form and melodiousness. Its deep emotion is presented in a restrained and aloof manner. This combination of qualities pervades her work with an ambiguity that belies its surface clarity and simplicity. Her worldview often seems correspondingly dualistic.

Works

Vienkārši vārdi (1937). Lietus lāse (1940). Mēness upe (1945). Zem augstiem kokiem (1951). Gaismas tuksneši (1951). Želastības gadi (1961). Pusvārdiem (1982). Numerous pieces in various collections and periodicals.
Translations: Samples of her work in *A Century of Latvian Poetry*, ed. and tr. W.K. Matthews (1957).

Bibliography

Gūtmane, Margita, ed., *Veronika Strēlerte: Rakstu krājums dzejnieces 70 gadu dzimšanas dienai 1982. gada 10. okt.* (Stockholm, 1982). Johansons, Andrejs, "Latvian Literature in Exile." *The Slavonic and East European Review* 30 (1952): 465–475. Rudzītis, Jānis, "Die in der Emigration entstandene lettische Literatur." *Acta Baltica* 6 (1966): 157–174. Also see Benjamiņš Jēgers, *Latviešu trimdas izdevumu bibliografija–Bibliography of Latvian Publications Published Outside Latvia, 1940–1960* (Sundbyberg, 1972; *1961–1970*, Sundbyberg, 1977; *1971–1980*, Stockholm, 1988).

Zoja Pavlovskis

Eva Strittmatter

Born 1930, Neuruppin, Germany
Genre(s): children's literature, poetry
Language(s): German

Eva Strittmatter was the daughter of a shop assistant. She studied Germanic philology in Berlin from 1947–1951. She was active in an East German writers group until 1953; from 1959–1960 she was the editor of the magazine *Neue Deutsche Literatur* (New German Literature). Between the years 1960–1972 she travelled eight times to the Soviet Union. Her poetry was well received in Moscow and in Novogorod. Pushkin was the prototype and model for her own poetry; she is not only fluent in Russian, but she has a deep love and respect for Russian culture. From 1952–1973 she engaged her talents in literary criticism.

In her works, Eva Strittmatter consciously avoids egocentricity although many of her poems are written in the first person. Critics of her works find her poetry too traditional and reminiscent of the nineteenth century. She seeks to encompass all of life and does not shy from history, politics, or polemics.

Works

Tinko [Tinko] (1956). *Brüderchn Vierbein* [Little Brother Fourlegs] (1959). *Vom Kater, der ein Mensch sein wollte* [About the Puss Who Wanted to Be Human] (1960). *Fünf Lieder für Singstimme* [Five Songs for the Singing Voice, with Music] (1970). *Ich mach ein Lied aus Stille* [I Make a Song from the Quietness] (1973). *Grossmütterchen Gutefrau und ihre Tiere* [Grandmother Goodwoman and Her Animals] (1974). *Ich schwing mich auf die Schaukel* [I Swing Myself on the Swing] (1974). *Mondschnee liegt auf des Wiesen* [Moonsnow Lies on the Meadows] (1975). *Jetzt wollen wir ein Liedchen singen* [Now We Want to Sing] (1976). *Die eine Rose überwältigt alles* [The One Rose Subdues Everything] (1977). *Briefe aus Schuzenhof* [Letters from Schulzenhof] (1977).

Krim [Crimea] (1980). *Poetic* [Poetics] (1980). *Zikadennächte* [Cicada Nights] (1980).

Bibliography

Franke, Konrad, *Die Literatur der Deutschen Demokratischen Republik* (Zürich und München, 1974). Lennartz, Franz, *Deutsche Schriftsteller des 20. Jahrhunderts im Spiegel der Kritik*. Band 3 (Stuttgart, 1984).

Brigitte Edith Archibald

Anna Strońska

Born March 14, 1931, Przemyśl, Poland
Genre(s): short story, novel, journalism
Language(s): Polish

A journalism graduate of Warsaw University, Strońska began her career in Cracow, writing for the *Gazeta Krakowska* (Cracow Gazette) between 1953 and 1963. In 1954 she married, and her daughter was born in 1956. After receiving first prize in a contest for reportages organized by the *Polityka* weekly, she then worked for it, living in Warsaw—where she still resides—until 1981. In 1982 she resigned from the Polish Writer's Union. In 1985 she joined the staff of the *Odrodzenie* (Rebirth) weekly as a *feuilletoniste*.

Strońska's journalism has the reflective strength of *belles lettres*. Its meditative, charged laconicism is also found in her short stories, e.g., "Palmy w kufrze" (1972; Palms in My Trunk) or her recent novel *Głuche rzeki* (1982; Unheard Currents), a political analysis of the failure of the "propaganda of success" of Poland in the 1970s to assuage the old, festering dissatisfaction with the workings of Party power, which would culminate in the unrest of August 1980. Throughout her work she is attracted to ordinary people who fail to perceive the extraordinariness of their lives. As the terminally ill, concentration camp survivors, or murderers under death sentence recount their experiences in a matter-of-fact tone, Strońska brings out the tension between extreme events and the air of the everyday. As she remarks when contemplating dying patients in "W wolnych chwilach przed śmiercią" (1978; In One's Spare Time Before Death): "As I lay on the neighboring hospital bed I could observe the marvelous calm of people who are very ordinary but deeply attuned to nature, to the biological calendar. There was nothing special about them, but they knew that the laws of the four seasons are true of more than just the corn."

Other books, such as *Tyle szczęscia dla szewców* (1977; All the More for the Woodworm) and *Podróz na kresy* (1979; A Trip to the Borderlands) record her travels in time and space through the former Ukrainian and Jewish areas of Galicia, a world that ceased to be when the Jews were exterminated, the Ukrainians expatriated, and a new border established for the Polish state. She is fascinated by the *kresy*, the borderlands of interwar Poland, by the marginality of the provinces. As in the work of the interwar Polish-Jewish writer Bruno Schulz, they appear as the native realm of kitsch, of naive and cruel childish fantasies. For a long time, she admits, she deliberately got off at the stations where few trains halted. Her travels abroad have yielded the recent *Ściśle prywatna Europa* (1986; A Strictly Personal Europe), inter alia, which treats West German life with an objectivity and insight rare amidst the general tendentiousness of Polish coverage of the German question. Here, as elsewhere, her formula is one of essayistic narration. Her passion for the peripheries and afterimages of cultures culminates in a sense of European culture as itself an increasingly marginal phenomenon.

Works

Okopy świętych Grójców (1964). *Na wysokich ojczyznach* (1965). *Niewolnicy z Niepołomic* (1965). *Głupi ślub* (1966). *Proszę nie podawać nazwiska* (1970). *Palmy w kufrze* (1972). *Panno piękna, piękny mój aniele* (1971). *Kup mi serce* (1975). *Zcie jakie jest* (1976). *Tyle szczęścia dla szewców* (1977). *W wolnych chwilach przed śmiercią* (1978). *Podróz na kresy* (1979). *Droga długa jak Rosja* (1979). *Motyw wschodni* (1981). *Głuche rzeki* (1982). *Ściśle prywatna Europa* (1986).

Irena I. Souness

Alessandra di Filippo Macinghi Strozzi

Born 1407, Florence, Italy; died 1471,
Florence
Genre(s): belle lettres
Language(s): Italian

Alessandra Macinghi, an intelligent and cultured Florentine humanist, married into one of the most influential business families in Florence with her alliance to Matteo Strozzi (1397–1435). Through their five children, particularly eldest son Filippo, the family continued the prestige and financial power exercised since the time of Matteo's grandfather Filippo. The Strozzi were one of the many Florentine families accumulating fortunes throughout Europe at the time and so laying the foundations of the great international, commercial, industrial, and financial center. In 1427, Matteo and Alessandra's taxable net worth of 4,396 florins marked them as one of the 247 wealthiest citizens, in the upper two-and-one-half percent of the Florentine population. The family members were long-standing and numerous: by 1351 there were twenty-eight Strozzi households residing in the parish of S. Pancrazio, in the quarter of *Leon rosso.* They matriculated in several major guilds, most frequently in the cloth importers', money changers', and wool guilds. Branches of the Strozzi business empire existed in Florence, Rome, and Naples, and transactions were primarily within Italy. The Strozzi family, as it outgrew its communal origins, ceased to be a clan, thus losing the tribal instinct that was once a source of social cohesion in corporate society and that was characteristic of Florentine society in general.

Matteo and Alessandra Strozzi had an avid interest in humanist learning, but political misfortune overshadowed the family. Matteo was exiled to Pesaro as a result of the political revolution following the return of Cosimo di Medici in 1434. In Pesaro where Matteo was confined, unable to liquidate Florentine land holdings to acquire capital, he and his family lived frugally. His residence was brief, for his exile was cut short by his death in 1435.

The twenty-nine-year-old pregnant Alessandra returned to Florence with her four small children, but as soon as her sons reached their middle teens, they were brought under the ban against their father and were compelled to leave. Their many years of exile were never regarded as anything other than a prolonged interval to be ended when the family could return to their native city. Impatiently waiting out that interval alone in Florence was Alessandra, whose subsistence was the small amount of real estate left by her husband. This she slowly liquidated for capital for her sons to make their fortune abroad. Despite the decline of her fortune, Alessandra, without wealth or political influence, maintained her status in Florentine society. Her daughters Caterina and Lesandra married into fine old patrician families, Caterina's marriage to Marco Parenti being particularly notable. A forceful woman, Alessandra provided firm guidance for her children; she could bully, entreat, and chide to get her way. She particularly emphasized the strong role men should play in relation to their wives, and generally favored her sons, filling them with ambition.

Perhaps Alessandra's most remarkable contributions were her numerous charming and literate letters to her sons, one of the most appealing social documents of the era. These communications, full of proverbs, folk wisdom, and piety, indicate her continued involvement with the family business, her astute perception in financial matters, and her literary expertise in these and other affairs. They also suggest the illegitimate use of power in Florentine politics, which was based on personal contacts and bribery. Sincere in their sentiment, profound in their religious faith, and candid in their content, they reflect an intelligence and broadly based knowledge which she imparted to her family, as well as a confirmation of her place in elite Florentine society.

When Alessandra died in 1471, her son Filippo received a letter of condolence from the King's son Alfonso, Duke of Calabria. No doubt it was a great loss to the family as well as to the society she so influenced.

Works

Lettere di una gentildonnna fiorentina del sec. XV ai figliuoli esuli, ed. C. Guasti, Firenze (1877; rpt. G. Papini, Lanciano, 1914, and by A. Dorel, Jena,

1927). *Una lettera della Alessandra Macinghi negli Strozzi* (I. Del Lungo, Firenze, 1890).

Bibliography

D'Ancona, A., *Varieta storiche e letterarie*, II Serie (Milano, 1885), pp. 222–238. D'Andrea, Maria, *Una gentildonna fiorentina del 1400* (Naples, 1907). *Dizionario Storico della Letteratura Italiana* (Turin, Milan, Florence, etc. 4th ed., 1960). Goldwaite, Richard A., *Private Wealth in Renaissance Florence: A Study of Four Families* (Princeton, 1968). Labalme, Patricia H., *Beyond their Sex: Learned Women of the European Past* (New York and London, 1980). Martines, Lauro, "A Way of Looking at Women in Renaissance Florence." *Journal of Medieval and Renaissance History* 4 (1974): 15–28.

Jean E. Jost

Lorenza Strozzi

Born 1514, Capalle, Italy; died 1591, Prato
Genre(s): hymn, poetry
Language(s): Latin

Zaccaria di Battista di Giovanni Strozzi, of the famous Florentine family, had five children. His fourth-born was named Francesca. As a very young child she was sent as a boarder ("in serbanza") to the Dominican convent of San Niccolò in Prato, a common practice in Florence in the sixteenth century. By the time she was seven, we are told by her nephew and biographer, Zaccaria Monti, she was well loved by the nuns of that convent. At age thirteen she entered San Niccolò officially, changing her name to Sister Lorenza, and by 1529 she had taken her vows. San Niccolò was a popular convent for the Strozzi women, and in 1529 a list of the professed nuns of the convent included five Strozzis, one of whom, Antonia, Lorenza's aunt, had been prioress, another, Maddalena, was then subprioress. Lorenza's older sister Elisabetta married, while her younger sister, Maria Salome, became a Franciscan nun in the convent of San Giorgio, also in Prato. Like her brother Ciriaco, who taught Greek and philosophy at the University of Bologna, and her other brother Francesco, a doctor of law, Lorenza had scholarly inclinations, which she was able to pursue in the convent while performing her normal duties. She was prioress a number of times, held other offices, and was closely associated with Catherina de' Ricci, a nun in San Niccolò who was later to be canonized.

It was clear from the time she was very young that Lorenza was exceptionally intelligent. While she was a school girl at the convent a special tutor, undoubtedly sent by her family, was brought in to give her lessons in Latin and Greek. When she was not at divine services Lorenza studied the classics, and by the time she was eighteen she was writing poetry in Latin herself. She seems to have known the famous religious reformers Bernardino Ochino and Pietro Martire Vermigli, both of whom later became Protestants and fled Italy. Like many of her contemporaries, while she was attracted by the desire for reform and the spirit of religious renewal, she remained a faithful Catholic. The strength of her faith is confirmed by the religious hymns she wrote and for which she became famous in her time.

The hymns are indebted primarily to Horace's odes and to famous liturgical songs for their meter, and there is one for each of the important feasts of the liturgical calender of the Florentine diocese. Individual compositions are preceded by references to their Horacian source. One hundred and four hymns, all in Latin, composed by 1587, were published at the Giunta Press in Florence in 1588; Lorenza dedicated them to the Bishop of Pistoia, Lattanzio de'Lattanzi, the prelate who had jurisdiction over the convents of Prato. Her hymns were later translated into French by Simeon Georges Pavillon, set to music by Jacques Maudint, and published in Paris in 1601 with a dedication written by her nephew Zaccaria Monti to the Queen of France, Lorenza's compatriot, Maria de' Medici. Lorenza Strozzi's hymns were sung in churches throughout Italy, and she is remembered and praised in the writing of many Tuscan literary historians and of Dominican scholars.

Works

Ven. Laurentiae Stroziae Monialis S. Dominici di Monasterio Divi Nicholai de Prato, in singula totius anni solemnia, Hymni . . . (1588); and again with

French translation by Simeon Georges Pavillon and music by Jacques Maudint (1601).

Bibliography

Bandini Buti, Maria, ed., *Poetesse e scrittrici*, II (*Enciclopedia biografica e bibliografica italiana*, Serie VI) (Rome, 1942), pp. 284–285. Masson, P.M., "Jacques Maudint et les 'Hymnes latines' de Lorenza Strozzi." *Revue de Musicologie* 9 (1925): 6–14, 59–69. Monti, Zaccaria, *Vita di Lorenza Strozzi religiosa domenicana* (Paris, 1510). Pierattini, Giovanna, "Suor Lorenza Strozzi, poetessa domenicana (1514–1591)." *Memorie domenicane* 59 (1942): 113–115, 142–145, 177–183; 60 (1943): 19–25.

Elissa B. Weaver

Karin Struck

Born May 14, 1947, Schlagtow bei Greifswalf, East Germany
Genre(s): novel
Language(s): German

After her family had relocated from East Germany to West Germany, Karin Struck finished her *Abitur* in 1966 and became a student of *Germanistik*, *Romanistik*, and *Psychology*, subjects she considered important for a career as a writer. During her student years she was totally engaged in the extra parliamentary opposition (APO) and the student movement for a democratic society (SDS), fighting against the restoration of her parental generation, against the consumerism of the affluent society, against Vietnam, and believing that a total politicization of society would lead to total change. She soon discovered, however, that all these movements, institutions, and ideologies, despite their revolutionary fervor, were unable to accommodate her own concerns: the demand for subjectivity, the primacy of individual existence, the priority of personal expression, and particularly the urgent importance of motherhood. With this confrontation she became one of the first spokespersons of the literature of New Subjectivity and women's writings.

Karin Struck's novels all reflect a continuous quest for radical authenticity, an involved and involving description of emotional turmoil. From the very first of her books she chose as her typical style the autobiographical form; it allows for the most intense, direct, and appellative discourse between the narrative "I" and reader. This seemingly self-revealing modus serves Struck's all-pervading typical queries into love and death, accounts that detail socially complex and sexually explicit relationships, accounts of motherhood that plead for a right-to-life stance, in which fertility is more important than marriage and accounts of death experiences from suicide to drug destructiveness. Form and contents of her writings meet in an overabundance of emotional outflow, dominated by an almost excessive female perspective. The titles of her novels reveal to a large degree her concerns. There have been public clashes between the author and feminist circles.

Works

Klassenliebe (1973). *Die Mutter* (1975). *Lieben* (1977). *Trennung* (1978). *Die Herberge* (1981). *Kindheitsende. Journal einer Krise* (1982). *Zwei Frauen* (1982). *Finale* (1984).

Bibliography

Alder, Hans, and Joachim Schrimpf, eds., *Karin Struck* (Frankfurt/Main, 1984).

Margaret Eifler

Marie Stuart

Born Linlithgow, Scotland; died 1587, London, England
Genre(s): poetry
Language(s): French

Daughter of the King of Scotland James V and of Marie of Lorraine, Marie Stuart was raised in France and married in 1558 to Francis II, heir to the throne of France. She became queen of France in 1559, but when her husband died the following year, she returned to reign in Scotland. Several plays and films have made her successive marriages and her decapitation, ordered by Elizabeth of England after nineteen years of prison, well known throughout four centuries.

A fervent Catholic, Marie Stuart was also an accomplished musician and a poet.

Bibliography

The Poems of Mary Queen of Scots (1873). Barbé, Louis, "Poésies françaises de Marie Stuart." *Livre* (1883). Malinowski, J., "Vers authentiques de la reine Marie Stuart." *Bull. Soc. Lot* (1884). Pawlowski, "Poésies françaises de la reine M.S." *Livre* (1883).

Marie-France Hilgar

Valja Stýblova

Born June 4, 1922, Kharbin, The Soviet Union
Genre(s): prose, children's literature
Lnguage(s): Czech

On finishing grammar school, Valja Stýblová studied piano, then entered the medical faculty of Charles University in Prague in 1945, later becoming head of the Neurological Clinic in Prague. She is currently also an Associate Professor in Medical Sciences at Charles University. As a novelist Stýblová incorporates in her work themes drawn from her professional milieu, emphasizing the moral aspect of everyday issues. She has received literary awards for her work which has been translated into English, German, Polish, Slovenian, and Byelorussian.

Works

Mne Soudila Noc [The Night Judged Me](1957). *Dům u Nemocnice* [A House Near the Hospital] (1959). *Moje Velká Víra* [My Great Belief] (1960). *Dopis Kláře* [Letter to Klara] (1963). *A' Bude Padat Hvězda* [When a Star Falls] (1966). *Nenávidím a Miluji* [I Hate and Love] (1969). *MSj Brácha* [My Brother] (1973). *Na Konci Aleje* [At the End of the Alley] (1979).

Warwick J. Rodden

María Aurelia Suárez de Deza

Born 1920, Buenos Aires, Argentina
Genre(s): drama
Language(s): Spanish

The daughter of Spaniards, María Isabel Suárez de Deza came to Spain permanently at age twelve and feels completely Spanish. Her plays, imaginative and poetic, show crimes of passion, savage environments, and the personification of teluric forces. Two of her plays won major prizes in the fifties: *Grito en el mar* (A Cry at Sea) and *Buenas noches* (Good Evening). The latter play concerns a woman who appeases a demented widower by saying "Good Evening" each afternoon in the role of the dead wife.

Works

Buenas noches [Good Evening] (1951).

Bibliography

O'Connor, Patricia W., "¿Quiénes son las dramaturgas españolas, y qué han escrito?" *Estreno* 10.2 (1984): 9–12. "Encuesta: ¿Por qué no estrenan las mujeres en España?" *Estreno* 10.2: 25. Pasero, Anne, "Woman's 'Second self' in María Isabel Suárez de Deza's *Buenas noches*." *Estreno* 16.1 (Spring 1990). O'Connor, Patricia W., *Dramaturgas españolas de hoy* (Madrid, 1989).

Patricia W. O'Connor

Sara Copia Sullam

Born 1588, Venice, Italy; died February 15, 1641, Venice
Genre(s): poetry, epistolary literature
Language(s): Italian

Born in Venice of a wealthy Jewish family, Sara Copia Sullam received an outstanding formal education which included not only a thorough knowledge of the Old Testament, of the sciences, of philosophy, theology and of classical literatures but also the study of Latin, Greek, Hebrew and Spanish. In the cultural milieu of Venice she became particularly familiar with Italian literature and culture. After her marriage to Ciacobbe Sullam in 1614, Sara became famous as the brilliant host of a literary salon distinguished by her critical spirit, by her gifts of conversation and by the literary personalities that frequented her home, such as Giovanni Basadonna, Baldassarre Bonifacio, Alessandro Berardelli, Gianfrancesco Corniani and Numidio Paluzzi.

Sara's fame and notoriety, however, are tied to the name of Ansaldo Cebà, a Genoese nobleman and monk who, in 1615, published the religious heroic epic poem *La Reina Ester*. Overwhelmed by the beauty of the composition, Sara wrote a complimentary letter to the author which marked the beginning of an epistolary correspondence that lasted for four years (1618–1622) and which took the form of letters and of sonnets. Sara praised Cebà for having chosen as heroine the tragic biblical Esther rather than drawing on traditional classical themes. Cebà, who unsuccessfully tried to convert Sara to the Christian faith, in 1623 published the 53 *lettere* that he had written to her but omitted from this publication those that Sara had written to him.

In 1621 Baldassarre Bonifacio, later Cardinal of Capodistria, published a small volume titled *Dell'immortalita' dell'anima* in which he attacked Sara by claiming that she denied the immortality of the soul. Sara replied the same year with a pamphlet, *Manifesto di Sarra Copia Silam Hebrea*, published in Venice, rejecting Baldassarre's accusation. Worthy of note is her friendship, in this period, with the Italian poet Leone Modena who in 1619 dedicated to Sara his tragedy *Esther* and even composed her epitaph. Although not much of her literary production remains, a volume of her collected sonnets appeared in 1887 in Bologna: *S.C. Sullam, Sonetti editi e inediti, raccolti insieme ad alquanti cenni biografici.*

Bibliography

Boccato, C., "Un episodio della vita di S.C.Sullam: il 'Manifesto sull'immortalita' dell'anima.'" *Rassegna mensile di Israel,* s. 3, 39 (1973): 633–646. Boccato, C., "Lettere di Ansaldo Cebà, genovese, a S.C. Sullam, poetessa del Ghetto di Venezia." *Rassegna mensile di Israel,* s. 3, 40 (1974): 169–191. Sarot, E., "Ansaldo Cebà and S.C. Sullam." *Italica* 31 (1954): 138–149.

Sandro Sticca

Sulpicia (1)

Flourished late 1st c. B.C., Rome
Genre(s): elegiac poetry
Language(s): Latin

Sulpicia was the niece and probably the ward of M. Valerius Messalla Corvinus, the eminent literary patron of the Augustan Age; his circle included, among others, Tibullus and Ovid. Sulpicia is the author of six short love elegies, that are preserved together with the works of Tibullus as part of the *Tibullianum Corpus* (Book IV.7–12). She is thus the only example of a *docta puella* whose works survive. The *doctae puellae* were the "learned" female companions of the elegists, often mentioned by Catullus, Ovid, Propertius, and others as an important element in their social and creative lives. While Sulpicia's extant works total only forty lines, they still manage to represent a wide variety of themes, for the most part traditional ones in elegy. All her poems deal with her love for an aristocratic Roman youth whom she addresses by the pseudonym Cerinthus. In them she exults over the consummation of their love (IV.7); laments that she must go to the country with Messalla to celebrate her birthday, rather than remain in the city with Cerinthus as she would prefer (IV.8); rejoices that Messalla has changed his plan, and that she will spend her birthday with Cerinthus after all (IV.9); complains of Cerinthus' unfaithfulness to her, with a woman she describes as sordid and of low class (IV.10); reports that she is ill with a fever but that her principal concern is whether Cerinthus really cares about her recovery (IV.11); and apologizes for her apparent coolness to him on one occasion (IV.12). Attempts have been made, as with Catullus' Lesbia sequence, to place these miscellaneous poems into some reasonably coherent chronological order; all such attempts must by their nature be based largely on subjective considerations. Critics are divided on the poetic merit of Sulpicia's works; but there is general agreement on their deeply felt emotion and sincerity. Some have professed to find, not only in the quality of the emotions expressed in Sulpicia's poems, but also in their syntax, metrics, and style, specifically "feminine" characteristics. In view of the smallness of the sampling, and because there is literally nothing else in Latin literature to compare with it, it is probably prudent to reserve judgment in this regard. This Sulpicia is not to be confused with another poet of the same name who lived about a century later (see the following item, Sulpicia [2]).

Bibliography

Currie, H. MacL., "The Poems of Sulpicia." *Aufstieg und Niedergand der römischen Welt* II.30.3 (1983), pp. 1751–1764, and bibliography. Kroll, W., in Pauly-Wissowa, *Realenzyklopädie* IV.A.1 (1931), cols. 879–880, s.v. Sulpicia (114). Santirocco, Matthew S., "Sulpicia Reconsidered." *Classical Journal* LXXIV (1979): 229–239. Schanz, M. and C. Hosius, *Geschichte der römischen Literatur* (Munich, 1935), vol. 2, pp. 189–191.

Paul Pascal

Sulpicia (2)

Flourished late 1st c. A.D., Rome
Genre(s): poetry
Language(s): Latin

Sulpicia's writings are not preserved, and little is known of her other than what can be deduced from two epigrams about her by the epigrammatist Martial (X.35, X.38, published in A.D. 95). From these it emerges that she was married to a man named Calenus, that the marriage was a phenomenally happy and durable one, and that Sulpicia wrote lyric poems about their love, and about their lovemaking, in an explicit and perhaps even ribald style. What may be the one fragment of her lyrics that survives (two lines of iambic senarii, quoted in somewhat garbled form in an ancient commentary on Juvenal VI.537) appears to bear this out. Martial compares Sulpicia favorably with Sappho. It is possible that her work survived until late antiquity, judging by references to it in Ausonius, Fulgentius, and Sidonius Apollinaris; but it is more likely that these references are simply based on the material in Martial. A satire of seventy lines dealing with the expulsion of the philosophers from Rome in the reign of Domitian has been attributed to Sulpicia on dubious grounds. This Sulpicia is not to be confused with another poet of the same name who lived about a century earlier (see the preceding item, Sulpicia [1]).

Bibliography

Kroll, W., in Pauly-Wissowa, *Realenzyklopädie* IV.A.1 (1931), cols. 880–882, s.v. Sulpicia (115). Schanz, M. and C. Hosius, *Geschichte der römischen Literatur* (Munich, 1935), vol. 2, pp. 560–561. Also see *Testimonia*, in Otto Jahn's edition of Juvenal; 4th edition by Friedrich Leo (Berlin, 1910).

Paul Pascal

Celia Suñol

Born 1899, Barcelona, Spain
Genre(s): novel, short story, translation
Language(s): Spanish, Catalan

Most of Suñol's life was spent in her native Barcelona, where she was raised in the early years of the century. Plagued by illness and lacking training for a career, she married but suffered psychological crises and the death of her first husband. After initial contacts with the feminist movement, she married again, but was widowed once more within a few years. To support her children, she worked as a barmaid, a seamstress, and finally as a translator. Many of these experiences are fictionalized against the background of Barcelona in the early decades of the twentieth century in her autobiographical first novel, *Primera part* (1948; First Part). This novel is significant for extra-literary reasons: Suñol was the first woman writer in Catalan to break the silence imposed by the Franco regime's prohibition of publishing in the vernacular, after a decade of outlaw status. Some of Suñol's work as a barmaid provided material for the ambience and certain characters portrayed in her second novel, *Bar* (written in 1949 but unpublished). *Bar* was prohibited by the censors because it ended with the protagonist's suicide, and suicide—as a mortal sin of which it was impossible to repent—was abhorrent to the regime. A collection of brief fiction, also with significant autobiographical substrata, is *L'home de les fires i altres contes* (1950; The Man of the Fairs, and Other Stories). Perhaps this is Suñol's most significant work as well as the most consciously feminist. In the title tale, the narrator-protagonist longs to devote herself to literature, but in the conflict between domestic duties and writing, creativity is overwhelmed by the pressing necessity to cook her children's meals. The unfinished story is saved for another day while the would-be writer devotes herself to cleaning and her kitchen. This story, and others like it, proved involuntarily prophetic, for notwithstanding awareness of her talent, Suñol abandoned writing to care for her children. Had this not been the case, current feminist writing in Catalan might have had a significant precursor, for Suñol's tone and themes resemble those of much later writers such as Núria Pompeia and Maria Antònia Oliver.

Works

L'home de les fires i altres contes (1950). Primera part (1948).

Janet Perez

Kerttu-Kaarina Suosalmi

Born September 9, 1921, Lahti, Finland
Genre(s): poetry, youth literature, short story, novel, drama
Language(s): Finnish

Kerttu-Kaarina Suosalmi is a versatile writer: her works include two early collections of poems of minor importance, five books for children and young people (new versions of the classical fairy-tale styles), several distinguished short stories, five novels, and several plays.

Suosalmi graduated from high school in 1943 and took a degree in sociology in 1946 at the High School of Social Sciences. She also studied Finnish literature and social policy at Helsinki University, and worked as a teacher. She is now a full-time writer, living near Lahti.

The small town, often with features reminiscent of her home town Lahti, is the chief milieu in Suosalmi's works. She does not write of the romance of the small town but of the conflicts concealed there. The characters in her novels come from the middle class: small business men, people in service jobs, minor officials. "I wanted to write about a man, unseen and unheard, who doesn't appear on the stage of life, who melts into the crowd," Suosalmi says. These followers of the middle road are often in the grip of extreme situations in her novels, reassessing their lives and relations to others. Decisive liberation may occur through the undergoing of childhood traumas; in the novel Venematka (1974; Boat Trip), there is a momentary flight back to childhood scenes.

Besides illustrating the psychological development of the individual, Suosalmi's novels provide a broad view of society about which they were written. Hyvin toimeentulevat ihmiset (1969; Prosperous People) has even been considered a report on the ideological state of the educated classes in the 1960s. Suosalmi's novels breathe the despair, the inertia of the middle classes. In particular she sharply describes educated men's ineffectiveness and inability to act rather than speak. The crucial conflict of her novels is the sensitive, aware person in an environment emphasizing increasingly materialistic values.

War interests Suosalmi in a broad sense, stimulated perhaps by Karl von Clausewitz's War. "War is in me," says a character in Suosalmi's most recent novel. Human life appears as a constant struggle for power and territory; all intercourse is warfare. Suosalmi markedly emphasizes individualism though her characters may be socially representative types. She does not accept the solution of withdrawing behind a collective morality but constantly demands greater self-awareness and personal decision.

Suosalmi has followed her own line, not turning aside to indulge in literary fashions. She constantly wrestles with the fundamental questions of existence. Her oeuvre is in a sense one big novel although her books are very different in form: her first novel Neitsyt (1964; Maiden) and Venematka (1974) are spare and highly controlled; Hyvin toimeentulevat ihmiset (1969) is more experimental; in Jeesuksen pieni soturi (1976; Jesus' Little Warrior), the writer uses for the first time the long monologue; Onnen metsämies (1982; Fortune's Hunter) is experimental in structure, deliberately incomplete, shapeless. As a narrator, Suosalmi is unusually intense and uncompromising. Her descriptions of the middle class are among the most durable of their kind in Finland. Her collection of short stories Rakas rouva (1979; Dear Mrs K.) is successful in catching the atmosphere of wartime from the viewpoints of a small town newspaperman and a station master.

Works

Poetry: Melanmitta [Paddle-length] (1950). Meren Maaria [Maaria of the Sea] (1952).

For children and young people: Uudenkuun juhla eli tarinoita vanhasta talosta [Feast of the New Moon or Tales of an Old House] (1955). Sadun lintu ja Takkutukka. Tarinoita pienistä tytöistä [The Fairytale Bird and Mophead. Tales of Little Girls] (1960). Tule takaisin, Menninkäinen! Satu [Gnome, Come

Back! A Fairy-tale] (1961). *Tehtävä UPT* [Task UPT] (1963). *Nyt saapuu Annamaria* [Annamaria is Coming Now] (1965). *Tummelin kevät* [Tummeli's Spring] (1976).

Short stories: *Synti* [Sin] (1957). *Rakas rouva* [Dear Mrs. K.] (1979).

Novels: *Neitsyt* [Maiden] (1964). *Hyvin toimeentulevat ihmiset* [Prosperous People] (1969). *Venematka* [Boat Trip] (1974). *Jeesuksen pieni soturi* [Jesus' Little Warrior] (1976). *Onnen metsämies* [Fortune's Hunter] (1982).

Plays: *Satahampaiset* [The Hundred-toothed] (1981).

Bibliography

Kuivasmäki, Riitta, ed., "Kirjailija Kerttu-Kaarina Suosalmi. Katsauksia ja analyysiharjoituksia Kerttu-Kaarina Suosalmen tuotannosta" [The Writer Suosalmi. Surveys and Analyses of Her Works]. Jyväskylä University Mimeo 12 (1980). Lassila, Eija, "Kerttu Kaarina Suosalmen romaanien maailmankatsomus" [World View in Novels of Suosalmi]. Oulu University Mimeo series, 8 (1984), Haavikko, Ritva, ed., *Miten kirjani ovat syntyneet 2* [How My Books Originated, 2] (1980), pp. 168–187. Niemi, Juhani, "Kerttu-Kaarina Suosalmi, maakylän Shakespeare" [Suosalmi, a Village Shakespeare], in *Kirjailijoita ja epäkirjailijoita* [Writers and Unwriters] (1983) pp. 49–56. Nupponen, Terttu, "Hyvin toimeentulevat ihmiset" [Prosperous People], in Mirjam Polkunen, ed., *Romaani ja tulkinta* [The Novel and the Interpretation] (1973), pp. 189–201. Viikari, Auli "The Search for Spontaneity. Conversation with Kerttu-Kaarina Suosalmi. An Extract from *Rakas rouva* [Dear Mrs. K.]. *Books from Finland* 21 (1980): 52–61. Viikari, Auli, Vastavirtaan/Onnen metsämies [Against the Stream/Fortune's Hunter]. *Parnasso* (1983): 130–141.

Päivi Karttunen

Margarete Susman

Born October 14, 1874, Hamburg, Germany;
died January 16, 1966
Genre(s): poetry, scholarship, novel,
philosophy
Language(s): German

Margarete Susman is the maiden name of Margarete von Bendemann-Susman. A German poet, writer, scholar, theorist, artist, public speaker, and socialist activist, her reputation rests mainly on her being a controversial woman philosopher of religion who spoke up for the Jews.

Susman was born to the family of a wealthy businessman in Hamburg in 1874. Her training as an artist began early. At the age of eight, she was sent to Zürich, where she attended a "*höhere Töchterschule.*" Her upbringing, a religious one with Protestant inclinations, was rather open-minded. In spite of her parents' liberal attitudes, however, she was not given a formal education. Instead, having undergone rigorous initial academic training under her father, she attended the Arts Academy in Düsseldorf and studied painting, where she met Eduard von Bendemann, a painter and art historian who later became her husband. While studying art in Paris, Munich, and Berlin, she also became a regular auditor in philosophy lectures, which proved to have a decisive impact on her career. She was a welcome guest in the seminars of Theodor Lipps and, especially, Georg Simmel, whom she rewarded with a book in her final years, *Die geistige Gestalt Georg Simmels* (1959; Georg Simmel's Mental Gestalt). These academic activities turned Susman into a great learner and scholar on her own.

In 1901, Susman made her debut as a lyrical poet with a volume of poems, *Mein Land* (My Land), though an earlier collection had been printed privately in 1892. Academic thinking obviously had no adverse affect on her creativity, for she turned out volume after volume of poetry. However, Susman was destined to claim her laurels off the beaten track: she decided to be a philosopher of religion when an article she contributed to the "Frankfurter Zeitung" (May 16, 1907) caused a great sensation. In her article, "Judentum und Kultur" (Jewry and Culture), she went against the grain by questioning the current tendency toward the solution of the problem of Jews. As a matter of principle, she proposed, the relationship between Jews and Germans had to be taken into consideration. The article was a point of departure for her. Thereafter, she devoted herself to articles, lectures, and books on religion, sociology, and psychology. The major concern of these efforts focused on the general question of the relationship between "God's people" (the Jews) and Christians and Germans in the history of ideas. In her most significant work, *Das Buch Hiob und das Schicksal des jüdischen Volkes* (1946; The Book of Job and the Fate of the Jewish People), she arrived at the most profound answer of her own: between the synagogue and the church, no barrier should ever exist.

Since her first article, Susman remained one of the most important contributors to the "Frankfurter Zeitung," for which she was a regular literary correspondent between 1900–1920. Her book, *Das Wesen der modern deutschen Lyrik* (The Nature of Modern German Lyrical Poetry), was a result of this activity. She had also been a long-time contributor to the "Morgan." In 1912, she published *Vom Sinn der Liebe* (Of the Desire of Love), a work appreciated by Scheler but rejected by Musil. After World War I and the dissolution of her marriage, reminiscences of which were given in *Ich habe viele Leben gelebt* (Much Life Have I Lived), she published a series of major works including *Frauen der Romantik* (1929, rev. 1960; Women of the Romantic Age); the book on Goethe and Charlotte von Stein, entitled *Deutung einer großen Liebe* (1951; Interpretation of a Great Love Affair); and the collection of essays, *Gestaltern und Kreise* (1954; Creator and Circles); *Vom Geheimnis der Freiheit* (1965; The Secret of Freedom).

In 1933, Susman immigrated to Zürich, where she was actively involved in the socialist-religious circle of the theologian Leonhard Ragaz ("Neue Wege. Blätter für den Kampf der Zeit"; New Paths—Papers for the Combat of the Time). Because of this, she was suspected to be an extreme leftist, and in 1937 she was banned from speaking and writing. As a result, she had to publish in part under the pseudonym of "Reiner" in Swiss newspapers and magazines. Susman continued to live in Zürich after the war. Although she lost her eyesight in her old age, Susman was still constantly at work until she died in 1966.

Susman was one of those German writers who, after withdrawing to a simplified order of life, remained unknown to or misunderstood by the general public. Seeking to reconcile the various strains of antitheses in herself, she received, ironically, both rejection and applause from the wrong people. In France, where such ambivalence was more readily appreciated, she was the only important German representative to attend the famous talks of Pontigny (1925–1928).

Her poetry is closely akin to the melancholy and weariness of the New Romantics; themes of an early expressionism are also present. For Susman, writing was also a part of the effort to cope with the world's problem in the interest of a new community. Owing to her determined will to action and dedication to the destiny of the time, and because of formal problems and on the grounds of the discussions with Karl Wolfskehl, at one point she withdrew copies of *Mein Land* from circulation. Susman's lyrical poetry is characterized by serious interrogations of and direct engagement with life. Mostly written in meditative blank verse, there is an original voice of her own throughout. Nevertheless, the volumes of poems including *Neue Gedichte* (1907; New Poems), *Die Liebenden* (1917; Loved Ones), *Lieder von Tod und Erlösung* (1922; Songs of Death and Redemption), and even the later collection *Aus sich wandelnder Zeit* (1955; From Changing Times) as well, can only be regarded as by-products of her entire output.

Her prose was derived from experience, with the evidence of a pure subjectivity identifying itself with the object. Whether on Kafka, Moses Mendelssohn, Franz Rosenzweig, Dostoyevsky, Nietzsche, or Goethe, her essays attend to suggestiveness rather than seek to provide mere information. The essays are in general philosophical, and one has to get used to her bold, deliberate, and occasionally irritating interpretations of the facts she was dealing with. She is fond of conjuring a host of images to invoke a call to action; hers is a rhetorically and rhythmically structured prose with intentions which she did not even seek to hide. Revolving around herself as a center, what her writing attempted to do was the expansion of personal existence to a wider circle of influence. Like Bloch, Buber, Gurewitsch, Landauer, Lukács, Rosenzweig, and Leopold Ziegler, over the years she played a decisive part through the "Frankfurter Zeitung" in contribution to the development of the spirit of revolution. Susman was also associated, closely or briefly, with well known figures such as Simmel, Groethuysen, Landauer, Rosenzweig, George, Wolfskehl, and (in her last years) Celan.

Susman's discursive writing was often intended to provoke the public. In her numerous articles and reviews, there is an acute attention to that which was new in her times. She sympathized, for instance, with the cause of Jewish women, particularly Berta Pappenheim. Writing had a special meaning to Susman, because her attempt to reconcile her role as a writer and as a wife and woman eventually failed. As her marriage broke to pieces, she underwent a state of psychological crisis. In a sense, she found a way out through literature and philosophy, for which she had a constant love. From these there issued, for her, such a great fascination that she was more than willing to be a spokeswoman of her time through her writing.

Works

Poetry: *Gedichte* (1892, privately printed). *Mein Land* (1901). *Neue Gedichte* (1907). *Die Liebenden* (1917). *Lieder von Tod und Erlösung* (1922). *Aus sich wandelnder Zeit*, anthology (1953).

Philosophy, critical studies, prose: *Vom Sinn der Liebe* (1912). *Das Wesen der modernen deutschen Lyrik* (1912). *Die Revolution und die Frau* (1918). *Das Kruzifix* (1922; novel). *Frauen der Romantik* (1929, 1960). *Das Buch Hiob und das Schicksal des jüdischen Volkes* (1946). *Deutung einer großen Liebe* (1951). *Gestalten und Kreise* (1954). *Deutung biblischer Gestalten* (1956). *Die geistige Gestalt Georg Simmels* (1959). *Ich habe viele Leben gelebt*, autobiographical reminiscences (1964). *Vom Geheimnis der Freiheit: Gesammelte Aufsätze 1914–1964*, selected essays, ed. Manfred Schlösser (1965).

Other works: [With H. Simon], *Philosophie der Romantik* by E. Kircher (1906). Introduction to *Brücke und Tür*, ed. M. Landmann (1957). Contributions to "Frankfurter Zeitung." Contributions to "Neue Wege. Blätter für den Kampf der Zeit." Contributions to "Morgan."

Bibliography

Brinker-Gabler, Gisela, ed., *Deutsche Literatur von Frauen*. 2 vols., Vol. II (Munich, 1988). Schlösser, Manfred, ed., *Auf gespaltenem Pfad–Für Margarete Susman*. Schlösser, Manfred, "Susman," in *Handbuch der deutschen Gegenwartsliteratur*, ed. Hermann Kunish, 2 vols., Vol. II (Munich, 1970). Schlösser, Manfred, "Susman," in *Lexikon der deutschsprachigen* (Munich, 1981). Schlösser, Manfred, ed., "Margarete Susman," in the "Dokumentarischer Teil" to *An den Wind geschrieben: Lyrik der Freiheit, 1933–1945*, ed. Manfred Schlösser (Darmstadt, 1961).

Balance Chow

Liūnė Sutema

(a.k.a. Zinaida Nagytė-Katiliškienė)

Born 1927, Ma'eikiai, Lithuania
Genre(s): poetry
Language(s): Lithuanian

Sutema withdrew to the West to escape the second Soviet occupation in 1944; she studied German literature and psychology in Innsbruck, Austria, and in Freiburg, Germany. In 1949 she married the Lithuanian writer Marius Katiliškis (pseudonym of Albinas Vaitkus) and became a widow in 1980. Sutema works as a nurse's aide in a home for the elderly and also teaches at a Lithuanian Saturday school in Lemont, Illinois.

Since her first book of verse, *Tebūnie tartum pasakoj* (1955; Let It Be as in a Fairy Tale), Sutema has published four more collections of increasingly tragic intensity. The greatest tension in her poetry arises from the confrontation of her own life, and that of her fellow Lithuanian refugees, with the trauma of exile and dispossession. There is an enemy stalking her verse— a barbaric force, easily recognized as Stalin's criminal empire in some of the poems, but assuming the quality of an almost metaphysical presence in some others. It invades the dreams of the exile, turning them into cold and silent nightmare visions of the lost homeland in which, as in Kafka's vision, things are terrible because they are there; they seem ordinary and yet have changed into some ghastly apparition of themselves. This evil force dispossesses the artist of language—the body of images, symbolic associations, turns of style, and value markers—the entire poetic tradition accumulated during the time when the country was free. Now, enslaved, this country no longer answers to any of the names the poets have called it. For the exiles, the additional calamity is the loss of their own relevance to the country, and also the loss of any relevance of the artistic language they had brought along to the realities of new places. In such a context, Sutema writes: "the words I brought with me / have no more things, / the things I brought with me / have no more names."

In this situation, Sutema's instinct for personal and moral survival as an artist has led her to seek a new kind of language for herself, one that could resurrect dead words into a new reality of exile while also restoring their relevance to the lost land of their birth. In some of her earlier collections, particularly *Nebėra nieko svetimo* (1962; Nothing is Alien Any More) there is optimism, a belief that a synthesis, or at least some symbiotic relationship between the new country and the old language, could be found that would alleviate the alienation of both. Perceiving the new world symbolically as a tree, Sutema wrote:

> Nothing is alien any more,
> the tree I'd never seen has grown
> and spread its branches in my eyes—
> the pattern of its stinging leaves
> is breathing now inside my palms. (p. 29)

In later poetry, the hope, or even the desire for such an organic unity with the soil of exile seems to fade away as it becomes increasingly evident to the poet that the burden of dead words and things is really but a small part of the entire existential anguish of the calamitous twentieth century weighing on the soul. Sutema then tries to turn her poetry into a radical declaration that one must cleanse, burn out, starve under a merciless desert sun all that there is in this nightmare of putrefying memory and pain of dispossession, and of all the helpless lies that the world has resorted to in the hope of accommodating itself somehow to the dumb force of the century's damnation. In her book *Badmetis* (1972; Time of Famine) Sutema discovers that great and shapeless evil of our epoch is not really an outside presence, but rather constitutes an integral part of ourselves, like some monstrous cancer taking over the functions of its host, the living organism. The cleansing conflagration then is acted out as a gigantic battle, a defense of one's own integrity against the "wolves" that turn out to be a part of oneself. More and more. Sutema's poetry acquires the vocabulary of defense, enclosure, secretiveness, stubborn resolve to endure, of fear of being overcome, of a sort of suicidal honesty that becomes a sacrificial act to free the soul.

In this grim topography of Sutema's verse, we do encounter many signs and symbols, themes and images from the folkloric dimension, from the "lyrical mythology" in Lithuanian mythical memory that has spun out its fairytales, songs, and visions. Even when she harshly refuses to forgive her century and asks not to be forgiven herself, there is this melodious undertone of gentle feeling from folklore, from little details of observed reality, from the heart, that gives a sort of lyrical dignity to her bitter confrontation with the tragic realities of her time.

Works

Tebūnie tartum pasakoj (1955). Nebėra nieko svetimo (1962). Bevardė šalis (1966). Badmetis (1972). Vendeta (1981).

Bibliography

Bilaišytė, Živilė, "Liūnės Sutemos daiktai ir 'od'iai." *Metmenys* 26 (1973). Mackus, Algimantas, "Nebėra nieko svetimo." *Metmenys* 5 (1962). Šilbajoris, R., "Image Development in the Poetry of Liūnė Sutema." *Lituanus* 34, No. 1 (1988).

R. Šilbajoris

Berta von Suttner

(a.k.a. B. Oulet)

Born July 9, 1843, Prague, Czechoslovakia;
    died June 21, 1914, Vienna, Austria
Genre(s): novel, short story, lyric, drama text,
    essay, autobiography
Language(s): German

Berta von Suttner's work brought her fame in the first place because of its themes and the engagement and the enthusiasm it conveys.

Berta von Suttner stems from an old prestigious family of the Austrian aristocracy. Her father was a high-ranking officer, her mother came from a family of poets and writers; she was born a Korner. The militaristic-aristocratic background of von Suttner and the political climate of the second half of the nineteenth century determined her career, the themes of her work and her engagement in antiwar propaganda.

Born in 1843, von Suttner married young and against the will of her family. Her husband was Arthus von Suttner, a writer of reputation and a member of the nobility himself. Husband and wife left Austria to escape the altercations with her parents and lived in Tiflis, now in the Soviet Union, where Arthur worked as an engineer and a war correspondent and Berta became a teacher. Later they moved back to Austria, where both became literarily and politically active. Both were independent, liberal thinkers, who could not agree with the contemporary socio-political climate. Arthur von Suttner joined his wife in her antiwar activities, while he himself was engaged in a league in Vienna, fighting antisemitism. In 1883, Berta's first novel had appeared, called *Inventarium einer Seele* (Inventory of a Soul). When her greatest success was published in 1889, she thus was already an established and accredited author. *Die Waffen nieder* (Lay Down Your Arms), became the basis for her world fame. The positive and negative letters of response, collected and preserved by Berta herself, have all been published in her *Memoiren* (Memoirs). Alfred Nobel congratulated her and asked her to work for him again, as she had been his personal secretary before she married Arthur, an offer that she declined. Leo Tolstoy compared the novel to Harriet Beecher Stowe's work, so that *Die Waffen nieder* received the unofficial subtitle "The 'Uncle Tom's Cabin' of the Peace Movement." Felix Dahn wrote a satire on the novel and attacked von Suttner for her antiwar propaganda. The Social Democrats, on the other hand, again tried to use her and her reputation for their own work. In 1891 she founded the Austrian Peace Society and supported Alfred Nobel in his efforts to establish a society in Germany in 1892. Between 1892 and 1899 von Suttner was the chief editor and publisher of the pacifist newspaper *Die Waffen nieder*, founded

an International League, and received in 1905, the first woman ever to do so, the Nobel Prize for Peace through the initiative of Nobel himself.

Her knowledge and the serious dedication to whatever she was doing are reflected in the novel *Mashinenzeitalter* (1899; Age of the Machine) and in the reaction to this work. Critics of the time were convinced that leading scholars and scientists had compiled the information. *Die Waffen nieder* became the most politically influential novel in Europe. The last printing appeared in 1914, shortly before World War I broke out. The book title can be regarded as a summary of her life and aspirations, and her battle cry until her death. The novel covers the time period between the childhood of the fictitious heroine and the Franco-German war in 1870/71. The fictitious autobiography carries traits of Berta's own life and has led readers to believe that Berta and the heroine must be identical. Except for the fact that Berta's husband did not die during the war, the background, the education of the heroine, the attitudes and expectations towards life and war, the lifestyle of the family and the heroine all parallel Berta's own life too much as not to see her behind her heroine. Looking back, the heroine remembers the past forty years of her life, especially the long list of battles and wars. It is as if "normal" life and the problems of everyday situations are completely irrelevant when it comes to fighting for the glory of the fatherland. The image of a perverted society, of a perverted age, is painted. The irony, the sarcasm, the wit with which Berta/Martha described the military enthusiasm of a seventeen-year-old girl is overwhelming. Berta's language and her ability to play with it are perfect. She involves the reader and allows him or her to feel with the heroine as she presents the pros and cons of warfare objectively and rationally. The novel is not only a sentimental story but also a thorough survey of the actual political and social conditions of the time. Here, as in other works, von Suttner proved that she was not only an idealistic woman but a serious and critical observer of her age and an educated witness of Europe's past.

Works

Novels and novellas: *Inventarium einer Seele* (1883). *Ein Manuskrip* (1884). *Ein schlechter Mensch* (1885). *Daniela Dormes* (1886). *Highlife* (1886). *Verkettungen* (1887). *Erzählte Lustspiele* (1888). *Schriftsteller-Roman* (1888). *Die Waffen nieder* (1889). *An der Riviera* (1892). *Eva Siebeck* (1892). *Die Tiefinnersten* (1893). *Trente-et-quarante* (1893). *Vor dem Gewitter* (1893). *Im Berghause* (1893). *Phantasie über "Gotha"* (1893). *Es Löwos* (1893). *Das Maschinenzeitalter* (1899). *Der Krieg und seine Bekämpfung* (1904). *Marthas Kinder* (1902). *Ketten und Verkettungen* (1904). *Briefe an einen Toten* (1904). *Babies siebente Liebe* (1905). *Stimmen und Gestalten* (1907). *Gesammelte Werke* (1907). *Der Menschheit Hochgedanken* (1911). *Rüstet ab!* (1960).

Short stories: *Doktor Hellmuths Donnerstage* (1892). *Krieg und Frieden* (1895). *Der Kaiser von Europa* (1897). *Schmetterlinge* (1897). *Franzl und Mirzl* (1905).

Essays: *Randglossen zur Zeitgeschichte* (1906). *Der Kampf um die Vermeidung des Weltkrieges* (1917). *Rüstung und Überrüstung* (1909). *Die Barbarisierung der Luft* (1912). *Aus der Werkstatt des Pazifismus* (1912). *Der Kampf um die Vermeidung des Weltkrieges* (1917).

Other: *Frühlingszeit, eine Lenzes-und Lebensgabe*, lyrics (1896). *Schach der Qual*, drama text (1898). *Die Haager Konferenz*, autobiography (1900). *Memoiren*, memoirs (1905).

Translations: *Lay Down Your Arms!* (1891). *Memoirs of Berta von Suttner* (1972).

Jutta Hagedorn

Henriette de Coligny, Comtesse de La Suze

Born 1618, Paris, France; died March 10, 1673
Genre(s): lyric poetry, letters
Language(s): French

The third of four children of Gaspard III de Coligny, maréchal-duc de Châtillon, and Anne de Polignac, Henriette was raised by a pious mother in an austerity thought fitting for one of France's most prominent reformed families. Related to the French royal family, and the House of Nassau, the Coligny daughters were sought as prestigious alliances: Henriette's sister Anne by George of Wurtemburg and Teck, and she herself by Thomas Hamilton, 3rd Earl of Haddington. After his premature death (February 1645) ended a short residence in war-torn England, where Queen Henrietta received her at Oxford, she returned to a marriage arranged by her mother (1647) to Gaspard de Champagne, comte de La Suze. Virtually cloistered by her husband at Belfort (Alsace), then Lumigny (Brie), the comtesse managed to establish permanent residence in their Marais *hôtel* only in 1653 after the comte's rearguard action in the Fronde failed and forced him into German exile. The marriage ended in a much-publicized divorce granted to the wife for cause of impotence by the Paris Parlement (1661). An equally publicized earlier conversion to Catholicism had been effected by a council of bishops assisted by her spiritual directors La Milletière and Père Léon, both of whom published accounts of it. Abjuration in high pomp (July 20, 1653) was ritually observed on the arms of the Queen and Gaston d'Orleans. From her scruples came the brief epigram "Oui, j'aime Charenton."

First sparked to write verse by a belated and brief period at the Hôtel de Rambouillet, whose spirit continued in her own circle, Mme de La Suze sought a succession of tutors beginning with the learned Urbain Chevreau and later including Montplaisir and Subligny. She received numerous poetic tributes, early on the "Vers pour Iris" sequence by Jacques (not Hercule) de Lacger, and she became in them "la dixième muse." But it was Madeleine de Scudéry, Pellison, and their group who most encouraged her writing with friendship and supported it in published compliments. An elaborate compliment to her elegies, which had been read out in the Académie de Castres, appeared in Book VIII of Scudéry's *Clélie*. Boileau's critical praise helped to consecrate the elegies, which remained through the eighteenth century her most often praised lyric mode. Admitted to *Le Parnasse français* by Tithon du Tillet, she retained her place there through the *Parnasse des Dames* (1773).

La Suze became queen of the *recueils collectifs*. Her single independent volume of verse (21 poems, 1666) collected the airs and madrigals, verse portraits and epigrams, *stances* and elegies that first appeared prominently (18 poems) in the collective volume produced by the Parisian bookseller Charles Sercy in 1653 and several times reedited, along with a prose portrait of the Grande Mademoiselle that originally figured in the album of *Portraits divers* (1659) published under her name. La Suze's was similarly used by the publisher Quinet for a new collection of "pièces galants" that after a first appearance in 1664 continued in expanded reeditions until the mid-eighteenth century to associate her name with the "new" and "le plus beau" of lyric poetry (1666, 1668, 1674, 1680, 1684; continued by Cavelier, 1691, 1698; by Trévoux, 1725, 1741, 1748). Among the 32 new poems in these and other anthologies, from 1667 through 1692, airs/*chansons* and elegies largely predominate. Her *oeuvre* is almost completely represented in the 1725 collection.

In the directness of her confessional expression of love, as in her independence in publishing, and her flamboyant pleasures (among which writing was prominent), the highly-born La Suze encouraged by her example younger women poets like Mlle Lheritier and Mme d'Esche. Although she remains the Doralise of Somaize's *Dictionaire des précieusses*, her airs and other short lyric pieces and especially her elegies contributed to the transformation of mid-seventeenth-century *préciosité*. Simplification of figures, conversational rhythms, and evident sensibility all would later seem more "natural" to Regency poets of *vers badins*.

Works

Poésies de Madame la Comtesse de La Suze (1666).
Recueil de pièces galantes, en prose et en vers, de Mme la Comtesse de La Suze (1664–1725).

Bibliography

Fukui, Y., *Raffinement précieux dans la poésie francaise du XVIIᵉ siècle* (1964). Goujet, Claude, *Bibliothèque francoise...*, vol. 17 (1716). Lachèvre, Frédéric, *Bibliographie des recueils collectifs de poésie publiés de 1597 à 1700*, vols. 2–3 (1903–1904). Magne, Emile, *Madame de La Suze (Henriette de Coligny) et la société précieuse* (1908). Niderst, Alain, *Madeleine de Scudéry, Paul Pellisson et leur monde* (1976).

Charles G.S. Williams

Karin Sveen

Born August 17, 1948, Ringsaker, Norway
Genre(s): short story, poetry, drama, novel
Language(s): both of the official languages of
Norway: Nynorsk (New Norwegian and
Bokmál (Dano Norwegian)

Karin Sveen has emerged as an important Norwegian writer in the 1980s. Born in a small rural town in Norway to working-class parents, she was educated as a teacher. Despite her education and present social position, she strongly identifies with the working class. This class consciousness is evident in her writing, as she often focuses on class differences in Norway. She currently lives in Hamar, Norway, and is active politically in the left wing in the Socialist Party (SV).

Sveen distanced herself from the social realists of the 1960s and early 1970s. While many of the central literary figures at this time believed they were creating a new form of literature for the working class, Sveen viewed the results as illusionary and unrealistic.

Sveen debuted with a collection of poems in 1975 (*Vinterhagen* [The Winter Garden]), followed closely by two more collections, *Mjøsa går* (1976; The Lake Mjosagar Flows) and *Den svarte hane* (1977; The Black Cock). The fact that the collections are written in New Norwegian, her regional dialect (from Hedemark), and Dano Norwegian, respectively, is witness to her linguistic versatility.

Døtre (1980; Daughter), a collection of short stories, gained widespread recognition and popularity in Norway. The thirteen stories in the collection deal with different aspects of motherhood and daughterhood: daughters' attempts to gain independence, mothers' difficulties in letting go, the barriers that mothers create for their own daughters and, at the same time, the disillusionments of motherhood for women who were themselves once daughters.

Sveen's first novel, *Utbryterdronninga* (1982; The Escape Queen), has been called a modern folk tale. It has a strong feminist message. There are elements of the fantastic, but they are firmly rooted in a realistic framework. A young girl, Marja, whose past is unknown, is found drifting in a boat by a childless couple who adopt her. She is confronted with the cruel and hostile world of adults and children and she learns to survive— not by adapting but by developing a strong identity of her own. Marja discovers her special talent as an escape artist, and when her talents become known to others she is viewed as both a hero and a witch.

Sveen's second novel, *Den reddende engel* (1984; The Saving Angel), is a sensitive and often humorous portrayal of the Norwegian society in the 1950s, seen through the eyes of a young girl. This girl (also called Marja) describes episodes from her early years growing up with her twin brother and under the care of a man whom we believe to be her father. The novel has some surprising twists and through the naive but observant eyes of Marja we gain insight into some of the social and psychological implications of class differences in Norway.

The language situation in Norway is complicated. Sveen is keenly aware of the connection between language and social class. In developing her characters she is able to unveil, through language, the strong class differences in Norway. Her prose is lyrical, despite the fact that she most often deals with common, everyday themes. Sveen's focus on the mother/daughter relationship and on the issue of parenthood in general has added to the debate of the 1980s surrounding these issues.

Works

Vinterhagen [The Winter Garden] (1975). *Mjøsa går* [The Lake (Mjøsa) Flows] (1976). *Den svarte hane* [The Black Cock] (1977). *Døtre* [Daughters] (1980). *Litt av et ord* [The Word] (1981), in *Så stor du er blitt* [You Have Gotten So Big]. *Utbryterdronninga* [The Escape Queen] (1982). *Snart 17* [Soon 17], script (1983). *Hanna* [Hanna], script (1984) *Den reddende engel* [The Saving Angel] (1984). *Kroppens sug, hjertets savn* [The Body's Urge, the Heart's Longing] (1985).
Translations: *Det gode hjertet* from *Døtre* [A Good Heart], in *An Everyday Story*, tr. and ed. Katherine Hanson (1984), pp. 203–209. *Litt av et ord* from *Så stor du er blitt* [The Word from *You Have Gotten So Big*], tr. Joan Tate. *The Norseman*, 5 (September 1985): 8–9.

Peggy Hagen

Karolina Světlá

Born February 24, 1830, Prague, Czechoslovakia; died September 7, 1899, Prague
Genres: short story, novel
Language(s): Czech

Svetlá, born Johanna Rotová, took the pseudonym by which she is known from the name of her husband's native town, Svetlá pod Ještědem. She became a leading figure in the important Maj literary movement in the 1860s and 1870s and is remembered as a pioneering feminist as well as a prose writer of considerable talent. Her sister Sofie Podlipská was also a writer.

Although she grew up in a solidly middle-class, Czech-German merchant's family, she rebelled early against her "philistine" background. In developing her role as an emancipated woman writer, Světlá was influenced by her older friend Bo'ena Němcová and by the writings of George Sand. Among her colleagues in the Maj group were Jan Neruda and Vítězslav Hálek. Her earliest works were published in journals associated with this group. During her thirty-year career, she published novels and stories on a wide range of subjects and in several narrative styles.

Much of her work, including stories about lost and searching young women and historical novels of old Prague, were considered by the next generation of writers and critics to be unrealistic and excessively romantic. However, her stories and novels based on the lives of people from the Liberec region of Northern Bohemia have retained a higher reputation through the years. In her frequent visits to this region, she studied the unique and well-preserved customs of its rural people and portrayed them in her books. However, critics have noted that these works in spite of their "picturesque" surface, actually deal with contemporary moral problems and with the personal experiences of Světlá. Among the most successful novels of this type are *Vesnický román* (1867; A Village Romance), *Kří' u potoka* (1868; The Cross by the Stream), and *Frantina* (1870).

Unlike her friend Bo'ena Němcová, Světlá was a "modern" Czech woman, critically analytical and involved in social issues of the day. She is historically important as a literary personality as well as a literary artist.

Works

Dvojí probuzení (1858). Sestry (1859). Společnice (1859). O krejčíkovic Ane'ce (1860). Zamítáni (1860). Láska k básníkovi (1860). Za májového večera (1860). První Češka (1861). Několik archů z rodinné kroniky (1862). Cikánka (1863). Ještě několik archů z rodinné kroniky (1863). Lesní panna (1863). Skalák (1863). Na úsvitě (1864). Lamač a jeho dcera (1864). Z tanečních hodin (1866). Rozcestí (1866). Vesnický román (1867). Kři'u potoka (1868). Kantůrčice (1869). Frantina (1870). Poslední paní Hlohovská (1870). Večer u koryta (1870). Hubička (1871). Mladsí bratr (1871). Černý Petříček (1871). Zvonečková královna (1872). Ten národ (1872). Námluvy (1872). Nemodlenec (1873). Nebo'ka Barbora (1873). Okam'ik (1873). Konec a počátek (1874). V zátiší (1878). Teta Vavřincová (1879). Divousové (1882). Miláček lidu svého (1882). Z vypravování staré 'ebračky (1884). V hlo'inách (1885). Poslední poustevnice (1886). Josefů Josef (1887). Větrně (1888). Za starých časů (1889). U sedmi Javorů (1890). Blázínek (1891).

Bibliography

Jurčinová, E., in *Podobizny spisovatelek svetové galerie* (1929). Novák, A., in *Posobiznv 'en* (1918). Nováková, T., *Karolina Světlá, její 'ivot a spisy* (1890). Šalda, F.X., in *Kritické projevy 8* (1956). Špičák, J., *Karolina Světlá* (1969).

Reference works: *Čeští spisovatelé desti století*, ed. R. Šťastný (1974) *Čeští spisovatelé 19. a počátku 20. století*, eds. K. Homolová, M. Otruba, and Z. Pešat.

Clinton Machann

Rů'ena Svobodová

(a.k.a. Čápcová)

Born July 10, 1868, Mikulovicí u Znojma, Czechoslovakia; died January 1, 1920, Prague
Genres: short story and novel
Language(s): Czech

Svobodová (nee Capkova) moved to Prague as a young girl after the death of her father, who was an administrator for a monastic order. In 1890, she married the writer F.X. Svoboda, who introduced her to the literary world. She surrounded herself with a circle of writers and artists, including Bo'ena Benešová. Her most important literary friendship was with the important Czech writer and critic F.X. Šalda, to whose journal she contributed.

The work of Svobodová is usually classified as impressionistic. In her novels and tales, she most often portrays young girls and sensitive women who experience a conflict between their dreams and reality or between girlhood and adulthood. Her heroines suffer from the indifference of their surroundings. In works such as *Přetí'eny klas* (1896; The Overburdened Stalk), these women want to rebel against their restricted lives and live independently, but they finally resign themselves to failure.

In later novels, for example, *Marné lásky* (1907; Vain Loves), Svobodová created a romantic woman who is able to defend herself against harsh reality and find an inner peace. However, *Černí myslivci* (1908; The Black Foresters), a cycle of tales centered on a princely hunting party, is sometimes considered to be her best work. In these stories, Svobodová expresses an ardent love of nature. *Pokojný dům* (1917; The Peaceful House) further illustrates her preoccupation with the "simple life" and is reminiscent of Bo'ena Němcová's work. Svobodová also wrote an interesting memoir entitled *Ráj* (1921; Paradise).

Svobodová is important in Czech literature for introducing a new awareness of the dreams and aspirations of women and children and for portraying delicate psychological states. However, many of her works soon lost their popularity and came to be judged as overrefined and unrealistic by critics.

Works

Na písčité půdě (1895). Ztroskotáno (1896). Povídky (1896). Přetí'ený klas (1896). V odlehlé dědině (1898). Zamotaná vlákna (1899). Milenky (1902). Pěšinkami srdce (1902). Plaméby a plamenky (1905). Marné lásky (1906). Černí myslivci (1908). Posvátné jaro (1912). Po svatební hostině (1916). Pokojný dům (1917). Hrdinné a bezpomocné dětství (1920). Ráj (1920). Zahrada irémská (1921).

Bibliography

Šalda, F.X., In memorium, R. Svobodové (1920). Sezima, K., in Podobizny a reliéfy (1927). Václavek, B., in Literární studie a podobizny (1962).

Reference works: Čeští spisovatelé deseti století, ed. R. Š<t&r>astný (1974). Čeští spisovatelé 19. a počátku 20. století, eds. K. Homolová, M. Otruba, and Z. Pešat (1982).

Clinton Machann

Hélène Swarth

Born October 25, 1859, Amsterdam, The
    Netherlands; died June 20 1941, Velp
Genre(s): poetry, short story, fairy tale
Language(s): French, Dutch

Hélène Swarth received a French education in Belgium (more specifically in Brussels) and initially wrote and published in French the collections Fleurs du rêve (1879; Dream Flowers) and Les printanières (1882; Spring Beauties); but under the influence of the Flemish impressionist poet and critic Pol de Mont with whom she corresponded extensively, she switched to Dutch—beginning in 1883 with Eenzame bloemen (Solitary Flowers) and Blauwe bloemen (Blue Flowers) in 1884. She quickly became a respected and admired compagnon de route of the literary generation of the 1880s whose principal representative, Willem Kloos, chiefly under the impression of her consummate ability to pair formal artistry to emotion and mood, hailed her as "the singing heart" of contemporary Dutch literature.

Though Swarth's poetry combines the romantic's responsiveness to nature and neo-religiosity with typical fin-de-siècle pessimist and decadent moods, the originality of her vast oeuvre lies in a delicately modulated, yet occasionally repetitive expression of her "alienated disposition . . . which apprehends everything—people, objects, events, landscapes—as being severed from its temporal relativity: everything is a symbol of a desperate defeat in a distant and inimical world" (Liebaers, 188).

While often neglected or underestimated in official Dutch and Flemish literary historiography, Swarth is, in many respects, a key figure in the literature of the Low Countries, having lived in both Belgium and Holland and integrating in her work Belgian French, Flemish, Dutch, and international sensibilities and influences—the latter to be sought mainly in the sphere of French and English romanticism and symbolism. Though few share the opinion of Jeroen Brouwers, the most recent biographer of Hélène Swarth, that she is "one of the greatest poetesses in Dutch literature" (13), the oeuvre of this "singing heart," both in its strengths and weaknesses, is a significant and original presence in Dutch and Belgian literary and cultural history.

Works

Poetry: Fleurs du rêve (1879). Les printanières (1882). These two early collections were reprinted collectively with Feuilles mortes as Première poésie (1902). Eenzame bloemen (1883). Blauwe bloemen (1884). Beelden en Stemmen (1887). Sneeuwvlokken (1888). Rouwviolen (1889). Liederen en gedichten (1890). Passiebloemen (1891). Poezie (1892). Nieuwe gedichten (1892). Verzen (1893). Bloesem en vrucht (1893). Blanke duiven (1895) Van vrouwenleed (1896). Diepe wateren (1897). Stille dalen (1898). Najaarsstemmen (1900). Octoberloover (1903). Nieuwe verzen (1906). Bleke luchten (1909). Herfstdraden (1910). Avondwolken (1911). Eenzame paden (1915). Late liefde (1919). Liederen en sonnetten (1919). Keurbundel (1919). Morgenrood (1929). Late rozen (1929). Avonddauw (1930). Natuurpoëzie (1930). Vrouwen (1935). Wijding (1936). Sorella (1942; posthumous).

Prose: Kindersprookjes (1886). Uit het meisjesleven (1890). Kleine schetsen (1893).

Letters: Herman Liebaers, ed. Brieven aan Pol de Mont (1964).

Bibliography

Anthology: Bloem, J.C., ed., Hélène Swarth. Het zingende hart (1952). Roest, Hans, ed., Hélène Swarth. Een mist van tranen (1969).

Biography and analysis: Brouwers, Jeroen, Hélène Swarth. Haar huwelijk met Frits Lapidoth, 1894–1910 (1985) extends Swarth's biography beyond the "Zuidnederlandse" (Belgian) years to her

"Noordnederlandse" (Netherlandic) years. Liebaers, Herman, *Hélène Swarths Zuidnederlandse jaren* (1964) contains a good bibliography of and about Swarth, pp. 213–229. See also the essays on Swarth in Maurits Basse, *Het aandeel der vrouw in de Nederlandse letterkunde* (1920–1921) vol. 2, pp. 29–61 and R. F. Lissens, *Het impressionisme in de Vlaamse letterkunde* (1934), pp. 101–116.

Reference works: Knuvelder, G.P.M., *Handboek tot de geschiedenis van de Nederlandse letterkunde*, vol. 4 (1976; 5th ed.), p. 239 and the entry in A.G.H. Bachrach et al., eds., *Moderne Encyclopedie der wereldliteratuur*, vol. 9 (1984).

Henk Vynckier

Anna Świrszczyńska

Born February 7, 1909, Warsaw, Poland; died
*   September 30, 1984, Cracow, Poland*
Genre(s): poetry, drama, children's literature
Language(s): Polish

In addition to creative writing, Świrszczyńska was an editor and literary director of a theater for the young. Although she began publishing before World War II, her wartime experiences strongly influenced her subsequent work. She was an active participant in the conspiracy against German occupation and in 1943 was awarded second prize for the play *Orfeusz* (Orpheus, not published until 1948). Another play, *Strzały na ulicy Długiej* (1948; Shots on Długa Street), depicts a dramatic rescue of prisoners, while *Śmierć w Kongo* (1963; Death in the Congo) also deals with struggle in that country.

Świrszczyńska's poetry combines modernistic techniques with mood-provoking yet simple imagery. *Czarne słowa* (1967; Black Words), for example, adopts the style of black poetry. The suffering she saw during the 1944 uprising in Warsaw is the subject of the widely acclaimed *Budowałam barykadę* (1974; Building the Barricade, English tr., 1979). Two volumes of her poetry deal with the lot of woman. *Jestem baba* (1972; I Am a Woman) explores biological as well as psychological aspects of female eroticism with fierce lucidity. So does her last published work, *Szczęśliwa jak psi ogon* (1978; Happy as a Dog's Tail), in which she examines her own life with an almost savage intensity and honesty.

Works

Poetry: *Wiersze i proza* [Poems and Prose] (1936). *Liryki zebrane* [Collected Lyrics] (1958). *Czarne słowa* [Black Words] (1967). *Wiatr* [Wind] (1970). *Jestem baba* [I Am a Woman] (1972). *Budowałam barykadę* [Building a Barricade] (1974). *Szczęśliwa jak psi ogon* [Happy as a Dog's Tail] (1978).

Plays: *Ostrożny* [The Cautious One] (1946). *Orfeusz* [Orpheus] (1947). *Strzały na ulicy Długiej* [Shots on Długa Street] (1948). *Odezwa na murze* [The Proclamation on the Wall] (1951). *Czerwone sztandary* [Red Banners, co-authored] (1951). *Życie i śmierć* [Life and Death] (1956). *Śmierć w Kongo* [Death in the Congo] (1963).

Children's literature: Over two dozen works for children.

Translations: *Building the Barricade*, tr. Magnus Jan Kryński and Robert A. Macguire (1979). *Postwar Polish Poetry; An Anthology*, tr. Czesław Miłosz et al., 3rd ed. (1983), pp. 57–71. *Contemporary East European Poetry; An Anthology*, tr. Emery George et al. (1983), pp. 105–107. *Introduction to Modern Polish Literature; An Anthology of Fiction and Poetry*, tr. Adam Gillon, Ludwik Krzyżanowski, et al., 2nd ed., with a New Poetry Sec. ed. by Adam Gillon and Krystyna Olszer (1982), p. 509.

Bibliography

Korzeniewska, Ewa, ed., *Słownik współczesnych pisarzy polskich*, vol. 3 (Warsaw, 1964). Zacharska, Jadwiga, "Świrszczyńska Anna," in *Literatura polska: Przewodnik encyklopedyczny*, ed. Julian Krzyżanowski. Vol. 2 (Warsaw, 1985).

Irene Suboczewski

Magda Szabó

Born October 5, 1917, Debrecen, Hungary
Genre(s): poetry, novel, children's literature,
*   drama, translation*
Language(s): Hungarian

Szabó was educated in Debrecen, where she earned a doctorate in Latin and Hungarian in 1940. Her dissertation, *A Romaikori szépségápolás* (The Cult of Beauty in the Roman Age), was later published. From 1940–1944 she was a secondary school teacher, and after 1945 she accepted a position in the ministry of culture. She returned to teaching between 1950 and

1959. After 1950, like so many other Hungarian writers, she did not or could not publish anything. This silence was broken in 1958, and the following year she left teaching to devote herself full time to writing. Szabó's first poems were published in *Magyarok* (Hungarians) and *Ujhold* (New Moon). The poetry volumes, *Bárány* (Lamb) and *Vissza az emberig* (Back to Man), document the tragedy of war. Her poetry is meditative and intellectual with a firm commitment to form. 1958 saw the publication of a third volume of poetry, *Neszek* (Sounds), and it was also the year her first novel, *Freskó* (Fresco), was published. For this she won the József Attila Prize in 1959.

Like so many of her generation, Szabó is interested in the decline of the old order and the effect of societal changes on women. In *Freskó* she presented the disintegration of a provincial clerical family. Her criticism is unusually harsh as she shows the failure of traditional moral values and blames this, as well as the conservatism of the provincial intelligentsia, for the demise of the family. *Az őz* (The Fawn) is more psychologically oriented as it studies the rivalry of two women, Eszter and Angela. The former is jealous of the ease with which Angela seems to gain everything, but in the end, when Eszter might have satisfaction, she finds that only hatred can fill her heart. Later novels, such as *Disznótor* (Pig Killing), *Pilátus* (Pilate), *Danaida* (Danaide), and *Katalin utca* (Katalin Street) also study loneliness through heroines who are generally passionate and suffering women. She uses the techniques of the modern novel, particularly the interior monologue; her sensitive and accurate understanding of psychological motivations, as well as her timely topics, make her a popular writer. As in her poetry, so in her prose style, a strong sense of form prevails.

Beginning with the sixties, her interest broadened and the themes of her novels reflect this wider view. In *Mózes egy, huszonkettő* (Moses One, Twenty-two) she examines the conflicts between the older and the younger generation. The differences between Eastern and Western Europeans and particularly the Eastern European's view of himself are the central themes of *A szemlélők* (The Spectators). *Ókút* (The Ancient Well) evokes the world of her childhood, and *Régimodi történet* (An Old-Fashioned Tale)

uses family reminiscences to evoke the life of a provincial town at the turn of the century. She is able to unite an inner realism and a historical distance in the characterization of her personae.

Her books for children and young people, while designed to be instructive, are popular with the readers. Many of her works, also, have been translated into German, English, and French among other languages. In addition to poetry and novels, she has written plays, film scripts and radio plays, and has several major translations to her credit. From English, she rendered Galsworthy, Shakespeare's *Two Gentlemen of Verona*, and Kyd's *Spanish Tragedy*. Her dramas, *Kígyo marás* (Snake-bite) and *Leleplezés* (Unveiling), were performed in Poland and in Yugoslavia in 1964.

Works

Poetry collections: *Bárány* (1947). *Vissza az emberig* (1947). *Neszek* [Sounds]. *Szilfán halat, összegyűjtött versek* [Fish on the Elm Tree, Collected Poems] (1975).

Novels: *Freskó* (1958). *Az őz* (1959; English ed., *The Fawn*, 1963). *Disznótor* (1960). *Pilátus* (1964). *A Danaida* (1964). *Katalin utca* (1969). *Mózes egy, huszonkettő* (1967). *A Szemlélők* (1973). *Ókút* (1970). *Régimodi történet* (1977).

Short stories: *Alvók futása* [Race of the Sleepers] (1967).

Juvenile novels: *Mondják meg Zsófinak* (1958; English ed., 1963, *Tell Sally*). *Sziget-kék* [Island-blue] (1959). *Álarcosbál* [The Masquerade-ball] (1961). *Születésnap* [The Birthday] (1962). *Abigél* [Abigail] (1978). *Tündér Lala* [Fairy Louis] (1965).

Children's books: *Bárány Boldizsár* [Who Lives Where], a verse tale (1958). *Marikáék háza* [Mary's House] (1959).

Plays: *Kígyó marás* (1960). *Leleplezés* (1962). *Fanny hagyomanyai* [The Posthumous Papers of Fanny] (1964). *Kiálts város* [Cry, City] (1973). *Az a szép, fényes nap* [That Beautiful, Bright Day] (1976). *A mérani fiú* [The Boy of Meran] (1980). *Béla király* [King Bela] (1984), collected in *Eleven képet a világnak* [A Living Picture for the World] (1966) and *Erők szerint* [According to Forces] (1980).

Film script: *Vöröstinta* [Red Ink] (1959).

Radio play: *A hallei kirurgus* [The Chirurgeon of Halle] (1963).

Critical essays: *Kívül a körön* [Outside the Circle] (1980).

Travelogues: *Hullámok kergetése* [The Pursuit of Waves] (1965). *Zeusz küszöbén* [On Zeus' Threshold] (1968).

Bibliography

Reviews and articles: Rákos, Sándor, *Ujhold* (1947). Szabo, Ede, *Magyarok* (1947). Lengyel, Balázs (1957) and Éva Katona (1963), *Élet és irodalom*. Nagy, László B., *Kritika* (1963). Bata, Imre, *Tiszatáj* (1963). Farago, Vilmos, "Egy büntudat története," in *Élet és irodalom* (1964). Béládi, Miklós, "Szabó Magda: *Freskó*," *Kortárs* (June 1958). Bessenyei, György, "Szabó Magda két regénye," *Kortárs* (May 1959). Herman, Istvan, "Szabó Magda drámája a Jókai színházban," *Kortárs* (May 1960). Tóth, Sándor, "Szabó Magda: *Szigetkek*" *Kortárs* (Feb. 1960). Illés, Jenö, "Jegyzetek Szabó Magda drámáiról," *Kortárs* (Jan. 1963). Benedek, Istvan, "Egy írónő tündöklése és a *Danaida*," *Kortárs* (Nov. 1964). Nagy, Péter, "Szabó Magda: *Freskó*," *Irodalomtörténet* (May 1959). Sík, Csaba, "Szabó Magda: *Neszek*," *Irodalomtörténet* (June 1960). Bor, Ambrus, "A kortárs szemével: Bor Ambrus Szabó Magdáról," *A Konyv* (1964).

Studies in critical anthologies: Kardos, László, "Szabó Magda: *Neszek*," in *Száz kritika* (Budapest, 1987). Konya, Judith, *Szabo Magda alkotasai es vallomasai tukreben* (Budapest, 1977).

Enikő Molnár Basa

Margit Szécsi

Born 1928, Budapest, Hungary
Genre(s): poetry
Language(s): Hungarian

Margit Szécsi, a daughter of the working class, received her education by virtue of postwar socialist reforms. After attending university in Budapest, she joined the editorial staff of the literary journal *Csillag* (Star), dedicated to opposing the politically dogmatic, hollow rhetoric that pervaded the literature of the day (a tendency dubbed "schematism" by its critics). Szécsi later left Budapest to work as a volunteer for Danube Ironworks on a project to build a steel mill complex. She returned to the capital to marry László Nagy, a poet who was one of the main exponents of the nationalistic *népi* (folk or populist) literary movement (in contrast to the *nyugat*—or Western influenced—movement that drew its inspiration from a wide range of continental sources).

Szécsi herself became one of the most significant voices within the populist literary movement. Her poetry grows from an indigenous oral tradition that includes Hungarian folk ballads, dirges, and highwayman's songs. It reflects the passion, drama, and high musicality of these forms. Virtuoso linguistic performances, her poems are replete with word games and anagrams; her particular innovation is the use of highly individualized, surrealistic imagery within the traditional folk forms.

Szécsi's poetry has been described as visionary realism or, alternatively, folk surrealism. Her poetic trademarks are her forceful affirmations of life and humanistic values combined with the articulation of violent internal conflicts. In Szécsi's poems, the public and private intersect. She conceives of art as a powerful moral force, and she continues to be vocal about the social and spiritual responsibilities of poetry. In her volumes *Papírkorona* (Paper Crown) and *A Sárkány és Lovagja* (The Dragon and his Knight), she speaks against antihumanism; in other volumes, such as *Szent Buborék* (Saint Bubble) and *Birodalom* (Empire), she addresses the problem of disintegrating communal attitudes in a socialist society.

Works

Március (1955). *Angyalok Strandja* (1956). *Páva a Tűzfalon* (1958). *A Trombitákat Összesőprik* (1965). *Új Heraldika*, collection (1967). *A Nagy Virágvágo Gép* (1969). *A Madaras Mérleg* (1972). *Szent Buborék* (1974). *Birodalom* (1976). *Mit Viszel, Folyó*, collection (1978). *A Szivárvány Kapujában* (1981). *Költő a Holdban*, collection (1984).

Bibliography

Beladi, Miklos, ed., *A Magyar irodalom tortenete, 1945–1975*, Vol. 1, "Irodalmi élet es irodalomkritika" (Budapest, 1981). Pomogats, Bela, ed., *Az újabb magyar irodalom, 1945–1981* (Budapest, 1981).

Gyorgyi Voros

Ewa Szelburg-Zarembina

*Born April 10, 1899, Bronowice, Poland; died
September 28, 1986, Warsaw, Poland*
*Genre(s): novel, short story, drama, poetry,
children's literature*
Language(s): Polish

Szelburg-Zarembina distinguished herself
by her contributions in the fields of education
and children's literature. She has more than five
dozen books and plays for children to her credit
as well as about a dozen primers and textbooks.
For these activities she was honored with four
awards. But in addition, this prolific writer produced a variety of adult works. Among the most
remarkable is the epic cycle of novels: *Wędrówka
Joanny* (1935; Joanna's Journey), *Ludzie z wosku*
(1936; Wax People), *Miasteczko aniołów* (1959;
Small Town of Angels), *Iskry na wiatr* (1963;
Windward the Sparks), and *Gaudeamus* (1968),
all five published collectively under the title
Rzeka kłamstwa (1968; River of Lies). The series
is a *Bildungsroman* relating the experiences of
the heroines Joanna and later her daughter
Salome, mainly from a psychological point of
view. The recurrent themes include adolescence,
friendship, love, loneliness, society. The style
can be described as expressionistic but also
contains elements of the uncanny and even demonic. For example, *Wędrówka Joanny* offers
wonderful descriptions of village landscapes, but
they do not resemble a typical Polish countryside.
Rather, they strike one as unfamiliar, almost
surreal. Here the real and fantastic, the conscious
and subconscious exist side by side. In *Iskry na
Wiatr*, the melodramatic and the grotesque alternate. Basically, history, environment, customs
are externals; another equally important reality is
the internal concerns of the human soul: love,
death, a sense of loss, sacrifice, and their psychological effects upon character and personality.

In the collection *Samotność* (1961; Solitude), the same eternal verities of life are revealed
in dramatic, often brutal, occurrences.

Works

Novels: *Polne grusze* [Wild Pears] (1924). *Ta, której
nie było* [The Absent Woman] (1925). *Dokąd?*
[Wither?] (1927). *Dziewczyna z zimorodkiem* [The
Girl with the Kingfisher] (1928). *Chusta św.
Weroniki* [The Kerchief of St. Veronica] (1930).
Wędrówka Joanny [Joanna's Journey] (1935).
Ludzie z wosku [Wax People] (1936). *Miasteczko
aniołów* [Small Town of Angels] (1959). *Zakochany
w miłości* [In Love with Love] (1961). *Iskry na wiatr*
[Windward the Sparks] (1963). *Imię jej Klara* [Her
Name Is Klara] (1964). *Gaudeamus* (1968). *I
otwarły się drzwi* [And the Doors Opened] (1971).
Short stories and essays: *Legendy żołnierskie*
[Soldiers' Legends] (1924). *Legendy Warszawy*
[Warsaw Legends] (1938). *Ziarno gorczyczne* [The
Mustard Seed] (1947). *Spotkania* [Encounters]
(1951). *W cieniu kolumny* [In the Pillar's Shadow]
(1954). *Krzyże z papieru* [Paper Crosses] (1955).
Samotność [Solitude] (1961).
Plays: *Ecce Homo* (1932). *Sygnaty* [Signals] (1933).
Poems: *Dzieci miasta* [Children of the City] (1935).
Młodość [Youth] (1948). *Matka i syn* [Mother and
Son] (1961).
Dozens of books and textbooks for children.

Bibliography

Klimowicz, Adam, *Szelburg-Zarembina* (Warsaw,
1966). Kuliczkowska, Krystyna, *Droga twórcza Ewy
Szelburg-Zarembiny; Szkic monograficzny*
(Cracow, 1965). Kuliczkowska, Krystyna,
"Szelburg-Zarembina Ewa," in *Literatura polska;
Przewodnik encyklopedyczny*, ed. Julian
Krzyżanowski. Vol. 2 (Warsaw, 1985). Szonert,
Ewa, "Z okazji sześciu tomów Szelburg-Zarembiny."
Kierunki (April 23, 1972): 7.

Irene Suboczewski

Bertha Szeps-Zuckerkandl

*Born 1893, Vienna, Austria; died 1945, Paris,
France*
Genre(s): article, translation, journalism
Language(s): German

Berta Zuckerkandl was a journalist and author. Her father, Morris Szeps, was the founder
of the liberal Viennese newspaper *Neues Wiener
Tagblatt*, which later became *Neues Wiener
Journal*. She contributed many articles to these
two journals and to the artistic periodicals *Ver
Sacrum* and *Die Kunst*. Berta Zuckerkandl was a
well-known champion not only of liberal political
ideas but also of new tendencies and movements

in art and theater of *fin de siècle* Vienna. She married Emil Zuckerkandl, professor of anatomy, who shared her liberal ideas and her interest in literature and art. In her salon in Döbling she received and encouraged many then-unknown personages of her time. It was in her salon that the idea of the artistic movement known as "The Secession" was first developed. She was a strong supporter of this movement as evidenced by her articles in *Ver Sacrum*, the journal that represented The Secession. Later she became one of the founders of the *Wiener Werkstätte*. In her salon she entertained, championed, and developed close friendships with Arthur Schnitzler, Hugo von Hofmannsthal, Herman Bahr, Peter Altenberg, Franz Werfel, Gustav Klimt, Oskar Kokoschka, Otto Wagner, Adolf Loos, Joseph Hoffmann, Auguste Rodin, Maurice Ravel, Max Reinhardt, Gustav Mahler, and others. Berta Zuckerkandl was fluent in French and, through her sister who had married Paul Clemenceau, she became acquainted with Georges Clemenceau. During and after the First World War, she served as the Austrian arbiter and courier to the French government seeking a separate peace. Among her literary output in addition to articles are many translations of French dramas.

Works

Polens Malkunst (1915). *Zeitkunst Wien 1901–1907. Ich erlebte fünfzig Jahre Weltgeschichte* (1939). *Österreich Intim, Erinnerungen 1892–1942* (1970).

Translations: *My Life History* [*Ich erlebte fünfzig Jahre Weltgeschichte*], tr. Roger Summerfield.

Bibliography

Clair, Jean, ed, *Vienne l'Apocalypse Joyeuse* (Paris, 1986), pp. 180, 558, 564, 567–568, 574. *Die Frau im Korsett, Wiener Frauenalltag zwischen Klischee und Wirklichkeit* (catalogue of exhibition at Hermesvilla, Vienna, April 1984–February 1985), pp. 174, 216. Johnston, William M., *The Austrian Mind* (Berkeley, 1972), pp. 35-6, 137. *Ver Sacrum, Die Zeitschrift der Wiener Secession 1898–1903* (catalogue of exhibition in Hermesvilla, Vienna, April 1982–March 1983), pp. 49, 54. Waissenberger, Robert, ed., *Wien 1870–1930: Traum und Wirklichkeit* (Vienna, 1984), pp. 111, 216.

M.A. Reiss

Wislawa Szymborska

Born July 2, 1923, Kornik, Poland
Genre(s): poetry
Language(s): Polish

According to Krynski and Maguire, Szymborska "is regarded as one of the three best representatives, since World War II, of the rich and ancient art of poetry in Poland" (and the only woman among them). They claim that the 10,000 copies of Szymborska's 1976 volume were sold out within a week. Unlike the other two poets who, the critics stress, "have by and large continued to cultivate their familiar territory, Szymborska constantly opens fresh themes and elaborates new techniques. Her verse shows the high seriousness, delightful inventiveness, and prodigality of imagination that we expect of first-rate poetry; and it bears the stamp of unmistakable originality."

Szymborska moved to Cracow from Kornik at the age of eight and has lived there ever since. She studied sociology and Polish literature at the Jagiellonian University and made her debut with the poem "Szukam slowa" (I Seek the Word) in *Walka* (Struggle), the 1945, no. 3 supplement to the Cracow newspaper *Dziennik polski* (Polish Daily). Officially criticized for writing "in a manner unintelligible to the masses" and "dwelling morbidly on the experiences of the war . . . at the expense of the new theme of building socialism" (Krynski and Maguire), her first volume of poetry, ready in 1948, was not published for four years until, apparently convinced that the times called for art to serve an important immediate goal, she rewrote it. Even though she sincerely tried to raise an authentic poetic voice in tune with the revolutionary era, she was found wanting. Her later publications included fewer and fewer poems on political themes and dealt more and more with lyrical subjects. She has won many literary prizes, written extensively on books by both Polish and foreign writers, and translated French poetry, mostly from the sixteenth and seventeenth centuries. She is poetry editor of the weekly *Zycie literackie* (Literary Life) in Cracow. The beautiful bilingual American publication of her seventy poems contains an extremely interesting and sensitively written introduction to her work and her ideas about poetry.

Works

Dlatego zyjemy [That's Why We Live] (1952, 1954). *Pytania zadawane sobie* [Questions Put to Myself] (1954). *Wolanie do Yeti* [Calling Out the Yeti] (1957). *Sol* [Salt] (1962). *Sto pociech* (1967). *Poezje wybrane* [Selected Poems], chosen and with introduction by the author (1967). *Poezje* [Poems] (1970, 1977). *Wszelki wypadek* (1972, 1975). *Wybor wierszy* [Selected Poems] (1973, 1979). *Tarsjusz i inne wiersze* [Tarsius and Other Poems] (1976). *Wielka liczba* [A Great Number] (1976, 1977).

Translations: *A Million Laughs. A Bright Hope* [*Sto pociech*], tr. Krynski and Maguire. *There But for the Grace* [*Wszelki wypadek*], tr. Krynski and Maguire.

Publications in periodicals abroad: *Les lettres nouvelles* (Paris, 1965). *The Literary Review* (New Jersey, 1967). *Micromegas* (Iowa City, 1968). *Wiadomosci* (London, 1968). *Monat* (Hamburg, 1970).

Poems in anthologies: *Anthologie de la poesie polonaise* (1965). *Lektion der Stille* (1959). *Neue polnische Lyrik* (1965). *Panorama moderner Lyrik* (1960). *Polish Writing Today* (1967). *Polnische Poesie des 20. Jahrhunderts* (1965). *Postwar Polish Poetry* (1965). *Vertige de bien vivre* (1962). *The New Polish Poetry. A bilingual collection*, compiled and edited by Milne Holton and Paul Vangelisti (1978). *Sounds, Feelings, and Thoughts: Seventy Poems by Wislawa Szymborska*, tr. and introd. by Magnus J. Krynski and Robert A. Maguire (1981).

Maya Peretz

T

Maila Talvio

Born October 17, 1871, Hartola, Finland; died
January 6, 1951, Helsinki
Genre(s): novel, short story, drama, speeches,
memoirs, autobiography
Language(s): Finnish

Maila Talvio is important both as a prose
writer and an influence on cultural policy in the
first decades of this century in Finland.

Talvio is chiefly a traditional realist but was
also influenced by Romanticism, mainly by Selma
Lagerlöf, and Expressionism. She began writing
in the 1890s with descriptions of the life of the
common people. The subject was familiar to her
since she had grown up on a remote farm in
Finland. She attended the Helsinki Finnish Girls'
School in the 1880s, and her work was instilled
with the patriotic spirit there. From the first it
was typical of her to teach and to moralize. For
example her novel *Pimeänpirtin hävitys* (1901;
The Destruction of Dark House) combined
criticism of upper-class life and revelation of the
oppression of tenant landholders in a manner
that caused a stir. She also wrote of the conditions
of the common people in Poland and Lithuania.
She became familiar with them during expeditions
of her husband—the scholar of Slavonic philology, J.J. Mikkola. Later she wrote of the world of
large inherited estates, with a touch of the feudal
romanticism of the Baltic countries. In the 1920s
she started the study of the history of Helsinki—
a pioneer work. Her novel trilogy *Itämeren tytär*
(1929–1936; Daughter of the Baltic) gave new
life to the Finnish historical novel. Some of the
events are based on what happened in her own
family.

Talvio published more than twenty novels
and a total of fifty-odd works. The leading
character in her works is usually a woman,
whose problem—often concealed—is childless-
ness and fear of giving birth. Women's education
is approached with reservations although Talvio
took a conspicuous part in student life due to her
husband's position. As a public figure from the
beginning of the twentieth century, she was an
admired public speaker and she held her own
literary salon. She championed many causes for
public good, including teetotalism. Her activity
and temperamental character gave rise to
defamatory articles and caricatures. During both
the First and Second World Wars, Talvio and her
husband were known for their German connections. She was one of the most conspicuous and
discussed Finnish women.

Works

Haapaniemen keinu [Haapaniemi Swing] (1895).
Nähtyä ja Tunnettua [Seen and Known] (1896).
Aili (1897). *Kaksi rakkautta* [Two Loves] (1898).
Suomesta pois [Away from Finland] (1899). *Johan
Ludig Runeberg* (1900). *Kansan seassa* [Among the
People] (1900). *Pimeänpirtin hävitys* [The De-
struction of Dark House] (1901). *Juha Joutsia*
(1903). *Muuan äiti* [A Mother] (1904).
Kauppaneuvoksen kuoltua [After the Tycoon's
Death] (1905). *Louhilinna* [Louhi Castle] (1906).
Puheita [Speeches] (1908). *Eri teitä* [Different
Roads] (1908) *Tähtien alla* [Under the Stars] (1910).
Anna Sarkoila (1910). *Kirjava keto* [Colorful Field]
(1912). *Hämähäkki* [Spider] (1912). *Elinan häät*
[Elina's Wedding] (1912). *Yölintu* [Nightbird]

(1913). *Kun meidän kaivosta vesi loppuu* [When There's No Water in our Well] (1913). *Talonhuijari* [Swindler of the House] (1913). *Huhtikuun Manta* [Manta of April] (1914). *Lempiäniemen tyttäret* [Daughters of Lempiäniemi] (1915). *Elämänleikki* [Life's Game] (1915). *Ruma ankanpoikanen* [The Ugly Duckling—Hans Christian Andersen] (1915). *Niniven lapset* [The Children of Niniveh] (1915). *Kultainen lyyra* [The Golden Lyre] (1916). *Elämän kasvot* [Life's Face] (1916). *Silmä yössä* [Eye of the Night] (1917). *Näkymätön kirjanpitäjä* [The Invisible Bookkeeper] (1918). *Yötä ja aamua* [Night and Morning] (1919). *Kurjet* [The Cranes] (1919). *Valkea huvila* [The White Villa] (1920). *Kihlasormus* [The Engagement Ring] (1921). *Kirkonkello* [The Church Bell] (1922). *Viimeinen laiva* [The Last Ship] (1922). *Opinsauna* [The Sauna of Learning] (1923). *Sydämet* [Hearts] (1924). *Jumalan puistot* [The Parks of God] (1927). *Hiljentykäämme* [Let Us Compose Ourselves] (1929). *Itämeren tytär I–III* [Daughter of the Baltic I–III] (1929–1936). *Ne 45,000* [Those 45,000] (1932). *Leipä-kulta* [Dear Bread] (1934). *Terveisiä* [Regards] (1936). *Linnoituksen iloiset rouvat* [The Merry Wives of the Fort] (1941). *Rukkaset ja kukkaset* [Mittens and Flowers] (1947). *Rakkauden riemut ja tuskat* [Love's Joys and Pains] (1949).

Bibliography

Koskenniemi, V.A., *Maila Talvio* (1946). Tuulio, Tyyni, *Maila Talvion vuosikymmenet I–II* [Talvio's Decades I–II] (1963–1965).

Liisi Huhtala

Tamar

(see: Renate Rubenstein)

Arcangela Tarabotti

(a.k.a. Galerana Baratotti)

Born 1604, Venice; died 1652, Venice, Italy
Genre(s): tract
Language(s): Italian

Elena Cassandra Tarabotti, born in Venice in 1604, became Sister Arcangela in the Benedictine convent of St. Anna, where she took the veil in 1620 and shortly afterwards, it is not known exactly when, took her final vows. She did not have a religious vocation and all of her life protested her confinement and that of other of women through her writing, much of which was published and known to a large community, even beyond the city of Venice. Her works are critical of family and state politics, which protected wealth and nobility by relegating potentially expensive daughters to a life of imprisonment and by denying them as well a good education. She exposed the hypocrisy of the fierce contemporary criticism of female vanity, pointing out that men were just as vain and suggesting that their concern was not so much for the virtue of their wives and daughters as for their money, which they would more readily spend on themselves and on the prostitutes with which they liberally associated. She argued for the merit of women and their right to attend to their beauty and adornment, one of the few areas of their lives in their control. Tarabotti wrote forcefully and convincingly, despite her lack of adequate formal training, and she unnerved her critics to the point that they mercilessly attacked her for the least evidence of literary shortcomings, indeed criticized her for typographical errors in a published work. She always responded promptly and fearlessly and seems to have had support and sympathy from many noblewomen and not a few erudite men.

Her first work, *La tirannia paterna* (Paternal Tyranny), written in her early years in the convent, decried the injustice of her situation, laying the blame on fathers and the State whose common interests were being served. This early work, somewhat transformed, was published posthumously in 1654 under a different title, *La simplicità ingannata* (Simplicity Deceived). Her second polemical tract, *L'Inferno monacale* (Convent Hell), on the misery of the lives of vocationless nuns, was never published, but its sequel, *Il paradiso monacale* (Convent Paradise), was, for obvious reasons. This latter work has been variously interpreted as expressing Sister Arcangela's repentance and acceptance of her religious vocation and, more convincingly, as a failed attempt to reconcile herself to that vocation, a failure that is expressed in conflicting attitudes and in a continuation, although attenuated, of her lifelong feminist polemic, an unfaltering defense of the merit of women. This polemic returns to the center of her attention in the works that followed, in the *Antisatira* (Antisatire), a reply to F. Buoninsegni's *Contro il lusso donnesco* (Against the Luxuries of Women), in her published letters, and in her response, *Che le donne siano della spetie degli uomini. Difesa delle donne* (That Women Are of the Same Species as Men. A Defense of Women) to the work of Acidalius Valens, an erudite German, the *Disputatio perjucunda qua anonimus probare nititur mulieres homines non esse* (A Most Delightful Disputation in Which an Anonymous [Author] Strives to Prove That Women Are Not Men), translated into Italian by Orazio Plata and published in 1595. Some historians have believed the Latin tract to be a joke though Arcangela did not and argued, or rather inveighed, against its heresy and its misogyny. The Church, too, took it seriously and put it on the Index for its heretical ideas in 1651. The *Antisatira* and the *Lettere* take up the defense of women, affirming that the ignorance of women derives from their having been deprived by men of an education. She refutes the argument that mixing men and women together in schools would lead women to sins of impurity, objecting that women cannot be held responsible for the lust of men. She argues for the "light of reason," a natural gift that has helped her overcome her educational handicap and permitted her to read with understanding, for example, the political works of Machiavelli, with, of course, the permission of her Superiors. She answers the accusation of vanity with counter accusations, often witty as well as accurate (for example, in answer to criticism of the excessively ornate dress of women, their exaggerated makeup, she replies that in contemporary fashion the "mustaches of men, that should fall down over the mouth to inhibit the production of obscene masculine language, are forced by iron and fire to rise menacingly towards the sky").

Besides being intelligent, clever, and combative, Arcangela Tarabotti was also ambitious; she wanted to be heard and appreciated. She corresponded with important men and women, dedicated her writing to some of them, and even sent a copy of her *Antisatira* to Cardinal Mazarin. Through her pen she made herself quite important for her time and condition, and scholars are now beginning to recognize what an extraordinary feat that was. She is the subject of a recent biography (Zanette, 1960), but it does not present her life and works clearly with the critical detachment she deserves. Her role as one of the early voices of Italian feminism has been firmly established and has begun to produce interesting analyses (Conti Odorisio, 1979; 1980) and to stimulate the scholarly interest she merits.

Works

[Baratotti, Galerana, pseud.], *La semplicità ingannata* (1654), written twenty years earlier and entitled *La tirannia paterna. L'inferno monacale*, unpublished, one ms. known to belong to the private collection of Count Giustiniani. *Il paradiso monacale* (1663 [1643]). *Antisatira*, publ. anonymously by DAT [donna Arcangela Tarabotti] in F. Buoninsegni, *Contro il lusso donnesco, satira menippea* (1644). *Lettere familiari e di complimento* (1650). *Che le donne siano della spetie degli uomini. Difesa delle donne di Galerana Barcitotti [pseud.] contro Horatio Plata* (1651).

Bibliography

Bandini Buti, Maria, ed., *Poetesse e scrittrici*, II (*Enciclopedia biografica e bibliografica italiana*, Serie VI) (Rome, 1942), p. 230. Conti Ororisio, Ginevra, *Donne e società nel Seicento* (Roma, 1979), esp. pp. 79–111, and selections from works of A.T. on 199–238. Conti Ororisio, Ginevra, *Storia dell'idea femminista in Italia* (Rome, 1980), pp. 35–49. Labalme, Patricia H., "Women's Roles in Early Modern Venice: An Exceptional Case" in *Beyond Their Sex: Learned Women of the European Past*, Patricia H. Labalme, ed. (New York, 1980), pp. 129–152, esp. 135–138, 149. Zanette, Emilio, *Suor Arcangela monaca del Seicento veneziano* (Rome-Venice, 1960).

Elissa B. Weaver

Pauline Mary Tarn

(see: Renée Vivien)

Sabine-Casimir-Amable Voïart Tastu

Born August 31, 1798, Metz, France; died
  January 11, 1885, Palaiseau
Genre(s): poetry, short fiction, pedagogy,
  literary history and criticism, travelogue
Language(s): French

The literary production of Amable Tastu falls into two somewhat overlapping phases, one "creative" and the other "professional": her lyric poetry, composed predominantly before her husband's financial difficulties, reflects characteristic features of French Romanticism. Her prose works, written under financial pressure, show how she adapted her talents to financial exigencies. In both periods, though, it is striking how successful her publications were, invariably going through many editions.

She was born in Metz, her father a public official and her mother the sister of the Minister of War under the First Republic. Her mother died when she was seven, an event that apparently reinforced her disposition to melancholy. She devoted much of her childhood and youth to reading and, encouraged by her father's second wife, steeped herself in the poetry of Gessner, Ossian, Bernardin de Saint-Pierre, and Chateaubriand. In 1809 she composed her first poem "Le Réséda" (The Mignonette) in honor of the Empress Josephine, and the work won her an audience with the Empress. In 1816 her father published another poem of hers, "Le Narcisse" (The Daffodil), in the journal *Le Mercure* without her knowledge. The eighteen-year-old protested to her father that she was confronted by the dilemma of marriage or work: if he wanted her poetry published, then he would have to accept her remaining single. Her father showed her letter of protest to the publisher of *Le Mercure*, Joseph Tastu, who promptly married the young woman. Their marriage seems to have been happy: they had one son, Eugène, who later became a French diplomat with assignments in Larnaca (Cyprus), Bagdad, Cairo, and eastern Europe. In 1820 and 1823 she won the "Silver Lily" (Lys d'argent) from the Académie des Jeux-Floraux (Academy of Floral Games), an academy founded in 1324 at Roussillon for the encouragement of poetry; the Académie des Jeux-Floraux at this time played an influential role in encouraging Romanticism in France; the significance of this award can be appreciated if one recalls that it was the Académie des Jeux-Floraux that first recognized Victor Hugo in 1819, the year before it recognized Amable Tastu, before comparable recognition from the Académie Française. Amable Tastu's status as a poet is further attested by the fact that she was asked to compose a poem in honor of the coronation of Charles X in 1824, "Les oiseaux du sacré" (The Birds of the Coronation). In 1826 her husband published her first collection of poetry. Three works stand out here: "L'Ange gardien" (The Guardian Angel), praised by Sainte-Beuve for its serene tone and for being a model of the "domestic elegy"; "Shakespeare," which presents selections from *Julius Caesar*, *Romeo and Juliet*, *King Lear*, and A *Midsummer Night's Dream* and which merits attention as part of the discovery of Shakespeare in France in the wake of Stendhal's *Racine et Shakespeare* (1823/25); and "A Victor Hugo," which must be viewed as one of the earliest tributes to the then-twenty-four-year-old poet. The Revolution of 1830 led to the gradual financial ruin of Joseph Tastu, and perhaps the fall of Charles X also had ramifications for the literary fortunes of the poet who had sung his coronation. In any event after 1830 a new phase in Amable Tastu's career began: she embarked on a series of publication ventures that stand in marked contrast to her earlier poetic works: a new translation of Robinson Crusoe (1835; reprinted 1839, 1845); children's literature; pedagogical treatises; historical writings; short fiction; literary criticism (her *Éloge de Mme. de Sévigné* [Praise of Madame de Sévigné] from 1840 was awarded a prize by the Académie Française and reprinted in subsequent editions of letters of Madame de Sévigné); literary history (her studies of both German and Italian literature were frequently reprinted throughout the nineteenth century); and travelogues. Following her husband's death in 1849, she joined her son during his various diplomatic assignments, at one time being the only European woman in Bagdad. In the course of these wanderings she lost her sight, which could only be partially restored later. She returned to Paris in 1865, experienced both the siege of Paris and the

Commune before she retired to Palaiseau where she died in 1885. Her early lyrical works bear reexamination; her literary criticism should be seen as part of more general movements.

Works

The following lists attempt to systematize the often contradictory listings found in the catalogues of the Bibliothèque Nationale, British Library, and National Union pre-1956 imprints. *Album poétique des jeunes personnes* [Poetic Album for Young People] (1861, 1869, 1876). *La Chevalerie française* [French Chivalry] (1821). *Chroniques de France* [Chronicles of France] (1820, 1829, 1831, 1837). *Cours d'histoire de France* [A Course on French History] (1836). *L'Éducation maternelle* [Maternal Education] (1835). *Éloge de Mme de Sévigné* (1840). *Les Enfants de la vallée d'Andlau, ou Notions familières sur la religion, la morale et les merveilles de la nature* (1837; English tr. as *Education, moral and religious, or familiar illustration of the importance of industry, sobriety, economy, kindness, benevolence, knowledge and piety, for children and youth*, tr. Rev. C. Newell 1842). *Le Livre de la jeunesse et de beauté* [The Book of Youth and Beauty] (1834). *Le Livre des Femmes, choix de morceaux extraits des meilleurs écrivains français sur le caractère, les moeurs et l'esprit des femmes* [The Book of Women, Choice of Selections from the Best French Authors on the Character, Behavior and Mind of Women] (1823). *Poésies* (1826, 5th edition, 1833). *Poésies nouvelles* (1835, 4th edition, 1839). *Prose* (1836). *Les Récits du maître d'école* [Tales of the Schoolmaster] (1844). *Soirées littéraires de Paris* [Literary Evenings in Paris] (1832). *Tableau de la littérature italienne* [Survey of Italian Literature] (1843). *Tableau de la littérature allemande* [Survey of German Literature] (1843, 1844). *Voyage en France* [Traveling in France] (1846). Under this title, a number of subsequent expanded editions wre published that collect many of Amable Tastu's scattered travelogue writings.

Bibliography

Grenier, Edouard, "Souvenirs littéraires." *Revue politique et littéraire (Revue bleue)* 52 (July 22, 1893): 107–111. Quérard, J.-M., "Tastu, Saine-Casimir-Amable Voïart." *La France littéraire* (Paris, 1838), v. 9, pp. 352–354. Sainte-Beuve, Charles, "Madame Tastu." *Portraits contemporains* (2nd ed., Paris, 1870), pp. 158–176 (originally in *La Revue des Deux-Mondes*, February 1835).

Earl Jeffrey Richards

Gina Teelen

(see: Tami Oelfken)

Telesilla

Fl. in 5th century B.C., Argos (Greece)
Genre(s): poetry
Language(s): Greek

Little is known of Telesilla's poetry, for only two complete lines and a few one-word fragments survive. The longest fragment (*PMG* 717) comes, apparently, from a choral hymn: "Artemis, o maidens, fleeing from Alpheus. . . ." Like several other women poets (Sappho, Corinna, Nossis, q.v.), Telesilla appears to have composed specifically for a female audience. Two later authors, Pausanias (2.20.8) and Plutarch (*Mul. virt.* 245c), tell us that her works were "renowned among women." She wrote of a famous temple of Artemis and also narrated myths about Apollo's childhood, about Niobe's tragic loss of her children, and possibly about the wedding of Zeus and Hera. The "Telesilleion" metre, named after her by Alexandrian scholars, is closely associated with marriage songs. Thus the evidence indicates that Telesilla's work treated mythic themes of paramount interest to female listeners.

Nevertheless, the single historical account of her represents her in a masculine and warlike capacity. According to Pausanias and the historian Socrates of Argos, cited in Plutarch (*Mul. virt.* 245C), Telesilla rallied the women of Argos to a successful defense of their city after its army had been destroyed by invading Spartans. Analysis of the source materials indicates that this story, though based upon a real Spartan victory over Argive troops, is itself simply a patriotic legend. An ancient commentator on Homer, however, reports that Telesilla composed a song celebrating noble valor. Such poetry may have prompted the creation of a tale about her own extraordinary military ability.

Works

Greek texts and German translations in Homeyer, H., *Dichterinnen des Altertums und des frühen Mittelalters*(Paderborn, 1979). Greek texts in *Poetae Melici Graeci*, ed. D.L. Page (Oxford, 1962). English translations in *Lyra Graeca* II, tr. J.M. Edmonds (Loeb Classical Library, Cambridge, Mass., 1958).

Bibliography

Kirkwood, G.M., *Early Greek Monody: The History of a Poetic Type* (Ithaca, 1974). Snyder, J.M., *The Woman and the Lyre* (Carbondale, Ill., 1989). Trypanis, C.A., *Greek Poetry from Homer to Seferis* (Chicago, 1981).

General references: *Cambridge History of Classical Literature I: Greek Literature*, eds. P.E. Easterling and B.M.W. Knox (Cambridge, 1985), p. 241. *Oxford Classical Dictionary* (Oxford, 1970), p. 1041. Pauly-Wissowa, *Real-Encyclopädie der klassischen Altertumswissenschaft*, supp. V, A.1 (Stuttgart, 1934), pp. 384–385.

Other references: Vidal-Naquet, P., "Slavery and the Rule of Women in Tradition, Myth and Utopia," in *Myth, Religion and Society*, ed. R.L. Gordon (Cambridge, 1981), pp. 191–192.

Marilyn B. Skinner

Madame de Tencin

Born 1682, Grenoble, France; died 1749
Genre(s): memoirs, novel, epistle
Language(s): French

The Marquise de Tencin was the sister of a well-known statesman, Cardinal Pierre Guerin de Tencin (1680–1758), archbishop of Lyon. Her name is also often mentioned in connection with Jean Le Rond d'Alembert, an illegitimate son fathered by a cavalry officer, the Chevalier Destouches. Although d'Alembert became a famous mathematician and was honored with membership in the French Academy, Madame de Tencin never acknowledged him as her son. Her salon was well attended by literary figures and "philosophes" of the eighteenth century. She had numerous sentimental entanglements and among her numerous affairs included the Regent of France.

Her writings often took a biographical tone; in *Le Siège de Calais*, for instance, she describes how a child is abandoned. Certain passages of *Mémoires de Comminge* remind us that Madame de Tencin was an unfrocked canoness. She left an impressive correspondence, describing many of the court intrigues from 1742 to 1757, published in 1790 under the title: *Correspondance du Cardinal de Tencin . . . et de Mme de Tencin, Sa Soeur, avec le Duc de Richelieu*. This epistolary collection was also published in Paris in 1823 by Chaumerot Jeune, with the letters of Madame de La Fayette and Madame de Villars.

Her complete works first appeared in 1786 in seven volumes, and included the *Anecdotes de la Cour du Règne d'Edouard I, Roi d'Angleterre*. The famous biographers Barbier and Quérard mention that most of her works were done in collaboration with Pont-de-Veyle and d'Argental. This is discussed in the book by Masson which also credits Madame de Tencin for two works attributed to Pont-de-Veyle, *Le Complaisant* and *Le Fat Puni*.

Another collection, with an interesting format, was the *Oeuvres Complètes de Mmes de La Fayette, de Tencin et de Fontaines*, first published in Paris by the widow Lepetit in 1820 and which included historical and literary notes on these three famous women.

There is also a possibility that Madame de Tencin may have translated a work by Charles Johnston (1767; *Chrisal, ou les Aventures d'une Guinee, Histoire Angloise*).

Works

Memoires du Comte de Comminge (1735). *La Religieuse Intéressée et Amoureuse* (1715). *Le Siège de Calais, Nouvelle Historique*, 2 vol. (1739). *Les Malheurs de l'Amour*, 2 vol. (1747). *Le Règne d'Edouard II* (1786). *Anecdotes de la Cour et du Règne d'Edouard II, Roi d'Angleterre* (1786). *Oeuvres Complètes*, 5 vols. (1825).

Bibliography

Green, Fr., *La Peinture des Moeurs de la Bonne Société dans le Roman Français de 1715 à 1761* (1924). Masson, P.-M., *Madame de Tencin (1682–1749)*. Servais, Etienne, *Le Genre Romanesque en France Depuis l'Apparition de la Nouvelle Héloise Jusqu'aux Approches de la Révolution* (1922).

Colette Michael

Nadezhda Teplova

*Born March 19, 1814, Moscow, Russia; died
June 16, 1848, Zvenigorod*
Genre(s): lyric poetry
Language(s): Russian

Nadezhda Teplova holds a minor but honorable place among the young poets who followed Pushkin into Russian literature. Her voice adds a rare feminine note to the poetry of the Golden Age. Born into a prosperous merchant family, she and her sister Serafima were encouraged early to express their gifts for music and literature. Teplova's first poem, published in *Damskii zhurnal* (Ladies' Magazine) when she was thirteen, attracted the attention of the Ukrainian poet and · historian, M.A. Maksimovich, who arranged for publication of her poetry in a wide range of journals.

Teplova's brief lyrics are technically proficient and exploit a wide variety of meters and forms. Their range of theme is narrow, and they are written in a minor key. She is good at finding correlatives for complex states of mind: religious faith close to mysticism, bitterness, resignation, grief at her husband's early death. Autumn with its "nature drear and cold" is her natural season ("Osen'," 1835). Only rarely does Teplova express a more positive frame of mind, as in "Pererozhdenie" (1835; Rebirth), where she likens an ecstatic mood to flying.

Like many of her fellow women writers, Teplova seems to have found the literary world inhospitable and regretted exposing her intimate thoughts to the public. Her bitter "Sovet" (1837; Advice) to a young woman poet was either to refrain from writing verse altogether ("Give up your lyre, give up and play no more") or at least to keep her verse to herself: "Where there's proud laurel, myrtle does not flourish!"

Works

Stikhotvoreniia (1833; 2nd, enlarged ed., 1838; 3rd, enlarged ed., 1860). *Poety 1820–1830kh godov*, vol. 1, L.Ia. Ginzburg, ed. (1972), pp. 580–592.

Translation: *Russian Literature Triquarterly* 9 (1974): 25–28.

Bibliography

Golitsyn, N.N., *Bibliograficheskii slovar' russkikh pisatel'nits.* (St. Petersburg, 1889; rpt., Leipzig, 1974), p. 244.

Mary F. Zirin

Teppo

(see: Wilhelmina "Minna" Ulrika [Johnson] Canth)

A. Terek

(see: Ol'ga Forsh)

Laura Terracina

Born 1519, Naples, Italy; died 1577
Genre(s): narrative and lyric poetry
Language(s): Italian

Laura Terracina was the most prolific woman poet of the Italian Renaissance. She was the daughter of Diana Onofra of Sorrento and of Paolo Terracina, a nobleman who held several offices at the Neapolitan court and died at the age of one hundred and ten. Laura did not receive a classical education but was encouraged in her poetic endeavors by Marcantonio Passero, a retired professor of the University of Padua, who kept a private register of Neapolitan poets, and by Lodovico Domenichi, a literary factotum and entrepreneur of the publishing business. The decade 1549–1559 was the happiest in her life: ensconced in the family residence in the then-pastoral as well as aristocratic district of Chiaia, Laura, in the bloom of her youth, savored the attention of the people who frequented the court, the university and the academies. For the Terracinas, staunch supporters of the monarchy, these were years of success. Laura's propensity for highly-placed men and women was strengthened during the street riots of 1547, when her entire family was threatened with extinction because of a tax imposed by her uncle Domenico. At the age of forty, she married a relative, Polidoro Terracina. The marriage was very unhappy, mostly on account of his obsessive jealousy. In the volumes published at this time and later, Laura laments her restricted life, her isolation, and the ingratitude of the powerful. Between 1570 and 1575, she travelled to Rome, perhaps in the hope of ingratiating herself with the Papal Court. Her last piece of writing is a letter dated November 30, 1577.

Most of Terracina's output can be seen as a poetic correspondence in the current Petrarchistic mode. About 80 poems were sent to as many literati of the peninsula, at least 200 more were addressed to members of the Neapolitan nobility. Thematic and stylistic commonplaces are used to praise the recipient and to celebrate private or public occasions. The metrical schemes are those of the sonnet, the *canzone*, the madrigal, the sestet, the octave, *terze rime*, and *capitoli*.

Relatively few are Laura's love poems. In her fourth volume, she evades the sexual entreaties of Alfonso Mantegna di Maida, professor of the Studium; when he finally turns his attention elsewhere, Terracina composes a poem in praise of the lady. Some poems of unrequited love maintain the male point of view and the manner of address to the beloved characteristic of Petrarchism. Modern scholars see them as a gauge of the degree of depersonalization present in the socialized applications of the lyric code. Most of Laura's poetry of courtship, however, is addressed to well-known women of high rank and was very probably written in the voice of and by request of male suitors. Other poems are complaints over the lover's betrayal in the person of fictional characters and can be easily traced to the popular genre of the "woman's lament."

The prevailing tone of Laura's poetry is deprecatory and moralistic. Contemporary society is upbraided for its greed, treachery, and ferocity. In the manner of Petrarch, she laments Italy's political upheavals and the devastations of cities and countryside brought about by invading armies. In a more personal vein, she expresses nostalgia for her past successes. Many poems written in her last years and never published belong to the genre of *rime spirituali*, much favored in the new religious climate of the Counter-Reformation. In her prayers and meditations on death, Terracina attains a level of intimate pathos.

A *Discorso sopra tutti i primi canti d'Orlando Furioso* (Summary of the Content of the First Cantos of *Orlando Furioso*) summarizes Ariosto's poem in 46 swift and graceful cantos interspersed with moralistic considerations. In Canto V, Laura upholds the intellectual equality of the sexes and attributes the limited achievements attained by her sex to the small number of women dedicated to literary work. First published by Giolito in 1549, the *Discorso* was reissued five times by him before 1561 and at least four more times by other publishers before the end of the century. In 1567, she wrote a second *Discorso*, this one about Ariosto's additional Cantos, when her reluctance was overcome by Valvassori, the publisher.

Exaggeratedly praised during her most productive years, Terracina outlived the popularity of the genres to which she had applied her facile vein. After her death, she became the butt of sexual and literary ridicule on the part of dyspeptic satirists. Most famous is the portrayal of her made by T. Boccalini in his *Ragguagli di Parnaso* (Reports from Parnassus). Her literary prolificity and pro-Spanish sympathies are here ferociously, though wittily, chastised in what is essentially an *ad feminam* attack of political nature. Since then, Terracina has scored very low in the scale of sixteenth-century poetic achievement. It is, therefore, a surprise to discover considerable facility and rhetorical skill in many of her verses. More recently she has been called a professional of literature, who capably answered the demands of a middle-brow public. As such, in a social-historical view of Renaissance literature, she fits the description given by her contemporary admirers as that of a "marvel of the female sex."

Works

Rime (1548). *Rime seconde* (1549). *Discorso sopra tutti i primi canti di Orlando Furioso* (1549). *Quarte rime* (1550). *Quinte rime* (1552). *Seste rime* (1558). *Sovra tutte le vedove di questa citta di Napoli* (1561). *La seconda parte de' Discorsi sopra le seconde stanze de' Canti d'Orlando Furioso* (1567).

Bibliography

Agnelli, G., and G. Ravegnani, *Annali delle edizioni ariostesche* II (Bologna, 1933), pp. 202–204. Borzelli, A., *Laura Terracina, poetessa napoletana del Cinquecento* (Napoli, 1924). Crescimbeni, G.M., *Istoria della volgar poesia* II (Venice, 1730), p. 351. Croce, B., "La casa di una poetessa" (1901). *Storie e leggende napoletane* (Bari, 1948), pp. 275–

289. *Dizionario biografico degli Italiani* V (Rome, 1960), pp. 61–63. Ferroni, G., and A. Quondam, *La locuzione artificiosa* (Rome, 1973), pp. 329–339. Gaspary, A., *Storia della letteratura italiana* II, tr. V. Rossi (Turin, 1981), pp. 137–155. Maroi, Lucia, *Laura Terracina napoletana del secolo XVI* (Napoli, 1913). Mazzarella di Cerreto, A., "Laura Terracina," in *Biografia degli uomini illustri del Regno di Napoli*, D. Martuscelli, ed. (Napoli, 1814). Quadrio, F.S., *Della storia e della ragione d'ogni poesia* II (Bologna, 1741), p. 249. Tiraboschi, G., *Storia della letteratura italiana* VII (Modena, 1793), p. 1184.

Rinaldina Russell

Juhani Tervapää

(see: Hella Maria Wuolijoki)

Maria Tesselschade

Born March 15, 1594, Amsterdam, The
Netherlands; died June 20, 1649, Amsterdam
Genre(s): poetry, letters
Language(s): Dutch

Maria Tesselschade Roemersdochter lived through the first half of the Dutch Golden Age, an era in which political power and economic prosperity were matched by intense cultural activity. She wrote poetry, including sonnets, and kept up a lively correspondence with some of the great writers and intellectuals of the time, such as Pieter Corneliszoon Hooft, Constantijn Huygens, and Caspar van Baerle or Barlaeus. Mostly written on the occasion of, or as a reaction to, private and public events, Tesselschade's letters and poems are not only fine examples of Dutch Renaissance literature (which was late in developing compared to Southern Europe); they also offer valuable insights into the bustling intellectual, literary, and religious climate of the young Dutch republic.

Her father, the wealthy grain merchant and poet Roemer Pieterszoon Visscher (1547–1620), had given her the middle name Tesselschade to "memorize" the heavy losses he suffered following a storm off the Frisian island Texel three months before she was born (*Tessel* is Texel; *Scha* is *schade*, or damage). Tesselschade (like her equally talented sister Anna Roemer Visscher) received an excellent education in the liberal arts. They knew both French and Italian, read foreign authors, wrote and translated, and were hostesses at the frequent gatherings of artists and intellectuals in their father's house. Later Tesselschade became a very welcome guest of the so-called *Muiderkring* or Muiden Circle, a rather loose group of literati, scholars, merchants, and holders of public office who met irregularly at the house of the poet and historiographer P.C. Hooft for poetry, music, and discussions.

Tesselschade's charm and her many accomplishments (singing, engraving, writing) attracted poets and artists. But in 1623 she married Allard Crombalgh, a naval officer with no literary or artistic pretensions. He died in 1634. As a widow in her forties, Tesselschade was still courted, half in jest, half in earnest, by two prominent members of the Muiden Circle. In 1641 or 1642, she converted to Catholicism, a courageous act of faith at a time when Roman Catholics were an unpopular minority. Both occasions characteristically gave rise to a lively poetic and epistolary exchange among Tesselschade and her friends. Faithful to the memory of her beloved husband, she never gave in to her "suitors," sending them level-headed and, often, witty replies. She countered the sometimes vicious attacks on her return to Rome with remarkable serenity and occasional playfulness.

A true child of the Renaissance, Tesselschade craftily explored the possibilities of the vernacular, making use of various rhyme schemes and prosodic patterns. She had a predilection for ingenious wordplay, complex imagery, and oblique allusions. An admirer of the Italian poet Marino, she did not keep her work free from frivolous punning and mannerisms.

Classical ideals prevail throughout her writing. The motto with which she occasionally signed her poems and letters, "Elck zyn Waerom"—"to each his why"—points toward her independent mind and her tolerance toward others. Her very aversion to intolerance and rigidity in religious and other matters may have turned her away from rigorous Calvinism, which, in her opinion, was seriously curtailing the freedom of the republic's citizens (including their freedom of religion). Tesselschade confronted grief—her own grief and that of others—with equanimity and stoic composure. In one of her most accomplished poems, a sonnet written on the death of the Lady of Sulekom, Huygens's wife, Tesselschade implored her friend to "confide to paper not to memory," since "paper was the weapon with which I fought the wish to die ere heaven could reclaim me."

Maria Tesselschade died in 1649, not only surviving her husband but also her two daughters and some of her closest friends. Though her beauty and talents had been extensively sung in poetry and prose during her lifetime, only a few of her own poems had actually been printed. More verse was published in various anthologies later in the century, but on the whole relatively little survived. Her work on a translation of Tasso's *Gerusalemme Liberata* is entirely lost except for one stanza. Among her most appreciated poems are the sonnet already mentioned, the beautifully solemn "Mary magdalen at the Feet of Jesus," emphasizing man's repentance and God's mercy, and "Onderscheyd tusschen een wilde, en een tamme zangster" (The Distinction Between a Wild and a Tame Singer), a crafted illustration of "the ars naturae aemula" theme.

Though Maria Tesselschade is generally not counted among the century's great, her work remains of interest today as one of the few testimonies of a highly intelligent, sensitive, and witty woman who participated, apparently with great zest, in the exciting cultural life of the Netherlands' most illustrious age.

Works

Een onwaerdeerlycke vrouw. Brieven en verzen van en aan Maria Tesselschade, ed. J.A. Worp (1918; rpt. 1976). *'t Hoge huis te Muiden. Teksten uit de Muiderkring*, ed. M.C.A. Van der Heijden, 2nd ed. (1978). Translations: Selected poems and letters, tr. R. Vanderauwera, in *Renaissance Women Writers*, ed. K.M. Wilson (1987).

Bibliography

Brachin, P., "Tesselschade, femme savante," in *Etudes de littérature néerlandaise* (1955). Damsteegt, B.C., "De schonckensonnetten," in *Tijdschrift voor Nederlandse Taal en Letteren* 96 (1980). Flinn, J.F., "La préciosité dans la littérature néerlandaise. L'oeuvre de Maria Tesselschade," in *Revue de Littérature Comparée* 40 (1966). Gosse, E.W., "A Dutch Poetess of the Seventeenth Century," in *Studies in the Literature of Northern Europe* (1879). Michels, L.C., *Filologische opstellen* (1957–1964). Minderaa, P., "Een omstreden gedicht van Tesselschade," in *Opstellen en voordrachten uit mijn hoogleraarstijd (1948–1964)* (1964). Minderaa, P., "Een geestige pennestrijd tussen Tesselschade en Huygens," in *Tijdschrift voor Levende Talen* 33 (1967). Scheltema, J., *Anna en Maria Tesselschade, de dochters van Roemer Visscher* (1978). Sterck, J.F.M., "Vondel—Eusebia—Tesselschade," in *Van Onzen Tijd* 11 (1910). Sterck, J.F.M., *Oorkonden over Vondel en zijn kring* (1918). Sterck, J.F.M., "Tessalica," in *Tijdschrift voor Nederlandse Taal en Letteren* 40 (1921). Vanderauwera, R., "Maria Tesselschade," in *Renaissance Women Writers*, ed. K.M. Wilson (1987). Van Gool, A., "Tessela—Thessala—Tesselschade." in *Vondeljaarboek 1949* (1949). Witstein, S.f., *Funeraire poëzie in de Nederlandse Renaissance* (1969).

General references: *Cassell's Encyclopaedia of World Literature. De Nederlandse en Vlaamse auteurs van middeleeuwen tot heden* (1985). Knuvelder, G.P., *Handboek tot de geschiedenis der Nederlandse letterkunde* 2 (1971). *Moderne encyclopedie van de wereldliteratuur* (1980–1984). *Winkler Prins Lexicon der Nederlandse letterkunde* (1986).

Ria Vanderauwera

Gerti Tetzner

Born 1936, Siegleben, Thüringen, Germany
Genre(s): novel
Language(s): German

Gerti Tetzner studied law and later attended the Johannes R. Becher institute for literature in Leipzig. Presently Tetzner resides in Leipzig and works as a free-lance writer. She received the Johannes R. Becher prize for her novel, *Karin W.*, which has also had much success in West Germany. *Karin W.*'s theme is the emancipation of women, and Tetzner's concern is the self-realization and the fulfillment of women independent of men.

Works
Karin W. (1974).

Bibliography
Emmerich, Wolfgang, *Kleine Literaturgeschichte der DDR* (Darmstadt, 1981). *Neue Literatur der Frauen.* Herausgegeben von Heinz Puknus (München, 1980).

Brigitte Edith Archibald

Anne Teyssiéras

Born 1945
Genre(s): poetry
Language(s): French

Anne Teyssiéras' first volume of poetry, aptly titled *Epervier ma solitude* (Sparrowhawk My Loneliness), was published in 1966 and followed soon by *Fragments pour une captive* (1969; Fragments for a Prisoner). The latter is an intense, compact collection centered upon an intimate though discreet elaboration of themes of disappearance and absence, waiting and possible future gesturing. A "hymn of Death," it struggles both with factors of (self-)imprisonment and devastation, and those of determination and invention. *L'Ecaille entre les eaux* (1975; The Shell Between the Waters), written under the sign of Artaud, shows just how difficult this struggle is: the bare, elegant texts swarm with unspeakableness, suffocation, pain and impotence, and, although the final section speaks of rebirth and maintains a sense of feasibility, it, too, is threatened with failure and cloaked in uncertainty.

Anne Teyssiéras' sixth volume, *Parallèles* (Parallels), appeared in 1976—it was to be republished in 1982 with *La Boule de cristal* (The Crystal Ball). *Parallèles* offers us poems of great emotional intensity, in which love and the poet's ceaseless interrogation of signs are repeatedly met with frustration and forced to the brink of "madness." The power of resistance is, however, great: death is not absolute, the (absent) other remains a "high keeper of my song," whilst the *hic et nunc* retains its vital compulsion: "I shall not wear mourning / Elsewhere summons me /

Here is my obligation wherein I cleanse a swamp." *Le Pays d'où j'irai* (1977; The Land from Where I Shall Go), liminally inspired by Michaux, betrays similar tensions: marginally more positive in tone and centered upon departure and future event, the volume nevertheless displays the many sober traces of the wretchedness and marredness of things as well as the exile wrought paradoxically by poetry itself. *Juste avant la nuit* (1979; Just Before Night) specifically articulates these paradoxes and tensions via a contrapuntal rhetoric in which the "intertwinement of speech" is delicately explored and enacted, and factors of poetic place and non-place, recognition and non-recognition, going and (non-)arrival, loss and regrowth are subtly and evocatively elaborated.

Les Clavicules de Minho (The Clavicles of Minho) was published in 1986. Taking up the interrogations Anne Teyssiéras began in part in *La Boule de cristal* (1982), "It is," she says, "the end consequence of a period of reflection on, if one wants, the result of the 'gropings' that went before." It is, at all events, both a powerfully felt and a brilliantly lucid assessment of the problematics of poetic voice and, indeed, all artistic expression. As such it stands alongside the writings of contemporaries such as Yves Bonnefoy, Michel Deguy and Bernard Noël. It happily avoids all pretentiousness and tendentiousness. Poetry and art, for Anne Teyssiéras, offer an oddly intransitive knowledge, a kind of "laughter . . . in response to all questions." They are predicated upon "belief," desire, "promise"; they hesitate between sense and non-sense; their "focusing" is illusory, their contact is with Nothingness. They are, one might say, living "deconstruction." The poet, as Anne Teyssiéras says, "seeks shelter in the eye of the cyclone, whereas you exhaust yourself at the fringes of non-sense." Poetry and art are thus "movement not achievement." Myth, she rightly argues, comes precisely from poetry's/art's "detour." Other forces, however, are infinitely greater, and, possibly, less mystifying: love, the forces of being beyond us, the "distant effusion" of which poetry and art are but an "echo." The latter are merely "the saliva of nothingness"—but "everything is in Nothingness"—and require our compassionate but lucid laughter to show both their skeletalness and their residual potential for illumination. *Les*

Clavicules de Minho gives us the revealed originality of Anne Teyssiéras as poet and theoretician.

Works

> *Epervier ma solitude* (1966). *Fragments pour une captive* (1969). *Cinq étapes pour une attente* (1971). *Dernier état* (1974). *L'Ecaille entre les eaux* (1975). *Parallèles* (1976). *Le Pays d'où j'irai* (1977). *Juste avant la nuit* (1979). *Parallèles, suivi de La Boule de cristal* (1982). *Poèmes en Kabbale* (1984). *Les Clavicules de Minho* (1986).

Michael Bishop

Thekla

(see: Ida von Reinsberg-Düringsfeld)

Victoria Theodorou

Born 1926 (1928?), Crete
Genre(s): poetry, memoirs
Language(s): Greek

Victoria Theodorou was born in Crete to a Cretan mother and a Yugoslavian father. She studied literature at the University of Athens. During and following World War II, she participated in the resistance movement and as a consequence was imprisoned for five years by the right-wing government that eventually came into power. During her imprisonment she wrote a journal of her wartime experiences. She eventually married and had two daughters. She lives in Athens.

Most of Theodorou's poetry is autobiographical and marked by bitterness as a result of her harsh experiences. Her purpose is to tell her side of the story, which until recently was not allowed to surface, and thus to set things "right." Her voice is the voice of the oppressed, but "the oppressed" in her poetry are usually the women who are cruelly and inhumanly treated by male figures of authority—jailers, policemen, prosecutors, judges. Theodorou's poems are attempts to make songs (laments?) out of life's pain, which is the advice Galateia Kazantzakē gave her when she was freed and allowed to go home, as she herself tells us in her poem "Galateia Kazantzakē" (in *Voreio Proasteio*).

In contrast to her earlier poetry, *To lagouto* (The Lute) takes us to pastoral settings and serene surroundings and offers an escape from the harshness of life.

Works

> *To lagouto* [The Lute] (1971). *Voreio Proasteio* [Northern Suburb]. *Stratopeda gynaikōn* [Women's Camps] (1975), ed. Victoria Theodorou (includes the journals of nine captive women).

Bibliography

> *Contemporary Greek Women Poets*, tr. Eleni Fourtouni (New Haven, Conn., 1978). *Four Greek Women: Love Poems.*, tr. Eleni Fourtouni (New Haven, Conn., 1982). Some of her work has been translated into Serbo-Croatian.

Helen Dendrinou Kolias

Theosebeia

(a.k.a. Theosebia Chemica, Theosobia)

Born 5th–6th century A.D., Greece
Genre(s): poetry
Language(s): Greek

Theosebeia wrote a poem in four hexameters lamenting the death of a famous doctor by the name of Ablabius. The poem is a sepulchral epigram which initially belonged to Agathias' collection of epigrams (sixth century A.D.) and later in the tenth century A.D. was incorporated in the Palatine (Greek) Anthology (7.559). Galen's name (court physician, second century A.D.) and Ablabius', which are mentioned in the poem, indicate a late imperial date of composition. It is not certain whether Theosebeia is the sister of Zosimus 1, the alchemist from Panoplis, and also the dedicatee of his 28-volume treatise on alchemy.

Theosebeia is inspired and strongly influenced by earlier epigrammatists, in particular by Asclepiades (third century B.C.) and Antipater of Sidon (flourished c. 120 B.C.) whose poems are also included in the Greek Anthology. The deified Virtue shearing her hair over the tomb of Ajax (*Anthologia Graeca* 7.145, 7.146) as she appears in the two earlier epigrammatists, becomes for Theosebeia the deified Healing Art (Akestoriē) shearing her hair on the tomb of

Ablabius. On the whole, the poem does not exhibit the typical characteristics seen in the other sepulchral epigrams of the Anthology, for example, some information about the dead man, his activities, the place of the burial or some address to the passer-by. No words of emotion are seen in these few lines, but on the contrary, what predominates is the objective and austere tone of the poem, reflected in its dry and unadorned style.

The name of the dedicatee, Ablabius, is most probably allegorical ("A-blabē" means without harm). Other examples in the *Anthologia Graeca* of made-up names which characterize the character or profession of the persons bearing them, reconfirm the above suggestion.

Bibliography

The text of Theosebeia's epigram is found in *Epigrammatum Anthologia Palatina*, ed. F. Dubner, vol. 1, bk. 7.559 (Paris, 1864). A Latin translation of the poem is found in *Anthologia Graeca Epigrammatum, Palatina cum Planudea*, ed. H. Stadtmveller, vol. 2 (Leipzig, 1899). An English translation of it is in the Loeb Classical Library, *Greek Anthology*, vol. 2 (Cambridge, Mass., Harvard Univ. Press, 1960), p. 301.
Martindale, J.R., *The Prosopography of the Later Roman Empire* (Cambridge, 1971), vol. 1, pp. 908 and 994; vol. 2, p. 1110. *Paulys Real-Encyclopadie der Klassischen Altertumswissenschaft* (Stuttgart, 1934), vol. 5, p. 2246.

A. Georgiadou

Theosebia Chemica

(see: Theosebeia)

Theosobia

(see: Theosebeia)

Thrakopoula (Thracian girl)

(see: Alexandra Papadopoulou)

Thyra

(see: Alfhild Agrell)

Tian

(see: Karoline von Günderrode)

Tibors

Born ca. first quarter 13th century
Genre(s): poetry
Language(s): Provençal

In all likelihood Tibors was the sister of the *troubadour* Raimbaut d'Aurenga. According to Bogin, a will, cited by Pattison, of Raimbaut d'Aurenga's mother (also named Tibors) links historical Tibors with Tibors of *razo*. Both Raimbaut's sisters were named Tibors; Bogin guesses this is probably the elder of the two, in part because she was the Tibors married to Bertrand des Baux, a patron of the troubadours.

Unfortunately, the only poetic composition we have by Tibors is a fragment of a *canso* found in one manuscript (H45) that begins "Bels dous amics, ben vos posc en ver dir." The fragment consists of eight lines rhyming *aabbccdd*. Dronke (*Women Writers*, p. 100) says of the *canso*: "Here there is no question of a woman's outcry . . . Nor is the love evoked by Tibors a one-sided, unrequited feeling . . . the persona in her lyric is self-assured; she expresses her joy in loving frankly, without grief or remorse. The tone is 'realistic' . . . yet the real is not allowed to appear indelicate. . . . It is the poet's attitude, open about her erotic wishes, and at the same time so measured and composed, which is unusual, and which has no exact parallel . . . in the lyrics of men troubadours."

Works

Eds., Schultz, p. 25; Raynouard, V, 447; Mahn, III, 321; Chabaneau, p. 300; Véran, p. 76; Boutiere-Schutz, pp. 498–499; Bogin, p. 80; Perkal-Balinsky, pp. 161–163.

Bibliography

Bec, P., "*Trobairitz* et chansons de femme: Contribution à la connaissance du lyrisme féminin au moyen âge." *CCM* 22 (1979): 235–262. Bogin, M., *The Women Troubadours* (New York, 1980). Boutière, J., and A.-H. Schutz, *Biographies des troubadours* (2nd. ed., Paris, 1964). Branciforti, F., *Il canzoniere di Lanfrancesco Cigala* (Florence, 1954). Bruckner, M., "Na Castelloza, *Trobairitz*, and Troubadour Lyric." *Romance Notes* 25 (1985): 1–15. Chabaneau, C., *Les biographies des troubadours en langue provençale in Histoire générale de Languedoc X* (Toulouse, 1885). Dronke, P., *Women Writers of the Middle Ages* (Cambridge, 1984). Mahn, C.A.F., *Die Werke der Troubadours in provenzalischer Sprache* (Berlin, 1846). Perkal-Balinsky, D., *The Minor Trobairitz*. Dissertation, Northwestern University, 1986. Raynouard, M., *Choix des poésies originales des troubadours*, 6 vols. (Osnabruck, 1966). de Riquer, M., *Los trovadores*, 3 vols. (Barcelona, 1975). Schultz, O., *Die Provenzalischen Dichterinnen* (Leipzig, 1888). Shapiro, M., "The Provençal *Trobairitz* and the Limits of Courtly Love." *Signs* 3 (1978): 560–571. Tavera, A., "A la recherche des troubadours maudits." *Sénéfiance* 5 (1978): 135–161. Véran, J., *Les poétesses provençales* (Paris, 1946).

Sarah Spence

Marie-Louise Tidick-Ulveling

Born 1892, Diekirch, Luxembourg; died 1989
Genre(s): novel, short story, lyric poetry
Language(s): German, Luxembourgish

Marie-Louise Tidick-Ulveling came from a cultured bourgeois family. She enjoyed a good education, but health problems prevented her from pursuing further studies. She was the wife of a well-known lawyer but lost her husband in the early years of their marriage. As a widow with a young child she had to accept a routine job to provide for herself and her child. During the Second World War she experienced the grief of seeing her only daughter arrested by the German occupants and of waiting in anguish for the Liberation and the return of her daughter Adeline.

Thus a personally felt grief met with a very vivid social sensitiveness. Although Marie-Louise Tidick-Ulveling was born into the privileged classes, she has always defended the cause of the socially less privileged. Her sense of justice, her yearning for progress, solidarity, and peace can be felt in her writings. In the last period of her creative activity, she also learned to experience the loneliness of ugliness, of disgrace, and of old age.

Marie-Louise Tidick-Ulveling writes poetry that bears the impress of tenderness and yet at times reveals a harsh ironic attack. In her historical novels she evokes scenes of the trials of so-called witches and of Luxembourg during the French Revolution with the purpose of accusing the narrow-mindedness of fanatics in order to claim the liberty of thought and to teach tolerance.

This woman writer exhibits an uncompromising heart and a virulent intelligence within a body impaired by old age.

Works

Funken der Hoffnung [Sparks of Hope] (1957). *Im Zeichen der Flamme* [Marked by Flames] (1961). *Erlebt und beobachtet* [Experienced and Observed] (1964). *Verworrene Wege* [Obscure Paths] (1965). *Traum und Wirklichkeit* [Dream and Reality] (1968). *Gesänge des Lebens* [Songs of Life] (1974). *Abglanz* [Reflection] (1978). *Von gestern für heute* [From Yesterday for Today] (1982).

Rosemarie Kieffer and Liliane Stomp-Erpelding

Ilse Tielsch

Born March 20, 1929, Hustopeče (formerly Auspitz) near Brno (formerly Brünn), Czechoslovakia
Genre(s): poetry, short story, novel, radio drama
Language(s): German

Ilse Tielsch is one of the most popular authors on the contemporary Austrian scene. She writes in a readily accessible style with conventional themes and forms and with a keen sense for what is topical in present-day society. Although her poetry is noteworthy, she is best known for her historical novels dealing with the Second World War and the immediate postwar period.

Tielsch was born in 1929 in southern Moravia, and her family was thus a part of the German minority in Czechoslovakia. She was ten years old when World War II broke out, and her teenage years were shaped by ensuing events. A few months before the end of the war the fifteen-year-old Ilse was sent on a train to relatives in Upper Austria, and she experienced first-hand the chaos as the refugees sought food and shelter in the war-torn country. After much moving around Tielsch studied journalism at the University of Vienna and received her doctorate in 1953. In 1950 she married Rudolf Tielsch, a medical doctor, and they have two children. Tielsch began writing in the mid-1960s, and the recognition she achieved in the 1970s became fame in the 1980s. Her works prior to 1979 appear under a hyphenated name, which she then shortened to Tielsch by dropping the family name Felzmann. Tielsch lives today as a freelance writer in Vienna, where she is a member of the PEN Club and co-editor of the literary journal *Podium*.

Tielsch's historical works begin with a short narrative, *Erinnerungen mit Bäumen* (1979; Reminiscences with Trees), and culminate in two lengthy novels, *Die Ahnenpyramide* (1980; The Ancestor Pyramid) and *Heimatsuchen* (1982; Searching for Home). *Erinnerungen* presents a quasi-biographical account of the events of 1945 from a present-day perspective. A trip to a writers' conference in Upper Austria serves as occasion for a trip into the past as the protagonist Anna visits the area where she had lived temporarily as a young girl more than three decades prior to the time of narration. The landscape becomes a soulscape as Anna recalls the war and the ensuing events. In contrast to the inferno of that time, the present narrative stance is reflective and meditative, and the titular designation "with Trees" articulates the metaphorical level of memory, raising also the question of continuity of identity between then and now.

Tielsch's major novels continue the theme of personal past interwoven with modern European history. *Ahnenpyramide* offers a family chronicle from a present-day perspective, looking back to the earliest mention of the family in church records in 1580 and extending to departure from the area in 1945. It is at the same time a social history of German enclaves in the Czech territories of Bohemia and Moravia, and it attempts to understand the historical relations between the Sudeten Germans and the native Slavic population. Realizing that "totality" is a utopian vision, the narrator points to the discontinuity of his-

toriography; and she presents realistic vignettes describing the everyday life and work of people in a small town, as based on documentary evidence culled from newspapers, photographs, and records of the time. The thematic center is the childhood of the protagonist, a thinly-veiled autobiographical figure named Anni F., and the events of her life between the ages of nine and sixteen are narrated in conjunction with the events of World War II between 1938 and 1945. Like an oscillograph the child registers the vibrations of a world run amok and plunging headlong toward destruction. The long expedition into the past is motivated by a search for the self, for "what we are began long before us." It is also an attempt to liberate the concept "home" (*Heimat*) from the odium of its nationalistic and imperialistic associations. Without idealization, sentimentality, or revisionism the narrator describes an era that is recognized as past and that stands as experience to be integrated into the present.

Heimatsuchen begins where the previous work left off at the end of the war in 1945 when the twelve million Germans living in the Sudetenland and other Eastern European countries were required to leave their homes and seek a new life elsewhere. The sixteen-year-old Anni and her family stand at the center as representative of the millions of refugees that poured into Austria as well as into East and West Germany. The work narrates the chaos of the times: the hardships and dangers of flight, cold, hunger, illness, and exhaustion, separation from and death of loved ones, search for a place to stay, the black market, suspicion and rejection by the indigenous population—and also the help and comfort that was offered and the hope for a new beginning. Without pathos or self-pity and also without bitterness or resentment the author presents a realistic, well-documented account of the time. Whereas the sociopolitical issue of the refugees, the "Heimatvertriebene," is a sensitive topic that had been virtually taboo for over three decades, Tielsch offers a reconciliatory book. While refusing to provide grist for the mill of right-wing politics, it illuminates the past in the true spirit of "Vergangenheitsbewältigung." The work is in some ways comparable to Christa Wolf's *Kindheitsmuster*, and although Tielsch's account is less subjective, it too constitutes an experiment in remembering. It is also an effort to understand the past and forgive its wrongdoings, and above all it is a cry against the repetition of history.

Tielsch has published several collections of short stories that demonstrate her superb stylistic ability even apart from the gripping material of recent history. *Ein Elefant in unserer Straße* (1977; An Elephant in Our Street) is a collection of satires on modern consumer society. With irony and humor the author parodies the drive for material wealth and social status, the grotesque manifestations of which, as indicated by the title, lead to absurdity and alienation. *Fremder Strand* (1984; Foreign Shore), set in the context of a trip to the North Sea, narrates the mid-life crisis of a typical modern woman. As wife, mother, and artist she had placed her family before her own professional ambitions; but with the children grown she finds herself estranged from her husband, alone and aging, and overwhelmed by the distance to her own self as well as to the ostensibly familiar outside world.

Since poetry has in general a more limited appeal than prose, Tielsch's poetry has been somewhat overshadowed by her large novels. But Tielsch would be a prominent author even if she had written only poetry, for her six lyric volumes have been well received. The breakthrough came in 1975 with *Regenzeit* (Rain Time), which was reprinted in 1981—a rare occurrence with poetry. Another volume, *Nicht beweisbar* (Not Provable), also appeared in 1981, and a further volume in 1986, *Zwischenbericht* (Interim Report). A development is noticeable over the past two decades away from the traditional certainties toward a more questioning, skeptical stance, as indicated also by the recent titles. Topics include childhood memories, landscapes, social criticism, and the hopes and fears attached to our fragile constructs. In short free-verse lines the author presents an amalgam of thought and feeling, experience and impression, often with a slight narrative line and a surprising twist at the end. The poems speak dynamically and directly, as indicated by the following self-commentary: "Metaphors don't save us when we fall" (from *Regenzeit*). Of course Tielsch also deploys metaphor very widely, but her images are readily understandable and stand in the service of life rather than art.

In contrast to the exclusiveness and elusiveness of hermetic poetry or experimental literature, Tielsch writes in a traditional realistic mode. The issues that concern her are practical and empirical rather than theoretical or abstract. If her work has not received full recognition from the literary establishment it is probably because it does not have the philosophical depth or aesthetic finesse associated with great literature. Tielsch's faith in the knowability of reality and in the adequacy of language to convey it stands in contrast to the modern tradition of language skepticism. On the other hand, Tielsch's books have reached a wider audience than many works in the intellectual tradition, and they stand as good literature for the general reading public.

Works

In meinem Orangengarten. Gedichte (1964). *Herbst, mein Segel. Gedichte* (1967). *Anrufung des Mondes. Gedichte* (1970). *Begegnung in einer steirischen Jausenstation. Drei Erzählungen* (1973). *Regenzeit. Gedichte* (1975; rpt. 1981). *Ein Elefant in unserer Straße oder Geschichten mit Paul. Satirische Erzählungen* (1977). *Erinnerungen mit Bäumen. Erzählung* (1979). *Südmährische Sagen* (1979). *Die Ahnenpyramide. Roman* (1980). *Nicht beweisbar. Gedichte* (1981). *Heimatsuchen. Roman* (1982). *Fremder Strand. Erzählung* (1984). *Zwischenbericht. Gedichte* (1986). *Der Solitär. Erzählungen* (1987).

Beth Bjorklund

Märta Eleonora Tikkanen

Born April 3, 1935, Helsinki, Finland
Genre(s): novel
Language(s): Swedish

Märta Tikkanen took a B.A. degree in humanities at Helsinki University in 1958, worked as a journalist and later as a secondary school teacher for several years, then became headmistress of a Citizens' Further Education Institute. Her second husband encouraged her writing. At first her writing seemed to emerge as one part of the dialogue in this marriage, the other being provided by her husband in his own novels.

Someone has described her novels as "reports from the innermost core of the kernel family."

Her first novel, *Nu imorron* (1970; Now Tomorrow), is an intense monologue, the ultimate purpose of which seems to be a search for the writer's self, and the autobiographical element recurs in her second novel, *Ingenmansland* (1972; No Man's Land). The first novel uses the first-person narrative throughout, describing a wife wanting a life of her own or at least a kind of total acceptance but unable to secure even enough time to read the newspaper. In the second novel the third-person narrative creates a certain distance between writer and work in debating the nature of freedom that the female protagonist seeks. In the time between these two novels, Märta Tikkanen had become acquainted with the American Women's Liberation movement and was definitely influenced by their ideas, but her female protagonist seems too naive and too isolated to be able to live up to any feminist ideals: she remains in a no-man's-land, but she is aware of the necessity of some kind of liberation for both partners. The works that earned her international fame were *Män kan inte våldtas* (1975; Men Cannot Be Raped) and *Århundradets kärlekssaga* (1978; The Love Story of This Century). The latter has been called a confessional poem and belongs in the genre of autobiographical stories that has dominated Swedish literature in Finland for some twenty years.

Her most recent work, *Rödluvan* (1986; Little Red Riding Hood), continues her constant focus on womanhood as well as her autobiographical line; it is a report obviously on her own maturing process through childhood and marriage, sorrow and liberation.

Märta Tikkanen has already offered many valid arguments in the ongoing debate on women and their new position. She is quite likely going to continue along these lines, as the issues involved seem to catch and keep her interest together with her analytical observation of her own self.

Works

Nu imorron [Now Tomorrow] (1970). *Ingenmansland* [No Man's Land] (1972). *Vem bryr sig om Doris Mihailov?* [Who Cares for Doris Miahilov?] (1974). *Män kan inte våldtas* [Men Cannot Be Raped] (1975) (translated into five languages, also English). [With Katarina Michelsson], *Mörkret som ger glädjen djup* [Darkness That Gives Joy Its Depth] (1981). *Sofias egen bok* [Sophy's Own Book]. *Rödluvan* (1986; Little Red Riding Hood). A few radio and television plays.

Bibliography

Articles, e.g., in *Hufvudstadsbladet* (September 14, 1986). Mazzarella, Merete, *Från Fredrika Runeberg till Märta Tikkanen* (Helsingfors, 1985). *Vem och vad?* Biografisk handbok (Helsingfors, 1986). Warburton, Thomas, *Åttio år finlandssvensk litteratur* (Helsingfors, 1984).

Gunnel Cleve

Anna Maria Tilschová

Born November 11, 1873, Prague, Czechoslovakia; died June 18, 1957, Dobříš
Genres: novel, short story
Language(s): Czech

Tilschová was born into a wealthy, middle-class family in Prague, where she lived most of her life. She married her cousin Emanuel Tilsch, who was a professor of law, and through him she met eminent scientists, writers, and artists. Her own attempts at poetry and drama were not published, but she gradually developed a career as a prose writer. Her early books of stories, *Sedmnáct povídek* (1904; Seventeen Stories) and *Na horách* (1905; Up in the Mountains), attracted little attention when they were published. About one decade later, however, her novels *Fany* (1915) and *Stará rodina* (1916; An Old Family) began to establish her reputation. They also introduced the theme to which she would return again and again: the rise and fall of Czech middle-class families. Her young protagonists attempt to liberate themselves from the confines of their world but usually fail. Finally, in the novel *Dědicové* (1924; The Heirs), the hero is able to break away, through the love of a simple girl, from the world of the "old family."

Tilschová is also noted for her sympathetic depiction of mine workers in *Haldy* (1927; Heaps) and for her portrayal of scientists, artists, and university professors in various stories and novels, especially the *roman a clef* entitled *Alma mater* (1933).

Today Tilschová is seen to occupy an important position in the development of the Czech realistic novel in the early twentieth century. Socialist critics see the "twilight of the bourgeois world" in her chronicles of fragmented life within middle-class society.

Works

Sedmnáct povídek (1904). Na horách (1905). Fany (1915). Stará rodina (1916). Synové (1918). Hříšnice a jiná próza (1918). Hoře z lásky (1921). Vykoupení (1923). Dědicové (1924). Cerná dáma a tři povídky (1924). Haldy (1927). Zlá tma (1928). Čert a láska (1929). Gita Turaja (1931). Alma mater (1933). Matky a dcery (1935). U modrého kohouta (1937). Tři kři'e (1940). Orlí hnízdo (1942). Návrat (1945).

Bibliography

Heřman, M., Anna Maria Tilschová (1949). Krejci, K., A.M. Tilschová (1959). Šalda, F.X., in Kritické projevy 10 (1957). Sezima, K., in Krystaly a prúsvity (1928).

Reference works: Čeští spisovatelé deseti století, ed. R. Š<t&>astný (1974), and Čeští spisovatelé 19. a počátku 20. století, eds. K. Homolová, M. Otruba, and Z. Pešat (1982).

Clinton Machann

Lia (Cecilia) Timmermans

Born August 9, 1920, Lier, Belgium
Genre(s): novel, biography, children's literature
Language(s): Dutch

Lia Timmermans is the eldest daughter of Felix Timmermans, Flanders' most widely read author during the two wars. Her works include three novels, a biography, and a vast collection of children's books. She received a licentiate in archaeology and antiquarian sciences from the Catholic University of Louvain and worked as a teacher of Dutch literature and history of art at the Lyceum St. Andre in Ostend till 1956. As a member of the Association of Flemish Authors, Writers for Young People, and Scriptores Catholici, she presented lectures throughout Flanders and the Netherlands based primarily on her famous father. In 1942, she married Lou Aspeslagh.

Timmermans published *Mijn Vader* (1951), a biography of Felix Timmermans, for which she received the Prize of the Best Biography presented by the Province of Antwerp. The first of her three novels, *De Ridder en zijn Gade* (1955), she strikingly and ironically depicts petit bourgeois narrow mindedness. *Verloren Zomerdag* (1959) deals with a completely different theme. Timmermans focuses on the inner life of a young girl who is confronted with the hypocrisy and disillusionment of adult life. In *Sabine Mardagas* (1963), she narrates the story of a young, mysterious, and sensitive woman who, even after her death, exercises a mesmerizing effect on her environment. The novel possesses a carefully built-up intrigue but is sometimes lacking in spontaneity and cogency.

In addition, Timmermans wrote a number of children's books and stories, the series *Janneke en Mieke* being the most famous. With uncomplicated characters and a fantastic plotline as main ingredients, Timmermans creates wonderful modern fairy tales that appeal to children of all ages. She also rewrote Greek legends and Russian and Bulgarian folk tales. Several of her works are tastefully illustrated by her sister Tonet Meyer-Timmermans.

Timmermans' three novels are romantic and often poetic in atmosphere. Although she is often compared to Van Schendel, another representative of the neo-romantic school, her work lacks the latter's creative power. She will be primarily remembered as a prolific and successful writer of children's literature; she created a highly colorful, folkloristic world reminiscent of the fictional creations of her father.

Works

Children's literature: *Van kat tot poes* (1960). *Sterretje* (1961). *Het kleine album van Martha* (1954). *Janneke en Mieke en de slimme rode kraai* (1963). *Janneke en Mieke en het glazen schipje* (1963). *Janneke en Mieke en het wonderhert* (1964). *Janneke en Mieke, Snuffel en Minetta* (1964). *Kerstvertellingen* (1964). *Janneke en Mieke en het geheimzinnige blauwe duifje* (1965). *Janneke en Mieke en het witte aapje* (1965). *Widdel en Waddel in het Circus* (1969). *Widdel en Waddel naar Dragoforal* (1970). *Vertelselkens van ons land. Uit de kindermond opgeschreven* (1971). *Het Gulden Vlies* (1971). *Het Gouden Visje* (1971). *De Gouden Appel* (1971).

Novels: *Mijn Vader* [biography] (1951). *De ridder en zijn gade* (1955). *Verloren zomerdag* (1959). *Sabine Mardagas* (1963).

Translations: *Mijn Vader* and *De Ridder en zijn Gade* are both translated in German.

Bibliography

Ceulaer de, Jose, *Te Gast Bij Nederlandse Auteurs* ('s Gravenhage, Rotterdam, 1966). Scheer, Lieve, "Romantiek en Berekening." *Dietsche Warande en Belfort* 1093 (1964): 350–357.

Dianne van Hoof

Timrava

(see: Bo'ena Slančíková)

Tina

(see: Kathinka [Katharina] Rosa Pauline Modesta Zitz-Halein)

Hans Owens Tochter Anna

(see: Anna Ovena Hoyers)

Viktoriia Tokareva

Born November 20, 1937, Leningrad, The Soviet Union
Genre(s): short story, tale, drama, script for film and television
Language(s): Russian

Tokareva published her first short stories in 1964 while still enrolled in the Leningrad Institute of Cinematography (VGIK—Vsesoiuznyi gosudarstvennyi institut kinematografii). After graduating from its scriptwriting department in 1967, Tokareva continued to write fiction while simultaneously authoring scripts for television and films, including *Vdovii parokhod* (Ship of Widows), based on I. Grekova's tale by the same name (see Elena Ventsel). A recipient of several

film awards, among them the Golden Prize at the Tenth Moscow International film festival, Tokareva has also gained considerable popularity in the last decade for her wryly witty fiction, some of which has appeared in the most respected literary journals and has been translated into foreign languages.

Tokareva defines her talent in ironic stories that have affinities with the satirical sketches of Nadezhda Teffi (1876–1952), Mikhail Zoshchenko (1895–1958), and Natal'ia Il'ina (1914–). Lightness of touch, brevity, and inconclusiveness characterize her laconic narratives, which are peppered with pseudo-syllogisms and mocking literary references. Their humor is underlaid with a profound seriousness that has surfaced increasingly in recent years. Tokareva's overriding concern is the search for a meaningful and authentic existence, a search undertaken in the teeth of human fallibility and discouraging external circumstances. Success and happiness for the most part recede into the inaccessible distance, for Tokareva's fictional world operates on the philosophical premise of discrepancy— between individuals, between aims and means, desires and actual possibilities, expectation and realization, intention and execution, style and essence, etc.

Although Tokareva occasionally assumes a masculine point of view, for her protagonist she favors a young or youthful heroine from whose calculatedly guileless perspective the narrative unfolds. This protagonist's amorous pursuits or familial problems, which underpin her efforts to find her appropriate goal or niche in life, provide the plot material and narrative momentum. Plot, however, often plays such a subordinate role as to create the impression that it exists solely to afford the distinctive voice of Tokareva's narrators opportunity for commentary. Indeed, it is above all the highly individualized narrative voice, dispensing ostensibly casual generalizations about life, that holds the key to Tokareva's art.

That voice typically adopts a breezy, ironic, self-deprecatory stance to the world and itself. It is ideally suited to Tokareva's beloved theme of the gap between illusion and reality, for which the dialogic cast of the heroine's constantly self-modifying presentation is a perfect vehicle. This double-voiced, bifocal perception of situations and events distances Tokreva's reflective, ingenuous protagonists, as well as the reader, from experiences that otherwise would seem unbearably painful, for the events *per se* in Tokareva's stories convey a gloomy picture of life. For instance, Tokareva has little that is positive or reassuring to divulge about relations between the sexes—one of her major themes—for both her women and men, but particularly the latter, are self-involved, foolish, insecure, and unhappy. They shuttle between impossible yearnings and brutal disappointments to which their gullibility is an unwitting accomplice (e.g., "Staraia sobaka" [An Old Dog], "Nichego osobennogo" [Nothing Special]). But Tokareva's wittily skeptical treatment of interaction between the sexes transforms melancholy insights into amusing scenarios. Tokareva clearly perceives the redemptive possibilities of an irony that places the world and one's niche in it in perspective, as indicated by her comments on the restorative function of humor: "Humor, of course, restores that which pathos destroys; when there is a great deal of it [humor], however, it in its turn starts to destroy. From chronic humor emerges cynicism, which makes life very convenient because then a person underestimates everything" ("Instruktor po plavaniiu" [The Swimming Instructor]). It is therefore crucial to Tokareva's world view and her literary purposes that she balance her humor, invariably relying on devices that both eschew and undercut extremes: those of *gradatio* or qualification, zeugma, false syllogisms, and deflation, mainly through the juxtaposition of the mythic or exalted with the banal. While not flinching from portraying heartbreaking dilemmas, Tokareva allows her personae to confront life's disillusionments buoyantly, with a readiness to embrace the future in a spirit of optimistic expectation, against all odds.

As Tokareva has grown older, her protagonists have aged correspondingly, a maturation that accounts for the increased frequency with which Tokareva's latest narratives tackle the problems of parenthood and of moral commitment and responsibility to others. Her recent play, *Ekspromt-Fantaziia* (Impromptu-Fantasy), which premiered at the Moscow Stanislavsky Theatre under the direction of A. Tovstonogov in 1983, examines the conflicting claims of love and duty beleaguering a young student of music who falls in love with her married teacher. While thematically traditional, the play, with its blend of music, drama, and fantasy, its absence of clearly defined beginning and of sharp distinction between rehearsal and performance, audience and performers, is fairly experimental in form. It also allows Tokareva to explore more extensively and through formal means her knowledgeable affection for music, which usually enters her fiction in the form of similes, metaphors, and comically eloquent references.

The stories comprising Tokareva's first anthology (1969) averaged about twelve pages in length. Moreover, many of them had appeared earlier in the literary journal *Iunost'* (Youth), which suggests that Tokareva was addressing herself to a young audience. By contrast, only a quarter of Tokareva's latest collection (1983) consists of short stories. The remainder is devoted to longer pieces of forty to fifty pages each, first published in such prestigious journals as *Novyi mir* (New World), and *Znamia* (The Banner). The difference implies that in the intervening years Tokareva has won a more sophisticated, adult readership and has gained stature in the world of Russian letters. Yet the wit, charm, human understanding, and deft handling of tone that make Tokareva one of the most readable as well as skillful contemporary practitioners of the short story still await adequate recognition in the tangible form of a full-scale study of her oeuvre.

Works

Prose collections: *O tom, chego ne bylo. Rasskazy* (1969). *Kogda stalo nemnozhko teplee* (1972). *Zanuda. Rasskazy* (1977). *Letaiushchie kacheli* (1978). *Michego osobennogo. Rasskazy* (1983). *Translations: Nichego osobennogo* [Nothing Special] (1981); *Meshdu nebom i zemlei* [Between Heaven and Earth] (1985) tr. Helen Goscilo, in *HERitage and HEResy: Recent Fiction by Russian Women* (1988).

Film and television scripts: *Dhentel'meni udachi* (1971). [With Georgii Daneliia], *Hopelessly Lost* (1972). [With G. Daneliia and R.L. Gabriadze] *Mimino. Kinostseranii* (1978). *Mezhdu nebom i zemlei.*

Play: *Ekspromt-fantaziia* (1982).

Bibliography

Lench, L., "Strannye, strannye liudi." *Literaturnaia gazeta* (February 11, 1970). Marchenko, A., "Vremia iskat' sebia." *Novyi mir* 10 (1972): 221–242. Marinova, Iuliia, "Fantaziia na temu liubvi: *Ekspromt-Fantaziia.*" *Sovetskii teatr* 1–2 (1983): 10–12 (review of *Ekspromt-Fantaziia*). Shtokman, I., "Mig povorota," *Druzhba narodov* 10 (1970): 275–276. Zelenko, N., "Ne kantovat'—smekh!" (review of *O tom, chego ne bylo*) *Sovremennaia kul'tura* (January 18, 1972).

Helena Goscilo

Luisa Sigea Toletana

(see: Luisa Sigea de Velasco)

Tat'iana Tolstaia

Born 1951, Leningrad, the Soviet Union
Genre(s): short story, drama, criticism
Language(s): Russian

A granddaughter of Aleksandr Nikolaevich Tolstoi (1882–1945), famous for his *Aelita* (1922–1923), *Peter the First* (1929–1945), and *The Road to Calvary* (1922–1941), Tolstaia has earned a name for herself among the literati only in the last year or so. She graduated in 1974 from the Department of Philology at the State University of Leningrad, a training that partially accounts for her inventive and rigorous attitude toward language. Although she whimsically claims to have dreamed since childhood of pursuing a nursing career, her attraction to literature manifested itself early in the several years she spent working at a publishing house after graduation. Her literary debut in 1983 with the excellent story "Na zolotom kryl'tse sideli" (1923; On the Golden Porch) unaccountably aroused little attention. But the publication of her longer narrative "Peter" just three years later in *New World* sparked lively enthusiasm in both Moscow and Leningrad. It established her reputation as an original and exciting young talent.

Tolstaia's stories focus on the isolation of the individual personality, the universal inability to grasp the essence of other human beings, and the indifference on the part of the overwhelming majority to the psychological complexity of others. Especially children and the elderly, situated at the two extremes of the age spectrum, suffer from the incomprehension and callousness of those around them. Many of Tolstaia's protagonists lead lives that go unnoticed or misunderstood. Victims of ridicule and condescension, they reside at the fringe of society, with scant opportunity for fulfillment or success.

Convinced that the significance of a life becomes partially revealed only after the person dies, Tolstaia treats the experience of death as a moment of epiphany in such works as "Na zolotom kryl'tse sideli," "Sonia," and "Svidanie s ptitsei" (Rendezvous with a Bird). Yet whatever insights death may vouchsafe, individual identity in Tolstaia's world eludes definition, being located somewhere in the interstices of seemingly irreconcilable contradictions. Children, whom Tolstaia frequently endows with bold imagination and unexpected insights, conceive of life as a miraculous adventure and thus appear particularly receptive to the inexplicable paradoxes inherent in human nature. Hence the girl in Tolstaia's first story sees her bookkeeping neighbor Uncle Pasha as a downtrodden husband, a happy lover, a helpless old man, a khalif, a prince, King Solomon, etc. Delight in provocative enigmas that reflect the mysterious nature of life and personality virtually disappears with adulthood, which is why Tolstaia tends to associate childhood with the Edenic state. "Na zolotom kryl'tse sideli," for example, explicitly equates childhood with the prelapsarian happiness of perceptions uncorrupted by commonplace forms and categories.

Tolstaia spotlights characters who range from the mildly unheroic to the unsettlingly pathetic. Since she entertains an unidealized, skeptical, even bleak, view of romantic love, her protagonists' amorous aspirations and involvements appear in a humorous or grotesque light. Elevated notions of love crumble under the assault of myopic delusions on the one hand and brute physicality on the other. In general Tolstaia's fictional universe is aggressively physical, populated by countless objects, bodies, and faces that she evokes vividly in striking metaphors and similes. Yet the relationship of Tolstaia's protagonists to this tangible reality is curiously unstable, and reality itself seems contingent, incessantly open to multiple interpretations.

Probably the single most distinctive aspect of Tolstaia's writing, her instantly identifiable signature (with the exception of her weakest effort, "Chistyi list" [Tabula Rasa], which by her own admission failed to come off), is her exuberant, condensed style. Above all, the prose of Tolstaia's eccentric narrators, descended from Laurence Sterne's and Nikolai Gogol's garrulous storytellers, pulses with iridescent vitality. Rife with contradictions and illogicalities, ellipses, erratic shifts from pathos to humor, flaunted lapses of memory side by side with perfect recall of apparently irrelevant and minute detail, this obtrusive narrative voice indulges in digressions, disclaimers, apostrophes, and exclamations as it freely mixes colloquialisms with elevated and poetic diction. Tolstaia's narrator disgorges a series of images startling in their originality and unexpectedness ("the garden waved its handkerchief," "the small change had slipped like minnows into the lining," "the calendar's viscous sleep," "the crystal of Sonia's foolishness"). Rather than serving a purely decorative function, these images tend to derive from a key concept that dominates the narrative. For instance, the opposition between material phenomena and intangibles around which the story "Sonia" revolves finds expression in a central image: "To chase after you would be like trying to catch butterflies by waving a shovel." That focal simile is sustained by the related images of dragonfly wings and dried forget-me-nots as well as by a consistent association between Sonia's spiritual qualities and the enamel dove of her brooch. The latter contrasts revealingly with the picture of "someone killing someone else" depicted on the brooch of Sonia's "snakelike" counterpart Ada, who is regularly portrayed against a backdrop of plenty, communicated through Tolstaia's list of food, furniture, etc. Many of Tolstaia's strongest effects, in fact, proceed from the interplay between the inner world of people's thoughts and emotions and the outer world of objects. And Tolstaia suggests the intricate nature of human relationship to the physical world of things through the device of animating objects and objectifying people.

Tolstaia's irrepressible humor manifests itself not only in the irony, grotesque portrayals, and comic formulations of her stories, but also in parody, as for example in a piece like "Uta-monogatari," a purported attempt to recreate a Japanese poetic genre, with amusing results. Her negative review of a book devoted to her grandfather shows another facet of Tolstaia—her capacity for outspoken, acerbic criticism, grounded in close textual analysis.

Given the limited quantity of Tolstaia's output thus far, a summary assessment of her abilities as a writer seems premature. But she gives every indication of possessing abundant creative powers in the sphere of short fiction.

Works

Stories: "Na zolotom kryl'tse sideli," in *Avrora* (1983). "Svidanie s ptitsei," in *Oktiabr'* (1983). "Sonia," in *Avrora* (1984) "Chistyi list," in *Neva* (1984). "Reka Okkarvil'," "Milaia Shura" and "Okhota na mamonta," *Oktiabr'* (1985). "Peter," *Novyi mir* (1986). "Poet i muza," "Fakir," "Serafim," in *Novyi mir* (1986). *Na zolotom kryl'tse sideli* (Moscow, 1987).

Translations: "Rendezvous with a bird" [Svidanie sptitsei], tr. Mary Fleming Zirin; "Sonia," tr. Nancy Condee; "Peter," tr. Mary Fleming Zirin, in *HERitage and HEResy: Recent Fiction by Russian Women*, ed. Helena Goscilo (1988). Volume of stories by Pantheon Books (forthcoming).

Parody: "Uta-monogatari," *Voprosy literatury* (1984).

Review article: "Kleem i nozhnitsami," *Voprosy literatury* (1983).

Bibliography

Condee, Nancy, *Newsletter* 17, Institute of Current World Affairs (June 1, 1986): 8–9. "Ten' na zakate." *Literaturnaia gazeta* (July 23, 1986): 7.

Helena Goscilo

Alexandra Tolstoy

*Born July 1, 1884, Yasnaya Polyana, Russia;
died September 26, 1979, Valley Cottage,
New York*
Genre(s): memoir, article, short story
Language(s): Russian

Alexandra Tolstoy was the youngest daughter of Leo Tolstoy. She was his faithful follower, close collaborator, literary executor, and editor of the definitive edition of his complete works. As a writer she became widely known through her memoirs of her famous father. One of the first books to appear was *Léon Tolstoi, mon père* (1916). Later she also began writing about her own extraordinary experiences, as in *I Worked for the Soviet* (1935). A number of books, short stories and articles that followed, particularly the book *Out of the Past*, which appeared posthumously in 1981, complete her lively reminiscences.

Alexandra Tolstoy spent her childhood at Tolstoy's family estate Yasnaya Polyana, in Russia. Like most children of the gentry she was educated at home. Music and foreign languages were particularly emphasized. A good deal of time was spent participating in various games, horseback riding, ice-skating, and the like. At the age of seventeen she became her father's secretary and lifelong disciple.

Alexandra Tolstoy's life was marked by a series of turbulent events of our century, especially World War I, during which she served as a nurse on the German and Turkish fronts and was twice decorated for service. The 1917 October revolution had the greatest impact. Under the new regime she worked at the Tolstoy Museum at Yasnaya Polyana and began the complete edition of Tolstoy's works. She rejected atheism, endured imprisonment, and finally in 1929 left for Japan. In 1931 she arrived in the United States of America where she lectured about her father and continued to write her memoirs. She also organized and became president of the Tolstoy Foundation (based at the Tolstoy Farm at Valley Cottage, N.Y.). Among its founders in 1939 were several prominent émigrés, including the last pre-revolutionary ambassador to the United States of America, B.A. Bakhmetev; the famed pilot B.V. Sergievsky; the developer of the helicopter, Igor Sikorsky, the historian M.I. Rostoytsey; the musician Serge Rachmaninov; and Tatiana Schaufuss, close friend of Alexandra Tolstoy and her constant collaborator. President Hoover became the honorary chairman. Under the leadership of Tolstoy the organization has assisted many ethnic and religious groups, rescued tens of thousands of oppressed Russians, and aided other refugees all over the world.

Parts of Tolstoy's memoirs appeared in a number of émigré periodicals. Not infrequently her books were first published in various translations. Among them were *Léon Tolstoi, mon père* (1933), *La mia vita col padre* (1933), *I Worked for the Soviet* (1935), and *Una vide de mi padre* (1958).

Two titles (*Otets, Zhizn' L'va Tolstogo* [1953] [1975; Engl. tr. *Tolstoy, A Life of My Father*] and *Doch'* [1979; Daughter]) best characterize her writing. Indeed, her memoirs could be divided into two parts. The subject of the first is her father, while she herself is the subject of the second part. The themes of her writings are many; they include literary life, childhood, family life, war, revolution, the new Soviet order, religious persecution under the Soviets, prisoners of war, refugees, America, the struggle for survival, adaptation, and—perhaps the most Tolstoyan of all themes—service to humanity.

Critics seem to agree about Alexandra Tolstoy's style; they praise her vivid descriptions, her keen sense of humor, and her gift for characterization. Although she wrote many articles and a number of short stories, memoirs constitute her dominant genre.

Works

Including translations: *Posmertnye khudozhestvennye proizvedeniya L'va Tolstogo*, 2 vol., ed. (1911). *Léon Tolstoi, mon père* (1916). *Tolstoys Fluchte und Tod* (1925–1933). *Tolstojs flugte og død* (1927). *Ob ukhode i smerti L.N. Tolstogo* (1928). [With Chertkov], *Polnoe sobranie sochinenii L'va Tolstogo*, 3 vols. (1929–1938). *Torusutoi no omoide* (1930). *The Tragedy of Tolstoy* (1933). *Ma vie avec mon père* (1933). *La mia vita col padre* (1933). *I worked for the Soviet* (1935). *Tolsztoj futása es halála*(193?). *Short, Short True Stories* (1949). *Otets, Zhizn' L'va Tolstogo* (1953). *Hayey avi*(1954). *Tolstoi, Min Feders Liv*

(1956?). *Una vida de mi padre* (1958). *Obrahchenie svobodnykh rossiyan iz svobodnogo mira, pervogo maya, 1959 goda* (1959). *Probleski vo t'me* (1965). *The Real Tolstoy* (Critique of Henri Troyat's book *Tolstoy*) (1968–1969). *A propos du "Tolstoi" d'Henri Troyat* (1969).

Chapters in books: "Home Leaving and Death," in Aymer Maude, *Family Views of Tolstoy* (1926). "Comment mon père écrivit *Guerre et Paix*," in *Guerre et Paix* (1957). "Léon Tolstoi, mon père, a l'époque où il écrivit *Résurrection*," in *Résurrection* (1959).

Articles and stories: "Iz vospominanii." *Sovremennyya zapiski*, Nos. 45–52 (1931–1933). "Otryvki vospominanii." *Sovremennyya zapiski*, Nos. 56–57 (1934–1936, 59–60, 62). "Predrazsvetnyi tuman." *Novyi Zhurnai* (1942). "Nikolka." *Opyty* (1955). "The Tolstoyans." *The Yale Review* (Winter 1978).

Bibliography

Yale Review (December 22, 1932). *New York Times Book Review* (April 26, 1942). *New York Herald Tribune* (August 15, 1948). *New Yorker* (March 15, 1952; March 22, 1952). *New York Times* (July 2, 1974). *Time* (October 8, 1979). *AB Bookman's Weekly* (October 22, 1979).

General references: *National Union Catalog* (Library of Congress). *World Biography* (1948). *Index Translation* (UNESCO, 1949–1979). *Who's Who* (1952, 1981). *Current Biography* (1953). *The Literatures of the World in English Translation* (1967). *Bibliographia Nazionale Italiana. Dictionary Catalog of the Slavonic Collection* (1974). *The Slavic Literatures. Contemporary Authors*, vols. 89–92 (1981).

Katherina Filips-Juswigg

G. Topîrceanu

(see: Otilia Cazimir)

Cecile Tormay

Born October 8, 1876, Budapest, Hungary;
died April 2, 1937, Mátraháza
Genre(s): novel, short story
Language(s): Hungarian

Founder and editor of *Napkelet*, leader of the Magyar Asszonyok Nemzeti Szövetsége (Hungarian Women's National Association), an association devoted to Christian and national goals, and prose writer, Tormay began her career by writing short stories. In 1911 her first novel, *Emberek a kövek között* (Stonecrop) appeared. It was also published abroad, and in 1914 she wrote what is considered her masterpiece, *A Régi haz* (The Old House), a generation-novel that depicts late nineteenth century Budapest. After 1919 she became committed to the conservative side and founded the conservative journal *Napkelet* (Sunrise) in 1929 partly to balance the liberal tendencies of *Nyugat* (West). Her novel, *Bujdosó könyv* (1921–1922; An Outlaw's Diary) shows the excesses of the brief Soviet-style dictatorship in Hungary in 1919. Her trilogy about the Tatar invasion of the thirteenth century, *Az Ósi küldött* (1934–1937; The Ancient Delegate), remained unfinished. Here as elsewhere in her work she used historical themes for a symbolic purpose.

In her first novel, Tormay portrayed the struggle of the elemental forces of nature with civilization: human fate, she implied, is decided by great natural powers. It is a fatalistic novel but also has nationalistic tendencies in the contrast of the wildness of the Slavic regions and the milder temperament of the Hungarian Plain. *Régi ház* studies the assimilation of the German bourgeoisie into Hungarian life through three generations in a manner reminiscent of Thomas Mann's *Buddenbrooks*.

Works

Apródszerelem [The Page's Love] (1900). *Apró bünök* [Minor Sins] (1905). *Emberek a kövek között* (1911). *Régi ház* (1914). *Viaszfigurák* (1918). *Bujdosó könyv* (1921–1922). *Az Ósi küldött* (1934). *A Fehér barát* (1937).

Translations: *Stonecrop* [*Emberek a kövek között*] (1922, 1923). *The Old House* [*Régi ház*] (1922). *An Outlaw's Diary* [*Bujdosó könyv*] (1923).

Bibliography

Gábor, Thurzo, "Tormay Cecile halálára." *Katolikus Szemle* (1937): 291–292. Hankiss, János, *Tormay Cecile* (Budapest: n.d). Horváth, János, "Tormay Cecile." *Budapesti Szemle* (1916): 310–316. Kardos, László, "*Az Ősi küldött.*" *Valóság* (May 1934): 77–78. Szerb, Antal, "Tormay Cecile." *Nyugat* (1937): I, 350–354.

Enikő Molnár Basa

Lucrezia Tornabuoni

Born 1425, Florence, Italy; died March 25, 1482, Florence
Genre(s): poetry
Language(s): Italian

Daughter of Francesco Tornabuoni and Francesca Pitti, Lucrezia became the wife of Piero di Cosimo de'Medici and hence the mother of Lorenzo. She was an influential figure in the Medici establishment, especially in matters affecting the vernacular. Herself something of a sacred poet, she sponsored several poets and commissioned Luigi Pulci to write *Il Morgante*. Her religious poetry has been recently published.

Bibliography

Pieroni, G. Levantini, "Lucrezia Tornabuoni, donna di Piero di Cosimo de' Medici." *Studi storici e letterarii* (Florence, 1893): 1–83. Jordan, Constance, *Pulci's "Morgante"* (Washington, 1986), pp. 17–18. Pezzarossa, Fulvio ed., *Poemetti sacri di Lucrezia Torna-buoni* (Florence, 1978).

Joseph Berrigan

Rita Tornborg

Born 1926, Poland
Genre(s): novel, short story, criticism
Language(s): Swedish

After a cosmopolitan youth with a multilingual background, Rita Tornborg came to her craft at the age of forty. She grew up in Polish-Jewish surroundings, but escaped to Sweden at the beginning of the Second World War in 1939. Seventeen years old, Rita faced a new cultural environment and the need to learn a new language. Eventually she married and had two children.

But it was not until 1970 that she felt ready to come out with her first novel, *Paukes gerilla* (Pauke's Guerilla), a story about the Polish resistance movement. Other novels soon followed at almost regular intervals.

It is not surprising to find Tornborg's unsteady youth and East European extrovert manner of expression reflected in her work. Writing in a manner that resembles that of Laurence Sterne's *Tristram Shandy*, her stories abound with digressions, reflections, and nota bene dialogues with the reader. Tornborg considers it "rigid to force things," or to obey a preconceived plan, which to her is "a violation of reality." According to Tornborg, the novel should develop as haphazardly as life tends to be and considers her stories collections of impressions and events carried along by a certain psychological development. Having experienced first-hand the political systems of both East and West, Tornborg considers life a mosaic. Her main concerns are personal freedom and peace. Often allegorical, her basic theme is modern man's struggle to resist the infringements on his liberty in his desire to give expression to his innate human needs and desires. Her stories have often been compared to the work of Isaac Bashevis Singer. Like him, she shows that special world-wise wisdom and humor so typical of Eastern European Jewish culture, which unfortunately was decimated so drastically during the Second World War.

Works

Paukes gerilla (1970). *Docent Åke Ternvall ser en syn* (1972). *Hansson och Goldmann* (1974). *Friedmans hus* (1976). *Salomos namnsdag* (1979). *Systrarna* (1982).

Translations: *Systrarna* [The Sisters], English tr. Bonniers Pocketbooks (1984). "The Naked Man," tr. Gary Jaekel, in *Supplement: in English* 3 (1985): 11–19.

Bibliography

Algulin, Ingemar, *Contemporary Swedish Prose* (Stockholm, 1983), pp. 69–70, 78, 94. Jaekel, Gary, "Mosaics in Words: An Interview With Rita Tornborg." *Supplement: in English* 3 (1985): 4–10.

Hanna Kalter Weiss

Alessandra Tornimparte

(see: Natalia Ginzburg)

Sophie Török

Born December 10, 1895, Budapest, Hungary;
died June 28, 1955, Budapest
Genre(s): poetry, novel, short story
Language(s): Hungarian

Ilona Tanner took the pen name of Sophie Török after the wife of Ferenc Kazinczy; she was a poet and wife of the poet and literary critic Mihály Babits and worked at the Budapest Library.

Török was among the young writers of *Nyugat*, where Babits noticed her writings. Her themes are the problems and psyche of women. In her poems she is very personal and lyrical, but in her prose works she studied the problems of working women. Her reactions to the death of her husband, who died of cancer of the larynx, are documented in *Sirató* (1948). Her works have been translated into French, German, and Italian.

Her career shows no great changes but reflects a progressive development and deepening of her emotional world. In *Asszony a karosszékben* (Woman in the Armchair) Margit Kaffka's example is perceivable, but Török is more unforgiving in her portrait. Her husband's influence can be seen in the theme of self-sacrifice for the loved one and in the searching dialogues. After Babits' death, her poems move towards free verse and swing between enthusiasm and despair: the psychological element becomes dominant. *Értem és helyetted* (1940; For Me and Instead of You) is almost a monologue, as she herself says: "there is no exterior world / any more, there is now only me!" ("Kísértet-óra"). Her final volume, *Sirató* (1948; Lament), is her best, for here dramatic tension in the second-person dialogue is present. The style is pure, and the feelings transcend the merely personal.

Works

Novel: *Hintz tanársegéd úr* (1934).
Stories: *Nem vagy igazi* (1939). *Boldog asszonyok* (1939).

Poems: *Asszonv a karosszékben* (1939). *Örömre születtél* (1934). *Értem és helyetted* (1940). *Sirató* (1948).
Some of her works have appeared in Italian, French, and German.

Bibliography

Csányi, László, "Kettős arckép. Babits Mihály és T.S. a *Beszélgetőfüzetek lapjain.*" *Kortárs* 11 (1980): 1806–1813. Gellért, Oszkár, *Csillag* (1955). Gyárgyai, Albert, *Nyugat* (1929). Kádár, Erzsebet, *Nyugat* (1939). Keresztúry, Dezső, *Nyugat* (1940). Kóháry, Sarolta, ed., *Babits Mihály és Török Sophie levelei, Kortárs* 9 (1978): 1424–1455. Kóháry, Sarolta, "Részlet, ami mégis az egész, T.S. Verse." *Uj Tükör* 52 (1978): 20. Lesznai, Anna, *Nyugat* (1934). Makay, Gusztáv, *Magyarok* (1949).

Enikő Molnár Basa

Josefina de la Torre

Born 1907, 1909, or 1910, Las Palmas, Canary Islands
Genre(s): poetry, novel
Language(s): Spanish

Josefina de la Torre was one of only two women included in Gerardo Diego's famous anthology, *Poesía española 1915–1931*, as a Generation of '27 poet. In addition to her poetry, for which she is principally known, she also experimented with a wide variety of other art forms, including instrumental and vocal music, acting and theatre production, and radio and recitation. Her older brother, Claudio de la Torre (1902), dramatist, novelist, and poet himself, encouraged her literary pursuits. Together they made a number of friends in the Generation of '27 circle, among them Rafael Alberti and Pedro Salinas. It was Salinas who became a major influence on Josefina de la Torre's work, motivating her to write a "light breeze of a poem," in Valbuena's opinion.

Salinas wrote the introduction to her first book of poetry, *Versos y Estampas*, published in 1927, and dedicated to her brother Claudio, when she was still in her teens. Considered the best poetry of her early years, her second book, *Poemas de la Isla* (1930), continues de la Torre's predilection for lyrical free verse and ocean and nature themes and imagery. Twenty-four years of silence followed these two exuberant and spontaneous books of poetry. In 1954, *Memorias de una estrella* appeared as a novel-of-the-week in a subscription series. Another fourteen years elapsed before *Marzo incompleto* was published. Predominantly "intimist," these poems are filled with incompletions, alienations, anxieties, fears, and contemplations on time, love, and death. Their technical starkness, devoid of poetic devices such as complex metaphor or rhyme scheme, creates an almost cathartic effect.

Josefina de la Torre is an exemplary Canarian poet in terms of her lyricism, her imagery, and her themes.

Works

Versos y Estampas (1927). *Poemas de la Isla* (1930). *Memorias de una estrella* (1954). *Marzo incompleto* (1968).

Bibliography

Artiles, Joaquín, *La Literatura Canaria* (Las Palmas De Gran Canaria, 1979). Galerstein, Carolyn L, ed., *Women Writers of Spain* (Westport, CT, 1986).

Rosetta Radtke

Maruja Torres

Born 1940s, Spain
Genre(s): essay, novel
Language(s): Spanish

Maruja Torres is well known in Spain for her contributions to journals such as *Pronto*, *Garbo*, *Fotogramas*, *Por favor*, *El País*, *Diario 16* and *Cambio 16*, where she has been writing since the 1960s.

Her first and only novel to date, *¿Oh es El! (Viaje fantástico hacia Julio Iglesias)* (1986; My, That's Him! [Fantastic Voyage Towards Julio Iglesias]), is a parody about the life of a journalist who is madly in love with the popular singer, Julio Iglesias. Life in the United States is satirized when she follows him on tour in order to write his biography. Torres' style is humorous and biting with sarcastic references to many aspects of popular journalism (horoscopes, gossip columns, advice letters, etc.). There is an implicit feminist message dealing with the conventions of sexual roles. This novel also has some charac-

teristics of the so-called "novela negra" or the detective story.

Works

¿Oh, es El! (Viaje fantástico hacia Julio Iglesias) (1986).

Bibliography

Harguindey, Angel S., "El triunfo de la ternura." *El País* (May 22, 1987): 21.

Concha Alborg

Erzsébet Tóth

Born 1951, Tatabanya, Hungary
Genre(s): poetry
Language(s): Hungarian

Erzsébet Tóth worked as an economist in Budapest until 1985 when she began to devote herself fully to her writing. In 1984 she visited the United States by invitation from the New York-based Committee for International Poetry. Her work, which has never been translated into English, has appeared regularly in numerous Hungarian journals, including *Mozgo Világ*, *Kortárs*, *Új Irás*, *Forrás*, and *Alföld*, as well as several anthologies, including *Madárúton: 45 Fiatal Költő* (1979) and *Szép Versek* (1980).

The critic Zoltán Kenyeres has written in *A Lélek Fényvűzése* that Erzsébet Tóth "is an elemental poet . . . she does not report her experiences, feeling and thoughts; rather, she radiates them." Indeed, Tóth is a poet of the nerve endings, whose highly personal, autobiographical work articulates the life of the emotions with expressionistic intensity and with little reference to the actual events or experiences that generate them. The almost painful emotional pitch of her poems, their combination of vulnerability and obstinacy, yearning and cynicism reflect a personality attuned to the political ironies of an economically successful but politically subservient Soviet satellite.

The mainstays of Erzsébet Tóth's work are nostalgia for childhood innocence, the emotional dislocations of adult life, and the suppressed violence and minute epiphanies of domesticity. Her sparsely punctuated free verse and prose poetry are sometimes addressed to family members, sometimes to shadowy, unnamed lovers, and sometimes to other poets and friends. The poems frequently juxtapose feverish, anxiety-ridden dream states with the bucolic natural elements of Budapest's gardens and backyards: fruit trees, birds, snow, the quality of light at dawn or at evening, the seasons.

The activity of poetry is, for Erzsébet Tóth, the clearest and most direct expression of life itself. In the introduction to her second volume, *Gyertyaszentelő* (Candlemas), Tóth wrote: ". . . I have written poems instead of doing so many things. Instead of many, many telephone calls, letters, travels. Instead of strolls through blossoms or snow. Instead of mirror-gazing. Instead of tears or love."

Works

Egy Végtelen Vers Közepe (1979). *Gyertyaszentelő* (1982).

Bibliography

Kenyeres, Zoltán, *A Lélek Fényvúzése* (Budapest, 1983), p. 478.

Gyorgyi Voros

Judit Tóth

Born May 21, 1936, Hungary
Genre(s): poetry, novel, translation
Language(s): Hungarian

Judit Tóth left Hungary in 1966 and she makes her home in Paris. A thorough, cosmopolitan erudition and the amalgamation of Hungarian and French themes characterize her poetry.

She studied Hungarian and French language and literature at the Eötvös University in Budapest. She has published her poems in three anthologies: *Partition Walls* (1963), *Two Cities* (1972), and *The Recalling of Space* (1975). Besides her activity as a poet, Tóth has also published a novel, *Runway* (1980), and earned a reputation as a translator of Hungarian poetry into French.

Her novel and many poems treat her experiences in Paris and in rural France. She has a strong faith in the humanist mission of her craft. The problems which preoccupy her are those of the present and the future of humankind: the dangers of urbanization, alienation in a world taken over by machines, and the increasing distance between people and nature.

Her verse reveals close familiarity with twentieth-century poetic experimentations with rhyme and rhythm. Her poems are often symbolic; the imagery has freshness and novelty in the context of Hungarian literature. In her poetic language she likes to reduce the number of verbs to a minimum; her tropes, thus, create an almost pictorial effect.

Works

Tűzfalak (1963). *Két város* (1972). *A tér visszahivása* (1975). *Kifutópálya* (1980).

Bibliography

Pomogáts, Béla, *Az ujabb magyar irodalom története* (Budapest, 1982).

Peter I. Barta

Flora Célestine Thérese Henriette Tristan

(a.k.a. Flore Tristan, Flore Tristan-Morcoso)

Born April 7, 1803, Paris, France; died November 14, 1844, Bordeaux
Genre(s): novel, essay, autobiography
Language(s): French

Tristan was a leading figure in the socialist and feminist movements in nineteenth century France. She was born to a wealthy Peruvian-Spanish nobleman and a French mother. After her father died, the French government refused to recognize the marriage, confiscated Tristan-Morcoso's property, and declared Flora illegitimate. Living in poverty and shunned by family, she went to work at age eighteen in a lithography shop. She eventually married the owner and had three children (one died). Chazal was an abusive alcoholic, and in 1825 Flora left him. To support her family she took a position as a ladies' companion, travelling to England several times during this nine year period. Harassed by her husband, barely able to eke out a living, and determined to receive her rightful share of her father's property and to be recognized by his family, she sailed to Peru unchaperoned. She failed to accomplish her goals, but her uncle did grant her a small pension which provided her a modicum of independence. Tristan's semi-autobiography, *Pérégrinations d'une paria* (1838; Peregrinations of a Pariah), described this voyage and her year spent in Peru; these experiences also provided the background for her novel, *Méphis* (1838).

Back in Paris in January 1835, she found that her husband had been awarded custody of their son and daughter; and that she had no legal recourse. When Chazal sexually assaulted his eleven year old daughter, Flora took him to court and won custody of the girl but not of her son. In 1838 Chazal shot Flora on a street in Paris. Finally she was able to obtain a legal separation and permission to use her own name. Still, she was not free to remarry. Forever bound to a man she despised by laws she considered discriminatory, Tristan began her campaign to crush the forces that oppressed women, workers, and the inarticulate masses. These injustices that affected her personally thrust Tristan into feminist and socialist activities to which she dedicated the rest of her life.

Tristan had already been in touch with the Fourierists and had attended regular meetings of the *Gazette des femmes* (Women's Gazette). She published several short articles on socialism and women; she also deluged the Chamber of Deputies with petitions for a revised divorce law and against capital punishment. In 1839 Tristan went to England to observe first-hand the conditions of the working class. Her observations were recorded in *Promenades dans Londres* (1840; Walks in London), which was acclaimed by socialists and republicans. Her most famous work, *l'Union ouvrière* (1843; The Workers' Union), contained her program which called for the working class to free itself from oppression; she was the first socialist to do this. Tristan's major purpose was to organize "the working class by means of a compact, solid, indissoluble Union." Five years before Marx's *Communist Manifesto* she saw workers as a distinct class and that their power lay in solidarity; "Isolated you are weak. . . . Union creates strength." Workers would tax themselves to establish 'Workers' Palaces' where their children would be educated and care given to injured and aged workers. Her program stressed the rights of workers: the right to work, to an education, and to political representation. Tristan wanted to reform the social order to allow for the full development of the individual personality. All of this would be accomplished without class conflict or violence, which she vehemently rejected.

Closely linked to emancipation of the worker was the liberation of women. An entire chapter of her book dealt with "The Necessity for Women's Emancipation," which, anomalously, was addressed to male workers whom she believed would lead the struggle to free women. As long as women remained enslaved, she insisted, workers could not be free. Though she stressed women's unique domestic role, she refused to confine them to family responsibilities. The subordination of women in marriage was her *bête noir*; she advocated the right of women to work for wages equal to men's and the right to divorce. Marriage was to be freely chosen and equality between spouses was essential to happiness in the home. Women should not be forced to sell themselves, as she had done, to gain security as this puts them on the same level as prostitutes. Her radical stance on freedom for women is clearly delineated in *L'émancipation de la femme; ou, Le testament de la paria* (1846; The Emancipation of Woman, or The Testament of a Pariah). Tristan argued forcefully that the emancipation of women was in the best interest of men. Her influence on notions of a universal union of workers and on feminism were truly remarkable. More than anyone else of her time she combined these two movements into one. Women and workers were everywhere exploited and enslaved by their powerlessness, ignorance, and poverty; if they would unite they could eradicate these evils.

Tristan had an overwhelming sense of mission; as the "Woman Messiah," she would lead the oppressed masses to freedom. She also felt isolated—she was, as she said, a pariah. Serious in purpose and determined to uplift the masses, she undertook an exhausting tour of France to spread her gospel. She contracted typhoid and died at Bordeaux at age forty-one. Tristan failed to create the Utopian socialist society she dreamed of, but her ideas survived and became part of modern socialist and feminist thought.

Works

Pérégrinations d'une paria, 2 vols. (1838). Méphis, novel (1838). A messieurs les membres de la Chambre des députés (1838?). Promenades des Londres (1840). l'Union ouvrière (1843). L'émancipation de la femme; ou Le testament de la paria (1846).

Bibliography

Baelen, Jean, Le vie de Flora Tristan: socialisme et feminisme au XIX siècle (1972). Brion, Hélène, Une méconnue. Flora Tristan; la vraie fondatrice de l'Internationale (1917). Collins, Marie, and Weil-Sayre, Sylvie, "Flora Tristan: Forgotten Feminist and Socialist." Nineteenth-Century French Studies (1973). Desanti, Dominique, A Women in Revolt: A Biography of Flora Tristan (1976). Gattey, C. N., Gauguin's Astonishing Grandmother: A Biography of Flora Tristan (1970). Leprohon, Pierre, Flora Tristan (1979). Moon, S. Joan, "Feminism and Socialism: The Utopian Synthesis of Flora Tristan," in Socialist Women, ed. Boxer and Quataert (1978). Morceaux choisis, précédés de La geste romantique de Flora Tristan, contée par Lucien Scheler pour le centenaire de 1848 (1948). Puech, J.-L., "Une romancière socialiste: Flora Tristan," La Revue socialiste (1914). Puech, J.L., La vie et l'oeuvre de Flora Tristan (1925). Recavarren de Zizold, C., La Mujer mesianica; Flora Tristan (1946). Rubel, M., "Flora Tristan et Karl Marx." Le Nef (1946). Sanchez, L. A., Una Mujer sola contra el mundo: Flora Tristan la pariah (1957). Tribert, M., "Feminisme et socialisme d'après Flora Tristan." Revue d'histoire économique et sociale (1921).

Jeanne A. Ojala

William T. Ojala

Flore Tristan

(see: Flora Célestine Thérese Henriette Tristan)

Flore Tristan-Morcoso

(see: Flora Célestine Thérese Henriette Tristan)

Carmen Troitiño

Born 1918, Madrid, Spain
Genre(s): drama
Language(s): Spanish

Troitiño holds a degree from the University of Madrid where she shared the interests in experimental theater of Alfonso Sastre, Alfonso Paso, Medardo Fraile and others. After her graduation from the university, she worked in Spain's National Theaters directing the most demanding of the foreign offerings (e.g., plays by O'Neill, Beckett, Ionesco, Williams, etc.). Although not a defender of women, she has touched upon problems relating to them. Si llevara agua . . . (Where There's Smoke . . .), a play concerning the evils of gossip and envy, won the Jacinto Benavente Prize in 1954. Y los hijos de tus hijos (Unto your Children's Children) explores from a psychological perspective the problems suffered by the children of prostitutes. She has been active as director and producer of major theatrical productions for the past thirty years and continues active in these areas.

Works

Pandereta [The Tambourine] (1949). Pasiones [Passions] (1952). Si llevara agua . . . [Where There's Smoke . . .] (1954). Y los hijos de tus hijos [Unto Your Children's Children] (1958).

Patricia W. O'Connor

Birgitta Trotzig

Born November 9, 1929, Göteborg, Sweden
Genre(s): novel, prose poetry, essay
Language(s): Swedish

Birgitta Trotzig (née Kjellén) has been called one of Sweden's "most important and original" contemporary writers because of her visionary perspective and aesthetic purity of style. She studied literature and art history at the University of Göteborg, then wrote critical essays on art and literature for some of Sweden's most important newspapers. Among them were Sydsvenska Dagbladet, Dagens Nyheter, and Afton-bladet. Her aesthetic writings also appeared in such collections as Endeavor and Proposal (1963), which contains her essays from 1955 to

1962. Topics discussed include Russian iconography, the painters Chagall and Soutine, and the philosopher Chardin. Literary journals such as *Bonniers Litterära Magasin* also published her essays. In 1949 she married the artist Ulf Trotzig. She moved to Paris, France, in 1955, but resides presently in Lund, Sweden.

Trotzig's work shows a strong ethical component that betrays personal involvement: "I write in order to understand life and thereby prepare myself for death," she once wrote. Part of this understanding derives from a contemplation of history. Therefore some of her novels aptly take the form of the *legend* or of the historical novel. Her first novel, *The Exposed* (1957; transl. into German, *Die Ausgesetzten*, 1967), is a legendary tale set in the last decade of the sixteenth century, when the province of Skaane was captured from Denmark by the Swedes and a merciless repatriation of the population ensued. Similarly, the novel *A Report from the Coast* (1961) takes the form of a medieval chronicle of the city of Aahus. The lives, deeds, beliefs, and prejudices of its leaders, citizens, and beggars are probed, and the picture that emerges is one of suffering humanity waiting for God's redemption. The novel's motifs are taken from stark contrasts such as light/darkness, birth/death, height/depth, and a supporting symbolism of transubstantiation and transcendence. Central to the novel is the theme that while yet in darkness and despair, humanity longs for redemption through Christ but is unable to recognize the truth. The Christ-symbolism is evident chiefly in the figure of the humpback Merete in whose deformed body a child grows as the result of rape—a ray of hope in the midst of evil. The perfectly formed child dies, however, as the first of a number of such deaths in the midst of want and disease. Merete is accused of having brought this evil upon the city. She is stoned to death and buried at sea. Biblical sentences (e.g., "who was the first to take up a stone") underscore the religious symbolism of the sacrificial lamb slain for the sins of others in the "flower month" of May. The novel's last sentence is both didactic and bitter: "This happened in Aahus on the east coast of Skaane in the year 1500 after Christ's birth. . . ."

Trotzig's development as a writer has been influenced by Spanish and Russian mystics, and by Walt Whitman, Selma Lagerlöf, Pär Lagerkvist, Kafka, and others.

Works

Ur de älskandes liv (1951). *Bilder* (1954). *De utsatta* (1957); German tr. Solita Felter, *Die Ausgesetzten* [1967]. *Ett landskap* (1959). *En berättelse fraan kusten* (1961). *Utkast och förslag* (1962). *Levande och döda* (1964). *Sveket* (1966). *Ordgränser* (1968). *Sjukdommen* (1972). *I kejsarens tid* (1975). *Jaget o världen* (1977). *Dirättelser* (1977). *Dykungens dotter* (1985).

Bibliography

Bäckström, L., *Under välfärdens yta* (1959). "B.T." *Svenskt Litteraturlexikon* (1964). Boyer, R., *Job mitt ibland oss: En studie över B.T.s verk* (Stockholm, 1978). Dahl, C., "Levande eller döda." *Bonniers Litterära Magasin* XXXIV: 642–653. D'Heurle, A., "The Image of Woman in the Fiction of B.T." *Scandinavian Studies* 55 (1983): 371–382. Ericsson, L.C., "Intervju med B.T." *Böckernas Värld* 2, No. 2: 11–14. Henmark, K., "Bristen och allvaret hos B.T." *Vaar lösen* LVI (1965): 108–115. Näsström, G., and Strömberg, M., *Den unga parnassen* (1956). Ohlsson, R. "B.T. och själens mörka natt." *Vaar lösen* 59 (1968): 653–659. Paillard, J., "Levande och döda." *Credo* XLVI (1965): 63–69. Sprogere, O., "Pateikt nepasakamo." *Dzimtenes Kalendars* (1985): 150–154. Vincent, M., "B.T.s Ordgränser—ett tolknings-förslag." *Samlaren* 92 (1971): 40–73. Vincent, M., "Kosmogoni och apokalyps: Tva intertextuella paragram i B.T.s 'Teologiska variationer.'" *Samlaren* 103 (1982): 17–27.

Helene M. Kastinger Riley

Marina Tsvetaeva

Born September 26, 1882, Moscow, Russia; died August 31, 1941, Elabuga, Soviet Union
Genre(s): poetry, prose
Language(s): Russian

Marina Tsvetaeva, one of the greatest Russian poets of the twentieth century, once wrote about herself: "I can be grasped only in terms of contrasts, i.e., of the simultaneous presence of everything. . . . I am many poets; as to how I've managed to harmonize all of them is my secret."

Her thoroughly disinterested poetic stance prevented her from siding with movements and ideologies. She spent her most productive years in the midst of constant literary and political struggles which she tended to regard as nonsensical. In her lifetime, her work was regarded as undesirable both abroad and in the Soviet Union by all except the greatest writers, among them Andrei Bely, Rainer Maria Rilke, Boris Pasternak, and Anna Akhmatova.

As a child she often felt unwanted by her family. Her upbringing, however, was intellectually very stimulating. Her father, a professor at the University of Moscow, founded one of Russia's best known museums. Her mother, a highly educated, cosmopolitan woman and a musician, had her learn the piano, which was to contribute considerably to the rhythmic novelty and musicality of her poetry. In 1912, she married Sergei Efron, a sickly and charming but rather talentless man. His inability to contribute to the family budget and his various political activities proved to be a heavy and tragic burden for Tsvetaeva. A devoted mother to her children, she had several love affairs with both men and women. After the October revolution in 1917, she was trapped in Moscow for five years. Her fragmentary documentary writings in *Omens of the Earth*, which was published only in excerpts, give a fascinating account of her experiences during this period. After one of her children starved to death, she joined her husband in the West in 1922. Following her initial success during her visit to Berlin and her three-year stay in Czechoslovakia, the family moved to Paris in 1925. Soon after her arrival, Tsvetaeva suggested in her essay *A Poet on Criticism* (1926) that only those who understand modern art can evaluate it. Her tone offended established figures in the emigre community. Her husband's pro-Soviet activities, in addition, resulted in her isolation and poverty in the years to come. Yielding to pressure from her family, she returned to Moscow in 1939, only to have all her relatives, except for her son, arrested (her husband was executed), and to find herself shunned by the Soviet literary elite. In August 1941, after Hitler attacked the Soviet Union, she was evacuated to Elabuga, where she committed suicide and where she is buried in an unmarked mass grave.

She started writing poetry at the age of six. Her first two collections of verse, *The Evening Album* (1910) and *The Magic Lantern* (1912), offer a myth-like evocation of childhood experiences. *The Evening Album* was received favorably by such established writers as Briusov and Gumilyov. Her poems in the collection *Mileposts I.* (1921) present a consecutive lyrical chronicle of the year 1916 in a diary format. Her use of more than one kind of foot in the line is a major innovation in Russian versification. Similarly novel is her simultaneous use of the archaic and colloquial dialects. A lyric chronicle of 1917, the year of two Russian revolutions, is offered in the collection *The Demesne of the Swans*, written between 1917 and 1921 and published in 1957. In her poetic diary, *Craft* (1923), personal themes merge with concerns about post-revolutionary Russia. This and another collection, *After Russia* (1928), represent the peak of Tsvetaeva's achievement. Inspired by her experiences in a provincial and philistine Czech town, she wrote perhaps her best work, the long, satirical poem, *The Pied Piper* (1925–1926), which is based on a German legend. The "Poem of the Staircase," written in 1926, is a lyrical narrative of the Paris squalor, in which the impoverished poet had to make her home. Also in Paris she wrote her two neoclassical verse tragedies, *Ariadne* (1927) and *Phaedre* (1928). Her only piece of prose fiction is the *Letter to an Amazon*, written in 1932, which examines lesbian love. In 1938–1939, before her return to the Soviet Union, she wrote her "Verses to Czechoslovakia," which voice her strong sympathies with the invaded people.

An uncommon wealth of topics, a ready receptiveness to foreign literatures, and the confident mastery of Russian culture highlight the literary activity of Marina Tsvetaeva. Her original prose, expansive correspondence and, in particular, the sonorous versification and strophic experimentation which typify her poetry finally started to receive due attention in the late 1950s in the Soviet Union and abroad. Even today, hitherto unnoticed aspects of Tsvetaeva's work and life are being uncovered.

Works

Izbrannye proizvedeniia [Selected Works] (1965).
Pis'ma k A. Teskovoi [Letters to A. Teskova] (1969).
Neizdannye pis'ma [Unpublished Letters] (1972).
Izbrannaia proze v dvukh tomakh [Selected Prose in Two Volumes] (1979). *Stikhotvoreniia i poemy v piati tomakh* [Poetry and Long Poems in Nine Volumes] (1980).
Translations: *Modern Russian Poetry*, eds. Vladimir Markov and Merill Sparks (1967), pp. 429–449. *Russian Poetry: The Modern Period* (1978), pp. 140–148. *Selected Poems*, tr. E. Feinstein (1981). *A Captive Spirit: Selected Prose*, tr. J.M. King (1980).

Bibliography

Gladkova, T.L., *Marina Cvetaeva: Bibliography* (Paris, 1982). Karlinsky, Simon, *Marina Tsvetaeva* (Cambridge, 1985). Lampl, Horst, ed., *Marina Cvetaeva: Studien und Materialen* (Wiener Slawistischer Almanach, Sonderband 3.) (Vienna, 1981). Razumovsky, Maria *Marina Tsvetaeva* (London, 1983).

Peter I. Barta

Felix Tuli

(see: Hella Maria Wuolijoki)

Mirjam Irene Tuominen

Born April 19, 1913, Kajana, Finland; died July 31, 1967, Helsinki, Finland
Genre(s): short story, essay, lyric poetry, translation
Language(s): Swedish

Mirjam Tuominen's interest in the soul in despair, in the psychology of mental breakdown, and in the walls separating man from fellow man is certainly not unique; however, few writers have approached these problems with such intensity or with such sympathy. Her concern with man's inner world sets her apart from most of her Finnish-Swedish contemporaries who were interested in the outer world of political and linguistic struggle.

Tuominen grew up in Ostrobothnia, received her bachelor's degree in 1935 and attended the Sorbonne in 1937. After her return to Finland, she married Torsten Korsström, whom she had met at seventeen, in 1939. They lived in Nykarleby, and their marriage produced two daughters; Tuominen left him in 1946 and moved to Helsinki. Plagued with "nervous" problems all her life, Tuominen never sought the help of a psychiatrist. Her conversion to Catholicism late in life gave her but brief respite from her "demons"; she died, having never found spiritual peace, in 1967.

Her short stories, spread among six collections, concern tormented human beings, dreamers and children; they examine in painful detail the mental and physical aspects of the dissolution of the psyche. When solace is to be found, it is usually in the form of a bleak, difficult religious experience that often brings death. Guilt and other moral issues also provide Tuominen with themes; the fight between spontaneity (her ideal) and the inhibitions that hamper it are also treated, as well as her fear of losing control. Of her short story collections, *Mörka gudar* (1944) and *Tvekan* (1947), a selection of previously published stories, are considered, stylistically speaking, her finest.

A shift occurs in her writing in the late 1940s. After World War II, she turned to Europe and in particular to Hölderlin and Rilke; her *oeuvre* includes Tuominen-colored translations of their poetry as well as an inner biography of Hölderlin. Under their influence she began writing her own poetry, as well as essays and "observations" that basically continue to examine, exhaustively, her original themes. However, now they have been expanded and linked to a more universal identity.

Tuominen, an intense, fearless yet desperate crusader into the deepest and most frightening elements of the human soul, will continue to be read for her short stories, which provide the reader with a dark yet truthful mirror.

Works

Short stories: *Tidig tvekan* (1938). *Murar* (1939). *Visshet* (1942). *Mörka gudar* (1944). (One of these short stories has been translated, *Kris* [1946]. *Besk brygd* (1947). *Tvekan, noveller i urval* (1947). Other prose: *Betraktelser* (1947). *Bliva ingen; prosa* (1949). *Stadier; essäer och översikter* (1949). *Tema med variationer* (1952). *Hölderlin, en inre biografi* (1960).

Poetry: *Monokord* (1954). *Under jorden sjönk* (1954). *Dikter III* (1956). *Vid gaitans* (1957).

Translations: "Slutet på depressionen" [The End of the Depression], tr. George C. Schoolfield, in *Swedo-Finnish Short Stories* (1974). . . . *Brev* (1957) (Translation of a selection of Rainer Maria Rilke's letters into Swedish).

Bibliography

Barck, Ghita, *Mirjam Irene Tuominen i liv och dikt* (Helsinki, 1983). Havu, I., *Finlands litteratur 1900–1950* (Nörnkrona, 195_?). Lindman-Strafford, Kerstin, *Fäder och döttrar* (Helsinki, 1986). Ljungdell, Ragna, "Att bliva ingen: Mirjam Tuominen's väg." *Ord och bild* 61 (1952): 269–277. Mazzarella, Merete, *Från Fredrika Runeberg till Märta Tikkanen* (Helsinki, 1985). Schoolfield, George C., *Swedo-Finnish Short Stories* (New York, 1974). Warburton, Thomas, "Vid förnimmelsegränsen." *Nya Argus* (1955). Warburton, Thomas, *Åttio år finlandssvensk litteratur* (Helsinki, 1984).

Kathy Saranpa Anstine

Evgeniia Tur

(see: Elizaveta Salhias de Tournemir)

Esther Tusquets

Born August 30, 1936, Barcelona, Spain
Genre(s): novel
Language(s): Spanish

Esther Tusquets was born on August 30, 1936, into a well-established Catalan family. She completed her secondary education in the *Colegio Alemán* in Barcelona (a Spanish version of a German High School) and later studied *Filosofía y Letras* (History) at the University of Barcelona and the University of Madrid. In 1960, she became the director of Editorial Lumen, a position which she still holds.

Born in the first year of Spain's convulsive Civil War, Tusquets' writing career was initiated much later—in the early years following Franco's death. This period in Spain is marked not only by an explosion of political parties, but also by a loosening of sexual and social taboos, and an artistic and literary boom. Tusquets' novels have attracted attention for their experimental and poetic qualities. Her erotic and heterodox feminist writing displays a penetrating engagement with various aspects of life. While her carefully circumscribed and intense psychological narrative has aptly been compared to Virginia Woolf's fiction, the latter's modernist epiphanies are rather more undermined than celebrated in Tusquets' work. Two major thematic strands, the illustrated Catalan upper-class and women's lives and loves, weave a complex narrative tapestry, combining the specificity of contemporary Barcelona with a universality that has prompted acclaim in Spain as well as the translation of her works into many languages.

Tusquets began her literary career until 1978, the year her first novel, *El mismo mar de todos los veranos* (The Same Sea of Every Summer), appeared. This work constitutes the beginning of a trilogy, continued by *El amor es un juego solitario* (1979; Love Is a Solitary Game), and completed by *Varada tras el último naufragio* (1980; Stranded After the Last Shipwreck). In 1981, she published a collection of short stories which are very closely interrelated, and another short story was published one year later in the collection of women's stories compiled by Ymelda Navajo entitled *Doce relatos de mujeres* (Twelve Stories by Women). Her last main work appeared in 1985 under the title *Para no volver* (To Not Return). She has also published a children's book *La conejita Marcela* (1979; Marcela, The Little Rabbit) and various articles in the magazine *Destino*. She is also an active collaborator for the most important newspaper in Barcelona, *La Vanguardia*.

The action of Tusquets' trilogy—as well as most of her narrative—is set in Barcelona, and her characters are part of the middle-class society that shows its mediocrity through its overall satisfaction with life. Tusquets' protagonists are women in search of their own identity, a search which leads them to a vast variety of homosexual and heterosexual experiences. The novels in the trilogy share, in addition to the theme of searching for oneself, the same protagonist, Elia. The first part of the trilogy, *El mismo mar de todos los veranos*, is written in the first person and could be considered as the first part of that search: the narrator, a professor of history, seeks to be reborn through a lesbian relationship. Clara, Elia's lover, will be the permanent companion throughout the different stages of Elia's search. Mythological and literary allusions are frequently used by Tusquets. The second volume of the trilogy, *El amor es un juego solitario*, deals with another form of quest. This time it is the desire to escape from a bourgeois, mediocre life which pushes middle-aged Elia to involve herself in a series of experiences with two adolescent lovers. Sexual experiences are, for a time, equated with love and fulfillment. This proves to be a temporary escape and not the solution to Elia's existential dilemmas. *Varada tras el último naufragio* concludes Elia's search. In this novel, the protagonist witnesses the end of her marriage and her false ideals of happiness and of idyllic wedlock, carefully learned during childhood through fairy tales and other myths. This time the search will be directed toward finding life and happiness in reality as opposed to fantasy. In this case, the search is a confrontation rather than an escape through sexual adventures.

Set in the snobbish Catalan society of Barcelona's elite, the novel explores the protagonist's menopausal crisis marked by the onset of old age, an estranged marriage and a re-evaluation of her life. Tusquets interrogates the role of females in society, focusing upon the protagonist's dislike of her mother and daughter in sharp contrast to her love for the young Clara, an androgynous alternative to traditional women and love relationships. The anatomical differences of lesbian sexuality (total body contact rather than more exclusively genital contact and the lack of dichotomy between penetrator and penetrated), as well as the ultimate equality between the lovers, implicitly undermines phallocentric ideology—underscored by the narrative's tenderness and feminine images. Although the protagonist fails to escape a prescribed wifely role, the dream-like erotic sequence in the novel's central section introduces a world of youthful hope—presaging different roles for other women, who, like Clara, can combine love, literature and political activism in a more daring way than her older counterparts. The juxtaposition between

the protagonist's (uneasy) acquiescence to cultural norms and her experience of otherness with Clara is paralleled by the structural counterpoint between the traditional framing story and the disruption of story expectations and literary norms in the long central portion of the novel. This strategy, along with the bold treatment of a forbidden subject matter, contributes to making this a very impressive novel.

In her next work, *Siete miradas en un mismo paisaje*, Tusquets continues with the main themes presented in earlier works. Here she chooses the short story as a means to analyze female psychological growth when faced with the expectations of society and of the family. The book is formed of seven stories which represent seven critical moments in the protagonist's (Sara's) life. Tusquets again explores homosexual as well as heterosexual love relationships and gives a sharp depiction of the social background against which Sara struggles. Tusquets' latest novel, *Para no volver* (1985), does not differ enormously from previous works from the point of view of content. Now, we truly witness a psychoanalytical search. This theme, which was omnipresent in other works, takes the form here of the relationship between the analyst and his patient, a middle-aged woman named Elena. The novel is a serious reflection on life and on the futility of success, suggesting that failure could be an almost desirable goal for human activity. Love and the suffering it entails are the only tools to understand oneself and others.

Tusquets is not a writer of plots; she is a writer of style. Her prose style, which has been called baroque, is indeed quite an achievement. Her writing is sumptuous, full of lyrical images and metaphors, and is both suggestive and sensual. She uses mainly the extended monologue to convey the autoanalysis her protagonists undergo. She is able to combine plasticity with cultural issues. Freud and Jung hide in almost every page. Her novels suggest the idea of a "life puzzle" that the protagonist must put together. Tusquets is a feminist writer in more ways than one: her feminism goes to remote corners of the feminine psyche. As in the case of other women writers in Spain, she deals with common themes such as love, mother-daughter relationships, and solitude. Yet, she goes a little farther; she treats feminine sexuality in a way rarely found in other novelists. Tusquets' protagonists may not like their present existence, but they do like their bodies. The female body is sometimes described through metaphor, other times less elliptically in sensuous, open, positive ways. This will possibly suggest paths to other writers' treatment of the too-often taboo subject of female sexuality.

Works

El mismo mar de todos los veranos (1978). *La conejita Marcela* (1979). *El amor es un juego solitario* (1980). *Varada tras el último naufragio* (1980). *Seite miradas en un mismo paisaje* (1981). "Las sutiles leyes de la simetría." *Doce relatos de mujeres* (1982). *Para no volver* (1985).

Bibliography

Bellver, Catherine, G., "The Language of Eroticism in the Novels of Esther Tusquets." *Anales de la literatura española contemporánea* 9, 1–3 (1984): 13–17. Claudín, Victor, "Esther Tusquets: conquista de la felicidad." *Camp de l'arpa* 71 (enero 1980): 48. Lee-Bonanno, Lucy, "The Quest for Personhood: An Expression of the Female Tradition in the Novels of Moix, Tusquets, Matute, and Alós." *DAI* 46 (1985): 3A. Diss., University of Kentucky, 1985. Ordóñez, Elizabeth, "The Barcelona Group: The Fiction of Alós, Moix, and Tusquets." *Letras femeninas* 6, no. 1 (Spring 1980): 47. Regazzoni, Susanna, "Cuatro novelistas españolas de hoy. Estudio y entrevistas." *Quaderni di Letterature Iberiche e Americane*, 2 (1984).

Coro Malaxecheverría

Marie Murphy

Aale Tynni

Born 1913, Kolppana, Ingermanland, Finland
Genre(s): poetry
Language(s): Finnish

After taking her bachelor's degree in 1936, Tynni was at first a teacher of Finnish, then became a free-lance writer. After her first collection, *Kynttilänsydän* (1938; Candlewick), she was considered to be continuing the work of Saima Harmaja, but in the course of time her originality has become more clearly apparent. Tynni has developed and polished metric verse in Finnish; her collections have appeared over five decades, and only in her later years has she given way to the movement towards free verse—not a change for the better in the opinion of some critics. Tynni has described herself as a "symbolist," but she has been more firmly classed as a "cultural poet." The term refers both to content and form. Tynni's themes come from cultural tradition: fairy tales, myth, history, and literature. And she has expressed herself in the form of old genres: folk song, ballad, romance, and dramatic monologue. Her poetry has also broadened the thematic range of poetry, especially in the direction of the fundamental experiences of a woman's life. Tynni's poetry is at times also polemic and committed though this may remain concealed beneath a historical disguise. Her high level of structure, together with the rhythm and melody of her language, have helped to make Tynni one of the most popular of Finnish poets. She is also a very assiduous translator of world poetry; her large anthology, *Tuhat laulujen vuotta* (A Thousand Years of Songs), contains translations of poetry from various European countries from the year 1000 up to the present day. In addition she has translated Shakespeare's sonnets, a selection of W.B. Yeats, and some of the French modernists.

Works

Kootut runot [Collected Poems] (1955, 1964, 1977). *Vihreys* [Greenness] (1979).

Bibliography

Sala, Kaarina "Maan sydän" [Heart of the Earth]. *Rivien takaa* [Behind the Lines] (1976).

Markku Envall

U

U.E.V. (Una ex Vocibus)

(see: Jacqueline E. van der Waals)

Julia Uceda

Born October 21, 1925, Sevilla, Spain
Genre(s): poetry
Language(s): Spanish

Julia Uceda's formative years were spent in the Andalusian city of Sevilla, where she received her doctorate from the University with a thesis on the poet José Luis Hidalgo. Later, she would also publish a study on Hidalgo. In 1966 she left to teach Spanish literature at Michigan State University for seven years. She has not lived in Sevilla since then. In an interview, she observed: "You have to understand what Sevilla was like in those years. [The Franco period] was a very difficult and destructive era, and if we survived . . . it was probably because we were too close to the situation and couldn't compare it to anything else. . . . Not only the poets of our generation left Sevilla, the university people too . . . because they realized how oppressive our situation was. They left for their own good. We were a very unlucky generation. . . ." Uceda would later move around, from the United States to Oviedo, Albacete, Ireland, and eventually back to Spain once more, where she resides and teaches in the northern province of Galicia. She has contributed steadily over the years to such journals as *Insula*, *Cal*, *Cuadernos Hispanoamericanos*, *Revista de Occidente*, and others. In addition, she now heads a small publishing house called Colección Esquío de Poesía.

Uceda has been regarded as part of the Generation of the 1950s, a group of Spanish poets noted especially for their social and political concerns and use of everyday language and imagery (Angel González, Manuel Mantero, Gloria Fuertes, Claudio Rodríguez, for example). Nevertheless, she possesses a poetic voice and spirit of her own, one which Manuel Mantero admiringly calls "strange," and which makes her difficult to categorize. Her poetry, which is always intimate and mysterious and yet never forgets the social context, has gravitated increasingly toward the metaphysical and existential.

Her first book, *Mariposa en cenizas* (Butterfly in Ashes), was published in 1959, but her poetry had been appearing regularly in small literary magazines and anthologies before that date. As she herself notes, she arrived "late" to poetry: late, yes, but with a surprising depth and purity of her poetic persona. This first book is basic for understanding her poetry, since it already contains some of the themes and the lyrical intellectualism of her more mature work. *Mariposa en cenizas*, though primarily love poetry, also deals with death and alienation, in poems like "Mariposa en cenizas" (Butterfly in Ashes) where she sees her death as "not yet ripe" in God's fields, and "La extraña" (The Stranger) where she senses herself radically cut off from another, mysterious existence.

Extraña juventud (1962; Strange Youth), a finalist for the prestigious Adonais Poetry Prize of 1961, develops the existentialist vein more fully, with an emphasis on the feeling of being both "strange" and "foreign," as the poet questions her own sense of authenticity and identity, pressured by mortality itself. "Julia Uceda," she asks herself, "what have you done with your shadow?" Her language, intense and strong, also opens out into wider concerns in this book, which is dedicated "to men of my time." *Extraña juventud* implicitly denounces a repressive and unjust political system, the inequalities, and the collective and individual alienation of Franco Spain.

By her third volume of poetry, *Sin mucha esperanza* (1966; Without Much Hope), Uceda had reached the end of one phase—what could be called "historical existentialism"—and the beginning of another, in which she takes a much more introspective and metaphysical turning. As in her earlier books, the poet, though intensely aware of man's social and political plight, never sets the collective over and against the individual. For her, "without the salvation of the individual we are lost." Thus such themes as loss of identity and freedom, alienation, lost childhood, exile, and death are treated together, merging singular and plural concerns into one. Particularly poignant are the poems "Eterno oleaje" (Eternal Wave) and "Una patria se ve desde la cumbre" (A Country Seen from Afar), in which images of inner and outer exile from "an impossible country" are juxtaposed.

Poemas de Cherry Lane (1968; Cherry Lane Poems) consists of fourteen poems, written in free verse and reflecting much of Uceda's experiences in the United States. This book, which at times approaches the hallucinatory in its imagery, has been called by one critic "fundamental" in the canon of Spanish post-war poetry. Her vision of reality is simply but profoundly expressed in this line from "Condenada al silencio" (Condemned to Silence): "Nada más natural. Nada más misterioso" (Nothing more natural. Nothing more mysterious).

Uceda's fifth book—*Campanas en Sansueña* (1977; Bells in Sansueña)—clearly anticipates her latest one, *Viejas voces secretas de la noche* (1981; Ancient Secret Voices of the Night), in its metaphysical and visionary search for illumination. For it is only the light, she writes, which, paradoxically, has substance. Reworking the traditional imagery of the dark side of the soul, Uceda seeks revelation in darkness, in the night

which possesses its own light, its own knowledge, or as she puts it, "la noche es caminar/ buscando ángulos de luz" (night is out walking/ searching for the angles of light). It is this powerful union of the intimate with the metaphysical which marks Uceda's poetry and makes her one of Spain's strongest and most singular poetic voices today.

Works

Mariposa en cenizas (1959). *Extraña juventud* (1962). *Sin mucha esperanza* (1966). *Poemas de Cherry Lane* (1968). *José Luis Hidalgo: Estudio y antología* (1970). *Campanas en Sansueña* (1977). *Viejas voces secretas de la noche* (1981).

Unpublished works: *Los andaluces.* Antología histórica de la poesía andaluza. *En elogio de la locura.* Narraciones.

Translations: *American Poetry Review* (Nov.-Dec. 1986). *Prairie Schooner* (Winter 1985). *Anthology of Magazine Verse and Yearbook of American Poetry, 1986–1988* ed. (1988). *New Orleans Review* (Spring 1987). *Touchstone* (Spring 1988). *Ulula* (1987).

Bibliography

Cano, J.L., "La poesía de Julia Uceda." *Insula* (May 1978). Mantero, M., "Julia Uceda y lo extraño." *Poesía española contemporánea* (1966). Molina Campos, E., "Nocturna luz de la poesía de Julia Uceda." *Nueva Estafeta* (Apr. 1982). Ruiz-Copete, J. de D., "Julia Uceda, o la poesía de la existencia." *Poetas de Sevilla* (1971).

General references: *Women Writers of Spain*, ed. C.L. Galerstein (1986).

Other references: *ABC* (Sept. 10, 1983). *Cal* (Jan. 1978). *Cuadernos de Agora* (Nov.–Dec. 1962). *Insula* (Nov. 1968).

Noël M. Valis

Acacia Uceta

Born 1927, Madrid, Spain
Genre(s): poetry
Language(s): Spanish

Uceta's works have appeared in numerous anthologies and have been translated into Portuguese, French, Italian and English. Her poetry has been awarded the following prizes: Contraluz, Ciudad de Cuenca, Fray Luis de Léon, Elisa

Soriano, Amigos de la Poesía de Valencia, and the Virgen del Carmen. Her short novels have also received the Sésamo and Cafe Gijón prizes. She has received fellowships from the Juan March Foundation and the Spanish Ministry of Culture. Her collections of poetry are noted for their lyricism and expressions of optimism and happiness.

Works

El corro de las horas (1961). *Quince años* novel (1962). *Frente a un muro de cal abrasadora* (1967). *Una hormiga tan sólo*, novel (1967). *Detrás de cada noche* (1970). *Al sur de las estrellas* (1976). *Cuenca, roca viva* (1980). *Intima dimensión* (1983).

Bibliography

Conde, Carmen, "Acacia Uceta." *Poesía Femenina Española Contemporánea* (Barcelona, 1967). Gatell, Angelina, "Acacia Uceta." *Mis primeras lecturas poéticas* (Barcelona, 1980). Miró, Emilio, "Poetisas Españolas Contemporáneas." *Revista de la Universidad de Madrid* XXIV, No. 95. Urbano, Victoria, "Entrevista a Acacia Uceta." *Letras Femeninas* XII, Nos. 1–2 (primavera-otoño 1986): 121–130.

Carolyn Galerstein

Dubravka Ugrešić

Born 1950, Kutina, Yugoslavia
Genre(s): novel, short story, criticism,
*   children's literature*
Language(s): Serbo-Croatian

Dubravka Ugrešić was born in Yugoslavia in 1950. She received her B.A. and M.A. in Russian literature from the University of Zagreb. She presently works at the Institute for the Theory of Literature and conducts research on the Russian *avant-garde.*

After two books for children, *Fili i Srećica* (Philip and Little Luck) and *Mali plamen* (A Small Flame), Ugrešić has published two novels—*Poza za prozu* (A Rose for Prose) in 1979 and *Štefica Cvek u raljama 'ivota* (Mary Brown in the Jaws of Life) in 1982. The novel has been turned into a scenario and successfully filmed. In 1983, Ugrešić published a collection of short stories *Život je bajka* (Life Is a Fairy-Tale) and co-authored the scenario for the movie *Za sreću je potrebno troje*

(Three Are Needed for Happiness) with Rajko Grlić. She has also published a book of essays on the contemporary Russian literature and is a co-editor of a series on the theory of *avant-garde* (*Pojmovnik avangarde*) with Aleksandar Flaker.

There are two main characteristics of Ugršić's writing: a strong formalist awareness that becomes obvious in her literary craftsmanship and narrative self-reflexiveness as well as the genderic markedness of her writing. Though Ugrešić is always very careful to avoid the label "feminist" or even "a woman writer," the topical concern of her texts as well as their intertextuality (the way in which they refer to literary and cultural tradition) mark them as feminist.

This was already obvious in her first novel, *The Pose for Prose*, which could be read as the allegory of a female author in the search for her own tradition. The novel starts with the desire of the author to attract and seduce her male friend by producing the sort of writing he would appreciate. The book thus turns into a parodic manuscript of different styles and genres of writing, none of them satisfactory to their recipient, Bublik.

Thus, disappointed at the end, the author swallows the metonimic Bublik—the Russian version of a croissant—reversing thus the economy of desire typical of Petrachian poetry and finds her own voice and her own identity in female gossip with her girl-friend over a cup of coffee.

The second novel, *Štefica Cvek u raljama 'ivota* (Mary Brown in the Jaws of Life), deals even more straightforwardly with a feminist issue. Subtitled "a patchwork story," the narrative is controlled by and organized around various sewing, cutting, and similar instructions typical of those in women's magazines. Within this framework, we follow the story of Štefica Cvek, a simple girl, a secretary, who escapes her trivial life only by taking fiction for reality, believing in the soap-opera plots her culture has surrounded her with. Thus, throughout the novel, by means of paraphrase, parody and montage, we are faced not only with a tragic-comic fate of a heroine but also with the stereotypes of our culture which the novel highlights and undermines.

The role of Dubravka Ugrešić on the contemporary literary scene is therefore a significant one. Differently from her male colleagues, which predominantly follow the models of genre literature, Dubravka Ugrešić's writing subverts and highlights these models in a manner new to Yugoslavian culture. If the main feminist concern is to point out and reevaluate the metaphors and stereotypes we live by, Ugrešić's writing can, in spite of its overt playfulness and formalism, be considered as an original attempt at achieving such a goal.

Works

Filip i Srećica. Mali plamen. Poza zaprozu (1979). Stefica Cvek u raljama 'ivota (1982). Život je bajka. [With Rajko Grlić], Za sreću je potrebno troje. [With Aleksandar Flaker], Pojmovnik avangarde.

Ljiljana Gjurgjan

Liesl Ujvary

Born October 10, 1939, Bratislava (formerly Pressburg), Czechoslovakia
Genre(s): photography, poetry, prose, radio drama, essay
Language(s): German

Liesl Ujvary is one of the most radical representatives of contemporary "experimental literature," the specifically Austrian avant-garde movement that originated with the Vienna Group in the late 1950s. Readers are often baffled by her texts, which defy genre classification and resist conformity with conventional literary norms. Ujvary seems to specialize in clichés and banalities, which, however, she turns around to expose the underlying thought processes. Behind the ostensible nonsense is a sharp mind and a keen observer of contemporary life in Western society.

Ujvary was born in Czechoslovakia of Austrian parents in 1939, and she retains her Austrian citizenship. She studied Slavic and Old Hebrew literature and art at the universities of Vienna and Zurich and received her doctorate from the University of Zurich in 1968. From 1965 to 1970 she taught Russian at a language institute in Zurich, and thereafter she spent a year teaching Russian in Tokyo; the following year, 1971–1972, she pursued postdoctoral studies at the University of Moscow. Since then she has lived as a free-lance writer in Vienna,

where she is a member of the Graz Authors' Association. From 1960 to 1963 she was married, and she has one daughter who grew up with her grandparents in Tyrol. Ujvary also works occasionally as translator and contributor to Austrian and German newspapers and radio stations.

Given Ujvary's advanced academic degrees and international cultural experience one may be inclined to look for erudite representations of it in the text; but in vain, for her works are not representational, and biographic experiences manifest themselves only indirectly. Sicher & Gut (1977; Safe & Good) and rosen, zugaben (1983; roses, additions) are her leading volumes of poetry, and their central theme is language itself. Language is seen less as a means of communication than as a barrier to it, and the shortcomings and absurdities of conventional talk are poetically foregrounded against an implicit background of total otherness. The short poems and prose pieces present phrases and slogans, statements and questions from everyday life arranged in a montage-like constellation to express the author's critical stance toward verbal behavior. The sentences are intentionally banal so that no traditional image arises, and the author deliberately avoids aesthetic effects. For example, "the sky is blue in Vienna / the sky is blue in Rome / the sky is blue in New Orleans / the sky is blue in Tokyo" (from "peter stuyvesant takes a trip") is obviously not a statement about particular cities but about the form of speaking itself. Whereas Sicher & Gut operates largely with such repetitions, rosen, zugaben presents short texts that look like poems but are written in a nondiscursive, highly experimental mode. Both works derive their power from the lack of convergence between superficial context and actual meaning.

Ujvary's basic philosophy is described more explicitly in her autobiographical prose work, Schöne Stunden (1984; Beautiful Hours). It gives an account of the author's development as a creative writer, which is equated with her development as a human being. Narration is in the form of an inner monologue in which two separate strains are nevertheless discernible. The first discusses the problem of the individual in a society that is seen as restrictive and dehumanizing; the second reflects the thoughts and feelings of the author as she writes. The "beautiful hours" of the ironic title are those in which she is entirely at one with herself, i.e., almost never. With wit but also with sadness Ujvary registers the distance between her utopian vision and the verbal norms that regiment our lives. The tension between the surface appearances and the various realities behind them is also the topic of her forthcoming prose work, *Geheimer Verkehr* (Secret Communication). Her radio plays, some of them written together with Bodo Hell, have been frequently broadcast by Austrian radio stations.

Ujvary writes in the tradition of radical language criticism stemming from Mauthner, Wittgenstein, and Kraus, and extending to the postwar Vienna Group and contemporary experimental writers. Language is weighed in the balance and found wanting. The intent is to question the epistemology behind the linguistic structures and thus to undermine the conventional certainties we all take for granted. Language, according to Ujvary, consists of verbal and graphic clichés that—particularly since the advent of modern media and advertising—intervene between the individual and his or her natural way of feeling. Language criticism is also sociopolitical criticism, for it specifically targets the normative behavior and ideological pressures foisted upon us by society. By showing the schematic, stereotypical forms of speech (and thus of thought) to which we are all enslaved, Ujvary hopes for emancipation to new and nonmanipulative modes of thought and communication. Ujvary's idealism vacillates between euphoria and disillusionment, but her lapidary reduction of formal means is in any case highly provocative.

Works

Ed., *Freiheit ist Freiheit. Inoffizielle sowjetische Dichtung* (1975). *Sicher & Gut* (1977). *Fotoroman Bisamberg* (1980). *rosen, zugaben* (1983). *Menschen & Pflanzen Porträts* (1983). *Schöne Stunden* (1984). *Geheimer Verkehr* (forthcoming).

Beth Bjorklund

Lesja Ukrajinka

(see: Ljarissa Kosac)

Leonora Christina Ulfeldt

Born July 8, 1621, Frederiksborg, Denmark;
died March 16, 1698, Maribo
Genre(s): autobiography, biography, poetry
Language(s): Danish, French, German

Born in 1621 as the daughter of King Christian IV and Kirstine Munk, Leonora Christina belonged to the educated, leisured aristocracy that dominated the cultural activities of her time. Yet Leonora Christina's autobiography, *Jammersminde* (published 1869; Memory of Woe), transcends the literature of seventeenth-century learned noblewomen not only in the suffering, the strength, and the courage of its author but also in its psychological and social realism.

Leonora Christina's marriage at fifteen to Corfits Ulfeldt, prime minister of Denmark until the death of Christian IV in 1648, catapulted her into innumerable political schemes and intrigues. The Ulfeldts' activities resulted first in exile and, in 1663, culminated in Leonora's imprisonment in Blaataarn (Blue Tower), where she remained for twenty-two years. Only after the death of her archenemy, the queen of Frederik III, was Leonora released in 1685. She spent her remaining years at Maribo Kloster.

The earliest writings of Leonora Christina include "Rejsen til Korsør" (1656; Journey to Korsør), a travelogue recounting the exiled Leonora's return to Denmark on behalf of her husband to seek reconciliation with the Danish king, and "Confrontationen i Malmø" (1659; The Confrontation in Malmø), Leonora's account of her legal defense of Ulfeldt, who was on trial for high treason against the Swedish king. The events of "Rejsen til Korsør" recur in *Den Franske Selvbiografi* (1673; The French Autobiography), intended for inclusion in Otto Sperling the Younger's never published *De Foeminis Doctis* (About Learned Women).

Leonora's masterpiece is *Jammersminde*, which describes her long incarceration in Blaataarn. Presenting her sufferings in religious terms by identifying with Job, Leonora recounts her day-to-day prison existence in a document of strength and dignity against all odds. Her vivid descriptions of characters and incidents at

Blaataarn point towards much later psychological realism and naturalism.

In a biography of (pre)historical female regents, *Haeltinners Pryd* (written 1674; The Ornaments of Heroines), Leonora celebrated the qualities with which she herself had been generously endowed. Of the three parts, on combative, faithful and virtuous, and steadfast heroines, respectively, only the first part survives.

Leonora Christina's *Jammersminde* remains unsurpassed in Danish literature as the autobiography of a woman who outshone her contemporaries, male and female, not only in riches and tragedies but also in intelligence, courage, and creativity. While her guilt or innocence is still being debated, the verdict on her literary mastery is unanimous.

Works

Den Franske Selvbiografi (1673; 1881). Jammersminde (1663–1685; 1869). Haeltinners Pryd (1684; 1977). Jammersminde og Andre Selvbiografiske Skrifter (1949).

Translations: Memoirs of Leonora Christina, Daughter of Christian IV of Denmark: Written During Her Imprisonment in the Blue Tower at Copenhagen 1663–1685, tr. F.E. Bunnett (1872).

Bibliography

Dalager, Stig, and Anne-Marie Mai, *Danske Kvindelige Forfattere* I (Copenhagen, 1982), pp. 35–64. Doctor, Jens Aage, "Sandhedens Rolle: Om Leonora Christinas Jammers Minde." *Kritik* 4.16 (1970): 5–36. Glismann, Otto, "Om Tilblivelsen af Leonora Christinas Jammers-minde." *Acta Philologica Scandinavica* 28.i–ii (1966): 75–102. Larsen, Finn S., "En Impressionist fra Baroktiden?" *Kritik* 7.25 (1973): 17–33. *Leonora Christina: Historien om en Heltinde. Acta Jutlandica* 58 (Aarhus, 1983). Includes bibliography. Liisberg, Bering, "The Diaries of Leonora Christine." *American-Scandinavian Review* 9 (June 1921): 383–393. Sverre, Lyngstad, "Leonora Christina," in *Women Writers of the 17th Century*, ed. K.M. Wilson (Athens, GA, 1988). Smith, S. Birket, *Leonora Christina Grevinde Ulfeldts Historie* I–II (Copenhagen, 1879–1881).

Clara Juncker

Regina Ullmann

Born December 14, 1884, St. Gallen,
    Switzerland; died January 1, 1961,
    Ebersberg, Bavaria
Genre(s): short story, poetry
Language(s): German

Regina Ullmann was born to parents of Jewish origin in St. Gallen, where her Austrian father was a well-to-do businessman. A dreamy, slow, difficult child, she suffered the loss of her father in 1887 and moved to Munich in 1902 with her mother and older sister. Here she fell in with a circle of avant-garde thinkers, poets, and literati—throughout her life she was to count eminent writers, among them Thomas Mann and Hans Carossa, among her acquaintances—and began developing the talent for story-telling that had already revealed itself in her childhood. Though she travelled frequently, Ullmann and her mother remained settled in the Munich area until 1935. In 1906 and 1908 she bore illegitimate daughters, who were raised by farmers in the vicinity of Munich, though Regina Ullmann visited them regularly and took charge of their education. 1908 also marks the beginning of Ullmann's friendship with the poet Rainer Maria Rilke, which had a profound influence on her writing and on her publishing career.

In 1911 Regina Ullmann converted to Catholicism. The years until 1935 were productive, though she periodically suffered from depressions and crises in her creative work and always lived in financially precarious circumstances, her various attempts at supporting herself (beekeeping and gardening among them) coming to naught. Expelled from the Deutscher Schriftsteller-Verband (German Writer's Association) because of her Jewish ancestry in 1935, she and her mother immigrated to Austria in 1936, where her mother died in the early days of 1938. Following the German occupation of Austria the same year, Regina Ullmann returned to Switzerland and found lodgings in a home run by nuns in St. Gallen, where she wrote and lived for the next twenty years. She died in Munich while visiting her daughter.

Regina Ullmann's work has never found a large following: it is in some ways as difficult and taciturn as the author herself. Although she was a born storyteller, the act of writing and the expectation that she live up to the calling of poet were constant obstacles in her path. While her early poems and prose pieces are in the neo-romantic vein—exalted expressions of feeling largely detached from descriptions of reality—her mature prose strikes a course between realism, symbolism, and deep piety that demands much of today's reader. Particularly fond of portraying peasant life, she often treats moments in the lives of the defenseless and powerless. An example is "Der goldene Griffel," a story based on a childhood memory, in which a slow and disturbed child's unexpected success in completing a schoolroom task leads not to the promised reward of a "golden" slate pencil but to a scolding for laziness and naughtiness. Ullmann is not sentimental, and her style is at times rough and imperfect; it wanders and breaks like Ullmann herself, restless, troubled, and clear-sighted.

Works

Feldpredigt. Dramatische Dichtung [Sermon in the Field, A Dramatic Poem] (1907, 1915). *Von der Erde des Lebens* [On the Earth of Life], prose poems (1910). *Gedichte* [Poems] (1919). *Die Landstrasse* [The Country Highway], short stories (1921). *Die Barockkirche, von einer Votivtafel herab gelesen, zugleich mit etlichen Volkserzählungen* [The Baroque Church, Interpreted from a Votive Tablet, and Including a Number of Folk Stories] (1925). *Vier Erzählungen* [Four Stories] (1930). *Vom Brot der Stillen.* 2 vols. [The Bread of the Silent], short stories (1932). *Der Apfel in der Kirche und andere Geschichten* [The Apple in the Church and Other Stories] (1934). *Der Engelskranz* [The Angelic Wreath], short stories (1942). *Madonna auf Glas und andere Geschichten* [Madonna on Glass and Other Stories] (1944). [Co-editor], *Erinnerungen an Rilke* [Remembrances of Rilke] (1945). *Der ehrliche Dieb und andere Geschichten* [The Honest Thief and Other Stories] (1946). "Sammlung der Vergesslichen. Ein Selbstporträt aus jüngsten Jahren, mit der Feder gezeichnet" [The Forgetful One's Anthology. A Recent Self-portrait Drawn with a Quill Pen]. *Gruss der Insel an Hans Carossa* (1948), pp. 221–236. *Von einem alten Wirtshausschild* [About an Old Sign at an Inn], short stories (1949). *Schwarze Kerze* [Black Candle], short stories (1954). *Gesammelte Werke.* 2 vols. [Collected Works] (1960, 1978, 1980). *Kleine Galerie. Eine Auswahl aus ihren Erzählungen* [Small Gallery. A Selection from Her Stories] (1975). *Erzählungen, Prosastücke, Gedichte.* 2 vols. [*Gesammelte Werke* but with bibliography, afterword, and biographical documents], Stories, Prose, Poems (1978). *Ausgewählte Erzählungen* [Selected Stories] (1979).

Bibliography

Binder, B., R. Schärer, und S. van den Bergh, "Regina Ullmann," in *Helvetische Steckbriefe. 47 Schriftsteller aus der deutschen Schweiz seit 1800*, ed. Zürcher Seminar für Literaturkritik und Werner Weber (Zürich, 1981), pp. 272–277. Delp, Ellen, *Regina Ullmann. Eine Biographie der Dichterin* (Zürich, 1962). Kemp, Friedhelm, "Nachwort." *Regina Ullman. Ausgewählte Erzählungen* (Frankfurt a.M., 1979), pp. 189–203. Kunisch, H., "Regina Ullmann." *Handbuch der deutschen Gegenwartsliteratur*, ed. Hermann Kunisch, Vol. 2, 2nd. ed. (Munich, 1970), pp. 263–264. LdS. 313–314 [excellent bibliography]. Matt, Beatrice von, "Schreiben aus eigenen Beständen. Zur Neuausgabe von Regina Ullmann's Werken." *Lesarten. Zur Schweizer Literatur von Walser bis Muschg* (1979; rpt. Zürich, 1985), pp. 40–46. Panthel, H.W., "Poetische Nekrologe zu Rainer Maria Rilkes Tod." *Literatur und Kritik* 201–202 (1986): 71–85. Rilke, Rainer Maria, *Briefwechsel mit Regina Ullmann und Ellen Delp*, ed. Walther Simon (Frankfurt a.M., 1987). Stephens, Don Steve, "Regina Ullmann. Biography, Literary Reception, Interpretation." Diss., U. of Texas at Austin, 1980 [DAI 41 (1981): 4727A]. Tappolet, Walther, *Regina Ullmann. Eine Einführung in ihre Erzählungen* (St. Gallen, 1955).

Ann Marie Rasmussen

Elisabeth von Ulmann (Meyer-Runge)

Born 1929, Kiel, Germany
Genre(s): poetry, prose poetry, sketch, short story, essay, drama, radio script
Language(s): German, Low German

Elisabeth von Ulmann stands out among the poets of younger generations through her disinclination to soliloquy and refusal to lose hope, the affirmative note in her works, and her wish to communicate. She does not belong to any group or movement. For works in Low German she uses the name of Meyer-Runge, with which she signed until 1984.

Elisabeth von Ulmann comes from a family with an artistic orientation: her grandfather was an architect and painter; her sister, a sculptor; her first husband, a painter. She stresses her capacity to work with visual artists and has published and exhibited in collaboration with Marie-Luise Blersch-Salden. She worked for some time in a bookstore as manager and as an actress during 25 years in Low German theaters. She was President of the Association of Low German Writers 1977–1980 and received the Freudenthal-Preis in 1978 and the Hamburger Literaturpreis für Kurzprosa in 1982. In 1983 she refused the AWMM (Luxembourg) prize for poetry. Several of her plays have been produced in Low Germany. She is the widow of the German-Baltic author Hellmuth v. Ulmann.

As her motto von Ulmann has chosen "poetic creation as existence." She writes remembering one remark often repeated by her father: "But this is insignificant." This may have helped to produce her extremely dense way of writing, admitting only the essential. There is never one superfluous word in her texts, and most words acquire additional meaning by their strategic position. She does not experiment with language for the sake of experimentation, although she molds it with remarkable skill, achieving great richness of tone and meaning. Hers is a poetry of commitment: commitment to mankind. Her verses reflect contemporary issues and concerns as do her prose poems and essays. One of her great themes is the fatherland, understood in the sense of "man's land." Man is the central axis of her work. Next to these great issues she gives much attention to small everyday happenings, often taken as a lesson: in beauty, in moral comportment.

In diesem Land (1980; In This Part of the Country) is the affirmation of her heritage, as a dweller of Low Germany, but also of the universe. Much attention is paid to natural phenomena, there is a close relationship with the earth. Poems in German and Low German alternate, achieving

great musical quality in the latter. *Wenn Kassandra wiederkehrte* (1981; After Cassandra Returned . . .) denounces the evils of "civilized" man who is forgetting human qualities. There is more irony in these lines, yet, hope never disappears. The first poem states: "We build / a small portrait of ourselves / into the infinite space of our world," confirming her ethical orientation. This book contains longer poems, new rhythms, and raises more complex issues. *Das Jahr gehört allen* (1984; The Year Belongs to All) intertwines prose and poetry in a series of stories of great sensitivity, the essence of which carries over into the interspersed poems. Delicate vignettes of nature contain great visual power. On the other hand, the exact placement of common but not necessarily very current words invites reflection. In some fragments a fairy-like atmosphere opens paths that go beyond the observed reality. The book is an incessant dialogue in which never a note of complaint is sounded, for "sadness is a sister of the mortal sins."

The quite unusual collection of letters between Meyer-Runge and her future husband, H.v. Ulmann (1984; We Must Become Our Own Country), represents a passionate discussion of one theme—fatherland and exile—in the manner of eighteenth-nineteenth-century literary epistles. In it, again, the capacity of condensation and the richness of language are quite extraordinary, and commitment to world problems is confirmed.

The poetry of von Ulmann shows that the most insignificant detail in everyday life can bring consolation. Setting out from the observation of a minute phenomenon—the song of a bird, a flower just opening—she relates it to the order of the universe, and often ends her poems with an ethical afterthought. Blank verse is her preferred choice; she does not burden her lines with complex imagery. She never uses pathos, but she does have a good sense of humor. The originality comes from within, arising from extraordinary precision in the choice of words that often seems to touch on magic.

Works

Rumpelstilzchen (1971). *Dem Traum vom Menschen nachgega genx* [In Pursuit of the Ideal Man] (1979). *Einsichtig* [Full of Insight] (1979). *In diesem Land* (1980). *Wenn Kassandra wiederkehrte* (1981). *Ok en Familiendag* [Also a Family-day] (1984). *Das Jahr gehört allen* (1984). *Heimat haben wir zu werden, ein Briefwechsel* [We Must Become Our Own Country] (1984). [Ed., with Siegfried Sichtermann], *Alltiet Ulenspegel* [Always Eulenspiegel] (1985). [Ed., with Hellmuth v. Ulmann], *Zeig mir einen Narren* [Show Me a Fool] (1987). *Irmgard B.* (1988). *En Fru von fuftig* [A Woman in her Fifties] (1988).

Translations: *Kasimir und Karoline*, tr. Odön von Horvath (1984).

Bibliography

Birkle, Marlies, "Mit dem Zungenschlag vom spitzen Stein an die Wahrheit herankommen." *Südwest Presse* (August 18, 1984). Eggers, Willi, "Laudatio am 30. September 1978 in Scheessel." *Preisträger der Jahre 1969–1978* (Rotenburg/Wümm, 1978), pp. 100–104. Hoffmann, Fernand, "Elisabeth Meyer-Runge: Auf keinen Fall zwischen zwei Stühlen." *Quickborn* 72–71 (1983): 3–13.

Birutė Ciplijauskaitė

Umiltà of Faenza

Born 1226, Faenza, Italy; died May 22, 1310, Florence
Genre(s): sermon, tractate, prayer, hymn
Language(s): Latin

Umiltà's given name was Rosanese; she was the only daughter of a noble family in Faenza. In her youth she underwent a religious conversion and wished to enter a convent; but her parents refused. When Rosanese's father died she was married to a nobleman named Ugolotto. For nine years she attempted to convince him to live a chaste life with her but to no avail. During this time she bore two sons, both of whom died shortly after their baptism, and she may have had other children as well. Finally Ugolotto became seriously ill, and his physicians advised him that he would die unless he abstained from sex. Rosanese then convinced Ugolotto, much against his will, to allow her to enter the convent of St. Perpetua near Faenza. She became a choir nun and he joined the same house as an extern brother. Rosanese then took the name Umiltà (Humility); she was twenty-five at the time. Her

conduct as a nun was exemplary, earning her the admiration of her sisters.

Umiltà was illiterate, but when the other sisters asked her to read at mealtime she miraculously "read" a marvelous sermon, which later could not be found in the book she had had before her. After this the convent provided her with a teacher who taught her to read and write.

Umiltà soon found that the convent was too lax for her taste and could not offer her the solitude she craved in order to devote her life to prayer. With the help of a miracle she escaped over the wall of the monastery, crossed a river, and walked to a nearby convent of the Order of St. Clare. The Abbess there placed Umiltà under the care of one of her relatives until a cell was built for her next to the church of St. Apollinaris in Faenza. She lived in this cell for the next twelve years.

Umiltà left her cell at the request of several clerics, among them the Abbot of the Greater Vallombrosan Order, who asked her to construct a monastery in Faenza. She founded a house and became its Abbess, an office she filled with great distinction. Later, in response to a vision of St. John the Evangelist she left her convent with several nuns (among them her close companion Blessed Margarita of Faenza [1230–1330]), obtained relics of the Evangelist, and built a church in his honor in Florence. Two years later she founded another convent in Florence, where she lived until her death.

Having miraculously healed herself of a tumor of the kidneys while at the convent of St. Perpetua, Umiltà soon became renowned as a healer and counselor, famous for her ability to detect unconfessed sins in others and for her eloquent preaching.

Nine of Umilta's sermons and fragments of several others, along with several of her prayers, have been preserved in an Italian *Life* edited by Giudiccius in 1632, and in the *Analecta*, based on this *Life* and written in the fourteenth century. Her works were for the most part dictated in Latin to one of her followers. Umiltà's writings as we have them are filled with extravagant praises of Christ and Mary, of her patron saint John the Evangelist, and of her two guardian angels. Her style is sensual, even erotic, and at times quite ornate, particularly in her descriptions of the

Virgin Mary and in her devotion to John the Evangelist, whom she calls her "sweetest Bridegroom."

Umiltà's sermons are usually meditative in tone and are often addressed to Christ, Mary, or St. John the Evangelist. She writes in the first person most of the time, occasionally using parables or extended allegories to illustrate a doctrinal point. The difficulty of her life and work and the support she receives from the divine realm are recurring themes.

Umiltà's Lauds were apparently well-received during her lifetime. They were still being used by the nuns of St. Salvio in the late fourteenth century and were translated into the vernacular. Her sermons also appear in the vernacular in the Italian *Life*.

Works

Sala, T., *Sermones S. Humilitatis de Faventia* (1884). Zama, Piero, *Santa Umiltà: La Vita e i "sermones"* (2nd ed., 1974).

Translations: Pioli, Richard J., tr. "St. Umiltà of Faenza, *Sermons*," in Elizabeth Alvilda Petroff, ed., *Medieval Women's Visionary Literature* (1986).

Bibliography

Acta Sanctorum collecta digesta illustrata, vol. XVIII (Brussels, 1643),, pp. 205–224. Petroff, Elizabeth, *Consolation of the Blessed* (Millerton, N.Y., 1979). Thurston, Herbert, S.J., and Donald Attwater, ed. and rev., *Butler's Lives of the Saints* (New York, 1956).

Lila F. Ralston

"Un femme chrestienne de Tornay"

(see: Marie Dentière)

"Un marchand de Genève"

(see: Marie Dentière)

Marie Under

Born March 27, 1883, Tallinn, Estonia; died September 25, 1980, Stockholm, Sweden
Genre(s): poetry, essays, translation
Language(s): Estonian

Born in what is now Soviet Estonia, Marie Under enjoyed the privilege of attending a German school, where she also studied Russian and French. Both her parents had come originally from Hiiumaa Island (Dagö) off the Estonian coast. Her father was a schoolteacher. Under had acquired the ability to read as early as age four and by age thirteen had commenced her career in poetry, writing in German initially. However, she was not to publish her first collection, *Sonetid* (Sonnets), until she was thirty-four.

The Estonian public was taken by surprise by the overt eroticism of Marie Under's first publication in 1917. The subjective, sensual treatment of love is continued in her next two verse collections, *Eelõitseng* (First Flowering) and *Sinine Puri* (The Azure Sail), both of which appeared in 1918. By this time Under had become the leading voice of the Siuru group of poets, referred to as both rebellious and colorful. European travel following World War I ultimately accounted for the influence of German Expressionist poetry in Under's subsequent work. She even translated into Estonian a selection of verse by George Heym, Franz Werfl, Ernst Stadler and Walter Hasenclever. Now her poetry had changed radically in its outlook and was marked by anxiety, inner conflict, and a preoccupation with hopelessness and death.

Marie Under had already received a number of literary prizes and seen her work translated into several languages by the appearance of her fourth and fifth collections of poems, *Verivalla* (1920; Bleeding Wound) and *Pärisosa* (1923; Heritage). Her most significant period of literary creativity is generally agreed to have commenced from the publication of *Hääl Varjust* (1927; Voice from the Shadows).

As a result of the second Soviet annexation of Estonia in 1944, Marie Under decided to flee to Sweden across the Baltic; in this self-imposed exile her poetic voice remained clear and powerful. Her subsequent publications are characterized by a language now more simple and direct.

Among other distinctions, Marie Under was elected to honorary membership of International PEN in 1937 and was repeatedly nominated for the Nobel Prize. As a distinguished translator she brought a total of twenty-six works into Estonian from German, English, French, and Russian, including *Doctor Zhivago* and Rilke's poetry. She also translated Goethe, Schiller, Ibsen, and Baudelaire. Her own original poetry has been translated into English, French, German, Russian, Swedish, and Finnish. Her critical essays were written largely in the 1920s.

Marie Under's total *oeuvre* amounts to around four hundred poems published over thirteen collections, spanning some six decades of literary creativity. It is justifiably argued that her voice has yet to be heard clearly in the West, at which time she would deservedly rank amongst the best six women poets in twentieth-century European literature.

Under easily claims to be Estonia's real national poet, and her poignant voice remains the clearest and most audible of all her contemporaries. Her themes range from nature and pantheism to biblical legends, her tone from the erotic to the indignant. Under constantly employs metaphor, comparison and symbol, and images of wind, sea, and fire. Her neoromantic verse, at times quasi-impressionistic and philosophical, conveys a suffering both personal and universal, an aesthetic ecstasy and an essentially extroverted spirituality. Marie Under's zest for life is balanced by a sometimes sombre introspection in poetry imbued with the alive, open senses of Estonia's most important poet.

Works

Sonetid [Sonnets] (1917). *Eelõitseng* [First Flowering] (1918). *Sinine Puri* [The Azure Sail] (1918). *Verivalla* [Bleeding Wound] (1920). *Pärisosa* [Heritage] (1923). *Hääl Varjust* [Voice from the Shadows] (1927). *Rõõm Uhest Ilusast Päevast* [Delight in a Beautiful Day] (1928). *Õnne Varjutus: Ballaadid ja Legendid* [Eclipse of Happiness: Ballads and Legends] (1929). *Lageda Taeva All* [Under the Open Sky] (1930). *Kivi Südamelt* [A Stone off the Heart] (1935). *Mureliku Suuga* [With Sor-

rowing Lips] (1942). *Sädemed Tuhas* [Sparks Under Ashes] (1954). *Ääremail* [On the Brink] (1963). Collections: *Ja Liha Sai Sõnaks* [And Flesh Turned into Word] (1936). *Kogutud Teosed* [Collected Works I–III] (1940). *Sõnasild* [Bridge of Words] (1945). *Südamik* [The Core] (1957). *Kogutud Luuletused* [Collected Poems] (1958). *Valitud Luuletused* [Selected Poems] (1958). Translations: *Modern Estonia Poetry*, 20 poems and ballads, tr. W.K. Matthews (1953). *The PEN in Exile I and II*, Selections (1954, 1966). *Child of Man*, tr. W.K. Matthews (1955).

Bibliography

Aspel, A., "Marie Under's Quest of Transcendence." (1969). Colby, Vineta, ed., *World Authors 1975–1980* (1985). Kõressaar, V., and Rannit, Aleksis, eds., *Estonian Poetry and Language: Studies in Honor of Ants Oras* (1965). Leitch, V.B., ed., *The Poetry of Estonia: Essays in Comparative Analysis* (1983). Nirk, Endel, *Estonian Literature: Historical Survey with Bibliographical Appendix* (1970). Oras, Ants, *Marie Under and Estonian Poetry* (1963). Rannit, Aleksis, *Tribute to Marie Under at Eighty* (1963). Rannit, Aleksis, "Marie Under and El Greco: An Attempt at Comparative Aesthetics." *Proceedings of the 7th International Congress of Aesthetics* (1977).

Warwick J. Rodden

Sigrid Undset

Born 1882, Kalundborg, Denmark; died 1949, Lillehammer, Norway
Genre(s): novel, essay, short story, poetry, drama, children's literature, biography
Language(s): Norwegian

In the English-speaking world there are few Norwegian authors whose popularity exceeds that of Sigrid Undset. She is best known for her trilogy *Kristin Lavransdatter* (1920–1922), an epic set in medieval Norway. Soon after it was written, this masterpiece was translated into numerous foreign languages (including English), and it became an international bestseller even before Undset was awarded the Nobel Prize for Literature in 1928.

Sigrid Undset was born in 1882 in Kalundborg, Denmark, at the home of her maternal grandfather, a chancery councillor of that small town. Her father, originally from Trondheim, was an archaeologist whose scholarship had earned him an international reputation, and Ingvald Undset kindled in his daughter an interest in history and the Middle Ages that was to bring her even greater renown. Other important influences from her childhood home included a fine library and a rich tradition of storytelling—folktales and legends but also purely imaginative stories. In 1884 the family moved to Kristiania (present-day Oslo), where Ingvald Undset had a position at the University Museum. For several years her father had suffered from poor health and in 1893, when Sigrid was only eleven years old, he died. The deep attachment Sigrid Undset felt toward her father was to later find expression in her fiction; the moving relationship between Kristin and her father, Lavrans (*Kristin Lavransdatter*), comes immediately to mind, and we have a second example in *Jenny* (1911), where the protagonist idolizes the father she lost during her childhood.

Making ends meet was difficult for a widow with three children, and Sigrid, the oldest child, felt a responsibility toward her mother and two younger sisters. She therefore decided not to pursue a university education but rather to enroll in a commercial college. She finished the program in one year and then took a job in an office where she remained for ten years. These were hardly lost or wasted years for Undset; she read a great deal during this period, both history and literature, and she was also writing. The first manuscript she completed and submitted to a publishing house was a story set in medieval Norway. It was rejected, but the editor nonetheless encouraged her to try her hand at something modern. This she did and in 1907 her first novel, *Fru Marta Oulie*, was published, thereby launching her career as a writer. The following year brought two more publications, and in 1909 she received a travel stipend which allowed her to quit her office job and travel to Italy.

In Rome Sigrid Undset met her future husband, the painter Anders Svarstad. They were married in 1912 in a civil ceremony in Antwerp and spent the first year of their marriage living abroad, in London and Rome. Between 1913 and 1919 Sigrid Undset gave birth to three children;

Svarstad had three children from a previous marriage and these children came periodically to live with their father and stepmother. Even while managing a busy household, Undset found time for her writing.

The novels and stories written before 1920 comprise the first phase of Undset's production. During this period Undset wrote about people and places she had observed firsthand: the setting is Kristiania; the time, the early years of this century; the people, ordinary middle-class citizens who shared Undset's workplace and neighborhood. In vivid and realistic prose Undset re-creates those sections of the capital city she had known as a child and young woman. She displays a fine ear for dialogue, even capturing the dialects within the city, and her character portrayals evidence human warmth and keen insight. The women in this early fiction are typically caught between their dreams for happiness and fulfillment and the reality of their situation with its inherent limitations. The Undset heroine believes in ideal love, and she longs to fall in love with a man in whom she can find fulfillment and to whom she can submit herself. These are ideals and expectations not easily realized; failure to do so cannot be blamed on circumstance or fate, however, for Undset insists that her characters possess a free will and that they are therefore morally responsible for their lives.

Jenny, in the novel bearing her name, is twenty-eight years old and has still not experienced love. An attractive and intelligent woman who has developed her talents as an artist, she nonetheless feels that she, as a woman, cannot find true fulfillment in her work, and so she longs for marriage and children. She chooses to match herself with a man who is not her equal, and this initial error leads to other and more serious mistakes. At the end of her life, she recognizes that she should have waited until she met the man who could claim her unreserved love and respect.

The trials and errors of Jenny and other female protagonists reflect the author's own quest for a set of values and norms that would endure the stress of great social change. Jenny had yearned to submit herself wholly to love, a husband and family, but as Undset continued to struggle and to search for some kind of authority, she looked more and more to religion and the church. The Lutheran Church, Norway's state church, did not answer her needs, and she eventually converted to Catholicism. In 1924 she was officially received into the Catholic Church. She and her husband had been separated since 1919 when she and the children moved to Lillehammer, and their marriage was now annulled.

The second phase of Undset's authorship coincides with her move to "Bjerkebæk," the name she gave her home in Lillehammer. This is the period of her great medieval epics, first *Kristin Lavransdatter* (1920–1922), followed by *Olav Audunssön i Hestviken* (1925–1927; The Master of Hestviken). Undset was a meticulous scholar and the historical authenticity of these novels has been well documented. (*The Master of Hestviken* takes place at the end of the thirteenth century, and *Kristin Lavransdatter* is set in the first half of the fourteenth.) Detailed descriptions of farm buildings and routine chores, of how people dressed and what they ate never seem dry or obtrusive, so artfully are they woven into the narrative. The political situation, the role of the church (Norway was Catholic until the Reformation), the family structure, customs and celebrations—these are also part of the fabric of the books.

Kristin Lavransdatter is unquestionably the more popular of the two to a large extent because, unlike *The Master of Hestviken*, the narrative centers around the main character, tracing her development from the time she is a child to her death as a mature woman. Kristin Lavransdatter stands out as one of the finest character portrayals in Norwegian literature. The novel's central conflict derives from Kristin's headstrong and sensuous nature: in following her desires, she thereby sets her own will against that of a higher authority. She challenges the authority first of her father and later her husband, and not until she is dying does she realize that in all these acts of independence and willfulness she has resisted the will of God.

Undset's Christian faith is reflected in everything she wrote after 1920. Following the medieval epics, she again wrote novels in a contemporary setting but now from a distinctly Catholic point of view. In *Gymnadenia* (1929; The

Wild Orchid) and *Den brændende busk* (1930; The Burning Bush) Undset depicts her protagonist's gradual conversion to Catholicism, and one assumes there is more than a trace of autobiography in these books.

Undset's production includes an impressive number of articles and essays, ranging from scholarly articles on Norwegian medieval history and portraits of Catholic saints, to essays on religious, moral and social issues and current political ideologies. She took a firm stand against both Communism and Nazism and, in fact, had been such an outspoken critic that when Norway was invaded by Nazi Germany in April 1940, she was advised to flee the country. She went first to Sweden and then crossed Siberia to Japan where she sailed to San Francisco. She remained in the United States until Norway was liberated in 1945 and during this time was an active diplomat for her country, writing articles and giving speeches all over America. She returned to Lillehammer in 1945 and two years later, on her birthday, King Haakon VII conferred upon her the Grand Cross of the Order of Saint Olav for service to her country.

Works

Novels: *Fru Marta Oulie* (1907). *Fortællingen om Viga-Ljot og Vigdis* (1910). *Jenny* (1911). *Vaaren* (1914). *Splinten av troldspeilet* (1917). *Kristin Lavransdatter* (trilogy): *Kransen* (1920). *Husfrue* (1921). *Korset* (1922). *Olav Audunssön i Hestviken* (1925). *Olav Audunssön og hans börn* (1927). *Gymnadenia* (1929). *Den brændene busk* (1930). *Ida Elisabeth* (1932). *Elleve aar* (1934). *Den trofaste hustru* (1936). *Madame Dorthea* (1939).

Short stories: *Den lykkelige alder* (1908). *Fattige skjæbner* (1912). *De kloge jomfruer* (1918).

Poetry: *Ungdom* (1910). *Ungdom. Dikt. Med forfatterens egne tegninger* (1986).

Books for children: *Fortællinger om Kong Artur og ridderne av det runde bord* (1915). *Sigurd og hans tapre venner*, tr. into Norwegian (1955).

Drama: *I grålysningen* (1952). *Prinsessene i berget det blå* (1973).

Biography: *Caterina av Siena* (1951).

Essays: *Et kvindesynspunkt* (1919). *Sankt Halvards liv, död og jærtegn* (1925). *Katholsk propaganda* (1927). *Etapper* (1929). *Hellig Olav, Norges konge* (1930). *Etapper. Ny række* (1933). *Norske helgener*

(1937). *Selvportretter og landskapsbilleder* (1938). *Tilbake til fremtiden* (1945). *Lykkelige dager* (1947). *Artikler og taler fra krigstiden*, ed. A.H. Winsnes (1952). *Kirke og klosterliv. Tre essays fra norsk middelalder*, intro. Hallvard Rieber-Mohn (1963). *Artikler og essays om litteratur*, ed. Jan Fr. Daniloff (1986).

Letters: *Kjære Dea*, ed. Christianne Undset Svarstad (1979). *Sigrid Undset skriver hjem: en vandring gjennom emigrantårene i Amerika*, ed. Arne Skouen (1982).

Originally published in English: *Sigurd and His Brave Companions. A Tale of Medieval Norway* (1943). *True and Untrue and Other Norse Tales* (1945).

Translations: *Jenny*, tr. W. Emmë (1921). *Kristin Lavransdatter: The Bridal Wreath*, tr. Charles Archer and J.S. Scott (1923). *The Mistress of Husaby*, tr. Charles Archer (1925). *The Cross*, tr. Charles Archer (1927). *The Master of Hestviken: The Axe*, tr. Arthur G. Chater (1928). *The Snake Pit*, tr. Arthur G. Chater (1929). *In the Wilderness*, tr. Arthur G. Chater (1929). *The Son Avenger*, tr. Arthur G. Chater (1930). (Single volume, *The Master of Hestviken*, was published in 1934.) *The Wild Orchid*, tr. Arthur G. Chater (1931). *The Burning Bush*, tr. Arthur G. Chater (1932). *Christmas and Twelfth Night. Reflections*, tr. E.C. Ramsden (1932). *Ida Elisabeth*, tr. Arthur G. Chater (1933). *Stages on the Road*, tr. Arthur G. Chater (1934). *Saga of Saints*, tr. E.C. Ramsden (1934). *The Longest Years*, tr. Arthur G. Chater (1935). *Gunnar's Daughter*, tr. Arthur G. Chater (1936). *The Faithful Wife*, tr. Arthur G. Chater (1937). *Images in a Mirror*, tr. Arthur G. Chater (1938). *Men, Women and Places*, tr. Arthur G. Chater (1939). *Madame Dorthea*, tr. Arthur G. Chater (1940). *Return to the Future*, tr. Henriette C.K. Naeseth (1942). *Happy Times in Norway*, tr. Joran Birkeland (1942). *Norway's Best Stories*, ed. Hanna Astrup Larsen (1927). *Four Stories*, tr. Naomi Walford (1959). *An Everyday Story. Norwegian Women's Fiction*, ed. Katherine Hanson (1984). "Gardens," tr. Sherrill Harbison. *Landscape* 30, no. 2 (1989).

Bibliography

Anker, Nini Roll, *Min venn Sigrid Undset* (Oslo, 1946). Bayerschmidt, Carl F., *Sigrid Undset* (New York, 1970). Bliksrud, Liv, *Natur og normer hos Sigrid Undset* (Oslo, 1988). Bonnevie, Mai Bente, et al., *Et annet språk. Analyser av norsk kvinnelitteratur* (Oslo, 1977). Brunsdale, Mitzi, *Sigrid Undset: Chronicler of Norway* (Oxford/New York, 1988). Budd, John, compiler, *Eight Scandinavian Novelists. Criticism and Reviews in English* (Westport, Conn, 1981). Deschamps, Nicole, *Sigrid Undset ou la Morale de la Passion* (Montreal, 1966). Dunn, Margaret Mary, "The Master of Hestviken: A New Reading." *Scandinavian Studies* (1966): 281–294; (1968): 210–224. Eide, Roar, Review. *Sigrid Undset i dag* (Oslo, 1982). *Scandinavica* (Norwich, 1985), p. 93. Engelstad, Carl Fr., *Mennesker og makter. Sigrid Undsets middealderromaner* (Oslo, 1940). Granaas, Rakel Christina, et al., *Kvinnesyntvisyn. En antologi om Sigrid Undset* (Oslo, 1985). Gustafson, Alrik, *Six Scandinavian Novelists* (Princeton, 1940; rpt. Minneapolis, 1966), pp. 286–361. Johnson, Pål Espolin, et al., *Sigrid Undset i dag* (Oslo, 1982). Krane, Borghild, *Sigrid Undset. Liv og meninger* (Oslo, 1970). *Kvinner og böker. Festskrift til Ellisiv Steen* (Oslo, 1978). Monroe, N. Elizabeth, *The Novel and Society* (Chapel Hill, N.C., 1941), pp. 39–87. Rasmussen, Janet E., "Dreams and Discontent: The Female Voice in Norwegian Literature." *Review of National Literatures. Norway*, vol. 12. (New York, 1983). Sæther, Astrid., Review. "Sigrid Undset: Reevaluations and Recollections." *Scandinavica*, vol. 23, no. 1 (Norwich, 1984). Steen, Ellisiv, *Kristin Lavransdatter. En estetisk studie* (Oslo, 1959). Thorn, Finn, *Sigrid Undset. Kristentro og kirkesyn* (Oslo, 1975). Winsnes, A.H., *Sigrid Undset: A Study in Christian Realism*, tr. P.G. Foote (New York, 1953).

Katherine Hanson

Johanna Charlotte Unzer

Born November 17, 1724, Halle an der Saale, Germany; died January 29, 1782, Altona
Genre(s): poetry, nonfiction
Language(s): German

Johanna Charlotte Unzer(in) is the only significant German woman writer of "anacreontic" poetry, publishing two volumes of poems, each with an expanded second edition. She is also one of very few German women in the eighteenth century who wrote books of nonfiction, producing popular accounts of philosophy and natural history for female readers.

Born in Halle an der Saale, a university town and center of pietism, Johanna Charlotte Ziegler came from a respectable family. Her father, who had studied with Johann Sebastian Bach, was an organist, composer and music teacher. Her mother came from a family of clock makers. Johanna Charlotte received a minimal education as a young girl, apparently learning some French, though not enough to read extensively in that language. When she was older, however, perhaps in her late teens, she began trying to make up for what she had missed. She was probably stimulated in this effort by her maternal uncle, Johann Gottlob Krüger, ten years her senior and a professor of medicine at the university, and by Johann August Unzer, two years her junior. This man, who was a student of her uncle in medicine and of her father in music, became her husband in 1751.

That was the most eventful year in her life. She made her literary debut, publishing three books at once. Her uncle moved away from Halle, and she, now that both parents were dead, married Unzer and moved from the provincial and deeply religious region of Thuringia to the far north of Germany, to Altona, a liberal Danish-controlled town next to Hamburg. Two years later, she was well established in her new surroundings, contributing poetry to two periodicals there, publishing an enlarged edition of her earlier poetry collection, being crowned poet laureate of the University of Helmstedt (where her uncle was now Vice-rector), and becoming an honorary member of two literary societies, the "Deutsche Gesellschaften" of Göttingen and Helmstedt. In 1754 she published a new volume of poetry. Immediately after this flurry of activity a long period of silence began. Two beloved and long-mourned infants died, and Unzer herself suffered from a sickness that lingered on for nine years. Finally, in 1766, she began publishing again. She must have been writing well before that date, however, because again three works appeared in one year, a new collection of poetry and revisions of both earlier volumes. The next year she published a revised version of her monumental book on philosophy, *The Fundamentals of Comprehensive Knowledge for Ladies*. From then on, for the fourteen years until her death at age fifty-seven, she published nothing

more, although she continued to be interested in literature, as is shown by her name on a subscription list (in 1773) for a novel by one of her famous contemporaries, Christoph Martin Wieland, and by her role as an agent collecting subscribers for Wieland's later venture into journalism with a monthly called *Der Teutscher Merkur*. Her husband, whose medical practice and literary activity showed no major interruptions during these decades, died seventeen years later.

Unzer first became known because of her ambitious undertaking for women readers, the composition of a popularized account of "comprehensive knowledge": it contained mostly philosophy, leavened with poems by various authors. For this long work (over 600 pages) Unzer relied on three sources, Christian Wolff for the sections on logic, Alexander Baumgarten for those on Metaphysics, and Krüger, her uncle, for those on science. It was extraordinary in eighteenth-century Germany for a woman to undertake a project of this kind. The follow-up volume, on the basics of natural history, seems to have been less successful. Her more lasting reputation rests however on her poetry. Johanna Charlotte Unzer-Zeigler accepted the conventions of wine, women, and song that characterized the Anacreontic poetry of her day and wrote drinking songs laden with pastoral allusions, songs of cheerful flirtation, rationalist odes and nature poems, and (least successfully) verse tales. Her first volume of poetry claims to be primarily joking (*Scherzhaft*), while the second, written after her marriage, contains poems she described as tender and moral. Many include illuminating autobiographical references and reflect Unzer's interest in philosophical issues and methods.

Works

Grundri einer Weltwei heit für das Frauenzimmer [Fundamentals of Comprehensive Knowledge for Ladies] (1751). *Grundri einer natürlichen Historie und eigentlichen Naturlehre für das Fraunenzimmer* (1751) [Fundamentals of Natural History and of Nature Study Itself for Ladies] (1751). *Versuch in Scherzgedichten* [Experiment in Witty Poems] (1751). *Versuch in sittlichen und zärtlichen Gedichtenx* [Experiment in moral and tender poems] (1754). *Fortgesetzte Versuche in* sittlichen und zärtlichen Gedichten [Continued experiments in moral and tender poems] (1766).

Bibliography

Brinker-Gabler, Gisela, ed., *Deutsche Dichterinnen vom 16. Jahrhundert bis zur Gegenwart. Gedichte und Lebensläufe* (Frankfurt, 1978), pp. 129–134. Dawson, Ruth P., "Selbstzähmung und weibliche Misogynie: Verserzählungen von Frauen im 18. Jahrhundert." *Der Widerspenstigen Zähmung. Studien zur bezwungenen Weiblichkeit in der Literatur vom Mittelalter bis zur Gegenwart*, ed. Sylvia Wallinger and Monika Jonas (Innsbruck, 1986), pp. 133–143. Friedrichs, Elisabeth, *Die deutschsprachigen Schriftstellerinnen des 18. und 19. Jahrhunderts. Ein Lexikon* (Stuttgart, 1981), p. 317. Gehring, Thomas, *Johanne Charlotte Unzer-Ziegler. 1725–1782. Ein Ausschnitt aus dem literarischen Leben in Halle, Göttingen und Altona* (Bern, 1973). (Europäische Hochschulschriften, Reihe I, Bd. 78.)

Ruth P. Dawson

Jarmila Urbánková

Born February 23, 1911, Horní Vilémovice, Czechoslovakia
Genre(s): poetry, children's literature, translation
Language(s): Czech

Jarmila Urbánková attended grammar school in Třebíč and Přerov, later graduating in philosophy from Brno University. After 1945 she worked at the Ministry of Information in Prague and then as a chief editor in the State Publishing House of Children's Books. Since 1957 she has specialized as a writer of poetry and literature for young people. Described as an important representative of contemporary Czech women's poetry, Urbánková is also noted as a translator of Shelly, Yavorov, J. Aldridge, A. Wilson, Pearl Buck and A.J. Cronin. She made her poetry début in 1932.

Works

Rozbité Zrcadlo [Broken Mirror] (1932). *Vetřný Čas* [Windy Time] (1937). *Slunečnice* [The Sunflower] (1942). *K Jitřnímu Prameni* [To the Fount of Dawn] (1955). *Krůpěje* [Drops] (1957). *Zpívající*

Pták [The Singing Bird] (1964). *Kotvy a Stébla* [Anchors and Straws] (1978).

Warwick J. Rodden

Ann-Marie de la Trimoille, Princesse des Ursines

Born 1642, Poitou, France; died December 5, 1722, Rome, Italy
Genre(s): letters
Language(s): French

Anne-Marie de la Trimoille, whose letters detail a fascinating portrait of a woman courtier in eclipse, was born in France sometime around 1642. She was the oldest daughter of Louis de la Tremoille, the duke of Noirmoutier, and Renée Julie Aubry. She wed her first husband, the Prince of Chalais, when seventeen. When he was exiled to Spain for killing a man in a duel, she followed him. They later went to Italy, where the Prince died. In 1675, she married a second time, to the Italian duke of Bracciano, Flavio Orsini. Soon afterward, she became a primary agent for French interests in Rome. After she was widowed a second time in 1698, she worked to bring about the union of the Spanish King Philip V and the French Princess Marie-Louise de Savoy (1701) whose *camera-mayor* she was. When the two married, she followed her charge to Philip's court.

In Spain, Anne-Marie exercised a considerable influence on the reigning couple. Despite the numerous conflicts that centered around her and those that arose between the Spanish armies and Louis XIV's representatives in Madrid, she saved Philip's crown for him more than once with her diplomatic skill and considerable energy. For this service, he was initially grateful. Her position at court was affirmed, and her influence showed no signs of waning upon the death of Marie-Louise on February 14, 1714. When he rewed, it was to a bride of her choice—Elisabeth Farnèse.

However, the situation was drastically altered during her first interview with the new queen on December 23, 1714. Chased from the royal presence, she was immediately exiled to France. Seven months later, she left her native land for

Holland, then for Gènes, and finally for Rome. She finished her life there in retreat, pensioned by the governments of both France and Spain, and in the thick of various political intrigues. She died in Rome on December 5, 1722.

The sole literary legacy that the Princesse des Ursins has given us is her voluminous correspondence with such personages as Madame de Maintenon and the maréchal de Villeroy. These letters, mostly written after her exile from Spain, leave a somewhat cryptic but fascinating account of an aged woman whose years at court have accustomed her to intrigue, injustice and the pressing need for discretion in life among the powerful. Although her style is simple, her revelations are guarded and at times so heavily veiled by indirection as to be indecipherable. Yet sadness and resignation, as well as the occasional spiritual note, forcefully express the princess' isolation. The woman who emerges is an aged, crafty courtier stripped of illusions, threatened by boredom, and burdened by her understanding of as well as her mistrust of courts and their creatures. Little emerges of her role as the powerful figure behind the Spanish throne, the agent of Louis XIV's international policy. She boasts of nothing, complains several times of the injustices against her, and speaks warmly of her closest friends, Madame de Maintenon and the late Queen Marie-Louise. Though her French is correct and refined, it is this combination of indirection and regret that leaves the most lasting impression. The Princesse des Ursine's letters provide an interesting portrait of a female courtier who, once a power, ended her life as a discarded relic of the Sun King's foreign policy.

Works

> *Correspondance avec Madame de Maintenon* [The Correspondence with Madame de Maintenon] (1826). *Correspondance avec le Maréchal de Villeroy* [The Correspondence with the Marshal Villeroy] (1806). *Lettres Inédites* [Unedited Letters] (1858).

Bibliography

Jal, Auguste, *Dictionnaire Critique et Biographie et d'Histoire* (rpt. New York, 1970), p. 1216. Saint Rene Taillandier, Madeline Marie Louis, *La Princesse des Ursines, une grande dame française à la cour d'Espagne sous Louis XIV* (Paris, 1926). Lalanne, Ludovic, *Dictionnaire Historique de la France* (rpt. New York, 1968).

Glenda Wall

V

V. V-an

(see: Vera Panova)

V.S.

(see: Vera Panova)

V.V.

(see: Vera Panova)

Aslaug Vaa

Born August 25, 1889, Rauland, Norway; died 1965
Genre(s): poetry, drama, criticism, translation
Language(s): Norwegian

Aslaug Vaa did not make her debut until she was forty-five years old, in 1934, but she nevertheless managed to create an important name for herself in modern Norwegian literature. In her writing she combines the local and the universal, the village and the world. In addition to the tradition-filled environment she grew up in, her early years of studies abroad, in Paris and Berlin, became an important foundation for her writing.

Her debut came in 1934 with the poetry collection *Nord i leite* (North in the Hills). In poetry, rich with human spirit, we find something which has always been characteristic for Aslaug Vaa as a poet: the juxtaposition of the traditional and the modern. Nature and the customs of the people in Telemark have provided the imagery in these poems. The poems frequently take place in the border land between dream and reality. In her next collection, *Skuggen og strendan* (1935; The Shadow and the Shores), she deals with the paradox of loneliness—unity and love as lust and longing but also as loneliness and hatred. In this, as well as in her third collection, *Villarkonn* (1936; Magic Potion), there are many reflective poems. Through her poetry Aslaug Vaa searches for the intuitive and the down-to-earth. Here we find sensitive feelings of nature and unforgettable images of folk life. In the collection, *På vegakanten* (1939; The Roadside), she approaches the outlook of the mystics. It is, however, the last three collections, *Fotefär* (1947; Footprints), *Skjenkarsveinens visur* (1954; The Servant's Songs), and *Bustader* (1963; Dwellings), that mark the highpoint of her career as a poet. The poems reveal a spirit always on the search for a deeper recognition of life. This motif is prevalent throughout her poetry. It seems to be the search more than goal that is the driving force, the vital base for her writing. The motif of searching can be seen in connection with another important theme: the erotic. The yearning for love is central in her poetry, and it is intimately connected with the motif of nature. Nature and the erotic completely melt together. Vaa more and more leans toward mysticism; from an uncomplicated experience of nature and life, she moves toward a mysticism in which the speculative and the reflective have a greater place. The French philosopher Pierre Teilhard de Chardin had a great influence on her, particularly his idea that there is a goal and a meaning both in the external development in creation and in the spiritual development in man.

Aslaug Vaa was, however, not only a poet. She was preoccupied with the art of theater, as well. Vaa had experienced both the theater of Max Reinhard and German expressionist theater when she lived in Berlin. Her first play, *Steinguden* (1938; The Stone God), is about a woman's spiritual liberation. After *Tjugendagen* (1947; The Last Day of Christmas), which presents pictures of life in a village, came *Honingfuglen og leoparden* (1965; The Honeybird and the Leopard), which takes its subject matter from African culture myth and was a result of her stay in Angola. Her play *Munkeklokka* (The Monk Clock) was not published until 1966. It was, however, performed at The Norwegian Theater (Det Norske Teateret) in the fall of 1950. It has folkloristic themes and is characterized by Vaa's strong interest in folk tradition. Man's struggle with the elemental forces in existence constitutes the dilemma she is preoccupied with in her plays. First and foremost, however, she is a poet, which is evident in her plays, as well, from their strong lyrical tone.

Despite her late debut, she managed to publish seven poetry collections, four plays, and innumerable articles in newspapers and journals. Her great knowledge of different countries' arts and cultures, her activity as a critic and translator, in addition to her own writings, has made her a source of inspiration for many artists.

Works

Nord i leite (1934). *Skuggen og strendan* (1935). *Villarkonn* (1936). *På vegakanten* (1939). *Fotefar* (1947). *Skjenkarseveinens visur* (1954). *Bustade* (1963). *Steinguden* (1938). *Tjugendagen* (1947). *Honingfuglen og leoparden* (1965). *Munkeklokka* (1966).

Bibliography

Maehle, Leif, "Aslaug Vaa og diktinga hennar." *Dikt i utval* (Oslo, 1964), pp. 207–232. Maehle, Leif, "Det lydde eit bod. Om Aslaug Vaa og diktinga hennar." *Frå bygda til verda* (Oslo, 1967), pp. 143–192. Ørjasaeter, Tore, "Kring diktingi til Aslaug Vaa." *Syn og Segn* (1943), pp. 277–286, 309–316. Østvedt, Einar, "Mennesker jeg møtte. Aslaug Vaa." *Årbok for Telemark* (1974), pp. 31–41. Shetelig, Kari, "Aslaug Vaa og dramaet." *Vinduet* (1954), pp. 63–68.

Frode Hermundsgard

Debora Vaarandi

Born October 1, 1916, Võru, Estonia
Genre(s): poetry, prose, translation
Language(s): Estonian

Debora Vaarandi graduated from Kuressaare secondary school in 1935 and was a student of the philosophy faculty of Tartu University from 1936–1940. On completion of her degree she became a journalist, working in Tallinn until 1946, when she turned to professional writing. Vaarandi mainly wrote poetry, also producing a book of short prose and essays in 1964 and a travel book in 1970. She has translated poetry from Russian, Finnish, and German and prose from Russian. Her own poetry has been extensively rendered in Russian and other Soviet languages. In 1954 Debora Vaarandi was awarded the title of Merited Writer of the Estonian S.S.R. and a Soviet Estonian Prize in 1965.

Works

Põleva Laotuse All [Under the Burning Sky] (1945). *Kohav Rand* [The Roaring Coast] (1948). *Selgel Hommikul* [On a Bright Morning] (1950). *Unistaja Aknal* [The Dreamer at the Window] (1959). *Rannalageda Leib* [The Bread of the Seaside Plain] (1965). *Luuletused* [Poems], anthology (1965). *Valik Luuletusi* [Selected Poems], anthology (1966). *Uuenevate Mälestuste Linnad* [Towns of Renewed Memories] (1964). *Välja Õuest Ja Väravast* [Beyond Your Yard and Gate] (1970).

Warwick J. Rodden

Lýdia Vadkerti-Gavorníková

Born March 30, 1932, Modra, Czechoslovakia
Genre(s): lyric poetry
Language(s): Slovak

Lýdia Vadkerti-Gavorníková (first published under the name Lýdia Vadkertiová) is probably the second leading woman poet in Slovakia today. She has also jointly translated poetry in several European languages.

Born into the family of a cabinetmaker who soon died, she grew up with her mother and stepfather in two small towns in western Slovakia. She graduated from an education college in Bratislava in 1951, then became a grade school teacher until 1962, when illness forced her retirement but gave her time to write. Three years later her first poems were published to considerable critical approval. Since 1978 she has worked as an editor.

Her first collection of poems, *Pohromnice* (Catastrophes) in 1966, is about the wine-growing region where she grew up, with its eternal symbolism of the grape, but also it echoes the personal stress of her father's death and mother's remarriage. The same motifs appear in her next collection, *Toto'nost'* (Identity) in 1970, but she includes poems on the various identities of women as maiden, wife, mother, widow, and aged woman. Vadkerti-Gavorníková's basic theme in all her poems is the value of human work and creativity. This theme appears in *Kameň a d'bán* (Stone and Jar) in 1973, where a stone represents persistent labor and a jar symbolizes art, and it is treated inversely in her series protesting the Vietnam war in the same volume. The collection *Trvanie* (Duration) in 1979 summarizes her previous motifs in recognizing the lasting worth of home, friendship, labor, and above all the continual human struggle for the good, the lasting struggle against darkness. Her latest collection, *Vino* (Wine) in 1982, parallels the pains and joys of human life with the process of grapes growing, being pressed, fermenting, and becoming true wine.

Vadkerti-Gavorníková's lyric poems are highly praised among contemporary Slovak poetry for their clarity, precision, and complex free-associative structure. She combines a feminine sensibility with a strongly intellectualized approach to her verse.

Works

Pohromnice [Catastrophes] (1966). *Toto'nost'* [Identity] (1970). *Kolovrátok* [Spinning Wheel] (1972). *Kameň a d'bán* [Stone and Jar] (1973). *Piesočna pieseň* [Sandy Song] (1977). *Trvanie* [Duration] (1979). *Precitnutie* [Awakening] (1982). *Vino* [Wine] (1982).

Translations: Macedonian: *Vino* (1987).

Bibliography

Hajko, Dalimír, *Sondy* (Bratislava, 1977), pp. 47–54. Mihalkovič, Jozef, Afterword to *Pohromnice* (2nd ed. Bratislava, 1984), pp. 59–64. Miko, František, *Od epiky k lyrike* (Bratislava, 1973), pp. 110–121.

General references: *Encyklopédia slovenských spisovateľov* II (Bratislava, 1984), pp. 220–221.

Norma L. Rudinsky

Judita Vaičiūnaitė

Born July 12, 1937, Kaunas, Lithuania
Genre(s): poetry, drama, translation
Language(s): Lithuanian

Vaičiūnaitė studied Lithuanian language and literature at the University of Vilnius, then worked for the newspaper *Literatūra ir menas* (Literature and Art) and presently is a free artist by profession.

Vaičiūnaitė has written verse plays and poems for children, and translated authors from several languages, among them works by the Russian poet Anna Akhmatova and Lewis Carroll's *Alice in Wonderland*. Her main strength, however, is in her lyrical verse, of which she has published some nine rather small volumes to date. Among them, the collections *Kaip 'alias vynas* (1962; Like the Green Wine), *Po šiaurės herbais* (1968; Under the Northern Coats of Arms), *Pakartojimai* (1971; Repetitions) and *Neu'mirštuolių mėnesį* (1977; In the Month of Forget-me-nots) might be counted as her best.

Her work can be seen through two main aspects, at first glance very different, but actually closely related. First, in Lithuania, where most poetry focuses on country life and relationships with nature, Vaičiūnaitė is known as an urban poet. Yet she neither worships the city, like the futurists have, nor does she howl from the depth of its slums, like Ginsburg. Her streets are intimate places that whisper the history embedded in their ancient walls into the ears of young lovers passing by as she herself wanders free around the old Baroque churches and antique shops of her ancient city of Vilnius, dreaming of passion and wine, and of going quietly insane with love among the arcades and in the squares where the fountains, flooded with sunlight, fill the heart with their diamond spray.

This very feeling of intimate devotion to color, light, textures and things that can be touched and dreamed about extends to the second, "mythological," aspect of Vaičiūnaitė's poetry. She attempts to compensate for the lack of extensive narrative myths in Lithuanian folklore by going back to the mists of prehistory. There she seeks an immediate, direct contact with the actual shapes and smells of a time out of mind, where a girl would sit on a stone in the cold morning dew and comb her coarse blond hair, listening to the drumbeat of horses racing by. Or else, she would look at a tiny amber god, long forgotten, lost among the shifting sands of the seashore, to divine its name and meaning to her own times. And she would find it in the fiery wheel of the sun turning ancient forests to amber, turning, turning again in the ancient grindstones and in the sun-decorated spindles of the women at their spinning wheels, and also in the spreading yellow fog full of the early sun on a village morning. The little god would speak in the humming of the bees bearing their amber honey, and flicker in the wax candles, and she would understand his plea: "preserve, do not forget."

In either aspect, and in the many other poems that are sunny with love, her poetry is both intimate and joyful, in some contrast to the voices of others drawing their breath in pain to tell the tragic story of their Lithuania, trampled in the march of history.

Works

Pavasario akvarelės, poems (1960). *Kap 'alias vynas*, poems (1962). *Per saulėtą gaubl<ai>*, poems (1964). *Vėtrungės*, poems (1966). *Po šiaurės herbais*, poems (1968). *Pakartojimai*, poems (1971). *Spalvoti piešiniai*, poems for children (1971). *Klajoklė saulė*, poems (1974). *Balkonas penktame aukšte*, poems for children (1976). *Neu'mirštuolių mėnes<ai>*, poems (1977). *Mėnulio gėlė*, fairytales and plays (1979). *Pavasario fleita*, plays (1980). *Šaligatvio pienės*, poems (1980). *Karuselės elnias*, poems for children (1981).

Bibliography

Baltakis, A., "Spalvingai, nuošird'iai, natūraliai," in A. Baltakis, *Poetų cechas* (1975). Kubilius, V., "Lyrinis herojus ir lyrinės akimirkos." *Pergalė* (1963). Nastopka, K., "Tarp dviejų erdvių" in K. Nastopka, *Šiuolaikinės poezijos problemos* (1977). Pakalniškis, R., "Mieste—'uvėdros ir kovarniai." *Pergalė* (1969). Šilbajoris, R., "Šviesa ir spalvos Juditos Vaičiūnaitės poezijoje." *Metmenys* (1971).

R. Šilbajoris

Eleni Vakalo

(see: Helenē Vakalo)

Helenē Vakalo

(a.k.a. Eleni Vakalo)

Born 1921, Constantinople
Genre(s): poetry, art criticism
Language(s): Greek

Helenē Vakalo studied archaeology at the University of Athens and art history at the Sorbonne in Paris. With her husband, the artist and stage designer George Vakalo, and others, she founded the School of Decorative Arts "Vakalo" in Athens in 1958, where she has been teaching art history. Since 1949 she has also been writing articles for newspapers and journals and has served as the art critic of *Ta Nea* and *Zygo* for many years.

She started writing poems in 1945 and has published thirteen poetry collections since then. She apparently has found a kindred spirit in Marianne Moore, the only poet she has translated into Greek. Translations of her own poetry have appeared in English, French and Russian anthologies.

Vakalo's poetry is highly personal and deliberately antilyrical. Except for her *Genealogia*, it can be described as surrealistic or post-surrealistic. She is one of the so-called "Poets of Essence," a group of poets who did most of their writing after World War II, the Nazi Occupation, and the Greek Civil War and had to deal with the ruins (physical and emotional) that were the result of those historical events and with the accompanying feelings of estrangement and alienation. Distrusting the senses, they chose to write in simple and direct language, avoiding ornamentation, the complexities of syntax, and the demands of form. Vakalo's poetry appears to be formless and prosaic; it is a poetry of nouns and verbs, with few adjectives and even fewer adverbs. This type of writing seems to be in agreement with her definition of what it is to be creative: to push things beyond the given shapes and forms. She is at the forefront of those Greek poets who experimented with new ways of writing and new ways of looking at the world.

Although Vakalo's language is simple, her poetry is highly subjective and requires of the reader a "suspension of disbelief" and a commitment to the journey that is each poem. But her entire *oeuvre* is a journey also, a larger journey, for the reader and for the poet. In her early poems Vakalo practiced a type of automatic writing while exploring the world of the subconscious. Starting with *To dasos* (The Forest), however, and reacting against sentimental writing, she has attempted to write a poetry "beyond lyricism," a poetry of essence. Like a blind person (*E ennoia ton typhlōn*—The Meaning of the Blind) who has to learn "to see" differently than other people, the poet tries to make her way through the forest (*To dasos*) of experience and distinguish essence from illusion before she arrives at an understanding of things (*O tropos na kindynevoume*— The Manner of Our Endangering), comes to terms with her own "archaeology" in *Genealogia* (Genealogy), and realizes that there are countless Madame Rodalinas (*Oi palavres tēs kyra-Rodalinas*—The Follies of Madame Rodalina) and that we all are both one of them and all of them.

Works

Themata kai parallages [Themes and Variations] (1945). *Anamnēseis apo mia ephialtikē politeia* [Recollections from a Nightmarish City] (1948). *Ste morphe ton theorēmaton* [In the Form of Theorems] (1951). *To dasos* [The Forest] (1954). *Toichographia* [Frescoes] (1956). *Hēmerologio tēs ēlikias* [Journal of Age] (1958). *Perigraphē tou sōmatos* [Description of the Body] (1959). *E ennoia tōn typhlōn* [The Meaning of the Blind] (1959). *O tropos na kindynevoume* [The Manner of Our Endangering] (1966). *Genealogia* [Genealogy] (1971). *Tou Kosmou* [Of the World] (1978). *Prin apo ton lyrismo* [Before Lyricism] (1981). *Oi palavres tēs kyra-Rodalinas* [The Follies of Madame Rodalina] (1985).

Translations: *The Charioteer: Annual Review of Modern Greek Culture* 15 (New York, 1974). *Contemporary Greek Poetry* tr., intro., biographies and notes by Kimon Friar (Athens, 1985). *Genealogy*, tr. Paul Merchant (1971; new and revised ed. 1977). *The Greeks. A Celebration of the Greek People through Poetry and Photographs*, ed., tr., with an epilogue by Kimon Friar. Commentary by Odysseus Elytis (New York, 1984). *Modern European Poetry*, ed. Willis Barnstone et al. (New York, 1966). Greek poems tr. Kimon Friar, in *Modern Poetry in Translation*, No. 4. *Modern Poetry in Translation*, 34. *Six Modern Greek Poets.*, ed. and tr. John Stathatos (London, 1975). *Resistance, Exile and Love. An Anthology of Post-War Greek Poetry*, tr. and ed. Nikos Spanias (New York, 1977).

Bibliography

Anagnostakē, Nora, *Magikes eikones: Epta dokimia, 1960–1965* (Thessalonikē, 1973). Anghelaki Rooke, Katerina, "A Note on Greek Poetry in the 1970s." *Modern Poetry in Translation* 34 (Summer, 1978). *Bulletin analytique de bibliographie hellenique, 1971* (Athens, 1971). *Columbia Dictionary of Modern European Literature* (eds. Jean-Albert Bédé and William B. Edgerton, 2nd ed. (New York, 1980). Decavalles, Adonis, "Modernity: The Third Stage, the New Poets." *The Charioteer* 20 (New York, 1974): 11–41. "Helenē Vakalo: To na kaneis treles pros ta exō einai san na theleis na toniseis oti eisai exairesē." *Diavazō* 139 (March 12, 1986). Friar, Kimon, "Eleni Vakalo: Beyond Lyricism." *Journal of the Hellenic Diaspora* IX, No. 4 (1982): 21–43. Politēs, Linos, *Historia tēs Neollēnikēs Logotechnias* (Athens, 1980). Vitti, Mario, *Storia della Letterature Neogreca* (Torino, 1971).

Helen Dendrinou Kolias

Katri Vala

(a.k.a. Pecka)

*Born September 11, 1901, Muonio, Finland;
died May 28, 1944, in Eksjö Sanatorium,
Sweden*
Genre(s): poetry, causery
Language(s): Finnish

Katri Vala graduated from high school and
was trained as a folk school teacher in 1922. She
worked as a teacher until the end of the 1920s,
when she became a free-lance writer. She returned
to teaching in the mid-1930s. She died in Sweden during the Second World War.

As a poet Katri Vala (née Wadenström)
discovered that free verse was her métier in
spring 1922. Her bold poetic imagery aroused
public attention before her first collection,
Kaukainen puutarha (1924; Faraway Garden),
had appeared. Critics considered her one of the
most artistically talented of the young generation
of poets. The Tulenkantajat (Torch Bearers)
group, whose early days are connected with
literary expressionism, began to take shape in
1924. Vala became a central figure and the most
important poet in the group. Her early collections
Kaukainen puutarha and *Sininen ovi* (1926; Blue
Door) aroused attention with their exoticism,
colorfulness, and ecstasy for life, but her work in
the twenties culminated in *Maan laiturilla* (1930;
On the Land Wharf). Her serious illness had
clarified and deepened the cosmic visions and
sense of death in this work.

After this Vala published two more collections. The pacifism and ideal of universal
brotherhood which she proclaimed in *Paluu*
(1934; Return) were connected with both the
writer's political activities and her earlier expressionist impulses. In her last collection,
Pesäpuu palaa (1942; The Nesting-tree Burns),
as in *Paluu*, Vala appears as a defender of the
child and a representative of social motherhood.
Since her death, her status as a poet and in
Finnish literature has become firmly established.
In her use of bold poetic imagery, Vala may be
considered a pioneer in the new modern Finnish
poetry after the First World War.

Works

Kaukainen puutarha [Faraway Garden] (1924).
Sininen ovi [Blue Door] (1926). *Maan laiturilla*
[On the Land Wharf] (1930). [With Elina Vaara
and Katri Suoranta], *Kolme* [Three], poetic anthology (1930). *Paluu* [Return] (1934). *Pesäpuu
palaa* [The Nesting-tree Burns] (1942). *Henki ja
aine eli yksinäisen naisen pölynimuri* [Spirit and
Matter or a Lonely Woman's Vacuum-Cleaner]
(1945). *Kootut runot* [Collected Poems] (1945).
Valikoima runoja [Selected Poems] (1958). *Kootut
runot* [Collected Poems] (1977).

Translations: Vala's poems translated into English
in anthologies: Allwood, Martin S., ed., *Twentieth
Century Scandinavian Poetry* (1950). Armstrong,
Robert, ed., *Finnish Odyssey* (1975). Ollilainen,
K.V., ed., *Singing Finland* (1956). Tompuri, Elli,
ed., *Voices from Finland* (1947).

Bibliography

Lassila, Pertti, *Uuden aikakauden runous* (Keuruu,
1987). Saarenheimo, Kerttu, *Katri Vala aikansa
kapinallinen* [Vala, a Rebel of Her Time] (Porvoo,
1984).

Ulla-Maija Juutila

Pilar de Valderrama

Born 1892; Madrid, Spain; died 1979
Genre(s): poetry, drama
Language(s): Spanish

Better known as the platonic love and muse
of Antonio Machado's later life, Valderrama
moved in important literary circles and was a
good friend of Concha Espina and Matilde Ras.
She prepared a small theater in her home where
works of Benavente and Azorín, among others,
were performed. She became disillusioned with
her marriage after learning of her husband's
infidelity and that a suicide had resulted. In her
major play, *El tercer mundo* (The World Beyond), she seems to sublimate the relationship
with Machado: the unhappy lovers, unable to
live together in this world, escape to a world of
the spirit where communication is complete.

Works

Las piedras de Horeb [The Rocks of Horeb] (1922).
Huerto cerrado [Closed Garden] (1928). *Esencias*
[Essences] (1930). *El tercer mundo* [The World

Beyond] (1934). *Holocausto* [The Holocaust] (1941).

Bibliography

Valderrama, Pilar de, *Sí, soy Guiomar* (Barcelona, 1981). Moreiro, José, *Guiomar, un amor imposible de Machado* (Madrid, 1983). Valencia, Juan, "Unión platónica de Machado y Guiomar en *El tercer mundo*." *Estreno* 10.2 (1984): 41–42.

Patricia W. O'Connor

Helena Valentí

Born 1940, Barcelona, Spain
Genre(s): novel, short story
Language(s): Catalan

Born to a bourgeois family in postwar Barcelona, Helena Valentí grew up under the Franco regime, experiencing the restrictions typical of the period in Spain. To escape this repression, she lived and studied in England, obtaining her doctor of literature degree from Cambridge University. Her marriage to an Englishman ended in divorce, and Valentí lived some five years of bohemian existence in London, during which she became active in the women's liberation movement. Returning to Catalonia in 1974, she lived for a time in Barcelona but soon moved to the coastal village of Cadaques. She has recently returned to Barcelona.

Valentí's first book, *L'amor adult* (1977; Adult Love), is a collection of thematically related stories with both autobiographical and feminist substrata. Motifs drawn from personal experience abound: the foreign female in England, the tolerant, enlightened British husband, posters advertising women's lib, quantities of gin, the feminist movement per se, and the "liberated" but not satisfied female. Additional themes include the unwanted pregnancy, hostility within matrimony, the lack of marital communication, frequent separations of lovers and spouses, and aggressively unconventional sexual behavior. Whatever common ground there may be among the eleven stories inheres in the use of the liberated woman as protagonist or central consciousness. A dominant note is the battle of the sexes, from which not even motherhood nor infancy provides a respite. Nearly all characters appear hypnotized by the mystique of their respective sexes and consequently suffer from inability to mature. Valentí's feminism in this collection is balanced without being unduly aggressive or defensive.

In *La solitud d'Anna* (1981; Anna's Loneliness), Valentí amplifies existential preoccupations implicit in the previous work. Anna is, as the title implies, an incarnation of existential solitude (the feminine lot). Masculine characters play strictly secondary roles and are portrayed as insensitive, indifferent, and ineffectual but necessary for procreation. Brutal, infantile, or criminal, they appear as exploiters, all but devoid of emotion, so lacking in understanding as to be unaware of their offenses against womankind. Anna decides to have an abortion, which spells the end of her relationship with her lover, Luis, after three years of living together. Luis disappears while Anna is in the clinic, leaving a handful of money. The novel holds out little hope for heterosexual love or for marriage as an institution.

La dona errant (1986; The Errant Woman) is a novel without beginning or end, a narrative whose action is directly melded to the daily adventure of people in the street. Somewhat as in a giant chess game without players, its pieces move regardless of their own wishes, as if impelled by mysterious cosmic forces. As a social commentary upon the contemporary generation of Spanish adolescents, the novel describes their search for a niche in the world and the disorientation resulting from having inherited from preceding generations various modes of conduct which they intuitively reject as erroneous. Concern with the "generation gap" in values is a major theme.

With three strong feminist statements to her credit to date, Valentí is one of the definitive voices of Catalan feminism in the 1980s. Her fiction is intelligently written and cosmopolitan in its outlook, and even when seemingly guilty of a certain dualistic conception of male and female characters, strikes a telling blow for openness, communication, and feminine self-sufficiency. Without limiting her focus to feminist issues and the war between the sexes, Valentí deals with broader philosophical questions and problems of contemporary society which transcend the matter of gender.

Works

L'amor adult (1977). La dona errant (1986). La solitud d'Anna (1981).

Bibliography

General references: Women Writers of Spain, ed. C.L. Galerstein (Westport, Conn., 1986).

Janet Perez

Marguerite Valette

(see: Rachilde)

Marie des Vallees

Born February 15, 1590, Saint-Sauveur
    Lendelin, France; died November 3, 1656,
    Coutance, Normandy
Genre(s): vision, text
Language(s): French

A mystic and a seer, she was in her lifetime the center of deep controversies. Considered by some to be possessed and diabolical, she was held by others—such as Saint Jean Eudes or Saint Grignion de Montfort—as an authentic mystic.

A village girl belonging to a poor family, she lost her father when she was twelve. Her mother married a butcher, Gilles Capolain, who ill-treated her until she fled and went to live with an aunt. Several suitors proposed to her, but she refused in order to follow her divine call.

She offered herself as an expiatory victim for the salvation of all sinners and asked God to suffer the pains of Hell for the redemption of all. She was then immersed into all kinds of trials. Obsessed by blasphemies, she felt terribly tormented by devils, spent days in prostration and sickness but kept praying and offering herself: "I do not know where I am," she said, "if I am, what I am." Denounced as a witch, she was exorcised several times by Church authorities and finally released as "a virtuous maid."

When people visited her, she gave the impression of being a cheerful, simple, and sane peasant woman, knowing the hearts and spiritual states of her visitors, and versant in the ways to conversion.

Her visions, inner words and counsels were always deeply symbolic. They were transmitted by witnesses who kept her pithy and racy style:

"The Sun" (i.e., God) "looks at us," she said. "The Earth" (i.e., men, all creatures and the whole Creation) "is going to clothe itself with flowers and fruit," an evocation of the final salvation and divine regeneration of everything Marie des Vallées kept praying for.

"You have married me on the Cross," she said to Jesus one day. "The violins of the wedding were the hammer-strokes. The wine of the nuptial banquet was the gall. The words of entertainment were the blasphemies. Are you not really my Spouse?" She heard Christ answer: "You are right. This is the way I have married you and all Mankind."

Her fundamental themes are: the absolute glory of God; the fusion—in His Love—of Justice and Mercy; Man's deification through self-surrender and self-annihilation for the flowering of a new man; Man's call to total compassion for everyone if he wants to respond to and correspond with the depths of love of Christ's heart; the announcement of the Age of the Spirit characterized by a great Tribulation and a Great Renovation and Jubilee: God will purify Mankind and all the Universe to transform them into a renewed beautiful and pure Creation that will manifest the triumph of Infinite Love.

The essential meaning of her mystic call may be grasped through this vision of hers. She saw herself in a hall, sitting close to Christ, among princesses and queens in rich array. She was also dressed as a queen. Christ seemed to be thoughtful. He was looking at a dress in a corner, all covered with vermin, dirt, and filth, as if he wished that one of the princesses should exchange her magnificent clothes for this dress. Marie des Vallées immediately got up and put on the ragged clothes. Then the Master of the House—Divine Love—arrived. He ordered her to get rid of these rags immediately. On her refusal, he commanded that she should be cast out into outer darkness, bound hand and foot, which was done. However Christ kept gazing at Marie and told her with ineffable love: "Wherever you are, my eyes will be set on you. I shall always be with you, even in Hell. I am with you in your tribulations and shall deliver and glorify you. Such is the explanation of the parable in the Gospel."

In the time of Jansenism, Marie des Vallées stands out in an original way as a herald of infinite Divine Mercy.

Works

No critical edition of her visions and texts has been published yet. One must consult the two books written by Saint Jean Eudes on the visionary of Coutances and partially transmitted through several manuscripts: (1) *La vie admirable de Marie des Vallées et des choses admirables qui se sont passées en elle*: The Quebec Manuscript (Laval University, Quebec); Manuscripts 11942, 11943, 11944, 11950 (Bibliothèque Nationale, Paris); (2) *Abrégé de la vie et de l'état de Marie des Vallées*: Manuscript 68 (Librairie Municipale, Cherbourg); Manuscript 6980 (Staatbibliothek, Vienna, Austria). One should also consult other manuscripts available in Paris and written by other witnesses: Bibliothèque Mazarine (Renty, no. 3177, favorable); Bibliothèque Nationale (M. de Launay-Huë, no. 14562, 14563/M. Le Pileur, no. 11949, both favorable; Dufour, Abbé d'Aulnay, no. 11947/Le Moine de Barbery, nę 11946, 11948, unfavorable).

Bibliography

Dermenghem, Emile, *La vie admirable et les révélations de Marie des Vallées*, d'après des textes inédits (Paris, 1926), 326 pages (with a rich bibliography). Milcent, Paul, *Un artisan du renouveau chrétien au XVIIème siècle, St. Jean Eudes* (Paris, 1985), 590 pages (with numerous long reference to Marie des Vallées, cf. pp. 134f, 147–161, 245, 263f., 301f, 313f, 316f, 324f, 488f, 558f).

Roland Maisonneuve

Marguerite de Valois

Born May 14, 1553, Saint-Germain-en-Laye, France; died March 27, 1615, Paris
Genre(s): memoirs, letters, poetry
Language(s): French

Born at Saint-Germain-en-Laye on May 14, 1553, Marguerite was the daughter of Henry II (1519–1559) and Catherine de Médicis (1519–1589). The niece of Marguerite of Savoy and the great niece of Marguerite of Angoulême, she was famous not only for her beauty but for her erudition and devotion to letters.

She was married by her brother Charles IX to Henry of Navarre, the future Henry IV (1553–1610), on August 18, 1572. The wedding occasioned the presence of many influential Protestants in Paris and was followed by a surprise attack on the Huguenots on the eve and feast day of St. Bartholomew. The Bartholomew Massacre, as it came to be known, was ordered by her brother Charles at the urging of their mother, Catherine de Médicis. The event made a strong impression on Marguerite, who later wrote an eye-witness account of it in her memoirs.

Cultivated, beautiful, and charismatic, Marguerite had had an extended liaison with the Duke of Guise before her marriage at the age of nineteen to Henry. Her sexual liberality became well-known among members of the Court, as did Henry's. The couple separated not long after the marriage began, sharing little more than a penchant for self-indulgence. During their long separation Marguerite sided with her brother the Duke of Alençon in a political matter against her husband, for which she was driven from the Court and even arrested in 1583. She withdrew to Nérac before establishing residence in the chateau of Usson in Auvergne from 1587 through 1605.

There were no children from the marriage, and after Henry's accession to the throne of France the Pope dissolved the marriage. Marguerite consented to the annulment but only in December of 1599, after the death of Gabrielle d'Estrées (1573–1599), Henry's mistress for eight years and the mother of the Dukes of Vendôme. Following the annulment Henry immediately married Marie de Médicis in 1600, an arrangement that seemed not to trouble Marguerite, who retained the title of Queen. She remained friends with Henry, who consulted her regularly on matters of state. She treated Marie as an equal.

She maintained a mansion in Paris, the cost of which was an annoyance to Henry, where she held a small court of poets and scholars. Like her aunt Marguerite of Savoy, she was the patron of Pierre de Ronsard (1524–1585). François Maynard (1582–1646), poet and member of the Académie Française, was her secretary and helped her in the writing of her own poetry. Her memoirs are addressed to Pierre de Bourdeilles Brantôme, the popular court figure who was smitten with her and who featured her in his *Vies des dames illustres*, a widely-circulated series of anecdotes dealing with court intrigue. Her letters reveal the same clear, exact style of her poetry and are among the best letters of the sixteenth century.

Marguerite, affectionately called La Reine Margot, died in her mansion at Paris on March 27, 1615. All her life she exhibited an almost equal attraction to piety and license, to rigor and decadence. Independent-minded from her youth, she was unaffected by popular opinion of her conduct.

Works

Les mémoires de la roine Margverite (1628). *Mémoires de la reyne Margerite*. Ed. nouv., plus correct (1665). Lauzun, Philippe, ed., *Lettres inedites de Marguerite de Valois 1579–1606)* (1886).

Translations: Codrington, Robert, *Memorialls of Margaret of Valoys* (London, 1649).

Bibliography

Chamberlin, Eric Russell, *Marguerite of Navarre* (New York, 1974). Erianger, Phillippe, *La reine Margot; ou, La rébellion* (Paris, 1972). Mariejol, Jean Hippolyte, *A Daughter of the Medicis* (London, New York, 1930). Saint-Poncy, *Histoire de Marguerite de Valois*, 2 vols. (Paris, 1887). Strage, Mark, *Women of Power* (New York, 1976).

Cory L. Wade

Terézia Vansová

(a.k.a. Johanka Georgiadesova, Milka S., Milka Zartovnicka, Nemophila, Neznama Velicina, P. Kronikar, P. Rokytovsky, Reseda, Terezka M.)

Born April 18, 1857, Zvolenská Slatina, then in Austro-Hungary; died October 10, 1942, Banská Bystrica, both towns now in Czechoslovakia
Genre(s): poetry, novel, novella, journalism
Language(s): German, Slovak

Terézia Vansová's German pieces of 1881–1882 are only imitative, but her documentarily detailed and romantically plotted two novels and numerous prose pieces represent the convergence of exalted "ladies' fiction" with the didactic realism used in the literary battle against political repression of the Slavs in Austria-Hungary before World War I.

Born into the family of Protestant minister Samuel Medvecký, Vansová was educated at home and in German and Magyar girls' schools until age fourteen. In 1875 she married Protestant minister Ján Vansa and moved to a small town parish in southern Slovakia. She founded the first Slovak women's magazine, *Dennica,* in 1898 and was its chief editor in 1898–1906 and 1910–1914. Her goal with the magazine was probably more nationalist than feminist, yet she remained throughout her life interested in women's issues. Her personal tolerance for literature different from her own allowed the magazine to become a haven for experimental works that had no other outlet in Hungary. After her husband's illness and retirement, she moved to the city of Banská Bystrica in 1911, where she remained an active writer for most of her life.

Vansová's first amateurish poetry, published in 1875 as *Moje piesne* (My Songs), was followed in 1881–1882 by German-language prose and poetry reacting to the death of her only son. Besides children's books, she wrote three Slovak plays: *Potopa* (Flood) in 1886, *V salóne speváčky* (In a Prima Donna's Salon) in 1889, and *Svedomie* (Conscience) in 1897. Her prose fiction, however, constitutes her only important work. Vansová's novel *Sirota Podhradských* (The Orphaned Daughter of the Podhradský Family) in 1889, which was the earliest novel by a Slovak woman writer, has a romantic and sentimental love plot, but the young heroine also shows surprising independence in her rejection of wealth and status. Historically, the novel catches the crisis period of capitalistic growth in Austria-Hungary in the 1870s. Vansová's many novellas also showed her effort to woo young Slovak women readers away from German and Magyar literature by providing in the Slovak language the exalted sentimentalism of the then popular novelists E. Marlitt (Eugenia John) and E. Courts-Mahler. In her late novel, *Kliatba* (Curse) in 1926, Vansová also added the element of horror and Gothic mystery by her fictionalization of a real Jack-the-Ripper type of murderer active in the early 1800s.

Vansová's magazine articles included many documentary and autobiographical prose pieces that she collected into historically interesting though somewhat rambling accounts of her husband's family in *Ján Vansa* in 1938 and her own travels to Prague in *Pani Georgiadesová na cestách* (Mrs. Georgiades and Her Travels) in 1930.

Like her contemporary Elena Maróthy-Šoltésová, Terézia Vansová is now remembered more for her nationalist and feminist editorial activity than for the aesthetic quality of her fiction. However, her work also has documentary value for its clear and detailed observation of her time.

Works

Sirota Podhradských [The Orphaned Daughter of the Podhradskýy Family] (1889). *Dve novelky* [Two Novellas] (1911). *Milku dajú na edukáciu* [Milka Is Sent Off to School] (1919). *Zobrané spisy* [Collected Works] (1919–1922). *Chovanica* [Ward] (1922). *Kliatba* [Curse] (1926). *Bo'enka, Divočka* (1927). *Ako zo svojh o* [As If One's Own] (1928). *Sestry* [Sisters] (1030). *Prsteň a iné novely* [Ring and Other Novellas] (1930). *Rozsobášeni* [Divorced] (1930). *Ilenin vydaj* [Ila's Wedding] (1933). *Zobrané spisy* [Collected Works] (1941–1947).

Translations: Czech: *Viola Podhradská* (1972).

Bibliography

Maróthy-Šoltésová, Elena, "Terézia Vansová." *Živena* I (1910): 6–7, 33–36. Mráz, Andrej, *Literárne dielo Terézie Vansovej* (Martin, 1937). Noge, Július, ed., "Terézia Vansová a jej dielo." *Drahé postavy* (Bratislava, 1978), pp. 439–458. Václavíková-Matulayová, Margita, *Život Terézie Vansovej* (Bratislava, 1937).

General references: *Dejiny slovenskej literatúry*, Vol. III (Bratislava, 1965), pp. 559–565. *Encyklopédia slovenských spisovateľov* (Bratislava, 1984), II, pp. 233–235. *Kindlers Literaturlexikon* (Zurich, 1964–1972).

Norma L. Rudinsky

Variag

(see: Zinaida Vengerova)

Inna Varlamova

Born 1922/23?, Leningrad, The Soviet Union
Genre(s): novel, short story, review, translation
Language(s): Russian

Varlamova's teenage years were peripatetic. In 1934 for political reasons her father was officially exiled from his native city of Leningrad, and thereafter the family moved from one area to another in search of a stable residence. World War II found Varlamova in the Urals, where, as the daughter of an "enemy of the people," she encountered difficulties in finding regular employment. After the war she worked in a soil laboratory during the construction of the Kakhov Hydroelectric Station, an experience that lies at the foundation of the stories assembled in *Zhivoi rodnik* (1957; A Live Spring) and *Okno* (1965; The Window).

After Stalin's death in 1953, Varlamova settled in Moscow, started a career as a journalist, and traveled about the country, partially to absorb impressions for the sketches and articles that she had begun publishing in 1955. In 1957 she turned to fiction, and produced the novels *Liubit'i verit'* (1959; To Love and Believe), *Ishchu tebia* (1964; I Search for You, 1964), and *Mnimaia zhizn'* (1978; A Counterfeit Life). The last is a highly autobiographical narrative set mainly in a cancer hospital. The personal drama of the heroine stricken with breast cancer is projected against the background of the 1960s' sociopolitical scene, which the novel captures in understated fashion. Varlamova's stories of the 1960s and 1970s, dealing with adjustment to change, divided loyalties, love, and integrity, appeared in the collections *Tret'ego ne dano* (1969; Tertium non datur) and *Dve liubvi* (1974; Two Loves).

Varlamova is not a very prolific writer. Stories or novellas afford a better vehicle for her talent than does the large-scale novel form, in which her besetting weakness is a certain slackness, a proclivity to include the inessential. Her writing in general combines telling detail with compassion, gentle humor, and a faith in human perseverance. If Varlamova's concern with human emotions and relations between men and women allies her with the majority of contemporary Russian women writers, she differs from them in at least one significant respect: she tends to focus not on the city, but on the northern and eastern outskirts of the Russian empire. In those works where the action takes place in these locales, she reproduces the regional dialects with skill and conviction (e.g., "Kovshik dlia chistoi vody" [1968; A Ladle for Pure Water], "Troe" [1968; A Threesome]).

In addition to her own fiction, Varlamova has published a number of translations from French and from languages of the minority Soviet republics. Her many reviews have appeared in the prestigious journals *Novyi mir* and *Literaturnoe obozrenie.*

Works

Novels and collections: *Zhivoi rodnik* (1957). *Liubit' i verit'* (1959). *My iz Novoi Kakhovki* (1961). *Ischu tebia* (1964). *Okno* (1965). *Tret-ego ne dano* (1969; a story in the collection entitled "Kovshik dlia chistoi vody" was translated into English as "Ladle for Pure Water" by Helena Goscilo, *Russian and Polish Women's Fiction* [Knoxville, 1985], pp. 181–198; it appeared in slightly different form in *The Barsukov Triangle*, ed. Carl and Ellendea Proferr [Ann Arbor, 1984], pp. 169–189). *Dve liubvi* (1974; a story in the collection entitled "Troe" was translated into English as "A Threesome" by Helena Goscilo, in *HERitage and HEResy: Recent Fiction by Russian Women* [Bloomington, 1988]). *Mnimaia zhizn'* (1978, tr. David Lowe, *A Counterfeit Life* [Ann Arbor, 1980]). Translations: Uri, L. *Proletarii. Roman* (1977) (French). Badmaev, A.B., *Reki nachinaiutsia s istokov. Roman* (1971) (Kalmyk). Paityk, A. *Naslednik Povest'* (1971) (Turkmen).

Bibliography

Levin, F., "Nado by po azimutu. . . ." *Literaturnaia gazeta* (September 25, 1968). Kantorovich, V., *Zametki pisatelia o sovremennom ocherke* (Moscow, 1962), pp. 207–216. Motyleva, T., "Chelovek poznaetsia v trude." *Oktiabr'* (Nov. 5, 1958).

Helena Goscilo

Zseni Várnai

Born May 25, 1890, Nagyvázsony, Hungary;
died October 16, 1981, Budapest,
Hungary
Genre(s): poetry, novels
Language(s): Hungarian

Várnai was a prolific Hungarian poet from the start of her career in the beginning of the century. Her belief in communism and her partisan affiliations with the politicized working class characterize her work.

She received an education in the College of Theatrical Art. Her verse often expresses personal sentiments—mainly of motherly love—as can be seen in her collection *To My Soldier Son* (1914). Yet many of her lyrical poems, like her purely programmatic verse, include the expression of her desire for "social justice." Her poetry became especially revolutionary at the time of the short-lived communist-led proletarian dictatorship in 1919. Her literary output of this period was published in the volume *Red Spring* (1919).

Várnai also wrote a few novels of an autobiographical nature: *Between the Sky and the Earth* (1941) and *As The Leaf in the Storm* (1943). She took a strong stand against Nazism and World War II. Her *Persecuted Poems* appeared in 1945. After the war, she enthusiastically welcomed the arrival of the communist worker state, in which she became a celebrated figure.

Her vision of the world is relatively simple. Many of her conventional rhymed, rhythmic poems are expressive and are informed by strong emotions.

Works

Katonafiamnak (1914). *Gracchusok anyja* (1916). *Anyasziv* (1918). *Vörös tavasz* (1919). *Ég és föld között* (1941). *Válogatott versei* (1942). *Mint viharban a falevél* (1943). *Üldözött versek* (1945). *Áldott asszonyok* (1947). *Feltámadás* (1959).

Bibliography

A Magyar Irodalom Története. 1945–1975 (Budapest, 1986). Pomogáts, Béla, *Az ujabb magyar irodalom története* (Budapest, 1982).

Peter I. Barta

Marja-Liisa Vartio

Born September 11, 1924, Sääminki, Finland;
died June 17, 1966, Savonlinna
Genre(s): poetry, short story, novel, radio
scripts
Language(s): Finnish

Marja-Liisa Orvokki Vartio died at the age of forty-two. Both of her parents were teachers; her mother was also a lay preacher and reciter. Vartio's upbringing was religious. Her parents divorced a few months before she was born; as a child she spent part of her time with her mother, part with her father. She graduated from high school in 1944. In 1950 she took a degree in art history. In 1945 she married the manager of an art shop, Valter Vertio; they divorced in 1955. She then married the writer Paavo Haavikko.

Vartio is said to have been a splendid teller of stories, who easily cast a spell over her listeners. This can be observed in her poems which are often long and narrative. The role of folk poetry and Finnish mythology in her verse is unique, particularly so at the time when she was writing. Vartio wrote both in an adapted *Kalevala* meter and in the free verse favored by the post-war modernists. Skillful use of rhythm and great gushes of imagery give an atmosphere of magic and incantation to her poetry.

Her collection of short stories, *Maan ja veden välillä* (1955; Between Earth and Water), is a bridge between poetry and prose. She has herself said that writing is by nature close to dreaming. Characteristics of her stories: timelessness, lack of comment, namelessness, metaphor, and a strongly suggestive atmosphere justify calling them dream stories. The real and unreal levels of her writing are not opposed but appear side by side; the best example of this is her story "Vatikaani" (The Vatican).

Vartio played her part in the renewing of prose writing in the 1950s. The attempt to achieve "objectivity" by means of more external description can be seen in her work. Vartio's narrator may leave the reader to provide conclusions and explanations. Irony and humor appear when the narrator and the characters approach matters in different ways. Vartio's narrative methods are versatile and interesting, with her use of viewpoint and free indirect discourse.

In her novels Vartio describes country folk, the upper classes, and the new suburban dwellers of the fifties, and in particular women. One of the principal themes in her work is the search for woman's identity, the attempt to break free from the demands set by her environment. The young girls in her novels *Mies kuin mies, tyttö kuin tyttö* (1958; Any Man, Any Girl) and *Tunteet* (1962; Feelings) strive hard to achieve a situation where they can decide things for themselves. Vartio's women do not always succeed in their endeavors. The longing for connection is great, human contacts are difficult, often only death provides the possibility of realizing something about another person in the world of her novels.

Dreams and fancies are important in Vartio's five novels. The tragedy of a character may be the inability to realize dreams, as in *Kaikki naiset näkevät unia* (1960; All Women Have Dreams), or the central character may be a person already dead who dominates the imaginations of others, as in *Se on sitten kevät* (1957; So It's Spring). Vartio's posthumous novel, *Hänen olivat linnut* (1967; Hers Were the Birds), an undisputed classic of modern Finnish literature, contains complex symbolism. The structure of the whole novel is built around a collection of birds which is an important departure point for both the plot and the meaning of the book. The fancies connected with the birds help the main characters to stay alive and maintain their connection to each other.

Works

Poetry: *Häät* [Wedding] (1952). *Seppele* [Wreath] (1953). *Runot ja proosarunot* [Poems and Prose Poems] (1966).

Short stories: *Maan ja veden välillä* [Between Earth and Water] (1955).

Novels: *Se on sitten kevät* [So It's Spring] (1957). *Mies kuin mies, tyttö kuin tyttö* [Any Man, Any Girl] (1958). *Kaikki naiset näkevät unia* [All Women Have Dreams] (1960). *Tunteet* [Feelings] (1962). *Hänen olivat linnut* [Hers Were the Birds] (1967).

Radio plays: *Säkki* [The Sack] (1959) in *Suomalaisia kuunelmia, 1952–1963* (Finnish Radio Plays), ed. Jyrki Mäntylä (1964). *Saara* (1964) in *Suomalaisia kuunelmia, 1964–1965*, ed. Jyrki Mäntylä (1966).

Translations: "The Vatican," a short story; three prose poems; two extracts from the novel *Hänen olivat linnut* [Hers Were the Birds], tr. Aili and Austin Flint, intro. Pirkko Alhoniemi, in *Books from Finland* (March 1986): 136–149.

Bibliography

Alhoniemi, Pirkko, "Marja-Liisa Vartion Hänen olivat. Aineksia ja rakenteen piirteitä" [V.'s *Hers Were the Birds*. Materials and Structural Features]. *Sananjalka* 13 (1971): 147–161. Also in Polkunen, Mirjam, ed., *Romaani ja tulkinta* [The Novel and the Interpretation] (1973), pp. 165–179. Alhoniemi, Pirkko, "Marja-Liisa Vartion Kaikki naiset näkevät unia ja Paavo Haavikon Toinen taivas ja maa rinnakkain." [Vartio's *All Women Have Dreams* and Paavo Haavikko's *Another Heaven and Earth* side by side]. *KTSV* 26 (1972): 9–23. Resume. Elovaara, Raili, "Eksistentialistisen vieraantumisen monumentti." [Monument of Existentialist Alienation] *Ajatus* 40 (1983): 195–213. Lippu, Hilkka, "Naisen identiteettikokemus Vartion lyriikassa" [Woman's Identity Experience in Vartio's Poetry], in *Noidannuolia.. Tutkijanaisten aikakirja*, ed. Auli Hakulinen (1985), pp. 102–114. Monola, Tuovi, "Aino Kallaksen ja Marja-Liisa Vartion proosarytmin vertailua. Kolmen prosakatkelman analyysi." [Comparison of Prose Rhythm of Aino Kallas and Vartio. Analysis of Three Prose Extracts.] *Publications of Helsinki University Phonetics Department* 28B (1976). Särkilahti, Sirkka-Liisa, "Marja-Liisa Vartion kertomataide" [Vartio's Art of Narration] (Tampere University, 1973). Särkilahti, Sirkka-Liisa, "Kvantitatiivista analyysia ja vertailua" [Vartio's Narrative Technique. Quantitative Analysis and Comparison] (Tampere University, 1975).

Päivi Karttunen

Vasalis

(a.k.a. Margaretha Droogleever Fortuyn-Leenmans)

Born February 2, 1909, s' Gravenhage, The Netherlands
Genre(s): poetry
Language(s): Dutch

Vasalis studied medicine at the University of Leiden and became a psychiatrist. Later she turned to writing and published some of her early poetry in the journal *Criterium*. This early poetry was romantic realism; it has a simple, lucid style. Her first volume of poetry, *Parken en woestijnen* (1940; Parks and Desert), won the Van der Hoogtprijs and has been reprinted twenty-eight times. The twenty-one poems in this collection deal with winter, death, and fear. She published *De vogel Phoenix* (The Bird Phoenix) in 1947. This is a melancholy twenty-two poem collection which shows the effects of war on her. In 1954 she published *Vergezichten en gezichten* (Vistas and Views). In these fifty-eight poems she becomes more abstract and takes a more optimistic philosophic view of life.

Works

Onweer [Thunderstorm] (1940). *Parken en woestijnen* [Parks and Deserts] (1940). *De vogel Phoenix* [The Bird Phoenix] (1947). *Vergezichten en gezichten* [Vistas and Views] (1954). *Kunstenaar en verzet* [Artistic and Opposed] (1958). *De dichter en de zee* [The Poet and the Sea] (1960).

Bibliography

Assche, Armand van, "M. Vasalis: De Psychische wereld van haar gedicten." *Algemen Tweemaandelijks Kultureel Tijdschrift* 22 (1979): 207–214. Binnendijk, D.A.M., Randschrift (1951). Kingstone, Basil D., "De Idioot in het bad: Five Versions and some Comments." *Canadian Journal of Netherlandic Studies* 4–5 (2–1) (1983 Fall): 50–53. Vries, H. de, *Vers tegen vers* (1949). "Dankwoord bij de aanvaarding van de P.C. Hooftprijs." *Tirade* 28 (290) (Jan.–Feb. 1984): 2–10.

Adolf von Württemberg

Paul Vasili

(see: Juliette Adam)

Vera Vel'tman

(see: Vera Panova)

Jacoba van (Catharina) Velde

Born May 10, 1913, 's-Gravenhage, The Netherlands; died September 7, 1985, Amsterdam
Genre(s): novel, translation
Language(s): Dutch

After an apprenticeship as a dancer (Catharina) Jacoba van Velde spent years in Paris and on the Spanish island of Mallorca. From the end of the second World War onward, she alternately lived in Paris and Amsterdam. Having first written in French, she obtained an international success with the Dutch novellette *De grote zaal* (1953; The Main Ward). Just like *Een blad in de wind* (1961; A Leaf in the Wind), it is a harrowing and hallucinating reflection on senescence and death. Jacoba van Velde was friendly with Beckett, and she translated his complete dramatic work into Dutch. She also translated plays by Ionesco, Genet, and Arrabal. The *Verrameld werk* (1987; Collected Works) add ten short stories to the titles already mentioned.

Works
De grote zaal (1953). Een blad in de wind (1961).

Bibliography
Dubois, P.H., *Het boek van nu* (1962). Schouten, D., *Vrij Nederland* (April 4, 1987). Visser, M., *MRC Handelsblad* (February 8, 1980) (interview).

Frank Joostens

Neznama Velicina

(see: Terézia Vansová)

Elisabeth-Céleste Vénard

(see: Céleste Mogador)

Zinaida Vengerova

(a.k.a. Variag)

Born 1867, Sveaborg, Russia; died 1941, New
    York City
Genre(s): literary criticism, translation
Language(s): Russian

Zinaida Vengerova played a central role in introducing literary modernism into Russia in the 1980s. She was also something of a cultural ambassador, writing articles for French, English, and German periodicals about Russian literature. She articulated the particular philosophical and psychological appeal that the modernist movement had for Russian women.

Vengerova came from a family of achievers. Her father, Afansaii, was a bank director in Minsk. Her mother, Paulina, became a published writer at the age of seventy with the appearance of her two-volume memoir describing life among prosperous Jews in nineteenth-century Russia (1908; *Memoiren einer Grossmutter, Bilder aus der Juden Russlands im 19 Jahrhundert*). Her older brother Semën became a leading historian of Russian literature and bibliographer. Her younger sister Izabella was a celebrated piano pedagogue who came to the United States in 1923, eventually teaching such pupils as Leonard Bernstein and Samuel Barber.

Vengerova received a particularly good education for a woman of her time. After graduation from a gymnasium in Minsk in 1881, she went to study foreign languages and literature in Vienna for a year. Returning to Russia, she enrolled in the Bestuzhev University courses for women where she specialized in history and literature. After graduation, she returned to Europe to attend lectures at the Sorbonne and to work in the British Museum library.

During her sojourn abroad, Vengerova began writing and publishing articles in the Russian press on Western European literature. From 1891 until 1908 she wrote a monthly column for *The Herald of Europe* in which she discussed the latest developments in Western European literary life. These articles were seminal in introducing modernism into Russia. Returning to St. Petersburg in the mid-nineties, Vengerova established close relations with the modernists grouped around *The Northern Herald* and later, Diaghilev's *The World of Art*. She wrote on Ibsen, Verlaine, Huysmanns, Anatole France, Maeterlinck, Ruskin, Verhaeren, Wilde, Romain Rolland, Hamsum, and others. Vengerova also promoted Western European modernists through her translation work. Her translations include Lou Andreas-Salomé on Nietzsche, Hauptmann, D'Annuncio, Paul Adam, Annie Besant, Gide, Conrad, Thomas Mann, Maupassant, Strindberg, Wells, Schnitzler, and G.B. Shaw. Vengerova's enthusiasm for modernism contrasted with her brother's more negative view and subjected her to hostility, even ridicule, on the part of other critics. Vengerova's career reached its height in 1913. By then she had published a three-volume collection of her criticism under the general title *Literary Characteristics* and a one-volume edition of her *Collected Works*.

The appeal of modernism to Vengerova included its emphasis on individual freedom, its rebellious attitude toward conventional values and behavior, its championing of spirituality and aestheticism. This appeal shaped her views on women which she discussed in two articles. "La femme russe" (1897) and "Feminism and Women's Freedom" (1898). The first of the two was written for the French magazine *Révue des révues* as part of a series on women in different countries. Vengerova idealizes Russian women, seeing in them the very embodiment of modernist preferences—their individualism, moral freedom, spirituality, and a keenly felt aestheticism. In the second article, she portrays Russian women as superior to French women because the former understand that freedom depends on an inner sense of self and not on political, legal, or economic externalities.

After the Revolution of 1917, Vengerova immigrated to the West, first to Berlin in 1922, and eventually to the United States, where she died in 1941. On her arrival in the U.S., she was able to continue her career for a couple of years. There is no record of any publications in the West after 1923. Sometime during this period she married the poetic and literary critic N.M. Minsky. Her last known article was for the Soviet series *Literary Heritage* in 1939.

Works

Literary Characteristics, 3 vols. (1897–1910). *Collected Works*, Vol. I (1913). "La femme russe." *Revue des revues* (September 15, 1897). "Lettres russes." *Mercure de France* (1897–1899). "Das jüngste Russland." *Magazin für die Litter. d. Auslands.* [Variag, pseud.], "Tolstoi's Life and Religion (1911) and "The Leader." *Fortnightly Review* (1911–1912)

Translations: Nonfiction, fiction, plays from German, English, Italian, French, and Spanish.

Bibliography

Berberova, Nina, *The Italics Are Mine* (New York, 1969), p. 586. Foster, Ludmila A., *Bibliography of Russian Literature in Exile*, 2 vols. (Boston, 1970). Narkevich, A.Iu., "Vengerova, Zinaida Afanas'eva." *Kratkaia literaturnaia èntsiklopediia*, 9 vols. (Moscow, 1962–1978), Vol. I (1962), p. 896. Pr., Ark., "Vengerova, Zinaida Afanas'evna." *Evreiskaia èntsiklopediia*, 16 vols. (St. Petersburg, 1906–1913), Vol. V (1911), p. 418. Vengerov, S.A., ed., "Vengerova, Zinaida Afanas'evna." *Istochniki slovaria russkikh pisatelei*, 4 vols. (St. Petersburg, 1900–1917), Vol. I (1900), pp. 534–535. Vengerov, S.A., ed., "Z. Vengerova, Avtobiograficheskaia spravka." *Russkaia literatura xx veka, 1890–1910*, 3 vols. (Moscow, 1914–1916), Vol. I (1914), pp. 135–138; "Z.A. Vengerova," Vol. II (1915), Book 5, pp. 156–159. "Vengerova, Zinaida Afanas'evna." *Novyi èntsiklopedicheskii slovar*(1911–1916), Vol. 10, pp. 12–131.

Charlotte Rosenthal

Maria Veniamin

(see: Nina Cassian)

Elena Ventsel

(a.k.a. I. Grekova)

Born March 1907, Tallin, Estonia, The Soviet Union
Genre(s): novel, novella, short story, children's literature, drama
Language(s): Russian

Unique among contemporary Russian women writers, Grekova is a respected mathematician, awarded the coveted Doctor of Sciences degree in 1954, author of a widely circulated textbook on probability theory, and from 1955 until 1967, a professor at Moscow's Zhukovskii Military Academy. Grekova was over fifty years old when she broke into print in 1962, under the tantalizing *nom de plume* that in French is the mathematical symbol for an unknown quantity. Although she has determinedly subordinated her literary activities to her career in mathematics, over the last two decades her reputation as a writer has steadily grown. Grekova's most characteristic narratives concern themselves with the harrowing daily routine of middle-aged, unmarried urban women torn between the conflicting demands of work and parenthood in modern Soviet society.

Grekova's first story, "Za prokhodnoi" (Behind the Checkpoint), appeared in 1962 in *Novyi mir* (New World), the journal with which her fiction is identified. Like several of her subsequent works, "Za prokhodnoi" depicts the professional strivings and personal relations of an educated milieu: a team of scientists apparently unconscious of or indifferent to the dire long-range consequences of their single-minded efforts to perfect a research project: the black box.

Her second narrative, "Damskii master" (1963; Ladies' Hairdresser), is one of her best, partly because of its nuanced language and tight structure. It dramatizes the interaction between two very dissimilar individuals: Kovaleva, the head of a computer institute and a single or divorced mother of two feckless teenage sons; and Vitalii, a talented young hairdresser who aspires to self-improvement and a better position in life through persistent but comically indiscriminate reading of recommended texts. The story sensitively depicts differences in class, education, generations, and gender, while also exposing the discrepancies between ideals and reality, intentions and actions.

Differences in generations likewise play a role in "Letom v gorode" (1965; One Summer in the City), where Grekova explores the issue of abortion as it affects a mother and daughter. Upon discovering that her illegitimate unmarried daughter plans to have an abortion, a middle-aged library director recalls her own decision of two decades ago to arrange precisely the same thing. The pregnant young woman owes her existence today to her mother's change of heart about committing an act that at that time was illegal. Here, as elsewhere, Grekova assumes a pro-natalist stance.

The publication of Grekova's "Na ispytaniiakh" (On Maneuvres) in *Novyi mir* in 1967 had serious consequences for the author and brought her unexpected notoriety. An unsparing close-up of the dismal life led by Red Army soldiers garrisoned in a drab little town, the story aroused heated reaction because of the unflattering light it cast on the military. As a result, Grekova resigned from the Zhukovskii Academy and was reassigned to another institution, while military personnel were denied access to the issue of the journal that carried the story. One of Grekova's most recent stories, entitled "Bez ulybok" (1986; Without Smiles), gives a thinly disguised, "fictionalized" account of the incident.

Since then, probably the most ambitious and certainly the most widely discussed of Grekova's works is *Vdovii parokhod* (Ship of Widows), published by *Novyi mir* in 1981. An intimate exploration of the peaks and valleys in the relationships of five widows who share a communal apartment during and after the second World War, the novella traces their struggles to earn a livelihood and to find something meaningful in an existence crippled by personal losses and practically devoid of men. The plot focusses on the superhuman efforts of the youngest member of the group to give her illegitimate son a security that she herself has never known. War and its effect on women's lives, women's contribution on the front, their responses to the gruelling trials of everyday communal living, their attitudes toward men, and their treatment of the younger generation— children born to or raised by women in wartime conditions—constitute the major themes of *Vdovii parokhod*. Received enthusiastically by readers and critics, the work was adapted for both stage and screen. Grekova and Lungin rewrote it as a two-act play that was produced at the Mossovet Theatre in Moscow in 1984, while Viktoriia Tokareva transformed it into a film scenario.

In the Soviet Union Grekova's reputation rests mainly on her skillful handling of language, especially her finely individualized speech; on her ability to capture the atmosphere and conditions that prevail in various professional milieus, without glossing over disagreeable details; and on recognizing the formative role of Russians' experiences during the devastation of the second World War. In the West, however, Grekova is regarded as a feminist, or at least an advocate for Russian women—a perception against which she has protested quite vehemently. The seeming conflict between the two images arises from the "mixed messages" transmitted by Grekova's narratives. On the one hand, Grekova endows her women with the virtues of courage, intelligence, dependability, resilience, and psychological depth. They hold important positions and fulfill professional obligations with conscientiousness and skill. More often than not, they are brutalized, abandoned, or simply disappointed by men, yet they always cope, usually with the support and practical help of other women. Female camaraderie is a powerful force in Grekova's fictional world, and it frequently has to compensate women for the absence of satisfying relationships with men. Grekova's heroines repeatedly find comfort and companionship with their mothers, daughters, or female friends. The majority of men encountered in Grekova's fiction do not measure up to their female counterparts. They tend to be timid or vicious, given to intractable egotism, self-delusion, posturing, and laziness. Their besetting sins are drinking and womanizing. Grekova's men remain "the other," and rarely emerge as complex and convincing figures. In fact, one of Grekova's main weaknesses lies in her rather perfunctory depiction of male characters.

If these traits incline one to assume that Grekova is a spokesman for women's rights, other, contrasting, tendencies in her oeuvre suggest precisely the opposite. Works like *Khoziaika gostinitsy* and *Vdovii parokhod*, for instance, implicitly affirm those values sanctioned by tradition and convention that feminism rejects or at the very least wishes to reexamine. Above all the cult of motherhood and the domestication of heterosexual relations that loom large in Grekova's fictional world indicate that Grekova has internalized several hoary assumptions about the two sexes. Her true heroines are the self-sacrificing nurturer, the wife or mistress who provides home comforts. The assumption that women by definition differ from men not only biologically but also in psychology and temperament informs all of Grekova's writing.

Among Grekova's assets as a writer are the psychological complexity of her female characters, the immediacy with which she conveys the texture of everyday contemporary life in the city, and the sensitive ear she displays for diverse modes and levels of speech. Her drawbacks are the sketchiness or vagueness of her male portraits, occasional lapses into bathos and banality, and flatness of narrative line and style. These flaws are especially apparent in her less successful pieces, such as "Malen'kii Garusov" (1970; Little Garusov) and "Kafedra" (1978; The Department).

By comparison with someone like Tolstaia, Grekova emerges as a comfortably traditional, even old-fashioned, writer who eschews experimentation. She occasionally disrupts the chronological flow of her narrative for a flashback or two, and in *Vdovii parokhod* she deploys Iurii Trifonov's favorite device of two narrators with divergent points of view. But that is more or less the extent of her flirtation with stylistic innovation. Partly because Grekova lacks a unique voice and also because she borrows liberally from nineteenth- and twentieth-century Russian writers (Dostoyvsky, Trifonov), her prose leaves one with the sensation of coming into contact with something familiar. Indeed, certain facets of Grekova's prose remind Western readers of women's fiction outside the Soviet Union, often leading them to draw misguided conclusions about Grekova's allegiances and intentions.

Works

"Za prokhodnoi" (1962). "Damskii master" [A Lady's Hairdresser] (1963), tr. Larry Gregg (1976); tr. Michel Petrov (1983). "Letom v gorode" [One Summer in the City] (1965), tr. Lauren Leighton (1984). "Na Ispytaniiakh" (1967). "Malen'kii Garusov" (1970). "Khoziaika gostinitsy" [Hotel Manager] (1976), tr. Michel Petrov (1978). *Vdovii parokhod* [Ship of Widows] (1981–1983), tr. Cathy Porter (1985). "V vagone" (1983). "Porogi" (1984). "Bez ulybok" (1986).

Collections: *Pod fonarem. Rasskazy* (1974). *Kafedra: Povesti* (1980).

Play: *Vdovii Parokhod*, with Lungin, performed at Mossovet Theatre (1984).

Children's literature: *Serezhka u okna: Stikhi* (1976). *Ania i Mania: Povest'* (1978).

Reviews: "Razvetleniia dorog." *Oktiabr'* 10 (1983). "Chudesa slova." *Literaturnaia gazeta* (February 27, 1985): 6.

Bibliography

Broyman, G., "Ploskoe bytopisatel'stvo i ego advokat." *Nash sovremennik* 9 (1965). Condee, Nancy, *Newsletter* to Institute of Current World Affairs 10 (Sept. 1985). Also brief sections in Brown, Edward J., *Russian Literature Since the Revolution* (Cambridge, MA, 1982). Svirski, Grigorii, *A History of Post-War Soviet Writing:*

The Literature of Moral Opposition, tr. Robert Dessaix and Michael Ulman (Ann Arbor, 1981). Al'tshuller, Mark, and Elena Dryzhakova, *Put' otrecheniia* (Tenafly, NJ, 1985). Dobin, E., "Khoziaika gostinitsy." *Literaturnoe obozrenie* 10 (1977). Gusarova, K., "'Strannye zhenshchiny' ili toska po garmonii." *Znamia* 9 (1979). Ianovskii, N., "S vekom naravne." *Sibirskie ogni* 3 (1963). Kamianov, V., "Sluzhba pamiati." *Novyi mir* 5 (1971). Kedrov, K., "Otkrovenie ili otkrovennost'?" *Literaturnaia gazeta* 5 (January 30, 1985). Khmel'nitskaia, G., "Mera chelovechnosti." *Neva* 2 (1982). Lakshin, V., "Pisatel', chitatel', kritik." *Novyi mir* 4 (1965). Mikhailova, L., "Puteshestvie za prokhodnoi." *Literaturnaia gazeta* (September 13, 1963). Pitliar, I., "Pod iarkim svetom fonaria." *Sem'ia i shkola* 9 (1966). Plotkin, L., "Puti reshenila voennoi temy." *Neva* 6 (1968).

Helena Goscilo

Laura Maria Caterina Bassi Verati

Born 1711, Bologna, Italy; died 1778, Bologna
Genre(s): scientific treatise, belles lettres
Language(s): Latin, French, Italian

Laura Bassi was an academic celebrated in her time for her vast cultural knowledge and proficiency in letters, philosophy, and science. Bassi was born in Bologna to Giovanni Bassi, an advocate, and Rosa Maria Cesari. Her first grammar teacher was Lorenzo Stegani, followed by Gaetano Tacconi, instructor of medicine, who taught logic, metaphysics, and natural philosophy. Her academic accomplishment was so great that by age twenty she was able to achieve a rank surprising to the public. The disputation "Concerning Universal Philosophical Things," which she presented on April 17, 1732 to the Cardinal Legate Girolamo Grimaldi, Archbishop Prospero Lambertini, and a multitude of literati, religious affiliates of every order, and members of the nobility, constituted an event of general interest and of great importance in her life.

Such was the impression aroused that in May of the same year she was conferred the Laureate in Philosophy with a solemn ceremony held in the hall of Hercules in the public Palazzo.

The college of Philosophy admitted her by acclamation and the Senate Academy conferred upon her a professional chair at the university. This encouraged Bassi to continue her thesis on natural bodies of water, elements of other bodies, and universal parts, following an *ex officio* readership on universal philosophy which she continued until her death.

Bassi was elected to many literary societies and carried on extensive correspondence with the most eminent European men of letters. She was well acquainted with classical literature as well as that of France and Italy. In 1738, she married the physician and medical lecturer Giuseppe Verati, with whom she had several children. She diligently provided for their education and care. Her most illustrious pupil, Lazzaro Spallanzani (1729–1799), was first educated by his father, who was an advocate, then sent to the Jesuit College at Reggio di Modena when fifteen, and finally attended the University of Bologna where he studied with Laura Bassi. His scientific interests have been attributed to her. Under her guidance, he studied natural philosophy and mathematics, as well as ancient and modern languages. After taking Orders, he became professor logic, metaphysics, and Greek at the Universities of Reggio, Modena, and Pavia.

Throughout her life, Bassi continued to deliver public lectures on experimental philosophy and physics. In 1776, she was given a professional chair in physics from the University of Bologna. Her remarkable achievements as well as great scientific accomplishments mark her as one of the most outstanding and influential women of the time.

Works

"De problemate quodam hydrometrico," in *De Bononiensi scientarium et artium Instituo atque Academia Commentarii* (Academicorum quorundam opuscola varia), IV, Bononiae (1757), pp. 61–73. "De Problemate quodam mechanico," ibid, pp. 74–79. *Philosophica studia* (1732).

Bibliography

Borsi, A., *Una gloria bolognese del sec. XVIII (Laura Bassi)* (Bologna, 1915). Cazzani, P., "I cento anni dell'Instituo magistrale 'Laura Bassi.'" *Studi e inediti per il primo centinario dell'Instituo magistrale*

Laura Bassi (Bologna, 1960), pp. 9–15; 43–52.
Comelli, G.B., "Laura Bassi e il suo primo trionfo."
Studi e Memorie per la storia dell'Universita di Bologna (Bologna, 1912). De Tipaldo, E., *Biografia degli italiani illustri* VII (Venice, 1840), p. 190 ff.
Fantuzzi, G., *Elogio della dottoressa Laura Maria Caterina Bassi Verati* (Bologna, 1778). Ferrucci, C.
Franceschi, "Vita di Laura Bassi Verati." *Prose e versi* (Florence, 1873), pp. 750–788. Garelli, A., *Lettere inedite alla celebre Laura Bassi scritte da illustri italiani e straniere* (Bologna, 1883). Masi, E., "Laura Bassi e il Voltaire." *Studi e ritratti* (Bologna, 1881).
Simeoni, L., *Storia dell'Universita di Bologna*, II, pp. 95, 114, 120. Tomassi, R., "Documenti riguardanti Laura Bassi conservati presso l'Archiginnasio."
L'Archignnasio LVII (1962), pp. 319–324.

Jean Jost

Anastasia Verbitskaia

Born February 11, 1861; died 1928
Genre(s): novel, drama, political commentary
Language(s): Russian

Verbitskaia, the prose writer, playwright and political commentator, is best remembered for her six-volume novel, *Kluchi Schastia* (1980–1913; The Keys to Happiness), which caused an uproar throughout Russia. Verbitskaia (neé Ziablova) was born into a family of landowning nobility. Her mother was descended from the famous Russian actor of the 1840s and 1850s, Pavel Mochalov. During her childhood years in Voronezh, her home was a gathering place for intelligentsia, actors, artists, and local writers. Upon completion of the Elisovetinskii Moscovskii Institute at age fifteen she turned to reading all the European classics as well as contemporary Russian popular fiction writers. Shel'gunov, Smirnova, and Boborikina seem to have enticed her to experiment with writing. She made a serious effort in copying V. Krestovsky (pseudonym of Nadezhda Zayonchkovskaya, 1824–1899) whose novels consistently reflected the ideas of the progressive wing of the Russian intelligentsia. Verbitskaia made use of her theme of suffering and lonely women who are not given the opportunity to apply their talents and idealism to a proper cause and themes of social protest for the good of people. She dealt with these themes most effectively in her plays prior to 1903.

Verbitskaia's determination to be independent and self-sufficient led her to take on various positions. She worked and studied at the Moscow Conservatory and was well on her way to becoming a successful opera singer. In 1882 she was married to A. Verbitski, who forced her to leave her studies and soon after demanded that she should help support his large family. She became the head of the political section at the *Russian Courier* in 1883, where she wrote numerous political commentaries. Over twelve other newspapers and journals carried her commentaries. It was only in 1894 that she began writing plays and novels continuously, perhaps in response to her unhappy family life and the growing political tensions in Russia.

Her earlier works, such as *Osvobodilas'* (1899; She Freed Herself), protest the false morals of Russian society and the position of women in it and challenge woman's place within the family. After 1905 she was more concerned with a new image for women and her association with man. She firmly preached what she believed—happiness for a woman cannot be achieved through the union with a man. She often developed her arguments through the use of Socialist and Darwinist ideologies. Verbitskaia's protagonists in *The Keys to Happiness* and *The Yoke of Love* (1914–1915) explore sex and free love, experience multiple affairs and even give birth to illegitimate children. All these hitherto unmentionables earned her the nickname "Sanin in a Skirt." Her protagonists became spokesmen of the multitude of political ideas that circulated in the post-1905 era. In her short stories, novels and plays she posed questions which were extremely important for Russian youth of the time: What is literature? What is life? What can one do for the future of humanity?

Verbitskaia's audience was extremely large and consisted mainly of Russian students who were attracted to "new ideas" and "new people." Her popularity rested more in the smaller cities and provinces than in Moscow or St. Petersburg. She prided herself on being more popular than Chekhov, Gorky, or Korolenko even though she was considered a second-rate writer or perhaps more aptly a writer of popular fiction. With the onset of the Russian Revolution in 1917, Verbitskaia's works were forbidden to be published, and many of her volumes were seized and destroyed. Despite urgings from Gorky and other writers that her works should be published because they were concerned with Socialist ideas, she was never published in Russian again.

Works

Razlad (1887). *Mirage* (1895). *Vavochka* (1898). *Osvobodilas'* (1899). *Prestuplenie Marii Ivanovny* (1899). *Sny Zhizni* (1899). *Po Novomy* (1902). *Istoria Odnoi Zhizni* (1903). *Chia Vina?* (1904). *Kluchi Schastia* (1908–1913). *Dukh Vremini* (1980). *Rasvet* (1909). *Igo lyubvi* (1914–1915).

Bibliography

Chukovskii, K., *Kniga o sovremenikh pisatelii* (1914), pp. 7–21, abbreviated version in his *Sobrannie sochenenii*, vol. 6 (1969), pp. 10–21. Kranikhfel'd, V., *V mire ideii i obrazov*, vol. 2 (1912), pp. 155–181. Pachmuss, Temira, *Women Writers in Russian Modernism* (1978), pp. 114–119.

Valeria Sajez

Verfasser der Alme

(see: Christiane Benedikte Eugenie Naubert)

Verfasser des Walther von Montbarry

(see: Christiane Benedikte Eugenie Naubert)

Marie-Madeleine, Pioche de la Vergne, Comtesse de Lafayette (or La Fayette)

Born 1634, Paris, France; died May 25, 1693, Paris
Genre(s): novels, novella, memoirs
Language(s): French

A major figure in the history of the novel, Mme de Lafayette is known primarily for *La Princesse de Clèves*, the greatest French novel of the seventeenth century and one of the acknowledged masterpieces of Western fiction.

Mme de Lafayette was born and raised in Paris and spent most of her adult life in the French capital. Christened Marie-Madeleine, Pioche de la Vergne, Mme de Lafayette was the first born of Marc Pioche, Sieur de La Vergne and Isabelle Pena, both from the lowest ranks of the nobility. Of her early years, little is known. Her father died in 1649, and a year later her mother married the Chevalier Renaud-René de Sévigné, whose elevated rank afforded both Mme de Lafayette and her mother entrée to the highest circles of the court. In 1650, Mme de Lafayette was made a lady-in-waiting to Anne of Austria, and in 1654 she made the acquaintance of Henriette-Anne Stuart (known as Henriette d'Angleterre), the future wife of Louis XIV's brother, Philippe de France, Duc d'Orléans. Mme de Lafayette was later to become the close companion of Henriette d'Angleterre and collaborate with her in the composition of her memoirs.

In 1655, Mme de Lafayette married Jean-François Motier, Comte de Lafayette, a widower twenty-eight years her senior and a member of a distinguished, albeit financially troubled, provincial family. From 1655 to 1660, the couple resided at the family chateau in the Auvergne, where Mme de Lafayette gave birth to two sons, Louis (1658) and Armand (1659). In 1660, Mme de Lafayette returned alone to Paris to tend to her husband's complicated legal suits, which she brought to a successful conclusion in 1662. Although she remained on good terms with her husband, the couple soon agreed that he would remain in the Auvergne, to oversee the family estate while she resided in Paris.

Once established in Paris, Mme de Lafayette became a regular member of court and intellectual circles. She remained a life-long friend of Mme de Sévigné, later recognized as one of the century's greatest letter-writers and gradually developed a deep and fast relationship with the Duc de la Rochefoucauld, author of the masterly *Maximes*. Her own literary career began with a novella titled *La Princesse de Montpensier*, published anonymously in 1662. This tale of a young woman's arranged marriage and illegitimate, ruinous passion was quite well received, and in ensuing years it was often praised for its *vraisemblance* and its rejection of the conventions of the heroic romances, so popular in the 1640s and 1650s, of Mlle de Scudéry and la Calprenède. In 1669, she began work on a romance, titled *Zaïde*, about Moors and Christians in medieval Spain, enlisting the help of La Rochefoucauld and Jean Regnalut de Segrais in the project. Volume one of *Zaïde* appeared in 1670 under Segrais' name, the second volume in 1671. Although a collaborative effort, this popular romance was clearly more Mme de Lafayette's work than anyone else's. During the 1670s, Mme de Lafayette assiduously researched the historical background for her masterpiece, *La Princesse de Clèves*, while working indefatigably for the advancement of her sons' careers. In 1678, *La Princesse de Clèves* was published anonymously, and for more than a year the novel was the center of conversation throughout Parisian intellectual circles. The novel's controversial confession scene, in which the Princesse begs her husband to help her overcome her passion for the Duc de Nemours, led the editors of the *Mercure Galant* to solicit letters from its readers evaluating the Princesse's decision—the first such literary survey in French letters. *La Princesse de Clèves* was the last of Mme de Lafayette's writings to be published during her lifetime. After her death in 1693, one short novella and two non-fictional works were published: *La Comtesse de Tende* (1724), probably written in the 1680s, although some scholars date it much earlier; *Histoire de Madame Henriette d'Angleterre* (1720), written in 1665 and 1669–1670; and *Mémoires de la Cour de France pour les années 1688 et 1689* (1731; Memoirs of the Court of France for the years 1688 and 1689).

La Princesse de Clèves is undoubtedly Mme de Lafayette's finest work, one whose psychological analysis and dramatic intensity are perhaps only equalled in the seventeenth century by the great tragedies of her contemporary Jean Racine. The novel was not, as was once thought, especially innovative in form, nor did it directly influence novelists of the eighteenth century; nevertheless, it was immediately recognized as a great work in its day, and it has continued to enjoy an unwavering preeminence in French literature to the present. Seventeenth- and eighteenth-century readers were impressed by the verisimilitude of Mme de Lafayette's treatment of passion. Later readers have been particularly struck by the acumen with which Mme de Lafayette exposes the complex motives of her characters, their divided alliances, ambiguous self-justifications, and obliquely erotic actions. All have been intrigued by the enigmatic Princesse—above all, by her singular confession to her husband and by her striking decision, after her husband's death, to reject the Duc de Nemours.

La Princesse de Montpensier and *La Comtesse de Tende*, although lesser works than *La Princesse de Clèves*, are well-crafted novellas whose merits have not been fully recognized. *La Princesse de Montpensier* combines historical fact and fiction in an ingenious fashion and subtly parallels the devastations of love and the upheavals of the state that attend the unfortunate passion of the Princesse. *La Comtesse de Tende*, Mme de Lafayette's most bitter and cynical work, portrays with laconic rigor the self-interest, callousness, and savagery of polite society; it also shows the real and brutal dangers aristocratic women were prey to once they entered into an illicit relationship.

The romance *Zaïde* shares the limitations of its genre, but given those constraints, it is a lively and at times psychologically astute tale which stands above most of the romances of the century. Of Mme de Lafayette's works of non-fiction, her *Histoire de Madame Henriette d'Angleterre* is the most interesting. The concluding narration of the death of Madame is one of the century's great instances of Neoclassical restraint and detachment in the expression of powerful feeling.

Works

Romans et nouvelles (La Princesse de Clèves, Zaïde, La Princesse de Montpensier and La Comtesse de Tende), ed. Émile Magne (1970). *Histoire de Madame Henriette d'Angleterre, La Princesse de Montpensier, La Comtesse de Tende*, ed. Claudine Herrmann (1979). *Correspondance de Madame de Lafayette*, ed. André Beaunier (1942).

Translations: *The Princess of Clèves*, tr. Nancy Mitford, rev. Leonard Tancock (1978). *The Comtesse de Tende* and selections from *The History of Madame Henriette d'Angleterre*, tr. Ronald Bogue, in *Baroque Women Writers*, ed. Katharina Wilson and Frank Warnke (1987).

Bibliography

Haig, Stirling, *Madame de Lafayette* (1970). [See Haig for bibliography]. Kamuf, Peggy, *Fictions of Feminine Desire* (1982), pp. 67–96. Magne, Émile, *Madame de Lafayette en ménage* (1926). Magne, Émile, *Le Coeur et L'Esprit de Madame de Lafayette* (1927). Scott, James, *Madame de Lafayette: A Selective Critical Bibliography* (1974).

Ronald Bogue

Angela Veronese

Born December 20, 1779, near Treviso, Italy;
died October 8, 1847, Padua
Genre(s): poetry, autobiography, novel
Language(s): Italian

Born in a small villa near the city of Treviso on December 20, 1779, Angela inherited from her father, Pietro Rinaldo Veronese—a gardener in the retinue of the aristocratic Venetian family of Grimani—her love for bucolic scenes and pastoral settings. Her early dislike for any kind of formal schooling soon turned to intellectual curiosity and activity. As she relates in her autobiography, "Notizie della sua vita," the change occurred when she attempted to decipher the inscriptions on the statues and on the paintings of the villa Albrizzi, near Treviso, where her father had been transferred. It was here that she made the acquaintance, over the years, of writers such as Isabella Albrizzi and even of major ones such as Cesarotti, Foscolo, and Pindemonte who came to appreciate the poetical ability of this lovely, talented, and "uneducated daughter of the woods." After her marriage to a young coachman, she moved with him to Padua and, having assumed the name of Aglaia, one of the graces, dedicated herself to the writing of poetical compositions in imitation of Jacopo Vittorelli, especially *canzonette* which are characterized by arcadian settings and sceneries where shepherds, shepherdesses, meadows, and fields abound. In 1813 she achieved some kind of recognition by being received in the Accademia degli Agiati of Rovereto. She died in Padua on October 8, 1847.

After disavowing the first poetical edition of her works that appeared in 1804 (*Varie poesie di Angela Veronese trivigiana*), she wrote a preface to the *Rime pastorali di Aglaja Anassillide* that was first printed in 1807 and then reprinted, with additions, in 1817. The year 1819 saw the publication of *Alcune poesie pastorali edite ed inedite* and in 1826 appeared *Versi di Aglaja Anassillide*, together with autobiographical information attached to it. From these "Notizie" we learn of her love for nature and of the early years in the life of this exceptional self-taught writer. In 1836 came her novel *Eurosia*, which, in a prose suffused with Romantic sentimentality and bucolic description, narrates the story of a farm girl seduced by a wealthy city man.

Works

Varie poesie di Angela Veronese trivigiana (1804). *Rime pastorali di Aglaja Anassillide* (1807). *Alcune poesie pastorali edite ed inedite* (1819). *Versi di Aglaja Anassillide* with "Notizie della sua vita" (1826). *Eurosia* (1836).

Bibliography

Costa-Zalessow, Natalia, *Scrittrici italiane dal XIII al XX secolo* (Ravenna, 1982), pp. 193–197. Stocchi, M. Pastore, ed., *A. Veronese. Notizie della sua vita scritte da lei medesima, Rime scelte* (Firenze, 1973).

Sandro Sticca

E.M. Vervliet

(see: Maria Rosseels)

Halldis Moren Vesaas

Born 1907, Trysil, Norway
Genre(s): poetry, children's literature, essay,
memoir
Language(s): Norwegian

Halldis Moren Vesaas was raised in Trysil, a community in the farm and forest region of eastern Norway. Growing up in the country did not mean she was deprived of books, however; her father was author Sven Moren and their home provided a stimulating environment for a girl who was already creating poems at age nine. In 1934 Halldis Moren married Tarjei Vesaas, one of Norway's finest novelists, and moved to Telemark, in the south central part of the country. Again, living in a rural community did not bring about cultural isolation or provincialism. To the contrary, Halldis Moren has played a leading role in Norwegian literary and cultural life, and the Vesaas home in Telemark has been a meeting place for authors from all over Scandinavia.

Halldis Moren Vesaas and her husband lived on a farm in Telemark, Norway during their marriage, creating a European cultural center in the middle of rural Norway. Writing in the minority language of nynorsk (New Norwegian), Halldis Moren Vesaas' talent was recognized already with her first work. Her warm and harmonious view of life is expressed in simple yet beautiful poetry. Love, not only of lover and child, but also of one's fellow human beings, as well as growth, symbolized by the tree, are common threads in Moren Vesaas' poetry. Even the poetry inspired by the occupation during World War II is characterized by its feeling of love and fellowship with other people.

The literary career of Halldis Moren Vesaas is extensive and varied, but there is no doubt that she has made her greatest contribution as a lyric poet. With her first volume of poems, *Harpe og dolk* (1929; Harp and Dagger), published when she was only twenty-two years old, Halldis Moren brought to Norwegian poetry a new voice and a new experience. Fully conscious of her identity as a woman, the poet expresses a joyful exuberance that is unmistakably feminine; she rejoices in her youth and confidently anticipates all that life has to offer.

Following a critically successful debut, Halldis Moren Vesaas produced six additional collections of poetry, and each of these volumes marks a stage in her personal development. Love is the central motif throughout Vesaas' production, and it grows both deeper and broader as the poet-woman matures. The erotic longings of the young woman are fulfilled, and the love experience develops into an intimate sharing with another person, *Strender* (1933; Shores). In *Lykkelege Hender* (1936; Joyful Hands), the love between woman and man is expanded to include their child; the joy of becoming a mother and the happiness derived from raising a child and making a home are subjects of poems in this collection.

Her next book, *Tung tids tale* (1945; Words from Difficult Days), reflects life in occupied Norway during World War II. She writes about everyday existence during this difficult time,

about how survival depended on reaching out to one's neighbor. The experience of war did not inspire Halldis Moren Vesaas to write patriotic verse; it rather impressed upon her the need to open her embrace to encompass all human beings. The tone in her final collection, *I ein annan skog* (1955; In Another Forest), is darker and more reflective. The poet expresses her concern for a world that must live under the cloud of the atomic bomb, and she admits to a growing awareness of death and human loneliness.

While the poems from her earlier collections are generally composed according to traditional metric patterns, her latter poems often display a freer verse form. It should also be mentioned that she writes in *nynorsk* (New Norwegian), Norway's second official language, which is based on the dialects of the mountain and fjord communities.

Halldis Moren Vesaas also has a considerable number of prose works to her credit. She has written several books for children and young adults. These are realistic stories in the everyday setting of rural Norway, and the author shows a warm sensitivity to the problems and difficulties young people face with their parents, their siblings, and their peers. She has recounted events from a rich and interesting life in three books of memoirs, one about her childhood home and two about her life with Tarjei Vesaas. An active translator of poetry and drama, she was awarded the Norwegian Translator's Prize in 1960 for her translation of Racine's *Phèdre*. And finally, rounding off the list of her remarkable contributions to Norwegian literature and culture is her unselfish service on advisory boards, countless committees, and editorial staffs.

Halldis Moren Vesaas holds a distinctive place in Norwegian literature in that she was the first to give poetic expression to a woman's realm of experience: her longings and joys, her sensibility, her everyday tasks and concerns.

Works

Poetry: *Harpe og dolk* (1929). *Morgonen* (1930). *Strender* (1933). *Lykkelege hender* (1936). *Tung tids tale* (1945). *Treet* (1947). *I ein annan skog* (1955).

Books for children and young adults: *Du får gjera det, du* (1935). *Den grönne hatten* (1939). *Hildegunn* (1942). *Tidlig på våren* (1949).
Memoirs: *Sven Moren og heimen hans* (1951). *I Midtbös bakkar* (1974). *Båten om dagen* (1976).
Critical essay: *Sett og levd* (1967).
Translations: *Modern Scandinavian Poetry*, ed. Martin Allwood (1982). *Twenty Contemporary Norwegian Poets*, ed. Terje Johanssen (1984).

Bibliography

Beyer, Edvard, ed., *Norges Litteratur Historie*, vol. 5 (Oslo, 1975). Killingbergtrö, Borghild, "Menneske og samfunn. Tre barneböker av Halldis Moren Vesaas." *Norsk Litterær Årbok* (Oslo, 1977). Mæhle, Leif, "'Alt det vi levande eig,' Halldis Moren Vesaas runder år." *Norsk Litterær Årbok* (Oslo, 1977). Skard, Sigmund, "Halldis Moren Vesaas sytti år." *Syn og Segn* (Oslo, 1977), pp. 451–462. Waagaard, Mari Beinset, "Halldis Moren Vesaas." *Norsk Litterær Årbok* (Oslo, 1966). Waagaard, Mari Beinset, "Forfatteren Halldis Moren Vesaas." *Syn og Segn* (Oslo, 1977), pp. 463–475.

Katherine Hanson and Margaret Hayford O'Leary

Lidia Ivanovna Veselitskaya

(a.k.a. V. Mikovlich)

Born 1857, Russia; died 1936
Genre(s): novel
Language(s): Russian

Lidia Ivanovna Veselitskaya, who wrote under the pseudonym V. Mikovlich, was a contemporary of Lev Tolstoy whose work she admired and with whom she corresponded. Like Tolstoy she was born into the nobility and became a critic of the middle classes. Parts of her mature novels are set in southern Russia where she was born. Veselitskaya was educated at the Pavlovsk Institute, a well-known and respected school for women in Russia. Later, Veselitskaya married an officer in the Russian army.

Veselitskaya's early works were volumes of stories for young people entitled *Family Evenings*, *In the Family*, and *Of Children's Reading*. Her later work consists of a trilogy published first in serial form surrounding an empty-headed young woman named Mimochka. In the first part

of the series entitled *Mimochka—Nev'sta*, Mimochka behaves passively as her struggling middle-class parents try to arrange her marriage to a handsome young officer who claims to be the sole heir of a wealthy, dying uncle. But when the young man (whose actual situation seems rather questionable to the reader) discovers the paltry amount of Mimochka's dowry, he quickly abandons her.

Mimochka is finally married by her mother to another man. Mimochka responds equally passively to her second suitor, and soon she is whisked away to Paris for her honeymoon.

The last half of the first novel is set in the Caucasus at health resorts where her mother takes her to recuperate from bearing a child and from a minor depression. Here Mimi acquires a lover, and we see her playing silly passionate games like Emma in *Madame Bovary*. Veselitskaya doesn't take her heroine very seriously; Mimochka is characterized as a shallow, opaque character, a total product of her middle-class upbringing with nothing redeeming in her character. She isn't intrinsically evil, but neither is she sympathetic. Mimochka's values are those Veselitskaya attributes to her social class.

Tolstoy once complimented Veselitskaya without meaning to when he commented, "the author must have been a man, as no woman would be so frank in writing of her own sex."

Works

Mimochka: I. Mimochka—Nev'sta; II. Mimochka na bodohk' (1982). *Mimochka otravit'cya*, in *Vestnik Evropy* (1893).
Translations: *Mimi's Marriage*, tr. C. Hagberg Wright, LLD (1915).

Nanette Jaynes

Iv. Vesen'ev

(see: Sofia Khvoshchinskaia)

Bea Vianen

Born November 6, 1935, Paramaribo, Surinam
Genre(s): poetry, novel
Language(s): Dutch, Sranan Tongo

The literature of Surinam, a former Dutch colony in the Caribbean, which gained independence from the Netherlands in 1975, has been late in developing compared to, say, the literatures of the English or French West Indies. Its contributors write in Dutch and, especially in the case of poetry, in Sranan, the English-based Creole language of Surinam. Bea Vianen, who writes mainly in Dutch, is one of Surinam literature's first women representatives and a controversial one as well.

Her life and work follow a pattern—departure, exile, return, disillusion—that is similar to the course taken by many contemporary Caribbean intellectuals. She was trained as a teacher in the Surinam capital, Paramaribo. She left for the Netherlands in 1957 where she first worked in education, contributed stories and poems to various Dutch periodicals, and finally devoted herself entirely to writing.

Her first novel *Sarnami, Hai* (1969), which was promptly accepted by one of the major Dutch publishing houses, received much critical acclaim. The protagonist of this absorbing story is a young Hindustani girl in search of her identity. Sita or S., because her full name is hardly ever mentioned, tries to collect information about her ancestry (her grandparents were among the last indentured workers "imported" from India), only to discover that she is burdened by things and traditions past. Like the young Bea Vianen (the novel is of autobiographical inspiration), S. comes to realize that for a Surinam woman to achieve personal freedom and independence, she must leave a milieu that is oppressive to her sex and reject the roles (wifehood, motherhood, submission) she is expected to play.

The title, which is Hindustani for "Surinam, I Am," is Sita's confirmation of her newly-won self-respect and a plea to Surinam to recognize her and, with her, all Hindustani women. Though Hindustanis are the numerical majority in Surinam, they are at the lower end of the social ladder. Bea Vianen, herself of mixed Hindustani and Creole descent, has repeatedly addressed the plight of the more "vulnerable" members of the Hindustani community—children, women, writers.

The theme of imprisonment and oppression, so well evoked in *Sarnami, Hai*, runs through all of Vianen's subsequent novels. In *Strafhok* (1971) (literally: "punishment cell" or "shed"), which combines a happily ending love story with the account of a revolt against class justice, Vianen's tone turned more militant. Surinam, in the author's view, is not the melting pot it professes to be, but a society full of "punishment cells" or "zones," social castes divided according to ethnic group, wealth, or religious and political affinity. Those who cross the dividing lines are punished, such as the black father who is convicted for killing a Dutch colonial civil servant who sexually assaulted his daughter, or the demonstrators whose collective defiance of the system could not but fail.

Interestingly, Vianen holds both the colonial oppressors and the oppressed responsible for maintaining this "punishment-zone" system. Such a stand makes her radically different from most other—nationalist—Surinam writers, and, at times, very much akin to the Trinidadian author V.S. Naipaul. Like Naipaul, whom she admires, Vianen has been severely criticized by her compatriots for exposing the pariochialism and lethargy of Caribbean society. Surinam, she contends, is suffering from intellectual poverty and a petty bourgeois mentality. One of the "victims" in *Strafhok*, a gay Creole teacher who is driven to suicide, speaks for her when he points out: "(Surinam stands) Detached from everything. Detached from all that's happening in the world. Small backward country. Cowardly people. Ignorant people. Scared people."

Like *Sarnami, hai*, in which Sita leaves her husband and child to study biology in Holland, or *Strafhok* where the Hindustani protagonist stands up to the system by marrying his Javanese girlfriend, Vianen's next novel, *Ik eet, ik eet, tot ik niet meer kan* (1972; I Eat, I Eat, till I Am Full), still holds out the hope of escape: three adolescent boys flee their lower-class boarding school, away from poverty, oppression and a sexually frustrated headmistress. Their future is uncertain, but the promised motherland is never far away.

From then on, however, a gloomier tone prevails. The author's disillusion with her own escape into European exile became the basis for *Het Paradijs van Oranje* (1973; The Paradise of Orange), while *Geen onderdelen* (1979; No Spare Parts), written and published after a six-year interval, was inspired by her abortive attempt at reintegrating in Surinam and her growing despair with the country's paralysis and chaos. The protagonists—coincidentally both writers—are well intentioned and want to work towards the full emancipation of their fellow countrymen and -women, either from without—Sirdjal in the ironical "Paradise of Orange," Holland—or from within—Astilla in Surinam, a badly organized country that fails to import "spare parts." Both are only half-assimilated in the community where they live and torn between two cultures. They are misunderstood and ridiculed, fail as "reformers," and, perhaps worse, as writers.

Vianen has also brought out collections of chiefly anecdotal and unpretentious poems treating the same themes as her novels, and she has published miscellaneous work in various Surinam journals. As a novelist she may not always have been entirely successful in mixing sustained plot with essayistic observations. The variety of characters and situations in her books, the realistic quality of her dialogues, the photographic and perceptive account of local customs and sensibilities (and of nature in her early work) make, however, a welcome change from the contemporary Dutch novel of small-scale domesticity.

In this Vianen seems to join other Caribbean writers (and Third-World authors in general) in renewing and broadening the scope of the literature of the former motherland. The fact that her work meets with mixed appreciation in her own country makes her persistence in showing Surinam, in all its complexity, including its ills, all the more courageous.

Works

Cautal (1965). *Sarnami, hai* (1969). *Strafhok* (1971). *Ik eet, ik eet, tot ik niet meer kan* (1972). *Het paradijs van Oranje* (1973). *Liggend stilstaan bij blijvende momenten* (1974). *Geen onderdelen* (1979). *Gedichten over de grens* (1987).

Bibliography

De Roo, J.B., *De tijd zal het leren. Analyse van Bea Vianens roman* Sarnami hai (1974). De Wispelaere, P., "Twee romans van Bea Vianen." *De Vlaamse Gids* 62 (1978). Eggink, C., "Het onbekende Suriname." *De Vlaamse Gids* 62 (1978). Geerts, L., "Wat is een Surinamer?" *De Vlaamse Gids* 62 (1978). Pos, H., "Inleiding tot de Surinaamse literatuur." *Tirade* 17 (1973). Roggeman, W.M., *Beroepsgeheim* 3 (1980). Rutgers, W., "De Surinaamse schrijfster Bea Vianen." *Ons Erfdeel* 23 (1980). Van Neck-Yoder, H., "The Theme of Imprisonment in Bea Vianen's Novels." *Journal of Caribbean Studies* 2 (1981).

General references: *Caribbean Writers. A Bio-Bibliographical-Critical Encyclopedia*, ed. D.E. Herdeck (1979). *De Nederlandse en Vlaamse auteurs van middeleeuwen tot heden* (1985). *Moderne encyclopedie van de wereldliteratuur* (1980–1984). *Winkler Prins Lexicon der Nederlandse letterkunde* (1986).

Ria Vanderauwera

Mme Louis-Charles Vieu

(see: Marie Robert Halt)

Frida Vigdorova

Born 1915; died 1965
Genre(s): prose
Language(s): Russian

After graduating from the literature department of the Moscow Pedagogical Institute, Frida Vigdorova became a journalist, pedagogue, and writer. During her time as a correspondent for Pravda in Tashkent, she came to know Anna Akhmatova and Lidia Chukovskaia. Her reputation as a journalist and writer spread, especially during the late 1950s and early 1960s, when she became a champion for the cause of justice with her writings for publications such as *Izvestiia*, *Komsomolskaia Pravda* and *Literaturnaia Gazeta*. Her last literary feat was the artistic documenting of the two trials of Joseph Brodsky (February 18 and March 13, 1964), for whom she arranged defense in court.

Unfortunately, much of Vigdorova's output remained unpublished, including *Devochki*

(Dnevnik Materi) (Little Girls [Diary of a Mother]), considered by Kornei Chukovsky as the best of its genre.

Works

Moi Klass [My Class] (1949). *Doroga v Zhizn* [The Way to Life] (1957). *Eto Moi Dom* [This Is My House] (1957).

Translation: *Diary of a Russian Schoolteacher* (1954, 1960, 1973).

Warwick J. Rodden

Anne de la Vigny

Born 1634, Vernon, France; died 1684, Paris
Genre(s): lyric poetry
Language(s): French

Anne de la Vigny's father was Michel de la Vigny, Louis XIII's physician and the author of two published treatises on medicine. Her talent for poetry manifested itself at an early age. Her father recognized it and is reported to have said, "Quand j'ai fait ma fille, je pensais faire mon fils, et quand j'ai fait mon fils, je pensais faire ma fille" ("When I made my daughter, I thought to make my son, and when I made my son, I thought to make my daughter").

When she moved to Paris as a young woman, la Vigny became a member of Mademoiselle de Scudéry's circle of friends. She associated with such figures as Descartes, Pellisson, Fléchier, and Ménage. There still exists a fragmentary correspondence of gallant compliments and return thrusts, characteristic of the *précieuse* esprit, between Fléchier and la Vigny. She died in Paris in 1684. Over her tomb is the inscription: "Munimenta Saxorum Sublimitas Ejus" ("Her sublimity, ramparts of stones").

La Vigny's poetry has never been gathered into a single volume. It is executed in a diversity of forms, including the couplet, the madrigal, and the ode, the latter being her favorite. Two of her most famous pieces are an ode to "Monseigneur le dauphin" and another addressed to Mademoiselle de Scudéry in honor of the prize for eloquence awarded her by the Academie Française.

Until a critical edition of her verse has been issued, it is difficult to access the full nature of la Vigny's accomplishments. From what is available, however, her style can be described as full of fire, and her thought as ingenious and concisely expressed. In fact, her verse clearly demonstrates the seriousness of her studies. The influence of Descartes, her favorite author, gave her poems a uniform severity, and Mademoiselle Descartes, the philosopher's niece, addressed a poem to her expressing what she felt sure would have been her uncle's approval. This intellectual rigor, an agreeable style, and an elegant form are the salient qualities of la Vigny's verse. They recommend her as an interesting candidate for further study.

Works

La Vigny's poems can be found in the various anthologies: *Recueil des vers choisis* [A Collection of Chosen Poems] (1745). *Bibliothéque Poétique* [A Library of Poets] (1745). *Annales Poétiques* [Poetic Annals]. *Chefs-d'oeuvre Poétiques des Dames Françaises* [Poetical Masterpieces by French Ladies] (1841). "Correspondance galante de Fléchier avec Mlle de la Vigne" [The Flirtatious Correspondence of Fléchier and Mlle de la Vigne]. *La Revue Rétrospective*, tome 1 (1838).

Bibliography

Deslandes, Raimond, "Anne de la Vigne" in *Poétes Normands* 1–4, ed. Louis Baratte. Frère, Eduoard, *Manuel du Bibliographe Normand*, Vol. II (1858, rpt. New York, 1963), p. 171. Grente, Georges, *Dictionnaire des lettres françaises XVII Siècle*, Vol. III (Paris, 1954).

Glenda Wall

Björg Vik

Born 1935, Oslo, Norway
Genre(s): short story, drama
Language(s): Norwegian

It is as a writer of short stories that Björg Vik has risen to her status as one of Norway's foremost contemporary authors. Before becoming a full-time writer of fiction, Vik studied journalism and for five years was a journalist for a newspaper in Porsgrunn, where she currently makes her home. Her journalistic skills are evident in her fiction, in her uncomplicated and realistic style, her precise and finely tuned use of language, and her ability to detect a story in even the most undramatic and ordinary situations.

Björg Vik's stories, then, are realistic depictions of ordinary people in everyday situations. These stories are generally (though not exclusively) about women in various stages of development, from childhood to old age. Vik's characters are often undergoing a transition or are faced with a personal crisis: The protagonist may be a child responding with fear and confusion to outbursts of anger and violence between parents; an adolescent yearning for the happiness and fulfillment denied her mother; a housewife and mother questioning the meaning of her existence; an elderly widow struggling to cope with loneliness. There is relatively little dramatic action in Vik's stories—the author is more interested in depicting the psyches of her characters and in exploring the nuances of their relationships with others. Björg Vik possesses a remarkable ability to enter into her characters and illuminate their innermost feelings and thoughts.

An undercurrent of longing—for love, personal fulfillment, freedom—runs throughout Vik's production. Female protagonists in her first three books long to experience love and warmth. They have a tendency to seek self-realization through love relationships with men and to equate freedom with sexual liberation. As Vik indicates in the title of her second collection, Nödrop fra en myk sofa (1966; Cry for Help from a Soft Sofa), the characters in these early stories belong to the upper-middle class and represent a traditional lifestyle.

In Kvinneakvariet (1972; An Aquarium of Women), Vik's concerns are more specifically feminist. To her gallery of characters have been added women and girls from the working class, professional women, and artists. While interpersonal relationships continue to be a major focus, the protagonist in these stories is awakening to the social and political factors influencing her life. She is beginning to perceive that male domination extends beyond the confines of her home and that personal freedom is consequently far more complicated than merely loosening the bonds of marriage. The problem of freedom is further explored in Vik's next collection, Fortellinger om frihet (1975; Stories of Freedom), and here there are several stories in which men are also shown to be victims of an impersonal, profit-oriented society.

With En håndful lengsel (1979; A Handful of Longing), one notes a thematic shift. The characters are still filled with a sense of longing, but the insight gained through sharpened perception has tempered their expectations and they often choose not to change their situations but to accept their lot and make the best of it. There is an aura of resignation over these stories that persists in Snart er det höst (1982; Soon It Will Be Autumn) and En gjenglemt petunia (1985; A Forgotten Petunia), Vik's most recent collections. Many of the protagonists in these latest stories feel they have freed themselves of false illusions; some of them are learning to deal with death; most of them have come to recognize their own loneliness as something inevitable.

Björg Vik has also had success as a dramatic writer of stage and radio plays. Her play To akter for fem kvinner (1974; Two Acts for Five Women) has been performed in all Scandinavian countries, Germany, and Austria; in addition, there have been two Off-Broadway productions. The subjects and themes of her dramatic pieces are much the same as in her prose fiction.

The recipient of many literary prizes in Norway, Björg Vik has also been nominated for the prestigious Nordic Council Literary Prize on three occasions. She is regarded as one of the finest short story writers not only in her native Norway but throughout Scandinavia.

Works

Novels: Gråt elskede mann (1970). Små nøkler store rom (1988).

Short stories: Söndag ettermiddag (1963). Nödrop fra en myk sofa (1966). Det grådige hjerte (1968). Kvinneakvariet (1972). Fortellinger om frihet (1975). En håndfull lengsel (1979). Snart er det höst (1982). En gjenglemt petunia (1985).

Drama: To akter for fem kvinner (1974). Hurra, det ble en pike! (1974). Sorgenfri (1978). Det trassige håp (1981). Fribillett til Soria Moria (1984).

Translations: Out of Season and Other Stories, tr. David McDuff and Patrick Browne (1983). An Aquarium of Women, tr. Janet Garton (1987). Slaves of Love and Other Norwegian Short Stories, ed. James McFarlane (1982). An Everyday Story. Norwegian Women's Fiction, ed. Katherine Hanson

(1984). *View from the Window. Norwegian Short Stories*, tr. Elizabeth Rokkan and Ingrid Weatherhead (1986). *Scandinavian Women Writers. An Anthology from the 1880s to the 1980s*, ed. Ingrid Clareus (1989). *Two Acts for Five Women*, performed in two Off-Broadway productions. *Free Pass to Soria Moria*, performed by Pan Viking company in New York, March 1987. *New Norwegian Plays*, tr. Janet Garton and Henning Sehmsdorf (1989).

Bibliography

Beyer, Edvard, ed., *Norges Litteratur Historie*, vol. 6 (Oslo, 1975). Engelstad, Irene, and Överland, Janneken, *Frihet til å skrive. Artikler om kvinnelitteratur fra Amalie Skram til Cecilie Löveid* (Oslo, 1981). Faldbakken, Knut, "Samtale med Björg Vik." *Vinduet*, nr. 1 (Oslo, 1976). Garton, Janet, "Om å snuble i sine egne lengsler. Björg Vik: *En håndfull lengsel.*" *Norsk Litterær Årbok* (Oslo, 1983). Överland, Janneken, "Det grådige hjertes ufrihet. Skisse til en forståelse av kvinneroller, seksualitet og ökonomi i Björg Viks forfatterskap." *Vinduet* 1 (Oslo, 1976). Rasmussen, Janet E., "Dreams and Discontent: The Female Voice in Norwegian Literature." *Review of National Literatures. Norway*, vol. 12 (New York, 1983). Rönning, Helge, ed., *Linjer i nordisk prosa. Norge 1965–1975* (Oslo, 1977). Waal, Carla, "The Norwegian Short Story: Björg Vik." *Scandinavian Studies* (1977), pp. 217–223.

Katherine Hanson

Bo'ena Viková-Kuněticka

Born 1862, Pardubice, Czechoslovakia; died Lobočany u Žatce
Genre(s): novel, drama, short story
Language(s): Czech

Vikova-Kunětická (born Novotná) at first studied acting, but after her marriage she turned to writing. Her works include essays on many current issues, most notably, as in *Dál* (1912; Onwards), feminist issues. Both before and after the founding of the Czechoslovak Republic in 1918, Viková-Kunětická was prominent in politics. She became the first Czech woman in Parliament.

Viková-Kunětická's early works, in the 1880s, are genre-pictures of idealized bourgeois family life. In the novels, woman's role in the family is more problematic. The heroines of *Po svatbě* (1892; After the Wedding) and *Minulost* (1895; The Past) commit suicide in remorse over their infidelities. In *Medřická* [1897], an unmarried mother argues (as Viková-Kunětická also argues in essays) for a woman's right to bring up children alone. This was Viková-Kunětická's most popular novel. In *Vzpoura* (1901; Rebellion), a young girl runs away from home with a student who preaches against all "old-fashioned" ties of love and family. The heroine finally rejects him and his philosophy, opting to keep their child. *Pán* (1905; The Squire) is a wife's protest against double standards for sexual freedom, a theme also treated in the play *Co bylo* (1902; What Was).

Unlike her novels, which tend to be heavy-handed, Viková-Kunětická's numerous short plays treat conflict between the sexes with humor. The only play still performed, *Cop* (1904; The Braid), satirizes outdated notions about the proper way to bring up girls. *Přítě'* (1901; Deadweight) contrasts an upright older generation with an egotistical younger generation. Unfair divorce laws are the target of *V jařmu* (1896; The Yoke). *Dospělé děti* (1909; Grown-Up Children) lampoons supporters of "open marriage." These and other plays are notable for witty dialogue.

Along with such Czech Realist writers of the 1890s and 1900s as Matěj Šimáček and Karel Scheinpflug, Viková-Kunětická treated literature primarily as an instrument for social reform and education. Her work was very popular in her own time but is little read today.

Works

Sebrané dílo [Collected Works] (1919–1922). For a complete list of works, see Voborník, pp. 41–50. English translations: "Spiritless," in *Czechoslovak Stories*, ed. Šárka B. Hrbková (rpt. New York, 1971), pp. 135–144. "Geese," in *The Best Continental Short Stories of 1927*, ed. Richard Eaton (New York, 1928), pp. 61–75.

Bibliography

Šalda, F.X., *Kritické projevy IV* (Prague, 1951). Voborník, Jan, *Bo'ena Viková-Kunětická* (Prague, 1934).

Nancy Cooper

Marie-Jeanne L'Héritier de Villandon

Born 1664, Paris, France; died February 24, 1734, Paris
Genre(s): poetry, short story, fairy tale
Language(s): French

Marie-Jeanne was the daughter of a playwright and was related to Charles Perrault, the famous author of fairy tales. She grew up in a studious and intellectual environment and started to write stories for the entertainment of her friends. After the death of Madeleine de Scudéry, she opened her salon twice a week to welcome all her friends.

The works of Marie-Jeanne L'Héritier de Villandon are well suited to literary salons: short stories, sonnets, and poems praising the king and royal family. She took part in the "Querelle des Anciens et Modernes," praising the "Modernes" with enthusiasm and defending women against their detractors. She expressed her feminist ideas in the *Triomphe de Madame Deshoulières* (1694) and in the *Apothéose de Mademoiselle de Scudéry* (1702).

Works

Marmoisan ou l'innocente tromperie [Marmoisan or the Innocent Cheating] (1695). *Oeuvres mêlées* [Selected Works] (1696). *Bigarrures ingénieuses* [Ingenious Variegations] (1696). *L'érudition enjouée* [Playful Erudition] (1703). *La tour ténébreuse et les jours lumineux* [The Dark Tower and Bright Days] (1705). *Mémoires de la duchesse de Longueville* (1709). *La Pompe dauphine* (1711). *Le tombeau de M. le Dauphin* [The Grave of the Dauphin] (1712). *Les caprices du destin* [The Capricious Destiny] (1718). *L'avare puni* [The Punished Spendthrift] (1729).

Bibliography

Hallays, A., *Les Perrault* (Paris, 1926).

Marie-France Hilgar

Madame de Villedieu

(a.k.a. Marie-Catherine Desjardins)

Born 1640 (?), France; died 1683
Genre(s): poetry, letters, novel, reviews, drama
Language(s): French

Neither Marie-Catherine Desjardins' place nor year of birth is certain: she was born perhaps in Alençon; she grew up until age fifteen in or around this Normandy town. Her death certificate, in 1683, gives her age as forty-five, but in a letter dated May 15, 1667, she claims that she has, "[. . .] the experience gained from twenty-seven years of life." She could have been born either in 1638 or in 1640.

In 1655, young Marie-Catherine fell in love with one of her cousins, handsome François Desjardins, a dashing cavalry lieutenant. Her father, Guillaume Desjardins, a stubborn, ill-tempered man, perpetually in debt due to bad business deals and grandiose schemes to amass wealth, went to court and succeeded in having the engagement broken. Outraged by this callous action, Catherine Ferrand, his wife, obtained a legal separation and moved to Paris, taking her two daughters with her. It is around this time that Marie-Catherine, in order to forget her grief over losing François, began to write verse.

In 1658, she met the man who was to become her lifelong love: Antoine de Boëssert de Villedieu, a lieutenant in the *Régiment de Picardie*. Six years later (she was twenty-four or twenty-six, depending on chronology), she and Villedieu signed before a priest a solemn promise to be married, just before Antoine sailed away with his regiment. Having written in 1664 a tragicomedy, *Le Favory*, which Molière was staging, Marie-Catherine insisted that she be known henceforth as "Madame de Villedieu" publicly and privately. She demanded that her name as the play's author be so changed, a whim that created conflict with and resentment among some of the actors. Not without difficulty, Molière persuaded her to change her mind.

Her relationship with Antoine de Villedieu was both intense and stormy. Marie-Catherine was very possessive, a trait that did not sit well with her lover. In 1667, he publicly denied any attachment or obligation he might have had toward her and sought to marry someone else, a decision that, although based partially on financial considerations, failed to affect her love, or rather, her obsession.

Marie-Catherine left France around that time for the Netherlands, officially to tend to a lawsuit she had pending there. She stayed awhile in Belgium, then went on to The Hague. Back in Belgium, she learned with dismay that her former lover had turned over (or, more likely, sold) her correspondence with him to the well-known Paris bookseller Barbin, who was about to publish it. Appalled that her most intimate—and passionate—declarations to Antoine were to become fodder for public curiosity, she begged her Parisian correspondent to stop Barbin. Too late: the best that could be done was to remove her name as author from the *privilège*.

On August 22, 1667, Antoine was killed at the siege of Lille. His death coincided with the losing of her Dutch lawsuit and with her own father's demise. Marie-Catherine was brokenhearted as well as penniless. She accepted the hospitality of the Duchess de Nemours, an early benefactress and protectress, at Neufchâtel, until the end of spring 1668. There she composed her first major novel, *Cléonice*. She also adopted permanently the name Madame de Villedieu from that time on, with the consent, indeed with the blessings, of Antoine's family.

Beginning in 1669, she made the name of Villedieu illustrious in the world of letters: a very prolific author, her works sold quite well until 1672, when her production slowed down due to a certain world weariness which induced her to seek the asylum of a convent. Monastic life, however, soon proved itself unsuitable to her independent nature, nor could she long bear the frustration of having to give up writing, especially poetry, an avocation deemed too secular for a nun. She left the convent in 1675.

In 1677, thirty-seven-year-old Marie-Catherine secretly wed fifty-five-year-old Claude-Nicolas de Chaste, likely more for reasons of convenience than for love. She bore him a son, Louis. Her husband died less than two years later, leaving her in financial difficulty despite a pension of 2,500 livres granted the young child by Louis XIV. Marie-Catherine retired with her son to the Desjardins family's country estate of Clinchemore where she died in 1683, having spent her twilight years in pious retreat. There is some evidence that she harbored Jansenist sympathies in the latter part of her life.

Works

Epigramme (1663). "Jouissance" (1658). *Alcidamie* (1661). *Recueil* (1662). *Manlius Torquatus*, a drame performed at the Hôtel de Bourgogne (1662). *Carrousel* for the *Dauphin* (1662). *Nitétis* (1663). "Lisandre" (1663). *Le Favory* (1664). "Carmente, histoire grecque" (1667). *Anaxandre* (1667). *Cléonice* (1668). *Nouveau recueil* (1668). *Relation d'une Revue des Troupes d'Amour* (1668). *Recueil de quelques lettres en relations galantes* (1668). *Amours des grands hommes* (1670). *Exilés de la Cour d'Auguste* (1670). *Fables et histoires allégoriques* (1671). *Mémoires de la vie d'Henriette-Sylvie de Molière* (1672). *Galanteries grenadines* (1672). *Nouvelles afriquaines* (1672). *Le Portefeuille* (1674). *Les Désordres de l'amour* (1674).

Bibliography

Cuénin, Micheline, *Roman et société sous Louis XIV: Madame de Villedieu (Marie-Catherine Desjardins 1640–1683)*, 2 vols. (Lille: Librairie Honoré Champion, 1979).

Francis Assaf

Gabrielle-Suzanne Barbot Gallon, dame de Villeneuve

(a.k.a. Mme. de Vxxx)

Born 1695(?); died December 29, 1755, Paris, France
Genre(s): "nouvelle," fairy tale, novel
Language(s): French

Mme de Villeneuve wrote the original version of "La Belle et la Bête," a tale which has become the French prototype of the eighteenth-century literary fairy tale. Yet for a long time Mme de Villeneuve did not receive due credit because her carefully constructed narrative of considerable length reached its wide distribution only in the severely abridged form included by Mme Leprince de Beaumont in her *Magasin des Enfants* of 1756.

The daughter of a nobleman of La Rochelle, Gabrielle-Suzanne Barbot married Jean-Baptiste Gallon de Villeneuve, a lieutenant-colonel of the French infantry. Finding herself without financial resources after her husband's death, Mme de Villeneuve sought to improve her lot through writing. She was rewarded with considerable success as her second full-length novel, *La Jardinière de Vincennes*, became a mid-century best seller. In contrast to the more prominent female authors of the first half of the century, like Mme de Graffigny or Mme de Tencin, whose personal flamboyance was coupled with public notoriety, Mme de Villeneuve pursued her life and literary career in relative obscurity. Her latter years were spent in the company of Crébillon père, Voltaire's arch-rival, whom—as Casanova reports—she assisted in his duties as royal censor while conducting the affairs of his household in general.

A review of the publishing history of Mme de Villeneuve's works suggests that, as a writer, she was decidedly aiming at commercial success, as she conformed in her literary expression to the dominant genre and style of the time, shifting from "nouvelle," to fairy tale, to novel. The "nouvelle" *Le Phénix conjugal* of 1734 depicts the fate of a young nobleman who is persecuted by his father for marrying a working-class girl. Her first book sets both the thematic and the formal parameters for her subsequent works; love and virtue, money and social class are the central issues of her fictional universe; multiple subplots and puzzle-effects characterize the construction of her narratives.

As the raging literary fashion of the declining seventeenth century—the fairy tale—underwent a short revival in the 1740s, Mme de Villeneuve published her two collections of tales. In *La Jeune Amériquaine ou les contes marins* (1740–1741) we find her masterpiece "La Belle et la Bête," set in the frame of a transatlantic sea voyage. There are few better-loved fairy tales than that of the young prince cursed to bear the likeness of a repulsive beast-like creature until he is released through the devoted love of an unselfish maiden. The second tale, "Les Nayades," elaborates the motif of the rivalry between the kind and the rude stepsister, who each receive the magical gifts they deserve. The third posthumous

tale, "Le Temps et la Patience" (1768), blends fairy tale with allegory as the reader follows the adventures of an errant princess and her exiled brothers.

Mme de Villeneuve's second collection of tales, *Les Belles Solitaires* (1745), is a puzzling work of uneven quality that seems to explore the nature of fictional discourse through concrete examples. A countess gives an autobiographical account improbable enough to be called fantasy and a marquise presents two fairy tales whose gratuitous invention is rendered plausible through logical explanation.

It is in her best and most successful novel, *La Jardiniere de Vincennes* (1753), that Mme de Villeneuve's feminist orientation becomes most visible. The heroine, an impoverished aristocratic widow, defies the reigning social order that disallows manual labor for the aristocracy. She resorts to work in order to bring up her children in dignity and independence. The plight of women's destiny is treated less optimistically in *Mesdemoiselles de Marsange* (1757), a somber tragedy set in motion by a young woman who challenges the patriarchal order that preordained her younger sister for the convent.

In Mme de Villeneuve's two other novels, the occasionally heavy-handed complications of the plot relegate most ideologic concerns to the background. *Le Beau-frère supposé* (1752) is a novel of pure intrigue and adventure, complete with abductions, blackmail, and murder, while the action of *Le Juge prévenu* (1754) revolves around the familiar issue of marriage across class barriers.

Despite certain stylistic flaws in her work, Mme de Villeneuve should be remembered as a woman and a writer who succeeded in conveying subtly and skillfully her distinct awareness of the social injustice produced by the aristocratic patriarchal ideology. Her brand of feminism, however, is decidedly undogmatic because she propounds pragmatism not only as an ultimate value but also as an effective means to bring about social change. Avoiding the trap of *sensibilité* that swept the century, Mme de Villeneuve presented an ideologically cohesive and consciously constructed narrative universe that relies on the reflection of social reality and not on the dissection of love.

Works

Le Phénix conjugal (1734). *La Jeune Amériquaine ou les Contes marins* (1740–1741). *Les Belles Solitaires* (1745). *Le Beau-frère supposé* (1752), *La Jardinière de Vincennes* (1753). *Le Juge prévenu* (1754). *Mesdemoiselles de Marsange* (1757). *Le Temps et la Patience* (1768).

Bibliography

Coulet, H., "Les Noces de la Bête." *Le Génie de la forme: Mélanges de langue et de littérature offerts à Jean Mourot* (Paris, 1982). Rémy, P., "Une Version méconnue de 'La Belle et la Bête.'" *Revue belge de philologie et d'histoire* (1957).

General references: La Porte, J. de, *Histoire littéraire des femmes françaises, ou Lettres historiques et critiques* IV (Paris, 1769). *Dictionnaire des lettres françaises*, ed. G. Grente III (Paris, 1960).

Barbara L. Cooper

Madame de Villeroy

(see: Madeleine de Laubespine)

Viola

(see: Kathinka [Katharina] Rosa Pauline Modesta Zitz-Halein)

Baba Vişa

(see: Smara)

Annie Vivanti

Born 1868, London, England; died 1942, Turin, Italy
Genre(s): poetry, novel, short story, travel literature, drama, essay
Language(s): Italian, English

Vivanti was born in London of a German mother, Anna Lindau, and an Italian father, Anselmo Vivanti, who was a political exile and a follower of Garibaldi and Mazzini. Annie arrived in Italy in 1887 and worked as a governess and as a voice teacher. After a failed debut in the theater she began to write poetry. Being put off by the Milan publisher, Treves, with the statement that he would publish her poetry only if prefaced by Carducci, Vivanti besieged the elderly and nationally acclaimed poet until he, succumbing to her charm and literary talents, wrote a preface that began this way: "In my poetic code, priests and women are forbidden to write poetry; I am not transgressing this article of law for any priest; but for her, I am." Her stormy friendship with Carducci lasted many years and inspired some of his best poems, later published in *Rime e ritmi* (Rhymes and Rhythms). In 1892, she married the Irish journalist and patriot John Chartres and moved to the United States with him and their daughter Vivien. She returned to Italy and to literature after twenty years and wrote some 16 works of fiction and non-fiction. Her last days were marred by her daughter's death in a London air raid and by her temporary internment at Arezzo with some British citizens. She died soon after, poor and alone.

Vivanti's poems—*Lirica* (1890; Lyrics)—depict her everyday experiences with colorful immediacy and show an approach to life that is practical and modern. They exhibit considerable thematic variety, from candid confessions of sudden and capricious loves to free-thinking, impish considerations about the existence of God. On the other hand, her novels—*Marion, artista da caffè concerto* (1891; Marion, Artist of the Cafè Chantant) and *I divoratori* (1911; The Devourers)—are populated by larger-than-life women, always beautiful, fascinating, sometimes vindictive and cruel, often heroically loyal. The artificiality of her characterizations and the theatricality of the situations are redeemed by a lively and humorous style and by the immediacy of a seemingly running chronicle. Several of her stories deal with contemporary events. In *Circe* (1912; Circe) she gave her version of a sensational trial. In the drama, *L'invasore* (1915; The Invader), soon turned into a novel with the title of *Vae Victis!* (1917; Woe to the Vanquished!), she described the circumstances of war and the ravages of a country invaded by the enemy.

Especially charming, and perhaps her best literary achievements, are two books of reminiscences and sketches: *Zingaresca* (1918; In Gypsy Style) and *Gioia!* (1912; Joy!) These are precise vignettes of her younger years and lovely recollections of her travels in many countries. The most memorable remain the delicate and affectionate sketches she drew of old Carducci and the spirited description of her attempt to run a ranch in Uvalde, Texas.

Works

Lirica (1890). Marion, artista di caffè concerto (1891). The Ruby Ring (1900). I divoratori (1910). Circe: il romanzo di Maria Tarnowska (1912). Giovanni Pascoli, la vita e le opere (1912). Winning Him Back (1914). L'invasore (1915); translated as The Outrage, 1918). Vae victis! (1917). Le bocche inutili (1918). Naja tripudians (1920). Gioia! (1921). Fosca, sorella di Messalina (1922). Sua altezza (1923). Terra di Cleopatra (1925). Perdonate Eglantina (1926). Mea culpa (1927). Zingaresca (1931). Salvate le nostre anime (1932). Oltre l'amore (1932). Il viaggio incantato (1933). Pancrazi, P., ed., Un amoroso incontro della fine Ottocento: lettere e ricordi di G., Carducci e A. Vivanti (1951).

Translations: The Devourers [I divoratori] (1910).

Bibliography

Borgese, G.A., La vita e il libro (Bologna, 1923), pp. 117–203. Cecchi, E., Letteratura italiana del Novecento (Milan, 1972), pp. 141, 1273–1275. Croce, B., Letteratura della Nuova Italia. IV (Bari, 1914), pp. 326–334. Croce, B., "Aggiunte alla Letteratura della Nuova Italia, XXXVI, Scrittrici." Critica (1938): 409–425. Pancrazi, P., Un amoroso incontro di fine Ottocento. Lettere e ricordi di G. Carducci e A. Vivanti (Florence, 1950). Ravegnani, G., I Contemporanei. I (Milan, 1960), pp. 99–113. Russo, L., I Narratori (Milan-Messina, 1955), pp. 269–270. Serra, R., Le lettere (Rome, 1920), pp. 122–123.

Rinaldina Russell

Renée Vivien

(a.k.a. Pauline Mary Tarn)

Born June 8, 1877, London, England; died
    November 18, 1909, Paris, France
Genre(s): poetry, prose poem, translation,
    novel, fairy tale, short story
Language(s): French

The problematic and uncertain facts concerning the birth and childhood of Renée Vivien (née Pauline Tarn) epitomize some of the complexities that the life and work of this figure represent. According to some biographers she was born in London, according to others, in Long Island in the United States as the child of a presumably English father and an American mother whose wealth derived mainly from the dry goods business. In 1898, the young Pauline escaped to Paris where she became a spirited and often scandalous member of the fin-de-siècle bohème. Her stormy lesbian relationships with, among others, Natalie Clifford Barney and Baroness Hélène Van Zuylen de Nyevelt—relationships that are reflected in her work and literary preferences—soon attracted the attention of the beau monde of turn of the century Paris. Her early death in 1909, at the age of thirty-three, of the combined effects of excessive alcohol use, nervous fatigue, and a final exhausting and mysterious lesbian affair, concludes the almost classic fin-de-siècle career of Renée Vivien.

In spite of her early death, Renée Vivien published an extensive oeuvre. Among her poetry, especially the collections Etudes et Préludes (1901), Cendres et Poussières (1902), Evocations (1903), her translation of Sappho's lyrics (1903) and the two collections of prose poems Brumes de Fjords (1902) and Du vert au violet (1903) deserve attention. Renée Vivien also published two volumes written in collaboration with Hélène V. Z. (Hélène Van Zuylen de Nyevelt) under the collective pseudonym of Paule Riversdale: L'Etre double (1904) and Netsuké (1904). Yet, Vivien is also the author of some intriguing prose texts such as the short fiction and lesbian fairy tales of La Dame à la Louve (1904), the quasi-autobiographical novel Une femme m'apparut (1904), and the only recently published Anne Boleyn (1982), a short narrative whose intended publication in 1909 was halted by the author's death.

The significance of the oeuvre of this woman writer who refused to be condemned to "the ugliness of men" resides in her ability to transform standard decadent and symbolist myths and themes in terms of her female and lesbian sensitivities and eroticism. Thus, the Baudelairian "delicate art of vice," the decadent's sense of artifice and predilection for autumnal moods, the symbolist's fascination with death, religion and mysticism, and classical Sapphic and modern lesbian motifs combined to form Vivien's private poetic universe. The dream of a new Lesbos—which Renée Vivien and Natalie C. Barney briefly tried to realize during their stay on Lesbos (Mytilene) in 1904 in the form of an artistic enclave for lesbian poets and intellectuals—is, in this respect, the feminist and lesbian counterpart of the male ivory tower of, e.g., Mallarmé's "soirées" or the more solitary "refined *thébaïde*" of J.-K. Huysmans' *Des Esseintes*. Although Renée Vivien has never gained widespread acceptance for either her literary talents or her militant views on the role of women, she has increasingly been the object of attention of both gay and feminist intellectuals and academic scholars of the *fin-de-siècle*.

Works

For Renée Vivien's collected poems, see *Poèmes de Renée Vivien*, 2 vols. (1923–1924) or the one volume facsimile reprint by Arno Press in 1975. Short fiction: *La Dame à la Louve* (1904). Novel: *Une femme m'apparut* (1904). Goujon, Jean-Paul, ed., *Anne Boleyn* (1982). Translations by R. Vivien: *Sapho* (1903). *Les Kitharèdes* (1904). *Sapho et huit poétesses grecques* (1909). English translations: Foster, Jeannette H., tr., *A Woman Appeared to Me* (1976). Porter, Margaret, and Catherine Kroger, tr., *The Muse of the Violets* (1977). Belgrade, Sandia, tr., *At the Sweet Hour of Hand-in-Hand* (1979). Jay, Karla, and Yvonne M. Klein, tr., *The Woman of the Wolf* (1983).

Bibliography

Lorenz, Paul, *Sapho 1900, Renée Vivien* (1977) is the most recent bibliography of Renée Vivien. See also the pages devoted to her life and works in Cooper, Clarissa, *Women Poets of the Twentieth Century in France* (1943); Foster, Jeannette, *Sex Variant Women in Literature* (1956); Barney, Natalie C., *Traits et portraits* (1963); Klaich, Dolores, *Woman Plus Woman* (1974); Benstock, Shari, *Women of the Left Bank: Paris 1900-1940* (1986); the Introductions in Jeannette H. Foster, tr., *A Woman Appeared to Me* (1976); and Karla Jay and Yvonne M. Klein, tr., *The Woman of the Wolf* (1983). For bibliography of and about R. Vivien, see Paul Lorenz, *Sapho 1900, Renée Vivien* (1977), pp. 187–185.

Henk Vynckier

Héliette de Vivonne

Born ca. 1560, France; died 1625, France
Genre(s): poetry
Language(s): French

Héliette de Vivonne was the daughter of Charles II Vivonne and of Renée de Vivonne, a relative of his. Her father's high position allowed her access to the French court and in 1571, she was already a lady in waiting. By 1578, she was attached to the retinue of Queen Louise of Lorraine, where she remained even after her marriage in 1580 to Louis IV de Montbéron, baron of Fontaines. Although a cousin of Brantôme, Héliette would probably have remained in total obscurity were it not for a supposed liaison with Philippe Desportes.

It is her relationship to Desportes that brings Héliette to the center of a controversy. That she is the woman whom Desportes celebrates as "Cléonice" in the majority of the sonnets of his *Derniers Amours* (Last Loves) is clear. But are certain anonymous poems found scattered in a seventeenth-century manuscript that also contains poems by Desportes and others writers of the period by Héliette or by another of Desportes' "mistresses," Madeleine de L'Aubespine? The corpus is slim: a few religious sonnets, some diverse pieces and a group of sonnets that seem to be occasioned by an affair with Desportes. These love sonnets are typical of the era; there is little depth of emotion and they make extensive use of stock themes. They are not, however, without merit for they reflect a mastery of the conceits of the period and a talent for versification.

Although Ronsard refers to Héliette as "savante," she was not known during her lifetime as a poet. Moreover, she would have been only fifteen or sixteen when the exchange of sonnets began. While this is not conclusive evidence against her, especially when one takes into account the early marriage age among the nobility, the sonnets often speak with a worldly, mature voice. The attribution of the poems to Héliette relies principally on manuscript evidence that identifies the author of the poems with two interlocked V's which could stand for Vivonne and the "Cléonice" sonnets which link her to Desportes.

Works

Poésies d'Héliette de Vivonne (1932).

Bibliography

Lachèvre, Frédéric, ed., Poésies d'Héliette de Vivonne (Paris, 1932).

Edith J. Benkov

Eva Vlamē

(a.k.a. Eva Vlami)

Born 1914, Galaxeidi, Greece; died 1974
Genre(s): novel
Language(s): Greek

Eva Vlamē was the daughter of a sea captain and grew up at the port city of Galaxeidi on the Corinthian Gulf. She was married to Panagēs Lekatsas.

Her first work, Galaxeidi, is a chronicle of a small town that at the time of sailing ships was a very important port. Its former greatness and importance, however, live on in the memory of its townspeople. Vlamē's language is simple, but the life she describes is colorful; her knowledge of the sea and ease with words make this a very interesting tale of a very special place. O Skeletovrachos, her second novel, is a novel about the tragic life of an old sea captain, Skeletovrachos, who refuses to admit that the steam engine is preferable to the sails. He takes it upon himself to sail the ocean to prove that sails are superior. He dies just after he looks out of his window and sees the first steamship come into his home port, which is, again, Galaxeidi. Skeletovrachos is a representative of the man who is tuned to a different time and is unable to deal with the changes of the modern world. Although he dies, he is not totally defeated, for there lingers in the reader's mind an appreciation for the things he considers important.

Ta oneira tēs Angelikas deals with the years 1912–1922 in a way that is obviously and rigidly allegorical. Ston argaleio tou phengariou is about an old woman living in a small village. Her son is killed in the war, but she does not recognize the fact of his death and lives as if he were alive. She makes arrangements for his "marriage," dresses "his bride" in a wedding gown, and finally kills her. The characters lack psychological depth and

development, and the reader may not be moved to identify either with the pathological condition of the mother or with the fate of the "daughter-in-law-to-be." However, the book's significance (as suggested by the Bulletin analytique de bibliographie hellenique) has to be found on the level of myth, specifically, the myth of Persephone.

Vlamē is creative with words and good at descriptions of places and people; her importance as a writer lies in the fact that in her first two works she recorded a way of life that in the minds of many people is synonymous with Greece: sea life. Her works can serve as documents of this type of life and thus as starting points for further writing.

O Skeletovrachos has been translated into Romanian, and Ston argaleio tou phengariou has been translated into German.

Works

To Galaxeidi, chronicle (1947). O Skeletovrachos, novel (1949). Ta oneira tēs Angelikas [The Dreams of Angelica], allegorical novel (1958). Ston argaleio tou phengariou [At the Loom of the Moon], novel (1963, 1970).

Bibliography

Bulletin analytique de bibliographie hellènique, t. XXI 1970 (Athens, 1973). Mirasgezē, Maria, Neoellēnikē Logotechnia (Athens, 1982). Sachinēs, Apostolos, Neoi Pezographoi: Eikosi chronia neollēnikēs pezographias 1945–1965 (Athens, 1965).

Helen Dendrinou Kolias

Eva Vlami

(see: Eva Vlamē)

Suzanne Voilquin

Born December 17, 1801, Paris, France; died
late 1876 or early 1877, near Paris
Genre(s): journalism, autobiography
Language(s): French

Suzanne Monnier Voilquin is best known for her autobiographical writings, particularly her Souvenirs d'une fille du peuple and more recently for her Mémoires d'une Saint-Simonienne en Russie, which remained unpublished until 1979. Most of the biographical information we now possess comes from her own accounts. She sometimes signed letters as "Jeanne," "Jenny," or "Jeanne S. Voilquin."

Suzanne was the third of four children, and the first daughter, of Parisian skilled workers. Her father was a hatter and an enthusiastic participant in revolutionary politics during the Revolution. She attended a convent school for a few years, then was briefly in apprenticeship when she suffered a breakdown and returned home. Her mother turned over responsibility for her new little sister Adrienne when Suzanne was nine years old. During her teens she lost her religious faith.

In her early twenties, Suzanne was courted, seduced, and abandoned by a young medical student who had promised marriage. She later married Eugène Voilquin, who promptly infected her with venereal disease, thus thwarting her dreams of motherhood. In 1830 she and Voilquin joined the Saint-Simonian sect, and in 1832 she affiliated with a group of young working women to edit a paper, *La Femme libre*, defending the cause of women within and beyond Saint-Simonian circles. This paper, under various names, published 40 issues in the course of two years. Suzanne and her husband separated in early 1833 (divorce was illegal in France), and he left France for Louisiana with another woman. Later that year Suzanne took up the study of homeopathic medicine.

In 1834 Suzanne cast her lot with the Saint-Simonians who were going to Egypt. She became the community's laundress in Cairo. During an outbreak of plague she apprenticed herself to several resident French doctors and declared she had discovered her true vocation. She then apprenticed medicine in an Egyptian military hospital. In May 1836 she bore a child, but it died within the month. She then left Cairo for France and returned to Paris nearly penniless.

By her own account, Suzanne earned a diploma in midwifery from the Paris Faculty of Medicine in November 1837 and returned to the study of homeopathic medicine. As a midwife she supported her aged father as well as herself and attempted to found an association to aid unwed mothers. In 1839 she went to Russia, to seek her fortune by earning enough money to become economically independent, but the Russian climate inflicted severe stress on her health. She returned to Paris in 1846, re-established her midwifery practice, and engaged in various unsuccessful but pioneering attempts to found institutions that would expedite the hiring of wetnurses, aid midwives, etc.

After the collapse of the Revolution in 1848, she left France for Louisiana with her father and niece to nurse her mortally ill sister Adrienne. She remained there until 1859, but no record of these years has come down to us.

In 1865 Suzanne published her *Souvenirs*. These autobiographical writings cover her life up to her 1839 departure for Russia. She then consolidated the letters she had written to her sister from Russia with the notion of keeping them safe "until women have their own archives." These letters miraculously survived and found their way to the Bibliothèque Marguerite Durand; they were published as *Mémoires* in 1979. Suzanne's later years were plagued by ill health and she reportedly died in a convalescent home outside Paris.

Suzanne Voilquin's contribution to literature and history lies in her distinctive contribution to women's journalism and in her two published volumes, the *Souvenirs* and the *Mémoires*. These published writings provide exceptional records of the adventurous life of a gifted and articulate working-class Frenchwoman, blessed with a keen sense of womanly dignity and a heightened consciousness of the injustice of women's lot in nineteenth-century French society.

Works

Ed., *La femme libre* (also published under the titles, *La Femme de l'avenir*, *La Femme nouvelle*, *Tribune des femmes*, *L'Apostolat des femmes*, 1832–1833). Préface de Suzanne à Claire Demar, *Ma Loi d'avenir* (1834; rpt. 1976). Two articles in *La Providence*, August and October 1838 [concerning Suzanne's project for an association to aid unwed mothers]. *Souvenirs d'une fille du peuple, ou la Saint-Simonienne en Egypte, 1834 à 1836* (1866; rpt. 1978, with introduction by Lydia Elhadad). *Mémoires d'une Saint-Simonienne en Russie, 1839–1846*, présenté et annoté par Maïté Albistur and Daniel Armogathe (1979).

Translations: Excerpt from *Souvenirs d'une fille du peuple* in *Victorian Women: A Documentary Ac-*

count of *Women's Lives in Nineteenth-Century England, France, and the United States* (1981), from an unpublished annotated translation of the *Souvenirs* by Elizabeth C. Altman.

Bibliography

Adler, Laure, *A l'aube du féminisme: les premières journalistes (1830–1850)* (Paris, 1979). Albistur, Maïté, and Daniel Armogathe, "Preface and Notes" to Voilquin's *Mémoires* (Paris, 1979). Alkana, Linda Anne Kelly, "Suzanne Voilquin, Feminist and Saint-Simonian." Ph.D. dissertation, University of California, Irvine, 1985. University Microfilms 85-16535. Bulciolu, M.T., *L'Ecole Saint-Simonienne et la femme: Notes et documents* (Pisa, 1980). Elhadad, Lydia, "Introduction" to Voilquin's *Souvenirs* (1978). Elhadad, Lydia, "Femmes prénommées: les prolétaires Saint-Simoniennes rédactrices de 'La Femme libre' 1832–1834." *Les Révoltes logiques*, nos. 4–5 (1977). Grépon, Marguerite, *Une Croisade pour un meilleur amour; histoire des Saint-Simoniennes* (Paris, 1967). d'Ivray, Jehan [pseud. Jeanne Fahmy Bey], *L'Avventure Saint-Simonienne et les femmes* (Paris, 1930). Moses, Claire G., *French Feminism in the Nineteenth Century* (Albany, N.Y., 1984). Rancière, Jacques, "Une femme encombrante (à propos de Suzanne Voilquin)." *Les Révoltes logiques*, nos. 8–9 (1979). Thibert, Marguerite, *Le Féminisme dans le socialisme français de 1830 à 1850* (Paris, 1926).

Karen Offen

Galina Evgenievna Volianskaia

(a.k.a. Galina Evgenievna Nikolaeva)

Born 1911, Usmana, W. Siberia; died 1963, Siberia(?)
Genre(s): novel, publicity, criticism, poetry
Language(s): Russian

Galina Volianskaia is probably one of the most outstanding representatives of socialist realism in the Soviet Union. She lived on a collective farm for a large portion of her life, a result of which is her intimate familiarity with the lifestyle and habits of the people in such farms. Her descriptions of this way of life and of agricultural matters are imbued with a vitality and force

rather uncommon to her genre. Volianskaia began writing in the late 1930s. She had completed her training at medical school but was kept from practicing because of a heart ailment. In 1942 she was serving in an evacuation hospital when she began sending her verses to the journal *Znamia* (The Banner). Her first small collection of poems, *Skvoz' ogon'* (Through Fire), was published in that journal in 1946. She turned to prose almost immediately after this, responding to an imperative of the Party for engaged literature. Her first novel, *Zhatva* (The Harvest), appeared in 1950, for which she was awarded the Stalin Prize in literature in 1951. Other prose works followed, perhaps most successful of which was *Povest' o direktore MTS i glavnom agronome* (1955; The Manager of an MTS and the Chief Agronomist). This story was subsequently made into a play, which ran for quite a long time both in the provinces and in the capitals. In the mid-fifties her second cycle of poems appeared, called *Cherez desjatiletie* (After a Decade). In the same period her theoretical article, "O specifike khudozhestvennoi literatury" (On the Specific Character of Artistic Literature) was also published. Thus the provincial writer entered a well-rounded field of literary activities. In her artistic prose, Volianskaia's strongest point is her descriptive power, which she displays from the very first. The genre she works in rather constrains individual psychological motivation—the "cause" explains the heroism, the plot, etc. Nonetheless, she produces interludes of beautifully described natural phenomena, such as a snow-storm or a country landscape. Moreover, emotions are fully integrated into the otherwise formulaic fabric of the glorification of workers, which relieves the monotony of the socialist realistic occupation.

Works

Skvoz' ogon', stikhi (1946). *Sobranie sochinenie*, 3 vols. (1972). *Sil'nee l'dov; dokumental'naia povest' o ledovykh kapitanakh M.V. i N.M. Nikolaevykh* (1963).

Translations: *Vypraveni o dvou kolchozech*, tr. R. Havrankova, in *Svet sovetu* (1950). *Harvest*, novel (1952). *La siega* (1952). *Two Collective Farms: The Tractor Kolkhoz* (1952). *The Newcomer; the Manager of an MTS and the Chief Agronomist*, tr. D. Skvirsky (1955?). *Das Geständnis*, Erzählung, tr. M. Brichmann (1956). *Der Direktor und der Agronom* (1958). *L'ingenieur Bakhirev*, tr. G. Soria (1960). *Dopo la lunga notte*, tr. P. Zveteremich (1962). *Schlacht unterwegs*, E. Zunk, tr. (1963).

Bibliography

"O specifike khudozhestvennoi literatury," *Voprosy filosofii* 6 (1953).

Christine Tomei

Genrikhovna von Notenberg

(a.k.a. Elena Guro)

Born 1877, St. Petersburg, Russia; died May 6, 1913, Usikirko, Finland
Genre(s): poetry, drama
Language(s): Russian

Elena Guro was a skilled painter as well as a poet. In 1890, at the age of thirteen, Guro was enrolled in the Society for the Encouragement of the Arts in St. Petersburg, where she studied drawing and painting. She was a professional painter as well as a poet.

In 1904 she made her graphic debut when she was asked by a publisher to illustrate George Sand's *Grandmother's Tales*, and in 1905 she made her literary debut with the publication of a prose work, "Rannaja vesna" (Early Spring), in *Sobranie molodikh pisatelei* (Collection of Young Writers). Around 1909 Guro and her husband, Mikhail Matiushin (1861–1934), formed an avant-garde group, "Soyuz molodezhi" (Union of Youth), in St. Petersburg but shortly left it because of differences of opinion. At about this time a small circle of literary friends gathered around Guro and Matiushin, which included, among others, Viktor Khlebnikov (1885–1922) and Vladimir Mayakovsky (1893–1930). By 1909 Guro was already an established writer and artist and an influence on Khlebnikov and Mayakovksy. This can be seen in the early years of the artistic development of both artists, especially in work that deals with the cityscape.

In 1909 a collection of her poetry, *Sharmanka* (The Organ Grinder), came out in St. Petersburg. In 1910 her work appeared in the Cubo-Futurist publication *Sadok sudei* (I and II [A Trap for Judges I and II]). And in 1912, her *Osenij son* (Autumn Dream), a play, was published with her own illustrations. Just before her death in 1913 she was collecting material for a book titled *Troe* (The Three), which was going to feature the poetry of Khlebnikov, Kruchenyckh, and Guro, with drawings by Malevich. This collection of work came out posthumously. The last publication of her work was in 1914. This book of poetry and illustrations by Guro was entitled *Nebesnye verbluzhata* (The Little Camels of the Sky). Her last work, *Bednyj ritzar* (Poor Knight), is still unpublished.

Her "Autumn Dream," a play, is her only symbolist work (1912). She greatly admired the work of Aleksandr Blok—his poem *To The Beautiful Lady* and his plays. She also admired Andrei Bely's *Symphonies*.

Her poetry is impressionistic, focusing on her observations of everyday life. In the winter months, when she was in St. Petersburg, her subject became the city life around her: she wrote about her impressions on her walks through St. Petersburg, the people around her, the shop windows. And in the summers, when she was in her dacha in Usikirko, she would focus her attention on nature and on her personal experience and perceptions of it. But her work is always concentrated on the moment, the life and things of the tangible world. Her Cubo-Futurist period began around 1909, when she brought into her poetry the faceted and fragmented style of the Cubists, at times even attempting to introduce the monochromatic color of early analytic Cubism, off-white, as can be seen in her poem "Liyen" (Languor). But her most experimental poem is "Finlandia," where she works with different sounds and creates a landscape through them.

For most of her adult life Guro suffered from leukemia and, because of this, was not able to participate fully in the avant-garde movement of the time. Elena Guro continued as long as she did because she was a firm believer in the rejuvenating powers of creativity and nature.

Works

Sharmanka (1909). *Sadok Sudei I* (1910). *Osennii son* (1912). *Sadok Sudei II* (1912). *Troe* (1913). *Nebesnye Verbluzhata* (1914). "Gorod" (1914).
Translations: O'Brien, Kevin, *The Little Camels of the Sky* (Ann Arbor, Michigan, 1983).

Bibliography

Gusman, Boris, *Sto Poetov* (Tverv, 1923). Jensen, Kjeld Bjornager, *Russian Futurism, Urbanism and Elena Guro* (Arhus, Denmark, 1977). Markov, Vladimir, *Russian Futurism: A History* (Berkeley, Calif., 1968). Mirsky, Dimitrii S., *Contemporary Russian Literature* (York, 1926).

Galina McGuire

Teresa Albarelli Vordoni

Born 1788, Verona, Italy; died 1870, Venice
Genre(s): poetry, letters, sermons
Language(s): Italian

A great literary talent, Teresa Verdoni wrote epistles and sermons in the manner of G. Gozzi and I. Pindemonte, as well as a poem in octaves entitled "Il Pellegreno dell' adige in Terrasanta." In 1834, she was proclaimed one of the new muses of the Italian Parnassus in Pisa. Her prose works span several volumes.

Bibliography

Enciclopedia Universal Ilustrada (Madrid and Barcelona: Espasa-Calpe, S.A., Bilboa).

Jean E. Jost

N. Vozdvizhensky

(see: Nadezhda Khvoshchinskaia)

Alena Vrbová

Born 1919, Starý Plzenec, Czechoslovakia
Genre(s): poetry, prose, translation
Language(s): Czech

After studying at the philosophical and medical faculties of Charles University in Prague and working for a number of years as a doctor in Mariánské Lázně, Alena Vrbová turned to full-time writing. She made her literary début with the poetry collection *Řeka Na Cestásh* (1942; A River on the Road) and produced her first prose work in 1944—*My Dva* (The Two of Us). In her latest two novels she draws on Czech history as the central theme.

Works

Poetry: *Řeka Na Cestách* [A River on the Road] (1942). *Svár* [Contention] (1946). *A' Do Krve* [Till It Bleeds] (1957). *Cervený Listář* [Red Notebook] (1960). *Sondy a Písně* [Probes and Songs] (1963). *Antigony* [Antigone] (1969). *Blýskání Na Časy* [Lightning for the Good Times] (1974). *Odkud Přichází Hudba* [Where the Music Comes From] (1976).

Prose: *My Dva* [The Two of Us] (1944). *Drsné Povídky* [Rough Stories] (1964). *Dálkové Povídky* [Distant Stories] (1967). *Znova v Monte Rose* [In Monte Rosa Again] (1971). *Ostnaté Povídky* [Spiky Stories] (1972). *Benátská* [Departure for Madras] (1975). *Všechny Krásy Světa* [All the Beauties of the World] (1979). *A' Na Západní Hranici* [As Far as the Western Frontier] (1979). *V Erbu Lvice* [A Lioness in the Coat-of-Arms] (1977). *Kdy' Kohout Dozpíval* [When the Cock Stopped Crowing] (1980).

Poetry: *Z Čista Jasna. Verše z Let 1937–1967* (1973).

Warwick J. Rodden

Henny de Vreede

(a.k.a. Mischa de Vreede)

Born September 17, 1936, Batavia (present-day Djakarta)
Genre(s): poetry, novel, children's literature
Language(s): Dutch

Born in the former Dutch East Indies of missionary parents, Mischa de Vreede came to the Netherlands in 1946 after spending four years of her childhood in Japanese internment camps. From a very young age she was determined to become a writer.

Her first collection of poetry, *Met huid en hand* (1959; With Skin and Hand), is a pun on the Dutch expression "met huid en haar" ("haar" means hair) meaning "completely" and was an instant success. One of the poems was awarded the Poetry Prize of the city of Amsterdam. The unpretentious free verse, lacking punctuation and capital letters and deriving its poetic effect from casual alliteration and repetition, was considered refreshing after the elaborate, experimental poetry of the fifties generation in the

Netherlands, the so-called "Vijftigers." De Vreede's emphatic "bodily" imagery was, however, directly inspired by the Vijftigers. Her motifs were loneliness, the search for love and affection and, most prominently, the yearning to merge with the beloved. The melodious "groot slaaplied" ("great cradlesong"), in which the author expressed her desire to return to the unborn state of union with her daughter Catelijne, figures in a great number of anthologies today.

Mischa de Vreede later turned to prose and published various novels chronicling the difficulties and tensions that occur in relationships between men and women. Her main character is invariably a woman, wife and/or mistress, often caught between a desire for security and a desire for freedom and noncommitment. The protagonist tends to identify emancipation with "being candid about sex"—a trait she shares with other heroines of feminist fiction written in the seventies. De Vreede's prose, like her poetry, is unpretentious, fluent and simple, mimicking the reflections and broodings of the heroine, whose preoccupation with domestic routines and actions is often painstakingly reported.

Onze eeuwige honger (1973; Our Eternal Hunger), advertised on the cover as "a shameless tearjerker," pictures a lonely woman desperately longing for sex and affection. She picks the wrong friend and ends up committing suicide. *13—Een meisjesboek* (1976; 13—A Girls' Book), *Eindelijk mezelf* (1977; Finally Myself), and *Over* (1980) are meant as a trilogy portraying women at different crucial stages in their lives: Lili at thirteen, experiencing sexual awakening; Agaath, at thirty-three, enjoying divorce, men and freedom, willfully deciding to have the child of her married lover; and the former nude model Margot, at fifty-three, winning back her philandering husband after a life of patience and acceptance. The more polished story "*Van jou houd ik*" (1982; It's You I love) turned out to be a commercial success. It portrays an adulterous young woman whose husband, a tabloid journalist, is interested more in other people's sex lives than in his own. At the end the heroine decides to record her "confession" on tape to be sure to get through to him, only to find out later that she mistakenly erased one of his interviews instead of registering her own words.

In 1983–1984, Mischa de Vreede was writer-in-residence at Ann Arbor, Michigan. Her critical view of American society is expressed in *Persoonlijk* (1986; Personally), a collection of autobiographical sketches and poetry, and in the novel *Bevroren* (1985; Frozen) in which a middle-aged woman tries to cope with her husband's death, the rift with her daughter and her disillusion with the United States. De Vreede is also a writer of children's books (with a slightly moralizing touch), and she has translated work by Bellow and Kosinsky.

The critical acclaim Mischa de Vreede won for her poetry was never matched later. Frequently attacked for being trendy, boring, and picturing characters that lack depth and substance, her popular feminist fiction has nevertheless earned her a steady readership. Her most compelling and intense writing to date remains, however, *Een hachelijk bestaan* (1974; A Hazardous Existence), an "autobiographic collage" of her experiences as a child in Japanese internment camps and as a twice-divorced young mother of two trying to eke out a living. While some of her novels may date easily, Mischa de Vreede should be credited for the candor with which she writes about herself. It invests her work with a unique sense of authenticity and vulnerability.

Works

Met huid en hand (1959). *Eindeloos* (1961). *Oorlog en liefde* (1963). *Binnen en buiten* (1968). *Onze eeuwige honger* (1973). *Een hachelijk bestaan* (1974). *Eindeloos en verder* (1975; revised edition of *Eindeloos* and *Oorlog en liefde*). *Oude mensen in kinderboeken: een onderzoek naar het beeld van oude mensen in de jeugdliteratuur* (1976). *13—Een meisjesboek* (1976). *Eindelijk mezelf* (1977). *Over* (1980). *Mijn reis* (1981). "*Van jou hou ik*" (1982). *Het leven een film* (1984). *Bevroren* (1985). (As Henny de Vreede) *De afspraak* (1985). *Persoonlijk* (1986).

Bibliography

Bibeb, *Veertien vrouwen. Interviews* (1980). Bousset, H., *Woord en schroom* (1977).
General references: *De Nederlandse en Vlaamse auteurs van middeleeuwen tot heden* (1985). *Winkler Prins Lexicon der Nederlandse letterkunde* (1986).

Other references: Spoor, C., "Mischa de Vreede 'Ik zeg alleen maar: schrijven spaart de psychiater uit'" (interview). *De Tijd* (December 30, 1977).

Ria Vanderauwera

Mischa de Vreede

(see: Henny de Vreede)

Johanna Petronella Vrugt

(a.k.a. Anna Blaman)

Born January 31, 1905, Rotterdam; died July 13, 1960, Rotterdam
Genre(s): novel, short story, poetry
Language(s): Dutch

Trained as a teacher but of delicate health, Anna Blaman (pseudonym of Johanna Vrugt) spent her life devoted to literature. For almost thirty years, she lived with her mother and sister in Rotterdam in her mother's boardinghouse. Rented rooms (not quite home, not quite hotel) and a middle-class environment would serve as the background for her characters, whose experiences are different versions of the same elementary conflicts: unfulfilled desire, insurmountable loss, despair, physical pain, and, above all, loneliness.

After writing poetry in the romantic-realistic vein fashionable at the time, Anna Blaman soon turned definitively to prose and published in various literary journals.

Her breakthrough as a novelist came with her second novel *Eenzaam avontuur* (1948; Lonely Adventure). The outspokenness with which she treated passion, jealousy, and eroticism, the homosexual subplot, and the complex literary structure all combined to make it an instant *succès de scandale*. A bookshop in Rotterdam staged a mock tribunal acquitting the book, while Anna Blaman refused the Van der Hoogt Prize because her candidness had been deplored in the jury report. Today Blaman's prose style seems to be rather suggestive and restrained and only mildly experimental.

In *Eenzaam avontuur* the beautiful Alide leaves her husband Kosta for the hairdresser Peps, clearly Alide's inferior in Kosta's eyes. Hopelessly obsessed by Alide, Kosta begins to write a detective story in which the relationship between the detective King and the poisoner Juliette soon mirrors that between Kosta and Alide. In the end, King/Kosta frees himself from Juliette/Alide, and the manuscript is torn up. The book can also be read as an autobiographical *roman à clef*. Kosta is a male disguise for the author herself. Alide was modeled after Alie Bosch, a nurse Anna Blaman had fallen in love with when treated for an supposedly fatal kidney disease in 1936. Almost a decade later, Alie Bosch "left" Anna Blaman for a dancing teacher. Like Kosta, Anna Blaman came to terms with this loss and betrayal by writing a book. The friendship between the two women was resumed later and lasted till Anna Blaman's death of a cerebral embolism in 1960.

Physical disease and the nursing care of women are recurring motifs in Anna Blaman's work. Alie Bosch (the source for the pen name *Anna Blaman?*) continued to be the main inspiration for the (either redeeming or destroying) women characters, such as Stella, who leaves the journalist Stefan in *Op leven en dood* (1954; A Matter of Life and Death), and Driekje, whom Kostiaan falls in love with after his unfaithful wife's death in the posthumous and unfinished novel *De verliezers* (1960; The Losers).

In the 1980s, Anna Blaman's lesbianism began to receive serious attention. An anonymous short story published in *De homosexuelen* (an anthology of 1939) about a myopic and sickly girl who falls in love with a beautiful yet unattainable young woman, was identified as Anna Blaman's and included in a recent collection of her short stories, *Droom in oorlogstijd* (1985; Dream in War Time). *Affaire B* (1985), a theatrical adaptation of *Eenzaam Avontuur* played by an all-women cast, emphasized the homosexual subplot.

Sometimes pictured as a sad and lonely woman living in the isolation of her mother's bleak guesthouse, Anna Blaman actually had many friends seeking her advice, took active part in the literary life of Rotterdam, and collaborated with the town's theater company as a dramaturge. She published various articles and gave lectures.

She spent short periods of time in France and was a great admirer of the French existentialists.

Her characters' attempt to understand the essence of man's existence amidst loneliness and despair and, failing to do so, to forge a life of acceptance, courage, and human dignity make Anna Blaman's work akin to that of her French contemporaries. She received the prose prize of the city of Amsterdam twice. The P.C. Hooft Prize awarded to her for her entire oeuvre in 1957 marked her recognition as a major modern Dutch novelist.

Works

> *Vrouw en vriend* (1941). *Ontmoeting met Selma* (1943). *Eenzaam avontuur* (1948). *De Kruisvaarder* (1950). *Ram Horna en andere verhalen* (1951). *Op leven en dood* (1954). *Overdag en andere verhalen* (1957). *De verliezers* (1960). *Verhalen* (1963). *Anna Blaman over zichzelf en anderen*, eds. A. Kossman and C. Lührs (1963). *Anna Blaman Fragmentarisch*, ed. Henk Struyker Boudier (1978). *In duizend vrezen*. Vier wagenspelen, Eds. A.J.M. Meinderts and M.A. Th. Zoetmulder (1983). *Droom in oorlogstijd,* ed. A. Meinderts (1985). *Drie Romans* (1985).
> Translations: *A Matter of Life and Death* [*Op leven en dood*], tr. A. Dixon (1974).

Bibliography

Anna Blaman. Informatie en herinneringen (Literair Moment) (1985). Dinaux, C.J.E., *Herzien bestek* (1974). Haasse, H. and Kossmann, A., *Anna Blaman. Twee lexingen* (1961). Lührs, C., *Mijn zuster Anna Blaman* (1976). *Schrijvers blootshoofds* (1956). *Schrijvers prentenboek* 8 (1962). Struyker Boudier, H.M.A., *Speurtocht naar een onbekende. A. Blaman en haar Eenzaam avontuur* (1973). Struyker Boudier, H.M.A., *Anna Blamans Op leven en dood* (1984). Van Marissing, L., "Anna Blaman en het literair existentialisme." *Te elfder ure* 21 (1974). General references: *Cassell's Encyclopaedia of World Literature. De Nederlandse en Vlaamse auteurs van middeleeuwen tot heden* (1985). Ross, L., in *Kritisch Lexicon van de Nederlandstalige Literatur na 1945* (1981). *Moderne encyclopedie van de wereldliteratuur* (1980–1984). *Winkler Prins Lexicon der Nederlandse letterkunde* (1986). Other references: Brunt, E., "De erfenis van Anna Blaman." *Haagse Post* (March 15, 1980). *Literama* 13 (special issue on Anna Blaman, Nov./Dec. 1978).

Ria Vanderauwera

Caroline Vuïet

(see: Caroline Wuïet, Baronne Auffdiener)

Ileana Vulpescu

Born 1932, Bratolovești (Dolj), Romania
Genre(s): novel, short story, lexicology, translation
Language(s): Romanian

Ileana Vulpescu graduated at the Bucharest University (Department of Philology) in 1958. Since 1959 she has worked at the Institute of Linguistics in Bucharest as a member in the team of lexicologists that revises, completes and publishes the prestigious Thesaurus dictionary of the Romanian language—*Dicţionarul limbii romăne.*

Vulpescu made her debut in *Familia* in 1966. In 1969 she published a volume of metaliterary short stories entitled *ș.a.m.d.* (a.s.o.) in which it is the narrative conventions and their ground rather than the stories which capture the author's attention.

Vulpescu's outstanding novel *Rămas bun* (1975; Leavetaking) tells a nineteenth-century Bucharest story of compulsive buying and selling of wives and husbands. The narration skillfully moves back and forth with physician Şerban's memories of, as he sells with no profit, his old, decayed, but once splendid house, and the four generations which had successively inhabited the house since the second quarter of the nineteenth century until the years immediately following the installation of the communist regime. After having built the house, Kir Costi Mavros, a rich Greek merchant in grain and cheese and owner of innumerable local tanneries and mills married, at forty-six, eighteen-year-old Melina Arghiropol, the intelligent and sturdy daughter of a poor Greek pretzel baker from Galaţi. Letting herself be bought, Melina had unconsciously hoped for an enhancement of her life, envisioning new outlets to her bursting vitality. She had to slowly understand, in twenty-four years of confinement spent with vampirically mean and sickly Mavros that in the buyer-seller marriage it is always the seller who loses in the end. When Costi dies, secretly passionate Melina, more than forty years old herself, becomes the rich and stylish merchant widow that impoverished aristocrat and universal broker Veta Krețulescu would like to pair with her dissipated young nephew Ienache Krețulescu. Ienache had spent in Paris the considerable fortunes of his father and mother and had returned to Bucharest a poor dandy. While melancholically accepting the role of the buyer this time, Melina will originally and convincingly combine in one person the strong undaunted owner of the money which has eaten her youth with the stoic aging wife who tries to minimize the harmful effects of the marriage mechanism she knows so well and to protect distracted, passive, and handsome Ienache against himself. She will die as she lived, lonely, lucid and firm, enjoining her husband to marry beautiful young Agripina whom she knows he loves. Agripina is both the opposite and the equivalent of Melina. As the youngest daughter of a ruined aristocratic family, she had been sold, at age fourteen, to rich, much older Sache Poenaru. Careless Sache, a gentle aesthete, will die a sudden death, seven years later, after having initiated his child-wife into the beauty of gracious tenderness and art but without having in the least ensured her future. Sache's daughters—who are both older than Agripina—seize the inheritance. Poor again, Agripina chooses freedom and love over the hunt of another rich husband with the help of forever available Veta Krețulescu. She will open a successful business as a *modiste*, live the forcedly adventurous life of an irresistible soft woman until she encounters Ienache, devote to him all the energies of her soul during two years of secret love and marry him after Melina's death, under the unavoidable brokerage of tireless old Veta. Like Melina, Agripina will know a shrinking, poisonous marriage. This time it is Ienache's mother, Catița Krețulescu, who destroys expected happiness around her. Agripina, who does not have Melina's clout and tenacity, will die leaving to daughter Luxița the task of trying to live her life alive. In contradistinction to elegant Melina

and poignant Agripina, Luxița is refreshingly ugly; like the first, whom she will often evoke, she is an energetic, clever and poised business woman who dominates father Ienache (turned, in the meantime, into an Oblomov-like compulsive eater), marries a decent husband and lives to be one hundred years old. The fourth generation, represented by Luța Șerban, the physician's mother, has lost the color and appeal of the previous ones.

Vulpescu's is a complex social novel in which the cynical symbiosis between an irresponsibly passive local aristocracy and the new, often Greek, bourgeoisie or the lazy confrontation between old and young generations mingle with the hopes and deceptions brought forth by the French and Romanian 1848 revolutions and by Cuza's post-Union attempts at social reform in a climate of nostalgic failure and careless vitality.

The author translated into Romanian works by Maurois, Simone de Beauvoir, A. Wurmser, A. Vollard, J. Defradas, J.R. Jimenez, J. Hamman and Samuel Pepys' *Journal*. She translated from Romanian into French works by Ioan Alexandru, Radu Boureanu, Constanța Buzea, Nina Cassian, Șt. Aug. Doinaș, Eugen Jebeleanu, Al. Philippide, Nichita Stănescu, Virgil Teodorescu, Romulus Vulpescu, etc.

Works

ș.a.m.d. [a.s.o.] (1969). *Rămas bun* [Leavetaking] (1975).

Bibliography

Popa, Marian, *Dicționar de literatură română contemporană* (2nd ed., Bucharest, 1977), p. 620.

Sanda Golopentia

Beb Vuyk

Born February 11, 1905, Delfshaven-Rotterdam, The Netherlands
Genre(s): short story, novel, children's literature
Language(s): Dutch

In her mid-twenties Beb Vuyk left the Netherlands, the country of her birth, to teach in the Dutch East Indies. Partly of Indian descent herself, she married in 1932 into a Molucca family. The East Indies became her new fatherland and the setting, if not the subject, of her writing. She spent the war years in a Japanese internment camp with her two sons. After the transfer of sovereignty (Dutch to Indonesian) in 1949, Vuyk and her husband, who had been confirmed nationalists, took out Indonesian citizenship. Their position as socialists and opponents of the Sukarno regime became untenable, however, and they returned to the Netherlands in 1958.

Beb Vuyk's early short stories (published in the Dutch journal *De Vrije Bladen*) were still written in the literary fashion of the 80s and 20s in Holland: the language was deliberately artificial, the tone solemn, and the metaphors often exaggerated and farfetched. Later Vuyk developed her own style: simple, natural, and rhythmic prose that has the authentic ring of the real storyteller.

All of Vuyk's work is inspired by her own life and experiences. Fascination with a rugged and venturesome pioneer's existence in the Moluccas—part of the colony that had seldom received attention in literature—underlies her first novel, *Duizend eilanden* (1937; A Thousand Islands), and the overtly autobiographical *Het laatste huis van de wereld* (1939; The Last House in the World). The duality between a life of adventure (inevitably burdened by bureaucracy) runs through both works. *Het laatste huis van de wereld*, which is based on letters Vuyk wrote her parents, is a gripping chronicle of the years she and her husband spent on the remote island of Buru trying to cultivate a paperbark tree plantation. The intensity of the couple's life is contrasted with their fear and panic in moments when the protective security of civilization is missed most as when the wife delivers her baby without proper medical assistance.

In her third and last novel, *Het hout van Bara* (1947; The Wood from Bara), Beb Vuyk fictionalizes her fight with a colonial civil servant who nearly bankrupted her and her husband. But the book, which was written in Japanese internment camps, transcends the traditional East Indian conflict between the colonial administration and the local population and addresses broader issues like injustice and abuse of power.

Vuyk's remaining work consists mainly of short stories (the form she mastered best) and travel reports. The stories collected in *Gerucht en geweld* (1959; Sound and Fury) are poignant comments on the meaningless violence and the atrocities she witnessed or heard of during the Japanese occupation and the Indonesian revolution. The social and cultural identity problem of the Indos—Western-educated East Indians of mixed descent (a group to whom Vuyk herself belonged through marriage)—is the main theme of two well-structured stories published under the title *De eigen wereld en die andere* (1969; Our Own World and the Other).

Beb Vuyk also published literary and journalistic work in Dutch progressive journals and papers (trying to explain the Indonesian point of view) and in the anti-Sukarno *Indonesian Raja*. (Her militant pro-Indonesian stance earned her many enemies in Holland.) She is the author of popular culinary columns and bestselling Indonesian cookbooks.

The critical response to Vuyk's literary work has been divided and hesitant. She is a slow and unprolific writer (claiming that life is more important for her than writing). Her aversion to descriptive prose and the absence of exoticizing and nostalgic elements in her writing—except for the travel book *Reis naar het "vaderland in de verte"* (1983; Journey to the "Fatherland in the Distance"), based on a visit to Indonesia in 1981–1982—put her outside the mainstream of both Dutch and Dutch East Indian literature. Only recently, since the publication of her collected works in 1972 (barely 500 pages) and the award of the prestigious Constantijn Huygens Prize in 1973, she has gained the doubtful reputation of "underestimated" author. She is now not only appreciated for her polished (for some, too polished) short stories but also for her engaging novels of adventure. She has been likened to writers like Kipling, Stevenson, and Conrad, much to Vuyk's own delight, for whom it is a belated recognition of her originality in contemporary Dutch letters.

Several of her stories, among them the children's book *De kinderen van Boeton Leon* (1949), have been translated into Indonesian. *Het laatste huis van de wereld*, considered her best work, was rendered into English for the

Library of the Indies, a series of Dutch colonial literature in translation.

Works

Vele namen (1932). Duizend eilanden (1937). Het laatste huis van de wereld (1939). De wilde groene geur van het avontuur (1941; 1962 as De wilde groene geur). Het hout van Bara (1947). De kinderen van Boeton Leon (1949). Gerucht en geweld (1959). De eigen wereld en die andere (1969). Een broer in Brazilië (1971). Verzameld werk (1972). Reis naar het "vaderland in de verte" (1983).

Translations: The Last House in the World [Het laatste huis van de wereld], tr. A. Lefevere and E.M. Beekman, in Two Tales of the East Indies (1983).

Bibliography

Beekman, E.M., Introduction to Two Tales of the East Indies (1983). Du Perron, E., Verzameld Werk 6 (1958). Nieuwenhuys, R., Oost-Indische Spiegel (1972). Ter Braak, M., Verzameld Werk 6 and 7 (1949–1951). Veenstra, J.H.W., "Beb Vuyks leven op avontuur." Ons Erfdeel 16 (1973). De Vlaamse Gids 69, No. 4 (1985; special issue).

General references: De Nederlandse en Vlaamse auteurs van middeleeuwen tot heden (1985). Kritisch Lexicon van de Nederlandstalige Literatuur na 1945 (article on Vuyk by E. Drayer). Moderne encyclopedie van de wereldliteratuur (1980–1984). Winkler Prins Lexicon der Nederlandse letterkunde (1986).

Ria Vanderauwera

Mme. de Vxxx

(see: Gabrielle-Suzanne Barbot Gallon, dame de Villeneuve)

Vyzandis

(see: Alexandra Papadopoulou)

W

Jacqueline E. van der Waals

(a.k.a. U.E.V. [Una ex Vocibus])

Born 1868; died 1922
Genre(s): poetry, novel, translation
Language(s): Dutch

The daughter of a Nobel Prize winner, Jacqueline van der Waals was well educated; in addition to Dutch, French, German, and English, she knew Swedish, Danish, Norse, and Italian. She wrote essays about Selma Lagerlöf, Ibsen, and Kierkegaard. She obtained a degree in history but found a teacher's existence hard to bear and instead went into practical social work.

She wrote one autobiographical novel, *Noortje Velt* (1907), whose protagonist is called Ursula Eleonora Velt (E.U.V.). In it she attempts to answer the question of how to find one's way in life despite isolation and uncertainty.

Her poetry is marked by a love of nature, the poet's relation to God, and a certain fascination with death as well as existential doubt and devotion to God. She saw poetry as a divine vocation and felt God's spirit in her when she was writing poetry. Her collections of poetry were so popular that they went through several reprints during her lifetime, something very unusual in the Netherlands.

She also wrote or translated a number of Christian hymns. Some of them, like "Wat de toekomst brengen moge" ("Whatever the Future May Bring"), are included in the Dutch *Liedboek voor de kerken* (Hymns for the Churches) and still sung.

Works

Verzen (1900). *Nieuwe verzen* (1909). *Laatste verzen* (1923). *Gebroken kleuren* (1939). *De mooiste gedichten van Jaqueline van der Waals* (1979). *Een bloemlezing uit haar werk* (1982). *Silhouetten* (1982). *Wat de toekomst brengen moge* (1982).

Bibliography

Moerman, Josien, *Lexicon Nederlandtalige auteurs* (1984), p. 255. Werkman, Hans, "Jacqueline van der Waals," in '*Tis vol van schatten hier*, vol. 1 (Amsterdam, 1986), pp. 197–198.

Maya Bijvoet

Elly de Waard

Born 1940
Genre(s): poetry, literary criticism, translation
Language(s): Dutch

Elly de Waard studied Dutch literature and was always interested in poetry but did not start writing seriously until after the death of her lover of many years, the nature poet Chr. van Geel (1917–1974).

Her poems have appeared in the literary journals *De Revisor*, *De Gids*, *Bzzlltin* and *Avenue literair*. She is a critic for the national newspapers *De Volkskrant* and *Vrij Nederland* and has published translations of poems by Emily Dickinson, *Westers* (1980; Occidentals).

She writes carefully chiseled verses about the universal themes of love, death, life, mother, longing, and the past. Initially in romantic poems full of memories of the deceased beloved, then about inner unrest, torment, and love, and lately more about language and poetry.

Works

Afstand (1978). Luwte (1979). Furie (1981). Strofen (1983).

Bibliography

Meulenbelt, Anja, ed., *Wie weegt de woorden. De auteur en haar werk* (Amsterdam, 1985), pp. 172–191, 229.

Maja Bijvoet

Melanie Waldor

Born June 28, 1796, Nantes, France; died
*   October 11, 1871, Paris*
Genre(s): poetry, novel, drama
Language(s): French

Melanie Waldor is known chiefly for her association with two of the great literary figures of the nineteenth century, Alexandre Dumas *père* and Victor Hugo. It was five years after her marriage to Francois Waldor in 1822 that she met and fell in love with the elder Dumas. Their love, detailed in a series of letters, lasted from 1827 to 1831. After the affair was over, Waldor was left to the "cold" love of her husband. This period was a most productive one, with four of her major works appearing in the next decade, including *Anna* (1833), *Poèsie du coeur* (1835; Poetry of the Heart), and *Pages de la vie intime* (1836; Pages of the Intimate Life). It is no coincidence that most of these works contain a Dumas-like hero. It was after this period that she became friends with Victor Hugo, an association that lasted into the early 1850s. Much of her latter work is in a comic vein, including two vaudevilles—*La tirelire de Jeanette* (1859; The Fate of Jeanette) and *La mère Grippetout* (1861; Mother Grippetout).

Works

L'Ecuyer Dauberon ou l'oratoire de Bonsecours (1831). Anna (1833). Poesie du coeur (1835). Richesse et pauvrete par Madame Wanderbuck (1835). Pages de la vie intime (1836). Alphonse et Juliette (1839). L'Ecole des jeunes filles (1841). Seance extraordinaire de la Societe de la Morale chretienne (1846). Louis Napoleon dans le Midi (1852). La tirelire de Jeanette (1859). La mère Grippetout (1861).

Bibliography

Lettres inedites de Mme. Waldor (1905). Schopp, Claude, *Lettres d'Alexandre Dumas a Melanie Waldor* (1982).

Stephen Wood

Wallādah bint al-Mustakfī

Born 994, southern Spain; died 1077 or 1091
Genre(s): lyric poetry
Language(s): Arabic

The immortality of this poet and patron of writers in Arab-dominated southern Spain has been preserved primarily by the poems of Ibn Zaidūn, one of which (his *qaṣīda* in *nūn*) the distinguished Spanish authority Emilio García-Gómez has called the most beautiful work of all Hispano-Arabic love poetry. Fragments of this poem appear anonymously in the famous *A Thousand and One Nights*.

Princess Wallādah (literally "fecund") was the daughter of the Calif of Cordova, Muhammad III al-Mustakfī, an abusive ruler whose seventeen-month reign ended when he was poisoned in 1025. At age thirty Wallādah inherited a fortune and made her home a popular gathering place for fellow writers. She enjoyed great notoriety and was a remarkable woman for her circumstances. The works of her contemporary, the renowned philosopher Ibn Hazam, and those of Ibn Bassām in the following generation, testify to her fame. She was reputed to be exceptionally beautiful, with light skin, blue eyes, and blondish-red hair. Historians report that her character was likewise exceptional—volatile, independent, and marked by extreme passions, as demonstrated by her defying precepts of the *Koran* (such as refusing to wear a veil), by her leaving the harem, by the verses she had embroidered on her robe ("I . . . bestow my kiss on him who craves it"), and by her possibly lesbian friendship with the poetess Muhga.

Wallādah's most tender and personal poems are those written in her late thirties, at the beginning of her intriguing and scandalous relationship with Ibn Zaidūn (1003–1071). These verses, using frequent images from nature, constitute a bold and exquisite confession of feminine passion: "I feel a love for you that, if felt by the stars, the sun would not shine." After only a few months, however, she became jealous of her black maid and rejected the poet to form a new alliance with the wealthy and influential vizier Abū '"mir ibn 'Abdūs. Although she never married, eventually she went to live in Ibn 'Abdūs' harem and lived to be quite old.

Wallādah's poems are significant for the insights they offer into a writer of remarkable creativity, intelligence, freedom, education, and stature. She was an accomplished poet in her own right; nevertheless, her few extant poems are published almost exclusively in collections of Ibn Zaidūn's works. Likewise, critical analyses of her verses are scant and appear most often in conjunction with his writings.

Bibliography

Cour, Auguste, *Un poète arabe d'Andalousie: Ibn Zaidoûn* (Constantine, 1920). García Gómez, Emilio, *Qaşīdas de Andalucía, puestas en verso castellano* (Madrid, 1940). Garulo, Teresa, *Dīwān de las poetisas de al-Andalus* (Madrid, 1985). González Palencia, Ángel, *Historia de la literatura arábigo-española* (2nd ed. Barcelona, 1945), pp. 67–72. Nykl, A.R., *Hispano-Arabic Poetry and Its Relations with the Old Provençal Troubadours* (Baltimore, 1946), pp. 106–121. Sobh, Mahmud, ed., *Poetisas arábigo-andaluzas* (Granada, 1986).

Lee Arthur Gallo

Judith Walter

(see: [Louise-Charlotte-Ernestine]
    Judith Gautier)

W.G.E. Walter

(see: Virginie Loveling)

Judith Walther

(see: [Louise-Charlotte-Ernestine]
    Judith Gautier)

Maxie Wander

Born 1933, Vienna, Austria; died 1977,
    Kleinmachnow/Berlin, East Germany
Genre(s): documentary literature, journal,
    letters
Language(s): German

Maxie Wander's work played a pivotal role in the development of the new body of women's literature produced in the German Democratic Republic (GDR) in the course of the 1970s. It contributed significantly to, and is itself emblematic of, the growing and, from mid-decade on, increasingly publicly articulated consciousness among GDR women of the ways in which their lives as citizens within a socialist state are shaped by sexual politics as well.

Born 1933 in Vienna, Wander worked as a secretary, photographer, and journalist; she wrote screenplays and short stories. In 1958 she moved to the GDR, where she lived with her husband, the Austrian writer Fred Wander, and their children until her death of cancer in 1977. As a writer, Wander became known primarily for two important documentations: *Guten Morgen, du Schöne. Protokolle nach Tonband* (1977; Good Morning, My Lovely. Tape-recorded Interviews), a documentary of GDR women's lives from the perspective of the 1970s, and *Tagebücher und Briefe* (1978; Journals and Letters), a record of her own life's journey through illness toward death.

Guten Morgen, du Schöne is a collection of minimally edited autobiographical sketches of seventeen contemporary GDR women. The women interviewed range in age from sixteen to seventy-four; they live a variety of different life styles; many of them are mothers; almost all of them work. Unlike previous "documentations" about life in the GDR, these stories are no longer measured by the standards of Socialist Realism; instead they are based on the authenticity of each individual's different and subjectively rendered experience. In its acknowledgement of difference and its insistently subjective definition of "truth," this collection of life stories by women speaking out in their own voices and unafraid to be critical of either their own or their society's shortcomings, marked a turning-point in the history of GDR women's culture. In her foreword "Berührung"

(In Touch) Christa Wolf describes *Guten Morgen, du Schöne* as exemplary of the belief in a concrete utopia that is at once a socialist and a feminist ideal; a society in which women and men are striving to live fully as human beings, subjects of a history they are in the process of shaping.

Wander's *Tagebücher und Briefe*, posthumously published and edited by her husband, recreates the texture of Wander's daily life as a woman and a writer and an Austrian expatriate in the GDR. Divided into three parts, the letter and diary selections span events from 1968 to 1977. Part I describes her treatment (mastectomy and radiation therapy) for breast cancer in 1976, her fear of pain and death and her struggle to come to terms with a body that has been mutilated. Part II records her engagement, emotionally, intellectually, and politically, with the lives of people around her. The immediacy of Wander's style makes palpable the intimacy of a life shared with family and friends: her unresolved grief over the fatal accident of her young daughter, the continuing balancing act of her marriage, the sustaining quality of her friendship with her colleague Christa Wolf. Part III tells a story of a life lived richly and fully, even as the writer is in the physical process of dying. Wander's writing is marked by an extraordinary degree of self-consciousness, always balanced between her writer's perception that life, in a sense, is a book, and her knowledge that writing itself grows out of the rich and complex materiality of common lives simply lived. This doubled sense of herself as both observer and participant in her own and other's lives blurs the boundary between autobiography and documentary in Wander's texts. As her reflections on death—her own and that of her child—show, living to her means being attentive to the significance of the minutia of everyday life: "Actually every woman is interesting when one has the energy to pay attention to her."

Works

> *Guten Morgen, du Schöne. Protokolle nach Tonband* [Good Morning, My Lovely: Tape-Recorded Interviews] (1977; West German ed.: *Guten Morgen, du Schöne. Frauen in der DDR* [1978]). [With Fred Wander], *Provenzalische Reise* [Visit to the Provence] (1978). *Tagebücher und Briefe* [Journals and Letters], ed. Fred Wander (1980;

West German ed.: *Leben wär' eine prima Alternative: Tagebuchaufzeichnungen und Briefe* [Life Would Be a Great Alternative: Journal Notes and Letters] [1980]).

Bibliography

Hilzinger, Sonja, *"Als ganzer Mensch zu leben . . ."* *Emanzipatorische Tendenzen in der neueren Frauen-Literatur der DDR* (Frankfurt, 1985), pp. 192–215. Lennox, Sara, "'Nun ja! Das nächste Leben geht aber heute an.' Prosa von Frauen und Frauenbefreiung in der DDR," in Peter-Uwe Hohendahl and Pat Herminghouse, eds., *Literatur der DDR in den siebziger Jahren* (Frankfurt/Main, 1983), pp. 224–258. Schröder, Claus B., "Gerammelt voll Leben." *Neue Deutsche Literatur* 4 (1978). Stahl, Sigrid, *Der Ausbruch des Subjekts aus gesellschaftlicher Konformität* (Frankfurt, 1984), pp. 209–225. Wolf, Christa, "Zum Tod von Maxie Wander." *Die Dimension des Autors: Christa Wolf Aufsätze, Essays, Gespräche, Reden.* Vol. 1 (Weimar, 1986), pp. 210–213.

Angelika Bammer

Ellen Warmond
(a.k.a. Pieternella Cornelia van Yperen)

Born 1930
Genre(s): poetry, novel
Language(s): Dutch

Ellen Warmond is known primarily as a poet. Her poetry is born out of a longing for stillness, fixity, equilibrium, and the absence of conscious ambition, which strikes an Oriental note in Dutch literature.

This longing is evident even in her earlier collections like *Weerszij van een wereld* (1957; On the Other Side of a World). In *Proeftuin* (1953; Garden) modern means of communication like letters, telephones, and radio stations are used as metaphors for the poet's suffocating sense of non-communication, her sense of being alienated and separate, alone in a void.

Warmte, een woonplaats (1961; Warmth, A Place to Live) contains her most beautiful love poems. Warmond states that one ought to build one's "place to live" in between love and one's awareness of it, not in love itself. But what man strives for is unattainable. The hero of "De

Nadagen van Prometheus" ("The Aftermath of Prometheus" in *Proeftuin*) must die when he is but two steps removed from the truth. Warmond's vision of skeptical humanism expresses itself in irony throughout.

With the years, she has felt an increasing need to turn inward and strive toward the annihilation of the will. She interrogates the silence that will give no answers. This is the closing of the mirror, as she calls it in *Gesloten spiegels* (1979; Closed Mirrors). These Oriental ideas, however, cannot eliminate Western reality, which keeps intruding in the poems.

This striving for simplicity and balance of thought and feeling is parallelled by an increased simplicity of form. Warmond's short poems are extremely concise and concentrated, containing but a few, very effective metaphors.

Works

Poetry: *Proeftuin* (1953). *Naar men zegt* (1955). *Weerszij van een wereld* (1957). *Warmte, een woonplaats* (1961). *Het struisvogelreservaat* (1963). *De huid als raakvlak* (1964). *Testbeeld voor koud klimaat* (1966). *Geen bloemen/geen bezoek* (1968). *Mens: een inventaris* (1969). *De groeten aan andersdenkenden* (1970). *Voorkeur/willekeur* (1972, work of thirty poets with E. Warmond's commentary). *Saluutschot met knaldemper* (1972). *Beestenboel* (1973). *Uitzicht op inzicht* (1974). *Gesloten spiegels* (1979). *Ordening* (1981). *Vragen stellen aan de stilte* (1984).

Prose: *Paspoort voor niemandsland* (1961). *Eeuwig duurt het langst* (1961). *Van kwaad tot erger* (1968).

Bibliography

Macken, Lieve, "Acrobatieën boven het veilige vangnet cerebraliteit." *Nieuw Vlaams Tijdschrift* 26 (1973): 133–145. Ouboter, C., "Dichterdriehoek." *Ontmoeting* XV (1962): 50–58. Vegt, Jan van der, "Skepsis in het kwadraat." *Ons Erfdeel* 14, iii: 114–115. Vegt, Jan van der, "Kijken in een gesloten spiegel: Notities bij de poëzie van Ellen Warmond." *Ons Erfdeel* 24(5) (Dec. 1981): 655–664.

Maya Bijvoet

Maria Waser

Born October 15, 1878, Herzogenbuchsee near Bern, Switzerland; died January 19, 1939, Zurich
Genre(s): novel, short story, autobiography, biography, poetry, letters
Language(s): German

Her father was the medical doctor Walther Krebs. She studied history and German literature at the Universities of Lausanne and Bern, Switzerland, and graduated with a Ph.D. From 1902 until 1904 she travelled in Italy and then worked as an editor for the cultural journal *Die Schweiz* (Switzerland) since 1904, founded by her teacher and later husband, the archeologist Otto Waser, in Zurich. She travelled widely through France, England, Germany, and Greece throughout her life.

Works

Die Politik von Bern, Solothurn und Basel 1466–1468 [Politics of Bern, Solothurn and Basel, 1466–1468], historical study (1902). *Henzi und Lessing* [Henzi and Lessing], literary study (1903). *Nachspiel zu Schuhmanns "Der Rose Pilgerfahrt"* [Epilogue to Schumann's "Rose's Pilgrimage"], study (1908). *Die Geschichte der Anna Waser* [Anna Waser's Story of Her Life], novel (1913; rpt. 1978). *Das Jätvreni*, short story (1917). *Scala Sancta* [Sacred Staircase], short story (1918). *Von der Liebe und vom Tod* [About Love and Death], short story (1920). *Wir Narren von Gestern* [We Fools of Yesterday] (1922). *Das Gespenst im Antistitium* [The Ghost in the Antistitium], short story (1924). *Wege zu Hodler* [Introduction to Hodler], study in art history (1927). *J. von Widmann* [*Die Schweizer im deutschen Geistesleben*, vol. 46 and 47], study (1927). *Der heilige Weg–Bekenntnis zu Hellas* [The Sacred Path—Dedications to Hellas] (1928). *Wende* [Turning Point], novel (1929). *Land unter Sternen* [Country Beneath the Stars), novel (1930). *Begegnung am Abend* [Encounter in the Evening] (1933). *Sinnbild des Lebens* [Symbol of Life], autobiography (1936). *Das besinnliche Blumenjahr* [The Meditative Year of Flowers), poems (1939). *Nachklang, aus dem Nachlaß ausgewählt von ihrem Gatten* [Reverberations, Posthumously Selected by Her Husband] (1944). *Gedichte, Briefe, Prose*

[Poems, Letters, Prose], ed. by Esther Gamper (1946).

Bibliography

Ammann-Meuring, F., "Eingebung und Gestaltung in Maria Wasers Prosawerk." *Schweizer Monatshefte* 25 (1945/46): 630–637. Brand, Olga, *Stilles Wirken, Schweizer Dichterinnen* (Zurich, 1949). Eberle, O., "Maria Waser." *Schweizer Rundschau* 28 (1928): 828. Fassbinder, K.M., "Von der Liebe und vom Leben." *Germania* 284 (1934). *12 Schweizer Dichter erzählen von ihrem Werk und aus ihrem Leben*, mit einer Einführung von Hermann Weilenmann (Zurich, 1934). Gamper, Esther, *Frühe Schatten—frühes Leuchten—Maria Wasers Jugendjahre* (Frauenfeld, 1945). Günther, Werner *Dichter der neueren Schweiz*, vol. 1 (Bern, 1963), pp. 452–487. Joachimi-Dege, Marie, "Maria Waser." *Die schöne Literatur* 29/30 (1928): 369–379. Küffer, Georg, *Maria Waser* (Berlin, 1971).

Albrecht Classen

Ella Wassenaar

(see: L. Post-Beukens)

Herbjørg Wassmo

Born December 6, 1942, Vesterålen, Norway
Genre(s): poetry, novel
Language(s): Norwegian (bokmål and dialect)

The first female Norwegian author to be awarded the prestigious Nordic Council Award for Literature, Herbjørg Wassmo has succeeded through both poetry and prose to portray the strength and courage of the women of coastal Norway.

Herbjørg Wassmo began her literary career in 1976 with two collections of poetry, making her prose debut in 1981 with the novel *Huset med den blinde glassveranda* (The House with the Blind Glass Veranda). Awarded the Norwegian Critics Award and nominated for the Nordic Council Award in the same year, *Huset med den blinde glassveranda* has been a tremendous success with the public as well as the critics. The first of three novels about Tora, *Huset med den blinde glassveranda*, is a sensitive portrait of a young girl who is the result of a brief romance between her mother, Ingrid, and a German soldier during the occupation of World War II. Now married to Henrik, a bitter alcoholic who had been crippled during the war, Ingrid works nights to support the family and is unable to protect Tora from Henrik's sexual abuse. Tora finds her only support from her aunt Rakel and Rakel's husband Simon. In *Det stumme rommet* (1983; The Mute Room) and *Hudløs himmel* (1986; Naked Sky), Wassmo continues Tora's story through adolescence as she leaves home and finally finds the courage to confide in Rakel, the only person who dares to stand up to Henrik. In 1986 Wassmo was awarded the Nordic Council Literature Prize for *Hudløs himmel*.

Veien å gå (1984; The Road to Take) is a documentary novel about a family forced to flee to Sweden during the occupation. As in her novels about Tora, Wassmo focuses on the fate of families, particularly women and children, the innocent victims of war. Wassmo's latest novel, *Dinas bok* (1989; Dina's Book) is set in North Norway during the 1800s.

Herbjørg Wassmo is one of the leading women writing in Norway and Europe today, and is praised by critics and the reading public alike for her narrative skill and psychological insight. Her books about Tora have been translated into eight languages, and a film is planned.

Works

Vingeslag [Wingbeat] (1976). *Flotid* [Flood Tide] (1977). *Huset med den blinde glassveranda* [The House with the Blind Glass Windows] (1981). *Det stumme rommet* [The Mute Room] (1983). *Junivinter* [June Winter] (1983). *Veien å gå* [The Road to Take] (1984). *Hudløs himmel* [Naked Sky] (1986). *Dinas bok* [Dina's Book] (1989).

Translations: *The House with the Blind Glass Windows*, tr. Roseann Lloyd and Allen Simpson (Seattle, 1987).

Bibliography

Amundsen, Jon, "Den blinde glassveranda. Litt om lyriske virkemidler i prosadiktningen." *Profil* 2/3 (1982): 38–39. Dahl, Willy, *Norges litteratur III: Tid og tekst 1935–1972* (Oslo, 1989), pp. 280, 299. Eriksen, Torunn, "Herbjørg Wassmo: Om en skadeskutt fugl i *Huset med den blinde* glassveranda." *Nordnorsk magasin* 5 (1982): 32–33, 35. Hareide, Jorunn, "Kampen for menneskeverd. Herbjørg Wassmo: *Huset med den blinde glassveranda.*" *Norsk Litterær årbok 1982*: 206–219. Matsson, Ragnar, "Två nordnorska romandebuter–en samhällsskildring och en ond fabel med ljudgestalter." *Horisont* 29.5/6 (1982): 104–106. Moe, Karin. "Liten morgenfugl–fortsettelsens problem. Om Herbjørg Wassmo *Det stumme rommet.*" *Nordisk profil* 1 (1983): 26–28. Norseng, Mary Kay, "A Child's Liberation of Space: Herbjørg Wassmo's *Huset med den blinde glassveranda.*" *Scandinavian Studies* 58.1 (1986): 48–66. Pettersen, Turid Barth, "Det stumme rop. Herbjørg Wassmo: *Det stumme rommet.*" *Vinduet* 37.4 (1983): 78–79. Simonsen, Malan, "Pristale for Herbjørg Wassmo. Nordisk Råds litteraturpris 1987." *Norsk Litterær Årbok 1987*: 9–11. Steinfeld, Torill, "Kropp og form: Herbjørg Wassmos *Huset med den blinde glassveranda.*" *Vinduet* 36.4 (1982): 53–55. Wassmo, Herbjørg. "Takketale." *Norsk Litterær Årbok 1987*: 12–15.

Margaret Hayford O'Leary

Ingeborg Weber-Kellermann

Born 1918, Berlin, Germany
Genre(s): scholarly monograph
Language(s): German

After having studied ethnology, anthropology, and paleontology, Ingeborg Weber-Kellermann obtained her doctorate in 1940 in Berlin. From 1946–1960, she was research associate at the German Academy of Sciences in Berlin. In 1960, she accepted a position in the field of European ethnology at the University of Marburg, where she has been a full professor for many years. The uniqueness of her research has been the application of methods from the social sciences in European ethnology.

With her publications *Die deutsche Familie. Versuch einer Sozialgeschichte* of 1974, which includes a wealth of visual and textual documentation; *Kindheit*, of 1979, which examines the clothing, housing, work, and play aspects of childhood, and the cultural and social history of Christmas, entitled *Das Weihnachtsfest*, she has made significant contributions towards an elucidation of German social history, especially of

the pre-industrial era. She became known to a wider public in 1983 through a television series of thirteen installments on German folk culture, in which she presents and interprets customs, costumes, and toys and games, drawing upon her extensive collection of toys and other folk objects.

Works

Josefsdorf. Lebensbild eines deutschen Dorfes in Slowenien (1942). *Deutsche Volkskunde zwischen Germanistik und Sozialwissenschaft* (1969). *Volksleben in Hessen* (1971). *Die deutsche Familie. Versuch einer Sozialgeschichte* (1976). *Die Familie: Geschichte, Geschichten und Bilder* (1979). *Das Weihnachtsfest. Eine Kultur–und Sozialgeschichte der Weihnachtszeit* (1978). *Was wir gespielt haben* (1981). *Die Kindheit: Kleidung, Wohnen, Arbeit und Spiel* (1979). *Frauenleben im 19. Jahrhundert* (1983). *Einführung in die Vokskunde und europäische Ethnologie* (1985).

Ingeborg Zeiträg

Simone Weil

(a.k.a. Émile Novis)

Born February 3, 1909, Paris, France; died
August 24, 1943, Ashford, England
Genre(s): political article, poetry, essay,
notebook
Language(s): French

Published political articles and poems under her own name and "Émile Novis" (anagram); her major works—essays and fragmentary writings on society and religion—appeared posthumously.

A political activist and the author of wide-ranging articles on society and its injustices, Simone Weil's private notebooks also contain some of the most powerful reflections on religious experience written in the twentieth century.

The daughter of cultivated agnostic Jews, Simone Weil was deeply influenced by Alain, her philosophy teacher at the Lycée Henri IV. At the École Normale Supérieure she gained a reputation for her left-wing sympathies. On graduating in 1931, the Ministry of Education posted her as a philosophy teacher to the remote town of Le Puy, where she irritated the authorities by participating in workers' demonstrations. The following year she was moved to Auxerre; the next, to Roanne (see *Leçons de philosophie de Simone Weil*, 1959). In 1934 she took a leave of absence in order to gain experience as a factory worker. When the Spanish Civil War broke out, she volunteered for noncombat duties. She returned to teaching, but ill-health forced her to take further leave. While visiting an Italian church in 1937, an experience of "something" stronger than herself compelled her to kneel for the first time in her life and awoke an interest in Christianity. During the war she lived with her parents in Marseille. Restless to participate in the Allied cause, she devised several plans (e.g., for the formation of a group of front-line nurses), none of which was accepted. Meanwhile, she was increasingly drawn to Catholicism and became a close friend of Father Perrin. In 1941 he arranged for her to take part in the grape harvest in the Ardèche, where she met Gustave Thibon. In 1942 she travelled with her parents to New York; from there she went alone to England, where she worked for the Free French forces. Crippled by ill-health, largely owing to self-deprivation, she died in a sanatorium aged thirty-four.

Throughout her life, Simone Weil was profoundly concerned with the relation between the individual and society. Within months of taking up her first teaching post, she became involved in a demonstration for higher wages for quarry workers. Although she was frail and suffered from excruciating headaches, she insisted on going down a mine and working with miners' equipment. In December 1933 she led a demonstration of 3000 miners through the streets of Saint-Étienne. The following year she spent doing exhausting piece-work in various factories, including Renault, an experience, she claimed, that marked her for life. Meanwhile she was writing articles for left-wing organs on workers' conditions and movements, industrial problems, social oppression, and pacifism. She distrusted the achievements of communism. In "Perspectives" (1933), starting from the premise that a state is not a workers' state if the workers in it are at the complete disposal of a bureaucratic elite, she argues that socialism must discover a closer union between manual and intellectual labor. Non-Stalinist Marxists praised the essay; Trotsky, to whom it was largely addressed, was stirred to

write an article in reply. The most important of her early essays, "Réflexions sur les causes de la liberté et de l'oppression sociale" (1934) was not published in her life. It has four parts: a critique of Marxism, an analysis of the nature of political oppression, a theoretical outline of a free society, and a lucid description of society and its ills. *L'Enracinement*, which she wrote in London in 1943, represents a synthesis of her later ideas. It discusses how to rebuild a just society in France after the liberation. Its axioms are that human rights are subservient to obligations incumbent on individuals and society alike, and that each individual has needs (*besoins de l'âme*) such as Order, Liberty, Obedience, Responsibility, Rootedness, etc. As a blueprint, these ideas are wildly impracticable; as theses, they merit consideration. Weil argues that an individual cannot realize his potential unless he actively participates in the life of a community rooted in long-standing traditions. (It was for this reason that she admired the twelfth-century Cathars.) Albert Camus, who was responsible for publishing the unfinished manuscript in 1949, was greatly impressed by it.

When Simone Weil died, her manuscripts were collected and edited by friends. Gustave Thibon, to whom she had given twelve of her private notebooks, was the first to compile a collection of *pensées* from them under the title *La Pesanteur et la Grâce*. Its publication in 1947 revealed a facet of her personality known previously only to close friends: the opinionated social philosopher was also a mystic dedicated to the annihilation of her ego in order to experience God.

"*L'Iliade*, ou le poème de la force" (1940–1941) bridges Weil's sociopolitical and religious thought. In her view, the "hero" of the poem is the impersonal "force" that turns a man into a thing and makes a corpse out of him. The greatness of Homer's epic lies in the fact that it does not take sides: it testifies. Her antipathy to Judaism, the Roman Empire, and the Christian Church as an institution stems from her view that each in its way has identified itself with force. In contrast, she admired the Gospels as the summum of Greek thought and as an expression of the antithesis of force: Grace. From 1938 onwards, she had repeated experiences that she described as Christ taking possession of her. In her notebooks, she strove to express the meaning that religious experience had for her. In 1942 she wrote a series of letters to Father Perrin explaining her commitment to Christianity as well as her reasons for refusing to be baptized. He published these in *Attente de Dieu* (1950), the most accessible of her works. Other collections of her often startling reflections on religion are *La Connaissance surnaturelle* (1950), *Intuitions pré-chrétiennes* and *Lettre à un religieux* (1951), *La Source grecque* (1953), and *Pensées sans ordre concernant l'amour de Dieu* (1962).

A tension of opposites conditions everything that Simone Weil was and wrote. A philosopher, she was drawn to physical labor. A Jew, she was drawn to Catholicism. A Catholic, she would not be baptized. Suspicious of the growth of individualism and the related loss of collective values, her writings constantly return to her own remarkable personality. The Marxist activist became one of the outstanding religious thinkers of her time, and this, in turn, deepened her sociopolitical ideas. Interest in her work has grown steadily since her death. Perhaps no other figure has written more impressively on both the individual in society and the individual and God.

Works

La Pesanteur et la Grâce (1947). L'Enracinement: Prélude à une déclaration des devoirs envers l'être humain (1949). Attente de Dieu (1950). La Conaissance surnaturelle (1950). Cahiers, 3 vols. (1951–1956; revised edition, 1970–1974). La Condition ouvrière (1951). Intuitions pré-chrétiennes (1951). Lettre à un religieux (1951). La Source grecque (1953). Oppression et Liberté (1955). Venise sauvée, tragédie en trois actes (1955). Écrits de Londres et dernières lettres (1957). Leçons de philosophie de Simone Weil: Roanne 1933–1934, ed. Anne Reynaud (1959). Écrits historiques et politiques (1960). Pensées sans ordre concernant l'amour de Dieu (1962). Sur la Science (1965). Poèmes, suivis de "Venise sauvée," Lettre de Paul Valéry (1968).

Translations: Waiting for God (1951). Gravity and Grace (1952). The Need for Roots (1952). Letter to a Priest (1953). The Notebooks of Simone Weil (1956). Intimations of Christianity (1957). Oppression and Liberty (1958). Selected Essays, 1934–1943 (1962). Seventy Letters (1965). On Science, Necessity and the Love of God (1968). First and Last Notebooks (1970). Gateway to God (1974). The Simone Weil Reader (1977). Lectures on Philosophy (1978). Simone Weil: An Anthology (1986).

Bibliography

Cabaud, Jacques, Simone Weil: A Fellowship in Love (1964). Davy, Marie-Magdeleine, Simone Weil (1956). Dujardin, Philippe, Simone Weil: Idéologie et politique (1975). Dunaway, John M., Simone Weil (1984). Friedman, Maurice, "Simone Weil," in To Deny our Nothingness: Contemporary Images of Man (1967), pp. 135–145. Hellman, John, Simone Weil: An Introduction to her Thought (1982). Kahn, Gilbert, ed., Simone Weil: Philosophe, historienne et mystique (1978). Little, J.P., Simone Weil: A Bibliography (1973; Supplement No. 1, 1979). McFarland, Dorothy Tuck, Simone Weil (1983). Perrin, J-M. and Gustave Thibon, Simone Weil telle que nous l'avons connue (1952). Pétrement, Simone, La Vie de Simone Weil, avec des lettres et d'autres textes inédits, 2 vols. (1973). Rees, Richard, Simone Weil: A Sketch for a Portrait (1966). White, George Abbott, ed., Simone Weil: Interpretations of a Life (1981). General references: Encyclopædia Brittanica (1974). Dictionnaire des Littératures de langues française (1984).

Terence Dawson

Sana Weinzieher

(see: Zuzanna Ginczanka)

Anna Elisabet Weirauch

(a.k.a. A.E. Ries or Reiss)

Born August 7, 1887, Galatz, Romania; died December 21, 1970, Berlin, Germany
Genre(s): novel, novella, young adult literature, film script
Language(s): German

A complicated and private person, Weirauch can be viewed as representative of one aspect of the "new woman" shaped by social, economic, and cultural forces in the twentieth century. She successfully created a life for herself in a society where a woman who was not in some way attached to a man only rarely achieved. In addition, she shared this life for almost six decades with another woman.

After her father's death in 1891, Weirauch's mother, an author, brought her two daughters to Germany. (Her two sons had died early in life.) Around the turn of the century, they moved to Berlin, where Anna Elisabet soon began studying acting. In 1906, she joined Max Reinhardt's famous ensemble at Berlin's Deutsches Theater where she performed through 1914.

Weirauch had tried her hand at playwriting in these years, but after the war ended, she discovered her real gift lay in writing prose. Clearly, she had been writing for some time already since four novels and three novellas were all published in 1919, the first year of her long career as an author. One of these was the first volume of a trilogy entitled *Der Skorpion* (1919, 1921, 1931; The Scorpion), which has become the work for which Weirauch is remembered today.

This three-volume *Entwicklungsroman* presents the story of Mette Rudloff as she learns and grows from the various loves she experiences for other females. The first volume portrays her from childhood through her early twenties. Although Olga, the woman she loves, does bend to social opprobria and commits suicide, Mette refuses to succumb to the prejudice and hostility heaped upon her. She pursues her own path toward happiness, no matter how difficult it proves. Over the course of the next two volumes, Mette learns about the lesbian and homosexual subculture, has several love affairs, and builds her own character so that, at the conclusion, she stands confident in the validity of her choices and at the same time hopeful and able to build a long-lasting relationship with another woman.

This work stands out from the vast amount of fiction depicting lesbian or homosexual characters during the Weimar Republic. It does not apply a medical theory to the origin and appearance of same-sex love, nor does Weirauch deem it necessary to supply "scientific" evidence to defend her characters. Seduction, psychological illness, the "Intermediate Sex"—none of this is critical here, although all of it plays a role within the text's discourse on sexuality. These aspects

evoked the enormous resonance of this work. The first edition of the initial volume quickly sold out. Readers, especially lesbian readers, praised the sympathetic—and true—depiction of lesbian characters which they found here. They begged Weirauch to tell more of Mette's story, a request she then granted twice over. The novels have been translated into several languages. In English alone, they have had seven editions in various forms.

No other work of hers approached the success of *Der Skorpion*. Her long and successful career, however, was based on her ability to tell a story which the public wanted to hear and which it could rather easily digest. She continued to publish during the Third Reich. To do so, Weirauch joined the *Reichsschrifttumskammer*, but she never joined the National Socialist Party. In 1933, she and her friend moved to Gastag in Upper Bavaria. After the war, they lived in Munich and, in 1961, they returned to Berlin. She was awarded the Golden Medal for Art and Science (date unknown).

Typical of Weirauch's work is a novel from 1939: *Das Rätsel Manuela* (The Puzzle Manuela). (The work has no relation to Christa Winsloe's novel *Das Mädchen Manuela* [The Child Manuela], published in Amsterdam in 1934, but one wonders whether Weirauch did not intend some connection to be made.) In this novel a chorus girl, Manuela Groot, becomes the object of the affections of a musical show's male star, Manfred. Manuela, of a healthy, morally upright, bourgeois background, replaces the show's female star, a wealthy foreigner named Marjorie Bruce. Having achieved fame, she assents to Manfred's offer of marriage, thus providing a suitably happy end to this escapist tale at a time when reality was taking quite a different shape.

Gifted with a talent for writing prose and plots that afforded easy accessibility and strong identification on the part of her readers, Weirauch's career spanned some of the most politically turbulent years in Germany's history. Yet that reality makes only brief appearances in her works. Much among her *oeuvre* can perhaps justly be labelled "trivial," but her trilogy *Der Skorpion* has found a secure place within the canon of literature that depicts homosexuality with veracity and with skill.

Works

Novels: *De kleine Dagmar* (1919). *Der Skorpion* (1919, 1921, 1931). *Der Tag der Artemis* (1919). *Sogno. Das Buch der Träume* (1919). *Anja. Die Geschichte einer unglücklichen Liebe* (1919). *Gewissen* (1920). *Die Gläserne Welt* (1921). *Agonie der Liedenschaft* (1922). *Ruth Meyer. Eine Fast alltägliche Geschichte* (1922). *Falk und die Felsen* (1923). *Edles Blut* (1923). *Höllenfahrt* (1923). *Nin van't Hell* (1924). *Tina und die Tänzerin* (1927). *Ungleiche Brüder* (1928). *Ein Herr in den besten Jahren* (1929). *Die Farrels* (1929). *Lotte* (1930). *Carmen an der Panke* (1931). *Denken Sie an Oliver* (1931). *Briefe in Baneiros Hand* (1932). *Schlange im Paradies* (1932). *Frau Kern* (1934). *Geheimnis um Petra* (1934). *Ein Mädchen ohne Furcht* (1935). *Das Haus in der Veenestraat* (1935). *Junger Mann mit Motorrad* (1935). *Mijnheer Corremans und seine Töchter* (1936). *Café-Edelweiss* (1936). *Der große Geiger* (1937). *Iduna auf Urlaub* (1937). *Martina wird mündig* (1937). *Das Rätsel Manuela* (1938). *Großgarage Tiedemann* (1939). *Donate und die Glückspilze* (1940). *Die entscheidende Stunde* (1940). *Die Geschichte mit Genia* (1941). *Die drei Schwestern Hahnemann* (1941). *Überhaupt kein Frau* (1941). *Einmal kommt die Stunde* (1942). *Wiedersehen auf Java* (1949). *Schicksale in der Coco-Bar. Ein Frauenroman* (1949). *Das Schiff in der Flasche* (1951). *Karin und Kathi* (1954). *Warum schweigst du?* (1954). *Die letzten Tage vor der Hochzeit* (1955). *Drei Monate, drei Wochen, und drei Tage* (1957). *Claudias großer Fall* (1957). *Der Mann gehört mir* (1958). *Und es begann so zauberhaft* (1959). *Mordprozeß Vehsemeyer* (1959). *Mit 21 beginnt das Leben* (1959). *Tanz um Till* (1960). *Uberfall bei Valentin* (1960). *Die gehemnisvolle Erbschaft* (1961). *Bella und Belinda* (1961). *Tante Zinnober und das Wasserschloß* (1961). *Die Flimfanny* (1962). *Ein Leben am Rande* (1965). *Anstatt der angekündigten Vorstellung* (1965).

Play: *Der Garten des Liebenden* (1921).

Film: *Es lebe die Liebe* (n.d.).

Translation: *The Scorpion*, Vols. 1–2 (1932), Vol. 3, *The Outcast* (1933).

Bibliography

Foster, Jeannette H., *Sex Variant Women in Literature* (n.p.: 1985), pp. 229–234. Jones, James W., "The 'Third Sex' in German Literature from the Turn of the Century to 1933." Ph.D. Diss., University of Wisconsin, 1986, pp. 630–648. Katz, Jonathan, *Gay/Lesbian Almanac* (New York, 1983), pp. 468–469. Schoppmann, Claudia, *Der Roman 'Der Skorpion' von Anna Elisabet Weirauch* (Berlin, 1986).

James W. Jones

Lina Wertmuller

Born August 14, 1923, Rome, Italy
Genre(s): film drama, novel
Language(s): Italian

Lina Wertmuller is known primarily as a film director, but, as she has written the screenplays for her movies as well as stage plays and one novel, she has also earned a reputation as a writer. She was born with the remarkably full name of Arcangela Felice Assunta Wertmuller von Elgg Spanol von Braueich, the daughter of Maria Santa Maria and Federico Wertmuller, a successful Roman attorney. Her great-great-grandfather, Baron Erich Wertmuller von Elgg, is said to have fled Zurich for Italy after killing a rival in a duel. By Lina Wertmuller's own account, her father was an autocrat who made domestic life miserable until her mother walked out on him after fifty years of marriage. Yet, he was also quietly anti-Fascist, protecting partisans and harboring a family of Jews in his own home. Lina Wertmuller herself has served on the central committee of the Italian Socialist Party. Her work reflects this socialist orientation and a certain feminism by keeping film audiences alive to the exploitation rampant in the society in which they live. Her writing nevertheless exhibits little programmatic content, and she is often ambivalent enough to outrage both socialists and feminists.

She began her career after studying stage directing in the dramatic academy of Pietro Sciaroff, who, along with Tatiana Pavlova, had introduced Stanislavsky's ideas to Italy. She spent a decade up to the early sixties in a wide variety of theatrical endeavors: acting, writing, directing, stage managing, and puppetry. She founded a short lived theater of her own, the "Arlecchino," then joined Maria Signorelli's touring puppet theater, doing a repertory of plays adapted from such authors as Franz Kafka (upsetting parents who expected fairy tales). She also worked with director Guido Salvini, director-actor Giorgio De Lullo, and finally Federico Fellini, whom she served as assistant on the movie *8 1/2*. Then, with partial backing from Fellini, she wrote and directed her first film, *I Basilischi* (The Lizards) produced in 1963. It portrays the youth of a Southern Italian town in their aimless lethargy which they occasionally punctuate with bursts of empty violence. It is nevertheless a strangely amusing film. It won the "Silver Sail" prize at the Lucarno Festival and a young director's award at Cannes.

In 1965, she wrote and directed her second feature film, *Questa volta, parliamo di uomini* (This Time, Let's Talk About Men, called simply *Let's Talk About Men* in its U.S. release), a group of four vignettes exploring abusive male-female relationships. It presents an array of styles, ranging from an almost farcical theatricality to serious realism, and overt surrealism. From the middle sixties on into the seventies, she wrote and directed a number of television musicals. They included *Il Giornalino di Gian Burasco* (1965; Gian Burasco's Diary), *Rita la zanzara* (1966; Rita the Mosquito), and *Non stuzzicate la zanzara* (1967; Don't Sting the Mosquito), all of them starring Rita Pavone. She returned to the stage in 1968, when Franco Zeffirelli directed her play *Due piu due non fan piu quattro* (Two Plus Two Don't Equal Four Any More) starring Giancarlo Giannini with sets by sculptor-designer Enrico Job, Lina Wertmuller's new husband. She has since worked often with both of these men, the one as lead actor, the other as art director.

In association with Giannini, she established her own production company, Liberty Films. The first result of this new enterprise was the 1972 film, *Mimi metallurgico ferito nell'onore* (Mimi, Metalworker, Wounded in His Honor), which appeared in the United States under the title *The Seduction of Mimi*. This film established both a pattern for Wertmuller and her reputation. Like her subsequent films, it is a story about a "little man." Mimi, played by Giannini, is a Sicilian worker caught up in maintaining his male honor and challenging the authority of the Mafia, only to find himself swallowed up in the "brotherhood." In 1973, her next film appeared:

Film d'amore e d'anarchia (released as *Love and Anarchy*). It, too, featured Giannini in the main role of Tunin. After seeing Fascists murder his friend, he comes to Rome to have vengeance by assassinating Mussolini. An anarchist prostitute helps him in his plans and he falls in love with another girl in the same brothel. Between the two, his plans go awry, he goes berserk, and the Fascist police beat him to death.

Wertmuller's films now came in rapid succession. In 1974 appeared *Tutto a posto, niente in ordine* (Everything in its Place, Nothing in Order, released as *All Screwed Up*) about Southern Italian workers who live in a commune in Milan as they become swallowed up in a bourgeois society of conspicuous consumption. In that same year another film appeared: *Travolti da un insolito destino nell'azzuro mare d'agosto* (Swept Away by an Unusual Fate upon an Azure August Sea, released simply as *Swept Away*) dealing with a curious reversal of social and sexual roles between a female ship passenger and a male deck hand once they find themselves shipwrecked and alone. Then in 1975 came *Pasqualino settebellezze* (Pasqualino Seven-Beauties, released as *Seven Beauties*). This was a considerable success, although highly controversial. It deals with prostitution in the fullest sense of the word: Pasqualino is a macho Neopolitan who has defended his seven ugly sisters against other macho types, but then goes to war, deserts the Fascist army, lands in a Nazi war camp, and ends up corrupted by the female prison commandant. He is finally welcomed back to Naples by his seven sisters, all of them now whores.

On the strength of these films, Warner Brothers signed Wertmuller to a contract which obligated her to produce four English language films. The first and only product of this agreement was *The End of the World in Our Usual Bed in a Night Full of Rain* (1978), the story of the marriage of a macho Italian Communist journalist (Giancarlo Giannini) and an American feminist photographer (Candice Bergen). It was generally regarded as a failure, enough so at the box office that Warner cancelled its contract.

In the next year, 1979, Wertmuller directed her own stage play, *Amore e magia nella cucina di mama* (Love and Magic in Mama's Kitchen) which she had begun in 1970 at the urging of Franco Zeffirelli. The play is based on the sensational 1945 trial of Leonarda Cianciuli, who had become unbalanced after the deaths of her twelve chidden at birth, murdered her best friends, and turned them into soap and candle wax, all in the fervent belief they would reappear reincarnated, more beautiful and more perfect than before. The play opened at the festival of Two Worlds in Spoleto, with scenery by Enrico Job. It played in Rome and was scheduled to open at Cafe La Mama in New York in April 1980. It was cancelled shortly before its announced appearance. Her next fiim appeared the same year, featuring Giannini, Marcello Mastroianni and Sofia Loren, a love triangle with the Mafia and Fascists on the periphery, all under the grand title, *Fatto di sangue fra due uomini per causa di una vedova. Si sospettano moventi politici* (Blood Feud Between Two Men Over a Widow. Political Motives Are Suspected, released in the United States as *Revenge* and in England as *Blood Feud*).

Wertmuller has continued to produce films. They include the 1983 *Scherzo del destino in aqquato dietro l'angolo come un brigante di strada* (A Twist of Fate Waiting in Ambush Around the Corner Like a Street Thief), about a government bureaucrat trapped in his bullet-proof, overdone limousine; *Sotto sotto* (1984; Softly, Softly), a marital farce satirizing the Catholic Church, sexual hangups, macho posturing, and the institution of marriage. Then, in 1986, two films appeared: *Un complicato intrigo di donne, vicoli e delitti* (A Complicated Intrigue of Women, Alleys and Crimes, released as *Camorra*), about a group of women taking on Naples' drug dealers and gangsters, and *Notte d'estate con profilo grecco, occhi a mandorla e odore di basilico* (Summer Night with Greek Profile, Almond-shaped Eyes and Scent of Basil) presenting the sexual fireworks that erupt when a wealthy, lusty woman kidnaps a political terrorist. Beyond these releases, she has also produced a novel, *La Testa di Alvise* (1981; published in English in 1982 as *The Head of Alvise*). It tells the story of Sammy Silverman's lifelong bitter hatred for Alvise Ottolenghi Portaleoni inspired by his awful sense of inferiority that began in their boyhood when the Italian Jew

saved the American Jew in a mad flight from Treblinka to Spain and on to New York. It ends now, forty years later, when the rich hack writer Sammy meets Nobel Prize author Alvise and thinks he kills him in a mad dance likened to Salome's over the head of John the Baptist.

Her work, taken generally, has addressed the difficulties people encounter trying to live together over against the odds of sexual and political entanglements that undercut integrity and purpose in human life. In an angular, nervous, and staccato style, she portrays life as a grotesque comedy.

Works

Films: *I Basilischi* (1963). *Questa volta, parliamo di uomini* (1965). *Mimi metallurgico ferito nell'onore* (1972). *Film d'amore e d'anarchia* (1973). *Tutto a posto, niente in ordine* (1974). *Travolti da un insolito destino nell'azzurro mare d'agosto* (1974). *Pasqualino Settebellezze* (1975). *The End of the World in Our Usual Bed in a Night Full of Rain* (1978). *Fatto di sangue fra due uomini a causa di una vedova. Si sospettano moventi politici* (1979). *Scherzo di destino in aqquato dietro un'agolo come un brigante di strada* (1983). *Sotto sotto* (1984). *Un complicato intrigo di donne, vicoli, e delitti* (1986). *Notte d'estate con profilo grecco, occhi a mandorla, e odore di basilico* (1986).

Published screenplays: *The Screenplays of Lina Wertmuller*, tr. John Simon (1977; includes *The Seduction of Mimi, Love and Anarchy, Swept Away*, and *Seven Beauties*).

Stage plays: *Due piu due non fan piu quattro* (1968). *Amore e magia nella cucina di mama* (1979).

Novel: *La testa di Alvise* (1981).

Bibliography

Bandanella, P., *Italian Cinema* (1983). Ferlita, Ernest and John R. May, *The Parables of Lina Wertmuller* (1977). Liehm, M., *Passion and Defiance: Film in Italy from 1942 to the Present* (1984). Smith, S., *Women Who Make Movies* (1975). Wakeman, John, ed., *World Film Directors* (1988).

Polixéna Wesselényi

Born 1801, Transylvania; died September 1,
1878, Aranyos-Gyéres, Transylvania
Genre(s): diary, travel notes, memoirs, eulogy
Language(s): Hungarian

Polixéna Wesselényi was born into one of the most distinguished families of Hungary and Transylvania, and she inherited the family sense of duty and patriotism. An ancestor, Ferenc Wesselényi, was a key figure in the failed conspiracy against Leopold II that had aimed at restoring the Constitutional rights of the Hungarian Estates, and a maternal uncle, Ádám Kendeffy, was one of the foremost patriots and statesmen of the previous generation. Her cousin, Miklós Wesselényi, also played an important role as an opposition politician in the Reform Era, working closely with Count István Széchenyi. His political views eventually resulted in imprisonment, and both Polixéna and John Paget were instrumental in unsuccessful attempts to spirit him out of the reach of the Habsburg authorities. Literary antecedents can also be found in her family: the first Polixéni Wesselényi wrote an elegy in memory of her father in 1759, and Zsuzsanna Wesselényi set down in writing her journey to Vienna in 1796, a journey she had undertaken to plead for the release of her brother.

Wesselényi married Baron Lászlo Bánffy, also of a distinguished Transylvanian family and one closely connected with the Wesselényis both through marriages and their sharing similar political views—he, as well as Polyxéna's family, were members of the liberal opposition who sought greater freedoms in Transylvania and Hungary. (At this time, Transylvania was governed as a separate province by the Habsburgs, with its own [seldom convened] Diet; the populace of both countries regarded themselves as sister-nations and one of their goals was the reunification of the country. This was also to become one of the major demands of the Revolution of 1848.) A daughter, Jozsefa, was born of this marriage. Though the marriage was no longer happy in 1834 when Polixéna set out on her journey to Italy, her husband did not oppose her plans, and her daughter and the governess (to whom she refers to as a friend) accompanied her. Even while absent, she kept up to date with events in her homeland and the activities of her family and friends in the Diet of 1834—the first one convened in 24 years—that ended in the proscription of Miklós Wesselényi for his bold move of publishing the proceedings of the Diet and publicizing the demands of the liberals. She met John Paget, an English gentleman who had taken a medical degree from the University of Edinburgh and was at the time on a tour of Europe. They travelled together for a while, but John Paget left for Hungary earlier, ostensibly to continue his studies but most likely on a political mission. He met with Széchenyi several times in the matter of getting Miklós Wesselényi out of the country to safety.

Wesselényi and Paget were married, probably in 1838; twin sons were born in 1841. One died as a child of twelve; the other, Oliver, in 1863 when only 22. His mother mourned him with a portrait and a brief eulogy. John Paget encouraged Wesselényi to write an account of her journey, based on the diary she had kept. The first part of her travels appeared duly under the title *Olaszhoni és Schweizi utazás* (Italian and Swiss Travels) in 1842; a second volume, recounting her travels in France and England, was never written, and the diary notes were most probably thrown into a pond on their property by Romanian insurgents during the Revolution of 1848–1849. Paget had also written a book, *Hungary and Transylvania* (1839), in which she had no small part. After they settled in Transylvania, Paget became very active in agricultural societies and wrote extensively in Hungarian professional journals. He introduced new stocks of livestock and new strains of plants on his lands, as well as the scientific methods of English farming, creating a model English-style estate. Polixéna's contribution to her husband's writing has always been acknowledged.

Little is known of her life upon their return to Transylvania in 1839 from the French and English trip that they had taken together. Paget was active in the Revolution of 1848–1849, and they were forced to flee numerous times before finally having to seek exile in England. Returning in 1855, they found their home plundered and the carefully tended farms destroyed, but they rebuilt along with everyone else.

Wesselényi's style was influenced by the diarists and memoir writers of Transylvania, for example Miklós Bethlen and Kelemen Mikes, as well as the language of the Protestant preachers. An equally important influence was the everyday speech of the various districts of Transylvania and the Partium, for she spent time in all these areas as a child and young woman. Since she also grew up at the time of the linguistic reforms of the nineteenth century, she was conscious of both style and language. She notes the variety and complexity of Italian as spoken by the simplest of the people, remarking also on the differences from city to city or region to region, and comments with some disapproval that Roman society does not use its own language at all, preferring French or English. And she is quite defensive when Pope Gregory XVI asks her whether they speak German in her native land; she answers that they speak their own language. To which he counters, "Latin?" and she has to reply, "No, Holy Father, Hungarian (Magyar)." Respect for the old man does not allow her to show even this much of a disagreement when he comments that all is quiet in her homeland and that the Emperor has graciously granted them a Diet—knowing full well that her husband and family are far from safe, the situation is quite turbulent, and that the Diet was the country's right, not an occasional privilege extended by the ruler.

In spite of the eclectic influences, Wesselényi's commonsense and good education enabled her to form a pleasant style that was rich and expressive then and has remained fresh to the present time. Beyond the consciously cultivated vocabulary, she was an accomplished stylist whose polished sentences reflect her command of not only Hungarian but also of Latin, French, English, German and Italian, all of which she spoke fluently and in whose literature she was well versed. But the travelogue gains its greatest value not from the form but the content: she recounts her adventures and makes her observations without calling undue attention to herself. The description of places and events is vivid, her comments on the art and architecture, on the antiquities and customs of the places she visits cultured and perceptive without being pedantic, and her characterization of the persons she describes, even if only in passing, captures the essence of these people.

The only other work left from Wesselényi is a brief eulogy on her son that accompanies his portrait, also painted by her. He is depicted in the uniform of Garibaldi's soldiers, and she notes the facts of his life: Born 1841 in Kolozsvár (now Cluj-Napoca, Romania) on September 5, at age 19, inspired by the love of freedom, he left King's College to join Garibaldi in Sicily enlisting in the Hungarian legion. In the battle of Volturno, as a sublieutenant, he captured eight cannon with his small band. General Türr embraced him on the battlefield and said that his country and his parents could be proud of him. Garibaldi made him a lieutenant. After five months service he was named a captain in the Piedmontese Army and decorated. Out of filial devotion, he left this promising career and returned to the university. The youth of Switzerland sent him a pair of pistols with the inscription, "To the Brave." He married in 1861, taking his relative, Ellen Paget, as his wife, returned to his country and became a farmer. One daughter was born in 1862. He died in 1863 on October 19. The values of Polixena's earlier life are not obscured in this account, for while she must have felt a mother's relief to know that her son was safe in Oxford and not on the Italian battlefields, it is also clear that she felt a Wesselényi pride that, in a few short months, her son had distinguished himself so well in the cause of freedom.

Works

Olaszhoni és Schweizi utazás (1842). *Olaszhoni és schweizi utazás*, ed. by János Győri and Zoltán Jékely, afterword by Zoltán Jékely. Magyar hírmondo (1981).

Bibliography

Balog, József, two studies in *Hungarian Quarterly* (1939/40). Fenyő, István, "A polgárosodás eszmevilága utirajzainkban 1848 elöt." *Két évtized* (Budapest, 1968). Gál, István, "Paget, Erdély angol honpolgára." *Pásztortűz* (September 1939). Gál, István, "Wesselényi Polixéna, az első magyar esztéta." *Müveszét* 7 (1972). Márki, Sándor, "Magyar nők utazásai." *Földrajzi közlemények* 17 (1889). Tóth, László, "Erdélyi biedermeier." *Széphalom* 12 (1941). V., I. [Imre Vachot?], "Regélő" of the *Pesti divatlap* (1843).

Enikő Molnár Basa

Minna Adelt Wettstein

Born May 1, 1867, Strasbourg, Germany; died
(unknown)
Genre(s): novel, travel and fashion literature
Language(s): German

Although most of her works are not available today and little is known of her life, Wettstein/Duc remains an important figure in the history of German literature due to her writings about the women's movement at the turn of the century. She was born in the border city of Strasbourg and was educated in France. She married a Swiss. Her first work, a novel entitled *Noli me tangere!* was published in 1887 and established her rather prolific career as an author of prose fiction. In addition, she contributed non-fiction pieces on the women's movement (e.g., *Macht Euch frei! Ein Wort an die deutschen Frauen* [1893; Liberate Yourselves! A Word to German Women]). She spent much of her adult life in Germany, especially in Berlin, where she edited the journal *Draisena. Blätter für Damenfahrten* (Draisena, Pages for Women's Trips) and published the *Berliner Modekorrespondenz* (Berlin Fashion Correspondent). Her love for travel, seen in *Draisena*, was further expressed in an extended trip to Egypt in 1907, and in a travel guide she wrote about Southern India and Burma in 1909.

Her name was brought to the attention of contemporary readers when her novel from 1901, *Sind es Frauen?* (Are These Women?), was republished by the feminist West German Amazonen Frauenverlag in 1976. This short novel, subtitled a "novel about the Third Sex," makes no apologies for women taking up careers and loving each other. Instead, the work polemicizes for the naturalness of such sexual preference and for the need of social change to accept the new roles women are creating for themselves. The novel follows the lives of a group of women college students in Geneva and centers in particular on the character of Minotschka Fernandoff. Her love for Countess Marta Kinzey provides a happy ending, which could be found in no other work in the rather extensive German fiction thematizing homosexual relationships during the Wilhelminian period. Although aesthetically inferior due to its overuse of sentiment, reliance on cliché, and use of a rather propagandistic voice, Duc's novel nevertheless takes an important step in the literary portrayal of the homosexual character in German literature for it emphatically defends the love between women and portrays a loving relationship which promises fulfillment.

Works

Novels: *Noli me tangere!* (1887). *Des Hauses Tausendkünstler* (1891). *Dreieinhalb Monate Fabrikarbeiterin* (1892). *Das Junggesellen Heim* (1895). *Sind es Frauen?* (1901). *Ich will!* (1902). *Des Pastors Liebe* (1902). *Und die Stein werden reden* (1906). *Indische Novellen* (1914).

Nonfiction: *Macht Euch frei!* (1893). *Meine Herren Kollegen* (1894). *Das Cocottentum der Kurorte* (1897). *Die Emmausfrage* (1905). As Mrs. M.A. Adelt-Duc: Tourist's Guide Books for the East (in English, German and French editions); German edition vol. I: *Süd-Indien und Burma* (1909).

Bibliography

Faderman, Lillian and Brigitte Eriksson, ed. and tr., *Lesbianism-Feminism in Turn-of-the-Century Germany* (Weatherby Lake, MO, 1980), pp. vi–ix, 1–21. Foster, Jeannette, *Sex Variant Women in Literature* (n.p.: 1985), pp. 220–221. Jones, James W., "The 'Third Sex' in German Literature from the Turn of the Cenury to 1933." Ph.D. Diss., University of Wisconsin, 1986, pp. 180–186.

James W. Jones

Fanny Wibmer

Born 1890, Innsbruck, Austria
Genre(s): novel, drama
Language(s): German

Wibmer went to school to the age of fourteen, at which point she began to work to earn her living. She married in 1912 and moved to Vienna where she lived for twenty years and had six children. She began her prolific literary career at the age of thirty-six with the publication of the dialect folk-tale *Das eigene Heim* (1929; One's Own Home). Wibmer's work reflects a Christian world-view with a strong didactic tendency. Her Roman Catholic belief in sin, atonement, and purification is evident in her earliest novels—*Die Hochzeiterin* (1930; The Bride), *Der brennende Dornbusch* (1930; The Burning Bush) and

Medardus Siegenwart. In 1934 she wrote *Die Pfaffin,* originally titled "Emerenzia." Here Wibmer recounts the life and eventual burning of the "witch" Emerenzia Pichlerin. Wibmer excels in an old-fashioned regional style using the dialect and expressions of the common people. Wibmer also wrote several historical novels: *Eine Frau trägt die Krone* (1937; A Woman Wears the Crown) dealing with Maria Theresa, *Der erste Landsknecht* (1940; The First Vassal) concerning the emperor Maximilian and *Graf und Herzog* (1954; Count and Duke) about Meinhard von Tirol. In addition to historical novels she wrote a peasant trilogy of regional novels spanning the time of the fourteenth to the twentieth century: *Die Dirnburg* (1949), *Auf Wolfsegg* (1949), and *Der Hochwalder* (1950). Her best-known peasant novel is *Die Sündenkrot* (1932), the story of a cleric whose unshakable faith overcomes various difficulties and dangers threatening his village and who is able through his faith to convert a former criminal. In addition to fiction, Wibmer wrote popular lay drama such as *Tiroler Krippenspiel* (1921; Tyrolean Nativity Play), *Die Sternsinger* (1930), and *Virgener Rosenkranzspiel* (1937). Most of Wibmer's work is realistic. She uses simple plots, clear dialogue, and regional speech. She often contrasts the fierce hereditary pride of the peasant with the innate weakness of the urban dweller. She believes that the sins of the father must be expiated by the next generation, and although she recognizes the presence of evil in the world, she feels strongly that evil can be overcome by God's mercy.

Works

Fiction: *Karl Müller's Lostag* (1929). *Die Hochzeiterin* (1930). *Der brennende Dornbusch* (1930). *Der Nussbaumer* (1931). *Medardus Siegenwart* (1931). *Die Sündenkrot* (1931). *Über den Berg* (1931). *Die drei Kristalle* (1932). *Das Marienglöckl von Leisach* (1932). *Emerenzia* (1934; later title is Die Pfaffin). *St. Notburg* (1935). *Ritter Florian Waldauf* (1936). *Eine Herztür ist zugefallen* (1936). *In stiller Abendstunde* (1936). *Eine Frau trägt die Krone* (1937). *Famile Holb* (1937). *Heimkehr zur Scholle* (1938). *Der Goldene Pflug* (1938). *Liebfrauenwunder* (1938). *Der Wieshofer* (1939). *Der erste Landsknecht* (1940). *Die Welserin* (1940). *Die Eibantochter* (1940). *Lisl Storm* (1941).

Der Kranz (1946). *Gewitter Über Aldein* (1947). *Der Galitzenschmied* (1949). *Die Dirnburg* (1949). *Auf Wolfsegg* (1949). *Der Hochwalder* (1950). *Der Perchtenstein* (1951). *Graf und Herzog* (1954). *Der heilige Berg* (1959). *Der Ritter von Presslab* (1960). **Drama:** *Das eigene Heim* (1929). *Das Sternsingerspiel* (1931). *Tiroler Krippenspiel* (1931). *Der Unfried Hirtenspiel* (1932). *Rosenkranzspiel* (1936). *Hochzeitsspiel* (1938). *Gericht des Herzens* (1950). *Der Fleck von Penk* (1951). *Der Schutzenbräutigam* (1952). *Der Hexenmeister* (1953). *Späte Sühne* (1953). *Aus dunklen Nachten* (1953). *Vierzig Minuten Verspätung* (1954). *Der Wildschütz* (1954). *Weinacht auf Hartegg* (1955). *Barbara wartet* (1955). *Das Opfer* (1955). *Die Nacht der Mutter* (1956). *Der Lindenhof* (1957). *Alles überwindet die Liebe* (1958). *Die Mondschau* (1960). *Heimlichkeiten* (1961). *Verloren gewonnen* (1961).

Bibliography

Langer, Norbert, *Dichter aus Österreich* (Wien, 1958), pp. 130ff. Schmidt, Adalber, *Dichtung und Dichter Österreichs im 19 und 20 Jahrhundert* II (Salzburg, 1964), p. 26.

M.A. Reiss

Martina Wied

(see: Alexandrine Martina Augusta Schnabl)

Gerhard Wieland

(see: Berta Lask)

Ottilie Wildermuth

Born February 22, 1817, Rottenburg, Würtemberg, Germany; died July 12, 1877, Tübingen.
Genre(s): short story, novella
Language(s): German

Ottilie Wildermuth's profuse writings were strongly influenced by her Swabian homeland. Born in Rottenburg, Würtemberg, in 1817 to Gottlieb and Leonore Rooschuz, Ottilie Wildermuth lived her entire life in this area of

Germany. In 1819 she began to attend school in Marbach, and at age sixteen went to the Katherinenstift in Stuttgart to learn the arts of household management. She met Dr. Johann David Wildermuth, language teacher at the high school in Tübingen and was married to him in 1843. She gave lessons to young women and founded a society that existed for thirty-eight years with the purpose of uplifting women.

Wildermuth was one of the most well-loved writers of women's stories of the period. Her stories, reflecting daily life in Schwabenland, emphasize the virtues of a faithful marriage and happy home. "Die alte Jungfer" (The Old Maid) was in 1847 the first of her stories to appear in a journal. For the next thirty years, she produced stories that appeared in journals and collections such as *Bilder und Geschichten aus Schwaben* (1852; Pictures and Stories from Schwabenland) which presents a "more or less realistic" look at life in Wildermuth's homeland. *Aus dem Frauenleben* (1855–1857; From a Woman's Life) and *Die Heimat der Frau* (1859; The Homeland of the Woman) are collections of stories that treat the theme of faithfulness and duty, not necessarily love, as the foundation of a marriage. Her works for children include *Aus der Kinderweit* (1854; From the Child's World), *Aus Schloss und Hütte* (1861; From Castle and Cottage), and *Aus Nord und Süd* (1874; From North and South). From 1870 she was also editor of *Der Jugendgarten* (Youth Garden), a journal of young people.

In 1871 Wildermuth was awarded a Gold Medalion for Art and Science. She died of a nervous disorder in 1877 and was honored a decade later with a monument in the city of Tübingen. Marbach founded a kindergarten in her honor, while Tübingen opened the Ottilie Wildermuth School on the fiftieth anniversary of her death.

Works

See Kosch, Pataky, ADB, *Gesammelte Werke* (10 vols. 1891–1894). *Werke* (8 vols. 1862).

Translations: *By Daylight*, tr. A. Pratt (1865). *Leon and Zephie, or the Little Wanderers*, tr. Anna B. Cooke (1865). *Stories for Little Folks*, tr. Anna B. Cooke (1866). *A Queen: A Story for Girls*, tr. Anna B. Cooke (1867, 1870, 1874). *Household Stories*, tr. E. Kimmont (1872). *The Little Sad Boy, or Who Is Best Off? A True Story* (189?).

Bibliography

Schmidt, Minna, *400 Outstanding Women of the World and the Costumology of their Time: The Authors* (Chicago, 1933). Willms, A., and A. Wildermuth, *Ottilie Wildermuths Leben (nach ihren eigenen Aufzeichnungem zusammengestellt und ergänzt)* (1888).

Ann Willison

Wilja

(see: Wilhelmina "Minna" Ulrika [Johnson] Canth)

Gertrud Wilker

Born March 18, 1924, Solothurn, Switzerland
Genre(s): novel, short story, radio drama,
*   children's literature, essay*
Language(s): German

Gertrud Wilker (née Hürsch) went to high school in Bern and studied German, psychology and art history in Bern and Zurich. After she had received her Ph.D., she worked as a librarian and teacher at a private school in Bern. She lived in the United States from 1962 to 1964. She presently lives in Wabern, Switzerland, where she works as a free-lance writer. She belongs to the Bern Association of Writers and the Group Olden. Gertrud Wilker became famous with her novel *Collages USA*, which reflects her experiences in the United States, where she felt homesick and alienated from her own country. She also thematized the process of poetic writing itself and discusses the author's distrust and criticism of his own work. Language is described as an independent and self-determining object once written down by the author.

She received the Prize of the Swiss Schiller Foundation in 1971 and the Award of the Bern Literary Commission in 1971 and 1978.

Works

Novels and short stories: *Der Drachen. Ein Gespräch* [The Dragon. A Talk] (1959). *Elegie auf die Zukunft* [Elegy on the Future] (1966). *Collages USA* (1968).

Einen Vater aus Wörtern machen [To Create a Father out of Words] (1970). *Altläger bei kleinem Feuer* [Old Experienced Campers at a Small Fire] (1971). *Jota* (1973). *Winterdorf* [Winter Village] (1977). *Blick auf meinesgleichen* [Look on People Like Myself] (1979). *Nachleben* [Life After Death] (1980). *Wolfsschatten* [In The Shadow of A Wolf] (1980).

Radio play: *Hörspiel-Sprechoper, Variationen über ein bekanntes Thema in der Originaltonart* [Radio-Play Talk Opera, Variations of a Well-Known Topic in the Original Voice] (1979).

Book for children: *Lesebuch, Kursbuch für Mädchen* [Story Book, Course Book for Girls] (1978).

Albrecht Classen

Marianne von Willemer

Born November 20, 1784, Linz, Austria; died December 6, 1860, Frankfurt am Main, Germany
Genre(s): poetry
Language(s): German

Willemer was a ballerina and actress in Frankfurt where the banker and privy counselor, Johann Jakob Willemer, was a director of the state theatre. Willemer, at that time a widower, took Willemer into his home in 1800 in order to protect her from the temptations of the stage. Willemer possessed remarkable social gifts, and she soon became the trusted friend of the family and the center of their social life. She was described as beautiful, talented, joyous, unaffected.

Goethe met Willemer in the summer of 1814 before her marriage to her foster father. At that time Goethe had read the collected poems of the Persian poet Hafis, and he was considering a similar collection in German. On his return to Frankfurt in 1815, Willemer became the inspiration for Suleika of the *West-östlicher Divan* (collection of verses of west and east); Goethe was Hatem. About the book of Suleika, Goethe wrote: "The shadow of earthly love reveals divine love." Love is celebrated as the creative force of the world, and Hatem is the giver and receiver of eternal love. Suleika appears as the inspiration and as the creator of poetry. Several of the poems in *Buch Suleika* were certainly written by

Willemer and several others partially by her: "Nimmer will ich dich verlieren"; "Ach, um deine feuchten Schwingen"; "Was bedeutet die Bewegung." Goethe said of the poem "Was bedeutet die Bewegung . . ." that it was the most beautiful poem ever composed by a German woman writer. The verses in memory of their last meeting are inscribed on the parapet of the castle in Heidelberg.

Bibliography

Bielschowsky, Albert, *Goethe, sein Leben und Seine Werke*, vol. 2 (Munich, 1913). Creizenach, Theodor, *Briefwechsel zwischen Goethe und Marianne v. Willemer* (Stuttgart, 1877). Grimm, Hermann, "Goethe und Suleika." *Preussische Jahrbücher*, vol. 24 (1869). Schmidt, Erich, "Marianne-Suleika." *charakteristiken* (Berlin, 1886).

Mary Gies Hatch

Dorrit Willumsen

Born August 31, 1940, Copenhagen, Denmark
Genre(s): novel, short story, poetry, drama
Language(s): Danish

Dorrit Willumsen can be classified as a modernist because she adeptly applies modernist stylistic techniques to modernist themes of alienation and depersonalization. There is, however, a pronounced fantastic element in her work, often leading critics to describe her bleak futuristic settings as science fictional.

Dorrit Willumsen grew up in a working-class neighborhood in Copenhagen and studied classical languages at the Metropolitan School in 1960. She took a variety of jobs before her first book, a short-story collection, *Knagen* (The Peg) was published in 1965, establishing her as an important modernist writer. She has won several Danish awards, including a State's Lifelong Grant in 1980, The Danish Academy's prize for literature in 1981, and the Critics Prize in 1984.

The encroachment of artificiality upon personality, whether through narcissism or rampant consumerism, is one of Willumsen's major themes, resulting in the proliferation of dolls, mannequins, and robots in her works. Abandoned children use their dolls as parent-surrogates, taking revenge upon them or otherwise externalizing their emotions in them. A little girl in *The krydderi acryl salær græshopper* (1970; Tea, Spice, Acrylic, Fee, Grasshopper) eats her doll after her father leaves, thereby becoming one with it. Adults have similar, if less innocent, relationships to "dolls." In "Modellen Coppelia" (1973; The Model Coppelia; the title story from the collection of the same name), the title character virtually turns herself into a wax mannequin in an attempt to avoid sex-role stereotyping by hanging on to her modelling job in order to keep her independence. *Programmet til kærlighed* (1981; Programmed for Love) features a female robot, "programmed for love," in other words, designed to be everything a man desires in a woman. In *Marie* (1983), Willumsen departs from her usual practice of depicting only fragments of lives in order to write a historical novel about Marie Tussaud, who survived the French Revolution by preserving the visages of its victims in wax. Another of Willumsen's major themes, sometimes found in combination with the first, is the relationship between men and women. Although a feminist, she is capable of seeing the oppressiveness of sex roles from both men's and women's points of view, and is pessimistic about easy solutions. In *Manden som påskud* (Man as an Excuse), which won the Danish Academy's prize in 1980, the male character, referred to only as "the man," is ostensibly in control; in fact he is really imprisoned in the authoritarian masculine roles he plays to his first and second wives, his daughters by each of them, and his mistress, all of whom are interested in him only as an excuse for their own development. The man becomes homeless, then dies. Each chapter of the novel is an interior monologue of one of the characters and expresses each viewpoint with understanding and sympathy. The lyrical prose frequently slips unabashedly into long sections of poetry. Willumsen's stylistic virtuosity, which draws on the fantastic as much as it does on modernism, has served her well in her depiction of the feelings and sensations of all human generations in all states of mind, from innocent child to schizophrenic adult. In one of her earlier works, *Da* (1968; Then), an intense long poem based upon her own childhood, she not only portrays the child's point of view, but the lives of four generations of relatives as well. In *Stranden* (1967; The Beach) and *Neonhaven* (1976; The Neon Garden) she depicts hallucinatory experiences, and the story "Hvis det virkelig var en film (1978; If It Really Were a Film, from the collection by the same name) is an interior monologue of a man who may or may not be a serial killer—his reality is so confused with the films he has seen that he doesn't seem to know for sure himself. Willumsen almost always gives us only fragments of experience, however, betraying a modernist lack of faith in continuity and skepticism about the relationship between cause and effect. Besides her formidable accomplishments in poetry and fiction, Willumsen has also worked successfully in the dramatic genre. Her first play was *Jomfru åben for kontakt* (1970; Virgin Open to Contact), which takes place in a supermarket. Also notable is the television program "Børn" (Children), which played in February 1982 in six parts, three of which were by Willumsen. The irony of this play is developed by having adults play the part of children.

Although labels like "modernist," "feminist," "science-fictional," "surrealistic," and "fantastic" are often attached to Willumsen's work, her real strength lies in her depiction of the individual's subjective response, whether to the artificial stimuli of a technological environment or to the rules and regulations of an earlier and supposedly simpler society. She is clearly rooted in European literary traditions, as is amply demonstrated in her use of the name "Coppelia," hearkening back to Hoffman, and her rewriting of Strindberg's "The Stronger." Her use of these themes updates them, however, showing their formal relevance to the present, in spite of the vast changes that have occurred since they were first used.

Works

"Børn" ["Children"], television screenplay (1985). *Caroline* (1985). *Da* [Then] (1968). *Glemslens Forår* [The Spring of Oblivion] (1988). *Hvis det virkelig var en film* [If It Really Were a Film] (1978). *Jomfru åben for kontakt* [Virgin Open to Contact], stage play (1970). *Knagen* [The Peg] (1965). *Kontakter* [Contacts] (1976). *Manden som påskud* [Man as an Excuse] (1980). *Marie: en roman om Marie Tussauds liv* [Marie: A Novel About the Life of Marie Tussaud] (1983). *Modellen Coppelia*

[The Model Coppelia] (1973). *Neonhaven* [The Neon Garden] (1976). *Ni liv* [Nine Lives] (1982). *Programmet til kaerlighed* [Programmed for Love] (1981). *Stranden* [The Beach] (1967). *Suk hjerte* [Sigh Heart] (1986). *The krydderi acryl salær græshopper* [Tea, Spice, Acrylic, Fee, Grasshopper] (1970). *Umage par* [Odd Couple] (1983). *En værtindes smil* [A Hostess's Smile] (1974).

Translations: *Bück Dich, Schneewittchen*, tr. Hans-Peter Naumann [German of *The krydderi acryl salær græshopper*] (1973). *If It Really Were a Film*, tr. Ann-Marie Rasmussen [English of *Hvis det virkelig var en film*] (1982). *Mannen som svepskäl*, tr. Jan Gehlin [Swedish of *Manden som påskud*] (1981). *Marie: A Novel About the Life of Marie Tussaud*, tr. Patricia Crampton (London, 1986). *Ongis*, tr. Maria Krysztofiak [Polish of *Da*] (1975).

Bibliography

Dalager, Stig, *Danske kvindelige forfattere: udvikling og perspektiv* (Copenhagen, 1982). *Dansk biografisk leksikon*, 3rd ed. (Copenhagen, 1979). Wamberg, Bodil, "I Am Only Afraid of Pure Angels." *Out of Denmark* (Copenhagen), pp. 89–102. Wamberg, Bodil, "Dorrit Willumsen." *Danske digtere i det 20. århundrede*, Vol. 5, ed. Torben Brøstrom and Mette Winge (Copenhagen, 1980–1982), pp. 244–258.

Kristine Anderson

Juliane Windhager

Born October 12, 1912, Bad Ischl, Austria;
died November 23, 1986, Salzburg
Genre(s): poetry, prose, radio drama
Language(s): German

Juliane Windhager is a *grand dame* of Austrian literature. Her work is traditional, but her voice is individual, characterized by both melancholy and charm. During her life-long career she distinguished herself primarily as a poet although her late prose work was also well received. Nature, as a principal poetic theme, is often fused with personal experience and childhood memories to create the poetic miniatures for which she is known.

When Windhager was born in 1912 the Hapsburg Monarchy was still on the throne, and her birthplace, Bad Ischl in Upper Austria, was the vacation spot for Emperor Franz Joseph. She attended school in Bad Ischl and in Pau, France. From 1939 until her death in 1986, she lived as a free-lance writer in Salzburg. Not the two world wars through which she lived but rather her childhood experiences and the values of that era seem to have been the formative influences on her life.

Her first two volumes of poetry, *Der linke Engel* (1959; The Left Angel) and *Die Disteltreppe* (1960; The Thistle Stairs), are characterized in part by traditional rhyme, rhythm, and stanzaic patterns. A departure therefrom is visible in *Talstation* (1967; Valley Stop), and her last book of poetry, *Schnee-Erwartung* (1979; Anticipation of Snow), is almost entirely in free verse. An analogous development is evident in her use of metaphor, progressing from traditional nineteenth-century images to original and unusual comparisons.

Her work reveals a careful observation of details in nature, which often conjure up memories of the past, and she writes of "the forgotten voice of the water under the snow." Her sense for concrete, lived experience does not preclude an openness to the fantastic, and she also writes of witches, angels, and other-worldly beings that break into human lives. *Schnee-Erwartung* includes poems about historical and mythological times and faraway places. Rather than relying on the exotic element for effect, however, she dissolves the narrative structure and transforms it into her own imaginary sequence of scenes and images.

At the age of seventy-two Windhager published a collection of short stories, *Ein Engel in Oulu* (1984; An Angel in Oulu). It contains realistic narratives of unusual situations, and the tension inheres in the relationship between imagination and reality. One of the best pieces is "Gras ist nicht blau" (Grass Is not Blue), describing the protest of a young peasant woman upon seeing a modern painting of her native village and thus broaching the question of representation in art. The title story tells of an angel who helped to put out a fire in the Finnish village of Oulu and who subsequently decided to stay there and become human. This balance between reality and fantasy, between self and world is characteristic of her work throughout.

Windhager's literary production is representative of an older sensibility. Before discounting it as provincial or trivial, however, one would do well to regard the historical context. Her best work appeared during the last two decades of her life, beginning when she was already over fifty. Perhaps that helps to explain her return to childhood memories as well as to traditional poetic themes such as nature and love. The experiences of a lifetime are given poetic treatment, and even the sadness is regarded from a reconciling distance. Perceived present and recalled past are inextricably intertwined, which perhaps only testifies to the enduring power of the past. It is, finally, the strength of the poetic language itself that makes Windhager's work stand out from that of numerous others of her time.

Works

Cordelia und das Erbe der Freien. Roman (1936). *Die Kassiansnacht. Novelle* (1942). *Der Friedtäter. Roman* (1948). *Der linke Engel. Gedichte* (1959). *Die Disteltreppe. Gedichte* (1960). *Staubflocken. Hörspiele* (1965). *Talstation. Gedichte* (1967). *Schnee-Erwartung. Gedichte* (1979). *Ein Engel in Oulu. Erzählungen* (1984).

Beth Bjorklund

Christa Winsloe

Born December 23, 1888, Darmstadt, Germany; died June 6 (or 10), 1944, Cluny, France
Genre(s): narrative prose, filmscript
Language(s): German

Winsloe fashioned her life against the grain of the expectations from her family and her society and created a body of fiction that portrays the difficulties felt by a woman who does not wish to conform.

The daughter of a German army officer, Christa Winsloe was educated at a strict girls' school in Potsdam and then sent to a finishing school in Switzerland. She had been educated to become an officer's wife; instead, she went to Schwabing, an area of Munich where many artists lived and pursued a career as a sculptress. Viewed as a dilettante, she achieved little success.

In 1913, she did indeed marry into the station expected of her. Her husband was the Hungarian Baron Ludwig Hatvany, who had made his fortune in sugar cane. At this time, Winsloe wrote a novel, *Das schwarze Schaf* (The Black Sheep), which she never published, perhaps because it mirrored her life too closely. It concerned a girl who is an outsider at school and in the art world where she seeks a career, but who discovers an entrance to the realm of acceptance through marriage to the right man.

Her real life took a different turn, however. Due to her husband's numerous affairs, Winsloe left him and returned to Munich where she pursued anew her artistic ambitions, this time sculpting only figures of animals. She also began to write for publication and soon contributed articles on cultural events to the Munich newspapers and to the prestigious *Querschnitt*, a journal of the arts. With her novella, *Männer kehren heim* (date unknown; Men Return Home), Winsloe began to voice the concern that would occupy the rest of her fiction, namely the question of sexual identity within a society stratified according to gender roles. During the First World War, a girl is attacked by several soldiers, and, to avoid future degradations, she wears her brother's clothes for the rest of the war.

In 1930, Winsloe created the work which made her name as a writer. In that year, her drama *Ritter Nérestan* (Knight Nérestan) premiered in Leipzig. It was a success but was retitled for its Berlin premiere as *Gestern und heute* (Yesterday and Today). Most well-known, however, is the film version, entitled *Mädchen in Uniform* (1931; Girls in Uniform). This work tells of the schoolgirl Manuela von Meinhardis who is forced into the strict confines of a Prussian girls' school. She finds solace and love in her relationship to one of her teachers, Fräulein von Bernburg. After performing the lead male role in the school play, Manuela has too much to drink and openly declares her love for her teacher. The headmistress views such feelings as "sinful" and "morbid" and decides Manuela must leave the school. Unable to face separation from her beloved, Manuela commits suicide. Two conclusions were filmed. In one, Manuela dies, but in the other she is saved by her classmates. This latter version was deemed unacceptable by

American censors. The former was for decades the only version shown in the United States.

The success of this work brought Winsloe's career as a sculptress to an end. In 1934, already in exile, she published the novelized version of this story, *Das Mädchen Manuela* (The Child Manuela). Here, too, Manuela commits suicide. The more erotic elements of the relationship between Manuela and Bernburg are downplayed, and Winsloe brings out Manuela's need for maternal love as the source of her attraction. Ultimately, however, all three versions do treat the love between two females extremely sympathetically and with extraordinary verisimilitude.

A turning point in her life seems to have been her love relationship with the American journalist Dorothy Thompson in 1932–1933. Winsloe accompanied Thompson to the United States, where, however, the latter decided she did not want to be part of a long-term lesbian relationship. Winsloe returned to Europe, settling in the south of France. Her novel, *Life Begins* (1935), published only in English, describes a young sculptress who gains the courage to attempt to live openly with the woman she loves. Her last novel, *Passagiere* (1938; Passengers), has lost that confidence. The heroine is on board a ship where no one knows her. She loses her identity, as a woman and as an individual, and achieves her goal of becoming part of the mass of passengers.

In the 1940s, Winsloe wrote several film scripts, including one for the German director G.W. Papst, *Jeunes filles en détresse*, about girls whose parents are divorced. Another, *Aiono* (1943), depicts a Finnish refugee who dresses in male clothing, a similar theme to that in her earlier novella.

Winsloe was active in the anti-fascist movement in France, even hiding refugees in the home she shared with her lover, the Swiss author Simone Gentet. They were murdered under circumstances that have never been fully explained. The official account attributes their deaths to the hand of a common thief.

Christa Winsloe is best known for her vivid evocation of the cruel repression exercised upon those who could not or would not fit into the narrow bounds drawn by a culture that proscribed behavior according to a strict code of the acceptable and the normal. In her life and her work, she struggled against those rules that denied the validity of any but the voice of the acceptable majority.

Works

Plays: *Ritter Nérestan* (1930). *Gestern und heute* (1930) (English tr., 1933, London and New York). *Der Schritt hinüber* (1940).

Novels: *Das Mädchen Manuela* (1934). *Life Begins* (1935; American title: *Girl Alone*, 1936). *Passeggiera* (1938).

Film: *Mädchen in Uniform* (1931). *Jeunes filles en détresse. Der Schritt hinüber* (1940). *Schicksal nach Wunsch* (1941). *Aiono* (1943).

Bibliography

Foster, Jeannette H., *Sex Variant Women in Literature* (n.p., 1985), pp. 236–238. Jones, James W., "The 'Third Sex' in German Literature from the Turn of the Century to 1933," Ph.D. Diss., University of Wisconsin, 1986, pp. 529–537. Katz, Jonathan, *Gay American History* (New York, 1976), pp. 556–562. Katz, Jonathan, *Gay/Lesbian Almanac* (New York, 1983), pp. 470–472, 479. Reinig, Christa, "Christa Reinig über Christa Winsloe." *Mädchen in Uniform* by Christa Winsloe (Munich, 1983), pp. 241–248. Rich, B. Ruby, "Mädchen in Uniform: From Repressive Tolerance to Erotic Liberation." *Jump Cut* 24/25: 44–50. Russo, Vito, *The Celluloid Closet* (New York, 1981), pp. 56–58. Sanders, Marion K., *Dorothy Thompson: A Legend in Her Time* (New York, 1974), pp. 188–193. Schlaeger, H., *Verfemte Dichterinnen. Verbrannt und vergessen*, in *Bücher*, ed. Brigitte Sonderheft (1983), pp. 22–25. Sheean, Vincent, *Dorothy and Red* (Boston, 1963), pp. 207–242.

James W. Jones

Anna Augusta Henrietta de Wit

Born November 25, 1864, Siboga, presently Sibolga, W. Sumatra, Indonesia; died February 9, 1939, Baarn, The Netherlands
Genre(s): novel, short story
Language(s): Dutch, English

Augusta de Wit was one of a growing group of Dutch authors whose writings reflected their experiences in the Dutch East-Indies, presently Indonesia, with which the Low Countries had had historic ties since the beginning of the six-teenth century. The publication of *Max Havelaar* by Eduard Douwes Dekker (pseud. Multatuli) in 1860 had marked the onset of a series of novels and tales that showed an appreciation of the culture of the far-away archipelago and portrayed the interactions between the Europeans, Eur-asians, and Asians living there.

Admittedly it was a difficult task to recreate this remote world on paper for a reading public that had never experienced the country first hand. Augusta de Wit was eminently qualified to do so. Born on West Sumatra, she had spent the first ten years of her life there. She then went to school in Holland, but returned to the Indies as a teacher and later revisited the islands periodi-cally as a journalist.

Unlike other authors of her time, de Wit does not view conditions and occurrences through the eyes of her European protagonists. Instead, the reader is lured into seeing situations as they appear to the Asians. This focus is enhanced by De Wit's unique style, which shows little influ-ence of European literary traditions but conjures up the story-telling tradition of the far-away islands. Thus her style creates an exotically ap-pealing atmosphere to the reader while the content presents such universal feelings as the pleasures of motherhood or the pride of the craftsman. And when the inevitable conflict between East and West arises, the Dutch readers, while recogniz-ing that they might have reacted the same as their countrymen in the story, will find themselves admitting that the Javanese reactions might not only be justified but are also consistent. In this way, Augusta de Wit succeeds in making her point in the aesthetically pleasing capsules of her tales.

Works

In Dutch: *Verborgen bronnen* [Hidden Sources] (1899). *Orpheus in de Dessa* [Orpheus in the Dessa] (1903). *De godin die wacht* [The Goddess Who Waits] (1903). *Het dure moederschap* [Motherhood Is Dear] (1907). *De drie vrouwen in het heilige woud* [The Three Women in the Sacred Grove], short stories (1920). *Natuur en menschen in Indie* [Nature and People in India], short stories (1914).

De wake bij de brug en andere verhalen [The Wake at the Bridge and Other Tales] (1918). *De avonturen van den muzikant* [The Adventures of the Musi-cian], short stories (1927). *Gods goochelaartjes* [God's Little Magicians], short stories (1932). *Java Facts and Fancies* (1984).

In English: *Island India* (1923). *Java Facts and Fancies* (1905; short stories).

Translation: "The Three Women in the Sacred Grove," *Insulinde, Selected Translations from Dutch Writers of Three Centuries on the Indonesian Archipelago*, ed. Cornelia N. Moore. *Asian Studies at Hawaii* 20 (Honolulu, 1978), pp. 76–99.

Bibliography

Borel, Henri, "Schoonheid in Indie." *De Gids* (1898). Deventer, C. Th. van "Drie Boeken over India." *De Gids* (1900). Netscher, Frans, "Augusta de Wit." *De Hollandse Lelie* (October 19, 1904). Nieuwenhuys, Rob, *Oost-Indische Spiegel* (Amsterdam, 1972), pp. 321–329. Zeyde, Marie H. van der, "Augusta de Wit in nuce." *Bundel opstellen van oudleerlingen aangeboden an Prof. Dr. C.G.N. de Vooys* (Groningen-Batavia, 1940), pp. 376f.

Cornelia N. Moore

Mina Witkojc

Born May 28, 1893, Burg (Spreewald), Germany; died 1975, Papitz (Kreis Cottbus), Germany
Genre(s): lyric poetry
Language(s): Lower Lusatian-Sorbian, used by the western Slavs isolated in Saxony and Brandenberg

One of the earliest women writers in the Lower Lusatian-Sorbian language used by Slavs isolated in a centuries-old enclave in the eastern provinces of Germany, Mina Witkojc wrote lyric poems identifying with the landscape of her native area and encouraging the sense of Slavic identity at a time when it appeared on the verge of extinction.

As the illegitimate daughter of a maidservant who soon died, Mina Witkojc had to take care of herself from childhood. After grade school she was a maid and factory worker in Berlin from 1907 to 1917, then a day laborer in Burg until

1922. From 1923 on, she devoted her great energy to the Sorbian national movement in the Germanized territory of Lower Lusatia as an editor of journals and calendars for the common people. Persecuted during the Nazi period of 1933–1945, she became a manual worker in Erfurt after her journal was confiscated, and she was briefly imprisoned and exiled from the Lusatian area. After the war she again was active in the Sorbian literary movement, and from 1947 to 1954 she lived in Czechoslovakia. From 1955 on she lived and wrote in Burg. Besides her own poetry she translated Pushkin, the Czechs Petr Bezruč and Bo'ena Němcová, as well as Slovak and German writers. She received the Ćišinski-Preis in 1964.

After publishing her first poems in the journal *Lu'ica*, she collected them in *Dolnoserbske basni* (1925; Lower Sorbian Poems). This was followed by *Wěnašk błośańskich kwětkow* (1934; A Wreath of Spreewald Flowers), and after the war by *K swětlu a slyńcu* (1955; To the Light and the Sun). Her work revived the tradition of nature lyrics and Sorbian national patriotism established by the poet and linguist Handrij Zejler in the nineteenth century. During the Weimar period and the 1930s in Lower Lusatia, she also spoke out against militarism and chauvinism, asking for national rights and also women's rights as is shown in her account of her life as an editor in *Po pucach Casnikarki* (1969; On the Path Taken by a *Casnik* Editor, 1969). Her terrible wartime experiences were movingly caught in *Erfurtske spomnješa* (1945; Recollections of Erfurt).

Besides her significance as one of the earliest women writers, Mina Witkojc's work against the Prussian and Nazi efforts to destroy the Sorbian sense of Slavic identity, made her a "Biblical voice in the wilderness," according to Marja Mlynkowa, whose *Ein Sommer der alten Frau* in 1970 was inspired by the life and work of Mina Witkojc.

Works

Dolnoserbske basni (1925). *Wěnašk błośańskich kwětkow* (1934). *Erfurtske spomnjesa* (1945). *K swětlu a slyńcu* (1955). *Po pucach Casnikarki* (1969).
Translations: Czech: *Erfurtské vzpominky* (1947).

Bibliography

Frinta, Antonín, *Lu'ičtí Srbové a jejich Písemnictvi* (Prague, 1955).
General references: *Lexikon deutschsprachiger Schriftsteller von den Anfängen bis zur Gegenwart.* Vol. 2 (Leipzig, 1974), p. 475. Lorenc, Kito, ed., *Serbska čitanka: Sorbisches Lesebuch* (Leipzig, 1981), pp. 476–477. *Mały słownik pisarzy zachodnio-słowiańskich i południowosłowiańskich* (Warsaw, 1973), p. 491.

Norma L. Rudinsky and Milan <Z&>itny

Włast

(see: Maria Komornicka)

Gabriele Wohmann

Born 1932, Darmstadt, West Germany
Genre(s): novel, short story, lyric poetry, drama
Language(s): German

Gabriele Wohmann studied German literature and music, taught from 1953–1956, and has been a very productive writer with about 50 or more books to her credit. Her narrative works are mostly very detailed observations of human interaction in daily life, of marriage partners, of children, of relatives, of neighbors, of lovers. All are situated into the dialectic of physical closeness and inner separation, into a daily routine filled with negative feelings, into a familiar private world that knows no communication. Wohmann does not explain the dismal nature of human relationships, the destructiveness, the loneliness, the psychosomatic illness, she simply describes acrimoniously, internalizing negativism into the distancing of inner monologues. The subjective expression of all characters does not invoke sympathy or empathy; it seems rather to get lost in the ironic minuteness of observation. One senses a narrowness, which does not point beyond, which lacks existential valor, which has deterministic features and is reductionist in nature.

Works

Mit einem Messer, short stories (1958). *Jetzt oder nie*, novel (1958). *Sieg über die Dämmerung*, short stories (1960). *Trinken ist das herrlichste*, short stories (1963). *Theater von innen*, essays (1966). *Abschied für länger*, novel (1965). *Die Bütows*, short stories (1967). *Ländliches Fest*, short stories (1968). *Ernste Absicht*, novel (1970). *Treibjagd*, short stories (1970). *Sonntag bei den Kreisands*, short story (1970). *Selbstverteidigung*, prose pieces (1971). *Der Fall Rufus*, story (1971). *Übersinnlich*, story (1972). *Habgier*, short stories (1973). *Paulinchen war allein zu Haus*, novel (1974). *Schönes Gehege*, novel (1975). *Ausflug mit der Mutter*, novel (1976). *Grund zur Aufregung*, lyric (1978). *Frühherbst in Badenweiler* (1978). *Paarlauf*, short stories (1979). *Ach wie gut, daß niemand weiß*, novel (1980). *Komm lieber Mai*, lyric (1981). *Das Glückspiel*, short stories (1981). *Jetzt und Nie*, novel (1981). *Einsamkeit*, short stories (1981). *Stolze Zeiten*, short story (1981). *Wir sind eine Familie*, short stories (1981). *Ein günstiger Tag*, short stories (1981). *Der Kürzeste Tag des Jahres*, short stories (1983). *Verliebt, oder?*, short stories (1983). *Passau, Gleis 3*, lyric (1984). *Ich lese, ich schreibe*, autobiographical essays (1984). *Der Irrgast*, short stories (1985).

Bibliography

Häntzschel, Günter, ed.: *Gabriele Wohmann* (Munich, 1982). Scheuffelen, Thomas, ed., *Gabriele Wohmann* (Darmstadt und Neuwied, 1977). Wellner, Klaus, *Leiden an der Familie* (Stuttgart, 1976).

Margaret Eifler

Christa Wolf

Born March 18, 1929, Landsberg/Warthe (now Gorzów, Poland)
Genre(s): novel, short story, essay, film script
Language(s): German

Christa Wolf's prose belongs to the most highly respected literature of the second half of this century. Not only has she won critical acclaim as novelist, short story writer, and essayist in both Germanies, her work is also widely read and respected in English translation.

From Wolf's earliest years, the political events of her times have directly affected her life and form the bases of her writing. She was four when Hitler became Chancellor, ten when the war began, and sixteen when her family fled their home, the small city of Landsberg, East of the Oder River (now the Eastern border of the GDR), settling in Mecklenburg, an area which became part of the Soviet zone. As a schoolgirl, Wolf participated in Nazi organizations and did not question the only ideology to which she had been exposed. However, after she had completed her *Abitur* (diploma granted when university prep examinations are passed) in 1949, she became an active member of the SED (the ruling party of the GDR). From 1949–1953, Wolf studied *Germanistik* at the Universities of Jena and Leipzig, where Hans Mayer, renowned scholar of literary history and philosophy, supervised her *Diplomarbeit*, "Problems of Realism in the Work of Hans Fallada."

In 1953, Wolf moved to East Berlin, which is still her home, and began working as reader for, then editor of, the journal, *Neue Deutsche Literatur*. She was also chief editor of the publishing house Neues Leben (until 1959) and reader for the Mitteldeutschen Verlag (publisher) in Halle (1959–1962). Since 1962, she has written full time, remaining, nevertheless, active in various writers' associations (an official in the writers' union, 1955–1977; member of PEN, GDR; member of the Academy of Arts, GDR), as well as being part of the Central Committee of the SED from 1963 through 1967. Wolf has received numerous, prestigious literary prizes from both Germanies including the Heinrich Mann Prize (1963); Wilhelm Raabe Prize of the City of Braunschweig (1972, declined); Theoodor Fontane Prize for Art and Literature (1972); Literature Prize of the Free Hanseatic City Bremen (1977); Georg Büchner Prize (1980).

Her earliest published work, "Moscow Novella" (1961), an idyllic German/Russian love story laced with reflections on Fascism and Socialism rightly evoked little literary stir. In contrast, Wolf's first novel, *Divided Heaven* (1963), a work stimulated by the erection of the Berlin Wall (the story is set in 1961), quickly sold out several printings, was widely translated, and made into a controversial film (1964). The plot is again both a romance and an argument for the values of Socialism. Rita, a pretty and intelligent young woman from a village in the GDR, falls in love with Manfred, a doctoral candidate in chemistry from Berlin (East); she goes to the city to be with him and begin studies to become a teacher. Before the semester starts, Rita finds work in a brigade that builds railroad cars and gets personally involved with the socialist production process; this aspect of the novel reflects Wolf's positive response to the late fifties' *Bitterfelder Weg* behest of Chancellor Ulbricht to intellectuals to participate in the reconstruction efforts of the state (Wolf herself worked in a factory for a time). Such aspects of *Divided Heaven* as long passages about worker relations and Rita's choosing her work brigade over a crass materialistic life with Manfred, who "deserts" to West Germany, reflect the conventions of socialist realism—the doyenne of the genre, Anna Seghers, had considerable influence on Wolf. But the book also shows promise of Wolf's developing individual style, particularly with respect to free flowing perspective change, passages of remembering, and intense self-reflection and questioning on the part of the heroine. Although the Wall itself is never mentioned, there were sufficient controversial topics touched on (for instance, the integration of ex-Fascists, the weaknesses of the socialist production system) to prevent Wolf from publishing for the next five years. Numerous GDR writers of the time suffered similar fates when they chose to write about the problems of East to West migration, for instance Uwe Johnson, who had to publish his *Speculations About Jacob* (1959) in the West. Publicly, officially sanctioned sources in the East focused on Wolf's tendency to "inwardness," condemning it as decadent.

The publication of her next major work, *The Quest for Christa T.* (1968), demonstrated that Wolf had clearly matured into a writer of considerable subtlety and merit. In her fiction, Wolf has tended to work backwards through her own biography. *Christa T.*, for example, reaches back to the period in which Wolf herself was a *Gymnasium* (secondary school) student and extends through the mid-sixties. The structure of the first-person narrator's reflections is not chronological, beginning instead with the title character

already dead; the perspective and time changes are more complicated than those of earlier works. Christa T., a friend of the narrator, embodies the concept of the individual striving for the right of subjective self-realization within the socialist state. Not the events of her life—study, teaching, marriage, children, death from leukemia—make her unique, but rather Christa T.'s constant refusal to stagnate and abnegate personal responsibility for the quality of her life. Christa's dynamic individualism contrasts with and yet affects the lives she touches, most profoundly that of the self-reflective narrator in her quest to comprehend Christa. In *Christa T.*, Wolf begins to define motifs suggested in *Divided Heaven* but central to this and future work: the question of what had become of the Hitler generation; the difficulty of saying "I" or the endless way to one's self; the possibility for a person (and thereby society) to change; the significance of the inner person; the lessons of history, in particular of the literary history of the nineteenth century; the necessity of remembering.

Following the initially unappreciative critical reception of *Christa T.*, Wolf published a series of conceptually experimental short stories and a collection of important literary-theoretical essays between 1969 and 1974. With these essays, *The Reader and the Writer*, she establishes an analytical basis for her own fiction, one that is grounded in her artistic philosophy that the dimension of self is essential for the presentation of truth in literature. The links between her essays and fiction continue into her most recent writing; through her fiction, her researches and theoretical concepts are imbued with life. A central principle of Wolf's writing is that of "subjective authenticity" ("Conversation with Hans Kaufmann," 1974). In a short essay, "Brecht and Others" (1966), she attests to the "determinative" influence this revolutionary author had had on her writing; pivotal for her is the concept that a literature that can capture the essence of modern social tensions has the possibility to change that society. By 1983, however, she had distanced herself from Brecht's aesthetic, suggesting that such objective definition as his tends to negate the potential of literature to express "the vital experience of countless subjects" ("Frankfurt Poetic Lectures").

Wolf's continuing concern with understanding what had made Fascism possible is reflected in the major novel, *A Model Childhood*, which appeared in 1976, a time of relative openness in the GDR to the exploration of its Fascist background (see, for example, Hermann Kant's *Der Aufenthalt*). Convinced that individual responsibility is a cornerstone of sociohistorical developments, Wolf, in keeping with her concept of authorial subjective authenticity, chose as the core of the work characters and events closely linked with those of her own family. The actual occurrence which is related is a trip in 1971 made by Wolf, her sixteen-year-old daughter, her husband, and her brother back to her birthplace, L. (Landsberg), now G. (Gorzów) in Poland. British critic Neal Ascherson aptly describes *A Model Childhood* as "a complex book of reminiscence and reflection." The complexity stems from the varied, free-flowing shifts in perspective and voice as well as in the chronological levels of the narrative. The events reach back to the Hitler years and involve the central character as a child, Nelly, referred to in the third person, the Wolf persona experiencing the trip and remembering her past, addressed as *du* (the familiar form of "you"), and the ongoing voice of the narrator, actually writing the story in the first person in active search for self-understanding, acutely aware of the necessity of the "candid 'I.'" In an attempt to hinder the falsification of history, the narrator assumes a further moral imperative by interlacing her text with real names and reports of contemporary events from November 1972 through May 1975, the period in which Wolf actually wrote the book. The question posed throughout: "How did we become what we are?" While paying indirect homage to Thomas Mann in certain passages (particularly to his "Mario and the Magician"), Wolf has clearly broken from traditional nineteenth-century narrative strictures; in *A Model Childhood* she adds her own voice to the innovative literary structures of the twentieth century, uniquely reflecting the complexity of contemporary reality.

Included among the theoretical concepts that Wolf has developed in her attempt to find "a new way to write" through "a new way to be in the world" are the re-examination of historical roots, especially those of the nineteenth-century romantics, where she finds the emergence of the intellectual woman in Germany, and the literary realization of the *Subjektwerden des Menschen* (presentation of human beings as subjects of literature rather than objects), while retaining artistic objectivity through epic distancing.

The 1979 novel *No Place on Earth* (the title in German is a play on the word *utopia*, no place) grew, for example, out of Wolf's essayistic considerations of the largely forgotten romantic author, Karoline von Günderode (1780–1806) and Heinrich von Kleist (1777–1811), a writer condemned as decadent in the GDR in line with Georg Lukác's theory of bourgeois writers. Wolf preceded her novel with considerable research re-evaluating the subjectivity of the romantics, the women in particular (see her excellent essay, "Der Schatten eines Traumes" [The Shadow of a Dream], introducing her edition of Günderode's works, 1979). In *No Place on Earth*, Wolf concentrates the action into a single afternoon, a fictive encounter of Günderode and Kleist at a tea. Karoline longs to have the right to assume the active role in life reserved for men in her times; Kleist protests the limitations on men's expression of their feelings. Wolf's suggestions for the breaking down of societal role barriers to achieve human wholeness and yet preserves unique female and male voices remind one of those of Virginia Woolf although she read Woolf only later. Wolf's own experience with the ingrained traditional sex-role prejudices in the GDR enters the narrative in the reiterated question "Who is speaking?" and in her concept of the "relationship and closeness" of writers' problems in the romantic period to those of the present. Additional researches in the nineteenth century are evidenced in her republication of Bettina von Arnim's *Die Günderode* with an essay Afterword, "A Letter About Bettina" (1980).

With her recent novel, *Cassandra* (1983), Wolf found a plot basis even farther removed from the present—in the prehistorical period of classical myth, a not uncommon setting for writers in the GDR (for example, Irmtraud Morgner, Anna Seghers, Erich Arendt, Peter Hacks). Wolf concentrates on a period building up to the Trojan War that she dubs *Vorkrieg*, that time when war is still preventable. She links her own fears about modern man's moral bankruptcy, self-destructive tendencies, especially with regard to nuclear armament, and her own frustrations as a writer trying to tell the truth, with the fate of Cassandra, cursed to foresee her people's fate but to be considered insane. (Wolf had introduced both "Cassandra" and "pre-war" in *A Model Childhood*.) *Cassandra* begins in the present with the narrator at the ruins of a Mycenean palace, the legendary place of Cassandra's execution after the Greeks had defeated Troy. Without transition Cassandra enters: "With this tale, I approach my own death." Her story unfolds as recollection and reflection in the brief time span between her arrival in the executioner's cart before the palace gates and her beheading at Clytemnestra's order. The "I" is thus distanced into a realm beyond the limitations of actual time or history, yet the text remains intensely personal, the theme of the fatality of the patriarchal power mentality frighteningly current. Wolf calls the work a *roman à clef* and documents its evolution exhaustively in the accompanying *Four Essays*.

The latter 1980s saw a progressively pessimistic view of humankind's future on Wolf's part. Her concern about the destructive tendencies of nations with relation to nature and armament culminated in the short work *Störfall* (1987), an autobiographically based, analytical interpretation of the Chernobyl debacle and the questions it raised about the direction humanity has chosen and the relation and responsibility of the individual to that direction within the context of his/her everyday reality.

Her most recent works of fiction, *Sommerstück* (1989; Summer Play) and *Was bleibt* (1990; What Remains), constitute reworkings of earlier manuscripts. Typically, each has as structuring center a reflective woman. *Sommerstück*, based on Wolf's own experiences between 1975 and 1983, when she wrote the original version, takes place in the Mecklenburg country home of the principal character, where close friends come, go, and interact. Wolf has called it "my most personal book," dealing with the intensely introspective theme through multi-perspective, third-person narrative and affirming personal bonds, reminiscent of Chekhov, and the bond with her *Heimat*. The state ostracism that she and other intellectuals were subjected as

a result of their protesting Wolf Biermann's expulsion (1976) from the GDR is not dealt with here. In contrast, *Was bleibt*, first written in 1979 (i.e., closer to the time Wolf was expelled from the executive committee of the Berlin Writers' Union as a result of having signed the "open letter" in support of Biermann) is a first-person narrative focusing on one day during the period when she was under surveillance by the State Security Police (Stasi). Both of these works of "association" stood in the center of media controversy surrounding Wolf in the months of transition from the Cold War to a unified Germany, *Sommerstück* because it had not been published ten years earlier.

Wolf's response to the events leading to the disappearance of the GDR as a political reality can be found in a collection of her texts written between November 1988 and March 3, 1990, and published as *Christa Wolf im Dialog: Aktuelle Texte* (1990; Current Texts). These speeches, interviews, and letters document a painful death of illusions and hope for a German socialist state. As in her other works, which question both past and present in relation to the future, Wolf continues to question, but the verb "become" ("Wie sind wir so geworden . . . ?"), which had characterized her *oeuvre*, has been replaced with a query about what of all that, which has *become*, has the possibility to *endure* ("Was wird wohl bleiben?"). The failures of the first generation of GDR idealists in dealing with their own history and their resultant failure to guide the second generation, the children of the 1950s and 1960s, to political responsibility is a dominant theme: "But the children of the parents, who were not able to establish real relationships with them, are now the young people who are leaving" (154). Wolf herself left the Socialist Union Party (Communist) in the latter part of 1989. As a writer, the concepts of hope and utopia continue to occupy her, and reflecting on her own writing of the later 1980s, she sees both deriving ultimately from "everyday life" rather than "theory" (162). The constant in Wolf's thinking is the necessity to analyze the "authenticity" of her own reality and to confront the dominant powers, whatever they be (168).

The ever-growing control and complexity of Wolf's narrative voice combines with her involvement with language use and philosophical development to fix her achievements among those of the outstanding writers in our times. In her search for expression of woman's subjective perspective, she explicitly rejects the historical tradition of subjugating women, in general, and the prevailing male literary standard, in particular. Western feminists, including writers and filmmakers, have long been positively influenced by her work. Wolf herself cites Ingeborg Bachmann and Marie-Luise Fleißer as forerunners of a new art form in which the writer rejects the role of object and finds new forms and the self-confidence in which to express herself as active subject. With her extensive involvement in political life, her world travels, and strong commitment to change without regard to political party, she serves as a model for those concerned with pushing back prevailing limits towards self-realization as writers and as individuals.

Works

Moskauer Novelle (1961). *Der geteilte Himmel Erzählung* (1963). *Nachdenken über Christa T.* (1968). *Lesen und Schreiben. Aufsätze und Betrachtungen* (1972). [With Gerhard Wolf], *Till Eulenspiegel. Erzählung für den Film* (1973). *Unter den Linden. 3 unwahrscheinliche Geschichten* (1974; rev. 1977). *Kindheitsmuster* (1976). *Fortgesetzter Versuch: Aufsätze, Gespräche, Essays* (1979). *Kein Ort. Nirgends* (1979). *Gesammelte Erzählungen:* "Blickwechsel," "Dienstag, der 27. September," "Juninachmittag," "Unter den Linden," "Neue Lebensansichten eines Katers." "Kleiner Ausflug nach H.," "Selbstversuch. Traktat zu einer Protokoll" (1980). *Lesen und Schreiben. Neue Sammlung* (1980). *Kein Ort. Nirgends/Karoline von Günderrode. Der Schatten eines Traumes,* ed. and intro. Christa Wolf (1981). *Kassandra. Erzählung und Frankfurter Poetik-Vorlesungen* (1983). [With Gerhard Wolf], *Ins Ungebundene gehet eine Sehnsucht. Gesprächsraum Romantik. Prosa, Essays* (1985). *Die Dimension des Autors. Essays und Aufsätze, Reden und Gespräche. 1959–1985* (1986). *Störfall. Nachrichten eines Tages* (1987). *Ansprachen. Reden, Briefe, Reflexionen* (1988). *Sommerstück* (1989). *DDR, Journal zur Novemberrevolution: August bis Dezember 1989: vom Ausreisen bis zum Einreißen der Mauer:*

Chronik (1989). *Was bleibt* (1990). *Christa Wolf im Dialog. Aktuelle Texte* (1990).

Screenplays: [With Gerhard Wolf], *Der geteilte Himmel* (1964). [With Gerhard Wolf], *Fräulein Schmetterling* (1965–66; never distributed). [With others], *Die Toten bleiben jung,* adaptation of the novel by Anna Seghers (1968). [With Gerhard Wolf], *Till Eulenspiegel. Eine historische Legende nach Motiven des Deutschen Volksbuches* (1975). [With Alfried Nehring], *Selbstversuch,* film for GDR TV (1990).

Translations: *Divided Heaven* [*Der geteilte Himmel*], tr. J. Becker (1965). *The Quest for Christa T.* [*Nachdenken über Christa T.*] (1970). *The Reader and the Writer: Essays, Sketches, Memories* [*Lesen und Schreiben*], tr. J. Becker (1977). *A Model Childhood* [*Kindheitsmuster*], tr. Molinaro/Rappolt (1980). *No Place on Earth* [*Kein Ort. Nirgends*], tr. J. van Heurck (1982). *Cassandra: A Novel and Four Essays* [*Kassandra und die Frankfurter Poetik-Vorlesungen*], tr. J. van Heurck (1984). *What Remains* [*Was bleibt*] (Farrar, Straus & Giroux, 1991). Excerpts of *What Remains* have been published in *Granta 33.* For translations of shorter works through 1982, see M. Gerber and J. Pouget, *Literature of the German Democratic Republic in English Translation. A Bibliography* (1984).

Bibliography

Arnold, H-L., ed., "Christa Wolf," secondary literature in German to April 1984, *Kritisches Literaturlexikon* (Munich, 1985). Drescher, Angela, ed., *Christa Wolf. Ein Arbeitsbuch. Studien, Dokumente, Bibliographie,* secondary literature in German to 1988 (Frankfurt am Main, 1990). Gruner, Petra, ed., *Agespaßt oder mündig? Briefe an Christa Wolf im Herbst 1989.* Nachwort, Jan Hofmann (Frankfurt am Main, 1990). Hilzinger, Sonja. *Christa Wolf* (Stuttgart: Mutzler, 1986). Hilzinger, S. "Christa Wolf," in *Deutsche Dichter: Gegenwart* (Stuttgart: Reclam, 1990). Hörnigk, Therese, *Christa Wolf: Eine Biographie* (Göttingen, 1989) *Erinnerte Zukunft.* 11 Studien zum Werk (Würzburg, 1990). "Christa Wolf zum 60. Geburtstag," in *Weimarer Beiträge* 3 (1989).

In English: Ascherson, Neal, "Growing up Nazi," review of *A Model Childhood,* in *New York Review of Books* (March 5, 1981). Buehler, George, *The Death of Socialist Realism in the Novels of Christa Wolf* (Frankfurt, Bern, New York, 1984). Buruma,

Ian, "There's No Place Like Heimat," *New York Review of Books* (Dec. 20, 1990). Fox, Thomas C., "Feminist Revisions: Christa Wolf's *Störfall*," in *The German Quarterly* (Summer/Fall, 1990). Hermann, Anne, *The Dialogic and Difference. "An/other Woman" in Virginia Woolf and Christa Wolf* (New York, 1989). Fries, Marilyn Sibley, ed., *Responses to Christa Wolf. Critical Essays*, includes list of English translations and selected secondary literature in English until 1988 (Detroit, 1989). Smith, Colin, *Tradition, art and society. Christa Wolf's Prose* (Essen, 1987). *The Fourth Dimension: Interviews with Christa Wolf*, tr. Hilary Pilkington; intro. Karin McPherson (London, 1990).

Sheila Johnson

Elizabeth Wolff-Bekker

Born July 24, 1738, Vlissingen, The Netherlands; died November 5, 1804, 's Gravenhage
Genre(s): poetry, novel, essay
Language(s): Dutch

Born in 1738 in Vlissingen, as the youngest child in a strict Calvinist merchant family, Elizabeth Bekker studied Latin and theology and early on in life developed a talent for literature. After an unsuccessful one night elopement with the ensign Matthijs Gargon, she had to suffer the censorship of the Calvinist bigots (Dutch: "fijnen") of Vlissingen, one of whom was her brother, whose moral and religious intolerance and hypocrisy she would combat all her life. In 1752, to escape from the unforgiving community of Vlissingen, she married Adriaan Wolff, a 52-year-old widower and minister at Beemster in the province. This "philosophical marriage"—as Betje Wolff called it—lasted 25 years till the death of Reverend Wolff in 1777. Yet, this pragmatic and generally uneventful marriage allowed Betje to bring to fruition her literary potential and within 15 years of her marriage, she achieved national recognition as one of Holland's most gifted but also most controversial authors. After the death of her husband in 1777, E. Wolff invited A. Deken (see also Deken, Agatha), with whom she had been acquainted since 1776, to stay at her house. Even though Deken and Wolff initially

pursued their literary careers individually, they soon started an intellectual collaboration that would last the rest of their lives. Together these two remarkable women wrote some of the most engaging and commercially successful literature of the Age of Enlightenment in Holland, and their novel *Historie van Mejuffrouw Sara Burgerhart* (1782; The History of Miss Sara Burgerhart) has been called "the first modern Dutch novel" (Knuvelder 191). In 1787, following the Prussian intervention in the conflict between the Patriotic and the Orangist parties, Wolff and Deken, who sympathized with the patriotic party, went into exile in Trévoux in France and, due to dire financial problems, did not return to Holland till 1797 when they moved to The Hague. Upon their return, they found Holland and the literary tastes of its readers changed. Wolff and Deken could not repeat their former literary triumphs and supported themselves mainly with translations and contributions from admirers and friends. They stayed together till Elizabeth's death on Nov. 5, 1804. Aagje died only eight days after the death of her life-long companion.

B. Wolff's earliest publications, two volumes of poetry entitled *Bespiegelingen over het genoegen* (Reflections on Joy) of 1763 and *Bespiegelingen over den staat der rechtheid* (Reflections on the State of Righteousness) of 1765, betray the influence of Alexander Pope and the philosophical poem in the neo-classical tradition. In 1769 follows *Walcheren*, a mixed epic and pastoral poem, about the region of Holland with the same name. The first really remarkable work by B. Wolff is the utopian *Holland in het jaar 2440* (Holland in the Year 2440), which was published anonymously in 1770 and which, in epistolary form and satirical tone, deals with the state, education, and the role of women in the Holland of the future. In 1772 Wolff continues her expert satirical attack on contemporary Dutch society with her *Zedenzang aan de Menschenliefde* (Moral Song to Human Love)—a spirited *riposte* to religious fundamentalists who saw the fire of the theatre of Amsterdam, in which several people died, as a sign of divine wrath. The same year she published *De menuet en de dominee's pruik* (The Menuet and the Reverend's Wig)—an amusing mock-epic and satirical narrative about the forced resignation of an elder of a local church who had been observed dancing at the wedding of his daughter. E. Wolff's didactic and reformist concerns resurface in her *Proeve over de opvoeding, aan de Nederlandsche moeders* (Essay Concerning Education. To the Mothers of Holland), which was published in 1780. The essay is prefaced with an introductory poem by A. Deken and as such testifies to the gradual development of their unified literary expression. The first real product of Wolff and Deken's collaboration, a three volume series of poems addressed to the poor of Holland which was entitled *Economische liedjes* (Domestic Songs), appeared in 1781. Yet, the lasting fame of this literary team depends on their first novel, *Historie van Mejuffrouw Sara Burgerhart* (The History of Miss Sara Burgerhart) of 1782. The novel's success was phenomenal (it achieved three editions in four years) and was soon translated into English and French. *The History* is a two-part epistolary novel and, though it betrays the influence of Samuel Richardson and Rousseau, the warning of its title page "Not Translated" (Dutch: "Niet Vertaalt") should be accepted fully. The novel is, indeed, entirely original in its detailed and perceptive portrayal of the Dutch middle class and its values, vices, triumphs, and miseries. The bigots who had caused so much hurt for Betje in her youth and whom she had already denounced vehemently in her previous writings were once again assaulted without pity in *Sara Burgerhart*. Yet the realism of this novel should be understood in terms of its didactic ramifications. As the authors indicate, the book is intended for the instruction and edification of young ladies: "Our main purpose is to prove: That an excess of vivacity, and a resulting desire for entertaining distractions—justified by Fashion and Luxury—often put the best girls in danger of falling into lamentable tragedies which will make them despised in the eyes of such who will never be able to be their equal in probity of heart and moral perfection."

In 1784–1785, Wolff and Deken followed up with *Historie van den heer Willem Leevend* (The History of Mister Willem Leevend), a novel in eight parts, which in its first two parts is as intense and captivating as their first novel but which becomes increasingly philosophical and long winded in the latter part of the novel, as the authors' didactic and speculative bent of mind seems to have overpowered their creative instincts. *Willem Leevend* was not as successful as *Sara Burgerhart* and marked the beginning of the decline of Wolff and Deken's popularity. During the ten years of their exile in Burgundy, they published *The Letters of Abraham Blankaart* (1787), a verse account of their stay in France entitled *Wandelingen door Bourgogne* (1789; Walks in Burgundy), and another epistolary novel, *The History of Miss Cornelia Wildschut* (1793–1796). Yet, none of these works was sufficient to keep alive the popularity of the absent authors with their native audience. Following their return to Den Haag in 1797, Wolff and Deken tried to remedy their financial woes, but the recently published *The History of Miss Cornelia Wildschut* did not appeal widely to the reading public, nor did the two-volume pseudo-autobiographical *Geschrift eener bejaarde vrouw* (The Writing of an Aged Woman) of 1802 bring them much relief.

Thanks to the outstanding scholarship of P.J. Buijnsters and others in the twentieth century, Betje Wolff and Aagje Deken have gained acceptance, after a century of neglect, as "a lasting presence in the history of our literature" (Knuvelder 205). Their wit, humor, refinement and progressive approach to such issues as the role of women, education, and religion at a time when women who had literary ambitions in Holland were almost exclusively confined to the role of what is known in Dutch literature as *zedendichtster*, i.e. moral poetess, are a source of continued fascination to the modern reader.

Works

Dyserinck, J. ed., *Brieven van Betje Wolff en Aagje Deken* (1904). Brandt Corstius, J.C., ed., *Lotje Roulin* (1954). Minderaa, P., ed., *De menuet en de dominees pruik* (1954). de Wolf, H.C., ed., *Proeve over de opvoeding, aan de Nederlandsche moeders* (1978). Huygens, G.W., ed., *Holland in het jaar 2440* (1978). Buijnsters, P.J., ed., *Historie van Mejuffrouw Sara Burgerhart*, 2 vols. (1980). Anthology: Vieu-Kuik, H.J., ed., *Keur uit het werk van Betje Wolff en Aagje Deken* (1969).

Bibliography

Biography: Ghijsen, H.C.M., "Aagje Deken in haar Amsterdamschen tijd 1741–1777." *De Gids* 3

(1970). Ghijsen, H.C.M., *Dapper vrouwenleven. Karakter-en levensbeeld van Betje Wolff en Aagje Deken* (1954). Minderaa, P., et al., eds., *Boeket voor Betje en Aagje. Van en over de schrijfsters Wolff en Deken* (1954). Naber, J.W.A., *Betje Wolff en Aagje Deken* (1913). Simons, P.H., *Wij beginnen te sympathiseren. Betje Wolf en Aagje Deken* (1970). Vieu-Kuik, H.J., *Het gebruik van Franse woorden door Wolff en Deken,* 2 vols. (1957).

Critical studies: Brachin, P., "Idylle et révolution: le séjour en France de Wolff et Deken (1788–1797)." *European Context, Studies in the History and Literature of the Netherlands, Presented to Theodoor Weevers* (1971), pp. 178–193. Brom, Gerard, "Wolff en Deken en de katholieken." *Vijf Studies* (1957). Buijnsters, P.J., "Tijd en plaats in de roman Sara Burgerhart." *Studia Neerlandica* 3 (1970): 20–32. Buijnsters, P.J., *Sara Burgerhart en de ontwikkeling van de Nederlandse roman in de 18e eeuw* (1971). de Vletter, A., *De opvoedkundige denkbeelden van van Betje Wolff en Aagje Deken* (1915). Ghijsen, H.C.M., *Betje Wolff in verband met het geestelijk leven van haar tijd, Jeugd en Huwelijksjaren* (1919). Romein-Verschoor, A., "Eva's tweede appel." *De Stem* (1939). van Betten, H., *Richardson in Holland and His Influence on Wolff and Deken's Novel* Sara Burgerhart. Diss., University of Southern California, 1971. van der Vliet, P., *Wolff en Deken's Brieven van Abraham Blankaart* (1982).

Reference works: Knuvelder, G.P.M., *Handboek tot de geschiedenis van de Nederlandse letterkunde,* vol. 3 (1973), pp. 190–205. Meijer, Reinder P., *The Literature of the Low Countries* (1971), pp. 173–179. For an exhaustive bibliography of Wolff and Deken, see P.J. Buijnsters, *Bibliografie der geschriften van en over Betje Wolff en Aagje Deken* (1979).

Henk Vynckier

Karoline von Wolzogen

Born February 3, 1763, Rudolfstadt, Germany; died January 11, 1847, Jena
Genre(s): novel, short story, biography, letters, drama
Language(s): German

Karoline von Wolzogen achieved a similar literary rank as the famous Rachel von Varnhagen, who established her name with the highly respected literary circle in Berlin, a center of the Older Romantic School. Karoline was born on February 3, 1763, in Rudolfstadt. At the age of sixteen she became engaged to Freiherr von Beulewitz. In 1783 she travelled to Vevey in Switzerland together with her mother and her sister Charlotte, who married Friedrich Schiller in 1790. Her fiancé Beulewitz accompanied them. On their trip they visited a relative, Henriette von Wolzogen, an important patron of Schiller. There Karoline met her future second husband, her cousin Wilhelm von Wolzogen. In Switzerland she also became acquainted with the famous physiologist Lavater. On her trip back she finally met Schiller himself in summer 1784 (see Schiller's letter to H. von Wolzogen June 7, 1784). Soon afterwards Karoline married von Beulewitz, but the marriage was not happy due to intellectual differences between them. At the same time she befriended Caroline von Dachröder and Karl von Dalberg, important personalities in their time, which compensated her for her unfortunate marriage. Since 1787 her contacts with Schiller intensified to a very close friendship. Then she separated from her husband and withdrew to Gaisburg near Cannstatt in Swabia. She published her *Briefe aus der Schweiz* (Letters from Switzerland) and the play *Der Leukadische Fels* (The Leucadian Rock) in 1792 in Schiller's journal *Neue Thalia*. She legally divorced her husband in 1794, and in fall of the same year, married her cousin Wilhelm von Wolzogen, with whom she moved to Weimar in 1797. She published, first anonymously, her novel *Agnes von Lilien* (Agnes from the Lilies) in 1796 in Schiller's journal *Die Horen*, which then appeared in Berlin in 1798 as a separate publication. Due to its popularity, the novel was reprinted two more times until 1800, and Ludwig Salomon edited it again in 1801 with a new introduction. Both brothers Schlegel took it for a production of Goethe, who was himself highly interested in it. Karoline's life and her marriage as well as her friendship with Schiller are closely reflected in the novel. Since 1799 when Schiller moved to Weimar, the von Wolzogen house became a literary center for all the great thinkers and poets in town, a town which was the center of German classical and Romantic literature at that time.

Here Goethe, Wieland, Fichte, Schelling and Wilhelm von Humboldt among others met. Even the Duke Karl August, his wife Luise and his mother, the Duchess Amalie, came and visited them. Two short stories: "Die Zigeuner" (The Gypsies) and "Walther und Nanny" (Walther and Nanny) appeared in Cotta's *Taschenkalender für Damen* in 1800–1802, the latter also in a separate Berlin printing in 1802. Since she had only one child, Adolf, who died in 1825 while hunting, and since her husband was on many diplomatic missions abroad, she had much leisure time to dedicate to her literary production. Her friend Schiller died in 1805, and her husband died in 1809. She withdrew from society but continued writing. She published two volumes of short stories in 1826, and in 1830 Schiller's biography: *Schillers Leben. Verfaßt aus Erinnerungen der Familie, seinen eigenen Briefen und den Nachrichten seines Freundes Körner* (Schiller's Life. Composed on the Basis of Memories of the Family, His Own Letters and News From His Friend Körner). She published the short story "Adele" in 1839 and her novel *Cordelia* in 1840, which again abounded in reflections on her life and contained little action. Her short story "Das neue Jahr" appeared in *Urania* in 1842. She began to work on other projects such as the novel *Alma* or the life of Dalberg, her old friend, but nothing was finished before her death on January 11, 1847. Among her other unpublished works are *Livre de plans* (Book with Projects), a collection of approximately 50 extended or only brief outlines of novels and short stories, which were written during the years of her friendship with Schiller in Weimar. According to her last will, a large part of her work was destroyed after her death, another part was published by Karl Hase in 1842, 2nd ed. in 1867, as *Literarischer Nachla der Frau Caroline von Wolzogen* (Unpublished Works By Ms. Caroline von Wolzogen), which includes a biography of Abeken, letters and notes from her diary.

Works

Briefe aus der Schweiz [Letters from Switzerland] (1792). *Der Leukadische Fels* [The Leucadian Rock] a play (1792).
Novels: *Agnes von Lilien* [Agnes from the Lilies] (1796, 1798, 1800, 1801). *Cordelia* (1840).

Short stories: *Die Zigeuner* [The Gypsies] (1800). *Walther und Nanny* [Walther and Nanny] (1802). *Adele* (1839). *Das neue Jahr* (1842).
Biography: *Schillers Leben. Verfat aus Erinnerungen der Familie, seinen eigenen Briefen und den Nachrichten seines Freundes Körner* [Schiller's Life. Composed out of Memories of the Family, His Own Letters and News From His Friend Körner] (1830).

Bibliography

Aner-Müller, E., *Schiller und die Schwestern von Lengefeld* (2nd ed., 1838). Bierbaum, H., *Karoline von Wolzogen*. Diss., Greifswald, 1909. Brock, St., *Karoline von Wolzogens "Agnes von Lilien."* Diss., Berlin, 1914. Calou, Thomas, *The Life and Works of Friedrich Schiller* (New York, 1901), pp. 5, 10, 206, 213, 256, 268. Kahn-Wallerstein, Carmen, *Die Frau im Schatten Schillers. Schwägerin Karoline von Wolzogen* (Bern, Munich, 1970). Kahn-Wallerstein, Carmen, "Karoline von Wolzogen, Ein Frauenbild aus Weimars klassischer Zeit." *Deutsche Rundschau* 81 (1955): 1277–1287. Scherer, Wilhelm, *A History of German Literature*, tr., vol. (Oxford, 1886), p. 232. *Schillers Leben und Werk in Daten und Bildern*, ed. Bernhard Zeller (Frankfurt, 1966), pp. 111–121, 155–157, 177–179 et al. von Wiese, Benno, *Friedrich Schiller* (Stuttgart, 1959), pp. 289–294 et al.

Albrecht Classen

Charlotte Worgitzky

Born 1934, Annaberg, Erzgebirge, Germany
Genre(s): novel, short story
Language(s): German

Charlotte Worgitzky is an actress in East Berlin and has published two novels and one volume of short stories, the latter listed below in second place.

Works

Die Unschuldigen (1975). *Vieräugig oder blind* (1978). *Meine ungeborenen Kinder* (1978).

Ute Marie Saine

Pauline Frederikke Worm

*Born November 29, 1825, Hyllested,
Denmark; died December 13, 1883,
Copenhagen*
Genre(s): novel, poetry, essay, lecture
Language(s): Danish

As an engaged, concerned teacher and school administrator, Pauline Frederikke Worm played an active role in the educational, cultural, and social debates of her day. Along with Louise Bjørnsen, Mathilde Fibiger, and Athalie Schwartz, Worm was an outspoken critic of the education afforded young women; she also spoke out on feminist and equal rights issues, on the untenable position of Danish governesses and private tutors, on the rising tide of Danish nationalism, based on the "spirit of 1848—the spirit of freedom, Danish identity, and Nordic unity" (*Dansk biografisk Leksikon*, 16, 51) and on the Danish resistance to German and Prussian political and military pressures, particularly evident after the War of 1864 and Denmark's loss of the Holstein-Schleswig Provinces. Pauline Worm has aptly and accurately described herself as a bit of a poet, perhaps a little more of a thinker, and even still more of a Valkyrie.

Pauline Frederikke Worm was born in Hyllested, Denmark, on November 29, 1825. She was the daughter of the parish priest of Kristrup (Randers area) Church, Peter Worm (1788–1865) and his wife, Louise Theodora Petrine Hjort (1800–1881). Pauline Worm received her first schooling from her father, then entered a girls' school in Randers in 1838. In 1841, when she was only just confirmed and barely sixteen years old, Worm became a teacher at the Randers school; she continued teaching in Randers until she accepted a post as private tutor in Præstø in 1847. In Præstø, Worm's significant talents for poetry and creative writing came to the fore, first in a poem in honor of the coronation of Frederik VII (in the nationalist journal *Fædrelandet*), and in a collection of poems, *En Krands af ni Blade* (1850; A Wreath of Nine Leaves), and, then, in her expansive, engaging *De fornuftige* I–II (1850; The Wise Ones I–II, published 1857). Worm wrote a response to Mathilde Fibiger's stimulating, thought-provoking letters on women's liberation, equal rights,

and education: *Tolv Breve af Clara Raphael* (Twelve Letters of Clara Raphael); Worm's response of 1851, *Fire Breve om Clara Raphael til en ung Pige fra hendes Søster* (Four Letters on Clara Raphael to a Young Girl from her Sister) generally supported Fibiger's thoughts on the status of women and the need to prepare for educational reform, but Worm's letters also recognized the importance of marriage and family. Worm's articles in *Fædrelandet*, "Om Kvindens Kald og Kvindens Opdragelse" (On the Calling and Education of Women), provided a more detailed explanation of her views and her concern for improved schooling as the very first goal of the feminist cause. In 1852, Worm received a degree in school administration and began her own school in Randers; from 1857 to 1863, she ran a similar school in Århus, where she was recognized for "her fine, just mind, [her] impracticality" (*DbL*16, 52), and her overwhelming, sometimes excessive, industry and endeavor. In 1859, Pauline Worm proposed a professional degree program enabling women to work as teachers in public schools; her recommendation was approved by the government, and women were allowed to pursue teaching as a viable, meaningful, rewarding career. In 1863, Worm sold her school and returned home to Randers, where she continued teaching and writing poetry; she contributed a poem in memory of Frederik VII (1863), several poems for Christian Winter's collection *Nye Digte af danske Digtere* (1864; New Poems by Danish Poets), and her own collection of poems, *Vaar og Høst* (1864, 2 ed. 1874; Spring and Autumn). Although shy, Worm became a very successful lecturer on feminist, historical, educational, and particularly, Danish nationalist causes. She wrote several articles on women in society and in the work force, and, as a proponent for equal rights for women, Worm joined *Dansk Kvindesamfund* (Society of Danish Women), "discussed . . . the possibility of organizing a university for women" (1875), and, through a written referendum campaign, sought to win support for the improvement of Danish naval defenses (1875–1876). From 1865 to 1868, Worm also engaged in volatile written exchanges with Vilhelm Beck, the leader of the *Indre Mission* (Home Mission); Worm's ideas concerning the Home Mission, inspired by N.F.S. Grundtvig, became the basis for her polemic *Den indre Mission under Vilhelm Beck. Et Nutids-og Fremtidsbillede* (1868; The Home Mission under Vilhelm Beck. A Current and Future Depiction). Worm also rose to defend Danish independence and integrity and Nordic unity in her poem "Forandrer Signalerne!" (1872; Change the Signals, *Fædrelandet*); she wrote against the conciliatory words of the Norwegian poet Bjørnstjerne Bjørnson, who urged peace and reconciliation with Germany. Worm's spirited national defense invoked poetic response from Andreas Munch ("Gjensvar," Response) and from no less a literary giant than Henrik Ibsen ("Nordens Signaler," Nordic Signals). Worm's last work, *En Brevvexling* (1878; A Correspondence), recorded only too clearly the difficulties women encountered in pursuing a literary career. Pauline Worm's efforts and literary accomplishments won her official recognition and honor: together with nine other women writers, Worm received a government bursary in 1883, the year she died, and a Worm endowment fund for young women teachers was established by friends and colleagues. Never married, Worm died in Copenhagen on December 13, 1883.

From a literary and social viewpoint, Pauline Worm's most important work is her lengthy, involved novel *De fornuftige*. The protagonist of the work, Alvilda, is the intelligent, promising, orphaned daughter of a cabinet official and his wife. As a dependent minor, Alvilda lives first with her aunt, then with a government-appointed official in the War Office, Minister Bigum, and his wife. What mainly concerned Worm in writing *De fornuftige* was the education of young women, and Alvilda became an illustration of the flaws in the Danish educational system: Alvilda enters school with a solid background from her parents, with a large measure of self-respect and concern for duty, hard work, and truth, but the system excludes Alvilda *a priori* from a meaningful and fair role in school and in the larger society, and society hardly values truth, mutual respect, and a meaningful role for each individual. Alvilda looks to art, to a career on the stage, as a means of "bringing her inner life to expression" (Dalager, 1, p. 191). In *De fornuftige*, Worm also describes marriage and family relations in changing social settings: Alvilda's own parents were linked "in a common land-based family structure where work [was the] integral element, where men's and women's work had equal value and equal respect . . . [where] marriage was based on mutual sensitive understanding." In the city, Alvilda meets a more negative marriage and family structure and a dissimilar work pattern, all based on the dependent woman in a marriage of security. In describing the young couple, Alvilda and Viggo of *De fornuftige*, Worm presents still another pattern of filial dedication, mutual respect, shared opinions and values, and innocent regard for personal qualities and attributes. The lively use of satire, the piquant sketches of secondary and central characters, the direct dialogue, and the intriguing dramatic sequences of *De fornuftige* all bring to mind the works of Charles Dickens: "It is surprising how cleverly Pauline Worm has mastered satire as an artistic medium [for] we do not find such comparable [mastery] among her women contemporaries" (Dalager, 1, p. 198). With *De fornuftige*, her essays, lectures, educational and social agenda, and her poetry, Pauline Worm was an admirable, persistent, and active Valkyrie, eagerly promoting a new meaningful, substantive education for young women and a new social respect for their talents, efforts, and work within Danish society.

Works

"Hyldestdigt, Frederik VIIs Tronbestigelse," *Fædrelandet* (1847). *En Krands af ni Blade: Digtsamling* (1850). *De fornuftige I–II* (1850, published 1857). *Fire Breve om Clara Raphael til en ung Pige af hendes Søster* (1851). "Om Kvindens Kald og Kvindens Opdragelse," *Fædrelandet* (1851). *Digte i Christian Winters Nye Digte af danske Digtere* (1864). *Vaar og Høst* (1864; 2 udg., 1874). *Den indre Mission under Vilhelm Beck. Et Nutids- og Fremtidsbillede* (1868). "Forandrer Signalerne," *Fædrelandet* (1872). *En Brevvexling* (1878).

Bibliography

Dalager, Stig, and Anne-Marie Mai, *Danske kvindelige forfattere 1. Fra Sophie Brahe til Mathilde Fibiger. Udvikling og perspektiv* (Copenhagen, 1983). *Dansk Litteraturhistorie, 6. Bannelse, folkelighed, individualisme 1848–1901* (Copenhagen, 1985). *Dansk biografisk Leksikon* 16, 3 udg. (1979). Dolleris, Andrea, *Pauline Worm*

(Copenhagen, 1921). Lassen, Carl C., *Otte nordiske kvinder* (Copenhagen, 1943), pp. 81–109.

Lanae Hjortsvang Isaacson

Liliane Wouters

Born 1930, Belgium
Genre(s): drama, poetry, translation
Language(s): French

Liliane Wouters is a prodigious and multi-talented force in contemporary Belgian letters. As a playwright, she has won acclaim for her comic spirit and mordant satire in such works as *La Porte* (1967; The Door) and *Vie et mort de mademoiselle Shakespeare* (1979; Life and Death of Miss Shakespeare). She has translated Flemish medieval and Renaissance literature, maintaining the richness and subtleties of the original in her French rendition. The mysticism and sensuality of older Flemish literature in turn infuses Liliane Wouter's own verse. The tensions, dichotomies, and melding of spiritual and physical experience is the dominant thematic of her four expansive volumes of poetry.

Her first volume, *La marche forcée* (1954; Forced March), contains imagery of quest, nomadism, and vain pilgrimage. *Le Bois sec* (1960; Dry Wood), includes baroquist imagery of the body as cage for the soul, imagery of physical sterility suggestive of spiritual dessication, and Manichaean imagery of Satan and God as coeval forces in the world. *Le gel* (1966; The Thaw) is rich in spatial metaphors for spiritual experience. Polar landscapes of the absolute are particularly recurrent. Sealed gardens are the setting for ambiguous mystico-physical unions with God or man. Metamorphosic states between life and death are explored, and the artist's role is evoked in grail imagery of wounding and healing. The recent poetry of *L'Aloès* (1983; The Aloe) has a more sensual cast and is concerned with suspension of time in amorous experience.

Liliane Wouter's poetry is her most important contribution to international letters. Her verse is strong, arresting, complex and varied. As an anthologist, Wouters has fostered the work of her contemporaries, conceiving of Belgian poetry as a *terre d'écarts*, "a world apart," noteworthy in its singularity.

Works

Drama: *Oscarine ou les tournesols* (1964). *La porte* (1967). *Vie et mort de Mademoiselle Shakespeare* (1979).
Poetry: *La marche forcée* (1954). *Le bois sec* (1960). *Le gel* (1966). *L'Aloès* (1983).
Anthologies: *Panorama de la poésie française de Belgique* (1976). *Terre d'Écarts* (1980).
Translations: *Les belles heures de Flandre* (1961). *Bréviaire des Pays Bas* (1973). *Guido Gezelle* (1965). *Reynart le goupil* (1974).

Donald Friedmann

Caroline Wuïet, Baronne Auffdiener

(a.k.a. Caroline Vuïet, Madame la baronne Caroline A . . ., née V . . . de M . . .; W . . .)

Born 1766 or 1770, Vienna, Austria; died ca. 1835, Paris, France
Genre(s): drama, romance, translation
Language(s): French

Born in Vienna, Carolina Wuïet was famous as a musical prodigy by the age of five. She attracted the attention of Marie-Antoinette, who became her sponsor. Her teachers included Beaumarchais, Greuze, and Grétry. Only the barest details are known of her life: her association with Marie-Antoinette led to her imprisonment during the Terror; she was released, went to England, and returned to Paris in 1797, where she was well received. In 1807 she married the German baron Auffdiener, accompanied him to Portugal, and returned to Paris after the French were defeated on the Iberian peninsula. After this time, she apparently earned a meager living giving music lessons. She retired to Saint-Cloud in the late 1820s, dying sometime around 1835 after becoming prematurely senile. In retrospect, perhaps her most important literary contribution lies in her having translated Anne Radcliffe.

Works

Sophie, comédie en un acte et en prose (1787). *Essai sur l'opinion publique, fragments de poésie fugitives, dedié à madame Bonaparte* (1800). *Mémoires de Bibiole, ou la Lanterne magique anglaise* (1803).

Esope au bal de l'Opéra, ou tout Paris en miniature, 2 vols. (1806). *Le Sterne de Mondego, ou le Français en Portugal* (1809). *Le couvent de Sainte-Catherine, ou les Moeurs du treizième siècle, Roman historique d'Anne Radcliffe,* traduit par madame la baronne Caroline A . . . . (1810).

Bibliography

Quérard, J.-M., "Wuĭet de M . . ., Caroline." *La France littéraire* (Paris, 1838), pp. 538–539. Souvestre, Emile, "Souvenirs de la République, Mémoires d'un bourgeois de Paris, Une femme célèbre." *Le Siècle* (April, 1841). "Wuĭet, Caroline," *Biographie universelle* [Michaud], vol. 45, p. 110.

Earl Jeffrey Richards

Hella Maria Wuolijoki

(a.k.a. Juhani Tervapää, Felix Tuli)

Born July 22, 1886, Valja-district of Estonia;
died February 2, 1954, Helsinki, Finland
Genre(s): drama, autobiography
Language(s): Estonian, Finnish

Hella Wuolijoki was born in the southern part of Estonia, in a district that was known as the birthplace of Estonian nationalism. The family moved to the city of Valga, where Hella started school in 1897. Four years later we find her in the Puśkin grammar school at Dorpat. She passed her matriculation exam and went to a university for women in St. Petersburg (Leningrad), a place she was admitted to only through influential contacts, and from there she asked for a transfer to the University of Helsinki to study folklore.

She spent her first summer in Finland in 1903 and returned to study at the university in 1904. The general Strike of 1905 in Finland changed her life entirely: she committed herself to socialism, to Finland, and to marriage, and the three were so intertwined that it would be hard to separate them. Her husband, Sulo Wuolijoki, was then a leading figure in the socialist student movement; they became engaged in 1906 and married two years later. After the parliamentary election of 1907, life became hard for young couples of the Wuolijoki-type. Following a fashion among young intellectuals of the day, they bought a house outside town and settled there when her husband had become a member of parliament. She had a daughter, and planned her first play. As soon as she had got hold of a nurse to take care of her daughter, she began to write the play. *Talon lapset* (The Children of the House) was printed in Estonia in 1913 and performed there at the Estonia Theatre in Reval (Tallinn) in the autumn of that year. Its first performance in Finland took place in February 1914. In both places it was immediately forbidden as being too revolutionary. At about this time she also decided to give up her plans for a doctorate. In 1913, she was asked to run in the election but refused. Her energetic studies of Marxist theories at this time did not in the least change her bourgeois attitudes and habits: she hated the office where she had to work and was not interested in a housewife's duties. For 17 years, 1915–1932, she worked in business, first for other people, then as a representative for the Finnish Government, trying to procure wheat from the United States, and finally operating on her own account. In the aftermath of the Civil War, she stated: "The year 1918 made me a Finn." At that time her drawing room was the meeting place of literary people and politicians alike. Her international business and political contacts and the flow of people who passed through her drawing room kept her and a good many Finnish politicians up to date on European points of view. Her husband was imprisoned for his political views, and she herself was considered a suspicious person.

In 1920 she bought a mansion, Marlebäck, and in the process of restoring it, she acquired the experience and insight that makes her Niskavuori-series of plays a description of genuine Finnish country life, mirroring the full specter of class and language differences and difficulties. She divorced her husband in 1923 and founded two businesses of her own in the same year. Both firms flourished until the Depression put an end to them in 1931. But she retained Marlebäck, and became in her own words "a capitalist employer with a Marxist view of the world and a belief in the bankruptcy of capitalism."

Her first play in the Niskavuori-series, *Niskavuoren naiset* (The Women of Niskavuori), was refused, and when finally accepted, people thought it might run for only two or three performances. It ran for a hundred performances and eventually brought in more cash than all the other plays at that theatre that season. The playwright used the pseudonym "Juhani Tervapää" and continued using it for the plays that followed during the next few years.

The Finnish Winter War began in 1939, and Hella Wuolijoki knew influential people both in the east and in the west. As things became critical, she offered to contact Madame Alexandra Kollontay in Stockholm and try to get her co-operation to bring about peace negotiations. She carried out this mission successfully and eventually helped secure peace. In April, immediately after the end of the war, she housed Bertolt Brecht and the people that accompanied him while they waited for visas to the United States. They produced a play together, which each of them, however, revised and re-named later. Hella Wuolijoki's version was called *Iso-Heikkilän isäntä* (The Farmer of Iso-Heikkilä).

Before World War II started, her plays were performed in many European countries, including England and Germany. But in 1941 Finland again had to defend herself, and this time Hella Wuolijoki was endangered. In 1943 she was imprisoned, accused of espionage and high treason, and given a life sentence, a sentence that the High Martial Court upheld in 1944. When the war ended, she was freed and immediately resumed her political activities. The first of the series of autobiographical works, written or at least drafted in prison, was published the same year: *Enkä ollut vanki* (And Prisoner I Was Not). In 1945 her memoirs, *Koulutyttönä Tartossa* (Schoolgirl in Dorpat), *Ylioppilasvuodet Helsinginssä* (The Student Years in Helsinki), and a few short plays appeared. In 1945 she was also appointed President of the Finnish Broadcasting Corporation, a post she held until 1949, when she was dismissed.

Before the parliamentary elections she published a lean volume called *Luottamukselliset neuvottelut Suomen ja Neuvostoliiton välillä vuosina 1938, –39, –40, –41* (Confidential Negotiations Between Finland and the U.S.S.R. in the Years 1938–1941). In the election she only gained deputy status, but due to a substitution later on, she actually became a member of parliament in 1946. In 1946, the play she wrote in cooperation with Brecht was published, *Iso-*Heikkilän isäntä ja hänen renkinsä Kalle* (The Farmer of Iso-Heikkilä and His Farmhand Kalle). She was not re-elected in 1948.

The fourth volume of her memoirs, *Kummituksia ja kajavia* (Ghosts and Gulls), was published in 1947. Then a few quiet years followed. Fortunately she was able to finish her Niskavuori-series of plays in 1953. Niskavuori is the name of the farm on which the events recounted take place. Within these plays she managed to cover almost every aspect of controversy and social debate going on in Finland at the time. The women of Niskavuori show a peculiar strength, which may be an unconscious transfer of the vital womanly strength she herself radiated. These plays seemed to be written out of the heart of the Finnish people, and they are still able to convey this impression of something most genuinely Finnish. The Estonian writer of these plays died on February 2, 1954. She was a colorful woman, always active, she loved social occasions and having lots of people around her. As a playwright she is a keen observer of character and capable of conveying the atmosphere and the feelings of the place and the people she describes. Her plays may seem purely realistic, but they also contain an almost mythic vigor. Her political activities may remain controversial for a long time; as a playwright she was and will remain one of the most popular ones in this century in Finland.

Works

In Estonian: *Talu lapsed* [The Children of the House] (1912). *Udutagused* (1914). *Koidula* [Lydia Koidula, Estonian writer, 1843–1886] (1932).
In Finnish: *Ministeri ja kommunisti* [The Minister and the Communist] (1936). *Laki ja Järjestys* [Law and Order] (1933). The Niskavuori-series of plays: *Niskavuoren naiset* [The Women of Niskavuori] (1936). *Niskavuoren leipä* [The Bread of Niskavuori] (1938). *Niskavuroen nuori emäntä* [The Young Mistress of Niskavuori] (1940). *Niskavuoren Heta* [Heta of Niskavuori] (1953). *Entäs nyt, Niskavuori* [What Next, Niskavuori?] (1953). *Palava maa* [The Burning Land] (1936). *Juurakon Hulda* [Hulda of Juurakko], filmed in the United States and given the film title *The Daughter of Parliament* (1937). *Justiina* (1937). *Naiset ja naamarit* [The Women and the Masks] (1937).

Vihreä kulta [Green Gold] (1938). *Vastamyrkky* [Antidote] (1939). *Kuningas hovinarrina* [The King as the Court's Jester], about the writer Eino Leino (1946). *Iso-Heikkilän isäntä ja hänen renkinsä Kalle* [The Farmer of Iso-Heikkilä and His Farm-hand Kalle], originally written in cooperation with Brecht (1947).

Memoirs: *Enkä ollut vanki* [And Prisoner I Was Not] (1944). *Koulutyttönä Tartossa* [Schoolgirl in Dorpat] (1945). *Yliopistovuodet Helsingissä* [The Student Years in Helsinki] (1945). *Kummituksia ja kajavia* [Ghosts and Gulls] (1947). *Minusta tuli liikenainen* [I Became a Business Woman] (1953).

Bibliography

Ammondt, Jukka, Unpublished licentiate thesis, University of Helsinki. Lounela, Pekka, *Hella Wuolijoki* (Porvoo, 1979). *Otavan iso tietosanakirja*, part 10. (Helsinki, 1965).

Gunnel Cleve

X

X

(see: Wilhelmina "Minna" Ulrika [Johnson] Canth)

Xanta

(see: Constanṭa Dunca-Ṣchiau)

Françoise Xénakis

Born September 27, 1930, France
Genre(s): novel
Language(s): French

Françoise Xénakis was born in the region of Sologne, which she calls "the very heart of Deep France." She is presently a literary critic and director of the cultural service for the newspaper *Le Matin.* She is married to the renowned composer Iannis Xénakis.

In her early novels the protagonists are always women whose lives seem cursed by destiny and whose loves are absolute. Though often politically oppressed they remain indomitable, courageous, and uncompromising. They are private women who feel so apart from all other people that they can confide in no one, not even with those they love. They are beautiful, intelligent and strong-willed while the male characters often stay in the background, undefined or weak.

Xénakis' last two novels are based on real-life characters; *Zut, on a encore oublié Madame Freud* (My, We Forgot Mrs. Freud Again) concerns the wives of famous men (Marx, Freud, Socrates, Hugo, Mahler) and the lives they led,

lives of sacrifices and courage. In *Mouche-toi Cléopâtre* (Blow Your Nose, Cleopatra) she depicts a queen, cheated and used by men, unhappy in her passion, motherhood and political ambitions. Although there is a tragic element in the condition of all her female characters, Xénakis endows them with a sense of humor which enables them to retain their strength and lucidity.

Works

Le Petit Caillou (1963). Aux lèvres pour que j'ai moins soif (1968). Elle lui dirait dans l'île (1970). Moi j'aime pas la mer (1972). Ecoute (1972). Et alors les morts pleureront (1974). L'écrivain ou la sixième roue du carosse (pamphlet) (1975). Le temps usé (1976) Des Dimanches et des Dimanches (1977). La natte coupée (1982). Zut, on a encore oublié Madame Freud (1985). Mouche -toi Cléopâtre (1986).

Translations: *Elle lui dirait dans l'île,* translated into English, German, Japanese, Danish, Dutch, Spanish, Portuguese. *Moi j'aime pas la mer,* translated into Japanese, German, Portuguese, Greek. *La natte coupée,* translated into Greek. *Zut, on a encore oublié Madame Freud,* translated into Japanese, Portuguese, Dutch, German, Greek.

More than thirty theatrical adaptations of *Elle lui dirait dans l'île,* and currently a film adaptation of *La natte coupée.*

Bibliography

Femme (April 1985). *Marie-Claire* (May 1985). *Lui* (March 26, 1985). *Elle* (October 14, 1986).

Michèle M. Magill

Adela Xenopol

Twentieth century
Genre(s): essay, journalism
Language(s): Romanian

A contributor to *Revista politică*, Adela Xenopol issued and directed the prestigious literary journal *Revista scriitoarei. Literatură, artă, chestiuni sociale* (Journal of the Woman Writer. Literature, Art, Social Issues, 1940, 1942–1943) which focussed upon female talent and represented a strong platform for constructive feminism. The journal had among its regular contributors many of the women writers of the time—Margareta Miller-Verghi, Claudia Millian, Hortensia Papadat-Bengescu, Ticu Archip, Mia Frollo, Constanţa Hodoş, Agatha Grigorescu, Sofia Nădejde, L. Sturdza-Bulandra—as well as a number of acclaimed male writers such as M. Sadoveanu, T. Arghezi, G. Bacovia, I. Minulescu, Liviu Rebreanu, A. Maniu, I. Pillat, Camil Petrescu, E. Jebeleanu.

Bibliography

Chiţimia, I.C. and Al. Dima, eds., *Dicţionar cronologic–Literatura romănă* (Bucharest, 1979), pp. 203, 322.

Sanda Golopentia

Kate Xucaro

(see: Kate Cukaro)

XYZ der Jüngere

(see: Luise Adelgunde Victoria Gottsched)

Y

Ekaterina Yossifova

Born 1941, Kyustendil, Bulgaria
Genre(s): poetry
Language(s): Bulgarian

After graduating from Sofia University in Russian, Ekaterina Yossifova worked as a teacher and journalist. Currently she is drama director for the Dramatic Theatre in her home town. Her poetry, rich in emotion and metaphor, has been translated into English, French, Russian, and Spanish.

Works

A Short Voyage (1969). Wind Blows at Night (1972). Dedication (1979).

Warwick J. Rodden

Marguerite Yourcenar

(a.k.a. Marguerite de Crayencour)

Born June 8, 1903, Brussels, Belgium
Genre(s): novel, short fiction, autobiographical texts, poetry, prose poems, essay, translations from Greek, English, and Japanese
Language(s): French

Born in Brussels of a French father and a Belgian mother who died ten days after her birth, Marguerite de Crayencour spent much of her childhood and subsequent life travelling: the North of France, England, Paris, Switzerland, Italy, Greece, etc. In 1939 she came to the United States upon the invitation of Grace Frick, a doctoral student at Yale, who became a life long companion and who translated many of her works into English. As a return to Europe was made impossible by the coming of World War II, she remained in the U.S. throughout the war years and became a part-time instructor at Sarah Lawrence—a position which she held intermittently till 1949. When in 1947 she became a U.S. citizen, she adopted her *nom de plume* Yourcenar, an incomplete anagram of Crayencour, as her legal name. In 1950 she and Grace Frick purchased "Petite Plaisance," a house on Mount Desert Island off the coast of Maine where Ms. Yourcenar still resides today.

Marguerite Yourcenar's career as a writer started at the age of eighteen, when, with the enthusiastic support of her father, she privately published a volume of poems entitled *Le Jardin des Chimères* (1921; The Garden of the Chimerae). A second privately published collection of poems, *Les Dieux ne sont pas morts* (The Gods Are Not Dead), followed one year later. Yet, the earliest work of Ms. Yourcenar's which the author still approves of today is the novel *Alexis ou le Traité du vain combat* (1929; Alexis or the Story of a Vain Struggle). Also noticeable among her early works are the novel *Denier du rêve* of 1934 (translated into English as *A Coin in Nine Hands*), the volume of prose poems *Feux* (1936; Fires), and her retellings of classical Arabic, Persian, Indian, and Chinese tales entitled *Nouvelles orientales* (1938; Oriental Tales). Fame came, however, in 1951, with *Mémoires d'Hadrien* (Memoirs of Hadrian), a novel about the Roman emperor Hadrian which was awarded the Prix Fémina-Vacaresco at the time of its publication and translated into English in 1954. She repeated her critical success in 1968 with *L'Oeuvre au noir* (The Work in Black), the story of an alchemist's physical and intellectual journeys in the Europe of the early Renaissance. Marguerite Yourcenar is also an accomplished playwright (her dramatic *oeuvre* has been published in two volumes, *Théâtre I* and *Théâtre II*), essayist (*The Dark Brain of Piranesi and Other Essays*, 1984, and *Mishima. A Vision of the Void*, 1986) and translator from Greek, English, and Japanese. Especially her translation of Virginia Woolf's *The Waves* (*Les Vagues*, 1937), of the Greek poet Cavafy (*Présentation critique de Constantin Cavafy [1863–1933]*, 1958), of negro spirituals (*Fleuve Profond, Sombre Rivière*, 1962) and her anthology of translations from classical Greek literature, *La Couronne et la Lyre* (1979; The Crown and the Lyre), deserve mention.

This prolific intellectual creativity could not but rouse interest in and admiration for Marguerite Yourcenar's *oeuvre* and, indeed, few honors have escaped her over the years. In 1970, she was elected to the Belgian Royal Academy of Language and Literature, in 1971 she received the Légion d'honneur, and in 1980 she became the first woman to be elected into the Académie Française. In 1981 followed an Honorary Doctorate from Harvard, and in 1982 membership in the American Academy of Arts and Letters. She also received numerous literary awards and prizes. Not all of these honors, however, came without controversy and especially her election into the French Academy was accompanied by a heated polemic between excited admirers and angry critics. Her critics referred to the fact that she relinquished her French citizenship in 1939 and that she had been living in the U.S. for several decades. Some members of the Academy were also disturbed that Ms. Yourcenar did not follow the traditional procedure for being elected into the Academy—a procedure which demands that candidates call on the members of the Academy and petition them for their vote. A few "Immortals" even maintained that, as in the past, no woman should be admitted to the exclusively male French Academy. Finally, there was the vexed question of which dress Ms. Yourcenar would wear during the induction ceremony as she objected to the traditional green and gold livery with sword and cocked hat.

The publication in 1982 of Marguerite Yourcenar's work in the prestigious *Bibliothèque de la Pléiade* with a first volume containing her novels and other prose fiction (*Oeuvres romanesques de Marguerite Yourcenar*), and the anticipated publication of her essayistic and biographical works in a second volume, signals her continuing public and critical success. A certain amount of literary image building, however, has seemed inescapable. American biographical sketches mention that Ms. Yourcenar became a U.S. citizen in 1947 (Farell and Farell; Horn), whereas the chronology of the *Pléiade* passes over this fact. Similarly, whereas American biographers review some of the controversial events surrounding her election into the French Academy, the French chronology neglects to mention these. In addition, Ms. Yourcenar submits her texts to continuous rewriting and does not hesitate to radically revamp or outright reject some of her earlier writings. In the preface to the *Pléiade* edition she states that "The duration of the literary labor coincides with that of the existence of the author himself." Thus the novel *La Nouvelle Eurydice* (1931; The New Euridice) has been excluded from the *Pléiade* edition, and she also announced in that preface her intention to exclude her study *Pindare* (1932) from the forthcoming second *Pléiade* volume.

The quality, however, of Ms. Yourcenar's work and its erudition, eclecticism, and cross-cultural richness have generally not been doubted. Her works succeed in merging asceticism and excess, refined skepticism and an avid search for absolute truths, classical myth and modern political discourse, and the East and the West. The author herself has often used the notion of "sympathetic magic" to describe the process which enables her to penetrate so thoroughly the mind of her characters—whether they be Roman emperors, Flemish alchemists, Chinese painters, Italian anti-fascist revolutionaries or classical heroes—and the complex historical and cultural frameworks within which they exist. Commenting on the *magnum opus* of Zeno, the protagonist of her *The Work in Black*, and the alchemists of the late Middle Ages and Renaissance during an interview, she stated, "in postulating a world in flux, a world which is perpetually coming into being, irrational *at least in appearance*, the philosophers of alchemy prefigured Hegel and contemporary physicists; this becoming world, they have also situated even more audaciously in the internal being of man" (P. de Rosbo, 125). It is this fluctuating world which is ever coming into being and dissolving again in the realm of history and in the inner being of man which she has tried to delineate and interpret in her complex *oeuvre*.

Works

Marguerite Yourcenar's novels, short fiction, and prose poems were published in 1982 in the *Bibliothèque de la Pléiade*, Yvon Bernier, ed., *Oeuvres romanesques de Marguerite Yourcenar*. This volume contains: *Alexis ou le Traité du vain combat* (1929); *Denier du rêve* (1934); the collection of prose poems *Feux* (1936); *Nouvelles orientales* (1938); *Le Coup de Grâce* (1939); *Mémoires d'Hadrien* (1951); *L'Oeuvre au noir* (1968); *Comme l'eau qui coule* (1982), and a collection of 3 novellas: *Anna, soror...*, *Un homme obscur*, and *Une belle matinée*. The early works *La Nouvelle Eurydice* (1931) and *La Mort conduit l'attelage* (1934) were excluded on the request of the author.

Poetry: *Les Charités d'Alcippe et autres poèmes* (1956).

Plays: *Le Dialogue dans le Marécage. Pièce en un acte* (1930). *Rendre à César. Pièce en trois actes* (1961). *La Petite Sirène. Divertissement dramatique d'après le conte de Hans-Christian Andersen* (1942; rpt. in *Théâtre I*; *Electre ou la Chute des masques* [1954]). *Le Mystère d'Alceste. Pièce en un acte* (1963). *Qui n'a pas son Minotaure? Divertissement sacré en dix scènes* (1963; rpt. in *Théâtre II*).

Biography: *Le Labyrinthe du monde, I: Souvenirs Pieux* (1974). *Le Labyrinthe du Monde, II: Archives du Nord* (1977).

Essays: *Les Songes et les sorts* (1938). *Sous Bénéfice d'inventaire* (1962). *Mishima ou la vision du vide* (1981). *Le Temps, ce grand sculpteur* (1983).

Translations: *Memoirs of Hadrian,* tr. Gabrielle Frick (1954). *Coup de Grâce,* tr. Gabrielle Frick (1957). *The Abyss,* tr. Gabrielle Frick (1976). *Fires,* tr. Dori Katz (1981). *The Alms of Alcippe,* tr. Edith R. Farrell (1982). *A Coin in Nine Hands,* tr. Dori Katz (1982). *Alexis,* tr. Walter Kaiser (1984). *Plays,* tr. Dori Katz (1984) (contains translations of all of the above six plays except *Le Dialogue dans le Marécage* and *Le Mystère d'Alceste*). *The Dark Brain of Piranesi and Other Essays,* tr. Richard Howard (1984). *Oriental Tales,* tr. Alberto Manguel (1985). *Mishima. A Vision of the Void,* tr. Alberto Manguel (1986).

Translations into French: Virginia Woolf, *Les Vagues* (1937). Henry James, *Ce Que Savait Maisie* (1947). *Présentation critique de Constantin Cavafy (1863–1933)* (1958). *Fleuve Profond, Sobre Rivière* (1962). *Présentation critique d'Hortense Flexner* (1970). *La Couronne et la Lyre* (1979). James Baldwin, *Le Coin des "Amen"* (1983). *Blues et Gospels* (1984). M. Yourcenar and Jun Shiragi, tr, Yukio Mishima, *Cinq Nô modernes* (1983).

Miscellaneous: *Discours de réception de Marguerite Yourcenar à l'Académie royale belge de langue et de littérature française* (1971). *Discours de réception à l'Académie française de Marguerite Yourcenar. Et réponse de Jean D'Ormesson* (1981). Marie Métailler and Marie-Magdeleine Brumagne, *Le Poudre de sourire, précédé de lettres de Marguerite Yourcenar de l'académie française* (1982) (contains two letters by M. Yourcenar). *Notre Dame des hirondelles. Contes de Noël,* collection of tales for children (1982).

Bibliography

Blot, Jean, *Marguerite Yourcenar* (1971). Spencer-Noël, Geneviève, *Zénon ou le thème de l'alchimie dans "L'Oeuvre au noir" de Marguerite Yourcenar* (1981). Farrell, C. Frederick, and Edith R. Farrell, *Marguerite Yourcenar in Counterpoint* (1983). Horn, Pierre, L. *Marguerite Yourcenar.* Twayne's World Authors Series (1985).

Interviews: de Rosbo, Patrick, *Entretiens radiophoniques avec Marguerite Yourcenar* (1972). Galey, Matthieu, *Les Yeux ouverts, Entretiens de Marguerite Yourcenar avec Matthieu Galey* (1980) [Arthur Goldhammer, tr., *With Open Eyes,* 1984].

Major articles and essays: Darbelnet, Jean, "Marguerite Yourcenar et la traduction littéraire." *Etudes littéraires* 12 (1979): 51–63. Whatley, Janet, "*Mémoires d'Hadrien*: A Manual for Princes." *University of Toronto Quarterly* 50 (1980–1981): 221–237. Horn, Pierre L. "Marguerite Yourcenar's *Le Labyrinthe du Monde*: A Modern Anti-Autobiography," in Donald L., Jennermann, ed., *The Writer and the Past* (Terre Haute, Ind. 1981), pp. 1–9. Peyre, Henri, "Marguerite Yourcenar. Independent, Imaginative and 'Immortal.'" *World Literature Today* 57 (1983): 191–195. Sándig, Brigitte,

"Mit offenen Augen: Zum Leben und Werk Marguerite Yourcenars." *Weimarer Beiträge* 33 (1985): 1739–1747.

For some reviews of her oeuvre, see Debra Popkin and Michael Popkin, eds., *Modern French Literature: A Library of Literary Criticism* (1977) vol. 2, pp. 505–510. For bibliography, see Yvon Bernier, ed., *Oeuvres romanesques de Marguerite Yourcenar* (1982) pp. 1219–1237. Horn, Pierre L., *Marguerite Yourcenar* (1985), pp. 111–117. The Hawthorne-Longfellow Library at Bowdoin College in Brunswick, Maine holds an extensive Yourcenar collection, see Robert R. Nunn and Edward J. Geary, *The Yourcenar Collection. A Descriptive Catalogue* (1984).

Henk Vynckier

Pieternella Cornelia van Yperen

(see: Ellen Warmond)

Zoya Osipovna Yurieff

Born August 24, 1922, Siemiatycze, Poland
Genre(s): essay, literary criticism
Language(s): Russian, Polish, German, English

Zoya Yurieff was educated in Poland, where she attended Russian secondary schools in Brest and Warsaw. Her studies at the University of Lvov were interrupted by World War II, but resumed at the University of Munich (1945–1946), at Barnard and Radcliffe Colleges (1947–1950), and were completed at Harvard University where she received her Ph.D. in Slavic literature and languages in 1956. Since 1959 she has been teaching Slavic literatures at various American institutions with a permanent full-professorship appointment (1974) at New York University.

Yurieff has distinguished herself as a keen literary critic concentrating on modernist Russian and Polish literature. Her book-length study of Józef Wittlin (1973) represents a conclusive evaluation of this eminent Polish writer's poetry and prose. Yurieff's essays and articles appear regularly in the best émigré literary journals as well as scholarly reviews in different countries.

They revolve around the most illustrious writers and poets of the Slavic Symbolist and Expressionist movements. Yurieff also has translated poetry by the Polish poet Kazimierz Wierzyński into Russian (1985), and her Polish versions of some of Pasternak's and Mandelshtam's poems were published by *Wiadomości* (Polish language journal) in London. She is currently completing three major works to be published in the near future: *Russian Symbolists as Critics, Julian Tuwim: A Devoted Believer in Words*, and *Andrei Belyi: Cosmos-in-Creation*.

Yurieff's original approaches to the complex poetics of Gogol, a direct precursor of the Russian Symbolists, of Andrei Belyi, Julian Tuwim, Józef Wittlin, and other innovative writers of the modern era rank her among the most perceptive and authoritative critics of Slavic literatures in the modern period.

Works

Books: *Joseph Wittlin* (1973). Kazimierz, Wierzynski, *Izbrannoe* [Selected Poetry], tr. from Polish. Intro. by Zbigniew Folejewski (1985). Translations of B. Pasternak's and Osip Mandelshtam's poems into Polish, *Wiadomości* (London, 1959).

Bibliography

Krzyzanowski, Jerzy R., "Zoya Yurieff. *Joseph Wittlin*." *Books Abroad*. (Norman, Oklahoma, Autumn, 1974). Vardaman, Enith, "Zoya Yurieff, *Joseph Wittlin*." *Slavic and East European Journal* (Fall, 1973). WK., "Amerykańska Monografia o Wittline" [American Monograph on Wittlin]. *Twórczość* [Creative Works] (May 1975). Cybulska, Maja Elzbieta, "W moich oczach" [In My View], *Tygodnik Powszechny* [The Common Weekly] (London, March 22, 1986). Stein, E., "V bezbrezhnom more zarubezhnoi poezii" [In the Boundless Sea of Émigré Poetry]. *Almanac-Panorama*, 276 (Los Angeles, July 25—August 1, 1986).

Articles: "Impressions from a Harvard Exhibit of the 'Tale of Igor's Campaign,'" *Novyj 'urnal* [The New Review], XXIX (1952). "Novolun'e," (On the Poetry of Kazimierz Wierzynski), *Novyj 'urnal* XXXIII (1953). "On Józef Wittlin's Creative Path." *Novyj 'urnal* XLVII (1956). "Annenskij o Gogole." *Novyj 'urnal* XLV (1956). "Remizov o Gogole." *Novyj 'urnal* LI (1957). "Hlasko, golos gneva i otčajanija." *Vol'naja mysl'* (Jan. 1960). "Poems of Georgij Ivanov" (in Polish), *Wiadomości* (1959). "Russian Literature." *McGraw-Hill Encyclopedia of Russia and the Soviet Union* (1961). "Slavic literatures." *American Oxford Encyclopedia* (New York: J.J. Little and Ives, 1966). "O'Shineli" Juliana Tuwima." *Orbis Scriptus*. For D. Tschi'ewskij, Festschrift zum 70. Geburtstag (1966). Introductory essay to a book of critical articles by Andrej Belyj, *Lug zelenyj* (New York: Johnson Reprint Corp., 1967), 45 pp. Necrology on Professor Waclaw Lednicki, *Novoe Russkoe Slovo* (November 9, 1967). "Kazimierz Wierzynski" (The Eclipse of the Moon Metaphor and Death). *Novyj 'urnal.* CVIII (1972). "Roman Ingarden," as a part of a panel (at the MLA meeting in Chicago, December 1971) devoted to Slavic and Western Literary Theories in contact, published in abbreviated form by the *Yearbook of Comparative and General Literature*, no. 21, 1972. "Poetry of Józef Wittlin" [Poezja Józefa Wittlina], *Wiadomości* (June 1975). "Józef Wittlin," necrology, *The New York Times* (March 1, 1976). "In Memoriam of Joseph Wittlin, 1896–1976." *The Polish Review* XXI, nos. 1–2, (1976). "Prishedshy: A. Bely and A. Chekhov," in *Andrey Bely: A Critical Review* (1978). Three entries on three Polish writers—Z. Nowakowski, G. Herling-Grudziński and Józef Wittlin—in the *Columbia Dictionary of Modern Literature*, 2nd ed., ed. by Jean-Albert Bede and W.B. Edgerton (New York: Columbia Univ. Press, 1980). "Odeżda i materija v cikle simfonij Andreja Belogo," *Bely Centenary Papers*, ed. by Boris Christa (1980). "Two Telegraphers: Notes on Andrei Belyi's 'Telegrafist' and Julian Tuwim's 'Piotr Plaksiń." *Poetica Slavica: Studies in Honor of Professor Zbigniew Folejewski* (1981). "Joseph Wittlin." *Encyclopedia of World Literature in the 20th Century*, vol. 4 (New York: Frederick Ungar Publishing Co., 2nd ed.) "The Myth of Orpheus in the works of A. Belyj, A. Blok and V. Ivanov," *American Contributions to the 1978 International Congress of Slavists*, ed. by V. Terras (1978). "Recurrent Water Imagery in the poetry of Masej Sednew," accepted for publication by *Queens Slavic Papers*, is now being translated into Belorussian. "The Green Myth and the Chalk Prism: on the Poetry of Oleg Ilyinsky," *Queens Slavic Papers* (in press). [With Dr. Valerie Filipp], "O poetike straxa v povesti Gogolja 'Vij', *Zapiski russkoj adademicheskoj gruppy v SSA/* Transactions of the Association of Russian-American Scholars in the USA, vol. XVIII (1984). "Kosmičeskaja tema v rannem tvorčestve Andreja Belogo," in *Andrej-Belyj-Symposium*, ed. Nina Kauchtschischwili (1984). "'Skučnaja—istorija' Čexova kak 'itie mučenika nauki, napisannoe im samim," v sbornik pamjati Prof. Ul'janova, pod red. V. Sechkareva (1987).

Marina Astman

Z

Zamani

(see: Astrid Roemer)

Gabriela Zapolska

Born 1857; died 1921, Lwów, Poland
Genre(s): drama, short story, novel
Language(s): Polish

Moralnosc Pani Dulskiej (1907; Mrs. Dulska's Morality) and *Panna Maliczewska* (1912; Miss Maliczewska) are her still immensely popular plays, exposing hypocritical ways of the middle class and men's abuse of women. Considered a rebel against male domination and extremely bitter in her harsh treatment of the male half of mankind, Zapolska also mocked and criticized women's dishonest and selfish ways (e.g., in her short story "Zabusia"). Unsuccessful in her career as an actress in Paris, she used her experience there to write her naturalist plays as well as short stories about the life of Polish emigres in France. Following the example of other Positivist Polish writers, she dealt with social and political issues in her plays set in a Jewish ghetto. A prolific writer, she is considered rather shallow, now recognized mainly for her skill as a playwright.

Works

Akwarele [Water Colors] (1885) *Kaska Kariatyda*, a novel about a country girl exploited in the city (1888). *Przedpiekle* [A Foretaste of Hell], a novel set at a pension for young ladies (1889). *Zaszumi las* [The Forest Will Whisper], a *roman à clef* about Polish revolutionaries in Paris (1899). *Sezonowa*

milosc [Love in the Season], a novel set in a mountain resort town (1905).

Maya Peretz

Faustina Zappi

Born 1679, Rome, Italy; died January 20,
1745, Rome
Genre(s): poetry
Language(s): Italian

Daughter of the painter Carlo Maratti, Faustina was born in Rome in 1679 where, at an early age, she began to frequent the artistic and literary society to which she was introduced by her father. In 1703 she gained wide notoriety for having successfully fought the attempt, on the part of the young duke Giangiorgio Sforza Cesarini, to kidnap her; for her heroic resistance her contemporaries bestowed on her the name of Lucrezia Romana. The very next year, 1704, she was made a member of Arcadia, taking the name of Aglauro Cidonia, and it was here that she met the poet Giambattista Zappi, whom she married in 1705. As a cultured lady of great beauty, interested in painting, music and poetry, her house became the meeting place for some of the most famous men of letters of the time, such as G.P. Zanotti and E. Manfredi. The period extending from 1705 to 1719 was the most fruitful of her poetical activity, resulting in some forty compositions dedicated variously to the celebration of domestic affection, such as the love for her husband and her grief upon his death in 1719 and that of her son Rinaldo, which occurred in 1711. Seven sonnets of her poetical corpus were written in praise of ancient Roman heroines: Porzia, Veturia, Claudia, Arria, Tuzia, Virginia and Lucrezia. After her husband's death, although she lived a secluded life, she did not abandon the pursuit of learning. Influenced by the poetry of Petrarch and Marino, the recurrent themes of her own poetry are love, grief and indignation, all rendered with psychological sincerity even though her literary production constitutes a kind of biography in verse form. More particularly, her poetry resents the influence of the Roman Arcadia, to which she belonged, and of the poetesses with whom she came in contact in that milieu: Petronilla Paolini Massimi and Teresa Grillo. After appearing in contemporary collections, Zappi's work, together with that of her husband, was published in 1723: *Rime dell'avvocato Giov. Battista Felice Zappi e di Faustina Maratti.* Faustina died in Rome on January 20, 1745.

Bibliography

Binni, Walter, *L'Arcadia e il Metastasio* (Florence, 1963), pp. 440–445. *Bruno Maier, Faustina Maratti, donna e rimatrice d'Arcadia* (Rome, 1954). Costa-Zalessow, Natalia, *Scrittrici italiane dal XIII al XX secolo* (Ravenna, 1982), pp. 172–178. Natali, Giulio, *Il Settecento* (Milan, 1955), pp. 148–149.

Sandro Sticca

Concha Zardoya

(a.k.a. Concha de Salamanca)

Born November 14, 1914, Valparaiso, Chile
Genre(s): poetry, short story, criticism
Language(s): Spanish

Concha Zardoya belongs chronologically to the generation of postwar Spanish poets; in theme and tone, however, her poetry bears little resemblance to that of the socially engaged women poets like Gloria Fuertes and Ángela Figuera Aymerich. Rather, in keeping with her training as a scholar and teacher, Zardoya writes on traditional lyric themes in a simpler, less rhetorical style. Her melancholy tone is reminiscent of the Renaissance elegies of Garcilaso de la Vega, and the classical purity and elegance of her diction recall the simple later style of Miguel Hernández, on whom Zardoya has written.

Though born in Chile, Concha Zardoya has lived and studied mainly in Spain and has studied and taught in the United States. She received her licentiate from the University of Madrid in 1947 and her Ph.D. in Spanish from the University of Illinois. She taught at Yale, Barnard College, and the University of Massachusetts at Boston and at Amherst. Now retired, she lives in Madrid.

While Zardoya's deceptively simple style gives her poetry a timelessness and grace, the nostalgic reflective stance of the speaker almost invariably sets up the situation of a person in the present looking back at a more favorable past. In *La casa deshabitada* (The Deserted House), dedicated "to those who are alone or lonely," the poet uses the recurring image of an abandoned house to represent the loneliness and isolation of the persona, who can only overcome her losses through the imagination: "The windows do not turn / in the absent wall. / I am anxious about departures / and half-dream that you are coming" ("Las ventanas"—"The Windows"). The brevity of these lines, which often consist of only three or four words, does not set up a staccato rhythm but rather focuses on each image and creates a melancholy sense of resignation to the ineluctable flow of impressions. Zardoya's recent poetry tends to be more experimental in form and structure. *Diotima y sus edades* is an "autobiography in four times": infancy, adolescence and youth, maturity, and the final stage. Each section traces through the perspective of Diotima actual events and experiences from the author's lifetime; the speaker, in direct, often austere language, does not present a single, coherent identity but uses the pronouns *I, you,* and *we* as subjects for the experiences, thereby effacing the distinctions between speaker and reader, past and present, here and there, and even the differences between author and persona: "When you write Diotima, you write Concha," the final poem concludes. In *Manhattan y otras latitudes,* the author turns toward a more concrete diction and a less fluid meter, as well as stressing social concerns, when she criticizes the superficiality and materialism of the modern metropolis.

In general, Zardoya's poetry and criticism are noteworthy for the sensitivity of their perceptions. Traditional in theme and subtle in formal innovation, her poems are never dry or derivative; their simplicity and restraint result from an effective synthesis of meticulous craftsmanship and profound creativity.

Works

Poetry: *Pájaros del Nuevo Mundo* [Birds of the New World] (1946). *Dominio del llanto* [Dominion of Tears] (1947). *La hermosura sencilla* [Simple Beauty] (1953). *Los signos* [The Signs] (1954). *El desterrado ensueño* [The Banished Dream] (1955). *Mirar al cielo es tu condena (Homenaje a Miguel Ángel)* [To Look at the Sky Is Your Penalty: Homage to Michaelangelo] (1957). *La casa deshabitada* [The Abandoned House] (1959). *Debajo de la luz* [Beneath the Light] (1959). *Elegias* [Elegies] (1961). *Corral de vivos y muertos (Poemas para espanoles)* [Corral of the Living and the Dead: Poems for Spaniards] (1965). *Donde el tiempo resbala: Romancero de Bélgica* [Where Time Slips: Remancero of Belgium] (1966). *Hondo Sur* [Deep South] (1968). *Los engaños de Tremont* [The Deceits of Tremont] (1971). *Las hiedras del tiempo* [The Ivies of Time] (1972). *El corazón y la sombra* [The Heart and the Shadow] (1977). *Diotima y sus edades (Autobiografía en cuatro tiempos)* [Diotima and Her Ages: Autobiography in Four Times] (1981). *Retorno a Margerit* [Return to Margerit] (1983). *Manhattan y otras latitudes* [Manhattan and Other Latitudes] (1983). *Forma de Esperanza* [Form of Hope] (1985).

Stories: (see written under the pseudonym "Concha de Salamanca"). *Cuentos del Antiguo Nilo: Las dos Tierras de Hapi* [Stories of the Ancient Nile: The Two Lands of Hapi] (1944). *Historias y leyendas españolas* [Spanish Stories and Legends] (1942–1946). *Historias y leyendas de Ultramar* [Stories and Legends from Overseas] (1942–1945).

Biography, criticism, literary history: *Miguel Hernández (1940–1942). Vida y obra. Bibliografía. Antología* [Miguel Hernández. Life and Work. Bibliography. Anthology] (1955). [With Carmen Iglesias], *Historia de la literatura norteamericana (1604–1950)* [History of North American Literature] (1956). *Poesia española contemporanea. Estudios temáticos y estilísticos* [Contemporary Spanish Poetry. Thematic and Stylistic Studies] (1961). *Verdad, belleza y expresión (Letras angloamericanas)* [Truth, Beauty, and Expression: Anglo-American Letters] (1967). *Poesia española del 98 y del 27. Estudios temáticos y estilísticos* [Spanish Poetry of the 98 Period and the 27 Period: Thematic and Stylistic Studies] (1968). *Poesia española del siglo XX* [Spanish Poetry of the Twentieth Century] (1974).

Translations: Walt Whitman: *Cantando a la primavera* [Singing to Spring] (1945). Walt Whitman: *Obras escogidas* [Selected Works] (1946). Charles Morgan: *Imagenes en un espejo* [Images in a Mirror] (1949).

Bibliography

Ciplijauskaité, Biruté, "Dos casas habitadas por la ausencia." *Sin Nombre* 9 (1979): 32–40. Duran, Manuel, "Concha Zardoya y su dolorido sentir." *Hispanofila* (1966): 59–61. Duran, Manuel, "La nota elegiaco en la poesía de Concha Zardoya." *Sin Nombre* 9 (1979): 52–59. Paraíso de Leal, Isabel, "Concha Zardoya, en su problematica realidad." *Sin Nombre* 9 (1979): 103–113.

Stephen Hale

Milka Zartovnicka

(see: Terézia Vansová)

Zyranna Zateli

Born 1951, Thessalonike, Greece
Genre(s): short story
Language(s): Greek

Zyranna Zateli is one of the youngest women fiction writers of Greece. She has published only two books so far, both collections of short stories, which enjoyed some popularity. The first one, *Persinē Arravoniastikia* (Last Year's Fiancée), has been reprinted four times since its first appearance in October of 1984. Her second collection, *Stēn Erēmia me Charē* (In Solitude Gracefully), was published in 1986.

The first collection includes nine stories; the second one consists of twenty-one stories and is divided in four parts: "Three Stories from the Beginning of the Century," "Six Stories from the Gardens of Pleasures," "Six Stories from the Middle of the Century and After," and "Six Stories from the Country of Luis de Camões."

The themes that seem to be running through Zateli's fiction are male and female relationships and the women's realization of their sexuality. For example, in one of the short stories of the first collection (the heroine is the same in almost every story), she explores a young teenager's incestuous sexual affair with her half-brother—who is not really her brother—and in another she narrates the same girl's initiation to adult sexuality—when she was merely a child—through a secret affair with her sister's finance. A third story tells of the girl's "engagement" to her male cat. However, in Zateli's fiction, death is always linked with the women's realization of sensuality and sexual pleasure. The male cat dies in a car accident; the sister's fiance dies of a heart attack; and the half-brother disappears forever in Australia.

As in Koutouzi's fiction, the stories are loosely connected, and the reader finds some of the characters mentioned in the first collection in the second one. The events taking place in each story often continue in the following piece, and this structure gives one the illusion of reading chapters of the same novel.

Even though Zyranna Zateli has only published the above collections, she is popular. Her exploration of female sexuality as well as her presentation of relationships between the two sexes is extremely intriguing.

Works

Persinē Arravoniastikia [Last Year's Fiancée] (1984). Stēn Erēmia me Charē [In Solitude Graciously] (1986).
Translations in English: "Birds," tr. Kay Cicellis. Translation: The Journal of Literary Translation XIV (Spring 1985): 28–38. "Dala" (Excerpt), tr. Aliki P. Dragona. Folio IX (1988): 14–16.

Aliki P. Dragona

Sidonia Hedwig Zäunemann

Born January 15, 1714, Erfurt, Germany; died December 11, 1740, near Plauen
Genre(s): poetry
Language(s): German

Sidonia Zäunemann is a forthright and ambitious poet whose life and work broke new ground for women. While growing up as the daughter of a notary in Erfurt, a small university town in central Germany, Zäunemann was inspired by the model of an older contemporary, the learned poet Mariana Ziegler. Determined not to be hampered by society's usual constraints upon women, she learned not only French but also Latin, she read history and also mythology, and she was familiar with the German poets of her time. But she was not only bookish; she was outspoken in her decision not to get married. She was one of the first middle-class women to descend into a mine, and she enjoyed riding horseback alone from Erfurt to Ilemenau in the mountains, where her sister lived. Sometimes on these exploits she wore men's clothing.

Zäunemann's poetry glorifies her ambition and adventurousness, it is oriented in many respects towards the aristocracy, and, although stressing her feeling of being under God's protection, it also shows her need to justify her unconventional behavior. While the poem that first drew attention to her was about a traditional poetic subject, war, in other work she deliberately sought new subjects, such as mining, and used new language as well, including the jargon of miners. She had a gift for vivid descriptions as though events occurred before her very eyes. While harshly criticized in some quarters for her deviation from the conventional female role, she was rewarded and encouraged in others, being the first woman to be crowned imperial poet by the University of Göttingen in 1738. Two years later she died on one of her rides, apparently drowning after her horse fell from a bridge.

Works

Poetische Rosen in Knospen [Poetic Roses in the Bud] (1738). Die von denen Faunen gepeitschte Laster [Vice Being Whipped by the Fauns] (1739). Translation: One poem in: Cocalis, Susan L., ed., The Defiant Muse. German Feminist Poems from the Middle Ages to the Present (New York, 1986).

Bibliography

Brinker-Gabler, Gisela, ed., Deutsche Dichterinnen vom 16. Jahrhundert bis zur Gegenwart. Gedichte und Lebensläufe (Frankfurt, 1978), pp. 121–128. Brinker-Gabler, Gisela, "Das weibliche Ich. Überlegungen zur Analyse von Werken weiblicher Autoren mit einem Beispiel aus dem 18. Jahrhundert; Sidonia Hedwig Zäunemann." Die Frau als Heldin und Autorin. Neue kritische Ansätze zur deutschen Literatur 10. Amherster kolloquium zur Deutschen Literatur (Bern, 1979). Brinker-Gabler, Gisela, ed., Deutsche Literatur von Frauen: Vom Mittelalter bis zum Ende des 18. Jahrhunderts (München, 1988), pp. 307–313. Friedrichs, Elisabeth, Die deutschsprachigen Schriftstellerinnen des 18. und 19. Jahrhunderts. Ein Lexikon (Stuttgart, 1981), p. 345. Lippert, W., "Zäunemann, Sidonia Hedwig." Allgemeine deutsche Biographie v. 44, p. 723–725.

Ruth P. Dawson

Kazimiera Zawistowska

Born January 17, 1870, Rasztowce, Podole,
    West Ukraine; died February 29, 1902,
    Kreków, Poland
Genre(s): poetry, translations
Language(s): Polish

Her father, Henryk Rawicz Jasienski, a lawyer, philosopher, and journalist, was stripped of his university degrees as well as his landed property for participation in the 1863 national uprising against the Russian rule over Poland, and her mother, Albertyna de domo Torosiewicz, born to a wealthy family of landowners of Armenian origin, was famous for her beauty and eccentric life style. Thanks to her mother's dowry, the family lived on a country estate, which would have been lost to them after her father's social and political activity and his financing of his numerous publications, if it weren't for their daughter's "good" marriage to a well-to-do landowner. Carefully educated at home, apart from her youthful voyage to Switzerland and Italy, and occasional visits to Lemberg (Lwów) and Cracow, the major cities of Galitzia where she lived on her husband's family estate called Supranowka, Zawistowska did not travel much. Born and raised in the country, she remained until the end under the influence of the charm of the land and its pagan folklore.

The future poet was influenced by the patriotic atmosphere of her childhood home but perhaps even more by her mother's independent ways. Her poetry is thoroughly feminine, dominated by women's preoccupations, problems, and concerns; for the first time in Polish literature, traditionally focused on social and national issues, a woman poet had the courage to make herself the subject and object of her work.

Her married life with Stanislaw Jastrzebiec-Zawistowski was exemplary; three children were born: a daughter who died only recently, and two sons, one of whom was killed as a soldier during the First World War, and the other who lived into his fifties. The poet's correspondence displays her life in a provincial setting full of longing for a larger society, for literary and artistic contacts, for a better access to books. The well-known poet and critic Zenon Przesmycki-Miriam served in her later years as a literary advisor. When she managed the trip to Cracow, she would meet Kazimierz Przerwa-Tetmajer, a famous poet of the period and the now-forgotten poet Stanislaw Wyrzykowski, both of whom were rumored to be romantically involved with her. The remaining diaries and letters prove that she had a gift of adjusting to the surrounding milieu but experienced provincial life as a drawback, often felt lonesome, and regretted the lack of opportunity for a more extensive education. Her sudden death at the age of thirty-two was called a suicide by Wyrzykowski (who in his diary constructed a legend of a tragic romance, with himself as its object and hero), and some other critics; the family attributed it to pneumonia.

Zawistowska made her debut probably in the Lemburg Courier in the last years of the nineteenth century, but no copies are known to be preserved. Her first volume of poetry, according to her husband prepared by the author herself, was published posthumously several months after her death, in 1903. Fourteen of her poems and some translations were published during the author's lifetime, in the years 1898–1901, in Cracow magazines. A supplement to the early volume was added in 1909. In 1923, Stanislaw Wyrzykowski published her "Poetry," with his own introduction, and Miriam's preface. The next publication was the 1969 Selected Poems (Wybor poezji) by the Warsaw Cztelnik.

Unlike other women poets of her time, Zawistowska did not start following the only existing model, Konopnicka. Her first school of poetry writing was translation, and until the end of her short life she was unsure whether she should not have devoted herself to it entirely. It was Miriam who first perceived the artistic value of her work and encouraged her to continue. According to some critics, had she abandoned it, Polish poetry would miss its earliest tone of daring eroticism which resounded later the most strongly in the voice of Jasnorzewska-Pawlikowska. Unlike the latter, Zawistowska is not well known among the general reading public nowadays. Her name does not appear in Milosz's *The History of Polish Literature.* Julian Krzyanowski claims that in her love poems, she "produced an abundance of cliches" and only praises those "faultlessly chiselled sonnets" in which she presented "some very expressive images of nature and scenes from the life of peasants." Jan Zygmunt Jakubowski, however, probably the best-known scholar of the Young Poland era, considers her the most talented among the poets of that period. Recent critiques call Zawistowska courageous and shocking for her time, and original in throwing the light on the multifaceted personality of a woman: her lyrical subject can be a femme fatale, a weak and defenseless female, as well as a man's conscious and even stronger partner, with similar problems of having to choose between life and art. Her poetry is not free from the mannerism of the period. Her glorification of the solitude of the soul, psychoanalytical symbolism and preoccupation with death viewed as peace and solution to all conflicts, are in harmony with the atmosphere of her times. So is her preoccupation with sin. In her two cycles entitled "Souls" and "Saints," the lyrical "I" functions as a narrator. The poems are like little pictures evolving around the central character of a woman. The heroines are drawn from history, myth, or the Bible, and referred to as "lionesses" or "tigresses" with their "tormented souls" in the "harlots' bosoms." Zawistowska calls them her "great loving ones" and divides them between "saints" and "sinners," the uniting character between the two groups being St. Mary Magdalene. The setting is usually medieval, and the general atmosphere of the poem is a sense of loss, presented more often than not as grief after lost love; but it is always love accompanied by blood, cruelty, crime, and death. The author does not condemn the "sinners," but she does judge them. Her Cleopatra, Herodias, Inez de Castro, Pompadour, St. Theresa or Agnes are presented as real women with believable, human motivations; if they sinned, their sins are viewed as a result of their inner experiences and suffering. None of these female characters is really evil, fascinated by sin; none is presented as demoniac. In this basically monothematic poetry, where love is elevated to the highest value, in spite of all her daring eroticism, which must have been shocking to the Polish readers of her time, the poet remains in agreement with the canons of traditional morality.

Works
Utwory zebrane [Collected Works], ed. and introd. by Lucyna Kozikowska-Kowalik (1982).

Bibliography
Jakubowski, J.Z., *Poetki Mlodej Polski* [Women Poets of the Young Poland] (Warsaw).
Krzyzanowsk, Julian, *A History of Polish Literature* (Warsaw, 1978).

Maya Peretz

María de Zayas y Sotomayor

Born September 12, 1590, Madrid, Spain; died 1661/1669 (?), Spain
Genre(s): short story
Language(s): Spanish

The life of María de Zayas is wrapped in mystery. Her father was a captain in the infantry and a member of the military order of Santiago; thus she evidently belonged to a distinguished Spanish family. Certainly the fictional world of her stories reflects aristocratic values and a cultivated mind. Zayas may have traveled with the Court to Valladolid (1601–1606) and, possibly, to Italy with the entourage of Count Lemos in 1610. But we cannot be sure of these facts. We do know she played an active part in the cultural life of Madrid, participating in literary academies and gatherings, writing encomiastic poems for her friends, and receiving high praise from such luminaries as Lope de Vega and Pérez de Montalbán. Did she marry? Bear children? Or was her life a solitary one? We do not know. But her stories disclose a strong personality, exceptionally sensitive to the effects of passion and the cruel, unjust treatment of women.

Zayas was already known for her verses and a play, *Traición en la amistad* (Treachery in

Friendship; published in Serrano y Sanz), by the time her first collection of *novellas* appeared in 1637. The ten stories included in *Novelas amorosas y ejemplares* (Exemplary Tales of Love) are: "Aventurarse perdiendo" (Nothing Ventured, Nothing Gained), "La burlada Aminta y Venganza del honor" (Aminta Deceived, or Honor Avenged), "El castigo de la miseria" (A Miser's Punishment), "El prevenido engañado" (The Foolish Wise Man), "La fuerza del amor" (The Power of Love), "El desengaño amando y Premio de la virtud" (The Deceits of Love, or Virtue's Reward), "Al fin se paga todo" (In the End We Always Pay), "El imposible vencido" (The Impossible Conquered), "El juez de su causa" (Judge and Jury), and "El jardín engañoso" (The Garden of Deceit). Ten years later, her second and last collection of stories appeared: *Parte segunda del Sarao y entretenimiento honesto, Desengaños amorosos* (The Second Part of an Evening's Honest Entertainments, or the Deceits of Love). The ten stories comprising her *Desengaños amorosos* are: "La esclava de su amante" (Her Lover's Slave), "La más infame venganza" (The Most Infamous Revenge), "El verdugo de su esposa" (His Wife's Executioner), "Tarde llega el desengaño" (A Tardy Lesson), "La inocencia castigada" (Innocence Castigated), "Amar sólo por vencer" (Love Conquers All), "Mal presagio casar lejos" (Beware of a Foreign Wedding), "El traidor contra su sangre" (Blood Betrayed), "La perseguida triunfante" (Virtue Triumphant), and "Estragos que causa el vicio" (The Wreckage of Sin).

Zayas's fictions were popular well into the eighteenth century. Subsequent Victorian hostility to her supposed libertine excesses persisted until fairly recently. While utilizing the conventional frame tale and topoi of love and honor lost, she turned escapist literature into a serious critique of counter-reformation values. Her feminist voice of dissent contrasts sharply with the more conformist, less daring narrations of Mariana de Carvajal. Readers loved her stories for their narrative deftness and for the extraordinary passion and vehemence brought to bear upon the frequently violent and cruel depiction of the darker side of Spanish culture. Zayas shunned a cultivated, rhetorical style, she said, because she wanted to be understood by everyone. Yet there is nothing simple either in the style or vision of María de Zayas's work. In her stories, women are guilty even when innocent, and punishment is extreme. Women are murdered, beaten, drained of their blood, even walled up to die an agonizingly protracted living death. When, for example, the married protagonist Inés of "La inocencia castigada" becomes the victim of a would-be seducer's hypnotic enchantment, both the character and the narrator claim her innocence, while her husband and family, believing she has dishonored them, plan an exemplary and horrorific punishment: to be walled up and barely kept alive for years. Zayas brilliantly plays out her narrative between the poles of fictional verisimilitude, or convention (the victim's hard-to-believe enchantment), and a dominant cultural code that demands "guilt." The reader, tempted at first to doubt Inés' innocence, is later appalled at her imprisoned, emaciated condition. Thus Zayas circumvents the cultural code, subverting it even as she imaginatively and dramatically exploits belief in that same code. Her fictions, which she fittingly called *maravillas*, or marvels, have drawn a new readership, intrigued by her capacity to create passion within artifice, violence, and other irrational acts within a conflicting framework of grace and repression.

Works

Novelas amorosas y ejemplares (1637). *Parte segunda del Sarao y entretenimiento honesto, Desengaños amorosos* (1647; modern eds. 1948, 1973, 1983, 1989).
Translations: *A Shameful Revenge and Other Stories* (1963; title story: "La más infame venganza") in *Women Writers of the Seventeenth Century*, ed. K. Wilson and F. Warnke (1989).

Bibliography

Cocozzella, P., "María de Zayas y Sotomayor: Writer of the Baroque 'Novela ejemplar,'" in *Women Writers of the Seventeenth Century*, ed. K. Wilson and F. Warnke (1989). Foa, S.M., *Feminismo y forma narrativa. Estudio del tema y las técnicas de María de Zayas* (1979). González de Amezúa, Agustín, Introd. *Novelas amorosas y ejemplares* (1948). Goytisolo, J., "El mundo erótico de María de Zayas." *Disidencias* (1977). Griswold, S.C. "Topoi and Rhetorical Distance: The Feminism of María de Zayas." *Revista de Estudios Hispánicos* 14:2 (1980). Ordóñez, E.J., "Woman and Her Text

in the Works of María de Zayas and Ana Caro."
Revista de Estudios Hispánicos 19:1 (1985).
Redondo Goicoechea, A., Introd. *Tres "Novelas amorosas y ejemplares" y tres "Desengaños amorosos"* (1989). Smith, P.J. "Writing Women in Golden Age Spain: Saint Teresa and María de Zayas." *MLN* 102 (1987). Welles, M.L., "María de Zayas y Sotomayor and her *novela cortesana:* a re-evaluation." *Bulletin of Hispanic Studies* 55 (1978). Yllera, A., Introd. *Desengaños amorosos* (1983).
General reference: *Diccionario de literatura española*, eds. G. Bleiberg and J. Marías (1972). Sainz de Robles, F.C., *Ensayo de un diccionario de mujeres célebres* (1959). Serrano y Sanz, M., *Apuntes para una biblioteca de escritoras españolas desde el año 1401 al 1833*, II (1905). *Women Writers of Spain*, ed. C.L. Galerstein (1986).

Noël M. Valis

Zelda

(see: Zelda Mishovsky)

Žemaitė

(a.k.a. Julija Beniuševičiūtė-
Žymantienė)

Born June 4, 1845 on the estate of Bukantė,
near Plungė, Lithuania; died December 7,
1921, Marijampolė, Lithuania
Genre(s): novella, short story, drama, essay,
journalism, children's literature
Language(s): Lithuanian

One of the classic writers of Lithuanian realism, Žemaitė (Julija Beniuševičiūtė), in her novellas, short stories, and sketches, gave a detailed and critical portrayal of rural Lithuanian life at the end of the nineteenth and the beginning of the twentieth centuries. She focused particularly on family relationships and on the status of women in the family. Other themes are the social and economic conflicts between the peasants and the landed gentry, the repressions of the Czarist regime, and the rising nationalist movement. In addition to their literary value, her works are of ethnographic interest for their accurate depictions of folk customs and traditions in the Lithuanian province of Samogitia.

The daughter of impoverished gentry, Beniuševičiūtė was raised in a family that emphasized class traditions and status. As was typical for the gentry of the time, her family spoke Polish, espoused Polish culture, and maintained a distance from the Lithuanian-speaking peasantry. At an early age she rejected these family attitudes, empathizing with the exploited peasants. Marriage to a commoner, Laurynas Žymantas, completed her estrangement from the gentry class. For the next 35 years she lived the difficult life of a farm-wife, struggling with poverty, engulfed by endless chores, and by the cares of child-raising. These experiences later provided her with raw material for her portrayals of peasant life. She began to write at the age of forty-nine, encouraged and aided by a patriotic student, Povilas Višinskis. Her lack of formal education was partly compensated for by extensive reading and by her keen observation of life. Her first prose work, "Rudens vakaras" (1894; Autumn Evening), was published in a farmers' almanac. After her husband's death, in about 1900, Žemaitė became active in the Lithuanian cultural resistance movement directed against the Russian Czarist regime. She also took part in early efforts for women's emancipation, participating in the first Lithuanian women's conference in 1907 and the first Russian women's conference in St. Petersburg in 1908. In 1912 she settled in Vilnius, working as administrator and editor for several journals. Her involvement in relief work during World War I led her to undertake a fund-raising journey to the United States in 1916. She remained there for five years, touring the Lithuanian communities in an effort to raise funds for war victims and refugees. Always sensitive to social injustice, she espoused the socialist movement while remaining skeptical of the Soviet revolution in Russia. Returning to Lithuania in 1921, she died that same year.

Žemaitė's best works are short sketches from everyday life, with particular attention to dialogue and description. Most of her subjects are derived from her own experience and keen observation of the country people surrounding her, whose defects she depicts in great variety: their predominantly materialistic orientation, illiteracy, passivity, and alcoholism. She denounces forced marriages based on economic calculations and shows great concern for lack of intimate family ties. On the other hand, she strongly criticizes the Polonized landlords and clergymen who exploit the naive peasant. Noteworthy, although not always organically incorporated, are her descriptions of nature. In them, she often transmits the peasants' point of view, which is not founded on aesthetic contemplation but on their relation to daily-life chores and farm inventory, thus showing nature to be the core of their lives. She excels even more in creating dynamic scenes consisting of almost pure dialogue. Her sharp pen equally chides the Russian occupant and the imposed administrative system. In all her writing, readers discern her acute class-consciousness. She tried her hand at drama, developing the same topics, but lack of technical knowledge was not easy to surmount, although the works had some success as did those she later produced in collaboration with Gabrielė Petkevičaitė-Bitė.

Among her best stories are those included in her first cycle of narratives entitled *Laimė nutekėjimo* (1896–1898; Marital Fortunes). A representative short story is "Marti" (Daughter-in-law), which depicts the fate of a young woman forced to marry into a backward, slovenly, and hard-hearted family. Efforts to reform the family prove futile and lead to her own demise. The daughter-in-law is caught between the traditional woman's stance–acceptance and resignation–and her desire to fight, which she, however, dismisses. In her, Žemaitė creates a very positive character (many of her women are morally and culturally superior to men), with a sensitivity that those surrounding her are lacking. Her personality is enhanced by almost lyrical descriptions of nature and, on the other hand, by extraordinarily dynamic scenes from daily life.

The denial of basic human rights to women, their mistreatment and exploitation by the patriarchal order, is explored further in the story "Topylis." In "Petras Kurmelis" she portrays the destructive forces of greed and narrow materialism that lead to loveless marriages and to moral decadence. While most of these works analyze negative family relationships, the stories "Sučiuptas velnias" (The Captured Devil) and "Sutkai" describe mutually supportive families in their struggles against a hostile environment. Narratives written in the years just prior to the 1905–1906 revolution present sharper social conflicts and stronger anti-Czarist sentiments. For instance, in the story "Prie dvaro" (1902; At the Estate) the peasants, embroiled in a dispute with local gentry, naively believe that the institutions of justice will uphold their rights. Concerned with the deprivations suffered by peasant children, Žemaitė wrote a number of stories about these children, such as "Kaip Jonelis raides pa'ino" (1914; How Johnny Learned His Letters). Her keen-eyed, unflinchingly honest perceptions of the world around her are especially evident in her prose sketches, such as those reflecting her impressions of the United States, in her unfinished autobiography, and in her extensive correspondence. Although not equal to her prose in quality, a number of her comedies and farces were popular with amateur theatrical groups during the early decades of the twentieth century.

Žemaitė's best prose is characterized by a laconic, energetic, often ironic style, the use of concrete vocabulary, and dramatically intense dialogues, finely tuned to the patterns of oral speech. Her language is colored by folk proverbs and by metaphors rooted in colloquial speech. Her less successful works are marred by tendentiousness, overt didacticism, and sentimentality. Her unique contribution to Lithuanian literature was her ability to depict broad social conditions and relationships through the portrayal of seemingly insignificant individual fates.

Works

Raštai [Collected Works], 4 vols. (1924–1931). *Rinktiniai raštai* [Selected Works], 4 vols. *Raštai* [Collected Works], 6 vols. (1956–1957). *Autobiografija* (1946). *Apie Ameriką* (1953).
Translations into English: "The Devil Captured," tr. Althea von Boskirk and Clark Mills, in *Selected Lithuanian Short Stories*, ed. Stepas Zobarskas (1963), pp. 15–30.

Bibliography

Būtėnas, J., *Žemaitė* (Kaunas, 1938); also *Žemaitė gyvenime ir kūryboje* (Vilnius, 1956). Doveika, K., ed., *Žemaitė*. Literatūra ir kalba 12 (Vilnius, 1972). Kelertas, Violeta, "Discourse Analysis of a Literary Narrative." *Oral and Written Narrative, Discourse*

Types and Functions. Diss. U. of Wisconsin, 1984, pp. 198–307. Rimantas, J., ed., *Žemaitė gyvenime ir kūryboje* (Vilnius, 1956). Sprindis, A., *Žemaitė* (Vilnius, 1986). Umbrasas, K., *Žemaitė. Biografija ir kūrybos ištakos* (Vilnius, 1975). Žiug'da, J., *Žemaitės kūryba* (Kaunas, 1936).

Audronė B. Willeke

Birutė Ciplijauskaite

Rosemarie Zeplin

Born 1939, Bützow, East Germany
Genre(s): novel
Language(s): German

The theme in all three of Zeplin's novels is the emancipation of woman. Zeplin juxtaposes the role of women with that of men in a predominantly masculine socialist society. The socialist state declares that both women and men will become truly free through the social revolution. And yet, according to Zeplin, there are still many areas of inequality between the sexes, especially in the area of love and sexuality. The women can attain the love of a partner, but they can never reach equality with them in love, thus, they remain shadows, without their own qualities, attributes, and characteristics.

Works

Schattenriss eines Liebhabers [Silhouette of a Lover] (1980). *Eine unvollkommene Betreuung* [An Imperfect Caretaking]. *Die kleine Seejungfrau* [The Little Seamaiden].

Bibliography

Kritik 81. Rezensionen zur DDR-Literatur. Herausgegeben von Eberhard Günther, Verner Liersch und Klaus Walter (Halle, Leipzig, 1981).

Brigitte Edith Archibald

Elisabeth Zernike

Born July 8, 1891, Amsterdam, The Netherlands; died March 12, 1982, Laren, Noord-Holland
Genre(s): novel, poetry
Language(s): Dutch

Elisabeth Zernike was the sister of the Nobel Prize-winning physicist Frits Zernike. Her prose narrative is rather unemotional, but it is occasionally punctuated by a passionate event. She began to publish poetry when she was in her sixties.

Works

Novels: *Het schamele deel* [The Poor Part] (1919). *Een vrouw als zig* [A Woman Like Her] (1920). *In de Salamaanderreeks* [In the Salamander Series] (1935). *Kinderspel* [Children's Game] (1921). *Het goede huis* [The Good House] (1923). *Zonderbok* [Special Goat] (1924). *De loop der dingen* [The Course of Things] (1930). *De gereede glimlach* [The Ready Smile] (1930). *Het buurmeisje* [The Girl Next Door] (1934). *Vriendschappen* [Friendships] (1935). *Het leven zonder einde* [Life Without End] (1936). *Morgen weer licht* [Bright Morning Weather] (1938). *Bruidstijd* [Bridal Days] (1940). *De schaatsentocht* [The Pond Plug] (1942). *De gast* [The Guest] (1947). *De erfenis* [The Legacy] (1950). *Bevrijding uit de jeugd* [Liberation from Youth] (1951). *De roep* [The Call] (1953). *Het harde paradijs* [The Hard Paradise] (1959). *Haar vreemdeling* [Her Stranger] (1961). *Kieren van de nacht* [Chinks in the Night] (1963).

Poetry: *Dralend afscheid* [Delayed Departure] (1950). *Het uur der stilte* [The Hour of Silence] (1952). *Kleine drieklank* [Small Triad] (1956).

Adolf von Württenberg

Yvette Z'Graggen

Born March 31, 1920, Geneva, Switzerland
Genre(s): novel, short story, journalism, radio journalism
Language(s): French

The only child of a German-Swiss dentist and a cosmopolitan Genevan mother, Yvette Z'Graggen was raised and educated in Geneva, where she took a "Maturité" (high school completion exam) in Latin. She later studied in Florence and worked as a secretary for the Red Cross in various European countries after the war before settling in the vicinity of Geneva, where she is a well-known journalist. Z'Graggen is divorced and has one daughter.

Z'Graggen's work articulates the experiences of ordinary people, particularly women. *Un été sans histoire* (1962), the story of a summer affair between an older, divorced woman and a young, struggling artist, avoids the cliches of romantic fiction through its precise and unsentimental tone. Z'Graggen's poise, her powers of observation, and skillful use of language make her autobiographical reflections, *Un temps de colère et d'amour* (1980), a fine study of female experience in three generations—her mother's, her own, and her daughter's.

Works

La Vie attendait [Life was Waiting], novel (1944). *L'Herbe d'octobre* [October's Grass], novel (1950). *Le Filet de l'oiseleur* [The Birdcatcher's Net], novel (1957). *Un été sans histoire* [An Uneventful Summer], novel (1962). *Chemins perdus* [Lost Roads], short stories (1971). *Un temps de colère et d'amour* [A Time of Anger and Love], novel (1980). *Les Années silencieuses* [The Silent Years] (1982). *Cornélia*, novel (1985).

Translations into German: *Das Netz des Vogelstellers* [*Le Filet de l'oiseleur*] (1959, 1962). *Ein Sommer ohne Geschichte* [*Un été sans histoire*] (1961). *Erwartung und Erfüllung* [*L'Herbe d'octobre*] (1963, 1965). *Zeit der Liebe, Zeit des Zorns* [*Un temps de colère et d'amour*] (1982, 1985).

Bibliography

L'Arrache-plume. Chroniques de littérature romande 1965–1980 (Lausanne, 1980; Geneva, 1980) (contains reviews of Y.Z.'s work). Pache, Jean, "Les temps d'un miroir. Esquisses pour un portrait d'Y.Z." *24 Heures* 29/30/31 (May 1982).

Ann Marie Rasmussen

Iulia Zhadovskaia

Born June 29, 1824; died July 23, 1883,
    Kostroma province, Russia
Genre(s): lyric poetry, fiction
Language(s): Russian

Iulia Zhadovskaia carried the tradition of Russian lyric poetry into the civic-minded mid-nineteenth century. She was born with no left arm and only a few rudimentary fingers on her right, but she overcame this handicap with a determination, charm, and intelligence which seem to have impressed all who knew her. Her mother died before she was two, and she was brought up by her maternal grandmother and her aunt, the minor poet Anna Gotovtseva. When she was sixteen, her autocratic father hired the future historian of Russian literature, Petr Perevlessky, to tutor Iulia. He was horrified when they fell in love, however, and refused to permit his noble daughter to marry the young plebeian. To console Iulia, he took her to Petersburg and introduced her into the literary circles of the mid-1840s.

There, under her own name or initials, Zhadovskaia began publishing poems that are still remarkable for the naked intensity with which she mourns her thwarted love ("Vse ty unosish', neshchadnoe vremia (1846; You take away everything, merciless time); "Da, ia vizhu—bezumstvo to bylo" (1856; Yes, I see—it was madness). A softer elegiac mood is reflected in nature verse ("Priblizhaiushchaiasia tucha" [The Approaching Storm-Cloud], in which: . . . "Before the grandeur of the storm / My soul's perturbation is stilled," 1845) and philosophical poems like "Na puti" (1856–1859; On My Way). Her diction is harsh, often deliberately unpoetic, and many of her poems have only proximate rhyme or none at all. These features, seen as defects by some mid-nineteenth century critics, stem from a mastery of technique as versatile as her emotional range is limited. Although Zhadovskaia found the conservatism of Moscow and the quiet of Iaroslavl' more compatible than the ferment of Petersburg, she was not unsympathetic to social concerns. She wrote a few poems suggesting that poetry has a civic function ("N.F. Shcherbine" [addressed to a fellow poet], 1857). In "Grustnaia kartina" (1847; A Sad

Picture) and "Niva" (1857; Grainfield), she depicted the hard life of the peasantry. Many of her poems were turned into popular or art songs. Mikhail Glinka wrote music for "Ty skoro menia pozabudesh'" (You'll soon forget me), and Aleksandr Dargomyzhsky set to music "Ia vse eshche ego, bezumnaia, liubliu" (Mad woman that I am, I can't stop loving him).

Zhadovskaia also produced prose tales of lovers thwarted by circumstance or social inequality. Titles like "Prostoi sluchai" (1847; A Simple Case), "Nepriniataia zhertva" (1848; A Sacrifice Refused), and "Sila proshedshego" (1851; The Force of the Past) indicate their general tone and themes. She was slow to master fiction. Her early tales alternate the telegraphic terseness of verse with passionate narratorial interpolation to produce an uneven, occasionally ludicrous, effect. Two later, more polished tales, published in Dostoyvsky's journal *Vremia* in 1861, "Zhenskaia istoriia" (A Woman's Story) and "Otstalaia" (Behind the Times), have strong female protagonists who manage to win happiness for themselves or others in the spirit of the "rational egotism" then being preached in radical circles. Zhadovskaia's most successful prose work was her largely autobiographical novel, *V storone ot bol'shogo sveta* (1857; Apart from the Great World); it was still in print over twenty-five years later.

In 1863 Zhadovskaia married a family friend, Dr. Karl Seven, and retired to Iaroslavl'. At about the same time she stopped writing, due both to failing health and to the fact that, as she told her cousin and ward Nastas'ia Fedorova, "love has vanished from my heart, and poetry has deserted me." After Zhadovskaia's death, her brother oversaw the publication of her complete works just in time to bring her lyric legacy to the attention of the nascent Symbolist movement. In 1887 Fedorova wrote the brief memoir which is the most reliable account of Zhadovskaia's life.

Works

Polnoe sobranie sochinenii, 4 vols. (1885–1886). Izbrannye stikhi (1958). Poety 1840–1850kh gg. (1972), pp. 271–293.

Bibliography

Bykov, P.B., "Iu. V. Zhadovskaia." *Drevniaia i Novaia Rossia* 9 (1877), pp. 71–74. Dobroliubov, N.A., "Stikhotvoreniia Iu. Zhadovskoi." *Sobranie sochinenii*, vol. 3 (Moscow-Leningrad, 1962), pp. 133–147. Fedorova, N., "Vospominanie ob Iu. V. Zhadovskoi." *Istoricheskii vestnik* 11 (1887), pp. 394–407. Golitsyn, N.N., Bibliograficheskii slovar' russkikh pisatel'nits (St. Petersburg, 1889; rpt. Leipzig, 1974), pp. 112–113. Iazykov, D.D., *Obzor zhizni i trudov pokoinykh russkikh pisatelei umershikh v 1883 godu* (St. Petersburg, 1886), pp. 33–34. *Istoriia russkoi literatury XIX v.: Bibliograficheskii slovar' russkikh pisatel'nits*, K.D. Muratova, ed. (Moscow-Leningrad, 1962), p. 325. Ivanov, I., "Poeziia i lichnost' Zhadovskoi," *Pochin: sb. Ob-va liubitelei rossiiskoi slovesnosti na 1896 god* (Moscow, 1896), pp. 270–283. *Kratkaja literaturnaja entsiklopedia*, vol. 2 (Moscow, 1964), cols. 905–906 (F.M. Ioffe). *Russkii biograficheskii slovar'*, vol. 7 (Petrograd, 1916), pp. 1–5 (B.L. Modzalevsky). Skabichevsky, A.M., "Pesnia o zhenskoi nevole." *Sochineniia*, vol. 2 (St. Petersburg, 1903), pp. 230–247.

Mary F. Zirin

Maria Zhukova

Born 1804, Nizhegorod province, Russia; died April 13, 1851, Saratov
Genre(s): fiction, travel sketch
Language(s): Russian

Zhukova began writing in the late 1830s and, with Elena Gan and Nadezhda Durova, was among the first women in Russia to publish a substantial body of prose fiction. Little is known about her life. Her talent as a watercolorist and the prominent role artists and works of art play in her stories suggest that she may have studied with teachers from the Academy of Art in Arzamas where she grew up. Judging from her fiction, her marriage to a local landowner was unhappy. Sometime after 1830 Zhukova separated from her husband and moved to St. Petersburg. For health reasons, between 1838 to 1842 she spent long periods in the milder climates of Europe.

Zhukova's first published work, *Vechera na Karpovke* (Evenings at Karpovka), was an untendentious, often humorous set of stories rich in details of the life of the provincial Russian nobility. It brought her instant fame. Her heroines are refreshingly unstereotyped. In

"Samopozhertvovznie," (1859; Self-Sacrifice), Liza, the poor young ward of a countess, became possibly the first independent woman in Russian fiction when, instead of fading under calumny, she returns home to found a girls' boarding school. Zhukova also used more conventionally Romantic themes and rhetoric: the son of a noble family, deprived of his birthright and true identity, has a near escape from incest ("Padaiushchaia zvezda" [1839; Falling Star]); a married woman makes the hard choice between love and fidelity to her marital vows ("Sud serdtsa" [1840; The Judgment of the Heart]). "Chernyi demon" (1840; The Black Demon) depicts a woman tainted by the Romantic affliction, more common in Russian male protagonists, of a cold intelligence that leads her to suspect and distrust all around her. Zhukova's feeling for the natural world is as genuine as her sympathy with her characters and her love of art, and she often uses extended landscape descriptions to retard a convoluted narrative and build suspense.

The critic Vissarion Belinsky found Zhukova's *Evenings* the epitome of popular light fiction—artless and prolix but enjoyable. The reader, he felt, could not help but respond to the conviction of her warm, engaging voice. Her closely observed, modest travel sketches of southern France and Nice were universally praised and widely read.

Works

Vechera na Karpovke, 2 vols. (1837–1838). Povesti, 2 vols. (1840). Ocherki iuzhnoi Frantsii i Nitstsy, 2 vols. (1844).

Bibliography

Belinksy, V.G., *Polnoe sobranie sochinenii*, 13 vols. (Moscow, 1959–1963), vol. 2, pp. 566–575; vol. 4, 110–118; vol. 8, 422–426. Golitsyn, N.N., *Bibliograficheskii slovar' russkikh pisatel' nits* (St. Petersburg, 1889; rpt. Leipzig, 1974), p. 115. *Handbook of Russian Literature*, Victor Terras, ed. (New Haven, 1985), p. 531 (Christine Tomei). *Istoriia russkoi literatury XIX v.: Bibliograficheskii ukazatel'*, K.D. Muratova, ed. (Moscow-Leningrad, 1962), p. 327. Konopleva, M.S., "M.S. Zhukova." *Golos minuvshego* 7 (1913), pp. 19–38. *Kratkaia literaturnaia entsiklopediia*, vol. 2 (Moscow, 1964), p. 954 (M.A. Sokolova).

Mary F. Zirin

K. Th. Zianitzka

(see: Kathinka [Katharina] Rosa Pauline Modesta Zitz-Halein)

Christiana Mariana Ziegler

Born ca. January 30, 1695, Frankfurt a.d. Oder, Germany; died May 1, 1760, Frankfurt a.M.
Genre(s): lyric poetry, prose text, libretto
Language(s): German

She was the daughter of the well-known Leipzig Mayor Franz Konrad Romanus (elected in 1701). After a few years in office, he was later accused of high crime against the state, but he died in prison before any trial was set up. Christiana married Heinrich Levin von Könitz in 1711 but only to be widowed after a few years. On January 22, 1715 she married the Officer Georg Friedrich von Ziegler auf Eckartsleben (near Gotha, today East Germany). Her second husband also died early and left her alone with two children, who did not survive their father for long. In 1722 she returned to Leipzig, where she met Johann Christoph Gottsched, later her mentor and principal supporter. Upon his recommendation she received an official diploma from the Faculty of the University of Wittemberg as an Imperial Poet Laureate on October 17, 1733, for her lyric poetry. On September 14, 1741, she married her third husband, the Professor for Philosophy in Frankfurt a.M., Wolf Balthasar Adolf von Steinwehr. She died in Frankfurt a.M. in 1760. Apart from her poetry, which is rather irrelevant today, she wrote several libretti for cantata by Johann Sebastian Bach. Bach, however, altered them quite substantially on his own and never used any libretti from her afterward although she included a few more in her later works. Her lyric poetry was first published in 1728 and 1729, then reprinted in 1731 at Leipzig. In the same year some of her public letters with moral and didactic content appeared. In 1735 followed *Der Mademoiselle Scudery scharfsinnige Unterredungen* (Mademoiselle Scudery's Sharp-Witted Discourse). In 1739 appeared a collection of various types of texts. She also translated from French into German *Essai de literature &*

morale des Abbé Trublet (Literary and Moral Essay by Abbé Trublet). After having twice received a prize for her poetry by the Deutsche Gesellschaft, she was also elected a member of the society in 1730.

Works

Versuch in gebundener Schreibart [Attempt in Lyric Poetry], 2 vols. (1728/29). *Moralische und vermischte Sendschreiben an einige ihrer vertrauten und guten Freunde gestellet* [Letters of Moral and Other Content to Some of Her Confidant and Good Friends] (1730). *Gedicht auf die Doktor-Promotion des gelehrten Frauenzimmers Laura Maria Catharina Bassi zu Bologne* [Poem on the Ph.D. Promotion of the Scholarly Woman Laura Maria Catharina Bassi at Bologna] (1932). *Gedicht auf das Absterben König Friedrich August von Polen und Kurfürsten von Sachsen* [Poem on the Death of King Frederick August of Poland and Duke Electorate of Saxony] (1733). *Vermischte Schriften, in gebundener und ungebundener Rede* [Various Works in Prose and Verse] (1739). *Aufsätze in den Schriften der Teutschen Gesellschaft zu Leipzig* (Essays in the Publications of the German Society in Leipzig].

Translations: *Der Madame Scudery scharfsinnige Unterredungen von Dingen, die zu einer wohl anständigen Aufführung gehören* [Mademoiselle Scudery's Sharp-Witted Discourse of Things Which Belong to a Well Mannered Behavior] (1735).

Bibliography

Finauer, Peter Paul, *Allgemeines historisches Verzeichnis gelehrter Frauenzimmer* (1761). Landsberg, Ernst, "Romanus." *Allgemeine Deutsche Biographie*, vol. 29 (Leipzig, 1889), pp. 100–102. Meusel, Johann Georg, *Lexikon der verstorbenen teutschen Schriftsteller*, vol. 15 (Leipzig, 1816; rpt. Hildesheim, 1968), p. 395. Rifkin, Joshua, "Ziegler, Christiana Mariane von." *The New Grove Dictionary*, vol. 20, ed. S. Sadie (London, Washington, D.C., Hong Kong, 1980), p. 678. Spitta, P., "Mariana von Ziegler und Johann Sebastian Bach." *Zur Musik* (Berlin, 1892), p. 93. Zander, F., "Die Dichter der Kantatentexte Johann Sebastian Bachs: Untersuchung zu ihrer Bestimmung." *Bach-Jahrbuch* 54 (1968), pp. 9–64.

Albrecht Classen

Aya Zikken

Born 1919
Genre(s): novel
Language(s): Dutch

The fact that she grew up in the former Dutch colony Indonesia has deeply influenced her work. She always contrasts the European world of thinking with the Oriental world of feeling. Her recent novels *Terug naar de atlasvlinder* (1981; Back to Atlasmoth) and *Eilanden van vroeger* (1982; Islands of the Past) describe a visit to the country of her youth.

Works

Het godgeschenk onbegrepen (1953). *Als wij groot zijn, dan misschien* (1954). *Alleen polenta vandaag* (1954). *De atlasvlinder* (1958). *Hut 277* (1962). *Geen wolf te zien* (1963). *Wees nieuwschierig en leef langer* (1966). *Gisteren gaat niet voorbij. Tempo doeloe* (1973). *Dwars door de spiegel* (1975). *Terug naar de atlasvlinder* (1981). *Eilanden van vroeger* (1982).

Bibliography

Moerman, Josien, ed., *Ik ben een God in 't diepst van mijn gedachten. Lexicon Nederlandstalige auteurs* (Utrecht, 1984), pp. 270–271.

Maya Bijvoet

Vytautė Žilinskaitė

Born December 12, 1930, Kaunas, Lithuania
Genre(s): satire, poetry, essay, drama, film
*   script, children's literature*
Language(s): Lithuanian

After graduating from the University of Vilnius in 1955 with a major in journalism, Žilinskaitė joined the editorial staff of a youth magazine and worked there for 12 years. The first sampling of her creative writing appeared in periodicals in the 1950s. Having started as a poet, she has later tried her hand in practically every genre, from fairy tales to film scripts and plays for puppet theater. Today she is best known for her satires and children's stories and dedicates full time to writing. She defines her creative work as "perpetual wrestling" with the bounty of objects encountered at every step.

The first satires, *Ne iš pirmo 'vilgsnio* (Not at First Sight), appeared in book form in 1962. The 1964 documentary narrative *Mano neapykanta stipresnė* (My Hatred Is Stronger), dealing with communist underground activities during the Nazi occupation, earned a prize in 1968 and again in 1972. In 1964 she was awarded a prize for her journalistic work. Her children's stories combine traditional fairy tale motives with modern situations. Endowed with psychological insight, they speak to the imagination while remaining on a realistic level. Written in a natural, not artificial "children's" language, they have an ethical dimension and invite the young readers to explore nature and the world of animals.

Most of her satires deal with everyday life in Lithuania: bureaucratic inefficiency, absurd situations, inflated egos, the system of bribing. In order to enjoy their full flavor one must know the conditions of life there. Žilinskaitė distinguishes herself by sharp wit, a biting tongue, and appropriate language to all social levels. Often the effects are achieved through juxtaposition or colorful dialogue. In some, the narrator is present as an observer and commentator. In many, a feminist stance is evident. *Paveikslas* (The Painting) adds a more universal note: a series of satires, "On the by-ways of myth," where mythological or classical subjects are deconstructed. Thus, "The short triumph of Judith" inverts/subverts the traditional story of Judith and Holophernes, re-telling it from Judith's point of view, as gracefully and pointedly as Christine Brückner re-shapes feminine figures of the past in her *Wenn du geredet hättest, Desdemona.* The story is told in first-person narration, addressing a young girl who is invited to sharpen her understanding of men's actions and the writing of history and to not despise woman's cunning.

Žilinskaitė participates often in writers' congresses in all Soviet republics and the satellite states, and has been translated into all East European languages as well as Finnish, Hindu, German, Mongolian, and Spanish.

Works

Nesustok, valandėle [Don't Stand Still, Moment] (1961). *Ne iš pirmo 'vilgsnio* [Not at First Sight] (1962). *Mano neapykanta stipresnė* (1964). *Ir aš o'ius ganiau* [I, Too, Was a Goat-heard] (1965). *Angelas virš miesto* [An Angel Above the City] (1967). *Mikė mil'inas* [Mike the Giant] (1967). *Melagių pilis* [The Castle of Liars] (1968). *Romantikos institutas* [The Institute of Romanticism] (1968). *Senelio Šalčio ūsai* [Uncle Cold's Whiskers] (1968). *Karuselėje* [In the Merry-go-round] (1970). *Paradoksai* [Paradoxes] (1973). *Kaktuso paslaptis* [The Secret of the Cactus] (1973). *Berniukas iš albumo* [The Boy from the Album] (1974). *Stebuklingas apsiausas* [The Miraculous Coat] (1977). *Robotas ir peteliškė* [The Robot and the Moth] (1978). *Satyros* [Satires] (1978). *Ledinė fėja* [Ice Fairy] (1979). *Paveikslas* (1981). *Gaid'io kalnas* [The Rooster's Mountain] (1981). *Kvaitulys* [Giddiness] (1984). *Kelionė į Tandadriką* [Voyage to Tandadriką] (1984).

Translations into English: "The Little Wooden Duck." *Soviet Literature* 8 (1979). "A Matter of Principle," "The Manuscript," tr. Eve Manning, in *Soviet Literature* 8 (1982). "The Tubeteika Affair," tr. Margaret Tate, in *Soviet Literature* 8 (1983). Two satires in APROPO 1 (1983). *The Robot and the Moth*, tr. Raissa Bobrova (1985).

Bibliography

Kalėda, Algis, *Komizmas lietuvių literatūroje* (Vilnius, 1984).

Birutė Ciplijauskaitė

Lidia Dmitrievna Zinov'eva-Annibal

Born February 17 (30), 1866; died October 1907, Zagor'e Mogilevskoj gubernii, Russia
Genre(s): drama, prose stories
Language(s): Russian

A Russian writer born into a noble family, Zinov'eva-Annibal married the Russian Symbolist poet, Vyacheslav Ivanov in Liverno, Italy. Returning to Russia, with Ivanov she organized the famous literary salon called the "Tower" where the Petersburg elite gathered regularly on Wednesday evenings starting in 1905. Her literary debut was with the play in verse *Kol'tsa* (1904; The Rings), which was badly received by the critics who overlooked her artistic goals and concentrated on the sensuality of the work.

Thereafter she wrote mostly prose stories as in her first collection, *Tragicheskii zverinets* (Tragic Menagerie). These stories revolve around her childhood memories and represent her greatest contribution to literature. The language is even and purposeful and there is a lyric quality well-designed for the themes of these remembrances. *Tridtsat' tri uroda* (1907; Thirty-three Abominations), an insightful if erotic evaluation of the self, exhibits one of Zinov'eva-Annibal's most powerful passions: exploring the process of liberating one's emotional nature. Through devotion to love and by only this means, one may attain the classical ideals of beauty and harmony.

During the 1905 revolution, she con-tributed to the illegal journal *Adskaia pochta* (Infernal Mail). Her last collection of stories, *Nyet!* (1908; No!), was published posthumously.

Works

Kol'tsa: drama v trekh dejstviakh, drama in three acts (1904). *Tragicheskii zverinets,* stories (1907). **Translations:** Pachmuss, T., *Women Writers in Russian Modernism* (1978).

Chris Tomei

Elisaveta Zirkowa

(a.k.a. Elisheva)

Born 1888, Russia; died 1949, Kinneret
Genre(s): poetry, short story, novel
Language(s): Hebrew

Elisheva, Russian by birth, was adopted by the Jewish people. She began her life along the banks of the Volga, and as a schoolgirl was a student in a gymnasium in Moscow. While in Moscow, she developed a friendship with several Jewish families, and this sparked her interest in both Jewish life and literature. She began studying the Hebrew language with the use of a Hebrew grammar given to her by her brother, an Orientalist. As she advanced in her studies she grew more and more attracted to the Zionist ideal, and she finally made her decision to convert to Judaism.

Whether Elisheva's conversion was genuine has been questioned by recent scholarship; however, friends and relatives asserted the reality of her experience at the time, and scholars of

her day have written of her devotion to her new people and fatherland, which must have come from her conversion to the beliefs and ways of her new people.

The first volume of poetry published by Elisheva was a small, sixteen-page volume written in Russian, *Tayniya Pyesni* (1919). In this volume she deals with her feelings of maladjustment, of being torn between two peoples, and her desperate need to merge with the new family she has chosen. She prefaces the volume with a quotation from Ruth 1:16, "Your people shall be my people, your god my God." Her passion for the Jewish life emerges in the intimate and somewhat drab verse of this volume.

Two other volumes of poetry, *Kos Ketanah* (A Small Cup) and *Haruzim* (Verses), are thin collections of short poems, mainly consisting of themes of nature and love. Most of Elisheva's poetry is not lyrical, but her short poems of nature certainly come the closest. In these poems she seems to reveal the very dwelling place of her soul, which is lost in the beauty of forests, streams, and the sacredness of the land itself. Elisheva sings of the beauty of the Kinneret and the majesty of the city of Jerusalem. The tone of her poems is not sorrowful or melancholy as with many Hebrew poets, but rather it seems to celebrate her acceptance in the "hallowed land of God" ("Green Pines"). At times she appears wistful for the past, for her native land, but her positive spirit shines through her exquisite Hebrew poetry.

Elisheva's prose deals mainly with two themes, alienation and love. In her first volume of prose, *Sippurim* (Stories), the short story "Nerot Shel Shabbat" (Sabbath Candles) depicts a young Gentile girl who falls in love with a Jew and develops a deep fascination for the rites of the Sabbath. They have a deeper meaning for the young girl as she studies their implications for humanity. In the same volume Elisheva reverses her story in "Malkah la-'Ivrim" (Queen of the Jews). Here a Jewish girl falls in love with a gentile young man and makes a sad attempt to lose her Jewish identity. In this pathetic process she also loses her lover. She has built a wall between them that can never be destroyed.

Another short story, published separately in 1928, embodies a similar theme. *Mikreh Tafel*

(Unimportant Incident) is a story about an assimilated girl who has acquired fluency in Russian and adapted to life in Russia. An old Jew moves to her town, is soon caught with the body of a child in a sack, and immediately is imprisoned. The town quickly adopts the cry of "Blood libel," and the growing antisemitism reaches even to the girl's best friend. The girl's relationship with her new people is not broken, but yet it is irreparably damaged.

Alienation was a reality for Elisheva's life, and it was constantly a topic for her writing. This theme is also encountered in her only novel, *Simtaot* (Alleys), about the struggle of a Hebrew writer and a Russian woman poet to retain their love. Even though much of this work came from her own biography (she was married to a Jew), Elisheva's ability to find sustaining imagery and language falls short in such a complex endeavor. Her poems and short stories develop her themes of love and alienation much better.

In 1925 Elisheva was able to capture much of the joy of nature and beauty of her beloved land as she and her Jewish husband, Simon Bichowsky, moved to Israel. It was in this land where she wrote much of her prose and continued to struggle with the alienation and loss of love she experienced. She finally found peace in her resting place on the banks of the Sea of Galilee in 1949.

Works

Tayniya Pyesni (1919). Kos Ketennah [A Small Cup] (1926). Haruzim [Verses] (1927). Sippurim [Stories] (1927). Meshorer ve-adam [Poet and Mankind] (1928–1929). Mikveh Tafel [Unimportant Incident] (1928–1929). Simtoat [Alleys] (1929).

Bibliography

Lubner, S.H., and L.V. Snowman, eds., *Stories and Poems [by] Elisheva* (London, 1933). Silberschlag, Eisig, *From Renaissance to Renaissance II: Hebrew Literature in the Land of Israel: 1870–1970* (New York, 1977). Waxman, Meyer, *A History of Jewish Literature*, vol. 4 (Cranbury, N.J., 1960).

JoAnne C. Juett

Martha Elisabeth Zitter(in)

Born 17th century
Genre(s): religious tracts
Language(s): German

We know next to nothing about Martha Elisabeth Zitter. She lived in the middle of the seventeenth century and was a member of the women's convent Weißfrauenkloster in Erfurt/Saxony (today East Germany). When she converted to the Lutheran belief, she was urged by her mother to expound on her reasons for the conversions in public. This *Scriptum*, which was to become a popular document for Protestants because of its analytic descriptions of a conversion from Catholicism to the new reformed belief, underwent five new editions from the original, printed in Jena. Later, however, Zitterin felt disappointed again with Protestantism and returned to her former church by entering a women's convent at Kitzingen in Northern Bavaria.

Bibliography

Paullini, Christian Franz, *Das hoch–und wohl-gelahrte deutsche Frauen-Zimmer* (Frankfurt-Leipzig, 1712).

Albrecht Classen

Kathinka (Katharina) Rosa Pauline Modesta Zitz-Halein

(a.k.a. K. Th. Zianitzka, Theophyle Christlieb, August Enders, Johann Golder, Dr. Schmid, Emmeline, Rosalbe, Stephanie, Tina, Viola; in newspapers also August, Emilie, Euginie, Pauline)

Born November 4, 1801, Mainz, Germany;
died March 8, 1877, Mainz
Genre(s): poetry, short story, journalism,
translation, novel
Language(s): German

As the daughter of a prominent Mainz businessman, Kathinka Zitz-Halein attended private schools and received a secular, enlightened education in the French language. With her mother's death and her father's increasing mental instability, she was forced to work three years as a governess. She later returned to Mainz to care for her younger sister and earned a living by selling embroidery and giving French lessons. At age seventeen, she became engaged to a Prussian officer, but the engagement was dissolved after ten years, and in 1837 she married Franz Zitz, a lawyer. Within two years the couple separated.

Kathinka Zitz-Halein was politically active in a wide variety of ways. Early in her career, she translated three of Victor Hugo's novels with political or social themes: *Marion de Lorme* (1833), *Triboulet, oder der Königs Hofnarr* (1835; based on The King Amuses Himself), and *Cromwell* (1835). Zitz-Halein's poems, published in literary journals and in collections, often express her support for a unified, democratic, and free Germany. She has been called the "poet laureate of the German Revolution." Perhaps her major contribution to the political campaigns before the revolution of 1848 were her articles published in the *Mannheimer Abendzeitung* opposing laws regarding marriage, divorce, and guardianship and calling for freedom from censorship. She was founder and first president of the Humania Association, the largest women's organization formed during the revolution.

Zitz-Halein's literary activities continued after the revolution as well. She produced numerous collections of short stories, which frequently served as a vehicle to call attention to social injustices. In the 1860s she wrote several novels, which presented romanticized versions of the lives of famous people such as Goethe (1863), Heine (1846), Rahel Varnhagen (1864), and Byron (1867).

Kathinka Zitz-Halein had a tremendous influence on her contemporaries through her political activities as organizer of the Humania Association and through her literary works.

Works

See Kosch, Brümmer, Pataky, ADB

Bibliography

Zucker, Stanley, "Female Political Opposition in Pre-1848 Germany: The Role of Kathinka Zitz-Halein," in *German Women in the Nineteenth Century: A Social History*, ed. John Fout (New York, 1984), pp. 133–150. Zucker, Stanley, "German Women and the Revolution of 1848: Kathinka Zitz-Halein and the Humania Association." *Central European History* 13 (1980), pp. 237–254; Brinker, pp. 212–217.

Ann Willison

Narcyza Żmichowska
(a.k.a. Gabryella)

Born March 4, 1819, Warsaw, Poland; died December 25, 1876, Warsaw, Poland
Genre(s): poetry, novel
Language(s): Polish

Although she has elicited little interest since her death, this talented woman was a leader in literary circles of her day. She has been referred to as an "emancipated woman" because of her independence in supporting herself as tutor throughout her unmarried life and her activism. An avid reader, she was influenced by both French and German writers and philosophers. She presided over a group of intellectual women who banded together for mutual support after the male population had been decimated by death, imprisonment, or exile following the unsuccessful 1830 uprising against Russian domination. Żmichowska's interests went beyond literature and included philosophy, social conditions, the lot of the peasantry, and the status of women. She was one of the guiding lights among the so-called "enthusiasts" who advocated reforms and improvements in society.

Her early writings are a melange of poetry and poetic prose containing lyrics and myths. They appeared in contemporary periodicals during the years 1839–1845. For her outspoken views against all forms of oppression, including the political, she was arrested and imprisoned in 1849.

She is best remembered for her novel *Poganka* (1846; The Pagan Woman). The nominal heroine is based on a woman in Polish society of the time and on the Greek courtesan and mistress of Pericles, Aspasia, famous for her beauty as well as her intelligence. Her amoral namesake in the novel uses her charm and beauty purely for selfish gratification, regardless of consequences to others. She comes to a deservedly unhappy end but not before she destroys the life of young Benjamin, who becomes inextricably and devastatingly enamored of her. Thus one of the themes is the pernicious effect of uncontrolled passion as opposed to genuine affection and devotion. The second theme is the equally dangerous self-absorption of the artist. Cyprian, Benjamin's brother, cynically disregards the latter's suffering in order to use him as model in his work. The novel is a mixture of the realistic and the fantastic, in which the influence of E.T.A. Hoffmann is recognizable.

The next novel, *Książka pamiątek* (1847; Book of Remembrances), also presents a character who comes to grief due to selfish ambition and brings ruin to others. The style here is entirely realistic. Although the author espouses the dignity of the peasants, a conflict between social classes appears unavoidable. *Biała róża* (1858; White Rose) is a social and psychological novel. The central female character struggles against an oppressive environment but finds relief only by escaping into a dream-like existence.

After another failed insurrection in 1863, Żmichowska abandoned all traces of romanticism to join the "positivists," most visibly in *Kasia i Marynka* (1869; Kasia and Marynka). This work deals with questions about love, family structure based on law, and heredity. It reflects in literary form scientific theories of the day. Along with other members of the positivist movement, Żmichowska placed hopes in human progress in science, especially anthropology and natural sciences.

Finally, toward the end of her life, Żmichowska wrote a novel in a totally realistic, dispassionate style. *Czy to powieść?* (1876; Is This a Novel?) is a family saga covering several generations and presenting the mores and cultural atmosphere of the respective periods.

Although a prolific writer, Żmichowska left much of her work unfinished and fragmentary. In addition, her strong self-criticism prevented her from publishing whatever she considered inadequate. However, a rich lode of letters published posthumously affirms her individuality and the originality of her thought.

Works

Poetry: *Już ku zachodniej pochylone stronie* [Already They Lean Westward] (1839). *Szczęście poety* [A Poet's Happiness] (1841). *Maina i Kościej* [Maina and Kościej] (1842). *Zagadnienie* [The Issue] (1842). *Niepewność. Znudzony* [Uncertainty. The Bored One] (1842). *Zwaliska Luksoru* [The Ruins of Luxor] (1842). *Fantazja* [Fantasy] (1843). *Lilia* [Lilia] (1843). *Ułam[ki] z pieśni gęślarza* [(Three) Fragment(s) from a Minstrel's Song] (printed separately in 1843 and 1844). *Przekleństwo* [The Curse] (1844). *Czemu mi smutno?* [Why Am I Sad?] (1844) *Wolne chwile Gabryelli* [Gabryella's Idle Moments] (1845). *Do moich dziewczynek* [To My Little Girls] (1853).

Novels and short prose: *Prządki* [Spinners] (1844). *Dańko z Jawuru* [Danko from Jawur] (1845). *Poganka* [The Pagan Woman] (1846). *Książka pamiątek* [Book of Remembrances] (1847). *Ostatnie chwile życia* [Life's Final Moments] (1857). *Biała róża* [White Rose] (1858). *Kasia i Marynka* [Kasia and Marynka] (1869). *Czy to powieść?* [Is This a Novel?] (1876).

Translations of Żmichowska's poetry were included in the following anthologies: Kirkconnell, Watson, tr., *A Golden Treasury of Polish Lyrics* (1936). Soboleski, Paul, comp., *Poets and Poetry of Poland; A Collection of Polish Verse*. 3rd ed. (1929).

Bibliography

Kleiner, Juliusz, *Zarys dziejów literatury polskiej od początków do 1918 r.* Reviewed and completed by Stefan Kawyn and others (Wrocław, 1968), pp. 390–393. Morzkowska Tyszkowa, Wanda, *Żmichowska wobec romantyzmu francuskiego* (Lwów, 1934). Panczyk, Halina, *Twórczość literacka Narcyzy Żmichowskiej (1819–1876).* Uniwersytet im. A. Mickiewicza w. Poznaniu. Prace Wydziału Filologicznego. Seria Filologia Polska No. 2 (Poznań, 1962). Stępień, Marian, "Żmichowska, Narcyza." *Literatura polska; Przewodnik encyklopedyczny*, ed. Julian Krzyżanowski. Vol. 2 (Warsaw, 1985).

Irene Suboczewski

Annemarie Zornack

Born March 12, 1932, Aschersleben in the Harz, West Germany
Genre(s): poetry, prose
Language(s): German

Annemarie Zornack attributes her lyrical beginnings to the doctor-poet William Carlos

Williams, whose simple yet strikingly memorable imagery inspired her dedication to everyday objects as the focal point of her poetry. She writes of the past and the present, of the significance of daily occurrences, resisting with the force of words the vulnerability of people and objects around her. With her verse, Zornack attempts to recreate chosen moments, to establish their connection with the past.

Although Zornack was educated as a nurse, both she and her husband Hans-Juergen Heise have achieved national recognition as poets. For almost 30 years, they have written from the vantage point of their home in the North German port city of Kiel. Notwithstanding the prevalence of the harbor theme, Zornack's work has been compared to the vignettes of the Viennese *fin-de-siecle* author Peter Altenberg. Her poetry is not prose-like, but, like Altenberg's prose, it is quintessentially impressionistic. Irony rescues her poetic impressions from romanticism: she explains that it offers her writing an escape from despair. Many critics cite in her verse the voice of the optimist. Other readers point to surrealistic elements in her poetry, noting the closeness of theme and the imagination. Zornack refers to thematic elements in her verse as memories that have been relocated in the present. She hopes to create "shining images," a reality transfigured, but not distorted by imagination.

Zornack's poetic relationship to her own childhood memories is significant for her writing, and she describes her use of childhood themes as a *Klappstulleneffekt*, a merging of memory and present experience like the layers of a double-decker sandwich. Similarly, Zornack's frequent inclusion of travel metaphors indicates not a longing for the exotic but rather a gaze directed toward home. Homecomings permeate her work, and, like her outreach to childhood memories from the distance of adulthood, distant locales provide not a destination but a place from which to return home.

The tone of Annemarie Zornack's poetry is spontaneous and conversational, and she favors the natural rhythm of speech and forms of direct address. She avoids punctuation, claiming that it separates and divides. She does not use capital letters (German nouns are capitalized), because she prefers to present all entities as equal.

Zornack's last three poetry volumes are published with original graphic designs—two by the Czech artist Guenter Dimmer and another by German artist Heinrich Richter.

Winner of the 1979 Friedrich-Hebbel prize for poetry, Annemarie Zornack's international reputation is beginning to form. She has been acclaimed as an artist who could prove the unacceptability of Theodor Adorno's assumption that poetry cannot be written after Auschwitz, since her approach to that genre is uniquely apolitical, almost ahistorical. Her verse, an artistic affirmation of daily life, has established for Zornack a leading place among German women writers of the eighties.

Works

Prose: [With Hans-Juergen Heise], *Der Macho und der Kampfhahn—Unterwegs in Spanien und Lateinamerika* (1987). [With Hans-Juergen Heise], *Die zwei Fluesse von Granada, Reiseprosa* (1976). Poetry: *kusshand, Gedichte*, with graphic art by Guenter Dimmer (1987). *Die langbeinige Zikade, Gedichte*, with graphic art by Guenter Dimmer (1985). *treibanker werfen, Gedichte*, with graphic art by Heinrich Richter (1982). *als das fernsehprogramm noch vorm kuechenfenster lief, Gedichte* (1979).

Minor works: *nichts weiter* (1976). *tagesanfaenge* (1972). *der steinschlaefer* (1972). *mobile* (1968). *zwei sommer* (1968).

Suzanne Shipley Toliver

Anna Radius Zuccari

(see: Neera)

Kate Zuccaro

(see: Kate Cukaro)

Loekie Zvonik

Born January 17, 1933, Ghent, Belgium
Genre(s): novel
Language(s): Flemish

Loekie Zvonik (Hermine Louise Marie Zvoniček), a member of the so-called "Silent

Generation" on the Flemish literary scene of the mid-seventies, was born of a Bohemian father and a Flemish mother of Walloon origin. From 1952 to 1956 she studied German and Dutch literature in Ghent. She was strongly impressed by the courses and the personality of professor Herman Uyttersprot, a well-known Kafka and Rilke specialist. So was her fellow student Dirk de Witte, a writer of fatalistic stories, who committed suicide in 1970. These data form the plot of Zvonik's autobiographical novel *Hoe heette de hoedenmaker?* (1975; How Was the Hatter Called?), awarded the yearly Prize for the Best Literary Debut. References to Rilke, Kafka, Hesse and Pavese and to the enigmatic cultural history of Vienna and Prague play a decisive role in this book. Zvonik counters the self-destructive impulses of her main character by a mythologized feminine vitality. This tendency has been reinforced in *Duizend jaar Thomas* (1979; Thomas, a Millennium), and *De eerbied en de angst van Uri en Ima Bosch* (1983; The Worship and the Terror of U. and I.B.), excessively marked by symbols of Christian apocalypticism and by neoconservative complaints about the decay of Western civilization.

Works

Hoe heette de hoedenmaker? (1975). Duizend jaar Thomas (1979). De eerbied en de angst van Uri en Ima Bosch (1983).

Bibliography

Special issue of the Flemish literary magazine *Yang* (1980). Schampaert, P., *Kritisch lexicon van de Nederlandstalige literatuur na 1945* (1982). Durnez, G., *Loekie Zvonik: een introductie* (1983).

Frank Joostens

Dikken Zwilgmeyer

(a.k.a. Inger Johanne)

Born 1853, Trondheim, Norway; died 1913, Norway
Genre(s): novel, short story, children's literature
Language(s): Norwegian

Dikken Zwilgmeyer was born Henrikke Barbara Wind Daae Zwilgmeyer in Trondheim,

Norway. Her family moved to Risør when she was around seven years old. This small southern seacoast town is characterized so well and so lovingly in many of Zwilgmeyer's children's books.

The twelve books in the Inger Johanne series represent the central portion of Zwilgmeyer's authorship for children. They span the years from 1890, when *Vi børn* by Inger Johanne, thirteen years old, was published, and 1911 when the last of these volumes, *Vi tre i hytten*, appeared.

Inger Johanne is a lively young girl, warm-hearted and impulsive and a leader among her playmates. Zwilgmeyer has captured Inger Johanne's personality in a style that is as fresh, direct, and impulsive as the voice of the adolescent Inger Johanne. Zwilgmeyer related the life Inger Johanne and her friends through the voice of Inger Johanne, without overt adult didacticism or moralizing.

Zwilgmeyer's adult literature exhibits an opposite tone and perspective to the charming, optimistic manner of her literature for children. *Som kvinder er*, six stories published in a collection in 1895, contains some of the most bitter descriptions of a woman's lot in all of Norwegian literature. *Ungt sind. En novelle* (1896) is concerned with all the doubt, anxiety, and despair in a young person awakening to sexuality and adult life.

Several of Dikken Zwilgmeyer's children's books have been translated into a number of languages, including English, and her Inger Johanne books are still read and enjoyed by Norwegian children. Zwilgmeyer was not recognized in her own lifetime as anything but a popular writer of children's books. However, in recent times her writing for adults has also been acknowledged and appreciated for its harshly realistic descriptions of the plight of women in turn-of-the-century Norway.

Works

Vi børn [We Children] (1890). *Karsten og jeg* [Karsten and I] (1891). *Fra vor by* [From Our Town] (1892). *Sommerferier* [Summer Vacations] (1894). *Barndom* [Childhood] (1895). *Som kvinder er* [As Women Are] (1895). *Ungt sind* [Young Mind] (1896). *Morsomme dager* [Amusing Days] (1896).

Hos onkel Max og tante Betty [At Uncle Max and Aunt Betty's] (1897). *Udenlands* [In Foreign Lands] (1898). *Fire kusiner* [Four Cousins] (1899). *Anniken Præstegaren* [Anniken Præstegaren] (1900). *Syvstjernen og andre historier* [The Seven Stars and Other Stories] (1900). *Frøken Lybæks pensionatskole* [Miss Lybaek's Boarding School] (1901). *Mægler Porsvold og andre historier* [Agent Porsvold and Other Stories] (1902). *Lille Jan Bluhme* [Johnny Blossom] (1903). *Kongsgaardsguttene* [The Boys from Kongsgaard] (1904). *Paul og Lollik* [Paul and Lollik] (1904). *Maja* [Maja] (1905). *Emerentze* [Emerentze] (1906). *Maren Ragna* [Maren Ragna] (1907). *Thekla* [Thekla] (1908). *Inger Johanne* [Inger Johanne] (1909). *Hos farfar paa Løvly og andre fortællinger for barn* [With Grandfather at Løvly and Other Stories for Children] (1910). *Vi tre i hytten* [We Three in the Hut] (1911). *Inger Johanne bøkene og andre fortellinger for gutter og piker. Mindeutgave i fem bind* [The Inger Johanne Books and Other Stories for Boys and Girls, memorial edition in five volumes] (1915–1916).

Translations: "An Everyday Story," tr. Katherine Hanson, in *An Everyday Story*, ed. Katherine Hanson (Seattle, 1984), pp. 38–45. *Four Cousins*, tr. Emilie Poulsson (1923). *Inger Johanne's Lively Doings*, tr. Emilie Poulsson (1926). *Johnny Blossom*, tr. Emilie Poulsson (1912; rpt. 1948). *What Happened to Inger Johanne*, tr. Emilie Poulsson (1919). *Visiting Grandfather and Eleven Other Stories*, tr. Klara Alice Holter (1900).

Bibliography

Hagemann, Sonja, *Barnelitteratur in Norge 1850–1914* (Oslo, 1974), pp. 176–197. Hareide, Jorunn, *Protest, desillusjonering, resignasjon. Dikken Zwilgmeyers forfatterskap for voksne* (Oslo, 1982).

Torild Homstad